CRIME IN THE UNITED STATES

CRIME IN THE UNITED STATES

2020

14th EDITION

EDITED BY SHANA HERTZ HATTIS

Bernan Press

Lanham • Boulder • New York • London

Published by Bernan Press
An imprint of The Rowman & Littlefield Publishing Group, Inc.
4501 Forbes Boulevard, Suite 200, Lanham, Maryland 20706
www.rowman.com
800-462-6420

6 Tinworth Street, London SE11 5AL, United Kingdom

ISBN: 978-1-64143-408-9
E-ISBN: 978-1-64143-409-6

CONTENTS

SECTION IV: PERSONS ARRESTED...309

LIST OF FIGURES

SECTION I

SUMMARY OF THE UNIFORM CRIME REPORTING (UCR) PROGRAM

SECTION I: SUMMARY OF THE UNIFORM CRIME REPORTING (UCR) PROGRAM

Bernan Press is proud to present its 14th edition of *Crime in the United States*. This title was formerly published by the Federal Bureau of Investigation (FBI), but is no longer available in printed form from the government. This edition contains final data from 2018, the most current year for which data is available.

This section describes the history of the UCR program, which collects the data used in *Crime in the United States*. It also examines the best way to use the data in this publication.

Currently, the UCR program includes four data collections:

- National Incident-Based Reporting System (NIBRS)— Provides detailed incident information on 52 offenses including the victims, offenders, and property stolen, recovered, or damaged. In addition, NIBRS collects arrest data for those offenses plus 10 others. In 2018, approximately 44 percent of the law enforcement agencies that participated in the UCR Program submitted their data via NIBRS. The populations of these agencies represented approximately 37 percent of the population covered by agencies that submitted data to the UCR Program. Of the 38 states that the FBI has certified to report via NIBRS, 17 states submitted 100 percent of their data via NIBRS; the other NIBRS-certified states submitted data through both NIBRS and the Summary Reporting System. Among states still working toward NIBRS-certification, a few agencies submitted NIBRS data through direct contributions to the FBI.

- Summary Reporting System (SRS)—Furnishes aggregate offense counts for 10 Part I offenses and arrest data for an additional 20 offenses. The historic data collection will give way to make UCR a NIBRS-only data collection by January 1, 2021.

- Law Enforcement Officers Killed and Assaulted (LEOKA) Program—Offers information about officers who were killed or assaulted while performing their duties. The information is published and used to help agencies develop polices to improve officer safety. More information about LEOKA and the accompanying data is available in Bernan Press's *Justice Statistics: An Extended Look at Crime in the United States*.

- Hate Crime Statistics Program—Provides information on crimes motivated by offenders' bias against race, gender, gender identity, religion, disability, sexual orientation, and ethnicity. These data are also collected via NIBRS.

About the UCR Program

The UCR program's primary objective is to generate reliable information for use in law enforcement administration, operation, and management; however, over the course of the program, its data has stood out as one of the country's leading social indicators.

The UCR program is a nationwide, cooperative statistical effort of more than 18,000 city, university and college, county, state, tribal, and federal law enforcement agencies voluntarily reporting data on crimes brought to their attention. Since 1930, the FBI has administered the UCR program and continued to assess and monitor the nature and type of crime in the nation. Criminologists, sociologists, legislators, municipal planners, the media, and other students of criminal justice use the data for varied research and planning purposes.

Note for Users

It is important for UCR data users to remember that the FBI's primary objective is to generate a reliable set of crime statistics for use in law enforcement administration, operation, and management. The FBI does not provide a ranking of agencies; instead, it provides alphabetical tabulations of states, metropolitan statistical areas, cities with over 10,000 inhabitants, suburban and rural counties, and selected colleges and universities. Law enforcement officials use these data for their designed purposes. Additionally, the public relies on these data for information about the fluctuations in levels of crime from year to year, while criminologists, sociologists, legislators, city planners, media outlets, and other students of criminal justice use them for a variety of research and planning purposes. Since crime is a sociological phenomenon influenced by a variety of factors, the FBI discourages data users from ranking agencies and using the data as a measurement of the effectiveness of law enforcement.

To ensure that data are uniformly reported, the FBI provides contributing law enforcement agencies with a handbook that explains how to classify and score offenses and provides uniform crime offense definitions. Acknowledging that offense definitions may vary from state to state, the FBI cautions agencies to report offenses according to the guidelines provided in the handbook, rather than by local or state statutes. Most agencies make a good faith effort to comply with established guidelines.

The UCR program publishes the statistics most commonly requested by data users. More information regarding the availability of UCR program data is available by telephone at (304) 625-4830, or by e-mail at ucr@fbi.gov.

Data requests via e-mail cannot be processed without the requester's full name, mailing address, and contact telephone number.

Variables Affecting Crime: Caution Against Ranking

Until data users examine all the variables that affect crime in a town, city, county, state, region, or college or university, they can make no meaningful comparisons. In each edition of *Crime in the United States*, many entities—including news media, tourism agencies, and other organizations with an interest in crime in the nation—use reported figures to compile rankings of cities and counties. However, these rankings are merely a quick choice made by that data user; they provide no insight into the many variables that mold the crime in a particular town, city, county, state, or region. Consequently, these rankings may lead to simplistic and/or incomplete analyses, which can create misleading perceptions and thus adversely affect cities, counties, and their residents.

Considering Other Characteristics of a Jurisdiction

To assess criminality and law enforcement's response from jurisdiction to jurisdiction, data users must consider many variables, some of which (despite having significant impact on crime) are not readily measurable or applicable among all locales. Geographic and demographic factors specific to each jurisdiction must be considered and applied in order to make an accurate and complete assessment of crime in that jurisdiction. Several sources of information are available to help the researcher explore the variables that affect crime in a particular locale. The U.S. Census Bureau data, for example, can help the user better understand the makeup of a locale's population. The transience of the population, its racial and ethnic makeup, and its composition by age and gender, educational levels, and prevalent family structures are all key factors in assessing and understanding crime.

Local chambers of commerce, planning offices, and similar entities provide information regarding the economic and cultural makeup of cities and counties. Understanding a jurisdiction's industrial/economic base, its dependence upon neighboring jurisdictions, its transportation system, its economic dependence on nonresidents (such as tourists and convention attendees), and its proximity to military installations, correctional institutions, and other types of facilities all contribute to accurately gauging and interpreting the crime known to and reported by law enforcement.

The strength (including personnel and other resources) and aggressiveness of a jurisdiction's law enforcement agency are also key factors in understanding the nature and extent of crime occurring in that area. Although information pertaining to the number of sworn and civilian employees can be found in this publication, it cannot be used alone as an assessment of the emphasis that a community places on enforcing the law. For example, one city may report more crime than another comparable city because its law enforcement agency identifies more offenses. Attitudes of citizens toward crime and their crime reporting practices—especially for minor offenses—also have an impact on the volume of crimes known to police.

Making Valid Crime Assessments

It is essential for all data users to become as well educated as possible about understanding and quantifying the nature and extent of crime in the United States and in the jurisdictions represented by law enforcement contributors to the UCR program. Valid assessments are possible only with careful study and analysis of the various unique conditions that affect each local law enforcement jurisdiction.

Some factors that are known to affect the volume and type of crime occurring from place to place are:

- Population density and degree of urbanization

- Variations in composition of population, particularly in the concentration of youth

- Stability of the population with respect to residents' mobility, commuting patterns, and transient factors

- Modes of transportation and highway systems

- Economic conditions, including median income, poverty level, and job availability

- Cultural factors and educational, recreational, and religious characteristics

- Family conditions, with respect to divorce and family cohesiveness

- Climate

- Effective strength of law enforcement agencies

- Administrative and investigative emphases of law enforcement

- Policies of other components of the criminal justice system (that is, prosecutorial, judicial, correctional, and probational policies)

- Residents' attitudes toward crime

- Crime reporting practices of residents

Although many of the listed factors equally affect the crime of a particular area, the UCR program makes no attempt to relate them to the data presented. **The data user is therefore cautioned against comparing statistical data of individual reporting units from cities, counties, metropolitan areas, states, or colleges or universities solely on the basis on their population coverage or student enrollment.** Until data users examine all the variables that affect crime in a town, city, county, state, region, or college or university, they can make no meaningful comparisons.

Historical Background

Since 1930, the FBI has administered the UCR program; the agency continues to assess and monitor the nature and type of crime in the nation. Data users look to the UCR program for various research and planning purposes.

Recognizing a need for national crime statistics, the International Association of Chiefs of Police (IACP) formed the Committee on Uniform Crime Records in the 1920s to develop a system of uniform crime statistics. After studying state criminal codes and making an evaluation of the recordkeeping practices in use, the committee completed a plan for crime reporting that became the foundation of the UCR program in 1929. The plan included standardized offense definitions for seven main offense classifications known as Part I crimes to gauge fluctuations in the overall volume and rate of crime. Developers also instituted the Hierarchy Rule as the main reporting procedure for what is now known as the Summary Reporting System of the UCR program.

Seven main offense classifications, known as Part I crimes, were chosen to gauge the state of crime in the nation. These seven offense classifications included the violent crimes of murder and non-negligent manslaughter, rape, robbery, and aggravated assault; also included were the property crimes of burglary, larceny-theft, and motor vehicle theft. By congressional mandate, arson was added as the eighth Part I offense category. Data collection for arson began in 1979.

During the early planning of the program, it was recognized that the differences among criminal codes precluded a mere aggregation of state statistics to arrive at a national total. Also, because of the variances in punishment for the same offenses in different states, no distinction between felony and misdemeanor crimes was possible. To avoid these problems and provide nationwide uniformity in crime reporting, standardized offense definitions were developed. Law enforcement agencies use these to submit data without regard for local statutes. UCR program offense definitions can be found in Appendix I.

In January 1930, 400 cities (representing 20 million inhabitants in 43 states) began participating in the UCR program. Congress enacted Title 28, Section 534, of the *United States Code* that same year, which authorized the attorney general to gather crime information. The attorney general, in turn, designated the FBI to serve as the national clearinghouse for the collected crime data. Since then, data based on uniform classifications and procedures for reporting have been obtained annually from the nation's law enforcement agencies.

Advisory Groups

Providing vital links between local law enforcement and the FBI for the UCR program are the Criminal Justice Information Systems Committees of the IACP and the National Sheriffs' Association (NSA). The IACP represents the thousands of police departments nationwide, as it has since the program began. The NSA encourages sheriffs throughout the country to participate fully in the program. Both committees serve the program in advisory capacities.

In 1988, a Data Providers' Advisory Policy Board was established. This board operated until 1993, when it combined with the National Crime Information Center Advisory Policy Board to form a single Advisory Policy Board (APB) to address all FBI criminal justice information services. The current APB works to ensure continuing emphasis on UCR-related issues. The Association of State Uniform Crime Reporting Programs (ASUCRP) focuses on UCR issues within individual state law enforcement associations and also promotes interest in the UCR program. These organizations foster widespread and responsible use of uniform crime statistics and lend assistance to data contributors.

Redesign of UCR

Although UCR data collection was originally conceived as a tool for law enforcement administration, the data were widely used by other entities involved in various forms of social planning by the 1980s. Recognizing the need for more detailed crime statistics, law enforcement called for a thorough evaluative study to modernize the UCR program. The FBI formulated a comprehensive three-phase redesign effort. The Bureau of Justice Statistics (BJS) agency in the Department of Justice responsible for funding criminal justice information projects, agreed to underwrite the first two phases. These phases were conducted by an independent contractor and structured to determine what, if any, changes should be made to the current program. The third phase would involve implementation of the changes identified.

The final report, the *Blueprint for the Future of the Uniform Crime Reporting Program*, was released in the summer of 1985. It specifically outlined recommendations for an expanded, improved UCR program to meet future informational needs. There were three recommended areas of enhancement to the UCR program:

- Offenses and arrests would be reported using an incident-based system

- Data would be collected on two levels. Agencies in level one would report important details about those offenses comprising the Part I crimes, their victims, and arrestees. Level two would consist of law enforcement agencies covering populations of more than 100,000 and a sampling of smaller agencies that would collect expanded detail on all significant offenses

- A quality assurance program would be introduced

In January 1986, Phase III of the redesign effort began, guided by the general recommendations set forth in the *Blueprint*. The FBI selected an experimental site to implement the redesigned program, while contractors developed new data guidelines and system specifications. Upon selecting the South Carolina Law Enforcement Division (SLED), which enlisted the cooperation of nine local law enforcement agencies, the FBI developed automated data capture specifications to adapt the SLED's state system to the national UCR program's standards, and the BJS funded the revisions. The pilot demonstration ran from March 1 through September 30, 1987, and resulted in further refinement of the guidelines and specifications.

From March 1 through March 3, 1988, the FBI held a national UCR conference to present the new system to law enforcement and to obtain feedback on its acceptability. Attendees of the conference passed three overall recommendations without dissent: first, that there be established a new, incident-based national crime reporting system; second, that the FBI manage this program, and third, that an Advisory Policy Board composed of law enforcement executives be formed to assist in directing and implementing the new program. Furthermore, attendees recommended that the implementation of national incident-based reporting proceed at a pace commensurate with the resources and limitations of contributing law enforcement agencies.

Establishing the NIBRS

From March 1988 through January 1989, the FBI developed and assumed management of the UCR program's National Incident-Based Reporting System (NIBRS), and by April 1989, the first test of NIBRS data was submitted to the national UCR program. Over the next few years, the national UCR program published information abouyt the rdesigned program in five documents:

- *Uniform Crime Reporting Handbook*, NIBRS Edition (1992) provides a nontechnical program overview focusing on definitions, policies, and procedures of the IBRS

- *Data Submission Specifications* (May 1992) is used by local and state systems personnel, who are responsible for preparing magnetic media for submission to the FBI

- *Approaches to Implementing an Incident-Based System* (July 1992) is a guide for system designers

- *Error Message Manual* (revised December 1999) contains designations of mandatory and optional data elements, data element edits, and error messages

- *Data Collection Guidelines* (revised August 2000) contains a system overview and descriptions of the offense codes, reports, data elements, and data values used in the system

As more agencies inquired about the NIBRS, the FBI, in May 2002, made the *Handbook for Acquiring a Records Management System (RMS) That Is Compatible with the NIBRS* available to agencies considering or developing automated incident-based records management systems. The handbook, developed under the sponsorship of the FBI and the BJS, provides instructions for planning and conducting a system acquisition and offers guidelines on preparing an agency for conversion to the new system and to the NIBRS.

Originally designed with 52 data elements, the redesigned NIBRS captures up to 57 data elements via 6 types of data segments: administrative, offense, victim property, offender, and arrestee. Although, in the late 1980s, the FBI committed to hold all changes to the NIBRS in abeyance until a substantial amount of contributors implemented the system, modifications have been necessary. The system's flexibility has allowed the collection of four additional pieces of information to be captured within an incident: bias-motivated offenses (1990), the presence of gang activity (1997), data for law enforcement officers killed and assaulted (2003), and data on cargo theft (2005). The system has also allowed the addition of new codes to further specify location types and property types (2010).

The FBI began accepting NIBRS data from a handful of agencies in January 1989. As more contributing law enforcement agencies become educated about the rich data available through incident-based reporting and as resources permit, more agencies are implementing the NIBRS. Based on the 2012 data submissions, 15 states submit all their data via the NIBRS and 32 state UCR Programs are certified for NIBRS participation.

Suspension of the *Crime Index* and the *Modified Crime Index*

In June 2004, the CJIS APB approved discontinuing the use of the *Crime Index* in the UCR program and its publications and directed the FBI to publish a violent crime total and a property crime total. The *Crime Index*, first published in *Crime in the United States* in 1960, was the title used for a simple aggregation of the seven main offense classifications (Part I offenses) in the Summary Reporting System. The Modified Crime Index was the number of Crime Index offenses plus arson.

For several years, the CJIS Division studied the appropriateness and usefulness of these indices and brought the matter before many advisory groups including the UCR Subcommittee of the CJIS APB, the ASUCRP, and a meeting of leading criminologists and sociologists hosted by the BJS. In short, the *Crime Index* and the *Modified Crime Index* were not true indicators of the degrees of criminality because they were always driven upward by the offense with the highest number, typically larceny-theft. The sheer volume of those offenses overshadowed more serious but less frequently committed offenses, creating a bias against a jurisdiction with a high number of larceny-thefts but a low number of other serious crimes such as murder and rape.

Recent Developments in UCR Program

In the fall of 2011, the APB recommended, and FBI Director Robert Mueller III approved, changing the definition of rape. Since 1929, in the SRS, rape had been defined as "the carnal knowledge of a female forcibly and against her will" (*UCR Handbook*, 2004, p. 19). Beginning with the 2013 data collection, the SRS definition for the violent crime of rape will be: "Penetration, no matter how slight, of the vagina or anus with any body part or object, or oral penetration by a sex organ of another person, without the consent of the victim." This definition can be found in the *Summary Reporting System [SRS] User Manual*, Version 1.0, dated June 20, 2013. The FBI is developing reporting options for law enforcement agencies to meet this requirement, which will be built into the redeveloped data collection system.

In addition to approving the new definition of rape for the SRS, the APB and Director Mueller approved removing the word "forcible" from the name of the offense and also replacing the phrase "against the person's will" with "without the consent of the victim" in other sex-related offenses in the SRS, the NIBRS, the Hate Crime Statistics Program, and Cargo Theft.

In response to a directive by the U.S. Government's Office of Management and Budget, the national UCR Program has expanded its data collection categories for race from four (White, Black, American Indian or Alaska Native, and Asian or Other Pacific Islander) to five (White, Black or African American, American Indian or Alaska Native, Asian, and Native Hawaiian or Other Pacific Islander). Also, the ethnicity categories have changed from "Hispanic" to "Hispanic or Latino" and from "Non-Hispanic" to "Not Hispanic or Latino." These changes are reflected in data presented from 2012.

The national UCR Program staff continues to develop data collection methods to comply with both the William Wilberforce Trafficking Victims Protection Reauthorization Act of 2008 and the Matthew Shepard and James Byrd, Jr. Hate Crime Prevention Act of 2009. As a result, the FBI began accepting data on human trafficking as well as data on crimes motivated by "gender and gender identity" bias and "crimes committed by, and crimes directed against, juveniles" from contributors in January 2013.

UCR Redevelopment Project Update

To streamline the program's database management and quality control activities, the FBI created the UCR Redevelopment Project (UCRRP). The UCRRP's goal is to improve the efficiency, usability, and maintainability of the UCR Program's submission processes, databases, and quality control activities. Through the UCRRP, the UCR Program will improve customer service by decreasing the time it takes to analyze data and by decreasing the time needed to release and publish crime data. The program will also enhance its external data query tool so that the public can view and analyze more published UCR data from the Internet.

Another major goal of the UCRRP is to reduce, to the point of elimination, the exchange of printed materials between submitting agencies and the FBI. Beginning with the 2013 data collections, all data was to be submitted electronically, and after July 2013, the UCR Program no longer accepted paper submissions or the electronic submission of documents (for example, Portable Document Format files). The UCRRP has begun working with agencies to help them adopt electronic submissions via the NIBRS, electronic SRS, or Extensible Markup Language.

Uniform Crime Reporting Program
Changes Definition of Rape

For the first time in the more than 80-year history of the Uniform Crime Reporting (UCR) Program, the FBI has changed the definition of a Part 1 offense. In December

2011, then FBI Director Robert S. Mueller, III, approved revisions to the UCR Program's definition of rape as recommended by the FBI's Criminal Justice Information Services (CJIS) Division Advisory Policy Board (APB), which is made up of representatives from all facets of law enforcement.

Beginning in 2013, rape is defined for Summary UCR purposes as, "Penetration, no matter how slight, of the vagina or anus with any body part or object, or oral penetration by a sex organ of another person, without the consent of the victim." The new definition updated the 80-year-old historical definition of rape which was "carnal knowledge of a female forcibly and against her will." Effectively, the revised definition expands rape to include both male and female victims and offenders, and reflects the various forms of sexual penetration understood to be rape, especially nonconsenting acts of sodomy, and sexual assaults with objects. Beginning in 2017, only this revised definition of rape was used.

"This new, more inclusive definition will provide us with a more accurate understanding of the scope and volume of these crimes," said Attorney General Eric Holder. Proponents of the new definition and of the omission of the term "forcible" say that the changes broaden the scope of the previously narrow definitions by capturing (1) data without regard to gender, (2) the penetration of any bodily orifice, penetration by any object or body part, and (3) offenses in which physical force is not involved. Now, for example, instances in which offenders use drugs or alcohol or incidents in which offenders sodomize victims of the same gender will be counted as rape for statistical purposes.

It has long been the UCR Program's mission to collect and publish data regarding the scope and nature of crime in the nation, including those for rape. Since the FBI began collecting data using the revised definition of rape in January 2013, program officials expected that the number of reported rapes would rise. According to David Cuthbertson, former FBI Assistant Director of the CJIS Division, "As we implement this change, the FBI is confident that the number of victims of this heinous crime will be more accurately reflected in national crime statistics."

Expanded Offense Tables

Expanded offense data are the details of the various offenses that the Uniform Crime Reporting Program collects beyond the count of how many crimes law enforcement agencies report. These details may include the type of weapon used in a crime, the type or value of items stolen, and so forth. Expanded homicide data provide supplemental details about murders such as the age, sex, and race of both the victim and the offender, the weapon used in the homicide, the circumstances surrounding the offense, and the relationship of the victim to the offender. In addition, expanded data includes trends (for example, 2-year comparisons) and rates per 100,000 inhabitants.

Expanded offense data, including expanded homicide data, are information collected in addition to the reports of the number of crimes known. As a result, law enforcement agencies can report an offense without providing the supplemental data about that offense. These additional tables can be found at https://ucr.fbi.gov/crime-in-the-u.s/2018/crime-in-the-u.s.-2018/topic-pages/expanded-offense.

About the Editor

Shana Hertz Hattis is a consulting writer-editor for Bernan Press. She holds a master of science in education degree in from Northwestern University and a bachelor's degree in journalism from the same university. She has previously edited *Vital Statistics of the United States: Births, Life Expectancy, Deaths, and Selected Health Data* and several volumes of *Crime in the United States* for Bernan.

SECTION II

OFFENSES KNOWN TO POLICE

VIOLENT CRIME

- MURDER

- RAPE

- ROBBERY

- AGGRAVATED ASSAULT

PROPERTY CRIME

- BURGLARY

- LARCENY-THEFT

- MOTOR VEHICLE THEFT

- ARSON

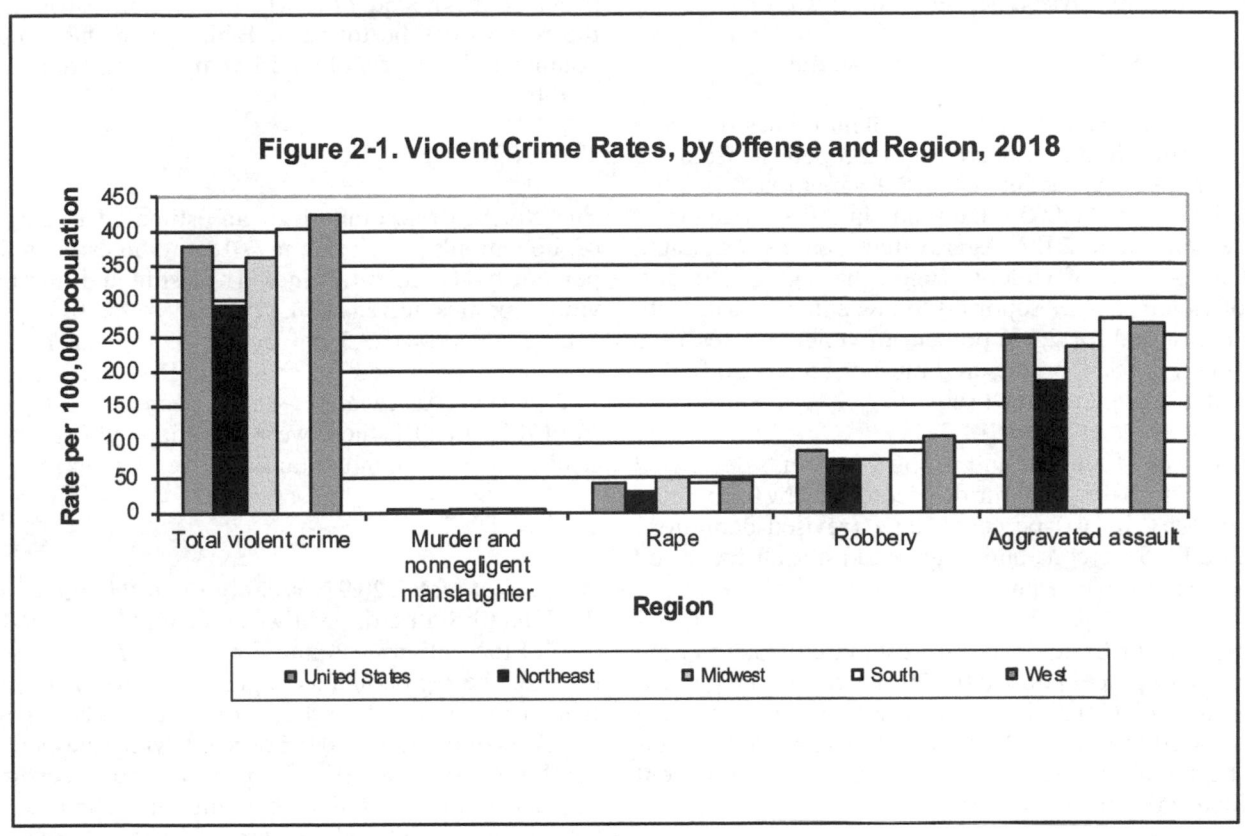

Figure 2-1. Violent Crime Rates, by Offense and Region, 2018

Definition

Violent crime consists of four offenses: murder and non-negligent manslaughter, rape, robbery, and aggravated assault. According to the Uniform Crime Reporting (UCR) program, run by the Federal Bureau of Investigation (FBI), violent crimes involve either the use of force or the threat of force.

Data Collection

The data presented in *Crime in the United States* reflect the Hierarchy Rule, which counts only the most serious offense in a multiple-offense criminal incident. In descending order of severity, the violent crimes are murder and non-negligent manslaughter, rape, robbery, and aggravated assault; these are followed by the property crimes of burglary, larceny-theft, and motor vehicle theft. Arson is also considered a property crime, but the Hierarchy Rule does not apply to the arson offense. In cases in which arson occurs in conjunction with another violent or property crime, the arson and the additional crime are reported. More information on the expanded violent crime tables (which are available online but not included in this publication) can be found in Section I.

Important Note: Rape Data

In 2013, the FBI UCR Program began collecting rape data under a revised definition within the Summary Reporting System. Previously, offense data for forcible rape were collected under the legacy UCR definition: the carnal knowledge of a female forcibly and against her will. Beginning with the 2013 data year, the term "forcible" was removed from the offense title, and the definition was changed. The revised UCR definition of rape is: penetration, no matter how slight, of the vagina or anus with any body part or object, or oral penetration by a sex organ of another person, without the consent of the victim. Attempts or assaults to commit rape are also included in the statistics presented here; however, statutory rape and incest are excluded.

In 2017, the FBI Director approved the recommendation to discontinue the reporting of rape data using the UCR legacy definition beginning in 2018. However, to maintain the 20-year trend in Table 1, national estimates for rape under the legacy definition are provided along with estimates under the revised definition for 2018.

National Volume, Trends, and Rate

In 2018, an estimated 1,206,836 violent crimes occurred in the United States, a decrease of 3.3 percent from the 2017 estimate. An estimated 368.9 violent crimes were committed per 100,000 inhabitants in 2018, a decline of 3.9 percent since 2017. Aggravated assaults accounted for 66.9 percent of violent crimes, the highest percentage of violent crimes reported to law enforcement. Robbery accounted for 23.46 percent of violent crimes, rape accounted for 8.4 percent, and murder accounted for 1.3 percent of violent crimes. (Table 1)

Occurrences of murder and robbery incidents decreased from 2017 to 2018, with murder decreasing by 0.7 percent and robbery by 4.0 percent. Rape (revised definition) increased 2.5 percent and aggravated assault increased 1.0 percent. (Tables 1 and 1A)

In longer-term trends, the 2018 estimated violent crime total was 4.7 percent above the 2014 level and 9.0 percent below the 2009 level. The 5-year and 10-year trend data also showed that the violent crime rate increased 2.0 percent between 2014 and 2018 and decreased 14.6 percent between 2009 and 2018. (Tables 1 and 1A)

In 2018, offenders used firearms in 72.7 percent of the nation's murders, 38.5 percent of robberies, and 26.1 percent of aggravated assaults. Although the largest percentage of murders were committed with firearms, weapons such as clubs and blunt objects accounted for more aggravated assaults (31.5 percent) than any other type of weapon. (Weapons data are not collected for rape offenses.) (Expanded Homicide Table 7, Expanded Offense Robbery Table 3, and Expanded Aggravated Assault Table; see https://ucr.fbi.gov/crime-in-the-u.s/2018/crime-in-the-u.s.-2018/tables/aggravated-assault.xls for more information)

Many violent crimes are committed by people in known relationships. Figure 2 shows the number of murder victims who knew their offender. In the figure, the relationship categories of husband and wife include common-law spouses and ex-spouses. The categories of mother, father, sister, brother, son, and daughter include stepparents, stepchildren, and stepsiblings. The category of "acquaintance" includes homosexual relationships and the composite category of other known-to-victim offenders.

Regional Offense Trends and Rate

The UCR program divides the United States into four regions: the Northeast, the South, the Midwest, and the West. (More details concerning geographic regions are provided in Appendix IV.) The population distribution of the regions can be found in Table 3, and the estimated volume and rate of violent crime by region are provided in Table 4.

THE NORTHEAST

The Northeast accounted for an estimated 17.2 percent of the nation's population in 2018 and an estimated 13.2 percent of its violent crimes. The estimated number of violent crimes decreased 4.4 percent from 2017 to 2018. Murder decreased 2.3 percent in the Northeast. However, rape increased 3.7 percent. Robberies declined 14.2 percent. Aggravated assaults decreased 1.1 percent from 2017. In 2018, there were an estimated 292.7 violent crimes per 100,000 inhabitants. (Tables 3 and 4)

THE MIDWEST

With an estimated 20.9 percent of the total population of the United States, the Midwest accounted for 19.8 percent of the nation's estimated number of violent crimes in 2018. The region had a 4.5 percent decrease in violent crime from 2017 to 2018. The estimated number of aggravated assaults decreased 0.5 percent, while the estimated number of robberies fell 17.9 percent and the estimated number of murders fell 9.1 percent. The estimated number of rapes increased 1.0 percent. The rate of violent crime per 100,000 inhabitants in the Midwest was 361.4, a decrease of 4.7 percent from 2017 to 2018. (Tables 3 and 4)

THE SOUTH

The South, the nation's most populous region, accounted for 38.1 percent of the nation's population in 2018. Approximately 40.5 percent of violent crimes in 2018 occurred in the South. Violent crime decreased 3.9 percent, while the estimated number of murders fell 5.3 percent and the estimated number of rapes rose 2.3 percent. Robberies dropped 12.6 percent, while aggravated assault increased by 1.8 percent. The estimated rate of violent crime in the South was 403.9 incidents per 100,000 inhabitants in 2018. (Tables 3 and 4)

THE WEST

With 23.8 percent of the nation's population in 2018, the West also accounted for an estimated 26.5 percent of the nation's violent crime. Violent crime in the West increased 0.3 percent from 2017 to 2018. Murders fell 7.4 percent, rapes increased 4.4 percent, robberies decreased 6.0 percent, and aggravated assault increased 2.5 percent. The region's violent crime rate in 2018 was 423.2 per 100,000 inhabitants. (Tables 3 and 4)

Community Types

The UCR program aggregates crime data into three community types: metropolitan statistical areas (MSAs), cities outside MSAs, and nonmetropolitan counties outside MSAs. Appendix IV provides additional information regarding community types. In 2018, approximately 86.0 percent of the nation's population lived in MSAs. Residents of cities outside MSAs accounted for 5.7 percent of the country's population, and residents living in nonmetropolitan counties accounted for 8.3 percent of the population. (Table 2)

In the areas reporting violent crimes to the UCR Program, approximately 88.8 percent of these crimes occurred in MSAs, while 5.5 percent occurred in cities outside MSAs and 4.1 percent occurred in nonmetropolitan counties. By community type, the violent crime rates were estimated at 397.8 incidents per 100,000 inhabitants in MSAs, 382.4 incidents per 100,000 inhabitants in cities outside MSAs, and 200.8 incidents per 100,000 inhabitants in nonmetropolitan counties. (Table 2)

Population Groups: Trends and Rates

In the UCR program, data are also aggregated into population groups; these groups are described in more detail in Appendix IV. The nation's cities had an overall decrease of 3.4 percent in the estimated number of violent crimes from 2017 to 2018. By city population group, cities with 25,000 to 49,999 inhabitants had the largest percentage decrease in the estimated number of violent crimes (7.3 percent). (Table 12)

The law enforcement agencies in the nation's cities collectively reported a rate of 451.5 violent crimes per 100,000 inhabitants in 2018. Law enforcement agencies in the subset of cities with 500,000 to 999,999 inhabitants reported the highest violent crime rate, 830.3 violent crimes per 100,000 inhabitants; the violent crime rate for all cities with 250,000 or more inhabitants was 768.5 per 100,000 inhabitants. Agencies in cities with 10,000 to 24,999 inhabitants reported the lowest violent crime rate (259.6 incidents per 100,000 inhabitants). Law enforcement agencies in the nation's metropolitan counties reported a collective violent crime rate of 253.9 per 100,000 inhabitants, while agencies in nonmetropolitan counties reported a collective rate of 204.6 violent crimes per 100,000 inhabitants. (Table 16)

MURDER

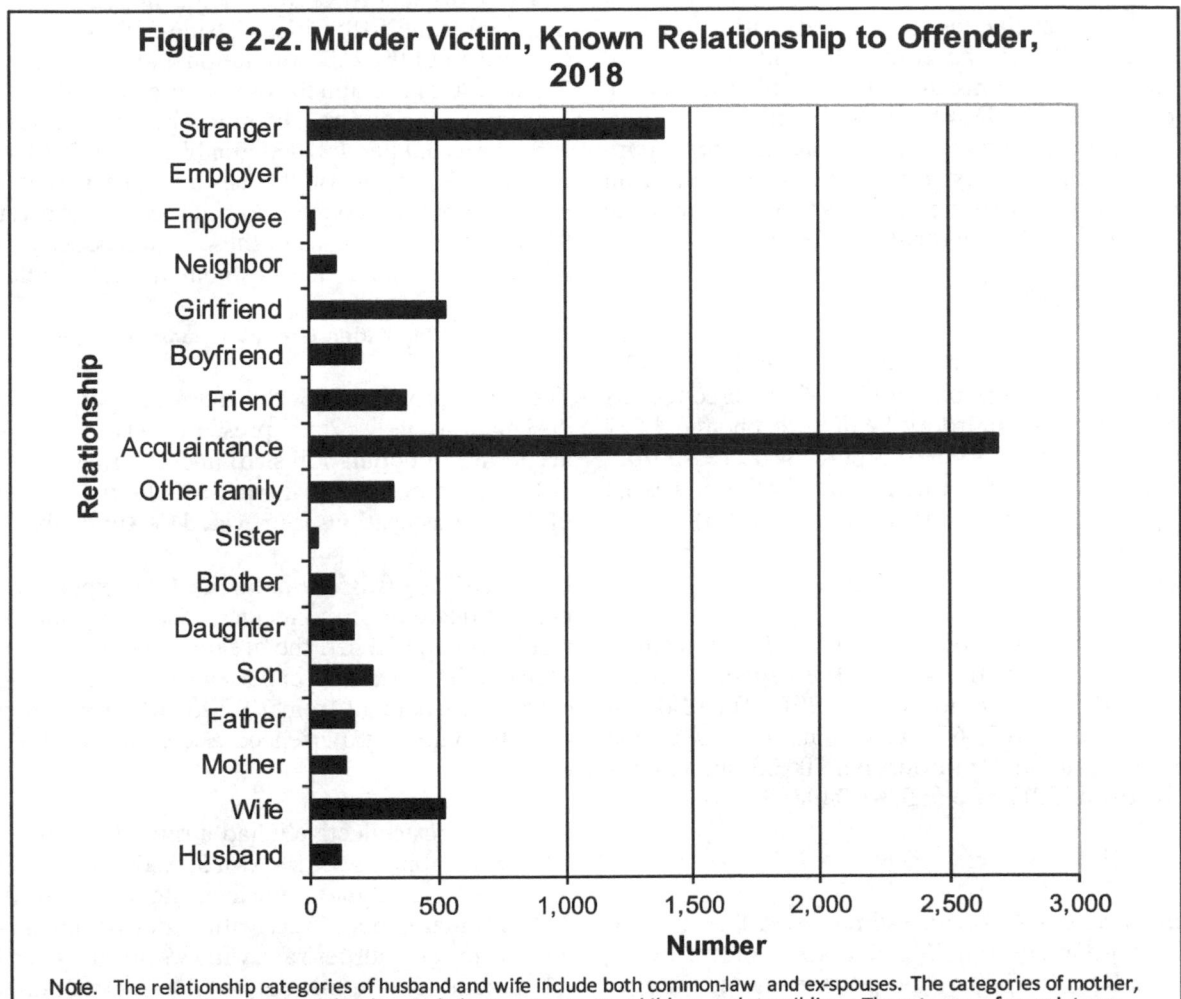

Figure 2-2. Murder Victim, Known Relationship to Offender, 2018

Note. The relationship categories of husband and wife include both common-law and ex-spouses. The categories of mother, father, sister, brother, son, and daughter include stepparents, stepchildren, and stepsiblings. The category of acquaintance includes homosexual relationships and the composite category of other known to victim. Approximately 6,992 victim-offender relationships were unknown.

Definition

The UCR program defines murder and non-negligent manslaughter as the willful (non-negligent) killing of one human being by another. The classification of this offense is based solely on police investigation, rather than on the determination of a court, medical examiner, coroner, jury, or other judicial body. The UCR program does not include the following situations under this offense classification: deaths caused by negligence, suicide, or accident; justifiable homicides; and attempts to murder or assaults to murder, which are considered aggravated assaults.

Data Collection/Supplementary Homicide Reports (SHR)

The UCR program's *Supplementary Homicide Report* (SHR) provides information about murder victims and offenders by age, sex, and race; the types of weapons used in the murders; the relationships of the victims to the offenders; and the circumstances surrounding the incident. Law enforcement agencies are asked to complete an SHR for each murder reported to the UCR program. Data from SHRs can be viewed in the Expanded Homicide Data section, found on the FBI Website: https://ucr.fbi.gov/crime-in-the-u.s/2018/crime-in-the-u.s.-2018/topic-pages/expanded-homicide. More information on these reports and the expanded homicide tables can be found in Section I. Highlights from these tables have been included below.

National Volume, Trends, and Rates

An estimated 16,214 persons were murdered nationwide in 2018. This number was a 6.2 percent decrease from the 2017 estimate, a 14.5 percent increase from the 2014 figure, and a 5.3 percent increase from the 2009 estimate. The 2018 murder rate, 5.0 offenses per 100,000 inhabitants, was a 6.8 percent decrease from the 2017 rate. Murder accounted for 1.3 percent of the overall estimated number of violent crimes in 2018. (Tables 1 and 1A)

Regional Offense Trends and Rates

The UCR program divides the United States into four regions: the Northeast, the South, the Midwest, and the West. (More details concerning geographic regions are provided in Appendix IV.) In 2018, 46.2 percent of murders were reported in the South, the country's most populous region. The Midwest reported 22.0 percent of all murders, while the West reported 19.9 percent and the Northeast reported 11.9 percent. (Table 3)

THE NORTHEAST

In 2018, the Northeast accounted for an estimated 17.2 percent of the nation's population and 11.9 percent of its estimated number of murders. With an estimated 1,922 murders, the Northeast saw a 2.3 percent decrease from its 2017 figure. The offense rate for the Northeast was 3.4 murders per 100,000 inhabitants. (Tables 3 and 4)

THE MIDWEST

The Midwest accounted for an estimated 20.9 percent of the nation's total population and 22.0 percent of the country's estimated number of murders in 2018. The Midwest reported an estimated 3,567 murders in 2018. The region experienced a rate of 5.2 murders per 100,000 inhabitants in 2018, below its 2017 rate of 5.8. (Tables 3 and 4)

THE SOUTH

The South accounted for an estimated 38.1 percent of the nation's population in 2018 and 46.2 percent of the nation's murders, the highest proportion among the four regions. The estimated 7,495 murders represented a 5.3 percent decrease from the 2017 figure. The region's estimated rate of 6.0 murders per 100,000 inhabitants represented a decrease of 6.2 percent from the estimated rate for 2017. (Tables 3 and 4)

THE WEST

The West accounted for an estimated 23.8 percent of the nation's population and 19.1 percent of the estimated number of murders in 2018. The West experienced an estimated 3,230 murders, a 7.4 percent increase from the 2017 estimate. The region's murder rate was 4.1 per 100,000 inhabitants. (Tables 3 and 4)

Community Types

The UCR program aggregates data for three community types: metropolitan statistical areas (MSAs), cities outside MSAs, and nonmetropolitan counties outside MSAs. (See Appendix IV for definitions.) In 2018, MSAs accounted for 86.0 percent of the nation's population and 89.0 percent of the estimated total number of murders. MSAs experienced a rate of 5.2 murders per 100,000 inhabitants in 2018. Cities outside MSAs accounted for 5.7 percent of the U.S. population and (with an estimated 727 murders) accounted for 4.4 percent of the estimated murders in the nation. The murder rate for cities outside MSAs was 3.9 per 100,000 inhabitants. In 2018, approximately 8.3 percent of the nation's population lived in nonmetropolitan counties outside MSAs. An estimated 912 murders took place in these counties, accounting for 5.5 percent of the nation's estimated total. (Table 2)

Population Groups: Trends and Rates

The UCR program uses the following population group designations in its data presentations: cities (grouped according to population size) and counties (classified as either metropolitan or nonmetropolitan). A breakdown of these classifications is provided in Appendix IV.

From 2017 to 2018, the nation's cities experienced a 6.7 percent decrease in homicides. Cities with under 10,000 residents experienced the greatest decrease, 9.4 percent. Metropolitan counties experienced a decrease in homicides of 4.1 percent from 2017 to 2018, while nonmetropolitan counties experienced a decrease of 2.0 percent. (Table 12)

In 2018, cities collectively had a rate of 5.8 murders per 100,000 inhabitants. Cities with 500,000 to 999,999 inhabitants had the highest murder rate (11.9 murders per 100,000 inhabitants). Cities with under 10,000 inhabitants had the lowest murder rate, with 2.9 murders per 100,000 inhabitants. The homicide rate for metropolitan counties was 3.4 murders per 100,000 inhabitants, while the rate for nonmetropolitan counties was 3.3 murders per 100,000 inhabitants. Suburban areas had a homicide rate of 3.0 per 100,000 inhabitants. (Table 16)

Supplementary Homicide Reports Data

VICTIMS/OFFENDERS

Based on 2018 supplemental homicide data (where the ages, sexes, or races of the murder victims were identified), 92.0 percent of victims were over 18 years of age, 20.0 percent were under 22 years of age, 8.0 percent were under 18 years of age, and the age of 1.0 percent of the victims was unknown. Of the 14,123 murder victims represented in the 2018 expanded tables whose gender was identified, 77.3 percent were male. Concerning race, 43.1 percent of victims were White, 52.4 percent were Black, and 2.8 percent were of other races. Race was unknown for 233 victims. For murders in which the gender of the offender was identified, 63.1 percent were males; the sex of offenders for 28.1 percent of homicides was unknown.

For the offenders for whom race was identified, 38.7 percent were Black, 29.9 percent were White, and 1.9 percent were other races; 4,821 offenders were of unknown race. (Expanded Homicide Data Tables 1, 2, and 3)

VICTIM-OFFENDER RELATIONSHIPS

For incidents in which the victim-offender relationship was specified (including the designation of "unknown"), 12.8 percent of victims were slain by family members, 9.9 percent were murdered by strangers, and 27.8 percent were killed by acquaintances (neighbor, friend, boyfriend, employer, etc.). The victim-offender relationship was unknown in 49.5 percent of incidents. (Expanded Homicide Data Table 10)

CIRCUMSTANCES/WEAPONS

Concerning the known circumstances surrounding murders, and including murders with unknown circumstances, 39.4 percent of victims were murdered during arguments (including romantic triangles) and brawls in 2018. Felony circumstances (rape, robbery, burglary, etc.) accounted for 24.5 percent of murders. Circumstances were unknown for 40.2 percent of reported homicides. Of the homicides for which the type of weapon was specified, 72.7 percent involved the use of firearms. Of the identified firearms used, handguns comprised 64.3 percent of the total. (Expanded Homicide Data Tables 8 and 12)

Justifiable Homicide

Certain willful killings must be reported as justifiable, or excusable, homicide. In the UCR program, justifiable homicide is defined as, and is limited to, the following:

- The killing of a felon by a peace officer in the line of duty

- The killing of a felon, during the commission of a felony, by a private citizen

Because these killings are determined by law enforcement investigation to be justifiable, they are tabulated separately from murder and nonnegligent manslaughter. Law enforcement reported 763 justifiable homicides in 2018. Of those, law enforcement officers justifiably killed 410 individuals, and private citizens justifiably killed 353 individuals. (Expanded Homicide Data Tables 14 and 15)

RAPE

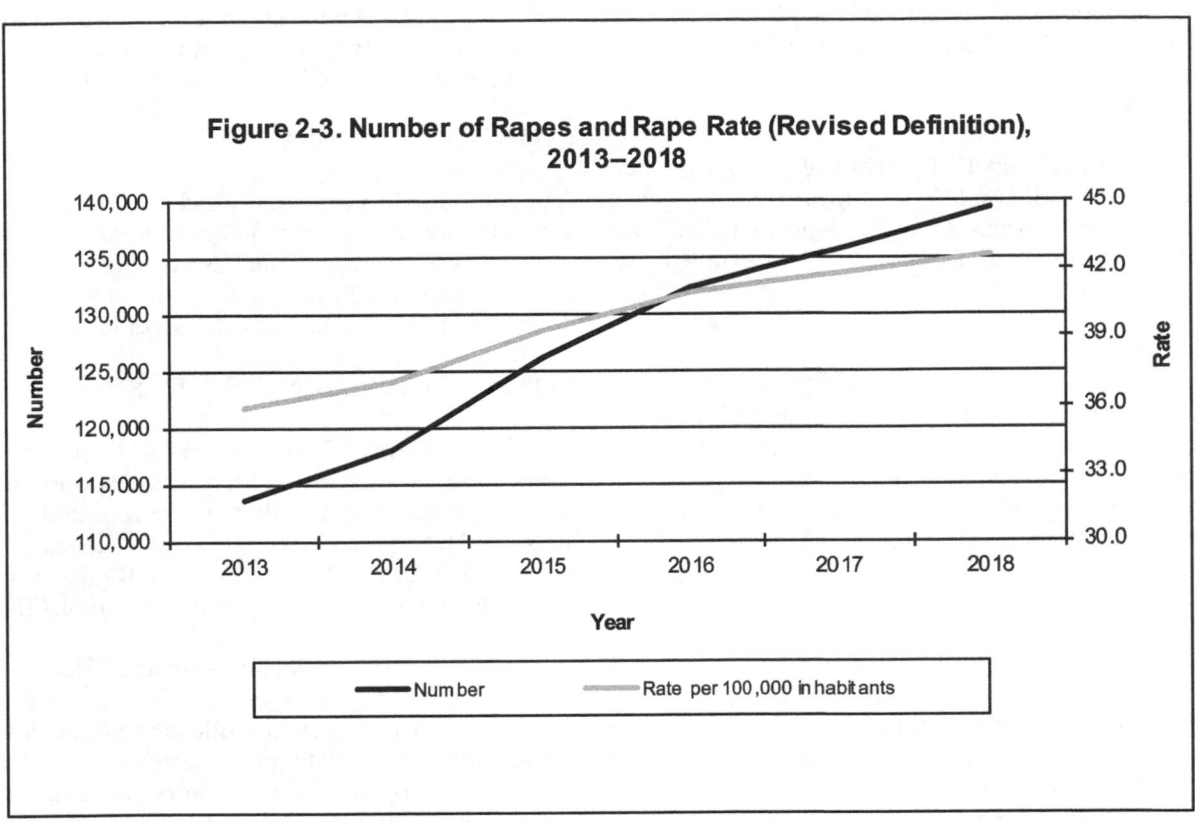

Figure 2-3. Number of Rapes and Rape Rate (Revised Definition), 2013–2018

Definition

In 2013, the FBI UCR Program began collecting rape data under a revised definition within the Summary Reporting System. Previously, offense data for forcible rape were collected under the legacy UCR definition: the carnal knowledge of a female forcibly and against her will. Beginning with the 2013 data year, the term "forcible" was removed from the offense title, and the definition was changed. The revised UCR definition of rape is: penetration, no matter how slight, of the vagina or anus with any body part or object, or oral penetration by a sex organ of another person, without the consent of the victim. Attempts or assaults to commit rape are also included in the statistics presented here; however, statutory rape and incest are excluded.

In 2016, the FBI Director approved the recommendation to discontinue the reporting of rape data using the UCR legacy definition beginning in 2017. However, to maintain the 20-year trend in Table 1, national estimates for rape under the legacy definition are provided along with estimates under the revised definition for 2017.

The UCR Program counts one offense for each victim of a rape, attempted rape, or assault with intent to rape, regardless of the victim's age. Non-consensual sexual relations involving a familial member is considered rape, not incest. All other crimes of a sexual nature are considered to be Part II offenses; as such, the UCR Program collects only arrest data for those crimes. The offense of statutory rape, in which no force is used but the female victim is under the age of consent, is included in the arrest total for the sex offenses category.

National Volume, Trends, and Rates

In 2018, the estimated number of rapes (revised definition), 139,380, increased 2.7 percent from the 2017 estimate. The estimated volume of rapes in 2018 was 18.1 percent higher than in the 2014 estimate. (Tables 1 and 1A)

Regional Offense Trends and Rates

The UCR program divides the United States into four regions: the Northeast, the South, the Midwest, and the

West. (More details concerning geographic regions are provided in Appendix IV) Regional analysis offers estimates of the volume of female rapes, the percent change from the previous year's estimate, and the rate of rape per 100,000 female inhabitants in each region.

NORTHEAST

The Northeast made up 17.2 percent of the U.S. population in 2018. An estimated 17,480 rapes—12.5 percent of the national total—occurred in the Northeast. This was an increase of 3.7 percent from the 2017 estimated figure. (Tables 3 and 4)

MIDWEST

The Midwest accounted for 20.9 percent of the U.S. population in 2018. Of all the rapes in the nation, 24.1 percent occurred in the Midwest in 2018. The 2018 estimate (33,628 rapes) represented an increase of 1.0 percent from the 2017 estimate. (Tables 3 and 4)

SOUTH

The South, the nation's most populous region, accounted for an estimated 38.1 percent of the nation's population in 2018; the region also accounted for an estimated 36.5 percent of the nation's estimated number of rapes. An estimated 50,833 victims reported rape in the South in 2018, up 2.3 percent from 2017. (Tables 3 and 4)

WEST

The West accounted for 23.8 percent of the nation's population in 2018. The region also accounted for 26.9 percent of the nation's total number of estimated rapes with an estimated 37,439 offenses. The West saw a 4.4 percent increase in rapes from 2017 to 2018. (Tables 3 and 4)

Community Types

Using the U.S. Office of Management and Budget's designations, the UCR program aggregates crime data by type of community in which the offenses occur: metropolitan statistical areas (MSAs), cities outside MSAs, and nonmetropolitan counties outside MSAs. (Appendix IV provides more detailed information about community types.)

MSAS

In 2018, MSAs accounted for 86.0 percent of the nation's population and 85.3 percent of the nation's estimated number of rapes (legacy definition). An estimated 119,842 victims were forcibly raped in metropolitan areas. (Table 2)

CITIES OUTSIDE MSAS

Cities outside MSAs are mostly incorporated areas that are served by city law enforcement agencies. Although accounting for only 5.8 percent of the U.S. population in 2018, cities outside MSAs accounted for 6.8 percent of the nation's estimated rapes (9,679 estimated offenses). (Table 2)

NONMETROPOLITAN COUNTIES

In 2018, approximately 8.3 percent of the nation's population lived in nonmetropolitan counties outside MSAs (counties made up of mostly non-incorporated areas that are served by non-city law enforcement agencies). Collectively, these areas had an estimated 9,841 rapes, representing 6.8 percent of the nation's estimated total. (Table 2)

Population Groups: Trends and Rates

The UCR program uses the following population group designations in its data presentations: cities (grouped according to population size) and counties (classified as either metropolitan or nonmetropolitan). A breakdown of these classifications is provided in Appendix IV.

From 2017 to 2018, the nation's cities experienced a 2.7 percent increase in rapes (see table notes for classification details). Cities with 1,000,000 or more inhabitants experienced the greatest increase (5.2 percent). Metropolitan counties experienced a 4.1 percent increase from 2017 to 2018, while nonmetropolitan counties experienced an increase of 0.2 percent. (Table 12)

In 2018, cities collectively had a rate of 48.0 rapes per 100,000 inhabitants. Cities with 250,000 to 499,999 inhabitants had the highest rate of rape (70.3 rapes per 100,000 inhabitants). Cities with 10,000 to 24,999 inhabitants had the lowest rate, with 36.6 rapes per 100,000 inhabitants. The rape rate for metropolitan counties was 34.4 per 100,000 inhabitants, and for nonmetropolitan counties, it was 40.7 per 100,000 inhabitants. Suburban areas had a rape rate of 33.5 per 100,000 inhabitants. (Table 16)

ROBBERY

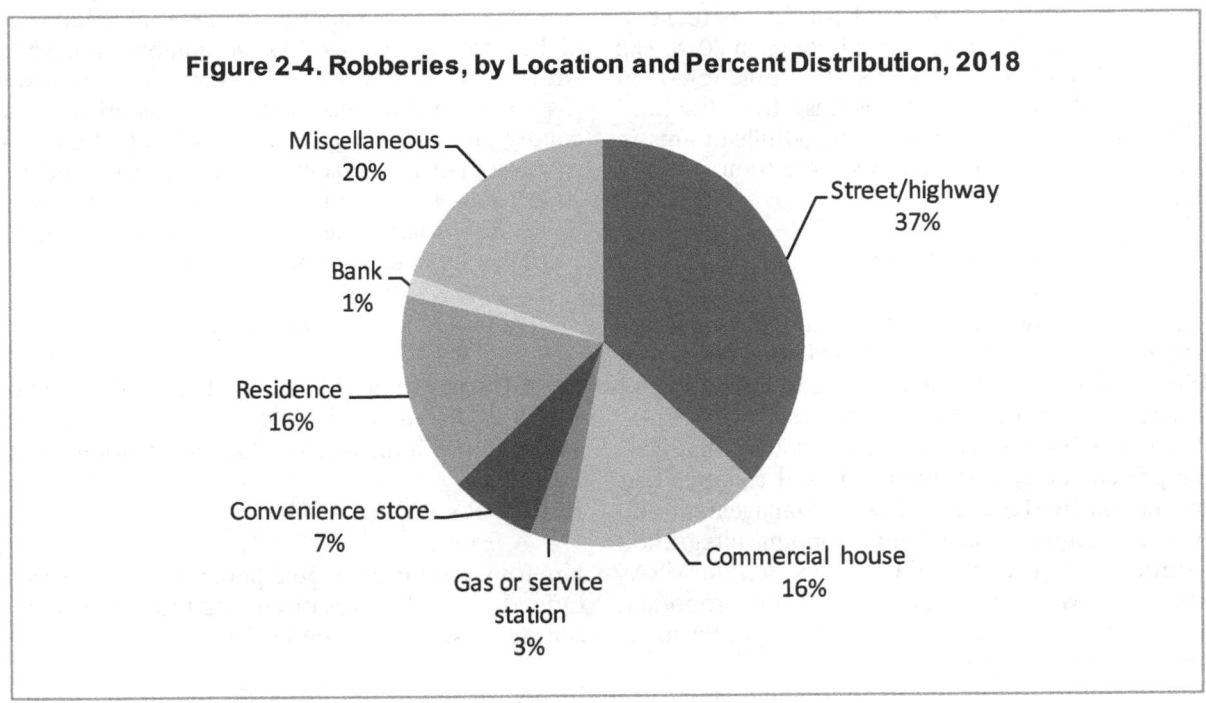

Figure 2-4. Robberies, by Location and Percent Distribution, 2018

Miscellaneous 20%

Bank 1%

Residence 16%

Convenience store 7%

Gas or service station 3%

Commercial house 16%

Street/highway 37%

Definition

The UCR program defines robbery as the taking or attempt to take anything of value from the care, custody, or control of a person or persons by force or threat of force or violence and/or by putting the victim in fear.

National Volume, Trends, and Rates

In 2018, the estimated robbery total (282,061) decreased 12.0 percent from the 2017 estimate. The 5-year robbery trend (2014 data compared with 2018 data) showed a decrease of 12.6 percent. The 2018 estimated robbery rate (86.2 per 100,000 inhabitants) showed a decrease of 12.6 percent when compared with the 2017 rate. (Tables 1 and 1A)

Regional Offense Trends and Rates

The UCR program divides the United States into four regions: the Northeast, the South, the Midwest, and the West. (More details concerning geographic regions are provided in Appendix IV.)

NORTHEAST

The Northeast, with an estimated 17.2 percent of the nation's population in 2018, accounted for 14.8 percent

of the nation's estimated number of robberies. The estimated number of robberies decreased 14.2 percent from 2017. The rate for this region was 74.6 robberies per 100,000 inhabitants, down from 86.9 robberies per 100,000 inhabitants in 2017. (Tables 3 and 4)

MIDWEST

The Midwest accounted for 20.9 percent of the total population of the United States and 17.8 percent of its estimated number of robberies in 2018. An estimated 50,269 robberies occurred in the Midwest in 2018, a 17.9 percent decrease from the estimated figure from 2017. The region's robbery rate was 73.6 robberies per 100,000 inhabitants in 2018. (Tables 3 and 4)

SOUTH

The South, the nation's most highly populated region, accounted for an estimated 38.1 percent of the nation's population and 37.9 percent of the nation's estimated number of robberies in 2018. Robberies accounted for an estimated 106,839 violent crimes in this region in 2018, representing a 12.6 percent decrease from the 2017 figure. The 2018 robbery rate in the South was 85.6 per 100,000 inhabitants, down 13.4 percent from 2017. (Tables 3 and 4)

WEST

The West was home to an estimated 23.8 percent of the nation's population and accounted for 29.5 percent of the nation's estimated number of robberies in 2018. The estimated number of robberies (83,106) in the region in 2018 represented a 6.0 percent decrease from the 2017 figure. The rate of robberies per 100,000 inhabitants in the West was 106.6, a 6.9 percent decrease from the 2017 rate. (Tables 3 and 4)

Community Types

The UCR program aggregates data for three community types: metropolitan statistical areas (MSAs), cities outside MSAs, and nonmetropolitan counties outside MSAs. MSAs include a central city or urbanized area with at least 50,000 inhabitants, as well as the county that contains the principal city and other adjacent counties that have, as defined by the U.S. Office of Management and Budget, a high degree of social and economic integration as measured through commuting. Cities outside MSAs are mostly incorporated areas, and nonmetropolitan counties are made up of mostly unincorporated areas served by non-city law enforcement.

In 2018, MSAs were home to an estimated 86.0 percent of the nation's population, and 95.1 percent of the nation's estimated number of robberies took place in these areas. Robberies in MSAs occurred at a rate of 96.6 per 100,000 inhabitants. Cities outside MSAs accounted for 5.7 percent of the U.S. population and accounted for 2.3 percent of the estimated number of robberies in the nation. The robbery rate for cities outside MSAs was 38.1 per 100,000 inhabitants. Nonmetropolitan counties made up 8.3 percent of the nation's estimated population and 0.9 percent of the nation's estimated robberies, at a rate of 12.4 robberies per 100,000 inhabitants. (Table 2)

Population Groups: Trends and Rates

The national UCR program aggregates data by various population groups, which include cities, metropolitan counties, and nonmetropolitan counties. A definition of these groups can be found in Appendix IV. The number of robberies in cities as a whole decreased by 11.6 percent between 2017 and 2018. Among the population groups and subsets labeled *city*, those cities with under 10,000 inhabitants had the greatest decrease in the number of robberies (14.8 percent). Nonmetropolitan counties had a 4.5 percent decrease in the estimated number of robberies, and metropolitan counties showed a 12.2 percent decrease. The number of robberies in suburban areas fell 13.5 percent. (Table 12)

Among the population groups, the nation's cities collectively had a rate of 114.9 robberies per 100,000 inhabitants. Of the population groups and subsets designated *city*, those with 500,000 to 999,999 inhabitants had the highest rate (239.8 per 100,000 inhabitants), while those with fewer than 10,000 inhabitants had the lowest rate (34.8 per 100,000 inhabitants) of robberies. Of the two county groups, metropolitan counties had a rate of 39.2 robberies per 100,000 inhabitants, while nonmetropolitan counties had a rate of 9.8 robberies per 100,000 inhabitants. Suburban areas had a robbery rate of 41.3 per 100,000 inhabitants. (Table 16)

Offense Analysis

The UCR program collects supplemental data about robberies to document the use of weapons, the dollar loss associated with the offense, and the location types.

ROBBERY BY WEAPON

Firearms were used in 38.2 percent of robberies in 2018. Offenders used knives or cutting instruments in 8.3 percent of these crimes. (Table 19)

LOSS BY DOLLAR VALUE

Based on the supplemental reports from law enforcement agencies, the average loss per robbery was $2,119. Average dollar losses were the highest for residences, which suffered an average loss of $4,600 per offense. Gas and service stations lost an average of $1,028 per offense. Commercial houses, which include supermarkets, department stores, and restaurants, had average losses of $1,546 per offense. An average of $4,303 was taken from banks. An average of $961 was lost in each offense against convenience stores. (Table 23)

ROBBERY TRENDS BY LOCATION

Among the location types, bank robberies had the greatest percentage decrease from 2017 to 2018, declining 18.2 percent. Robberies that occurred on streets and highways decreased 15.0 percent. (Table 23)

By location type, the greatest proportion of robberies in 2018 occurred on streets and highways (36.3 percent). Robbers targeted commercial houses in 16.1 percent of offenses and also struck residences in 16.1 percent of offenses. Convenience stores accounted for 7.0 percent of robberies, followed by gas and service stations (3.2 percent) and banks (1.6 percent). (Table 23)

AGGRAVATED ASSAULT

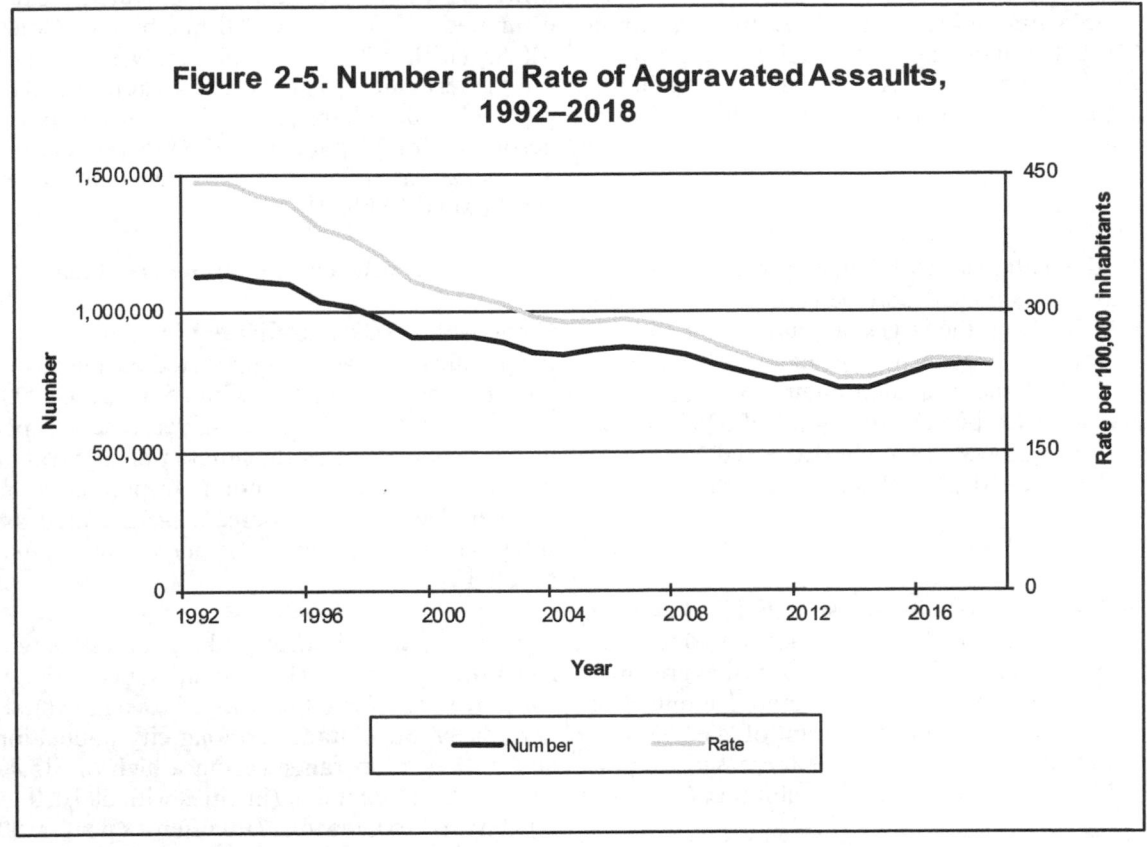

Figure 2-5. Number and Rate of Aggravated Assaults, 1992–2018

Definition

The UCR program defines aggravated assault as an unlawful attack by one person upon another for the purpose of inflicting severe or aggravated bodily injury. This type of assault is usually accompanied by the use of a weapon or by other means likely to produce death or great bodily harm. Attempted aggravated assaults that involve the display or threat of a gun, knife, or other weapon are included in this crime category because serious personal injury would likely result if these assaults were completed. When aggravated assault and larceny-theft occur together, the offense falls under the category of robbery.

National Volume, Trends, and Rates

In 2018, estimated occurrences of aggravated assaults totaled 807,410, a 0.4 percent decrease from the 2017 figure and a 0.6 percent decline when compared with the estimate for 2009. The estimated rate of aggravated assault in 2018 was 246.8 per 100,000 inhabitants, a 6.8 percent decrease from 2009. (Tables 1 and 1A)

Among the four types of violent crime offenses (murder, rape, robbery, and aggravated assault), aggravated assault typically has the highest rate of occurrence. This trend continued in 2018. (Table 1)

Regional Offense Trends and Rates

The UCR program divides the United States into four regions: the Northeast, the South, the Midwest, and the West. (More details concerning geographic regions are provided in Appendix IV.)

NORTHEAST

The region with the smallest proportion of the nation's population (an estimated 17.2 percent in 2018) also accounted for the smallest proportion of the nation's estimated number of aggravated assaults (12.8 percent). Occurrences of aggravated assault decreased 1.1 percent from 2017 to 2018, dropping to an estimated 102,967 incidents. The region continued to have the lowest aggravated assault rate in the nation, at 183.5 incidents per 100,000 inhabitants. (Tables 3 and 4)

MIDWEST

With 20.9 percent of the nation's total population in 2018, the Midwest accounted for approximately 19.7

percent of the nation's estimated number of aggravated assaults. Occurrences of this offense decreased 0.5 percent from the estimated total for 2017, dropping to an estimated 159,423 incidents. The region's aggravated assault rate, at 233.4 incidents per 100,000 inhabitants, represented a 0.7 percent decrease from the 2017 rate. (Tables 3 and 4)

SOUTH

The South, the nation's most highly populated region, accounted for an estimated 38.1 percent of the nation's population in 2018 and the largest amount of the nation's estimated number of aggravated assaults (42.0 percent). From 2017 to 2018, the estimated number of aggravated assaults decreased 1.8 percent to a total of 338,715 incidents. The rate of aggravated assaults decreased 2.7 percent to 271.5 incidents per 100,000 inhabitants. (Tables 3 and 4)

WEST

In 2018, the West was home to an estimated 23.8 percent of the nation's population. The region accounted for 25.6 percent of the nation's estimated number of aggravated assaults. From 2017 to 2018, the estimated number of offenses increased 2.5 percent to a total of 206,305 incidents. The rate of aggravated assaults increased 1.6 percent to 264.5 incidents per 100,000 inhabitants. (Tables 3 and 4)

Community Types

The UCR program aggregates data for three community types: metropolitan statistical areas (MSAs), cities outside MSAs, and nonmetropolitan counties outside MSAs. MSAs include a central city or urbanized area with at least 50,000 inhabitants, as well as the county that contains the principal city and other adjacent counties that have a high degree of social and economic integration as measured through commuting. Cities outside MSAs are mostly incorporated areas, and nonmetropolitan counties are made up of mostly unincorporated areas. (For additional information about community types, see Appendix IV.)

In 2018, 86.0 percent of the nation's population lived in MSAs, where the rate of aggravated assault was an estimated 253.5 per 100,000 inhabitants. Cities outside MSAs (with 5.7 percent of the U.S. population) had the highest rate of aggravated assault at 288.6 offenses per 100,000 inhabitants. Nonmetropolitan counties accounted for 8.3 percent of the U.S. population and had an offense rate of 148.9 aggravated assaults per 100,000 inhabitants. (Table 2)

Population Groups: Trends and Rates

Cities with 500,000 to 999,999 inhabitants experienced the greatest increase in aggravated assaults from 2017 to 2018 (0.9 percent). Cities with 25,000 to 49,999 inhabitants experienced the greatest decrease, 6.3 percent. In metropolitan counties, the number of aggravated assaults declined 0.3 percent; in nonmetropolitan counties, this number decreased 2.1 percent. Aggravated assaults in suburban areas decreased 1.4 percent from 2017 to 2018. (Table 12)

Aggravated assault occurred at an estimated rate of 250.0 offenses per 100,000 inhabitants nationwide. The collective rate for cities was 283.9 aggravated assaults per 100,000 inhabitants. Among city population groups and subsets, rates ranged from a high of 515.4 offenses per 100,000 inhabitants (in cities with 500,000 to 999,999 inhabitants) to a low of 171.0 offenses per 100,000 inhabitants (in cities with 25,000 to 49,999 inhabitants). The aggravated assault rate was 178.0 in metropolitan counties and 152.0 in nonmetropolitan counties. It was 164.0 in suburban areas. (Table 16)

Offense Analysis

AGGRAVATED ASSAULT BY WEAPON

Of the aggravated assault offenses for which law enforcement agencies provided expanded data in 2018, 25.2 percent involved personal weapons (such as hands, feet, and fists); 26.1 percent were committed with firearms; 17.3 percent involved knives or other cutting instruments; and 31.5 percent involved other weapons. (Table 19)

PROPERTY CRIME

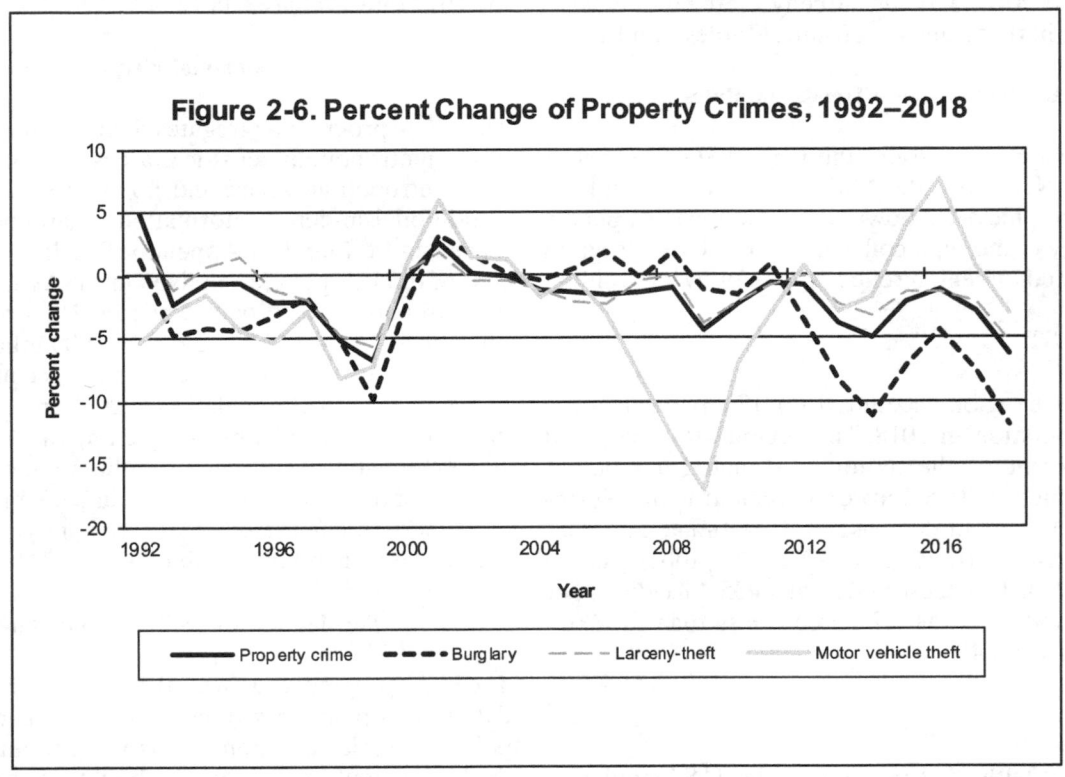

Figure 2-6. Percent Change of Property Crimes, 1992–2018

Definition

The UCR program's definition of property crime includes the offenses of burglary, larceny-theft, motor vehicle theft, and arson. The object of theft-type offenses is the taking of money or property without the use of force or threat of force against the victims. Property crime includes arson because the offense involves the destruction of property; however, arson victims may be subjected to force. Because of limited participation and the varying collection procedures conducted by local law enforcement agencies, only limited data are available for arson. Arson statistics are included in the trend, clearance, and arrest tables in *Crime in the United States*, but they are not included in any estimated volume data. More information on the expanded arson tables (which are available online but not included in this publication) can be found in Section I.

Data Collection

The data presented in *Crime in the United States* reflect the Hierarchy Rule, which counts only the most serious offense in a multiple-offense criminal incident. In descending order of severity, the violent crimes are murder and non-negligent manslaughter, rape, robbery, and aggravated assault; these are followed by the property crimes of burglary, larceny-theft, and motor vehicle theft. The Hierarchy Rule does not apply to the offense of arson.

National Volume, Trends, and Rates

An estimated 7,196,045 property crimes were committed in the United States in 2018, representing a 6.3 percent decrease from the 2017 (2-year trend) estimate, a 12.3 percent decrease from the 2014 (5-year trend) estimate, and a 22.9 percent decrease from the 2009 (10-year trend) estimate. (Tables 1 and 1A)

From 2017 to 2018, motor vehicle theft decreased 3.1 percent; from 2014 to 2018, it increased 9.0 percent, and from 2009 to 2018, it decreased 5.9 percent. Larceny-theft decreased 17.7 percent from 2009 to 2018, 10.2 percent from 2014 to 2018, and 5.4 percent from 2017 to 2018. Burglary in 2018 declined 44.2 percent from 2009, 28.2 percent from 2014, and 11.9 percent from 2017. (Tables 1 and 1A)

The estimated property crime rate per 100,000 inhabitants in 2018 was 2,199.5 incidents per 100,000 people, a 6.9 percent decrease from the 2017 rate, a 14.6 percent decrease from the 2014 rate, and a 27.7 percent decrease from the 2009 rate. The rate of burglaries per 100,000 residents fell 47.6 percent from 2009 to 2018. The motor vehicle theft rates per 100,000 residents fell 11.7 percent from 2009 to 2018, and the larceny-theft rate declined 17.7 percent in that same timeframe. (Tables 1 and 1A)

Regional Offense Trends and Rates

The UCR program separates the United States into four regions: the Northeast, the Midwest, the South, and the West. (Geographic breakdowns can be found in Appendix IV.) Property crime data collected by the UCR program and aggregated by region reflected the following results.

NORTHEAST

The Northeast region accounted for 17.2 percent of the nation's population in 2018. The region also accounted for 11.2 percent of the nation's estimated number of property crimes in 2018. Law enforcement in the Northeast saw a 7.6 percent decrease in the estimated number of property crimes from 2017 to 2018. The property crime rate for the Northeast, estimated at 1,435.4 incidents per 100,000 inhabitants, was 7.7 percent less than the 2017 rate. (Tables 3 and 4)

MIDWEST

The Midwest, with 20.9 percent of the U.S. population in 2018, accounted for 19.1 percent of the nation's estimated number of property crimes. Law enforcement in the Midwest saw the number of property crimes decrease 8.0 percent from 2017 to 2018. The rate of property crime in the Midwest in 2018, estimated at 2,016.7 incidents per 100,000 inhabitants, represented an 8.2 percent decrease from the 2017 rate. (Tables 3 and 4)

SOUTH

The South, the nation's most populous region, accounted for 38.1 percent of the U.S. population in 2018. The region also accounted for an estimated 42.2 percent of the nation's property crimes. The South experienced a 6.1 percent decrease in its estimated number of property crimes from 2017 to 2018. The 2018 property crime rate, an estimated 2,433.3 incidents per 100,000 inhabitants, dropped 7.0 percent from the 2017 rate. (Tables 3 and 4)

WEST

In 2018, the West accounted for 23.8 percent of the nation's population. The West also accounted for 27.5 percent of the nation's estimated number of property crimes. From 2017 to 2018, the estimated number of property crimes in this region decreased 5.0 percent. The estimated

property crime rate in the West in 2018, 2,535.4 incidents per 100,000 inhabitants, was a 5.8 percent decrease from the 2017 rate. (Tables 3 and 4)

Community Types

The UCR program aggregates data by three community types: metropolitan statistical areas (MSAs), cities outside metropolitan areas, and nonmetropolitan counties. (Additional in-depth information regarding community types can be found in Appendix IV.) In 2018, 86.0 percent of the U.S. population lived in MSAs and accounted for 87.6 percent of property crimes. The property crime rate for MSAs was 2,277.2 per 100,000 inhabitants. Cities outside metropolitan areas, which accounted for 5.7 percent of the total population in 2018 and 6.3 percent of property crimes, had a property crime rate of 2,638.6 per 100,000 inhabitants. Nonmetropolitan counties, with 8.3 percent of the nation's population in 2018 and 3.8 percent of property crimes, had a property crime rate of 1,094.3 per 100,000 inhabitants. (Table 2)

Population Groups: Trends and Rates

The UCR program organizes the agencies that contribute data into population groups, which include cities, metropolitan counties, and nonmetropolitan counties. (Appendix IV provides further details about these groups.) From 2017 to 2018, law enforcement in the nation's cities collectively reported a 6.1 percent decrease in the number of property crimes. All city groups experienced decreases in the number of property crimes; cities with under 10,000 residents had the greatest decline, 9.5 percent. Metropolitan counties also experienced a decrease of 7.4 percent from 2017 to 2018, while property crime in nonmetropolitan counties dropped 9.2 percent. (Table 12)

The nation's cities collectively had a property crime rate of 2,579.9 incidents per 100,000 inhabitants in 2018. Nonmetropolitan counties had a rate of 1,072.9 incidents per 100,000 inhabitants, and metropolitan counties had a rate of 1,473.0 incidents per 100,000 inhabitants. The rate was 1,665.6 in suburban areas. (Table 16)

Offense Analysis

The estimated dollar loss attributing to property crimes in 2018 was $16.4 billion. In 2018, the average dollar value per motor vehicle stolen in the United States was $8,407. The average dollar value of property taken during burglaries was $2,799, and during larceny-thefts, $1,153. (Tables 1 and 23) Arson had an average dollar loss of $17,406. Arsons of industrial/manufacturing structures had the highest average dollar loss ($100,578). (Expanded Arson Table 2)

BURGLARY

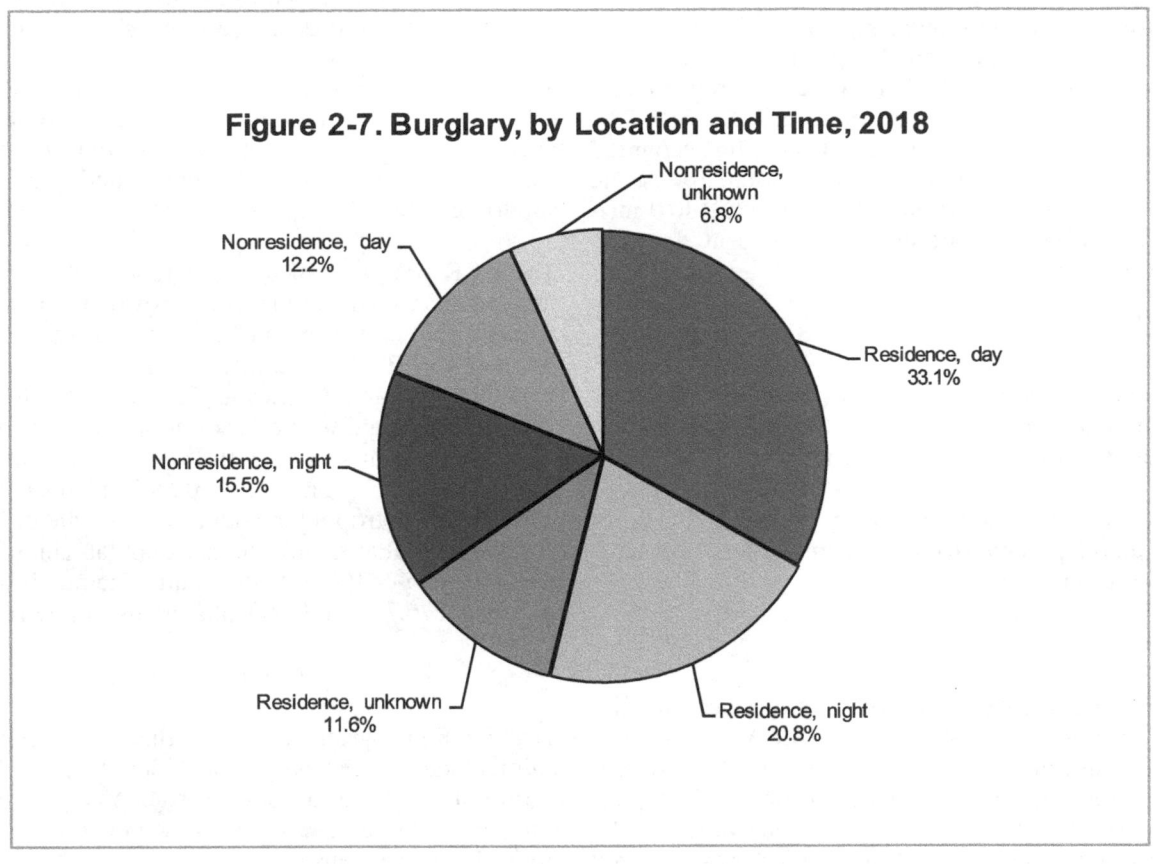

Figure 2-7. Burglary, by Location and Time, 2018

Nonresidence, unknown
6.8%

Nonresidence, day
12.2%

Residence, day
33.1%

Nonresidence, night
15.5%

Residence, unknown
11.6%

Residence, night
20.8%

Definition

The UCR program defines burglary as the unlawful entry of a structure to commit a felony or theft. To classify an offense as a burglary, the use of force to gain entry need not have occurred. The program has three subclassifications for burglary: forcible entry, unlawful entry where no force is used, and attempted forcible entry. The UCR definition of "structure" includes, but is not limited to, apartments, barns, house trailers or houseboats (when used as permanent dwellings), offices, railroad cars (but not automobiles), stables, and vessels (such as ships).

National Volume, Trends, and Rate

In 2018, there were an estimated 1,230,149 burglaries—a decrease of 11.9 percent when compared with 2017 data. There was a decrease of 28.2 percent in the number of burglaries in 2018 when compared with the 2014 estimate, and a decrease of 44.2 percent when compared with the 2009 estimate. Burglary accounted for 17.1 percent of the estimated number of property crimes committed in 2018. The burglary rate for the United States in 2018 was 376.0 incidents per 100,000 inhabitants, a 12.5 percent decrease from the 2017 rate. (Tables 1 and 1A)

Regional Offense Trends and Rates

The UCR program divides the United States into four regions: the Northeast, the Midwest, the South, and the West. (Details regarding these regions can be found in Appendix IV.) An analysis of burglary data by region showed the following details.

NORTHEAST

In 2018, 17.2 percent of the nation's population lived in the Northeast. This region accounted for 8.8 percent of the estimated total number of burglary offenses in the nation in 2018. The region's burglary rate, an estimated 192.7 offenses per 100,000 inhabitants, represented a decrease of 15.3 percent from the 2017 rate. (Tables 3 and 4)

MIDWEST

The Midwest accounted for 20.9 percent of the nation's population in 2018. This region accounted for 19.2 percent of the nation's estimated number of burglaries. In this region, the estimated number of burglaries dropped 13.6 percent from 2017 to 2018. The Midwest had a burglary rate of 345.4 offenses per 100,000 inhabitants, a 13.8 percent decrease from the 2017 rate. (Tables 3 and 4)

SOUTH

The South, the nation's most highly populated region (38.1 percent of all inhabitants), had the most burglaries in 2018 (an estimated 548,927); however, this represented a 12.6 percent drop from its estimate in 2017. With 38.1 percent of the nation's population, this region accounted for 44.6 percent of all burglaries in the United States. The estimated rate of burglary in the South was 440.0 incidents per 100,000 inhabitants, a 13.4 percent decrease from the 2017 rate. (Tables 3 and 4)

WEST

The West accounted for 23.8 percent of the nation's population in 2018. This region accounted for an estimated 27.4 percent of the nation's burglaries. The region's burglary rate was 432.3, an 9.3 percent decrease from the 2017 rate. The total number of burglaries (337,171) represented an 8.5 percent decrease from the 2017 estimate. (Tables 3 and 4)

Community Types

The UCR program aggregates data by three community types: metropolitan statistical areas (MSAs), cities outside MSAs, and nonmetropolitan counties. (See Appendix IV for more information regarding community types.) In 2018, 86.0 percent of the U.S. population lived in MSAs, and an estimated 83.9 percent of all burglaries occurred in this type of community. Inhabitants of cities outside MSAs accounted for 5.7 percent of the total population in 2018 and 6.7 percent of the estimated number of burglaries; nonmetropolitan counties, with 8.3 percent of the U.S. population, accounted for 6.6 percent of all burglaries. The burglary rates per 100,000 inhabitants were 373.0 in MSAs, 485.5 in cities outside MSAs, and 331.8 in nonmetropolitan counties. (Table 2)

Population Groups: Trends and Rates

In addition to analyzing data by region and community type, the UCR program aggregates crime statistics by population groups. Cities are categorized into six groups based on the number of inhabitants; counties are categorized into two groups, metropolitan and nonmetropolitan. (Appendix IV offers further details regarding these population groups.)

An examination of data from law enforcement agencies showed that the nation's cities experienced a collective 11.5 percent decrease in burglaries from 2017 to 2018. Burglaries decreased in all city groups and subsets, with cities under 10,000 inhabitants posting the greatest decrease (14.6 percent). The volume of burglaries decreased 13.9 percent in metropolitan counties, 13.8 percent in nonmetropolitan counties, and 14.3 percent in suburban areas. (Table 12)

The UCR program calculates burglary rates for population groups from the information provided by participating agencies that submitted all 12 months of offense data for the year. In 2018, the nation's cities had 404.9 offenses per 100,000 inhabitants. Cities with 500,000 to 999,999 inhabitants had the highest burglary rate at 645.6 incidents per 100,000 inhabitants. Cities with 25,000 to 49,999 inhabitants had the lowest burglary rate—312.9 incidents per 100,000 inhabitants. Metropolitan counties had a rate of 288.6 per 100,000 inhabitants, and nonmetropolitan counties had a rate of 314.9 per 100,000 inhabitants. The rate in suburban areas was 276.7 per 100,000 inhabitants. (Table 16)

Offense Analysis

The UCR program requests that participating law enforcement agencies provide details regarding the nature of burglaries in their jurisdictions, such as type of entry, type of structure, time of day, and dollar loss associated with each offense.

Of all burglaries in 2018, 56.7 percent involved forcible entry, 36.7 percent were unlawful entries (without force), and 6.6 percent comprised forcible entry attempts. (Table 19)

Victims of burglary offenses suffered an estimated $3.4 billion in lost property in 2018; overall, the average dollar loss per burglary offense was $2,799. (Tables 1 and 23)

As in the past, burglars targeted residences more often than nonresidential structures. In 2018, burglaries of residential properties accounted for 65.5 percent of all burglary offenses. Of the burglaries for which time of day could be established, most burglaries of residences (33.1 percent of all reported burglaries) occurred during the day, while most burglaries of nonresidential structures (15.5 percent of all reported burglaries) occurred at night. (Table 23)

LARCENY-THEFT

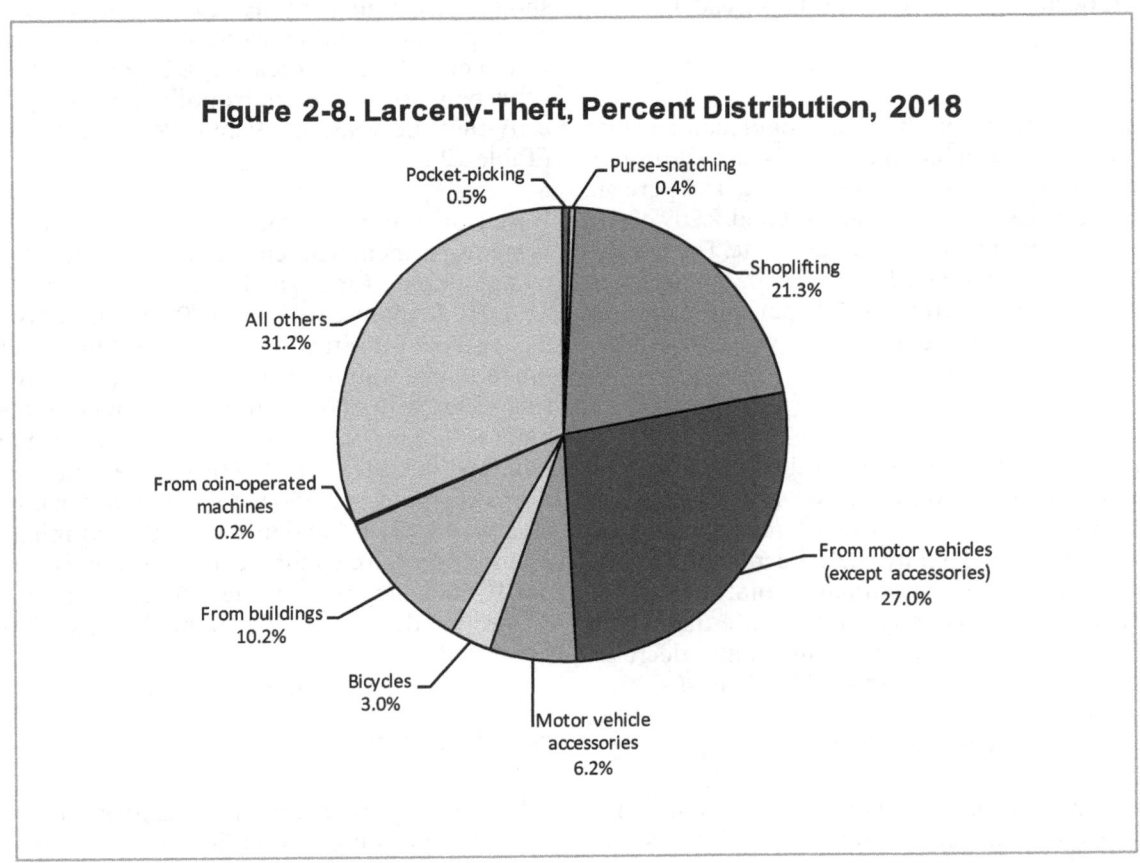

Figure 2-8. Larceny-Theft, Percent Distribution, 2018

- Pocket-picking 0.5%
- Purse-snatching 0.4%
- Shoplifting 21.3%
- All others 31.2%
- From coin-operated machines 0.2%
- From buildings 10.2%
- Bicycles 3.0%
- Motor vehicle accessories 6.2%
- From motor vehicles (except accessories) 27.0%

Definition

The UCR program defines larceny-theft as the unlawful taking, carrying, leading, or riding away of property from the possession or constructive possession of another. Examples are thefts of bicycles, motor vehicle parts and accessories, shoplifting, pocket picking, or the stealing of any property or article not taken by force and violence or by fraud. Attempted larcenies are included. Embezzlement, confidence games, forgery, check fraud, and so on, are excluded from this category.

National Volume, Trends, and Rates

Larceny-thefts accounted for an estimated 72.5 percent of property crimes in 2018—an estimated 5,217,055 larceny-thefts nationwide. The estimated number of larceny-thefts declined 5.4 from 2017 to 2018. The 2018 estimate showed a 10.2 percent decline from the 2014 data and a 17.7 percent decline from the 2009 estimate. The trend data also showed decreases in the larceny-theft rates per 100,000 inhabitants during these periods. The rate of larceny-thefts declined 6.0 percent from 2017 to 2018 and 22.8 percent from 2009 to 2018. (Tables 1 and 1A)

Regional Offense Trends and Rates

The UCR program defines four regions within the United States: the Northeast, the Midwest, the South, and the West. (See Appendix IV for a geographical description of each region.)

NORTHEAST

The Northeast was the region with the smallest proportion (17.2 percent) of the U.S. population in 2018. The region also experienced the fewest larceny-thefts in the country, accounting for only 12.3 percent of all larceny-thefts. The estimated number of offenses in 2018 (642,606) represented a 6.6 percent decline from 2017, and the estimated rate—1,145.2 incidents per 100,000 inhabitants—also represented a 6.6 percent decline. (Tables 3 and 4)

MIDWEST

With 20.9 percent of the U.S. population in 2018, the Midwest accounted for an estimated 19.4 percent of the nation's larceny-thefts (the same proportion as in 2017). The estimated number of offenses (1,010,073) declined

7.1 percent compared with the 2017 data, and the estimated rate of occurrence (1,478.7 incidents per 100,000 inhabitants) declined 7.3 percent. (Tables 3 and 4)

SOUTH

With nearly two-fifths of the U.S. population in 2018 (38.1 percent), the South had the nation's highest proportion of larceny-theft offenses: an estimated 42.4 percent. (Estimated offenses in this region totaled 2,209,438, a 5.2 percent decrease from the 2017 estimate. The South's larceny-theft rate—estimated at 1,771.0 offenses per 100,000 inhabitants—decreased 6.1 percent from the 2017 estimate. (Tables 3 and 4)

WEST

In 2018, an estimated 23.8 percent of the U.S. population lived in the West. This region was also where 26.0 percent of the nation's estimated number of larceny-thefts took place. Occurrences of larceny-theft decreased 3.8 percent from 2017 to 2018 to an estimated total of 1,354,938 offenses. The region's larceny-theft rate, estimated at 1,737.2 offenses per 100,000 inhabitants, was a decrease of 4.6 percent from the 2017 rate. (Tables 3 and 4)

Community Types

The UCR program aggregates data for three community types: metropolitan statistical areas (MSAs), cities outside MSAs, and nonmetropolitan counties outside MSAs. MSAs include a central city or urbanized area with at least 50,000 inhabitants, as well as the county that contains the principal city and other adjacent counties that share a high degree of social and economic integration as measured through commuting. Cities outside MSAs are mostly incorporated areas, and nonmetropolitan counties are composed of unincorporated areas. (See Appendix IV for more information regarding community types.)

In 2018, MSAs were home to an estimated 86.0 percent of the nation's population and experienced 88.0 percent of the nation's larceny-theft incidents. Cities outside MSAs accounted for 5.7 percent of the U.S. population and 6.5 percent of larceny-theft offenses. Nonmetropolitan counties, which were home to 8.3 percent of the nation's population, accounted for 3.2 percent of the estimated number of larceny-theft offenses. The larceny-theft rates per 100,000 inhabitants were 1,658.9 in MSAs, 1,994.9 in cities outside MSAs, and 654.9 in nonmetropolitan counties. (Table 2)

Population Groups: Trends and Rates

In cities, collectively, occurrences of larceny-theft decreased 5.2 percent between 2017 and 2018. Cities with under 10,000 inhabitants experienced the greatest decrease (9.1 percent). Larceny-theft continued to show decline in counties and suburban areas—nonmetropolitan counties experienced the greatest drop in larceny thefts, decreasing 8.2 percent, followed by suburban areas and metropolitan counties, with larceny-theft decreasing 6.9 and 5.9 percent, respectively. (Table 12)

Based on reports of larceny-theft offenses from U.S. law enforcement agencies that submitted 12 months of complete data for 2018, this offense occurred at a rate of 1,610.5 offenses per 100,000 inhabitants. The collective rate for cities was 1,900.8 offenses per 100,000 inhabitants. Among city population groups and subsets, cities with 500,000 to 999,000 inhabitants had the highest larceny-theft rate, 2,718.6 incidents per 100,000 inhabitants. Cities with 10,000 to 24,999 inhabitants had the lowest rate, at 1,750.6. In metropolitan counties, the rate was 1,031.6 incidents per 100,000 inhabitants; in nonmetropolitan counties, the rate was 649.5 incidents per 100,000 inhabitants. The rate in suburban areas was 1,241.3 incidents per 100,000 inhabitants. (Table 16)

Offense Analysis

DISTRIBUTION

Table 23 provides a further breakdown of larceny-theft offenses, including shoplifting, thefts from buildings, thefts of motor vehicle accessories, thefts of bicycles, thefts from coin-operated machines, purse snatching, and pocket picking. The "all other" category, which includes the less-defined types of larceny-theft, accounted for 31.2 percent of all offenses in 2018.

LOSS BY DOLLAR VALUE

Larceny-theft offenses cost victims an estimated $6.0 billion dollars in 2018. The average value of property stolen was $1,153 per offense, $146 more than in 2017. Larceny-theft from buildings had the highest average dollar loss per offense at $1,610. Thefts from motor vehicles (except accessories) had an average dollar loss of $994 per offense; thefts of motor vehicle accessories, $648; purse snatching, $718; pocket picking, $1,169; thefts from coin-operated machines, $851; thefts of bicycles, $546; and shoplifting, $304. (Tables 1 and 23)

Offenses in which the stolen property was valued at more than $200 accounted for 46.7 percent of all larceny-thefts in 2018. Table 23 provides further analysis, including the average dollar value per offense of all offenses in the overall category of property crime. (Table 23)

MOTOR VEHICLE THEFT

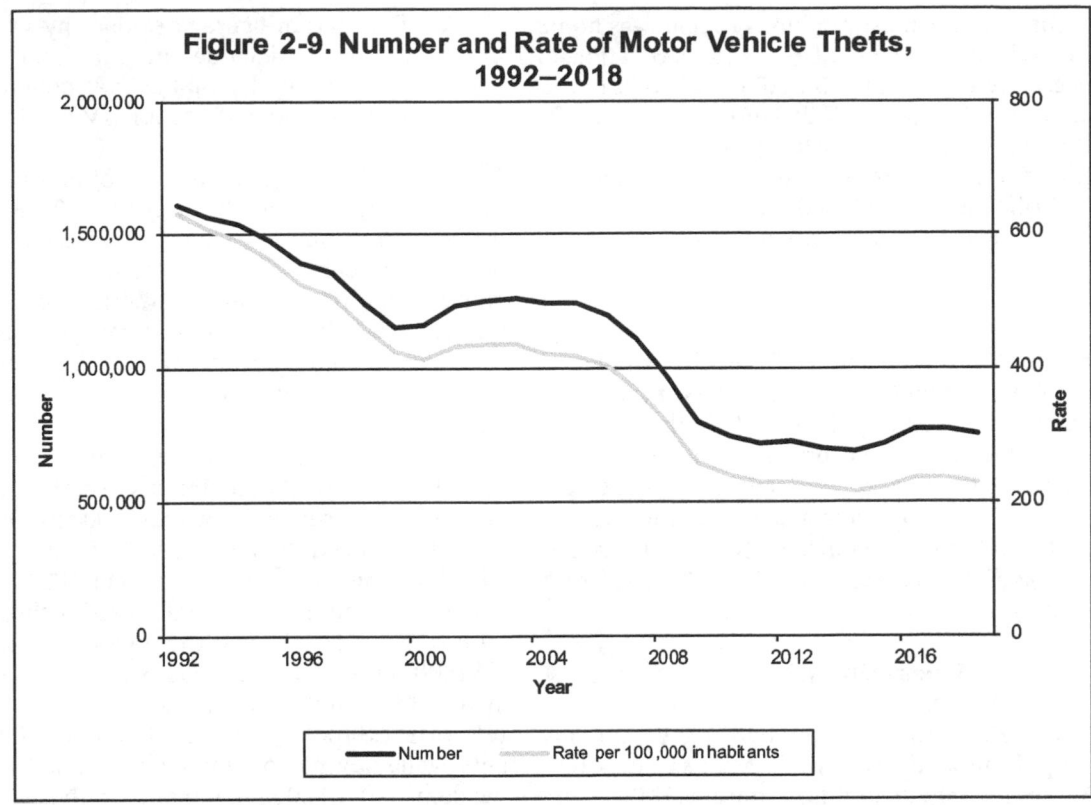

Figure 2-9. Number and Rate of Motor Vehicle Thefts, 1992–2018

Definition

The UCR program defines motor vehicle theft as the theft or attempted theft of a motor vehicle. The offense includes the stealing of automobiles, trucks, buses, motorcycles, snowmobiles, etc. The taking of a motor vehicle for temporary use by a person or persons with lawful access is excluded.

National Volume, Trends, and Rates

In 2018, an estimated 748,841 motor vehicle thefts took place in the United States. The estimated number of motor vehicle thefts decreased 3.1 percent when compared with data from 2017 but increased 9.0 percent when compared with 2014 figures. Occurrences decreased 5.9 percent when compared with 2009 figures. (Tables 1 and 1A)

The estimated rate of motor vehicle theft in 2018 was 228.9 incidents per 100,000 inhabitants. The 2018 rate was 3.7 percent less than the 2017 rate, 6.3 percent higher than the 2014 rate, and 11.7 percent lower than the 2009 rate. (Tables 1 and 1A)

Regional Offense Trends and Rates

In order to analyze crime by geographic area, the UCR program divides the United States into four regions:

the Northeast, the Midwest, the South, and the West. (Appendix IV provides a map delineating the regions.) This section provides a regional overview of motor vehicle theft.

NORTHEAST

The Northeast accounted for an estimated 17.2 percent of the nation's population in 2018. The region also accounted for an estimated 7.3 percent of its motor vehicle thefts. An estimated 54,709 motor vehicle thefts occurred in the Northeast in 2018, a 3.5 percent drop in occurrences from 2017. The estimated rate of 97.5 motor vehicle thefts per 100,000 inhabitants in the Northeast in 2018 represented a 3.6 percent decline from the 2017 rate. (Tables 3 and 4)

MIDWEST

An estimated 20.9 percent of the country's population resided in the Midwest in 2018. The region accounted for 17.6 percent of the nation's motor vehicle thefts. The Midwest had an estimated 131,562 motor vehicle thefts in 2018, a decrease of 3.8 percent from the previous year's total. The motor vehicle theft rate was estimated at 192.6 motor vehicles stolen per 100,000 inhabitants, a decrease of 4.0 percent from the 2017 rate. (Tables 3 and 4)

SOUTH

The South, the nation's most populous region, was home to an estimated 38.1 percent of the U.S. population in 2018 and accounted for 37.0 percent of the nation's motor vehicle thefts. The estimated 277,259 motor vehicle thefts in the South was up 0.9 percent from the 2017 estimate. Motor vehicles in the South were stolen at an estimated rate of 222.2 offenses per 100,000 inhabitants in 2018, a rate that was static from 2017. (Tables 3 and 4)

WEST

With approximately 23.8 percent of the U.S. population in 2018, the West accounted for the highest percentage (38.1 percent) of all motor vehicle thefts in the nation in 2018. An estimated 285,311 motor vehicle thefts occurred in this region. This number represented a 6.4 percent decrease from the previous year's estimate. The region's 2018 rate of 365.8 motor vehicles stolen per 100,000 inhabitants was 7.2 percent lower than the 2017 rate. (Tables 3 and 4)

Community Types

The UCR program aggregates data by three community types: metropolitan statistical areas (MSAs), cities outside MSAs, and nonmetropolitan counties. MSAs are areas that include a principal city or urbanized area with at least 50,000 inhabitants and the county that contains the principal city and other adjacent counties that have, as defined by the U.S. Office of Management and Budget, a high degree of economic and social integration.

In 2018, the vast majority (86.0 percent) of the U.S. population resided in MSAs, where approximately 91.1 percent of motor vehicle thefts occurred. For 2018, the UCR program estimated an overall rate of 245.3 motor vehicles stolen per 100,000 MSA inhabitants. Cities outside MSAs, with 5.7 percent of the U.S. population, accounted for 3.7 percent of motor vehicle thefts, and nonmetropolitan counties, with 8.3 percent of the population, accounted for 3.6 percent of motor vehicle thefts. The UCR program estimated a 2018 rate of 158.2 motor vehicles stolen for every 100,000 inhabitants in cities outside MSAs and a rate of 107.6 motor vehicles stolen per 100,000 inhabitants in nonmetropolitan counties. (Table 2)

Population Groups: Trends and Rates

The UCR program aggregates data by various population groups, which include cities, metropolitan counties, and nonmetropolitan counties. (A definition of these groups can be found in Appendix IV.)

In cities, collectively, the number of motor vehicle thefts decreased 3.2 percent from 2017 to 2018. Occurrences dropped in all subsets. Cities with 50,000 to 99,999 residents experienced the greatest decline at 5.5 percent. Nonmetropolitan counties experienced a decrease of 0.7 percent, suburban areas experienced a decrease of 3.1 percent, and metropolitan counties experienced a decrease of 3.0 percent. (Table 12)

In 2018, cities had a collective motor vehicle theft rate of 274.2 per 100,000 inhabitants. Among the population groups and subsets, cities with 500,000 to 999,999 inhabitants experienced the highest rate of motor vehicle thefts with 506.2 motor vehicle thefts per 100,000 inhabitants. Conversely, the nation's smallest cities, those with populations under 10,000, had the lowest rate of motor vehicle theft with 137.5 incidents per 100,000 in population. Within the county groups, metropolitan counties had a rate of 152.8 motor vehicles stolen per 100,000 inhabitants, while nonmetropolitan counties had a rate of 108.5 incidents per 100,000 inhabitants. Suburban areas had a rate of 147.6 per 100,000 inhabitants. (Table 16)

Offense Analysis

Based on the reports of law enforcement agencies, the UCR program estimated the combined value of motor vehicles stolen nationwide in 2018 at $6.3 billion. In 2018, the average dollar value per motor vehicle stolen in the United States was $8,407. (Tables 1 and 23) Automobiles were, by far, the most frequently stolen vehicles, accounting for 74.9 percent of all vehicles stolen. Trucks and buses accounted for 15.9 percent of stolen vehicles, and other vehicles accounted for 9.3 percent of stolen vehicles. (Expanded Motor Vehicle Theft Table)

By type of vehicle, automobiles were stolen at a rate of 177.8 cars per 100,000 inhabitants in 2018. Trucks and buses were stolen at a rate of 37.4 vehicles per 100,000 inhabitants, and other types of vehicles were stolen at a rate of 22.0 vehicles per 100,000 inhabitants. (Table 19)

ARSON

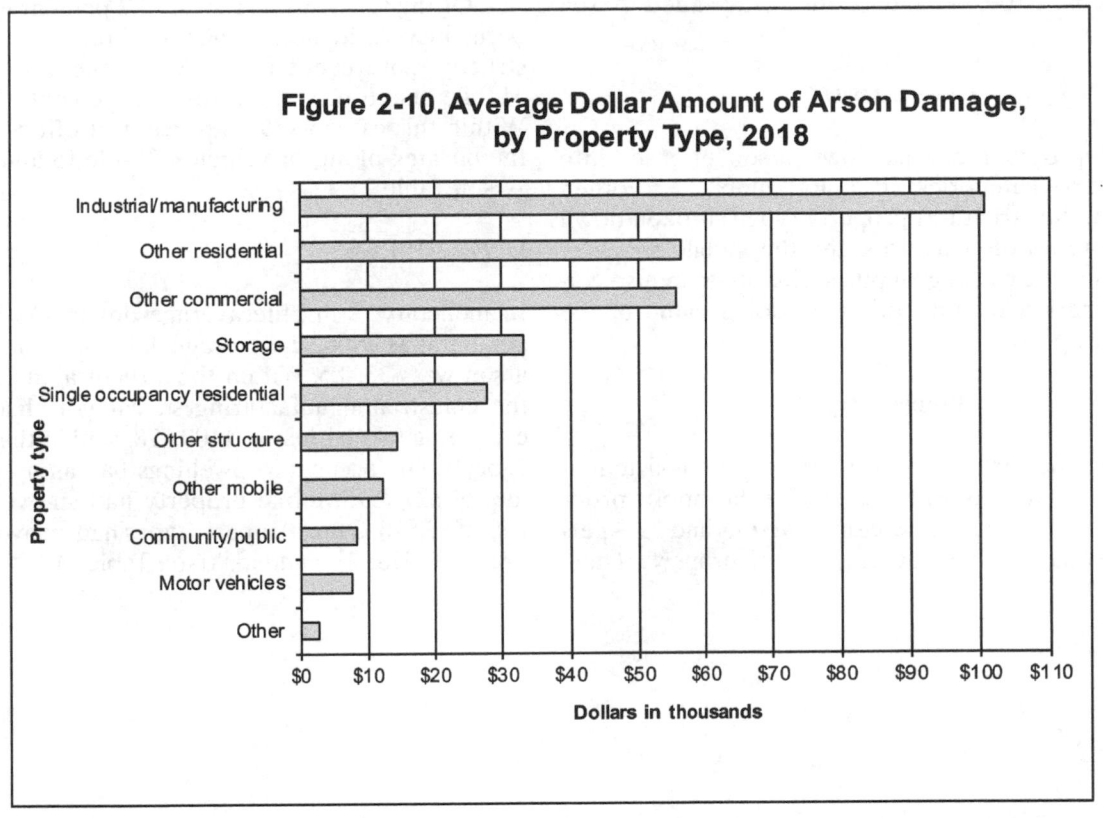

Figure 2-10. Average Dollar Amount of Arson Damage, by Property Type, 2018

Definition

The UCR program defines arson as any willful or malicious burning or attempt to burn (with or without intent to defraud) a dwelling house, public building, motor vehicle, aircraft, or personal property of another, etc.

Data Collection

Only fires that investigators determined were willfully set (not fires labeled as "suspicious" or "of unknown origin") are included in this arson data collection. Points to consider regarding arson statistics include:

National offense rates per 100,000 inhabitants (found in Tables 1, 2, and 4) do not include arson data; the FBI presents rates for arson separately. Arson rates are calculated based upon data received from all law enforcement agencies that provide the UCR program with data for 12 complete months.

Arson data collection does not include estimates for arson, because the degree of reporting arson offenses varies from agency to agency. Because of this unevenness of reporting, arson offenses are excluded from Tables 1 through 7, all of which contain offense estimations.

The number of arsons reported by individual law enforcement agencies is available in Tables 8 through 11. Arson trend data (which indicate year-to-year changes) can be found in Tables 12 through 15.

Population Groups: Trends and Rates

The number of arsons reported in cities 2018 was 9.5 percent lower than the number reported in 2017. Among the population groups labeled *city*, the subset with 500,000 to 999,999 inhabitants reported the largest decrease (13.9 percent). Agencies in the nation's metropolitan counties reported an 11.0 percent decrease in the number of arsons, while those in nonmetropolitan counties reported a 9.9 percent decrease from 2017 to 2018. Those in suburban areas reported a 12.1 percent decline. (Table 12)

Arson rates in this paragraph were based on information received from 13,856 agencies that provided 12 months of complete arson data to the UCR program. An examination of data indicated that in 2018, the highest rate among city groups and subsets—25.1 arsons per 100,000 inhabitants—was reported in cities with 500,000 to 999,999 inhabitants. Cities with 10,000 to 24,999 inhabitants had the lowest rate of arson at 8.5 per 100,000 inhabitants. Metropolitan counties had 8.7 arsons per 100,000 inhabitants, and nonmetropolitan counties had 9.1 arsons per 100,000 inhabitants. The rate in suburban areas was 8.6 arsons per 100,000 inhabitants. (Expanded Arson Table 1)

Offense Analysis

The UCR program breaks down arson offenses into three property categories: structural, mobile, and other. In addition, the structural property type is broken down into seven types of structures, and the mobile property type consists of two subgroupings. The program also collects information on the estimated dollar value of the damaged property.

Property Type

Arsons for the structural property type consisted of 44.0 percent of arsons, while arsons for the mobile property type comprised 24.2 percent of arsons and 31.8 percent of arsons involved other types of property (such as crops, timber, fences, etc.). Of the arsons involving structures, 63.9 percent involved residential properties. Of the residential arsons, 73.7 percent were single-occupancy residences. Approximately 20.2 percent of structures were not in use when the arson occurred. Mobile arsons accounted for 24.2 percent of all arsons. Within this category, 93.8 percent of offenses involved the burning of motor vehicles. (Table 15 and Expanded Arson Table 2)

DOLLAR LOSS

In monetary terms, the average dollar loss in 2018 for arson was $17,406. The average dollar loss for a structural arson was $33,485. Within the structural arson category, the industrial/manufacturing subcategory had the highest average dollar loss at $100,578. Within that same category, single-occupancy dwellings had an average dollar loss of $27,751. Mobile property had an average dollar loss of $7,816. Other property types had an average dollar loss of $2,478. (Expanded Arson Table 2)

Table 1. Crime in the United States, by Volume and Rate Per 100,000 Inhabitants, 1999–2018

(Number, rate per 100,000 population.)

Year	Population[1]	Violent crime[2]		Murder and nonnegligent manslaughter		Rape (revised definition)[3]		Rape (legacy definition)[4]		Robbery		Aggravated assault	
		Number	Rate	Number	Rate	Number	Rate	Number	Rate	Number	Rate	Number	Rate
1999	272,690,813	1,426,044	523.0	15,522	5.7	X	X	89,411	32.8	409,371	150.1	911,740	334.3
2000	281,421,906	1,425,486	506.5	15,586	5.5	X	X	90,178	32.0	408,016	145.0	911,706	324.0
2001[5]	285,317,559	1,439,480	504.5	16,037	5.6	X	X	90,863	31.8	423,557	148.5	909,023	318.6
2002	287,973,924	1,423,677	494.4	16,229	5.6	X	X	95,235	33.1	420,806	146.1	891,407	309.5
2003	290,788,976	1,383,676	475.8	16,528	5.7	X	X	93,883	32.3	414,235	142.5	859,030	295.4
2004	293,656,842	1,360,088	463.2	16,148	5.5	X	X	95,089	32.4	401,470	136.7	847,381	288.6
2005	296,507,061	1,390,745	469.0	16,740	5.6	X	X	94,347	31.8	417,438	140.8	862,220	290.8
2006	299,398,484	1,435,123	479.3	17,309	5.8	X	X	94,472	31.6	449,246	150.0	874,096	292.0
2007	301,621,157	1,422,970	471.8	17,128	5.7	X	X	92,160	30.6	447,324	148.3	866,358	287.2
2008	304,059,724	1,394,461	458.6	16,465	5.4	X	X	90,750	29.8	443,563	145.9	843,683	277.5
2009	307,006,550	1,325,896	431.9	15,399	5.0	X	X	89,241	29.1	408,742	133.1	812,514	264.7
2010	309,330,219	1,251,248	404.5	14,722	4.8	X	X	85,593	27.7	369,089	119.3	781,844	252.8
2011	311,587,816	1,206,005	387.1	14,661	4.7	X	X	84,175	27.0	354,746	113.9	752,423	241.5
2012	313,873,685	1,217,057	387.8	14,856	4.7	X	X	85,141	27.1	355,051	113.1	762,009	242.8
2013	316,497,531	1,168,298	369.1	14,319	4.5	113,695	35.9	82,109	25.9	345,093	109.0	726,777	229.6
2014	318,907,401	1,153,022	361.6	14,164	4.4	118,027	37.0	84,864	26.6	322,905	101.3	731,089	229.2
2015	320,896,618	1,199,310	373.7	15,883	4.9	126,134	39.3	91,261	28.4	328,109	102.2	764,057	238.1
2016	323,405,935	1,250,162	386.6	17,413	5.4	132,414	40.9	96,970	30.0	332,797	102.9	802,982	248.3
2017[6]	325,147,121	1,247,917	383.8	17,294	5.3	135,666	41.7	99,708	30.7	320,596	98.6	810,319	249.2
2018	327,167,434	1,206,836	368.9	16,214	5.0	139,380	42.6	101,151	30.9	282,061	86.2	807,410	246.8

Table 1. Crime in the United States, by Volume and Rate Per 100,000 Inhabitants, 1999–2018—Continued

(Number, rate per 100,000 population.)

Year	Property crime		Burglary		Larceny-theft		Motor vehicle theft	
	Number	Rate	Number	Rate	Number	Rate	Number	Rate
1999	10,208,334	3,743.6	2,100,739	770.4	6,955,520	2,550.7	1,152,075	422.5
2000	10,182,584	3,618.3	2,050,992	728.8	6,971,590	2,477.3	1,160,002	412.2
2001[5]	10,437,189	3,658.1	2,116,531	741.8	7,092,267	2,485.7	1,228,391	430.5
2002	10,455,277	3,630.6	2,151,252	747.0	7,057,379	2,450.7	1,246,646	432.9
2003	10,442,862	3,591.2	2,154,834	741.0	7,026,802	2,416.5	1,261,226	433.7
2004	10,319,386	3,514.1	2,144,446	730.3	6,937,089	2,362.3	1,237,851	421.5
2005	10,174,754	3,431.5	2,155,448	726.9	6,783,447	2,287.8	1,235,859	416.8
2006	10,019,601	3,346.6	2,194,993	733.1	6,626,363	2,213.2	1,198,245	400.2
2007	9,882,212	3,276.4	2,190,198	726.1	6,591,542	2,185.4	1,100,472	364.9
2008	9,774,152	3,214.6	2,228,887	733.0	6,586,206	2,166.1	959,059	315.4
2009	9,337,060	3,041.3	2,203,313	717.7	6,338,095	2,064.5	795,652	259.2
2010	9,112,625	2,945.9	2,168,459	701.0	6,204,601	2,005.8	739,565	239.1
2011	9,052,743	2,905.4	2,185,140	701.3	6,151,095	1,974.1	716,508	230.0
2012	9,001,992	2,868.0	2,109,932	672.2	6,168,874	1,965.4	723,186	230.4
2013	8,651,892	2,733.6	1,932,139	610.5	6,019,465	1,901.9	700,288	221.3
2014	8,209,010	2,574.1	1,713,153	537.2	5,809,054	1,821.5	686,803	215.4
2015	8,024,115	2,500.5	1,587,564	494.7	5,723,488	1,783.6	713,063	222.2
2016	7,928,530	2,451.6	1,516,405	468.9	5,644,835	1,745.4	767,290	237.3
2017[6]	7,682,988	2,362.9	1,397,045	429.7	5,513,000	1,695.5	772,943	237.7
2018	7,196,045	2,199.5	1,230,149	376.0	5,217,055	1,594.6	748,841	228.9

Note: Although arson data are included in the trend and clearance tables, sufficient data are not available to estimate totals for this offense. Therefore, no arson data are published in this table.
X = Not applicable.
1 Populations are U.S. Census Bureau provisional estimates as of July 1 for each year except 2000 and 2010, which are decennial census counts.   2 The violent crime figures include the offenses of murder, rape (legacy definition), robbery, and aggravated assault.   3 The figures shown in this column for the offense of rape were estimated using the revised UCR definition of rape.   4 The figures shown in this column for the offense of rape were estimated using the legacy UCR definition of rape.   5 The murder and nonnegligent homicides that occurred as a result of the events of September 11, 2001, are not included in this table.   6 The crime figures have been adjusted.

Table 1A. Crime in the United States, Percent Change in Volume and Rate Per 100,000 Inhabitants for 2 Years, 5 Years, and 10 Years, 2009–2018

(Percent change.)

Year	Violent crime		Murder and nonnegligent manslaughter		Rape (revised definition)[2]		Rape (legacy definition)[3]		Robbery		Aggravated assault		Property crime		Burglary		Larceny-theft		Motor vehicle theft	
	Number[1]	Rate	Number	Rate	Number	Rate	Number	Rate	Number	Rate	Number	Rate	Number	Rate	Number	Rate	Number	Rate	Number	Rate
2009–2018	-3.3	-3.9	-6.2	-6.8	+2.7	+2.1	+1.4	+0.8	-12.0	-12.6	-0.4	-1.0	-6.3	-6.9	-11.9	-12.5	-5.4	-6.0	-3.1	-3.7
2014–2018	+4.7	+2.0	+14.5	+11.6	+18.1	+15.1	+19.2	+16.2	-12.6	-14.9	+10.4	+7.7	-12.3	-14.6	-28.2	-30.0	-10.2	-12.5	+9.0	+6.3
2017–2018	-9.0	-14.6	+5.3	-1.2	X	X	+13.3	+6.4	-31.0	-35.2	-0.6	-6.8	-22.9	-27.7	-44.2	-47.6	-17.7	-22.8	-5.9	-11.7

X = Not applicable.   1 The violent crime figures include the offenses of murder, rape (legacy definition), robbery, and aggravated assault.   2 The figures shown in this column for the offense of rape were estimated using the revised UCR definition of rape.   3 The figures shown in this column for the offense of rape were estimated using the legacy UCR definition of rape.

Table 2. Crime, by Community Type, 2017–2018

(Number, rate per 100,000 population, percent.)

Area	Population[1]	Violent crime[2]	Murder and nonnegligent manslaughter	Rape[3]	Robbery	Aggravated assault	Property crime	Burglary	Larceny-theft	Motor vehicle theft
United States	327,167,434	1,245,065	16,214	139,380	282,061	807,410	7,196,045	1,230,149	5,217,055	748,841
Rate per 100,000 inhabitants		380.6	5.0	42.6	86.2	246.8	2,199.5	376.0	1,594.6	228.9
Metropolitan Statistical Area	281,259,303									
Area actually reporting[4]	98.2	1,105,433	14,428	118,836	268,371	703,798	6,305,123	1,032,441	4,590,178	682,504
Estimated total	100.0	1,118,920	14,575	119,842	271,561	712,942	6,404,896	1,049,087	4,665,845	689,964
Rate per 100,000 inhabitants		397.8	5.2	42.6	96.6	253.5	2,277.2	373.0	1,658.9	245.3
Cities Outside Metropolitan Areas	18,699,875									
Area actually reporting[4]	90.7	68,036	711	9,439	6,461	51,425	452,123	82,867	341,223	28,033
Estimated total	100.0	71,517	727	9,697	7,126	53,967	493,416	90,789	373,036	29,591
Rate per 100,000 inhabitants		382.4	3.9	51.9	38.1	288.6	2,638.6	485.5	1,994.9	158.2
Cities Outside Metropolitan Areas	27,208,256									
Area actually reporting[4]	92.0	50,616	889	9,527	2,595	37,605	273,319	80,962	165,134	27,223
Estimated total	100.0	54,628	912	9,841	3,374	40,501	297,733	90,273	178,174	29,286
Rate per 100,000 inhabitants		200.8	3.4	36.2	12.4	148.9	1,094.3	331.8	654.9	107.6

Note: Although arson data are included in the trend and clearance tables, sufficient data are not available to estimate totals for this offense. Therefore, no arson data are published in this table.

1 Population figures are U.S. Census Bureau provisional estimates as of July 1, 2018.   2 The violent crime figures include the offenses of murder, rape (revised definition), robbery, and aggravated assault.   3 The figures shown in this column for the offense of rape were estimated using the revised Uniform Crime Reporting definition of rape.   4 The percentage reported under "Area actually reporting" is based upon the population covered by agencies providing 3 months or more of crime reports to the FBI.

Table 3. Crime in the United States, Population and Offense Distribution, by Region, 2018

(Percent distribution.)

Region	Population	Violent crime	Murder and nonnegligent manslaughter	Rape (revised definition)[1]	Robbery	Aggravated assault	Property crime	Burglary	Larceny-theft	Motor vehicle theft
United States[2]	100.0	100.0	100.0	100.0	100.0	100.0	100.0	100.0	100.0	100.0
Northeast	17.2	13.2	11.9	12.5	14.8	12.8	11.2	8.8	12.3	7.3
Midwest	20.9	19.8	22.0	24.1	17.8	19.7	19.1	19.2	19.4	17.6
South	38.1	40.5	46.2	36.5	37.9	42.0	42.2	44.6	42.4	37.0
West	23.8	26.5	19.9	26.9	29.5	25.6	27.5	27.4	26.0	38.1

Note. Although arson data are included in the trend and clearance tables, sufficient data are not available to estimate totals for this offense. Therefore, no arson data are published in this table.   1 The figures shown in the rape column were calculated using the revised Uniform Crime Reporting (UCR) definition of rape.   2 Because of rounding, the percentages may not add to 100.0.

Table 4. Crime in the United States,[1] by Region, Geographic Division, and State, 2017–2018

(Number, rate per 100,000 population, percent.)

Area	Population[2]	Violent crime[3]		Murder and nonnegligent manslaughter		Rape[4]		Robbery	
		Number	Rate	Number	Rate	Number	Rate	Number	Rate
United States[5,6]									
2017	325,147,121	1,283,875	394.9	17,294	5.3	135,666	41.7	320,596	98.6
2018	327,167,434	1,245,065	380.6	16,214	5.0	139,380	42.6	282,061	86.2
Percent change		-3.0	-3.6	-6.2	-6.8	+2.7	+2.1	-12.0	-12.6
Northeast									
2017	56,072,676	171,696	306.2	1,967	3.5	16,864	30.1	48,745	86.9
2018	56,111,079	164,216	292.7	1,922	3.4	17,480	31.2	41,847	74.6
Percent change		-4.4	-4.4	-2.3	-2.4	+3.7	+3.6	-14.2	-14.2
New England									
2017	14,802,967	40,316	272.4	351	2.4	4,846	32.7	8,951	60.5
2018	14,853,290	37,992	255.8	290	2.0	4,998	33.6	7,448	50.1
Percent change		-5.8	-6.1	-17.4	-17.7	+3.1	+2.8	-16.8	-17.1
Connecticut									
2017	3,573,880	8,190	229.2	105	2.9	850	23.8	2,813	78.7
2018	3,572,665	7,411	207.4	83	2.3	840	23.5	2,194	61.4
Percent change		-9.5	-9.5	-21.0	-20.9	-1.2	-1.1	-22.0	-22.0
Maine									
2017	1,335,063	1,610	120.6	23	1.7	470	35.2	249	18.7
2018	1,338,404	1,501	112.1	24	1.8	446	33.3	228	17.0
Percent change		-6.8	-7.0	+4.3	+4.1	-5.1	-5.3	-8.4	-8.7
Massachusetts									
2017	6,863,246	24,318	354.3	172	2.5	2,199	32.0	4,874	71.0
2018	6,902,149	23,337	338.1	136	2.0	2,410	34.9	4,143	60.0
Percent change		-4.0	-4.6	-20.9	-21.4	+9.6	+9.0	-15.0	-15.5
New Hampshire									
2017	1,349,767	2,642	195.7	13	1.0	619	45.9	441	32.7
2018	1,356,458	2,349	173.2	21	1.5	534	39.4	359	26.5
Percent change		-11.1	-11.5	+61.5	+60.7	-13.7	-14.2	-18.6	-19.0
Rhode Island									
2017	1,056,486	2,474	234.2	21	2.0	454	43.0	474	44.9
2018	1,057,315	2,317	219.1	16	1.5	481	45.5	454	42.9
Percent change		-6.3	-6.4	-23.8	-23.9	+5.9	+5.9	-4.2	-4.3
Vermont									
2017	624,525	1,082	173.3	17	2.7	254	40.7	100	16.0
2018	626,299	1,077	172.0	10	1.6	287	45.8	70	11.2
Percent change		-0.5	-0.7	-41.2	-41.3	+13.0	+12.7	-30.0	-30.2
Middle Atlantic									
2017	41,269,709	131,380	318.3	1,616	3.9	12,018	29.1	39,794	96.4
2018	41,257,789	126,224	305.9	1,632	4.0	12,482	30.3	34,399	83.4
Percent change		-3.9	-3.9	+1.0	+1.0	+3.9	+3.9	-13.6	-13.5
New Jersey									
2017	8,888,543	20,604	231.8	324	3.6	1,505	16.9	7,895	88.8
2018	8,908,520	18,537	208.1	286	3.2	1,424	16.0	6,364	71.4
Percent change		-10.0	-10.2	-11.7	-11.9	-5.4	-5.6	-19.4	-19.6
New York									
2017	19,590,719	70,746	361.1	550	2.8	6,297	32.1	20,122	102.7
2018	19,542,209	68,495	350.5	562	2.9	6,575	33.6	18,187	93.1
Percent change		-3.2	-2.9	+2.2	+2.4	+4.4	+4.7	-9.6	-9.4
Pennsylvania									
2017	12,790,447	40,030	313.0	742	5.8	4,216	33.0	11,777	92.1
2018	12,807,060	39,192	306.0	784	6.1	4,483	35.0	9,848	76.9
Percent change		-2.1	-2.2	+5.7	+5.5	+6.3	+6.2	-16.4	-16.5
Midwest[5]									
2017	68,156,035	258,578	379.4	3,922	5.8	33,279	48.8	61,226	89.8
2018	68,308,744	246,887	361.4	3,567	5.2	33,628	49.2	50,269	73.6
Percent change		-4.5	-4.7	-9.1	-9.3	+1.0	+0.8	-17.9	-18.1
East North Central									
2017	46,878,905	180,226	384.5	2,898	6.2	23,156	49.4	46,868	100.0
2018	46,931,883	171,888	366.2	2,613	5.6	23,467	50.0	38,477	82.0
Percent change		-4.6	-4.7	-9.8	-9.9	+1.3	+1.2	-17.9	-18.0
Illinois									
2017	12,786,196	55,777	436.2	983	7.7	5,424	42.4	17,731	138.7
2018	12,741,080	51,490	404.1	884	6.9	5,859	46.0	14,208	111.5
Percent change		-7.7	-7.4	-10.1	-9.8	+8.0	+8.4	-19.9	-19.6
Indiana									
2017	6,660,082	26,307	395.0	413	6.2	2,612	39.2	7,035	105.6
2018	6,691,878	25,581	382.3	438	6.5	2,370	35.4	5,939	88.7
Percent change		-2.8	-3.2	+6.1	+5.5	-9.3	-9.7	-15.6	-16.0
Michigan									
2017	9,976,447	44,883	449.9	569	5.7	7,110	71.3	6,508	65.2
2018	9,995,915	44,918	449.4	551	5.5	7,690	76.9	5,656	56.6
Percent change		+0.1	-0.1	-3.2	-3.4	+8.2	+7.9	-13.1	-13.3
Ohio									
2017	11,664,129	34,621	296.8	741	6.4	5,833	50.0	11,224	96.2
2018	11,689,442	32,723	279.9	564	4.8	5,300	45.3	9,185	78.6
Percent change		-5.5	-5.7	-23.9	-24.1	-9.1	-9.3	-18.2	-18.3

Table 4. Crime in the United States,[1] by Region, Geographic Division, and State, 2017–2018—Continued

(Number, rate per 100,000 population, percent.)

Area	Aggravated assault		Property crime		Burglary		Larceny-theft		Motor vehicle theft	
	Number	Rate	Number	Rate	Number	Rate	Number	Rate	Number	Rate
United States[5,6,7]										
2017	810,319	249.2	7,682,988	2,362.9	1,397,045	429.7	5,513,000	1,695.5	772,943	237.7
2018	807,410	246.8	7,196,045	2,199.5	1,230,149	376.0	5,217,055	1,594.6	748,841	228.9
Percent change	-0.4	-1.0	-6.3	-6.9	-11.9	-12.5	-5.4	-6.0	-3.1	-3.7
Northeast										
2017	104,120	185.7	872,031	1,555.2	127,621	227.6	687,693	1,226.4	56,717	101.1
2018	102,967	183.5	805,435	1,435.4	108,120	192.7	642,606	1,145.2	54,709	97.5
Percent change	-1.1	-1.2	-7.6	-7.7	-15.3	-15.3	-6.6	-6.6	-3.5	-3.6
New England										
2017	26,168	176.8	228,239	1,541.8	36,877	249.1	173,141	1,169.6	18,221	123.1
2018	25,256	170.0	207,956	1,400.1	30,647	206.3	159,890	1,076.5	17,419	117.3
Percent change	-3.5	-3.8	-8.9	-9.2	-16.9	-17.2	-7.7	-8.0	-4.4	-4.7
Connecticut										
2017	4,422	123.7	63,646	1,780.9	8,906	249.2	47,418	1,326.8	7,322	204.9
2018	4,294	120.2	60,055	1,681.0	7,948	222.5	44,724	1,251.8	7,383	206.7
Percent change	-2.9	-2.9	-5.6	-5.6	-10.8	-10.7	-5.7	-5.6	+0.8	+0.9
Maine										
2017	868	65.0	20,142	1,508.7	3,337	250.0	16,012	1,199.3	793	59.4
2018	803	60.0	18,173	1,357.8	2,713	202.7	14,683	1,097.1	777	58.1
Percent change	-7.5	-7.7	-9.8	-10.0	-18.7	-18.9	-8.3	-8.5	-2.0	-2.3
Massachusetts										
2017	17,073	248.8	97,977	1,427.6	16,916	246.5	73,573	1,072.0	7,488	109.1
2018	16,648	241.2	87,196	1,263.3	13,862	200.8	66,728	966.8	6,606	95.7
Percent change	-2.5	-3.0	-11.0	-11.5	-18.1	-18.5	-9.3	-9.8	-11.8	-12.3
New Hampshire										
2017	1,569	116.2	18,550	1,374.3	2,554	189.2	15,087	1,117.7	909	67.3
2018	1,435	105.8	16,935	1,248.5	1,847	136.2	14,219	1,048.2	869	64.1
Percent change	-8.5	-9.0	-8.7	-9.2	-27.7	-28.0	-5.8	-6.2	-4.4	-4.9
Rhode Island										
2017	1,525	144.3	18,585	1,759.1	3,219	304.7	13,882	1,314.0	1,484	140.5
2018	1,366	129.2	17,561	1,660.9	2,810	265.8	13,220	1,250.3	1,531	144.8
Percent change	-10.4	-10.5	-5.5	-5.6	-12.7	-12.8	-4.8	-4.8	+3.2	+3.1
Vermont										
2017	711	113.8	9,339	1,495.4	1,945	311.4	7,169	1,147.9	225	36.0
2018	710	113.4	8,036	1,283.1	1,467	234.2	6,316	1,008.5	253	40.4
Percent change	-0.1	-0.4	-14.0	-14.2	-24.6	-24.8	-11.9	-12.1	+12.4	+12.1
Middle Atlantic										
2017	77,952	188.9	643,792	1,560.0	90,744	219.9	514,552	1,246.8	38,496	93.3
2018	77,711	188.4	597,479	1,448.2	77,473	187.8	482,716	1,170.0	37,290	90.4
Percent change	-0.3	-0.3	-7.2	-7.2	-14.6	-14.6	-6.2	-6.2	-3.1	-3.1
New Jersey										
2017	10,880	122.4	140,086	1,576.0	23,891	268.8	104,025	1,170.3	12,170	136.9
2018	10,463	117.4	125,156	1,404.9	19,232	215.9	94,887	1,065.1	11,037	123.9
Percent change	-3.8	-4.0	-10.7	-10.9	-19.5	-19.7	-8.8	-9.0	-9.3	-9.5
New York										
2017	43,777	223.5	293,390	1,497.6	34,928	178.3	245,093	1,251.1	13,369	68.2
2018	43,171	220.9	281,507	1,440.5	31,137	159.3	237,233	1,214.0	13,137	67.2
Percent change	-1.4	-1.1	-4.1	-3.8	-10.9	-10.6	-3.2	-3.0	-1.7	-1.5
Pennsylvania										
2017	23,295	182.1	210,316	1,644.3	31,925	249.6	165,434	1,293.4	12,957	101.3
2018	24,077	188.0	190,816	1,489.9	27,104	211.6	150,596	1,175.9	13,116	102.4
Percent change	+3.4	+3.2	-9.3	-9.4	-15.1	-15.2	-9.0	-9.1	+1.2	+1.1
Midwest[5]										
2017	160,151	235.0	1,497,290	2,196.9	273,100	400.7	1,087,436	1,595.5	136,754	200.6
2018	159,423	233.4	1,377,566	2,016.7	235,931	345.4	1,010,073	1,478.7	131,562	192.6
Percent change	-0.5	-0.7	-8.0	-8.2	-13.6	-13.8	-7.1	-7.3	-3.8	-4.0
East North Central										
2017	107,304	228.9	979,344	2,089.1	184,078	392.7	709,853	1,514.2	85,413	182.2
2018	107,331	228.7	902,564	1,923.1	158,284	337.3	663,365	1,413.5	80,915	172.4
Percent change	*	-0.1	-7.8	-7.9	-14.0	-14.1	-6.5	-6.7	-5.3	-5.4
Illinois										
2017	31,639	247.4	255,108	1,995.2	43,355	339.1	190,860	1,492.7	20,893	163.4
2018	30,539	239.7	246,264	1,932.8	39,080	306.7	187,591	1,472.3	19,593	153.8
Percent change	-3.5	-3.1	-3.5	-3.1	-9.9	-9.5	-1.7	-1.4	-6.2	-5.9
Indiana										
2017	16,247	243.9	158,932	2,386.3	29,799	447.4	114,395	1,717.6	14,738	221.3
2018	16,834	251.6	145,838	2,179.3	25,268	377.6	105,242	1,572.7	15,328	229.1
Percent change	+3.6	+3.1	-8.2	-8.7	-15.2	-15.6	-8.0	-8.4	+4.0	+3.5
Michigan										
2017	30,696	307.7	179,839	1,802.6	35,833	359.2	124,410	1,247.0	19,596	196.4
2018	31,021	310.3	165,280	1,653.5	31,651	316.6	116,178	1,162.3	17,451	174.6
Percent change	+1.1	+0.9	-8.1	-8.3	-11.7	-11.8	-6.6	-6.8	-10.9	-11.1
Ohio										
2017	16,823	144.2	280,557	2,405.3	57,521	493.1	202,320	1,734.5	20,716	177.6
2018	17,674	151.2	254,496	2,177.1	48,186	412.2	186,401	1,594.6	19,909	170.3
Percent change	+5.1	+4.8	-9.3	-9.5	-16.2	-16.4	-7.9	-8.1	-3.9	-4.1

Table 4. Crime in the United States,[1] by Region, Geographic Division, and State, 2017–2018—Continued

(Number, rate per 100,000 population, percent.)

Area	Population[2]	Violent crime[3]		Murder and nonnegligent manslaughter		Rape[4]		Robbery	
		Number	Rate	Number	Rate	Number	Rate	Number	Rate
Wisconsin									
2017	5,792,051	18,638	321.8	192	3.3	2,177	37.6	4,370	75.4
2018	5,813,568	17,176	295.4	176	3.0	2,248	38.7	3,489	60.0
Percent change		-7.8	-8.2	-8.3	-8.7	+3.3	+2.9	-20.2	-20.5
West North Central[5]									
2017	21,277,130	78,352	368.2	1,024	4.8	10,123	47.6	14,358	67.5
2018	21,376,861	74,999	350.8	954	4.5	10,161	47.5	11,792	55.2
Percent change[5]		-4.3	-4.7	-6.8	-7.3	+0.4	-0.1	-17.9	-18.3
Iowa[5]									
2017	3,143,637	9,038	287.5	98	3.1	1,305	41.5	1,269	40.4
2018	3,156,145	7,893	250.1	54	1.7	976	30.9	932	29.5
Percent change		-12.7	-13.0	-44.9	-45.1	-25.2	-25.5	-26.6	-26.8
Kansas									
2017	2,910,689	11,654	400.4	134	4.6	1,504	51.7	1,633	56.1
2018	2,911,505	12,782	439.0	113	3.9	1,567	53.8	1,543	53.0
Percent change		+9.7	+9.6	-15.7	-15.7	+4.2	+4.2	-5.5	-5.5
Minnesota									
2017	5,568,155	13,345	239.7	114	2.0	2,405	43.2	3,627	65.1
2018	5,611,179	12,369	220.4	106	1.9	2,462	43.9	2,944	52.5
Percent change		-7.3	-8.0	-7.0	-7.7	+2.4	+1.6	-18.8	-19.5
Missouri									
2017	6,108,612	32,450	531.2	599	9.8	2,737	44.8	6,362	104.1
2018	6,126,452	30,758	502.1	607	9.9	2,912	47.5	5,197	84.8
Percent change		-5.2	-5.5	+1.3	+1.0	+6.4	+6.1	-18.3	-18.5
Nebraska									
2017	1,917,575	5,979	311.8	42	2.2	1,191	62.1	1,020	53.2
2018	1,929,268	5,494	284.8	44	2.3	1,233	63.9	756	39.2
Percent change		-8.1	-8.7	+4.8	+4.1	+3.5	+2.9	-25.9	-26.3
North Dakota									
2017	755,176	2,133	282.5	10	1.3	406	53.8	183	24.2
2018	760,077	2,133	280.6	18	2.4	397	52.2	158	20.8
Percent change		-0.6		+80.0	+78.8	-2.2	-2.8	-13.7	-14.2
South Dakota									
2017	873,286	3,753	429.8	27	3.1	575	65.8	264	30.2
2018	882,235	3,570	404.7	12	1.4	614	69.6	262	29.7
Percent change		-4.9	-5.8	-55.6	-56.0	+6.8	+5.7	-0.8	-1.8
South[6,7]									
2017	123,598,424	524,545	424.4	7,918	6.4	49,678	40.2	122,178	98.9
2018	124,753,948	503,882	403.9	7,495	6.0	50,833	40.7	106,839	85.6
Percent change		-3.9	-4.8	-5.3	-6.2	+2.3	+1.4	-12.6	-13.4
South Atlantic[6,7]									
2017	64,641,801	252,228	390.2	4,033	6.2	21,428	33.1	62,109	96.1
2018	65,322,408	242,051	370.5	3,925	6.0	22,499	34.4	54,312	83.1
Percent change		-4.0	-5.0	-2.7	-3.7	+5.0	+3.9	-12.6	-13.5
Delaware									
2017	957,078	4,377	457.3	51	5.3	351	36.7	1,082	113.1
2018	967,171	4,097	423.6	48	5.0	338	34.9	866	89.5
Percent change		-6.4	-7.4	-5.9	-6.9	-3.7	-4.7	-20.0	-20.8
District of Columbia[6]									
2017	695,691	6,976	1,002.7	116	16.7	444	63.8	2,625	377.3
2018	702,455	6,996	995.9	160	22.8	450	64.1	2,415	343.8
Percent change		+0.3	-0.7	+37.9	+36.6	+1.4	+0.4	-8.0	-8.9
Florida									
2017	20,976,812	85,606	408.1	1,057	5.0	7,936	37.8	18,597	88.7
2018	21,299,325	81,980	384.9	1,107	5.2	8,438	39.6	16,884	79.3
Percent change		-4.2	-5.7	+4.7	+3.1	+6.3	+4.7	-9.2	-10.6
Georgia									
2017	10,413,055	37,118	356.5	681	6.5	2,646	25.4	9,844	94.5
2018	10,519,475	34,355	326.6	642	6.1	2,651	25.2	8,279	78.7
Percent change		-7.4	-8.4	-5.7	-6.7	+0.2	-0.8	-15.9	-16.7
Maryland									
2017	6,024,891	30,321	503.3	558	9.3	1,712	28.4	11,189	185.7
2018	6,042,718	28,320	468.7	490	8.1	1,979	32.8	9,716	160.8
Percent change		-6.6	-6.9	-12.2	-12.4	+15.6	+15.3	-13.2	-13.4
North Carolina[7]									
2017	10,270,800	38,043	370.4	622	6.1	1,944	18.9	9,884	96.2
2018	10,383,620	39,210	377.6	628	6.0	2,633	25.4	8,423	81.1
Percent change		+3.1	+1.9	+1.0	-0.1	+35.4	+34.0	-14.8	-15.7
South Carolina									
2017	5,021,219	25,412	506.1	380	7.6	2,576	51.3	3,884	77.4
2018	5,084,127	24,825	488.3	392	7.7	2,434	47.9	3,553	69.9
Percent change		-2.3	-3.5	+3.2	+1.9	-5.5	-6.7	-8.5	-9.7
Virginia									
2017	8,465,207	17,811	210.4	470	5.6	3,026	35.7	4,331	51.2
2018	8,517,685	17,032	200.0	391	4.6	2,924	34.3	3,604	42.3
Percent change		-4.4	-5.0	-16.8	-17.3	-3.4	-4.0	-16.8	-17.3
West Virginia									
2017	1,817,048	6,564	361.2	98	5.4	793	43.6	673	37.0
2018	1,805,832	5,236	289.9	67	3.7	652	36.1	572	31.7
Percent change		-20.2	-19.7	-31.6	-31.2	-17.8	-17.3	-15.0	-14.5

Table 4. Crime in the United States,[1] by Region, Geographic Division, and State, 2017–2018—Continued

(Number, rate per 100,000 population, percent.)

Area	Aggravated assault Number	Rate	Property crime Number	Rate	Burglary Number	Rate	Larceny-theft Number	Rate	Motor vehicle theft Number	Rate
Wisconsin										
2017	11,899	205.4	104,908	1,811.2	17,570	303.3	77,868	1,344.4	9,470	163.5
2018	11,263	193.7	90,686	1,559.9	14,099	242.5	67,953	1,168.9	8,634	148.5
Percent change	-5.3	-5.7	-13.6	-13.9	-19.8	-20.1	-12.7	-13.1	-8.8	-9.2
West North Central[5]										
2017	52,847	248.4	517,946	2,434.3	89,022	418.4	377,583	1,774.6	51,341	241.3
2018	52,092	243.7	475,002	2,222.0	77,647	363.2	346,708	1,621.9	50,647	236.9
Percent change	-1.4	-1.9	-8.3	-8.7	-12.8	-13.2	-8.2	-8.6	-1.4	-1.8
Iowa[5]										
2017	6,366	202.5	65,652	2,088.4	14,711	468.0	45,441	1,445.5	5,500	175.0
2018	5,931	187.9	53,385	1,691.5	11,127	352.6	37,571	1,190.4	4,687	148.5
Percent change	-6.8	-7.2	-18.7	-19.0	-24.4	-24.7	-17.3	-17.6	-14.8	-15.1
Kansas										
2017	8,383	288.0	79,387	2,727.4	13,102	450.1	58,891	2,023.3	7,394	254.0
2018	9,559	328.3	76,686	2,633.9	12,537	430.6	56,305	1,933.9	7,844	269.4
Percent change	+14.0	+14.0	-3.4	-3.4	-4.3	-4.3	-4.4	-4.4	+6.1	+6.1
Minnesota										
2017	7,199	129.3	122,430	2,198.8	18,828	338.1	93,602	1,681.0	10,000	179.6
2018	6,857	122.2	111,874	1,993.8	16,185	288.4	85,561	1,524.8	10,128	180.5
Percent change	-4.8	-5.5	-8.6	-9.3	-14.0	-14.7	-8.6	-9.3	+1.3	+0.5
Missouri										
2017	22,752	372.5	173,380	2,838.3	30,086	492.5	123,356	2,019.4	19,938	326.4
2018	22,042	359.8	162,173	2,647.1	27,257	444.9	115,101	1,878.8	19,815	323.4
Percent change	-3.1	-3.4	-6.5	-6.7	-9.4	-9.7	-6.7	-7.0	-0.6	-0.9
Nebraska										
2017	3,726	194.3	43,856	2,287.1	6,513	339.6	32,064	1,672.1	5,279	275.3
2018	3,461	179.4	40,126	2,079.9	5,246	271.9	30,006	1,555.3	4,874	252.6
Percent change	-7.1	-7.7	-8.5	-9.1	-19.5	-19.9	-6.4	-7.0	-7.7	-8.2
North Dakota										
2017	1,534	203.1	16,653	2,205.2	2,947	390.2	11,944	1,581.6	1,762	233.3
2018	1,560	205.2	15,507	2,040.2	2,724	358.4	11,008	1,448.3	1,775	233.5
Percent change	+1.7	+1.0	-6.9	-7.5	-7.6	-8.2	-7.8	-8.4	+0.7	+0.1
South Dakota										
2017	2,887	330.6	16,588	1,899.5	2,835	324.6	12,285	1,406.8	1,468	168.1
2018	2,682	304.0	15,251	1,728.7	2,571	291.4	11,156	1,264.5	1,524	172.7
Percent change	-7.1	-8.0	-8.1	-9.0	-9.3	-10.2	-9.2	-10.1	+3.8	+2.8
South[6,7]										
2017	344,771	278.9	3,232,483	2,615.3	627,770	507.9	2,329,978	1,885.1	274,735	222.3
2018	338,715	271.5	3,035,624	2,433.3	548,927	440.0	2,209,438	1,771.0	277,259	222.2
Percent change	-1.8	-2.7	-6.1	-7.0	-12.6	-13.4	-5.2	-6.1	+0.9	*
South Atlantic[6,7]										
2017	164,658	254.7	1,623,573	2,511.6	295,986	457.9	1,197,511	1,852.5	130,076	201.2
2018	161,315	247.0	1,513,936	2,317.6	253,831	388.6	1,132,713	1,734.0	127,392	195.0
Percent change	-2.0	-3.1	-6.8	-7.7	-14.2	-15.1	-5.4	-6.4	-2.1	-3.1
Delaware										
2017	2,893	302.3	23,430	2,448.1	3,960	413.8	18,108	1,892.0	1,362	142.3
2018	2,845	294.2	22,481	2,324.4	3,158	326.5	17,847	1,845.3	1,476	152.6
Percent change	-1.7	-2.7	-4.1	-5.1	-20.3	-21.1	-1.4	-2.5	+8.4	+7.2
District of Columbia[6]										
2017	3,791	544.9	29,736	4,274.3	1,809	260.0	25,340	3,642.4	2,587	371.9
2018	3,971	565.3	30,724	4,373.8	1,788	254.5	26,343	3,750.1	2,593	369.1
Percent change	+4.7	+3.7	+3.3	+2.3	-1.2	-2.1	+4.0	+3.0	+0.2	-0.7
Florida										
2017	58,016	276.6	527,125	2,512.9	88,835	423.5	395,375	1,884.8	42,915	204.6
2018	55,551	260.8	486,017	2,281.8	71,933	337.7	372,919	1,750.8	41,165	193.3
Percent change	-4.2	-5.7	-7.8	-9.2	-19.0	-20.3	-5.7	-7.1	-4.1	-5.5
Georgia										
2017	23,947	230.0	297,651	2,858.4	55,363	531.7	216,252	2,076.7	26,036	250.0
2018	22,783	216.6	270,738	2,573.7	45,369	431.3	200,609	1,907.0	24,760	235.4
Percent change	-4.9	-5.8	-9.0	-10.0	-18.1	-18.9	-7.2	-8.2	-4.9	-5.9
Maryland										
2017	16,862	279.9	134,705	2,235.8	23,526	390.5	97,657	1,620.9	13,522	224.4
2018	16,135	267.0	122,864	2,033.3	18,892	312.6	91,835	1,519.8	12,137	200.9
Percent change	-4.3	-4.6	-8.8	-9.1	-19.7	-19.9	-6.0	-6.2	-10.2	-10.5
North Carolina[7]										
2017	25,593	249.2	265,483	2,584.8	65,247	635.3	184,119	1,792.6	16,117	156.9
2018	27,526	265.1	258,979	2,494.1	62,290	599.9	179,057	1,724.4	17,632	169.8
Percent change	+7.6	+6.4	-2.4	-3.5	-4.5	-5.6	-2.7	-3.8	+9.4	+8.2
South Carolina										
2017	18,572	369.9	160,368	3,193.8	31,165	620.7	114,931	2,288.9	14,272	284.2
2018	18,446	362.8	153,421	3,017.6	29,473	579.7	109,616	2,156.0	14,332	281.9
Percent change	-0.7	-1.9	-4.3	-5.5	-5.4	-6.6	-4.6	-5.8	+0.4	-0.8
Virginia										
2017	9,984	117.9	152,515	1,801.7	18,524	218.8	123,812	1,462.6	10,179	120.2
2018	10,113	118.7	141,885	1,665.8	15,574	182.8	115,533	1,356.4	10,778	126.5
Percent change	+1.3	+0.7	-7.0	-7.5	-15.9	-16.4	-6.7	-7.3	+5.9	+5.2
West Virginia										
2017	5,000	275.2	32,560	1,791.9	7,557	415.9	21,917	1,206.2	3,086	169.8
2018	3,945	218.5	26,827	1,485.6	5,354	296.5	18,954	1,049.6	2,519	139.5
Percent change	-21.1	-20.6	-17.6	-17.1	-29.2	-28.7	-13.5	-13.0	-18.4	-17.9

Table 4. Crime in the United States,[1] by Region, Geographic Division, and State, 2017–2018—Continued

(Number, rate per 100,000 population, percent.)

Area	Population[2]	Violent crime[3]		Murder and nonnegligent manslaughter		Rape[4]		Robbery	
		Number	Rate	Number	Rate	Number	Rate	Number	Rate
East South Central									
2017	19,027,451	87,362	459.1	1,412	7.4	7,504	39.4	17,559	92.3
2018	19,112,813	84,091	440.0	1,296	6.8	7,061	36.9	15,318	80.1
Percent change		-3.7	-4.2	-8.2	-8.6	-5.9	-6.3	-12.8	-13.2
Alabama									
2017	4,875,120	25,469	522.4	419	8.6	2,001	41.0	4,233	86.8
2018	4,887,871	25,399	519.6	383	7.8	1,996	40.8	4,076	83.4
Percent change		-0.3	-0.5	-8.6	-8.8	-0.2	-0.5	-3.7	-4.0
Kentucky									
2017	4,453,874	10,292	231.1	265	5.9	1,817	40.8	2,967	66.6
2018	4,468,402	9,467	211.9	244	5.5	1,707	38.2	2,457	55.0
Percent change		-8.0	-8.3	-7.9	-8.2	-6.1	-6.4	-17.2	-17.5
Mississippi									
2017	2,989,663	7,661	256.2	190	6.4	658	22.0	2,492	83.4
2018	2,986,530	6,999	234.4	171	5.7	537	18.0	1,595	53.4
Percent change		-8.6	-8.5	-10.0	-9.9	-18.4	-18.3	-36.0	-35.9
Tennessee									
2017	6,708,794	43,940	655.0	538	8.0	3,028	45.1	7,867	117.3
2018	6,770,010	42,226	623.7	498	7.4	2,821	41.7	7,190	106.2
Percent change		-3.9	-4.8	-7.4	-8.3	-6.8	-7.7	-8.6	-9.4
West South Central									
2017	39,929,172	184,955	463.2	2,473	6.2	20,746	52.0	42,510	106.5
2018	40,318,727	177,740	440.8	2,274	5.6	21,273	52.8	37,209	92.3
Percent change		-3.9	-4.8	-8.0	-8.9	+2.5	+1.5	-12.5	-13.3
Arkansas									
2017	3,002,997	16,996	566.0	249	8.3	2,140	71.3	1,998	66.5
2018	3,013,825	16,384	543.6	216	7.2	2,196	72.9	1,594	52.9
Percent change		-3.6	-3.9	-13.3	-13.6	+2.6	+2.2	-20.2	-20.5
Louisiana									
2017	4,670,818	25,986	556.3	576	12.3	1,850	39.6	5,385	115.3
2018	4,659,978	25,049	537.5	530	11.4	2,085	44.7	4,568	98.0
Percent change		-3.6	-3.4	-8.0	-7.8	+12.7	+13.0	-15.2	-15.0
Oklahoma									
2017	3,932,640	17,989	457.4	243	6.2	2,220	56.5	3,007	76.5
2018	3,943,079	18,380	466.1	206	5.2	2,299	58.3	2,791	70.8
Percent change		+2.2	+1.9	-15.2	-15.5	+3.6	+3.3	-7.2	-7.4
Texas									
2017	28,322,717	123,984	437.8	1,405	5.0	14,536	51.3	32,120	113.4
2018	28,701,845	117,927	410.9	1,322	4.6	14,693	51.2	28,256	98.4
Percent change		-4.9	-6.1	-5.9	-7.2	+1.1	-0.3	-12.0	-13.2
West									
2017	77,319,986	329,056	425.6	3,487	4.5	35,845	46.4	88,447	114.4
2018	77,993,663	330,080	423.2	3,230	4.1	37,439	48.0	83,106	106.6
Percent change		+0.3	-0.6	-7.4	-8.2	+4.4	+3.5	-6.0	-6.9
Mountain									
2017	24,184,624	106,432	440.1	1,225	5.1	14,188	58.7	21,933	90.7
2018	24,552,385	107,602	438.3	1,090	4.4	14,729	60.0	18,817	76.6
Percent change		+1.1	-0.4	-11.0	-12.4	+3.8	+2.3	-14.2	-15.5
Arizona									
2017	7,048,876	35,647	505.7	422	6.0	3,622	51.4	7,440	105.5
2018	7,171,646	34,058	474.9	369	5.1	3,638	50.7	6,523	91.0
Percent change		-4.5	-6.1	-12.6	-14.1	+0.4	-1.3	-12.3	-13.8
Colorado									
2017	5,615,902	20,901	372.2	222	4.0	4,021	71.6	3,868	68.9
2018	5,695,564	22,624	397.2	210	3.7	4,070	71.5	3,797	66.7
Percent change		+8.2	+6.7	-5.4	-6.7	+1.2	-0.2	-1.8	-3.2
Idaho									
2017	1,718,904	4,111	239.2	42	2.4	755	43.9	222	12.9
2018	1,754,208	3,983	227.1	35	2.0	791	45.1	200	11.4
Percent change		-3.1	-5.1	-16.7	-18.3	+4.8	+2.7	-9.9	-11.7
Montana									
2017	1,053,090	3,937	373.9	41	3.9	639	60.7	234	22.2
2018	1,062,305	3,974	374.1	34	3.2	551	51.9	269	25.3
Percent change		+0.9	+0.1	-17.1	-17.8	-13.8	-14.5	+15.0	+14.0
Nevada									
2017	2,972,405	16,663	560.6	266	8.9	1,896	63.8	4,841	162.9
2018	3,034,392	16,420	541.1	202	6.7	2,329	76.8	3,862	127.3
Percent change		-1.5	-3.5	-24.1	-25.6	+22.8	+20.3	-20.2	-21.9
New Mexico									
2017	2,093,395	16,300	778.6	144	6.9	1,244	59.4	3,732	178.3
2018	2,095,428	17,949	856.6	167	8.0	1,354	64.6	2,830	135.1
Percent change		+10.1	+10.0	+16.0	+15.9	+8.8	+8.7	-24.2	-24.2
Utah									
2017	3,103,118	7,515	242.2	74	2.4	1,758	56.7	1,498	48.3
2018	3,161,105	7,368	233.1	60	1.9	1,753	55.5	1,236	39.1
Percent change		-2.0	-3.8	-18.9	-20.4	-0.3	-2.1	-17.5	-19.0
Wyoming									
2017	578,934	1,358	234.6	14	2.4	253	43.7	98	16.9
2018	577,737	1,226	212.2	13	2.3	243	42.1	100	17.3
Percent change		-9.7	-9.5	-7.1	-7.0	-4.0	-3.8	+2.0	+2.3

Table 4. Crime in the United States,[1] by Region, Geographic Division, and State, 2017–2018—Continued

(Number, rate per 100,000 population, percent.)

Area	Aggravated assault		Property crime		Burglary		Larceny-theft		Motor vehicle theft	
	Number	Rate	Number	Rate	Number	Rate	Number	Rate	Number	Rate
East South Central										
2017	60,887	320.0	520,465	2,735.3	113,073	594.3	361,317	1,898.9	46,075	242.2
2018	60,416	316.1	488,440	2,555.6	100,002	523.2	340,326	1,780.6	48,112	251.7
Percent change	-0.8	-1.2	-6.2	-6.6	-11.6	-12.0	-5.8	-6.2	+4.4	+4.0
Alabama										
2017	18,816	386.0	143,774	2,949.1	31,270	641.4	99,707	2,045.2	12,797	262.5
2018	18,944	387.6	137,700	2,817.2	28,841	590.1	95,747	1,958.9	13,112	268.3
Percent change	+0.7	+0.4	-4.2	-4.5	-7.8	-8.0	-4.0	-4.2	+2.5	+2.2
Kentucky										
2017	5,243	117.7	95,899	2,153.2	20,535	461.1	65,006	1,459.5	10,358	232.6
2018	5,059	113.2	87,695	1,962.6	17,190	384.7	60,244	1,348.2	10,261	229.6
Percent change	-3.5	-3.8	-8.6	-8.9	-16.3	-16.6	-7.3	-7.6	-0.9	-1.3
Mississippi										
2017	4,321	144.5	82,764	2,768.3	22,449	750.9	55,968	1,872.1	4,347	145.4
2018	4,696	157.2	71,766	2,403.0	20,839	697.8	46,627	1,561.2	4,300	144.0
Percent change	+8.7	+8.8	-13.3	-13.2	-7.2	-7.1	-16.7	-16.6	-1.1	-1.0
Tennessee										
2017	32,507	484.5	198,028	2,951.8	38,819	578.6	140,636	2,096.3	18,573	276.8
2018	31,717	468.5	191,279	2,825.4	33,132	489.4	137,708	2,034.1	20,439	301.9
Percent change	-2.4	-3.3	-3.4	-4.3	-14.7	-15.4	-2.1	-3.0	+10.0	+9.1
West South Central										
2017	119,226	298.6	1,088,445	2,725.9	218,711	547.7	771,150	1,931.3	98,584	246.9
2018	116,984	290.1	1,033,248	2,562.7	195,094	483.9	736,399	1,826.4	101,755	252.4
Percent change	-1.9	-2.8	-5.1	-6.0	-10.8	-11.7	-4.5	-5.4	+3.2	+2.2
Arkansas										
2017	12,609	419.9	94,419	3,144.2	22,369	744.9	64,795	2,157.7	7,255	241.6
2018	12,378	410.7	87,793	2,913.0	19,193	636.8	61,487	2,040.2	7,113	236.0
Percent change	-1.8	-2.2	-7.0	-7.4	-14.2	-14.5	-5.1	-5.4	-2.0	-2.3
Louisiana										
2017	18,175	389.1	157,272	3,367.1	34,135	730.8	112,042	2,398.8	11,095	237.5
2018	17,866	383.4	152,661	3,276.0	31,132	668.1	109,993	2,360.4	11,536	247.6
Percent change	-1.7	-1.5	-2.9	-2.7	-8.8	-8.6	-1.8	-1.6	+4.0	+4.2
Oklahoma										
2017	12,519	318.3	113,611	2,888.9	28,749	731.0	72,546	1,844.7	12,316	313.2
2018	13,084	331.8	113,364	2,875.0	26,858	681.1	73,217	1,856.8	13,289	337.0
Percent change	+4.5	+4.2	-0.2	-0.5	-6.6	-6.8	+0.9	+0.7	+7.9	+7.6
Texas										
2017	75,923	268.1	723,143	2,553.2	133,458	471.2	521,767	1,842.2	67,918	239.8
2018	73,656	256.6	679,430	2,367.2	117,911	410.8	491,702	1,713.1	69,817	243.2
Percent change	-3.0	-4.3	-6.0	-7.3	-11.6	-12.8	-5.8	-7.0	+2.8	+1.4
West										
2017	201,277	260.3	2,081,184	2,691.7	368,554	476.7	1,407,893	1,820.9	304,737	394.1
2018	206,305	264.5	1,977,420	2,535.4	337,171	432.3	1,354,938	1,737.2	285,311	365.8
Percent change	+2.5	+1.6	-5.0	-5.8	-8.5	-9.3	-3.8	-4.6	-6.4	-7.2
Mountain										
2017	69,086	285.7	669,796	2,769.5	121,057	500.6	468,273	1,936.2	80,466	332.7
2018	72,966	297.2	627,402	2,555.4	106,424	433.5	444,756	1,811.5	76,222	310.4
Percent change	+5.6	+4.0	-6.3	-7.7	-12.1	-13.4	-5.0	-6.4	-5.3	-6.7
Arizona										
2017	24,163	342.8	204,999	2,908.3	37,722	535.1	148,251	2,103.2	19,026	269.9
2018	23,528	328.1	191,974	2,676.8	31,532	439.7	141,303	1,970.3	19,139	266.9
Percent change	-2.6	-4.3	-6.4	-8.0	-16.4	-17.8	-4.7	-6.3	+0.6	-1.1
Colorado										
2017	12,790	227.7	152,032	2,707.2	22,618	402.7	107,470	1,913.7	21,944	390.7
2018	14,547	255.4	152,163	2,671.6	21,371	375.2	109,119	1,915.9	21,673	380.5
Percent change	+13.7	+12.1	+0.1	-1.3	-5.5	-6.8	+1.5	+0.1	-1.2	-2.6
Idaho										
2017	3,092	179.9	28,557	1,661.3	5,837	339.6	20,570	1,196.7	2,150	125.1
2018	2,957	168.6	25,636	1,461.4	4,940	281.6	18,732	1,067.8	1,964	112.0
Percent change	-4.4	-6.3	-10.2	-12.0	-15.4	-17.1	-8.9	-10.8	-8.7	-10.5
Montana										
2017	3,023	287.1	27,294	2,591.8	3,623	344.0	21,073	2,001.1	2,598	246.7
2018	3,120	293.7	26,518	2,496.3	3,257	306.6	20,465	1,926.5	2,796	263.2
Percent change	+3.2	+2.3	-2.8	-3.7	-10.1	-10.9	-2.9	-3.7	+7.6	+6.7
Nevada										
2017	9,660	325.0	78,320	2,634.9	20,049	674.5	45,459	1,529.4	12,812	431.0
2018	10,027	330.4	73,985	2,438.2	17,743	584.7	44,338	1,461.2	11,904	392.3
Percent change	+3.8	+1.7	-5.5	-7.5	-11.5	-13.3	-2.5	-4.5	-7.1	-9.0
New Mexico										
2017	11,180	534.1	81,865	3,910.6	17,872	853.7	52,284	2,497.6	11,709	559.3
2018	13,598	648.9	71,657	3,419.7	16,088	767.8	45,390	2,166.1	10,179	485.8
Percent change	+21.6	+21.5	-12.5	-12.6	-10.0	-10.1	-13.2	-13.3	-13.1	-13.2
Utah										
2017	4,185	134.9	86,201	2,777.9	11,780	379.6	64,955	2,093.2	9,466	305.0
2018	4,319	136.6	75,156	2,377.5	9,968	315.3	57,460	1,817.7	7,728	244.5
Percent change	+3.2	+1.3	-12.8	-14.4	-15.4	-16.9	-11.5	-13.2	-18.4	-19.9
Wyoming										
2017	993	171.5	10,528	1,818.5	1,556	268.8	8,211	1,418.3	761	131.4
2018	870	150.6	10,313	1,785.1	1,525	264.0	7,949	1,375.9	839	145.2
Percent change	-12.4	-12.2	-2.0	-1.8	-2.0	-1.8	-3.2	-3.0	+10.2	+10.5

Table 4. Crime in the United States,[1] by Region, Geographic Division, and State, 2017–2018—Continued

(Number, rate per 100,000 population, percent.)

Area	Population[2]	Violent crime[3]		Murder and nonnegligent manslaughter		Rape[4]		Robbery	
		Number	Rate	Number	Rate	Number	Rate	Number	Rate
Pacific									
2017	53,135,362	222,624	419.0	2,262	4.3	21,657	40.8	66,514	125.2
2018	53,441,278	222,478	416.3	2,140	4.0	22,710	42.5	64,289	120.3
Percent change		-0.1	-0.6	-5.4	-5.9	+4.9	+4.3	-3.3	-3.9
Alaska									
2017	739,786	6,338	856.7	62	8.4	1,074	145.2	952	128.7
2018	737,438	6,526	885.0	47	6.4	1,192	161.6	896	121.5
Percent change		+3.0	+3.3	-24.2	-24.0	+11.0	+11.3	-5.9	-5.6
California									
2017	39,399,349	178,597	453.3	1,830	4.6	14,724	37.4	56,625	143.7
2018	39,557,045	176,982	447.4	1,739	4.4	15,505	39.2	54,326	137.3
Percent change		-0.9	-1.3	-5.0	-5.4	+5.3	+4.9	-4.1	-4.4
Hawaii									
2017	1,424,203	3,577	251.2	39	2.7	567	39.8	1,077	75.6
2018	1,420,491	3,532	248.6	36	2.5	625	44.0	946	66.6
Percent change		-1.3	-1.0	-7.7	-7.5	+10.2	+10.5	-12.2	-11.9
Oregon[6]									
2017	4,146,592	11,629	280.4	105	2.5	1,992	48.0	2,474	59.7
2018	4,190,713	11,966	285.5	82	2.0	1,975	47.1	2,549	60.8
Percent change		+2.9	+1.8	-21.9	-22.7	-0.9	-1.9	+3.0	+1.9
Washington									
2017	7,425,432	22,483	302.8	226	3.0	3,300	44.4	5,386	72.5
2018	7,535,591	23,472	311.5	236	3.1	3,413	45.3	5,572	73.9
Percent change		+4.4	+2.9	+4.4	+2.9	+3.4	+1.9	+3.5	+1.9
Puerto Rico									
2017	3,325,001	7,762	233.4	679	20.4	209	6.3	3,055	91.9
2018	3,195,153	6,417	200.8	639	20.0	198	6.2	2,271	71.1
Percent change		-17.3	-14.0	-5.9	-2.1	-5.3	-1.4	-25.7	-22.6

Table 4. Crime in the United States,[1] by Region, Geographic Division, and State, 2017–2018—Continued

(Number, rate per 100,000 population, percent.)

Area	Aggravated assault		Property crime		Burglary		Larceny-theft		Motor vehicle theft	
	Number	Rate	Number	Rate	Number	Rate	Number	Rate	Number	Rate
Pacific										
2017	132,191	248.8	1,411,388	2,656.2	247,497	465.8	939,620	1,768.4	224,271	422.1
2018	133,339	249.5	1,350,018	2,526.2	230,747	431.8	910,182	1,703.1	209,089	391.2
Percent change	+0.9	+0.3	-4.3	-4.9	-6.8	-7.3	-3.1	-3.7	-6.8	-7.3
Alaska										
2017	4,250	574.5	26,203	3,542.0	4,167	563.3	17,782	2,403.7	4,254	575.0
2018	4,391	595.4	24,339	3,300.5	3,979	539.6	16,364	2,219.0	3,996	541.9
Percent change	+3.3	+3.6	-7.1	-6.8	-4.5	-4.2	-8.0	-7.7	-6.1	-5.8
California										
2017	105,418	267.6	987,063	2,505.3	176,679	448.4	642,019	1,629.5	168,365	427.3
2018	105,412	266.5	941,618	2,380.4	164,632	416.2	621,775	1,571.8	155,211	392.4
Percent change	*	-0.4	-4.6	-5.0	-6.8	-7.2	-3.2	-3.5	-7.8	-8.2
Hawaii										
2017	1,894	133.0	40,392	2,836.1	5,549	389.6	29,574	2,076.5	5,269	370.0
2018	1,925	135.5	40,772	2,870.3	5,631	396.4	29,492	2,076.2	5,649	397.7
Percent change	+1.6	+1.9	+0.9	+1.2	+1.5	+1.7	-0.3	*	+7.2	+7.5
Oregon[6]										
2017	7,058	170.2	122,524	2,954.8	17,415	420.0	88,091	2,124.4	17,018	410.4
2018	7,360	175.6	121,278	2,894.0	16,304	389.1	88,418	2,109.9	16,556	395.1
Percent change	+4.3	+3.2	-1.0	-2.1	-6.4	-7.4	+0.4	-0.7	-2.7	-3.7
Washington										
2017	13,571	182.8	235,206	3,167.6	43,687	588.3	162,154	2,183.8	29,365	395.5
2018	14,251	189.1	222,011	2,946.2	40,201	533.5	154,133	2,045.4	27,677	367.3
Percent change	+5.0	+3.5	-5.6	-7.0	-8.0	-9.3	-4.9	-6.3	-5.7	-7.1
Puerto Rico										
2017	3,819	114.9	31,176	937.6	7,949	239.1	19,633	590.5	3,594	108.1
2018	3,309	103.6	24,851	777.8	5,486	171.7	15,658	490.1	3,707	116.0
Percent change	-13.4	-9.8	-20.3	-17.0	-31.0	-28.2	-20.2	-17.0	+3.1	+7.3

Note: Although arson data are included in the trend and clearance tables, sufficient data are not available to estimate totals for this offense. Therefore, no arson data are published in this table.
* = Less than one-tenth of 1 percent.
1 The previous year's crime figures have been adjusted.   2 Population figures are U.S. Census Bureau provisional estimates as of July 1, 2018.   3 The violent crime figures include the offenses of murder, rape (revised definition), robbery, and aggravated assault.   4 The figures shown in this column for the offense of rape were estimated using the revised Uniform Crime Reporting (UCR) definition of rape. See chapter notes for more detail.   5 Limited data for 2018 were available for Iowa.   5 Includes offenses reported by the Metro Transit Police and the District of Columbia Fire and Emergency Medical Services: Arson Investigation Unit.   6 This state's agencies submitted rape data according to the legacy UCR definition of rape.

Table 5. Crime in the United States, by State and Area, 2018

(Number, percent, rate per 100,000 population.)

Area	Population	Violent crime[1]	Murder and nonnegligent manslaughter	Rape[2]	Robbery	Aggravated assault	Property crime	Burglary	Larceny-theft	Motor vehicle theft
Alabama										
Metropolitan statistical area	3,709,622									
Area actually reporting	94.3%	20,207	322	1,530	3,608	14,747	108,373	22,178	75,625	10,570
Estimated total	100.0%	20,570	324	1,546	3,649	15,051	110,384	22,615	77,059	10,710
Cities outside metropolitan areas	531,555									
Area actually reporting	93.1%	3,477	40	242	312	2,883	19,161	3,685	13,976	1,500
Estimated total	100.0%	3,644	40	242	316	3,046	19,996	3,817	14,634	1,545
Nonmetropolitan counties	646,694									
Area actually reporting	91.9%	1,090	17	203	68	802	6,737	2,238	3,710	789
Estimated total	100.0%	1,185	19	208	111	847	7,320	2,409	4,054	857
State total	4,887,871	25,399	383	1,996	4,076	18,944	137,700	28,841	95,747	13,112
Rate per 100,000 inhabitants		519.6	7.8	40.8	83.4	387.6	2,817.2	590.1	1,958.9	268.3
Alaska										
Metropolitan statistical area	343,648									
Area actually reporting	100.0%	4,127	30	645	772	2,680	17,021	2,293	11,560	3,168
Cities outside metropolitan areas	127,692									
Area actually reporting	97.1%	994	5	199	77	713	4,119	642	3,128	349
Estimated total	100.0%	1,012	5	203	77	727	4,164	646	3,165	353
Nonmetropolitan counties	266,098									
Area actually reporting	100.0%	1,387	12	344	47	984	3,154	1,040	1,639	475
State total	737,438	6,526	47	1,192	896	4,391	24,339	3,979	16,364	3,996
Rate per 100,000 inhabitants		885.0	6.4	161.6	121.5	595.4	3,300.5	539.6	2,219.0	541.9
Arizona										
Metropolitan statistical area	6,820,581									
Area actually reporting	99.3%	28,938	325	3,297	6,409	18,907	183,308	29,518	135,712	18,078
Estimated total	100.0%	29,054	326	3,314	6,448	18,966	184,427	29,730	136,514	18,183
Cities outside metropolitan areas	124,445									
Area actually reporting	96.3%	4,684	38	313	55	4,278	5,937	1,326	3,847	764
Estimated total	100.0%	4,707	38	313	55	4,301	6,057	1,345	3,944	768
Nonmetropolitan counties	226,620									
Area actually reporting	100.0%	297	5	11	20	261	1,490	457	845	188
State total	7,171,646	34,058	369	3,638	6,523	23,528	191,974	31,532	141,303	19,139
Rate per 100,000 inhabitants		474.9	5.1	50.7	91.0	328.1	2,676.8	439.7	1,970.3	266.9
Arkansas										
Metropolitan statistical area	1,902,947									
Area actually reporting	99.7%	11,659	150	1,420	1,266	8,823	61,777	12,699	43,799	5,279
Estimated total	100.0%	11,690	150	1,423	1,270	8,847	61,850	12,731	43,826	5,293
Cities outside metropolitan areas	504,175									
Area actually reporting	91.1%	2,590	39	396	252	1,903	16,156	3,944	11,238	974
Estimated total	100.0%	2,833	40	406	289	2,098	17,899	4,394	12,465	1,040
Nonmetropolitan counties	606,703									
Area actually reporting	84.9%	1,782	26	361	35	1,360	7,137	1,870	4,507	760
Estimated total	100.0%	1,861	26	367	35	1,433	8,044	2,068	5,196	780
State total	3,013,825	16,384	216	2,196	1,594	12,378	87,793	19,193	61,487	7,113
Rate per 100,000 inhabitants		543.6	7.2	72.9	52.9	410.7	2,913.0	636.8	2,040.2	236.0
California										
Metropolitan statistical area	38,726,576									
Area actually reporting	99.9%	173,383	1,684	15,067	53,895	102,737	925,205	160,267	611,972	152,966
Estimated total	100.0%	173,393	1,684	15,067	53,895	102,747	925,308	160,286	612,051	152,971
Cities outside metropolitan areas	265,831									
Area actually reporting	100.0%	1,536	14	174	245	1,103	8,198	1,633	5,615	950
Nonmetropolitan counties	564,638									
Area actually reporting	100.0%	2,053	41	264	186	1,562	8,112	2,713	4,109	1,290
State total	39,557,045	176,982	1,739	15,505	54,326	105,412	941,618	164,632	621,775	155,211
Rate per 100,000 inhabitants		447.4	4.4	39.2	137.3	266.5	2,380.4	416.2	1,571.8	392.4
Colorado										
Metropolitan statistical area	4,986,493									
Area actually reporting	95.1%	20,718	191	3,670	3,670	13,187	138,757	19,300	98,778	20,679
Estimated total	100.0%	20,778	191	3,684	3,687	13,216	139,506	19,331	99,444	20,731
Cities outside metropolitan areas	339,737									
Area actually reporting	94.9%	1,058	5	233	55	765	9,108	1,172	7,386	550
Estimated total	100.0%	1,090	5	234	70	781	9,462	1,224	7,682	556
Nonmetropolitan counties	369,334									
Area actually reporting	91.5%	718	14	144	15	545	2,952	774	1,860	318
Estimated total	100.0%	756	14	152	40	550	3,195	816	1,993	386
State total	5,695,564	22,624	210	4,070	3,797	14,547	152,163	21,371	109,119	21,673
Rate per 100,000 inhabitants		397.2	3.7	71.5	66.7	255.4	2,671.6	375.2	1,915.9	380.5
Connecticut										
Metropolitan statistical area	2,980,253									
Area actually reporting	100.0%	6,995	72	728	2,123	4,072	56,246	7,239	42,122	6,885
Cities outside metropolitan areas	112,751									
Area actually reporting	100.0%	117	3	26	31	57	1,648	203	1,321	124
Nonmetropolitan counties	479,661									
Area actually reporting	100.0%	299	8	86	40	165	2,161	506	1,281	374
State total	3,572,665	7,411	83	840	2,194	4,294	60,055	7,948	44,724	7,383
Rate per 100,000 inhabitants		207.4	2.3	23.5	61.4	120.2	1,681.0	222.5	1,251.8	206.7

Table 5. Crime in the United States, by State and Area, 2018—Continued

(Number, percent, rate per 100,000 population.)

Area	Population	Violent crime[1]	Murder and nonnegligent manslaughter	Rape[2]	Robbery	Aggravated assault	Property crime	Burglary	Larceny-theft	Motor vehicle theft
Delaware										
Metropolitan statistical area	967,171									
Area actually reporting	100.0%	4,097	48	338	866	2,845	22,481	3,158	17,847	1,476
Cities outside metropolitan areas	None									
Nonmetropolitan counties	None									
State total	967,171	4,097	48	338	866	2,845	22,481	3,158	17,847	1,476
Rate per 100,000 inhabitants		423.6	5.0	34.9	89.5	294.2	2,324.4	326.5	1,845.3	152.6
District of Columbia[3]										
Metropolitan statistical area	702,455									
Area actually reporting	100.0%	6,996	160	450	2,415	3,971	30,724	1,788	26,343	2,593
Cities outside metropolitan areas	None									
Nonmetropolitan counties	None									
District total	702,455	6,996	160	450	2,415	3,971	30,724	1,788	26,343	2,593
Rate per 100,000 inhabitants		995.9	22.8	64.1	343.8	565.3	4,373.8	254.5	3,750.1	369.1
Florida										
Metropolitan statistical area	20,609,181									
Area actually reporting	99.9%	79,202	1,074	8,200	16,638	53,290	472,759	68,481	364,004	40,274
Estimated total	100.0%	79,241	1,074	8,201	16,647	53,319	473,080	68,545	364,237	40,298
Cities outside metropolitan areas	141,401									
Area actually reporting	95.0%	810	12	58	103	637	4,289	855	3,200	234
Estimated total	100.0%	829	12	58	104	655	4,439	908	3,288	243
Nonmetropolitan counties	548,743									
Area actually reporting	100.0%	1,910	21	179	133	1,577	8,498	2,480	5,394	624
State total	21,299,325	81,980	1,107	8,438	16,884	55,551	486,017	71,933	372,919	41,165
Rate per 100,000 inhabitants		384.9	5.2	39.6	79.3	260.8	2,281.8	337.7	1,750.8	193.3
Georgia										
Metropolitan statistical area	8,732,372									
Area actually reporting	96.6%	28,495	548	2,260	7,501	18,186	223,556	36,007	165,559	21,990
Estimated total	100.0%	29,161	559	2,290	7,650	18,662	229,661	36,903	170,274	22,484
Cities outside metropolitan areas	622,684									
Area actually reporting	88.7%	2,563	45	169	473	1,876	21,036	3,707	16,424	905
Estimated total	100.0%	2,662	45	170	481	1,966	23,282	4,005	18,341	936
Nonmetropolitan counties	1,164,419									
Area actually reporting	93.5%	2,470	38	191	148	2,093	16,905	4,231	11,407	1,267
Estimated total	100.0%	2,532	38	191	148	2,155	17,795	4,461	11,994	1,340
State total	10,519,475	34,355	642	2,651	8,279	22,783	270,738	45,369	200,609	24,760
Rate per 100,000 inhabitants		326.6	6.1	25.2	78.7	216.6	2,573.7	431.3	1,907.0	235.4
Hawaii										
Metropolitan statistical area	1,148,121									
Area actually reporting	100.0%	2,886	30	454	857	1,545	33,970	4,328	24,758	4,884
Cities outside metropolitan areas	None									
Nonmetropolitan counties	272,370									
Area actually reporting	100.0%	646	6	171	89	380	6,802	1,303	4,734	765
State total	1,420,491	3,532	36	625	946	1,925	40,772	5,631	29,492	5,649
Rate per 100,000 inhabitants		248.6	2.5	44.0	66.6	135.5	2,870.3	396.4	2,076.2	397.7
Idaho										
Metropolitan statistical area	1,300,470									
Area actually reporting	100.0%	3,152	19	644	178	2,311	20,923	3,861	15,487	1,575
Cities outside metropolitan areas	181,635									
Area actually reporting	95.7%	404	4	77	5	318	2,502	522	1,802	178
Estimated total	100.0%	414	4	79	11	320	2,561	527	1,838	196
Nonmetropolitan counties	272,103									
Area actually reporting	98.3%	401	12	67	7	315	2,128	546	1,389	193
Estimated total	100.0%	417	12	68	11	326	2,152	552	1,407	193
State total	1,754,208	3,983	35	791	200	2,957	25,636	4,940	18,732	1,964
Rate per 100,000 inhabitants		227.1	2.0	45.1	11.4	168.6	1,461.4	281.6	1,067.8	112.0
Illinois										
Metropolitan statistical area	11,305,797									
Area actually reporting	92.1%	47,266	865	5,050	13,857	27,494	218,713	33,314	167,160	18,239
Estimated total	100.0%	48,003	873	5,171	14,007	27,952	225,321	34,316	172,338	18,667
Cities outside metropolitan areas	814,261									
Area actually reporting	83.2%	2,357	6	475	161	1,715	13,966	2,681	10,760	525
Estimated total	100.0%	2,668	6	515	174	1,973	16,018	3,132	12,290	596
Nonmetropolitan counties	621,022									
Area actually reporting	89.7%	737	5	159	25	548	4,396	1,454	2,644	298
Estimated total	100.0%	819	5	173	27	614	4,925	1,632	2,963	330
State total	12,741,080	51,490	884	5,859	14,208	30,539	246,264	39,080	187,591	19,593
Rate per 100,000 inhabitants		404.1	6.9	46.0	111.5	239.7	1,932.8	306.7	1,472.3	153.8
Indiana										
Metropolitan statistical area	5,228,617									
Area actually reporting	84.4%	21,358	363	1,976	5,307	13,712	114,723	20,173	81,982	12,568
Estimated total	100.0%	22,320	383	2,027	5,396	14,514	124,342	21,936	89,268	13,138
Cities outside metropolitan areas	540,439									
Area actually reporting	59.0%	788	15	98	93	582	8,140	1,055	6,521	564
Estimated total	100.0%	1,119	26	104	141	848	13,533	1,496	11,259	778

Table 5. Crime in the United States, by State and Area, 2018—Continued

(Number, percent, rate per 100,000 population.)

Area	Population	Violent crime[1]	Murder and nonnegligent manslaughter	Rape[2]	Robbery	Aggravated assault	Property crime	Burglary	Larceny-theft	Motor vehicle theft
Nonmetropolitan counties	922,822									
Area actually reporting	51.4%	622	15	121	33	453	4,260	1,178	2,640	442
Estimated total	100.0%	2,142	29	239	402	1,472	7,963	1,836	4,715	1,412
State total	6,691,878	25,581	438	2,370	5,939	16,834	145,838	25,268	105,242	15,328
Rate per 100,000 inhabitants		382.3	6.5	35.4	88.7	251.6	2,179.3	377.6	1,572.7	229.1
Iowa[4]										
Metropolitan statistical area	1,929,318									
Area actually reporting	90.7%	4,345	40	589	612	3,104	33,142	6,717	23,433	2,992
Estimated total	100.0%	4,951	44	635	759	3,513	37,029	7,342	26,305	3,382
Cities outside metropolitan areas	572,110									
Area actually reporting	85.7%	1,903	7	218	77	1,601	11,322	2,379	8,173	770
Estimated total	100.0%	2,175	7	241	144	1,783	13,090	2,665	9,476	949
Nonmetropolitan counties	654,717									
Area actually reporting	97.0%	700	3	95	12	590	2,833	1,050	1,471	312
Estimated total	100.0%	767	3	100	29	635	3,266	1,120	1,790	356
State total	3,156,145	7,893	54	976	932	5,931	53,385	11,127	37,571	4,687
Rate per 100,000 inhabitants		250.1	1.7	30.9	29.5	187.9	1,691.5	352.6	1,190.4	148.5
Kansas										
Metropolitan statistical area	2,018,178									
Area actually reporting	83.8%	8,495	88	999	1,127	6,281	49,894	7,590	36,811	5,493
Estimated total	100.0%	10,105	88	1,162	1,376	7,479	58,412	8,830	43,142	6,440
Cities outside metropolitan areas	571,274									
Area actually reporting	95.4%	1,899	17	298	126	1,458	14,140	2,545	10,585	1,010
Estimated total	100.0%	1,957	17	298	145	1,497	14,738	2,644	11,069	1,025
Nonmetropolitan counties	322,053									
Area actually reporting	96.6%	708	8	105	13	582	3,466	1,054	2,057	355
Estimated total	100.0%	720	8	107	22	583	3,536	1,063	2,094	379
State total	2,911,505	12,782	113	1,567	1,543	9,559	76,686	12,537	56,305	7,844
Rate per 100,000 inhabitants		439.0	3.9	53.8	53.0	328.3	2,633.9	430.6	1,933.9	269.4
Kentucky										
Metropolitan statistical area	2,659,106									
Area actually reporting	99.7%	7,130	144	944	2,104	3,938	66,119	11,452	47,079	7,588
Estimated total	100.0%	7,135	144	945	2,106	3,940	66,231	11,478	47,148	7,605
Cities outside metropolitan areas	534,383									
Area actually reporting	97.5%	911	17	235	238	421	12,313	2,479	8,797	1,037
Estimated total	100.0%	912	17	236	238	421	12,437	2,496	8,890	1,051
Nonmetropolitan counties	1,274,913									
Area actually reporting	100.0%	1,420	83	526	113	698	9,027	3,216	4,206	1,605
State total	4,468,402	9,467	244	1,707	2,457	5,059	87,695	17,190	60,244	10,261
Rate per 100,000 inhabitants		211.9	5.5	38.2	55.0	113.2	1,962.6	384.7	1,348.2	229.6
Louisiana										
Metropolitan statistical area	3,921,292									
Area actually reporting	97.2%	21,501	481	1,864	4,256	14,900	131,877	25,979	95,308	10,590
Estimated total	100.0%	22,029	487	1,880	4,326	15,336	135,727	26,788	98,151	10,788
Cities outside metropolitan areas	274,151									
Area actually reporting	80.8%	1,454	25	89	156	1,184	8,835	2,132	6,415	288
Estimated total	100.0%	1,577	25	89	159	1,304	10,371	2,360	7,719	292
Nonmetropolitan counties	464,535									
Area actually reporting	96.7%	1,416	18	116	83	1,199	6,373	1,936	3,987	450
Estimated total	100.0%	1,443	18	116	83	1,226	6,563	1,984	4,123	456
State total	4,659,978	25,049	530	2,085	4,568	17,866	152,661	31,132	109,993	11,536
Rate per 100,000 inhabitants		537.5	11.4	44.7	98.0	383.4	3,276.0	668.1	2,360.4	247.6
Maine										
Metropolitan statistical area	794,794									
Area actually reporting	100.0%	887	12	230	170	475	11,228	1,452	9,347	429
Cities outside metropolitan areas	256,583									
Area actually reporting	100.0%	322	2	112	33	175	4,473	627	3,675	171
Nonmetropolitan counties	287,027									
Area actually reporting	100.0%	292	10	104	25	153	2,472	634	1,661	177
State total	1,338,404	1,501	24	446	228	803	18,173	2,713	14,683	777
Rate per 100,000 inhabitants		112.1	1.8	33.3	17.0	60.0	1,357.8	202.7	1,097.1	58.1
Maryland										
Metropolitan statistical area	5,893,251									
Area actually reporting	100.0%	27,945	488	1,932	9,646	15,879	120,507	18,359	90,082	12,066
Cities outside metropolitan areas	51,354									
Area actually reporting	100.0%	228	2	17	55	154	1,545	290	1,226	29
Nonmetropolitan counties	98,113									
Area actually reporting	100.0%	147	0	30	15	102	812	243	527	42
State total	6,042,718	28,320	490	1,979	9,716	16,135	122,864	18,892	91,835	12,137
Rate per 100,000 inhabitants		468.7	8.1	32.8	160.8	267.0	2,033.3	312.6	1,519.8	200.9
Massachusetts										
Metropolitan statistical area	6,873,328									
Area actually reporting	97.5%	22,924	136	2,377	4,068	16,343	85,784	13,762	65,538	6,484
Estimated total	100.0%	23,216	136	2,393	4,141	16,546	86,714	13,807	66,319	6,588
Cities outside metropolitan areas	28,747									
Area actually reporting	100.0%	121	0	17	2	102	481	55	408	18

Table 5. Crime in the United States, by State and Area, 2018—Continued

(Number, percent, rate per 100,000 population.)

Area	Population	Violent crime[1]	Murder and nonnegligent manslaughter	Rape[2]	Robbery	Aggravated assault	Property crime	Burglary	Larceny-theft	Motor vehicle theft
Nonmetropolitan counties	74									
Area actually reporting	98.8%	0	0	0	0	0	0	0	0	0
Estimated total	100.0%	0	0	0	0	0	1	0	1	0
State total	6,902,149	23,337	136	2,410	4,143	16,648	87,196	13,862	66,728	6,606
Rate per 100,000 inhabitants		338.1	2.0	34.9	60.0	241.2	1,263.3	200.8	966.8	95.7
Michigan										
Metropolitan statistical area	8,193,112									
Area actually reporting	98.8%	39,962	513	5,988	5,514	27,947	144,783	27,577	100,875	16,331
Estimated total	100.0%	40,037	514	5,999	5,521	28,003	145,166	27,653	101,165	16,348
Cities outside metropolitan areas	578,160									
Area actually reporting	98.0%	1,729	10	623	70	1,026	9,729	1,163	8,147	419
Estimated total	100.0%	1,743	10	625	81	1,027	9,869	1,168	8,258	443
Nonmetropolitan counties	1,224,643									
Area actually reporting	99.2%	3,124	27	1,065	46	1,986	10,171	2,822	6,690	659
Estimated total	100.0%	3,138	27	1,066	54	1,991	10,245	2,830	6,755	660
State total	9,995,915	44,918	551	7,690	5,656	31,021	165,280	31,651	116,178	17,451
Rate per 100,000 inhabitants		449.4	5.5	76.9	56.6	310.3	1,653.5	316.6	1,162.3	174.6
Minnesota										
Metropolitan statistical area	4,367,933									
Area actually reporting	98.6%	10,564	85	1,988	2,848	5,643	94,250	12,953	72,415	8,882
Estimated total	100.0%	10,564	85	1,988	2,848	5,643	94,250	12,953	72,415	8,882
Cities outside metropolitan areas	564,597									
Area actually reporting	99.7%	1,182	12	294	79	797	11,817	1,612	9,535	670
Estimated total	100.0%	1,182	12	294	79	797	11,841	1,613	9,557	671
Nonmetropolitan counties	678,649									
Area actually reporting	100.0%	623	9	180	17	417	5,783	1,619	3,589	575
State total	5,611,179	12,369	106	2,462	2,944	6,857	111,874	16,185	85,561	10,128
Rate per 100,000 inhabitants		220.4	1.9	43.9	52.5	122.2	1,993.8	288.4	1,524.8	180.5
Mississippi										
Metropolitan statistical area	1,437,099									
Area actually reporting	75.9%	2,942	114	208	854	1,766	30,690	6,285	21,574	2,831
Estimated total	100.0%	3,735	138	256	1,049	2,292	39,700	7,943	28,430	3,327
Cities outside metropolitan areas	557,101									
Area actually reporting	37.9%	1,031	28	68	200	735	8,504	2,425	5,715	364
Estimated total	100.0%	1,698	28	152	370	1,148	17,844	5,437	11,810	597
Nonmetropolitan counties	992,330									
Area actually reporting	20.7%	368	5	47	50	266	2,840	1,262	1,394	184
Estimated total	100.0%	1,566	5	129	176	1,256	14,222	7,459	6,387	376
State total	2,986,530	6,999	171	537	1,595	4,696	71,766	20,839	46,627	4,300
Rate per 100,000 inhabitants		234.4	5.7	18.0	53.4	157.2	2,403.0	697.8	1,561.2	144.0
Missouri										
Metropolitan statistical area	4,592,956									
Area actually reporting	99.8%	25,819	537	2,372	4,985	17,925	131,128	20,841	92,909	17,378
Estimated total	100.0%	25,822	537	2,372	4,988	17,925	131,163	20,850	92,926	17,387
Cities outside metropolitan areas	650,579									
Area actually reporting	98.5%	2,486	27	327	164	1,968	20,341	3,153	15,940	1,248
Estimated total	100.0%	2,503	27	327	164	1,985	20,506	3,154	16,095	1,257
Nonmetropolitan counties	882,917									
Area actually reporting	100.0%	2,433	43	213	45	2,132	10,504	3,253	6,080	1,171
State total	6,126,452	30,758	607	2,912	5,197	22,042	162,173	27,257	115,101	19,815
Rate per 100,000 inhabitants		502.1	9.9	47.5	84.8	359.8	2,647.1	444.9	1,878.8	323.4
Montana										
Metropolitan statistical area	382,078									
Area actually reporting	100.0%	1,589	14	181	183	1,211	14,400	1,671	11,176	1,553
Cities outside metropolitan areas	224,421									
Area actually reporting	100.0%	1,216	8	212	63	933	6,250	700	4,997	553
Nonmetropolitan counties	455,806									
Area actually reporting	99.3%	1,162	12	158	20	972	5,845	885	4,275	685
Estimated total	100.0%	1,169	12	158	23	976	5,868	886	4,292	690
State total	1,062,305	3,974	34	551	269	3,120	26,518	3,257	20,465	2,796
Rate per 100,000 inhabitants		374.1	3.2	51.9	25.3	293.7	2,496.3	306.6	1,926.5	263.2
Nebraska										
Metropolitan statistical area	1,255,602									
Area actually reporting	99.8%	4,418	39	914	681	2,784	31,051	3,872	22,973	4,206
Estimated total	100.0%	4,429	39	915	683	2,792	31,141	3,882	23,040	4,219
Cities outside metropolitan areas	347,118									
Area actually reporting	92.9%	773	2	252	50	469	6,773	963	5,357	453
Estimated total	100.0%	805	2	253	72	478	7,211	1,017	5,721	473
Nonmetropolitan counties	326,548									
Area actually reporting	84.6%	260	3	65	1	191	1,641	347	1,112	182
Estimated total	100.0%	260	3	65	1	191	1,774	347	1,245	182
State total	1,929,268	5,494	44	1,233	756	3,461	40,126	5,246	30,006	4,874
Rate per 100,000 inhabitants		284.8	2.3	63.9	39.2	179.4	2,079.9	271.9	1,555.3	252.6
Nevada										
Metropolitan statistical area	2,759,691									
Area actually reporting	100.0%	15,629	186	2,198	3,805	9,440	70,268	16,758	42,000	11,510

Table 5. Crime in the United States, by State and Area, 2018—Continued

(Number, percent, rate per 100,000 population.)

Area	Population	Violent crime[1]	Murder and nonnegligent manslaughter	Rape[2]	Robbery	Aggravated assault	Property crime	Burglary	Larceny-theft	Motor vehicle theft
Cities outside metropolitan areas	48,497									
Area actually reporting	100.0%	256	6	45	22	183	993	230	684	79
Nonmetropolitan counties	226,204									
Area actually reporting	100.0%	535	10	86	35	404	2,724	755	1,654	315
State total	3,034,392	16,420	202	2,329	3,862	10,027	73,985	17,743	44,338	11,904
Rate per 100,000 inhabitants		541.1	6.7	76.8	127.3	330.4	2,438.2	584.7	1,461.2	392.3
New Hampshire										
Metropolitan statistical area	854,544									
Area actually reporting	99.2%	1,530	15	304	259	952	10,324	1,026	8,747	551
Estimated total	100.0%	1,535	15	304	259	957	10,473	1,031	8,887	555
Cities outside metropolitan areas	459,985									
Area actually reporting	93.6%	728	5	209	72	442	5,960	738	4,929	293
Estimated total	100.0%	766	5	216	96	449	6,165	754	5,117	294
Nonmetropolitan counties	41,929									
Area actually reporting	93.4%	39	1	13	2	23	237	52	171	14
Estimated total	100.0%	48	1	14	4	29	297	62	215	20
State total	1,356,458	2,349	21	534	359	1,435	16,935	1,847	14,219	869
Rate per 100,000 inhabitants		173.2	1.5	39.4	26.5	105.8	1,248.5	136.2	1,048.2	64.1
New Jersey										
Metropolitan statistical area	8,908,520									
Area actually reporting	100.0%	18,537	286	1,424	6,364	10,463	125,156	19,232	94,887	11,037
Cities outside metropolitan areas	None									
Nonmetropolitan counties	None									
State total	8,908,520	18,537	286	1,424	6,364	10,463	125,156	19,232	94,887	11,037
Rate per 100,000 inhabitants		208.1	3.2	16.0	71.4	117.4	1,404.9	215.9	1,065.1	123.9
New Mexico										
Metropolitan statistical area	1,408,549									
Area actually reporting	92.5%	12,522	107	909	2,419	9,087	52,221	10,979	32,955	8,287
Estimated total	100.0%	13,376	111	936	2,527	9,802	53,954	11,465	34,013	8,476
Cities outside metropolitan areas	394,037									
Area actually reporting	96.0%	2,820	33	227	252	2,308	13,827	3,289	9,359	1,179
Estimated total	100.0%	2,836	33	229	255	2,319	14,284	3,406	9,687	1,191
Nonmetropolitan counties	292,842									
Area actually reporting	97.4%	1,701	23	187	41	1,450	3,302	1,172	1,627	503
Estimated total	100.0%	1,737	23	189	48	1,477	3,419	1,217	1,690	512
State total	2,095,428	17,949	167	1,354	2,830	13,598	71,657	16,088	45,390	10,179
Rate per 100,000 inhabitants		856.6	8.0	64.6	135.1	648.9	3,419.7	767.8	2,166.1	485.8
New York										
Metropolitan statistical area	18,197,801									
Area actually reporting	99.7%	65,791	535	5,597	17,953	41,706	263,956	28,097	223,311	12,548
Estimated total	100.0%	65,840	535	5,603	17,961	41,741	264,695	28,169	223,958	12,568
Cities outside metropolitan areas	502,454									
Area actually reporting	97.4%	1,242	11	285	174	772	8,916	1,373	7,308	235
Estimated total	100.0%	1,278	12	296	176	794	9,222	1,421	7,559	242
Nonmetropolitan counties	841,954									
Area actually reporting	100.0%	1,377	15	676	50	636	7,590	1,547	5,716	327
State total	19,542,209	68,495	562	6,575	18,187	43,171	281,507	31,137	237,233	13,137
Rate per 100,000 inhabitants		350.5	2.9	33.6	93.1	220.9	1,440.5	159.3	1,214.0	67.2
North Carolina[5]										
Metropolitan statistical area	8,401,289									
Area actually reporting	89.1%	29,429	396	1989	6,340	20,704	190,073	42,468	134,375	13,230
Estimated total	100.0%	32,996	456	2,140	7,449	22,951	210,122	46,893	148,551	14,678
Cities outside metropolitan areas	586,242									
Area actually reporting	86.2%	2,842	66	122	566	2,088	22,507	5,258	16,180	1,069
Estimated total	100.0%	3,174	68	135	633	2,338	25,766	5,983	18,566	1,217
Nonmetropolitan counties	1,396,089									
Area actually reporting	95.3%	2,909	99	342	327	2,141	22,190	9,060	11,454	1,676
Estimated total	100.0%	3,040	104	358	341	2,237	23,091	9,414	11,940	1,737
State total	10,383,620	39,210	628	2,633	8,423	27,526	258,979	62,290	179,057	17,632
Rate per 100,000 inhabitants		377.6	6.0	25.4	81.1	265.1	2,494.1	599.9	1,724.4	169.8
North Dakota										
Metropolitan statistical area	379,498									
Area actually reporting	100.0%	1,164	11	233	121	799	9,331	1,538	6,924	869
Cities outside metropolitan areas	188,093									
Area actually reporting	99.8%	765	7	120	32	606	4,574	807	3,135	632
Estimated total	100.0%	766	7	120	32	607	4,582	808	3,141	633
Nonmetropolitan counties	192,486									
Area actually reporting	100.0%	203	0	44	5	154	1,594	378	943	273
State total	760,077	2,133	18	397	158	1,560	15,507	2,724	11,008	1,775
Rate per 100,000 inhabitants		280.6	2.4	52.2	20.8	205.2	2,040.2	358.4	1,448.3	233.5
Ohio										
Metropolitan statistical area	9,376,628									
Area actually reporting	90.1%	28,724	537	4,341	8,382	15,464	199,224	39,060	143,262	16,902
Estimated total	100.0%	29,748	537	4,511	8,829	15,871	215,783	40,774	157,031	17,978
Cities outside metropolitan areas	1,018,281									
Area actually reporting	80.9%	1,562	15	421	249	877	21,458	3,433	17,179	846
Estimated total	100.0%	1,643	16	429	254	944	25,677	4,001	20,747	929

Table 5. Crime in the United States, by State and Area, 2018—Continued

(Number, percent, rate per 100,000 population.)

Area	Population	Violent crime[1]	Murder and nonnegligent manslaughter	Rape[2]	Robbery	Aggravated assault	Property crime	Burglary	Larceny-theft	Motor vehicle theft
Nonmetropolitan counties	1,294,533									
Area actually reporting	86.0%	1,301	11	359	102	829	11,326	2,990	7,401	935
Estimated total	100.0%	1,332	11	360	102	859	13,036	3,411	8,623	1,002
State total	11,689,442	32,723	564	5,300	9,185	17,674	254,496	48,186	186,401	19,909
Rate per 100,000 inhabitants		279.9	4.8	45.3	78.6	151.2	2,177.1	412.2	1,594.6	170.3
Oklahoma										
Metropolitan statistical area	2,621,457									
Area actually reporting	99.9%	14,233	162	1,708	2,432	9,931	82,153	18,608	53,054	10,491
Estimated total	100.0%	14,233	162	1,708	2,432	9,931	82,153	18,608	53,054	10,491
Cities outside metropolitan areas	731,666									
Area actually reporting	99.3%	3,082	31	421	317	2,313	23,573	5,537	16,165	1,871
Estimated total	100.0%	3,085	31	421	317	2,316	23,677	5,556	16,248	1,873
Nonmetropolitan counties	589,956									
Area actually reporting	97.9%	1,053	13	169	42	829	7,384	2,640	3,828	916
Estimated total	100.0%	1,062	13	170	42	837	7,534	2,694	3,915	925
State total	3,943,079	18,380	206	2,299	2,791	13,084	113,364	26,858	73,217	13,289
Rate per 100,000 inhabitants		466.1	5.2	58.3	70.8	331.8	2,875.0	681.1	1,856.8	337.0
Oregon										
Metropolitan statistical area	3,518,314									
Area actually reporting	99.3%	10,262	65	1,707	2,296	6,194	105,007	13,343	76,678	14,986
Estimated total	100.0%	10,313	65	1,713	2,310	6,225	105,339	13,359	76,960	15,020
Cities outside metropolitan areas	311,614									
Area actually reporting	95.0%	893	8	154	144	587	10,648	1,602	8,227	819
Estimated total	100.0%	923	8	158	158	599	11,119	1,660	8,618	841
Nonmetropolitan counties	360,785									
Area actually reporting	84.3%	603	8	91	34	470	4,118	1,086	2,425	607
Estimated total	100.0%	730	9	104	81	536	4,820	1,285	2,840	695
State total	4,190,713	11,966	82	1,975	2,549	7,360	121,278	16,304	88,418	16,556
Rate per 100,000 inhabitants		285.5	2.0	47.1	60.8	175.6	2,894.0	389.1	2,109.9	395.1
Pennsylvania										
Metropolitan statistical area	11,353,779									
Area actually reporting	99.7%	36,145	745	3,830	9,605	21,965	175,929	24,132	139,309	12,488
Estimated total	100.0%	36,160	745	3,830	9,606	21,979	176,290	24,146	139,655	12,489
Cities outside metropolitan areas	642,834									
Area actually reporting	98.9%	1,751	13	164	142	1,432	7,172	1,019	5,921	232
Estimated total	100.0%	1,757	13	164	142	1,438	7,233	1,021	5,980	232
Nonmetropolitan counties	810,447									
Area actually reporting	100.0%	1,275	26	489	100	660	7,293	1,937	4,961	395
State total	12,807,060	39,192	784	4,483	9,848	24,077	190,816	27,104	150,596	13,116
Rate per 100,000 inhabitants		306.0	6.1	35.0	76.9	188.0	1,489.9	211.6	1,175.9	102.4
Puerto Rico										
Metropolitan statistical area	3,079,741									
Area actually reporting	100.0%	6,181	614	191	2,239	3,137	24,202	5,273	15,259	3,670
Cities outside metropolitan areas	115,412									
Area actually reporting	100.0%	236	25	7	32	172	649	213	399	37
Total	3,195,153	6,417	639	198	2,271	3,309	24,851	5,486	15,658	3,707
Rate per 100,000 inhabitants		200.8	20.0	6.2	71.1	103.6	777.8	171.7	490.1	116.0
Rhode Island										
Metropolitan statistical area	1,057,315									
Area actually reporting	100.0%	2,317	16	481	454	1,366	17,561	2,810	13,220	1,531
Cities outside metropolitan areas	None									
Nonmetropolitan counties	None									
State total	1,057,315	2,317	16	481	454	1,366	17,561	2,810	13,220	1,531
Rate per 100,000 inhabitants		219.1	1.5	45.5	42.9	129.2	1,660.9	265.8	1,250.3	144.8
South Carolina										
Metropolitan statistical area	4,347,374									
Area actually reporting	98.8%	20,355	306	2,060	3,050	14,939	127,824	23,029	92,348	12,447
Estimated total	100.0%	20,541	306	2,074	3,075	15,086	129,023	23,215	93,322	12,486
Cities outside metropolitan areas	203,525									
Area actually reporting	97.0%	2,028	32	133	287	1,576	10,512	2,169	7,820	523
Estimated total	100.0%	2,061	32	133	292	1,604	10,661	2,185	7,947	529
Nonmetropolitan counties	533,228									
Area actually reporting	96.3%	2,158	54	226	183	1,695	13,312	3,927	8,100	1,285
Estimated total	100.0%	2,223	54	227	186	1,756	13,737	4,073	8,347	1,317
State total	5,084,127	24,825	392	2,434	3,553	18,446	153,421	29,473	109,616	14,332
Rate per 100,000 inhabitants		488.3	7.7	47.9	69.9	362.8	3,017.6	579.7	2,156.0	281.9
South Dakota										
Metropolitan statistical area	420,829									
Area actually reporting	99.1%	1,623	7	339	176	1,101	9,378	1,556	6,849	973
Estimated total	100.0%	1,638	7	342	178	1,111	9,470	1,569	6,918	983
Cities outside metropolitan areas	219,614									
Area actually reporting	96.0%	1,587	2	231	40	1,314	4,504	633	3,508	363
Estimated total	100.0%	1,608	2	231	47	1,328	4,604	645	3,590	369
Nonmetropolitan counties	241,792									
Area actually reporting	82.8%	183	3	29	3	148	817	213	522	82
Estimated total	100.0%	324	3	41	37	243	1,177	357	648	172

Table 5. Crime in the United States, by State and Area, 2018—Continued

(Number, percent, rate per 100,000 population.)

Area	Population	Violent crime[1]	Murder and nonnegligent manslaughter	Rape[2]	Robbery	Aggravated assault	Property crime	Burglary	Larceny-theft	Motor vehicle theft
State total	882,235	3,570	12	614	262	2,682	15,251	2,571	11,156	1,524
Rate per 100,000 inhabitants		404.7	1.4	69.6	29.7	304.0	1,728.7	291.4	1,264.5	172.7
Tennessee										
Metropolitan statistical area	5,297,542									
Area actually reporting	99.9%	36,817	451	2,379	6,916	27,071	160,578	26,609	116,881	17,088
Estimated total	100.0%	36,817	451	2,379	6,916	27,071	160,578	26,609	116,881	17,088
Cities outside metropolitan areas	483,479									
Area actually reporting	100.0%	2,646	14	186	190	2,256	17,352	2,813	13,213	1,326
Nonmetropolitan counties	988,989									
Area actually reporting	100.0%	2,763	33	256	84	2,390	13,349	3,710	7,614	2,025
State total	6,770,010	42,226	498	2,821	7,190	31,717	191,279	33,132	137,708	20,439
Rate per 100,000 inhabitants		623.7	7.4	41.7	106.2	468.5	2,825.4	489.4	2,034.1	301.9
Texas										
Metropolitan statistical area	25,601,190									
Area actually reporting	98.2%	109,688	1,228	13,483	27,686	67,291	631,017	105,140	459,349	66,528
Estimated total	100.0%	109,839	1,228	13,496	27,703	67,412	632,569	105,409	460,517	66,643
Cities outside metropolitan areas	1,443,676									
Area actually reporting	93.4%	4,859	42	617	447	3,753	30,004	6,785	21,596	1,623
Estimated total	100.0%	5,065	42	638	454	3,931	31,297	7,099	22,520	1,678
Nonmetropolitan counties	1,656,979									
Area actually reporting	98.4%	2,985	52	554	98	2,281	15,328	5,321	8,529	1,478
Estimated total	100.0%	3,023	52	559	99	2,313	15,564	5,403	8,665	1,496
State total	28,701,845	117,927	1,322	14,693	28,256	73,656	679,430	117,911	491,702	69,817
Rate per 100,000 inhabitants		410.9	4.6	51.2	98.4	256.6	2,367.2	410.8	1,713.1	243.2
Utah										
Metropolitan statistical area	2,830,802									
Area actually reporting	99.4%	6,631	53	1,615	1,201	3,762	69,225	9,095	52,857	7,273
Estimated total	100.0%	6,639	53	1,616	1,202	3,768	69,483	9,128	53,065	7,290
Cities outside metropolitan areas	149,423									
Area actually reporting	89.6%	364	4	78	15	267	3,076	390	2,469	217
Estimated total	100.0%	397	4	81	27	285	3,280	412	2,642	226
Nonmetropolitan counties	180,880									
Area actually reporting	90.9%	310	3	56	7	244	2,179	401	1,573	205
Estimated total	100.0%	332	3	56	7	266	2,393	428	1,753	212
State total	3,161,105	7,368	60	1,753	1,236	4,319	75,156	9,968	57,460	7,728
Rate per 100,000 inhabitants		233.1	1.9	55.5	39.1	136.6	2,377.5	315.3	1,817.7	244.5
Vermont										
Metropolitan statistical area	220,420									
Area actually reporting	100.0%	384	4	117	26	237	3,412	493	2,852	67
Cities outside metropolitan areas	190,773									
Area actually reporting	100.0%	402	1	95	34	272	3,183	452	2,638	93
Nonmetropolitan counties	215,106									
Area actually reporting	100.0%	291	5	75	10	201	1,441	522	826	93
State total	626,299	1,077	10	287	70	710	8,036	1,467	6,316	253
Rate per 100,000 inhabitants		172.0	1.6	45.8	11.2	113.4	1,283.1	234.2	1,008.5	40.4
Virginia										
Metropolitan statistical area	7,466,029									
Area actually reporting	99.9%	15,054	334	2,428	3,384	8,908	127,888	13,142	104,914	9,832
Estimated total	100.0%	15,056	334	2,428	3,384	8,910	127,900	13,145	104,921	9,834
Cities outside metropolitan areas	244,617									
Area actually reporting	97.8%	640	18	95	123	404	6,088	752	5,033	303
Estimated total	100.0%	645	18	96	124	407	6,201	761	5,134	306
Nonmetropolitan counties	807,039									
Area actually reporting	100.0%	1,331	39	400	96	796	7,784	1,668	5,478	638
State total	8,517,685	17,032	391	2,924	3,604	10,113	141,885	15,574	115,533	10,778
Rate per 100,000 inhabitants		200.0	4.6	34.3	42.3	118.7	1,665.8	182.8	1,356.4	126.5
Washington										
Metropolitan statistical area	6,769,023									
Area actually reporting	98.6%	21,866	214	3,094	5,400	13,158	204,842	36,088	142,637	26,117
Estimated total	100.0%	21,919	214	3,099	5,415	13,191	205,202	36,129	142,935	26,138
Cities outside metropolitan areas	308,505									
Area actually reporting	92.8%	944	4	209	95	636	10,638	1,922	7,728	988
Estimated total	100.0%	979	4	211	114	650	11,011	2,008	7,997	1,006
Nonmetropolitan counties	458,063									
Area actually reporting	100.0%	574	18	103	43	410	5,798	2,064	3,201	533
State total	7,535,591	23,472	236	3,413	5,572	14,251	222,011	40,201	154,133	27,677
Rate per 100,000 inhabitants		311.5	3.1	45.3	73.9	189.1	2,946.2	533.5	2,045.4	367.3
West Virginia										
Metropolitan statistical area	1,164,452									
Area actually reporting	81.9%	3,193	40	446	251	2,456	17,785	3,837	12,480	1,468
Estimated total	100.0%	3,677	45	492	418	2,722	20,085	4,105	14,123	1,857
Cities outside metropolitan areas	175,743									
Area actually reporting	54.3%	342	2	24	17	299	1,625	204	1,341	80
Estimated total	100.0%	490	2	35	77	376	4,071	482	3,332	257
Nonmetropolitan counties	465,637									
Area actually reporting	86.7%	917	19	109	26	763	2,445	758	1,417	270
Estimated total	100.0%	1,069	20	125	77	847	2,671	767	1,499	405

Table 5. Crime in the United States, by State and Area, 2018—Continued

(Number, percent, rate per 100,000 population.)

Area	Population	Violent crime[1]	Murder and nonnegligent manslaughter	Rape[2]	Robbery	Aggravated assault	Property crime	Burglary	Larceny-theft	Motor vehicle theft
State total	1,805,832	5,236	67	652	572	3,945	26,827	5,354	18,954	2,519
Rate per 100,000 inhabitants		289.9	3.7	36.1	31.7	218.5	1,485.6	296.5	1,049.6	139.5
Wisconsin										
Metropolitan statistical area	4,343,699									
Area actually reporting	98.2%	15,155	153	1,737	3,414	9,851	74,000	11,575	54,598	7,827
Estimated total	100.0%	15,159	153	1,738	3,417	9,851	74,030	11,575	54,628	7,827
Cities outside metropolitan areas	640,432									
Area actually reporting	99.5%	1,194	10	290	54	840	10,935	1,048	9,477	410
Estimated total	100.0%	1,194	10	290	54	840	11,005	1,048	9,547	410
Nonmetropolitan counties	829,437									
Area actually reporting	100.0%	823	13	220	18	572	5,651	1,476	3,778	397
State total	5,813,568	17,176	176	2,248	3,489	11,263	90,686	14,099	67,953	8,634
Rate per 100,000 inhabitants		295.4	3.0	38.7	60.0	193.7	1,559.9	242.5	1,168.9	148.5
Wyoming										
Metropolitan statistical area	178,207									
Area actually reporting	81.3%	384	5	102	27	250	4,582	712	3,463	407
Estimated total	100.0%	496	6	110	54	326	5,107	859	3,769	479
Cities outside metropolitan areas	239,201									
Area actually reporting	91.9%	456	4	91	14	347	3,795	465	3,125	205
Estimated total	100.0%	476	4	91	29	352	4,120	488	3,386	246
Nonmetropolitan counties	160,329									
Area actually reporting	89.1%	220	3	38	3	176	958	174	708	76
Estimated total	100.0%	254	3	42	17	192	1,086	178	794	114
State total	577,737	1,226	13	243	100	870	10,313	1,525	7,949	839
Rate per 100,000 inhabitants		212.2	2.3	42.1	17.3	150.6	1,785.1	264.0	1,375.9	145.2

Note: Although arson data are included in the trend and clearance tables, sufficient data are not available to estimate totals for this offense. Therefore, no arson data are published in this table.
1 The violent crime figures include the offenses of murder, rape (revised definition), robbery, and aggravated assault.   2 The figures shown in the rape (revised definition) column were estimated using the revised Uniform Crime Reporting (UCR) definition of rape. See chapter notes for more detail.   3 Includes offenses reported by the Metro Transit Police and the Arson Investigation Unit of the District of Columbia Fire and Emergency Medical Services.   4 Limited data for 2018 were available for Iowa.   5 This state's agencies submitted rape data according to the legacy UCR definition of rape.

Table 6. Crime in the United States, by Selected Metropolitan Statistical Area, 2018

(Number, percent, rate per 100,000 population.)

Area	Population	Violent crime	Murder and nonnegligent manslaughter	Rape[1]	Robbery	Aggravated assault	Property crime	Burglary	Larceny-theft	Motor vehicle theft
Abilene, TX M.S.A.[2]	170,417									
Includes Callahan, Jones, and Taylor Counties										
City of Abilene	122,480	591	8	97	104	382	3,528	734	2,561	233
Total area actually reporting	100.0%	670	9	109	112	440	4,025	910	2,846	269
Rate per 100,000 inhabitants		393.2	5.3	64.0	65.7	258.2	2,361.9	534.0	1,670.0	157.8
Akron, OH M.S.A.[3]	704,283									
Includes Portage3 and Summit Counties										
City of Akron	197,690	1,704	38	221	387	1,058	7,159	1,740	4,701	718
Total area actually reporting	96.2%	2,509	45	336	495	1,633	15,101	2,883	11,194	1,024
Estimated total	100.0%	2,547	45	343	514	1,645	15,677	2,927	11,687	1,063
Rate per 100,000 inhabitants		361.6	6.4	48.7	73.0	233.6	2,226.0	415.6	1,659.4	150.9
Albany, GA M.S.A.	147,142									
Includes Dougherty, Lee, Terrell, and Worth Counties										
City of Albany	72,594	809	15	28	113	653	3,704	760	2,666	278
Total area actually reporting	97.9%	1,069	17	45	139	868	5,402	1,134	3,909	359
Estimated total	100.0%	1,072	17	45	140	870	5,495	1,138	3,995	362
Rate per 100,000 inhabitants		728.5	11.6	30.6	95.1	591.3	3,734.5	773.4	2,715.1	246.0
Albany-Schenectady-Troy, NY M.S.A.	871,741									
Includes Albany, Rensselaer, Saratoga, Schenectady, and Schoharie Counties										
City of Albany	98,322	823	12	52	209	550	3,147	432	2,585	130
City of Schenectady	65,550	620	1	57	136	426	2,106	353	1,542	211
City of Troy	49,491	283	1	22	93	167	1,411	250	1,082	79
Total area actually reporting	99.8%	2,472	19	334	544	1,575	16,477	1,977	13,797	703
Estimated total	100.0%	2,473	19	334	544	1,576	16,496	1,978	13,815	703
Rate per 100,000 inhabitants		283.7	2.2	38.3	62.4	180.8	1,892.3	226.9	1,584.8	80.6
Albuquerque, NM M.S.A.[3]	915,468									
Includes Bernalillo, Sandoval, Torrance, and Valencia Counties										
City of Albuquerque[2]	560,235	7,646	69	479	1,979	5,119	34,619	6,378	21,625	6,616
Total area actually reporting	100.0%	9,930	87	641	2,181	7,021	41,440	7,964	25,989	7,487
Rate per 100,000 inhabitants		1,084.7	9.5	70.0	238.2	766.9	4,526.6	869.9	2,838.9	817.8
Alexandria, LA M.S.A.	152,464									
Includes Grant and Rapides Parishes										
City of Alexandria	47,238	685	12	17	128	528	3,973	996	2,694	283
Total area actually reporting	98.8%	1,174	16	70	157	931	6,414	1,732	4,246	436
Estimated total	100.0%	1,182	16	70	157	939	6,449	1,740	4,272	437
Rate per 100,000 inhabitants		775.3	10.5	45.9	103.0	615.9	4,229.9	1,141.3	2,802.0	286.6
Allentown-Bethlehem-Easton, PA-NJ M.S.A.	841,039									
Includes Warren County, NJ and Carbon, Lehigh, and Northampton Counties, PA										
City of Allentown, PA	121,743	412	11	49	183	169	2,821	463	2,100	258
City of Bethlehem, PA	75,809	207	1	32	50	124	1,281	217	1,008	56
Total area actually reporting	100.0%	1,380	16	208	347	809	12,097	1,706	9,695	696
Rate per 100,000 inhabitants		164.1	1.9	24.7	41.3	96.2	1,438.3	202.8	1,152.7	82.8
Altoona, PA M.S.A.	122,830									
Includes Blair County										
City of Altoona	43,840	165	3	67	27	68	686	188	464	34
Total area actually reporting	100.0%	284	3	88	32	161	1,317	285	987	45
Rate per 100,000 inhabitants		231.2	2.4	71.6	26.1	131.1	1,072.2	232.0	803.5	36.6
Amarillo, TX M.S.A.[2]	266,043									
Includes Armstrong, Carson, Oldham, Potter,[2] and Randall Counties										
City of Amarillo	201,082	1,622	12	199	305	1,106	8,433	1,527	5,996	910
Total area actually reporting	100.0%	1,757	13	235	312	1,197	9,116	1,685	6,458	973
Rate per 100,000 inhabitants		660.4	4.9	88.3	117.3	449.9	3,426.5	633.4	2,427.4	365.7
Anchorage, AK M.S.A.	309,917									
Includes Anchorage Municipality and Matanuska-Susitna Borough										
City of Anchorage	291,992	3,824	26	613	717	2,468	14,389	2,068	9,498	2,823
Total area actually reporting	100.0%	3,916	26	620	729	2,541	15,548	2,180	10,359	3,009
Rate per 100,000 inhabitants		1,263.6	8.4	200.1	235.2	819.9	5,016.8	703.4	3,342.5	970.9
Ann Arbor, MI M.S.A.	371,644									
Includes Washtenaw County										
City of Ann Arbor	122,571	270	2	55	45	168	1,932	215	1,650	67
Total area actually reporting	100.0%	1,199	13	245	147	794	5,560	843	4,382	335
Rate per 100,000 inhabitants		322.6	3.5	65.9	39.6	213.6	1,496.1	226.8	1,179.1	90.1
Anniston-Oxford, AL M.S.A.	114,180									
Includes Calhoun County										
City of Anniston	21,592	646	7	43	68	528	1,696	413	1,131	152
City of Oxford	17,000	54	0	1	9	44	746	89	633	24
Total area actually reporting	99.3%	829	8	55	96	670	3,180	695	2,276	209

Table 6. Crime in the United States, by Selected Metropolitan Statistical Area, 2018—Continued

(Number, percent, rate per 100,000 population.)

Area	Population	Violent crime	Murder and nonnegligent manslaughter	Rape[1]	Robbery	Aggravated assault	Property crime	Burglary	Larceny-theft	Motor vehicle theft
Estimated total	100.0%	829	8	55	96	670	3,184	695	2,280	209
Rate per 100,000 inhabitants		726.0	7.0	48.2	84.1	586.8	2,788.6	608.7	1,996.8	183.0
Appleton, WI M.S.A.	237,722									
Includes Calumet and Outagamie Counties										
City of Appleton	74,931	165	0	26	23	116	1,151	131	973	47
Total area actually reporting	100.0%	341	2	67	28	244	2,491	277	2,104	110
Rate per 100,000 inhabitants		143.4	0.8	28.2	11.8	102.6	1,047.9	116.5	885.1	46.3
Asheville, NC M.S.A.[3]	460,823									
Includes Buncombe, Haywood, Henderson, and Madison Counties[3]										
City of Asheville[3]	93,186		12		148	392	4,798	691	3,707	400
Total area actually reporting	99.2%	1,221	16	118	218	869	10,211	2,289	7,023	899
Estimated total	100.0%	1,227	16	118	218	875	10,320	2,312	7,104	904
Rate per 100,000 inhabitants		266.3	3.5	25.6	47.3	189.9	2,239.5	501.7	1,541.6	196.2
Atlanta-Sandy Springs-Alpharetta, GA M.S.A.[2]	5,962,282									
Includes Barrow, Bartow, Butts, Carroll, Cherokee, Clayton, Cobb, Coweta,[2] Dawson, DeKalb, Douglas, Fayette, Forsyth, Fulton, Gwinnett, Haralson, Heard, Henry, Jasper, Lamar, Meriwether, Morgan, Newton, Paulding, Pickens, Pike, Rockdale, Spalding, and Walton Counties										
City of Atlanta	496,106	3,814	88	245	1,099	2,382	23,091	3,082	16,701	3,308
City of Sandy Springs	108,654	128	2	10	43	73	2,015	301	1,553	161
City of Alpharetta	67,051	42	1	10	16	15	1,204	103	1,060	41
City of Marietta	61,675	214	3	27	74	110	1,948	228	1,554	166
Total area actually reporting	97.8%	18,890	340	1,553	5,577	11,420	151,018	23,109	111,517	16,392
Estimated total	100.0%	19,120	341	1,558	5,611	11,610	153,531	23,483	113,475	16,573
Rate per 100,000 inhabitants		320.7	5.7	26.1	94.1	194.7	2,575.0	393.9	1,903.2	278.0
Atlantic City-Hammonton, NJ M.S.A.	265,451									
Includes Atlantic County										
City of Atlantic City	38,271	276	7	11	131	127	1,181	116	994	71
City of Hammonton	14,311	9	0	0	5	4	149	30	111	8
Total area actually reporting	100.0%	692	16	46	234	396	5,895	884	4,814	197
Rate per 100,000 inhabitants		260.7	6.0	17.3	88.2	149.2	2,220.7	333.0	1,813.5	74.2
Auburn-Opelika, AL M.S.A	164,783									
Includes Lee County										
City of Auburn	65,585	240	4	16	29	191	1,396	115	1,206	75
City of Opelika	30,822	168	5	13	31	119	1,214	143	991	80
Total area actually reporting	100.0%	859	12	59	80	708	3,812	556	2,947	309
Rate per 100,000 inhabitants		521.3	7.3	35.8	48.5	429.7	2,313.3	337.4	1,788.4	187.5
Augusta-Richmond County, GA-SC M.S.A.[4]	604,618									
Includes Burke, Columbia, Lincoln, McDuffie, and Richmond Counties, GA and Aiken and Edgefield Counties, SC										
Total area actually reporting	96.5%	1,619	63	184	354	1,018		2,947		1,237
Estimated total	100.0%	1,696	63	192	363	1,078		3,042		1,261
Rate per 100,000 inhabitants		280.5	10.4	31.8	60.0	178.3		503.1		208.6
Austin-Round Rock-Georgetown, TX M.S.A.[2]	2,172,348									
Includes Bastrop, Caldwell, Hays, Travis, and Williamson2 Counties										
City of Austin	973,344	3,720	32	787	1,021	1,880	33,655	4,549	26,568	2,538
City of Round Rock	127,354	154	1	34	29	90	2,494	288	2,148	58
City of Georgetown	74,709	78	0	22	10	46	731	92	595	44
City of San Marcos[2]	66,157	263	1	83	42	137	1,415	270	1,044	101
Total area actually reporting	99.9%	6,329	53	1,322	1,279	3,675	50,376	7,371	39,508	3,497
Estimated total	100.0%	6,330	53	1,322	1,279	3,676	50,389	7,374	39,517	3,498
Rate per 100,000 inhabitants		291.4	2.4	60.9	58.9	169.2	2,319.6	339.4	1,819.1	161.0
Bakersfield, CA M.S.A.	893,851									
Includes Kern County										
City of Bakersfield	385,609	1,895	31	113	811	940	16,097	4,025	9,295	2,777
Total area actually reporting	100.0%	5,289	101	382	1,365	3,441	30,268	7,993	16,221	6,054
Rate per 100,000 inhabitants		591.7	11.3	42.7	152.7	385.0	3,386.2	894.2	1,814.7	677.3
Baltimore-Columbia-Towson, MD M.S.A.	2,799,376									
Includes Anne Arundel, Baltimore, Carroll, Harford, Howard, and Queen Anne's Counties and Baltimore City										
City of Baltimore	605,436	11,100	309	361	5,066	5,364	27,217	6,048	16,794	4,375
Total area actually reporting	100.0%	20,179	373	1,073	7,234	11,499	69,161	11,192	50,513	7,456
Rate per 100,000 inhabitants		720.8	13.3	38.3	258.4	410.8	2,470.6	399.8	1,804.4	266.3
Bangor, ME M.S.A.	151,827									
Includes Penobscot County										
City of Bangor	31,746	56	4	4	15	33	1,300	89	1,151	60
Total area actually reporting	100.0%	112	5	20	29	58	2,476	275	2,106	95
Rate per 100,000 inhabitants		73.8	3.3	13.2	19.1	38.2	1,630.8	181.1	1,387.1	62.6

Table 6. Crime in the United States, by Selected Metropolitan Statistical Area, 2018—Continued

(Number, percent, rate per 100,000 population.)

Area	Population	Violent crime	Murder and nonnegligent manslaughter	Rape[1]	Robbery	Aggravated assault	Property crime	Burglary	Larceny-theft	Motor vehicle theft
Barnstable Town, MA M.S.A.	213,058									
Includes Barnstable County										
City of Barnstable	44,015	166	1	20	8	137	462	85	363	14
Total area actually reporting	100.0%	677	2	113	28	534	2,345	502	1,752	91
Rate per 100,000 inhabitants		317.8	0.9	53.0	13.1	250.6	1,100.6	235.6	822.3	42.7
Baton Rouge, LA M.S.A.	852,689									
Includes Ascension, Assumption, East Baton Rouge, East Feliciana, Iberville, Livingston, Pointe Coupee, St. Helena, West Baton Rouge, and West Feliciana Parishes										
City of Baton Rouge	224,790	2,067	79	74	727	1,187	11,965	2,686	8,329	950
Total area actually reporting	99.3%	4,507	127	251	1,061	3,068	30,469	5,899	22,824	1,746
Estimated total	100.0%	4,532	127	251	1,061	3,093	30,578	5,923	22,906	1,749
Rate per 100,000 inhabitants		531.5	14.9	29.4	124.4	362.7	3,586.1	694.6	2,686.3	205.1
Battle Creek, MI M.S.A	134,139									
Includes Calhoun County										
City of Battle Creek	60,615	600	6	85	69	440	1,958	467	1,414	77
Total area actually reporting	100.0%	894	7	154	82	651	3,873	837	2,862	174
Rate per 100,000 inhabitants		666.5	5.2	114.8	61.1	485.3	2,887.3	624.0	2,133.6	129.7
Bay City, MI M.S.A.	103,965									
Includes Bay County										
City of Bay City	32,953	231	0	43	28	160	732	162	524	46
Total area actually reporting	100.0%	366	7	98	38	223	1,411	275	1,050	86
Rate per 100,000 inhabitants		352.0	6.7	94.3	36.6	214.5	1,357.2	264.5	1,010.0	82.7
Beaumont-Port Arthur, TX M.S.A.[2]	398,704									
Includes Hardin, Jefferson, and Orange Counties										
City of Beaumont	119,368	1,265	13	96	358	798	4,516	961	3,145	410
City of Port Arthur	55,643	390	13	20	96	261	1,445	504	807	134
Total area actually reporting	99.9%	2,208	31	206	520	1,451	9,286	2,299	6,059	928
Estimated total	100.0%	2,209	31	206	520	1,452	9,294	2,301	6,064	929
Rate per 100,000 inhabitants		554.0	7.8	51.7	130.4	364.2	2,331.1	577.1	1,520.9	233.0
Beckley, WV M.S.A	117,329									
Includes Fayette and Raleigh Counties										
City of Beckley	16,234	147	3	24	11	109	836	136	669	31
Total area actually reporting	95.7%	371	6	63	17	285	2,090	458	1,514	118
Estimated total	100.0%	387	6	63	21	297	2,225	471	1,631	123
Rate per 100,000 inhabitants		329.8	5.1	53.7	17.9	253.1	1,896.4	401.4	1,390.1	104.8
Bellingham, WA M.S.A	225,272									
Includes Whatcom County										
City of Bellingham	90,208	204	0	34	53	117	3,346	459	2,722	165
Total area actually reporting	97.6%	420	2	79	80	259	5,553	978	4,268	307
Estimated total	100.0%	438	2	81	85	270	5,679	990	4,377	312
Rate per 100,000 inhabitants		194.4	0.9	36.0	37.7	119.9	2,521.0	439.5	1,943.0	138.5
Bend, OR M.S.A.	191,547									
Includes Deschutes County										
City of Bend	97,403	162	1	21	26	114	2,079	164	1,822	93
Total area actually reporting	100.0%	344	1	56	50	237	3,863	414	3,219	230
Rate per 100,000 inhabitants		179.6	0.5	29.2	26.1	123.7	2,016.7	216.1	1,680.5	120.1
Billings, MT M.S.A.	181,264									
Includes Carbon, Stillwater, and Yellowstone Counties										
City of Billings	110,397	598	8	54	108	428	5,276	685	3,796	795
Total area actually reporting	100.0%	776	10	72	116	578	6,360	838	4,593	929
Rate per 100,000 inhabitants		428.1	5.5	39.7	64.0	318.9	3,508.7	462.3	2,533.9	512.5
Binghamton, NY M.S.A.	236,403									
Includes Broome and Tioga Counties										
City of Binghamton	44,876	326	3	40	75	208	1,893	427	1,407	59
Total area actually reporting	100.0%	640	7	141	112	380	4,881	808	3,909	164
Rate per 100,000 inhabitants		270.7	3.0	59.6	47.4	160.7	2,064.7	341.8	1,653.5	69.4
Bismarck, ND M.S.A.	128,877									
Includes Burleigh, Morton, and Oliver Counties										
City of Bismarck	74,644	223	2	46	24	151	2,034	254	1,570	210
Total area actually reporting	100.0%	391	2	70	30	289	3,063	449	2,240	374
Rate per 100,000 inhabitants		303.4	1.6	54.3	23.3	224.2	2,376.7	348.4	1,738.1	290.2
Blacksburg-Christiansburg, VA M.S.A.	167,435									
Includes Giles, Montgomery, and Pulaski Counties and Radford City										
City of Blacksburg	44,853	41	0	20	4	17	322	28	285	9
City of Christiansburg	22,444	43	0	15	2	26	532	34	485	13
Total area actually reporting	100.0%	335	1	125	25	184	2,689	329	2,249	111
Rate per 100,000 inhabitants		200.1	0.6	74.7	14.9	109.9	1,606.0	196.5	1,343.2	66.3

Table 6. Crime in the United States, by Selected Metropolitan Statistical Area, 2018—Continued

(Number, percent, rate per 100,000 population.)

Area	Population	Violent crime	Murder and nonnegligent manslaughter	Rape[1]	Robbery	Aggravated assault	Property crime	Burglary	Larceny-theft	Motor vehicle theft
Bloomington, IL M.S.A.	171,896									
Includes McLean County										
City of Bloomington	78,097	339	9	68	37	225	1,193	196	909	88
Total area actually reporting	100.0%	515	11	123	59	322	2,436	364	1,946	126
Rate per 100,000 inhabitants		299.6	6.4	71.6	34.3	187.3	1,417.1	211.8	1,132.1	73.3
Bloomington, IN M.S.A.	168,926									
Includes Monroe and Owen Counties										
City of Bloomington	85,730	463	2	47	76	338	2,275	465	1,678	132
Total area actually reporting	87.7%	586	3	85	80	418	3,399	646	2,529	224
Estimated total	100.0%	611	4	86	81	440	3,607	712	2,660	235
Rate per 100,000 inhabitants		361.7	2.4	50.9	47.9	260.5	2,135.3	421.5	1,574.7	139.1
Bloomsburg-Berwick, PA M.S.A	83,914									
Includes Columbia and Montour Counties										
City of Bloomsburg Town	14,145	35	0	4	0	31	194	27	161	6
City of Berwick	10,030	37	0	8	2	27	181	19	156	6
Total area actually reporting	98.1%	156	0	25	3	128	929	118	786	25
Estimated total	100.0%	156	0	25	3	128	953	119	809	25
Rate per 100,000 inhabitants		185.9	0.0	29.8	3.6	152.5	1,135.7	141.8	964.1	29.8
Boise City, ID M.S.A.	730,260									
Includes Ada, Boise, Canyon, Gem, and Owyhee Counties										
City of Boise	229,265	635	1	173	51	410	4,627	638	3,725	264
Total area actually reporting	100.0%	1,782	9	394	103	1,276	11,455	2,007	8,546	902
Rate per 100,000 inhabitants		244.0	1.2	54.0	14.1	174.7	1,568.6	274.8	1,170.3	123.5
Boston-Cambridge-Newton, MA-NH M.S.A.	4,879,088									
Includes the Metropolitan Divisions of Boston, MA; Cambridge-Newton-Framingham, MA; and Rockingham County-Strafford County, NH										
City of Boston, MA	694,673	4,324	56	278	1,172	2,818	14,007	1,853	11,000	1,154
City of Cambridge, MA	114,881	339	0	27	102	210	2,068	255	1,704	109
City of Newton, MA	89,505	58	0	3	5	50	629	72	540	17
City of Framingham, MA	72,510	253	0	21	18	214	820	123	635	62
City of Waltham, MA	62,655	117	0	13	11	93	561	90	431	40
Total area actually reporting	98.8%	13,783	93	1,433	2,627	9,630	56,555	7,352	44,867	4,336
Estimated total	100.0%	13,878	93	1,439	2,655	9,691	56,956	7,376	45,203	4,377
Rate per 100,000 inhabitants		284.4	1.9	29.5	54.4	198.6	1,167.3	151.2	926.5	89.7
Boston, MA M.D.	2,030,758									
Includes Norfolk, Plymouth, and Suffolk Counties										
Total area actually reporting	97.6%	8,165	67	718	1,752	5,628	28,224	3,608	22,402	2,214
Estimated total	100.0%	8,241	67	724	1,776	5,674	28,592	3,632	22,710	2,250
Rate per 100,000 inhabitants		405.8	3.3	35.7	87.5	279.4	1,407.9	178.8	1,118.3	110.8
Cambridge-Newton-Framingham, MA M.D.	2,407,742									
Includes Essex and Middlesex Counties										
Total area actually reporting	99.7%	5,034	18	576	791	3,649	23,502	3,302	18,319	1,881
Estimated total	100.0%	5,053	18	576	795	3,664	23,535	3,302	18,347	1,886
Rate per 100,000 inhabitants		209.9	0.7	23.9	33.0	152.2	977.5	137.1	762.0	78.3
Rockingham County-Strafford County, NH M.D.	440,588									
Includes Rockingham and Strafford Counties										
Total area actually reporting	100.0%	584	8	139	84	353	4,829	442	4,146	241
Rate per 100,000 inhabitants		132.6	1.8	31.5	19.1	80.1	1,096.0	100.3	941.0	54.7
Boulder, CO M.S.A.[5]	326,642									
Includes Boulder County										
City of Boulder	108,380	292	0	39	39	214	3,666	386	3,035	245
Total area actually reporting	100.0%	882	2	201	95	584		1,073		717
Rate per 100,000 inhabitants		270.0	0.6	61.5	29.1	178.8		328.5		219.5
Bowling Green, KY M.S.A.	177,116									
Includes Allen, Butler, Edmonson, and Warren Counties										
City of Bowling Green	68,268	208	6	59	64	79	3,312	414	2,681	217
Total area actually reporting	100.0%	276	7	80	73	116	4,190	724	3,172	294
Rate per 100,000 inhabitants		155.8	4.0	45.2	41.2	65.5	2,365.7	408.8	1,790.9	166.0
Bridgeport-Stamford-Norwalk, CT M.S.A.[2]	936,667									
Includes Fairfield County										
City of Bridgeport[2]	146,819	945	11	83	325	526	2,833	588	1,647	598
City of Stamford	132,007	218	3	21	64	130	2,120	228	1,655	237
City of Norwalk	89,442	252	1	13	49	189	1,347	147	1,082	118
City of Danbury	85,818	133	0	21	40	72	1,163	128	926	109
City of Stratford	52,472	53	0	6	21	26	1,080	132	833	115
Total area actually reporting	100.0%	1,756	16	178	547	1,015	12,541	1,633	9,399	1,509
Rate per 100,000 inhabitants		187.5	1.7	19.0	58.4	108.4	1,338.9	174.3	1,003.5	161.1

Table 6. Crime in the United States, by Selected Metropolitan Statistical Area, 2018—Continued

(Number, percent, rate per 100,000 population.)

Area	Population	Violent crime	Murder and nonnegligent manslaughter	Rape[1]	Robbery	Aggravated assault	Property crime	Burglary	Larceny-theft	Motor vehicle theft
Brownsville-Harlingen, TX M.S.A.[2]	424,884									
Includes Cameron County										
City of Brownsville[2]	184,461	694	2	12	141	539	4,834	553	4,142	139
City of Harlingen[2]	65,525	272	2	49	50	171	2,792	455	2,262	75
Total area actually reporting	99.8%	1,408	5	172	217	1,014	10,859	1,697	8,816	346
Estimated total	100.0%	1,409	5	172	217	1,015	10,871	1,700	8,824	347
Rate per 100,000 inhabitants		331.6	1.2	40.5	51.1	238.9	2,558.6	400.1	2,076.8	81.7
Brunswick, GA M.S.A.	118,723									
Includes Brantley, Glynn, and McIntosh Counties										
City of Brunswick	16,431	175	2	4	42	127	862	176	627	59
Total area actually reporting	100.0%	433	7	35	93	298	3,272	682	2,367	223
Rate per 100,000 inhabitants		364.7	5.9	29.5	78.3	251.0	2,756.0	574.4	1,993.7	187.8
Buffalo-Cheektowaga, NY M.S.A.	1,115,731									
Includes Erie and Niagara Counties										
City of Buffalo	258,219	2,692	57	167	907	1,561	9,852	2,271	6,707	874
City of Cheektowaga Town	77,648	189	0	17	71	101	2,156	259	1,810	87
Total area actually reporting	98.2%	4,132	61	391	1,278	2,402	23,030	4,012	17,571	1,447
Estimated total	100.0%	4,151	61	393	1,282	2,415	23,281	4,038	17,788	1,455
Rate per 100,000 inhabitants		372.0	5.5	35.2	114.9	216.5	2,086.6	361.9	1,594.3	130.4
Burlington, NC M.S.A.[3]	164,044									
Includes Alamance County[3]										
City of Burlington[3]	53,385		4		61	349	1,877	481	1,303	93
Total area actually reporting	84.6%	572	4	36	74	458	3,106	873	2,088	145
Estimated total	100.0%	661	5	43	91	522	3,898	1,029	2,683	186
Rate per 100,000 inhabitants		402.9	3.0	26.2	55.5	318.2	2,376.2	627.3	1,635.5	113.4
Burlington-South Burlington, VT M.S.A.	220,420									
Includes Chittenden, Franklin, and Grand Isle Counties										
City of Burlington	42,212	115	1	22	10	82	837	120	704	13
City of South Burlington	19,318	32	1	17	1	13	572	51	520	1
Total area actually reporting	100.0%	384	4	117	26	237	3,412	493	2,852	67
Rate per 100,000 inhabitants		174.2	1.8	53.1	11.8	107.5	1,548.0	223.7	1,293.9	30.4
California-Lexington Park, MD M.S.A.	112,779									
Includes St. Mary's County										
Total area actually reporting	100.0%	250	2	36	57	155	1,913	446	1,391	76
Rate per 100,000 inhabitants		221.7	1.8	31.9	50.5	137.4	1,696.2	395.5	1,233.4	67.4
Canton-Massillon, OH M.S.A.	399,725									
Includes Carroll and Stark Counties										
City of Canton	70,605	845	3	98	189	555	3,790	970	2,517	303
City of Massillon	32,361	75	0	30	17	28	747	118	595	34
Total area actually reporting	84.3%	1,214	7	199	261	747	8,444	1,871	6,070	503
Estimated total	100.0%	1,267	7	209	282	769	9,523	2,020	6,928	575
Rate per 100,000 inhabitants		317.0	1.8	52.3	70.5	192.4	2,382.4	505.3	1,733.2	143.8
Cape Coral-Fort Myers, FL M.S.A.	757,462									
Includes Lee County										
City of Cape Coral	187,869	267	3	17	51	196	2,701	413	2,110	178
City of Fort Myers	82,805	582	11	53	146	372	2,285	376	1,652	257
Total area actually reporting	100.0%	2,126	40	276	454	1,356	10,803	1,802	7,938	1,063
Rate per 100,000 inhabitants		280.7	5.3	36.4	59.9	179.0	1,426.2	237.9	1,048.0	140.3
Cape Girardeau, MO-IL M.S.A.	96,774									
Includes Alexander County, IL and Bollinger and Cape Girardeau Counties, MO										
City of Cape Girardeau, MO	39,303	192	5	14	52	121	1,537	250	1,214	73
Total area actually reporting	97.7%	287	8	26	57	196	2,104	394	1,594	116
Estimated total	100.0%	290	8	27	57	198	2,132	399	1,615	118
Rate per 100,000 inhabitants		299.7	8.3	27.9	58.9	204.6	2,203.1	412.3	1,668.8	121.9
Carson City, NV M.S.A.	54,555									
Includes Carson City										
Total area actually reporting	100.0%	199	1	43	13	142	785	173	533	79
Rate per 100,000 inhabitants		364.8	1.8	78.8	23.8	260.3	1,438.9	317.1	977.0	144.8
Casper, WY M.S.A.	79,631									
Includes Natrona County										
City of Casper	58,200	117	2	60	4	51	1,630	327	1,165	138
Total area actually reporting	100.0%	176	3	72	4	97	2,006	427	1,389	190
Rate per 100,000 inhabitants		221.0	3.8	90.4	5.0	121.8	2,519.1	536.2	1,744.3	238.6
Chambersburg-Waynesboro, PA M.S.A.	154,702									
Includes Franklin County										
City of Chambersburg	20,962	60	0	4	13	43	577	73	479	25
City of Waynesboro	10,920	13	0	4	3	6	189	27	155	7
Total area actually reporting	97.4%	257	3	62	29	163	1,876	344	1,460	72
Estimated total	100.0%	259	3	62	29	165	1,916	345	1,499	72
Rate per 100,000 inhabitants		167.4	1.9	40.1	18.7	106.7	1,238.5	223.0	969.0	46.5

Table 6. Crime in the United States, by Selected Metropolitan Statistical Area, 2018—Continued

(Number, percent, rate per 100,000 population.)

Area	Population	Violent crime	Murder and nonnegligent manslaughter	Rape[1]	Robbery	Aggravated assault	Property crime	Burglary	Larceny-theft	Motor vehicle theft
Champaign-Urbana, IL M.S.A.	225,961									
Includes Champaign and Piatt Counties										
City of Champaign	88,326	602	7	72	83	440	1,998	276	1,637	85
City of Urbana	42,029	150	2	24	57	67	1,233	198	1,012	23
Total area actually reporting	99.0%	958	10	163	160	625	4,396	738	3,501	157
Estimated total	100.0%	960	10	163	160	627	4,426	744	3,523	159
Rate per 100,000 inhabitants		424.9	4.4	72.1	70.8	277.5	1,958.7	329.3	1,559.1	70.4
Charleston, WV M.S.A.	261,601									
Includes Boone, Clay, Jackson, Kanawha, and Lincoln Counties										
City of Charleston	47,470	331	10	50	48	223	2,853	660	1,947	246
Total area actually reporting	78.8%	1,052	20	140	68	824	6,548	1,467	4,372	709
Estimated total	100.0%	1,177	22	152	113	890	6,983	1,523	4,642	818
Rate per 100,000 inhabitants		449.9	8.4	58.1	43.2	340.2	2,669.3	582.2	1,774.5	312.7
Charleston-North Charleston, SC M.S.A.	792,638									
Includes Berkeley, Charleston, and Dorchester Counties										
City of Charleston	137,092	415	10	57	89	259	2,848	360	2,163	325
City of North Charleston	112,840	1,039	25	77	302	635	6,567	880	4,985	702
Total area actually reporting	99.0%	3,010	61	277	594	2,078	20,394	3,018	15,193	2,183
Estimated total	100.0%	3,045	61	279	599	2,106	20,650	3,046	15,416	2,188
Rate per 100,000 inhabitants		384.2	7.7	35.2	75.6	265.7	2,605.2	384.3	1,944.9	276.0
Charlotte-Concord-Gastonia, NC-SC M.S.A.[3]	2,597,260									
Includes Anson, Cabarrus, Gaston, Iredell, Lincoln, Mecklenburg, Rowan, and Union Counties, NC[3] and Chester, Lancaster, and York Counties, SC										
City of Charlotte-Mecklenburg, NC[3]	931,235		59		1,761	4,408	34,881	5,670	26,186	3,025
City of Concord, NC[3]	94,022		3		40	50	1,679	201	1,414	64
City of Gastonia, NC[3]	77,316		7		140	378	3,839	624	2,919	296
City of Rock Hill, SC	74,049		3		61	246	2,794	325	2,263	206
Total area actually reporting	99.0%	10,422	136	155	2,614	7,517	70,283	12,897	52,180	5,206
Estimated total	100.0%	11,087	136	717	2,631	7,603	71,158	13,046	52,879	5,233
Rate per 100,000 inhabitants		426.9	5.2	27.6	101.3	292.7	2,739.7	502.3	2,036.0	201.5
Charlottesville, VA M.S.A.	218,409									
Includes Albemarle, Buckingham, Fluvanna, Greene, and Nelson Counties and Charlottesville City										
City of Charlottesville	48,585	174	1	36	30	107	1,161	116	961	84
Total area actually reporting	100.0%	414	3	125	57	229	3,192	350	2,649	193
Rate per 100,000 inhabitants		189.6	1.4	57.2	26.1	104.8	1,461.5	160.2	1,212.9	88.4
Chattanooga, TN-GA M.S.A.	560,236									
Includes Catoosa, Dade, and Walker Counties, GA and Hamilton, Marion, and Sequatchie Counties, TN										
City of Chattanooga, TN	180,397	1,891	19	149	310	1,413	10,930	1,441	8,065	1,424
Total area actually reporting	97.5%	2,925	29	209	387	2,300	18,010	2,681	13,070	2,259
Estimated total	100.0%	2,944	29	209	387	2,319	18,201	2,726	13,213	2,262
Rate per 100,000 inhabitants		525.5	5.2	37.3	69.1	413.9	3,248.8	486.6	2,358.5	403.8
Chicago-Naperville-Elgin, IL-IN-WI M.S.A.[4,5]	9,503,981									
Includes the Metropolitan Divisions of Chicago-Naperville-Evanston, IL; Elgin, IL; Gary, IN; and Lake County-Kenosha County, IL-WI										
City of Chicago, IL	2,719,151	27,357	563	1,798	9,684	15,312	86,513	11,686	64,695	10,132
City of Naperville, IL[4]	148,457	102	0	29	21	52		163		39
City of Elgin, IL	113,060	235	3	48	57	127	1,713	172	1,455	86
City of Gary, IN	75,426	374	40	33	145	156	2,723	703	1,564	456
City of Evanston, IL	74,780	140	3	6	47	84	1,702	289	1,358	55
City of Schaumburg, IL	74,169	61	0	15	22	24	1,516	75	1,393	48
City of Bolingbrook, IL	75,451	112	1	23	17	71	592	60	477	55
City of Skokie, IL	63,849	172	0	15	37	120	1,606	206	1,348	52
City of Des Plaines, IL	58,155	39	1	6	12	20	725	65	623	37
City of Hoffman Estates, IL	51,514	48	1	14	9	24	417	45	349	23
Total area actually reporting	96.4%		755	3,739						
Estimated total	100.0%		762	3,829						
Rate per 100,000 inhabitants			8.0	40.3						
Chicago-Naperville-Evanston, IL M.D.[4,5]	7,167,753									
Includes Cook, DuPage, Grundy, McHenry, and Will Counties,										
Total area actually reporting	97.5%		655	3,052	11,650					14,041
Estimated total	100.0%		659	3,106	11,721					14,220
Rate per 100,000 inhabitants			9.2	43.3	163.5					198.4
Elgin, IL M.D.	766,519									
Includes DeKalb, Kane, and Kendall Counties										
Total area actually reporting	98.4%	1,277	9	278	214	776	7,942	979	6,638	325
Estimated total	100.0%	1,297	9	281	217	790	8,122	1,004	6,782	336
Rate per 100,000 inhabitants		169.2	1.2	36.7	28.3	103.1	1,059.6	131.0	884.8	43.8

Table 6. Crime in the United States, by Selected Metropolitan Statistical Area, 2018—Continued

(Number, percent, rate per 100,000 population.)

Area	Population	Violent crime	Murder and nonnegligent manslaughter	Rape[1]	Robbery	Aggravated assault	Property crime	Burglary	Larceny-theft	Motor vehicle theft
Gary, IN M.D.[5]	700,510									
Includes Jasper, Lake, Newton, and Porter Counties										
Total area actually reporting	88.6%		68	158		663	13,620	1,764	10,448	1,408
Estimated total	100.0%		69	167		752	14,929	1,961	11,465	1,503
Rate per 100,000 inhabitants			9.8	23.8		107.4	2,131.2	279.9	1,636.7	214.6
Lake County-Kenosha County, IL-WI M.D.[4,5]	869,199									
Includes Lake County, IL and Kenosha County, WI										
Total area actually reporting	91.9%	1,343	23	251	357	712		1,341		
Estimated total	100.0%	1,483	25	275	392	791		1,498		
Rate per 100,000 inhabitants		170.6	2.9	31.6	45.1	91.0		172.3		
Chico, CA M.S.A.	228,880									
Includes Butte County										
City of Chico	94,273	611	2	86	106	417	2,403	327	1,761	315
Total area actually reporting	100.0%	1,214	10	152	178	874	5,824	1,242	3,762	820
Rate per 100,000 inhabitants		530.4	4.4	66.4	77.8	381.9	2,544.6	542.6	1,643.7	358.3
Cincinnati, OH-KY-IN M.S.A.[2]	2,212,114									
Includes Dearborn, Franklin, Ohio, and Union Counties, IN; Boone, Bracken, Campbell, Gallatin, Grant, Kenton, and Pendleton Counties, KY; and Brown, Butler, Clermont, Hamilton, and Warren Counties, OH										
City of Cincinnati, OH	301,952	2,535	57	293	897	1,288	13,710	2,978	9,422	1,310
Total area actually reporting	86.9%	4,733	85	847	1,437	2,364	41,496	6,850	31,502	3,144
Estimated total	100.0%	4,982	86	873	1,492	2,531	45,584	7,454	34,770	3,360
Rate per 100,000 inhabitants		225.2	3.9	39.5	67.4	114.4	2,060.7	337.0	1,571.8	151.9
Clarksville, TN-KY M.S.A.	302,027									
Includes Christian and Trigg Counties, KY and Montgomery and Stewart Counties, TN										
City of Clarksville, TN	156,264	1,041	15	81	130	815	4,514	598	3,572	344
Total area actually reporting	100.0%	1,333	19	120	167	1,027	7,140	1,289	5,277	574
Rate per 100,000 inhabitants		441.4	6.3	39.7	55.3	340.0	2,364.0	426.8	1,747.2	190.0
Cleveland, TN M.S.A.	123,241									
Includes Bradley and Polk Counties										
City of Cleveland	44,954	412	0	22	32	358	2,512	384	1,908	220
Total area actually reporting	100.0%	664	1	33	44	586	3,826	674	2,748	404
Rate per 100,000 inhabitants		538.8	0.8	26.8	35.7	475.5	3,104.5	546.9	2,229.8	327.8
Coeur d'Alene, ID M.S.A.	161,890									
Includes Kootenai County										
City of Coeur d'Alene	51,650	188	2	54	19	113	972	141	760	71
Total area actually reporting	100.0%	370	5	79	28	258	2,518	418	1,929	171
Rate per 100,000 inhabitants		228.6	3.1	48.8	17.3	159.4	1,555.4	258.2	1,191.5	105.6
College Station-Bryan, TX M.S.A.[2]	261,699									
Includes Brazos, Burleson, and Robertson Counties										
City of College Station	116,565	237	1	76	30	130	2,422	285	1,988	149
City of Bryan	85,152	332	2	55	53	222	2,073	373	1,561	139
Total area actually reporting	100.0%	713	5	166	93	449	5,617	916	4,337	364
Rate per 100,000 inhabitants		272.5	1.9	63.4	35.5	171.6	2,146.4	350.0	1,657.2	139.1
Colorado Springs, CO M.S.A.	735,368									
Includes El Paso and Teller Counties										
City of Colorado Springs	471,124	2,617	32	483	515	1,587	15,752	2,727	10,626	2,399
Total area actually reporting	98.6%	3,405	44	680	570	2,111	19,217	3,316	13,024	2,877
Estimated total	100.0%	3,430	44	687	578	2,121	19,485	3,323	13,266	2,896
Rate per 100,000 inhabitants		466.4	6.0	93.4	78.6	288.4	2,649.7	451.9	1,804.0	393.8
Columbia, MO M.S.A.	208,160									
Includes Boone, Cooper, and Howard Counties										
City of Columbia	123,586	446	5	89	104	248	3,483	549	2,648	286
Total area actually reporting	100.0%	606	9	110	116	371	4,879	743	3,715	421
Rate per 100,000 inhabitants		291.1	4.3	52.8	55.7	178.2	2,343.9	356.9	1,784.7	202.2
Columbia, SC M.S.A.	833,205									
Includes Calhoun, Fairfield, Kershaw, Lexington, Richland, and Saluda Counties										
City of Columbia	133,540	986	16	90	224	656	6,753	1,006	4,979	768
Total area actually reporting	99.9%	4,731	61	419	724	3,527	29,202	4,814	20,968	3,420
Estimated total	100.0%	4,732	61	419	724	3,528	29,212	4,816	20,975	3,421
Rate per 100,000 inhabitants		567.9	7.3	50.3	86.9	423.4	3,506.0	578.0	2,517.4	410.6
Columbus, IN M.S.A.	82,793									
Includes Bartholomew County										
City of Columbus	47,595	76	0	46	26	4	1,706	180	1,411	115
Total area actually reporting	100.0%	123	0	67	31	25	2,180	255	1,752	173
Rate per 100,000 inhabitants		148.6	0.0	80.9	37.4	30.2	2,633.1	308.0	2,116.1	209.0
Columbus, OH M.S.A.	2,106,940									
Includes Delaware, Fairfield, Franklin, Hocking, Licking, Madison, Morrow, Perry, Pickaway, and Union Counties										

Table 6. Crime in the United States, by Selected Metropolitan Statistical Area, 2018—Continued

(Number, percent, rate per 100,000 population.)

Area	Population	Violent crime	Murder and nonnegligent manslaughter	Rape[1]	Robbery	Aggravated assault	Property crime	Burglary	Larceny-theft	Motor vehicle theft
City of Columbus	892,576	4,416	99	820	1,922	1,575	31,512	6,271	21,323	3,918
Total area actually reporting	93.7%	5,775	129	1,217	2,221	2,208	51,370	9,423	36,982	4,965
Estimated total	100.0%	5,951	129	1,247	2,300	2,275	53,769	9,669	38,958	5,142
Rate per 100,000 inhabitants		282.4	6.1	59.2	109.2	108.0	2,552.0	458.9	1,849.0	244.1
Corpus Christi, TX M.S.A.[2]	430,731									
Includes Nueces and San Patricio Counties										
City of Corpus Christi	328,614	2,488	24	295	515	1,654	11,975	2,146	8,913	916
Total area actually reporting	97.4%	2,991	32	339	538	2,082	14,290	2,628	10,600	1,062
Estimated total	100.0%	3,012	32	342	541	2,097	14,525	2,662	10,785	1,078
Rate per 100,000 inhabitants		699.3	7.4	79.4	125.6	486.8	3,372.2	618.0	2,503.9	250.3
Corvallis, OR M.S.A.	91,791									
Includes Benton County										
City of Corvallis	58,491	94	0	28	25	41	1,835	185	1,580	70
Total area actually reporting	100.0%	139	1	36	30	72	2,587	290	2,196	101
Rate per 100,000 inhabitants		151.4	1.1	39.2	32.7	78.4	2,818.4	315.9	2,392.4	110.0
Crestview-Fort Walton Beach-Destin, FL M.S.A.	276,692									
Includes Okaloosa and Walton Counties										
City of Crestview	24,293	86	1	14	21	50	702	137	516	49
City of Fort Walton Beach	22,263	69	1	13	7	48	655	82	515	58
Total area actually reporting	99.7%	872	12	124	61	675	5,339	874	4,078	387
Estimated total	100.0%	875	12	124	62	677	5,363	879	4,095	389
Rate per 100,000 inhabitants		316.2	4.3	44.8	22.4	244.7	1,938.3	317.7	1,480.0	140.6
Cumberland, MD-WV M.S.A.	97,589									
Includes Allegany County, MD and Mineral County, WV										
City of Cumberland, MD	19,555	146	0	11	30	105	881	231	630	20
Total area actually reporting	98.5%	291	2	21	44	224	1,805	431	1,294	80
Estimated total	100.0%	297	2	21	46	228	1,845	435	1,328	82
Rate per 100,000 inhabitants		304.3	2.0	21.5	47.1	233.6	1,890.6	445.7	1,360.8	84.0
Dallas-Fort Worth-Arlington, TX M.S.A.[2]	7,458,118									
Includes the Metropolitan Divisions of Dallas-Plano-Irving and Fort Worth-Arlington-Grapevine[2]										
City of Dallas[2]	1,362,465	10,422	155	828	3,987	5,452	44,266	9,065	25,541	9,660
City of Fort Worth	893,756	4,482	58	482	1,116	2,826	25,433	4,504	17,957	2,972
City of Arlington	400,920	1,784	7	203	360	1,214	11,780	1,509	9,033	1,238
City of Plano	289,897	402	5	77	112	208	4,955	671	3,911	373
City of Irving	243,940	510	10	55	218	227	5,759	712	4,327	720
City of Denton	139,262	439	2	124	97	216	3,228	404	2,600	224
City of Richardson	119,480	135	2	18	52	63	2,522	364	1,944	214
City of Grapevine	55,130	87	0	7	16	64	1,288	91	1,061	136
Total area actually reporting	99.6%	26,124	328	3,357	7,717	14,722	165,937	26,825	116,661	22,451
Estimated total	100.0%	26,178	328	3,362	7,725	14,763	166,519	26,917	117,108	22,494
Rate per 100,000 inhabitants		351.0	4.4	45.1	103.6	197.9	2,232.7	360.9	1,570.2	301.6
Dallas-Plano-Irving, TX M.D.[2]	5,001,330									
Includes Collin, Dallas, Denton, Ellis, Hunt, Kaufman, and Rockwall Counties										
Total area actually reporting	99.9%	17,688	241	2,216	5,851	9,380	109,087	18,048	74,577	16,462
Estimated total	100.0%	17,694	241	2,216	5,851	9,386	109,150	18,062	74,620	16,468
Rate per 100,000 inhabitants		353.8	4.8	44.3	117.0	187.7	2,182.4	361.1	1,492.0	329.3
Fort Worth-Arlington-Grapevine, TX M.D.[2]	2,456,788									
Includes Johnson, Parker, Tarrant, and Wise Counties										
Total area actually reporting	98.9%	8,436	87	1,141	1,866	5,342	56,850	8,777	42,084	5,989
Estimated total	100.0%	8,484	87	1,146	1,874	5,377	57,369	8,855	42,488	6,026
Rate per 100,000 inhabitants		345.3	3.5	46.6	76.3	218.9	2,335.1	360.4	1,729.4	245.3
Dalton, GA M.S.A.	144,471									
Includes Murray and Whitfield Counties										
City of Dalton	33,831	93	0	11	21	61	987	119	787	81
Total area actually reporting	99.6%	297	1	22	33	241	2,435	499	1,730	206
Estimated total	100.0%	297	1	22	33	241	2,444	499	1,739	206
Rate per 100,000 inhabitants		205.6	0.7	15.2	22.8	166.8	1,691.7	345.4	1,203.7	142.6
Danville, IL M.S.A.	77,051									
Includes Vermilion County										
City of Danville	31,203	559	12	53	103	391	1,508	379	1,052	77
Total area actually reporting	98.4%	717	16	93	117	491	2,303	636	1,550	117
Estimated total	100.0%	718	16	93	117	492	2,319	639	1,562	118
Rate per 100,000 inhabitants		931.9	20.8	120.7	151.8	638.5	3,009.7	829.3	2,027.2	153.1
Daphne-Fairhope-Foley, AL M.S.A.	217,171									
Includes Baldwin County										
City of Daphne	26,618	36	0	6	8	22	463	42	404	17
City of Fairhope	21,688	43	0	16	3	24	537	57	449	31
City of Foley	18,740	48	2	6	7	33	755	90	643	22
City of Gulf Shores	12,014	24	0	3	2	19	497	53	419	25
Total area actually reporting	100.0%	565	3	72	70	420	4,010	556	3,263	191
Rate per 100,000 inhabitants		260.2	1.4	33.2	32.2	193.4	1,846.5	256.0	1,502.5	87.9

Table 6. Crime in the United States, by Selected Metropolitan Statistical Area, 2018—Continued

(Number, percent, rate per 100,000 population.)

Area	Population	Violent crime	Murder and nonnegligent manslaughter	Rape[1]	Robbery	Aggravated assault	Property crime	Burglary	Larceny-theft	Motor vehicle theft
Dayton-Kettering, OH M.S.A.[2]	804,790									
Includes Greene, Miami, and Montgomery Counties										
City of Dayton	140,094	1,291	37	167	403	684	6,323	1,697	3,831	795
City of Kettering	55,038	54	0	19	16	19	838	168	631	39
Total area actually reporting	95.7%	2,496	60	470	667	1,299	19,241	3,755	13,631	1,855
Estimated total	100.0%	2,555	60	485	706	1,304	19,726	3,770	14,026	1,930
Rate per 100,000 inhabitants		317.5	7.5	60.3	87.7	162.0	2,451.1	468.4	1,742.8	239.8
Decatur, IL M.S.A.	104,649									
Includes Macon County										
City of Decatur	71,625	358	9	30	84	235	2,050	618	1,325	107
Total area actually reporting	99.0%	407	9	36	86	276	2,529	712	1,698	119
Estimated total	100.0%	408	9	36	86	277	2,543	715	1,708	120
Rate per 100,000 inhabitants		389.9	8.6	34.4	82.2	264.7	2,430.0	683.2	1,632.1	114.7
Deltona-Daytona Beach-Ormond Beach, FL M.S.A.	657,657									
Includes Flagler and Volusia Counties										
City of Daytona Beach	69,030	764	8	17	91	648	3,358	384	2,750	224
City of Ormond Beach	43,315	131	0	12	16	103	1,367	184	1,088	95
City of DeLand	33,384	182	2	2	43	135	1,256	185	993	78
Total area actually reporting	100.0%	2,237	25	171	314	1,727	14,614	2,216	11,366	1,032
Rate per 100,000 inhabitants		340.1	3.8	26.0	47.7	262.6	2,222.1	337.0	1,728.3	156.9
Detroit-Warren-Dearborn, MI M.S.A.[5]	4,325,220									
Includes the Metropolitan Divisions of Detroit-Dearborn-Livonia and Warren-Troy-Farmington Hills										
City of Detroit	671,275	13,478	261	988	2,309	9,920	28,897	7,440	15,003	6,454
City of Warren	135,160	688	4	108	121	455	2,808	581	1,688	539
City of Dearborn	94,022	314	1	36	82	195	1,871	233	1,438	200
City of Livonia	93,740	138	0	34	19	85	1,313	111	1,092	110
City of Troy	84,221	52	1	8	11	32	1,157	94	1,011	52
City of Farmington Hills	81,239	69	1	16	9	43	681	85	554	42
City of Southfield	73,418	204	2	36	48	118	1,509	262	1,049	198
City of Taylor	61,037	366	1	54	48	263	1,346	276	946	124
City of Pontiac	59,817	799	14	58	96	631	1,286	412	779	95
City of Novi	60,378	43	2	6	3	32	532	33	481	18
Total area actually reporting	100.0%	23,144	345	2,618	3,556	16,625			49,050	11,168
Rate per 100,000 inhabitants		535.1	8.0	60.5	82.2	384.4			1,134.0	258.2
Detroit-Dearborn-Livonia, MI M.D.	1,748,511									
Includes Wayne County										
Total area actually reporting	100.0%	17,516	293	1,582	2,916	12,725	47,367	10,476	28,355	8,536
Rate per 100,000 inhabitants		1,001.8	16.8	90.5	166.8	727.8	2,709.0	599.1	1,621.7	488.2
Warren-Troy-Farmington Hills, MI M.D.[5]	2,576,709									
Includes Lapeer, Livingston, Macomb, Oakland, and St. Clair Counties										
Total area actually reporting	100.0%	5,628	52	1,036	640	3,900			20,695	2,632
Rate per 100,000 inhabitants		218.4	2.0	40.2	24.8	151.4			803.2	102.1
Dothan, AL M.S.A.	148,181									
Includes Geneva, Henry, and Houston Counties										
City of Dothan	67,260	656	9	26	78	543	2,745	550	2,002	193
Total area actually reporting	99.7%	892	11	49	100	732	4,108	886	2,909	313
Estimated total	100.0%	892	11	49	100	732	4,111	886	2,912	313
Rate per 100,000 inhabitants		602.0	7.4	33.1	67.5	494.0	2,774.3	597.9	1,965.2	211.2
Dover, DE M.S.A.	178,138									
Includes Kent County										
City of Dover	37,778	301	4	20	43	234	1,810	58	1,663	89
Total area actually reporting	100.0%	757	6	82	92	577	3,804	410	3,206	188
Rate per 100,000 inhabitants		425.0	3.4	46.0	51.6	323.9	2,135.4	230.2	1,799.7	105.5
Duluth, MN-WI M.S.A.	288,923									
Includes Carlton, Lake, and St. Louis Counties, MN and Douglas County, WI										
City of Duluth, MN	86,048	308	1	45	66	196	3,688	472	3,013	203
Total area actually reporting	100.0%	605	4	119	99	383	7,550	1,192	5,841	517
Rate per 100,000 inhabitants		209.4	1.4	41.2	34.3	132.6	2,613.2	412.6	2,021.6	178.9
East Stroudsburg, PA M.S.A.	167,618									
Includes Monroe County										
Total area actually reporting	100.0%	352	6	87	39	220	2,892	485	2,285	122
Rate per 100,000 inhabitants		210.0	3.6	51.9	23.3	131.3	1,725.4	289.3	1,363.2	72.8
Eau Claire, WI M.S.A.[2]	168,407									
Includes Chippewa and Eau Claire[2] Counties										
City of Eau Claire[2]	68,923	199	0	58	23	118	1,688	292	1,332	64
Total area actually reporting	100.0%	306	2	108	28	168	2,851	462	2,259	130
Rate per 100,000 inhabitants		181.7	1.2	64.1	16.6	99.8	1,692.9	274.3	1,341.4	77.2
El Centro, CA M.S.A.	182,590									
Includes Imperial County										

Table 6. Crime in the United States, by Selected Metropolitan Statistical Area, 2018—Continued

(Number, percent, rate per 100,000 population.)

Area	Population	Violent crime	Murder and nonnegligent manslaughter	Rape[1]	Robbery	Aggravated assault	Property crime	Burglary	Larceny-theft	Motor vehicle theft
City of El Centro	44,609	126	1	12	29	84	1,625	439	1,076	110
Total area actually reporting	95.9%	645	6	40	83	516	4,293	1,090	2,726	477
Estimated total	100.0%	655	6	40	83	526	4,396	1,109	2,805	482
Rate per 100,000 inhabitants		358.7	3.3	21.9	45.5	288.1	2,407.6	607.4	1,536.2	264.0
Elizabethtown-Fort Knox, KY M.S.A.[5]	150,452									
Includes Hardin, Larue, and Meade Counties										
City of Elizabethtown	30,180	64	3	17	22	22	400	124	207	69
Total area actually reporting	100.0%	171	7	48	53	63			1,081	222
Rate per 100,000 inhabitants		113.7	4.7	31.9	35.2	41.9			718.5	147.6
Elmira, NY M.S.A.	83,485									
Includes Chemung County										
City of Elmira	27,556	70	3	0	21	46	702	131	553	18
Total area actually reporting	100.0%	134	3	19	25	87	1,304	198	1,073	33
Rate per 100,000 inhabitants		160.5	3.6	22.8	29.9	104.2	1,562.0	237.2	1,285.3	39.5
El Paso, TX M.S.A.[2]	848,016									
Includes El Paso and Hudspeth2 Counties										
City of El Paso	688,442	2,554	23	405	376	1,750	10,365	1,107	8,441	817
Total area actually reporting	100.0%	2,925	32	464	404	2,025	12,022	1,393	9,688	941
Rate per 100,000 inhabitants		344.9	3.8	54.7	47.6	238.8	1,417.7	164.3	1,142.4	111.0
Enid, OK M.S.A.	61,489									
Includes Garfield County										
City of Enid	50,214	173	3	34	17	119	1,428	370	975	83
Total area actually reporting	100.0%	188	3	39	17	129	1,577	415	1,065	97
Rate per 100,000 inhabitants		305.7	4.9	63.4	27.6	209.8	2,564.7	674.9	1,732.0	157.8
Erie, PA M.S.A.	273,386									
Includes Erie County										
City of Erie	96,758	299	11	39	91	158	1,880	420	1,355	105
Total area actually reporting	100.0%	638	17	109	117	395	4,339	718	3,455	166
Rate per 100,000 inhabitants		233.4	6.2	39.9	42.8	144.5	1,587.1	262.6	1,263.8	60.7
Eugene-Springfield, OR M.S.A.	378,307									
Includes Lane County										
City of Eugene	170,771	661	3	119	171	368	5,503	813	4,148	542
City of Springfield	62,786	182	2	36	31	113	2,120	211	1,754	155
Total area actually reporting	99.1%	1,176	5	195	224	752	9,671	1,437	7,307	927
Estimated total	100.0%	1,186	5	196	227	758	9,752	1,440	7,368	944
Rate per 100,000 inhabitants		313.5	1.3	51.8	60.0	200.4	2,577.8	380.6	1,947.6	249.5
Evansville, IN-KY M.S.A.[5]	316,135									
Includes Posey, Vanderburgh, and Warrick Counties, IN and Henderson County, KY										
City of Evansville	118,765	675	10	91	156	418	5,301	714	4,078	509
Total area actually reporting	98.0%	1,005	13	144	205	643			5,899	736
Estimated total	100.0%	1,009	13	144	205	647			5,997	737
Rate per 100,000 inhabitants		319.2	4.1	45.6	64.8	204.7			1,897.0	233.1
Fairbanks, AK M.S.A.	33,731									
Includes Fairbanks North Star Borough										
City of Fairbanks	31,635	193	4	21	43	125	1,354	111	1,089	154
Total area actually reporting	100.0%	211	4	25	43	139	1,473	113	1,201	159
Rate per 100,000 inhabitants		625.5	11.9	74.1	127.5	412.1	4,366.9	335.0	3,560.5	471.4
Fargo, ND-MN M.S.A.	244,233									
Includes Clay County, MN and Cass County, ND										
City of Fargo, ND	124,906	522	5	105	63	349	3,931	695	2,927	309
Total area actually reporting	100.0%	686	6	141	78	461	5,964	1,029	4,474	461
Rate per 100,000 inhabitants		280.9	2.5	57.7	31.9	188.8	2,441.9	421.3	1,831.9	188.8
Farmington, NM M.S.A.	126,691									
Includes San Juan County										
City of Farmington	45,364	593	8	81	70	434	1,769	434	1,189	146
Total area actually reporting	100.0%	1,520	9	152	84	1,275	2,798	726	1,822	250
Rate per 100,000 inhabitants		1,199.8	7.1	120.0	66.3	1,006.4	2,208.5	573.0	1,438.1	197.3
Fayetteville-Springdale-Rogers, AR M.S.A.[5]	525,272									
Includes Benton, Madison, and Washington[5] Counties										
City of Fayetteville	87,008	496	1	81	60	354	3,768	444	2,894	430
City of Springdale	80,895	388	3	94	31	260	2,702	357	2,078	267
City of Rogers	68,026	294	2	78	23	191	1,925	189	1,636	100
City of Bentonville	51,607	106	0	28	5	73	705	110	568	27
Total area actually reporting	100.0%	2,027	14	455	138	1,420			9,042	1,133
Rate per 100,000 inhabitants		385.9	2.7	86.6	26.3	270.3			1,721.4	215.7
Flagstaff, AZ M.S.A.	142,927									
Includes Coconino County										
City of Flagstaff	72,852	342	2	37	40	263	2,465	178	2,234	53
Total area actually reporting	100.0%	572	5	72	48	447	3,548	355	3,095	98
Rate per 100,000 inhabitants		400.2	3.5	50.4	33.6	312.7	2,482.4	248.4	2,165.4	68.6

Table 6. Crime in the United States, by Selected Metropolitan Statistical Area, 2018—Continued

(Number, percent, rate per 100,000 population.)

Area	Population	Violent crime	Murder and nonnegligent manslaughter	Rape[1]	Robbery	Aggravated assault	Property crime	Burglary	Larceny-theft	Motor vehicle theft
Flint, MI M.S.A.	405,750									
Includes Genesee County										
City of Flint	95,677	1,739	32	130	189	1,388	2,584	796	1,488	300
Total area actually reporting	100.0%	2,772	38	338	275	2,121	7,380	1,675	5,002	703
Rate per 100,000 inhabitants		683.2	9.4	83.3	67.8	522.7	1,818.9	412.8	1,232.8	173.3
Florence, SC M.S.A.	205,828									
Includes Darlington and Florence Counties										
City of Florence	37,819	362	8	18	72	264	2,462	375	1,935	152
Total area actually reporting	98.8%	1,529	33	135	214	1,147	8,008	1,794	5,632	582
Estimated total	100.0%	1,540	33	136	216	1,155	8,076	1,806	5,682	588
Rate per 100,000 inhabitants		748.2	16.0	66.1	104.9	561.1	3,923.7	877.4	2,760.6	285.7
Florence-Muscle Shoals, AL M.S.A.	146,974									
Includes Colbert and Lauderdale Counties										
City of Florence	39,925	206	4	23	30	149	1,663	282	1,215	166
City of Muscle Shoals	14,143	86	2	7	7	70	800	115	620	65
Total area actually reporting	99.8%	438	11	54	50	323	3,456	608	2,517	331
Estimated total	100.0%	438	11	54	50	323	3,457	608	2,518	331
Rate per 100,000 inhabitants		298.0	7.5	36.7	34.0	219.8	2,352.1	413.7	1,713.2	225.2
Fond du Lac, WI M.S.A.	102,729									
Includes Fond du Lac County										
City of Fond du Lac	42,777	101	4	29	14	54	1,012	78	887	47
Total area actually reporting	100.0%	145	4	40	17	84	1,358	140	1,151	67
Rate per 100,000 inhabitants		141.1	3.9	38.9	· 16.5	81.8	1,321.9	136.3	1,120.4	65.2
Fort Collins, CO M.S.A.	349,357									
Includes Larimer County										
City of Fort Collins	168,163	392	3	28	39	322	3,701	357	3,163	181
Total area actually reporting	100.0%	772	5	120	60	587	6,994	790	5,822	382
Rate per 100,000 inhabitants		221.0	1.4	34.3	17.2	168.0	2,002.0	226.1	1,666.5	109.3
Fort Smith, AR-OK M.S.A.	250,116									
Includes Crawford, Franklin, and Sebastian Counties, AR and Sequoyah County, OK										
City of Fort Smith, AR	88,290	707	9	86	97	515	4,265	711	3,268	286
Total area actually reporting	99.7%	1,306	14	180	112	1,000	7,116	1,451	5,175	490
Estimated total	100.0%	1,312	14	181	113	1,004	7,127	1,456	5,179	492
Rate per 100,000 inhabitants		524.6	5.6	72.4	45.2	401.4	2,849.5	582.1	2,070.6	196.7
Fort Wayne, IN M.S.A.	409,063									
Includes Allen and Whitley Counties										
City of Fort Wayne	267,634	1,024	40	131	307	546	7,007	1,006	5,453	548
Total area actually reporting	92.2%	1,234	41	167	347	679	8,033	1,206	6,180	647
Estimated total	100.0%	1,266	42	168	348	708	8,405	1,282	6,462	661
Rate per 100,000 inhabitants		309.5	10.3	41.1	85.1	173.1	2,054.7	313.4	1,579.7	161.6
Fresno, CA M.S.A.										
Includes Fresno County										
City of Fresno	531,818	2,953	32	170	909	1,842	17,787	2,949	12,473	2,365
Total area actually reporting	100.0%	5,893	54	350	1,171	4,318	27,426	5,905	17,532	3,989
Rate per 100,000 inhabitants		595.3	5.5	35.4	118.3	436.2	2,770.4	596.5	1,770.9	402.9
Gadsden, AL M.S.A.	102,492									
Includes Etowah County										
City of Gadsden	35,204	372	3	24	47	298	2,495	409	1,831	255
Total area actually reporting	92.8%	522	6	63	49	404	3,258	648	2,257	353
Estimated total	100.0%	546	6	64	56	420	3,422	670	2,392	360
Rate per 100,000 inhabitants		532.7	5.9	62.4	54.6	409.8	3,338.8	653.7	2,333.8	351.2
Gainesville, FL M.S.A.	327,771									
Includes Alachua, Gilchrist, and Levy Counties										
City of Gainesville	133,400	989	5	169	222	593	5,229	510	4,287	432
Total area actually reporting	99.8%	2,335	17	313	347	1,658	8,976	1,587	6,663	726
Estimated total	100.0%	2,338	17	313	348	1,660	8,997	1,592	6,677	728
Rate per 100,000 inhabitants		713.3	5.2	95.5	106.2	506.5	2,744.9	485.7	2,037.1	222.1
Gainesville, GA M.S.A.[2]	201,865									
Includes Hall County										
City of Gainesville	41,368	158	1	20	36	101	1,280	163	1,027	90
Total area actually reporting	100.0%	433	5	75	65	288	3,130	522	2,290	318
Rate per 100,000 inhabitants		214.5	2.5	37.2	32.2	142.7	1,550.5	258.6	1,134.4	157.5
Gettysburg, PA M.S.A.	102,358									
Includes Adams County										
City of Gettysburg	7,637	30	0	6	2	22	89	19	70	0
Total area actually reporting	100.0%	133	3	32	12	86	635	121	500	14
Rate per 100,000 inhabitants		129.9	2.9	31.3	11.7	84.0	620.4	118.2	488.5	13.7
Glens Falls, NY M.S.A.	123,394									
Includes Warren and Washington Counties										
City of Glens Falls	14,403	24	1	6	2	15	150	13	133	4

Table 6. Crime in the United States, by Selected Metropolitan Statistical Area, 2018—Continued

(Number, percent, rate per 100,000 population.)

Area	Population	Violent crime	Murder and nonnegligent manslaughter	Rape[1]	Robbery	Aggravated assault	Property crime	Burglary	Larceny-theft	Motor vehicle theft
Total area actually reporting	97.9%	167	2	82	12	71	1,203	138	1,036	29
Estimated total	100.0%	168	2	82	12	72	1,233	141	1,062	30
Rate per 100,000 inhabitants		136.1	1.6	66.5	9.7	58.3	999.2	114.3	860.7	24.3
Grand Forks, ND-MN M.S.A.	102,144									
Includes Polk County, MN and Grand Forks County, ND										
City of Grand Forks, ND	57,662	148	4	28	21	95	1,410	216	1,068	126
Total area actually reporting	100.0%	211	4	53	25	129	1,968	297	1,495	176
Rate per 100,000 inhabitants		206.6	3.9	51.9	24.5	126.3	1,926.7	290.8	1,463.6	172.3
Grand Island, NE M.S.A.	76,086									
Includes Hall, Howard, and Merrick Counties										
City of Grand Island	51,768	241	1	46	21	173	1,505	222	1,185	98
Total area actually reporting	100.0%	277	1	52	22	202	1,676	253	1,308	115
Rate per 100,000 inhabitants		364.1	1.3	68.3	28.9	265.5	2,202.8	332.5	1,719.1	151.1
Grand Junction, CO M.S.A.	152,438									
Includes Mesa County										
City of Grand Junction	62,974	275	3	57	17	198	2,733	291	2,282	160
Total area actually reporting	99.2%	459	4	90	26	339	3,999	559	3,177	263
Estimated total	100.0%	463	4	90	27	342	4,078	564	3,246	268
Rate per 100,000 inhabitants		303.7	2.6	59.0	17.7	224.4	2,675.2	370.0	2,129.4	175.8
Grand Rapids-Kentwood, MI M.S.A.	1,075,204									
Includes Ionia, Kent, Montcalm, and Ottawa Counties										
City of Grand Rapids	200,428	1,313	5	141	319	848	3,830	679	2,881	270
City of Kentwood	52,192	193	0	28	37	128	1,100	183	850	67
Total area actually reporting	99.9%	3,551	26	965	511	2,049	14,806	2,394	11,485	927
Estimated total	100.0%	3,558	26	966	512	2,054	14,823	2,399	11,494	930
Rate per 100,000 inhabitants		330.9	2.4	89.8	47.6	191.0	1,378.6	223.1	1,069.0	86.5
Grants Pass, OR M.S.A.	86,901									
Includes Josephine County										
City of Grants Pass	37,814	135	3	27	29	76	1,342	143	1,019	180
Total area actually reporting	100.0%	236	5	39	37	155	1,753	251	1,168	334
Rate per 100,000 inhabitants		271.6	5.8	44.9	42.6	178.4	2,017.2	288.8	1,344.1	384.3
Greeley, CO M.S.A.[4]	314,239									
Includes Weld County										
City of Greeley	107,325	424	2	78	64	280	2,739	418	2,041	280
Total area actually reporting	97.4%	791	6	155	82	548		812		591
Estimated total	100.0%	813	6	161	88	558		822		610
Rate per 100,000 inhabitants		258.7	1.9	51.2	28.0	177.6		261.6		194.1
Green Bay, WI M.S.A.[2]	322,146									
Includes Brown, Kewaunee, and Oconto Counties										
City of Green Bay	105,281	483	1	78	56	348	1,798	250	1,448	100
Total area actually reporting	100.0%	675	1	152	65	457	3,715	479	3,047	189
Rate per 100,000 inhabitants		209.5	0.3	47.2	20.2	141.9	1,153.2	148.7	945.8	58.7
Greensboro-High Point, NC M.S.A.[3]	766,708									
Includes Guilford, Randolph, and Rockingham Counties[3]										
City of Greensboro[3]	293,298		37		536	1,207	9,831	2,117	7,035	679
City of High Point[3]	112,526		19		116	517	3,682	590	2,812	280
Total area actually reporting	99.8%	3,279	66	198	774	2,241	19,834	4,343	14,103	1,388
Estimated total	100.0%	3,281	66	198	774	2,243	19,878	4,352	14,136	1,390
Rate per 100,000 inhabitants		427.9	8.6	25.8	101.0	292.5	2,592.6	567.6	1,843.7	181.3
Greenville, NC M.S.A.[3]	180,583									
Includes Pitt County[3]										
City of Greenville[3]	93,235		5		109	327	2,707	475	2,121	111
Total area actually reporting	99.1%	749	7	45	146	551	4,120	858	3,078	184
Estimated total	100.0%	753	7	45	147	554	4,169	868	3,115	186
Rate per 100,000 inhabitants		417.0	3.9	24.9	81.4	306.8	2,308.6	480.7	1,725.0	103.0
Gulfport-Biloxi, MS M.S.A.[3]	415,723									
Includes Hancock, Harrison, Jackson, and Stone Counties										
City of Gulfport	72,402	387	4	26	86	271	3,662	528	2,844	290
City of Biloxi	46,148	149	1	23	52	73	2,577	619	1,773	185
Total area actually reporting	89.7%	983	17	126	225	615	13,354	2,417	9,832	1,105
Estimated total	100.0%	1,026	23	129	235	639	14,720	2,583	10,991	1,146
Rate per 100,000 inhabitants		246.8	5.5	31.0	56.5	153.7	3,540.8	621.3	2,643.8	275.7
Hagerstown-Martinsburg, MD-WV M.S.A.	283,596									
Includes Washington County, MD and Berkeley and Morgan Counties, WV										
City of Hagerstown, MD	40,384	255	5	27	102	121	1,052	242	709	101
City of Martinsburg, WV	17,428	55	0	10	6	39	540	69	456	15
Total area actually reporting	99.6%	782	10	74	152	546	4,056	821	2,995	240

Table 6. Crime in the United States, by Selected Metropolitan Statistical Area, 2018—Continued

(Number, percent, rate per 100,000 population.)

Area	Population	Violent crime	Murder and nonnegligent manslaughter	Rape[1]	Robbery	Aggravated assault	Property crime	Burglary	Larceny-theft	Motor vehicle theft
Estimated total	100.0%	785	10	74	152	549	4,085	824	3,020	241
Rate per 100,000 inhabitants		276.8	3.5	26.1	53.6	193.6	1,440.4	290.6	1,064.9	85.0
Hammond, LA M.S.A.	132,841									
Includes Tangipahoa Parish										
City of Hammond	20,550	299	0	32	57	210	2,124	622	1,385	117
Total area actually reporting	95.0%	1,113	9	87	152	865	5,197	1,516	3,283	398
Estimated total	100.0%	1,128	9	87	152	880	5,364	1,544	3,420	400
Rate per 100,000 inhabitants		849.1	6.8	65.5	114.4	662.4	4,037.9	1,162.3	2,574.5	301.1
Hanford-Corcoran, CA M.S.A.	148,619									
Includes Kings County										
City of Hanford	56,805	274	2	32	41	199	1,264	145	945	174
City of Corcoran	21,487	75	0	8	11	56	380	88	214	78
Total area actually reporting	100.0%	784	5	81	86	612	2,701	505	1,777	419
Rate per 100,000 inhabitants		527.5	3.4	54.5	57.9	411.8	1,817.4	339.8	1,195.7	281.9
Harrisburg-Carlisle, PA M.S.A.	574,520									
Includes Cumberland, Dauphin, and Perry Counties										
City of Harrisburg	49,147	531	15	72	190	254	1,252	259	806	187
City of Carlisle	19,335	18	1	7	7	3	145	8	133	4
Total area actually reporting	100.0%	1,494	21	278	332	863	6,986	946	5,632	408
Rate per 100,000 inhabitants		260.0	3.7	48.4	57.8	150.2	1,216.0	164.7	980.3	71.0
Harrisonburg, VA M.S.A.	135,460									
Includes Rockingham County and Harrisonburg City										
City of Harrisonburg	54,869	110	4	17	12	77	834	98	711	25
Total area actually reporting	100.0%	185	5	39	14	127	1,540	246	1,241	53
Rate per 100,000 inhabitants		136.6	3.7	28.8	10.3	93.8	1,136.9	181.6	916.1	39.1
Hartford-East Hartford-Middletown, CT M.S.A.[2]	1,019,309									
Includes Hartford, Middlesex, and Tolland Counties										
City of Hartford	123,117	1,313	21	53	355	884	4,435	605	3,089	741
City of East Hartford	50,184	117	1	21	61	34	1,206	185	831	190
City of Middletown	46,314	36	1	3	8	24	584	78	431	75
Total area actually reporting	100.0%	2,419	29	235	719	1,436	21,084	2,625	15,876	2,583
Rate per 100,000 inhabitants		237.3	2.8	23.1	70.5	140.9	2,068.5	257.5	1,557.5	253.4
Hilton Head Island-Bluffton, SC M.S.A.	219,523									
Includes Beaufort and Jasper Counties										
City of Bluffton	22,578	50	1	2	5	42	252	25	206	21
Total area actually reporting	100.0%	884	10	74	119	681	3,896	667	2,930	299
Rate per 100,000 inhabitants		402.7	4.6	33.7	54.2	310.2	1,774.8	303.8	1,334.7	136.2
Hinesville, GA M.S.A.	80,804									
Includes Liberty and Long Counties										
City of Hinesville	33,163	147	1	8	33	105	1,201	218	953	30
Total area actually reporting	95.2%	331	5	14	40	272	1,650	347	1,229	74
Estimated total	100.0%	335	5	14	41	275	1,771	353	1,340	78
Rate per 100,000 inhabitants		414.6	6.2	17.3	50.7	340.3	2,191.7	436.9	1,658.3	96.5
Homosassa Springs, FL M.S.A.	146,209									
Includes Citrus County										
Total area actually reporting	100.0%	345	2	19	42	282	2,104	369	1,505	230
Rate per 100,000 inhabitants		236.0	1.4	13.0	28.7	192.9	1,439.0	252.4	1,029.3	157.3
Hot Springs, AR M.S.A.	98,904									
Includes Garland County										
City of Hot Springs	37,006	194	6	29	46	113	2,592	740	1,651	201
Total area actually reporting	100.0%	546	6	64	60	416	4,183	1,406	2,436	341
Rate per 100,000 inhabitants		552.1	6.1	64.7	60.7	420.6	4,229.4	1,421.6	2,463.0	344.8
Houma-Thibodaux, LA M.S.A.	208,782									
Includes Lafourche and Terrebonne Parishes										
City of Houma	33,226	158	3	19	30	106	1,625	173	1,366	86
City of Thibodaux	14,745	68	3	3	12	50	534	44	470	20
Total area actually reporting	98.8%	691	13	67	84	527	6,089	868	4,920	301
Estimated total	100.0%	702	13	67	84	538	6,134	878	4,954	302
Rate per 100,000 inhabitants		336.2	6.2	32.1	40.2	257.7	2,938.0	420.5	2,372.8	144.6
Houston-The Woodlands-Sugar Land, TX M.S.A.2,[5]	7,020,685									
Includes Austin, Brazoria, Chambers, Fort Bend,[2] Galveston, Harris,[5] Liberty, Montgomery, and Waller Counties										
City of Houston[2]	2,344,966	24,062	276	1,261	8,761	13,764	94,033	16,317	65,767	11,949
City of Sugar Land	89,919	82	0	15	45	22	1,537	186	1,288	63
City of Baytown	77,539	302	2	35	94	171	2,911	384	2,028	499
City of Conroe	87,544	219	3	50	49	117	2,183	284	1,763	136
City of Galveston	50,896	265	7	82	70	106	1,539	176	1,110	253
Total area actually reporting	99.8%		440	3,091	12,404		182,598	31,095	129,441	22,062
Estimated total	100.0%		440	3,094	12,408		182,869	31,137	129,651	22,081
Rate per 100,000 inhabitants			6.3	44.1	176.7		2,604.7	443.5	1,846.7	314.5

Table 6. Crime in the United States, by Selected Metropolitan Statistical Area, 2018—Continued

(Number, percent, rate per 100,000 population.)

Area	Population	Violent crime	Murder and nonnegligent manslaughter	Rape[1]	Robbery	Aggravated assault	Property crime	Burglary	Larceny-theft	Motor vehicle theft
Idaho Falls, ID M.S.A.	148,685									
Includes Bonneville, Butte, and Jefferson Counties										
City of Idaho Falls	61,643	206	0	43	12	151	960	282	597	81
Total area actually reporting	100.0%	318	2	58	15	243	1,641	453	1,052	136
Rate per 100,000 inhabitants		213.9	1.3	39.0	10.1	163.4	1,103.7	304.7	707.5	91.5
Indianapolis-Carmel-Anderson, IN M.S.A.	2,048,700									
Includes Boone, Brown, Hamilton, Hancock, Hendricks, Johnson, Madison, Marion, Morgan, Putnam, and Shelby Counties										
City of Indianapolis	877,584	11,170	162	677	3,081	7,250	36,237	7,842	23,448	4,947
City of Carmel	94,128	43	0	14	10	19	716	53	603	60
City of Anderson	54,925	227	5	78	71	73	2,340	520	1,622	198
Total area actually reporting	87.0%	12,840	185	935	3,399	8,321	51,316	9,657	35,335	6,324
Estimated total	100.0%	13,142	191	948	3,417	8,586	54,163	10,175	37,510	6,478
Rate per 100,000 inhabitants		641.5	9.3	46.3	166.8	419.1	2,643.8	496.7	1,830.9	316.2
Ithaca, NY M.S.A	103,272									
Includes Tompkins County										
City of Ithaca	31,145	72	0	9	26	37	815	62	738	15
Total area actually reporting	100.0%	147	0	59	30	58	1,727	188	1,509	30
Rate per 100,000 inhabitants		142.3	0.0	57.1	29.0	56.2	1,672.3	182.0	1,461.2	29.0
Jackson, MI M.S.A.	158,748									
Includes Jackson County										
City of Jackson	32,602	366	6	68	43	249	1,387	195	1,068	124
Total area actually reporting	100.0%	777	12	202	61	502	3,474	507	2,715	252
Rate per 100,000 inhabitants		489.5	7.6	127.2	38.4	316.2	2,188.4	319.4	1,710.3	158.7
Jackson, TN M.S.A.	178,110									
Includes Chester, Crockett, Gibson, and Madison Counties										
City of Jackson	66,848	670	9	29	102	530	2,866	447	2,197	222
Total area actually reporting	100.0%	1,084	15	58	149	862	4,566	887	3,293	386
Rate per 100,000 inhabitants		608.6	8.4	32.6	83.7	484.0	2,563.6	498.0	1,848.9	216.7
Jacksonville, FL M.S.A.	1,528,141									
Includes Baker, Clay, Duval, Nassau, and St. Johns Counties										
City of Jacksonville	903,213	5,381	110	535	1,323	3,413	30,112	4,909	22,262	2,941
Total area actually reporting	100.0%	6,916	123	735	1,524	4,534	40,049	6,631	29,672	3,746
Rate per 100,000 inhabitants		452.6	8.0	48.1	99.7	296.7	2,620.8	433.9	1,941.7	245.1
Jacksonville, NC M.S.A.[3]	194,966									
Includes Onslow County[3]										
City of Jacksonville[3]	71,715		3	45	160	1,763	337	1,334	92
Total area actually reporting	100.0%	514	9	49	77	379	4,335	1,101	3,024	210
Rate per 100,000 inhabitants		263.6	4.6	25.1	39.5	194.4	2,223.5	564.7	1,551.0	107.7
Janesville-Beloit, WI M.S.A.[2]	162,672									
Includes Rock County[2]										
City of Janesville[2]	64,471	167	1	41	28	97	1,800	282	1,454	64
City of Beloit	36,746	171	1	38	41	91	979	125	815	39
Total area actually reporting	100.0%	389	2	94	74	219	3,440	574	2,728	138
Rate per 100,000 inhabitants		239.1	1.2	57.8	45.5	134.6	2,114.7	352.9	1,677.0	84.8
Jefferson City, MO M.S.A.[2]	151,557									
Includes Callaway, Cole, Moniteau, and Osage Counties										
City of Jefferson City[2]	42,856	151	5	37	27	82	1,277	131	1,053	93
Total area actually reporting	100.0%	353	6	60	34	253	2,707	476	2,028	203
Rate per 100,000 inhabitants		232.9	4.0	39.6	22.4	166.9	1,786.1	314.1	1,338.1	133.9
Johnson City, TN M.S.A.	202,463									
Includes Carter, Unicoi, and Washington Counties										
City of Johnson City	66,795	274	1	24	38	211	2,622	290	2,143	189
Total area actually reporting	100.0%	665	5	51	60	549	4,837	769	3,666	402
Rate per 100,000 inhabitants		328.5	2.5	25.2	29.6	271.2	2,389.1	379.8	1,810.7	198.6
Johnstown, PA M.S.A.	131,500									
Includes Cambria County										
City of Johnstown	20,877	240	5	26	32	177	620	190	406	24
Total area actually reporting	98.0%	359	5	44	39	271	1,558	310	1,194	54
Estimated total	100.0%	360	5	44	39	272	1,584	311	1,219	54
Rate per 100,000 inhabitants		273.8	3.8	33.5	29.7	206.8	1,204.6	236.5	927.0	41.1
Jonesboro, AR M.S.A.	132,617									
Includes Craighead and Poinsett Counties										
City of Jonesboro	77,134	425	4	57	57	307	3,143	1,150	1,825	168
Total area actually reporting	98.6%	653	8	102	68	475	4,278	1,446	2,587	245
Estimated total	100.0%	664	8	103	69	484	4,305	1,458	2,597	250
Rate per 100,000 inhabitants		500.7	6.0	77.7	52.0	365.0	3,246.2	1,099.4	1,958.3	188.5

Table 6. Crime in the United States, by Selected Metropolitan Statistical Area, 2018—Continued

(Number, percent, rate per 100,000 population.)

Area	Population	Violent crime	Murder and nonnegligent manslaughter	Rape[1]	Robbery	Aggravated assault	Property crime	Burglary	Larceny-theft	Motor vehicle theft
Kahului-Wailuku-Lahaina, HI M.S.A.	166,102									
Includes Maui County										
Total area actually reporting	100.0%	435	5	114	53	263	5,084	751	3,640	693
Rate per 100,000 inhabitants		261.9	3.0	68.6	31.9	158.3	3,060.8	452.1	2,191.4	417.2
Kalamazoo-Portage, MI M.S.A.	265,316									
Includes Kalamazoo County										
City of Kalamazoo	76,020	1,008	7	117	159	725	3,825	842	2,646	337
City of Portage	49,175	117	0	29	15	73	1,442	171	1,196	75
Total area actually reporting	99.2%	1,562	10	235	225	1,092	8,952	1,745	6,515	692
Estimated total	100.0%	1,572	10	236	226	1,100	8,978	1,752	6,529	697
Rate per 100,000 inhabitants		592.5	3.8	89.0	85.2	414.6	3,383.9	660.3	2,460.8	262.7
Kankakee, IL M.S.A.	108,593									
Includes Kankakee County										
City of Kankakee	26,032	230	4	35	47	144	871	143	682	46
Total area actually reporting	99.7%	349	6	65	58	220	2,017	341	1,564	112
Estimated total	100.0%	349	6	65	58	220	2,021	342	1,567	112
Rate per 100,000 inhabitants		321.4	5.5	59.9	53.4	202.6	1,861.1	314.9	1,443.0	103.1
Kennewick-Richland, WA M.S.A.	296,791									
Includes Benton and Franklin Counties										
City of Kennewick	82,687	158	3	36	35	84	2,126	293	1,680	153
City of Richland	57,450	127	0	17	18	92	1,281	177	1,039	65
Total area actually reporting	100.0%	597	11	108	98	380	5,625	936	4,244	445
Rate per 100,000 inhabitants		201.2	3.7	36.4	33.0	128.0	1,895.3	315.4	1,430.0	149.9
Killeen-Temple, TX M.S.A.[2]	447,912									
Includes Bell, Coryell, and Lampasas Counties										
City of Killeen	148,007	577	7	117	146	307	3,336	854	2,233	249
City of Temple	75,706	236	12	70	51	103	1,940	342	1,408	190
Total area actually reporting	99.0%	1,244	24	264	254	702	8,577	1,794	6,207	576
Estimated total	100.0%	1,249	24	264	254	707	8,631	1,806	6,245	580
Rate per 100,000 inhabitants		278.8	5.4	58.9	56.7	157.8	1,926.9	403.2	1,394.2	129.5
Kingsport-Bristol, TN-VA M.S.A.	305,997									
Includes Hawkins and Sullivan Counties, TN and Scott and Washington Counties and Bristol City, VA										
City of Kingsport, TN	53,465	404	4	21	43	336	2,801	348	2,164	289
City of Bristol, TN	26,863	151	0	18	16	117	857	117	656	84
Total area actually reporting	100.0%	1,099	14	101	90	894	7,578	1,231	5,535	812
Rate per 100,000 inhabitants		359.2	4.6	33.0	29.4	292.2	2,476.5	402.3	1,808.8	265.4
Kingston, NY M.S.A.	175,637									
Includes Ulster County										
City of Kingston	23,077	70	0	11	12	47	477	80	372	25
Total area actually reporting	92.0%	272	4	90	21	157	1,929	286	1,567	76
Estimated total	100.0%	285	4	92	23	166	2,100	304	1,715	81
Rate per 100,000 inhabitants		162.3	2.3	52.4	13.1	94.5	1,195.6	173.1	976.4	46.1
Knoxville, TN M.S.A.	859,416									
Includes Anderson, Blount, Campbell, Knox, Loudon, Morgan, Roane, and Union Counties										
City of Knoxville	188,653	1,508	20	132	249	1,107	8,827	1,374	6,379	1,074
Total area actually reporting	100.0%	3,545	32	352	367	2,794	19,358	3,318	13,752	2,288
Rate per 100,000 inhabitants		412.5	3.7	41.0	42.7	325.1	2,252.5	386.1	1,600.2	266.2
Kokomo, IN M.S.A.	82,284									
Includes Howard County										
City of Kokomo	57,804	364	4	42	70	248	1,426	309	1,036	81
Total area actually reporting	98.7%	392	4	44	70	274	1,559	357	1,112	90
Estimated total	100.0%	398	4	44	72	278	1,593	363	1,136	94
Rate per 100,000 inhabitants		483.7	4.9	53.5	87.5	337.9	1,936.0	441.2	1,380.6	114.2
La Crosse-Onalaska, WI-MN M.S.A.	137,410									
Includes Houston County, MN and La Crosse County, WI										
City of La Crosse, WI	51,901	145	1	41	22	81	1,924	260	1,600	64
City of Onalaska, WI	18,841	6	0	0	0	6	415	22	386	7
Total area actually reporting	100.0%	189	1	48	23	117	2,732	347	2,298	87
Rate per 100,000 inhabitants		137.5	0.7	34.9	16.7	85.1	1,988.2	252.5	1,672.4	63.3
Lafayette, LA M.S.A.	490,305									
Includes Acadia, Iberia, Lafayette, St. Martin, and Vermilion Parishes										
City of Lafayette	127,592	681	9	21	158	493	5,882	1,019	4,485	378
Total area actually reporting	83.1%	1,835	38	101	260	1,436	12,889	2,852	9,084	953
Estimated total	100.0%	2,288	44	117	330	1,797	16,069	3,540	11,389	1,140
Rate per 100,000 inhabitants		466.6	9.0	23.9	67.3	366.5	3,277.3	722.0	2,322.8	232.5
Lafayette-West Lafayette, IN M.S.A.	229,919									
Includes Benton, Carroll, Tippecanoe, and Warren Counties										

Table 6. Crime in the United States, by Selected Metropolitan Statistical Area, 2018—Continued

(Number, percent, rate per 100,000 population.)

Area	Population	Violent crime	Murder and nonnegligent manslaughter	Rape[1]	Robbery	Aggravated assault	Property crime	Burglary	Larceny-theft	Motor vehicle theft
City of Lafayette	72,904	338	4	34	62	238	2,623	502	1,979	142
City of West Lafayette	46,906	31	0	8	7	16	401	23	367	11
Total area actually reporting	83.0%	419	4	57	75	283	3,796	691	2,917	188
Estimated total	100.0%	480	5	60	83	332	4,270	798	3,253	219
Rate per 100,000 inhabitants		208.8	2.2	26.1	36.1	144.4	1,857.2	347.1	1,414.8	95.3
Lake Charles, LA M.S.A.	208,685									
Includes Calcasieu and Cameron Parishes										
City of Lake Charles	77,852	575	6	55	134	380	3,777	1,845	1,638	294
Total area actually reporting	96.9%	1,137	12	133	179	813	9,783	3,260	5,798	725
Estimated total	100.0%	1,143	12	133	179	819	9,968	3,289	5,952	727
Rate per 100,000 inhabitants		547.7	5.8	63.7	85.8	392.5	4,776.6	1,576.1	2,852.1	348.4
Lake Havasu City-Kingman, AZ M.S.A.	210,037									
Includes Mohave County										
City of Lake Havasu City	54,678	88	2	20	6	60	830	155	615	60
City of Kingman	29,669	118	1	5	15	97	1,152	174	898	80
Total area actually reporting	97.7%	507	8	51	72	376	5,484	1,384	3,642	458
Estimated total	100.0%	522	8	53	77	384	5,664	1,422	3,771	471
Rate per 100,000 inhabitants		248.5	3.8	25.2	36.7	182.8	2,696.7	677.0	1,795.4	224.2
Lakeland-Winter Haven, FL M.S.A.	698,853									
Includes Polk County										
City of Lakeland	109,616	361	8	47	106	200	3,417	477	2,737	203
City of Winter Haven	42,268	236	0	31	27	178	1,032	148	797	87
Total area actually reporting	100.0%	2,072	24	193	286	1,569	12,335	2,214	9,131	990
Rate per 100,000 inhabitants		296.5	3.4	27.6	40.9	224.5	1,765.0	316.8	1,306.6	141.7
Lancaster, PA M.S.A.	545,657									
Includes Lancaster County										
City of Lancaster	59,761	419	2	96	92	229	1,580	164	1,332	84
Total area actually reporting	100.0%	966	12	196	166	592	6,093	750	5,077	266
Rate per 100,000 inhabitants		177.0	2.2	35.9	30.4	108.5	1,116.6	137.4	930.4	48.7
Lansing-East Lansing, MI M.S.A.	548,858									
Includes Clinton, Eaton, Ingham, and Shiawassee Counties										
City of Lansing	117,380	1,301	8	149	182	962	3,557	868	2,252	437
City of East Lansing	48,880	107	1	34	13	59	807	91	536	180
Total area actually reporting	99.9%	2,320	15	485	281	1,539	9,821	1,831	7,014	976
Estimated total	100.0%	2,322	15	485	281	1,541	9,828	1,833	7,018	977
Rate per 100,000 inhabitants		423.1	2.7	88.4	51.2	280.8	1,790.6	334.0	1,278.7	178.0
Laredo, TX M.S.A.	277,538									
Includes Webb County										
City of Laredo	264,214	890	10	145	141	594	6,367	692	5,506	169
Total area actually reporting	100.0%	969	10	156	145	658	6,662	795	5,698	169
Rate per 100,000 inhabitants		349.1	3.6	56.2	52.2	237.1	2,400.4	286.4	2,053.1	60.9
Las Vegas-Henderson-Paradise, NV M.S.A.[5]	2,236,094									
Includes Clark County										
City of Las Vegas Metropolitan Police Department	1,644,390	9,949	120	1,610	2,690	5,529	46,673	11,968	26,756	7,949
City of Henderson	309,586	583	15	65	217	286	6,072	1,042	4,349	681
Total area actually reporting	100.0%		169	1,854	3,386		59,722	14,704	35,073	9,945
Rate per 100,000 inhabitants			7.6	82.9	151.4		2,670.8	657.6	1,568.5	444.7
Lawton, OK M.S.A.	126,316									
Includes Comanche and Cotton Counties										
City of Lawton	93,140	840	7	90	122	621	3,338	1,023	2,011	304
Total area actually reporting	100.0%	878	7	100	122	649	3,738	1,174	2,209	355
Rate per 100,000 inhabitants		695.1	5.5	79.2	96.6	513.8	2,959.2	929.4	1,748.8	281.0
Lebanon, PA M.S.A.	140,510									
Includes Lebanon County										
City of Lebanon	25,816	83	2	12	12	57	469	75	372	22
Total area actually reporting	100.0%	250	4	34	23	189	1,510	230	1,232	48
Rate per 100,000 inhabitants		177.9	2.8	24.2	16.4	134.5	1,074.7	163.7	876.8	34.2
Lewiston, ID-WA M.S.A.	63,627									
Includes Nez Perce County, ID and Asotin County, WA										
City of Lewiston, ID	32,949	48	0	14	6	28	1,007	140	804	63
Total area actually reporting	100.0%	88	1	24	12	51	1,553	255	1,205	93
Rate per 100,000 inhabitants		138.3	1.6	37.7	18.9	80.2	2,440.8	400.8	1,893.9	146.2
Lewiston-Auburn, ME M.S.A.	107,743									
Includes Androscoggin County										
City of Lewiston	36,170	84	2	15	22	45	598	89	486	23
City of Auburn	23,031	50	0	13	6	31	765	56	698	11
Total area actually reporting	100.0%	162	2	40	29	91	1,650	201	1,395	54
Rate per 100,000 inhabitants		150.4	1.9	37.1	26.9	84.5	1,531.4	186.6	1,294.7	50.1
Lexington-Fayette, KY M.S.A.	518,324									
Includes Bourbon, Clark, Fayette, Jessamine, Scott, and Woodford Counties										

Table 6. Crime in the United States, by Selected Metropolitan Statistical Area, 2018—Continued

(Number, percent, rate per 100,000 population.)

Area	Population	Violent crime	Murder and nonnegligent manslaughter	Rape[1]	Robbery	Aggravated assault	Property crime	Burglary	Larceny-theft	Motor vehicle theft
City of Lexington	325,579	982	22	243	422	295	10,329	1,523	7,755	1,051
Total area actually reporting	99.9%	1,240	24	306	492	418	15,043	2,339	11,332	1,372
Estimated total	100.0%	1,240	24	306	492	418	15,048	2,340	11,335	1,373
Rate per 100,000 inhabitants		239.2	4.6	59.0	94.9	80.6	2,903.2	451.5	2,186.9	264.9
Lima, OH M.S.A.[3]	102,857									
Includes Allen County										
City of Lima	36,948	240	3	47	68	122	1,664	479	1,087	98
Total area actually reporting	93.8%	291	5	58	86	142	2,855	648	2,066	141
Estimated total	100.0%	300	5	60	93	142	2,943	650	2,139	154
Rate per 100,000 inhabitants		291.7	4.9	58.3	90.4	138.1	2,861.3	631.9	2,079.6	149.7
Lincoln, NE M.S.A.	335,032									
Includes Lancaster and Seward Counties										
City of Lincoln	288,589	1,045	6	283	162	594	8,307	1,182	6,694	431
Total area actually reporting	99.4%	1,100	6	321	163	610	8,758	1,247	7,047	464
Estimated total	100.0%	1,108	6	322	164	616	8,820	1,254	7,093	473
Rate per 100,000 inhabitants		330.7	1.8	96.1	49.0	183.9	2,632.6	374.3	2,117.1	141.2
Little Rock-North Little Rock-Conway, AR M.S.A.[5]	742,751									
Includes Faulkner, Grant, Lonoke, Perry, Pulaski, and Saline Counties										
City of Little Rock	199,288	2,882	40	218	371	2,253	13,049	2,079	9,850	1,120
City of North Little Rock	66,424	494	13	16	97	368	2,287	431	1,567	289
City of Conway	66,720	361	5	50	56	250	2,229	248	1,881	100
Total area actually reporting	100.0%	5,482	68	491	662	4,261			20,691	2,522
Rate per 100,000 inhabitants		738.1	9.2	66.1	89.1	573.7			2,785.7	339.5
Logan, UT-ID M.S.A.	140,265									
Includes Franklin County, ID and Cache County, UT										
City of Logan, UT	51,508	70	1	35	3	31	852	145	675	32
Total area actually reporting	91.7%	126	1	72	5	48	1,273	211	1,001	61
Estimated total	100.0%	126	1	72	5	48	1,424	230	1,127	67
Rate per 100,000 inhabitants		89.8	0.7	51.3	3.6	34.2	1,015.2	164.0	803.5	47.8
Longview, TX M.S.A.[2], [5]	283,875									
Includes Gregg, Harrison,[2] Rusk, and Upshur Counties										
City of Longview	81,660	326	8	53	46	219	2,506	584	1,722	200
Total area actually reporting	99.3%	945	19	111	97	718		1,562		534
Estimated total	100.0%	948	19	111	97	721		1,568		536
Rate per 100,000 inhabitants		333.9	6.7	39.1	34.2	254.0		552.4		188.8
Longview, WA M.S.A.	107,998									
Includes Cowlitz County										
City of Longview	37,720	110	2	36	21	51	1,350	230	948	172
Total area actually reporting	100.0%	256	2	80	35	139	2,553	482	1,763	308
Rate per 100,000 inhabitants		237.0	1.9	74.1	32.4	128.7	2,363.9	446.3	1,632.4	285.2
Los Angeles-Long Beach-Anaheim, CA M.S.A.	13,325,181									
Includes the Metropolitan Divisions of Anaheim-Santa Ana-Irvine and Los Angeles-Long Beach-Glendale										
City of Los Angeles	4,029,741	30,126	258	2,528	10,327	17,013	101,267	15,988	67,963	17,316
City of Long Beach	470,445	3,284	30	219	979	2,056	11,922	2,328	7,315	2,279
City of Anaheim	354,743	1,192	7	142	407	636	8,702	1,408	5,921	1,373
City of Santa Ana	335,403	1,571	21	230	499	821	6,390	910	3,931	1,549
City of Irvine	288,052	160	0	40	53	67	3,659	621	2,840	198
City of Glendale	204,724	202	1	24	77	100	3,110	454	2,390	266
City of Torrance	146,968	267	2	35	107	123	2,702	468	1,951	283
City of Pasadena	143,448	547	7	47	174	319	2,928	663	1,959	306
City of Orange	141,108	160	3	12	73	72	2,478	478	1,700	300
City of Costa Mesa	114,358	344	3	75	110	156	3,792	515	2,975	302
City of Burbank	105,041	229	0	18	77	134	2,625	276	2,135	214
City of Carson	92,895	435	5	14	131	285	1,971	345	1,181	445
City of Santa Monica	92,674	797	7	60	278	452	4,732	662	3,835	235
City of Newport Beach	86,276	124	1	31	29	63	2,073	397	1,513	163
City of Tustin	81,243	122	0	15	49	58	1,874	243	1,506	125
City of Gardena	60,423	326	7	16	160	143	1,306	289	702	315
City of Arcadia	59,151	76	1	8	41	26	1,420	372	969	79
City of Fountain Valley	56,433	52	0	1	21	30	1,496	194	1,185	117
Total area actually reporting	100.0%	65,929	619	5,466	21,683	38,161	299,404	52,037	198,376	48,991
Rate per 100,000 inhabitants		494.8	4.6	41.0	162.7	286.4	2,246.9	390.5	1,488.7	367.7
Anaheim-Santa Ana-Irvine, CA M.D.	3,191,133									
Includes Orange County										
Total area actually reporting	100.0%	7,362	49	977	2,203	4,133	61,590	9,485	44,526	7,579
Rate per 100,000 inhabitants		230.7	1.5	30.6	69.0	129.5	1,930.0	297.2	1,395.3	237.5
Los Angeles-Long Beach-Glendale, CA M.D.	10,134,048									
Includes Los Angeles County										
Total area actually reporting	100.0%	58,567	570	4,489	19,480	34,028	237,814	42,552	153,850	41,412
Rate per 100,000 inhabitants		577.9	5.6	44.3	192.2	335.8	2,346.7	419.9	1,518.1	408.6

Table 6. Crime in the United States, by Selected Metropolitan Statistical Area, 2018—Continued

(Number, percent, rate per 100,000 population.)

Area	Population	Violent crime	Murder and nonnegligent manslaughter	Rape[1]	Robbery	Aggravated assault	Property crime	Burglary	Larceny-theft	Motor vehicle theft
Lubbock, TX M.S.A.[2]	319,795									
Includes Crosby,[2] Lubbock, and Lynn Counties										
City of Lubbock	257,372	2,565	13	239	443	1,870	11,743	2,312	8,228	1,203
Total area actually reporting	99.2%	2,649	14	263	447	1,925	12,642	2,490	8,883	1,269
Estimated total	100.0%	2,652	14	263	447	1,928	12,675	2,497	8,906	1,272
Rate per 100,000 inhabitants		829.3	4.4	82.2	139.8	602.9	3,963.5	780.8	2,784.9	397.8
Lynchburg, VA M.S.A.	261,837									
Includes Amherst, Appomattox, Bedford, and Campbell Counties and Lynchburg City										
City of Lynchburg	81,603	275	8	33	41	193	1,627	181	1,278	168
Total area actually reporting	100.0%	527	14	91	57	365	3,535	498	2,706	331
Rate per 100,000 inhabitants		201.3	5.3	34.8	21.8	139.4	1,350.1	190.2	1,033.5	126.4
Macon-Bibb County, GA M.S.A.	228,018									
Includes Bibb, Crawford, Jones, Monroe, and Twiggs Counties										
Total area actually reporting	100.0%	1,069	28	66	287	688	8,682	1,924	6,094	664
Rate per 100,000 inhabitants		468.8	12.3	28.9	125.9	301.7	3,807.6	843.8	2,672.6	291.2
Madera, CA M.S.A.	156,529									
Includes Madera County										
City of Madera	66,098	399	6	37	92	264	1,346	241	898	207
Total area actually reporting	100.0%	896	12	70	113	701	2,969	794	1,728	447
Rate per 100,000 inhabitants		572.4	7.7	44.7	72.2	447.8	1,896.8	507.3	1,103.9	285.6
Madison, WI M.S.A.[2]	661,678									
Includes Columbia, Dane, Green, and Iowa Counties										
City of Madison	258,455	1,043	5	116	240	682	6,722	1,061	5,129	532
Total area actually reporting	100.0%	1,605	10	218	313	1,064	11,715	1,721	9,166	828
Rate per 100,000 inhabitants		242.6	1.5	32.9	47.3	160.8	1,770.5	260.1	1,385.3	125.1
Manchester-Nashua, NH M.S.A.	413,956									
Includes Hillsborough County										
City of Manchester	111,422	661	4	65	144	448	2,878	333	2,382	163
City of Nashua	88,596	124	1	57	19	47	1,144	85	991	68
Total area actually reporting	98.3%	946	7	165	175	599	5,495	584	4,601	310
Estimated total	100.0%	951	7	165	175	604	5,644	589	4,741	314
Rate per 100,000 inhabitants		229.7	1.7	39.9	42.3	145.9	1,363.4	142.3	1,145.3	75.9
Manhattan, KS M.S.A.	132,035									
Includes Geary, Pottawatomie, and Riley Counties										
Total area actually reporting	100.0%	425	5	72	39	309	2,171	303	1,720	148
Rate per 100,000 inhabitants		321.9	3.8	54.5	29.5	234.0	1,644.3	229.5	1,302.7	112.1
Mankato, MN M.S.A.[2]	101,446									
Includes Blue Earth[2] and Nicollet Counties										
City of Mankato[2]	42,606	140	0	24	17	99	1,418	164	1,178	76
Total area actually reporting	100.0%	205	1	47	22	135	1,977	290	1,580	107
Rate per 100,000 inhabitants		202.1	1.0	46.3	21.7	133.1	1,948.8	285.9	1,557.5	105.5
Mansfield, OH M.S.A.	120,208									
Includes Richland County										
City of Mansfield	45,941	237	3	60	57	117	2,087	434	1,577	76
Total area actually reporting	98.5%	319	3	101	68	147	3,409	661	2,607	141
Estimated total	100.0%	326	3	102	70	151	3,507	671	2,691	145
Rate per 100,000 inhabitants		271.2	2.5	84.9	58.2	125.6	2,917.4	558.2	2,238.6	120.6
McAllen-Edinburg-Mission, TX M.S.A.[2]	870,548									
Includes Hidalgo County										
City of McAllen	144,363	122	0	39	26	57	3,856	203	3,598	55
City of Edinburg	92,391	304	2	78	50	174	3,248	418	2,756	74
City of Mission	85,368	94	0	35	27	32	1,594	150	1,380	64
Total area actually reporting	99.3%	2,344	12	465	341	1,526	20,117	2,796	16,633	688
Estimated total	100.0%	2,355	12	466	342	1,535	20,226	2,812	16,720	694
Rate per 100,000 inhabitants		270.5	1.4	53.5	39.3	176.3	2,323.4	323.0	1,920.6	79.7
Medford, OR M.S.A.	219,676									
Includes Jackson County										
City of Medford	82,800	403	2	33	93	275	4,463	471	3,633	359
Total area actually reporting	100.0%	737	3	73	127	534	8,016	1,049	6,338	629
Rate per 100,000 inhabitants		335.5	1.4	33.2	57.8	243.1	3,649.0	477.5	2,885.2	286.3
Memphis, TN-MS-AR M.S.A.2, [3]	1,343,002									
Includes Crittenden County, AR; DeSoto, Marshall, Tate, and Tunica[3] Counties, MS; and Fayette, Shelby, and Tipton Counties, TN										
City of Memphis, TN	652,226	12,674	186	491	3,050	8,947	41,779	8,494	28,835	4,450
Total area actually reporting	94.8%	15,190	225	666	3,380	10,919	55,382	11,033	38,698	5,651
Estimated total	100.0%	15,344	231	680	3,416	11,017	57,361	11,377	40,209	5,775
Rate per 100,000 inhabitants		1,142.5	17.2	50.6	254.4	820.3	4,271.1	847.1	2,994.0	430.0

Table 6. Crime in the United States, by Selected Metropolitan Statistical Area, 2018—Continued

(Number, percent, rate per 100,000 population.)

Area	Population	Violent crime	Murder and nonnegligent manslaughter	Rape[1]	Robbery	Aggravated assault	Property crime	Burglary	Larceny-theft	Motor vehicle theft
Merced, CA M.S.A.	272,901									
Includes Merced County										
City of Merced	83,659	465	1	30	116	318	2,219	387	1,404	428
Total area actually reporting	100.0%	1,548	9	74	232	1,233	6,761	1,412	4,050	1,299
Rate per 100,000 inhabitants		567.2	3.3	27.1	85.0	451.8	2,477.5	517.4	1,484.1	476.0
Miami-Fort Lauderdale-Pompano Beach, FL M.S.A.	6,241,618									
Includes the Metropolitan Divisions of Fort Lauderdale-Pompano Beach-Sunrise, Miami-Miami Beach-Kendall, and West Palm Beach-Boca Raton-Boynton Beach										
City of Miami	473,047	2,978	46	131	828	1,973	16,837	2,057	13,136	1,644
City of Fort Lauderdale	182,150	1,006	20	73	350	563	9,050	1,366	6,814	870
City of Pompano Beach	112,045	876	6	91	312	467	4,307	608	3,121	578
City of West Palm Beach	111,659	1,026	27	77	354	568	4,249	578	3,290	381
City of Boca Raton	100,162	205	2	28	80	95	2,361	277	1,894	190
City of Sunrise	95,812	186	2	21	57	106	2,350	187	1,998	165
City of Miami Beach	92,928	871	5	96	279	491	6,947	646	5,902	399
City of Deerfield Beach	81,371	329	3	21	110	195	2,490	422	1,737	331
City of Boynton Beach	79,142	477	4	21	134	318	2,964	256	2,423	285
City of Delray Beach	69,970	409	6	27	84	292	2,522	279	2,038	205
City of Jupiter	66,457	132	0	15	31	86	959	84	814	61
City of Doral	63,680	77	2	14	12	49	1,464	108	1,235	121
City of Palm Beach Gardens	55,999	83	2	14	25	42	1,409	125	1,210	74
City of Coral Gables	51,716	68	1	14	20	33	1,225	128	1,035	62
Total area actually reporting	100.0%	26,694	385	2,111	7,258	16,940	173,588	19,669	136,923	16,996
Rate per 100,000 inhabitants		427.7	6.2	33.8	116.3	271.4	2,781.1	315.1	2,193.7	272.3
Fort Lauderdale-Pompano Beach-Deerfield Beach, FL M.D.	1,962,248									
Includes Broward County										
Total area actually reporting	100.0%	7,094	96	629	2,095	4,274	51,803	6,286	39,998	5,519
Rate per 100,000 inhabitants		361.5	4.9	32.1	106.8	217.8	2,640.0	320.3	2,038.4	281.3
Miami-Miami Beach-Kendall, FL M.D.	2,786,840									
Includes Miami-Dade County										
Total area actually reporting	100.0%	13,735	198	916	3,653	8,968	86,869	9,181	69,349	8,339
Rate per 100,000 inhabitants		492.9	7.1	32.9	131.1	321.8	3,117.1	329.4	2,488.4	299.2
West Palm Beach-Boca Raton-Boynton Beach, FL M.D.	1,492,530									
Includes Palm Beach County										
Total area actually reporting	100.0%	5,865	91	566	1,510	3,698	34,916	4,202	27,576	3,138
Rate per 100,000 inhabitants		393.0	6.1	37.9	101.2	247.8	2,339.4	281.5	1,847.6	210.2
Michigan City-La Porte, IN M.S.A.	109,795									
Includes La Porte County										
City of Michigan City	30,999	230	3	13	50	164	1,373	189	1,080	104
City of La Porte	21,630	111	0	11	21	79	495	91	360	44
Total area actually reporting	95.9%	422	3	29	77	313	2,262	399	1,679	184
Estimated total	100.0%	448	3	31	84	330	2,401	422	1,780	199
Rate per 100,000 inhabitants		408.0	2.7	28.2	76.5	300.6	2,186.8	384.4	1,621.2	181.2
Midland, MI M.S.A.	83,544									
Includes Midland County										
City of Midland	41,961	55	1	19	1	34	354	36	306	12
Total area actually reporting	100.0%	119	1	55	1	62	618	101	490	27
Rate per 100,000 inhabitants		142.4	1.2	65.8	1.2	74.2	739.7	120.9	586.5	32.3
Midland, TX M.S.A.	174,780									
Includes Martin and Midland Counties										
City of Midland	140,072	403	5	60	59	279	2,764	378	2,108	278
Total area actually reporting	100.0%	555	9	69	70	407	3,445	482	2,557	406
Rate per 100,000 inhabitants		317.5	5.1	39.5	40.1	232.9	1,971.0	275.8	1,463.0	232.3
Milwaukee-Waukesha, WI M.S.A.[2]	1,579,729									
Includes Milwaukee, Ozaukee, Washington, and Waukesha Counties										
City of Milwaukee	595,619	8,416	99	489	2,279	5,549	17,699	4,259	8,851	4,589
City of Waukesha	72,672	92	2	37	13	40	750	83	618	49
Total area actually reporting	100.0%	9,631	113	690	2,606	6,222	32,859	5,611	21,636	5,612
Rate per 100,000 inhabitants		609.7	7.2	43.7	165.0	393.9	2,080.0	355.2	1,369.6	355.3
Minneapolis-St. Paul-Bloomington, MN-WI M.S.A.[2]	3,619,258									
Includes Anoka, Carver, Chisago, Dakota, Hennepin, Isanti, Le Sueur, Mille Lacs, Ramsey,[2] Scott, Sherburne, Washington, and Wright Counties, MN and Pierce and St. Croix Counties, WI										
City of Minneapolis, MN	428,261	3,395	31	432	1,184	1,748	16,750	3,089	11,471	2,190
City of St. Paul, MN	309,756	1,941	15	277	560	1,089	10,082	1,909	5,877	2,296

Table 6. Crime in the United States, by Selected Metropolitan Statistical Area, 2018—Continued

(Number, percent, rate per 100,000 population.)

Area	Population	Violent crime	Murder and nonnegligent manslaughter	Rape[1]	Robbery	Aggravated assault	Property crime	Burglary	Larceny-theft	Motor vehicle theft
City of Bloomington, MN	86,279	165	2	51	44	68	2,592	158	2,304	130
City of Plymouth, MN	79,559	44	2	12	9	21	904	165	702	37
City of Eagan, MN	66,981	59	2	18	16	23	1,289	88	1,148	53
City of Eden Prairie, MN	64,917	39	1	15	7	16	873	65	784	24
City of Minnetonka, MN	53,573	28	1	12	4	11	810	105	674	31
City of Edina, MN	52,544	23	1	7	10	5	803	101	677	25
Total area actually reporting	99.9%	9,167	70	1,660	2,638	4,799	78,165	10,649	59,705	7,811
Estimated total	100.0%	9,171	70	1,661	2,641	4,799	78,195	10,649	59,735	7,811
Rate per 100,000 inhabitants		253.4	1.9	45.9	73.0	132.6	2,160.5	294.2	1,650.5	215.8
Missoula, MT M.S.A.	118,931									
Includes Missoula County										
City of Missoula	74,300	333	2	65	42	224	3,521	379	2,944	198
Total area actually reporting	100.0%	413	2	83	47	281	4,131	497	3,380	254
Rate per 100,000 inhabitants		347.3	1.7	69.8	39.5	236.3	3,473.4	417.9	2,842.0	213.6
Mobile, AL M.S.A.[6]	430,335									
Includes Mobile and Washington Counties										
City of Mobile[6]	245,475	1,613	26	168	378	1,041	12,094	2,568	8,442	1,084
Total area actually reporting	100.0%	2,266	37	202	469	1,558	16,744	3,803	11,206	1,735
Rate per 100,000 inhabitants		526.6	8.6	46.9	109.0	362.0	3,890.9	883.7	2,604.0	403.2
Modesto, CA M.S.A.	548,464									
Includes Stanislaus County										
City of Modesto	215,822	1,904	16	105	420	1,363	7,727	1,109	5,420	1,198
Total area actually reporting	100.0%	3,160	40	190	811	2,119	15,300	2,696	10,018	2,586
Rate per 100,000 inhabitants		576.2	7.3	34.6	147.9	386.4	2,789.6	491.6	1,826.6	471.5
Monroe, LA M.S.A.[2]	202,029									
Includes Morehouse, Ouachita,[2] and Union Parishes										
City of Monroe	48,291	677	4	28	147	498	3,278	749	2,358	171
Total area actually reporting	97.5%	1,454	11	87	237	1,119	8,834	2,368	5,984	482
Estimated total	100.0%	1,464	11	87	237	1,129	8,963	2,390	6,089	484
Rate per 100,000 inhabitants		724.6	5.4	43.1	117.3	558.8	4,436.5	1,183.0	3,013.9	239.6
Monroe, MI M.S.A.	149,626									
Includes Monroe County										
City of Monroe	19,754	114	0	25	11	78	383	66	295	22
Total area actually reporting	97.0%	380	2	114	34	230	1,851	395	1,310	146
Estimated total	100.0%	388	2	116	37	233	1,899	399	1,353	147
Rate per 100,000 inhabitants		259.3	1.3	77.5	24.7	155.7	1,269.2	266.7	904.3	98.2
Montgomery, AL M.S.A.	373,669									
Includes Autauga, Elmore, Lowndes, and Montgomery Counties										
City of Montgomery	198,662	1,216	29	39	391	757	8,480	2,052	5,456	972
Total area actually reporting	99.6%	1,712	39	112	480	1,081	12,727	2,805	8,608	1,314
Estimated total	100.0%	1,712	39	112	480	1,081	12,735	2,805	8,616	1,314
Rate per 100,000 inhabitants		458.2	10.4	30.0	128.5	289.3	3,408.1	750.7	2,305.8	351.6
Morristown, TN M.S.A.	141,820									
Includes Grainger, Hamblen, and Jefferson Counties										
City of Morristown	29,884	242	0	22	14	206	1,388	164	1,131	93
Total area actually reporting	100.0%	534	1	53	37	443	3,032	531	2,201	300
Rate per 100,000 inhabitants		376.5	0.7	37.4	26.1	312.4	2,137.9	374.4	1,552.0	211.5
Mount Vernon-Anacortes, WA M.S.A.	127,401									
Includes Skagit County										
City of Mount Vernon	35,550	99	2	16	26	55	1,308	233	964	111
City of Anacortes	17,130	30	0	8	3	19	380	64	308	8
Total area actually reporting	100.0%	248	4	39	46	159	3,633	695	2,672	266
Rate per 100,000 inhabitants		194.7	3.1	30.6	36.1	124.8	2,851.6	545.5	2,097.3	208.8
Muncie, IN M.S.A.	114,803									
Includes Delaware County										
City of Muncie	68,406	219	1	40	80	98	2,281	407	1,434	440
Total area actually reporting	100.0%	281	1	59	83	138	2,760	513	1,756	491
Rate per 100,000 inhabitants		244.8	0.9	51.4	72.3	120.2	2,404.1	446.9	1,529.6	427.7
Muskegon, MI M.S.A.	174,304									
Includes Muskegon County										
City of Muskegon	38,125	245	7	39	31	168	1,717	321	1,226	170
Total area actually reporting	100.0%	754	14	154	92	494	5,676	774	4,521	381
Rate per 100,000 inhabitants		432.6	8.0	88.4	52.8	283.4	3,256.4	444.1	2,593.7	218.6
Myrtle Beach-Conway-North Myrtle Beach, SC-NC M.S.A.3,[5]	477,881									
Includes Brunswick County, NC3 and Horry County, SC										
City of Myrtle Beach, SC	33,687	473	4	64	129	276	3,553	410	2,883	260
City of Conway, SC	24,784	141	1	15	22	103	960	164	748	48

Table 6. Crime in the United States, by Selected Metropolitan Statistical Area, 2018—Continued

(Number, percent, rate per 100,000 population.)

Area	Population	Violent crime	Murder and nonnegligent manslaughter	Rape[1]	Robbery	Aggravated assault	Property crime	Burglary	Larceny-theft	Motor vehicle theft
City of North Myrtle Beach, SC[5]	16,688	105	1	28	16	60		192	782	
Total area actually reporting	98.3%	1,852	30	292	312	1,218		2,560	10,425	
Estimated total	100.0%	1,910	30	326	315	1,239		2,612	10,613	
Rate per 100,000 inhabitants		399.7	6.3	68.2	65.9	259.3		546.6	2,220.8	
Napa, CA M.S.A.	140,489									
Includes Napa County										
City of Napa	80,145	269	0	56	46	167	1,241	258	814	169
Total area actually reporting	100.0%	683	1	84	67	531	2,033	405	1,387	241
Rate per 100,000 inhabitants		486.2	0.7	59.8	47.7	378.0	1,447.1	288.3	987.3	171.5
Naples-Marco Island, FL M.S.A.	380,429									
Includes Collier County										
City of Naples	22,308	9	0	0	2	7	320	19	277	24
City of Marco Island	18,122	6	0	0	1	5	98	11	82	5
Total area actually reporting	100.0%	913	9	109	141	654	4,228	535	3,449	244
Rate per 100,000 inhabitants		240.0	2.4	28.7	37.1	171.9	1,111.4	140.6	906.6	64.1
Nashville-Davidson–Murfreesboro–Franklin, TN M.S.A.[4]	1,913,148									
Includes Cannon, Cheatham, Davidson, Dickson, Macon, Maury, Robertson, Rutherford,[4] Smith, Sumner, Trousdale, Williamson, and Wilson Counties										
City of Metropolitan Nashville Police Department	686,492	7,641	91	480	2,116	4,954	27,537	3,627	20,828	3,082
City of Murfreesboro	140,702	613	11	77	107	418	4,417	649	3,458	310
City of Franklin	80,825	119	0	19	9	91	982	77	850	55
Total area actually reporting	100.0%	11,462	150	879	2,465	7,968		6,551	37,424	
Rate per 100,000 inhabitants		599.1	7.8	45.9	128.8	416.5		342.4	1,956.1	
New Bern, NC M.S.A.[3]	124,530									
Includes Craven, Jones, and Pamlico Counties[3]										
City of New Bern[3]	29,600		0		27	81	940	195	718	27
Total area actually reporting	88.8%	298	1	28	45	224	2,483	740	1,622	121
Estimated total	100.0%	330	1	31	49	249	2,760	814	1,809	137
Rate per 100,000 inhabitants		265.0	0.8	24.9	39.3	200.0	2,216.3	653.7	1,452.7	110.0
New Haven-Milford, CT M.S.A.	805,875									
Includes New Haven County										
City of New Haven	131,181	1,105	10	60	320	715	5,111	749	3,688	674
City of Milford	54,754	37	0	1	25	11	1,119	193	846	80
Total area actually reporting	100.0%	2,377	24	200	765	1,388	19,635	2,615	14,424	2,596
Rate per 100,000 inhabitants		295.0	3.0	24.8	94.9	172.2	2,436.5	324.5	1,789.9	322.1
New Orleans-Metairie, LA M.S.A.[4]	1,275,532									
Includes Jefferson, Orleans, Plaquemines, St. Bernard, St. Charles, St. James, St. John the Baptist, and St. Tammany Parishes										
City of New Orleans	396,374	4,611	147	681	1,219	2,564	18,063	2,027	13,042	2,994
Total area actually reporting	100.0%	7,191	198	882	1,713	4,398		4,757		4,258
Rate per 100,000 inhabitants		563.8	15.5	69.1	134.3	344.8		372.9		333.8
Niles, MI M.S.A.	154,218									
Includes Berrien County										
City of Niles	11,154	70	0	18	14	38	273	49	196	28
Total area actually reporting	100.0%	810	5	154	92	559	3,124	631	2,257	236
Rate per 100,000 inhabitants		525.2	3.2	99.9	59.7	362.5	2,025.7	409.2	1,463.5	153.0
North Port-Sarasota-Bradenton, FL M.S.A.	819,882									
Includes Manatee and Sarasota Counties										
City of North Port	67,682	117	4	34	18	61	1,186	132	1,026	28
City of Sarasota	57,718	337	3	22	82	230	1,877	301	1,442	134
City of Bradenton	57,647	388	1	30	76	281	1,564	227	1,258	79
City of Venice	23,362	25	0	1	2	22	323	38	269	16
Total area actually reporting	100.0%	2,751	29	248	440	2,034	14,937	2,205	11,851	881
Rate per 100,000 inhabitants		335.5	3.5	30.2	53.7	248.1	1,821.8	268.9	1,445.5	107.5
Norwich-New London, CT M.S.A.[2]	176,337									
Includes New London County										
City of Norwich[2]	39,318	108	0	35	27	46	498	93	362	43
City of New London	26,995	122	2	30	39	51	568	113	388	67
Total area actually reporting	100.0%	365	3	93	78	191	2,662	314	2,191	157
Rate per 100,000 inhabitants		207.0	1.7	52.7	44.2	108.3	1,509.6	178.1	1,242.5	89.0
Ocala, FL M.S.A.	357,538									
Includes Marion County										
City of Ocala	59,505	405	7	58	106	234	2,871	406	2,286	179
Total area actually reporting	100.0%	1,475	29	244	199	1,003	7,428	1,611	5,175	642
Rate per 100,000 inhabitants		412.5	8.1	68.2	55.7	280.5	2,077.5	450.6	1,447.4	179.6
Ocean City, NJ M.S.A.	91,732									
Includes Cape May County										
City of Ocean City	11,138	5	0	0	0	5	283	33	249	1

Table 6. Crime in the United States, by Selected Metropolitan Statistical Area, 2018—Continued

(Number, percent, rate per 100,000 population.)

Area	Population	Violent crime	Murder and nonnegligent manslaughter	Rape[1]	Robbery	Aggravated assault	Property crime	Burglary	Larceny-theft	Motor vehicle theft
Total area actually reporting	100.0%	185	1	23	37	124	1,919	321	1,557	41
Rate per 100,000 inhabitants		201.7	1.1	25.1	40.3	135.2	2,092.0	349.9	1,697.3	44.7
Odessa, TX M.S.A.	159,752									
Includes Ector County										
City of Odessa	119,545	1,049	8	118	104	819	2,996	504	2,123	369
Total area actually reporting	100.0%	1,215	12	123	125	955	4,574	794	3,153	627
Rate per 100,000 inhabitants		760.6	7.5	77.0	78.2	597.8	2,863.2	497.0	1,973.7	392.5
Ogden-Clearfield, UT M.S.A.	677,282									
Includes Box Elder, Davis, Morgan, and Weber Counties										
City of Ogden	87,616	417	5	74	81	257	3,218	500	2,319	399
City of Clearfield	31,558	59	0	15	8	36	462	68	341	53
Total area actually reporting	99.9%	1,136	11	356	168	601	12,125	1,899	9,143	1,083
Estimated total	100.0%	1,137	11	356	168	602	12,146	1,902	9,159	1,085
Rate per 100,000 inhabitants		167.9	1.6	52.6	24.8	88.9	1,793.3	280.8	1,352.3	160.2
Oklahoma City, OK M.S.A.[2]	1,397,950									
Includes Canadian, Cleveland, Grady, Lincoln, Logan, McClain, and Oklahoma Counties										
City of Oklahoma City	652,865	5,663	52	542	1,082	3,987	26,298	6,000	16,668	3,630
Total area actually reporting	100.0%	7,402	72	859	1,333	5,138	43,021	9,568	28,012	5,441
Rate per 100,000 inhabitants		529.5	5.2	61.4	95.4	367.5	3,077.4	684.4	2,003.8	389.2
Olympia-Lacey-Tumwater, WA M.S.A.	285,879									
Includes Thurston County										
City of Olympia	52,312	246	1	38	50	157	2,020	320	1,473	227
City of Lacey	50,844	96	4	15	17	60	1,374	190	1,087	97
City of Tumwater	23,405	84	1	15	9	59	703	155	481	67
Total area actually reporting	100.0%	751	8	110	101	532	6,385	1,434	4,314	637
Rate per 100,000 inhabitants		262.7	2.8	38.5	35.3	186.1	2,233.5	501.6	1,509.0	222.8
Orlando-Kissimmee-Sanford, FL M.S.A.	2,566,617									
Includes Lake, Orange, Osceola, and Seminole Counties										
City of Orlando	286,679	2,282	39	200	628	1,415	13,803	1,619	10,965	1,219
City of Kissimmee	72,894	288	3	26	58	201	1,839	285	1,419	135
City of Sanford	60,154	421	5	57	83	276	2,133	356	1,661	116
Total area actually reporting	99.9%	11,359	139	1,281	2,390	7,549	62,884	10,424	47,582	4,878
Estimated total	100.0%	11,367	139	1,281	2,392	7,555	62,946	10,438	47,625	4,883
Rate per 100,000 inhabitants		442.9	5.4	49.9	93.2	294.4	2,452.5	406.7	1,855.6	190.3
Owensboro, KY M.S.A.	118,844									
Includes Daviess, Hancock, and McLean Counties										
City of Owensboro	59,686	160	2	42	59	57	2,638	453	1,945	240
Total area actually reporting	100.0%	180	4	49	63	64	3,097	582	2,228	287
Rate per 100,000 inhabitants		151.5	3.4	41.2	53.0	53.9	2,605.9	489.7	1,874.7	241.5
Oxnard-Thousand Oaks-Ventura, CA M.S.A.	851,810									
Includes Ventura County										
City of Oxnard	211,737	801	14	66	327	394	5,055	704	3,568	783
City of Thousand Oaks	129,319	126	14	30	30	52	1,480	236	1,127	117
City of Ventura	111,272	445	2	54	117	272	3,482	481	2,667	334
City of Camarillo	68,218	78	0	16	21	41	841	110	663	68
Total area actually reporting	100.0%	2,048	35	256	639	1,118	14,659	2,235	10,774	1,650
Rate per 100,000 inhabitants		240.4	4.1	30.1	75.0	131.2	1,720.9	262.4	1,264.8	193.7
Palm Bay-Melbourne-Titusville, FL M.S.A.	595,540									
Includes Brevard County										
City of Palm Bay	112,902	404	9	64	43	288	2,109	402	1,583	124
City of Melbourne	82,844	601	5	65	101	430	2,941	440	2,357	144
City of Titusville	46,650	289	3	24	45	217	1,397	322	918	157
Total area actually reporting	100.0%	2,214	29	216	336	1,633	12,754	2,262	9,612	880
Rate per 100,000 inhabitants		371.8	4.9	36.3	56.4	274.2	2,141.6	379.8	1,614.0	147.8
Panama City, FL M.S.A.	185,593									
Includes Bay County										
City of Panama City	37,318	234	2	4	45	183	2,150	423	1,467	260
Total area actually reporting	100.0%	760	7	72	98	583	5,974	1,173	4,301	500
Rate per 100,000 inhabitants		409.5	3.8	38.8	52.8	314.1	3,218.9	632.0	2,317.4	269.4
Pensacola-Ferry Pass-Brent, FL M.S.A.	493,023									
Includes Escambia and Santa Rosa Counties										
City of Pensacola	52,672	285	1	36	56	192	2,012	261	1,646	105
Total area actually reporting	100.0%	1,971	13	286	311	1,361	11,449	2,174	8,484	791
Rate per 100,000 inhabitants		399.8	2.6	58.0	63.1	276.1	2,322.2	441.0	1,720.8	160.4
Peoria, IL M.S.A.[4]	404,570									
Includes Fulton, Marshall, Peoria, Stark, Tazewell, and Woodford Counties										
City of Peoria	112,595	860	22	68	201	569	4,509	890	3,197	422
Total area actually reporting	84.3%	1,396	26	206	244	920		1,593		590

Table 6. Crime in the United States, by Selected Metropolitan Statistical Area, 2018—Continued

(Number, percent, rate per 100,000 population.)

Area	Population	Violent crime	Murder and nonnegligent manslaughter	Rape[1]	Robbery	Aggravated assault	Property crime	Burglary	Larceny-theft	Motor vehicle theft
Estimated total	100.0%	1,484	27	219	255	983		1,741		643
Rate per 100,000 inhabitants		366.8	6.7	54.1	63.0	243.0		430.3		158.9
Philadelphia-Camden-Wilmington, PA-NJ-DE-MD M.S.A.	6,088,470									
Includes the Metropolitan Divisions of Camden, NJ; Montgomery County-Bucks County-Chester County, PA; Philadelphia, PA; and Wilmington, DE-MD-NJ										
City of Philadelphia, PA	1,586,916	14,420	351	1,095	5,262	7,712	49,145	6,497	36,968	5,680
City of Camden, NJ	73,140	1,198	23	64	355	756	2,219	458	1,242	519
City of Wilmington, DE	71,157	1,099	23	14	358	704	3,502	567	2,483	452
Total area actually reporting	100.0%	24,901	540	1,966	8,030	14,365	118,959	16,167	92,645	10,147
Rate per 100,000 inhabitants		409.0	8.9	32.3	131.9	235.9	1,953.8	265.5	1,521.6	166.7
Camden, NJ M.D.	1,233,912									
Includes Burlington, Camden, and Gloucester Counties										
Total area actually reporting	100.0%	3,003	48	250	915	1,790	21,451	3,813	16,274	1,364
Rate per 100,000 inhabitants		243.4	3.9	20.3	74.2	145.1	1,738.5	309.0	1,318.9	110.5
Montgomery County-Bucks County-Chester County, PA M.D.	1,978,598									
Includes Bucks, Chester, and Montgomery Counties										
Total area actually reporting	100.0%	2,374	54	328	508	1,484	22,207	2,212	19,016	979
Rate per 100,000 inhabitants		120.0	2.7	16.6	25.7	75.0	1,122.4	111.8	961.1	49.5
Philadelphia, PA M.D.	2,151,872									
Includes Delaware and Philadelphia Counties										
Total area actually reporting	100.0%	16,434	394	1,187	5,809	9,044	58,066	7,643	43,947	6,476
Rate per 100,000 inhabitants		763.7	18.3	55.2	270.0	420.3	2,698.4	355.2	2,042.3	300.9
Wilmington, DE-MD-NJ M.D.	724,088									
Includes New Castle County, DE; Cecil County, MD; and Salem County, NJ										
Total area actually reporting	100.0%	3,090	44	201	798	2,047	17,235	2,499	13,408	1,328
Rate per 100,000 inhabitants		426.7	6.1	27.8	110.2	282.7	2,380.2	345.1	1,851.7	183.4
Phoenix-Mesa-Chandler, AZ M.S.A.	4,861,204									
Includes Maricopa and Pinal Counties										
City of Phoenix	1,653,080	12,110	132	1,086	3,112	7,780	57,732	10,479	39,438	7,815
City of Mesa	504,873	1,837	17	238	417	1,165	10,024	1,563	7,598	863
City of Chandler	255,986	606	4	146	123	333	5,430	658	4,455	317
City of Scottsdale	254,961	422	7	122	87	206	5,683	711	4,700	272
City of Tempe	188,543	913	5	176	189	543	7,802	1,017	6,247	538
City of Casa Grande	56,479	346	1	32	34	279	1,478	228	1,144	106
Total area actually reporting	99.9%	21,687	222	2,406	4,772	14,287	126,788	20,991	92,472	13,325
Estimated total	100.0%	21,690	222	2,406	4,772	14,290	126,815	20,992	92,496	13,327
Rate per 100,000 inhabitants		446.2	4.6	49.5	98.2	294.0	2,608.7	431.8	1,902.7	274.2
Pine Bluff, AR M.S.A	89,619									
Includes Cleveland, Jefferson, and Lincoln Counties										
City of Pine Bluff	42,195	679	15	37	97	530	2,278	665	1,380	233
Total area actually reporting	100.0%	789	20	61	103	605	3,065	954	1,808	303
Rate per 100,000 inhabitants		880.4	22.3	68.1	114.9	675.1	3,420.0	1,064.5	2,017.4	338.1
Pittsburgh, PA M.S.A.	2,327,716									
Includes Allegheny, Armstrong, Beaver, Butler, Fayette, Washington, and Westmoreland Counties										
City of Pittsburgh	302,544	1,751	57	121	696	877	9,125	1,341	7,055	729
Total area actually reporting	99.2%	6,380	127	601	1,368	4,284	32,667	4,555	26,251	1,861
Estimated total	100.0%	6,391	127	601	1,369	4,294	32,893	4,564	26,467	1,862
Rate per 100,000 inhabitants		274.6	5.5	25.8	58.8	184.5	1,413.1	196.1	1,137.0	80.0
Pittsfield, MA M.S.A.	125,593									
Includes Berkshire County										
City of Pittsfield	42,298	356	3	43	35	275	1,196	464	661	71
Total area actually reporting	88.7%	556	5	63	50	438	2,147	690	1,349	108
Estimated total	100.0%	581	5	63	55	458	2,191	690	1,387	114
Rate per 100,000 inhabitants		462.6	4.0	50.2	43.8	364.7	1,744.5	549.4	1,104.4	90.8
Pocatello, ID M.S.A.	93,951									
Includes Bannock and Power Counties										
City of Pocatello	55,317	209	1	21	13	174	1,568	339	1,100	129
Total area actually reporting	100.0%	274	1	31	15	227	2,387	433	1,778	176
Rate per 100,000 inhabitants		291.6	1.1	33.0	16.0	241.6	2,540.7	460.9	1,892.5	187.3
Portland-South Portland, ME M.S.A.[2]	535,224									
Includes Cumberland, Sagadahoc, and York Counties										
City of Portland	66,997	192	2	49	49	92	1,626	169	1,370	87
City of South Portland	25,557	36	0	9	4	23	455	54	388	13

Table 6. Crime in the United States, by Selected Metropolitan Statistical Area, 2018—Continued

(Number, percent, rate per 100,000 population.)

Area	Population	Violent crime	Murder and nonnegligent manslaughter	Rape[1]	Robbery	Aggravated assault	Property crime	Burglary	Larceny-theft	Motor vehicle theft
Total area actually reporting	100.0%	613	5	170	112	326	7,102	976	5,846	280
Rate per 100,000 inhabitants		114.5	0.9	31.8	20.9	60.9	1,326.9	182.4	1,092.3	52.3
Portland-Vancouver-Hillsboro, OR-WA M.S.A.	2,489,355									
Includes Clackamas, Columbia, Multnomah, Washington, and Yamhill Counties, OR and Clark and Skamania Counties, WA										
City of Portland, OR	657,260	3,418	25	438	1,056	1,899	35,884	4,444	24,508	6,932
City of Vancouver, WA	177,580	819	3	150	155	511	5,852	789	3,987	1,076
City of Hillsboro, OR	109,121	287	0	61	54	172	2,077	208	1,651	218
City of Beaverton, OR	98,616	189	2	59	40	88	2,039	191	1,587	261
City of Tigard, OR	53,880	114	0	30	33	51	1,558	180	1,277	101
Total area actually reporting	99.5%	7,405	48	1,377	1,748	4,232	71,193	9,064	49,785	12,344
Estimated total	100.0%	7,446	48	1,382	1,759	4,257	71,444	9,077	50,006	12,361
Rate per 100,000 inhabitants		299.1	1.9	55.5	70.7	171.0	2,870.0	364.6	2,008.8	496.6
Port St. Lucie, FL M.S.A.	480,458									
Includes Martin and St. Lucie Counties										
City of Port St. Lucie	193,137	218	2	26	31	159	1,851	256	1,523	72
Total area actually reporting	100.0%	1,200	21	177	208	794	6,598	965	5,275	358
Rate per 100,000 inhabitants		249.8	4.4	36.8	43.3	165.3	1,373.3	200.9	1,097.9	74.5
Poughkeepsie-Newburg-Middletown, NY M.S.A.	666,032									
Includes Dutchess and Orange Counties										
City of Poughkeepsie	30,580	216	4	26	59	127	494	85	374	35
City of Newburgh	28,282	329	2	24	102	201	657	141	475	41
City of Middletown	27,885	110	0	20	28	62	510	71	421	18
City of Woodbury Town	11,114	7	0	1	3	3	416	0	414	2
Total area actually reporting	99.8%	1,311	11	251	277	772	8,093	898	6,920	275
Estimated total	100.0%	1,311	11	251	277	772	8,109	899	6,935	275
Rate per 100,000 inhabitants		196.8	1.7	37.7	41.6	115.9	1,217.5	135.0	1,041.2	41.3
Prescott Valley-Prescott, AZ M.S.A.	232,771									
Includes Yavapai County										
City of Prescott Valley	45,337	67	1	10	5	51	776	73	676	27
City of Prescott	43,172	136	2	11	2	121	896	107	749	40
Total area actually reporting	100.0%	605	7	68	22	508	3,777	589	2,969	219
Rate per 100,000 inhabitants		259.9	3.0	29.2	9.5	218.2	1,622.6	253.0	1,275.5	94.1
Providence-Warwick, RI-MA M.S.A.	1,620,470									
Includes Bristol County, MA and Bristol, Kent, Newport, Providence, and Washington Counties, RI										
City of Providence, RI	180,169	819	10	109	248	452	5,679	931	4,196	552
City of Warwick, RI	80,380	73	1	27	9	36	1,372	136	1,178	58
Total area actually reporting	99.5%	4,582	23	695	804	3,060	24,805	4,203	18,519	2,083
Estimated total	100.0%	4,603	23	696	808	3,076	24,843	4,204	18,550	2,089
Rate per 100,000 inhabitants		284.1	1.4	43.0	49.9	189.8	1,533.1	259.4	1,144.7	128.9
Provo-Orem, UT M.S.A.	633,113									
Includes Juab and Utah Counties										
City of Provo	117,986	207	2	70	22	113	2,090	209	1,747	134
City of Orem	99,221	69	1	20	12	36	1,827	152	1,576	99
Total area actually reporting	100.0%	556	5	203	47	301	8,610	889	7,226	495
Rate per 100,000 inhabitants		87.8	0.8	32.1	7.4	47.5	1,359.9	140.4	1,141.3	78.2
Pueblo, CO M.S.A.	167,573									
Includes Pueblo County										
City of Pueblo	111,756	1,110	9	185	220	696	6,231	1,224	3,947	1,060
Total area actually reporting	100.0%	1,162	10	186	234	732	7,352	1,451	4,679	1,222
Rate per 100,000 inhabitants		693.4	6.0	111.0	139.6	436.8	4,387.3	865.9	2,792.2	729.2
Punta Gorda, FL M.S.A.	185,327									
Includes Charlotte County										
City of Punta Gorda	20,170	11	0	1	2	8	330	28	290	12
Total area actually reporting	100.0%	361	2	32	19	308	2,093	255	1,724	114
Rate per 100,000 inhabitants		194.8	1.1	17.3	10.3	166.2	1,129.4	137.6	930.2	61.5
Racine, WI M.S.A.[2]	196,249									
Includes Racine County										
City of Racine	77,373	435	8	54	81	292	1,662	347	1,196	119
Total area actually reporting	100.0%	518	8	59	93	358	2,744	521	2,054	169
Rate per 100,000 inhabitants		264.0	4.1	30.1	47.4	182.4	1,398.2	265.5	1,046.6	86.1
Rapid City, SD M.S.A.	140,572									
Includes Meade and Pennington Counties										
City of Rapid City	75,290	492	2	99	65	326	2,194	428	1,502	264
Total area actually reporting	100.0%	713	2	184	68	459	3,123	626	2,151	346
Rate per 100,000 inhabitants		507.2	1.4	130.9	48.4	326.5	2,221.6	445.3	1,530.2	246.1
Reading, PA M.S.A.	418,275									
Includes Berks County										
City of Reading	88,466	621	19	53	221	328	1,984	603	1,192	189

Table 6. Crime in the United States, by Selected Metropolitan Statistical Area, 2018—Continued

(Number, percent, rate per 100,000 population.)

Area	Population	Violent crime	Murder and nonnegligent manslaughter	Rape[1]	Robbery	Aggravated assault	Property crime	Burglary	Larceny-theft	Motor vehicle theft
Total area actually reporting	100.0%	989	23	103	284	579	5,452	1,062	4,042	348
Rate per 100,000 inhabitants		236.4	5.5	24.6	67.9	138.4	1,303.4	253.9	966.3	83.2
Redding, CA M.S.A.	178,909									
Includes Shasta County										
City of Redding	92,068	620	2	87	96	435	3,433	613	2,281	539
Total area actually reporting	100.0%	1,163	13	137	127	886	5,131	1,182	3,020	929
Rate per 100,000 inhabitants		650.1	7.3	76.6	71.0	495.2	2,867.9	660.7	1,688.0	519.3
Reno, NV M.S.A.	469,042									
Includes Storey and Washoe Counties										
City of Reno	252,341	1,636	6	174	303	1,153	6,053	1,073	3,930	1,050
Total area actually reporting	100.0%	2,408	16	301	406	1,685	9,761	1,881	6,394	1,486
Rate per 100,000 inhabitants		513.4	3.4	64.2	86.6	359.2	2,081.1	401.0	1,363.2	316.8
Richmond, VA M.S.A.	1,279,968									
Includes Amelia, Charles City, Chesterfield, Dinwiddie, Goochland, Hanover, Henrico, King and Queen, King William, New Kent, Powhatan, Prince George, and Sussex Counties and Colonial Heights, Hopewell, Petersburg, and Richmond Cities										
City of Richmond	229,927	1,190	52	77	428	633	8,807	1,121	6,518	1,168
Total area actually reporting	100.0%	3,064	100	354	808	1,802	27,596	3,176	21,972	2,448
Rate per 100,000 inhabitants		239.4	7.8	27.7	63.1	140.8	2,156.0	248.1	1,716.6	191.3
Riverside-San Bernardino-Ontario, CA M.S.A.[2]	4,595,416									
Includes Riverside and San Bernardino Counties										
City of Riverside	331,022	1,686	14	150	543	979	10,226	1,470	6,911	1,845
City of San Bernardino	217,986	2,906	49	153	974	1,730	9,014	2,226	4,594	2,194
City of Ontario	177,542	670	6	106	231	327	4,584	723	2,858	1,003
City of Corona	170,041	263	6	46	119	92	3,264	488	2,185	591
City of Temecula	116,411	139	0	4	60	75	2,711	429	1,964	318
City of Chino	91,535	259	1	25	67	166	2,216	407	1,508	301
City of Redlands	71,954	264	5	64	82	113	2,491	326	1,842	323
City of Palm Desert	53,567	91	0	6	21	64	1,989	329	1,530	130
Total area actually reporting	100.0%	17,937	220	1,479	5,306	10,932	112,378	21,681	69,078	21,619
Rate per 100,000 inhabitants		390.3	4.8	32.2	115.5	237.9	2,445.4	471.8	1,503.2	470.4
Roanoke, VA M.S.A.	314,160									
Includes Botetourt, Craig, Franklin, and Roanoke Counties and Roanoke and Salem Cities										
City of Roanoke	100,042	427	12	48	103	264	4,434	488	3,579	367
Total area actually reporting	100.0%	739	22	126	149	442	7,472	842	6,044	586
Rate per 100,000 inhabitants		235.2	7.0	40.1	47.4	140.7	2,378.4	268.0	1,923.9	186.5
Rochester, MN M.S.A.[2]	219,724									
Includes Dodge, Fillmore, Olmsted, and Wabasha[2] Counties										
City of Rochester	117,037	227	5	58	41	123	2,435	353	1,952	130
Total area actually reporting	100.0%	312	6	83	48	175	3,101	504	2,424	173
Rate per 100,000 inhabitants		142.0	2.7	37.8	21.8	79.6	1,411.3	229.4	1,103.2	78.7
Rochester, NY M.S.A.	1,057,448									
Includes Livingston, Monroe, Ontario, Orleans, Wayne, and Yates Counties										
City of Rochester	207,701	1,615	29	131	516	939	7,036	1,178	5,285	573
Total area actually reporting	99.7%	2,718	44	452	720	1,502	18,593	2,810	14,760	1,023
Estimated total	100.0%	2,720	44	452	720	1,504	18,632	2,814	14,794	1,024
Rate per 100,000 inhabitants		257.2	4.2	42.7	68.1	142.2	1,762.0	266.1	1,399.0	96.8
Rockford, IL M.S.A.	335,289									
Includes Boone and Winnebago Counties										
City of Rockford	146,196	2,027	23	133	346	1,525	5,368	1,169	3,752	447
Total area actually reporting	99.0%	2,487	35	252	394	1,806	7,954	1,683	5,687	584
Estimated total	100.0%	2,490	35	252	394	1,809	7,998	1,691	5,720	587
Rate per 100,000 inhabitants		742.6	10.4	75.2	117.5	539.5	2,385.4	504.3	1,706.0	175.1
Rocky Mount, NC M.S.A.[3]	145,982									
Includes Edgecombe and Nash Counties[3]										
City of Rocky Mount[3]	54,085		13		87	320	1,577	424	1,053	100
Total area actually reporting	93.3%	578	18	35	116	409	2,630	793	1,677	160
Estimated total	100.0%	609	18	37	120	434	2,932	856	1,902	174
Rate per 100,000 inhabitants		417.2	12.3	25.3	82.2	297.3	2,008.5	586.4	1,302.9	119.2
Sacramento-Roseville-Folsom, CA M.S.A.	2,332,284									
Includes El Dorado, Placer, Sacramento, and Yolo Counties										
City of Sacramento	507,037	3,329	36	102	1,052	2,139	15,417	2,751	9,783	2,883
City of Roseville	137,706	299	3	28	133	135	3,252	428	2,543	281
City of Folsom	78,916	85	1	20	29	35	1,245	245	918	82
City of Rancho Cordova	74,863	272	3	26	74	169	1,388	257	934	197
City of West Sacramento	54,215	225	1	17	92	115	1,412	224	931	257

Table 6. Crime in the United States, by Selected Metropolitan Statistical Area, 2018—Continued

(Number, percent, rate per 100,000 population.)

Area	Population	Violent crime	Murder and nonnegligent manslaughter	Rape[1]	Robbery	Aggravated assault	Property crime	Burglary	Larceny-theft	Motor vehicle theft
Total area actually reporting	100.0%	8,754	86	682	2,456	5,530	50,411	8,922	33,827	7,662
Rate per 100,000 inhabitants		375.3	3.7	29.2	105.3	237.1	2,161.4	382.5	1,450.4	328.5
Saginaw, MI M.S.A.	191,213									
Includes Saginaw County										
City of Saginaw	48,302	783	11	48	86	638	886	376	420	90
Total area actually reporting	100.0%	1,264	18	159	113	974	3,001	751	2,035	215
Rate per 100,000 inhabitants		661.0	9.4	83.2	59.1	509.4	1,569.5	392.8	1,064.3	112.4
Salem, OR M.S.A.[3]	430,201									
Includes Marion[3] and Polk Counties										
City of Salem	172,022	719	5	56	177	481	7,170	934	5,338	898
Total area actually reporting	100.0%	1,236	10	145	258	823	13,428	1,797	9,986	1,645
Rate per 100,000 inhabitants		287.3	2.3	33.7	60.0	191.3	3,121.3	417.7	2,321.2	382.4
Salinas, CA M.S.A.	437,653									
Includes Monterey County										
City of Salinas	158,590	981	19	100	321	541	4,304	897	2,180	1,227
Total area actually reporting	100.0%	1,750	27	197	483	1,043	9,030	1,767	5,416	1,847
Rate per 100,000 inhabitants		399.9	6.2	45.0	110.4	238.3	2,063.3	403.7	1,237.5	422.0
Salisbury, MD-DE M.S.A.	408,178									
Includes Sussex County, DE and Somerset, Wicomico, and Worcester Counties, MD										
City of Salisbury, MD	33,183	272	3	21	74	174	1,548	195	1,312	41
Total area actually reporting	100.0%	1,413	10	150	232	1,021	9,150	1,711	7,138	301
Rate per 100,000 inhabitants		346.2	2.4	36.7	56.8	250.1	2,241.7	419.2	1,748.7	73.7
Salt Lake City, UT M.S.A.	1,223,475									
Includes Salt Lake and Tooele Counties										
City of Salt Lake City	202,633	1,480	10	245	414	811	12,516	1,601	9,422	1,493
Total area actually reporting	99.9%	4,513	33	903	958	2,619	44,779	5,695	33,636	5,448
Estimated total	100.0%	4,514	33	903	958	2,620	44,796	5,697	33,649	5,450
Rate per 100,000 inhabitants		368.9	2.7	73.8	78.3	214.1	3,661.4	465.6	2,750.3	445.5
San Angelo, TX M.S.A.[2]	121,589									
Includes Irion,[2] Sterling,[2] and Tom Green Counties										
City of San Angelo	101,084	373	2	82	52	237	3,383	583	2,567	233
Total area actually reporting	100.0%	401	3	101	52	245	3,718	701	2,756	261
Rate per 100,000 inhabitants		329.8	2.5	83.1	42.8	201.5	3,057.8	576.5	2,266.7	214.7
San Antonio-New Braunfels, TX M.S.A.2,[4]	2,516,781									
Includes Atascosa, Bandera, Bexar, Comal,[4] Guadalupe, Kendall, Medina, and Wilson Counties										
City of San Antonio	1,539,328	9,647	107	1,346	1,767	6,427	61,478	9,118	46,271	6,089
City of New Braunfels[2]	82,739	241	2	43	22	174	1,197	215	892	90
Total area actually reporting	99.9%		135	1,818	2,021		77,793	12,085	58,321	7,387
Estimated total	100.0%		135	1,818	2,021		77,809	12,089	58,332	7,388
Rate per 100,000 inhabitants			5.4	72.2	80.3		3,091.6	480.3	2,317.7	293.5
San Diego-Chula Vista-Carlsbad, CA M.S.A.	3,346,474									
Includes San Diego County										
City of San Diego	1,436,495	5,360	35	605	1,439	3,281	27,416	3,752	18,482	5,182
City of Chula Vista	274,370	835	6	79	256	494	3,611	585	2,338	688
City of Carlsbad	116,739	243	1	39	52	151	2,100	299	1,649	152
City of Poway	50,346	65	1	11	10	43	509	92	380	37
Total area actually reporting	100.0%	11,414	85	1,162	2,976	7,191	56,699	8,292	38,819	9,588
Rate per 100,000 inhabitants		341.1	2.5	34.7	88.9	214.9	1,694.3	247.8	1,160.0	286.5
San Francisco-Oakland-Berkeley, CA M.S.A.	4,747,868									
Includes the Metropolitan Divisions of Oakland-Berkeley-Livermore, San Francisco-San Mateo-Redwood City, and San Rafael										
City of San Francisco	889,282	6,144	46	354	3,165	2,579	49,214	5,322	39,675	4,217
City of Oakland	430,230	5,480	70	448	2,624	2,338	23,190	2,394	15,725	5,071
City of Berkeley	123,735	586	1	65	353	167	5,381	829	4,004	548
City of San Mateo	105,839	285	0	25	88	172	2,163	590	1,360	213
City of Livermore	91,612	186	0	33	58	95	1,696	212	1,329	155
City of Redwood City	88,161	177	0	45	53	79	1,254	172	912	170
City of Pleasanton	84,992	110	0	6	57	47	1,445	156	1,177	112
City of San Ramon	76,569	43	0	4	21	18	786	103	631	52
City of Walnut Creek	70,587	109	2	3	35	69	2,249	303	1,812	134
City of South San Francisco	67,973	181	0	22	56	103	1,444	257	1,002	185
City of San Rafael	59,254	257	2	32	107	116	1,695	277	1,050	368
Total area actually reporting	100.0%	22,443	196	1,820	10,332	10,095	155,896	19,033	114,842	22,021
Rate per 100,000 inhabitants		472.7	4.1	38.3	217.6	212.6	3,283.5	400.9	2,418.8	463.8
Oakland-Berkeley-Livermore, CA M.D.	2,825,431									
Includes Alameda and Contra Costa Counties										
Total area actually reporting	100.0%	13,828	132	1,097	6,334	6,265	86,407	10,403	60,430	15,574
Rate per 100,000 inhabitants		489.4	4.7	38.8	224.2	221.7	3,058.2	368.2	2,138.8	551.2

Table 6. Crime in the United States, by Selected Metropolitan Statistical Area, 2018—Continued

(Number, percent, rate per 100,000 population.)

Area	Population	Violent crime	Murder and nonnegligent manslaughter	Rape[1]	Robbery	Aggravated assault	Property crime	Burglary	Larceny-theft	Motor vehicle theft
San Francisco-San Mateo-Redwood City, CA M.D.	1,662,338									
Includes San Francisco and San Mateo Counties										
Total area actually reporting	100.0%	8,087	59	659	3,831	3,538	64,795	7,808	51,096	5,891
Rate per 100,000 inhabitants		486.5	3.5	39.6	230.5	212.8	3,897.8	469.7	3,073.7	354.4
San Rafael, CA M.D.	260,099									
Includes Marin County										
Total area actually reporting	100.0%	528	5	64	167	292	4,694	822	3,316	556
Rate per 100,000 inhabitants		203.0	1.9	24.6	64.2	112.3	1,804.7	316.0	1,274.9	213.8
San Jose-Sunnyvale-Santa Clara, CA M.S.A.	2,006,271									
Includes San Benito and Santa Clara Counties										
City of San Jose	1,047,305	4,444	28	615	1,593	2,208	25,753	4,539	13,510	7,704
City of Sunnyvale	155,637	255	1	43	71	140	2,541	424	1,764	353
City of Santa Clara	128,682	208	1	33	74	100	3,741	429	2,860	452
City of Mountain View	82,518	157	0	13	59	85	2,103	276	1,659	168
City of Milpitas	79,895	87	0	11	45	31	1,934	243	1,435	256
City of Palo Alto	67,560	72	0	5	30	37	1,513	234	1,197	82
City of Cupertino	61,078	72	0	18	14	40	956	183	720	53
Total area actually reporting	100.0%	6,304	33	869	2,135	3,267	46,073	7,540	28,213	10,320
Rate per 100,000 inhabitants		314.2	1.6	43.3	106.4	162.8	2,296.4	375.8	1,406.2	514.4
San Luis Obispo-Paso Robles, CA M.S.A.	283,198									
Includes San Luis Obispo County										
City of San Luis Obispo	47,885	192	1	55	33	103	1,809	242	1,493	74
City of Paso Robles	32,228	43	0	13	7	23	797	133	610	54
Total area actually reporting	100.0%	746	3	122	72	549	5,569	1,079	4,169	321
Rate per 100,000 inhabitants		263.4	1.1	43.1	25.4	193.9	1,966.5	381.0	1,472.1	113.3
Santa Cruz-Watsonville, CA M.S.A.	275,614									
Includes Santa Cruz County										
City of Santa Cruz	65,680	390	1	34	66	289	2,905	336	2,308	261
City of Watsonville	54,513	243	1	18	50	174	1,330	196	785	349
Total area actually reporting	100.0%	989	5	103	173	708	7,530	1,064	5,509	957
Rate per 100,000 inhabitants		358.8	1.8	37.4	62.8	256.9	2,732.1	386.0	1,998.8	347.2
Santa Fe, NM M.S.A.	149,630									
Includes Santa Fe County										
City of Santa Fe	84,176	333	5	32	89	207	3,388	1,380	1,786	222
Total area actually reporting	100.0%	592	6	42	115	429	4,111	1,720	2,147	244
Rate per 100,000 inhabitants		395.6	4.0	28.1	76.9	286.7	2,747.4	1,149.5	1,434.9	163.1
Santa Maria-Santa Barbara, CA M.S.A.	448,173									
Includes Santa Barbara County										
City of Santa Maria	108,100	497	6	60	159	272	1,932	377	979	576
City of Santa Barbara	92,630	415	1	77	89	248	2,333	261	1,894	178
Total area actually reporting	100.0%	1,493	11	229	322	931	7,633	1,322	5,203	1,108
Rate per 100,000 inhabitants		333.1	2.5	51.1	71.8	207.7	1,703.1	295.0	1,160.9	247.2
Santa Rosa-Petaluma, CA M.S.A.	503,136									
Includes Sonoma County										
City of Santa Rosa	176,325	823	3	149	147	524	3,118	547	2,179	392
City of Petaluma	61,289	197	0	31	27	139	889	153	668	68
Total area actually reporting	100.0%	1,985	9	312	268	1,396	7,167	1,375	5,109	683
Rate per 100,000 inhabitants		394.5	1.8	62.0	53.3	277.5	1,424.5	273.3	1,015.4	135.7
Savannah, GA M.S.A.[2]	392,726									
Includes Bryan, Chatham, and Effingham Counties										
City of Savannah-Chatham Metropolitan	242,265	982	28	85	267	602	5,960	884	4,420	656
Total area actually reporting	100.0%	1,516	36	141	368	971	10,688	1,632	7,980	1,076
Rate per 100,000 inhabitants		386.0	9.2	35.9	93.7	247.2	2,721.5	415.6	2,032.0	274.0
Scranton–Wilkes-Barre, PA M.S.A.	553,684									
Includes Lackawanna, Luzerne, and Wyoming Counties										
City of Scranton	77,827	811	2	43	62	704	1,505	340	1,080	85
City of Wilkes-Barre	40,710	210	4	30	85	91	965	204	707	54
Total area actually reporting	99.3%	1,913	21	204	249	1,439	7,524	1,328	5,816	380
Estimated total	100.0%	1,914	21	204	249	1,440	7,569	1,330	5,859	380
Rate per 100,000 inhabitants		345.7	3.8	36.8	45.0	260.1	1,367.0	240.2	1,058.2	68.6
Seattle-Tacoma-Bellevue, WA M.S.A.2, [3]	3,946,150									
Includes the Metropolitan Divisions of Seattle-Bellevue-Kent and Tacoma-Lakewood										
City of Seattle	742,759	5,052	32	292	1,649	3,079	38,246	7,985	26,219	4,042
City of Tacoma	215,687	1,869	17	198	503	1,151	11,362	1,912	7,573	1,877
City of Bellevue	146,913	194	0	27	82	85	4,294	519	3,395	380
City of Kent	129,870	452	5	92	196	159	5,953	854	3,949	1,150
City of Everett	111,091	373	5	55	110	203	4,683	650	3,077	956
City of Renton	102,749	331	5	53	110	163	4,915	542	3,447	926
City of Auburn	82,381	360	1	59	120	180	3,334	605	2,116	613
City of Redmond	65,827	89	1	6	32	50	1,854	186	1,577	91
City of Lakewood	60,694	393	9	34	80	270	2,818	486	1,939	393

Table 6. Crime in the United States, by Selected Metropolitan Statistical Area, 2018—Continued

(Number, percent, rate per 100,000 population.)

Area	Population	Violent crime	Murder and nonnegligent manslaughter	Rape[1]	Robbery	Aggravated assault	Property crime	Burglary	Larceny-theft	Motor vehicle theft
Total area actually reporting	100.0%	14,167	131	1,575	4,165	8,296	131,458	23,368	89,577	18,513
Rate per 100,000 inhabitants		359.0	3.3	39.9	105.5	210.2	3,331.3	592.2	2,270.0	469.1
Seattle-Bellevue-Kent, WA M.D.[2,3]	3,053,639									
Includes King[2,3] and Snohomish Counties										
Total area actually reporting	100.0%	10,160	83	1,138	3,244	5,695	102,149	17,815	70,180	14,154
Rate per 100,000 inhabitants		332.7	2.7	37.3	106.2	186.5	3,345.2	583.4	2,298.2	463.5
Tacoma-Lakewood, WA M.D.	892,511									
Includes Pierce County										
Total area actually reporting	100.0%	4,007	48	437	921	2,601	29,309	5,553	19,397	4,359
Rate per 100,000 inhabitants		449.0	5.4	49.0	103.2	291.4	3,283.9	622.2	2,173.3	488.4
Sebastian-Vero Beach, FL M.S.A.	156,733									
Includes Indian River County										
City of Sebastian	25,672	31	0	4	3	24	279	35	232	12
City of Vero Beach	17,172	34	3	7	8	16	415	71	332	12
Total area actually reporting	100.0%	329	12	38	51	228	2,398	395	1,884	119
Rate per 100,000 inhabitants		209.9	7.7	24.2	32.5	145.5	1,530.0	252.0	1,202.0	75.9
Sebring-Avon Park, FL M.S.A.	103,440									
Includes Highlands County										
City of Sebring	10,741	80	0	6	6	68	431	95	326	10
Total area actually reporting	100.0%	314	2	44	39	229	2,394	568	1,736	90
Rate per 100,000 inhabitants		303.6	1.9	42.5	37.7	221.4	2,314.4	549.1	1,678.3	87.0
Sheboygan, WI M.S.A.	115,368									
Includes Sheboygan County										
City of Sheboygan	48,195	183	0	27	10	146	826	89	715	22
Total area actually reporting	100.0%	237	0	49	13	175	1,355	146	1,167	42
Rate per 100,000 inhabitants		205.4	0.0	42.5	11.3	151.7	1,174.5	126.6	1,011.5	36.4
Sherman-Denison, TX M.S.A.[2]	132,282									
Includes Grayson County										
City of Sherman	42,448	147	0	29	28	90	1,068	224	778	66
City of Denison	24,623	92	2	17	12	61	467	101	312	54
Total area actually reporting	98.4%	355	3	75	49	228	2,137	501	1,443	193
Estimated total	100.0%	357	3	75	49	230	2,165	507	1,463	195
Rate per 100,000 inhabitants		269.9	2.3	56.7	37.0	173.9	1,636.7	383.3	1,106.0	147.4
Shreveport-Bossier City, LA M.S.A.	397,965									
Includes Bossier, Caddo, and De Soto Parishes										
City of Shreveport	190,808	1,588	49	123	335	1,081	9,884	1,832	7,241	811
City of Bossier City	69,551	576	4	46	60	466	2,998	387	2,313	298
Total area actually reporting	100.0%	2,399	57	186	413	1,743	14,900	2,727	10,882	1,291
Rate per 100,000 inhabitants		602.8	14.3	46.7	103.8	438.0	3,744.0	685.2	2,734.4	324.4
Sioux Falls, SD M.S.A.	265,074									
Includes Lincoln, McCook, Minnehaha, and Turner Counties										
City of Sioux Falls	180,335	788	5	121	107	555	5,288	652	4,092	544
Total area actually reporting	98.7%	896	5	150	107	634	6,122	917	4,601	604
Estimated total	100.0%	911	5	153	109	644	6,214	930	4,670	614
Rate per 100,000 inhabitants		343.7	1.9	57.7	41.1	243.0	2,344.3	350.8	1,761.8	231.6
South Bend-Mishawaka, IN-MI M.S.A.[2]	322,244									
Includes St. Joseph County, IN and Cass County, MI										
City of South Bend, IN[2]	102,397	1,064	9	67	277	711	4,406	970	2,956	480
City of Mishawaka, IN	49,310	114	4	15	48	47	2,525	248	2,032	245
Total area actually reporting	87.1%	1,357	19	129	346	863	8,247	1,598	5,803	846
Estimated total	100.0%	1,430	20	138	355	917	8,661	1,678	6,117	866
Rate per 100,000 inhabitants		443.8	6.2	42.8	110.2	284.6	2,687.7	520.7	1,898.3	268.7
Spokane-Spokane Valley, WA M.S.A.	558,298									
Includes Spokane and Stevens Counties										
City of Spokane	218,222	1,742	8	351	297	1,086	15,439	2,130	11,631	1,678
City of Spokane Valley	99,020	346	1	79	59	207	4,165	484	3,328	353
Total area actually reporting	99.9%	2,435	13	530	383	1,509	24,428	3,598	18,411	2,419
Estimated total	100.0%	2,436	13	530	383	1,510	24,433	3,600	18,413	2,420
Rate per 100,000 inhabitants		436.3	2.3	94.9	68.6	270.5	4,376.3	644.8	3,298.1	433.5
Springfield, IL M.S.A.	207,537									
Includes Menard and Sangamon Counties										
City of Springfield	114,623	955	9	93	216	637	5,487	1,195	4,044	248
Total area actually reporting	97.6%	1,232	10	128	234	860	6,587	1,497	4,732	358
Estimated total	100.0%	1,237	10	128	234	865	6,650	1,509	4,779	362
Rate per 100,000 inhabitants		596.0	4.8	61.7	112.8	416.8	3,204.2	727.1	2,302.7	174.4
Springfield, MA M.S.A.	703,308									
Includes Franklin, Hampden and Hampshire Counties										
City of Springfield	155,179	1,534	19	104	475	936	4,089	910	2,752	427

Table 6. Crime in the United States, by Selected Metropolitan Statistical Area, 2018—Continued

(Number, percent, rate per 100,000 population.)

Area	Population	Violent crime	Murder and nonnegligent manslaughter	Rape[1]	Robbery	Aggravated assault	Property crime	Burglary	Larceny-theft	Motor vehicle theft
Total area actually reporting	95.6%	3,477	26	408	692	2,351	12,536	2,562	9,068	906
Estimated total	100.0%	3,508	26	409	698	2,375	12,591	2,563	9,114	914
Rate per 100,000 inhabitants		498.8	3.7	58.2	99.2	337.7	1,790.3	364.4	1,295.9	130.0
Springfield, MO M.S.A.	465,708									
Includes Christian, Dallas, Greene, Polk, and Webster Counties										
City of Springfield	168,537	2,218	16	333	295	1,574	11,830	1,975	8,385	1,470
Total area actually reporting	100.0%	2,620	25	409	330	1,856	15,905	2,738	11,337	1,830
Rate per 100,000 inhabitants		562.6	5.4	87.8	70.9	398.5	3,415.2	587.9	2,434.4	393.0
Springfield, OH M.S.A.	134,171									
Includes Clark County										
City of Springfield	59,016	336	13	21	143	159	3,141	699	2,204	238
Total area actually reporting	92.6%	375	13	25	152	185	3,810	850	2,705	255
Estimated total	100.0%	398	13	29	163	193	4,069	868	2,924	277
Rate per 100,000 inhabitants		296.6	9.7	21.6	121.5	143.8	3,032.7	646.9	2,179.3	206.5
State College, PA M.S.A.	163,729									
Includes Centre County										
City of State College	58,781	20	0	1	5	14	448	32	411	5
Total area actually reporting	100.0%	161	2	71	11	77	1,344	143	1,178	23
Rate per 100,000 inhabitants		98.3	1.2	43.4	6.7	47.0	820.9	87.3	719.5	14.0
Staunton, VA M.S.A.	122,240									
Includes Augusta County and Staunton and Waynesboro Cities										
City of Staunton	24,584	46	1	7	11	27	608	63	523	22
Total area actually reporting	100.0%	211	5	51	32	123	1,896	312	1,442	142
Rate per 100,000 inhabitants		172.6	4.1	41.7	26.2	100.6	1,551.0	255.2	1,179.6	116.2
St. Cloud, MN M.S.A.	198,828									
Includes Benton and Stearns Counties										
City of St. Cloud	68,282	262	1	56	49	156	2,575	297	2,089	189
Total area actually reporting	100.0%	355	5	85	51	214	4,348	489	3,564	295
Rate per 100,000 inhabitants		178.5	2.5	42.8	25.7	107.6	2,186.8	245.9	1,792.5	148.4
St. George, UT M.S.A.[2]	170,464									
Includes Washington County										
City of St. George	86,202	196	3	48	19	126	1,388	228	1,049	111
Total area actually reporting	98.3%	311	3	85	23	200	2,503	416	1,898	189
Estimated total	100.0%	317	3	86	24	204	2,572	425	1,951	196
Rate per 100,000 inhabitants		186.0	1.8	50.5	14.1	119.7	1,508.8	249.3	1,144.5	115.0
St. Joseph, MO-KS M.S.A.[2,3]	126,765									
Includes Doniphan County, KS and Andrew, Buchanan,[2] and DeKalb Counties, MO										
City of St. Joseph, MO2,[3]	76,409		8		65	301	3,768	716	2,491	561
Total area actually reporting	99.8%	589	9	164	72	344	4,382	852	2,897	633
Estimated total	100.0%	589	9	164	72	344	4,386	853	2,899	634
Rate per 100,000 inhabitants		464.6	7.1	129.4	56.8	271.4	3,459.9	672.9	2,286.9	500.1
St. Louis, MO-IL M.S.A.[2,4,5,7]	2,806,936									
Includes Bond, Calhoun, Clinton, Jersey, Macoupin, Madison, Monroe, and St. Clair Counties, IL and Franklin,[2] Jefferson, Lincoln,[5] St. Charles, St. Louis, and Warren Counties and St. Louis City, MO										
City of St. Louis, MO	306,875	5,525	187	309	1,452	3,577	18,142	2,979	12,413	2,750
City of St. Charles, MO	70,925	147	7	33	19	88	1,610	134	1,321	155
Total area actually reporting	97.9%	12,687	360	1,163	2,603	8,561			46,749	
Estimated total	100.0%	12,775	361	1,176	2,619	8,619			47,411	
Rate per 100,000 inhabitants		455.1	12.9	41.9	93.3	307.1			1,689.1	
Stockton, CA M.S.A.	748,303									
Includes San Joaquin County										
City of Stockton	313,158	4,383	33	193	1,205	2,952	11,800	2,329	7,417	2,054
Total area actually reporting	100.0%	5,950	52	288	1,656	3,954	22,123	4,231	14,163	3,729
Rate per 100,000 inhabitants		795.1	6.9	38.5	221.3	528.4	2,956.4	565.4	1,892.7	498.3
Sumter, SC M.S.A.	140,650									
Includes Clarendon and Sumter Counties										
City of Sumter	39,898	366	4	12	53	297	1,873	376	1,411	86
Total area actually reporting	100.0%	955	10	40	103	802	4,790	1,144	3,306	340
Rate per 100,000 inhabitants		679.0	7.1	28.4	73.2	570.2	3,405.6	813.4	2,350.5	241.7
Syracuse, NY M.S.A.	641,425									
Includes Madison, Onondaga, and Oswego Counties										
City of Syracuse	143,129	1,006	23	92	285	606	4,420	831	3,083	506
Total area actually reporting	99.0%	1,697	30	332	354	981	11,288	1,674	8,797	817
Estimated total	100.0%	1,703	30	333	355	985	11,368	1,682	8,867	819
Rate per 100,000 inhabitants		265.5	4.7	51.9	55.3	153.6	1,772.3	262.2	1,382.4	127.7

Table 6. Crime in the United States, by Selected Metropolitan Statistical Area, 2018—Continued

(Number, percent, rate per 100,000 population.)

Area	Population	Violent crime	Murder and nonnegligent manslaughter	Rape[1]	Robbery	Aggravated assault	Property crime	Burglary	Larceny-theft	Motor vehicle theft
Tallahassee, FL M.S.A.	384,355									
Includes Gadsden, Jefferson, Leon, and Wakulla Counties										
City of Tallahassee	192,443	1,404	16	213	307	868	8,695	1,379	6,549	767
Total area actually reporting	99.6%	2,143	27	281	382	1,453	12,672	2,273	9,362	1,037
Estimated total	100.0%	2,148	27	281	383	1,457	12,713	2,282	9,391	1,040
Rate per 100,000 inhabitants		558.9	7.0	73.1	99.6	379.1	3,307.6	593.7	2,443.3	270.6
Tampa-St. Petersburg-Clearwater, FL M.S.A.	3,135,589									
Includes Hernando, Hillsborough, Pasco, and Pinellas Counties										
City of Tampa	392,945	1,598	27	100	332	1,139	6,576	1,047	5,069	460
City of St. Petersburg	265,942	1,660	21	133	368	1,138	8,784	1,206	6,832	746
City of Clearwater	116,504	510	6	95	105	304	3,087	345	2,564	178
City of Largo	85,568	322	3	66	72	181	2,593	282	2,126	185
City of Pinellas Park	53,383	224	3	41	57	123	2,423	247	2,037	139
Total area actually reporting	99.7%	9,588	119	1,207	1,722	6,540	57,991	8,016	45,564	4,411
Estimated total	100.0%	9,608	119	1,208	1,726	6,555	58,164	8,047	45,694	4,423
Rate per 100,000 inhabitants		306.4	3.8	38.5	55.0	209.1	1,855.0	256.6	1,457.3	141.1
Texarkana, TX-AR M.S.A.[5]	150,172									
Includes Little River and Miller[5] Counties, AR and Bowie County, TX										
City of Texarkana, TX	37,460	171	3	28	45	95	1,914	348	1,427	139
Total area actually reporting	100.0%	583	5	87	99	392			3,219	331
Rate per 100,000 inhabitants		388.2	3.3	57.9	65.9	261.0			2,143.5	220.4
The Villages, FL M.S.A.	130,254									
Includes Sumter County										
Total area actually reporting	100.0%	227	8	23	16	180	1,151	263	729	159
Rate per 100,000 inhabitants		174.3	6.1	17.7	12.3	138.2	883.7	201.9	559.7	122.1
Toledo, OH M.S.A.	644,005									
Includes Fulton, Lucas, Ottawa, and Wood Counties										
City of Toledo	275,023	2,333	37	239	477	1,580	10,222	2,802	6,712	708
Total area actually reporting	88.4%	2,700	41	340	552	1,767	15,773	3,520	11,369	884
Estimated total	100.0%	2,781	41	355	595	1,790	17,181	3,652	12,537	992
Rate per 100,000 inhabitants		431.8	6.4	55.1	92.4	277.9	2,667.8	567.1	1,946.7	154.0
Topeka, KS M.S.A.	232,183									
Includes Jackson, Jefferson, Osage, Shawnee, and Wabaunsee Counties										
City of Topeka	126,399	766	14	84	254	414	6,560	973	4,851	736
Total area actually reporting	98.1%	1,001	22	117	261	601	8,251	1,333	6,013	905
Estimated total	100.0%	1,028	22	117	265	624	8,373	1,370	6,080	923
Rate per 100,000 inhabitants		442.8	9.5	50.4	114.1	268.8	3,606.2	590.1	2,618.6	397.5
Trenton-Princeton, NJ M.S.A.	370,436									
Includes Mercer County										
City of Trenton	83,753	973	16	40	342	575	2,467	772	1,318	377
City of Princeton	31,856	11	0	0	3	8	224	43	169	12
Total area actually reporting	100.0%	1,318	22	92	432	772	6,687	1,423	4,689	575
Rate per 100,000 inhabitants		355.8	5.9	24.8	116.6	208.4	1,805.2	384.1	1,265.8	155.2
Tucson, AZ M.S.A.	1,037,852									
Includes Pima County										
City of Tucson	537,392	3,958	47	504	1,224	2,183	26,623	3,257	20,798	2,568
Total area actually reporting	99.5%	4,728	57	613	1,411	2,647	38,215	4,965	29,857	3,393
Estimated total	100.0%	4,747	57	616	1,417	2,657	38,425	5,009	30,008	3,408
Rate per 100,000 inhabitants		457.4	5.5	59.4	136.5	256.0	3,702.4	482.6	2,891.4	328.4
Tulsa, OK M.S.A.	994,764									
Includes Creek, Okmulgee, Osage, Pawnee, Rogers, and Wagoner Counties										
City of Tulsa	403,147	4,294	60	422	830	2,982	21,893	4,800	13,834	3,259
Total area actually reporting	100.0%	5,618	79	689	955	3,895	33,024	7,240	21,242	4,542
Rate per 100,000 inhabitants		564.8	7.9	69.3	96.0	391.6	3,319.8	727.8	2,135.4	456.6
Tuscaloosa, AL M.S.A.	252,822									
Includes Greene, Hale, Pickens, and Tuscaloosa Counties										
City of Tuscaloosa	101,764	514	5	47	140	322	4,415	753	3,347	315
Total area actually reporting	89.6%	947	10	87	198	652	7,331	1,426	5,295	610
Estimated total	100.0%	1,002	10	90	203	699	7,708	1,536	5,536	636
Rate per 100,000 inhabitants		396.3	4.0	35.6	80.3	276.5	3,048.8	607.5	2,189.7	251.6
Twin Falls, ID M.S.A.	111,002									
Includes Jerome and Twin Falls Counties										
City of Twin Falls	49,908	225	0	39	7	179	1,180	190	912	78
Total area actually reporting	100.0%	334	1	61	11	261	1,788	380	1,291	117
Rate per 100,000 inhabitants		300.9	0.9	55.0	9.9	235.1	1,610.8	342.3	1,163.0	105.4
Tyler, TX M.S.A.[2]	229,669									
Includes Smith County										

Table 6. Crime in the United States, by Selected Metropolitan Statistical Area, 2018—Continued

(Number, percent, rate per 100,000 population.)

Area	Population	Violent crime	Murder and nonnegligent manslaughter	Rape[1]	Robbery	Aggravated assault	Property crime	Burglary	Larceny-theft	Motor vehicle theft
City of Tyler	106,159	412	7	71	82	252	3,133	386	2,596	151
Total area actually reporting	100.0%	737	16	136	92	493	4,830	876	3,604	350
Rate per 100,000 inhabitants		320.9	7.0	59.2	40.1	214.7	2,103.0	381.4	1,569.2	152.4
Urban Honolulu, HI M.S.A.[2]	982,019									
Includes Honolulu County										
Total area actually reporting	100.0%	2,451	25	340	804	1,282	28,886	3,577	21,118	4,191
Rate per 100,000 inhabitants		249.6	2.5	34.6	81.9	130.5	2,941.5	364.2	2,150.5	426.8
Utica-Rome, NY M.S.A.	287,286									
Includes Herkimer and Oneida Counties										
City of Utica	60,413	381	6	45	88	242	1,914	328	1,492	94
City of Rome	32,298	49	0	9	13	27	540	116	411	13
Total area actually reporting	97.4%	727	7	218	113	389	4,690	749	3,757	184
Estimated total	100.0%	733	7	219	114	393	4,779	758	3,834	187
Rate per 100,000 inhabitants		255.1	2.4	76.2	39.7	136.8	1,663.5	263.8	1,334.6	65.1
Vallejo, CA M.S.A.	446,656									
Includes Solano County										
City of Vallejo	122,974	942	8	103	349	482	4,508	2,456	975	1,077
Total area actually reporting	100.0%	2,110	18	239	653	1,200	11,894	3,368	6,285	2,241
Rate per 100,000 inhabitants		472.4	4.0	53.5	146.2	268.7	2,662.9	754.0	1,407.1	501.7
Victoria, TX M.S.A.	100,184									
Includes Goliad and Victoria Counties										
City of Victoria	67,766	280	4	51	46	179	1,885	358	1,440	87
Total area actually reporting	100.0%	370	7	74	47	242	2,352	503	1,715	134
Rate per 100,000 inhabitants		369.3	7.0	73.9	46.9	241.6	2,347.7	502.1	1,711.9	133.8
Vineland-Bridgeton, NJ M.S.A.	149,815									
Includes Cumberland County										
City of Vineland	60,330	258	1	22	59	176	2,021	399	1,564	58
City of Bridgeton	24,386	203	5	12	107	79	720	163	510	47
Total area actually reporting	100.0%	663	10	50	218	385	4,571	899	3,522	150
Rate per 100,000 inhabitants		442.5	6.7	33.4	145.5	257.0	3,051.1	600.1	2,350.9	100.1
Virginia Beach-Norfolk-Newport News, VA-NC M.S.A.[3,4]	1,764,232									
Includes Camden, Currituck and Gates Counties, NC[3] and Gloucester, Isle of Wight, James City, Mathews, Southampton, and York Counties and Chesapeake, Franklin, Hampton, Newport News, Norfolk, Poquoson, Portsmouth, Suffolk, Virginia Beach, and Williamsburg Cities, VA										
City of Virginia Beach, VA	451,001	528	7	81	174	266	7,772	584	6,611	577
City of Norfolk, VA	244,347	1,134	36	117	321	660	8,463	703	6,972	788
City of Newport News, VA	178,734	942	24	89	187	642	5,148	693	3,961	494
City of Hampton, VA[4]	133,965	316	16	24	120	156		491		231
City of Portsmouth, VA	94,218	749	20	44	203	482	4,977	958	3,651	368
Total area actually reporting	99.3%	5,386	122	573	1,287	3,404	42,290	4,800	34,312	3,178
Estimated total	100.0%	5,413	122	586	1,288	3,417	42,430	4,841	34,398	3,191
Rate per 100,000 inhabitants		306.8	6.9	33.2	73.0	193.7	2,405.0	274.4	1,949.7	180.9
Visalia, CA M.S.A.	464,028									
Includes Tulare County										
City of Visalia	134,224	450	3	107	138	202	3,978	748	2,701	529
Total area actually reporting	100.0%	1,587	26	201	359	1,001	11,682	2,259	7,220	2,203
Rate per 100,000 inhabitants		342.0	5.6	43.3	77.4	215.7	2,517.5	486.8	1,555.9	474.8
Waco, TX M.S.A.[2]	270,144									
Includes Falls and McLennan Counties										
City of Waco[2]	138,091	878	3	129	122	624	4,851	1,194	3,329	328
Total area actually reporting	97.9%	1,232	5	209	151	867	7,165	1,594	5,066	505
Estimated total	100.0%	1,239	5	209	151	874	7,239	1,611	5,116	512
Rate per 100,000 inhabitants		458.6	1.9	77.4	55.9	323.5	2,679.7	596.3	1,893.8	189.5
Walla Walla, WA M.S.A.	61,042									
Includes Walla Walla County										
City of Walla Walla	32,906	128	0	25	12	91	1,194	162	972	60
Total area actually reporting	100.0%	180	1	30	14	135	1,660	252	1,319	89
Rate per 100,000 inhabitants		294.9	1.6	49.1	22.9	221.2	2,719.4	412.8	2,160.8	145.8
Warner Robins, GA M.S.A.	182,049									
Includes Houston and Peach Counties										
City of Warner Robins	75,668	444	8	63	86	287	4,200	726	3,258	216
Total area actually reporting	100.0%	755	9	82	122	542	6,482	1,097	5,035	350
Rate per 100,000 inhabitants		414.7	4.9	45.0	67.0	297.7	3,560.6	602.6	2,765.7	192.3
Washington-Arlington-Alexandria, DC-VA-MD-WV M.S.A.	6,281,155									
Includes the Metropolitan Divisions of Frederick-Gaithersburg-Rockville, MD and Washington-Arlington-Alexandria, DC-VA-MD-WV										

Table 6. Crime in the United States, by Selected Metropolitan Statistical Area, 2018—Continued

(Number, percent, rate per 100,000 population.)

Area	Population	Violent crime	Murder and nonnegligent manslaughter	Rape[1]	Robbery	Aggravated assault	Property crime	Burglary	Larceny-theft	Motor vehicle theft
City of Washington, D.C.	702,455	6,613	160	445	2,157	3,851	29,993	1,786	25,658	2,549
City of Alexandria, VA	162,588	260	4	24	78	154	2,482	128	1,967	387
City of Frederick, MD	72,299	285	3	27	74	181	1,490	139	1,301	50
Total area actually reporting	99.9%	16,630	314	1,999	5,295	9,022	104,021	8,653	86,179	9,189
Estimated total	100.0%	16,635	314	1,999	5,296	9,026	104,064	8,659	86,214	9,191
Rate per 100,000 inhabitants		264.8	5.0	31.8	84.3	143.7	1,656.8	137.9	1,372.6	146.3
Frederick-Gaithersburg-Rockville, MD M.D.	1,315,236									
Includes Frederick and Montgomery Counties										
Total area actually reporting	100.0%	2,069	22	352	647	1,048	16,662	1,780	13,992	890
Rate per 100,000 inhabitants		157.3	1.7	26.8	49.2	79.7	1,266.8	135.3	1,063.8	67.7
Washington-Arlington-Alexandria, DC-VA-MD-WV M.D.	4,965,919									
Includes District of Columbia; Calvert, Charles, and Prince George's Counties, MD; Arlington, Clarke, Culpeper, Fairfax, Fauquier, Loudoun, Madison, Prince William, Rappahannock, Spotsylvania, Stafford, and Warren Counties and Alexandria, Fairfax, Falls Church, Fredericksburg, Manassas, and Manassas Park Cities, VA; and Jefferson County, WV										
Total area actually reporting	99.9%	14,561	292	1,647	4,648	7,974	87,359	6,873	72,187	8,299
Estimated total	100.0%	14,566	292	1,647	4,649	7,978	87,402	6,879	72,222	8,301
Rate per 100,000 inhabitants		293.3	5.9	33.2	93.6	160.7	1,760.0	138.5	1,454.4	167.2
Watertown-Fort Drum, NY M.S.A.	111,731									
Includes Jefferson County										
City of Watertown	25,525	175	0	65	19	91	904	130	755	19
Total area actually reporting	100.0%	254	0	106	21	127	1,740	242	1,456	42
Rate per 100,000 inhabitants		227.3	0.0	94.9	18.8	113.7	1,557.3	216.6	1,303.1	37.6
Wausau-Weston, WI M.S.A.	163,751									
Includes Lincoln and Marathon Counties										
City of Wausau	38,682	119	1	21	11	86	626	94	491	41
Total area actually reporting	100.0%	229	2	59	12	156	1,516	242	1,206	68
Rate per 100,000 inhabitants		139.8	1.2	36.0	7.3	95.3	925.8	147.8	736.5	41.5
Weirton-Steubenville, WV-OH M.S.A.	117,330									
Includes Jefferson County, OH and Brooke and Hancock Counties, WV										
City of Weirton, WV	18,542	9	0	2	0	7	166	21	137	8
City of Steubenville, OH	17,913	55	1	2	20	32	958	72	870	16
Total area actually reporting	82.3%	168	2	11	22	133	1,380	164	1,174	42
Estimated total	100.0%	223	2	17	44	160	1,973	214	1,680	79
Rate per 100,000 inhabitants		190.1	1.7	14.5	37.5	136.4	1,681.6	182.4	1,431.9	67.3
Wenatchee, WA M.S.A.	120,009									
Includes Chelan and Douglas Counties										
City of Wenatchee	34,169	100	0	20	17	63	851	97	698	56
Total area actually reporting	100.0%	176	3	35	21	117	2,012	373	1,492	147
Rate per 100,000 inhabitants		146.7	2.5	29.2	17.5	97.5	1,676.5	310.8	1,243.2	122.5
Wheeling, WV-OH M.S.A.	140,198									
Includes Belmont County, OH and Marshall and Ohio Counties, WV										
City of Wheeling, WV	26,855	229	1	16	12	200	321	81	219	21
Total area actually reporting	80.6%	361	4	51	18	288	975	207	713	55
Estimated total	100.0%	423	4	59	43	317	1,416	243	1,063	110
Rate per 100,000 inhabitants		301.7	2.9	42.1	30.7	226.1	1,010.0	173.3	758.2	78.5
Wichita, KS M.S.A.	638,135									
Includes Butler, Harvey, Sedgwick, and Sumner Counties										
City of Wichita	391,726	4,622	38	378	572	3,634	22,011	3,412	15,826	2,773
Total area actually reporting	97.3%	5,213	49	475	617	4,072	26,663	4,349	19,123	3,191
Estimated total	100.0%	5,271	49	484	631	4,107	27,006	4,409	19,383	3,214
Rate per 100,000 inhabitants		826.0	7.7	75.8	98.9	643.6	4,232.0	690.9	3,037.4	503.7
Wichita Falls, TX M.S.A.	150,750									
Includes Archer, Clay, and Wichita Counties										
City of Wichita Falls	104,738	387	5	78	139	165	3,234	602	2,381	251
Total area actually reporting	95.4%	503	6	109	145	243	3,901	815	2,769	317
Estimated total	100.0%	518	6	110	146	256	3,992	840	2,826	326
Rate per 100,000 inhabitants		343.6	4.0	73.0	96.8	169.8	2,648.1	557.2	1,874.6	216.3
Williamsport, PA M.S.A.	113,393									
Includes Lycoming County										
City of Williamsport	28,331	71	1	11	12	47	646	84	543	19
Total area actually reporting	100.0%	194	3	33	15	143	1,314	179	1,092	43
Rate per 100,000 inhabitants		171.1	2.6	29.1	13.2	126.1	1,158.8	157.9	963.0	37.9
Wilmington, NC M.S.A.[3]	293,180									
Includes New Hanover and Pender Counties[3]										

Table 6. Crime in the United States, by Selected Metropolitan Statistical Area, 2018—Continued

(Number, percent, rate per 100,000 population.)

Area	Population	Violent crime	Murder and nonnegligent manslaughter	Rape[1]	Robbery	Aggravated assault	Property crime	Burglary	Larceny-theft	Motor vehicle theft
City of Wilmington[3]	120,920		9		145	580	3,639	954	2,467	218
Total area actually reporting	99.1%	1,041	11	75	182	773	6,264	1,534	4,403	327
Estimated total	100.0%	1,048	11	76	183	778	6,342	1,550	4,461	331
Rate per 100,000 inhabitants		357.5	3.8	25.9	62.4	265.4	2,163.2	528.7	1,521.6	112.9
Winchester, VA-WV M.S.A.	138,929									
Includes Frederick County and Winchester City, VA and Hampshire County, WV										
City of Winchester, VA	28,128	93	0	38	15	40	692	86	567	39
Total area actually reporting	99.7%	187	0	58	23	106	1,966	230	1,624	112
Estimated total	100.0%	188	0	58	23	107	1,976	231	1,633	112
Rate per 100,000 inhabitants		135.3	0.0	41.7	16.6	77.0	1,422.3	166.3	1,175.4	80.6
Worcester, MA-CT M.S.A.	871,779									
Includes Windham County, CT and Worcester County, MA										
City of Worcester, MA	186,188	1,271	4	49	290	928	3,979	849	2,790	340
Total area actually reporting	92.7%	2,773	11	281	416	2,065	9,935	1,751	7,462	722
Estimated total	100.0%	2,893	11	289	446	2,147	10,327	1,770	7,792	765
Rate per 100,000 inhabitants		331.9	1.3	33.2	51.2	246.3	1,184.6	203.0	893.8	87.8
Yakima, WA M.S.A.	252,019									
Includes Yakima County	96									
City of Yakima	93,959	421	16	49	121	235	3,343	625	2,212	506
Total area actually reporting	96.0%	681	25	87	156	413	6,913	1,377	4,502	1,034
Estimated total	100.0%	715	25	90	166	434	7,142	1,404	4,689	1,049
Rate per 100,000 inhabitants		283.7	9.9	35.7	65.9	172.2	2,833.9	557.1	1,860.6	416.2
York-Hanover, PA M.S.A.	447,168									
Includes York County										
City of York	44,170	450	20	7	130	293	1,137	197	710	230
City of Hanover	15,653	49	1	2	13	33	437	30	396	11
Total area actually reporting	100.0%	1,125	24	98	198	805	6,059	731	4,898	430
Rate per 100,000 inhabitants		251.6	5.4	21.9	44.3	180.0	1,355.0	163.5	1,095.3	96.2
Yuba City, CA M.S.A.	173,299									
Includes Sutter and Yuba Counties										
City of Yuba City	67,035	264	1	35	75	153	1,846	234	1,356	256
Total area actually reporting	100.0%	669	8	82	149	430	4,351	838	2,748	765
Rate per 100,000 inhabitants		386.0	4.6	47.3	86.0	248.1	2,510.7	483.6	1,585.7	441.4
Yuma, AZ M.S.A.	210,913									
Includes Yuma County										
City of Yuma	96,121	491	9	37	55	390	2,041	407	1,417	217
Total area actually reporting	100.0%	673	26	58	64	525	3,655	857	2,344	454
Rate per 100,000 inhabitants		319.1	12.3	27.5	30.3	248.9	1,732.9	406.3	1,111.4	215.3
Aguadilla-Isabela, Puerto Rico M.S.A.	289,735									
Includes Aguada, Aguadilla, Anasco, Isabela, Lares, Moca, Rincon, San Sebastian, and Utuado Municipios										
Total area actually reporting	100.0%	367	10	22	51	284	1,580	490	1,006	84
Rate per 100,000 inhabitants		126.7	3.5	7.6	17.6	98.0	545.3	169.1	347.2	29.0
Arecibo, Puerto Rico M.S.A.	174,271									
Includes Arecibo, Camuy, Hatillo, and Quebradillas Municipios										
Total area actually reporting	100.0%	269	17	9	55	188	926	184	645	97
Rate per 100,000 inhabitants		154.4	9.8	5.2	31.6	107.9	531.4	105.6	370.1	55.7
Guayama, Puerto Rico M.S.A.	73,000									
Includes Arroyo, Guayama, and Patillas Municipios										
Total area actually reporting	100.0%	157	7	7	28	115	377	105	264	8
Rate per 100,000 inhabitants		215.1	9.6	9.6	38.4	157.5	516.4	143.8	361.6	11.0
Mayaguez, Puerto Rico M.S.A.	95,409									
Includes Hormigueros, Las Marias, and Mayaguez Municipios										
Total area actually reporting	100.0%	124	16	6	21	81	544	104	398	42
Rate per 100,000 inhabitants		130.0	16.8	6.3	22.0	84.9	570.2	109.0	417.2	44.0
Ponce, Puerto Rico M.S.A.	216,479									
Includes Adjuntas, Juana Diaz, Ponce, and Villalba Municipios										
Total area actually reporting	100.0%	454	50	12	118	274	1,585	293	1,232	60
Rate per 100,000 inhabitants		209.7	23.1	5.5	54.5	126.6	732.2	135.3	569.1	27.7
San German, Puerto Rico M.S.A.	121,078									
Includes Cabo Rojo, Lajas, Sabana Grande, and San German Municipios										

Table 6. Crime in the United States, by Selected Metropolitan Statistical Area, 2018—Continued

(Number, percent, rate per 100,000 population.)

Area	Population	Violent crime	Murder and nonnegligent manslaughter	Rape[1]	Robbery	Aggravated assault	Property crime	Burglary	Larceny-theft	Motor vehicle theft
Total area actually reporting	100.0%	135	7	8	19	101	441	138	282	21
Rate per 100,000 inhabitants		111.5	5.8	6.6	15.7	83.4	364.2	114.0	232.9	17.3
San Juan-Bayamon-Caguas, Puerto Rico M.S.A.	2,023,237									
Includes Aguas Buenas, Aibonito, Barceloneta, Barranquitas, Bayamon, Caguas, Canovanas, Carolina, Catano, Cayey, Ceiba, Ciales, Cidra, Comerio, Corozal, Dorado, Fajardo, Florida, Guaynabo, Gurabo, Humacao, Juncos, Las Piedras, Loiza, Luquillo, Manati, Maunabo, Morovis, Naguabo, Naranjito, Orocovis, Rio Grande, San Juan, San Lorenzo, Toa Alta, Toa Baja, Trujillo Alto, Vega Alta, Vega Baja, and Yabucoa Municipios										
Total area actually reporting	100.0%	4,544	497	120	1,930	1,997	18,445	3,850	11,252	3,343
Rate per 100,000 inhabitants		224.6	24.6	5.9	95.4	98.7	911.7	190.3	556.1	165.2
Yauco, Puerto Rico M.S.A.	86,532									
Includes Guanica, Guayanilla, Penuelas, and Yauco Municipios										
Total area actually reporting	100.0%	131	10	7	17	97	304	109	180	15
Rate per 100,000 inhabitants		151.4	11.6	8.1	19.6	112.1	351.3	126.0	208.0	17.3

1 The figures shown in this column for the offense of rape were reported using only the revised Uniform Crime Reporting (UCR) definition of rape. See the chapter notes for further explanation.   2 Because of changes in the state/local agency's reporting practices, figures are not comparable to previous years' data.   3 One or more agency(s) within this Metropolitan Statistical Area submitted rape data classified according to the legacy UCR definition. See the chapter notes for further explanation.   4 The FBI determined that the agency's data were overreported. Consequently, those data are not included in this table.   5 The FBI determined that the agency did not follow national UCR Program guidelines for reporting an offense. Consequently, this figure is not included in this table.   6 The population for the city of Mobile, Alabama, includes 55,819 inhabitants from the jurisdiction of the Mobile County Sheriff's Department.   7 The FBI determined that the agency did not follow national UCR Program guidelines for reporting an offense. Consequently, this figure is not included in this table.

Table 7. Offense Analysis, United States, 2014–2018

(Number.)

Classification	2014	2015	2016	2017[1]	2018
Murder	14,164	15,883	17,413	17,294	16,214
Rape[2]	118,027	126,134	132,414	135,666	139,380
Robbery[3]	322,905	328,109	332,797	320,596	282,061
By location					
Street/highway	132,269	130,724	129,337	119,180	102,433
Commercial house	45,273	47,229	50,785	49,654	45,274
Gas or service station	8,072	8,916	9,708	9,603	8,888
Convenience store	17,380	18,661	20,656	21,048	19,702
Residence	54,120	54,142	55,102	51,260	45,534
Bank	5,939	5,691	5,914	5,441	4,474
Miscellaneous	59,853	62,747	61,296	64,410	55,756
Burglary[3]	1,713,153	1,587,564	1,516,405	1,397,045	1,230,149
By location					
Residence (dwelling)	1,253,915	1,136,664	1,054,470	939,509	805,427
Residence, night	349,441	328,736	311,805	285,358	256,072
Residence, day	669,364	594,668	543,930	474,495	406,741
Residence, unknown	235,111	213,260	198,735	179,656	142,614
Nonresidence (store, office, etc.)	459,238	450,900	461,935	457,536	424,722
Nonresidence, night	188,010	189,167	199,741	200,859	190,066
Nonresidence, day	167,749	159,177	159,630	157,375	150,496
Nonresidence, unknown	103,480	102,556	102,564	99,302	84,161
Larceny-theft (except motor vehicle theft)[3]	5,809,054	5,723,488	5,644,835	5,513,000	5,217,055
By type					
Pocket-picking	31,213	31,208	27,648	31,026	27,247
Purse-snatching	23,479	23,144	22,671	21,961	20,055
Shoplifting	1,247,199	1,276,575	1,179,137	1,144,948	1,113,439
From motor vehicles (except accessories)	1,332,924	1,373,720	1,477,587	1,477,684	1,406,493
Motor vehicle accessories	408,545	399,452	415,590	407,017	323,361
Bicycles	209,762	205,600	184,546	174,803	156,589
From buildings	712,073	664,381	605,765	586,612	532,874
From coin-operated machines	13,328	13,020	12,349	12,014	11,478
All others	1,830,531	1,736,388	1,719,542	1,656,937	1,625,523
By value					
Under $50	2,687,591	2,613,333	2,561,619	2,529,654	2,438,851
$50 to $200	1,306,350	1,278,027	1,221,246	1,169,612	1,116,776
Over $200	1,815,113	1,832,128	1,861,970	1,813,734	1,661,372
Motor vehicle theft	686,803	713,063	767,290	772,943	748,841

1 The crime figures have been adjusted.   2 The figures shown for this offense of rape were estimated using the revised Uniform Crime Reporting (UCR) definition of rape. See chapter notes for more detail.   3 Because of rounding, the number of offenses may not add to the total.

Table 8. Offenses Known to Law Enforcement, by Selected State and City, 2018

(Number.)

State/city	Population	Violent crime	Murder and nonnegligent manslaughter	Rape[1]	Robbery	Aggravated assault	Property crime	Burglary	Larceny-theft	Motor vehicle theft	Arson[2]
ALABAMA											
Abbeville	2,551	18	0	2	0	16	49	14	33	2	
Adamsville	4,323	19	0	1	4	14	289	42	230	17	
Alabaster	33,501	92	0	2	10	80	579	56	497	26	
Albertville	21,428	24	0	6	10	8	802	194	492	116	
Alexander City	14,548	314	2	5	15	292	610	92	484	34	
Aliceville	2,315	9	0	0	1	8	24	7	16	1	
Andalusia	8,753	82	1	6	6	69	467	76	368	23	
Anniston	21,592	646	7	43	68	528	1,696	413	1,131	152	
Ardmore	1,428	5	0	0	1	4	35	15	18	2	
Ashford	2,145	4	0	0	0	4	32	2	24	6	
Ashland	1,918	52	0	0	1	51	57	16	35	6	
Athens	26,177	13	3	0	8	2	768	110	630	28	
Auburn	65,585	240	4	16	29	191	1,396	115	1,206	75	
Bay Minette	9,304	73	0	3	3	67	250	35	196	19	
Bayou La Batre	2,500	36	0	4	5	27	305	70	203	32	
Birmingham	210,564	4,025	88	180	941	2,816	13,295	2,555	8,988	1,752	145
Boaz	9,678	74	0	3	3	68	364	68	259	37	
Brent	4,853	18	0	2	2	14	96	25	66	5	
Brewton	5,212	31	0	3	1	27	175	19	132	24	
Brilliant	867	3	0	0	0	3	29	7	19	3	
Brookwood	1,861	7	0	1	2	4	103	27	54	22	
Calera	14,334	265	2	10	6	247	429	164	242	23	
Camden	1,824	26	1	1	0	24	85	28	55	2	
Carrollton	961	4	0	0	0	4	13	4	7	2	
Cedar Bluff	1,794	1	0	0	0	1	20	3	16	1	
Chatom	1,200	8	0	0	0	8	34	5	25	4	
Cherokee	999	1	0	0	0	1	19	2	13	4	
Childersburg	4,870	64	2	1	2	59	197	43	141	13	
Clayton	2,854	4	0	0	0	4	25	8	15	2	
Coaling	1,661	6	0	2	1	3	55	15	33	7	
Columbiana	4,720	64	0	1	2	61	113	15	89	9	
Cottonwood	1,251	2	0	0	0	2	10	4	6	0	
Cullman	15,470	32	1	5	6	20	629	64	521	44	
Dadeville	3,091	22	0	2	4	16	110	18	81	11	
Daleville	5,096	8	0	0	0	8	56	12	39	5	
Daphne	26,618	36	0	6	8	22	463	42	404	17	
Dauphin Island	1,274	4	0	0	0	4	57	17	35	5	
Decatur	54,207	228	1	31	58	138	2,308	445	1,692	171	
Demopolis	6,770	51	0	4	2	45	241	55	175	11	
Dothan	68,530	670	9	27	80	554	2,799	561	2,041	197	
Eclectic	1,022	10	0	1	0	9	41	12	27	2	
Elba	3,864	20	0	1	4	15	113	31	73	9	
Enterprise	28,464	127	1	11	18	97	809	208	538	63	
Eufaula	11,905	75	1	9	10	55	469	109	333	27	
Eutaw	2,656	31	1	0	5	25	87	31	46	10	
Fairfield	10,625	224	8	3	75	138	855	284	489	82	
Fairhope	21,688	43	0	16	3	24	537	57	449	31	
Falkville	1,243	10	0	1	0	9	28	8	16	4	
Fayette	4,313	10	0	1	0	9	85	12	66	7	
Florence	39,925	206	4	23	30	149	1,663	282	1,215	166	
Foley	18,740	48	2	6	7	33	755	90	643	22	
Fultondale	9,312	46	0	3	8	35	366	42	300	24	
Fyffe	1,018	5	0	0	0	5	28	0	22	6	
Gadsden	35,204	372	3	24	47	298	2,495	409	1,831	255	
Gardendale	13,907	94	1	3	9	81	347	33	292	22	
Geraldine	900	3	0	1	0	2	33	8	15	10	
Glencoe	5,151	8	1	2	1	4	87	31	46	10	
Greenville	7,564	109	0	3	3	103	342	36	293	13	
Guin	2,260	6	0	1	0	5	46	9	30	7	
Gulf Shores	12,014	24	0	3	2	19	497	53	419	25	
Guntersville	8,462	52	2	1	8	41	550	79	430	41	
Hamilton	6,611	23	0	4	1	18	187	45	124	18	
Hanceville	3,423	9	0	5	3	1	98	13	74	11	
Harpersville	1,721	7	0	1	1	5	32	7	19	6	
Hartford	2,587	16	0	2	0	14	55	8	39	8	
Hartselle	14,385	61	0	3	2	56	353	57	269	27	
Headland	4,706	5	0	1	1	3	89	16	71	2	
Helena	19,387	61	0	3	0	58	131	16	97	18	
Henagar	2,354	1	0	0	0	1	35	8	25	2	
Hokes Bluff	4,267	3	0	0	0	3	49	11	33	5	
Homewood	25,523	75	0	7	35	33	956	138	750	68	
Hueytown	15,367	71	0	7	3	61	531	72	430	29	
Irondale	12,486	74	1	5	7	61	350	84	236	30	
Jackson	4,733	20	1	4	1	14	175	29	141	5	
Jacksonville	12,534	85	0	3	4	78	433	107	300	26	
Jasper	13,512	74	0	7	8	59	1,035	125	822	88	
Killen	969	1	0	0	0	1	20	2	16	2	
Kimberly	3,246	7	0	3	0	4	27	1	21	5	
Lanett	6,245	88	0	13	14	61	492	96	348	48	
Leesburg	1,021	4	0	0	1	3	35	13	17	5	
Leighton	705	3	0	0	1	2	38	13	20	5	
Level Plains	2,023	7	0	1	0	6	68	24	36	8	

Table 8. Offenses Known to Law Enforcement, by Selected State and City, 2018—Continued

(Number.)

State/city	Population	Violent crime	Murder and nonnegligent manslaughter	Rape[1]	Robbery	Aggravated assault	Property crime	Burglary	Larceny-theft	Motor vehicle theft	Arson[2]
Lincoln	6,725	71	0	3	5	63	336	56	239	41	
Littleville	985	0	0	0	0	0	8	3	3	2	
Livingston	3,317	18	1	0	2	15	42	6	36	0	
Maplesville	702	3	0	1	0	2	12	4	7	1	
Margaret	4,870	9	0	1	0	8	43	11	28	4	
McIntosh	221	6	0	0	0	6	25	5	18	2	
Midland City	2,387	13	0	2	2	9	70	20	43	7	
Millbrook	15,410	44	0	7	6	31	728	82	607	39	
Mobile[3]	245,475	1,613	26	168	378	1,041	12,094	2,568	8,442	1,084	55
Montgomery	198,662	1,216	29	39	391	757	8,480	2,052	5,456	972	
Moody	13,134	56	1	1	2	52	206	34	151	21	
Morris	1,987	2	0	1	0	1	31	9	15	7	
Moulton	3,229	7	0	3	0	4	76	32	40	4	
Mountain Brook	20,373	16	0	2	7	7	228	47	175	6	
Mount Vernon	1,491	10	0	1	1	8	34	5	26	3	
Muscle Shoals	14,143	86	2	7	7	70	800	115	620	65	
New Hope	2,846	14	0	2	0	12	71	16	44	11	
Newton	1,457	7	0	1	0	6	33	6	26	1	
Northport	25,353	89	1	19	20	49	772	123	610	39	
Odenville	3,781	15	0	3	0	12	43	9	27	7	
Ohatchee	1,157	2	0	0	0	2	11	6	4	1	
Oneonta	6,646	17	0	2	1	14	218	20	176	22	
Opelika	30,822	168	5	13	31	119	1,214	143	991	80	
Orange Beach	6,116	15	1	8	0	6	226	13	206	7	
Owens Crossroads	2,002	6	0	0	1	5	20	5	12	3	
Oxford	21,149	67	0	1	11	55	928	111	787	30	
Ozark	14,358	148	1	2	7	138	619	88	493	38	
Parrish	938	11	0	3	3	5	40	16	21	3	
Pelham	23,785	36	0	3	8	25	404	39	330	35	
Phenix City	36,668	235	7	51	75	102	1,326	243	927	156	
Piedmont	4,583	23	1	3	8	11	102	22	74	6	
Pine Hill	870	7	1	2	0	4	26	7	13	6	
Pleasant Grove	10,105	16	0	2	1	13	127	17	102	8	
Prattville	35,697	83	1	8	34	40	1,221	126	1,003	92	
Prichard	21,615	263	7	4	46	206	930	309	478	143	
Rainbow City	9,546	1	0	0	0	1	50	11	30	9	
Red Bay	3,075	7	0	3	0	4	62	13	43	6	
Reform	1,577	10	0	2	1	7	14	5	8	1	
Riverside	2,306	6	0	1	0	5	39	8	26	5	
Roanoke	5,914	41	0	2	2	37	130	15	106	9	
Rogersville	1,226	8	0	1	1	6	30	11	16	3	
Saraland	14,704	51	1	8	6	36	490	61	388	41	
Satsuma	6,153	16	0	0	2	14	77	19	52	6	
Scottsboro	14,443	193	0	8	5	180	671	93	549	29	
Sheffield	8,914	73	1	14	7	51	446	95	312	39	
Snead	841	2	0	0	0	2	28	6	17	5	
Southside	8,774	15	0	5	0	10	65	22	36	7	
Spanish Fort	8,923	33	0	6	5	22	246	14	230	2	
Steele	1,074	3	0	1	0	2	10	2	7	1	
Sulligent	1,835	9	0	2	0	7	60	15	42	3	
Sumiton	2,348	2	0	0	1	1	47	9	34	4	
Summerdale	1,467	24	0	2	0	22	64	16	43	5	
Sylacauga	12,186	77	3	13	10	51	614	98	481	35	
Talladega	15,341	124	4	8	10	102	805	179	556	70	
Tallassee	4,650	43	1	3	4	35	276	43	211	22	
Tarrant	6,175	109	1	0	16	92	368	86	253	29	
Taylor	2,399	0	0	0	0	0	7	0	5	2	
Thomasville	3,909	23	0	2	1	20	160	26	119	15	
Thorsby	2,061	6	0	0	0	6	16	1	10	5	
Town Creek	1,044	4	0	1	1	2	16	3	11	2	
Triana	544	5	0	1	0	4	23	13	8	2	
Trinity	2,165	10	0	3	2	5	25	8	13	4	
Troy	19,159	303	6	7	28	262	961	192	713	56	
Trussville	22,096	113	0	6	7	100	654	38	604	12	
Tuscaloosa	101,764	514	5	47	140	322	4,415	753	3,347	315	
Tuscumbia	8,370	26	0	2	3	21	281	49	206	26	
Union Springs	3,510	49	0	3	7	39	184	66	101	17	
Uniontown	2,271	18	1	0	3	14	60	14	33	13	
Valley	9,230	54	2	14	12	26	483	74	371	38	
Vance	1,626	3	0	0	0	3	19	4	13	2	
Vestavia Hills	34,368	30	0	0	3	27	435	83	313	39	
Warrior	3,213	10	0	1	2	7	49	9	27	13	
Wedowee	796	4	0	0	0	4	44	11	29	4	
Wetumpka	8,377	28	1	6	6	15	366	32	321	13	
York	2,245	19	0	0	1	18	16	5	7	4	
ALASKA											
Anchorage	291,992	3,824	26	613	717	2,468	14,389	2,068	9,498	2,823	58
Bethel	6,509	99	0	31	6	62	57	15	30	12	4
Bristol Bay Borough	843	0	0	0	0	0	9	2	2	5	0
Cordova	2,179	6	0	0	0	6	12	3	9	0	0
Craig	1,285	8	0	1	0	7	25	5	19	1	0
Dillingham	2,365	32	0	9	1	22	44	7	31	6	1

Table 8. Offenses Known to Law Enforcement, by Selected State and City, 2018—Continued

(Number.)

State/city	Population	Violent crime	Murder and nonnegligent manslaughter	Rape[1]	Robbery	Aggravated assault	Property crime	Burglary	Larceny-theft	Motor vehicle theft	Arson[2]
Fairbanks	31,635	193	4	21	43	125	1,354	111	1,089	154	4
Haines	2,508	3	0	0	0	3	16	4	12	0	0
Homer	5,797	12	0	0	2	10	216	24	182	10	0
Juneau	31,922	264	1	41	37	185	1,550	294	1,125	131	5
Kenai	7,888	62	1	19	1	41	561	49	462	50	0
Ketchikan	8,300	25	1	6	4	14	410	38	348	24	1
Kodiak	5,995	48	0	12	0	36	259	81	156	22	0
Kotzebue	3,273	106	1	19	12	74	140	20	92	28	1
Nome[4]	3,874	103	0	39	1	63	37	5	26	6	0
North Pole	2,096	11	0	1	0	10	62	1	59	2	1
North Slope Borough	9,743	148	1	14	3	130	89	27	54	8	0
Palmer	7,403	26	0	3	2	21	244	12	215	17	0
Petersburg	3,262	10	0	0	1	9	77	15	56	6	0
Seward	2,850	6	0	0	0	6	74	10	61	3	0
Sitka	8,588	21	0	0	4	17	227	17	196	14	0
Skagway	1,177	0	0	0	0	0	9	1	8	0	0
Soldotna	4,731	18	0	1	5	12	167	8	152	7	2
Unalaska	4,546	17	0	3	0	14	49	5	34	10	2
Valdez	3,845	5	0	3	0	2	68	11	55	2	0
Wasilla	10,522	61	0	1	10	50	637	92	470	75	4
Wrangell	2,521	1	0	1	0	0	23	1	18	4	0
ARIZONA											
Apache Junction	41,245	81	0	0	16	65	773	118	575	80	5
Avondale	85,204	286	6	20	73	187	2,739	384	2,111	244	18
Buckeye	71,318	125	1	30	16	78	1,348	171	1,113	64	1
Bullhead City	40,354	149	1	20	34	94	1,444	362	945	137	4
Camp Verde	11,249	31	0	3	3	25	212	53	142	17	0
Casa Grande	56,479	346	1	32	34	279	1,478	228	1,144	106	6
Chandler	255,986	606	4	146	123	333	5,430	658	4,455	317	15
Chino Valley	11,840	42	1	3	1	37	179	33	132	14	0
Clarkdale	4,367	4	0	0	0	4	46	11	29	6	0
Coolidge	12,815	37	0	2	10	25	433	66	331	36	5
Eagar	4,876	9	0	1	0	8	38	4	31	3	1
El Mirage	35,733	77	1	15	12	49	933	397	448	88	11
Eloy	19,549	81	0	8	2	71	351	70	252	29	6
Flagstaff	72,852	342	2	37	40	263	2,465	178	2,234	53	48
Florence	25,987	34	0	2	0	32	127	16	105	6	0
Fredonia	1,300	5	1	0	0	4	11	5	3	3	1
Gilbert	247,463	234	2	75	32	125	3,273	406	2,715	152	16
Glendale	249,799	1,167	9	110	325	723	10,186	1,641	7,491	1,054	62
Globe	7,330	157	3	2	3	149	541	76	418	47	3
Goodyear	82,159	203	2	35	33	133	2,081	358	1,624	99	0
Hayden	970	5	0	0	0	5	39	20	16	3	1
Holbrook	5,048	18	0	0	1	17	189	44	130	15	2
Jerome	456	1	0	0	0	1	10	3	7	0	0
Kearny	2,116	5	0	1	0	4	25	4	20	1	2
Kingman	29,669	118	1	5	15	97	1,152	174	898	80	15
Lake Havasu City	54,678	88	2	20	6	60	830	155	615	60	5
Marana	46,447	33	0	7	5	21	1,076	62	962	52	7
Maricopa	48,660	93	1	13	7	72	489	57	399	33	0
Mesa	504,873	1,837	17	238	417	1,165	10,024	1,563	7,598	863	12
Miami	1,764	18	0	0	2	16	26	21	5	0	1
Nogales	19,973	41	2	0	0	39	610	82	392	136	0
Oro Valley	44,844	17	0	6	3	8	610	67	525	18	0
Page	7,576	79	0	7	4	68	387	34	330	23	5
Paradise Valley	14,519	3	0	1	1	1	196	46	141	9	0
Parker	3,060	6	0	0	1	5	116	38	63	15	0
Payson	15,549	63	0	3	4	56	403	94	292	17	3
Peoria	170,177	388	3	57	68	260	3,241	519	2,505	217	6
Phoenix	1,653,080	12,110	132	1,086	3,112	7,780	57,732	10,479	39,438	7,815	242
Pinetop-Lakeside	4,371	48	1	0	1	46	110	14	93	3	0
Prescott	43,172	136	2	11	2	121	896	107	749	40	5
Prescott Valley	45,337	67	1	10	5	51	776	73	676	27	1
Quartzsite	3,695	15	0	1	1	13	105	24	71	10	2
Safford	9,657	32	0	0	3	29	282	46	219	17	2
Sahuarita	29,896	38	0	8	6	24	348	42	281	25	0
San Luis	33,074	8	1	3	1	3	472	56	317	99	0
Scottsdale	254,961	422	7	122	87	206	5,683	711	4,700	272	17
Show Low	11,156	59	0	7	0	52	427	60	350	17	0
Sierra Vista	42,574	104	0	26	14	64	1,121	153	923	45	2
Snowflake-Taylor	9,971	36	0	0	0	36	178	59	106	13	3
Somerton	16,380	19	0	2	1	16	218	63	121	34	4
Springerville	1,955	2	1	0	0	1	18	3	13	2	0
St. Johns	3,510	21	0	3	1	17	48	11	37	0	2
Superior	3,095	7	0	0	0	7	75	17	54	4	21
Surprise	136,611	165	7	21	37	100	2,103	239	1,672	192	5
Tempe	188,543	913	5	176	189	543	7,802	1,017	6,247	538	12
Thatcher	5,048	0	0	0	0	0	70	12	56	2	0
Tolleson	7,305	61	3	3	23	32	671	213	376	82	3
Tombstone	1,283	3	0	0	0	3	22	1	19	2	1
Tucson	537,392	3,958	47	504	1,224	2,183	26,623	3,257	20,798	2,568	158
Wellton	3,003	6	3	1	0	2	31	13	15	3	0

Table 8. Offenses Known to Law Enforcement, by Selected State and City, 2018—Continued

(Number.)

State/city	Population	Violent crime	Murder and nonnegligent manslaughter	Rape[1]	Robbery	Aggravated assault	Property crime	Burglary	Larceny-theft	Motor vehicle theft	Arson[2]
Wickenburg	7,042	25	0	4	0	21	128	29	71	28	1
Willcox	3,465	9	0	0	1	8	159	43	107	9	2
Williams	3,176	13	0	1	1	11	85	10	74	1	0
Winslow	9,361	83	1	8	9	65	410	64	326	20	1
Yuma	96,121	491	9	37	55	390	2,041	407	1,417	217	18
ARKANSAS											
Alexander	3,078	16	2	1	1	12	76	20	47	9	0
Alma	5,772	40	0	12	3	25	245	36	199	10	0
Altus	735	1	0	1	0	0	11	5	6	0	0
Amity	678	3	0	0	0	3	8	1	4	3	0
Arkadelphia	10,647	45	0	12	4	29	256	43	204	9	0
Ashdown	4,389	16	0	5	1	10	120	24	93	3	0
Ash Flat	1,090	2	0	0	0	2	16	1	15	0	0
Atkins	3,041	7	0	4	1	2	80	19	59	2	1
Austin	3,508	7	0	2	2	3	25	14	10	1	0
Bald Knob	2,879	11	0	3	0	8	90	28	57	5	1
Barling	4,972	24	0	6	0	18	92	13	77	2	1
Batesville	10,782	46	0	11	4	31	311	48	249	14	1
Bay	1,806	1	0	1	0	0	19	4	15	0	0
Beebe	8,268	29	0	7	1	21	280	43	224	13	3
Bella Vista	28,798	53	0	23	0	30	193	30	157	6	0
Benton[5]	36,556	182	1	17	22	142			1,124	105	5
Bentonville	51,607	106	0	28	5	73	705	110	568	27	2
Berryville	5,470	14	0	7	1	6	191	51	136	4	1
Bethel Heights	2,825	2	0	1	0	1	14	4	7	3	0
Blytheville	13,843	137	6	4	22	105	837	117	696	24	0
Bono	2,405	21	0	8	0	13	39	11	28	0	0
Booneville	3,837	5	0	4	0	1	92	19	71	2	0
Bradford	742	4	0	1	0	3	23	2	19	2	0
Brinkley	2,658	40	1	4	5	30	124	32	86	6	1
Brookland	3,582	8	0	2	1	5	43	8	33	2	0
Bryant	20,738	32	0	2	2	28	889	38	794	57	0
Bull Shoals	1,943	9	0	1	0	8	53	14	39	0	0
Cabot	26,459	39	0	10	7	22	403	92	278	33	0
Caddo Valley	591	2	0	1	0	1	31	4	24	3	0
Camden	10,880	127	0	16	10	101	488	155	313	20	3
Caraway	1,253	5	0	1	0	4	13	2	11	0	0
Carlisle	2,177	6	0	3	0	3	48	7	35	6	0
Cave Springs	4,981	1	0	1	0	0	32	6	25	1	0
Cedarville	1,401	1	0	0	0	1	12	4	7	1	0
Centerton	14,791	59	0	26	0	33	130	30	97	3	0
Charleston	2,458	3	0	1	0	2	20	3	17	0	0
Cherokee Village	4,637	12	0	3	0	9	81	35	41	5	0
Cherry Valley	593	3	0	0	0	3	7	2	4	1	0
Clarksville	9,679	26	0	10	3	13	348	46	293	9	1
Clinton	2,471	4	0	1	0	3	94	16	77	1	0
Conway	66,720	361	5	50	56	250	2,229	248	1,881	100	3
Corning	3,102	4	0	1	0	3	39	14	25	0	0
Cotter	935	5	0	0	0	5	21	10	11	0	1
Crossett	4,920	26	2	6	2	16	223	86	128	9	4
Damascus	372	0	0	0	0	0	6	0	6	0	0
Danville	2,422	1	0	0	0	1	12	4	6	2	0
Dardanelle	4,535	16	0	7	0	9	124	40	76	8	0
Decatur	1,814	15	0	9	0	6	50	11	34	5	1
De Queen	6,588	19	0	1	1	17	155	44	107	4	2
Des Arc	1,618	9	0	5	0	4	34	8	25	1	0
DeWitt	3,058	39	0	3	0	36	115	42	65	8	3
Diamond City	794	0	0	0	0	0	3	2	1	0	0
Diaz	1,215	2	0	0	0	2	17	6	9	2	1
Dover	1,411	1	0	0	0	1	31	7	22	2	0
Dumas	4,179	12	0	0	5	7	41	18	21	2	2
El Dorado[5]	17,916			11	27	158	1,069	576	437	56	2
Elkins	3,111	8	0	1	0	7	23	3	20	0	0
Eudora	1,970	20	0	1	0	19	53	19	33	1	1
Eureka Springs	2,073	20	0	3	1	16	109	29	69	11	0
Fairfield Bay	2,189	7	0	3	0	4	60	16	43	1	2
Farmington	7,032	16	0	3	1	12	86	19	62	5	1
Fayetteville	87,008	496	1	81	60	354	3,768	444	2,894	430	5
Flippin	1,324	5	0	2	0	3	116	23	91	2	0
Fordyce	3,852	46	0	3	5	38	154	41	110	3	3
Forrest City	14,144	132	3	4	18	107	882	154	552	176	11
Fort Smith	88,290	707	9	86	97	515	4,265	711	3,268	286	17
Gassville	2,145	8	0	1	0	7	87	19	64	4	1
Gentry	3,842	6	0	4	0	2	21	0	14	7	0
Gosnell	3,225	19	0	0	0	19	33	11	21	1	1
Gravette	3,328	18	0	4	0	14	84	14	67	3	0
Green Forest	2,682	16	0	6	2	8	52	17	25	10	1
Greenland	1,422	7	0	2	0	5	14	3	8	3	0
Greenwood	9,454	18	0	3	0	15	37	7	29	1	0
Greers Ferry	854	0	0	0	0	0	12	2	9	1	0
Gurdon	2,080	17	0	1	0	16	35	13	20	2	1
Hamburg	2,672	9	0	1	1	7	24	14	10	0	0

Table 8. Offenses Known to Law Enforcement, by Selected State and City, 2018—Continued

(Number.)

State/city	Population	Violent crime	Murder and nonnegligent manslaughter	Rape[1]	Robbery	Aggravated assault	Property crime	Burglary	Larceny-theft	Motor vehicle theft	Arson[2]
Harrison	13,100	65	0	6	10	49	468	80	357	31	2
Haskell	4,649	19	0	9	0	10	36	2	32	2	0
Hazen	1,372	0	0	0	0	0	16	7	7	2	0
Heber Springs	6,929	18	0	6	1	11	199	44	148	7	1
Helena-West Helena	10,477	157	8	4	19	126	471	160	293	18	4
Highfill	663	0	0	0	0	0	0	0	0	0	0
Highland	1,104	7	0	2	0	5	28	6	19	3	0
Hope	9,744	75	0	8	12	55	392	78	294	20	2
Hot Springs	37,006	194	6	29	46	113	2,592	740	1,651	201	7
Hoxie	2,611	8	0	4	0	4	16	5	9	2	0
Hughes	1,254	8	0	2	1	5	21	9	12	0	2
Jacksonville	28,530	331	2	10	35	284	1,322	271	916	135	6
Jericho	111	0	0	0	0	0	3	2	1	0	0
Johnson	3,716	9	0	1	0	8	80	27	43	10	1
Jonesboro	77,134	425	4	57	57	307	3,143	1,150	1,825	168	11
Judsonia	1,988	8	0	2	0	6	22	7	15	0	0
Kensett	1,629	3	0	1	0	2	30	5	22	3	0
Lake City	2,507	4	0	1	1	2	24	4	14	6	0
Lakeview	713	0	0	0	0	0	19	4	15	0	0
Lake Village	2,293	14	0	0	7	7	86	30	56	0	0
Lamar	1,729	4	0	2	0	2	14	5	9	0	0
Lavaca	2,464	9	0	5	0	4	29	8	20	1	0
Leachville	1,766	5	0	2	0	3	25	4	18	3	0
Lewisville	1,133	4	0	0	0	4	23	9	14	0	0
Lincoln	2,489	27	0	4	1	22	51	14	34	3	2
Little Flock	2,787	10	0	3	0	7	35	9	21	5	0
Little Rock	199,288	2,882	40	218	371	2,253	13,049	2,079	9,850	1,120	57
Lonoke	4,247	34	0	5	2	27	145	29	109	7	1
Lowell	9,522	18	0	2	3	13	114	37	68	9	0
Luxora	1,044	0	0	0	0	0	3	0	2	1	0
Magnolia[5]	11,425	22	2	2	7	11		0	258	13	3
Mammoth Spring	931	0	0	0	0	0	1	0	1	0	0
Marianna	3,492	28	1	2	3	22	207	76	112	19	3
Marion	12,426	125	0	13	20	92	500	143	322	35	2
Marked Tree	2,493	20	0	1	3	16	57	17	39	1	1
Marmaduke	1,260	3	0	0	0	3	30	5	24	1	2
Maumelle	18,356	47	1	2	5	39	326	78	226	22	2
Mayflower	2,511	11	0	4	1	6	76	29	44	3	0
McCrory	1,532	11	0	8	0	3	22	1	20	1	0
McGehee	3,775	10	0	3	1	6	67	21	44	2	0
McRae	665	2	0	1	0	1	5	0	4	1	0
Mena	5,546	14	1	7	1	5	208	25	177	6	0
Menifee	312	1	0	0	0	1	1	0	1	0	0
Mineral Springs	1,160	0	0	0	0	0	13	5	8	0	1
Monticello	9,630	53	2	11	8	32	301	64	216	21	1
Morrilton	6,633	9	0	3	1	5	288	18	260	10	3
Mountainburg	614	1	0	0	0	1	31	2	22	7	0
Mountain Home	12,315	22	3	7	0	12	590	54	515	21	1
Mountain View	2,867	19	0	5	0	14	103	22	79	2	1
Mulberry	1,640	11	0	1	1	9	48	13	33	2	1
Murfreesboro	1,542	5	0	2	0	3	24	6	17	1	1
Nashville	4,454	18	0	6	0	12	156	13	138	5	1
Newport	7,654	67	0	4	7	56	358	84	266	8	2
Norfork	528	0	0	0	0	0	4	0	3	1	0
North Little Rock	66,424	494	13	16	97	368	2,287	431	1,567	289	10
Ola	1,219	6	0	1	0	5	18	0	12	6	0
Osceola	6,819	158	1	8	9	140	314	127	159	28	4
Paris	3,379	31	0	3	1	27	88	30	47	11	0
Pea Ridge	5,873	20	0	5	1	14	112	13	98	1	1
Perryville	1,432	1	0	0	0	1	32	3	28	1	0
Piggott	3,575	6	0	2	0	4	41	16	24	1	1
Pine Bluff	42,195	679	15	37	97	530	2,278	665	1,380	233	56
Plainview	584	0	0	0	0	0	0	0	0	0	0
Plumerville	775	5	0	3	0	2	11	2	9	0	1
Pocahontas	6,478	32	0	11	1	20	291	39	229	23	1
Pottsville	3,246	5	0	1	0	4	26	12	14	0	0
Prairie Grove	5,921	11	0	1	1	9	141	18	121	2	0
Quitman	719	3	0	0	0	3	33	3	30	0	0
Redfield	1,578	1	0	0	0	1	20	3	15	2	0
Rogers	68,026	294	2	78	23	191	1,925	189	1,636	100	6
Russellville	29,455	114	0	22	9	83	904	124	705	75	3
Salem	1,605	5	0	1	0	4	14	4	10	0	0
Sheridan	4,922	15	0	9	2	4	173	23	139	11	0
Sherwood	31,284	180	1	15	14	150	978	229	685	64	4
Siloam Springs[5]	17,102	78	0	19	3	56			267	56	3
Springdale	80,895	388	3	94	31	260	2,702	357	2,078	267	11
Star City	2,099	13	0	1	1	11	54	13	35	6	0
St. Charles	211	2	0	1	0	1	2	1	1	0	0
Sulphur Springs	543	2	0	0	0	2	11	5	5	1	0
Swifton	738	0	0	0	0	0	5	1	4	0	0
Texarkana	30,300	200	0	22	44	134	1,256	196	984	76	3
Trumann	7,071	56	3	6	2	45	364	53	295	16	1
Tuckerman	1,708	7	0	1	0	6	18	10	6	2	0

Table 8. Offenses Known to Law Enforcement, by Selected State and City, 2018—Continued

(Number.)

State/city	Population	Violent crime	Murder and nonnegligent manslaughter	Rape[1]	Robbery	Aggravated assault	Property crime	Burglary	Larceny-theft	Motor vehicle theft	Arson[2]
Tyronza	746	0	0	0	0	0	10	1	8	1	0
Van Buren	23,608	134	1	16	3	114	771	220	487	64	1
Vilonia	4,648	6	0	2	0	4	60	19	40	1	0
Waldron	3,375	14	0	8	0	6	108	45	60	3	2
Walnut Ridge	5,013	14	0	4	0	10	75	19	53	3	3
Ward	5,278	37	0	12	0	25	106	23	79	4	0
Warren	5,608	25	1	4	1	19	130	51	69	10	1
West Fork	2,623	11	1	3	0	7	32	5	25	2	0
West Memphis	24,668	486	16	26	55	389	1,262	357	795	110	7
White Hall	4,987	4	0	0	1	3	85	42	37	6	0
Wilson	845	1	1	0	0	0	11	2	8	1	0
Wynne	7,907	70	0	15	7	48	325	54	261	10	8
CALIFORNIA											
Adelanto	34,429	239	0	25	40	174	610	175	336	99	19
Agoura Hills	20,744	27	0	5	8	14	274	64	186	24	3
Alameda	79,951	184	1	13	75	95	2,123	196	1,576	351	18
Albany	20,379	37	1	2	28	6	608	69	492	47	3
Alhambra	85,718	193	3	14	88	88	1,930	328	1,346	256	16
Aliso Viejo	52,183	43	0	11	10	22	445	66	348	31	1
Alturas	2,501	24	0	0	3	21	76	27	38	11	1
American Canyon	20,339	56	0	8	13	35	405	54	311	40	0
Anaheim	354,743	1,192	7	142	407	636	8,702	1,408	5,921	1,373	27
Anderson	10,433	64	1	6	12	45	388	89	201	98	4
Angels Camp	3,808	10	0	0	0	10	80	22	50	8	0
Antioch	112,956	602	7	56	213	326	3,330	641	2,087	602	92
Apple Valley	73,631	227	5	17	55	150	1,459	279	917	263	15
Arcadia	59,151	76	1	8	41	26	1,420	372	969	79	5
Arcata	18,073	64	1	15	14	34	665	89	512	64	12
Arroyo Grande	18,244	24	0	3	3	18	286	37	225	24	4
Artesia	16,959	82	1	3	34	44	335	107	180	48	1
Arvin	21,560	207	3	7	27	170	382	89	172	121	20
Atascadero	30,716	99	0	15	9	75	428	63	330	35	3
Atherton	7,285	5	0	3	2	0	107	31	73	3	0
Atwater	29,565	179	2	6	21	150	910	163	561	186	16
Auburn	14,094	72	0	3	9	60	192	51	123	18	3
Avalon	3,769	4	0	1	0	3	41	9	27	5	0
Avenal	12,084	44	1	2	1	40	118	43	57	18	0
Azusa	50,393	193	3	25	63	102	1,122	221	716	185	9
Bakersfield	385,609	1,895	31	113	811	940	16,097	4,025	9,295	2,777	275
Baldwin Park	76,541	287	3	35	71	178	1,386	240	843	303	1
Banning	31,451	135	6	17	28	84	531	191	217	123	0
Barstow	24,095	285	2	14	96	173	1,102	348	584	170	32
Bear Valley	5,500	5	0	1	0	4	118	5	113	0	0
Beaumont	48,559	208	1	17	24	166	871	163	570	138	3
Bell	35,857	184	3	10	45	126	495	120	266	109	0
Bellflower	77,937	335	4	25	118	188	1,688	331	963	394	10
Bell Gardens	42,845	117	2	6	53	56	633	85	306	242	4
Belmont	27,325	40	0	10	10	20	424	58	336	30	1
Belvedere	2,134	0	0	0	0	0	11	4	6	1	0
Benicia	28,536	34	0	7	17	10	382	71	229	82	2
Berkeley	123,735	586	1	65	353	167	5,381	829	4,004	548	31
Beverly Hills	34,557	106	0	14	42	50	1,757	405	1,282	70	5
Big Bear	5,296	36	1	4	3	28	171	44	109	18	1
Biggs	1,712	10	0	0	2	8	34	9	20	5	0
Bishop	3,744	41	0	6	4	31	232	26	201	5	0
Blythe	19,517	71	1	6	23	41	684	213	440	31	35
Bradbury	1,100	2	0	0	0	2	13	9	4	0	0
Brawley	26,590	154	1	4	18	131	657	112	494	51	19
Brea	43,279	83	1	7	29	46	1,293	159	1,068	66	5
Brentwood	64,118	152	1	7	39	105	1,317	211	1,021	85	1
Brisbane	4,786	9	0	1	1	7	93	39	51	3	1
Broadmoor	4,440	14	2	1	5	6	78	24	36	18	0
Buellton	5,176	3	0	0	0	3	51	4	41	6	0
Buena Park	83,336	257	0	17	74	166	2,583	265	1,977	341	2
Burbank	105,041	229	0	18	77	134	2,625	276	2,135	214	8
Burlingame	30,959	58	0	9	19	30	921	177	684	60	4
Calabasas	24,309	26	0	8	3	15	363	81	269	13	0
Calexico	40,596	87	0	6	19	62	1,064	320	576	168	40
California City	14,051	47	4	2	8	33	393	196	137	60	0
Calimesa	8,953	12	0	0	3	9	202	36	129	37	0
Calistoga	5,289	10	0	3	2	5	62	15	39	8	1
Camarillo	68,218	78	0	16	21	41	841	110	663	68	3
Campbell	41,853	119	0	11	37	71	1,379	235	976	168	25
Canyon Lake	11,314	12	0	3	0	9	101	22	56	23	1
Capitola	10,218	26	0	5	9	12	507	28	458	21	3
Carlsbad	116,739	243	1	39	52	151	2,100	299	1,649	152	14
Carmel	3,921	11	0	0	0	11	96	20	73	3	0
Carpinteria	13,712	22	0	0	2	20	212	36	148	28	0
Carson	92,895	435	5	14	131	285	1,971	345	1,181	445	11
Cathedral City	55,056	172	2	22	39	109	717	188	283	246	6
Central Marin	35,033	40	0	10	19	11	723	193	503	27	0
Ceres	49,101	228	1	13	74	140	1,452	325	792	335	19

Table 8. Offenses Known to Law Enforcement, by Selected State and City, 2018—Continued

(Number.)

State/city	Population	Violent crime	Murder and nonnegligent manslaughter	Rape[1]	Robbery	Aggravated assault	Property crime	Burglary	Larceny-theft	Motor vehicle theft	Arson[2]
Cerritos	51,307	162	0	13	91	58	1,794	372	1,259	163	3
Chico	94,273	611	2	86	106	417	2,403	327	1,761	315	66
Chino	91,535	259	1	25	67	166	2,216	407	1,508	301	6
Chino Hills	81,177	77	1	8	17	51	1,079	242	747	90	3
Chowchilla	18,551	42	3	1	4	34	293	81	144	68	5
Chula Vista	274,370	835	6	79	256	494	3,611	585	2,338	688	20
Citrus Heights	88,603	324	1	47	86	190	2,478	410	1,739	329	12
Claremont	36,178	66	1	15	19	31	930	227	646	57	5
Clayton	12,330	1	0	0	1	0	146	11	128	7	0
Clearlake	15,037	109	4	16	21	68	506	188	220	98	7
Cloverdale	8,826	19	0	6	4	9	138	22	106	10	0
Clovis	111,759	221	1	46	36	138	2,438	358	1,932	148	6
Coachella	46,115	104	1	5	40	58	1,143	123	766	254	4
Coalinga	16,593	73	2	3	8	60	244	73	144	27	3
Colma	1,524	37	0	0	18	19	359	32	309	18	0
Colton	55,203	184	11	11	77	85	1,600	324	851	425	14
Colusa	5,961	11	1	1	1	8	80	24	42	14	0
Commerce	12,961	128	1	9	48	70	995	108	646	241	7
Compton	97,775	1,174	22	38	424	690	2,559	362	1,349	848	58
Concord	130,855	473	3	49	200	221	4,126	446	3,124	556	18
Corcoran	21,487	75	0	8	11	56	380	88	214	78	2
Corning	7,580	40	1	2	4	33	287	78	169	40	2
Corona	170,041	263	6	46	119	92	3,264	488	2,185	591	21
Coronado	24,491	18	0	2	3	13	314	32	262	20	0
Costa Mesa	114,358	344	3	75	110	156	3,792	515	2,975	302	17
Cotati	7,509	36	0	4	4	28	101	19	71	11	1
Covina	48,557	188	2	28	67	91	1,117	291	653	173	3
Crescent City	6,245	35	0	2	8	25	220	18	199	3	5
Cudahy	24,114	90	4	5	32	49	187	26	88	73	4
Culver City	39,335	188	0	6	109	73	1,756	246	1,417	93	0
Cupertino	61,078	72	0	18	14	40	956	183	720	53	7
Cypress	49,223	58	0	14	25	19	704	146	478	80	5
Daly City	107,928	242	3	38	103	98	1,528	221	1,130	177	8
Dana Point	34,019	69	0	7	13	49	504	73	395	36	0
Danville	45,202	16	0	0	10	6	326	53	251	22	1
Davis	69,486	117	2	21	44	50	1,690	232	1,366	92	9
Delano	53,141	238	10	13	44	171	1,437	319	656	462	73
Del Mar	4,391	14	0	3	2	9	118	26	78	14	0
Del Rey Oaks	1,696	2	0	0	1	1	59	16	40	3	0
Desert Hot Springs	28,991	309	3	22	56	228	638	292	179	167	8
Diamond Bar	56,821	58	2	7	30	19	936	360	521	55	5
Dinuba	24,411	184	0	9	28	147	597	77	427	93	4
Dixon	20,472	53	1	3	14	35	368	35	278	55	4
Dorris	902	3	0	0	0	3	12	7	3	2	0
Dos Palos	5,518	71	0	3	0	68	201	69	99	33	6
Downey	113,277	367	5	14	185	163	2,615	439	1,570	606	15
Duarte	21,816	62	0	5	19	38	403	49	287	67	1
Dublin	63,463	108	0	6	47	55	1,188	96	1,005	87	2
Dunsmuir	1,572	9	1	1	0	7	23	9	12	2	0
East Palo Alto	29,991	141	3	13	55	70	567	84	300	183	3
Eastvale	64,642	63	1	5	29	28	956	147	678	131	0
El Cajon	104,497	515	5	31	191	288	2,269	353	1,544	372	18
El Centro	44,609	126	1	12	29	84	1,625	439	1,076	110	8
El Cerrito	25,793	171	0	3	101	67	1,314	167	1,045	102	9
Elk Grove	174,651	414	1	40	93	280	2,359	321	1,859	179	10
El Monte	116,464	362	6	35	149	172	2,242	482	1,256	504	20
El Segundo	16,881	62	0	11	22	29	714	202	448	64	3
Emeryville	12,016	170	0	9	120	41	2,014	98	1,761	155	6
Encinitas	63,700	114	0	16	21	77	795	145	567	83	3
Escalon	7,653	21	0	2	3	16	124	25	87	12	0
Escondido	153,073	535	4	64	159	308	2,736	357	1,891	488	12
Etna	718	0	0	0	0	0	0	0	0	0	0
Eureka	27,174	197	3	26	64	104	1,491	231	1,055	205	28
Exeter	10,583	16	0	2	3	11	279	49	193	37	0
Fairfax	7,620	6	0	1	1	4	116	21	90	5	0
Fairfield	117,883	587	4	78	176	329	3,280	404	2,300	576	29
Farmersville	10,806	45	3	1	8	33	190	48	116	26	4
Ferndale	1,373	6	0	1	0	5	20	8	12	0	0
Fillmore	15,928	39	1	7	7	24	135	27	94	14	1
Firebaugh	8,438	45	0	4	5	36	111	23	66	22	0
Folsom	78,916	85	1	20	29	35	1,245	245	918	82	8
Fontana	213,964	709	8	63	195	443	3,218	542	1,773	903	10
Fort Bragg	7,317	31	0	7	6	18	314	34	266	14	7
Fort Jones	690	7	0	0	0	7	10	3	4	3	0
Fortuna	12,228	46	0	3	9	34	352	61	257	34	6
Foster City	34,993	35	0	6	5	24	376	59	300	17	3
Fountain Valley	56,433	52	0	1	21	30	1,496	194	1,185	117	1
Fowler	6,627	22	0	1	6	15	107	52	46	9	0
Fremont	238,024	502	3	55	216	228	4,687	720	3,284	683	22
Fresno	531,818	2,953	32	170	909	1,842	17,787	2,949	12,473	2,365	264
Fullerton	141,132	332	3	66	107	156	3,660	329	2,856	475	16
Galt	26,548	96	0	11	21	64	462	66	347	49	6
Gardena	60,423	326	7	16	160	143	1,306	289	702	315	8

Table 8. Offenses Known to Law Enforcement, by Selected State and City, 2018—Continued

(Number.)

State/city	Population	Violent crime	Murder and nonnegligent manslaughter	Rape[1]	Robbery	Aggravated assault	Property crime	Burglary	Larceny-theft	Motor vehicle theft	Arson[2]
Garden Grove	174,661	507	4	54	163	286	4,040	613	2,815	612	15
Gilroy	59,033	209	0	37	75	97	1,609	188	1,040	381	7
Glendale	204,724	202	1	24	77	100	3,110	454	2,390	266	11
Glendora	52,727	122	0	23	26	73	1,523	222	1,179	122	5
Goleta	31,284	42	0	4	10	28	352	75	233	44	0
Gonzales	8,521	11	0	1	4	6	74	11	30	33	0
Grand Terrace	12,672	37	0	6	17	14	254	55	166	33	0
Grass Valley	13,004	70	0	1	14	55	517	81	386	50	1
Greenfield	17,680	97	3	4	14	76	193	41	108	44	3
Gridley	6,612	80	0	5	1	74	250	49	191	10	3
Grover Beach	13,694	28	1	5	4	18	249	45	180	24	4
Guadalupe	7,411	11	0	1	3	7	51	16	23	12	1
Gustine	5,890	38	0	2	1	35	95	24	56	15	1
Hanford	56,805	274	2	32	41	199	1,264	145	945	174	7
Hawaiian Gardens	14,474	81	0	4	24	53	250	56	143	51	1
Hawthorne	88,372	617	0	37	232	348	1,705	294	1,064	347	5
Hayward	162,881	669	3	85	364	217	4,770	545	2,849	1,376	21
Healdsburg	11,917	20	0	1	4	15	223	30	174	19	0
Hemet	86,047	432	7	25	144	256	2,863	574	1,754	535	29
Hercules	25,750	30	0	0	16	14	350	82	240	28	0
Hermosa Beach	19,737	30	0	3	5	22	477	130	316	31	0
Hesperia	95,519	406	2	32	126	246	2,035	444	1,228	363	19
Hidden Hills	1,930	0	0	0	0	0	15	4	9	2	0
Highland	55,651	208	1	7	62	138	1,143	242	636	265	11
Hillsborough	11,580	9	0	2	0	7	90	44	42	4	0
Hollister	38,930	98	1	13	16	68	496	62	334	100	2
Holtville	6,695	15	0	3	1	11	84	19	53	12	1
Hughson	7,627	7	0	0	2	5	88	17	60	11	0
Huntington Beach	203,428	429	1	83	106	239	3,993	525	3,158	310	24
Huntington Park	58,922	429	2	38	214	175	1,800	256	954	590	16
Huron	7,396	96	0	4	3	89	49	18	10	21	15
Imperial	17,976	9	0	2	1	6	77	18	38	21	0
Imperial Beach	27,569	79	0	3	18	58	352	63	201	88	1
Indian Wells	5,467	1	0	0	0	1	132	28	90	14	0
Indio	91,346	495	2	47	112	334	2,242	405	1,362	475	11
Industry	203	87	2	3	50	32	979	161	681	137	3
Inglewood	110,726	683	15	51	312	305	2,744	450	1,636	658	12
Ione	7,848	5	0	0	0	5	56	13	38	5	0
Irvine	288,052	160	0	40	53	67	3,659	621	2,840	198	9
Irwindale	1,467	12	0	0	6	6	194	44	115	35	1
Isleton	851	0	0	0	0	0	24	14	9	1	0
Jackson	4,752	29	0	2	3	24	128	27	93	8	3
Jurupa Valley	107,605	332	6	11	84	231	2,839	399	1,548	892	1
Kensington	5,400	2	0	0	0	2	48	13	30	5	0
Kerman	15,128	59	1	5	21	32	358	84	218	56	0
King City	14,228	32	1	7	5	19	175	53	93	29	2
Kingsburg	12,089	40	0	5	7	28	306	129	124	53	2
La Canada Flintridge	20,436	13	0	2	4	7	330	86	231	13	0
Lafayette	26,827	10	0	0	5	5	231	23	191	17	0
Laguna Beach	23,202	90	0	5	9	76	443	60	340	43	4
Laguna Hills	31,474	55	0	5	15	35	402	97	277	28	4
Laguna Niguel	66,806	81	0	2	21	58	640	104	480	56	2
Laguna Woods	16,219	10	0	1	2	7	108	11	84	13	0
La Habra	62,769	111	1	5	45	60	1,155	190	800	165	2
La Habra Heights	5,415	6	0	1	2	3	66	22	43	1	0
Lake Elsinore	68,451	161	2	2	55	102	1,919	258	1,329	332	3
Lake Forest	85,302	159	1	14	36	108	761	139	510	112	10
Lakeport	4,763	27	0	1	5	21	175	48	114	13	0
Lake Shastina	2,563	2	0	1	0	1	5	0	5	0	0
Lakewood	81,097	270	2	23	118	127	1,848	275	1,347	226	5
La Mesa	60,442	160	1	13	67	79	1,049	157	760	132	6
La Mirada	49,175	89	1	6	22	60	829	128	580	121	3
Lancaster	160,818	1,193	7	94	298	794	3,805	1,001	2,074	730	28
La Palma	15,747	20	0	0	5	15	334	84	227	23	1
La Puente	40,390	162	3	16	41	102	501	96	258	147	2
La Quinta	41,849	42	1	1	20	20	1,154	174	896	84	2
La Verne	32,656	87	0	18	11	58	742	129	538	75	1
Lawndale	33,121	129	3	10	30	86	348	61	185	102	1
Lemon Grove	27,364	155	2	6	52	95	468	67	309	92	3
Lemoore	26,626	188	0	18	20	150	385	69	264	52	1
Lincoln	48,364	35	0	13	12	10	418	83	291	44	4
Lindsay	13,542	34	1	0	8	25	214	30	129	55	3
Livermore	91,612	186	0	33	58	95	1,696	212	1,329	155	8
Livingston	14,301	41	0	1	13	27	308	82	173	53	4
Lodi	66,416	277	9	12	88	168	1,701	359	1,000	342	14
Loma Linda	24,319	40	0	7	10	23	608	125	385	98	1
Lomita	20,770	66	1	6	11	48	312	64	201	47	0
Lompoc	43,719	218	1	26	32	159	951	178	629	144	14
Long Beach	470,445	3,284	30	219	979	2,056	11,922	2,328	7,315	2,279	127
Los Alamitos	11,629	8	0	1	3	4	156	54	78	24	0
Los Altos	30,989	13	0	4	3	6	284	80	188	16	0
Los Altos Hills	8,656	7	0	0	2	5	48	29	17	2	2
Los Angeles	4,029,741	30,126	258	2,528	10,327	17,013	101,267	15,988	67,963	17,316	1,654

Table 8. Offenses Known to Law Enforcement, by Selected State and City, 2018—Continued

(Number.)

State/city	Population	Violent crime	Murder and nonnegligent manslaughter	Rape[1]	Robbery	Aggravated assault	Property crime	Burglary	Larceny-theft	Motor vehicle theft	Arson[2]
Los Banos	39,651	144	1	7	37	99	1,071	244	659	168	4
Los Gatos	30,899	10	0	2	6	2	459	58	360	41	0
Lynwood	71,315	426	9	22	180	215	1,438	228	656	554	21
Madera	66,098	399	6	37	92	264	1,346	241	898	207	15
Malibu	12,911	37	1	9	9	18	380	74	277	29	1
Mammoth Lakes	8,118	19	0	2	3	14	82	9	71	2	1
Manhattan Beach	36,038	57	1	8	27	21	844	113	684	47	2
Manteca	81,080	256	0	18	97	141	2,288	386	1,522	380	15
Marina	22,511	49	1	4	14	30	317	41	240	36	2
Martinez	38,699	73	0	10	32	31	524	73	346	105	0
Marysville	12,459	112	0	11	26	75	533	72	332	129	11
Maywood	27,612	87	2	10	26	49	302	72	107	123	0
McFarland	15,475	61	2	10	6	43	212	69	68	75	8
Mendota	11,476	86	0	5	6	75	197	50	78	69	0
Menifee	92,540	155	3	9	46	97	1,945	331	1,282	332	1
Menlo Park	34,694	43	1	9	9	24	606	110	470	26	1
Merced	83,659	465	1	30	116	318	2,219	387	1,404	428	62
Mill Valley	14,418	9	0	1	4	4	196	44	137	15	0
Milpitas	79,895	87	0	11	45	31	1,934	243	1,435	256	4
Mission Viejo	96,419	113	0	5	24	84	937	157	702	78	5
Modesto	215,822	1,904	16	105	420	1,363	7,727	1,109	5,420	1,198	62
Monrovia	37,128	69	2	10	31	26	914	121	723	70	1
Montague	1,401	12	0	1	1	10	26	16	8	2	2
Montclair	39,648	239	1	37	72	129	1,646	337	990	319	18
Montebello	63,291	218	6	10	109	93	1,643	619	548	476	86
Monterey	28,744	112	0	18	35	59	1,143	204	859	80	3
Monterey Park	61,160	124	0	4	73	47	1,589	356	1,017	216	2
Monte Sereno	3,606	0	0	0	0	0	19	8	8	3	0
Moorpark	37,121	33	0	7	7	19	261	55	188	18	1
Moraga	17,866	12	0	2	2	8	94	12	75	7	0
Moreno Valley	209,145	775	9	30	293	443	6,161	1,101	3,854	1,206	11
Morgan Hill	46,142	52	1	0	17	34	740	125	501	114	1
Morro Bay	10,692	36	0	3	4	29	135	16	113	6	0
Mountain View	82,518	157	0	13	59	85	2,103	276	1,659	168	7
Mount Shasta	3,289	11	0	1	1	9	47	7	28	12	0
Murrieta	114,706	92	2	16	35	39	1,412	234	952	226	2
Napa	80,145	269	0	56	46	167	1,241	258	814	169	30
National City	61,763	306	2	22	101	181	1,167	127	748	292	8
Needles	5,030	59	0	6	2	51	202	74	99	29	12
Nevada City	3,146	13	0	3	2	8	112	21	72	19	0
Newark	48,276	97	1	20	39	37	1,318	180	969	169	7
Newman	11,525	19	3	1	7	8	134	25	71	38	0
Newport Beach	86,276	124	1	31	29	63	2,073	397	1,513	163	3
Norco	26,716	63	0	4	19	40	675	123	442	110	0
Norwalk	106,158	449	9	23	132	285	1,948	438	1,116	394	13
Novato	56,577	97	1	10	19	67	773	118	564	91	8
Oakdale	23,504	48	0	9	18	21	555	109	375	71	4
Oakland	430,230	5,480	70	448	2,624	2,338	23,190	2,394	15,725	5,071	245
Oakley	42,655	42	1	1	9	31	508	90	323	95	2
Oceanside	177,464	669	9	69	158	433	3,836	526	2,845	465	16
Ojai	7,597	6	0	1	3	2	68	12	50	6	1
Ontario	177,542	670	6	106	231	327	4,584	723	2,858	1,003	27
Orange	141,108	160	3	12	73	72	2,478	478	1,700	300	19
Orange Cove	9,682	25	1	2	5	17	94	30	42	22	0
Orinda	20,020	9	0	1	7	1	110	30	69	11	0
Orland	7,697	25	0	3	6	16	121	22	82	17	0
Oroville	19,186	112	4	10	32	66	982	152	623	207	9
Oxnard	211,737	801	14	66	327	394	5,055	704	3,568	783	41
Pacifica	39,339	71	0	20	16	35	402	70	304	28	1
Pacific Grove	15,788	23	0	9	2	12	312	44	252	16	0
Palmdale	158,177	591	4	43	161	383	2,442	513	1,426	503	20
Palm Desert	53,567	91	0	6	21	64	1,989	329	1,530	130	4
Palm Springs	48,644	274	3	35	81	155	2,078	522	1,281	275	5
Palo Alto	67,560	72	0	5	30	37	1,513	234	1,197	82	8
Palos Verdes Estates	13,559	6	0	1	4	1	104	33	69	2	0
Paradise	26,755	65	0	15	5	45	279	109	125	45	0
Paramount	55,023	329	3	19	137	170	1,427	213	871	343	5
Parlier	15,356	111	3	9	18	81	335	108	124	103	9
Pasadena	143,448	547	7	47	174	319	2,928	663	1,959	306	22
Paso Robles	32,228	43	0	13	7	23	797	133	610	54	2
Patterson	22,363	53	0	0	8	45	387	45	224	118	2
Perris	79,238	214	5	7	78	124	2,000	248	1,036	716	5
Petaluma	61,289	197	0	31	27	139	889	153	668	68	6
Pico Rivera	63,602	228	4	9	77	138	1,159	231	614	314	5
Piedmont	11,478	21	0	1	10	10	195	47	124	24	1
Pinole	19,509	70	0	0	29	41	747	83	605	59	2
Pismo Beach	8,323	30	0	3	3	24	439	129	295	15	1
Pittsburg	73,462	422	3	53	130	236	1,679	251	1,010	418	20
Placentia	52,324	120	0	10	20	90	904	243	548	113	2
Placerville	11,018	54	0	17	9	28	278	47	189	42	2
Pleasant Hill	35,252	57	1	3	32	21	1,584	134	1,373	77	1
Pleasanton	84,992	110	0	6	57	47	1,445	156	1,177	112	4
Pomona	153,496	877	17	76	361	423	4,697	903	2,764	1,030	34

Table 8. Offenses Known to Law Enforcement, by Selected State and City, 2018—Continued

(Number.)

State/city	Population	Violent crime	Murder and nonnegligent manslaughter	Rape[1]	Robbery	Aggravated assault	Property crime	Burglary	Larceny-theft	Motor vehicle theft	Arson[2]
Porterville	59,394	209	3	15	52	139	1,561	320	935	306	3
Port Hueneme	22,417	61	0	4	18	39	421	86	280	55	11
Poway	50,346	65	1	11	10	43	509	92	380	37	4
Rancho Cordova	74,863	272	3	26	74	169	1,388	257	934	197	1
Rancho Cucamonga	179,114	290	1	51	112	126	3,854	625	2,831	398	15
Rancho Mirage	18,463	24	0	0	5	19	708	133	513	62	0
Rancho Palos Verdes	42,464	32	0	6	5	21	389	120	240	29	0
Rancho Santa Margarita	48,918	46	0	3	6	37	316	43	261	12	9
Red Bluff	14,315	165	2	24	20	119	719	151	451	117	14
Redding	92,068	620	2	87	96	435	3,433	613	2,281	539	9
Redlands	71,954	264	5	64	82	113	2,491	326	1,842	323	41
Redondo Beach	68,048	171	4	14	53	100	1,452	249	1,071	132	3
Redwood City	88,161	177	0	45	53	79	1,254	172	912	170	8
Reedley	25,809	105	3	13	10	79	289	91	128	70	6
Rialto[4]	104,173	543	5	45	195	298	3,038	544	1,850	644	20
Richmond	110,982	1,046	17	32	375	622	4,353	383	2,285	1,685	43
Ridgecrest	29,055	171	1	31	15	124	500	123	316	61	13
Rio Dell	3,413	8	0	3	2	3	61	14	41	6	1
Rio Vista	9,268	21	0	2	2	17	118	32	63	23	1
Ripon	15,878	10	0	3	5	2	225	27	184	14	2
Riverbank	25,035	24	0	0	13	11	447	67	326	54	0
Riverside	331,022	1,686	14	150	543	979	10,226	1,470	6,911	1,845	73
Rocklin	65,969	52	0	13	16	23	952	172	699	81	6
Rohnert Park	43,129	222	0	40	22	160	745	112	549	84	4
Rolling Hills	1,885	0	0	0	0	0	5	1	4	0	0
Rolling Hills Estates	8,249	8	1	3	2	2	108	33	67	8	2
Rosemead	54,661	194	1	12	87	94	1,274	288	702	284	5
Roseville	137,706	299	3	28	133	135	3,252	428	2,543	281	21
Ross	2,487	1	0	1	0	0	24	7	17	0	0
Sacramento	507,037	3,329	36	102	1,052	2,139	15,417	2,751	9,783	2,883	146
Salinas	158,590	981	19	100	321	541	4,304	897	2,180	1,227	31
San Bernardino	217,986	2,906	49	153	974	1,730	9,014	2,226	4,594	2,194	75
San Bruno	43,621	123	0	20	38	65	984	116	775	93	19
San Clemente	65,509	114	0	9	28	77	900	140	697	63	3
Sand City	395	8	0	0	3	5	111	8	96	7	0
San Diego	1,436,495	5,360	35	605	1,439	3,281	27,416	3,752	18,482	5,182	187
San Dimas	34,463	80	1	11	22	46	751	152	534	65	6
San Fernando	24,869	102	0	3	37	62	312	51	162	99	0
San Francisco	889,282	6,144	46	354	3,165	2,579	49,214	5,322	39,675	4,217	288
San Gabriel	40,637	136	0	9	51	76	691	172	453	66	3
Sanger	25,287	88	1	15	13	59	362	110	188	64	2
San Jacinto	48,830	132	2	1	70	59	1,461	287	935	239	0
San Jose	1,047,305	4,444	28	615	1,593	2,208	25,753	4,539	13,510	7,704	121
San Juan Capistrano	36,295	84	0	9	12	63	351	96	215	40	1
San Leandro	91,359	473	1	22	299	151	3,584	439	2,333	812	27
San Luis Obispo	47,885	192	1	55	33	103	1,809	242	1,493	74	21
San Marcos	98,088	202	0	18	61	123	1,052	167	740	145	5
San Marino	13,358	11	0	1	2	8	203	84	118	1	3
San Mateo	105,839	285	0	25	88	172	2,163	590	1,360	213	6
San Pablo	31,403	180	0	14	99	67	979	114	531	334	6
San Rafael	59,254	257	2	32	107	116	1,695	277	1,050	368	16
San Ramon	76,569	43	0	4	21	18	786	103	631	52	6
Santa Ana	335,403	1,571	21	230	499	821	6,390	910	3,931	1,549	57
Santa Barbara	92,630	415	1	77	89	248	2,333	261	1,894	178	16
Santa Clara	128,682	208	1	33	74	100	3,741	429	2,860	452	11
Santa Clarita	216,589	292	4	43	94	151	2,437	582	1,560	295	26
Santa Cruz	65,680	390	1	34	66	289	2,905	336	2,308	261	53
Santa Fe Springs	18,241	105	1	6	39	59	991	176	651	164	8
Santa Maria	108,100	497	6	60	159	272	1,932	377	979	576	24
Santa Monica	92,674	797	7	60	278	452	4,732	662	3,835	235	21
Santa Paula	30,456	90	1	3	32	54	458	99	318	41	0
Santa Rosa	176,325	823	3	149	147	524	3,118	547	2,179	392	26
Santee	58,781	109	0	13	31	65	886	113	701	72	11
Saratoga	31,023	22	0	7	6	9	237	97	127	13	1
Sausalito	7,167	9	0	0	0	9	201	13	179	9	1
Scotts Valley	11,998	17	0	6	2	9	191	42	137	12	3
Seal Beach	24,356	39	0	9	20	10	601	70	493	38	14
Seaside	34,303	92	0	13	23	56	445	41	333	71	4
Sebastopol	7,705	15	1	2	5	7	164	71	84	9	0
Selma	24,979	240	3	23	16	198	725	239	344	142	3
Shafter	19,986	44	0	6	8	30	544	138	285	121	12
Sierra Madre	11,055	7	0	0	0	7	95	34	59	2	0
Signal Hill	11,711	86	0	10	37	39	690	107	471	112	4
Simi Valley	127,222	214	0	46	56	112	1,491	253	1,118	120	2
Solana Beach	13,524	23	1	2	3	17	206	62	123	21	0
Soledad	26,313	70	1	5	10	54	101	17	53	31	1
Solvang	6,013	6	0	1	1	4	52	12	35	5	0
Sonoma	11,173	44	0	4	5	35	164	23	133	8	0
Sonora	4,851	27	0	8	8	11	286	40	228	18	5
South El Monte	21,113	126	1	7	33	85	621	145	313	163	5
South Gate	95,570	634	1	34	192	407	2,364	343	1,376	645	15
South Lake Tahoe	22,060	182	3	9	22	148	454	114	279	61	7
South Pasadena	25,924	32	0	2	19	11	522	103	360	59	0

Table 8. Offenses Known to Law Enforcement, by Selected State and City, 2018—Continued

(Number.)

State/city	Population	Violent crime	Murder and nonnegligent manslaughter	Rape[1]	Robbery	Aggravated assault	Property crime	Burglary	Larceny-theft	Motor vehicle theft	Arson[2]
South San Francisco	67,973	181	0	22	56	103	1,444	257	1,002	185	5
Stallion Springs	2,645	1	0	1	0	0	17	2	14	1	0
Stanton	38,618	135	0	10	42	83	618	94	401	123	5
St. Helena	6,251	9	0	0	1	8	47	11	31	5	1
Stockton	313,158	4,383	33	193	1,205	2,952	11,800	2,329	7,417	2,054	191
Suisun City	29,859	93	1	13	18	61	627	54	483	90	5
Sunnyvale	155,637	255	1	43	71	140	2,541	424	1,764	353	8
Susanville	15,017	197	0	8	11	178	274	84	177	13	3
Sutter Creek	2,584	1	0	0	0	1	39	5	29	5	0
Taft	9,449	72	0	1	6	65	338	105	190	43	0
Tehachapi	12,402	82	0	19	12	51	276	71	155	50	3
Temecula	116,411	139	0	4	60	75	2,711	429	1,964	318	2
Temple City	36,484	64	0	7	22	35	472	212	216	44	0
Thousand Oaks	129,319	126	14	30	30	52	1,480	236	1,127	117	4
Tiburon	9,195	7	0	0	2	5	77	15	62	0	0
Torrance	146,968	267	2	35	107	123	2,702	468	1,951	283	9
Tracy	91,988	199	4	31	61	103	2,331	261	1,772	298	17
Truckee	16,609	17	0	2	3	12	143	42	85	16	2
Tulare	64,509	251	3	24	61	163	1,818	325	1,143	350	6
Tulelake	991	0	0	0	0	0	6	1	3	2	0
Turlock	74,267	420	7	29	130	254	2,233	351	1,447	435	45
Tustin	81,243	122	0	15	49	58	1,874	243	1,506	125	5
Twentynine Palms	26,755	81	1	16	16	48	278	111	136	31	7
Ukiah	16,037	95	1	15	11	68	284	76	149	59	26
Union City	76,198	261	1	15	89	156	1,653	246	1,170	237	10
Upland	77,453	290	2	13	109	166	2,072	500	1,297	275	3
Vacaville	101,146	230	2	22	63	143	2,158	163	1,804	191	12
Vallejo	122,974	942	8	103	349	482	4,508	2,456	975	1,077	40
Ventura	111,272	445	2	54	117	272	3,482	481	2,667	334	32
Vernon	113	27	1	1	13	12	383	82	195	106	3
Victorville	123,343	809	9	63	258	479	2,718	631	1,386	701	32
Villa Park	5,904	0	0	0	0	0	57	21	34	2	0
Visalia	134,224	450	3	107	138	202	3,978	748	2,701	529	23
Vista	102,742	330	5	32	104	189	1,497	266	926	305	2
Walnut	30,343	22	0	4	9	9	483	217	228	38	0
Walnut Creek	70,587	109	2	3	35	69	2,249	303	1,812	134	1
Waterford	9,018	20	0	0	6	14	114	27	53	34	0
Watsonville	54,513	243	1	18	50	174	1,330	196	785	349	14
Weed	2,682	26	0	2	4	20	82	13	62	7	0
West Covina	107,806	292	1	25	150	116	2,513	385	1,735	393	8
West Hollywood	37,478	301	3	40	127	131	2,100	240	1,762	98	20
Westlake Village	8,459	12	1	0	6	5	200	36	156	8	1
Westminster	91,821	286	2	26	117	141	2,433	425	1,739	269	8
Westmorland	2,291	12	1	0	0	11	28	6	21	1	1
West Sacramento	54,215	225	1	17	92	115	1,412	224	931	257	15
Wheatland	3,892	3	0	0	0	3	49	9	29	11	1
Whittier	87,055	233	1	23	99	110	2,225	367	1,527	331	11
Wildomar	37,626	48	1	0	19	28	724	136	456	132	0
Williams	5,380	22	0	1	3	18	81	28	43	10	3
Willits	4,875	21	0	10	5	6	72	15	32	25	3
Windsor	27,654	74	0	7	6	61	249	42	190	17	2
Winters	7,371	9	0	2	3	4	118	17	94	7	0
Woodlake	7,700	25	0	2	1	22	107	25	69	13	5
Woodland	60,679	220	1	16	67	136	1,602	252	1,146	204	25
Yorba Linda	68,794	44	0	6	12	26	812	185	561	66	5
Yountville	2,921	2	0	1	0	1	33	5	28	0	0
Yreka	7,573	37	0	2	2	33	221	38	164	19	0
Yuba City	67,035	264	1	35	75	153	1,846	234	1,356	256	11
Yucaipa	54,001	101	0	12	29	60	822	160	473	189	3
Yucca Valley	21,895	85	2	8	21	54	340	83	204	53	5
COLORADO											
Alamosa	9,955	56	0	12	9	35	552	79	450	23	5
Arvada	120,631	272	0	53	48	171	3,544	366	2,679	499	18
Aspen	7,465	12	0	9	0	3	289	12	267	10	0
Ault	1,792	0	0	0	0	0	0	0	0	0	0
Aurora	372,824	2,716	17	387	631	1,681	11,122	1,723	7,189	2,210	53
Avon	6,565	42	0	9	0	33	120	13	102	5	0
Basalt	4,219	3	0	1	0	2	33	2	30	1	0
Bayfield	2,738	4	0	1	0	3	29	2	23	4	0
Black Hawk	128	5	0	3	1	1	221	6	203	12	0
Boulder	108,380	292	0	39	39	214	3,666	386	3,035	245	21
Bow Mar	982	0	0	0	0	0	9	1	6	2	0
Brighton	41,613	114	0	33	11	70	1,135	114	860	161	4
Broomfield	70,307	82	0	18	14	50	1,707	156	1,403	148	4
Brush	5,347	6	0	4	1	1	84	17	53	14	0
Buena Vista	2,842	0	0	0	0	0	40	2	35	3	0
Burlington	3,057	8	0	2	0	6	61	8	49	4	0
Calhan	835	2	0	0	0	2	7	1	6	0	0
Canon City	16,557	94	0	20	7	67	757	96	623	38	4
Carbondale	6,882	7	0	2	1	4	57	3	50	4	0
Castle Rock	64,526	36	0	17	1	18	969	99	805	65	2
Centennial	111,646	202	2	47	28	125	1,958	268	1,493	197	7

Table 8. Offenses Known to Law Enforcement, by Selected State and City, 2018—Continued

(Number.)

State/city	Population	Violent crime	Murder and nonnegligent manslaughter	Rape[1]	Robbery	Aggravated assault	Property crime	Burglary	Larceny-theft	Motor vehicle theft	Arson[2]
Center	2,282	10	0	0	2	8	46	8	36	2	2
Cherry Hills Village	6,740	0	0	0	0	0	47	3	39	5	0
Colorado Springs	471,124	2,617	32	483	515	1,587	15,752	2,727	10,626	2,399	126
Columbine Valley	1,469	0	0	0	0	0	6	2	4	0	0
Commerce City	57,474	385	0	66	45	274	1,826	269	1,231	326	8
Cortez	8,738	28	0	1	3	24	239	9	221	9	0
Craig	8,848	23	0	5	0	18	316	43	259	14	4
Crested Butte	1,668	2	0	0	0	2	11	1	9	1	0
Cripple Creek	1,206	14	0	1	1	12	70	4	62	4	0
Dacono	5,774	7	0	5	0	2	65	8	53	4	0
Del Norte	1,563	1	0	0	0	1	36	22	13	1	0
Delta	8,819	19	0	3	2	14	415	79	311	25	5
Denver	720,745	5,262	65	717	1,211	3,269	26,464	3,982	17,207	5,275	116
Dillon	971	0	0	0	0	0	32	4	26	2	0
Durango	18,717	81	1	10	2	68	661	55	568	38	3
Eagle	6,921	25	0	3	0	22	84	5	72	7	2
Eaton	5,355	5	0	1	1	3	38	5	23	10	1
Edgewater	5,328	16	1	1	10	4	327	16	280	31	0
Elizabeth	1,416	6	1	1	0	4	16	2	13	1	0
Englewood	35,029	83	0	8	26	49	2,139	173	1,640	326	10
Erie	25,233	25	0	3	3	19	258	26	217	15	0
Estes Park	6,399	14	0	3	0	11	47	6	37	4	0
Evans	20,744	108	0	16	9	83	423	66	290	67	7
Federal Heights	12,929	86	2	9	12	63	554	65	373	116	3
Firestone	14,419	18	0	8	0	10	122	9	95	18	1
Florence	3,919	4	0	0	0	4	57	5	48	4	0
Fort Collins	168,163	392	3	28	39	322	3,701	357	3,163	181	13
Fort Lupton	8,273	4	0	1	0	3	78	0	50	28	0
Fort Morgan	11,267	38	1	23	2	12	300	35	235	30	6
Fountain	30,367	120	1	30	12	77	632	83	443	106	3
Fraser/Winter Park	2,320	6	0	0	0	6	90	9	78	3	0
Frederick[6]	13,390	4	3	0	0	1		1		2	0
Frisco	3,196	15	0	4	0	11	92	6	72	14	0
Fruita	13,390	30	0	5	2	23	217	51	159	7	3
Glendale	5,293	46	0	8	6	32	838	33	742	63	1
Glenwood Springs	10,022	35	1	16	2	16	473	40	403	30	2
Golden	20,768	44	0	16	2	26	537	49	441	47	2
Granby	2,110	0	0	0	0	0	26	1	24	1	1
Grand Junction	62,974	275	3	57	17	198	2,733	291	2,282	160	22
Greeley	107,325	424	2	78	64	280	2,739	418	2,041	280	19
Green Mountain Falls	699	1	0	0	0	1	2	2	0	0	0
Greenwood Village	15,989	94	0	9	7	78	728	85	581	62	3
Gunnison	6,627	21	0	7	1	13	131	14	108	9	3
Haxtun	909	0	0	0	0	0	7	1	6	0	0
Hayden	1,952	3	0	0	0	3	23	1	22	0	0
Holyoke	2,199	2	0	0	1	1	18	2	15	1	0
Hotchkiss	922	4	0	3	0	1	19	10	7	2	0
Hugo	746	0	0	0	0	0	8	3	2	3	0
Idaho Springs	1,792	15	0	7	1	7	68	4	59	5	0
Ignacio	733	3	0	0	0	3	14	6	8	0	0
Johnstown	16,490	9	0	6	0	3	222	15	184	23	1
Lafayette	28,914	60	0	13	7	40	711	100	557	54	3
La Junta	6,867	34	0	12	1	21	328	83	227	18	1
Lakeside	8	0	0	0	0	0	168	0	164	4	0
La Salle	2,385	1	0	0	1	0	38	9	25	4	0
Leadville	2,785	4	0	0	1	3	30	2	28	0	0
Limon	1,937	4	0	1	0	3	4	1	2	1	0
Littleton	48,632	43	2	7	17	17	1,560	221	1,136	203	5
Log Lane Village	867	0	0	0	0	0	10	1	9	0	0
Lone Tree	13,933	43	0	4	11	28	1,010	57	922	31	1
Longmont	95,534	415	1	118	39	257	2,586	344	1,938	304	30
Louisville[5]	21,545	16	0	3	2	11		54		38	1
Loveland	78,192	201	1	51	14	135	1,749	189	1,455	105	15
Manitou Springs	5,365	10	0	2	0	8	57	14	39	4	0
Meeker	2,274	3	0	1	0	2	25	5	18	2	1
Milliken	7,238	3	0	2	1	0	35	5	25	5	1
Monte Vista	4,136	17	0	3	1	13	189	46	137	6	0
Montrose	19,335	66	0	13	5	48	894	110	729	55	2
Mountain View	541	0	0	0	0	0	20	3	16	1	0
Mountain Village	1,405	0	0	0	0	0	21	1	20	0	0
Mount Crested Butte	849	0	0	0	0	0	12	0	12	0	0
Nederland	1,554	1	0	1	0	0	26	6	17	3	0
New Castle	4,863	11	1	3	0	7	39	2	33	4	1
Northglenn	39,383	145	2	35	18	90	1,302	116	920	266	7
Oak Creek	933	4	0	0	0	4	20	4	15	1	0
Olathe	1,809	0	0	0	0	0	8	1	5	2	0
Ouray	1,015	0	0	0	0	0	13	1	11	1	0
Pagosa Springs	1,974	4	0	1	1	2	70	4	64	2	0
Palisade	2,693	8	0	1	0	7	32	11	19	2	1
Parachute	1,120	10	0	1	1	8	31	6	23	2	1
Parker	55,573	55	0	17	17	21	781	122	595	64	4
Platteville	3,887	3	0	1	0	2	48	10	32	6	1
Pueblo	111,756	1,110	9	185	220	696	6,231	1,224	3,947	1,060	76

Table 8. Offenses Known to Law Enforcement, by Selected State and City, 2018—Continued

(Number.)

State/city	Population	Violent crime	Murder and nonnegligent manslaughter	Rape[1]	Robbery	Aggravated assault	Property crime	Burglary	Larceny-theft	Motor vehicle theft	Arson[2]
Rangely	2,323	3	0	1	0	2	3	1	1	1	0
Rifle	9,711	40	0	12	1	27	231	19	185	27	0
Salida	5,951	6	0	1	0	5	121	16	100	5	1
Severance	4,454	16	0	2	0	14	36	12	22	2	1
Sheridan	6,159	52	0	7	11	34	543	47	424	72	1
Silt	3,160	3	0	0	0	3	31	3	25	3	0
Silverthorne	4,775	9	0	4	1	4	129	12	100	17	0
Springfield	1,358	5	0	0	0	5	8	1	4	3	0
Steamboat Springs	13,100	17	0	3	0	14	264	22	232	10	1
Sterling	13,928	88	1	23	2	62	487	74	381	32	3
Telluride	2,456	4	0	0	2	2	53	9	43	1	0
Thornton	139,697	378	5	147	72	154	4,647	504	3,417	726	18
Timnath	4,174	1	0	1	0	0	108	19	88	1	0
Trinidad	7,947	43	0	5	5	33	340	73	247	20	3
Vail	5,511	19	0	2	1	16	205	21	179	5	0
Walsh	509	1	0	0	0	1	0	0	0	0	0
Westminster	113,751	318	8	46	80	184	3,669	333	2,646	690	24
Wheat Ridge	31,452	76	0	11	12	53	1,031	90	722	219	7
Windsor	26,441	6	0	1	0	5	163	23	134	6	2
Woodland Park	7,709	16	0	2	0	14	143	14	121	8	1
Wray	2,368	1	0	0	0	1	1	0	1	0	0
Yuma	3,509	3	0	2	0	1	13	4	8	1	0
CONNECTICUT											
Ansonia	18,751	25	0	7	11	7	442	29	353	60	2
Avon	18,379	4	0	2	0	2	186	18	155	13	0
Berlin	20,593	15	0	2	4	9	281	31	215	35	0
Bethel	19,974	4	0	1	0	3	144	15	116	13	0
Bloomfield	21,541	60	0	6	13	41	573	35	473	65	1
Branford	28,121	17	0	0	4	13	476	24	401	51	0
Bridgeport[4]	146,819	945	11	83	325	526	2,833	588	1,647	598	16
Bristol	60,184	62	0	7	29	26	970	140	706	124	2
Brookfield	17,230	5	0	0	1	4	158	8	143	7	2
Canton	10,298	1	0	1	0	0	70	13	51	6	0
Cheshire	29,337	5	0	0	1	4	244	26	190	28	0
Clinton	12,917	2	0	1	0	1	323	35	271	17	0
Coventry	12,438	10	0	4	1	5	90	13	66	11	0
Cromwell	13,950	7	0	3	1	3	251	30	208	13	0
Danbury	85,818	133	0	21	40	72	1,163	128	926	109	8
Darien	22,050	4	1	0	1	2	259	13	218	28	0
Derby	12,535	38	0	3	20	15	291	40	216	35	1
East Hampton	12,893	11	0	3	1	7	87	12	64	11	0
East Hartford	50,184	117	1	21	61	34	1,206	185	831	190	3
East Haven	28,805	21	1	3	8	9	593	60	434	99	1
East Lyme	18,744	8	1	3	1	3	88	12	72	4	0
Easton	7,590	0	0	0	0	0	25	0	22	3	1
East Windsor	11,425	17	0	4	4	9	362	44	296	22	1
Enfield	44,574	55	1	6	8	40	687	144	491	52	0
Fairfield	62,452	34	0	1	12	21	955	97	791	67	0
Farmington	25,602	14	0	4	5	5	555	40	495	20	0
Glastonbury	34,593	20	0	3	3	14	456	76	327	53	2
Granby	11,367	3	0	0	0	3	79	13	64	2	0
Greenwich	63,075	6	0	2	0	4	396	48	286	62	1
Groton	9,051	23	0	5	1	17	110	25	79	6	1
Groton Long Point	510	0	0	0	0	0	1	0	1	0	0
Groton Town	29,372	37	0	8	2	27	383	23	341	19	2
Guilford	22,268	11	0	3	0	8	320	32	271	17	0
Hamden	61,234	205	1	3	51	150	1,168	134	911	123	4
Hartford	123,117	1,313	21	53	355	884	4,435	605	3,089	741	70
Ledyard	14,808	8	0	1	2	5	52	8	43	1	0
Madison	18,184	0	0	0	0	0	111	14	87	10	0
Manchester	57,884	101	0	21	36	44	1,275	103	1,039	133	0
Meriden	59,792	215	1	15	60	139	1,216	191	860	165	5
Middlebury	7,746	3	0	0	2	1	70	8	50	12	0
Middletown	46,314	36	1	3	8	24	584	78	431	75	0
Milford	54,754	37	0	1	25	11	1,119	193	846	80	0
Monroe	19,653	10	0	5	4	1	105	11	85	9	0
Naugatuck	31,400	26	0	8	4	14	502	48	406	48	3
New Britain	72,630	310	1	30	84	195	2,014	223	1,372	419	16
New Canaan	20,461	0	0	0	0	0	101	12	79	10	0
New Haven	131,181	1,105	10	60	320	715	5,111	749	3,688	674	18
Newington	30,382	21	0	7	6	8	780	48	662	70	1
New London	26,995	122	2	30	39	51	568	113	388	67	3
New Milford	26,956	20	2	5	1	12	263	5	246	12	2
Newtown	28,015	6	0	1	2	3	122	11	96	15	0
North Branford	14,179	9	0	5	0	4	146	18	111	17	0
North Haven	23,703	13	0	3	4	6	524	95	393	36	1
Norwalk	89,442	252	1	13	49	189	1,347	147	1,082	118	5
Norwich[4]	39,318	108	0	35	27	46	498	93	362	43	8
Old Saybrook	10,117	5	0	1	0	4	48	5	42	1	0
Orange	14,002	7	0	2	4	1	465	52	376	37	0
Plainfield	15,049	22	0	6	2	14	74	6	53	15	0
Plainville[4]	17,701	34	1	3	3	27	509	50	424	35	1

Table 8. Offenses Known to Law Enforcement, by Selected State and City, 2018—Continued

(Number.)

State/city	Population	Violent crime	Murder and nonnegligent manslaughter	Rape[1]	Robbery	Aggravated assault	Property crime	Burglary	Larceny-theft	Motor vehicle theft	Arson[2]
Plymouth	11,646	11	0	2	4	5	151	13	120	18	0
Portland	9,340	7	0	0	0	7	60	11	40	9	0
Putnam	9,325	27	0	7	1	19	99	21	74	4	1
Redding	9,242	2	0	1	0	1	28	5	21	2	0
Ridgefield	25,260	1	0	0	1	0	64	3	53	8	0
Rocky Hill	20,163	6	0	5	1	0	265	29	206	30	0
Seymour	16,589	10	0	2	5	3	153	14	113	26	0
Shelton	41,657	23	0	8	7	8	286	67	185	34	2
Simsbury	25,164	5	0	0	2	3	150	21	112	17	0
Southington	43,960	32	1	13	9	9	734	86	590	58	1
South Windsor	25,968	14	0	4	2	8	358	64	267	27	0
Stamford	132,007	218	3	21	64	130	2,120	228	1,655	237	5
Stonington	18,602	13	0	4	1	8	164	26	134	4	1
Stratford	52,472	53	0	6	21	26	1,080	132	833	115	2
Suffield	15,688	2	0	1	0	1	77	32	38	7	0
Thomaston	7,563	11	0	5	2	4	81	16	57	8	0
Torrington	34,286	46	0	6	12	28	564	85	448	31	0
Trumbull	36,167	46	0	10	18	18	850	79	721	50	1
Vernon	29,304	21	0	7	8	6	367	75	263	29	0
Wallingford	44,680	30	0	1	1	28	597	123	439	35	0
Waterbury	108,378	481	9	58	200	214	4,252	546	2,868	838	17
Waterford	18,937	11	0	3	0	8	329	8	319	2	0
Watertown	21,631	21	1	1	11	8	491	63	383	45	0
West Hartford	63,085	45	1	2	41	1	1,742	195	1,409	138	1
West Haven	54,738	105	1	23	38	43	1,175	120	915	140	0
Weston	10,351	0	0	0	0	0	27	0	25	2	0
Westport	28,278	3	0	1	0	2	241	22	208	11	0
Wethersfield	26,127	23	0	6	10	7	384	62	255	67	1
Willimantic	17,691	29	0	9	11	9	136	25	90	21	3
Wilton	18,654	5	0	2	0	3	154	16	127	11	0
Winchester	10,669	8	0	7	1	0	97	21	67	9	0
Windsor	28,867	27	0	4	18	5	783	51	688	44	1
Windsor Locks	12,560	10	1	2	5	2	171	43	108	20	0
Wolcott	16,666	8	0	2	5	1	240	55	146	39	0
Woodbridge	8,832	2	1	0	1	0	148	11	116	21	1
DELAWARE											
Bethany Beach	1,224	1	0	0	0	1	64	3	61	0	0
Blades	1,444	1	0	0	1	0	23	6	16	1	0
Bridgeville	2,368	4	0	0	1	3	33	3	28	2	0
Camden	3,497	12	0	0	3	9	145	4	139	2	1
Cheswold	1,596	3	0	0	1	2	22	1	20	1	0
Clayton	3,297	16	0	1	1	14	29	6	20	3	0
Dagsboro	902	0	0	0	0	0	27	2	24	1	0
Delaware City	1,835	10	0	1	0	9	30	3	27	0	0
Delmar	1,810	6	0	2	2	2	52	24	27	1	1
Dewey Beach	388	7	0	1	0	6	24	4	20	0	0
Dover	37,778	301	4	20	43	234	1,810	58	1,663	89	3
Ellendale	439	2	0	0	0	2	8	0	7	1	0
Elsmere	6,033	25	0	2	6	17	95	32	48	15	0
Felton	1,414	3	0	0	0	3	25	2	22	1	0
Georgetown	7,419	39	0	5	9	25	378	43	323	12	1
Greenwood	1,116	4	0	3	0	1	16	5	10	1	0
Harrington	3,659	41	0	4	6	31	105	21	78	6	0
Laurel	4,394	43	0	2	10	31	180	33	144	3	0
Lewes	3,134	7	0	0	0	7	65	15	49	1	0
Middletown	22,350	64	1	4	15	44	437	44	386	7	0
Milford	11,301	85	0	5	16	64	565	48	499	18	0
Millsboro	4,439	11	0	5	1	5	179	13	161	5	0
Milton	2,966	0	0	0	0	0	47	16	30	1	0
Newark	34,207	100	0	21	20	59	667	58	576	33	0
New Castle	5,351	17	0	1	6	10	224	24	184	16	0
Newport	1,038	5	0	0	3	2	23	3	18	2	0
Ocean View	2,146	2	0	0	0	2	24	7	17	0	0
Rehoboth Beach	1,522	9	0	1	2	6	146	13	131	2	0
Seaford	7,876	64	0	7	18	39	420	65	349	6	1
Selbyville	2,494	9	0	0	2	7	56	13	40	3	0
Smyrna	11,791	50	0	7	8	35	268	45	205	18	0
South Bethany	519	0	0	0	0	0	7	0	7	0	0
Wilmington	71,157	1,099	23	14	358	704	3,502	567	2,483	452	4
Wyoming	1,531	5	0	0	1	4	13	4	8	1	0
DISTRICT OF COLUMBIA											
Washington	702,455	6,613	160	445	2,157	3,851	29,993	1,786	25,658	2,549	
FLORIDA											
Alachua	10,123	54	2	1	6	45	263	37	204	22	2
Altamonte Springs	44,664	136	0	21	37	78	1,446	142	1,211	93	5
Apalachicola	2,306	5	0	0	0	5	22	6	16	0	0
Apopka	53,106	218	0	30	51	137	1,508	303	1,106	99	3
Arcadia	8,082	46	0	1	5	40	151	69	70	12	0
Atlantic Beach	13,750	30	0	3	5	22	246	27	206	13	0
Atlantis	2,151	5	0	2	0	3	44	5	36	3	1

Table 8. Offenses Known to Law Enforcement, by Selected State and City, 2018—Continued

(Number.)

State/city	Population	Violent crime	Murder and nonnegligent manslaughter	Rape[1]	Robbery	Aggravated assault	Property crime	Burglary	Larceny-theft	Motor vehicle theft	Arson[2]
Auburndale	16,358	36	0	6	9	21	578	90	463	25	0
Aventura	38,544	82	1	6	41	34	1,963	71	1,822	70	0
Bal Harbour Village	3,116	3	0	1	0	2	73	2	70	1	0
Bartow	19,954	114	0	10	20	84	756	132	581	43	2
Bay Harbor Islands	6,074	3	0	0	1	2	87	3	75	9	0
Belleair	4,121	1	0	0	0	1	74	14	52	8	0
Belleair Beach	1,617	1	0	0	0	1	17	3	12	2	0
Belleair Bluffs	2,123	1	0	0	1	0	28	5	23	0	0
Belle Glade	19,877	206	2	13	44	147	787	134	582	71	6
Belle Isle	7,151	9	0	0	5	4	78	20	44	14	0
Belleview	5,026	24	1	4	6	13	247	73	160	14	0
Biscayne Park	3,199	5	0	0	0	5	65	18	45	2	0
Blountstown	2,446	14	0	0	1	13	40	7	31	2	0
Boca Raton	100,162	205	2	28	80	95	2,361	277	1,894	190	5
Bonifay	2,712	7	0	0	0	7	22	17	5	0	5
Bowling Green	2,918	6	1	0	0	5	63	23	36	4	0
Boynton Beach	79,142	477	4	21	134	318	2,964	256	2,423	285	1
Bradenton	57,647	388	1	30	76	281	1,564	227	1,258	79	7
Bradenton Beach	1,284	2	0	0	0	2	47	5	41	1	0
Bunnell	2,939	43	0	1	3	39	95	25	63	7	0
Cape Coral	187,869	267	3	17	51	196	2,701	413	2,110	178	2
Casselberry	28,744	152	3	18	31	100	946	120	770	56	3
Center Hill	1,435	3	0	0	0	3	9	1	5	3	0
Chattahoochee	3,039	15	0	3	2	10	72	13	34	25	0
Chiefland	2,172	4	0	0	0	4	188	92	93	3	0
Chipley	3,516	10	0	1	0	9	78	8	70	0	0
Clearwater	116,504	510	6	95	105	304	3,087	345	2,564	178	5
Clermont	36,233	58	1	9	10	38	723	93	605	25	2
Clewiston	7,807	37	1	2	10	24	193	64	126	3	1
Cocoa	18,739	141	6	5	53	77	1,021	157	804	60	7
Cocoa Beach	11,807	41	0	4	8	29	407	25	354	28	0
Coconut Creek	62,237	89	1	13	16	59	1,027	99	826	102	1
Cooper City	36,896	36	0	10	9	17	433	50	353	30	0
Coral Gables	51,716	68	1	14	20	33	1,225	128	1,035	62	2
Coral Springs	134,640	209	1	35	55	118	2,027	195	1,684	148	1
Crescent City	1,540	7	0	2	1	4	123	58	54	11	0
Crestview	24,293	86	1	14	21	50	702	137	516	49	1
Cross City	1,714	3	0	0	0	3	26	6	19	1	0
Cutler Bay	45,807	97	1	6	33	57	1,278	84	1,113	81	1
Dade City	7,238	37	0	6	5	26	225	35	186	4	1
Dania Beach	32,376	209	2	15	62	130	1,210	163	889	158	1
Davenport	4,849	6	0	0	0	6	72	26	42	4	0
Davie	107,120	270	0	24	63	183	2,763	238	2,233	292	2
Daytona Beach	69,030	764	8	17	91	648	3,358	384	2,750	224	7
Daytona Beach Shores	4,549	9	0	3	3	3	157	18	128	11	0
Deerfield Beach	81,371	329	3	21	110	195	2,490	422	1,737	331	7
DeFuniak Springs	6,646	17	0	2	0	15	94	11	79	4	0
DeLand	33,384	182	2	2	43	135	1,256	185	993	78	3
Delray Beach	69,970	409	6	27	84	292	2,522	279	2,038	205	3
Doral	63,680	77	2	14	12	49	1,464	108	1,235	121	0
Dunedin	36,723	52	1	15	6	30	652	66	554	32	0
Dunnellon	1,808	5	0	0	2	3	88	19	69	0	0
Eatonville	2,289	45	1	2	2	40	129	28	87	14	2
Edgewater	22,643	25	0	1	5	19	410	65	306	39	3
Edgewood	2,996	4	0	0	1	3	66	12	49	5	0
El Portal	2,503	3	0	0	0	3	49	15	29	5	0
Eustis	21,182	39	4	2	21	12	522	101	374	47	1
Fellsmere	5,803	14	0	0	4	10	60	5	49	6	0
Fernandina Beach	12,411	19	0	7	1	11	280	30	229	21	1
Flagler Beach	5,152	3	0	0	0	3	79	14	58	7	0
Florida City	12,284	375	10	8	99	258	875	94	727	54	0
Fort Lauderdale	182,150	1,006	20	73	350	563	9,050	1,366	6,814	870	12
Fort Myers	82,805	582	11	53	146	372	2,285	376	1,652	257	5
Fort Pierce	46,109	283	7	23	66	187	1,184	197	872	115	6
Fort Walton Beach	22,263	69	1	13	7	48	655	82	515	58	2
Fruitland Park	9,093	23	1	0	1	21	181	77	103	1	0
Gainesville	133,400	989	5	169	222	593	5,229	510	4,287	432	6
Golden Beach	972	0	0	0	0	0	16	6	7	3	0
Graceville	2,188	4	0	0	0	4	29	14	14	1	0
Greenacres City	41,174	159	2	18	26	113	836	89	678	69	1
Green Cove Springs	8,130	32	0	5	3	24	180	34	140	6	2
Groveland	14,342	24	0	10	4	10	190	49	129	12	0
Gulf Breeze	6,642	8	0	3	1	4	89	5	82	2	0
Gulfport	12,424	15	0	2	3	10	398	47	319	32	1
Gulf Stream	888	0	0	0	0	0	3	1	2	0	0
Haines City	24,887	36	1	3	12	20	528	71	424	33	0
Hallandale Beach	40,222	217	1	23	64	129	1,296	140	1,032	124	3
Havana	1,659	4	0	0	0	4	25	4	14	7	0
Hialeah	241,778	533	2	35	149	347	5,355	407	4,239	709	5
Hialeah Gardens	24,510	30	0	4	2	24	517	39	395	83	1
Highland Beach	3,838	3	1	0	0	2	24	1	19	4	0
High Springs	6,147	13	0	2	1	10	82	19	62	1	0
Hillsboro Beach	2,038	2	0	0	1	1	16	4	11	1	0

Table 8. Offenses Known to Law Enforcement, by Selected State and City, 2018—Continued

(Number.)

State/city	Population	Violent crime	Murder and nonnegligent manslaughter	Rape[1]	Robbery	Aggravated assault	Property crime	Burglary	Larceny-theft	Motor vehicle theft	Arson[2]
Holly Hill	12,302	63	0	3	9	51	495	90	357	48	0
Hollywood	155,503	363	5	37	109	212	4,343	520	3,253	570	5
Holmes Beach	4,325	3	0	0	0	3	46	11	33	2	0
Homestead	71,314	714	4	42	260	408	2,282	280	1,841	161	3
Howey-in-the-Hills	1,176	1	0	1	0	0	13	4	9	0	0
Hypoluxo	2,799	3	0	1	1	1	56	8	40	8	0
Indialantic	2,920	2	0	0	1	1	39	5	34	0	1
Indian Creek Village	93	0	0	0	0	0	0	0	0	0	0
Indian Harbour Beach	8,617	2	0	0	2	0	93	14	79	0	1
Indian River Shores	4,280	0	0	0	0	0	21	7	10	4	0
Indian Rocks Beach	4,308	6	0	1	0	5	87	10	70	7	0
Indian Shores	3,809	6	0	1	0	5	30	2	25	3	0
Jacksonville	903,213	5,381	110	535	1,323	3,413	30,112	4,909	22,262	2,941	76
Jacksonville Beach	23,842	143	1	18	36	88	915	67	786	62	0
Jasper	3,894	4	0	0	4	0	81	11	62	8	0
Jennings	872	1	0	0	0	1	11	4	5	2	0
Juno Beach	3,682	5	0	0	2	3	46	6	40	0	0
Jupiter	66,457	132	0	15	31	86	959	84	814	61	1
Jupiter Inlet Colony	459	0	0	0	0	0	1	0	1	0	0
Jupiter Island	922	1	0	0	1	0	7	1	6	0	0
Kenneth City	5,111	10	0	1	2	7	143	23	117	3	1
Key Biscayne	13,299	5	0	0	1	4	90	12	68	10	0
Key Colony Beach	837	0	0	0	0	0	13	3	10	0	0
Key West	25,286	100	0	18	10	72	808	74	652	82	2
Kissimmee	72,894	288	3	26	58	201	1,839	285	1,419	135	7
Lady Lake	15,517	16	0	0	2	14	227	27	178	22	0
Lake Alfred	6,084	9	0	0	1	8	91	29	59	3	0
Lake City	12,182	148	1	15	22	110	858	133	697	28	1
Lake Clarke Shores	3,632	7	0	0	1	6	50	13	35	2	0
Lake Hamilton	1,418	10	0	0	4	6	50	15	31	4	1
Lake Helen	2,802	7	0	0	2	5	16	3	13	0	0
Lakeland	109,616	361	8	47	106	200	3,417	477	2,737	203	0
Lake Mary	16,896	36	0	7	4	25	270	46	211	13	2
Lake Park	8,716	75	2	3	28	42	825	84	685	56	0
Lake Placid	2,282	14	0	1	3	10	109	17	91	1	1
Lake Wales	16,349	57	0	12	7	38	369	30	315	24	2
Lake Worth	38,577	369	4	39	134	192	1,153	242	784	127	8
Lantana	12,006	91	0	12	25	54	612	29	534	49	1
Largo	85,568	322	3	66	72	181	2,593	282	2,126	185	16
Lauderdale-by-the-Sea	6,615	15	0	1	8	6	120	17	91	12	0
Lauderdale Lakes	36,575	312	2	21	92	197	1,209	154	890	165	1
Lauderhill	72,694	551	13	54	134	350	2,313	394	1,651	268	6
Lawtey	722	2	0	0	0	2	2	1	1	0	0
Leesburg	23,029	175	1	23	31	120	1,214	186	942	86	1
Lighthouse Point	11,372	12	0	1	4	7	173	14	149	10	0
Live Oak	6,902	38	0	0	8	30	116	58	52	6	0
Longboat Key	7,351	2	0	1	1	0	54	2	51	1	0
Longwood	15,273	46	1	4	6	35	441	75	342	24	2
Lynn Haven	21,285	28	1	5	0	22	202	39	150	13	0
Madeira Beach	4,427	26	0	4	1	21	140	7	123	10	0
Madison	2,775	1	0	0	0	1	15	5	10	0	0
Maitland	17,846	37	0	4	4	29	303	67	215	21	1
Manalapan	469	1	0	1	0	0	15	0	10	5	0
Mangonia Park	2,026	45	0	7	16	22	196	14	166	16	0
Marco Island	18,122	6	0	0	1	5	98	11	82	5	0
Margate	59,186	98	1	4	37	56	997	103	793	101	1
Marianna	7,251	85	3	9	6	67	133	51	80	2	1
Mascotte	5,693	37	1	0	4	32	91	16	62	13	1
Medley	898	17	0	0	4	13	203	26	142	35	0
Melbourne	82,844	601	5	65	101	430	2,941	440	2,357	144	13
Melbourne Beach	3,304	1	0	0	0	1	15	4	11	0	0
Melbourne Village	703	0	0	0	0	0	23	0	23	0	0
Mexico Beach	1,217	4	0	1	0	3	28	2	24	2	1
Miami	473,047	2,978	46	131	828	1,973	16,837	2,057	13,136	1,644	56
Miami Beach	92,928	871	5	96	279	491	6,947	646	5,902	399	11
Miami Gardens	114,670	816	24	17	228	547	4,530	456	3,608	466	16
Miami Lakes	31,323	33	3	4	10	16	653	44	518	91	0
Miami Shores	10,673	34	1	2	16	15	523	59	421	43	0
Miami Springs	14,508	48	1	3	11	33	446	65	334	47	0
Midway	3,368	1	0	1	0	0	16	0	15	1	0
Milton	10,158	18	0	5	4	9	195	64	119	12	0
Minneola	11,859	19	0	3	3	13	114	22	83	9	0
Miramar	143,103	337	6	39	84	208	2,128	208	1,644	276	5
Monticello	2,380	7	1	0	1	5	49	29	19	1	0
Mount Dora	14,179	67	0	7	11	49	548	82	465	1	0
Naples	22,308	9	0	0	2	7	320	19	277	24	0
Neptune Beach	7,317	13	0	0	3	10	108	14	86	8	0
New Port Richey	16,459	160	0	10	25	125	599	112	455	32	0
New Smyrna Beach	26,937	96	1	2	9	84	684	132	492	60	1
Niceville	15,621	23	0	0	2	21	187	19	162	6	0
North Bay Village	8,499	11	0	0	2	9	123	12	91	20	0
North Lauderdale	44,650	246	1	17	50	178	805	120	591	94	1
North Miami	62,585	524	3	26	158	337	2,329	331	1,727	271	7

Table 8. Offenses Known to Law Enforcement, by Selected State and City, 2018—Continued

(Number.)

State/city	Population	Violent crime	Murder and nonnegligent manslaughter	Rape[1]	Robbery	Aggravated assault	Property crime	Burglary	Larceny-theft	Motor vehicle theft	Arson[2]
North Miami Beach	44,485	323	6	23	115	179	1,683	257	1,318	108	2
North Palm Beach	13,214	12	0	0	5	7	105	12	79	14	0
North Port	67,682	117	4	34	18	61	1,186	132	1,026	28	0
North Redington Beach	1,486	0	0	0	0	0	14	1	12	1	0
Oakland	3,066	8	0	1	2	5	56	16	30	10	0
Oakland Park	45,564	277	1	18	92	166	1,606	261	1,157	188	1
Ocala	59,505	405	7	58	106	234	2,871	406	2,286	179	19
Ocean Ridge	1,966	3	0	0	0	3	27	6	13	8	0
Ocoee	48,128	162	2	12	39	109	1,430	265	1,098	67	3
Okeechobee	5,740	21	0	2	10	9	244	30	202	12	0
Oldsmar	14,763	31	0	7	5	19	336	17	306	13	0
Opa Locka	16,663	391	8	7	88	288	880	169	574	137	0
Orange City	11,805	45	1	8	13	23	782	79	672	31	1
Orange Park	8,750	23	1	4	4	14	179	26	142	11	0
Orlando	286,679	2,282	39	200	628	1,415	13,803	1,619	10,965	1,219	13
Ormond Beach	43,315	131	0	12	16	103	1,367	184	1,088	95	0
Oviedo	41,937	66	0	23	10	33	374	68	293	13	2
Pahokee	6,305	49	4	4	7	34	174	40	120	14	1
Palatka	10,365	110	3	3	14	90	630	64	542	24	0
Palm Bay	112,902	404	9	64	43	288	2,109	402	1,583	124	7
Palm Beach	8,837	13	0	1	2	10	98	11	77	10	0
Palm Beach Gardens	55,999	83	2	14	25	42	1,409	125	1,210	74	1
Palm Beach Shores	1,260	6	0	0	1	5	58	32	24	2	0
Palmetto	13,807	72	0	6	5	61	439	63	351	25	1
Palmetto Bay	24,890	42	0	5	12	25	711	85	607	19	2
Palm Springs	25,146	126	0	6	41	79	981	113	780	88	3
Panama City	37,318	234	2	4	45	183	2,150	423	1,467	260	3
Panama City Beach	12,935	110	2	20	21	67	960	90	866	4	1
Parker	4,614	15	0	2	2	11	145	32	103	10	1
Parkland	33,760	38	17	1	2	18	240	19	180	41	0
Pembroke Park	6,674	54	1	0	23	30	282	39	217	26	1
Pembroke Pines	173,053	314	1	26	74	213	3,333	232	2,861	240	2
Pensacola	52,672	285	1	36	56	192	2,012	261	1,646	105	3
Perry	6,926	90	3	2	4	81	258	71	175	12	1
Pinellas Park	53,383	224	3	41	57	123	2,423	247	2,037	139	8
Plantation	95,204	239	1	15	83	140	2,706	265	2,172	269	2
Plant City	39,305	186	0	13	26	147	1,198	130	958	110	4
Pompano Beach	112,045	876	6	91	312	467	4,307	608	3,121	578	5
Ponce Inlet	3,272	8	0	1	0	7	61	10	42	9	0
Port Orange	64,208	25	1	1	6	17	1,397	166	1,166	65	1
Port Richey	2,855	15	0	1	7	7	193	18	165	10	0
Port St. Joe	3,593	8	0	0	0	8	22	8	13	1	0
Port St. Lucie	193,137	218	2	26	31	159	1,851	256	1,523	72	4
Punta Gorda	20,170	11	0	1	2	8	330	28	290	12	0
Quincy	7,476	74	4	3	14	53	273	104	153	16	5
Redington Beaches	1,487	1	0	0	0	1	15	0	14	1	0
Riviera Beach	34,991	413	9	18	65	321	1,333	212	970	151	3
Rockledge	27,852	61	0	7	6	48	408	72	309	27	1
Royal Palm Beach	39,253	61	2	7	9	43	759	24	690	45	1
Safety Harbor	17,985	24	0	7	2	15	227	25	190	12	1
Sanford	60,154	421	5	57	83	276	2,133	356	1,661	116	2
Sanibel	7,498	2	0	2	0	0	69	11	58	0	0
Sarasota	57,718	337	3	22	82	230	1,877	301	1,442	134	11
Satellite Beach	11,197	3	0	0	0	3	41	12	27	2	0
Sea Ranch Lakes	749	0	0	0	0	0	10	0	10	0	0
Sebastian	25,672	31	0	4	3	24	279	35	232	12	1
Sebring	10,741	80	0	6	6	68	431	95	326	10	2
Seminole	18,795	24	0	5	8	11	604	31	544	29	2
Sewall's Point	2,221	0	0	0	0	0	5	0	5	0	0
South Bay	5,198	21	1	0	9	11	87	20	54	13	1
South Daytona	13,038	56	0	1	9	46	319	81	200	38	1
South Miami	12,365	41	0	3	13	25	487	91	375	21	2
South Palm Beach	1,453	0	0	0	0	0	2	1	1	0	0
South Pasadena	5,141	7	0	0	1	6	120	5	115	0	0
Southwest Ranches	8,046	3	0	0	0	3	128	8	103	17	0
Springfield	9,514	37	0	4	6	27	283	70	182	31	1
Starke	5,361	44	0	0	6	38	149	15	124	10	0
St. Augustine	14,427	93	0	14	14	65	571	67	476	28	1
St. Augustine Beach	7,120	18	0	1	1	16	114	19	93	2	0
St. Cloud	53,560	76	0	16	10	50	666	123	504	39	5
St. Pete Beach	9,693	23	0	5	5	13	281	17	250	14	0
St. Petersburg	265,942	1,660	21	133	368	1,138	8,784	1,206	6,832	746	27
Stuart	16,689	50	0	6	6	38	493	56	428	9	1
Sunny Isles Beach	22,563	34	0	6	10	18	302	27	245	30	0
Sunrise	95,812	186	2	21	57	106	2,350	187	1,998	165	1
Surfside	5,878	6	0	1	0	5	102	10	88	4	0
Sweetwater	21,181	17	0	0	8	9	341	18	297	26	0
Tallahassee	192,443	1,404	16	213	307	868	8,695	1,379	6,549	767	6
Tamarac	66,454	206	3	24	54	125	1,239	145	985	109	1
Tampa	392,945	1,598	27	100	332	1,139	6,576	1,047	5,069	460	41
Tarpon Springs	25,603	51	2	10	4	35	530	43	462	25	3
Tavares	17,318	48	1	7	8	32	250	95	152	3	0
Temple Terrace	26,777	67	0	10	16	41	571	103	430	38	0

Table 8. Offenses Known to Law Enforcement, by Selected State and City, 2018—Continued

(Number.)

State/city	Population	Violent crime	Murder and nonnegligent manslaughter	Rape[1]	Robbery	Aggravated assault	Property crime	Burglary	Larceny-theft	Motor vehicle theft	Arson[2]
Tequesta	6,161	2	0	0	0	2	35	14	19	2	0
Titusville	46,650	289	3	24	45	217	1,397	322	918	157	5
Treasure Island	6,972	11	0	2	2	7	179	19	150	10	0
Trenton	2,106	6	2	1	1	2	24	7	16	1	0
Umatilla	3,786	5	0	1	0	4	94	22	67	5	0
Valparaiso	4,936	8	0	0	0	8	44	22	17	5	0
Venice	23,362	25	0	1	2	22	323	38	269	16	0
Vero Beach	17,172	34	3	7	8	16	415	71	332	12	0
Village of Pinecrest	19,854	26	0	1	12	13	473	39	409	25	0
Virginia Gardens	2,486	3	0	0	0	3	31	4	23	4	0
Wauchula	4,927	12	0	2	1	9	166	48	107	11	0
Welaka	701	1	0	0	0	1	15	3	12	0	0
Wellington	66,080	81	0	10	17	54	832	44	709	79	1
West Melbourne	22,665	27	2	1	3	21	550	53	467	30	0
West Miami	8,486	11	0	0	4	7	78	22	43	13	0
Weston	71,744	41	1	10	8	22	374	49	277	48	1
West Palm Beach	111,659	1,026	27	77	354	568	4,249	578	3,290	381	20
West Park	15,297	109	2	4	28	75	490	59	361	70	3
White Springs	768	6	0	1	1	4	21	4	15	2	0
Wildwood	7,120	33	1	5	3	24	222	78	130	14	1
Williston	2,702	20	0	2	6	12	110	14	88	8	0
Wilton Manors	12,941	54	0	1	14	39	427	53	354	20	3
Windermere	3,478	2	0	0	0	2	32	15	16	1	0
Winter Garden	44,921	155	0	13	31	111	1,018	171	791	56	1
Winter Haven	42,268	236	0	31	27	178	1,032	148	797	87	7
Winter Park	31,323	60	0	13	12	35	767	120	599	48	7
Winter Springs	37,137	57	1	13	6	37	274	56	199	19	0
Zephyrhills	15,504	47	0	10	7	30	612	66	526	20	3
GEORGIA											
Abbeville	2,772	0	0	0	0	0	8	1	7	0	0
Acworth	23,028	24	1	5	4	14	503	33	449	21	0
Adairsville[4]	4,879	8	0	1	2	5	110	17	76	17	0
Alamo	3,408	1	0	0	0	1	18	4	14	0	0
Alapaha	667	1	0	0	0	1	5	1	4	0	
Albany	72,594	809	15	28	113	653	3,704	760	2,666	278	26
Alma[4]	3,486	25	1	0	3	21	198	65	123	10	1
Alpharetta	67,051	42	1	10	16	15	1,204	103	1,060	41	2
Alto	1,178	0	0	0	0	0	15	3	11	1	0
Americus	15,184	130	2	4	37	87	921	151	736	34	3
Aragon	1,249	0	0	0	0	0	0	0	0	0	0
Arcade	1,905	9	0	1	0	8	59	16	39	4	0
Arlington	1,375	5	0	0	1	4	32	7	20	5	0
Ashburn	3,623	32	1	0	7	24	107	16	84	7	2
Atlanta	496,106	3,814	88	245	1,099	2,382	23,091	3,082	16,701	3,308	90
Attapulgus	429	0	0	0	0	0	0	0	0	0	0
Auburn	7,706	7	0	0	0	7	134	13	106	15	0
Austell	7,301	52	0	0	8	44	168	25	125	18	
Avondale Estates	3,205	5	0	2	3	0	70	10	58	2	0
Bainbridge	12,033	91	0	7	15	69	456	93	346	17	2
Ball Ground	2,147	0	0	0	0	0	13	0	12	1	0
Baxley	4,718	73	1	3	8	61	388	67	293	28	0
Blackshear	3,526	32	0	2	0	30	193	51	137	5	0
Blairsville	610	0	0	0	0	0	6	0	6	0	0
Blakely	4,603	41	0	3	0	38	99	29	67	3	0
Bloomingdale	2,767	4	0	0	0	4	51	5	44	2	0
Blue Ridge	1,418	4	0	0	0	4	29	4	23	2	0
Blythe	704	0	0	0	0	0	0	0	0	0	0
Bowdon	2,107	8	0	0	1	7	48	7	37	4	0
Braselton[4]	11,537	1	0	0	0	1	65	6	52	7	0
Braswell	384	0	0	0	0	0	0	0	0	0	0
Bremen	6,456	10	1	0	1	8	362	38	315	9	0
Brookhaven	54,138	187	1	13	82	91	1,456	283	1,063	110	7
Brooklet	1,647	2	0	0	1	1	10	1	8	1	
Brunswick	16,431	175	2	4	42	127	862	176	627	59	5
Buchanan	1,166	9	0	0	0	9	39	2	35	2	0
Byron	5,258	2	0	0	1	1	153	27	115	11	0
Cairo	9,407	21	1	0	3	17	320	80	224	16	0
Camilla	5,016	19	0	1	2	16	179	40	129	10	0
Canon	831	0	0	0	0	0	2	0	2	0	0
Canton	28,685	34	0	4	6	24	668	39	596	33	0
Carrollton	27,189	160	1	19	26	114	1,122	129	951	42	2
Cave Spring	1,131	4	0	0	0	4	12	5	6	1	0
Cedartown	9,959	59	1	5	12	41	487	98	362	27	0
Centerville	7,795	31	0	0	5	26	342	26	301	15	0
Chatsworth	4,301	7	0	0	0	7	24	1	23	0	0
Chattahoochee Hills	2,982	5	0	2	0	3	50	9	40	1	0
Chickamauga	3,149	7	0	0	2	5	52	12	37	3	0
Clarkesville	1,843	8	0	0	0	8	37	13	23	1	0
Clarkston	12,957	63	1	7	33	22	415	108	257	50	1
Claxton	2,240	4	0	0	2	2	92	16	67	9	0
Clayton	2,264	9	0	3	0	6	69	12	53	4	0
Cleveland	3,956	8	0	1	0	7	212	17	194	1	0

Table 8. Offenses Known to Law Enforcement, by Selected State and City, 2018—Continued

(Number.)

State/city	Population	Violent crime	Murder and nonnegligent manslaughter	Rape[1]	Robbery	Aggravated assault	Property crime	Burglary	Larceny-theft	Motor vehicle theft	Arson[2]
Cochran	4,882	11	0	1	0	10	153	15	134	4	0
College Park	15,034	156	0	6	51	99	1,035	142	686	207	4
Colquitt	1,863	12	0	1	0	11	60	22	38	0	0
Commerce	6,927	28	0	1	3	24	137	17	100	20	0
Coolidge	524	0	0	0	0	0	1	1	0	0	0
Cordele	10,669	64	2	9	3	50	561	147	402	12	0
Cornelia	4,278	17	0	0	0	17	169	25	143	1	1
Covington	14,178	51	0	9	16	26	666	78	525	63	0
Cuthbert	3,585	1	0	0	1	0	48	16	32	0	0
Dallas	13,496	37	0	0	13	24	303	59	217	27	0
Dalton	33,831	93	0	11	21	61	987	119	787	81	2
Danielsville	587	0	0	0	0	0	16	3	12	1	0
Darien	1,836	2	0	0	1	1	72	19	49	4	0
Davisboro	1,704	0	0	0	0	0	2	0	2	0	0
Dawson	4,103	18	0	0	6	12	115	23	87	5	0
Decatur	24,491	41	3	2	19	17	576	61	476	39	1
Demorest	1,951	1	0	1	0	0	21	6	14	1	0
Dillard	369	1	0	0	0	1	4	1	3	0	0
Doerun	753	0	0	0	0	0	9	3	6	0	0
Donalsonville	2,524	2	0	0	0	2	53	9	44	0	0
Doraville	10,625	53	0	1	32	20	637	73	487	77	0
Douglasville	34,076	193	0	9	41	143	1,841	138	1,612	91	6
Dublin	15,756	127	5	5	25	92	774	151	584	39	0
Duluth	29,882	20	0	2	9	9	537	75	437	25	1
Dunwoody	50,095	79	1	6	34	38	2,032	155	1,786	91	0
East Ellijay	573	6	0	0	2	4	142	5	130	7	
Eastman	5,038	42	0	7	9	26	435	71	356	8	0
East Point	35,486	441	5	23	175	238	4,260	531	3,145	584	0
Eatonton	6,614	34	0	1	5	28	180	46	127	7	0
Edison	1,459	0	0	0	0	0	4	2	2	0	0
Elberton[4]	4,300	39	0	2	4	33	219	44	170	5	0
Ellaville	1,874	10	0	0	1	9	14	3	11	0	0
Ellijay	1,733	5	0	3	0	2	59	5	51	3	0
Emerson	1,610	12	0	0	0	12	65	4	53	8	1
Eton	923	1	0	0	0	1	22	8	14	0	0
Fairburn	15,904	52	1	3	16	32	660	104	486	70	0
Fayetteville	18,042	29	0	7	14	8	467	30	410	27	0
Fitzgerald	8,673	43	0	2	15	26	458	78	365	15	0
Flowery Branch	7,760	22	0	0	0	22	92	13	78	1	0
Folkston	4,664	17	0	0	0	17	98	30	64	4	0
Forest Park	20,024	134	3	8	61	62	962	175	690	97	2
Forsyth	4,082	11	1	0	1	9	182	31	134	17	0
Fort Oglethorpe	9,912	35	0	1	3	31	539	26	473	40	0
Fort Valley	8,675	93	1	1	11	80	262	53	193	16	0
Franklin	953	0	0	0	0	0	20	1	17	2	0
Franklin Springs[4]	1,161	0	0	0	0	0	11	1	9	1	0
Gainesville	41,368	158	1	20	36	101	1,280	163	1,027	90	1
Glennville	5,083	4	1	0	1	2	83	25	56	2	0
Gordon	1,869	7	0	0	0	7	26	4	20	2	0
Graham	295	0	0	0	0	0	0	0	0	0	0
Grantville	3,250	8	0	4	1	3	58	10	44	4	0
Gray	3,188	6	0	1	0	5	38	6	32	0	0
Greensboro	3,354	20	0	0	3	17	84	12	67	5	0
Greenville	838	4	0	1	2	1	19	3	16	0	0
Griffin	22,707	261	1	16	34	210	1,080	213	825	42	2
Grovetown	14,543	14	1	1	3	9	186	55	123	8	0
Hagan	982	0	0	0	0	0	10	2	6	2	0
Hahira	2,988	5	0	0	0	5	86	11	72	3	0
Hampton	7,841	16	0	0	4	12	106	14	88	4	0
Hapeville	6,607	49	0	2	29	18	737	75	594	68	0
Harlem	3,214	8	0	0	5	3	32	11	21	0	0
Hartwell	4,468	30	0	0	2	28	210	17	188	5	0
Hazlehurst	4,143	17	0	1	0	16	183	38	139	6	0
Helen	547	3	0	1	0	2	45	5	38	2	0
Hiawassee	916	5	0	0	0	5	21	2	17	2	0
Hinesville	33,163	147	1	8	33	105	1,201	218	953	30	5
Hiram	4,046	10	0	2	2	6	287	16	259	12	16
Hoboken	529	0	0	0	0	0	0	0	0	0	0
Hogansville	3,116	5	0	0	2	3	134	20	108	6	0
Holly Springs	12,369	3	0	0	0	3	123	9	107	7	1
Homeland	909	0	0	0	0	0	0	0	0	0	0
Homerville[4]	2,394	15	0	0	1	14	104	27	70	7	0
Irwinton	548	0	0	0	0	0	0	0	0	0	0
Ivey	912	0	0	0	0	0	11	3	8	0	0
Jackson	5,101	18	0	1	5	12	172	23	141	8	0
Jacksonville	132	0	0	0	0	0	0	0	0	0	0
Jasper	3,896	11	0	2	1	8	236	18	210	8	0
Jefferson	11,394	12	0	1	2	9	151	21	121	9	0
Jesup	9,698	36	0	1	7	28	524	81	409	34	0
Johns Creek	85,446	34	1	4	12	17	532	90	427	15	2
Jonesboro	4,760	22	0	1	7	14	251	14	219	18	0
Kennesaw	34,907	57	0	16	11	30	428	41	354	33	0
Kingston	655	0	0	0	0	0	15	0	15	0	0

Table 8. Offenses Known to Law Enforcement, by Selected State and City, 2018—Continued

(Number.)

State/city	Population	Violent crime	Murder and nonnegligent manslaughter	Rape[1]	Robbery	Aggravated assault	Property crime	Burglary	Larceny-theft	Motor vehicle theft	Arson[2]
LaFayette	7,210	11	0	0	0	11	327	23	299	5	0
LaGrange	30,611	130	5	3	42	80	1,408	149	1,199	60	0
Lake City	2,838	14	1	0	7	6	139	17	112	10	0
Lake Park	909	2	0	0	0	2	13	1	12	0	0
Lavonia	2,163	20	0	1	4	15	101	13	79	9	0
Leary	577	0	0	0	0	0	0	0	0	0	0
Leslie	369	0	0	0	0	0	2	0	2	0	0
Lilburn	12,847	47	1	2	25	19	407	50	326	31	0
Locust Grove	6,852	13	2	3	2	6	405	31	360	14	0
Loganville	12,308	16	0	1	9	6	320	21	287	12	0
Lookout Mountain	1,565	0	0	0	0	0	19	5	14	0	0
Louisville	2,209	16	0	1	3	12	115	8	104	3	0
Ludowici	2,289	3	0	0	1	2	12	1	10	1	
Lumber City	1,247	0	0	0	0	0	9	1	8	0	0
Lumpkin	1,162	0	0	0	0	0	0	0	0	0	0
Lyons	4,284	10	0	1	0	9	33	15	18	0	0
Madison	4,098	11	0	1	3	7	134	21	111	2	0
Manchester	3,966	17	0	1	2	14	123	30	88	5	0
Marietta	61,675	214	3	27	74	110	1,948	228	1,554	166	4
Maysville	1,956	2	0	0	0	2	18	1	17	0	0
McDonough	25,151	37	1	7	7	22	662	64	560	38	0
McIntyre	602	1	0	0	0	1	10	5	5	0	0
Metter	3,981	7	0	1	3	3	112	27	82	3	1
Midville	258	0	0	0	0	0	0	0	0	0	0
Midway	2,026	1	0	0	0	1	54	7	43	4	0
Milledgeville	18,620	66	0	5	17	44	764	103	617	44	2
Millen	2,769	30	0	0	1	29	101	24	75	2	0
Milton	39,848	11	0	4	3	4	288	19	261	8	
Molena	372	0	0	0	0	0	0	0	0	0	0
Monroe	13,573	89	4	6	15	64	629	89	506	34	1
Montezuma	3,030	18	1	0	5	12	79	24	53	2	0
Morrow	7,632	34	0	0	23	11	760	33	671	56	0
Moultrie	14,136	73	2	8	24	39	707	88	585	34	0
Mountain City	1,076	0	0	0	0	0	0	0	0	0	0
Mount Airy	1,307	4	0	0	0	4	4	2	1	1	0
Mount Zion	1,811	2	0	0	0	2	9	3	6	0	1
Nahunta	1,065	0	0	0	0	0	7	0	6	1	0
Nashville	4,839	41	0	4	2	35	199	45	144	10	
Newnan	39,830	182	3	10	29	140	1,052	142	855	55	4
Newton	593	0	0	0	0	0	1	0	1	0	0
Norcross[4]	17,089	81	1	3	37	40	569	78	419	72	0
Norman Park	976	3	0	1	0	2	12	6	5	1	0
Oak Park	474	0	0	0	0	0	19	5	12	2	0
Oakwood	4,179	13	1	1	3	8	182	18	158	6	0
Ocilla	3,653	20	0	0	4	16	108	19	86	3	0
Oglethorpe	1,160	4	0	0	1	3	23	6	16	1	0
Omega	1,221	7	0	0	0	7	40	3	37	0	0
Oxford	2,250	4	0	0	1	3	26	2	18	6	0
Palmetto	4,752	11	0	0	0	11	92	23	54	15	0
Peachtree City	35,374	18	0	4	5	9	466	37	394	35	1
Pelham	3,511	31	3	0	5	23	119	50	62	7	0
Pembroke	2,581	5	1	0	1	3	45	11	33	1	0
Pine Lake	770	3	0	0	2	1	64	0	61	3	0
Pine Mountain	1,383	4	0	0	1	3	37	11	22	4	0
Plains	720	1	0	0	0	1	3	2	0	1	0
Pooler	24,656	24	0	3	11	10	758	52	636	70	0
Port Wentworth	9,105	31	1	6	4	20	120	14	89	17	
Powder Springs	15,214	33	0	0	2	31	285	24	240	21	0
Ray City	1,065	3	0	0	1	2	20	6	12	2	
Remerton	1,097	13	0	4	2	7	64	14	44	6	
Reynolds	991	0	0	0	0	0	2	1	1	0	0
Rincon	10,039	13	1	5	1	6	314	32	279	3	0
Ringgold	3,600	28	0	0	3	25	165	14	141	10	
Roberta	970	6	0	0	2	4	21	2	19	0	
Rochelle	1,104	1	0	0	1	0	41	12	29	0	0
Rockmart	4,281	38	0	4	6	28	339	93	234	12	0
Rossville	3,967	29	0	2	5	22	324	48	236	40	
Roswell	95,677	126	0	18	39	69	1,500	174	1,215	111	1
Sandersville	5,527	20	0	1	4	15	224	24	197	3	1
Sandy Springs	108,654	128	2	10	43	73	2,015	301	1,553	161	3
Sardis	967	0	0	0	0	0	22	5	16	1	
Savannah-Chatham Metropolitan	242,265	982	28	85	267	602	5,960	884	4,420	656	12
Senoia	4,352	1	0	0	0	1	33	4	29	0	0
Shiloh	476	0	0	0	0	0	0	0	0	0	0
Smyrna	57,498	117	0	6	38	73	1,459	146	1,117	196	
Snellville	19,947	64	1	0	8	55	795	38	717	40	
Social Circle	4,517	9	1	0	1	7	75	22	47	6	0
Sparks	2,012	10	0	1	2	7	87	23	62	2	0
Sparta	1,232	6	0	0	1	5	11	2	9	0	
Springfield	4,192	8	0	2	0	6	88	16	65	7	0
Statesboro	31,819	110	3	13	37	57	845	159	651	35	7
Statham	2,722	7	0	0	3	4	43	9	28	6	

Table 8. Offenses Known to Law Enforcement, by Selected State and City, 2018—Continued

(Number.)

State/city	Population	Violent crime	Murder and nonnegligent manslaughter	Rape[1]	Robbery	Aggravated assault	Property crime	Burglary	Larceny-theft	Motor vehicle theft	Arson[2]
Stone Mountain	6,447	33	1	0	9	23	177	43	121	13	
Summerville	4,275	0	0	0	0	0	44	0	40	4	0
Suwanee	20,227	29	0	10	7	12	523	50	452	21	1
Swainsboro	7,501	57	0	3	14	40	347	31	304	12	0
Sylvania	2,433	13	0	1	7	5	136	39	90	7	1
Talbotton	843	7	0	0	2	5	14	2	12	0	0
Tallapoosa	3,159	21	0	1	0	20	115	30	73	12	0
Temple	4,462	4	0	1	0	3	85	14	60	11	0
Tennille	1,977	8	1	1	0	6	28	0	24	4	
Thomaston	8,703	46	0	4	10	32	458	57	380	21	0
Thomasville	18,507	33	4	1	9	19	860	206	624	30	0
Thunderbolt	2,697	1	0	0	0	1	40	6	27	7	0
Toccoa	8,310	36	1	3	3	29	460	66	386	8	0
Toomsboro	426	1	0	0	0	1	2	2	0	0	
Trenton	2,224	6	0	0	1	5	55	5	46	4	
Tunnel Hill	873	0	0	0	0	0	16	3	13	0	0
Tybee Island	3,148	9	0	2	0	7	161	17	142	2	
Tyrone	7,390	1	0	0	0	1	108	14	89	5	
Uvalda	583	0	0	0	0	0	0	0	0	0	0
Vidalia	10,488	65	2	1	17	45	493	88	380	25	0
Vienna	3,663	18	2	3	2	11	74	14	60	0	0
Villa Rica	15,536	57	1	7	6	43	583	64	491	28	2
Wadley	1,896	11	0	0	1	10	47	25	19	3	
Warm Springs	399	0	0	0	0	0	0	0	0	0	0
Warner Robins	75,668	444	8	63	86	287	4,200	726	3,258	216	19
Warrenton	1,714	14	0	1	2	11	30	6	21	3	
Warwick	393	0	0	0	0	0	3	1	2	0	0
Waverly Hall	756	0	0	0	0	0	5	1	3	1	0
Waycross	13,771	71	3	8	20	40	770	117	627	26	2
Waynesboro	5,462	29	1	3	3	22	176	37	133	6	
West Point	3,766	24	1	0	5	18	175	40	125	10	0
Willacoochee	1,373	3	0	0	1	2	31	13	18	0	
Winterville	1,239	0	0	0	0	0	15	5	9	1	0
Woodstock	32,850	42	0	3	5	34	491	18	449	24	0
Wrens	1,974	16	0	0	3	13	53	23	29	1	
Zebulon	1,174	0	0	0	0	0	6	1	3	2	0
HAWAII											
Honolulu[4]	982,019	2,451	25	340	804	1,282	28,886	3,577	21,118	4,191	258
IDAHO											
Aberdeen	1,943	2	0	0	0	2	20	4	16	0	0
Bellevue	2,368	5	0	0	0	5	13	7	6	0	0
Blackfoot	11,910	40	0	5	0	35	315	108	187	20	1
Boise	229,265	635	1	173	51	410	4,627	638	3,725	264	40
Bonners Ferry	2,618	4	0	0	0	4	23	4	18	1	0
Buhl	4,399	15	0	2	0	13	82	21	58	3	1
Caldwell	55,936	183	0	9	11	163	1,202	239	829	134	6
Chubbuck	14,998	55	0	8	2	45	678	70	583	25	0
Coeur d'Alene	51,650	188	2	54	19	113	972	141	760	71	8
Cottonwood	926	0	0	0	0	0	3	0	3	0	0
Emmett	6,871	15	0	1	0	14	68	11	49	8	2
Filer	2,813	6	0	0	0	6	11	2	6	3	0
Fruitland	5,308	4	0	1	1	2	68	33	32	3	0
Garden City	12,025	82	0	11	6	65	354	74	254	26	9
Gooding	3,433	5	0	1	0	4	32	7	22	3	0
Grangeville	3,168	15	0	2	0	13	29	9	20	0	0
Hailey	8,334	14	0	0	0	14	21	7	10	4	0
Heyburn	3,364	3	0	1	0	2	24	3	20	1	0
Idaho Falls	61,643	206	0	43	12	151	960	282	597	81	5
Jerome	11,738	31	0	9	4	18	179	33	135	11	0
Kellogg	2,074	13	0	4	0	9	60	15	40	5	1
Ketchum	2,771	8	0	0	0	8	25	4	20	1	0
Kimberly	3,943	6	1	1	0	4	26	6	19	1	2
Lewiston	32,949	48	0	14	6	28	1,007	140	804	63	3
McCall	3,413	13	0	6	0	7	85	19	63	3	1
Meridian	103,774	165	2	42	14	107	1,260	171	1,041	48	10
Middleton	7,762	11	0	3	0	8	35	11	19	5	0
Montpelier	2,517	1	0	0	0	1	37	7	28	2	0
Moscow	25,339	13	0	4	0	9	394	55	328	11	1
Mountain Home	14,220	38	0	8	0	30	260	47	192	21	1
Nampa	95,386	268	5	80	11	172	2,424	439	1,730	255	9
Parma	2,123	8	0	1	1	6	52	25	25	2	0
Payette	7,430	16	0	7	0	9	99	16	68	15	0
Pocatello	55,317	209	1	21	13	174	1,568	339	1,100	129	5
Post Falls	34,144	69	0	7	5	57	578	77	472	29	4
Preston	5,411	7	0	4	0	3	37	12	23	2	0
Rathdrum	8,508	5	0	0	2	3	94	27	53	14	0
Rexburg	28,765	5	0	2	0	3	135	7	127	1	0
Rigby	4,076	6	0	0	1	5	42	7	31	4	0
Rupert	5,845	15	0	4	1	10	96	28	64	4	0
Salmon	3,103	15	0	0	0	15	25	11	14	0	0
Shelley	4,412	2	0	1	0	1	62	7	49	6	0

Table 8. Offenses Known to Law Enforcement, by Selected State and City, 2018—Continued

(Number.)

State/city	Population	Violent crime	Murder and nonnegligent manslaughter	Rape[1]	Robbery	Aggravated assault	Property crime	Burglary	Larceny-theft	Motor vehicle theft	Arson[2]
Soda Springs	3,036	10	0	6	0	4	22	7	14	1	1
Spirit Lake	2,378	5	0	0	0	5	39	16	21	2	1
Sun Valley	1,443	1	0	1	0	0	10	4	6	0	0
Twin Falls	49,908	225	0	39	7	179	1,180	190	912	78	7
Wendell	2,692	8	0	1	0	7	33	9	20	4	0
Wilder	1,748	2	0	0	0	2	7	2	4	1	0
ILLINOIS											
Addison	36,791	61	1	18	6	36	464	65	361	38	4
Albany	876	1	0	1	0	0	6	2	4	0	0
Aledo	3,455	0	0	0	0	0	26	3	23	0	0
Alexis	789	0	0	0	0	0	15	7	4	4	0
Algonquin	31,156	27	0	7	4	16	265	18	243	4	0
Alsip	19,050	24	2	0	16	6	427	66	329	32	1
Altamont	2,274	2	0	1	0	1	38	13	25	0	1
Alton	26,563	171	8	26	25	112	994	228	703	63	8
Amboy	2,323	5	0	2	0	3	7	4	3	0	0
Anna	4,155	14	0	2	2	10	147	26	118	3	3
Annawan	852	1	0	0	0	1	8	0	8	0	0
Antioch	14,201	20	0	8	2	10	165	12	150	3	0
Arcola	2,878	7	0	0	0	7	7	5	2	0	0
Arlington Heights	75,688	28	0	10	6	12	628	68	535	25	1
Aroma Park	695	1	0	0	1	0	15	6	8	1	0
Arthur	2,248	3	0	0	1	2	15	5	10	0	0
Ashland	1,203	1	0	1	0	0	4	2	2	0	0
Ashton	898	0	0	0	0	0	2	2	0	0	0
Assumption	1,083	2	0	0	0	2	9	6	3	0	0
Athens	1,901	0	0	0	0	0	16	4	9	3	0
Auburn	4,695	2	0	0	0	2	7	2	5	0	0
Aurora	201,364	538	4	68	94	372	2,301	319	1,860	122	9
Aviston	2,117	2	0	2	0	0	1	1	0	0	0
Bannockburn	1,579	0	0	0	0	0	19	2	17	0	0
Barrington	10,293	1	0	0	1	0	124	9	111	4	0
Barrington Hills	4,219	1	0	0	0	1	23	3	20	0	0
Barry	1,256	0	0	0	0	0	11	6	5	0	0
Bartlett	41,140	21	0	5	8	8	169	11	150	8	2
Bartonville	6,221	16	0	5	2	9	200	37	151	12	0
Batavia	26,614	34	0	9	5	20	369	21	333	15	2
Beardstown	5,507	58	0	1	0	57	160	32	122	6	0
Beecher	4,486	4	0	2	0	2	25	4	21	0	0
Belgium	386	0	0	0	0	0	2	2	0	0	0
Belleville	41,283	171	2	38	41	90	1,261	284	890	87	12
Belvidere	25,121	60	0	18	2	40	270	51	206	13	1
Bensenville	18,324	20	0	11	4	5	272	26	225	21	0
Berkeley	5,119	5	0	1	1	3	49	6	40	3	0
Berwyn	55,391	191	1	54	54	82	818	99	629	90	6
Bethalto	9,300	5	0	0	1	4	81	15	62	4	0
Bethany	1,265	1	0	0	1	0	11	7	4	0	0
Bloomingdale	22,008	32	0	1	5	26	488	36	448	4	0
Bloomington	78,097	339	9	68	37	225	1,193	196	909	88	5
Blue Island	23,310	93	1	10	32	50	288	68	168	52	0
Bluffs	660	1	0	0	0	1	1	1	0	0	0
Bolingbrook	75,451	112	1	23	17	71	592	60	477	55	3
Bourbonnais	18,388	33	0	7	2	24	154	16	130	8	1
Bradley	15,271	17	0	3	3	11	442	31	403	8	2
Braidwood	6,217	11	0	5	0	6	45	9	33	3	2
Breese	4,491	2	0	0	0	2	28	0	28	0	0
Bridgeview	16,317	30	0	3	8	19	319	31	270	18	1
Brighton	2,136	1	0	0	0	1	5	1	3	1	0
Broadview	7,761	19	0	2	12	5	330	28	278	24	0
Brooklyn	706	7	0	1	3	3	18	3	11	4	0
Brookport	904	1	0	0	0	1	11	2	9	0	1
Buffalo Grove	41,182	7	0	2	1	4	268	42	216	10	0
Bunker Hill	1,680	1	0	0	0	1	22	5	16	1	1
Burbank	28,771	60	0	5	21	34	242	38	184	20	3
Burr Ridge	10,852	3	0	0	0	3	190	17	162	11	0
Byron	3,588	1	0	1	0	0	34	3	31	0	0
Cahokia	14,004	75	2	14	14	45	604	169	383	52	18
Calumet City	36,560	187	5	36	107	39	980	205	586	189	4
Cambridge	2,090	2	0	0	0	2	7	1	6	0	0
Campton Hills	11,305	1	0	0	0	1	17	2	15	0	0
Carbondale	25,816	111	0	27	26	58	760	114	613	33	10
Carlinville	5,499	21	0	3	1	17	230	37	187	6	2
Carlyle	3,175	6	0	0	0	6	44	1	42	1	0
Carol Stream	40,019	33	0	7	10	16	411	48	336	27	2
Carpentersville	38,220	34	0	10	17	7	496	48	433	15	2
Carrollton	2,434	15	0	1	0	14	25	5	18	2	0
Carterville	5,873	13	0	5	1	7	58	17	40	1	0
Carthage	2,466	2	0	1	0	1	23	6	16	1	0
Cary	17,830	20	0	7	4	9	110	17	91	2	0
Casey	2,649	8	0	2	0	6	21	7	13	1	0
Caseyville	4,038	38	0	6	1	31	50	8	33	9	0
Catlin	1,958	0	0	0	0	0	3	3	0	0	0

Table 8. Offenses Known to Law Enforcement, by Selected State and City, 2018—Continued

(Number.)

State/city	Population	Violent crime	Murder and nonnegligent manslaughter	Rape[1]	Robbery	Aggravated assault	Property crime	Burglary	Larceny-theft	Motor vehicle theft	Arson[2]
Centralia	12,372	157	1	28	19	109	499	151	296	52	5
Centreville	4,969	19	1	0	3	15	201	50	96	55	0
Champaign	88,326	602	7	72	83	440	1,998	276	1,637	85	10
Channahon	12,837	9	0	4	0	5	58	15	42	1	0
Charleston	20,878	29	0	8	3	18	61	24	36	1	1
Chatham	12,770	18	0	6	3	9	82	8	71	3	0
Chenoa	3,142	2	0	0	0	2	7	4	3	0	0
Cherry Valley	3,067	9	1	1	0	7	238	12	225	1	1
Chester	8,505	16	0	3	2	11	14	5	3	6	0
Chicago	2,719,151	27,357	563	1,798	9,684	15,312	86,513	11,686	64,695	10,132	438
Chicago Heights[6]	29,832	260	2	32	106	120			214	105	2
Chicago Ridge	14,167	18	0	2	9	7	358	15	328	15	0
Chillicothe	6,153	21	0	3	1	17	99	23	69	7	2
Christopher	2,717	15	0	0	0	15	19	2	16	1	0
Cicero	82,310	314	4	34	127	149	1,770	364	1,295	111	16
Clarendon Hills	8,751	7	0	0	0	7	42	9	31	2	0
Clinton	6,927	8	0	7	1	0	203	68	135	0	0
Coal City[6]	5,338	5	0	0	0	5		3		1	0
Coal Valley	3,782	9	0	4	0	5	73	8	61	4	0
Cobden	1,094	6	0	1	0	5	8	0	8	0	0
Colchester	1,306	0	0	0	0	0	1	0	1	0	0
Cortland	4,342	2	0	0	0	2	28	5	23	0	0
Country Club Hills	16,565	71	3	11	21	36	589	68	468	53	1
Cowden	575	0	0	0	0	0	5	1	4	0	0
Crest Hill	21,221	42	1	16	9	16	203	29	148	26	0
Crete	8,147	17	0	2	1	14	132	16	108	8	1
Crystal Lake	40,345	38	0	12	4	22	648	37	602	9	0
Dallas City	880	2	0	0	0	2	3	2	1	0	0
Dana	153	0	0	0	0	0	0	0	0	0	0
Danvers	1,110	0	0	0	0	0	2	0	2	0	0
Danville	31,203	559	12	53	103	391	1,508	379	1,052	77	15
Darien	22,054	25	2	10	1	12	231	23	199	9	0
Decatur	71,625	358	9	30	84	235	2,050	618	1,325	107	23
Deer Creek	668	3	0	1	1	1	13	9	4	0	0
Deerfield	19,049	4	1	1	1	1	137	16	115	6	0
DeKalb	43,064	228	0	45	31	152	1,105	125	939	41	6
Delavan	1,612	2	0	0	0	2	44	22	21	1	0
De Soto	1,534	3	0	0	0	3	12	2	10	0	0
Des Plaines	58,155	39	1	6	12	20	725	65	623	37	2
Diamond	2,505	0	0	0	0	0	1	0	0	1	0
Divernon	1,124	0	0	0	0	0	6	0	5	1	0
Dixon	15,129	32	0	23	0	9	222	22	196	4	0
Downers Grove	49,626	49	0	15	9	25	563	71	466	26	3
Downs	970	2	0	1	0	1	5	0	5	0	0
Dupo	3,844	4	0	0	0	4	82	17	59	6	0
Du Quoin	5,770	14	0	2	0	12	43	13	22	8	0
Dwight	4,009	5	0	0	2	3	38	1	30	7	0
East Alton	6,073	29	0	13	7	9	231	33	186	12	0
East Dubuque	1,592	3	0	0	1	2	17	3	13	1	0
East Dundee	3,243	2	0	0	1	1	32	8	21	3	0
East Peoria	22,640	114	1	37	8	68	584	93	482	9	0
East St. Louis[6]	26,630	317	23	22	51	221		198		100	24
Edinburg	1,026	14	0	2	0	12	12	1	8	3	0
Edwardsville	25,054	13	0	0	5	8	185	14	168	3	0
Effingham	12,624	43	0	12	5	26	340	41	281	18	0
Elburn	5,900	0	0	0	0	0	13	6	7	0	0
Eldorado	3,975	12	0	0	3	9	87	32	50	5	0
Elgin	113,060	235	3	48	57	127	1,713	172	1,455	86	7
Elizabeth	729	0	0	0	0	0	5	1	4	0	0
Elk Grove Village	32,723	23	0	3	9	11	485	35	391	59	3
Elmhurst	47,025	23	0	6	9	8	445	63	372	10	0
Elmwood	2,054	2	0	0	0	2	10	3	7	0	0
Elmwood Park	24,486	54	0	6	16	32	250	53	182	15	2
Elwood	2,262	4	0	0	0	4	17	1	11	5	0
Energy	1,127	0	0	0	0	0	17	3	12	2	0
Erie	1,519	0	0	0	0	0	6	2	3	1	0
Eureka	5,335	11	0	2	0	9	34	2	30	2	0
Evanston	74,780	140	3	6	47	84	1,702	289	1,358	55	6
Evergreen Park	19,497	54	0	4	19	31	921	30	883	8	2
Fairfield	5,013	21	0	5	1	15	85	8	74	3	0
Fairmont City	2,466	3	0	1	0	2	15	6	6	3	0
Fairmount	612	0	0	0	0	0	3	0	3	0	0
Fairview Heights	16,516	67	1	18	6	42	695	56	615	24	1
Farmersville	684	0	0	0	0	0	0	0	0	0	0
Farmington	2,257	6	0	1	0	5	27	6	21	0	0
Findlay	639	0	0	0	0	0	1	0	1	0	0
Fisher	1,973	2	0	1	0	1	30	8	22	0	0
Fithian	462	0	0	0	0	0	0	0	0	0	0
Flora	4,856	7	0	0	0	7	97	1	93	3	1
Flossmoor	9,315	11	0	1	3	7	244	15	215	14	0
Forest Park	13,919	66	1	6	32	27	531	70	415	46	0
Forest View	685	0	0	0	0	0	36	5	24	7	0
Fox Lake	10,535	17	0	4	3	10	256	33	215	8	0

Table 8. Offenses Known to Law Enforcement, by Selected State and City, 2018—Continued

(Number.)

State/city	Population	Violent crime	Murder and nonnegligent manslaughter	Rape[1]	Robbery	Aggravated assault	Property crime	Burglary	Larceny-theft	Motor vehicle theft	Arson[2]
Fox River Grove	4,639	9	0	1	0	8	62	9	51	2	3
Frankfort	19,184	9	0	1	0	8	187	21	154	12	2
Franklin Park	17,968	47	0	14	6	27	242	67	151	24	4
Freeburg	4,246	2	0	0	1	1	29	7	18	4	0
Freeport	23,887	49	1	20	7	21	572	89	468	15	5
Fulton	3,288	9	0	0	0	9	48	9	36	3	0
Galena	3,198	1	0	0	0	1	85	12	71	2	0
Geneva	22,082	6	0	0	1	5	154	27	125	2	0
Genoa	5,225	12	0	5	0	7	65	3	60	2	0
Georgetown	3,265	16	1	3	1	11	72	17	49	6	0
Germantown	1,278	2	0	0	0	2	18	0	18	0	0
Gibson City	3,292	11	0	3	0	8	8	3	5	0	0
Gifford	1,100	0	0	0	0	0	3	0	3	0	0
Gilberts	8,254	3	0	1	0	2	20	2	18	0	0
Gilman	1,687	1	0	0	0	1	53	5	48	0	0
Girard	2,003	14	0	3	1	10	14	4	9	1	0
Glasford	976	1	0	0	0	1	1	1	0	0	0
Glen Carbon	12,991	9	0	0	0	9	129	14	114	1	0
Glendale Heights	34,030	18	0	0	12	6	397	32	332	33	2
Glen Ellyn	28,079	21	0	8	5	8	217	27	179	11	3
Glenview	48,088	34	0	7	5	22	422	60	331	31	1
Glenwood	8,864	11	0	0	6	5	55	21	30	4	0
Godley	746	0	0	0	0	0	6	3	1	2	0
Golf	499	0	0	0	0	0	3	0	3	0	0
Goodfield	999	0	0	0	0	0	27	1	26	0	0
Grafton	636	0	0	0	0	0	22	5	16	1	0
Grand Ridge	525	0	0	0	0	0	0	0	0	0	0
Grandview	1,400	2	0	0	0	2	24	7	17	0	0
Granite City	28,593	219	1	34	36	148	729	283	316	130	13
Grantfork	331	1	0	0	0	1	3	1	1	1	0
Grayslake	20,943	27	0	5	3	19	168	28	134	6	0
Greenfield	995	4	0	0	0	4	12	2	9	1	0
Greenup	1,487	2	0	0	0	2	29	6	22	1	0
Greenville	6,723	14	1	0	2	11	100	10	83	7	1
Gurnee	30,698	44	0	17	14	13	1,085	53	1,007	25	1
Hainesville	3,640	0	0	0	0	0	46	5	39	2	0
Hamel	814	0	0	0	0	0	7	4	2	1	0
Hampshire	6,466	11	0	1	0	10	23	13	10	0	0
Hampton	1,807	2	0	0	0	2	9	3	5	1	0
Hanover Park	37,971	43	0	7	12	24	194	35	147	12	0
Harrisburg	8,697	49	0	7	5	37	325	111	207	7	2
Hartford	1,359	2	0	1	0	1	24	2	22	0	0
Harvard	9,144	8	0	3	0	5	64	4	58	2	0
Havana	3,046	29	0	8	2	19	59	5	50	4	0
Hawthorn Woods	8,504	0	0	0	0	0	40	2	36	2	0
Hazel Crest	13,811	52	2	7	25	18	424	85	273	66	1
Henning	236	0	0	0	0	0	0	0	0	0	0
Henry	2,247	5	0	1	0	4	30	2	27	1	0
Herrin	12,930	35	0	5	7	23	376	92	264	20	1
Hickory Hills	13,934	16	1	2	4	9	189	20	157	12	1
Highland	9,812	9	0	2	1	6	79	9	63	7	0
Highland Park	29,764	24	0	3	2	19	198	26	150	22	1
Highwood	5,307	4	0	1	1	2	33	0	33	0	0
Hillsboro	6,016	28	0	6	1	21	74	13	58	3	0
Hillsdale	510	0	0	0	0	0	1	0	0	1	0
Hinckley	2,045	0	0	0	0	0	20	3	17	0	0
Hinsdale	17,831	2	0	2	0	0	98	23	60	15	0
Hodgkins	1,897	1	0	0	0	1	299	5	292	2	0
Hoffman Estates	51,514	48	1	14	9	24	417	45	349	23	0
Homer	1,168	0	0	0	0	0	0	0	0	0	0
Homer Glen	24,638	9	0	1	2	6	149	31	107	11	1
Hometown	4,263	3	0	0	2	1	15	3	12	0	0
Homewood	19,056	46	1	9	23	13	786	55	678	53	2
Hoopeston	5,078	21	0	6	2	13	155	53	95	7	2
Hudson	1,823	0	0	0	0	0	4	1	3	0	0
Huntley	27,637	9	0	0	1	8	99	8	89	2	0
Ina	2,349	4	0	0	0	4	9	0	9	0	0
Indian Head Park	3,782	1	0	0	0	1	27	4	22	1	0
Indianola	263	0	0	0	0	0	0	0	0	0	0
Itasca	9,531	7	0	4	1	2	103	15	80	8	0
Jacksonville	18,320	65	0	7	6	52	519	72	435	12	2
Jerseyville	8,238	10	0	2	0	8	96	27	60	9	0
Johnsburg	6,313	2	0	2	0	0	112	5	102	5	0
Joliet	148,553	486	8	44	122	312	2,312	449	1,726	137	49
Justice	12,822	7	0	1	2	4	29	4	21	4	0
Kankakee	26,032	230	4	35	47	144	871	143	682	46	11
Kansas	720	0	0	0	0	0	0	0	0	0	0
Kenilworth	2,521	0	0	0	0	0	15	5	7	3	0
Kewanee	12,413	35	0	7	0	28	489	39	425	25	6
Kildeer	4,060	1	0	0	0	1	52	6	45	1	0
Kincaid	1,397	4	0	1	0	3	18	6	11	1	0
Kingston	1,170	0	0	0	0	0	7	0	6	1	0
Lacon	1,760	4	0	0	0	4	16	3	13	0	0

Table 8. Offenses Known to Law Enforcement, by Selected State and City, 2018—Continued

(Number.)

State/city	Population	Violent crime	Murder and nonnegligent manslaughter	Rape[1]	Robbery	Aggravated assault	Property crime	Burglary	Larceny-theft	Motor vehicle theft	Arson[2]
Ladd	1,208	3	0	0	0	3	2	0	2	0	0
La Grange	15,583	15	0	0	5	10	153	16	134	3	1
La Grange Park	13,411	5	0	0	2	3	62	16	46	0	0
La Harpe	1,161	0	0	0	0	0	3	3	0	0	0
Lake Bluff	5,654	1	0	0	1	0	43	7	36	0	0
Lake In the Hills	28,924	32	0	19	2	11	117	14	101	2	1
Lakemoor	6,046	6	0	2	0	4	21	2	19	0	0
Lake Villa	8,726	9	1	4	0	4	33	3	29	1	0
Lakewood	3,945	4	0	0	0	4	21	2	19	0	0
Lake Zurich	19,930	5	0	1	1	3	259	18	238	3	0
Lanark	1,340	0	0	0	0	0	1	0	1	0	0
Lansing	27,904	88	2	13	45	28	1,525	116	1,301	108	2
La Salle	9,051	0	0	0	0	0	103	9	92	2	0
Leland	921	0	0	0	0	0	2	0	2	0	0
Leland Grove	1,486	0	0	0	0	0	1	0	0	1	0
Lemont	17,224	22	0	13	1	8	142	15	113	14	0
Lenzburg	488	0	0	0	0	0	4	1	3	0	1
Le Roy	3,541	7	0	1	0	6	30	8	21	1	0
Lexington	2,045	1	0	1	0	0	1	1	0	0	0
Lincoln	13,724	52	0	5	2	45	253	38	204	11	2
Lincolnwood	12,467	15	0	0	5	10	380	40	317	23	3
Lindenhurst	14,450	13	1	8	1	3	58	6	48	4	0
Lisle	22,966	16	0	4	5	7	106	20	74	12	0
Litchfield	6,747	5	0	2	1	2	217	26	188	3	3
Loami	753	1	0	0	0	1	13	3	8	2	0
Lockport	25,510	17	0	2	5	10	177	31	137	9	3
Lombard	43,794	52	1	15	4	32	856	59	781	16	2
Loves Park	23,301	86	0	24	13	49	456	71	354	31	1
Lovington	1,061	3	0	3	0	0	18	3	15	0	1
Lyons	10,563	11	2	2	2	5	115	9	96	10	0
Machesney Park	22,627	57	0	15	7	35	416	57	341	18	1
Macomb	18,124	56	1	19	2	34	228	36	185	7	1
Mahomet	8,672	10	0	5	0	5	56	12	43	1	0
Malta	1,159	0	0	0	0	0	2	0	2	0	0
Manhattan	7,879	2	0	0	0	2	26	4	20	2	0
Manteno	8,996	9	0	4	0	5	159	18	139	2	0
Maple Park	1,327	1	0	1	0	0	8	2	6	0	0
Marengo	7,470	3	0	2	0	1	54	8	43	3	0
Marine	920	1	0	0	0	1	2	1	1	0	0
Marissa	1,820	22	0	0	0	22	36	17	17	2	0
Maroa	1,720	1	0	0	0	1	22	6	15	1	0
Marquette Heights	2,669	4	0	2	1	1	16	1	13	2	1
Marseilles	4,869	8	0	2	3	3	58	16	37	5	2
Marshall	3,851	4	0	0	0	4	25	3	19	3	0
Martinsville	1,113	1	0	0	0	1	5	1	4	0	0
Maryville	7,954	9	0	0	2	7	53	10	38	5	0
Mascoutah	8,078	7	0	4	1	2	87	7	78	2	0
Mason City	2,159	11	0	7	0	4	26	6	19	1	0
Mattoon	17,794	99	0	17	1	81	281	102	179	0	4
Maywood	23,573	135	4	20	57	54	570	120	345	105	4
McCook	223	0	0	0	0	0	19	4	12	3	0
McCullom Lake	1,009	1	0	0	0	1	1	1	0	0	0
McHenry	26,893	48	0	20	3	25	288	26	241	21	0
McLean	799	0	0	0	0	0	5	1	4	0	0
Melrose Park	25,164	85	0	7	27	51	316	68	176	72	4
Mendota	7,062	10	0	7	0	3	61	14	41	6	0
Merrionette Park	1,879	3	0	0	0	3	38	9	26	3	0
Metropolis	6,076	33	0	7	2	24	359	68	273	18	1
Midlothian	14,607	26	1	1	19	5	330	64	236	30	0
Milan	5,046	17	0	0	1	16	98	31	62	5	0
Milledgeville	957	1	0	0	0	1	9	4	5	0	0
Minonk	1,996	0	0	0	0	0	20	2	15	3	0
Mokena	20,507	11	0	2	4	5	295	31	240	24	0
Moline	42,051	228	2	33	24	169	1,050	190	780	80	8
Momence	3,127	4	0	0	1	3	45	13	26	6	1
Monmouth	9,042	31	0	1	4	26	212	40	160	12	2
Montgomery	19,897	17	0	2	5	10	287	20	262	5	2
Monticello	5,557	11	0	0	0	11	28	4	24	0	1
Morris	14,798	16	0	4	5	7	238	13	212	13	0
Morrison	4,054	10	0	2	0	8	61	12	48	1	0
Morrisonville	1,011	0	0	0	0	0	5	0	5	0	0
Morton	16,302	18	0	4	1	13	103	27	74	2	0
Morton Grove	23,123	10	0	2	2	6	285	55	218	12	0
Mount Carmel	6,931	17	0	0	0	17	123	21	102	0	0
Mount Morris	2,803	1	0	0	1	0	16	3	13	0	0
Mount Olive	1,956	1	0	0	0	1	22	1	21	0	0
Mount Prospect	53,888	32	0	7	11	14	558	55	486	17	3
Mount Pulaski	1,484	0	0	0	0	0	1	1	0	0	0
Mount Vernon	14,914	228	0	27	18	183	773	168	585	20	7
Mount Zion	5,816	5	0	0	1	4	51	11	38	2	0
Moweaqua	1,712	3	0	3	0	0	13	6	4	3	0
Mundelein	31,436	27	0	15	1	11	183	22	148	13	1
Murphysboro	7,511	53	0	9	4	40	231	82	144	5	0

Table 8. Offenses Known to Law Enforcement, by Selected State and City, 2018—Continued

(Number.)

State/city	Population	Violent crime	Murder and nonnegligent manslaughter	Rape[1]	Robbery	Aggravated assault	Property crime	Burglary	Larceny-theft	Motor vehicle theft	Arson[2]
Naperville[6]	148,457	102	0	29	21	52		163		39	0
Neoga	1,623	3	0	1	1	1	12	2	9	1	0
New Athens	1,903	3	0	0	0	3	24	4	20	0	0
New Baden	3,268	7	0	1	1	5	36	0	33	3	8
New Berlin	1,329	0	0	0	0	0	8	4	3	1	0
New Lenox	26,905	35	0	13	7	15	299	17	272	10	1
Newton	2,848	5	0	2	0	3	26	11	12	3	0
Niles	29,433	34	1	5	11	17	605	63	514	28	2
Nokomis	2,124	9	0	4	0	5	31	6	24	1	0
Normal	54,525	119	2	35	21	61	985	119	843	23	0
Norridge	14,416	20	0	0	9	11	413	26	373	14	0
Norris City	1,203	10	0	0	0	10	9	0	9	0	0
North Aurora	18,470	24	0	6	4	14	240	14	220	6	1
Northbrook	33,424	6	0	3	1	2	512	67	431	14	0
Northfield	5,472	3	1	1	0	1	82	19	58	5	0
Northlake	12,369	10	0	1	6	3	268	14	250	4	0
North Pekin	1,543	0	0	0	0	0	19	3	16	0	0
North Riverside	6,548	20	1	0	4	15	448	10	401	37	0
North Utica	1,343	2	0	0	0	2	2	1	1	0	0
Oak Brook	8,103	10	0	3	3	4	552	22	514	16	0
Oakbrook Terrace	2,164	2	0	0	0	2	85	5	78	2	0
Oak Forest	27,644	37	0	5	12	20	304	48	222	34	0
Oak Lawn	55,996	81	0	11	24	46	758	74	671	13	3
Oak Park[5]	52,313		2	16	97				1,176	65	2
Oakwood	1,523	1	0	1	0	0	13	5	8	0	0
Oblong	1,381	3	0	0	0	3	10	1	9	0	0
O'Fallon	29,354	81	1	28	11	41	543	76	456	11	2
Okawville	1,368	2	0	0	0	2	22	6	16	0	0
Olney	8,919	45	0	11	5	29	371	70	289	12	5
Olympia Fields	4,878	7	0	1	4	2	353	17	327	9	0
Onarga	1,276	2	0	0	0	2	12	6	5	1	0
Orion	1,810	3	0	0	0	3	13	1	12	0	0
Orland Park	59,064	20	1	1	5	13	1,015	29	963	23	2
Oswego	35,478	17	0	8	2	7	298	10	284	4	2
Ottawa	18,096	15	0	1	2	12	310	45	259	6	5
Palatine	68,648	28	1	11	7	9	358	26	317	15	0
Palestine	1,285	9	0	1	0	8	30	8	20	2	0
Palos Heights	12,385	3	0	0	2	1	135	11	114	10	0
Palos Hills	17,338	18	0	2	3	13	84	8	68	8	0
Palos Park	4,822	0	0	0	0	0	63	4	57	2	0
Paris	8,253	61	0	10	1	50	162	91	59	12	0
Park City	7,504	11	0	6	2	3	86	8	68	10	0
Park Forest	21,636	61	1	4	24	32	344	75	218	51	7
Park Ridge	37,490	21	0	2	4	15	341	51	273	17	4
Pawnee	2,667	1	0	1	0	0	0	0	0	0	0
Paxton	4,180	11	0	3	0	8	48	18	28	2	0
Pekin[6]	32,541	136	1	37	16	82		127		25	4
Peoria	112,595	860	22	68	201	569	4,509	890	3,197	422	50
Peoria Heights	5,828	18	0	7	0	11	90	21	49	20	0
Peotone	4,152	3	0	2	0	1	23	4	19	0	0
Peru	9,770	10	0	5	1	4	149	12	133	4	1
Phoenix	1,944	8	0	2	5	1	44	9	29	6	0
Pierron	562	0	0	0	0	0	0	0	0	0	0
Pinckneyville	5,358	4	0	0	0	4	34	5	29	0	0
Pingree Grove	8,867	3	0	3	0	0	48	1	47	0	0
Pittsfield	4,397	7	1	3	0	3	31	8	22	1	0
Plainfield	44,525	54	0	14	7	33	328	34	275	19	0
Plano	11,692	9	0	4	1	4	72	8	61	3	1
Pleasant Hill	928	0	0	0	0	0	24	5	19	0	0
Pleasant Plains	800	0	0	0	0	0	6	1	5	0	0
Pontiac	11,795	40	0	0	4	36	172	21	149	2	1
Pontoon Beach	5,640	13	0	0	3	10	68	5	53	10	0
Posen	5,903	14	0	1	6	7	116	14	82	20	0
Potomac	711	2	0	1	0	1	3	2	1	0	0
Princeton	7,538	22	0	11	1	10	160	26	128	6	0
Prophetstown	1,959	0	0	0	0	0	1	1	0	0	0
Prospect Heights	16,167	25	0	5	3	17	82	11	61	10	0
Quincy	40,249	252	1	51	14	186	1,288	216	1,022	50	3
Rankin	528	0	0	0	0	0	0	0	0	0	0
Rantoul	12,741	35	1	18	14	2	349	92	243	14	1
Red Bud	3,505	4	0	0	0	4	26	13	12	1	0
Richmond	1,926	11	0	3	1	7	20	4	15	1	0
Richton Park	13,485	55	0	7	27	21	331	40	235	56	0
Ridge Farm	828	0	0	0	0	0	14	3	11	0	0
Riverdale	13,322	99	5	11	41	42	377	88	237	52	2
River Forest	11,125	14	0	0	6	8	233	32	193	8	0
Riverside	8,723	13	0	5	4	4	91	11	77	3	0
Riverton	3,427	12	0	3	0	9	41	10	26	5	0
Riverwoods	3,619	2	0	1	1	0	22	3	16	3	0
Robbins	5,506	38	2	3	5	28	57	8	26	23	3
Rochester	3,733	2	0	0	0	2	18	2	14	2	0
Rockdale	1,939	4	0	0	0	4	6	1	3	2	0
Rock Falls	8,844	11	0	2	0	9	89	23	61	5	0

Table 8. Offenses Known to Law Enforcement, by Selected State and City, 2018—Continued

(Number.)

State/city	Population	Violent crime	Murder and nonnegligent manslaughter	Rape[1]	Robbery	Aggravated assault	Property crime	Burglary	Larceny-theft	Motor vehicle theft	Arson[2]
Rockford	146,198	2,027	23	133	346	1,525	5,368	1,169	3,752	447	64
Rock Island	37,985	99	1	3	19	76	986	166	688	132	11
Rockton	7,443	9	0	3	0	6	184	9	173	2	0
Rolling Meadows	23,970	15	0	3	3	9	284	19	258	7	0
Romeoville	39,625	58	1	10	15	32	431	42	361	28	2
Roscoe	10,466	10	0	0	1	9	93	23	66	4	0
Roselle	22,799	9	0	6	1	2	206	24	172	10	1
Rosemont	4,143	42	0	10	8	24	411	8	396	7	0
Round Lake	18,454	18	0	0	3	15	108	14	84	10	0
Round Lake Beach	27,534	34	0	7	6	21	509	36	461	12	1
Round Lake Heights	2,689	7	0	0	1	6	12	1	11	0	0
Round Lake Park	7,740	23	0	0	5	18	49	8	39	2	2
Roxana	1,455	4	0	2	0	2	35	3	32	0	0
Ruma	308	0	0	0	0	0	4	0	4	0	0
Rushville	2,936	6	0	2	0	4	46	7	37	2	0
Salem	7,131	18	0	6	1	11	342	42	287	13	1
Sandoval	1,214	7	0	3	0	4	50	14	32	4	28
Sandwich	7,382	7	0	2	0	5	9	5	2	2	0
San Jose	607	0	0	0	0	0	2	0	0	2	0
Sauget	148	2	1	0	1	0	47	7	28	12	0
Sauk Village[5]	10,436		3	16	23		271	103	135	33	1
Savanna	2,818	14	0	3	0	11	98	28	66	4	1
Schaumburg	74,169	61	0	15	22	24	1,516	75	1,393	48	1
Schiller Park	11,617	17	0	2	6	9	219	18	178	23	1
Seneca	2,255	13	0	0	0	13	40	8	32	0	0
Shannon	697	0	0	0	0	0	4	0	4	0	0
Shawneetown	1,113	5	0	0	0	5	13	7	6	0	0
Sherman	4,782	3	0	1	0	2	21	6	15	0	0
Shiloh	13,167	22	0	12	4	6	159	32	121	6	2
Shorewood	17,482	14	0	6	1	7	101	9	88	4	1
Sidell	579	0	0	0	0	0	0	0	0	0	0
Silvis	7,578	32	0	3	3	26	174	39	123	12	0
Skokie	63,849	172	0	15	37	120	1,606	206	1,348	52	7
Sleepy Hollow	3,314	2	0	0	0	2	8	0	8	0	0
Smithton	3,822	1	0	0	0	1	8	3	5	0	0
Somonauk	1,878	1	0	0	0	1	5	3	2	0	0
South Barrington	5,040	0	0	0	0	0	105	6	86	13	0
South Beloit	7,642	13	3	0	4	6	102	17	80	5	0
South Chicago Heights	4,077	19	1	1	8	9	151	6	138	7	0
South Elgin	22,627	24	0	13	3	8	97	12	85	0	0
South Holland	21,690	68	2	19	31	16	541	89	352	100	0
South Pekin	1,098	0	0	0	0	0	36	9	24	3	0
South Roxana	1,968	7	0	4	0	3	25	8	13	4	0
Springfield	114,623	955	9	93	216	637	5,487	1,195	4,044	248	40
Spring Grove	5,718	4	0	0	0	4	45	3	40	2	0
Spring Valley	5,196	8	0	1	0	7	90	11	79	0	0
Stanford	585	0	0	0	0	0	0	0	0	0	0
St. Charles	32,764	45	1	11	5	28	232	32	189	11	0
Steger	9,388	25	0	5	6	14	247	48	185	14	1
St. Elmo	1,378	4	0	0	0	4	10	1	7	2	0
Sterling	14,674	34	0	25	3	6	436	42	373	21	1
Stickney	6,680	2	0	0	2	0	52	6	40	6	1
Stockton	1,730	1	0	0	0	1	21	5	16	0	1
Stonington	859	1	0	0	1	0	0	0	0	0	0
Streator	13,038	31	1	22	1	7	302	25	270	7	7
Sullivan	4,459	46	0	1	0	45	49	4	44	1	0
Summit	11,310	40	0	9	15	16	241	25	186	30	0
Swansea	13,506	14	1	2	4	7	192	38	145	9	2
Sycamore	18,095	10	0	3	2	5	172	14	155	3	1
Taylorville	10,565	7	0	0	2	5	134	21	107	6	0
Thayer	664	0	0	0	0	0	3	0	3	0	0
Thornton	2,457	6	0	2	2	2	38	10	25	3	0
Tilton	2,565	17	0	4	4	9	58	11	45	2	0
Tinley Park	56,638	23	0	2	9	12	694	79	582	33	0
Tolono	3,447	5	0	3	0	2	23	9	12	2	0
Toluca	1,286	3	0	0	0	3	9	2	7	0	0
Tower Lakes	1,246	0	0	0	0	0	6	4	2	0	0
Trenton	2,605	3	0	2	1	0	18	4	11	3	0
Troy	10,216	13	0	3	0	10	81	24	50	7	0
Tuscola	4,399	28	0	0	2	26	74	12	58	4	0
Urbana	42,029	150	2	24	57	67	1,233	198	1,012	23	8
Valmeyer	1,257	2	0	0	0	2	9	2	7	0	0
Vandalia	7,009	24	0	7	1	16	159	27	127	5	0
Vernon Hills	26,429	15	0	4	7	4	295	20	271	4	2
Vienna	1,729	0	0	0	0	0	14	2	9	3	0
Villa Park	21,806	27	0	8	7	12	232	25	191	16	1
Viola	891	0	0	0	0	0	0	0	0	0	0
Virden	3,344	10	0	3	0	7	131	35	88	8	0
Walnut	1,324	0	0	0	0	0	4	1	3	0	0
Warren	1,319	3	0	0	0	3	0	0	0	0	0
Warrensburg	1,133	2	0	1	0	1	4	1	3	0	0
Warrenville	13,280	13	0	6	2	5	108	11	92	5	0
Washington	17,048	30	0	5	1	24	193	36	153	4	1

Table 8. Offenses Known to Law Enforcement, by Selected State and City, 2018—Continued

(Number.)

State/city	Population	Violent crime	Murder and nonnegligent manslaughter	Rape[1]	Robbery	Aggravated assault	Property crime	Burglary	Larceny-theft	Motor vehicle theft	Arson[2]
Waterloo	10,408	13	0	7	0	6	73	10	62	1	0
Watseka	4,868	9	0	5	1	3	136	22	112	2	0
Waukegan[5,6]	87,530	355	11	20	150	174		296			
Waverly	1,220	0	0	0	0	0	11	3	8	0	0
Wayne	2,442	0	0	0	0	0	5	1	4	0	0
Westchester	16,423	19	0	2	9	8	172	41	126	5	2
West Chicago	27,174	34	2	13	6	13	245	28	200	17	0
West City	648	5	0	0	0	5	96	3	93	0	0
Western Springs	13,554	2	0	0	1	1	154	13	139	2	2
West Frankfort	7,921	2	0	0	2	0	242	95	127	20	2
Westmont	24,766	19	0	8	3	8	270	39	217	14	3
Westville	3,017	14	0	5	2	7	58	22	30	6	0
Wheaton	53,418	39	0	16	8	15	629	64	554	11	2
Wheeling	38,687	27	1	13	1	12	322	53	257	12	0
White Hall	2,352	8	0	3	1	4	30	11	18	1	1
Williamsville	1,496	2	0	1	0	1	2	1	1	0	0
Willow Springs	5,639	4	0	0	0	4	31	5	26	0	0
Wilmette	27,467	13	0	0	0	13	259	61	186	12	0
Winfield	9,762	10	2	5	0	3	33	4	25	4	0
Winnebago	2,973	3	0	2	0	1	31	3	25	3	0
Winnetka	12,518	3	0	2	0	1	108	15	85	8	0
Winthrop Harbor	6,727	12	0	4	1	7	23	4	16	3	0
Witt	852	0	0	0	0	0	7	1	6	0	0
Wood Dale	13,800	10	0	3	3	4	191	22	161	8	0
Woodridge	33,681	32	0	6	12	14	392	32	338	22	4
Wood River	10,210	59	0	15	10	34	528	56	440	32	0
Woodstock	25,353	24	0	10	2	12	298	27	266	5	0
Worth	10,642	26	0	11	7	8	123	21	92	10	1
Yates City	659	1	0	1	0	0	8	1	7	0	0
Yorkville	19,751	18	0	8	3	7	200	17	178	5	2
Zion	23,885	148	4	36	45	63	721	129	553	39	4
INDIANA											
Albion	2,324	16	1	0	1	14	36	3	30	3	
Anderson	54,925	227	5	78	71	73	2,340	520	1,622	198	
Auburn	13,220	7	0	1	4	2	169	27	133	9	0
Bargersville	7,695	12	0	0	2	10	122	4	113	5	0
Batesville	6,616	7	0	2	0	5	67	11	47	9	0
Bedford	13,282	16	0	6	0	10	283	25	238	20	0
Berne	4,155	0	0	0	0	0	33	1	30	2	0
Bloomington	85,730	463	2	47	76	338	2,275	465	1,678	132	
Bluffton	10,046	20	0	1	2	17	167	8	150	9	1
Boonville	6,318	16	0	2	0	14	143	10	125	8	
Bremen	4,507	16	0	0	0	16	53	13	35	5	0
Brownsburg	26,525	33	1	3	6	23	264	18	219	27	0
Cannelton	1,496	2	0	0	0	2	10	2	8	0	0
Carmel	94,128	43	0	14	10	19	716	53	603	60	
Cedar Lake	12,602	7	0	4	1	2	193	24	159	10	
Chesterton	13,561	11	0	2	2	7	111	10	94	7	
Clinton	4,707	29	0	0	1	28	140	25	113	2	0
Columbus	47,595	76	0	46	26	4	1,706	180	1,411	115	5
Crawfordsville	16,207	71	0	5	4	62	342	48	266	28	0
Crown Point	29,884	6	1	1	2	2	335	12	306	17	0
Cumberland	5,739	23	1	0	18	4	104	15	80	9	
Decatur	9,585	17	0	2	1	14	134	10	114	10	0
Dyer	15,880	10	0	1	6	3	133	11	111	11	0
Edinburgh	4,607	17	0	3	2	12	469	30	433	6	0
Elkhart	52,659	624	7	31	56	530	1,869	360	1,231	278	13
Ellettsville	6,740	17	0	0	2	15	55	9	42	4	0
Elwood	8,405	9	0	4	5	0	187	30	149	8	2
Evansville	118,765	675	10	91	156	418	5,301	714	4,078	509	
Fairmount	2,771	9	0	0	0	9	16	14	0	2	
Fishers	94,035	46	1	12	8	25	815	35	712	68	3
Fort Wayne	267,634	1,024	40	131	307	546	7,007	1,006	5,453	548	40
Frankfort[5]	15,744		0		2	7	469	47	402	20	0
Franklin	25,288	129	0	8	7	114	708	51	637	20	2
Gary	75,426	374	40	33	145	156	2,723	703	1,564	456	21
Goshen	33,386	47	0	18	17	12	1,128	174	853	101	5
Greenwood	58,312	83	1	2	17	63	1,777	92	1,544	141	0
Griffith	16,050	8	0	1	4	3	381	43	319	19	0
Hagerstown	1,678	2	0	1	0	1	6	0	6	0	0
Hammond	76,050	365	4	48	128	185	2,652	359	2,002	291	17
Hartford City	5,736	8	0	0	0	8	59	9	44	6	0
Highland[5]	22,428		0	1		10	567	29	492	46	1
Hobart	28,101	71	4	5	10	52	1,112	74	997	41	3
Huntingburg	6,135	32	0	4	3	25	85	27	54	4	0
Indianapolis	877,584	11,170	162	677	3,081	7,250	36,237	7,842	23,448	4,947	229
Jeffersonville	47,709	65	3	25	23	14	1,239	164	905	170	3
Kendallville	9,850	52	0	2	2	48	270	22	212	36	
Kokomo	57,804	364	4	42	70	248	1,426	309	1,036	81	8
Lafayette	72,904	338	4	34	62	238	2,623	502	1,979	142	10
Lake Station	11,880	31	0	3	11	17	321	35	253	33	4
La Porte	21,630	111	0	11	21	79	495	91	360	44	2

Table 8. Offenses Known to Law Enforcement, by Selected State and City, 2018—Continued

(Number.)

State/city	Population	Violent crime	Murder and nonnegligent manslaughter	Rape[1]	Robbery	Aggravated assault	Property crime	Burglary	Larceny-theft	Motor vehicle theft	Arson[2]
Lawrence	49,093	210	5	15	87	103	1,083	185	754	144	5
Lawrenceburg	5,033	30	0	2	1	27	117	6	103	8	
Lowell	9,711	1	0	0	0	1	21	1	19	1	
Marion	28,116	128	9	7	33	79	1,038	132	827	79	1
Michigan City	30,999	230	3	13	50	164	1,373	189	1,080	104	5
Mishawaka	49,310	114	4	15	48	47	2,525	248	2,032	245	14
Muncie	68,406	219	1	40	80	98	2,281	407	1,434	440	
Munster	22,596	21	0	1	16	4	375	16	348	11	1
Nappanee	6,864	4	0	2	2	0	97	24	67	6	0
New Whiteland	6,182	0	0	0	0	0	44	19	22	3	0
Noblesville	63,315	59	1	20	14	24	589	45	516	28	0
North Vernon	6,694	12	0	5	2	5	164	16	148	0	0
Peru	10,973	51	0	3	1	47	370	46	309	15	0
Plainfield	33,668	93	1	16	12	64	794	69	655	70	
Plymouth	9,948	5	0	2	2	1	218	24	187	7	0
Portage	36,646	68	0	17	7	44	740	60	641	39	
Porter	4,812	1	0	0	0	1	28	2	19	7	0
Portland	6,132	14	0	1	0	13	80	2	73	5	0
Rensselaer	5,864	25	1	6	0	18	185	31	153	1	0
Rushville	6,009	4	0	2	0	2	212	45	152	15	0
Sellersburg	8,935	5	0	0	1	4	90	7	62	21	0
Seymour	19,681	41	0	3	5	33	995	71	856	68	1
Shelbyville	19,075	215	0	3	6	206	563	67	443	53	
South Bend[4]	102,397	1,064	9	67	277	711	4,406	970	2,956	480	44
South Whitley	1,745	2	0	0	0	2	13	2	11	0	0
Speedway	12,187	35	0	5	14	16	522	54	431	37	1
St. John	17,615	3	0	1	0	2	111	15	89	7	0
Tell City	7,313	16	0	3	1	12	115	12	94	9	1
Tipton	5,072	18	0	1	1	16	45	10	29	6	0
Valparaiso	33,610	37	0	9	4	24	402	39	350	13	
Westfield	41,037	11	0	6	2	3	390	21	360	9	1
West Lafayette	46,906	31	0	8	7	16	401	23	367	11	0
Westville	5,664	7	0	0	0	7	23	5	17	1	0
Whitestown	9,388	6	0	0	1	5	101	7	80	14	0
Whiting	4,802	13	1	1	7	4	153	6	132	15	0
Winchester	4,689	0	0	0	0	0	227	35	181	11	1
Zionsville	27,185	0	0	0	0	0	60	7	52	1	0
IOWA[7]	NA	NA	NA	NA	NA	NA	NA	NA	NA	NA	NA
KANSAS											
Abilene	6,315	14	0	5	0	9	99	22	69	8	1
Alta Vista	419	0	0	0	0	0	0	0	0	0	0
Anthony	2,115	7	0	0	0	7	56	14	40	2	0
Argonia	479	0	0	0	0	0	2	0	2	0	0
Arkansas City	11,791	50	0	7	1	42	510	87	390	33	1
Atchison	10,589	43	0	8	2	33	269	39	216	14	1
Atwood	1,196	1	0	0	0	1	11	5	6	0	0
Auburn	1,221	0	0	0	0	0	0	0	0	0	0
Augusta	9,387	18	0	3	5	10	324	33	262	29	1
Basehor	6,239	7	0	0	1	6	68	7	52	9	0
Baxter Springs	3,919	9	0	1	0	8	121	23	90	8	0
Bel Aire	8,092	8	0	2	0	6	156	35	113	8	1
Belle Plaine	1,568	3	0	0	0	3	8	2	5	1	0
Belleville	1,885	3	0	0	0	3	38	10	26	2	2
Beloit	3,695	9	0	0	2	7	42	10	28	4	0
Benton	872	2	0	1	1	0	10	2	6	2	0
Bronson	310	0	0	0	0	0	0	0	0	0	0
Bucklin	792	0	0	0	0	0	0	0	0	0	0
Burlington[5]	2,537	9	0	3	2	4			53	3	0
Caney	2,000	2	0	0	1	1	8	2	5	1	0
Carbondale	1,357	0	0	0	0	0	41	9	31	1	0
Cheney	2,180	3	0	1	0	2	36	5	27	4	0
Cherryvale	2,154	9	4	1	0	4	53	20	31	2	0
Clay Center	3,930	19	0	0	0	19	68	12	51	5	0
Clearwater	2,529	1	0	0	0	1	44	8	34	2	0
Coffeyville	9,375	57	0	8	5	44	472	108	342	22	0
Colony	409	0	0	0	0	0	0	0	0	0	0
Columbus	3,066	10	0	0	0	10	64	10	48	6	1
Concordia	5,059	16	0	0	1	15	122	23	96	3	1
Council Grove	2,030	4	0	1	0	3	14	4	9	1	0
Derby	23,842	37	1	11	4	21	505	54	416	35	4
Dodge City	27,756	90	2	13	5	70	592	102	454	36	4
Edwardsville	4,505	13	0	2	1	10	113	26	75	12	2
El Dorado	12,960	28	0	3	3	22	383	94	243	46	9
Elkhart	1,825	6	0	0	0	6	9	1	6	2	0
Ellinwood	1,992	8	0	0	0	8	27	6	18	3	0
Ellsworth	3,044	4	0	0	0	4	36	6	26	4	1
Emporia	24,698	28	0	17	0	11	429	49	368	12	0
Fort Scott	7,779	37	0	3	1	33	259	53	184	22	3
Frontenac	3,409	3	0	1	0	2	54	12	40	2	0
Galena	2,871	12	0	0	0	12	104	21	71	12	7
Garden City	26,902	123	0	27	15	81	608	65	499	44	2

Table 8. Offenses Known to Law Enforcement, by Selected State and City, 2018—Continued

(Number.)

State/city	Population	Violent crime	Murder and nonnegligent manslaughter	Rape[1]	Robbery	Aggravated assault	Property crime	Burglary	Larceny-theft	Motor vehicle theft	Arson[2]
Gardner	21,945	56	0	9	3	44	308	28	262	18	2
Garnett	3,231	9	0	1	0	8	64	18	38	8	1
Grandview Plaza	1,627	5	0	2	0	3	64	17	35	12	0
Great Bend	15,251	112	2	10	6	94	577	131	410	36	3
Havensville	155	0	0	0	0	0	0	0	0	0	0
Haysville	11,343	46	2	12	5	27	283	33	233	17	4
Herington[5]	2,305	5	0	0	0	5			38	3	1
Hesston	3,791	5	0	0	0	5	37	4	31	2	0
Hiawatha	3,132	13	0	9	0	4	116	15	88	13	0
Hillsboro	2,829	3	0	0	1	2	40	14	16	10	0
Hoisington	2,539	7	1	1	0	5	46	6	36	4	0
Holton	3,258	12	0	2	0	10	80	10	68	2	0
Horton	1,687	2	0	0	0	2	23	9	14	0	0
Hoxie	1,194	0	0	0	0	0	4	0	4	0	0
Hugoton	3,816	2	0	0	0	2	9	0	8	1	0
Humboldt	1,783	0	0	0	0	0	31	4	22	5	0
Hutchinson	40,573	166	1	31	18	116	1,624	356	1,151	117	16
Independence[5]	8,629	62	1	9	3	49			383	32	3
Iola	5,306	33	2	13	1	17	209	69	130	10	0
Lake Quivira	939	0	0	0	0	0	4	0	3	1	0
Lansing	12,043	30	0	5	7	18	136	42	82	12	0
Larned	3,828	9	0	1	0	8	92	31	52	9	0
Leavenworth	36,331	345	1	31	43	270	1,130	247	783	100	10
Leawood	35,070	27	0	1	3	23	543	76	428	39	0
Lenexa	54,349	107	0	11	12	84	838	99	661	78	2
Lindsborg	3,247	3	0	1	0	2	40	12	27	1	0
Little River	524	0	0	0	0	0	1	0	1	0	0
Lyons	3,540	21	0	1	0	20	12	4	7	1	0
Maize	4,735	12	0	2	0	10	93	17	70	6	2
Marysville	3,268	5	0	0	0	5	53	10	39	4	0
McPherson[6]	13,211	23	1	4	5	13				21	1
Meade	1,610	0	0	0	0	0	10	0	10	0	0
Minneapolis	1,949	2	0	1	0	1	20	5	14	1	0
Montezuma	943	0	0	0	0	0	0	0	0	0	0
Moran	511	0	0	0	0	0	0	0	0	0	0
Mound City	680	0	0	0	0	0	0	0	0	0	0
Mount Hope	804	0	0	0	0	0	7	1	5	1	0
Mulvane	6,391	9	0	3	0	6	163	12	135	16	1
Neodesha	2,292	8	0	1	1	6	43	11	27	5	0
Newton	18,830	131	0	24	9	98	560	92	429	39	8
Norton	2,760	5	0	1	0	4	39	14	24	1	1
Oberlin	1,730	3	0	0	0	3	19	8	11	0	0
Olathe	139,154	305	2	80	26	197	1,957	147	1,639	171	7
Osage City	2,777	2	0	1	0	1	41	6	33	2	4
Osawatomie	4,278	7	0	1	0	6	72	8	59	5	0
Oswego	1,703	0	0	0	0	0	18	2	14	2	0
Ottawa	12,300	63	0	11	1	51	313	37	238	38	3
Overland Park	193,877	440	3	120	78	239	3,739	379	3,017	343	22
Paola	5,574	4	0	1	0	3	134	10	119	5	2
Park City	7,785	24	0	6	0	18	161	41	105	15	0
Parsons	9,664	91	1	6	6	78	345	80	251	14	5
Peabody	1,111	3	0	1	1	1	20	11	6	3	0
Plainville	1,832	3	1	0	0	2	1	0	1	0	0
Pratt	6,737	28	0	4	0	24	132	22	98	12	1
Rose Hill	3,986	5	0	2	0	3	58	14	41	3	1
Russell	4,454	25	0	7	0	18	83	10	62	11	1
Sabetha	2,569	0	0	0	0	0	29	3	22	4	0
Scott City	3,854	6	0	0	0	6	29	4	24	1	0
Sedgwick	1,661	4	0	0	0	4	18	5	12	1	0
Seneca	2,044	10	0	0	0	10	37	4	28	5	1
Shawnee	65,983	165	3	25	14	123	1,076	139	791	146	8
Sterling	2,214	1	0	0	0	1	31	8	18	5	1
St. Francis	1,301	1	0	0	0	1	13	4	2	7	0
St. George	1,028	0	0	0	0	0	6	1	5	0	0
Tonganoxie	5,508	6	0	1	0	5	59	3	47	9	0
Topeka	126,399	766	14	84	254	414	6,560	973	4,851	736	7
Ulysses	5,878	10	0	0	2	8	48	20	22	6	0
Valley Center	7,370	6	0	3	0	3	83	14	60	9	0
Walton	235	0	0	0	0	0	0	0	0	0	0
Wamego	4,748	19	0	1	1	17	103	13	81	9	0
Wellsville	1,803	5	0	0	0	5	19	3	15	1	0
Westwood	2,276	2	0	0	1	1	60	2	50	8	0
Wichita	391,726	4,622	38	378	572	3,634	22,011	3,412	15,826	2,773	139
Winfield	12,072	22	0	6	1	15	524	95	394	35	5
KENTUCKY											
Adairville	878	0	0	0	0	0	1	0	1	0	0
Alexandria	9,583	1	0	0	0	1	144	12	122	10	0
Anchorage	2,448	0	0	0	0	0	13	1	11	1	0
Ashland	20,525	30	0	8	5	17	774	122	608	44	2
Auburn	1,377	2	0	0	1	1	2	1	1	0	0
Audubon Park	1,506	0	0	0	0	0	36	3	29	4	0
Augusta	1,141	2	0	0	0	2	16	3	12	1	0

Table 8. Offenses Known to Law Enforcement, by Selected State and City, 2018—Continued

(Number.)

State/city	Population	Violent crime	Murder and nonnegligent manslaughter	Rape[1]	Robbery	Aggravated assault	Property crime	Burglary	Larceny-theft	Motor vehicle theft	Arson[2]
Barbourville	3,094	21	0	4	7	10	85	14	48	23	0
Bardstown[5]	13,244	26	0	7	11	8			233	27	1
Beattyville	1,192	2	0	0	0	2	13	4	1	8	0
Beaver Dam	3,587	6	0	1	1	4	30	1	23	6	0
Bellefonte	836	0	0	0	0	0	3	1	1	1	0
Bellevue	5,746	4	0	1	1	2	80	6	69	5	0
Benton	4,495	1	1	0	0	0	142	29	108	5	0
Berea	15,893	20	1	6	6	7	326	67	214	45	0
Bloomfield	1,061	1	0	0	1	0	5	0	3	2	0
Bowling Green	68,268	208	6	59	64	79	3,312	414	2,681	217	2
Brandenburg	2,852	1	0	0	0	1	26	6	12	8	1
Brodhead	1,179	0	0	0	0	0	4	0	2	2	0
Brownsville	832	0	0	0	0	0	6	1	4	1	0
Burnside	905	2	0	0	0	2	22	4	14	4	0
Cadiz	2,637	4	0	0	0	4	62	15	41	6	0
Calvert City	2,513	3	0	1	0	2	43	9	32	2	0
Campbellsville	11,503	32	0	5	16	11	522	121	370	31	1
Carlisle	1,957	2	0	2	0	0	5	2	2	1	0
Carrollton	3,820	2	0	0	0	2	36	9	20	7	1
Catlettsburg	1,766	1	0	0	1	0	37	11	22	4	0
Cave City	2,425	6	0	1	0	5	23	9	11	3	0
Centertown	436	0	0	0	0	0	2	1	1	0	0
Central City	5,746	3	0	1	0	2	56	4	49	3	0
Clay City	1,098	0	0	0	0	0	1	0	1	0	0
Clinton	1,277	0	0	0	0	0	10	4	5	1	0
Coal Run Village	1,502	1	0	0	1	0	23	2	21	0	0
Cold Spring	6,430	4	0	0	3	1	112	12	99	1	0
Columbia	4,927	2	0	0	0	2	13	2	8	3	0
Corbin	7,267	15	3	4	7	1	164	39	101	24	3
Covington	40,448	164	5	37	66	56	1,097	200	763	134	7
Cynthiana	6,362	12	0	2	5	5	109	25	72	12	0
Danville	16,801	34	0	17	7	10	283	80	176	27	3
Dawson Springs	2,665	4	0	0	3	1	43	20	18	5	0
Dayton	5,464	6	0	1	0	5	95	23	60	12	1
Dry Ridge	2,220	1	0	0	0	1	33	3	29	1	0
Eddyville	2,569	2	0	0	0	2	41	7	32	2	0
Edgewood	8,736	6	0	3	2	1	61	6	54	1	0
Edmonton	1,583	1	0	0	0	1	27	8	16	3	0
Elizabethtown	30,180	64	3	17	22	22	400	124	207	69	6
Elkton	2,106	5	0	0	1	4	31	13	18	0	1
Elsmere	8,680	11	0	4	2	5	92	13	68	11	1
Eminence	2,581	0	0	0	0	0	3	0	3	0	0
Erlanger	22,993	22	0	6	6	10	186	38	130	18	1
Evarts	816	1	0	0	0	1	4	1	2	1	0
Falmouth	2,100	1	0	0	1	0	33	9	22	2	1
Flatwoods	7,136	6	0	2	2	2	24	8	14	2	0
Flemingsburg	2,822	3	0	2	0	1	45	5	32	8	0
Florence	32,701	59	1	21	19	18	1,240	100	1,065	75	4
Fort Mitchell	8,260	4	0	2	1	1	62	12	45	5	0
Fort Thomas	16,274	6	0	3	1	2	68	8	56	4	0
Fort Wright	5,737	8	0	4	2	2	66	5	54	7	0
Frankfort	27,664	71	3	19	25	24	1,052	197	763	92	0
Franklin[5]	8,829	22	0	4	9	9	80	22	249	18	1
Fulton	2,175	3	0	1	1	1	80	22	55	3	2
Georgetown	34,351	62	1	14	22	25	992	124	787	81	0
Glasgow	14,411	33	0	4	5	24	452	111	314	27	4
Graymoor-Devondale	2,981	0	0	0	0	0	38	10	26	2	0
Grayson	3,983	11	0	0	4	7	43	10	29	4	3
Greensburg	2,101	5	0	0	1	4	24	6	17	1	0
Greenville	4,239	1	0	1	0	0	19	4	12	3	0
Guthrie	1,388	2	0	0	1	1	2	0	0	2	0
Harlan	1,526	8	0	2	3	3	32	11	20	1	0
Harrodsburg	8,399	3	0	1	0	2	96	25	55	16	1
Hazard	5,035	12	0	4	5	3	144	18	111	15	2
Henderson[5]	28,618	95	2	20	30	43			549	88	3
Heritage Creek	1,147	0	0	0	0	0	1	0	1	0	0
Highland Heights	7,112	2	0	1	1	0	66	16	47	3	0
Hillview	9,163	8	0	3	2	3	99	10	72	17	0
Hodgenville	3,223	5	0	2	0	3	47	6	33	8	1
Hopkinsville	30,606	85	2	19	25	39	997	228	701	68	3
Horse Cave	2,366	0	0	0	0	0	1	0	1	0	0
Hurstbourne Acres	1,909	0	0	0	0	0	17	1	14	2	0
Independence	28,052	23	0	13	1	9	154	30	109	15	0
Indian Hills	3,002	0	0	0	0	0	20	8	12	0	0
Irvine	2,330	4	1	2	0	1	17	11	4	2	1
Irvington	1,173	1	0	0	0	1	5	1	3	1	0
Jackson	2,029	1	0	1	0	0	55	10	44	1	0
Jamestown	1,790	0	0	0	0	0	11	5	6	0	0
Jeffersontown[5]	27,443	44	2	7	26	9			409	97	0
Junction City	2,300	1	0	0	0	1	6	3	3	0	0
La Grange	8,995	5	0	2	2	1	147	23	105	19	2
Lakeside Park-Crestview Hills	6,107	1	0	0	0	0	141	9	130	2	0
Lancaster	3,866	8	0	0	1	7	59	20	34	5	1

Table 8. Offenses Known to Law Enforcement, by Selected State and City, 2018—Continued

(Number.)

State/city	Population	Violent crime	Murder and nonnegligent manslaughter	Rape[1]	Robbery	Aggravated assault	Property crime	Burglary	Larceny-theft	Motor vehicle theft	Arson[2]
Lawrenceburg	11,378	4	0	2	1	1	142	31	87	24	0
Lebanon	5,668	23	0	3	5	15	85	22	48	15	0
Lebanon Junction	1,957	0	0	0	0	0	7	2	3	2	0
Leitchfield	6,914	14	0	5	1	8	194	51	126	17	1
Lewisburg	804	0	0	0	0	0	3	2	1	0	0
Lewisport	1,710	0	0	0	0	0	0	0	0	0	0
Lexington	325,579	982	22	243	422	295	10,329	1,523	7,755	1,051	50
Liberty	2,105	1	0	0	0	1	12	5	4	3	0
Livingston	217	0	0	0	0	0	0	0	0	0	0
London	8,008	18	0	0	7	11	271	32	187	52	1
Louisa	2,405	2	0	0	1	1	40	11	22	7	0
Ludlow	4,502	9	0	4	3	2	74	17	53	4	1
Madisonville[5]	18,959	37	0	9	9	19			169	33	7
Manchester	1,343	5	0	0	2	3	14	2	8	4	0
Marion	2,916	6	0	5	0	1	71	22	48	1	0
Martin	562	0	0	0	0	0	3	2	1	0	0
Mayfield	9,819	35	0	3	10	22	454	87	349	18	1
Maysville	8,770	19	0	5	5	9	276	46	211	19	0
Middlesboro	9,360	13	0	3	4	6	424	47	348	29	1
Millersburg	796	0	0	0	0	0	15	5	9	1	0
Monticello	6,101	6	0	1	1	4	74	24	39	11	2
Morehead	7,869	4	0	1	0	3	169	15	143	11	0
Morganfield	3,454	0	0	0	0	0	24	11	12	1	0
Morgantown	2,425	2	0	0	0	2	16	10	6	0	0
Mount Sterling	7,253	14	0	3	5	6	271	33	222	16	3
Mount Vernon	2,437	4	0	0	1	3	24	9	9	6	0
Mount Washington	14,704	12	0	3	2	7	131	29	84	18	2
Muldraugh	984	1	0	0	1	0	14	0	12	2	0
Munfordville	1,651	0	0	0	0	0	16	4	6	6	0
Murray[5]	19,402	23	0	9	2	12			403	21	0
Newport	14,972	46	1	8	23	14	569	70	451	48	0
Nicholasville	30,922	60	0	11	18	31	824	146	632	46	6
Northfield	1,061	0	0	0	0	0	9	2	7	0	0
Oak Grove	7,232	30	0	6	6	18	310	50	229	31	0
Olive Hill	1,569	0	0	0	0	0	18	6	8	4	0
Owensboro	59,686	160	2	42	59	57	2,638	453	1,945	240	9
Owenton	1,541	0	0	0	0	0	4	0	4	0	0
Owingsville	1,575	1	0	1	0	0	10	3	6	1	0
Paducah[5]	24,933	93	2	27	24	40			1,044	80	10
Paintsville	4,061	10	0	1	0	9	25	5	16	4	0
Paris	9,809	13	0	2	3	8	214	42	163	9	1
Park Hills	2,982	2	0	1	0	1	23	4	15	4	0
Pikeville	6,641	12	0	7	0	5	300	50	244	6	1
Pineville	1,716	2	0	1	1	0	29	13	15	1	0
Pioneer Village	2,914	1	0	0	1	0	19	2	14	3	0
Powderly	736	1	0	0	0	1	2	0	2	0	0
Prestonsburg	3,404	2	0	0	0	2	28	8	15	5	0
Princeton	6,075	10	0	3	3	4	281	114	154	13	0
Prospect	4,956	1	0	0	0	1	41	3	37	1	0
Providence	2,994	1	0	0	0	1	21	6	14	1	0
Raceland	2,347	0	0	0	0	0	3	1	2	0	0
Radcliff[5]	22,576	82	1	27	25	29			612	62	5
Richmond	35,952	66	1	18	17	30	1,066	204	781	81	1
Russell	3,203	4	0	1	1	2	69	12	54	3	0
Russell Springs	2,588	8	1	4	2	1	74	12	49	13	0
Russellville	7,088	17	0	6	4	7	213	53	154	6	2
Salyersville	1,745	0	0	0	0	0	3	1	2	0	0
Science Hill	696	0	0	0	0	0	3	0	3	0	0
Scottsville	4,478	6	0	2	1	3	162	51	105	6	0
Sebree	1,535	2	0	0	0	2	1	0	0	1	0
Shelbyville	16,138	20	2	5	5	8	273	52	197	24	0
Shepherdsville	12,391	26	0	8	7	11	257	47	163	47	1
Shively	15,876	55	1	5	23	26	578	87	379	112	0
Simpsonville	2,871	1	0	0	1	0	94	3	88	3	0
Somerset	11,453	30	1	9	11	9	247	54	145	48	2
Southgate	3,908	7	0	2	2	3	40	8	30	2	0
Springfield	3,157	2	0	0	0	2	17	5	9	3	0
Stamping Ground	782	1	0	1	0	0	3	0	2	1	0
Stanford	3,617	2	0	0	0	2	36	18	10	8	0
Stanton	2,642	2	0	1	0	1	88	27	56	5	0
St. Matthews[5]	18,228	37	0	2	21	14			740	83	0
Taylor Mill	6,781	4	0	2	1	1	51	6	37	8	0
Taylorsville	1,262	1	0	1	0	0	15	5	8	2	0
Tompkinsville	2,267	3	0	0	0	3	4	1	3	0	0
Trenton	374	0	0	0	0	0	2	1	1	0	0
Uniontown	943	3	0	1	0	2	33	9	23	1	0
Vanceburg	1,403	0	0	0	0	0	8	2	6	0	0
Versailles	26,552	27	0	10	6	11	391	92	273	26	2
Villa Hills	7,455	2	0	1	1	0	41	9	29	3	0
Vine Grove	6,237	2	0	1	1	0	93	46	40	7	0
Warsaw	1,693	1	0	0	0	1	3	0	3	0	0
West Buechel	1,287	3	0	0	3	0	79	4	59	16	0
West Liberty	3,342	0	0	0	0	0	8	2	5	1	0

Table 8. Offenses Known to Law Enforcement, by Selected State and City, 2018—Continued

(Number.)

State/city	Population	Violent crime	Murder and nonnegligent manslaughter	Rape[1]	Robbery	Aggravated assault	Property crime	Burglary	Larceny-theft	Motor vehicle theft	Arson[2]
West Point	858	0	0	0	0	0	10	3	7	0	0
Whitesburg	1,885	0	0	0	0	0	2	0	2	0	0
Wilder	3,068	8	1	2	0	5	37	3	27	7	0
Williamsburg	5,299	11	3	1	2	5	45	12	28	5	2
Williamstown	3,932	0	0	0	0	0	24	8	10	6	0
Wilmore	6,406	4	0	2	1	1	56	8	46	2	0
Woodburn	375	0	0	0	0	0	0	0	0	0	0
Worthington	1,519	0	0	0	0	0	8	3	5	0	0
LOUSIANA											
Abbeville	12,279	89	6	4	7	72	241	78	160	3	0
Addis	5,505	7	0	0	3	4	0	0	0	0	0
Alexandria	47,238	685	12	17	128	528	3,973	996	2,694	283	0
Baker	13,487	44	1	4	8	31	335	42	285	8	1
Ball	4,018	5	0	0	0	5	13	6	4	3	0
Bastrop	10,270	138	3	2	16	117	1,006	342	635	29	0
Baton Rouge	224,790	2,067	79	74	727	1,187	11,965	2,686	8,329	950	153
Berwick	4,537	1	0	0	0	1	67	23	41	3	0
Blanchard	3,168	1	0	0	0	1	60	19	34	7	0
Bogalusa	11,730	124	1	6	14	103	584	175	377	32	1
Bossier City	69,551	576	4	46	60	466	2,998	387	2,313	298	4
Breaux Bridge	8,349	28	0	1	4	23	595	133	439	23	0
Broussard	12,672	52	4	0	10	38	500	150	339	11	0
Brusly	2,773	1	0	0	1	0	18	6	9	3	0
Carencro	9,174	22	1	1	5	15	262	37	219	6	0
Church Point	4,440	49	0	4	5	40	215	38	167	10	0
Clinton	1,516	5	0	0	0	5	13	2	11	0	0
Covington	10,658	30	0	1	4	25	223	13	203	7	0
Crowley	12,779	228	5	9	15	199	916	234	640	42	1
Cullen	1,088	0	0	0	0	0	0	0	0	0	0
Denham Springs	9,761	44	2	2	5	35	669	115	551	3	0
De Ridder	10,820	10	1	3	0	6	301	75	213	13	3
Epps	820	0	0	0	0	0	0	0	0	0	0
Erath	2,083	13	0	0	0	13	29	4	24	1	0
Eunice	10,073	44	2	3	11	28	487	95	377	15	0
Farmerville	3,805	23	0	0	2	21	155	35	112	8	0
Ferriday	3,256	10	0	0	4	6	83	37	45	1	0
Fisher	221	0	0	0	0	0	0	0	0	0	0
Florien	607	2	0	0	1	1	1	0	0	1	0
Folsom	860	2	0	0	0	2	5	1	2	2	0
Franklin	6,874	52	2	0	4	46	273	110	153	10	1
Franklinton	3,771	36	1	4	3	28	137	25	107	5	2
French Settlement	1,175	4	0	0	0	4	12	3	8	1	0
Georgetown	324	0	0	0	0	0	1	1	0	0	0
Golden Meadow	1,985	2	0	0	0	2	8	8	0	0	0
Gonzales	10,916	62	1	2	7	52	775	60	691	24	2
Gramercy	3,382	9	0	1	1	7	99	11	84	4	0
Greensburg	659	26	0	0	0	26	34	10	22	2	0
Greenwood	3,183	12	0	0	1	11	65	12	38	15	0
Gretna	17,965	86	1	4	10	71	555	62	461	32	0
Hammond	20,550	299	0	32	57	210	2,124	622	1,385	117	2
Harahan	9,424	12	0	1	4	7	106	17	81	8	1
Haughton	3,425	15	0	1	0	14	89	41	34	14	0
Houma	33,226	158	3	19	30	106	1,625	173	1,366	86	5
Ida	208	0	0	0	0	0	0	0	0	0	0
Independence	1,911	25	0	1	1	23	124	19	93	12	0
Iowa	3,322	19	0	0	3	16	139	45	89	5	0
Jena	3,379	2	0	0	0	2	17	1	16	0	0
Jennings	9,949	19	0	1	1	17	187	18	169	0	0
Kaplan	4,529	13	0	3	0	10	39	14	25	0	0
Kenner	67,556	155	2	34	42	77	2,040	145	1,742	153	2
Kinder	2,404	1	0	0	0	1	98	13	79	6	0
Krotz Springs	1,221	8	0	0	1	7	36	4	30	2	0
Lafayette	127,592	681	9	21	158	493	5,882	1,019	4,485	378	20
Lake Arthur	2,757	11	0	3	0	8	78	12	65	1	0
Lake Charles	77,852	575	6	55	134	380	3,777	1,845	1,638	294	0
Lake Providence	3,551	24	0	0	0	24	9	7	2	0	0
Leesville	5,999	61	0	12	7	42	375	51	313	11	1
Lutcher	3,266	12	3	1	1	7	41	8	31	2	0
Mandeville	12,371	16	0	1	3	12	217	24	185	8	0
Mansfield	4,741	34	0	1	1	32	184	58	125	1	0
Many	2,714	13	0	1	0	12	78	17	61	0	0
Marion	750	1	0	0	0	1	12	3	9	0	0
Marksville	5,450	106	0	0	4	102	395	113	275	7	0
Minden	12,215	18	0	2	6	10	251	44	195	12	0
Monroe	48,291	677	4	28	147	498	3,278	749	2,358	171	14
Moreauville	889	0	0	0	0	0	0	0	0	0	0
Morgan City	11,066	96	3	6	8	79	535	192	339	4	0
Natchitoches	17,981	159	4	8	14	133	1,141	308	785	48	6
New Orleans[6]	396,374	4,611	147	681	1,219	2,564	18,063	2,027	13,042	2,994	0
Norwood	299	0	0	0	0	0	0	0	0	0	0
Oak Grove	1,581	7	0	1	0	6	77	13	63	1	0
Oil City	995	3	0	0	0	3	8	0	8	0	0

Table 8. Offenses Known to Law Enforcement, by Selected State and City, 2018—Continued

(Number.)

State/city	Population	Violent crime	Murder and nonnegligent manslaughter	Rape[1]	Robbery	Aggravated assault	Property crime	Burglary	Larceny-theft	Motor vehicle theft	Arson[2]
Olla	1,362	1	0	0	0	1	0	0	0	0	0
Opelousas	16,262	348	9	18	54	267	1,180	379	747	54	4
Patterson	5,964	26	0	0	5	21	157	7	147	3	1
Pearl River	2,641	26	0	0	1	25	64	10	48	6	0
Pineville	14,415	91	0	7	7	77	796	152	609	35	0
Plaquemine	6,660	32	2	1	0	29	209	44	163	2	0
Pollock	478	0	0	0	0	0	0	0	0	0	0
Ponchatoula	7,369	76	1	6	5	64	435	78	339	18	0
Port Allen	5,011	27	1	1	1	24	112	22	83	7	1
Port Vincent	751	0	0	0	0	0	0	10	10	0	0
Rayne[6]	8,184	21	0	0	3	18	196	23	170	3	0
Rayville[6]	3,557		0	0	0			4		0	0
Ringgold	1,396	0	0	0	0	0	0	0	0	0	0
Ruston	22,274	82	0	7	8	67	628	131	489	8	0
Scott	8,810	15	1	0	0	14	159	43	102	14	0
Shreveport	190,808	1,588	49	123	335	1,081	9,884	1,832	7,241	811	104
Sibley	1,161	0	0	0	0	0	2	1	1	0	0
Slidell	27,973	87	3	11	17	56	815	115	660	40	0
Springhill	4,891	8	0	0	0	8	141	2	139	0	0
St. Gabriel	7,399	65	0	2	2	61	54	18	34	2	0
Sulphur	20,250	95	1	13	16	65	879	138	691	50	1
Tallulah	6,777	21	0	1	0	20	23	6	16	1	2
Thibodaux	14,745	68	3	3	12	50	534	44	470	20	1
Vidalia	3,948	7	0	0	3	4	179	18	156	5	0
Ville Platte	7,130	11	1	0	7	3	566	139	409	18	0
Walker	6,286	59	0	1	4	54	432	40	384	8	1
Washington	940	0	0	0	0	0	2	1	1	0	0
Welsh	3,230	50	1	2	0	47	100	18	76	6	0
West Monroe	12,594	103	0	9	20	74	1,008	193	765	50	2
Westwego	8,551	22	0	4	6	12	171	39	117	15	1
White Castle	1,750	22	1	1	0	20	74	30	42	2	0
Wilson	552	0	0	0	0	0	0	0	0	0	0
Winnfield	4,376	73	0	3	0	70	205	59	140	6	0
Youngsville	14,370	12	1	3	1	7	221	35	176	10	0
Zachary	17,884	110	0	7	12	91	624	62	535	27	0
MAINE											
Ashland	1,214	1	0	0	0	1	30	8	16	6	0
Auburn	23,031	50	0	13	6	31	765	56	698	11	5
Augusta	18,523	60	0	21	10	29	618	63	530	25	0
Baileyville	1,446	6	0	1	0	5	9	0	8	1	0
Bangor	31,746	56	4	4	15	33	1,300	89	1,151	60	2
Bar Harbor	5,464	4	1	1	0	2	55	2	52	1	0
Bath	8,293	5	0	3	0	2	153	17	134	2	1
Belfast	6,765	5	0	1	0	4	94	31	58	5	0
Berwick	7,738	3	0	2	0	1	69	19	47	3	0
Biddeford	21,519	64	0	16	9	39	673	75	573	25	4
Boothbay Harbor	2,193	2	0	1	0	1	21	2	16	3	0
Brewer	8,984	12	0	3	7	2	266	7	253	6	0
Bridgton	5,391	6	0	3	0	3	56	9	45	2	0
Brunswick	20,672	28	0	13	5	10	361	34	317	10	2
Bucksport	4,914	1	0	0	0	1	37	5	32	0	0
Buxton	8,285	9	0	1	1	7	64	9	51	4	0
Calais	2,970	5	0	2	1	2	89	12	77	0	0
Camden	4,856	0	0	0	0	0	14	0	13	1	0
Cape Elizabeth	9,358	1	0	1	0	0	43	8	35	0	0
Caribou	7,617	5	0	0	1	4	83	13	57	13	0
Carrabassett Valley	777	0	0	0	0	0	12	0	12	0	0
Clinton	3,342	3	0	2	0	1	28	2	25	1	0
Cumberland	8,274	2	0	0	1	1	17	5	12	0	0
Damariscotta	2,134	0	0	0	0	0	44	1	41	2	0
Dexter	3,707	2	0	1	0	1	40	10	26	4	0
Dixfield	2,465	0	0	0	0	0	41	20	21	0	0
Dover-Foxcroft	4,023	3	0	0	0	3	60	9	49	2	0
East Millinocket	2,929	1	0	0	0	1	22	5	16	1	0
Eastport	1,258	0	0	0	0	0	20	12	8	0	0
Eliot	6,651	0	0	0	0	0	47	9	37	1	0
Ellsworth	8,008	6	0	4	1	1	182	9	173	0	0
Fairfield	6,539	7	0	2	1	4	102	14	82	6	0
Falmouth	12,307	7	0	2	3	2	87	8	76	3	0
Farmington	7,617	5	0	2	0	3	87	12	71	4	1
Fort Fairfield	3,279	3	0	0	1	2	20	8	8	4	0
Fort Kent	3,895	1	1	0	0	0	27	2	23	2	0
Freeport[4]	8,542	4	0	2	0	2	110	5	104	1	0
Fryeburg	3,437	7	0	2	1	4	47	10	34	3	0
Gardiner	5,673	1	0	0	1	0	50	5	43	2	0
Gorham	17,609	4	0	0	2	2	93	20	72	1	2
Gouldsboro	1,745	0	0	0	0	0	4	1	3	0	0
Greenville	1,588	2	0	0	0	2	24	3	20	1	0
Hallowell	2,363	2	0	1	0	1	14	1	13	0	0
Hampden	7,336	2	1	0	0	1	45	7	35	3	0
Holden	3,061	2	0	0	0	2	26	7	19	0	0
Houlton	5,770	19	0	3	0	16	125	8	111	6	0

Table 8. Offenses Known to Law Enforcement, by Selected State and City, 2018—Continued

(Number.)

State/city	Population	Violent crime	Murder and nonnegligent manslaughter	Rape[1]	Robbery	Aggravated assault	Property crime	Burglary	Larceny-theft	Motor vehicle theft	Arson[2]
Islesboro	568	0	0	0	0	0	3	3	0	0	0
Jay	4,606	9	0	2	0	7	54	10	38	6	0
Kennebunk	11,463	6	0	1	1	4	51	9	41	1	0
Kennebunkport	3,632	1	0	0	0	1	28	3	23	2	0
Kittery	9,755	11	0	4	1	6	107	10	95	2	0
Lewiston	36,170	84	2	15	22	45	598	89	486	23	4
Limestone	2,174	1	0	0	0	1	38	17	19	2	0
Lincoln	4,891	1	0	0	0	1	93	29	63	1	0
Lisbon	8,869	9	0	6	0	3	71	9	59	3	0
Livermore Falls	3,120	5	0	1	0	4	47	7	36	4	0
Machias	2,086	8	0	2	1	5	33	8	24	1	0
Madawaska	3,750	0	0	0	0	0	23	5	17	1	0
Mechanic Falls	2,973	6	0	2	0	4	38	5	32	1	1
Mexico	2,600	13	0	9	0	4	153	26	125	2	0
Milbridge	1,286	0	0	0	0	0	11	2	9	0	0
Millinocket	4,264	2	0	1	0	1	50	17	32	1	0
Milo	2,262	1	0	1	0	0	21	4	15	2	0
Monmouth	4,103	2	0	2	0	0	13	2	11	0	0
Newport	3,273	6	0	2	1	3	60	18	40	2	0
North Berwick	4,707	0	0	0	0	0	23	3	15	5	0
Norway	4,948	5	0	2	0	3	56	13	43	0	1
Oakland	6,253	2	0	1	0	1	55	7	45	3	2
Ogunquit	925	0	0	0	0	0	24	5	19	0	0
Old Orchard Beach	8,890	23	0	3	4	16	162	9	143	10	1
Old Town	7,450	5	0	2	1	2	129	17	111	1	0
Orono	11,451	10	0	4	1	5	90	11	75	4	0
Oxford	4,049	2	0	2	0	0	135	19	113	3	0
Paris	5,145	3	0	1	1	1	84	11	73	0	0
Phippsburg	2,246	1	0	0	0	1	6	0	6	0	0
Pittsfield	3,999	0	0	0	0	0	19	2	17	0	1
Portland	66,997	192	2	49	49	92	1,626	169	1,370	87	11
Presque Isle	8,997	22	0	4	1	17	262	46	210	6	1
Rangeley	1,150	1	0	1	0	0	10	1	9	0	0
Richmond	3,423	8	1	1	0	6	11	4	7	0	0
Rockland	7,171	4	0	2	0	2	147	7	135	5	0
Rockport	3,384	0	0	0	0	0	15	0	15	0	0
Rumford	5,712	13	0	6	2	5	183	17	160	6	0
Sabattus	5,057	1	0	1	0	0	18	3	12	3	0
Saco	19,628	21	1	6	4	10	309	48	251	10	2
Sanford[4]	21,062	56	1	22	9	24	568	76	469	23	5
Scarborough	20,072	7	0	3	0	4	253	15	230	8	3
Searsport	2,668	4	0	1	0	3	26	14	9	3	0
Skowhegan	8,223	25	0	13	1	11	258	31	221	6	3
South Berwick	7,500	7	0	5	0	2	27	2	24	1	1
South Portland	25,557	36	0	9	4	23	455	54	388	13	3
Southwest Harbor	1,779	0	0	0	0	0	25	4	21	0	0
Thomaston	2,772	0	0	0	0	0	45	3	40	2	0
Topsham	8,780	4	0	0	2	2	95	20	72	3	0
Van Buren	2,002	0	0	0	0	0	21	3	16	2	0
Veazie	1,819	1	0	0	0	1	12	3	9	0	0
Waldoboro	5,015	5	0	0	1	4	44	14	27	3	0
Washburn	1,550	1	0	0	0	1	3	2	0	1	0
Waterville	16,729	30	0	13	5	12	536	50	469	17	2
Wells	10,412	6	0	1	0	5	79	9	63	7	0
Westbrook	18,915	33	0	8	11	14	358	52	293	13	1
Wilton	3,939	8	0	3	0	5	23	7	15	1	0
Windham	18,230	9	0	0	2	7	220	36	178	6	0
Winslow	7,589	7	0	3	2	2	86	10	71	5	2
Winter Harbor	514	0	0	0	0	0	4	1	2	1	0
Winthrop	6,007	1	0	0	0	1	73	26	45	2	0
Wiscasset	3,678	0	0	0	0	0	26	2	24	0	0
Yarmouth	8,510	3	0	3	0	0	32	7	24	1	0
York	13,170	8	0	3	0	5	91	21	70	0	0
MARYLAND											
Aberdeen	16,210	116	0	8	24	84	314	48	256	10	0
Annapolis	39,461	215	1	27	47	140	910	133	722	55	3
Baltimore	605,436	11,100	309	361	5,066	5,364	27,217	6,048	16,794	4,375	138
Baltimore City Sheriff		0	0	0	0	0	0	0	0	0	0
Bel Air	10,027	23	0	2	10	11	231	8	219	4	1
Berlin	4,660	2	0	0	1	1	69	9	58	2	0
Berwyn Heights	3,300	14	0	2	11	1	49	6	42	1	0
Bladensburg	9,518	56	0	4	13	39	330	46	233	51	0
Boonsboro	3,569	0	0	0	0	0	21	5	16	0	0
Bowie	59,356	80	1	3	26	50	817	82	686	49	0
Brentwood	3,513	4	0	0	3	1	41	11	22	8	0
Brunswick	6,322	12	0	0	1	11	84	15	65	4	0
Cambridge	12,364	128	1	3	24	100	602	156	437	9	4
Capitol Heights	4,587	19	0	1	6	12	51	14	21	16	0
Centreville	4,844	9	0	2	1	6	27	1	26	0	1
Chestertown	5,035	20	0	1	5	14	83	16	65	2	0
Cheverly	6,519	21	0	0	10	11	131	22	100	9	0
Chevy Chase Village	2,094	0	0	0	0	0	42	7	33	2	0

Table 8. Offenses Known to Law Enforcement, by Selected State and City, 2018—Continued

(Number.)

State/city	Population	Violent crime	Murder and nonnegligent manslaughter	Rape[1]	Robbery	Aggravated assault	Property crime	Burglary	Larceny-theft	Motor vehicle theft	Arson[2]
Colmar Manor	1,476	13	0	0	5	8	34	6	27	1	0
Cottage City	1,375	1	0	0	1	0	27	7	16	4	0
Crisfield	2,587	7	0	1	0	6	7	2	5	0	0
Cumberland	19,555	146	0	11	30	105	881	231	630	20	6
Delmar	3,227	11	0	0	3	8	64	20	44	0	0
Denton	4,485	11	0	1	2	8	132	14	113	5	3
District Heights	6,062	16	0	0	6	10	34	13	16	5	0
Easton	16,550	36	1	9	15	11	400	48	348	4	5
Edmonston	1,508	5	0	0	2	3	33	1	25	7	0
Elkton	15,681	199	0	11	56	132	989	160	777	52	4
Fairmount Heights	1,545	6	0	0	4	2	39	8	19	12	0
Federalsburg	2,656	15	0	2	3	10	98	20	76	2	0
Forest Heights	2,588	0	0	0	0	0	47	16	25	6	0
Frederick	72,299	285	3	27	74	181	1,490	139	1,301	50	10
Frostburg	8,591	19	0	0	3	16	137	39	94	4	0
Fruitland	5,349	19	0	0	4	15	260	16	243	1	0
Glenarden	6,258	8	0	0	3	5	63	13	35	15	0
Greenbelt	23,661	116	3	14	56	43	722	87	563	72	2
Greensboro	1,882	5	0	0	3	2	28	3	25	0	0
Hagerstown	40,384	255	5	27	102	121	1,052	242	709	101	17
Hampstead	6,364	4	0	0	1	3	48	5	41	2	2
Hancock	1,546	3	0	0	0	3	9	1	6	2	0
Havre de Grace	13,655	32	1	5	6	20	217	40	165	12	
Hurlock	2,023	4	0	0	1	3	79	13	65	1	1
Hyattsville	18,448	79	0	3	50	26	927	49	818	60	0
Landover Hills	1,679	9	0	0	6	3	91	20	56	15	0
La Plata	9,449	41	0	0	10	31	312	21	278	13	4
Laurel	26,038	115	3	10	48	54	929	74	777	78	0
Lonaconing	1,120	0	0	0	0	0	0	0	0	0	0
Luke	60	0	0	0	0	0	0	0	0	0	0
Manchester	4,837	0	0	0	0	0	13	4	9	0	0
Morningside	1,594	3	0	0	1	2	30	6	18	6	0
Mount Airy	9,434	4	0	0	2	2	85	13	65	7	0
Mount Rainier	8,198	35	0	5	19	11	270	15	214	41	0
New Carrollton	13,115	40	1	1	14	24	181	51	109	21	1
North East	3,642	7	0	0	3	4	68	4	58	6	1
Oakland	1,829	4	0	0	0	4	64	7	55	2	0
Ocean City	6,950	83	0	5	14	64	832	114	701	17	0
Ocean Pines	12,244	14	0	2	1	11	52	12	39	1	0
Oxford	601	0	0	0	0	0	2	1	0	1	0
Perryville	4,424	14	0	0	3	11	110	22	87	1	0
Pocomoke City	4,044	10	0	3	5	2	155	32	119	4	
Princess Anne	3,600	39	0	3	10	26	129	30	94	5	1
Ridgely	1,638	1	0	0	1	0	20	4	13	3	2
Rising Sun	2,800	7	0	0	1	6	34	12	22	0	0
Riverdale Park	7,330	45	0	0	13	32	174	10	129	35	1
Rock Hall	1,263	1	0	0	0	1	3	0	3	0	0
Salisbury	33,183	272	3	21	74	174	1,548	195	1,312	41	11
Seat Pleasant	4,857	49	2	0	12	35	131	15	88	28	1
Smithsburg	2,977	2	0	0	0	2	15	2	12	1	0
Snow Hill	2,044	0	0	0	0	0	30	2	27	1	0
St. Michaels	1,028	3	0	1	1	1	34	8	26	0	0
Sykesville	3,941	44	0	0	0	44	13	3	10	0	0
Takoma Park	18,049	57	0	4	18	35	393	54	315	24	0
Taneytown	6,795	0	0	0	0	0	49	2	47	0	1
Thurmont	6,712	8	0	2	3	3	39	6	33	0	0
University Park	2,670	5	0	0	4	1	19	5	12	2	0
Upper Marlboro	676	0	0	0	0	0	7	2	4	1	0
Westminster	18,603	84	0	0	22	62	579	75	481	23	1
MASSACHUSETTS											
Abington	16,443	41	0	5	3	33	147	18	107	22	0
Acton	24,038	26	1	7	2	16	156	27	125	4	0
Acushnet	10,576	19	0	5	1	13	69	21	42	6	0
Adams	8,036	23	1	1	2	19	96	32	60	4	1
Agawam	28,955	105	0	14	12	79	428	142	268	18	0
Amesbury	17,623	32	0	8	2	22	143	18	117	8	1
Amherst	40,242	120	0	27	2	91	175	43	121	11	3
Andover	36,324	7	0	4	1	2	173	27	139	7	1
Aquinnah	329	0	0	0	0	0	2	0	2	0	0
Arlington	45,876	34	0	2	9	23	191	41	144	6	0
Ashburnham	6,335	6	0	1	0	5	24	4	17	3	0
Ashland	17,860	22	0	4	0	18	90	8	73	9	0
Athol	11,721	57	0	7	4	46	143	19	121	3	1
Attleboro	44,719	98	0	23	8	67	529	70	432	27	4
Auburn	16,771	29	1	3	1	24	318	28	281	9	3
Avon	4,514	4	0	0	3	1	64	10	50	4	
Ayer	8,246	36	0	2	4	30	69	10	50	9	1
Barnstable	44,015	166	1	20	8	137	462	85	363	14	3
Becket	1,716	3	0	0	0	3	15	5	10	0	
Bedford	14,319	7	0	1	1	5	58	9	48	1	0
Belchertown	15,165	25	0	3	0	22	78	11	63	4	0
Bellingham	17,184	19	0	4	2	13	210	17	185	8	1

Table 8. Offenses Known to Law Enforcement, by Selected State and City, 2018—Continued

(Number.)

State/city	Population	Violent crime	Murder and nonnegligent manslaughter	Rape[1]	Robbery	Aggravated assault	Property crime	Burglary	Larceny-theft	Motor vehicle theft	Arson[2]
Belmont	26,700	5	0	1	0	4	167	52	107	8	0
Berkley	6,748	7	0	0	0	7	19	6	9	4	0
Berlin	3,222	3	0	2	1	0	33	4	28	1	0
Bernardston	2,108	4	0	0	0	4	22	7	12	3	0
Beverly	42,114	42	0	3	3	36	243	24	208	11	0
Billerica	44,482	37	0	4	7	26	171	39	123	9	2
Blackstone	9,345	3	0	1	1	1	37	11	22	4	0
Bolton	5,335	0	0	0	0	0	33	9	22	2	0
Boston	694,673	4,324	56	278	1,172	2,818	14,007	1,853	11,000	1,154	
Bourne	19,894	46	0	5	1	40	266	99	157	10	0
Boxborough	6,634	5	0	2	0	3	16	1	14	1	1
Boxford	8,355	2	0	2	0	0	20	0	20	0	0
Boylston	4,674	3	0	1	0	2	13	7	5	1	0
Braintree	37,345	52	0	0	8	44	487	49	409	29	2
Brewster	9,831	31	0	9	0	22	68	10	55	3	2
Bridgewater	27,584	57	0	4	1	52	116	29	81	6	0
Brockton	95,922	868	9	72	182	605	2,071	267	1,496	308	7
Brookline	59,199	56	0	5	9	42	632	71	540	21	0
Burlington	27,562	40	0	11	5	24	378	21	346	11	0
Cambridge	114,881	339	0	27	102	210	2,068	255	1,704	109	7
Canton	23,709	81	0	4	4	73	118	7	98	13	1
Carlisle	5,289	1	0	1	0	0	22	3	19	0	0
Carver	11,743	30	0	8	2	20	70	6	59	5	0
Charlton	13,652	13	0	0	1	12	88	11	69	8	1
Chatham	6,174	9	0	1	1	7	54	10	43	1	0
Chelmsford	35,264	31	0	4	2	25	381	32	335	14	0
Chelsea	40,974	277	0	39	60	178	584	78	428	78	1
Chilmark	923	0	0	0	0	0	9	0	9	0	0
Clinton	14,009	10	0	0	2	8	18	1	17	0	0
Cohasset	8,665	6	0	0	1	5	56	8	48	0	0
Concord	19,459	8	0	3	0	5	111	8	100	3	0
Dalton	6,556	14	0	4	0	10	30	5	20	5	0
Danvers	27,703	54	0	5	6	43	420	53	351	16	2
Dartmouth	34,322	66	2	12	5	47	458	55	383	20	1
Dedham	25,437	7	0	0	2	5	339	12	294	33	0
Deerfield	5,012	7	0	1	1	5	59	12	41	6	0
Dennis	13,872	63	0	8	1	54	231	55	164	12	0
Douglas	8,925	20	0	1	1	18	20	4	14	2	0
Dover	6,104	0	0	0	0	0	11	1	9	1	0
Dracut	31,917	41	0	3	4	34	277	48	208	21	1
Dudley	11,807	24	0	7	1	16	33	7	24	2	1
Dunstable	3,407	4	0	1	0	3	18	6	11	1	0
Duxbury	16,049	7	0	0	0	7	92	18	74	0	1
East Bridgewater	14,558	22	0	2	1	19	94	15	70	9	0
Eastham	4,871	10	0	3	1	6	66	8	57	1	0
Easthampton	16,050	34	0	5	2	27	122	26	88	8	0
East Longmeadow	16,398	28	0	4	6	18	262	40	212	10	0
Easton	25,225	45	0	15	3	27	173	27	135	11	0
Edgartown	4,357	27	0	4	1	22	91	11	78	2	0
Egremont	1,202	2	0	0	0	2	2	0	2	0	
Erving	1,762	6	0	1	0	5	23	8	13	2	0
Everett	47,005	173	1	17	36	119	685	140	472	73	1
Fairhaven	16,076	55	0	8	2	45	293	53	229	11	2
Fall River	89,475	908	1	76	118	713	1,361	388	764	209	20
Falmouth	31,033	109	0	22	3	84	329	97	211	21	0
Fitchburg	40,836	238	2	32	36	168	526	110	376	40	2
Foxborough	17,667	44	0	5	2	37	154	20	128	6	0
Framingham	72,510	253	0	21	18	214	820	123	635	62	5
Franklin	33,156	5	0	2	0	3	85	4	77	4	0
Freetown	9,404	24	0	4	1	19	67	9	47	11	1
Gardner	20,704	92	0	21	4	67	364	64	271	29	1
Georgetown	8,757	2	0	0	0	2	45	8	36	1	3
Gill	1,498	4	0	2	0	2	16	3	12	1	0
Gloucester	30,356	72	0	8	3	61	216	33	167	16	2
Goshen	1,067	0	0	0	0	0	3	0	3	0	0
Grafton	18,900	21	0	0	2	19	61	13	42	6	0
Granby	6,347	7	0	3	0	4	41	8	29	4	0
Great Barrington	6,821	18	0	2	3	13	53	5	45	3	0
Greenfield	17,443	101	0	21	10	70	325	50	261	14	1
Groton	11,462	11	0	3	1	7	36	5	30	1	0
Groveland	6,833	0	0	0	0	0	18	2	13	3	0
Hadley	5,347	34	0	4	1	29	122	9	111	2	0
Halifax	7,901	4	0	1	0	3	94	13	79	2	1
Hamilton	8,088	2	0	0	0	2	26	7	18	1	0
Hampden	5,213	5	0	1	0	4	23	2	18	3	0
Hanover	14,521	2	0	1	0	1	120	6	110	4	0
Hanson	10,858	30	0	4	1	25	58	12	42	4	2
Hardwick	3,029	6	0	0	0	6	31	6	23	2	0
Harvard	6,572	4	0	1	0	3	76	8	68	0	1
Harwich	12,130	24	0	4	2	18	125	32	90	3	0
Hatfield	3,302	4	0	0	2	2	22	9	12	1	0
Haverhill	64,012	358	2	18	32	306	895	186	615	94	3
Hingham	23,588	37	0	7	0	30	180	20	152	8	0

Table 8. Offenses Known to Law Enforcement, by Selected State and City, 2018—Continued

(Number.)

State/city	Population	Violent crime	Murder and nonnegligent manslaughter	Rape[1]	Robbery	Aggravated assault	Property crime	Burglary	Larceny-theft	Motor vehicle theft	Arson[2]
Holbrook	11,052	23	0	2	3	18	110	17	85	8	0
Holland	2,502	2	1	0	0	1	12	4	8	0	0
Holliston	14,924	12	0	0	0	12	40	5	35	0	0
Holyoke	40,470	391	1	40	62	288	1,640	246	1,275	119	9
Hopedale	5,984	2	0	2	0	0	16	4	10	2	0
Hopkinton	18,516	2	0	0	1	1	30	0	29	1	0
Hudson	20,060	48	0	13	3	32	90	6	84	0	0
Ipswich	14,107	14	0	1	0	13	74	13	59	2	1
Kingston	13,700	26	0	2	1	23	102	9	86	7	0
Lakeville	11,525	14	0	2	1	11	114	28	78	8	0
Lancaster	8,074	15	0	0	0	15	53	12	36	5	1
Lawrence	80,669	500	5	29	71	395	934	129	583	222	
Lee	5,694	17	0	2	2	13	83	15	67	1	0
Leicester	11,435	35	0	8	2	25	142	11	124	7	0
Lenox	4,941	11	0	5	0	6	78	8	70	0	0
Leominster	41,727	219	0	17	12	190	824	125	670	29	1
Lexington	34,050	8	0	1	0	7	113	24	88	1	1
Lincoln	6,839	5	0	2	0	3	25	1	24	0	0
Littleton	10,292	9	0	1	0	8	56	6	48	2	0
Longmeadow	15,898	15	0	6	0	9	183	33	145	5	0
Lowell	111,989	363	4	24	105	230	1,718	354	1,147	217	15
Ludlow	21,590	46	1	2	2	41	228	47	169	12	1
Lunenburg	11,498	18	0	3	0	15	180	30	144	6	0
Lynn	94,558	563	3	51	140	369	1,359	187	954	218	5
Lynnfield	13,141	4	0	1	1	2	93	4	86	3	1
Malden	61,469	180	0	8	35	137	588	63	451	74	0
Manchester-by-the-Sea	5,428	6	0	2	2	2	11	2	8	1	0
Mansfield	24,050	34	0	6	1	27	205	35	159	11	0
Marblehead	20,652	20	0	3	1	16	102	12	88	2	0
Marion	5,134	9	0	1	0	8	50	7	40	3	0
Marlborough	40,052	167	0	36	17	114	456	53	378	25	2
Marshfield	25,922	33	0	5	1	27	83	14	66	3	0
Mashpee	14,215	47	0	7	2	38	134	12	119	3	0
Mattapoisett	6,369	12	0	2	0	10	36	12	23	1	0
Maynard	10,744	21	0	4	0	17	52	6	42	4	0
Medford	57,997	73	0	6	9	58	548	85	414	49	2
Medway	13,406	21	0	4	1	16	73	7	64	2	0
Melrose	28,552	15	0	1	1	13	146	22	115	9	0
Mendon	6,130	4	0	0	0	4	31	4	24	3	0
Merrimac	6,993	4	0	2	1	1	26	10	14	2	0
Methuen	50,676	44	0	2	10	32	486	52	384	50	1
Middleboro	25,125	111	0	16	6	89	215	37	166	12	4
Middleton	9,991	17	0	0	0	17	48	6	40	2	0
Milford	29,056	61	0	18	2	41	233	19	192	22	1
Millbury	13,802	19	0	1	1	17	155	22	124	9	1
Millville	3,260	0	0	0	0	0	19	3	15	1	1
Milton	27,642	12	0	3	2	7	60	23	29	8	0
Monson	8,890	22	0	4	1	17	51	27	21	3	2
Montague	8,235	58	0	5	2	51	95	22	71	2	1
Nahant	3,513	6	0	0	1	5	7	1	6	0	0
Nantucket	11,388	37	0	9	1	27	225	21	193	11	0
Natick	36,717	56	0	19	1	36	419	27	382	10	0
Needham	31,264	16	1	2	2	11	144	7	134	3	1
New Bedford	95,106	603	3	45	166	389	2,425	491	1,753	181	18
New Braintree	1,028	1	0	0	0	1	4	0	3	1	0
Newbury	7,135	9	0	3	0	6	28	7	19	2	0
Newburyport	18,146	18	0	8	0	10	121	9	105	7	0
Newton	89,505	58	0	3	5	50	629	72	540	17	2
Norfolk	11,872	1	0	0	0	1	21	2	18	1	0
North Adams	12,858	100	1	3	7	89	421	112	290	19	1
Northampton	28,587	113	1	24	7	81	540	108	414	18	1
North Andover	31,394	35	1	9	2	23	173	10	151	12	3
North Attleboro	29,208	28	0	7	2	19	357	27	323	7	0
Northborough	15,124	0	0	0	0	0	111	5	103	3	0
Northbridge	16,759	27	0	7	3	17	186	25	148	13	0
Northfield	2,982	4	0	2	0	2	15	5	10	0	0
North Reading	15,849	16	0	0	1	15	44	6	35	3	0
Norton	19,983	14	0	0	0	14	23	6	13	4	0
Norwell	11,144	9	0	2	0	7	51	6	42	3	0
Norwood	29,267	39	0	9	7	23	265	23	214	28	1
Oak Bluffs	4,699	25	0	0	0	25	74	9	62	3	0
Oakham	1,952	3	0	0	1	2	11	2	8	1	0
Orleans	5,809	8	0	0	1	7	72	3	69	0	0
Oxford	14,015	33	0	7	5	21	171	10	151	10	2
Palmer	12,320	57	1	6	4	46	98	15	70	13	0
Paxton	4,888	3	0	0	1	2	14	1	12	1	0
Peabody	53,209	159	0	17	11	131	532	93	402	37	0
Pelham	1,326	1	0	1	0	0	2	1	1	0	0
Pembroke	18,446	15	0	4	0	11	86	8	75	3	0
Pepperell	12,234	13	0	3	1	9	41	5	32	4	1
Pittsfield	42,298	356	3	43	35	275	1,196	464	661	71	8
Plainville	9,281	10	0	0	1	9	62	6	52	4	0
Plymouth	60,349	230	0	42	17	171	519	85	411	23	3

Table 8. Offenses Known to Law Enforcement, by Selected State and City, 2018—Continued

(Number.)

State/city	Population	Violent crime	Murder and nonnegligent manslaughter	Rape[1]	Robbery	Aggravated assault	Property crime	Burglary	Larceny-theft	Motor vehicle theft	Arson[2]
Plympton	2,988	5	0	0	1	4	26	6	19	1	0
Princeton	3,458	0	0	0	0	0	7	2	5	0	0
Provincetown	2,960	18	0	6	0	12	96	16	78	2	0
Quincy	94,388	352	0	32	49	271	1,190	261	860	69	4
Randolph	34,535	108	0	14	18	76	456	74	349	33	1
Raynham	14,320	27	0	1	1	25	235	20	198	17	0
Reading	26,293	5	0	0	2	3	144	24	112	8	1
Rehoboth	12,268	8	0	0	0	8	97	14	76	7	0
Revere	54,296	259	0	32	33	194	885	99	700	86	1
Rochester	5,623	7	0	0	1	6	25	3	20	2	0
Rockport	7,284	5	0	2	0	3	13	3	10	0	0
Rowley	6,392	9	0	2	0	7	29	6	21	2	0
Rutland	8,803	18	0	1	0	17	27	4	21	2	0
Salem	43,634	83	0	5	22	56	824	96	688	40	0
Salisbury	9,567	20	0	4	0	16	90	16	54	20	1
Sandwich	20,248	23	0	10	1	12	102	17	81	4	1
Saugus	28,471	66	0	4	9	53	370	34	303	33	0
Scituate	18,761	15	0	4	0	11	63	8	54	1	0
Seekonk	15,820	26	0	2	3	21	267	20	230	17	0
Sharon	18,373	13	0	2	3	8	51	10	39	2	1
Shelburne	1,842	0	0	0	0	0	18	5	12	1	0
Sherborn	4,351	8	0	1	1	6	23	3	19	1	0
Shirley	7,724	10	0	0	1	9	31	6	18	7	0
Shrewsbury	37,631	4	0	1	1	2	114	10	94	10	1
Somerset	18,166	39	1	7	1	30	155	14	130	11	1
Somerville	82,161	177	0	21	43	113	1,020	160	750	110	1
Southampton	6,254	11	0	0	0	11	28	4	22	2	0
Southborough	10,187	11	0	5	1	5	23	2	19	2	0
Southbridge	16,933	89	1	6	9	73	304	55	237	12	1
South Hadley	17,799	24	0	1	3	20	251	78	160	13	0
Southwick	9,810	17	0	2	1	14	70	16	51	3	0
Spencer	11,989	18	0	2	0	16	69	14	49	6	0
Springfield	155,179	1,534	19	104	475	936	4,089	910	2,752	427	20
Sterling	8,181	7	0	0	0	7	32	9	21	2	0
Stockbridge	1,900	3	0	1	0	2	26	5	20	1	0
Stoneham	22,135	33	0	3	2	28	243	68	166	9	1
Stoughton	28,729	76	0	4	12	60	327	38	259	30	3
Stow	7,171	5	0	1	0	4	35	12	19	4	0
Sturbridge	9,626	24	1	2	2	19	115	15	91	9	0
Sudbury	19,037	21	0	7	0	14	63	3	58	2	1
Sunderland	3,638	4	0	0	1	3	23	4	18	1	0
Sutton	9,527	15	0	1	1	13	67	17	45	5	0
Swampscott	15,380	9	0	3	1	5	170	25	138	7	0
Swansea	16,619	29	0	1	4	24	193	20	157	16	0
Taunton	57,304	243	0	18	35	190	356	84	248	24	3
Templeton	8,156	15	0	1	1	13	27	8	16	3	0
Tewksbury	31,561	82	0	22	7	53	345	33	293	19	1
Tisbury	4,131	24	0	4	0	20	57	12	44	1	0
Topsfield	6,628	6	0	0	0	6	16	2	14	0	0
Townsend	9,600	9	0	0	0	9	48	14	29	5	0
Truro	2,004	5	0	0	0	5	18	6	11	1	0
Tyngsboro	12,499	20	0	4	0	16	53	8	33	12	0
Upton	7,979	5	0	3	0	2	21	3	15	3	0
Wakefield	27,447	42	0	12	5	25	175	15	152	8	1
Wales	1,902	1	1	0	0	0	8	0	7	1	0
Walpole	25,204	42	0	3	4	35	262	34	220	8	0
Waltham	62,655	117	0	13	11	93	561	90	431	40	0
Ware	9,850	46	1	1	4	40	153	15	130	8	1
Wareham	22,747	160	0	17	15	128	384	57	299	28	2
Watertown	36,320	29	0	9	3	17	283	38	230	15	0
Wayland	14,088	1	0	0	0	1	1	0	1	0	0
Webster	17,051	108	1	16	10	81	206	52	129	25	1
Wellesley	29,681	12	0	3	1	8	124	11	113	0	0
Wellfleet	2,733	5	0	1	0	4	31	4	27	0	0
Wenham	5,299	3	0	0	0	3	14	2	12	0	0
Westborough	19,226	17	0	6	2	9	181	38	132	11	0
West Boylston	8,103	11	1	1	2	7	56	7	46	3	0
West Bridgewater	7,272	6	0	0	1	5	86	7	70	9	0
Westfield	41,854	111	0	16	8	87	464	78	362	24	2
Westford	24,649	12	0	3	0	9	64	10	54	0	1
Westminster	7,835	13	0	3	0	10	49	4	44	1	1
West Newbury	4,694	2	0	0	0	2	16	3	11	2	0
Weston	12,264	5	0	3	0	2	45	4	39	2	0
Westport	15,959	33	0	7	2	24	115	39	72	4	1
West Springfield	28,802	168	0	26	26	116	1,020	138	821	61	3
West Tisbury	2,920	8	0	0	0	8	23	2	20	1	0
Westwood	16,267	10	0	3	0	7	136	8	122	6	0
Weymouth	57,069	160	1	14	20	125	514	46	437	31	3
Whately	1,559	2	0	0	0	2	9	2	6	1	0
Whitman	15,093	38	0	5	2	31	111	15	87	9	1
Wilbraham	14,760	22	0	5	1	16	170	45	121	4	0
Williamsburg	2,493	3	0	1	0	2	31	13	16	2	0
Williamstown	7,845	5	0	2	1	2	79	4	75	0	0

Table 8. Offenses Known to Law Enforcement, by Selected State and City, 2018—Continued

(Number.)

State/city	Population	Violent crime	Murder and nonnegligent manslaughter	Rape[1]	Robbery	Aggravated assault	Property crime	Burglary	Larceny-theft	Motor vehicle theft	Arson[2]
Wilmington	24,005	20	0	0	3	17	125	16	100	9	1
Winchendon	10,933	38	0	9	0	29	149	19	112	18	1
Winchester	23,036	6	1	1	0	4	112	21	87	4	0
Winthrop	18,783	28	0	6	2	20	112	24	82	6	1
Woburn	39,895	46	0	6	8	32	377	35	312	30	1
Worcester	186,188	1,271	4	49	290	928	3,979	849	2,790	340	9
Wrentham	11,952	5	0	2	0	3	218	11	195	12	0
Yarmouth	23,269	113	1	17	7	88	291	48	227	16	5
MICHIGAN											
Addison Township	6,598	1	0	0	0	1	15	1	13	1	0
Adrian	20,624	115	0	38	12	65	474	108	344	22	1
Adrian Township	6,264	8	0	5	0	3	13	2	9	2	0
Akron	374	2	0	1	0	1	4	3	1	0	0
Albion	8,241	69	0	8	5	56	304	68	220	16	7
Allegan	5,051	12	0	5	1	6	45	3	38	4	0
Allen Park	27,020	68	0	9	12	47	500	46	411	43	3
Alma	8,944	21	0	5	2	14	105	19	83	3	1
Almont	2,820	15	0	8	0	7	38	16	18	4	0
Alpena	9,934	41	0	12	3	26	194	25	166	3	0
Ann Arbor	122,571	270	2	55	45	168	1,932	215	1,650	67	7
Argentine Township	6,526	3	0	1	0	2	21	6	15	0	0
Armada	1,734	3	0	1	0	2	10	2	8	0	0
Auburn Hills	23,579	94	0	15	6	73	530	30	482	18	2
Au Gres	835	0	0	0	0	0	3	0	3	0	0
Augusta	905	0	0	0	0	0	16	4	12	0	0
Bad Axe	2,933	0	0	0	0	0	81	5	73	3	1
Bancroft	497	3	0	3	0	0	0	0	0	0	0
Bangor	1,831	15	0	2	0	13	53	5	45	3	1
Baroda-Lake Township	3,826	8	0	3	0	5	26	8	14	4	0
Barryton	353	0	0	0	0	0	1	0	1	0	0
Barry Township	3,476	6	0	3	0	3	31	9	18	4	0
Bath Township	12,984	14	0	9	1	4	106	21	77	8	0
Battle Creek	60,615	600	6	85	69	440	1,958	467	1,414	77	16
Bay City	32,953	231	0	43	28	160	732	162	524	46	6
Beaverton	1,047	7	0	2	0	5	10	2	8	0	0
Belding	5,737	16	0	9	0	7	70	9	56	5	2
Belleville	3,855	10	0	5	0	5	57	5	52	0	0
Bellevue	1,285	1	0	0	0	1	4	1	3	0	0
Benton Harbor	9,836	213	3	27	28	155	422	101	264	57	4
Benton Township	14,382	231	1	26	36	168	857	94	694	69	5
Berkley	15,382	5	0	0	0	5	87	7	76	4	0
Berrien Springs-Oronoko Township	8,961	17	0	3	0	14	83	11	63	9	0
Beverly Hills	10,450	5	0	0	1	4	57	4	52	1	0
Big Rapids	10,369	24	0	5	1	18	86	8	72	6	0
Birch Run	1,465	4	0	0	0	4	86	3	77	6	0
Birmingham	21,295	10	0	3	3	4	137	26	104	7	0
Blackman Township	36,884	97	0	39	13	45	1,321	165	1,098	58	5
Blissfield	3,261	8	0	0	0	8	11	3	8	0	0
Bloomfield Hills	4,009	2	0	0	0	2	24	3	20	1	0
Bloomfield Township	42,199	21	0	2	2	17	327	35	283	9	2
Boyne City	3,741	10	0	6	1	3	89	2	82	5	0
Brandon Township	15,962	13	0	7	0	6	50	13	33	4	0
Breckenridge	1,273	1	0	0	0	1	14	2	12	0	0
Bridgeport Township	9,853	40	0	3	2	35	138	58	72	8	1
Bridgman	2,231	3	0	2	0	1	17	2	13	2	0
Brighton	7,635	11	0	4	4	3	102	6	93	3	1
Bronson	2,297	6	0	2	0	4	65	15	46	4	0
Brown City	1,238	2	0	1	0	1	22	1	21	0	0
Brownstown Township	31,912	78	1	9	10	58	281	41	205	35	1
Buchanan	4,293	19	0	1	2	16	91	8	79	4	0
Buena Vista Township	8,146	86	0	6	3	77	139	45	73	21	2
Burton	28,464	127	1	25	16	85	685	134	483	68	5
Cadillac	10,455	68	0	18	10	40	226	35	179	12	3
Calumet	694	2	0	2	0	0	18	3	15	0	0
Cambridge Township	5,656	1	0	1	0	0	23	5	15	3	0
Canton Township	92,055	134	0	24	11	99	986	56	898	32	8
Capac	1,831	13	0	0	0	13	19	7	10	2	0
Carleton	2,364	7	0	2	1	4	13	3	10	0	0
Caro	3,993	12	0	4	0	8	76	5	67	4	0
Carrollton Township	5,675	18	0	5	1	12	57	18	36	3	1
Carson City	1,112	3	0	1	0	2	13	0	12	1	1
Caseville	729	1	0	1	0	0	10	3	7	0	0
Caspian-Gaastra	1,166	1	0	0	0	1	1	1	0	0	0
Cass City	2,281	9	0	4	0	5	49	7	40	2	0
Center Line	8,275	35	0	11	2	22	173	17	121	35	0
Charlevoix	2,491	11	0	7	0	4	37	5	29	3	0
Charlotte	9,053	24	0	8	2	14	239	19	212	8	0
Cheboygan	4,690	15	0	7	0	8	125	15	109	1	0
Chelsea	5,248	3	0	0	2	1	41	5	35	1	0
Chesaning	2,251	3	0	2	0	1	13	2	9	2	0
Chesterfield Township	45,686	59	0	7	3	49	630	62	546	22	4

Table 8. Offenses Known to Law Enforcement, by Selected State and City, 2018—Continued

(Number.)

State/city	Population	Violent crime	Murder and nonnegligent manslaughter	Rape[1]	Robbery	Aggravated assault	Property crime	Burglary	Larceny-theft	Motor vehicle theft	Arson[2]
Chikaming Township	3,094	3	0	2	0	1	32	5	26	1	1
Chocolay Township	5,936	7	0	0	0	7	21	5	15	1	0
Clare	3,055	13	0	5	0	8	51	5	41	5	0
Clarkston	926	0	0	0	0	0	3	1	1	1	0
Clawson	11,962	12	0	3	1	8	69	13	56	0	0
Clayton Township	7,121	7	0	1	0	6	31	8	17	6	0
Clay Township	8,849	13	0	1	2	10	62	5	54	3	1
Clinton	2,281	2	0	0	0	2	13	2	9	2	0
Clinton Township	101,279	322	3	58	23	238	1,422	163	1,102	157	10
Clio	2,491	4	0	1	0	3	38	4	30	4	0
Coldwater	10,736	49	0	21	2	26	312	52	244	16	1
Coleman	1,193	0	0	0	0	0	2	0	2	0	0
Coloma Township	6,369	10	0	4	0	6	109	19	87	3	1
Colon	1,157	2	0	1	0	1	15	2	11	2	0
Columbia Township	7,356	17	0	1	1	15	74	5	65	4	0
Commerce Township	39,023	15	0	1	4	10	195	28	163	4	2
Constantine	2,103	16	0	8	2	6	36	8	26	2	0
Corunna	3,359	3	0	0	0	3	21	4	15	2	0
Covert Township	2,849	16	1	4	2	9	36	13	21	2	0
Croswell	2,267	11	1	5	0	5	29	4	25	0	2
Crystal Falls	1,365	5	0	4	0	1	33	1	30	2	0
Davison	4,893	10	0	4	0	6	55	9	42	4	0
Davison Township	19,177	40	0	11	0	29	171	36	125	10	2
Dearborn	94,022	314	1	36	82	195	1,871	233	1,438	200	7
Dearborn Heights	55,495	243	0	20	39	184	911	235	557	119	9
Decatur	1,737	19	0	2	0	17	46	5	34	7	0
Denton Township	5,384	3	0	1	0	2	63	5	58	0	0
Detroit	671,275	13,478	261	988	2,309	9,920	28,897	7,440	15,003	6,454	853
DeWitt	4,742	3	0	0	0	3	25	2	22	1	0
DeWitt Township	15,194	18	0	10	1	7	127	33	89	5	0
Dryden Township	4,744	3	0	2	0	1	33	4	28	1	0
Durand	3,296	9	0	3	0	6	56	6	43	7	1
East Grand Rapids	11,886	6	0	2	2	2	122	19	95	8	0
East Jordan	2,343	2	0	2	0	0	39	5	32	2	0
East Lansing	48,880	107	1	34	13	59	807	91	536	180	6
Eastpointe	32,526	222	1	33	45	143	1,063	170	605	288	8
Eaton Rapids	5,194	15	0	3	1	11	52	4	46	2	0
Eau Claire	603	0	0	0	0	0	4	0	3	1	0
Ecorse	9,184	96	1	5	13	77	294	79	171	44	5
Elkton	751	0	0	0	0	0	9	0	9	0	0
Elsie	977	1	0	1	0	0	1	0	1	0	0
Emmett Township	11,619	42	0	5	2	35	606	57	525	24	2
Escanaba	12,169	41	0	15	0	26	337	20	309	8	1
Essexville	3,306	1	0	0	0	1	15	3	12	0	0
Evart	1,860	12	0	3	0	9	32	5	25	2	0
Fair Haven Township	1,038	1	0	1	0	0	0	0	0	0	0
Farmington	10,605	20	0	3	0	17	58	2	51	5	0
Farmington Hills	81,239	69	1	16	9	43	681	85	554	42	3
Fennville	1,419	1	0	1	0	0	7	1	6	0	0
Fenton	11,225	17	0	7	2	8	207	21	173	13	1
Ferndale	20,095	39	0	6	7	26	341	52	243	46	0
Flat Rock	9,967	26	2	1	3	20	144	14	119	11	1
Flint	95,677	1,739	32	130	189	1,388	2,584	796	1,488	300	29
Flint Township	30,378	266	0	34	32	200	1,214	186	951	77	12
Flushing	7,890	11	0	6	1	4	94	8	83	3	0
Flushing Township	10,179	5	0	2	0	3	45	12	30	3	3
Forsyth Township	6,199	27	1	9	0	17	48	10	36	2	0
Fowlerville	2,953	6	0	6	0	0	53	6	47	0	0
Frankenmuth	5,290	5	0	2	1	2	69	6	54	9	0
Frankfort	1,279	0	0	0	0	0	13	2	10	1	0
Franklin	3,266	3	0	1	0	2	9	2	7	0	0
Fraser	14,626	23	0	6	3	14	198	17	159	22	1
Fremont	4,008	7	0	1	1	5	151	11	137	3	1
Fruitport Township	14,168	15	0	3	4	8	544	20	513	11	1
Gaines Township	6,100	3	0	0	0	3	24	6	16	2	1
Galien	535	0	0	0	0	0	0	0	0	0	0
Garden City	26,520	105	0	21	7	77	241	79	140	22	3
Garfield Township	829	0	0	0	0	0	0	0	0	0	0
Gaylord	3,693	23	0	8	0	15	256	7	244	5	1
Genesee Township	20,447	73	0	12	9	52	256	58	162	36	1
Gerrish Township	2,919	5	0	2	1	2	16	5	8	3	1
Gibraltar	4,474	6	0	1	0	5	34	5	27	2	0
Gladstone	4,721	4	0	0	0	4	45	6	35	4	0
Gladwin	2,874	17	0	2	0	15	65	15	48	2	2
Grand Beach	282	0	0	0	0	0	3	0	3	0	0
Grand Blanc	7,841	4	0	1	0	3	72	7	63	2	0
Grand Blanc Township	36,489	49	0	16	2	31	448	55	363	30	2
Grand Haven	10,984	21	1	9	0	11	173	21	143	9	0
Grand Ledge	7,804	7	0	5	1	1	82	9	72	1	0
Grand Rapids	200,428	1,313	5	141	319	848	3,830	679	2,881	270	37
Grandville	16,057	28	0	13	4	11	516	33	461	22	1
Grant	882	5	0	1	0	4	24	4	19	1	0
Grayling	1,837	13	0	1	0	12	59	14	43	2	0

Table 8. Offenses Known to Law Enforcement, by Selected State and City, 2018—Continued

(Number.)

State/city	Population	Violent crime	Murder and nonnegligent manslaughter	Rape[1]	Robbery	Aggravated assault	Property crime	Burglary	Larceny-theft	Motor vehicle theft	Arson[2]
Green Oak Township	18,874	25	0	10	1	14	140	25	108	7	0
Greenville	8,437	42	0	19	2	21	283	33	241	9	1
Grosse Ile Township	10,128	3	0	1	0	2	34	2	28	4	0
Grosse Pointe	5,157	6	0	4	0	2	90	7	76	7	0
Grosse Pointe Farms	9,116	6	0	1	1	4	90	14	73	3	0
Grosse Pointe Park	11,069	0	0	0	0	0	175	17	150	8	0
Grosse Pointe Shores	2,907	0	0	0	0	0	9	0	7	2	0
Grosse Pointe Woods	15,497	13	0	2	5	6	225	41	172	12	0
Hamburg Township	22,024	10	0	4	0	6	67	10	54	3	0
Hampton Township	9,458	18	1	7	2	8	97	15	76	6	4
Hamtramck	21,668	166	1	7	42	116	493	117	292	84	7
Hancock	4,545	8	0	2	0	6	26	4	20	2	0
Harbor Beach	1,591	6	0	1	0	5	30	1	29	0	0
Harbor Springs	1,205	1	0	0	0	1	8	0	8	0	0
Harper Woods	13,674	128	0	11	27	90	677	92	470	115	2
Hart	2,101	12	0	2	0	10	145	12	130	3	0
Hastings	7,310	14	2	8	0	4	159	15	138	6	0
Hazel Park	16,501	53	2	9	12	30	284	38	217	29	5
Highland Park	10,794	188	5	12	34	137	344	58	200	86	8
Highland Township	20,137	15	0	2	1	12	99	27	63	9	1
Hillsdale	8,120	21	0	9	0	12	103	28	70	5	1
Holland	33,405	142	1	37	15	89	728	106	579	43	1
Holly	6,170	7	0	2	1	4	48	9	39	0	2
Houghton	7,914	7	0	3	0	4	116	3	112	1	0
Howell	9,532	26	0	11	0	15	112	8	97	7	0
Hudson	2,221	8	0	2	0	6	39	5	32	2	0
Huntington Woods	6,328	4	0	3	0	1	35	3	31	1	1
Huron Township	15,930	34	0	9	2	23	120	27	78	15	0
Imlay City	3,579	7	0	3	0	4	38	6	30	2	0
Independence Township	36,925	16	1	0	2	13	191	37	146	8	0
Inkster	24,334	262	9	40	43	170	656	242	312	102	9
Ionia	11,170	48	0	33	0	15	120	14	101	5	0
Iron Mountain	7,327	3	0	3	0	0	9	0	9	0	0
Iron River	2,818	6	0	1	0	5	59	23	35	1	3
Ironwood	4,915	2	0	1	0	1	50	3	44	3	0
Ishpeming	6,441	19	0	4	0	15	75	7	63	5	0
Ishpeming Township	3,528	0	0	0	0	0	3	1	2	0	0
Jackson	32,602	366	6	68	43	249	1,387	195	1,068	124	29
Jonesville	2,206	7	0	2	1	4	90	4	85	1	0
Kalamazoo	76,020	1,008	7	117	159	725	3,825	842	2,646	337	23
Kalamazoo Township	24,623	98	1	21	8	68	660	147	433	80	4
Kalkaska	2,068	2	0	2	0	0	22	1	21	0	0
Keego Harbor	3,465	10	3	0	1	6	34	3	29	2	0
Kentwood	52,192	193	0	28	37	128	1,100	183	850	67	3
Kinde	418	0	0	0	0	0	0	0	0	0	0
Kingsford	4,960	11	0	7	0	4	31	2	29	0	0
Kinross Township	7,432	2	0	1	0	1	16	3	10	3	0
Laingsburg	1,277	4	0	1	0	3	13	4	7	2	0
Lake Angelus	309	0	0	0	0	0	0	0	0	0	0
Lake Linden	969	2	0	0	0	2	1	0	1	0	0
Lake Odessa	2,031	2	0	2	0	0	4	1	3	0	0
Lake Orion	3,118	3	0	0	0	3	30	5	25	0	0
Lakeview	1,005	1	0	1	0	0	32	4	27	1	0
Lansing	117,380	1,301	8	149	182	962	3,557	868	2,252	437	22
Lansing Township	8,213	67	1	14	15	37	525	82	405	38	0
Lapeer	8,697	37	1	12	2	22	267	29	226	12	2
Lapeer Township	5,036	0	0	0	0	0	11	4	7	0	2
Lathrup Village	4,130	6	0	2	3	1	33	5	26	2	0
Laurium	1,924	4	0	0	0	4	10	3	7	0	0
Lawton	1,847	4	0	1	0	3	38	9	27	2	0
Lennon	484	1	0	0	0	1	8	5	3	0	0
Leslie	1,889	2	0	0	1	1	15	7	8	0	0
Lexington	1,107	3	0	1	0	2	7	0	6	1	0
Lincoln Park	36,466	208	0	17	31	160	1,023	195	724	104	3
Lincoln Township	14,585	12	0	4	0	8	177	62	111	4	1
Linden	3,884	4	0	2	1	1	18	4	14	0	0
Litchfield	1,336	2	0	1	0	1	11	3	7	1	0
Livonia	93,740	138	0	34	19	85	1,313	111	1,092	110	4
Lowell	4,138	9	0	3	0	6	84	4	76	4	2
Ludington	8,058	34	0	18	2	14	109	13	94	2	1
Luna Pier	1,408	2	0	0	1	1	11	1	10	0	0
Lyon Township[5]	20,815	14	0	1	0	13			91	5	0
Mackinac Island	467	3	0	2	0	1	97	3	94	0	0
Mackinaw City	794	7	0	1	1	5	24	4	19	1	0
Madison Heights	30,100	89	1	11	19	58	435	53	347	35	3
Madison Township	8,341	15	0	2	0	13	126	5	115	6	1
Manistee	6,091	28	0	9	1	18	118	19	96	3	1
Manistique	2,907	7	0	2	0	5	48	4	41	3	0
Marenisco Township	1,626	0	0	0	0	0	0	0	0	0	0
Marine City	4,083	3	0	1	0	2	28	2	22	4	1
Marlette	1,757	3	0	1	0	2	16	1	13	2	0
Marquette	20,529	23	0	10	0	13	204	14	175	15	1
Marshall	6,986	11	0	5	1	5	134	10	120	4	0

Table 8. Offenses Known to Law Enforcement, by Selected State and City, 2018—Continued

(Number.)

State/city	Population	Violent crime	Murder and nonnegligent manslaughter	Rape[1]	Robbery	Aggravated assault	Property crime	Burglary	Larceny-theft	Motor vehicle theft	Arson[2]
Marysville	9,674	9	0	1	0	8	70	7	59	4	3
Mason	8,431	26	0	6	0	20	143	15	124	4	0
Mattawan	1,971	5	0	1	0	4	44	9	31	4	0
Mayville	888	1	0	0	0	1	7	0	7	0	0
Melvindale	10,291	68	1	9	10	48	243	58	163	22	5
Memphis	1,190	0	0	0	0	0	6	1	5	0	0
Mendon	854	1	0	1	0	0	10	1	9	0	0
Menominee	8,089	23	0	14	0	9	135	14	117	4	0
Meridian Township	43,072	98	1	26	15	56	1,090	115	919	56	3
Metamora Township	4,279	3	0	0	0	3	26	7	15	4	0
Metro Police Authority of Genesee County	19,887	42	1	6	6	29	268	39	207	22	2
Michiana	181	0	0	0	0	0	8	3	5	0	0
Midland	41,961	55	1	19	1	34	354	36	306	12	0
Milan	6,079	10	0	5	0	5	72	13	51	8	1
Milford	16,808	10	0	5	1	4	67	14	49	4	0
Millington	1,000	3	0	3	0	0	9	0	8	1	0
Monroe	19,754	114	0	25	11	78	383	66	295	22	2
Montague	2,350	2	0	1	0	1	27	1	26	0	0
Montrose Township	7,459	11	0	3	1	7	47	10	34	3	1
Morenci	2,159	10	0	0	0	10	45	18	21	6	0
Morrice	894	1	0	0	0	1	10	2	7	1	0
Mount Morris	2,860	24	0	7	1	16	64	12	50	2	0
Mount Morris Township	20,295	137	4	27	6	100	401	136	205	60	2
Mount Pleasant	25,828	76	0	25	3	48	323	40	271	12	4
Munising	2,186	6	0	3	0	3	43	6	36	1	2
Muskegon	38,125	245	7	39	31	168	1,717	321	1,226	170	19
Muskegon Heights	10,720	240	5	14	39	182	630	129	420	81	11
Muskegon Township	17,879	40	0	10	5	25	781	77	670	34	0
Napoleon Township	6,751	4	0	1	0	3	34	9	25	0	0
Nashville	1,660	13	0	3	0	10	24	2	22	0	0
Negaunee	4,554	3	0	2	0	1	40	2	37	1	0
Newaygo	2,043	7	0	4	0	3	69	5	61	3	0
New Baltimore	12,423	8	0	2	0	6	57	3	52	2	0
New Buffalo	1,875	0	0	0	0	0	11	4	7	0	0
New Era	442	0	0	0	0	0	5	1	4	0	0
New Lothrop	557	0	0	0	0	0	0	0	0	0	0
Niles	11,154	70	0	18	14	38	273	49	196	28	2
Northfield Township	8,741	12	0	4	0	8	98	25	60	13	0
North Muskegon	3,794	1	0	0	0	1	81	3	74	4	0
Northville	5,992	5	0	1	1	3	40	3	35	2	0
Northville Township	28,939	21	0	2	5	14	302	34	263	5	2
Norton Shores	24,578	37	1	11	4	21	695	77	600	18	1
Norway	2,746	0	0	0	0	0	0	0	0	0	0
Novi	60,378	43	2	6	3	32	532	33	481	18	0
Oakland Township	19,495	4	0	1	1	2	30	7	21	2	1
Oak Park	29,688	83	1	11	16	55	455	69	337	49	2
Olivet	1,695	4	0	2	0	2	19	5	14	0	0
Ontwa Township-Edwardsburg	6,493	29	0	3	3	23	124	45	70	9	1
Orchard Lake	2,465	3	0	0	0	3	20	4	16	0	0
Orion Township	36,193	20	0	1	2	17	200	17	164	19	0
Oscoda Township	6,771	16	0	5	0	11	79	24	51	4	1
Otisville	822	0	0	0	0	0	2	0	2	0	0
Otsego	4,000	16	0	12	0	4	53	7	43	3	0
Ovid	1,618	1	0	0	0	1	3	0	1	2	0
Owendale	225	0	0	0	0	0	1	0	1	0	0
Owosso	14,455	76	0	8	5	63	169	41	119	9	2
Oxford	3,561	3	0	0	0	3	8	0	8	0	0
Oxford Township	19,139	12	0	2	0	10	81	10	67	4	1
Paw Paw	3,404	11	0	4	1	6	185	28	144	13	1
Peck	591	0	0	0	0	0	0	0	0	0	0
Pentwater	849	1	0	0	0	1	13	1	12	0	0
Perry	2,085	2	0	1	1	0	21	3	15	3	0
Petoskey	5,733	11	0	3	0	8	53	4	45	4	1
Pinckney	2,479	8	0	5	0	3	10	3	7	0	0
Pinconning	1,241	0	0	0	0	0	17	0	16	1	0
Pittsfield Township	39,314	76	1	25	9	41	582	54	493	35	0
Plainwell	3,810	15	0	3	2	10	65	9	53	3	0
Pleasant Ridge	2,470	1	0	1	0	0	24	0	21	3	0
Plymouth	9,142	7	0	5	0	2	74	9	54	11	1
Plymouth Township	27,032	24	0	9	2	13	165	19	132	14	0
Pontiac	59,817	799	14	58	96	631	1,286	412	779	95	17
Portage	49,175	117	0	29	15	73	1,442	171	1,196	75	4
Port Austin	622	0	0	0	0	0	6	0	6	0	0
Port Huron	28,907	230	1	36	18	175	746	156	540	50	12
Portland	3,927	8	0	7	0	1	43	6	32	5	0
Port Sanilac	579	0	0	0	0	0	0	0	0	0	0
Potterville	2,678	4	0	1	0	3	29	3	23	3	1
Prairieville Township	3,509	0	0	0	0	0	10	3	7	0	0
Quincy	1,610	3	0	0	0	3	28	3	21	4	0
Raisin Township	7,716	2	0	1	0	1	26	5	19	2	0
Redford Township	46,899	302	2	34	54	212	1,044	223	626	195	5
Reed City	2,380	9	0	4	1	4	23	1	19	3	0

Table 8. Offenses Known to Law Enforcement, by Selected State and City, 2018—Continued

(Number.)

State/city	Population	Violent crime	Murder and nonnegligent manslaughter	Rape[1]	Robbery	Aggravated assault	Property crime	Burglary	Larceny-theft	Motor vehicle theft	Arson[2]
Reese	1,372	0	0	0	0	0	7	4	3	0	0
Richfield Township, Genesee County	8,325	14	0	5	0	9	58	15	37	6	0
Richfield Township, Roscommon County	3,633	1	0	1	0	0	7	2	4	1	0
Richland	807	2	0	2	0	0	15	0	14	1	0
Richland Township, Saginaw County	3,934	7	0	2	0	5	10	6	4	0	0
Richmond	5,918	18	0	3	0	15	40	4	35	1	0
River Rouge	7,426	41	1	4	4	32	171	31	116	24	10
Riverview	12,058	14	0	2	0	12	116	10	83	23	2
Rochester	13,075	8	0	1	1	6	48	4	43	1	0
Rochester Hills	74,669	53	1	9	8	35	442	47	369	26	1
Rockford	6,345	7	0	3	0	4	59	3	54	2	0
Rockwood	3,169	1	0	0	0	1	12	0	11	1	0
Rogers City	2,676	2	0	2	0	0	47	3	43	1	0
Romeo	3,623	2	0	1	0	1	31	2	28	1	0
Romulus	23,389	190	0	28	18	144	532	107	358	67	2
Roosevelt Park	3,793	3	0	1	2	0	336	1	323	12	0
Roseville	47,524	187	1	26	41	119	1,528	148	1,229	151	4
Rothbury	445	1	0	0	0	1	7	0	7	0	0
Royal Oak	59,383	56	0	11	4	41	481	64	380	37	0
Saginaw	48,302	783	11	48	86	638	886	376	420	90	11
Saginaw Township	39,198	79	1	18	13	47	796	80	679	37	7
Saline	9,358	13	0	3	2	8	76	5	69	2	0
Sand Lake	532	0	0	0	0	0	12	0	10	2	0
Sandusky	2,515	7	0	2	0	5	66	5	61	0	0
Saugatuck-Douglas	2,312	4	0	1	0	3	33	2	28	3	0
Sault Ste. Marie	13,557	30	0	12	1	17	225	21	193	11	1
Schoolcraft	1,566	0	0	0	0	0	23	0	20	3	0
Scottville	1,218	2	0	0	1	1	53	1	49	3	0
Sebewaing	1,638	3	2	1	0	0	9	1	8	0	0
Shelby	2,019	2	0	2	0	0	28	1	26	1	0
Shelby Township	79,878	119	1	45	4	69	500	69	395	36	6
Shepherd	1,503	0	0	0	0	0	11	2	9	0	0
Southfield	73,418	204	2	36	48	118	1,509	262	1,049	198	3
Southgate	28,959	46	0	13	8	25	789	70	668	51	4
South Haven	4,340	24	0	7	3	14	276	33	237	6	1
South Lyon	11,803	12	0	1	0	11	40	6	33	1	0
South Rockwood	1,657	0	0	0	0	0	7	1	4	2	0
Sparta	4,380	11	0	7	0	4	61	8	53	0	0
Spring Arbor Township	8,044	5	2	0	0	3	12	5	7	0	0
Springfield Township	14,423	11	0	2	1	8	54	16	32	6	0
Springport Township	2,144	1	0	0	0	1	7	1	4	2	0
Stanton	1,430	0	0	0	0	0	13	3	9	1	0
St. Charles	1,910	2	0	0	0	2	31	8	22	1	0
St. Clair	5,316	27	0	5	1	21	49	6	39	4	0
St. Clair Shores	59,618	132	1	17	16	98	591	85	451	55	4
Sterling Heights	133,055	240	2	42	19	177	1,334	139	1,073	122	2
St. Ignace	2,311	5	0	3	0	2	36	6	27	3	0
St. Johns	7,890	10	0	6	0	4	40	10	29	1	0
St. Joseph	8,364	26	0	5	3	18	185	20	158	7	2
St. Joseph Township	9,773	7	0	0	1	6	88	12	70	6	1
St. Louis	7,274	15	0	13	0	2	58	5	48	5	1
Stockbridge	1,237	1	0	1	0	0	9	1	8	0	0
Sturgis	10,796	61	0	29	2	30	259	32	207	20	0
Sumpter Township	9,362	8	1	0	0	7	63	17	41	5	1
Sylvan Lake	1,860	3	0	1	0	2	32	5	26	1	0
Tawas	4,487	6	0	3	1	2	55	2	52	1	0
Taylor	61,037	366	1	54	48	263	1,346	276	946	124	12
Tecumseh	8,363	7	1	2	0	4	56	11	42	3	0
Thomas Township	11,488	8	0	0	0	8	68	14	51	3	0
Three Rivers	7,673	57	0	13	2	42	301	25	260	16	1
Tittabawassee Township	9,819	10	0	5	0	5	47	10	33	4	0
Traverse City	15,630	74	0	22	4	48	253	27	219	7	1
Trenton	18,176	22	0	7	1	14	104	18	69	17	0
Troy	84,221	52	1	8	11	32	1,157	94	1,011	52	2
Tuscarora Township	2,928	1	0	1	0	0	45	4	34	7	0
Ubly	800	1	0	1	0	0	11	1	10	0	0
Unadilla Township	3,465	9	0	3	0	6	22	7	15	0	1
Union City	1,564	2	0	1	0	1	42	3	39	0	0
Utica	4,949	11	0	3	4	4	174	8	164	2	0
Van Buren Township	28,210	86	0	18	9	59	540	87	417	36	4
Vassar	2,543	12	0	9	0	3	18	4	13	1	0
Vernon	776	0	0	0	0	0	2	0	2	0	0
Vicksburg	3,443	11	0	3	0	8	53	6	44	3	1
Walker	25,010	63	1	28	12	22	522	46	449	27	1
Walled Lake	7,170	9	1	1	0	7	44	5	37	2	0
Warren	135,160	688	4	108	121	455	2,808	581	1,688	539	13
Waterford Township	73,066	146	3	47	18	78	750	172	529	49	4
Watervliet	1,658	8	0	0	1	7	10	1	8	1	0
Wayland	4,260	22	0	7	1	14	62	24	38	0	0
Wayne	16,862	132	1	19	15	97	266	70	167	29	7

Table 8. Offenses Known to Law Enforcement, by Selected State and City, 2018—Continued

(Number.)

State/city	Population	Violent crime	Murder and nonnegligent manslaughter	Rape[1]	Robbery	Aggravated assault	Property crime	Burglary	Larceny-theft	Motor vehicle theft	Arson[2]
West Bloomfield Township	65,928	38	0	6	3	29	386	38	335	13	2
West Branch	2,051	2	0	1	0	1	32	4	27	1	0
Westland	81,438	316	0	88	42	186	1,234	221	905	108	10
White Cloud	1,377	7	0	2	0	5	43	2	38	3	1
Whitehall	2,741	9	0	2	0	7	45	1	44	0	1
White Lake Township	31,236	13	0	4	0	9	266	13	242	11	0
White Pigeon	1,521	3	0	2	0	1	19	3	12	4	0
Williamston	3,924	2	0	0	0	2	25	4	19	2	0
Wixom	13,876	26	0	4	1	21	169	19	134	16	2
Wolverine Lake	4,686	10	0	3	1	6	20	4	16	0	0
Woodhaven	12,435	12	1	5	1	5	117	7	100	10	1
Wyandotte	24,862	61	0	6	8	47	397	55	276	66	0
Wyoming	76,498	350	3	85	52	210	1,477	229	1,110	138	6
Yale	1,883	6	0	0	0	6	16	6	10	0	0
Ypsilanti	21,298	186	4	32	36	114	612	161	406	45	2
Zeeland	5,567	11	0	5	0	6	97	18	77	2	0
Zilwaukee	1,538	0	0	0	0	0	10	6	3	1	0
MINNESOTA											
Aitkin	1,998	2	0	2	0	0	56	4	51	1	0
Akeley	438	0	0	0	0	0	16	2	13	1	0
Albany	2,711	0	0	0	0	0	3	1	2	0	0
Albert Lea	17,655	26	0	3	3	20	466	145	296	25	1
Alexandria[4]	13,759	51	0	15	3	33	390	43	319	28	1
Annandale	3,389	1	0	0	0	1	86	4	81	1	0
Anoka	17,574	27	0	10	3	14	393	42	326	25	1
Appleton	1,333	5	0	0	0	5	33	4	26	3	0
Apple Valley	52,922	63	1	25	15	22	956	93	830	33	6
Arlington	2,141	0	0	0	0	0	17	1	14	2	0
Atwater	1,115	0	0	0	0	0	1	0	1	0	0
Austin	24,935	66	1	8	9	48	544	91	417	36	1
Avon	1,573	0	0	0	0	0	10	2	5	3	0
Babbitt	1,510	1	0	0	0	1	6	1	4	1	0
Barnesville	2,586	1	0	1	0	0	0	0	0	0	0
Baxter	8,372	9	0	3	0	6	160	4	155	1	0
Bayport	3,774	0	0	0	0	0	17	2	12	3	0
Becker	4,880	9	0	8	0	1	24	4	20	0	0
Belgrade/Brooten	1,523	2	0	0	0	2	11	2	8	1	0
Belle Plaine	7,189	5	0	4	0	1	76	8	61	7	0
Bemidji	15,528	79	0	9	9	61	1,094	70	964	60	1
Benson	3,072	1	0	0	0	1	0	0	0	0	0
Big Lake	11,036	11	0	2	0	9	53	1	47	5	0
Blackduck	768	3	0	1	0	2	10	3	3	4	0
Blaine	65,649	64	0	22	16	26	1,705	156	1,472	77	5
Blooming Prairie	1,980	2	0	0	0	2	2	0	2	0	0
Bloomington	86,279	165	2	51	44	68	2,592	158	2,304	130	5
Blue Earth[4]	3,112	0	0	0	0	0	36	9	26	1	0
Bovey	789	1	0	0	0	1	0	0	0	0	0
Braham	1,788	0	0	0	0	0	2	0	2	0	0
Brainerd	13,404	61	0	17	3	41	453	70	360	23	2
Breckenridge	3,200	8	1	0	0	7	68	10	55	3	0
Breezy Point	2,390	1	0	0	0	1	6	0	6	0	0
Breitung Township	608	2	0	0	0	2	1	0	1	0	0
Brooklyn Center	31,128	117	1	29	50	37	1,065	109	803	153	3
Brooklyn Park	81,263	302	1	47	79	175	2,465	328	1,893	244	7
Brownton	727	0	0	0	0	0	4	4	0	0	0
Buffalo	16,304	17	0	9	0	8	317	19	292	6	1
Buffalo Lake	680	1	0	0	0	1	3	0	3	0	0
Burnsville	61,592	114	1	10	24	79	1,613	186	1,317	110	2
Caledonia	2,736	0	0	0	0	0	3	0	2	1	0
Cambridge	8,905	9	0	0	1	8	310	24	269	17	0
Canby	1,688	1	0	0	0	1	4	1	3	0	0
Cannon Falls	4,060	5	0	1	0	4	84	10	66	8	0
Centennial Lakes	11,062	11	0	3	2	6	148	13	128	7	0
Champlin	25,304	26	0	6	3	17	234	16	202	16	1
Chaska	26,962	21	0	9	3	9	227	27	192	8	0
Chisholm	4,908	4	0	0	0	4	48	5	37	6	1
Clara City	1,287	2	0	2	0	0	1	0	1	0	0
Cleveland	717	0	0	0	0	0	10	2	8	0	0
Cloquet	11,911	12	0	1	1	10	181	8	155	18	0
Cold Spring/Richmond	5,572	2	0	1	0	1	37	0	35	2	0
Coleraine	1,970	1	0	0	0	1	19	0	18	1	0
Columbia Heights	21,119	57	0	11	18	28	504	63	363	78	3
Coon Rapids	62,818	83	0	23	28	32	1,322	149	1,110	63	4
Corcoran	5,988	4	0	2	0	2	52	11	36	5	0
Cottage Grove	37,102	25	0	6	3	16	546	58	468	20	2
Crookston	7,779	19	0	10	0	9	159	26	120	13	1
Crosby	2,338	7	1	3	0	3	73	7	66	0	1
Crosslake	2,266	0	0	0	0	0	7	3	3	1	0
Crystal	23,310	34	0	7	9	18	487	33	409	45	1
Danube	457	0	0	0	0	0	9	0	8	1	0
Dawson/Boyd	1,549	2	0	1	0	1	8	1	7	0	0
Dayton	5,970	2	0	0	0	2	56	11	37	8	0

Table 8. Offenses Known to Law Enforcement, by Selected State and City, 2018—Continued

(Number.)

State/city	Population	Violent crime	Murder and nonnegligent manslaughter	Rape[1]	Robbery	Aggravated assault	Property crime	Burglary	Larceny-theft	Motor vehicle theft	Arson[2]
Deephaven	3,951	1	0	0	0	1	45	2	42	1	0
Deer River	933	1	0	0	0	1	32	0	32	0	0
Detroit Lakes	9,289	19	0	10	2	7	270	32	231	7	0
Dilworth	4,474	6	0	2	0	4	208	18	174	16	0
Duluth	86,048	308	1	45	66	196	3,688	472	3,013	203	10
Dundas	1,544	1	0	0	0	1	18	4	12	2	0
Eagan	66,981	59	2	18	16	23	1,289	88	1,148	53	0
Eagle Lake[4]	3,129	2	0	1	0	1	20	3	16	1	0
East Grand Forks	8,632	7	0	0	0	7	87	9	70	8	1
East Range	3,614	6	0	4	0	2	52	10	40	2	0
Eden Prairie	64,917	39	1	15	7	16	873	65	784	24	9
Eden Valley	1,033	0	0	0	0	0	0	0	0	0	0
Edina	52,544	23	1	7	10	5	803	101	677	25	1
Elko New Market	4,809	2	0	0	0	2	22	3	19	0	0
Elk River	24,724	29	0	7	4	18	429	62	339	28	1
Ely	3,377	3	0	1	0	2	33	6	26	1	0
Eveleth	3,609	6	0	0	1	5	100	20	58	22	0
Fairfax	1,130	3	0	2	0	1	27	0	25	2	0
Fairmont[4]	10,053	12	0	3	0	9	244	35	197	12	0
Faribault	23,806	77	1	15	13	48	423	75	323	25	3
Farmington	23,355	13	0	3	1	9	174	28	133	13	0
Fergus Falls	13,839	30	1	4	2	23	488	70	392	26	0
Floodwood	520	0	0	0	0	0	10	1	7	2	0
Foley	2,635	4	0	0	0	4	56	7	47	2	0
Frazee	1,397	7	0	3	0	4	17	1	15	1	0
Fridley	27,943	85	1	23	27	34	1,014	112	817	85	1
Fulda	1,222	0	0	0	0	0	8	7	1	0	0
Gaylord	2,211	12	0	1	0	11	34	7	27	0	0
Gilbert	1,796	5	0	0	0	5	86	14	69	3	4
Glencoe	5,480	6	0	1	0	5	65	12	49	4	0
Glenwood	2,523	1	0	0	0	1	12	2	9	1	0
Golden Valley	21,688	22	0	7	5	10	410	36	344	30	0
Goodview	4,125	4	0	2	0	2	74	25	41	8	0
Grand Rapids	11,297	9	0	4	0	5	145	8	127	10	0
Granite Falls	2,712	3	0	0	0	3	92	24	66	2	1
Hallock	898	0	0	0	0	0	0	0	0	0	0
Hastings	22,799	42	0	6	3	33	412	49	331	32	1
Hawley	2,209	2	0	0	0	2	2	1	1	0	0
Hector	1,047	0	0	0	0	0	13	1	12	0	0
Hermantown	9,525	10	0	4	2	4	412	47	350	15	0
Hibbing	15,998	44	1	13	4	26	182	26	133	23	2
Hill City	586	0	0	0	0	0	14	5	9	0	0
Hokah	549	0	0	0	0	0	2	0	2	0	0
Hopkins	18,838	32	0	7	7	18	334	52	262	20	0
Houston	958	0	0	0	0	0	0	0	0	0	0
Howard Lake	2,066	1	0	0	0	1	2	0	2	0	0
Hutchinson	13,862	28	0	13	1	14	227	17	202	8	0
International Falls	5,933	8	0	3	0	5	58	4	49	5	0
Inver Grove Heights	35,592	90	1	19	14	56	560	68	424	68	2
Isanti	5,787	4	0	1	1	2	111	11	96	4	0
Isle	801	2	0	0	0	2	55	4	48	3	0
Janesville[4]	2,259	6	0	3	0	3	22	8	12	2	0
Jordan	6,375	4	0	3	0	1	45	2	42	1	1
Kasson	6,444	1	0	0	0	1	8	0	7	1	1
Keewatin	1,021	0	0	0	0	0	10	1	8	1	0
Kimball	795	0	0	0	0	0	0	0	0	0	0
La Crescent	5,012	2	0	0	0	2	22	1	21	0	0
Lake City[4]	5,116	1	0	1	0	0	59	4	53	2	0
Lake Crystal[4]	2,487	1	0	0	0	1	30	17	12	1	0
Lakefield	1,615	0	0	0	0	0	12	2	10	0	0
Lakes Area	9,679	20	0	12	0	8	150	20	126	4	1
Lake Shore	1,052	1	0	0	0	1	13	1	11	1	0
Lakeville	64,914	39	0	13	6	20	532	46	458	28	1
Lamberton	768	0	0	0	0	0	0	0	0	0	0
Lauderdale	2,549	5	0	2	0	3	66	7	49	10	0
Le Center	2,469	0	0	0	0	0	19	2	17	0	0
Lester Prairie	1,710	2	0	0	0	2	10	5	5	0	0
Le Sueur	4,004	2	0	2	0	0	29	4	23	2	0
Lewiston	1,557	1	0	0	0	1	7	0	7	0	0
Lino Lakes	21,577	12	0	6	3	3	181	20	149	12	0
Litchfield	6,615	8	0	2	0	6	84	8	68	8	2
Little Falls	8,683	12	0	2	1	9	171	20	139	12	0
Long Prairie	3,305	7	0	4	0	3	55	3	51	1	0
Lonsdale	4,038	0	0	0	0	0	11	2	9	0	0
Madelia	2,228	6	0	2	0	4	24	4	18	2	0
Madison Lake[4]	1,183	0	0	0	0	0	1	1	0	0	0
Mankato[4]	42,606	140	0	24	17	99	1,418	164	1,178	76	2
Maple Grove	72,502	44	0	14	8	22	1,117	65	1,014	38	3
Mapleton[4]	1,696	1	0	1	0	0	15	4	11	0	0
Maplewood[4]	41,339	90	0	18	32	40	1,859	206	1,492	161	8
Marshall	13,713	25	0	10	3	12	250	35	204	11	0
McGregor	364	0	0	0	0	0	0	0	0	0	0
Medina	6,721	2	0	1	0	1	74	3	71	0	0

Table 8. Offenses Known to Law Enforcement, by Selected State and City, 2018—Continued

(Number.)

State/city	Population	Violent crime	Murder and nonnegligent manslaughter	Rape[1]	Robbery	Aggravated assault	Property crime	Burglary	Larceny-theft	Motor vehicle theft	Arson[2]
Melrose	3,622	2	0	0	0	2	25	2	23	0	0
Menahga[4]	1,315	0	0	0	0	0	6	0	6	0	0
Mendota Heights	11,381	16	0	1	2	13	207	33	166	8	1
Milaca	2,880	13	0	2	1	10	58	3	48	7	0
Minneapolis	428,261	3,395	31	432	1,184	1,748	16,750	3,089	11,471	2,190	76
Minneota	1,368	2	0	1	0	1	1	1	0	0	0
Minnetonka	53,573	28	1	12	4	11	810	105	674	31	3
Minnetrista	10,357	4	0	1	0	3	84	13	67	4	0
Montevideo	5,101	4	0	1	0	3	62	34	26	2	0
Montgomery	2,950	1	0	1	0	0	27	3	21	3	0
Moorhead	43,657	61	0	9	10	42	1,024	131	815	78	2
Moose Lake	2,795	4	0	0	0	4	43	2	39	2	0
Morris	5,300	10	0	3	0	7	50	8	40	2	0
Mounds View[4]	13,235	23	0	9	8	6	449	44	364	41	1
Mountain Lake	2,054	0	0	0	0	0	4	0	4	0	0
Nashwauk	945	1	0	0	0	1	4	1	2	1	0
New Brighton[4]	22,978	25	0	6	9	10	564	69	460	35	0
New Hope	21,168	14	0	1	4	9	396	66	301	29	1
New Prague	7,884	5	0	3	0	2	91	10	74	7	0
New Richland[4]	1,184	0	0	0	0	0	11	2	9	0	0
New Ulm	13,202	9	0	4	0	5	162	13	144	5	2
New York Mills	1,228	1	0	1	0	0	1	1	0	0	0
Nisswa	2,045	1	0	0	0	1	1	0	1	0	0
North Branch	10,511	12	0	3	0	9	246	25	211	10	0
Northfield	20,535	28	0	18	1	9	199	25	170	4	2
North Mankato	13,794	19	0	8	0	11	144	16	125	3	1
North St. Paul	12,588	15	0	6	6	3	220	35	158	27	1
Oakdale	28,178	37	0	17	9	11	663	53	558	52	5
Oak Park Heights	4,991	6	0	3	1	2	196	8	177	11	0
Olivia	2,328	4	0	3	0	1	57	4	49	4	1
Onamia	858	6	0	3	0	3	36	6	27	3	0
Orono	20,225	6	0	3	1	2	118	23	93	2	0
Ortonville	1,788	2	0	0	0	2	28	7	17	4	0
Osakis[4]	1,700	2	0	2	0	0	21	4	16	1	0
Osseo	2,820	1	0	0	0	1	4	0	2	2	0
Owatonna	25,829	26	0	3	6	17	438	56	344	38	0
Parkers Prairie	998	0	0	0	0	0	6	1	4	1	0
Park Rapids	4,046	13	0	4	1	8	291	22	254	15	1
Paynesville	2,503	4	2	1	0	1	14	4	8	2	0
Pelican Rapids	2,467	3	0	1	0	2	4	1	2	1	0
Pequot Lakes	2,321	0	0	0	0	0	94	2	92	0	0
Perham	3,484	6	0	1	1	4	12	0	11	1	0
Pike Bay	1,673	0	0	0	0	0	6	2	4	0	0
Pillager	467	0	0	0	0	0	28	1	25	2	0
Pine River	925	0	0	0	0	0	64	2	59	3	0
Plainview[4]	3,284	10	0	0	0	10	26	4	21	1	0
Plymouth	79,559	44	2	12	9	21	904	165	702	37	4
Preston	1,295	2	0	0	0	2	3	2	0	1	0
Princeton	4,666	6	0	2	0	4	164	7	146	11	0
Prior Lake	26,925	40	0	10	8	22	574	30	520	24	1
Proctor	3,058	5	0	3	0	2	98	11	81	6	1
Ramsey	27,023	27	0	10	3	14	349	44	280	25	0
Red Wing	16,405	40	1	10	5	24	427	53	356	18	0
Redwood Falls	4,952	15	0	4	0	11	160	7	147	6	1
Renville	1,178	2	0	1	0	1	9	1	7	1	0
Rice	1,354	0	0	0	0	0	7	1	6	0	0
Richfield	36,300	81	1	12	32	36	771	100	596	75	3
Robbinsdale	14,629	49	0	8	12	29	232	34	157	41	0
Rochester	117,037	227	5	58	41	123	2,435	353	1,952	130	3
Rogers	13,257	10	0	3	1	6	236	20	203	13	0
Roseau	2,704	9	0	3	0	6	21	2	19	0	0
Rosemount	24,707	16	0	9	1	6	187	34	143	10	0
Roseville	36,701	86	0	9	27	50	1,829	176	1,567	86	2
Rushford	1,713	0	0	0	0	0	0	0	0	0	0
Sartell	18,014	11	0	3	2	6	301	23	264	14	0
Sauk Centre	4,389	8	0	4	0	4	61	8	51	2	0
Sauk Rapids	13,853	6	1	1	1	3	283	33	242	8	1
Savage	32,029	36	0	14	5	17	433	39	377	17	3
Shakopee	41,424	75	1	25	8	41	810	81	683	46	2
Sherburn[4]	1,089	1	0	0	0	1	5	2	2	1	0
Silver Bay	1,753	0	0	0	0	0	0	0	0	0	0
Silver Lake	820	3	0	1	0	2	13	3	8	2	1
Slayton	2,004	4	0	0	0	4	2	1	1	0	0
Sleepy Eye	3,378	7	1	3	0	3	23	6	14	3	0
South Lake Minnetonka	12,731	3	0	1	0	2	88	32	55	1	0
South St. Paul	20,260	46	0	10	8	28	505	98	362	45	3
Springfield	2,006	0	0	0	0	0	0	0	0	0	0
Spring Grove	1,276	0	0	0	0	0	22	1	20	1	0
Spring Lake Park	6,515	27	0	10	7	10	291	34	234	23	1
St. Anthony	9,205	19	0	4	7	8	206	31	164	11	1
Staples	2,947	2	0	0	0	2	46	4	40	2	0
Starbuck	1,246	4	0	0	0	4	64	21	42	1	0
St. Charles	3,759	6	0	1	1	4	68	9	57	2	0

Table 8. Offenses Known to Law Enforcement, by Selected State and City, 2018—Continued

(Number.)

State/city	Population	Violent crime	Murder and nonnegligent manslaughter	Rape[1]	Robbery	Aggravated assault	Property crime	Burglary	Larceny-theft	Motor vehicle theft	Arson[2]
St. Cloud	68,282	262	1	56	49	156	2,575	297	2,089	189	10
St. Francis	7,728	10	0	5	1	4	118	15	96	7	0
Stillwater	19,467	18	0	4	1	13	151	28	117	6	0
St. James	4,375	10	2	5	0	3	84	14	65	5	0
St. Joseph	7,212	4	0	2	0	2	69	8	54	7	0
St. Louis Park[4]	49,595	70	0	19	22	29	1,227	119	1,015	93	2
St. Paul	309,756	1,941	15	277	560	1,089	10,082	1,909	5,877	2,296	110
St. Paul Park	5,409	6	1	1	0	4	100	12	75	13	0
St. Peter[4]	12,012	14	0	5	2	7	152	14	131	7	3
Thief River Falls	8,865	16	0	3	1	12	207	25	178	4	0
Tracy	2,049	2	0	0	0	2	8	0	8	0	0
Twin Valley	778	0	0	0	0	0	0	0	0	0	0
Two Harbors	3,486	2	0	0	0	2	10	4	6	0	0
Virginia	8,458	35	0	9	3	23	293	36	238	19	0
Wabasha[4]	2,475	2	0	0	0	2	46	9	36	1	0
Wadena[4]	4,076	4	0	1	0	3	76	4	62	10	3
Waite Park	7,512	29	0	2	4	23	752	33	682	37	3
Walker	930	1	0	0	0	1	46	1	39	6	0
Warroad	1,758	2	0	0	0	2	11	1	10	0	0
Waseca[4]	8,918	7	0	2	0	5	190	32	153	5	1
Waterville	1,866	3	0	1	0	2	17	1	16	0	0
Wayzata	6,582	6	0	1	0	5	130	18	104	8	0
Wells[4]	2,176	4	0	0	0	4	7	4	3	0	0
West Concord	774	2	0	0	0	2	7	3	4	0	0
West Hennepin	5,663	5	0	0	0	5	43	10	31	2	0
West St. Paul	19,798	74	0	18	15	41	960	102	791	67	0
Wheaton	1,303	2	0	2	0	0	24	5	19	0	0
White Bear Lake	26,187	37	0	9	7	21	704	132	519	53	1
Willmar	19,635	55	0	16	3	36	499	69	399	31	0
Windom	4,401	8	1	3	0	4	68	11	54	3	0
Winona	26,840	43	0	18	5	20	615	60	543	12	0
Winsted	2,280	2	0	0	0	2	23	6	17	0	0
Woodbury	70,900	50	0	14	9	27	941	103	806	32	0
Worthington	13,309	35	0	14	1	20	111	19	82	10	1
Wyoming	7,900	9	0	2	1	6	63	11	44	8	0
Zumbrota	3,428	2	0	0	1	1	47	13	32	2	0
MISSISSIPPI											
Ackerman	1,444	2	0	0	0	2	34	14	19	1	1
Batesville[6]	7,212		0	0		17	321	41	274	6	2
Biloxi	46,148	149	1	23	52	73	2,577	619	1,773	185	5
Booneville[8]	8,688		0		14	10	124	84	33	7	
Brandon[4]	24,283	30	0	5	5	20	186	30	152	4	0
Brookhaven	12,125	93	7	2	17	67	346	195	128	23	0
Byram	11,692	18	0	1	10	7	283	28	236	19	0
Clinton	25,137	15	1	0	10	4	538	65	459	14	0
D'Iberville	11,928	15	0	6	4	5	827	47	756	24	0
Edwards	1,006	17	0	0	1	16	37	17	20	0	0
Florence[8]	4,468		0		0	1	15	1	11	3	0
Fulton[8]	4,019		0		2	10	166	36	123	7	
Gautier	18,501	62	1	7	11	43	573	115	406	52	0
Gulfport	72,402	387	4	26	86	271	3,662	528	2,844	290	16
Hattiesburg[4,5]	46,461	92	0	20	21	51			1,591	156	4
Horn Lake[8]	27,238	28	0	1	18	9	650	110	516	24	5
Iuka[8]	2,955		0		0	4	65	11	53	1	0
Jackson[8]	166,024		78		476	598	7,855	2,073	4,726	1,056	74
Laurel	18,486	103	1	16	32	54	870	271	559	40	3
Leakesville[8]	896		0		0	1	4	2	1	1	0
Madison	25,832	18	0	0	2	16	241	7	231	3	0
Meridian	37,500	155	4	16	51	84	1,477	400	963	114	7
Ocean Springs	17,726	36	1	2	11	22	589	69	484	36	3
Oxford[5]	24,369		0		6	10	666	81	568	17	1
Pascagoula	21,654	73	3	12	26	32	1,325	187	1,076	62	9
Pass Christian	6,082	6	0	1	3	2	139	39	99	1	0
Petal	10,656	0	0	0	0	0	59	25	28	6	0
Southaven	54,772	68	1	0	26	41	1,633	226	1,291	116	6
Starkville[4,6]	25,559	43	1	2	7	33		390		19	1
Summit[8]	1,593		0		1	0	41	23	15	3	0
Vicksburg[8]	22,298		9		15	91	1,140	199	869	72	3
Waveland[6]	6,343		0		1	2	328	26	289	13	0
West Point	10,593	33	1	3	2	27	273	105	168	0	2
Wiggins[8]	4,561		0		5	3	221	48	165	8	0
MISSOURI											
Adrian	1,599	3	0	0	0	3	40	4	32	4	2
Advance	1,348	2	0	0	0	2	21	7	13	1	0
Alma	384	0	0	0	0	0	1	1	0	0	0
Anderson	1,975	6	0	0	0	6	50	9	36	5	0
Annapolis	341	0	0	0	0	0	4	3	1	0	0
Appleton City	1,064	2	0	0	0	2	16	10	5	1	0
Arbyrd	473	0	0	0	0	0	1	0	0	1	0
Arnold	21,151	22	0	6	4	12	767	40	673	54	0
Ash Grove	1,448	0	0	0	0	0	17	4	11	2	0

Table 8. Offenses Known to Law Enforcement, by Selected State and City, 2018—Continued

(Number.)

State/city	Population	Violent crime	Murder and nonnegligent manslaughter	Rape[1]	Robbery	Aggravated assault	Property crime	Burglary	Larceny-theft	Motor vehicle theft	Arson[2]
Ashland	3,956	6	0	0	0	6	49	2	44	3	0
Aurora	7,478	74	0	4	7	63	349	61	261	27	1
Ava	2,883	10	0	0	1	9	83	9	66	8	0
Ballwin	30,151	9	0	2	0	7	245	20	205	20	0
Bates City	216	1	1	0	0	0	5	0	3	2	1
Battlefield	6,218	1	0	0	1	0	41	8	33	0	0
Bella Villa	736	3	0	1	0	2	7	0	6	1	0
Belle	1,490	4	0	0	0	4	14	5	8	1	0
Bellefontaine Neighbors	10,597	100	4	2	20	74	462	169	208	85	0
Bellflower	358	0	0	0	0	0	2	0	1	1	0
Bel-Nor	1,453	6	0	2	0	4	27	7	16	4	0
Bel-Ridge	2,661	31	1	4	3	23	116	21	76	19	2
Bernie	1,904	0	0	0	0	0	21	2	18	1	0
Bertrand	756	0	0	0	0	0	15	10	5	0	0
Bethany	3,107	2	0	1	0	1	73	28	38	7	0
Billings	1,100	1	0	0	0	1	14	2	10	2	0
Blackburn	237	0	0	0	0	0	1	1	0	0	0
Blue Springs	55,277	134	4	29	17	84	1,599	148	1,296	155	
Bolivar	10,966	30	0	10	3	17	443	48	363	32	1
Bonne Terre	7,305	8	0	1	0	7	46	6	22	18	0
Boonville	8,434	12	0	0	3	9	162	26	127	9	1
Bourbon	1,598	6	0	1	0	5	46	13	30	3	0
Bowling Green	5,577	32	0	0	2	30	86	5	79	2	1
Branson	11,589	85	0	10	10	65	1,224	129	999	96	3
Branson West	450	2	0	0	0	2	96	5	91	0	0
Braymer	849	0	0	0	0	0	1	0	0	1	0
Breckenridge Hills	4,612	20	1	2	6	11	131	25	87	19	0
Brentwood	7,991	15	0	2	7	6	355	20	319	16	0
Bridgeton	11,663	68	1	6	19	42	680	67	557	56	1
Brookfield	4,291	14	0	2	2	10	77	17	58	2	3
Buckner	3,053	3	0	1	0	2	67	25	40	2	0
Buffalo	3,057	14	0	2	1	11	129	14	99	16	0
Bunker	388	3	0	0	0	3	4	2	2	0	0
Butler	4,025	8	0	4	0	4	104	16	77	11	5
Butterfield Village	472	0	0	0	0	0	0	0	0	0	0
Byrnes Mill	3,016	2	0	1	0	1	17	2	11	4	0
Cabool	2,119	5	0	1	0	4	35	8	27	0	0
California	4,425	3	0	0	0	3	55	8	46	1	1
Calverton Park	1,276	6	1	0	0	5	26	9	13	4	0
Camden	185	0	0	0	0	0	0	0	0	0	0
Camdenton	4,106	10	0	5	0	5	197	18	167	12	1
Cameron	9,736	18	0	5	0	13	174	19	154	1	
Campbell	1,858	10	0	0	0	10	16	1	12	3	0
Canalou	306	0	0	0	0	0	1	1	0	0	0
Canton	2,335	15	0	5	0	10	45	7	33	5	0
Cape Girardeau	39,303	192	5	14	52	121	1,537	250	1,214	73	9
Carl Junction	7,921	0	0	0	0	0	128	23	93	12	0
Carrollton	3,508	33	0	1	0	32	40	12	24	4	0
Carterville	1,919	5	0	1	0	4	32	7	22	3	0
Caruthersville	5,640	70	2	3	8	57	270	82	177	11	0
Cassville	3,311	20	0	1	0	19	257	19	233	5	1
Center	506	0	0	0	0	0	2	0	1	1	0
Centralia	4,255	12	0	1	1	10	71	9	56	6	0
Charleston	5,599	37	0	2	2	33	115	17	94	4	0
Chesterfield	47,602	22	0	3	2	17	732	56	654	22	0
Chillicothe	9,699	30	0	5	1	24	151	39	101	11	0
Clarkson Valley	2,610	0	0	0	0	0	12	2	10	0	0
Clarkton	1,189	1	0	1	0	0	5	0	4	1	0
Claycomo	1,496	3	0	0	0	3	41	6	31	4	1
Clayton	16,935	25	0	3	4	18	265	50	199	16	0
Cleveland	660	0	0	0	0	0	0	0	0	0	0
Clever	2,743	2	0	0	0	2	17	3	14	0	0
Clinton	8,897	49	1	9	2	37	355	77	248	30	0
Cole Camp	1,106	0	0	0	0	0	10	0	10	0	0
Columbia	123,586	446	5	89	104	248	3,483	549	2,648	286	7
Concordia	2,362	1	0	0	0	1	25	8	12	5	0
Conway	773	0	0	0	0	0	7	0	5	2	0
Corder	398	0	0	0	0	0	0	0	0	0	0
Cottleville	5,670	5	0	0	0	5	15	0	15	0	0
Country Club Hills	1,258	10	0	0	3	7	43	10	26	7	0
Crestwood[9]	11,864	15	0	0	1	14		6	160		0
Creve Coeur	18,831	22	0	0	11	11	289	39	228	22	0
Crocker	1,022	2	1	0	0	1	19	5	12	2	0
Crystal City	4,726	12	0	2	0	10	157	14	128	15	0
Cuba	3,302	5	0	0	0	5	146	17	124	5	0
Delta	439	0	0	0	0	0	0	0	0	0	0
Desloge	4,861	15	1	0	1	13	250	11	234	5	0
Des Peres	8,601	11	0	0	4	7	583	16	550	17	0
Dexter	7,839	5	1	1	1	2	215	61	146	8	0
Diamond	928	2	0	0	0	2	6	0	6	0	0
Dixon	1,429	17	0	1	1	15	36	6	26	4	0
Doolittle	602	1	0	0	0	1	7	0	7	0	0
Duenweg	1,348	0	0	0	0	0	30	5	17	8	0

Table 8. Offenses Known to Law Enforcement, by Selected State and City, 2018—Continued

(Number.)

State/city	Population	Violent crime	Murder and nonnegligent manslaughter	Rape[1]	Robbery	Aggravated assault	Property crime	Burglary	Larceny-theft	Motor vehicle theft	Arson[2]
Duquesne	1,736	2	0	0	0	2	87	15	59	13	0
East Lynne	304	0	0	0	0	0	1	1	0	0	0
Edgar Springs	194	0	0	0	0	0	2	0	2	0	0
Edmundson	831	1	0	0	1	0	66	8	43	15	0
Eldon	4,632	16	0	2	2	12	100	11	86	3	0
El Dorado Springs	3,568	9	0	1	0	8	205	34	156	15	3
Ellington	922	2	0	0	0	2	1	0	0	1	1
Ellisville	9,842	10	0	1	1	8	102	8	86	8	0
Eminence	582	0	0	0	0	0	1	1	0	0	1
Eureka	10,626	11	0	0	1	10	130	15	105	10	0
Excelsior Springs	11,626	22	0	11	2	9	351	55	273	23	0
Exeter	771	0	0	0	0	0	3	0	2	1	0
Fair Grove	1,473	6	0	1	0	5	28	4	22	2	0
Fairview	379	0	0	0	0	0	0	0	0	0	0
Farber	315	0	0	0	0	0	0	0	0	0	0
Farmington	18,740	29	0	2	6	21	621	65	524	32	0
Fayette	2,713	2	0	1	0	1	25	7	17	1	0
Ferguson	20,663	129	2	4	46	77	946	149	647	150	0
Ferrelview	872	0	0	0	0	0	0	0	0	0	0
Festus	12,092	56	0	3	1	52	202	26	156	20	0
Fleming	125	0	0	0	0	0	0	0	0	0	0
Flordell Hills	801	16	0	0	2	14	35	10	22	3	0
Florissant	51,326	115	7	5	36	67	1,079	162	772	145	2
Fordland	842	2	0	0	0	2	14	2	11	1	0
Foristell	578	3	0	0	1	2	32	1	29	2	0
Forsyth	2,437	6	0	0	0	6	55	3	49	3	0
Frankford	317	0	0	0	0	0	4	1	3	0	0
Fredericktown	4,014	23	0	1	1	21	103	20	77	6	1
Frontenac	3,875	3	0	0	0	3	73	8	62	3	0
Fulton	12,856	29	0	1	2	26	500	138	333	29	2
Gallatin	1,759	4	0	0	0	4	14	3	10	1	0
Gideon	985	2	0	0	1	1	8	3	5	0	0
Gladstone	27,382	116	2	14	20	80	660	134	432	94	5
Glendale	5,881	3	0	1	0	2	32	2	28	2	0
Goodman	1,244	2	0	0	0	2	8	4	3	1	0
Gower	1,476	2	0	0	1	1	12	3	7	2	0
Grain Valley	14,165	25	0	9	2	14	201	24	151	26	3
Granby	2,100	5	0	0	1	4	71	14	53	4	0
Grandview	25,256	173	4	11	30	128	924	150	645	129	6
Greenfield	1,309	6	0	1	0	5	16	2	13	1	0
Green Ridge	498	0	0	0	0	0	0	0	0	0	0
Hamilton	1,694	2	0	0	0	2	13	1	11	1	0
Hannibal	17,545	102	0	24	3	75	896	91	757	48	2
Hardin	534	1	0	0	0	1	2	0	2	0	0
Harrisonville[4]	10,113	36	0	3	2	31	298	58	219	21	0
Hartville	606	0	0	0	0	0	4	0	2	2	0
Hawk Point	691	2	0	0	0	2	9	1	8	0	0
Hayti	2,644	27	0	5	3	19	152	44	99	9	17
Hazelwood	25,234	99	2	7	29	61	734	104	514	116	0
Henrietta	355	1	0	1	0	0	2	0	2	0	0
Herculaneum	4,067	15	0	0	1	14	68	7	56	5	0
Hermann	2,327	6	0	0	0	6	39	13	23	3	1
Higginsville	4,606	3	0	1	0	2	58	9	45	4	0
Hillsdale	1,567	14	2	0	3	9	19	14	0	5	0
Holden	2,232	5	0	1	1	3	59	12	40	7	0
Hollister[6]	4,561	4	0	0	0	4			77	0	0
Holts Summit	4,599	21	0	0	0	21	39	3	33	3	0
Hornersville	613	0	0	0	0	0	9	5	4	0	0
Houston	2,091	7	0	0	1	6	97	19	76	2	0
Howardville	346	0	0	0	0	0	0	0	0	0	0
Huntsville	1,512	2	0	0	0	2	3	0	3	0	0
Iberia	745	0	0	0	0	0	2	1	0	1	0
Independence	117,368	521	10	70	105	336	6,115	704	4,203	1,208	15
Indian Point	519	0	0	0	0	0	0	0	0	0	0
Ironton	1,389	0	0	0	0	0	20	4	16	0	0
Jackson	15,101	19	0	1	0	18	179	22	147	10	3
Jasper	942	2	0	0	0	2	9	3	6	0	1
Jefferson City[4]	42,856	151	5	37	27	82	1,277	131	1,053	93	5
Jonesburg	705	1	0	0	0	1	15	3	11	1	0
Kahoka	1,987	7	0	4	0	3	9	1	8	0	0
Kansas City	493,115	7,842	137	403	1,637	5,665	21,236	3,717	13,305	4,214	216
Kearney	10,300	6	0	3	0	3	149	16	120	13	0
Kennett	10,326	50	0	6	9	35	654	153	471	30	4
Kimberling City	2,306	12	0	0	0	12	41	9	31	1	0
Kimmswick	151	0	0	0	0	0	0	0	0	0	0
Kirksville	17,539	44	0	10	1	33	507	73	412	22	1
Kirkwood	27,670	30	2	2	5	21	381	34	335	12	0
Knob Noster	2,763	2	0	0	0	2	45	7	35	3	0
Laddonia	500	0	0	0	0	0	7	3	4	0	0
Ladue	8,625	5	0	0	1	4	112	17	86	9	0
La Grange	915	1	1	0	0	0	5	1	4	0	0
Lake Lafayette	332	1	0	0	0	1	4	1	3	0	0
Lake Lotawana	2,119	2	0	0	0	2	18	0	16	2	0

Table 8. Offenses Known to Law Enforcement, by Selected State and City, 2018—Continued

(Number.)

State/city	Population	Violent crime	Murder and nonnegligent manslaughter	Rape[1]	Robbery	Aggravated assault	Property crime	Burglary	Larceny-theft	Motor vehicle theft	Arson[2]
Lake Ozark	1,822	4	0	0	0	4	61	2	59	0	0
Lakeshire	1,397	1	0	0	0	1	9	1	6	2	0
Lake St. Louis	16,134	12	0	2	1	9	248	16	223	9	0
Lake Tapawingo	725	2	0	0	0	2	11	1	9	1	0
Lake Waukomis	932	1	0	0	0	1	0	0	0	0	0
Lake Winnebago	1,175	0	0	0	0	0	5	0	5	0	0
Lamar	4,303	8	0	6	1	1	156	39	116	1	0
Lanagan	416	0	0	0	0	0	4	1	3	0	2
Lathrop	2,028	4	0	1	0	3	22	3	15	4	0
Laurie	935	0	0	0	0	0	42	5	37	0	0
Lawson	2,382	3	0	0	0	3	27	5	20	2	1
Leadington	606	2	0	0	0	2	15	6	6	3	0
Leadwood	1,165	5	0	2	0	3	30	9	17	4	0
Lebanon	14,622	57	2	8	2	45	731	104	562	65	2
Lee's Summit	98,144	118	2	24	25	67	2,105	208	1,718	179	0
Lexington	4,531	16	0	1	1	14	10	3	4	3	1
Liberty	31,842	93	0	6	6	81	511	69	383	59	1
Licking	3,094	4	0	1	1	2	30	7	22	1	0
Lincoln	1,179	7	0	0	0	7	32	3	29	0	0
Linn	1,517	0	0	0	0	0	14	3	10	1	0
Lone Jack	1,266	7	0	0	0	7	4	0	3	1	0
Louisiana	3,282	2	0	0	0	2	43	5	36	2	0
Lowry City	610	0	0	0	0	0	2	0	2	0	0
Macon	5,368	11	0	3	0	8	126	15	109	2	0
Malden	3,943	25	2	0	4	19	57	21	31	5	0
Manchester	18,114	16	0	3	2	11	267	13	242	12	0
Mansfield	1,249	3	0	2	0	1	92	7	79	6	0
Maplewood	8,130	48	0	3	14	31	700	28	636	36	0
Marble Hill	1,483	2	0	0	0	2	10	1	9	0	0
Marceline[4]	2,122	8	0	1	0	7	24	9	15	0	0
Marionville	2,186	16	0	4	0	12	43	12	27	4	0
Marshall[4]	12,655	29	1	8	2	18	300	48	236	16	0
Marshfield	7,442	7	0	3	0	4	222	31	183	8	0
Marston	456	1	0	0	0	1	2	0	2	0	0
Martinsburg	300	0	0	0	0	0	0	0	0	0	0
Maryland Heights	26,930	93	2	23	15	53	692	59	579	54	2
Maryville	11,716	7	0	3	0	4	169	17	132	20	0
Matthews	606	3	0	0	0	3	5	1	4	0	0
Maysville	1,067	0	0	0	0	0	3	1	2	0	0
Memphis	1,864	3	0	2	0	1	16	2	13	1	0
Merriam Woods	1,858	0	0	0	0	0	8	2	2	4	0
Mexico	11,507	14	0	1	5	8	289	44	234	11	0
Milan	1,799	1	0	0	0	1	19	5	10	4	0
Miner	947	43	0	0	1	42	53	12	37	4	0
Moberly	13,750	120	2	3	1	114	253	38	199	16	0
Moline Acres	2,382	24	0	1	5	18	128	16	83	29	1
Monett	8,984	29	0	5	2	22	274	40	216	18	1
Monroe City	2,424	15	0	0	0	15	39	10	26	3	1
Montgomery City	2,630	4	0	1	0	3	66	13	52	1	0
Morehouse	880	0	0	0	0	0	4	2	1	1	0
Moscow Mills	3,004	4	0	2	1	1	38	5	31	2	0
Mound City	1,026	1	0	0	0	1	13	8	5	0	0
Mountain Grove	4,659	26	0	0	1	25	99	15	71	13	1
Mountain View	2,645	2	0	0	0	2	80	18	57	5	1
Mount Vernon	4,525	2	0	1	0	1	123	14	103	6	2
Napoleon	212	0	0	0	0	0	1	0	0	1	0
Neosho	12,057	29	0	2	6	21	526	100	388	38	0
Nevada	8,116	44	0	2	4	38	472	78	370	24	3
Newburg	435	0	0	0	0	0	1	0	1	0	0
New Florence	705	0	0	0	0	0	3	1	2	0	0
New Franklin	1,074	0	0	0	0	0	0	0	0	0	0
New Haven	2,076	6	0	2	0	4	22	11	10	1	2
New London	973	4	0	0	0	4	14	0	13	1	0
Niangua	423	0	0	0	0	0	0	0	0	0	0
Nixa	21,653	26	0	1	3	22	249	27	200	22	3
Noel	1,815	6	0	2	0	4	23	2	16	5	1
North Kansas City	4,552	44	0	2	10	32	386	23	311	52	1
Northmoor	347	8	0	1	0	7	10	2	4	4	0
Northwoods	4,404	25	1	0	4	20	111	43	53	15	
Oak Grove	8,151	16	0	1	2	13	207	42	143	22	0
Oakland	1,368	0	0	0	0	0	11	0	11	0	0
Odessa	5,184	8	0	0	1	7	68	11	52	5	0
O'Fallon	88,763	145	0	14	2	129	952	54	839	59	1
Old Monroe	282	0	0	0	0	0	0	0	0	0	0
Olivette	7,843	16	0	0	5	11	110	8	97	5	0
Oregon	754	1	0	0	0	1	7	1	6	0	0
Oronogo	2,578	9	0	0	0	9	27	3	22	2	0
Orrick	802	2	0	0	0	2	1	0	0	1	0
Osage Beach	4,582	23	0	1	0	22	266	28	231	7	0
Osceola	895	3	0	0	0	3	10	4	5	1	0
Owensville	2,576	5	0	0	1	4	80	10	65	5	0
Ozark	20,203	41	0	5	3	33	436	33	368	35	1
Pacific	7,241	9	0	1	1	7	151	15	122	14	0

Table 8. Offenses Known to Law Enforcement, by Selected State and City, 2018—Continued

(Number.)

State/city	Population	Violent crime	Murder and nonnegligent manslaughter	Rape[1]	Robbery	Aggravated assault	Property crime	Burglary	Larceny-theft	Motor vehicle theft	Arson[2]
Pagedale	3,292	49	2	0	14	33	113	23	77	13	1
Palmyra	3,598	1	0	0	0	1	95	2	87	6	0
Parkville	6,963	13	0	4	2	7	124	21	94	9	0
Peculiar	5,192	2	0	1	0	1	117	17	95	5	0
Perry	694	0	0	0	0	0	1	0	0	1	0
Perryville[4]	8,495	41	0	9	1	31	224	21	190	13	1
Pevely	5,883	34	0	5	4	25	166	20	131	15	1
Piedmont	1,947	4	0	0	0	4	24	6	18	0	0
Pierce City	1,302	3	0	0	0	3	27	7	18	2	1
Pilot Grove	760	3	0	0	0	3	3	0	3	0	0
Pilot Knob	718	1	0	0	0	1	10	1	9	0	0
Pineville	790	0	0	0	0	0	0	0	0	0	0
Platte City	4,979	4	0	0	0	4	50	5	34	11	0
Plattsburg	2,262	3	0	1	1	1	16	5	10	1	0
Pleasant Hill[6]	8,606		0	1	0		119	17	87	15	0
Pleasant Valley	3,059	5	0	1	0	4	31	6	19	6	0
Poplar Bluff	17,074	85	2	15	19	49	1,163	210	854	99	1
Portageville[4]	3,019	12	0	4	1	7	57	9	43	5	0
Potosi	2,623	8	0	2	0	6	181	22	150	9	0
Purdy	1,096	4	0	1	0	3	30	7	20	3	1
Queen City	607	0	0	0	0	0	0	0	0	0	0
Qulin	453	1	0	0	0	1	9	1	8	0	0
Raymore	21,452	9	0	2	3	4	474	26	423	25	1
Raytown	29,173	153	7	17	48	81	1,295	258	817	220	2
Reeds Spring	880	0	0	0	0	0	0	0	0	0	0
Republic	16,495	43	0	4	1	38	311	24	263	24	2
Rich Hill	1,323	2	0	0	0	2	1	0	0	1	0
Richland	1,759	7	0	3	0	4	53	21	26	6	1
Richmond	5,636	31	0	2	0	29	240	43	185	12	2
Richmond Heights	8,342	22	0	2	5	15	445	15	398	32	0
Risco	315	0	0	0	0	0	1	0	0	1	0
Riverview	2,772	48	3	1	9	35	114	33	60	21	0
Rockaway Beach	866	1	0	0	0	1	1	1	0	0	0
Rock Hill	4,599	3	0	0	1	2	53	6	45	2	0
Rock Port	1,212	3	0	0	0	3	15	1	12	2	0
Rogersville	3,739	3	0	0	0	3	53	16	30	7	0
Rolla	20,385	121	0	30	7	84	683	102	547	34	5
Rosebud	406	1	0	1	0	0	11	7	3	1	0
Salem	4,910	5	0	2	0	3	159	12	141	6	0
Sarcoxie	1,296	4	0	0	0	4	45	8	28	9	0
Savannah	5,202	6	0	1	2	3	57	11	42	4	1
Scott City	4,486	10	0	3	0	7	86	16	62	8	0
Sedalia	21,590	183	1	11	10	161	944	118	774	52	3
Seligman	844	1	0	0	0	1	19	3	15	1	0
Seneca	2,389	4	0	0	1	3	57	10	41	6	0
Seymour	2,003	7	0	1	0	6	93	14	74	5	0
Shrewsbury	6,108	19	2	2	3	12	207	10	193	4	0
Sikeston	16,129	97	2	16	14	65	644	118	498	28	0
Silex	301	0	0	0	0	0	0	0	0	0	0
Smithville	10,012	10	0	3	2	5	153	15	114	24	0
Sparta	1,907	2	0	0	0	2	13	4	9	0	0
Springfield	168,537	2,218	16	333	295	1,574	11,830	1,975	8,385	1,470	55
St. Ann	12,698	36	1	2	5	28	275	28	210	37	1
St. Charles	70,925	147	7	33	19	88	1,610	134	1,321	155	6
St. Clair	4,702	53	0	0	1	52	256	22	208	26	0
Steele	1,991	11	1	2	2	6	62	17	42	3	0
Steelville	1,677	6	0	2	0	4	91	20	67	4	1
Ste. Genevieve	4,443	3	0	0	0	3	68	4	64	0	0
Stewartsville	734	0	0	0	0	0	0	0	0	0	0
St. James	4,059	3	0	1	0	2	128	12	104	12	1
St. John	6,344	15	1	0	7	7	185	26	131	28	2
St. Joseph[4,8]	76,409		8		65	301	3,768	716	2,491	561	10
St. Louis	306,875	5,525	187	309	1,452	3,577	18,142	2,979	12,413	2,750	188
St. Marys	346	3	0	0	0	3	1	0	1	0	0
Stover	1,063	10	0	0	0	10	15	2	11	2	0
St. Peters	57,838	106	0	19	14	73	1,248	89	1,091	68	11
Strafford	2,408	5	0	0	1	4	63	13	47	3	0
St. Robert	6,006	29	0	1	2	26	319	43	267	9	0
Sugar Creek	3,303	15	0	1	0	14	127	15	79	33	0
Sullivan	7,156	22	0	2	4	16	352	92	230	30	1
Summersville	491	0	0	0	0	0	0	0	0	0	0
Sunset Hills	8,492	11	0	0	2	9	156	15	131	10	0
Tarkio	1,453	0	0	0	0	0	8	3	4	1	0
Thayer	2,136	11	0	0	1	10	38	12	24	2	0
Tipton	3,387	13	0	0	0	13	5	2	2	1	0
Town and Country	11,154	2	0	1	1	0	132	9	111	12	0
Trenton	5,800	13	0	0	0	13	97	30	58	9	0
Troy	12,226	26	0	2	0	24	244	26	199	19	0
Truesdale	813	2	0	0	0	2	6	1	5	0	0
Union	11,710	52	1	7	0	44	533	59	426	48	7
University City	34,438	108	1	6	41	60	1,147	138	902	107	5
Urbana	414	0	0	0	0	0	0	0	0	0	0
Van Buren	820	4	0	0	0	4	12	6	6	0	0

Table 8. Offenses Known to Law Enforcement, by Selected State and City, 2018—Continued

(Number.)

State/city	Population	Violent crime	Murder and nonnegligent manslaughter	Rape[1]	Robbery	Aggravated assault	Property crime	Burglary	Larceny-theft	Motor vehicle theft	Arson[2]
Vandalia	4,215	7	0	1	0	6	34	7	26	1	0
Velda City	1,378	17	1	1	2	13	42	17	21	4	0
Verona	608	0	0	0	0	0	4	0	3	1	0
Versailles	2,426	6	0	1	1	4	52	2	49	1	1
Viburnum	665	1	0	0	0	1	4	0	2	2	0
Vienna	588	4	0	0	0	4	16	4	12	0	0
Vinita Park	11,003	144	13	3	44	84	592	136	375	81	1
Walnut Grove	807	0	0	0	0	0	0	0	0	0	0
Warrensburg[4]	20,355	78	1	15	6	56	692	105	534	53	3
Warrenton	8,283	62	1	14	2	45	369	56	298	15	0
Warsaw	2,184	13	0	2	0	11	74	8	62	4	0
Warson Woods	1,915	0	0	0	0	0	19	1	17	1	0
Washburn	436	0	0	0	0	0	2	0	1	1	0
Washington	13,964	34	0	11	1	22	526	35	453	38	1
Waynesville	5,275	14	1	6	1	6	81	14	61	6	1
Webb City	11,379	10	0	0	2	8	309	15	274	20	0
Webster Groves	22,873	25	0	6	6	13	164	34	116	14	4
Wellington	795	1	0	0	0	1	8	1	2	5	0
Wellsville	1,132	1	0	0	0	1	4	1	3	0	0
Wentzville	41,057	106	0	16	5	85	427	45	369	13	2
West Plains	12,277	44	0	5	3	36	585	96	451	38	0
Wheaton	690	0	0	0	0	0	0	0	0	0	0
Willard	5,447	15	0	1	1	13	52	8	42	2	0
Willow Springs[5]	2,110		0	3	2		77	7	62	8	0
Winfield	1,461	0	0	0	0	0	14	1	12	1	0
Winona	1,299	8	0	0	0	8	15	3	9	3	1
Woodson Terrace	4,032	25	1	4	6	14	162	11	73	78	0
Wright City	3,777	6	0	4	1	1	31	4	24	3	1
MONTANA											
Baker	1,960	2	0	1	0	1	5	0	5	0	0
Belgrade	8,724	20	1	9	0	10	184	11	160	13	0
Billings	110,397	598	8	54	108	428	5,276	685	3,796	795	16
Bozeman	48,101	104	0	32	7	65	885	50	778	57	6
Bridger	760	0	0	0	0	0	7	1	4	2	0
Chinook	1,256	0	0	0	0	0	10	1	7	2	0
Colstrip	2,324	4	0	0	0	4	12	3	9	0	0
Columbia Falls	5,456	8	0	0	2	6	84	7	68	9	0
Columbus	2,046	5	0	0	0	5	44	1	33	10	0
Cut Bank	3,013	25	0	2	2	21	115	10	98	7	0
Deer Lodge	2,902	7	0	2	0	5	18	3	9	6	0
Dillon	4,281	16	0	3	0	13	26	0	22	4	0
East Helena	2,075	8	0	0	1	7	66	5	49	12	0
Ennis	936	0	0	0	0	0	2	1	1	0	0
Eureka	1,106	4	0	0	0	4	11	1	7	3	0
Fort Benton	1,450	3	0	0	0	3	7	1	5	1	0
Glasgow	3,325	14	0	2	1	11	43	4	36	3	2
Glendive	5,132	11	0	2	0	9	36	11	23	2	0
Hamilton	4,794	21	0	6	2	13	170	13	148	9	0
Havre	9,821	39	0	11	3	25	316	31	259	26	1
Helena	31,898	196	2	55	11	128	1,694	184	1,374	136	8
Hot Springs	565	0	0	0	0	0	3	0	3	0	0
Kalispell	23,700	72	0	11	3	58	675	63	576	36	3
Laurel	6,800	15	0	0	0	15	136	12	116	8	0
Lewistown	5,899	27	0	3	0	24	77	11	59	7	0
Libby	2,698	3	0	1	0	2	81	6	74	1	1
Livingston	7,608	46	0	8	0	38	212	15	185	12	0
Manhattan	1,787	15	0	0	0	15	15	4	9	2	0
Miles City	8,496	17	0	2	0	15	159	15	132	12	0
Missoula	74,300	333	2	65	42	224	3,521	379	2,944	198	13
Plains	1,101	5	0	0	0	5	13	4	7	2	0
Polson	4,928	40	0	11	1	28	176	25	139	12	0
Red Lodge	2,310	6	0	2	0	4	42	2	37	3	0
Ronan City	2,110	17	0	1	1	15	64	5	55	4	0
Sidney	6,490	42	0	4	0	38	89	17	67	5	2
Stevensville	2,011	12	0	1	0	11	22	8	14	0	0
St. Ignatius	838	0	0	0	0	0	4	0	4	0	0
Thompson Falls	1,386	7	0	2	0	5	40	2	35	3	0
Troy	907	3	0	0	0	3	14	2	11	1	0
West Yellowstone	1,379	4	0	0	0	4	26	1	24	1	0
Whitefish	7,801	9	0	1	0	8	130	16	110	4	1
Wolf Point	2,782	14	0	1	3	10	47	2	43	2	0
NEBRASKA											
Alliance	8,122	9	0	3	0	6	130	32	90	8	0
Ashland	2,586	0	0	0	0	0	11	1	10	0	0
Aurora	4,488	1	0	0	0	1	36	8	26	2	0
Bayard	1,130	2	0	2	0	0	5	0	4	1	0
Beatrice	12,244	33	0	22	3	8	293	47	222	24	1
Bellevue	53,683	113	4	44	23	42	983	112	734	137	2
Bennington	1,532	0	0	0	0	0	9	1	7	1	0
Blair	8,103	8	0	3	1	4	128	17	96	15	1
Boys Town	631	6	0	4	0	2	31	0	30	1	

Table 8. Offenses Known to Law Enforcement, by Selected State and City, 2018—Continued

(Number.)

State/city	Population	Violent crime	Murder and nonnegligent manslaughter	Rape[1]	Robbery	Aggravated assault	Property crime	Burglary	Larceny-theft	Motor vehicle theft	Arson[2]
Broken Bow	3,546	4	0	0	2	2	31	2	29	0	0
Central City	2,918	3	0	2	0	1	10	1	8	1	0
Chadron	5,621	9	0	4	1	4	94	17	70	7	1
Columbus	23,257	26	0	8	7	11	357	43	289	25	1
Cozad	3,791	15	0	5	0	10	17	2	13	2	1
Crete	7,185	36	0	10	0	26	117	9	103	5	1
Emerson	798	0	0	0	0	0	2	0	2	0	0
Falls City	4,167	2	0	0	0	2	43	10	29	4	0
Fremont	26,465	59	0	32	3	24	534	105	393	36	5
Gering	8,291	14	0	5	1	8	113	14	91	8	2
Gothenburg	3,458	1	0	1	0	0	47	5	37	5	0
Grand Island	51,768	241	1	46	21	173	1,505	222	1,185	98	5
Hastings	24,963	51	0	21	7	23	830	107	639	84	3
Holdrege	5,432	5	0	3	0	2	65	2	57	6	0
Imperial[4]	2,061	0	0	0	0	0	10	0	6	4	0
Kearney	34,261	85	0	35	3	47	801	109	650	42	9
Kimball	2,342	4	1	0	0	3	9	2	6	1	
La Vista	17,177	16	1	8	0	7	270	19	209	42	4
Lexington	9,996	10	0	4	1	5	141	11	122	8	0
Lincoln	288,589	1,045	6	283	162	594	8,307	1,182	6,694	431	
Madison	2,352	2	0	0	0	2	12	2	9	1	0
McCook	7,518	21	0	7	0	14	129	35	87	7	0
Minden	2,981	8	0	5	0	3	47	5	37	5	0
Mitchell	1,654	2	0	1	0	1	4	1	3	0	0
Nebraska City	7,316	29	0	4	1	24	221	20	190	11	1
Neligh	1,501	0	0	0	0	0	7	0	7	0	
Norfolk	24,458	29	0	9	2	18	444	23	397	24	1
North Platte	23,774	97	1	8	11	77	1,006	193	742	71	4
Ogallala	4,512	12	0	2	1	9	130	15	110	5	1
Omaha	469,351	2,628	22	403	456	1,747	16,314	1,848	11,343	3,123	
O'Neill	3,625	11	0	8	2	1	17	4	11	2	
Ord	2,097	9	0	2	0	7	17	3	11	3	0
Papillion	19,588	39	1	9	2	27	367	6	342	19	2
Plainview	1,189	0	0	0	0	0	7	0	7	0	
Plattsmouth	6,444	14	0	8	1	5	113	12	97	4	0
Ralston	7,535	11	0	8	0	3	130	15	95	20	0
Schuyler	6,210	12	0	5	0	7	38	3	32	3	0
Scottsbluff	16,029	55	0	16	3	36	486	85	370	31	0
Seward	7,209	3	0	2	0	1	71	11	53	7	1
Sidney	6,602	16	0	2	1	13	133	10	120	3	0
South Sioux City	12,845	24	0	8	1	15	389	21	332	36	0
St. Paul	2,347	0	0	0	0	0	13	2	10	1	0
Superior	1,848	3	0	1	0	2	21	2	19	0	
Tekamah	1,709	4	0	1	0	3	24	4	20	0	
Tilden	929	0	0	0	0	0	0	0	0	0	
Valentine	2,791	11	0	2	1	8	35	5	26	4	1
Valley[4]	2,334	2	0	0	1	1	34	7	24	3	
Wahoo	4,464	3	0	1	0	2	42	5	31	6	0
West Point	3,335	0	0	0	0	0	16	0	16	0	0
York	7,875	6	0	3	0	3	240	11	223	6	
NEVADA											
Boulder City	16,112	13	1	2	1	9	147	50	81	16	0
Carlin	2,319	35	0	1	0	34	22	8	10	4	0
Elko	20,764	95	3	18	17	57	443	113	297	33	
Henderson	309,586	583	15	65	217	286	6,072	1,042	4,349	681	22
Las Vegas Metropolitan Police Department	1,644,390	9,949	120	1,610	2,690	5,529	46,673	11,968	26,756	7,949	83
Lovelock	1,775	11	0	1	0	10	39	24	14	1	0
Mesquite	19,055	32	0	14	3	15	298	61	204	33	0
North Las Vegas	246,951	2,386	33	150	443	1,760	5,202	1,326	2,677	1,199	20
Reno	252,341	1,636	6	174	303	1,153	6,053	1,073	3,930	1,050	16
Sparks	102,354	508	4	68	87	349	2,440	570	1,536	334	19
West Wendover	4,290	42	0	16	2	24	77	17	52	8	0
Winnemucca	7,832	10	1	0	1	8	181	48	110	23	8
NEW HAMPSHIRE											
Alexandria	1,611	3	0	1	0	2	15	0	15	0	0
Allenstown	4,365	10	0	4	1	5	35	6	26	3	0
Alstead	1,902	1	0	1	0	0	1	1	0	0	0
Alton	5,353	9	0	6	0	3	52	3	46	3	0
Amherst	11,232	6	1	3	0	2	127	5	119	3	1
Antrim	2,673	5	0	2	0	3	13	2	9	2	0
Ashland	2,056	1	0	0	1	0	39	5	30	4	0
Atkinson	6,970	3	0	0	1	2	19	3	16	0	0
Auburn	5,564	2	0	1	0	1	31	10	21	0	1
Barnstead	4,674	20	0	4	0	16	45	4	36	5	0
Barrington	9,122	6	0	5	0	1	33	9	20	4	0
Bartlett	2,784	3	0	1	0	2	28	3	25	0	0
Bedford	22,640	12	0	3	1	8	190	2	183	5	1
Belmont	7,329	12	0	1	4	7	148	21	119	8	0
Bennington	1,483	6	0	2	2	2	11	2	8	1	0
Berlin	10,263	16	1	7	0	8	103	22	75	6	2

Table 8. Offenses Known to Law Enforcement, by Selected State and City, 2018—Continued

(Number.)

State/city	Population	Violent crime	Murder and nonnegligent manslaughter	Rape[1]	Robbery	Aggravated assault	Property crime	Burglary	Larceny-theft	Motor vehicle theft	Arson[2]
Bethlehem	2,550	2	0	1	0	1	25	7	17	1	1
Boscawen	4,022	7	0	3	0	4	38	7	29	2	0
Bow	7,860	2	0	0	0	2	44	4	35	5	1
Bradford	1,690	2	0	1	0	1	10	2	8	0	0
Brentwood	4,740	1	0	0	0	1	29	2	24	3	0
Bristol	3,047	4	0	1	0	3	30	3	27	0	2
Brookline	5,351	6	0	1	0	5	12	3	8	1	1
Campton	3,281	14	0	4	1	9	58	9	48	1	3
Candia	3,959	0	0	0	0	0	14	2	12	0	0
Canterbury	2,434	3	0	0	0	3	21	1	17	3	0
Carroll	730	3	0	0	0	3	9	1	8	0	0
Center Harbor	1,109	0	0	0	0	0	17	7	9	1	1
Charlestown	4,988	17	0	0	1	16	25	5	19	1	0
Chester	5,201	5	0	0	1	4	30	4	25	1	1
Chichester	2,661	0	0	0	0	0	21	5	14	2	0
Claremont	12,930	58	1	20	8	29	247	22	215	10	1
Colebrook	2,117	5	0	1	0	4	21	5	16	0	0
Concord	43,071	103	0	25	17	61	849	106	709	34	6
Conway	10,153	18	0	9	1	8	204	16	182	6	0
Cornish	1,621	0	0	0	0	0	1	0	1	0	0
Dalton	870	0	0	0	0	0	1	0	0	1	0
Danville	4,595	0	0	0	0	0	11	0	10	1	0
Deerfield	4,536	3	0	0	0	3	33	4	27	2	0
Deering	1,938	0	0	0	0	0	17	3	13	1	1
Derry	33,724	45	1	9	12	23	315	37	252	26	4
Dover	31,600	35	4	11	4	16	353	24	318	11	6
Dublin	1,531	0	0	0	0	0	11	5	5	1	0
Dunbarton	2,829	2	0	0	0	2	22	5	15	2	0
Durham	16,813	11	0	9	0	2	53	9	44	0	0
East Kingston	2,437	0	0	0	0	0	1	1	0	0	0
Effingham	1,458	3	0	1	0	2	10	2	8	0	0
Enfield	4,536	4	0	2	0	2	20	6	13	1	0
Epping	7,114	15	0	1	2	12	92	3	88	1	0
Epsom	4,707	4	0	1	0	3	24	5	15	4	0
Exeter	15,305	15	1	5	2	7	114	6	106	2	1
Farmington	6,902	7	0	3	1	3	107	21	75	11	0
Fitzwilliam	2,343	1	0	1	0	0	11	3	6	2	0
Franconia	1,101	2	0	1	0	1	7	1	6	0	0
Franklin	8,621	20	0	3	2	15	83	19	61	3	1
Freedom	1,532	0	0	0	0	0	9	4	1	4	0
Fremont	4,821	6	0	3	0	3	33	9	24	0	0
Gilford	7,216	8	0	3	2	3	119	14	96	9	3
Gilmanton	3,757	4	0	2	0	2	13	4	9	0	0
Goffstown	17,978	24	0	6	2	16	134	12	109	13	0
Gorham	2,578	0	0	0	0	0	55	5	49	1	0
Grantham	2,954	2	0	0	0	2	6	2	3	1	0
Greenland	4,139	1	0	0	0	1	15	2	13	0	0
Hampstead	8,696	2	0	1	1	0	47	5	38	4	0
Hampton	15,679	34	0	6	3	25	159	13	139	7	0
Hampton Falls	2,380	8	0	6	0	2	22	4	16	2	0
Hancock	1,639	2	0	0	0	2	6	0	6	0	0
Hanover	11,519	8	0	5	0	3	96	10	86	0	1
Haverhill	4,557	14	0	4	0	10	89	3	84	2	0
Henniker	4,948	6	0	3	0	3	25	5	19	1	0
Hillsborough	5,936	18	1	5	2	10	77	9	62	6	0
Hinsdale	3,855	11	0	1	0	10	111	14	92	5	1
Holderness	2,091	2	0	0	1	1	24	1	22	1	0
Hollis	7,851	0	0	0	0	0	40	2	35	3	1
Hooksett	14,283	18	1	3	2	12	207	17	187	3	2
Hopkinton	5,680	0	0	0	0	0	31	2	25	4	0
Hudson	25,232	25	0	3	3	19	246	27	203	16	1
Jackson	824	1	0	0	0	1	8	4	4	0	0
Jaffrey	5,232	16	0	2	0	14	37	7	29	1	0
Keene	22,870	46	0	13	9	24	560	38	511	11	1
Kensington	2,135	1	0	1	0	0	3	1	2	0	0
Kingston	6,308	5	0	0	1	4	19	4	14	1	1
Laconia	16,658	40	0	11	11	18	554	75	436	43	1
Lancaster	3,226	8	0	3	0	5	37	4	28	5	1
Lebanon	13,578	22	0	8	2	12	236	19	205	12	1
Lee	4,435	3	0	0	0	3	19	4	15	0	0
Lincoln	1,772	4	0	2	0	2	42	5	35	2	0
Lisbon	1,574	1	0	1	0	0	14	2	11	1	2
Litchfield	8,535	6	0	0	0	6	56	8	48	0	1
Littleton	5,872	7	0	4	1	2	140	19	110	11	0
Londonderry	26,627	39	0	11	3	25	194	22	157	15	3
Loudon	5,523	3	0	0	0	3	38	6	29	3	0
Lyndeborough	1,720	0	0	0	0	0	9	0	8	1	0
Madbury	1,850	0	0	0	0	0	7	0	7	0	0
Madison	2,561	0	0	0	0	0	11	2	8	1	1
Manchester	111,422	661	4	65	144	448	2,878	333	2,382	163	21
Marlborough	2,054	0	0	0	0	0	12	4	8	0	0
Mason	1,422	0	0	0	0	0	4	2	2	0	0
Meredith	6,446	15	0	4	0	11	88	22	63	3	2

Table 8. Offenses Known to Law Enforcement, by Selected State and City, 2018—Continued

(Number.)

State/city	Population	Violent crime	Murder and nonnegligent manslaughter	Rape[1]	Robbery	Aggravated assault	Property crime	Burglary	Larceny-theft	Motor vehicle theft	Arson[2]
Merrimack	25,683	6	0	0	1	5	148	12	130	6	0
Middleton	1,820	1	0	0	0	1	13	1	11	1	0
Milford	15,497	8	0	3	0	5	94	6	83	5	1
Milton	4,636	5	0	2	0	3	53	12	35	6	1
Mont Vernon	2,555	3	0	1	0	2	7	1	6	0	1
Moultonborough	4,098	1	0	0	0	1	24	0	22	2	0
Nashua	88,596	124	1	57	19	47	1,144	85	991	68	15
New Boston	5,706	3	0	1	0	2	15	3	11	1	0
Newbury	2,211	1	0	1	0	0	15	2	11	2	0
New Castle	988	0	0	0	0	0	2	0	1	1	0
New Durham	2,680	6	0	1	0	5	45	5	30	10	0
Newfields	1,736	1	0	1	0	0	3	0	3	0	0
New Hampton	2,215	2	0	0	0	2	21	6	14	1	0
Newington	800	2	0	0	0	2	106	1	103	2	0
New Ipswich	5,302	7	0	3	0	4	31	12	17	2	1
New London	4,405	1	0	0	0	1	29	3	23	3	0
Newmarket	9,160	15	0	5	0	10	48	10	37	1	1
Newport	6,347	12	0	5	2	5	100	9	84	7	0
Newton	4,995	3	0	2	0	1	19	2	15	2	0
Northfield	4,864	12	0	2	1	9	48	10	35	3	0
North Hampton	4,510	4	0	2	0	2	47	6	38	3	0
Northumberland	2,112	3	0	1	0	2	23	1	22	0	1
Northwood	4,326	2	0	0	0	2	31	7	21	3	1
Nottingham	5,130	5	0	3	0	2	10	1	8	1	0
Ossipee	4,335	8	0	2	0	6	59	11	46	2	0
Pelham	13,795	13	0	6	0	7	96	32	62	2	0
Pembroke	7,157	21	0	8	0	13	68	8	55	5	0
Peterborough	6,536	5	0	2	0	3	77	9	63	5	0
Pittsburg	806	0	0	0	0	0	3	2	1	0	0
Pittsfield	4,101	7	0	0	0	7	18	2	15	1	0
Plaistow	7,773	7	0	0	5	2	178	6	168	4	0
Plymouth	6,722	12	0	2	1	9	103	6	92	5	1
Portsmouth	22,038	36	0	9	3	24	341	22	302	17	3
Raymond	10,485	10	0	4	0	6	54	5	46	3	0
Rindge	6,235	5	0	1	2	2	67	10	55	2	6
Rochester	30,947	117	1	12	15	89	902	82	775	45	0
Rollinsford	2,567	1	0	1	0	0	20	1	18	1	0
Rye	5,501	5	0	1	0	4	28	1	26	1	0
Salem	29,297	30	0	6	13	11	475	20	443	12	0
Sanbornton	2,992	5	0	1	1	3	22	6	16	0	0
Sandown	6,501	2	0	0	0	2	21	1	18	2	0
Sandwich	1,332	2	0	0	0	2	14	6	8	0	0
Seabrook	8,941	16	1	0	4	11	155	11	136	8	0
Somersworth	11,920	30	0	8	8	14	319	21	283	15	2
South Hampton	827	1	0	0	0	1	2	1	1	0	0
Springfield	1,329	0	0	0	0	0	0	0	0	0	0
Strafford	4,132	0	0	0	0	0	11	3	6	2	0
Stratham	7,484	5	0	1	1	3	35	4	29	2	0
Sugar Hill	572	0	0	0	0	0	0	0	0	0	0
Sunapee	3,462	1	0	0	0	1	15	0	15	0	0
Tamworth	3,009	3	0	2	0	1	19	2	17	0	1
Thornton	2,492	1	0	0	0	1	15	1	14	0	0
Tilton	3,581	9	0	1	1	7	186	16	161	9	0
Troy	2,072	1	0	0	0	1	23	3	18	2	0
Tuftonboro	2,372	2	0	1	0	1	18	1	15	2	0
Wakefield	5,708	10	0	4	0	6	53	8	40	5	0
Warner	2,924	1	0	1	0	0	27	2	21	4	0
Washington	1,103	1	0	0	0	1	8	1	7	0	0
Waterville Valley	242	0	0	0	0	0	19	2	16	1	0
Weare	8,990	3	0	1	1	1	33	10	19	4	0
Webster	1,923	1	0	0	0	1	14	4	9	1	0
Whitefield	2,201	1	0	0	0	1	12	2	10	0	1
Wilton	3,704	2	0	1	0	1	28	4	23	1	0
Winchester	4,160	3	0	0	0	3	44	6	37	1	0
Windham	14,811	5	0	1	2	2	52	8	40	4	1
Wolfeboro	6,286	15	2	8	0	5	43	5	37	1	0
Woodstock	1,362	2	0	1	0	1	13	4	8	1	0
NEW JERSEY											
Aberdeen Township	18,378	11	0	2	2	7	163	18	137	8	0
Absecon	8,252	17	1	1	5	10	181	16	159	6	0
Allendale	6,865	3	0	1	0	2	30	4	23	3	0
Allenhurst	488	0	0	0	0	0	7	0	4	3	0
Allentown	1,809	0	0	0	0	0	5	1	4	0	0
Alpha	2,288	1	0	1	0	0	38	6	32	0	0
Alpine	1,873	1	0	1	0	0	24	4	11	9	0
Andover Township	5,936	2	0	0	0	2	14	4	9	1	0
Asbury Park	15,717	174	3	10	54	107	653	101	538	14	1
Atlantic City	38,271	276	7	11	131	127	1,181	116	994	71	1
Atlantic Highlands	4,302	1	0	0	0	1	40	2	38	0	0
Audubon	8,599	0	0	0	0	0	296	28	262	6	0
Audubon Park	997	4	0	0	0	4	11	4	6	1	0
Avalon	1,258	2	0	0	0	2	138	7	130	1	0

Table 8. Offenses Known to Law Enforcement, by Selected State and City, 2018—Continued

(Number.)

State/city	Population	Violent crime	Murder and nonnegligent manslaughter	Rape[1]	Robbery	Aggravated assault	Property crime	Burglary	Larceny-theft	Motor vehicle theft	Arson[2]
Avon-by-the-Sea	1,780	1	0	0	0	1	31	3	26	2	0
Barnegat Light	580	0	0	0	0	0	12	1	11	0	0
Barnegat Township	22,777	13	0	5	1	7	120	25	92	3	0
Barrington	6,661	5	0	0	0	5	113	16	94	3	1
Bay Head	971	0	0	0	0	0	17	3	13	1	0
Bayonne	66,824	114	0	12	47	55	773	97	587	89	3
Beach Haven	1,169	0	0	0	0	0	118	3	114	1	0
Beachwood	11,146	6	0	1	5	0	130	19	111	0	0
Bedminster Township	8,126	1	0	0	1	0	34	5	26	3	0
Belleville	36,075	62	0	1	17	44	589	87	414	88	0
Bellmawr	11,312	8	0	0	1	7	158	28	122	8	0
Belmar	5,666	6	0	3	2	1	83	16	63	4	0
Belvidere	2,592	1	0	0	0	1	47	18	27	2	0
Bergenfield	27,684	1	0	0	1	0	76	12	60	4	0
Berkeley Heights Township	13,646	4	0	1	0	3	60	14	38	8	0
Berkeley Township	41,331	25	0	6	6	13	378	68	300	10	0
Berlin	7,495	13	0	2	0	11	123	12	103	8	1
Berlin Township	5,532	4	0	1	1	2	163	15	144	4	1
Bernards Township	26,813	2	0	0	1	1	87	13	66	8	0
Bernardsville	7,742	1	0	0	0	1	39	2	36	1	0
Beverly	2,497	7	0	1	0	6	44	20	22	2	0
Blairstown Township	5,787	3	0	0	0	3	30	16	13	1	0
Bloomfield	50,777	50	2	1	19	28	647	71	488	88	1
Bloomingdale	8,211	1	0	0	0	1	37	6	30	1	0
Bogota	8,499	2	1	0	1	0	45	8	34	3	0
Boonton	8,236	7	0	1	2	4	94	11	79	4	0
Boonton Township	4,299	2	0	1	1	0	24	3	20	1	0
Bordentown City	3,823	3	0	0	2	1	23	7	11	5	0
Bordentown Township	12,323	14	0	3	3	8	99	15	72	12	0
Bound Brook	10,360	13	0	2	9	2	114	33	75	6	0
Bradley Beach	4,214	1	0	1	0	0	55	2	53	0	0
Branchburg Township	14,577	4	0	2	0	2	80	5	70	5	0
Brick Township	74,712	65	0	12	8	45	904	113	768	23	4
Bridgeton	24,386	203	5	12	107	79	720	163	510	47	2
Bridgewater Township	45,050	16	0	0	9	7	331	53	265	13	0
Brielle	4,719	0	0	0	0	0	23	4	14	5	0
Brigantine	8,896	1	0	0	0	1	129	23	105	1	0
Brooklawn	1,904	16	0	3	6	7	132	8	116	8	0
Buena	4,405	5	0	0	1	4	72	13	58	1	0
Burlington City	9,817	37	1	1	10	25	211	60	139	12	0
Burlington Township	22,857	35	0	7	10	18	274	45	218	11	0
Butler	7,679	0	0	0	0	0	50	11	37	2	0
Byram Township	7,925	3	0	1	0	2	45	4	40	1	0
Caldwell	7,999	5	0	2	0	3	49	16	31	2	0
Califon	1,068	0	0	0	0	0	0	0	0	0	0
Camden County Police Department	73,140	1,198	23	64	355	756	2,219	458	1,242	519	40
Cape May	3,463	4	0	1	0	3	72	8	62	2	0
Cape May Point	277	0	0	0	0	0	2	1	1	0	0
Carlstadt	6,252	6	0	0	2	4	87	5	79	3	0
Carney's Point Township	7,655	16	0	4	7	5	86	23	60	3	1
Carteret	23,921	45	1	4	15	25	295	35	236	24	2
Cedar Grove Township	12,566	4	0	0	2	2	86	17	63	6	0
Chatham	8,793	0	0	0	0	0	39	5	30	4	0
Chatham Township	10,288	0	0	0	0	0	33	2	26	5	0
Cherry Hill Township	70,578	92	0	0	57	35	2,026	148	1,839	39	1
Chesilhurst	1,617	3	0	0	0	3	47	22	19	6	1
Chester	1,643	0	0	0	0	0	6	0	6	0	0
Chesterfield Township	7,567	0	0	0	0	0	14	0	13	1	0
Chester Township	7,809	0	0	0	0	0	22	5	14	3	0
Cinnaminson Township	16,630	14	0	3	3	8	286	42	237	7	0
Clark Township	16,079	4	0	0	2	2	227	7	213	7	0
Clayton	8,624	10	0	1	3	6	70	7	58	5	0
Clementon	4,887	11	0	0	8	3	139	45	87	7	0
Cliffside Park	25,001	15	0	5	4	6	150	17	121	12	0
Clifton	85,732	97	1	3	43	50	1,354	162	1,096	96	1
Clinton	2,699	1	0	0	0	1	13	5	7	1	0
Clinton Township	12,824	1	0	1	0	0	50	15	34	1	0
Closter	8,691	1	0	0	0	1	58	1	49	8	0
Collingswood	13,843	30	0	3	13	14	279	51	200	28	2
Colts Neck Township	9,944	8	5	0	1	2	51	8	29	14	1
Cranbury Township	3,900	0	0	0	0	0	37	1	35	1	0
Cranford Township	24,353	7	0	0	2	5	145	7	131	7	0
Cresskill	8,862	1	0	0	0	1	47	11	25	11	0
Deal	730	2	0	0	0	2	23	2	12	9	0
Delanco Township	4,509	5	0	3	2	0	47	12	32	3	0
Delaware Township	4,461	1	0	0	0	1	14	2	9	3	0
Delran Township	16,579	8	0	3	2	3	176	26	143	7	0
Demarest	4,977	0	0	0	0	0	21	2	10	9	0
Denville Township	16,737	2	0	1	1	0	90	7	77	6	1
Deptford Township	30,137	47	2	8	22	15	1,153	163	954	36	0
Dover	17,982	26	0	1	10	15	187	32	141	14	1
Dumont	17,825	5	0	0	2	3	49	6	43	0	0

Table 8. Offenses Known to Law Enforcement, by Selected State and City, 2018—Continued

(Number.)

State/city	Population	Violent crime	Murder and nonnegligent manslaughter	Rape[1]	Robbery	Aggravated assault	Property crime	Burglary	Larceny-theft	Motor vehicle theft	Arson[2]
Dunellen	7,328	3	0	0	1	2	97	14	82	1	0
Eastampton Township	5,940	6	0	1	2	3	59	13	42	4	0
East Brunswick Township	48,342	32	0	4	8	20	632	70	553	9	0
East Greenwich Township	10,504	4	0	0	0	4	68	12	50	6	0
East Hanover Township	11,084	2	0	0	0	2	106	16	83	7	0
East Newark	2,740	1	0	0	1	0	44	4	30	10	0
East Orange	64,625	333	6	21	133	173	904	168	522	214	9
East Rutherford	9,941	14	0	3	3	8	148	15	123	10	0
East Windsor Township	27,401	18	0	5	8	5	171	7	160	4	1
Eatontown	12,364	30	0	10	8	12	277	17	255	5	0
Edgewater	12,318	13	0	0	3	10	137	3	127	7	0
Edgewater Park Township	8,713	15	0	1	3	5	6	126	31	75	20	0
Edison Township	101,309	120	2	8	44	66	1,147	166	899	82	4
Egg Harbor City	4,162	9	0	0	4	5	122	35	85	2	0
Egg Harbor Township	43,276	62	1	4	10	47	902	114	765	23	5
Elizabeth	129,080	897	3	43	386	465	4,002	602	2,655	745	7
Elk Township	4,116	1	0	0	0	1	34	7	26	1	1
Elmer	1,301	0	0	0	0	0	4	0	4	0	0
Elmwood Park	20,277	33	0	0	14	19	342	37	284	21	0
Elsinboro Township	968	0	0	0	0	0	9	3	5	1	1
Emerson	7,679	2	0	0	0	2	36	2	32	2	0
Englewood	28,988	85	0	6	19	60	281	45	215	21	0
Englewood Cliffs	5,395	1	0	0	0	1	62	17	38	7	0
Englishtown	1,959	6	0	2	0	4	20	2	15	3	0
Essex Fells	2,109	0	0	0	0	0	15	0	11	4	0
Evesham Township	45,354	34	0	0	11	23	506	53	445	8	1
Ewing Township	36,142	69	0	13	18	38	685	113	511	61	3
Fairfield Township, Essex County	7,528	7	0	0	2	5	176	9	149	18	1
Fair Haven	5,927	1	0	0	0	1	23	1	19	3	0
Fair Lawn	33,413	19	2	0	4	13	304	39	255	10	0
Fairview	14,428	35	0	0	25	10	144	29	109	6	0
Fanwood	7,768	1	0	0	1	0	32	7	25	0	0
Far Hills	918	1	0	1	0	0	6	1	4	1	0
Fieldsboro	529	1	0	0	0	1	11	3	6	2	0
Flemington	4,627	4	0	1	2	1	64	10	50	4	0
Florence Township	12,748	13	0	3	2	8	89	30	55	4	0
Florham Park	11,602	3	0	0	2	1	65	8	53	4	0
Fort Lee	37,729	22	0	3	6	13	271	32	220	19	1
Franklin	4,735	5	1	3	0	1	37	1	36	0	0
Franklin Lakes	11,191	1	0	0	1	0	59	7	46	6	0
Franklin Township, Gloucester County	16,225	9	0	0	3	6	236	52	171	13	6
Franklin Township, Hunterdon County	3,238	0	0	0	0	0	30	3	27	0	0
Franklin Township, Somerset County	66,624	48	1	12	17	18	670	114	504	52	1
Freehold Borough	11,873	16	0	1	7	8	129	41	81	7	0
Freehold Township	34,896	41	2	5	9	25	451	26	410	15	0
Frenchtown	1,363	1	0	0	0	1	0	0	0	0	0
Galloway Township	36,467	73	0	2	8	63	399	90	295	14	1
Garfield	32,203	79	0	11	27	41	585	61	480	44	1
Garwood	4,370	1	0	0	0	1	32	5	26	1	0
Gibbsboro	2,211	4	0	0	1	3	28	12	16	0	0
Glassboro	19,938	38	0	3	10	25	327	69	250	8	3
Glen Ridge	7,622	1	0	0	1	0	158	24	121	13	0
Glen Rock	11,937	0	0	0	0	0	49	1	47	1	1
Gloucester City	11,167	34	0	0	13	21	269	47	204	18	0
Gloucester Township	63,198	78	5	10	24	39	945	90	839	16	3
Green Brook Township	7,138	10	0	0	2	8	94	21	61	12	0
Greenwich Township, Gloucester County	4,769	7	0	0	1	6	68	7	56	5	0
Greenwich Township, Warren County	5,510	0	0	0	0	0	99	6	93	0	0
Guttenberg	11,602	28	1	5	10	12	99	20	74	5	0
Hackensack	44,926	116	0	15	28	73	649	36	578	35	0
Hackettstown	9,530	5	0	1	1	3	46	2	40	4	0
Haddonfield	11,253	6	0	1	1	4	100	21	78	1	0
Haddon Heights	7,497	3	0	0	1	2	41	12	28	1	0
Haddon Township	14,500	19	0	0	13	6	247	37	199	11	1
Haledon	8,363	15	0	0	1	14	120	23	89	8	0
Hamburg	3,109	1	0	0	0	1	11	1	10	0	0
Hamilton Township, Atlantic County	26,380	57	2	3	13	39	857	98	736	23	4
Hamilton Township, Mercer County	87,889	116	4	12	50	50	1,700	325	1,296	79	3
Hammonton	14,311	9	0	0	5	4	149	30	111	8	0
Hanover Township	14,583	4	0	2	1	1	161	10	143	8	0
Harding Township	3,824	0	0	0	0	0	18	5	11	2	0
Hardyston Township	7,823	7	0	1	0	6	38	9	27	2	1
Harrington Park	4,802	0	0	0	0	0	13	7	3	3	0
Harrison	18,058	41	1	5	11	24	373	45	259	69	0
Harrison Township	12,915	2	0	1	1	0	67	13	53	1	0

Table 8. Offenses Known to Law Enforcement, by Selected State and City, 2018—Continued

(Number.)

State/city	Population	Violent crime	Murder and nonnegligent manslaughter	Rape[1]	Robbery	Aggravated assault	Property crime	Burglary	Larceny-theft	Motor vehicle theft	Arson[2]
Harvey Cedars	338	0	0	0	0	0	24	3	21	0	0
Hasbrouck Heights	12,163	1	0	0	0	1	51	0	51	0	0
Haworth	3,463	0	0	0	0	0	12	1	11	0	0
Hawthorne	18,874	2	0	0	2	0	177	28	139	10	0
Hazlet Township	19,970	23	0	4	4	15	208	13	187	8	0
Helmetta	2,198	0	0	0	0	0	8	0	8	0	0
High Bridge	3,528	4	0	0	0	4	21	8	13	0	0
Highland Park	13,989	8	1	0	1	6	166	20	141	5	0
Highlands	4,794	1	0	0	0	1	28	4	24	0	0
Hightstown	5,289	1	0	1	0	0	34	6	28	0	0
Hillsborough Township	39,796	15	0	6	1	8	240	46	190	4	2
Hillsdale	10,484	3	0	0	1	2	41	3	37	1	0
Hillside Township	22,078	41	0	2	22	17	540	72	372	96	0
Hi-Nella	855	1	0	1	0	0	10	1	9	0	0
Hoboken	55,096	119	0	4	23	92	862	99	726	37	0
Ho-Ho-Kus	4,139	1	0	0	0	1	31	10	20	1	0
Holland Township	5,128	4	0	2	0	2	9	2	6	1	0
Holmdel Township	16,621	4	0	2	0	2	129	6	108	15	2
Hopatcong	14,183	6	0	0	0	6	42	3	33	6	0
Hopewell Borough	1,921	0	0	0	0	0	6	1	5	0	0
Hopewell Township	18,000	8	0	5	1	2	76	18	58	0	0
Howell Township	52,672	36	0	4	8	24	351	61	282	8	1
Independence Township	5,495	3	0	2	0	1	10	5	3	2	0
Interlaken	798	0	0	0	0	0	5	5	0	0	0
Irvington	54,220	354	5	24	218	107	1,277	229	656	392	0
Island Heights	1,652	3	0	1	1	1	12	1	11	0	0
Jackson Township	56,706	27	1	7	4	15	360	73	263	24	3
Jamesburg	6,006	5	0	1	2	2	56	10	45	1	0
Jefferson Township	21,071	5	0	0	0	5	84	16	64	4	0
Jersey City	270,175	1,233	17	89	458	669	4,781	988	3,190	603	20
Keansburg	9,766	33	0	4	10	19	160	24	132	4	0
Kearny	42,339	38	0	1	10	27	677	61	547	69	0
Kenilworth	8,249	9	0	3	2	4	114	4	99	11	0
Keyport	7,065	17	1	0	5	11	87	15	64	8	0
Kinnelon	10,080	1	0	0	0	1	25	13	11	1	0
Lacey Township	28,654	18	0	5	2	11	257	30	221	6	0
Lake Como	1,710	2	0	1	0	1	16	3	13	0	0
Lakehurst	2,672	9	0	0	3	6	30	4	25	1	0
Lakewood Township	102,915	129	0	2	30	97	779	145	588	46	8
Lambertville	3,811	2	0	0	0	2	44	5	34	5	0
Laurel Springs	1,856	2	0	0	0	2	22	5	16	1	0
Lavallette	1,824	1	0	0	0	1	22	1	21	0	0
Lawnside	2,875	6	0	0	4	2	122	16	103	3	0
Lawrence Township, Mercer County	32,644	30	0	6	6	18	596	54	529	13	1
Lebanon Township	6,070	3	0	0	0	3	28	13	15	0	0
Leonia	9,175	3	0	0	0	3	74	28	41	5	0
Lincoln Park	10,308	0	0	0	0	0	60	6	49	5	0
Linden	42,806	122	1	16	39	66	1,126	143	943	40	1
Lindenwold	17,204	111	2	16	40	53	455	103	328	24	3
Linwood	6,822	4	1	0	2	1	53	12	40	1	0
Little Egg Harbor Township	21,087	4	1	0	1	2	241	38	194	9	2
Little Falls Township	14,306	16	0	0	0	16	113	17	83	13	0
Little Ferry	10,895	7	0	0	0	7	94	17	67	10	0
Little Silver	5,898	2	0	0	0	2	34	3	27	4	0
Livingston Township	29,820	23	0	2	3	18	277	22	238	17	1
Loch Arbour	181	0	0	0	0	0	4	1	3	0	0
Lodi	24,720	28	0	3	9	16	254	37	184	33	1
Logan Township	5,844	5	0	0	3	2	115	12	96	7	0
Long Beach Township	3,029	3	0	0	0	3	59	5	53	1	1
Long Branch	30,750	124	3	7	24	90	639	94	514	31	2
Long Hill Township	8,587	3	0	0	1	2	43	2	37	4	0
Longport	873	0	0	0	0	0	5	0	3	2	0
Lopatcong Township	8,384	1	0	1	0	0	67	6	59	2	0
Lower Alloways Creek Township	1,676	1	0	0	0	1	7	1	6	0	0
Lower Township	21,617	35	1	6	7	21	163	38	118	7	1
Lumberton Township	12,253	10	1	0	5	4	212	8	194	10	0
Lyndhurst Township	22,384	12	0	2	3	7	168	12	138	18	0
Madison	15,832	3	0	1	1	1	76	6	68	2	1
Magnolia	4,237	9	0	0	3	6	85	16	62	7	0
Mahwah Township	26,501	3	0	2	0	1	98	7	79	12	1
Manalapan Township	40,150	13	0	7	2	4	218	36	165	17	0
Manasquan	5,903	7	0	0	2	5	60	5	50	5	0
Manchester Township	42,939	15	1	1	2	11	238	48	185	5	6
Mansfield Township, Burlington County	8,577	3	0	0	2	1	61	9	46	6	1
Mansfield Township, Warren County	7,431	1	0	1	0	0	82	8	72	2	0
Mantoloking	249	0	0	0	0	0	11	2	6	3	0
Mantua Township	14,772	7	0	0	3	4	190	41	136	13	0
Manville	10,308	18	0	6	3	9	214	10	191	13	2
Maple Shade Township	18,772	38	0	8	10	20	305	55	226	24	1

Table 8. Offenses Known to Law Enforcement, by Selected State and City, 2018—Continued

(Number.)

State/city	Population	Violent crime	Murder and nonnegligent manslaughter	Rape[1]	Robbery	Aggravated assault	Property crime	Burglary	Larceny-theft	Motor vehicle theft	Arson[2]
Maplewood Township	24,635	22	1	2	12	7	394	43	291	60	0
Margate City	6,045	9	0	1	1	7	135	43	92	0	0
Marlboro Township	40,338	25	0	1	1	23	271	37	206	28	2
Matawan	8,864	0	0	0	0	0	10	0	9	1	0
Maywood	9,763	4	0	0	3	1	68	9	55	4	0
Medford Lakes	3,995	1	0	1	0	0	21	3	17	1	0
Medford Township	23,558	47	0	2	3	42	176	25	146	5	0
Mendham	4,905	0	0	0	0	0	24	4	18	2	0
Mendham Township	5,757	0	0	0	0	0	12	6	5	1	0
Merchantville	3,712	4	0	0	0	4	64	20	41	3	0
Metuchen	14,262	5	0	0	3	2	128	20	102	6	0
Middlesex Borough	13,704	11	0	1	3	7	100	13	81	6	1
Middle Township	18,358	51	0	9	12	30	394	79	301	14	3
Middletown Township	65,469	14	0	1	2	11	388	32	334	22	4
Midland Park	7,313	1	0	1	0	0	37	0	36	1	0
Millburn Township	20,250	8	0	0	8	0	369	27	325	17	0
Milltown	7,099	2	0	0	2	0	113	3	110	0	0
Millville	27,837	127	3	7	44	73	1,217	149	1,041	27	3
Mine Hill Township	3,534	0	0	0	0	0	16	4	8	4	0
Monmouth Beach	3,231	0	0	0	0	0	26	5	17	4	1
Monroe Township, Gloucester County	36,498	47	2	7	12	26	462	105	335	22	0
Monroe Township, Middlesex County	45,597	5	0	1	0	4	158	16	128	14	0
Montclair	38,893	37	3	10	5	19	502	110	350	42	2
Montgomery Township	23,515	7	0	0	0	7	97	43	50	4	0
Montvale	8,729	0	0	0	0	0	20	0	19	1	0
Montville Township	21,396	4	0	1	0	3	173	16	124	33	0
Moonachie	2,774	4	0	2	0	2	58	3	53	2	0
Moorestown Township	20,510	13	0	1	5	7	251	30	208	13	0
Morris Plains	5,509	3	0	1	1	1	61	2	59	0	0
Morristown	18,860	30	0	2	9	19	202	14	177	11	0
Morris Township	22,183	6	0	0	1	5	120	25	91	4	0
Mountain Lakes	4,308	0	0	0	0	0	43	7	23	13	0
Mountainside	6,925	2	0	0	0	2	53	4	40	9	0
Mount Arlington	5,914	1	0	0	0	1	25	2	22	1	0
Mount Ephraim	4,565	6	0	0	5	1	200	19	172	9	0
Mount Holly Township	9,658	38	0	12	7	19	231	17	207	7	1
Mount Laurel Township	41,629	52	0	6	17	29	664	51	579	34	1
Mount Olive Township	28,994	6	0	1	1	4	77	15	59	3	0
Mullica Township	6,005	6	0	0	1	5	71	33	31	7	0
National Park	2,934	0	0	0	0	0	35	2	31	2	0
Neptune City	4,694	10	0	1	1	8	141	9	130	2	0
Neptune Township	27,825	106	2	4	24	76	851	92	749	10	3
Netcong	3,182	3	0	2	1	0	14	1	12	1	0
Newark	282,258	2,069	75	150	689	1,155	5,674	832	2,827	2,015	38
New Brunswick	56,577	309	2	30	142	135	1,210	230	907	73	6
Newfield	1,535	0	0	0	0	0	14	2	11	1	0
New Hanover Township	7,504	0	0	0	0	0	2	0	2	0	0
New Milford	16,701	5	0	1	0	4	52	11	39	2	1
New Providence	13,283	0	0	0	0	0	65	7	53	5	0
Newton	7,824	11	0	0	1	10	81	8	72	1	1
North Arlington	15,868	5	0	0	2	3	148	9	120	19	0
North Bergen Township	63,166	98	0	19	27	52	435	70	302	63	0
North Brunswick Township	42,205	53	0	5	24	24	683	90	562	31	0
North Caldwell	6,716	0	0	0	0	0	14	0	12	2	0
Northfield	8,324	8	0	0	2	6	78	29	47	2	0
North Haledon	8,469	3	0	1	1	1	32	6	26	0	0
North Hanover Township	7,518	6	0	0	0	6	22	5	17	0	0
North Plainfield	21,834	39	1	7	18	13	338	54	272	12	0
Northvale	4,965	2	0	0	0	2	5	0	5	0	0
North Wildwood	3,816	13	0	2	1	10	167	23	144	0	0
Norwood	5,836	0	0	0	0	0	15	0	14	1	0
Nutley Township	28,596	27	0	2	4	21	197	27	149	21	0
Oakland	13,102	7	0	0	0	7	48	4	44	0	0
Oaklyn	3,934	10	0	0	5	5	140	37	99	4	0
Ocean City	11,138	5	0	0	0	5	283	33	249	1	0
Ocean Gate	2,001	1	0	0	0	1	30	8	22	0	0
Oceanport	5,742	4	0	0	0	4	47	11	33	3	0
Ocean Township, Monmouth County	26,947	20	0	1	8	11	586	66	505	15	1
Ocean Township, Ocean County	9,045	1	0	0	1	0	54	8	45	1	0
Ogdensburg	2,262	1	0	1	0	0	3	0	2	1	0
Old Bridge Township	66,321	28	0	1	12	15	490	49	393	48	0
Old Tappan	5,998	1	0	0	0	1	22	2	12	8	0
Oradell	8,243	6	0	4	0	2	25	4	18	3	0
Orange City	30,449	226	6	10	154	56	772	188	411	173	4
Oxford Township	2,446	0	0	0	0	0	12	2	9	1	0
Palisades Park	20,888	17	0	1	10	6	130	34	80	16	0
Palmyra	7,198	12	0	3	1	8	152	16	130	6	0
Paramus	26,744	24	0	3	12	9	1,067	24	1,015	28	0
Park Ridge	8,858	3	0	0	0	3	15	6	9	0	0

Table 8. Offenses Known to Law Enforcement, by Selected State and City, 2018—Continued

(Number.)

State/city	Population	Violent crime	Murder and nonnegligent manslaughter	Rape[1]	Robbery	Aggravated assault	Property crime	Burglary	Larceny-theft	Motor vehicle theft	Arson[2]
Parsippany-Troy Hills Township	52,447	29	1	4	6	18	362	53	279	30	0
Passaic	70,435	406	1	7	167	231	1,298	170	943	185	5
Paterson	146,893	1,076	13	49	532	482	3,564	797	2,326	441	8
Paulsboro	5,812	16	2	0	8	6	196	59	128	9	0
Peapack-Gladstone	2,588	0	0	0	0	0	19	10	9	0	0
Pemberton Borough	1,331	2	0	0	2	0	28	2	24	2	0
Pemberton Township	27,212	90	1	0	25	64	547	215	304	28	2
Pennington	2,554	1	0	1	0	0	5	0	5	0	0
Pennsauken Township	35,420	101	0	5	41	55	909	298	564	47	2
Penns Grove	4,790	33	3	4	8	18	180	36	135	9	3
Pennsville Township	12,378	6	0	1	0	5	236	21	209	6	1
Pequannock Township	15,177	3	0	0	0	3	93	17	72	4	0
Perth Amboy	52,347	165	1	0	53	111	721	126	530	65	1
Phillipsburg	14,395	44	0	12	15	17	295	56	230	9	3
Pine Beach	2,148	2	0	1	1	0	21	4	17	0	0
Pine Hill	10,431	25	0	0	9	16	162	45	114	3	3
Pine Valley	11	0	0	0	0	0	0	0	0	0	0
Piscataway Township	57,342	54	0	6	18	30	425	70	320	35	1
Pitman	8,696	4	1	0	1	2	48	9	38	1	0
Plainfield	50,820	195	5	4	99	87	820	141	597	82	9
Plainsboro Township	23,243	10	0	0	0	10	118	12	102	4	0
Pleasantville	20,799	92	1	19	33	39	306	99	195	12	3
Plumsted Township	8,460	1	0	0	0	1	53	22	28	3	0
Pohatcong Township	3,217	1	0	0	1	0	146	5	140	1	0
Point Pleasant	18,474	14	0	0	2	12	115	22	92	1	0
Point Pleasant Beach	4,472	3	0	0	0	3	64	5	59	0	0
Pompton Lakes	11,062	15	0	0	0	15	89	24	62	3	0
Princeton	31,856	11	0	0	3	8	224	43	169	12	2
Prospect Park	5,893	5	0	1	3	1	95	17	66	12	0
Rahway	30,113	34	0	4	9	21	245	44	163	38	1
Ramsey	15,126	2	0	0	0	2	106	8	96	2	1
Randolph Township	25,552	2	0	0	0	2	128	14	106	8	0
Raritan	8,098	1	0	0	0	1	59	5	54	0	0
Raritan Township	22,092	5	0	0	2	3	95	8	84	3	1
Readington Township	15,941	2	1	0	0	1	82	16	60	6	0
Red Bank	12,128	21	1	0	6	14	162	14	139	9	0
Ridgefield	11,329	3	0	0	1	2	68	7	57	4	0
Ridgefield Park	13,028	13	0	0	2	11	99	9	88	2	0
Ridgewood	25,429	5	0	1	0	4	155	22	130	3	0
Ringwood	12,303	6	0	1	0	5	48	15	29	4	0
Riverdale	4,293	0	0	0	0	0	93	5	85	3	0
River Edge	11,611	0	0	0	0	0	64	6	56	2	0
Riverside Township	7,875	7	0	0	1	6	15	8	6	1	0
Riverton	2,698	2	0	0	0	2	35	4	30	1	0
River Vale Township	10,157	1	0	0	0	1	24	2	19	3	1
Robbinsville Township	14,710	2	1	0	1	0	59	10	47	2	0
Rochelle Park Township	5,648	1	0	0	1	0	73	8	62	3	0
Rockaway	6,388	0	0	0	0	0	54	5	48	1	0
Rockaway Township	25,328	6	0	0	3	3	294	14	269	11	0
Rockleigh	526	1	0	0	0	1	0	0	0	0	0
Roseland	5,867	1	0	0	0	1	31	6	19	6	0
Roselle	21,787	45	0	0	14	31	281	53	203	25	1
Roselle Park	13,698	5	0	0	4	1	104	6	91	7	0
Roxbury Township	23,010	1	0	1	0	0	127	9	111	7	0
Rumson	6,835	1	0	0	0	1	26	3	13	10	0
Runnemede	8,261	7	0	0	2	5	208	53	147	8	2
Rutherford	18,617	19	0	1	3	15	164	22	132	10	0
Saddle Brook Township	14,037	1	0	0	0	1	192	2	187	3	0
Saddle River	3,230	0	0	0	0	0	29	4	17	8	0
Salem	4,726	43	2	2	9	30	221	75	129	17	11
Sayreville	45,062	44	0	3	6	35	301	31	236	34	3
Scotch Plains Township	24,423	10	0	1	2	7	171	36	127	8	0
Sea Bright	1,379	2	0	1	0	1	5	2	3	0	0
Sea Girt	1,766	4	0	0	2	2	32	2	24	6	0
Sea Isle City	2,061	3	0	0	3	0	103	23	80	0	0
Seaside Heights	2,872	26	1	1	6	18	215	38	173	4	0
Seaside Park	1,526	0	0	0	0	0	26	1	25	0	0
Secaucus	20,482	30	0	0	14	16	526	32	473	21	0
Ship Bottom	1,129	0	0	0	0	0	23	4	19	0	0
Shrewsbury	4,170	1	0	0	0	1	85	10	72	3	0
Somerdale	5,484	13	0	0	6	7	175	32	138	5	0
Somers Point	10,436	14	0	3	6	5	246	30	209	7	0
Somerville	12,326	16	0	2	5	9	131	24	101	6	0
South Amboy	8,764	6	0	0	1	5	97	19	68	10	1
South Bound Brook	4,621	4	0	2	1	1	28	5	21	2	0
South Brunswick Township	46,340	23	0	5	7	11	276	46	219	11	1
South Hackensack Township	2,473	6	1	0	3	2	63	6	51	6	0
South Harrison Township	3,118	0	0	0	0	0	13	3	8	2	0
South Orange Village	16,880	22	0	0	10	12	293	38	229	26	0
South Plainfield	24,238	23	0	0	5	18	397	34	339	24	1
South River	16,159	19	0	3	2	14	122	16	102	4	2
South Toms River	3,740	7	0	0	1	6	43	5	35	3	0

Table 8. Offenses Known to Law Enforcement, by Selected State and City, 2018—Continued

(Number.)

State/city	Population	Violent crime	Murder and nonnegligent manslaughter	Rape[1]	Robbery	Aggravated assault	Property crime	Burglary	Larceny-theft	Motor vehicle theft	Arson[2]
Sparta Township	18,694	5	0	0	1	4	54	6	41	7	0
Spotswood	8,364	1	0	0	0	1	61	7	53	1	0
Springfield Township, Burlington County	3,280	1	0	0	1	0	26	5	19	2	1
Springfield Township, Union County	17,762	4	0	0	1	3	144	22	113	9	0
Spring Lake	2,958	0	0	0	0	0	41	4	35	2	0
Spring Lake Heights	4,607	1	0	0	1	0	17	1	11	5	0
Stafford Township	27,141	15	0	1	1	13	183	13	162	8	1
Stanhope	3,306	2	0	0	1	1	18	0	17	1	0
Stone Harbor	816	0	0	0	0	0	63	8	54	1	0
Stratford	6,913	6	0	1	3	2	77	11	65	1	0
Summit	22,125	7	0	2	5	0	143	9	120	14	0
Surf City	1,174	0	0	0	0	0	12	1	11	0	0
Swedesboro	2,557	1	0	0	1	0	14	1	12	1	0
Tavistock	5	0	0	0	0	0	1	0	1	0	0
Teaneck Township	40,939	45	0	10	13	22	419	79	322	18	2
Tenafly	14,742	4	0	0	1	3	37	9	21	7	0
Teterboro	68	1	0	0	0	1	137	0	132	5	0
Tewksbury Township	5,825	0	0	0	0	0	12	3	8	1	0
Tinton Falls	17,754	5	0	0	1	4	182	15	164	3	0
Toms River Township	92,191	55	1	19	10	25	1,317	171	1,112	34	1
Totowa	10,666	12	1	1	0	10	219	12	198	9	0
Trenton	83,753	973	16	40	342	575	2,467	772	1,318	377	14
Tuckerton	3,336	1	0	0	0	1	36	14	21	1	0
Union Beach	5,469	7	0	1	0	6	24	2	20	2	0
Union City	69,950	233	2	0	76	155	1,078	95	894	89	0
Union Township	58,861	45	0	1	24	20	954	96	767	91	1
Upper Saddle River	8,330	0	0	0	0	0	25	1	15	9	0
Ventnor City	10,182	17	3	0	5	9	259	54	199	6	1
Vernon Township	22,057	1	0	0	0	1	100	12	82	6	0
Verona	13,437	0	0	0	0	0	89	15	68	6	0
Vineland	60,330	258	1	22	59	176	2,021	399	1,564	58	9
Voorhees Township	29,071	42	0	12	10	20	375	35	322	18	1
Waldwick	10,019	2	0	0	0	2	47	8	34	5	0
Wallington	11,676	5	0	0	2	3	120	8	108	4	0
Wall Township	25,955	6	0	0	0	6	262	36	225	1	0
Wanaque	11,960	11	0	0	2	9	71	1	70	0	0
Warren Township	15,951	3	0	1	1	1	52	10	28	14	0
Washington	6,535	4	0	0	0	4	47	19	28	0	0
Washington Township, Bergen County	9,299	0	0	0	0	0	29	6	20	3	0
Washington Township, Gloucester County	47,024	66	1	1	10	54	554	73	463	18	0
Washington Township, Morris County	18,484	7	0	3	0	4	50	6	39	5	0
Washington Township, Warren County	6,434	2	0	1	0	1	50	9	39	2	0
Watchung	5,939	1	0	0	1	0	395	17	374	4	0
Waterford Township	10,641	7	0	1	1	5	64	9	51	4	0
Wayne Township	54,340	64	0	0	13	51	986	75	875	36	5
Weehawken Township	15,567	23	0	0	7	16	223	24	182	17	0
Wenonah	2,201	3	0	0	0	3	13	7	4	2	0
Westampton Township	8,752	18	0	7	6	5	144	27	109	8	1
West Amwell Township	2,757	2	0	1	0	1	16	7	9	0	0
West Caldwell Township	10,912	2	0	0	0	2	68	5	57	6	0
West Cape May	1,015	1	0	0	0	1	13	3	10	0	0
West Deptford Township	20,889	19	0	2	4	13	290	73	203	14	0
Westfield	30,011	4	0	0	2	2	217	24	167	26	0
West Long Branch	7,957	3	0	0	2	1	101	9	86	6	0
West Milford Township	26,560	10	0	2	0	8	158	23	127	8	2
West New York	54,095	138	1	7	61	69	567	92	449	26	1
West Orange	48,071	91	1	13	24	53	615	81	462	72	0
Westville	4,121	5	0	0	2	3	118	22	84	12	0
West Wildwood	561	0	0	0	0	0	6	1	4	1	0
West Windsor Township	28,277	11	0	2	3	6	298	48	243	7	1
Westwood	11,219	11	0	1	0	10	57	20	36	1	0
Wharton	6,482	2	0	0	0	2	69	10	57	2	0
Wildwood	5,035	40	0	1	10	29	314	39	269	6	0
Wildwood Crest	3,116	7	0	0	0	7	61	19	42	0	0
Willingboro Township	32,124	112	0	9	23	80	476	152	297	27	4
Winfield Township	1,514	1	0	0	1	0	8	5	3	0	0
Winslow Township	38,382	64	3	20	8	33	512	143	357	12	6
Woodbridge Township	100,884	113	0	6	32	75	1,554	142	1,325	87	6
Woodbury	9,746	53	1	0	28	24	423	65	328	30	0
Woodbury Heights	2,944	0	0	0	0	0	52	4	43	5	0
Woodcliff Lake	5,844	0	0	0	0	0	20	3	13	4	0
Woodland Park	12,799	10	0	2	2	6	149	16	127	6	0
Woodlynne	2,902	11	0	0	4	7	43	5	31	7	0
Wood-Ridge	9,105	7	0	0	1	6	83	5	77	1	0
Woodstown	3,447	2	0	0	0	2	46	30	14	2	0
Woolwich Township	12,636	0	0	0	0	0	50	3	43	4	0
Wyckoff Township	17,161	6	0	1	1	4	84	9	70	5	1

Table 8. Offenses Known to Law Enforcement, by Selected State and City, 2018—Continued

(Number.)

State/city	Population	Violent crime	Murder and nonnegligent manslaughter	Rape[1]	Robbery	Aggravated assault	Property crime	Burglary	Larceny-theft	Motor vehicle theft	Arson[2]
NEW MEXICO											
Alamogordo	31,332	96	2	10	5	79	1,022	129	818	75	
Albuquerque[4]	560,235	7,646	69	479	1,979	5,119	34,619	6,378	21,625	6,616	107
Angel Fire	1,072	8	0	3	0	5	24	13	11	0	
Anthony	9,313	41	0	6	0	35	41	15	15	11	
Aztec	6,538	36	0	5	1	30	146	39	88	19	
Bayard	2,166	11	0	0	0	11	36	16	15	5	
Belen	7,061	161	0	1	12	148	362	69	260	33	
Bernalillo	9,841	110	0	6	6	98	278	78	174	26	
Bloomfield	7,922	127	1	11	1	114	109	36	64	9	
Bosque Farms	3,789	22	0	1	1	20	46	5	27	14	
Capitan	1,402	5	0	0	0	5	18	11	5	2	
Carlsbad	29,158	148	4	22	14	108	844	99	635	110	
Cimarron	887	11	0	0	0	11	14	8	4	2	
Clayton	2,735	5	0	0	0	5	8	3	4	1	
Cloudcroft	689	5	2	0	0	3	10	2	8	0	
Corrales	8,577	3	0	0	0	3	43	7	30	6	
Deming	14,094	141	0	10	9	122	734	232	451	51	
Dexter	1,242	0	0	0	0	0	2	0	0	2	
Edgewood	3,911	15	0	0	1	14	105	37	58	10	
Estancia	1,581	3	0	0	0	3	14	11	3	0	
Eunice	2,961	4	0	0	1	3	27	7	14	6	
Farmington	45,364	593	8	81	70	434	1,769	434	1,189	146	
Gallup	21,980	338	1	18	65	254	1,515	351	1,000	164	
Grants	8,982	19	1	0	6	12	135	68	59	8	
Hatch	1,607	10	0	0	0	10	32	6	24	2	
Hobbs	38,320	251	1	34	24	192	1,579	310	1,134	135	
Hope	105	0	0	0	0	0	4	4	0	0	
Hurley	1,199	3	0	0	0	3	11	9	2	0	
Las Cruces[4]	102,203	413	5	56	39	313	3,627	526	2,817	284	7
Las Vegas	13,084	111	2	12	10	87	457	108	316	33	
Logan	962	2	0	2	0	0	11	0	11	0	
Lordsburg	2,421	18	0	0	0	18	27	15	10	2	
Los Alamos	18,883	24	0	5	0	19	110	20	88	2	
Los Lunas	15,568	189	0	3	19	167	681	109	487	85	
Lovington	11,175	15	0	0	2	13	271	105	133	33	
Magdalena	874	9	0	0	0	9	21	5	14	2	
Mesilla	1,826	0	0	0	0	0	0	0	0	0	
Milan	3,644	5	0	0	1	4	12	7	4	1	
Moriarty	1,777	4	0	0	1	3	54	18	28	8	
Peralta	3,572	15	0	0	0	15	48	13	27	8	
Portales	11,768	66	3	5	6	52	306	130	156	20	
Questa	1,749	0	0	0	0	0	3	0	3	0	
Raton	5,960	13	0	2	5	6	161	59	88	14	
Red River	466	2	0	0	1	1	17	11	6	0	
Rio Rancho	97,394	197	4	18	29	146	1,595	238	1,194	163	
Roswell	47,678	396	2	44	30	314	2,008	398	1,456	154	
Ruidoso	7,718	29	1	6	2	20	226	96	119	11	
Ruidoso Downs	2,557	20	0	1	0	19	134	37	91	6	
Santa Clara	1,786	1	0	0	0	1	28	13	13	2	
Santa Fe	84,176	333	5	32	89	207	3,388	1,380	1,786	222	
Santa Rosa	2,691	14	0	0	0	14	63	15	46	2	
San Ysidro	197	2	0	0	1	1	3	2	1	0	
Socorro	8,363	59	0	0	3	56	415	88	295	32	
Springer	903	2	0	0	1	1	6	4	0	2	
Taos	5,662	29	0	3	5	21	437	105	302	30	
Taos Ski Valley	67	0	0	0	0	0	0	0	0	0	
Tatum	813	0	0	0	0	0	1	0	1	0	
Texico	1,113	11	0	0	0	11	6	1	2	0	
Truth or Consequences	5,875	30	0	0	0	30	144	34	96	14	
Tularosa	2,939	8	1	2	0	5	101	49	51	1	
NEW YORK											
Adams Village	1,757	0	0	0	0	0	2	1	1	0	0
Addison Town and Village	2,490	3	0	1	0	2	15	2	11	2	0
Afton Village	794	0	0	0	0	0	0	0	0	0	0
Akron Village	2,872	1	0	0	0	1	10	5	5	0	0
Albany	98,322	823	12	52	209	550	3,147	432	2,585	130	21
Albion Village	5,878	24	0	9	2	13	162	30	125	7	0
Alexandria Bay Village	1,054	1	0	0	0	1	9	1	8	0	0
Alfred Village	4,022	6	0	1	2	3	16	6	10	0	0
Allegany Village	1,702	2	0	0	0	2	10	1	9	0	0
Amherst Town	121,343	145	0	25	49	71	1,766	192	1,531	43	2
Amityville Village	9,526	8	0	0	2	6	99	6	84	9	0
Amsterdam	17,737	25	0	6	7	12	201	45	148	8	1
Angelica Village	827	0	0	0	0	0	1	0	1	0	0
Arcade Village	1,951	3	0	1	0	2	15	1	13	1	0
Ardsley Village	4,614	1	0	1	0	0	27	4	23	0	0
Asharoken Village	650	0	0	0	0	0	2	1	1	0	0
Attica Village	2,426	2	0	0	0	2	5	1	4	0	0
Auburn	26,570	137	0	20	26	91	718	85	602	31	1
Bainbridge Village	1,304	0	0	0	0	0	2	1	1	0	0

Table 8. Offenses Known to Law Enforcement, by Selected State and City, 2018—Continued

(Number.)

State/city	Population	Violent crime	Murder and nonnegligent manslaughter	Rape[1]	Robbery	Aggravated assault	Property crime	Burglary	Larceny-theft	Motor vehicle theft	Arson[2]
Baldwinsville Village	7,976	2	0	0	0	2	51	1	48	2	0
Ballston Spa Village	5,329	3	2	0	0	1	28	6	22	0	0
Barker	510	0	0	0	0	0	0	0	0	0	
Batavia	14,565	63	3	7	14	39	370	61	290	19	1
Beacon	14,241	26	0	2	11	13	190	40	142	8	2
Bedford Town	18,034	4	0	0	0	4	41	1	40	0	1
Belmont Village	913	0	0	0	0	0	0	0	0	0	0
Bethlehem Town	35,704	27	0	8	3	16	498	28	465	5	0
Binghamton	44,876	326	3	40	75	208	1,893	427	1,407	59	9
Black River	1,274	0	0	0	0	0	4	2	2	0	0
Blooming Grove Town	11,888	8	0	1	0	7	81	25	48	8	0
Bolton Town	2,258	0	0	0	0	0	5	3	2	0	0
Boonville Village	2,022	4	0	0	0	4	12	1	11	0	0
Brant Town	2,073	0	0	0	0	0	14	4	8	2	0
Brewster	2,371	2	0	0	1	1	8	0	8	0	0
Briarcliff Manor Village	8,044	0	0	0	0	0	16	3	10	3	1
Brighton Town	36,470	32	0	9	15	8	613	62	537	14	0
Brockport Village	8,290	14	0	2	1	11	83	9	71	3	1
Brownville Village	1,110	0	0	0	0	0	3	0	3	0	0
Buchanan Village	2,282	0	0	0	0	0	2	0	2	0	0
Buffalo	258,219	2,692	57	167	907	1,561	9,852	2,271	6,707	874	157
Cairo Town	6,404	3	0	0	0	3	36	12	23	1	0
Caledonia Village	2,140	0	0	0	0	0	2	0	1	1	0
Cambridge Village	1,809	2	0	1	0	1	13	2	10	1	1
Camden Village	2,184	0	0	0	0	0	19	3	16	0	0
Camillus Town and Village	24,462	14	0	2	2	10	275	17	249	9	0
Canajoharie Village	2,129	6	0	0	0	6	14	4	10	0	0
Canandaigua	10,252	24	0	8	1	15	194	22	167	5	1
Canastota Village	4,536	5	0	1	0	4	40	2	36	2	0
Canisteo Village	2,156	0	0	0	0	0	18	1	17	0	0
Canton Village	6,510	3	0	0	1	2	29	4	25	0	0
Cape Vincent Village	711	0	0	0	0	0	0	0	0	0	0
Carmel Town	34,382	17	0	0	3	14	132	22	105	5	0
Carroll Town	3,347	0	0	0	0	0	6	1	5	0	0
Carthage Village	3,392	5	0	3	0	2	45	7	35	3	0
Catskill Village	3,803	11	0	2	0	9	131	6	124	1	0
Cattaraugus Village	916	0	0	0	0	0	1	1	0	0	0
Cayuga Heights Village	3,753	0	0	0	0	0	8	0	8	0	0
Cazenovia Village	2,842	1	0	0	0	1	35	3	30	2	0
Central Square Village	1,768	1	0	0	0	1	51	4	47	0	0
Centre Island Village	414	2	0	0	1	1	2	0	2	0	0
Chatham Village	1,642	0	0	0	0	0	1	0	1	0	0
Cheektowaga Town	77,648	189	0	17	71	101	2,156	259	1,810	87	3
Chester Town	8,053	3	0	0	0	3	18	0	16	2	0
Cicero Town	28,992	11	0	2	0	9	218	12	191	15	0
Clarkstown Town	81,994	71	0	15	17	39	1,209	43	1,143	23	0
Clayton Village	1,860	0	0	0	0	0	6	0	6	0	0
Clyde Village	1,976	3	0	0	0	3	27	3	23	1	0
Cobleskill Village	4,534	3	0	1	2	0	125	7	117	1	2
Coeymans Town	7,416	7	0	0	0	7	71	9	56	6	1
Cohoes	16,979	46	1	5	9	31	195	25	157	13	1
Colchester Town	1,978	0	0	0	0	0	16	4	11	1	0
Cold Spring Village	1,966	1	0	0	0	1	9	0	9	0	1
Colonie Town	79,842	80	0	3	25	52	1,856	130	1,678	48	1
Cooperstown Village	1,757	1	0	0	0	1	4	1	3	0	0
Corning	10,643	52	0	19	7	26	244	47	190	7	0
Cornwall-on-Hudson Village	2,935	1	0	1	0	0	9	1	8	0	0
Cortland	18,631	28	1	7	6	14	316	66	241	9	1
Coxsackie Village	2,658	1	0	0	0	1	3	1	2	0	0
Crawford Town	9,217	7	0	1	1	5	84	19	64	1	1
Cuba Town	3,110	3	0	2	0	1	38	4	34	0	0
Dansville Village	4,433	3	0	1	0	2	85	14	69	2	1
Deerpark Town	7,759	6	0	1	0	5	63	13	50	0	1
Delhi Village	3,116	2	0	0	0	2	36	4	32	0	0
Depew Village	15,159	12	0	4	3	5	250	47	194	9	0
Deposit Village	1,542	0	0	0	0	0	9	3	6	0	0
DeWitt Town	25,268	34	2	3	8	21	584	64	500	20	0
Dexter Village	1,029	0	0	0	0	0	1	1	0	0	0
Dobbs Ferry Village	11,182	3	0	0	1	2	93	6	83	4	0
Dolgeville Village	2,084	1	0	0	0	1	7	1	6	0	0
Dryden Village	2,201	1	0	1	0	0	34	4	30	0	0
Dunkirk	11,755	24	0	0	8	16	170	48	117	5	0
Durham Town	2,656	0	0	0	0	0	6	0	6	0	0
East Aurora-Aurora Town	13,900	1	0	0	0	1	79	8	69	2	0
Eastchester Town	20,452	4	0	0	4	0	90	10	79	1	0
East Fishkill Town	29,623	9	0	5	0	4	136	17	112	7	0
East Greenbush Town	16,331	12	0	0	3	9	404	39	357	8	0
East Hampton Town	19,992	11	0	2	1	8	176	16	159	1	1
East Hampton Village	1,130	1	0	0	0	1	35	2	31	2	0
East Rochester Village	6,580	11	0	3	5	3	96	13	78	5	0
Eden Town	7,667	0	0	0	0	0	34	3	30	1	0
Ellenville Village	4,023	13	2	3	2	6	69	15	52	2	1
Ellicott Town	5,060	7	0	0	3	4	162	19	138	5	0

Table 8. Offenses Known to Law Enforcement, by Selected State and City, 2018—Continued

(Number.)

State/city	Population	Violent crime	Murder and nonnegligent manslaughter	Rape[1]	Robbery	Aggravated assault	Property crime	Burglary	Larceny-theft	Motor vehicle theft	Arson[2]
Ellicottville	1,583	0	0	0	0	0	10	0	10	0	0
Elmira	27,556	70	3	0	21	46	702	131	553	18	3
Elmira Heights Village	3,865	3	0	0	1	2	58	10	45	3	0
Elmira Town	5,665	1	0	0	0	1	1	0	0	1	0
Elmsford Village	5,379	4	0	1	1	2	17	1	11	5	0
Endicott Village	12,754	70	0	17	14	39	397	62	327	8	2
Evans Town	16,220	22	0	7	1	14	177	31	138	8	2
Fairport Village	5,388	1	0	1	0	0	22	4	17	1	1
Fallsburg Town	12,207	15	0	1	2	12	109	41	66	2	0
Fishkill Town	21,529	10	0	2	3	5	161	10	146	5	0
Fishkill Village	2,112	2	0	0	1	1	27	0	27	0	0
Floral Park Village	16,131	8	0	1	4	3	46	8	31	7	0
Florida Village	2,872	1	0	0	0	1	4	0	3	1	0
Fort Plain Village	2,218	20	1	8	1	10	104	25	75	4	0
Frankfort Village	2,454	0	0	0	0	0	14	2	10	2	0
Franklinville Village	1,649	0	0	0	0	0	7	0	7	0	0
Fredonia Village	10,475	7	0	0	4	3	159	20	136	3	0
Freeport Village	43,597	70	0	2	26	42	422	23	371	28	0
Friendship Town	1,889	1	0	1	0	0	3	0	2	1	0
Fulton City	11,244	8	0	1	5	2	396	66	324	6	1
Garden City Village	22,749	10	0	0	3	7	358	26	321	11	0
Gates Town	28,717	56	1	6	18	31	823	64	706	53	0
Geddes Town	10,177	7	0	0	2	5	215	16	193	6	0
Geneseo Village	8,184	4	0	3	1	0	86	9	77	0	1
Geneva	12,841	31	0	8	8	15	221	58	160	3	1
Glen Cove	27,574	4	0	0	4	0	111	7	102	2	0
Glen Park Village	490	0	0	0	0	0	0	0	0	0	0
Glens Falls	14,403	24	1	6	2	15	150	13	133	4	1
Glenville Town	21,670	19	0	5	2	12	293	13	272	8	0
Gloversville	14,860	83	0	29	9	45	363	39	310	14	2
Goshen Town	8,703	2	0	0	0	2	42	9	28	5	0
Goshen Village	5,373	5	0	1	1	3	37	2	34	1	0
Gowanda Village	2,609	6	0	0	0	6	35	4	29	2	0
Granville Village	2,446	1	0	0	0	1	21	6	15	0	0
Great Neck Estates Village	2,898	0	0	0	0	0	0	0	0	0	0
Greece Town	96,650	189	1	30	52	106	2,040	291	1,654	95	1
Greene Village	1,432	0	0	0	0	0	10	1	9	0	0
Green Island Village	2,602	7	0	5	0	2	32	6	26	0	0
Greenport Town	4,362	1	0	0	0	1	165	0	164	1	0
Greenwich Village	1,721	0	0	0	0	0	10	0	10	0	0
Groton Village	2,357	4	0	1	0	3	30	2	26	2	0
Guilderland Town	34,260	27	0	8	6	13	687	31	652	4	0
Hamburg Town	46,490	41	0	0	8	33	888	93	785	10	6
Hamburg Village	9,735	8	0	0	0	8	97	18	76	3	0
Hamilton Village	4,091	1	0	1	0	0	9	3	6	0	0
Hammondsport Village	626	0	0	0	0	0	6	0	6	0	0
Hancock Village	944	3	0	1	0	2	13	4	9	0	0
Harriman Village	2,461	3	0	0	1	2	28	1	25	2	0
Harrison Town	28,741	0	0	0	0	0	101	12	89	0	0
Hastings-on-Hudson Village	8,030	2	0	0	0	2	77	1	73	3	1
Hempstead Village	56,059	322	4	9	114	195	589	106	369	114	
Highland Falls Village	3,838	2	1	0	0	1	16	3	13	0	0
Highlands Town	8,328	1	0	0	0	1	4	1	3	0	0
Holley Village	1,691	2	0	0	0	2	19	3	15	1	0
Homer Village	3,104	0	0	0	0	0	5	1	2	0	0
Hoosick Falls Village	3,386	6	0	2	0	4	36	9	23	4	0
Hornell	8,161	4	0	0	2	2	112	6	105	1	0
Horseheads Village	6,464	0	0	0	0	0	95	7	87	1	0
Hudson	6,173	32	1	7	0	24	162	31	128	3	1
Hudson Falls Village	7,071	10	0	3	1	6	43	6	35	2	0
Huntington Bay Village	1,436	0	0	0	0	0	2	0	2	0	0
Hyde Park Town	21,046	9	0	2	3	4	91	19	70	2	2
Ilion Village	7,736	21	0	1	4	16	163	24	132	7	0
Independence Town	1,149	1	0	0	0	1	3	1	2	0	0
Inlet Town	307	0	0	0	0	0	1	0	1	0	0
Interlaken Village	605	0	0	0	0	0	0	0	0	0	0
Irondequoit Town	50,212	91	0	14	30	47	922	132	736	54	5
Irvington Village	6,631	2	1	0	0	1	17	1	16	0	0
Ithaca	31,145	72	0	9	26	37	815	62	738	15	1
Jamestown	29,384	227	1	48	28	150	817	191	602	24	7
Johnson City Village	14,418	63	3	12	12	36	596	84	493	19	3
Johnstown	8,265	13	0	4	3	6	150	11	137	2	0
Jordan Village	1,310	0	0	0	0	0	1	1	0	0	0
Kenmore Village	15,178	14	0	0	5	9	185	20	159	6	0
Kensington Village	1,192	0	0	0	0	0	0	0	0	0	0
Kent Town	13,326	1	0	0	0	1	51	4	45	2	1
Kings Point Village	5,299	0	0	0	0	0	11	2	8	1	0
Kingston	23,077	70	0	11	12	47	477	80	372	25	2
Kirkland Town	8,355	0	0	0	0	0	6	1	4	1	0
Lackawanna	17,904	70	0	11	14	45	315	71	215	29	1
Lake Success Village	3,170	1	0	0	1	0	23	5	16	2	0
Lakewood-Busti	7,260	1	0	0	0	1	355	41	311	3	0
Lancaster Town	37,776	21	0	9	1	11	405	40	356	9	0

Table 8. Offenses Known to Law Enforcement, by Selected State and City, 2018—Continued

(Number.)

State/city	Population	Violent crime	Murder and nonnegligent manslaughter	Rape[1]	Robbery	Aggravated assault	Property crime	Burglary	Larceny-theft	Motor vehicle theft	Arson[2]
Larchmont Village	6,200	2	0	1	0	1	75	6	68	1	0
Le Roy Village	4,161	6	0	1	0	5	56	13	43	0	1
Lewisboro Town	12,823	0	0	0	0	0	0	0	0	0	0
Lewiston Town and Village	15,922	13	0	3	1	9	155	18	103	34	7
Liberty Village	4,092	20	0	5	2	13	161	23	134	4	0
Little Falls	4,684	11	0	1	0	10	60	15	43	2	1
Liverpool Village	2,238	0	0	0	0	0	19	2	17	0	0
Lloyd Harbor Village	3,697	1	0	0	0	1	11	2	8	1	0
Lloyd Town	10,510	9	0	5	0	4	75	3	71	1	0
Long Beach	33,801	29	0	0	6	23	80	5	71	4	0
Lowville Village	3,347	9	0	2	0	7	22	3	17	2	0
Lynbrook Village	19,745	12	0	0	2	10	105	8	84	13	0
Macedon Town and Village	8,960	3	0	1	0	2	92	10	77	5	0
Malone Village	5,641	8	0	5	0	3	107	10	97	0	0
Malverne Village	8,626	2	0	0	1	1	17	2	13	2	0
Mamaroneck Town	12,336	0	0	0	0	0	75	11	62	2	0
Mamaroneck Village	19,496	13	1	0	2	10	127	24	99	4	0
Manchester Village	1,630	0	0	0	0	0	0	0	0	0	0
Manlius Town	24,417	18	0	3	4	11	260	36	216	8	0
Marcellus Village	1,755	0	0	0	0	0	11	0	11	0	0
Marlborough Town	8,663	5	0	0	0	5	37	11	22	4	0
Maybrook Village	3,667	3	0	0	0	3	8	0	7	1	0
Mechanicville	5,118	11	0	0	1	10	41	8	31	2	0
Medina Village	5,687	12	0	2	3	7	96	23	71	2	0
Menands Village	3,940	5	0	0	2	3	139	10	127	2	0
Middleport Village	1,756	1	0	0	0	1	28	2	24	2	0
Middletown	27,885	110	0	20	28	62	510	71	421	18	3
Monroe Village	8,665	4	0	0	2	2	88	6	79	3	0
Montgomery Town	9,122	8	0	1	1	6	30	9	18	3	0
Montgomery Village	4,682	0	0	0	0	0	15	1	13	1	0
Monticello Village	6,414	35	1	4	7	23	141	32	103	6	0
Moravia Village	1,212	0	0	0	0	0	3	0	3	0	0
Moriah Town	3,532	0	0	0	0	0	0	0	0	0	0
Mount Morris Village	2,821	6	0	0	2	4	53	5	48	0	0
Mount Pleasant Town	26,506	14	0	2	3	9	206	30	174	2	0
Mount Vernon	68,889	351	6	27	100	218	975	122	734	119	4
Nassau Village	1,105	2	0	0	0	2	5	0	3	2	1
Newark Village	8,864	29	0	10	3	16	248	24	222	2	0
New Berlin Town	1,512	0	0	0	0	0	10	1	9	0	0
Newburgh	28,282	329	2	24	102	201	657	141	475	41	8
Newburgh Town	31,200	34	0	2	10	22	978	43	926	9	0
New Castle Town	18,197	1	0	0	1	0	53	8	44	1	0
New Hartford Town and Village	20,232	5	0	2	1	2	691	33	650	8	0
New Paltz Town and Village	14,075	20	0	5	2	13	145	12	131	2	
New Rochelle	80,340	98	3	8	22	65	666	55	578	33	0
New Windsor Town	28,137	40	0	2	2	36	329	33	287	9	0
New York	8,523,171	46,113	295	2,814	12,962	30,042	128,051	10,837	111,680	5,534	
New York Mills Village	3,265	0	0	0	0	0	33	5	25	3	0
Niagara Falls	48,225	418	2	24	124	268	1,962	297	1,507	158	15
Niagara Town	8,014	17	0	3	3	11	252	19	221	12	0
Niskayuna Town	22,486	23	0	4	5	14	390	36	342	12	0
Nissequogue Village[5]	1,751	0	0	0	0	0		1		1	0
Norfolk Town	4,420	0	0	0	0	0	1	0	0	1	0
North Castle Town	12,454	6	0	2	1	3	55	6	46	3	0
North Greenbush Town	12,216	9	0	1	1	7	156	18	136	2	0
Northport Village	7,362	0	0	0	0	0	25	3	22	0	0
North Tonawanda	30,325	46	1	16	11	18	400	38	337	25	7
Norwich	6,656	31	1	16	1	13	170	14	154	2	0
Norwood Village	1,571	1	0	0	0	1	12	4	7	1	0
Ogdensburg	10,629	32	1	6	11	14	395	80	310	5	1
Ogden Town	20,288	8	0	1	3	4	195	23	167	5	0
Old Brookville Village	2,220	0	0	0	0	0	33	7	23	3	0
Old Westbury Village	4,763	5	0	0	1	4	31	6	18	7	0
Olean	13,615	44	0	9	4	31	403	41	353	9	2
Olive Town	4,303	0	0	0	0	0	11	2	9	0	0
Oneida	10,940	53	0	16	5	32	377	37	330	10	2
Oneonta City	14,073	33	0	9	2	22	191	43	146	2	2
Orchard Park Town	29,760	28	0	8	5	15	331	30	295	6	0
Oriskany Village	1,353	0	0	0	0	0	8	1	7	0	0
Ossining Village	25,452	15	0	0	7	8	188	12	171	5	0
Oswego City	17,370	36	0	6	7	23	455	36	394	25	0
Owego Village	3,898	10	0	3	2	5	147	18	122	7	0
Oxford Village	1,382	0	0	0	0	0	3	0	3	0	0
Palmyra Village	3,345	3	0	0	1	2	9	0	8	1	0
Peekskill	24,365	50	1	5	9	35	224	11	207	6	0
Pelham Manor Village	5,660	9	0	0	2	7	150	8	140	2	0
Pelham Village	7,036	6	0	0	2	4	60	4	54	2	0
Penn Yan Village	4,946	3	0	0	0	3	69	6	63	0	1
Perry Village	3,474	10	0	4	1	5	55	7	46	2	0
Philmont Village	1,279	0	0	0	0	0	10	1	9	0	0
Phoenix Village	2,250	0	0	0	0	0	18	4	14	0	0
Piermont Village	2,585	0	0	0	0	0	6	1	5	0	0
Pine Plains Town	2,427	0	0	0	0	0	5	3	2	0	0

Table 8. Offenses Known to Law Enforcement, by Selected State and City, 2018—Continued

(Number.)

State/city	Population	Violent crime	Murder and nonnegligent manslaughter	Rape[1]	Robbery	Aggravated assault	Property crime	Burglary	Larceny-theft	Motor vehicle theft	Arson[2]
Plattekill Town	10,235	0	0	0	0	0	31	6	22	3	0
Plattsburgh City	19,651	35	0	9	5	21	312	32	274	6	1
Pleasantville Village	7,352	2	0	0	1	1	38	4	33	1	0
Port Chester Village	29,814	22	0	1	12	9	185	9	164	12	1
Port Dickinson Village	1,553	0	0	0	0	0	19	8	11	0	0
Port Jervis	8,599	24	0	3	9	12	164	36	128	0	1
Portville Village	961	0	0	0	0	0	0	0	0	0	0
Port Washington	19,555	6	0	1	2	3	188	10	170	8	1
Potsdam Village	9,723	5	0	1	1	3	104	3	101	0	0
Poughkeepsie	30,580	216	4	26	59	127	494	85	374	35	5
Pound Ridge Town	5,257	2	0	1	0	1	46	3	43	0	0
Pulaski Village	2,249	0	0	0	0	0	23	1	21	1	0
Quogue Village	1,019	1	0	0	1	0	23	2	19	2	0
Ramapo Town	95,068	75	0	16	15	44	538	34	483	21	1
Rensselaer City	9,249	11	0	1	4	6	87	15	67	5	0
Rhinebeck Village	2,589	0	0	0	0	0	28	0	27	1	0
Riverhead Town	33,812	50	0	3	25	22	603	72	514	17	1
Rochester	207,701	1,615	29	131	516	939	7,036	1,178	5,285	573	85
Rockville Centre Village	24,960	20	0	0	8	12	180	16	156	8	0
Rome	32,298	49	0	9	13	27	540	116	411	13	1
Rotterdam Town	29,882	37	0	3	10	24	909	80	803	26	1
Rye	16,050	6	0	0	1	5	56	6	46	4	0
Rye Brook Village	9,622	0	0	0	0	0	46	7	34	5	0
Sackets Harbor Village	1,432	0	0	0	0	0	0	0	0	0	0
Sag Harbor Village	2,310	0	0	0	0	0	0	0	0	0	0
Sands Point Village	2,926	0	0	0	0	0	10	1	8	1	0
Saranac Lake Village	5,265	6	0	4	0	2	30	1	29	0	0
Saratoga Springs	28,237	63	1	9	8	45	468	44	397	27	1
Scarsdale Village	18,214	2	0	0	2	0	123	13	105	5	1
Schenectady	65,550	620	1	57	136	426	2,106	353	1,542	211	26
Schodack Town	11,747	11	0	2	4	5	48	5	40	3	0
Schoharie Village	820	0	0	0	0	0	0	0	0	0	0
Scotia Village	7,700	10	0	2	2	6	107	11	86	10	1
Seneca Falls Town	8,670	7	0	2	0	5	200	16	180	4	0
Sherburne Village	1,307	1	0	0	1	0	10	0	10	0	0
Sherrill	3,031	0	0	0	0	0	6	1	5	0	0
Shortsville Village	1,422	0	0	0	0	0	0	0	0	0	0
Sidney Village	3,621	7	0	2	0	5	97	12	84	1	0
Skaneateles Village	2,486	0	0	0	0	0	17	4	12	1	0
Sleepy Hollow Village	10,267	0	0	0	0	0	1	0	1	0	0
Sodus Village	1,719	1	0	1	0	0	3	1	2	0	0
Solvay Village	6,307	16	0	3	2	11	108	13	86	9	0
Southampton Town	51,231	52	0	11	8	33	523	66	428	29	1
Southampton Village	3,335	0	0	0	0	0	53	4	47	2	0
South Glens Falls Village	3,628	6	0	1	0	5	53	11	41	1	0
South Nyack Village	3,556	2	0	0	2	0	34	4	27	3	0
Southold Town	20,092	17	0	3	4	10	216	38	171	7	0
Spring Valley Village	32,909	120	0	24	36	60	403	29	364	10	1
Stillwater Town	7,302	2	0	0	1	1	12	1	11	0	0
St. Johnsville Village	1,665	2	0	0	0	2	16	4	12	0	0
Stony Point Town	15,667	5	0	0	0	5	51	5	46	0	0
Syracuse	143,129	1,006	23	92	285	606	4,420	831	3,083	506	35
Tarrytown Village	11,617	7	1	0	4	2	41	10	29	2	0
Theresa Village	801	0	0	0	0	0	0	0	0	0	0
Ticonderoga Town	4,853	16	1	6	0	9	33	4	28	1	3
Tonawanda	14,868	27	0	10	4	13	245	35	205	5	1
Tonawanda Town	57,256	89	0	6	24	59	763	110	623	30	3
Troy	49,491	283	1	22	93	167	1,411	250	1,082	79	16
Trumansburg Village	1,818	1	0	1	0	0	9	2	7	0	0
Tuckahoe Village	6,677	3	0	0	2	1	15	0	12	3	0
Tupper Lake Village	3,503	5	0	2	2	1	62	8	51	3	0
Tuxedo Park Village	603	1	0	0	0	1	10	5	5	0	0
Tuxedo Town	2,924	1	0	1	0	0	6	2	3	1	0
Ulster Town	12,600	13	1	2	0	10	232	15	212	5	2
Utica	60,413	381	6	45	88	242	1,914	328	1,492	94	17
Vernon Village	1,170	1	0	0	1	0	9	1	8	0	0
Vestal Town	28,223	18	0	3	1	14	521	20	489	12	0
Walden Village	6,727	8	0	1	0	7	61	6	55	0	0
Wallkill Town	29,123	47	0	8	13	26	541	52	480	9	0
Warsaw Village	3,317	13	0	0	0	13	59	9	49	1	0
Warwick Town	18,450	9	0	1	0	8	120	20	94	6	1
Washingtonville Village	5,755	2	0	1	0	1	38	1	37	0	0
Waterloo Village	4,906	4	0	1	0	3	57	9	47	1	1
Watertown	25,525	175	0	65	19	91	904	130	755	19	7
Watervliet	10,115	36	0	3	5	28	225	38	183	4	0
Watkins Glen Village	1,929	0	0	0	0	0	19	1	17	1	0
Waverly Village	4,123	7	0	1	0	6	15	0	14	1	0
Wayland Village	1,769	0	0	0	0	0	2	0	2	0	0
Webb Town	1,795	0	0	0	0	0	0	0	0	0	0
Webster Town and Village	45,023	35	0	7	8	20	361	51	301	9	1
Weedsport Village	1,724	0	0	0	0	0	6	0	6	0	0
Wellsville Village	4,420	14	0	0	0	14	67	3	63	1	1
West Carthage Village	1,981	1	0	1	0	0	14	1	12	1	0

Table 8. Offenses Known to Law Enforcement, by Selected State and City, 2018—Continued

(Number.)

State/city	Population	Violent crime	Murder and nonnegligent manslaughter	Rape[1]	Robbery	Aggravated assault	Property crime	Burglary	Larceny-theft	Motor vehicle theft	Arson[2]
Westfield Village	3,012	1	0	1	0	0	9	2	6	1	0
Westhampton Beach Village	1,819	3	0	1	1	1	46	4	41	1	1
West Seneca Town	45,721	62	0	15	13	34	628	112	505	11	0
Whitesboro Village	3,655	0	0	0	0	0	17	3	14	0	0
Whitestown Town	9,175	2	0	2	0	0	28	3	19	6	0
Windham Town	1,671	0	0	0	0	0	2	0	2	0	0
Wolcott Village	1,613	0	0	0	0	0	9	0	9	0	0
Woodbury Town	11,114	7	0	1	3	3	416	0	414	2	0
Woodridge Village	779	3	0	2	0	1	22	9	13	0	0
Woodstock Town	5,819	2	0	0	0	2	60	5	55	0	0
Yonkers	202,827	706	1	31	213	461	1,771	270	1,344	157	6
Yorktown Town	37,101	14	0	4	1	9	185	16	166	3	2
Yorkville Village	2,600	3	0	0	0	3	32	6	26	0	0
Youngstown Village	1,892	0	0	0	0	0	2	0	2	0	0
NORTH CAROLINA[8]											
Aberdeen	7,821		0		5	9	232	40	187	5	2
Albemarle	15,991		2		22	95	853	176	634	43	8
Apex	52,577		0		15	35	663	74	577	12	2
Archdale	11,529		1		6	20	235	49	166	20	0
Asheboro	25,922		1		18	98	1,168	214	891	63	2
Asheville	93,186		12		148	392	4,798	691	3,707	400	13
Atlantic Beach	1,493		0		3	7	92	38	52	2	0
Ayden	5,162		0		2	14	149	31	111	7	0
Beaufort	4,178		1		0	9	135	46	84	5	1
Belmont	12,331		0		8	31	550	45	476	29	0
Benson	3,795		0		1	25	154	34	108	12	4
Biltmore Forest	1,432		0		0	0	17	3	14	0	0
Biscoe	1,675		0		0	0	195	4	189	2	0
Blowing Rock	1,267		0		1	0	21	3	18	0	0
Boone	19,524		0		5	13	289	53	230	6	1
Brevard	7,921		0		2	12	151	23	122	6	0
Burgaw	4,147		1		0	9	155	36	117	2	0
Burlington	53,385		4		61	349	1,877	481	1,303	93	0
Butner	7,803		0		4	26	177	59	112	6	1
Carolina Beach	6,352		0		3	15	144	23	112	9	3
Carrboro	21,841		2		12	17	407	98	280	29	0
Carthage	2,488		0		1	9	80	17	54	9	0
Cary	170,518		0		37	68	1,666	247	1,357	62	5
Chadbourn	1,730		1		4	11	63	8	51	4	0
Charlotte-Mecklenburg	931,235		59		1,761	4,408	34,881	5,670	26,186	3,025	157
China Grove	4,209		0		2	3	80	18	58	4	0
Chocowinity	792		0		1	2	16	8	8	0	0
Clayton	22,258		0		5	22	417	58	352	7	5
Cleveland	876		0		0	2	25	3	17	5	0
Columbus	991		0		0	0	38	5	31	2	0
Concord	94,022		3		40	50	1,679	201	1,414	64	1
Conover	8,391		0		7	9	299	61	219	19	0
Creedmoor	4,576		0		1	5	93	33	58	2	0
Davidson	12,954		0		0	12	127	18	106	3	0
Drexel	1,858		0		0	0	33	7	21	5	0
Duck	387		0		0	1	32	14	18	0	0
Durham	273,759		33		723	1,125	9,755	2,238	6,688	829	35
Eden	14,952		1		14	52	530	146	361	23	5
Edenton	4,671		0		5	47	145	29	107	9	0
Elizabeth City	17,629		3		14	78	939	208	689	42	5
Emerald Isle	3,685		0		1	14	189	87	93	9	0
Farmville	4,712		0		4	27	129	43	81	5	1
Fletcher	8,392		0		1	4	128	58	61	9	1
Forest City	7,175		0		12	24	555	165	361	29	1
Four Oaks	2,106		0		0	12	56	8	40	8	0
Gastonia	77,316		7		140	378	3,839	624	2,919	296	16
Gibsonville	7,193		0		2	9	70	34	35	1	0
Granite Falls	4,653		0		2	4	293	7	271	15	0
Greensboro	293,298		37		536	1,207	9,831	2,117	7,035	679	76
Greenville	93,235		5		109	327	2,707	475	2,121	111	5
Havelock	19,870		0		8	18	530	183	332	15	2
Henderson	14,780		10		65	193	804	248	519	37	8
Hickory	40,701		3		39	118	1,884	300	1,390	194	4
Highlands	942		0		0	3	54	19	31	4	0
High Point[6]	112,526		19		116	517	3,682	590	2,812	280	
Hillsborough	7,323		0		5	24	310	34	265	11	2
Holly Ridge	2,584		0		0	5	36	13	21	2	0
Holly Springs	37,008		0		1	18	267	33	226	8	1
Hope Mills	16,219		0		28	76	681	84	580	17	0
Huntersville	57,677		4		14	56	884	157	691	36	3
Jacksonville	71,715		3		45	160	1,763	337	1,334	92	3
Jonesville	2,226		0		2	16	123	34	86	3	2
Kannapolis	49,750		2		31	76	968	190	711	67	4
Kernersville	24,571		1		14	52	970	111	820	39	2
King	6,911		0		2	12	302	15	284	3	1
Kings Mountain	10,808		0		7	30	400	78	308	14	9
Kinston	20,341		3		38	185	1,305	313	943	49	8

Table 8. Offenses Known to Law Enforcement, by Selected State and City, 2018—Continued

(Number.)

State/city	Population	Violent crime	Murder and nonnegligent manslaughter	Rape[1]	Robbery	Aggravated assault	Property crime	Burglary	Larceny-theft	Motor vehicle theft	Arson[2]
Kitty Hawk	3,529		0		0	4	125	24	99	2	0
Lake Lure	1,148		0		0	0	5	1	4	0	0
Leland	21,008		1		2	24	320	59	257	4	1
Lenoir	17,904		0		12	39	845	197	549	99	0
Lexington	18,754		0		26	93	489	113	335	41	6
Lillington	3,639		0		3	8	130	27	103	0	0
Louisburg	3,549		0		5	22	137	25	105	7	2
Madison	2,119		0		1	3	57	12	44	1	0
Mars Hill	2,157		0		0	2	14	2	10	2	0
Marshville	2,728		0		1	10	117	39	73	5	0
Matthews	32,873		2		22	42	949	95	801	53	2
Mayodan	2,399		0		1	1	113	13	99	1	0
Maysville	950		0		0	4	13	6	6	1	0
Mint Hill	27,375		0		13	45	471	99	345	27	1
Mocksville	5,303		0		1	4	165	36	124	5	1
Mooresville	38,340		0		17	55	1,018	99	885	34	2
Morehead City	9,393		0		6	25	396	60	330	6	2
Mount Gilead	1,159		0		3	0	61	15	40	6	0
Mount Holly	15,940		1		2	20	302	68	210	24	5
Murfreesboro	2,984		0		3	1	61	19	40	2	0
Murphy	1,640		1		1	8	175	25	135	15	0
Nags Head	2,925		0		1	6	138	49	89	0	0
New Bern	29,600		0		27	81	940	195	718	27	2
Newport	4,691		1		1	3	50	13	35	2	0
Newton	13,121		0		8	58	453	136	302	15	6
North Topsail Beach	723		2		0	0	35	19	15	1	0
North Wilkesboro	4,277		0		2	15	125	1	112	12	1
Ocean Isle Beach	624		0		1	2	45	28	17	0	0
Oxford	8,793		0		10	58	411	98	298	15	0
Pilot Mountain	1,427		0		0	3	42	4	34	4	0
Pinebluff	1,515		0		0	1	19	7	10	2	0
Pinehurst	16,213		0		0	15	111	33	77	1	0
Pine Knoll Shores	1,330		0		0	1	21	6	15	0	0
Pittsboro	4,289		0		1	13	114	13	99	2	0
Plymouth	3,448		0		3	33	146	40	97	9	4
Raeford	4,976		1		4	21	150	57	90	3	1
Ramseur	1,690		0		2	4	78	22	53	3	0
Randleman	4,133		0		0	1	141	32	104	5	0
Reidsville	13,774		2		21	81	693	121	521	51	5
Richlands	1,719		0		0	0	21	3	18	0	0
Robbins	1,212		0		0	4	26	6	18	2	0
Rockingham	8,754		2		6	43	602	133	450	19	3
Rockwell	2,146		0		2	2	27	5	17	5	0
Rocky Mount	54,085		13		87	320	1,577	424	1,053	100	9
Rowland	1,010		0		3	1	47	21	25	1	2
Roxboro	8,284		2		9	62	318	83	221	14	0
Rutherfordton	4,014		0		1	0	158	14	139	5	1
Salisbury	33,901		6		72	158	1,579	313	1,139	127	5
Sanford	29,483		5		20	39	782	160	587	35	2
Scotland Neck	1,880		0		0	8	42	14	26	2	0
Selma	6,776		2		7	35	239	85	134	20	1
Shallotte	4,183		0		2	3	229	23	197	9	0
Siler City	8,225		1		9	55	369	71	280	18	1
Smithfield	12,507		0		12	37	454	64	372	18	1
Snow Hill	1,516		0		3	7	53	10	43	0	1
Southern Pines	14,271		4		9	20	312	62	243	7	0
Spencer	3,254		0		4	12	99	29	65	5	0
Stanley	3,727		0		1	7	123	30	86	7	0
Star	855		0		0	0	18	4	12	2	0
St. Pauls	2,344		0		4	4	68	24	43	1	0
Surf City	2,412		0		0	4	151	6	142	3	0
Swansboro	3,292		0		0	14	127	15	110	2	0
Thomasville	26,591		0		26	57	1,009	252	695	62	1
Trent Woods	4,064		0		0	0	18	8	9	1	0
Troy	3,275		1		2	11	81	18	63	0	0
Valdese	4,427		0		0	9	54	8	35	11	0
Wake Forest	44,318		0		16	33	653	61	577	15	1
Waynesville	9,991		0		6	48	517	80	395	42	3
Weaverville	3,946		0		2	0	141	0	136	5	0
Whispering Pines	3,348		0		0	0	17	3	14	0	0
Whiteville	5,401		1		11	44	471	122	325	24	5
Wilkesboro	3,482		0		4	4	255	23	221	11	0
Wilmington	120,920		9		145	580	3,639	954	2,467	218	9
Wilson	49,367		5		75	170	1,719	408	1,153	158	8
Windsor	3,259		0		0	10	34	4	27	3	0
Wingate	4,034		1		1	3	68	35	28	5	1
Winterville	9,712		0		3	11	90	19	62	9	0
Woodfin	6,541		0		2	10	116	53	52	11	3
Wrightsville Beach	2,558		0		1	11	100	28	71	1	0
Yadkinville	2,879		0		1	10	90	15	72	3	2
Youngsville	1,331		0		0	2	28	4	24	0	0

Table 8. Offenses Known to Law Enforcement, by Selected State and City, 2018—Continued

(Number.)

State/city	Population	Violent crime	Murder and nonnegligent manslaughter	Rape[1]	Robbery	Aggravated assault	Property crime	Burglary	Larceny-theft	Motor vehicle theft	Arson[2]
NORTH DAKOTA											
Arnegard	158	0	0	0	0	0	0	0	0	0	0
Belfield	1,006	0	0	0	0	0	8	2	6	0	0
Berthold	503	2	0	0	0	2	3	0	2	1	0
Beulah	3,288	1	0	0	0	1	8	0	8	0	0
Bismarck	74,644	223	2	46	24	151	2,034	254	1,570	210	3
Bowman	1,661	2	0	0	0	2	18	2	13	3	0
Burlington	1,227	1	0	1	0	0	5	1	3	1	0
Cavalier	1,264	1	0	0	0	1	6	1	4	1	0
Devils Lake	7,314	17	0	6	3	8	282	28	231	23	0
Dickinson	22,878	56	1	10	3	42	500	34	418	48	0
Ellendale	1,158	2	0	1	0	1	6	1	5	0	0
Emerado	453	0	0	0	0	0	12	1	10	1	0
Fargo	124,906	522	5	105	63	349	3,931	695	2,927	309	10
Fessenden	449	0	0	0	0	0	5	2	3	0	0
Grafton	4,216	8	0	1	0	7	98	20	71	7	0
Grand Forks	57,662	148	4	28	21	95	1,410	216	1,068	126	1
Harvey	1,715	2	0	1	0	1	8	1	6	1	0
Hazen	2,366	0	0	0	0	0	3	1	2	0	0
Jamestown	15,378	40	1	10	5	24	341	74	247	20	0
Kenmare	1,027	1	0	0	0	1	6	3	3	0	0
Killdeer	1,219	1	0	0	0	1	20	1	17	2	0
Lincoln	3,956	2	0	0	0	2	14	3	10	1	0
Lisbon	2,063	1	0	0	0	1	32	0	30	2	1
Mandan	22,743	82	0	6	6	70	690	105	476	109	3
Medora	135	0	0	0	0	0	0	0	0	0	0
Minot	48,829	134	0	21	18	95	1,011	213	623	175	6
Napoleon	773	0	0	0	0	0	1	0	1	0	0
New Town	2,626	4	0	0	0	4	17	1	10	6	1
Northwood	897	1	0	0	0	1	3	0	2	1	0
Oakes	1,703	2	0	0	0	2	12	1	9	2	0
Powers Lake	284	0	0	0	0	0	2	0	2	0	0
Ray	813	0	0	0	0	0	5	1	3	1	0
Rolla	1,314	1	0	1	0	0	15	5	5	5	0
Rugby	2,679	2	0	1	0	1	29	6	21	2	0
Stanley	2,883	3	1	0	0	2	4	0	3	1	0
Steele	716	1	0	0	0	1	2	0	2	0	0
Surrey	1,453	3	0	0	0	3	10	2	3	5	0
Thompson	1,014	0	0	0	0	0	0	0	0	0	0
Tioga	1,542	5	0	3	0	2	14	3	11	0	0
Valley City	6,423	16	0	3	1	12	146	27	112	7	0
Wahpeton	7,836	11	0	3	0	8	198	12	170	16	1
Watford City	7,931	36	0	4	0	32	122	8	103	11	0
West Fargo	37,385	67	0	15	2	50	527	105	391	31	0
Williston	27,390	142	0	15	2	125	776	102	597	77	0
Wishek	927	0	0	0	0	0	4	0	4	0	0
OHIO											
Ada	5,556	1	0	0	0	1	19	6	13	0	0
Akron	197,690	1,704	38	221	387	1,058	7,159	1,740	4,701	718	82
Alliance	21,723	43	1	8	5	29	515	79	423	13	9
Amberley Village	3,783	0	0	0	0	0	15	0	15	0	0
Amelia	4,994	2	0	1	0	1	60	6	52	2	0
American Township	12,094	2	0	0	1	1	144	4	133	7	0
Amherst	12,100	11	0	2	2	7	187	23	163	1	0
Archbold	4,302	3	0	0	0	3	37	4	33	0	0
Ashland	20,446	20	0	9	1	10	369	56	305	8	2
Ashville	4,162	2	0	1	0	1	46	6	39	1	0
Athens	25,356	31	0	2	3	26	453	49	389	15	1
Aurora	16,047	10	1	2	1	6	148	11	135	2	0
Austintown	35,029	42	0	4	13	25	667	67	575	25	0
Barberton	26,060	94	2	14	19	59	833	137	662	34	2
Barnesville	4,064	0	0	0	0	0	13	1	11	1	0
Batavia	1,674	3	0	1	1	1	42	1	38	3	0
Bath Township, Summit County	9,689	2	0	0	1	1	136	12	121	3	0
Bazetta Township	5,565	3	0	0	2	1	135	6	127	2	0
Beachwood	11,681	11	1	3	4	3	289	25	259	5	0
Beavercreek	47,203	40	1	20	2	17	1,145	74	1,028	43	1
Beaver Township	6,437	2	0	0	0	2	58	8	50	0	0
Bedford	12,587	27	0	1	6	20	182	34	124	24	0
Bedford Heights	10,574	20	0	3	8	9	223	50	136	37	1
Bellaire	4,083	8	0	2	1	5	55	13	40	2	0
Bellbrook	7,256	6	0	5	1	0	52	4	46	2	0
Bellefontaine	13,137	12	1	1	1	9	282	25	257	0	0
Bellville	1,867	0	0	0	0	0	25	1	24	0	0
Belpre	6,402	5	0	1	1	3	88	17	66	5	0
Berea	18,838	10	0	2	3	5	116	13	95	8	0
Bethel	2,796	10	0	1	2	7	63	2	59	2	0
Bexley	13,893	13	1	3	4	5	398	94	287	17	0
Blanchester	4,246	3	0	0	3	0	159	12	108	39	0
Blue Ash	12,227	14	1	9	2	2	247	20	217	10	0
Bluffton	4,117	4	0	3	0	1	36	1	34	1	0
Bowling Green	32,017	24	0	9	6	9	386	32	346	8	0

Table 8. Offenses Known to Law Enforcement, by Selected State and City, 2018—Continued

(Number.)

State/city	Population	Violent crime	Murder and nonnegligent manslaughter	Rape[1]	Robbery	Aggravated assault	Property crime	Burglary	Larceny-theft	Motor vehicle theft	Arson[2]
Brecksville	13,652	10	0	4	1	5	44	11	32	1	0
Bridgeport	1,756	3	1	1	0	1	24	6	17	1	0
Brimfield Township	10,330	5	0	1	2	2	232	18	205	9	0
Broadview Heights	19,236	2	0	0	0	2	18	1	16	1	0
Brooklyn[8]	10,759		0		14	4	566	35	508	23	1
Brunswick	34,954	22	0	2	0	20	173	21	149	3	1
Brunswick Hills Township	10,418	4	0	2	1	1	30	2	25	3	0
Bucyrus	11,741	30	0	7	1	22	354	65	286	3	1
Butler Township	7,802	16	0	2	7	7	438	78	335	25	0
Cambridge[8]	10,369		1		2	11	396	53	330	13	1
Campbell	7,844	8	0	1	3	4	37	14	22	1	0
Canal Fulton	5,450	4	0	1	0	3	46	11	35	0	0
Canfield	7,220	3	0	2	0	1	49	1	48	0	0
Canton	70,605	845	3	98	189	555	3,790	970	2,517	303	19
Carey	3,564	1	0	0	0	1	7	3	4	0	0
Carlisle	5,393	4	0	0	1	3	23	6	13	4	0
Centerville	23,757	8	0	3	0	5	292	30	252	10	2
Chagrin Falls	3,973	3	0	0	0	3	15	2	13	0	0
Chardon	5,174	3	0	0	0	3	94	2	91	1	0
Chillicothe	21,441	104	0	10	21	73	1,622	220	1,345	57	4
Cincinnati[6]	301,952	2,535	57	293	897	1,288	13,710	2,978	9,422	1,310	
Circleville	13,993	43	1	16	6	20	530	72	431	27	1
Clayton	13,209	5	0	0	3	2	135	11	101	23	0
Clay Township, Montgomery County	4,238	1	1	0	0	0	21	8	13	0	0
Clearcreek Township	15,765	4	0	0	0	4	48	7	41	0	0
Cleveland	384,666	5,576	86	461	1,772	3,257	16,970	4,658	9,342	2,970	165
Cleveland Heights	44,413	93	3	11	48	31	711	63	552	96	5
Clyde	6,182	4	0	2	2	0	98	18	76	4	0
Coitsville Township	1,331	3	0	0	1	2	25	12	12	1	2
Coldwater	4,515	8	1	6	0	1	35	0	35	0	0
Columbiana	6,218	5	0	0	0	5	33	5	25	3	0
Columbus[6]	892,576	4,416	99	820	1,922	1,575	31,512	6,271	21,323	3,918	
Commercial Point	1,636	0	0	0	0	0	15	4	11	0	0
Conneaut	12,616	19	0	5	0	14	256	51	200	5	0
Cortland	6,759	1	0	0	0	1	60	3	56	1	0
Covington	2,666	0	0	0	0	0	17	4	13	0	0
Crestline	4,396	4	0	0	0	4	46	17	26	3	0
Cuyahoga Falls	49,201	57	0	18	8	31	1,040	73	933	34	1
Danville	1,003	0	0	0	0	0	24	4	17	3	0
Dayton	140,094	1,291	37	167	403	684	6,323	1,697	3,831	795	44
Deer Park	5,671	2	0	0	1	1	37	2	33	2	0
Defiance	16,620	25	0	15	0	10	313	46	254	13	5
Delaware	39,944	64	1	31	12	20	601	78	496	27	4
Delphos[8]	6,954		1		1	1	144	7	134	3	0
Dennison	2,607	2	0	1	0	1	8	1	7	0	0
Dover	12,752	11	0	4	4	3	97	16	74	7	0
Dublin	48,570	29	1	11	6	11	413	84	311	18	0
East Cleveland	17,127	112	4	7	52	49	311	98	115	98	17
Eastlake	18,111	7	0	0	2	5	399	32	351	16	1
Englewood	13,474	14	0	6	5	3	400	27	362	11	3
Euclid	47,048	291	6	27	86	172	1,224	196	864	164	6
Evendale	2,863	2	0	0	1	1	192	7	177	8	1
Fairborn	33,604	106	2	26	15	63	673	144	494	35	9
Fairfax	1,709	0	0	0	0	0	309	4	304	1	0
Fairfield	42,568	84	2	11	13	58	909	97	762	50	3
Fairfield Township	22,789	19	0	4	4	11	681	45	626	10	2
Fairview Park	16,248	16	0	2	3	11	140	17	116	7	1
Fayette	1,246	0	0	0	0	0	12	2	9	1	0
Findlay	41,351	90	5	37	12	36	1,043	145	872	26	3
Fredericktown	2,498	1	0	0	0	1	34	8	26	0	0
Fremont[8]	16,125		0		7	13	870	244	612	14	0
Gahanna	35,596	31	1	10	11	9	588	70	484	34	5
Galion	9,957	17	0	5	2	10	220	26	190	4	1
Gallipolis	3,402	18	0	4	3	11	327	44	269	14	1
Garrettsville	2,315	2	0	1	0	1	22	1	21	0	0
Gates Mills	2,234	1	0	0	1	0	9	3	6	0	0
Geneva-on-the-Lake	1,202	8	0	0	0	8	33	8	23	2	0
Georgetown	4,282	6	1	0	0	5	109	20	83	6	0
Germantown	5,499	2	0	0	0	2	50	5	42	3	1
Girard	9,304	28	0	2	2	24	232	44	177	11	1
Glouster	1,806	3	0	1	0	2	31	13	18	0	0
Goshen Township, Clermont County	16,177	11	0	5	0	6	154	30	110	14	0
Goshen Township, Mahoning County	3,110	5	0	0	0	5	56	16	35	5	0
Grafton	5,953	2	0	0	0	2	31	5	25	1	1
Grandview Heights	7,977	3	0	1	2	0	112	15	89	8	0
Granville	5,787	4	0	2	0	2	22	6	16	0	0
Greenfield	4,543	13	0	3	1	9	135	31	84	20	1
Greenhills	3,595	1	0	0	0	1	14	2	12	0	0
Greenville	12,707	48	0	17	8	23	226	37	159	30	17
Grove City	41,833	43	0	11	19	13	1,156	83	1,039	34	4

Table 8. Offenses Known to Law Enforcement, by Selected State and City, 2018—Continued

(Number.)

State/city	Population	Violent crime	Murder and nonnegligent manslaughter	Rape[1]	Robbery	Aggravated assault	Property crime	Burglary	Larceny-theft	Motor vehicle theft	Arson[2]
Groveport	5,656	25	0	2	3	20	128	17	103	8	1
Hamilton	62,059	315	5	47	114	149	2,686	644	1,851	191	42
Hamilton Township, Warren County	23,330	11	0	6	0	5	91	8	74	9	1
Harrison	11,513	2	0	0	1	1	156	10	139	7	0
Hartville	3,036	1	1	0	0	0	54	2	51	1	0
Heath	10,774	25	1	7	2	15	546	66	461	19	3
Highland Heights[8]	8,438		0		0	2	89	5	83	1	0
Hilliard	37,184	35	0	10	8	17	242	46	180	16	3
Hillsboro	6,499	15	1	3	1	10	136	19	108	9	0
Hinckley Township	8,029	4	0	1	1	2	21	5	11	5	0
Holland	1,645	8	0	0	7	1	513	3	508	2	0
Howland Township	16,449	10	0	3	3	4	350	46	299	5	0
Huber Heights	37,969	57	2	17	16	22	916	107	731	78	5
Hudson	22,242	1	0	0	0	1	126	16	104	6	0
Huron	6,893	1	0	1	0	0	68	6	62	0	0
Independence	7,135	12	0	2	4	6	125	12	111	2	1
Indian Hill	5,883	1	0	1	0	0	39	8	28	3	0
Ironton	10,666	25	0	10	5	10	340	50	179	111	0
Jackson	6,231	3	0	0	2	1	161	17	140	4	0
Jackson Township, Mahoning County	2,026	5	0	1	0	4	44	7	34	3	0
Jackson Township, Montgomery County	3,674	4	0	2	0	2	18	7	10	1	0
Jackson Township, Stark County	40,416	84	1	23	22	38	1,111	156	933	22	4
Jamestown	2,098	2	0	0	2	0	43	11	30	2	0
Johnstown	5,054	4	0	3	0	1	32	0	32	0	0
Kent	30,065	36	0	3	9	24	421	79	330	12	3
Kenton	8,114	29	0	10	5	14	313	54	256	3	4
Kettering	55,038	54	0	19	16	19	838	168	631	39	8
Kirtland	6,819	0	0	0	0	0	28	3	25	0	0
Kirtland Hills	641	0	0	0	0	0	0	0	0	0	0
Lakemore	3,074	2	0	0	1	1	102	11	88	3	1
Lakewood	50,078	58	2	5	27	24	674	102	522	50	3
Lancaster	40,498	116	0	44	21	51	1,687	262	1,369	56	10
Lawrence Township	8,273	6	0	2	0	4	65	17	45	3	0
Lebanon[4]	20,696	41	0	21	3	17	365	36	311	18	0
Lexington	4,666	1	0	0	0	1	9	0	9	0	0
Liberty Township	11,456	25	0	3	6	16	200	30	163	7	1
Lima	36,948	240	3	47	68	122	1,664	479	1,087	98	19
Lisbon	2,653	4	0	1	1	2	20	2	16	2	0
Lithopolis	1,651	0	0	0	0	0	19	1	17	1	0
Lockland	3,462	11	0	0	4	7	70	12	48	10	0
Logan	7,059	28	1	8	4	15	384	44	328	12	0
London	10,175	20	0	5	2	13	239	34	192	13	2
Lordstown	3,252	1	0	0	0	1	40	7	29	4	0
Loudonville	2,621	5	0	4	0	1	38	1	36	1	0
Louisville	9,347	9	0	0	0	9	142	26	112	4	1
Loveland	12,876	5	0	1	0	4	102	17	81	4	0
Lyndhurst	13,519	14	0	0	2	12	154	12	142	0	0
Macedonia	12,056	3	0	0	2	1	271	5	264	2	1
Madison Township, Franklin County	19,241	19	0	3	2	14	148	34	97	17	1
Madison Township, Lake County	15,626	11	0	1	0	10	224	28	196	0	0
Mansfield	45,941	237	3	60	57	117	2,087	434	1,577	76	17
Mariemont	3,438	3	0	0	0	3	30	1	26	3	0
Marietta	13,618	25	0	7	2	16	265	26	229	10	1
Marion	35,885	101	1	39	26	35	940	288	598	54	8
Martins Ferry	6,624	15	0	5	1	9	81	17	57	7	0
Mason	33,583	6	0	1	2	3	264	21	235	8	0
Massillon	32,361	75	0	30	17	28	747	118	595	34	3
Maumee	13,720	18	0	2	3	13	340	43	286	11	1
Mayfield Heights	18,648	5	0	0	1	4	113	3	109	1	0
McArthur	1,646	2	0	1	0	1	37	7	25	5	1
McConnelsville	1,775	3	0	2	0	1	25	5	19	1	1
Mechanicsburg	1,589	0	0	0	0	0	20	3	16	1	0
Medina	26,128	27	1	7	3	16	272	16	256	0	0
Medina Township	9,004	7	0	3	1	3	93	1	87	5	0
Mentor	47,118	41	1	17	7	16	709	40	654	15	0
Mentor-on-the-Lake	7,399	9	0	0	1	8	52	5	46	1	1
Miamisburg	19,954	49	0	13	15	21	443	66	342	35	1
Miami Township, Clermont County	42,493	34	0	13	3	18	448	48	392	8	0
Miami Township, Montgomery County	29,065	45	0	9	17	19	897	65	798	34	1
Middlefield[8]	2,707		0		0	0	53	2	50	1	1
Middleport	2,435	3	0	0	0	3	15	7	8	0	0
Milford	6,914	7	0	2	1	4	191	6	176	9	0
Milton Township	2,446	2	0	0	1	1	24	7	17	0	0
Mingo Junction	3,236	59	0	0	1	58	26	10	15	1	0
Mogadore[8]	3,821		0		0	1	42	9	30	3	0

Table 8. Offenses Known to Law Enforcement, by Selected State and City, 2018—Continued

(Number.)

State/city	Population	Violent crime	Murder and nonnegligent manslaughter	Rape[1]	Robbery	Aggravated assault	Property crime	Burglary	Larceny-theft	Motor vehicle theft	Arson[2]
Monroe	16,310	15	0	2	2	11	407	24	373	10	1
Montgomery	10,807	7	0	2	1	4	97	6	88	3	0
Montpelier	3,934	9	0	6	0	3	170	35	126	9	2
Montville Township	11,831	2	0	0	0	2	49	3	46	0	0
Mount Orab	3,485	8	0	2	0	6	104	1	61	42	0
Mount Vernon	16,607	20	0	7	1	12	510	52	457	1	1
Munroe Falls	5,064	1	0	0	0	1	30	2	28	0	0
Napoleon	8,236	14	0	3	3	8	135	17	111	7	0
Navarre	1,893	4	0	0	1	3	23	4	19	0	0
Nelsonville	5,278	8	0	0	4	4	185	46	121	18	0
New Albany	11,192	2	0	1	0	1	82	10	71	1	0
Newark	49,687	152	4	35	34	79	2,166	485	1,530	151	28
New Boston	2,103	10	0	1	3	6	340	23	309	8	1
Newcomerstown[8]	3,756		0		2	10	50	12	30	8	0
New Franklin	14,157	4	1	0	0	3	120	38	74	8	0
New Lebanon	3,983	6	0	0	0	6	102	22	74	6	0
New Lexington	4,697	14	0	5	1	8	112	18	86	8	0
New Philadelphia	17,445	7	0	1	1	5	212	7	202	3	0
New Richmond	2,683	10	0	3	2	5	41	4	34	3	0
Newton Falls	4,516	15	0	5	0	10	84	8	76	0	0
Newtown	2,664	0	0	0	0	0	27	2	24	1	0
Niles	18,370	43	1	9	12	21	505	81	408	16	0
North Canton	17,265	19	0	5	1	13	267	39	209	19	0
Northfield	3,668	5	0	0	3	2	36	1	33	2	0
North Olmsted	31,653	13	0	3	7	3	397	50	327	20	0
North Ridgeville	34,025	9	0	2	2	5	97	26	66	5	0
North Royalton	30,324	15	2	6	1	6	122	22	92	8	1
Northwood	5,421	12	0	1	5	6	153	20	123	10	0
Norton	12,003	11	0	2	0	9	215	35	161	19	0
Norwalk	16,800	14	0	3	5	6	311	43	255	13	1
Norwood	19,976	55	0	9	21	25	738	108	592	38	1
Oak Hill	1,512	0	0	0	0	0	21	6	15	0	0
Oberlin	8,262	17	1	8	3	5	184	30	151	3	2
Olmsted Falls	8,912	0	0	0	0	0	20	3	14	3	0
Olmsted Township	13,425	2	1	0	0	1	28	4	20	4	0
Ontario	6,056	3	0	0	1	2	325	5	316	4	0
Oregon	19,922	31	0	11	5	15	630	61	552	17	1
Orrville	8,472	16	0	7	0	9	68	22	45	1	1
Ottawa	4,346	1	0	0	0	1	7	0	6	1	0
Ottawa Hills	4,472	0	0	0	0	0	36	4	30	2	0
Owensville	821	2	0	0	0	2	9	4	5	0	0
Oxford	23,038	23	0	14	2	7	463	63	387	13	5
Oxford Township	2,210	1	0	0	0	1	25	7	17	1	0
Parma	78,968	124	3	39	14	68	846	176	604	66	6
Pepper Pike	6,309	4	0	1	0	3	33	3	29	1	0
Perrysburg	21,585	9	0	6	3	0	240	23	217	0	0
Perrysburg Township	12,935	8	2	2	1	3	133	25	105	3	0
Perry Township, Columbiana County	4,324	0	0	0	0	0	11	6	5	0	0
Perry Township, Franklin County	3,773	1	0	0	0	1	38	4	33	1	0
Pickerington	20,716	28	0	6	9	13	264	27	230	7	1
Pierce Township	11,669	10	0	4	1	5	307	15	279	13	1
Pioneer	1,399	1	0	0	0	1	20	4	14	2	0
Piqua	21,056	45	0	28	9	8	806	123	653	30	7
Poland Township	11,888	2	0	1	0	1	31	14	16	1	0
Poland Village	2,432	1	0	0	1	0	9	3	6	0	0
Port Clinton	5,899	13	0	5	3	5	176	43	128	5	0
Portsmouth	20,473	118	1	14	33	70	1,021	213	720	88	1
Powell	13,455	6	0	3	2	1	109	15	91	3	0
Reminderville	4,381	1	0	0	0	1	25	2	23	0	0
Reynoldsburg	38,126	88	3	22	34	29	942	104	758	80	5
Richmond Heights	10,414	37	2	0	12	23	179	33	106	40	0
Riverside	25,083	25	0	3	4	18	287	74	183	30	3
Rocky River	20,253	3	0	0	0	3	65	9	55	1	0
Ross Township	8,879	4	0	2	0	2	63	11	50	2	1
Russell Township	5,216	0	0	0	0	0	5	0	5	0	0
Sabina	2,546	1	0	1	0	0	62	12	47	3	1
Sagamore Hills	10,956	0	0	0	0	0	30	5	24	1	0
Salem	11,710	22	0	5	3	14	414	34	370	10	0
Salineville	1,228	1	0	0	1	0	21	2	18	1	1
Sandusky	24,700	71	0	19	21	31	920	198	682	40	1
Sebring	4,217	4	1	1	0	2	79	11	66	2	0
Seven Hills	11,662	3	0	1	0	2	52	11	39	2	0
Shawnee Township	12,061	12	0	5	1	6	104	20	78	6	0
Sheffield Lake	8,954	6	1	2	1	2	69	14	54	1	1
Shelby	8,984	13	0	6	1	6	215	36	174	5	1
Sidney	20,537	54	0	28	12	14	688	114	547	27	3
Solon	22,948	10	0	2	0	8	210	24	181	5	1
Somerset	1,459	1	0	0	0	1	6	1	4	1	0
South Bloomfield	1,998	0	0	0	0	0	23	2	18	3	0
South Euclid	21,539	31	0	7	8	16	518	59	424	35	0
South Russell	3,781	0	0	0	0	0	4	1	3	0	0

Table 8. Offenses Known to Law Enforcement, by Selected State and City, 2018—Continued

(Number.)

State/city	Population	Violent crime	Murder and nonnegligent manslaughter	Rape[1]	Robbery	Aggravated assault	Property crime	Burglary	Larceny-theft	Motor vehicle theft	Arson[2]
Springboro	18,789	4	0	1	0	3	101	17	76	8	1
Springfield	59,016	336	13	21	143	159	3,141	699	2,204	238	
Springfield Township, Mahoning County	6,448	4	0	3	1	0	68	20	47	1	1
Springfield Township, Summit County	14,572	46	0	15	12	19	667	100	540	27	2
Steubenville	17,913	55	1	2	20	32	958	72	870	16	8
St. Marys	8,127	6	0	0	0	6	88	25	61	2	0
Stow	34,762	26	0	12	7	7	510	65	441	4	1
Streetsboro	16,411	10	1	0	0	9	215	23	184	8	0
Strongsville	44,819	12	0	0	3	9	642	41	585	16	1
Struthers	10,193	11	0	3	5	3	141	31	104	6	1
Sugarcreek Township	8,412	10	0	2	1	7	228	12	214	2	0
Swanton	3,900	1	0	0	0	1	46	11	34	1	0
Sylvania Township	29,574	49	0	5	6	38	658	67	570	21	1
Tallmadge	17,550	20	0	10	7	3	290	76	200	14	3
Tiffin	17,492	2	0	1	0	1	458	48	404	6	5
Tipp City	9,995	5	0	3	0	2	155	35	111	9	0
Toledo[10]	275,023	2,333	37	239	477	1,580	10,222	2,802	6,712	708	
Toronto	4,776	6	1	2	0	3	14	7	7	0	0
Trotwood	24,380	165	6	25	39	95	893	197	524	172	7
Troy	25,960	33	0	8	6	19	535	64	450	21	1
Twinsburg	18,983	12	1	1	3	7	109	16	87	6	0
Uhrichsville	5,343	3	0	1	1	1	40	5	30	5	1
Uniontown	3,349	6	0	0	0	6	80	18	58	4	0
Union Township, Clermont County	48,187	35	0	15	8	12	951	73	842	36	2
University Heights	12,981	21	0	3	11	7	217	15	187	15	0
Upper Arlington	35,572	10	2	1	5	2	391	79	303	9	1
Upper Sandusky	6,497	7	0	2	0	5	138	23	114	1	6
Urbana	11,337	22	0	9	0	13	363	45	308	10	3
Utica	2,220	3	0	0	0	3	18	5	11	2	0
Vandalia[4]	15,023	31	0	12	16	3	286	65	193	28	1
Van Wert	10,631	30	0	10	2	18	319	47	268	4	0
Vermilion	10,436	4	0	1	1	2	132	18	113	1	0
Village of Leesburg	1,301	3	0	0	1	2	34	5	27	2	0
Wadsworth	23,744	26	1	3	4	18	371	31	329	11	0
Waite Hill	457	0	0	0	0	0	0	0	0	0	0
Wapakoneta	9,771	8	0	5	0	3	161	15	141	5	0
Warren	39,280	245	4	41	64	136	1,500	508	922	70	8
Warren Township	5,110	21	0	1	1	19	76	26	44	6	0
Washington Court House	14,210	23	0	8	6	9	489	72	403	14	2
Waterville	5,490	0	0	0	0	0	21	1	18	2	0
Wauseon	7,345	9	0	2	0	7	213	24	188	1	2
Waverly	4,295	5	2	0	0	3	74	1	69	4	0
Wellston	5,506	11	0	3	1	7	154	33	116	5	0
West Carrollton	12,893	36	0	10	9	17	261	57	182	22	1
West Chester Township	62,063	64	0	23	17	24	1,279	137	1,105	37	2
Westerville	40,225	46	3	19	5	19	717	47	648	22	3
West Jefferson	4,375	3	0	1	0	2	50	2	48	0	0
West Union	3,141	4	0	1	0	3	15	9	4	2	0
Whitehall	19,024	119	2	14	52	51	1,074	181	810	83	11
Whitehouse	4,823	4	0	3	0	1	22	2	18	2	0
Wickliffe	12,734	9	0	0	3	6	155	16	132	7	2
Willard	6,022	8	0	3	0	5	243	24	212	7	0
Williamsburg	2,564	7	0	2	3	2	52	1	45	6	0
Willoughby	22,949	30	1	4	7	18	385	55	309	21	2
Wilmington	12,386	17	0	5	2	10	703	86	603	14	2
Windham	2,199	1	0	0	0	1	18	3	14	1	0
Wintersville	3,700	1	0	0	0	1	45	9	36	0	1
Woodlawn	3,298	7	0	0	0	7	86	3	77	6	0
Wooster	26,688	87	1	35	11	40	797	152	618	27	7
Wyoming	8,554	4	0	0	2	2	76	8	65	3	0
Xenia	26,691	71	4	17	8	42	789	126	636	27	7
Yellow Springs	3,768	6	0	2	1	3	77	16	60	1	0
Youngstown	64,282	428	23	28	150	227	2,285	825	1,262	198	129
Zanesville	25,371	120	1	31	16	72	946	139	749	58	8
OKLAHOMA											
Achille	531	0	0	0	0	0	0	0	0	0	0
Ada	17,339	84	0	12	14	58	640	139	462	39	3
Allen	929	0	0	0	0	0	10	1	7	2	0
Altus	18,712	43	0	11	4	28	385	119	240	26	5
Alva	5,112	6	0	1	0	5	57	23	29	5	0
Amber	456	0	0	0	0	0	1	1	0	0	0
Anadarko	6,598	71	2	6	14	49	272	60	195	17	5
Antlers	2,300	4	0	0	3	1	10	4	5	1	0
Apache	1,411	6	0	0	0	6	22	9	11	2	0
Ardmore	24,817	159	0	19	17	123	1,083	229	779	75	2
Arkoma	1,894	0	0	0	0	0	6	1	2	3	0
Atoka	3,086	7	0	0	1	6	111	43	56	12	2
Avant	302	0	0	0	0	0	1	1	0	0	0
Barnsdall	1,160	4	0	1	0	3	8	4	3	1	1

Table 8. Offenses Known to Law Enforcement, by Selected State and City, 2018—Continued

(Number.)

State/city	Population	Violent crime	Murder and nonnegligent manslaughter	Rape[1]	Robbery	Aggravated assault	Property crime	Burglary	Larceny-theft	Motor vehicle theft	Arson[2]
Bartlesville	36,473	103	1	18	12	72	1,213	290	835	88	10
Beaver	1,391	0	0	0	0	0	2	0	2	0	0
Beggs	1,245	2	0	2	0	0	15	6	7	2	0
Bernice	577	4	0	0	0	4	12	5	7	0	0
Bethany	19,448	49	1	10	10	28	577	133	363	81	6
Big Cabin	252	1	0	0	0	1	13	1	11	1	0
Binger	642	0	0	0	0	0	3	0	3	0	0
Bixby	27,654	34	0	9	5	20	419	60	325	34	2
Blackwell	6,684	20	1	3	0	16	111	38	65	8	2
Blanchard	8,886	5	0	1	0	4	120	30	68	22	0
Boise City	1,071	1	0	0	0	1	6	3	1	2	0
Bokoshe	492	4	0	0	1	3	4	0	4	0	0
Boley	1,176	0	0	0	0	0	1	1	0	0	0
Bristow	4,214	7	0	0	0	7	105	23	68	14	1
Broken Arrow	109,663	156	3	50	28	75	2,283	292	1,800	191	6
Broken Bow	4,069	19	0	3	2	14	282	79	186	17	3
Cache	2,864	6	0	2	0	4	43	21	16	6	1
Caddo	1,076	0	0	0	0	0	5	1	2	2	1
Calera	2,338	6	0	1	2	3	32	17	13	2	0
Caney	198	3	0	2	0	1	7	2	5	0	0
Canton	594	1	0	0	0	1	9	2	5	2	0
Carnegie	1,664	4	0	2	0	2	22	9	11	2	0
Carney	662	0	0	0	0	0	4	1	3	0	0
Cashion	864	2	0	1	0	1	3	1	1	1	0
Catoosa	7,006	43	0	8	4	31	385	40	266	79	2
Cement	484	0	0	0	0	0	8	0	6	2	0
Chandler	3,127	6	0	1	1	4	53	14	35	4	0
Chattanooga	448	0	0	0	0	0	3	1	1	1	1
Checotah	3,138	11	0	0	1	10	112	12	93	7	0
Chelsea	1,913	3	0	2	0	1	56	11	42	3	0
Cherokee	1,568	3	0	3	0	0	19	5	11	3	0
Chickasha	16,314	63	3	9	8	43	436	113	273	50	5
Choctaw	12,724	21	1	2	1	17	210	44	139	27	0
Chouteau	2,076	7	0	0	0	7	69	21	33	15	0
Claremore	18,748	47	0	9	3	35	558	92	432	34	1
Clayton	793	1	0	0	0	1	7	3	3	1	0
Cleveland	3,164	4	0	0	0	4	11	3	4	4	0
Clinton	9,163	58	0	12	7	39	203	55	123	25	2
Coalgate	1,827	1	0	1	0	0	9	0	7	2	0
Colcord	836	0	0	0	0	0	19	3	11	5	0
Collinsville	7,098	9	0	4	2	3	97	21	68	8	1
Comanche	1,554	7	0	0	0	7	28	13	13	2	0
Cordell	2,757	1	0	0	0	1	41	20	19	2	0
Covington	538	0	0	0	0	0	0	0	0	0	0
Coweta	9,706	20	0	1	4	15	154	33	102	19	1
Crescent	1,539	4	0	1	0	3	22	4	15	3	1
Cushing	7,687	22	0	5	2	15	257	54	177	26	0
Cyril	1,032	1	0	0	0	1	13	1	8	4	0
Davenport	823	6	0	0	0	6	14	5	5	4	0
Davis	2,861	8	0	1	1	6	93	36	54	3	0
Del City	21,859	172	3	12	35	122	1,062	201	739	122	4
Depew	483	2	0	0	1	1	13	0	12	1	0
Dewar	862	1	0	0	0	1	7	2	5	0	0
Dewey	3,477	10	1	1	0	8	78	24	48	6	1
Dibble	862	3	0	0	1	2	13	1	9	3	0
Dickson	1,252	0	0	0	0	0	8	2	5	1	0
Drumright	2,832	3	0	0	0	3	65	21	39	5	1
Duncan	22,351	39	1	5	5	28	692	223	431	38	8
Durant	18,043	53	0	4	4	45	911	194	659	58	4
Earlsboro	647	2	0	0	0	2	4	1	2	1	0
Edmond[4]	93,557	127	0	25	13	89	1,424	266	1,064	94	4
Eldorado	415	0	0	0	0	0	0	0	0	0	0
Elgin	3,279	0	0	0	0	0	1	0	1	0	0
Elk City	11,544	7	0	1	0	6	231	36	177	18	0
Elmore City	711	0	0	0	0	0	14	4	9	1	0
El Reno[4]	19,272	43	2	5	8	28	341	65	233	43	3
Enid	50,214	173	3	34	17	119	1,428	370	975	83	4
Erick	993	1	0	0	0	1	0	0	0	0	0
Eufaula	2,898	11	0	5	0	6	81	21	49	11	0
Fairfax	1,287	3	0	0	0	3	16	11	5	0	0
Fairview	2,623	6	0	1	0	5	27	10	11	6	0
Fletcher	1,139	0	0	0	0	0	4	0	1	3	0
Forest Park	1,080	1	0	1	0	0	4	1	2	1	0
Fort Gibson	4,021	7	0	1	0	6	49	10	35	4	0
Fort Towson	492	4	0	0	0	4	24	7	16	1	0
Frederick	3,603	15	0	3	3	9	119	44	65	10	0
Gans	300	0	0	0	0	0	0	0	0	0	0
Geary	1,271	4	0	0	0	4	40	15	21	4	0
Glenpool	14,273	66	0	15	4	47	215	51	136	28	0
Goodwell	1,307	3	0	1	0	2	15	6	9	0	0
Gore	945	7	0	0	0	7	16	7	8	1	0
Grandfield	949	1	0	0	0	1	7	3	4	0	0
Granite	1,972	2	0	0	0	2	7	2	5	0	0

Table 8. Offenses Known to Law Enforcement, by Selected State and City, 2018—Continued

(Number.)

State/city	Population	Violent crime	Murder and nonnegligent manslaughter	Rape[1]	Robbery	Aggravated assault	Property crime	Burglary	Larceny-theft	Motor vehicle theft	Arson[2]
Grove	7,122	13	0	4	1	8	251	45	185	21	3
Guthrie	11,519	39	0	6	2	31	339	86	225	28	1
Guymon	11,546	11	1	3	0	7	121	29	87	5	1
Harrah	6,504	15	0	4	1	10	141	38	92	11	0
Hartshorne	1,952	6	1	0	1	4	39	18	18	3	0
Haskell	1,940	0	0	0	0	0	2	0	2	0	0
Healdton	2,708	3	0	0	0	3	29	14	11	4	2
Heavener	3,272	8	0	0	0	8	34	12	19	3	0
Hennessey	2,223	3	0	2	0	1	11	2	8	1	0
Henryetta	5,628	9	0	5	0	4	142	31	97	14	2
Hinton	3,247	3	0	0	0	3	36	5	25	6	0
Hobart	3,476	3	0	0	1	2	47	21	25	1	0
Holdenville	5,514	7	1	0	1	5	84	36	33	15	0
Hollis	1,872	6	0	0	0	6	53	15	37	1	6
Hominy	3,412	3	0	1	0	2	50	23	22	5	0
Hooker	1,923	6	0	1	0	5	9	6	3	0	0
Howe	788	2	0	0	0	2	3	1	2	0	0
Hulbert	593	0	0	0	0	0	0	0	0	0	0
Hydro	943	1	0	0	0	1	7	3	3	1	0
Idabel	6,860	32	3	7	1	21	384	98	276	10	7
Jay	2,532	5	0	1	0	4	69	19	42	8	1
Jenks	23,473	26	1	7	3	15	307	108	185	14	1
Jennings	359	1	0	1	0	0	9	2	5	2	1
Jones	3,159	5	0	0	0	5	48	17	28	3	0
Kellyville	1,159	2	0	1	0	1	15	2	13	0	0
Kiefer	2,010	4	0	2	0	2	35	8	24	3	0
Kingfisher	4,912	10	0	3	0	7	102	20	74	8	0
Kingston	1,644	0	0	0	0	0	9	2	6	1	0
Konawa	1,232	9	0	1	0	8	41	18	19	4	1
Krebs	1,931	10	0	2	0	8	59	20	31	8	0
Lahoma	629	0	0	0	0	0	1	0	1	0	0
Lamont	400	1	0	0	0	1	3	0	2	1	0
Langley	819	4	0	0	1	3	24	7	14	3	1
Langston	1,845	5	0	2	1	2	9	5	4	0	0
Lawton	93,140	840	7	90	122	621	3,338	1,023	2,011	304	21
Lexington	2,150	8	0	1	1	6	52	11	36	5	0
Lindsay	2,818	7	0	0	0	7	93	41	44	8	0
Locust Grove	1,392	5	0	0	0	5	26	7	12	7	1
Lone Grove	5,090	2	0	0	0	2	31	11	16	4	1
Luther	1,772	2	0	1	0	1	13	3	9	1	0
Madill	3,957	4	1	1	1	1	152	9	141	2	0
Mangum	2,746	8	0	1	0	7	27	8	16	3	0
Mannford	3,195	11	0	2	1	8	25	12	9	4	0
Marietta	2,751	8	0	4	0	4	60	8	42	10	1
Marlow	4,410	5	0	2	1	2	129	40	83	6	1
Maud	1,064	2	0	1	0	1	15	5	10	0	0
Maysville	1,225	5	0	0	0	5	31	10	19	2	0
McAlester	17,999	115	0	22	8	85	1,031	201	772	58	0
McCurtain	508	0	0	0	0	0	14	7	5	2	1
McLoud	4,708	12	1	1	2	8	59	17	33	9	1
Medicine Park	454	2	0	0	0	2	4	1	1	2	0
Meeker	1,163	6	0	0	0	6	16	8	8	0	0
Miami	13,162	55	0	12	2	41	439	147	268	24	8
Midwest City	57,710	180	2	21	50	107	1,795	335	1,263	197	8
Minco	1,635	1	0	0	0	1	8	1	5	2	0
Moore	62,453	108	2	23	27	56	1,314	278	893	143	5
Mooreland	1,204	0	0	0	0	0	9	2	3	4	0
Morris	1,445	2	0	1	1	0	10	7	2	1	0
Mounds	1,253	3	0	0	0	3	16	4	12	0	2
Mountain View	740	0	0	0	0	0	4	3	1	0	0
Muldrow	3,203	28	0	5	0	23	95	20	65	10	4
Muskogee	37,659	377	1	32	66	278	1,536	474	924	138	6
Mustang	21,809	30	0	8	1	21	231	46	158	27	3
Nash	198	0	0	0	0	0	0	0	0	0	0
Newcastle	10,266	8	0	4	0	4	240	69	123	48	1
Newkirk	2,207	10	1	3	1	5	42	16	24	2	0
Nichols Hills	3,912	2	0	0	1	1	82	12	56	14	0
Nicoma Park	2,492	2	0	0	0	2	59	10	31	18	0
Ninnekah	1,037	0	0	0	0	0	7	2	2	3	0
Noble	6,772	15	0	2	2	11	124	32	75	17	1
Norman	124,577	336	3	79	56	198	3,466	535	2,573	358	4
North Enid	928	1	0	1	0	0	11	1	10	0	0
Nowata	3,635	8	0	1	1	6	79	19	50	10	1
Oilton	1,015	0	0	0	0	0	7	3	2	2	0
Okarche	1,338	0	0	0	0	0	8	2	4	2	0
Okemah	3,190	16	0	4	0	12	124	32	75	17	1
Oklahoma City	652,936	5,663	52	542	1,082	3,987	26,298	6,000	16,668	3,630	66
Okmulgee	11,919	62	0	15	9	38	548	130	380	38	7
Olustee	567	2	0	0	0	2	4	2	1	1	0
Oologah	1,172	0	0	0	0	0	0	0	0	0	0
Owasso	37,220	65	1	15	12	37	856	78	714	64	2
Paoli	617	0	0	0	0	0	1	0	1	0	0
Pauls Valley	6,180	23	0	7	2	14	297	68	215	14	0

Table 8. Offenses Known to Law Enforcement, by Selected State and City, 2018—Continued

(Number.)

State/city	Population	Violent crime	Murder and nonnegligent manslaughter	Rape[1]	Robbery	Aggravated assault	Property crime	Burglary	Larceny-theft	Motor vehicle theft	Arson[2]
Pawhuska	3,349	13	0	5	0	8	68	27	37	4	1
Pawnee	2,128	10	0	1	1	8	55	18	34	3	2
Perkins	2,842	2	1	1	0	0	88	20	56	12	0
Perry	4,908	8	0	1	0	7	84	19	62	3	0
Piedmont	8,080	5	0	1	1	3	19	4	13	2	1
Pocola	4,072	7	1	1	0	5	12	0	7	5	1
Ponca City	24,066	169	1	31	27	110	951	305	612	34	9
Pond Creek	834	0	0	0	0	0	3	1	2	0	0
Porum	707	1	0	0	0	1	1	1	0	0	0
Poteau	8,913	36	1	10	5	20	412	96	298	18	1
Prague	2,415	4	0	0	0	4	52	18	31	3	0
Pryor Creek	9,369	66	0	5	3	58	209	41	126	42	1
Purcell	6,470	32	0	7	4	21	254	71	164	19	1
Quinton	985	9	0	0	0	9	11	5	6	0	0
Ramona	550	0	0	0	0	0	13	4	5	4	0
Ringling	977	3	0	0	1	2	21	3	16	2	0
Roland	3,794	8	0	2	2	4	80	12	64	4	1
Rush Springs	1,254	4	0	1	0	3	33	19	14	0	1
Salina	1,385	8	0	1	0	7	21	3	11	7	0
Sallisaw	8,427	16	1	4	1	10	258	34	212	12	0
Sand Springs	20,056	19	0	5	5	9	683	82	525	76	1
Sapulpa	20,948	42	0	6	5	31	529	131	303	95	0
Savanna	653	2	0	0	0	2	34	12	18	4	0
Sawyer	315	0	0	0	0	0	1	0	1	0	0
Sayre	4,508	7	0	1	1	5	58	21	25	12	1
Seiling	862	0	0	0	0	0	4	1	2	1	0
Seminole	7,237	11	1	1	1	8	135	31	94	10	0
Shady Point	993	0	0	0	0	0	2	1	0	1	0
Shattuck	1,284	0	0	0	0	0	6	2	4	0	0
Shawnee	31,422	424	2	28	27	367	1,616	409	1,042	165	1
Skiatook	8,020	19	0	8	0	11	220	50	149	21	3
Snyder	1,295	3	0	0	0	3	17	4	11	2	0
South Coffeyville	748	1	0	0	0	1	14	1	9	4	0
Sparks	171	0	0	0	0	0	2	1	1	0	0
Spencer	4,009	15	0	1	4	10	75	24	32	19	0
Sperry	1,315	4	0	1	0	3	47	20	18	9	0
Spiro	2,164	3	0	0	0	3	14	6	8	0	0
Sportsmen Acres	309	0	0	0	0	0	0	0	0	0	0
Stigler	2,742	10	0	2	0	8	71	13	53	5	1
Stillwater	50,445	168	0	38	12	118	959	179	729	51	11
Stilwell	4,007	22	0	5	3	14	207	35	141	31	4
Stonewall	476	4	0	2	1	1	6	3	2	1	0
Stratford	1,541	1	0	0	0	1	21	9	8	4	1
Stringtown	402	1	0	0	0	1	2	1	1	0	0
Stroud	2,747	3	0	2	0	1	85	27	43	15	1
Sulphur	5,005	16	0	3	1	12	139	30	94	15	1
Tahlequah	16,877	23	1	0	11	11	685	93	544	48	2
Talala	275	0	0	0	0	0	1	1	0	0	0
Talihina	1,076	0	0	0	0	0	13	3	6	4	0
Tecumseh	6,628	18	0	0	1	17	182	64	93	25	3
Texhoma	939	2	0	0	0	2	2	0	0	2	0
Thackerville	483	0	0	0	0	0	4	0	4	0	0
The Village	9,475	28	0	4	3	21	248	48	186	14	0
Thomas	1,200	0	0	0	0	0	1	0	1	0	0
Tipton	772	2	0	0	0	2	9	4	5	0	0
Tishomingo	3,077	4	0	1	1	2	29	11	18	0	1
Tonkawa	3,040	6	0	2	0	4	44	19	23	2	0
Tryon	501	1	0	1	0	0	3	1	2	0	0
Tulsa	403,147	4,294	60	422	830	2,982	21,893	4,800	13,834	3,259	223
Tupelo	311	1	0	1	0	0	6	1	5	0	0
Tushka	304	0	0	0	0	0	7	2	4	1	0
Tuttle	7,318	23	0	3	0	20	167	42	110	15	1
Tyrone	778	0	0	0	0	0	8	2	5	1	0
Union City	2,125	1	0	0	0	1	29	7	16	6	2
Valley Brook	774	5	0	2	0	3	26	4	15	7	0
Valliant	734	1	0	0	0	1	9	5	2	2	0
Velma	596	0	0	0	0	0	0	0	0	0	0
Verden	525	2	0	0	0	2	16	5	9	2	0
Verdigris	4,580	1	0	1	0	0	50	3	42	5	0
Vian	1,363	6	0	0	1	5	32	9	20	3	0
Vici	708	0	0	0	0	0	0	0	0	0	0
Vinita	5,348	4	0	0	0	4	88	26	55	7	2
Wagoner	8,986	25	0	2	0	23	188	47	126	15	2
Wakita	332	0	0	0	0	0	6	2	4	0	0
Walters	2,399	4	0	0	0	4	51	21	25	5	0
Warner	1,605	5	0	2	0	3	12	2	10	0	0
Warr Acres	10,372	43	0	6	6	31	386	158	176	52	0
Washington	662	0	0	0	0	0	2	1	0	1	0
Watonga	2,848	5	0	2	0	3	35	8	24	3	0
Watts	308	0	0	0	0	0	3	1	1	1	0
Waukomis	1,314	0	0	0	0	0	13	4	7	2	0
Waurika	1,937	3	0	0	0	3	5	0	5	0	0
Waynoka	931	3	0	1	0	2	12	3	6	3	0

Table 8. Offenses Known to Law Enforcement, by Selected State and City, 2018—Continued

(Number.)

State/city	Population	Violent crime	Murder and nonnegligent manslaughter	Rape[1]	Robbery	Aggravated assault	Property crime	Burglary	Larceny-theft	Motor vehicle theft	Arson[2]
Weatherford	11,981	25	0	5	5	15	251	53	186	12	0
Weleetka	969	5	0	0	0	5	27	8	14	5	0
West Siloam Springs	867	2	0	0	1	1	75	3	56	16	0
Westville	1,534	5	0	0	1	4	65	11	48	6	2
Wetumka	1,192	1	0	0	0	1	20	7	11	2	0
Wewoka	3,300	15	0	2	0	13	88	39	41	8	2
Wilburton	2,615	9	0	0	0	9	80	33	43	4	0
Wilson	1,707	7	0	0	1	6	23	10	7	6	0
Wister	1,056	1	0	0	0	1	23	4	19	0	0
Woodward	12,323	35	1	15	2	17	329	96	204	29	2
Wright City	736	0	0	0	0	0	11	4	4	3	0
Wyandotte	329	0	0	0	0	0	12	4	7	1	0
Wynnewood	2,218	3	0	0	0	3	18	7	11	0	1
Wynona	434	0	0	0	0	0	0	0	0	0	0
Yale	1,200	8	0	0	1	7	31	9	17	5	1
Yukon	27,452	48	0	8	2	38	524	83	412	29	4
OREGON											
Ashland	21,269	38	0	5	7	26	701	59	611	31	3
Aumsville	4,186	6	0	0	1	5	53	9	36	8	0
Baker City	9,779	19	0	5	2	12	324	47	262	15	2
Banks	2,031	3	0	2	0	1	21	2	19	0	0
Beaverton	98,616	189	2	59	40	88	2,039	191	1,587	261	17
Bend	97,403	162	1	21	26	114	2,079	164	1,822	93	15
Black Butte		0	0	0	0	0	6	1	5	0	0
Brookings	6,453	31	0	6	1	24	121	20	88	13	1
Canby	17,914	45	0	11	3	31	260	21	226	13	3
Cannon Beach	1,733	0	0	0	0	0	41	21	19	1	0
Carlton	2,168	1	0	0	1	0	29	7	22	0	0
Central Point	18,402	35	0	2	5	28	462	55	383	24	5
Coburg	1,117	4	0	2	0	2	9	2	6	1	0
Coos Bay	16,343	46	0	7	8	31	775	111	621	43	7
Coquille	3,909	11	1	0	1	9	74	14	54	6	0
Cornelius	12,580	32	0	8	6	18	297	27	240	30	7
Corvallis	58,491	94	0	28	25	41	1,835	185	1,580	70	28
Cottage Grove	10,241	27	0	4	4	19	415	28	344	43	8
Dallas	16,561	45	0	8	2	35	492	45	425	22	3
Eagle Point	9,236	20	0	1	2	17	235	23	202	10	1
Eugene	170,771	661	3	119	171	368	5,503	813	4,148	542	45
Florence	9,016	11	0	3	1	7	287	23	247	17	2
Forest Grove	24,560	42	1	14	1	26	435	42	363	30	6
Gearhart	1,613	0	0	0	0	0	14	1	10	3	0
Gervais	2,742	4	0	1	0	3	32	3	22	7	0
Grants Pass	37,814	135	3	27	29	76	1,342	143	1,019	180	17
Gresham	111,797	472	0	67	115	290	3,823	486	2,072	1,265	11
Hermiston	17,517	42	1	1	7	33	584	83	457	44	2
Hillsboro	109,121	287	0	61	54	172	2,077	208	1,651	218	12
Hood River	7,767	9	0	1	0	8	278	15	231	32	2
Hubbard	3,549	4	0	0	0	4	41	1	38	2	1
Independence	10,280	13	0	2	1	10	175	23	138	14	1
Jacksonville	2,910	8	0	1	0	7	56	4	49	3	0
Keizer	39,727	85	0	11	14	60	888	94	689	105	3
King City	4,014	8	0	1	3	4	62	10	51	1	2
Klamath Falls	22,242	91	1	8	14	68	744	106	507	131	7
La Grande	13,186	12	0	5	0	7	264	44	202	18	8
Lake Oswego	39,557	20	0	11	4	5	530	115	387	28	7
Lincoln City	8,998	57	0	9	7	41	473	133	305	35	1
Madras	6,919	13	0	2	6	5	253	29	203	21	3
Manzanita	659	1	0	1	0	0	12	2	8	2	0
McMinnville	34,669	84	0	16	13	55	1,064	98	924	42	6
Medford	82,800	403	2	33	93	275	4,463	471	3,633	359	42
Milton-Freewater	7,021	25	0	1	5	19	151	33	100	18	3
Milwaukie	20,873	36	0	14	6	16	309	52	207	50	2
Molalla	9,322	7	0	2	2	3	182	14	152	16	1
Monmouth	10,457	13	0	2	0	11	144	13	116	15	2
Mount Angel	3,559	3	0	0	1	2	43	7	31	5	0
Myrtle Creek	3,483	7	0	0	1	6	62	8	48	6	0
Newberg-Dundee	27,122	42	0	19	4	19	394	33	329	32	5
Newport	10,684	30	0	5	7	18	346	50	285	11	10
North Bend	9,705	29	3	2	8	16	409	66	321	22	7
North Plains	2,190	11	0	3	0	8	23	3	17	3	0
Nyssa[4,8]	3,166		0		0	6	82	30	39	13	
Ontario	10,958	56	1	8	12	35	577	56	462	59	4
Oregon City	36,918	134	0	13	13	108	868	76	671	121	10
Pendleton	16,681	44	0	9	5	30	451	46	358	47	4
Philomath	4,787	10	0	1	0	9	56	12	42	2	0
Phoenix	4,597	9	0	2	2	5	242	30	202	10	0
Portland[5]	657,260	3,418	25	438	1,056	1,899	35,884	4,444	24,508	6,932	
Prineville	10,184	43	0	9	2	32	371	75	279	17	2
Rainier	1,992	0	0	0	0	0	38	7	26	5	0
Redmond	30,597	73	0	17	14	42	1,106	100	926	80	10
Reedsport	4,117	8	0	1	0	7	167	33	120	14	2
Rockaway Beach	1,414	5	0	0	0	5	57	20	35	2	0

Table 8. Offenses Known to Law Enforcement, by Selected State and City, 2018—Continued

(Number.)

State/city	Population	Violent crime	Murder and nonnegligent manslaughter	Rape[1]	Robbery	Aggravated assault	Property crime	Burglary	Larceny-theft	Motor vehicle theft	Arson[2]
Rogue River	2,318	2	0	1	0	1	57	10	42	5	0
Roseburg	22,366	58	1	16	17	24	1,338	157	1,097	84	14
Salem	172,022	719	5	56	177	481	7,170	934	5,338	898	53
Scappoose	7,345	13	0	5	3	5	62	8	48	6	2
Silverton	10,477	12	0	2	1	9	214	31	160	23	0
Springfield	62,786	182	2	36	31	113	2,120	211	1,754	155	16
Stayton	8,195	19	0	1	0	18	321	27	266	28	6
St. Helens	13,800	21	0	9	1	11	204	13	175	16	3
Sunriver		3	0	0	0	3	57	6	48	3	1
Sutherlin	8,052	25	0	7	3	15	203	31	156	16	4
Sweet Home	9,712	16	0	3	5	8	498	44	429	25	1
Talent	6,556	11	0	1	0	10	143	13	112	18	0
The Dalles	15,740	33	0	12	5	16	466	82	347	37	9
Tigard	53,880	114	0	30	33	51	1,558	180	1,277	101	6
Tillamook	5,295	23	0	4	5	14	190	24	158	8	2
Toledo	3,625	3	0	2	0	1	23	3	20	0	1
Tualatin	27,671	60	2	14	14	30	729	69	596	64	1
Turner	2,131	2	0	1	0	1	21	5	16	0	0
Umatilla	7,162	4	0	1	0	3	64	16	41	7	1
Vernonia	2,251	6	0	0	0	6	11	1	10	0	0
Warrenton	5,688	24	0	0	6	18	277	20	245	12	2
West Linn	26,934	24	0	4	3	17	234	33	192	9	2
Winston	5,463	14	0	2	4	8	170	24	128	18	1
Woodburn	26,031	111	0	11	31	69	962	116	741	105	5
Yamhill	1,175	0	0	0	0	0	21	1	18	2	0
PENNSYLVANIA											
Abington Township, Montgomery County	55,631	44	1	6	12	25	949	66	852	31	3
Adamstown	1,857	3	0	0	0	3	14	1	12	1	0
Adams Township, Butler County	14,105	3	0	0	0	3	46	3	42	1	0
Adams Township, Cambria County	5,581	0	0	0	0	0	11	1	8	2	0
Akron	4,015	7	0	1	0	6	34	6	24	4	0
Albion	1,466	0	0	0	0	0	13	4	8	1	0
Alburtis	2,663	3	0	0	1	2	5	0	5	0	0
Aldan	4,157	3	0	0	1	2	100	9	87	4	1
Aleppo Township	1,876	0	0	0	0	0	4	0	3	1	0
Aliquippa	8,946	50	1	1	5	43	81	25	45	11	0
Allegheny Township, Blair County	6,573	37	0	2	0	35	60	7	52	1	2
Allegheny Township, Westmoreland County	8,093	7	0	0	0	7	73	7	64	2	0
Allentown	121,743	412	11	49	183	169	2,821	463	2,100	258	9
Altoona	43,840	165	3	67	27	68	686	188	464	34	9
Ambler	6,532	9	1	1	2	5	80	6	72	2	0
Ambridge	6,679	89	2	1	7	79	182	26	139	17	1
Amity Township	13,076	4	0	1	0	3	84	23	56	5	0
Annville Township	4,968	35	0	2	4	29	44	4	39	1	0
Apollo	1,536	4	0	2	0	2	8	3	5	0	0
Archbald	6,947	14	0	0	0	14	55	13	42	0	1
Armagh Township	3,810	2	0	0	0	2	5	1	4	0	0
Arnold	4,868	47	0	0	9	38	186	41	132	13	1
Ashland	2,680	4	0	0	1	3	36	8	25	3	0
Ashley	2,709	11	1	0	2	8	35	6	28	1	0
Ashville	210	0	0	0	0	0	0	0	0	0	0
Aspinwall	2,722	1	0	0	0	1	17	1	15	1	0
Aston Township	16,708	6	0	1	1	4	164	16	139	9	1
Athens	3,192	8	0	5	0	3	38	3	35	0	0
Athens Township	5,079	13	0	4	1	8	138	3	135	0	0
Avalon	4,569	18	1	2	0	15	55	11	41	3	0
Avis	1,500	0	0	0	0	0	0	0	0	0	0
Avoca	2,625	0	0	0	0	0	24	4	18	2	0
Avondale	1,422	0	0	0	0	0	0	0	0	0	0
Avonmore Boro	953	1	0	0	0	1	0	0	0	0	0
Baden	3,928	8	0	0	0	8	27	5	22	0	0
Baldwin Borough	19,586	17	0	2	7	8	104	14	80	10	0
Baldwin Township	1,932	2	0	0	0	2	12	2	10	0	0
Bally	1,275	0	0	0	0	0	0	0	0	0	0
Bangor	5,222	13	0	1	0	12	51	8	41	2	0
Beaver	4,320	19	0	0	4	15	48	4	41	3	0
Beaver Falls	9,588	40	1	3	9	27	230	20	200	10	2
Beaver Meadows	832	0	0	0	0	0	0	0	0	0	0
Bedford	2,709	5	0	0	0	5	21	4	17	0	0
Bedminster Township	7,241	3	0	1	0	2	15	0	15	0	0
Bell Acres	1,387	0	0	0	0	0	7	1	6	0	0
Bellefonte	6,325	1	0	0	0	1	30	3	26	1	1
Bellevue	8,130	21	0	0	3	18	183	34	140	9	0
Bellwood	1,735	1	0	0	0	1	10	2	8	0	0
Ben Avon	1,750	0	0	0	0	0	11	0	11	0	0
Ben Avon Heights	364	0	0	0	0	0	0	0	0	0	0
Bensalem Township	60,588	70	4	5	35	26	1,292	110	1,107	75	7

Table 8. Offenses Known to Law Enforcement, by Selected State and City, 2018—Continued

(Number.)

State/city	Population	Violent crime	Murder and nonnegligent manslaughter	Rape[1]	Robbery	Aggravated assault	Property crime	Burglary	Larceny-theft	Motor vehicle theft	Arson[2]
Bentleyville	2,492	5	0	0	1	4	7	2	4	1	0
Benton Area	1,928	0	0	0	0	0	9	0	9	0	0
Berlin	1,973	4	0	0	0	4	6	1	5	0	0
Bern Township	7,025	5	0	3	0	2	59	6	48	5	0
Bernville	956	0	0	0	0	0	1	0	1	0	0
Berwick	10,030	37	0	8	2	27	181	19	156	6	0
Bessemer	1,062	1	0	0	0	1	0	0	0	0	0
Bethel Park	32,417	11	0	0	2	9	282	16	261	5	0
Bethel Township, Berks County	4,154	0	0	0	0	0	15	4	10	1	0
Bethel Township, Delaware County	9,219	6	0	1	0	5	62	8	52	2	0
Bethlehem	75,809	207	1	32	50	124	1,281	217	1,008	56	5
Bethlehem Township	23,983	18	0	7	4	7	323	19	290	14	2
Biglerville	1,213	0	0	0	0	0	4	0	4	0	0
Birdsboro	5,167	3	0	1	0	2	33	5	24	4	0
Birmingham Township	4,201	0	0	0	0	0	17	4	11	2	0
Blacklick Township	1,890	0	0	0	0	0	0	0	0	0	0
Blairsville	3,248	11	0	1	1	9	48	3	43	2	1
Blair Township	4,503	3	0	0	0	3	26	6	20	0	0
Blakely	6,201	6	0	0	0	6	39	4	33	2	0
Blawnox	1,391	0	0	0	0	0	3	0	1	2	0
Bloomsburg Town	14,145	35	0	4	0	31	194	27	161	6	1
Blossburg	1,478	2	0	0	0	2	2	1	1	0	0
Bonneauville	1,824	3	0	0	0	3	6	0	6	0	0
Boyertown	4,058	2	0	0	1	1	64	9	50	5	2
Brackenridge	3,168	4	0	0	1	3	45	5	39	1	0
Braddock	2,110	15	1	1	6	7	53	14	35	4	0
Braddock Hills	1,824	0	0	0	0	0	3	0	3	0	0
Bradford	8,244	84	0	5	2	77	208	21	183	4	2
Bradford Township	4,724	11	0	2	1	8	21	6	15	0	1
Branch Township	1,747	0	0	0	0	0	0	0	0	0	0
Brecknock Township, Berks County	4,640	3	0	0	0	3	18	2	13	3	0
Brentwood	9,364	21	0	0	4	17	80	6	73	1	0
Briar Creek Township	2,974	8	0	1	0	7	23	2	21	0	0
Bridgeport	4,596	15	1	7	2	5	65	5	58	2	0
Bridgeville	5,005	6	0	1	1	4	56	9	47	0	0
Bridgewater	772	4	0	0	0	4	9	1	8	0	0
Brighton Township	8,297	15	0	4	4	7	37	1	34	2	0
Bristol	9,618	31	5	0	12	14	112	21	91	0	0
Bristol Township	53,684	95	4	15	40	36	973	96	782	95	5
Brockway	2,004	6	0	1	0	5	17	5	12	0	0
Brookhaven	8,042	19	0	0	13	6	131	7	117	7	1
Brookville	3,807	4	0	1	1	2	19	0	19	0	0
Brownsville	2,238	4	0	2	0	2	27	8	17	2	0
Bryn Athyn	1,409	2	0	0	0	2	5	1	4	0	0
Buckingham Township	20,311	1	0	0	0	1	70	9	57	4	0
Buffalo Township	7,294	11	0	0	0	11	34	3	30	1	0
Buffalo Valley Regional	12,660	4	0	0	3	1	75	10	65	0	1
Burgettstown	1,320	5	0	0	0	5	18	2	14	2	0
Bushkill Township	8,528	26	0	1	0	25	25	2	22	1	0
Butler	13,017	40	3	1	8	28	347	56	271	20	2
Butler Township, Butler County	16,542	25	0	3	2	20	431	17	411	3	4
Butler Township, Luzerne County	9,788	8	0	2	0	6	71	14	54	3	1
Butler Township, Schuylkill County	5,625	0	0	0	0	0	16	8	8	0	0
Caernarvon Township, Berks County	4,129	14	0	1	1	12	89	6	82	1	0
California	6,738	18	0	5	1	12	72	10	61	1	0
Callery	384	0	0	0	0	0	0	0	0	0	0
Caln Township	14,316	39	0	0	3	36	272	18	241	13	0
Cambria Township	5,768	7	0	0	1	6	50	0	49	1	0
Cambridge Springs	2,648	2	0	0	0	2	2	1	1	0	0
Camp Hill	7,946	2	0	0	2	0	56	1	55	0	0
Canonsburg	8,815	13	0	0	3	10	62	0	62	0	0
Canton	1,881	10	0	1	0	9	8	0	7	1	0
Carbondale	8,386	14	0	6	4	4	65	8	55	2	1
Carlisle	19,335	18	1	7	7	3	145	8	133	4	1
Carmichaels	455	0	0	0	0	0	1	0	1	0	0
Carnegie	7,888	11	0	0	2	9	136	19	110	7	0
Carrolltown	796	5	0	1	0	4	3	0	3	0	0
Carroll Township, Washington County	5,481	21	0	0	1	20	24	7	17	0	1
Carroll Township, York County	6,440	2	0	0	1	1	53	17	35	1	0
Carroll Valley	3,928	1	0	0	1	0	20	4	16	0	0
Cass Township	1,877	4	0	0	0	4	4	3	1	0	0
Castle Shannon	8,153	6	0	0	0	6	53	8	42	3	0
Catasauqua	6,619	10	0	2	3	5	101	10	82	9	1
Catawissa	1,484	7	0	1	0	6	16	2	14	0	0
Cecil Township	12,633	2	0	0	0	2	54	2	46	6	0
Center Township	11,439	38	0	0	3	35	324	9	311	4	2
Centerville	3,159	11	0	0	0	11	35	9	24	2	2

Table 8. Offenses Known to Law Enforcement, by Selected State and City, 2018—Continued

(Number.)

State/city	Population	Violent crime	Murder and nonnegligent manslaughter	Rape[1]	Robbery	Aggravated assault	Property crime	Burglary	Larceny-theft	Motor vehicle theft	Arson[2]
Central Berks Regional	13,309	20	0	4	3	13	201	22	169	10	0
Central Bucks Regional	15,584	9	1	1	3	4	83	1	78	4	0
Chambersburg	20,962	60	0	4	13	43	577	73	479	25	4
Charleroi Regional	6,519	26	0	4	5	17	136	13	121	2	0
Chartiers Township	7,937	3	0	1	1	1	49	5	37	7	0
Cheltenham Township	37,501	70	4	4	31	31	995	117	842	36	2
Cherry Tree	340	1	0	0	0	1	0	0	0	0	0
Chester	34,087	474	18	11	159	286	1,151	352	624	175	13
Chester Township	4,102	49	1	0	10	38	98	21	56	21	0
Chippewa Township	7,995	2	0	0	0	2	162	5	153	4	0
Christiana	1,175	0	0	0	0	0	15	7	6	2	0
Churchill	2,928	4	0	0	0	4	19	0	17	2	0
Clairton	6,587	23	0	0	13	10	146	44	85	17	0
Clarion	5,316	3	0	0	2	1	17	1	14	2	1
Clarks Summit	6,210	3	0	0	0	3	47	14	33	0	0
Clearfield	5,874	36	0	5	3	28	186	5	179	2	0
Cleona	2,197	0	0	0	0	0	6	2	4	0	0
Clifton Heights	6,709	37	0	2	4	31	121	15	94	12	0
Clymer	1,272	1	0	0	1	0	10	0	10	0	0
Coaldale	2,150	6	0	0	0	6	11	0	11	0	0
Coal Township	10,329	57	1	1	1	54	163	18	141	4	0
Cochranton	1,090	1	0	0	0	1	2	0	2	0	0
Colebrookdale District	6,014	7	0	1	0	6	98	5	89	4	0
Collegeville	5,134	0	0	0	0	0	37	5	29	3	1
Collier Township	8,324	4	0	0	2	2	114	9	96	9	0
Collingdale	8,793	64	0	1	10	53	270	34	209	27	0
Colonial Regional	17,966	6	0	0	1	5	448	30	403	15	1
Columbia	10,436	19	0	4	4	11	176	21	146	9	2
Colwyn	2,551	13	1	2	1	9	59	1	51	7	1
Conemaugh Township, Cambria County	1,854	6	0	0	0	6	4	0	4	0	0
Conemaugh Township, Somerset County	6,865	6	0	0	1	5	20	7	13	0	0
Conewago Township, Adams County	7,184	6	0	1	1	4	54	8	46	0	0
Conewango Township	3,362	23	0	2	0	21	90	11	76	3	0
Conneaut Lake Regional	3,482	0	0	0	0	0	16	2	11	3	0
Connellsville	7,331	36	1	4	9	22	264	43	214	7	0
Conoy Township	3,484	11	0	0	1	10	14	1	13	0	1
Conshohocken	8,081	5	0	0	0	5	88	9	75	4	1
Conway	2,090	2	0	0	0	2	23	2	17	4	0
Conyngham	1,860	0	0	0	0	0	0	0	0	0	0
Coopersburg	2,509	3	0	1	1	1	29	2	26	1	0
Coplay	3,274	3	0	0	0	3	34	6	27	1	0
Coraopolis	5,510	25	0	2	4	19	129	18	106	5	0
Cornwall	4,326	2	2	0	0	0	0	0	0	0	0
Corry	6,311	42	0	4	2	36	157	14	136	7	3
Coudersport	2,430	11	0	2	1	8	6	2	4	0	0
Courtdale	722	0	0	0	0	0	3	0	3	0	0
Covington Township	2,243	7	0	0	0	7	43	5	38	0	0
Crafton	6,223	8	0	0	2	6	165	4	156	5	0
Cranberry Township	31,154	8	1	0	4	3	302	11	286	5	0
Crescent Township	2,569	11	0	0	0	11	12	1	11	0	0
Cresson	1,576	2	0	0	0	2	12	2	10	0	0
Cresson Township	2,536	1	0	0	0	1	16	0	16	0	0
Croyle Township	2,232	0	0	0	0	0	7	2	5	0	0
Cumberland Township, Adams County	6,236	12	0	2	0	10	26	4	21	1	0
Cumberland Township, Greene County	6,221	6	0	0	0	6	89	10	77	2	1
Cumru Township	15,387	13	0	0	9	4	170	26	135	9	1
Curwensville	2,397	14	0	4	0	10	37	3	32	2	2
Dallas	2,753	0	0	0	0	0	29	3	25	1	0
Dallas Township	9,259	7	0	1	2	4	51	4	45	2	0
Dalton	1,190	2	0	0	0	2	13	3	10	0	0
Danville	4,621	14	0	0	0	14	69	6	61	2	0
Darby	10,702	149	1	17	37	94	346	46	251	49	2
Darby Township	9,282	19	1	0	2	16	125	9	108	8	2
Darlington Township	1,880	0	0	0	0	0	16	5	11	0	0
Delano Township	421	0	0	0	0	0	0	0	0	0	0
Delaware Water Gap	730	0	0	0	0	0	0	0	0	0	0
Delmont	2,570	0	0	0	0	0	13	1	12	0	0
Denver	3,881	4	0	2	1	1	34	8	25	1	1
Derry Township, Dauphin County	25,131	40	0	1	1	38	379	41	326	12	2
Dickson City	5,761	24	0	0	3	21	246	11	232	3	0
Donegal Township	3,252	3	0	0	0	3	18	0	18	0	0
Donora	4,584	9	0	1	1	7	31	6	25	0	0
Dormont	8,347	17	0	0	4	13	67	15	39	13	0
Douglass Township, Berks County	3,597	0	0	0	0	0	29	6	22	1	0
Douglass Township, Montgomery County	10,644	8	0	0	0	8	50	5	39	6	0

Table 8. Offenses Known to Law Enforcement, by Selected State and City, 2018—Continued

(Number.)

State/city	Population	Violent crime	Murder and nonnegligent manslaughter	Rape[1]	Robbery	Aggravated assault	Property crime	Burglary	Larceny-theft	Motor vehicle theft	Arson[2]
Downingtown	7,933	9	0	0	2	7	162	20	134	8	5
Doylestown Township	17,430	15	0	2	1	12	141	5	131	5	2
Dublin Borough	2,149	4	0	0	0	4	6	0	3	3	0
DuBois	7,409	15	0	3	2	10	136	14	119	3	1
Duboistown	1,180	0	0	0	0	0	4	0	4	0	0
Dunbar	993	0	0	0	0	0	0	0	0	0	0
Duncansville	1,174	2	0	1	0	1	6	0	6	0	0
Dunmore	12,933	23	0	5	0	18	169	33	131	5	0
Dunnstable Township	1,011	0	0	0	0	0	0	0	0	0	0
Dupont	2,670	4	0	0	0	4	19	5	14	0	0
Duquesne	5,544	58	3	3	20	32	163	48	95	20	1
Duryea	4,857	9	0	1	0	8	37	7	27	3	0
Earl Township	7,243	2	0	1	0	1	48	10	35	3	0
East Bangor	1,705	2	0	0	0	2	6	0	6	0	0
East Berlin	1,539	0	0	0	0	0	3	0	3	0	0
East Brandywine Township	8,765	7	0	1	1	5	38	3	33	2	0
East Cocalico Township	10,569	8	0	2	0	6	63	9	51	3	0
East Conemaugh	1,416	14	0	0	0	14	7	4	3	0	1
East Coventry Township	6,778	1	0	1	0	0	40	5	31	4	0
East Deer Township	1,450	1	0	0	0	1	23	5	16	2	0
Eastern Adams Regional	7,379	9	0	0	0	9	40	7	32	1	1
Eastern Pike Regional	4,604	12	0	5	1	6	134	12	118	4	0
East Fallowfield Township	7,584	9	0	3	0	6	19	10	9	0	0
East Franklin Township	3,854	0	0	0	0	0	33	0	33	0	0
East Greenville	2,991	0	0	0	0	0	17	8	8	1	0
East Hempfield Township	24,694	32	1	7	7	17	244	18	219	7	0
East Lampeter Township	17,133	9	1	3	2	3	457	24	429	4	1
East Lansdowne	2,670	9	0	0	2	7	79	14	56	9	0
East Marlborough Township	7,416	0	0	0	0	0	15	0	15	0	0
East McKeesport	2,636	10	0	0	1	9	13	4	7	2	1
East Norriton Township	14,085	43	0	1	2	40	267	23	237	7	0
Easton	27,158	69	0	9	18	42	388	38	325	25	1
East Pennsboro Township	21,750	11	0	5	3	3	113	12	100	1	0
East Petersburg	4,526	2	0	0	1	1	32	9	22	1	0
East Pikeland Township	7,345	4	1	0	1	2	34	1	32	1	0
East Rochester	537	0	0	0	0	0	29	0	28	1	0
East Taylor Township	2,513	3	0	1	0	2	5	1	4	0	0
Easttown Township	10,668	17	0	2	0	15	56	4	51	1	2
East Union Township	1,586	3	0	0	0	3	3	0	3	0	0
East Vincent Township	7,232	0	0	0	0	0	33	4	29	0	0
East Washington	1,822	7	0	1	0	6	24	7	15	2	0
East Whiteland Township	12,085	3	0	0	1	2	107	14	89	4	0
Ebensburg	3,093	2	0	1	0	1	35	2	27	6	0
Economy	9,205	2	0	0	0	2	89	1	87	1	0
Eddystone	2,412	24	0	0	3	21	239	9	225	5	1
Edgewood	3,022	2	0	0	1	1	84	8	73	3	0
Edgeworth	1,653	2	0	0	0	2	1	0	0	1	0
Edinboro	5,902	4	0	0	2	2	57	12	44	1	0
Edwardsville	4,687	22	0	4	1	17	102	4	96	2	0
Elderton	342	0	0	0	0	0	0	0	0	0	0
Elizabeth	1,980	11	0	0	1	10	9	3	4	2	0
Elizabethtown	11,591	21	4	3	3	11	88	5	82	1	0
Elizabeth Township	13,087	9	0	3	0	6	63	10	50	3	1
Elkland	1,736	6	0	2	0	4	25	3	18	4	2
Ellwood City	7,445	10	0	1	3	6	120	20	95	5	0
Emlenton Borough	576	0	0	0	0	0	11	2	9	0	0
Emmaus	11,490	7	0	1	5	1	164	23	129	12	1
Emporium	1,851	3	0	0	0	3	27	4	22	1	0
Emsworth	2,379	1	0	0	0	1	7	1	6	0	0
Ephrata	13,956	23	0	0	2	21	175	22	148	5	1
Ephrata Township	10,465	10	0	1	1	8	155	6	148	1	1
Erie	96,758	299	11	39	91	158	1,880	420	1,355	105	55
Etna	3,348	5	0	0	2	3	55	3	49	3	0
Evans City-Seven Fields Regional	4,488	1	0	0	0	1	33	6	26	1	0
Everett	1,737	2	0	0	0	2	19	3	16	0	0
Everson	760	1	0	0	0	1	1	1	0	0	0
Exeter	5,580	12	0	1	0	11	73	8	64	1	0
Exeter Township, Berks County	25,956	24	0	4	8	12	247	24	213	10	0
Exeter Township, Luzerne County	2,358	2	0	2	0	0	11	2	8	1	0
Fairfield	513	2	0	0	0	2	2	0	2	0	0
Fairview Township, Luzerne County	4,485	0	0	0	0	0	25	1	24	0	0
Fairview Township, York County	17,555	39	0	6	3	30	137	16	111	10	0
Falls Township, Bucks County	33,854	42	1	10	11	20	448	40	363	45	5
Farrell	4,651	48	1	3	3	41	120	32	81	7	5
Fawn Township	2,326	4	0	0	0	4	21	5	16	0	0
Fayette City	570	0	0	0	0	0	0	0	0	0	0
Ferguson Township	19,551	8	0	2	2	4	88	17	67	4	0
Ferndale	1,503	0	0	0	0	0	1	0	1	0	0
Findlay Township	5,867	9	0	1	0	8	43	7	34	2	0

Table 8. Offenses Known to Law Enforcement, by Selected State and City, 2018—Continued

(Number.)

State/city	Population	Violent crime	Murder and nonnegligent manslaughter	Rape[1]	Robbery	Aggravated assault	Property crime	Burglary	Larceny-theft	Motor vehicle theft	Arson[2]
Fleetwood	4,087	16	0	0	1	15	56	9	47	0	0
Folcroft	6,615	32	0	3	9	20	128	15	101	12	0
Ford City	2,788	0	0	0	0	0	3	0	3	0	0
Forest City	1,770	3	0	0	0	3	20	2	18	0	0
Forest Hills	6,331	5	0	0	1	4	68	7	52	9	0
Forks Township	15,545	8	0	3	0	5	98	8	89	1	0
Forty Fort	4,092	5	0	0	2	3	27	3	24	0	0
Forward Township	3,295	2	0	0	0	2	12	3	7	2	0
Foster Township, McKean County	4,080	2	0	1	0	1	21	1	20	0	0
Foster Township, Schuylkill County	244	2	0	0	0	2	7	1	6	0	0
Fountain Hill	4,721	7	0	0	1	6	130	23	101	6	0
Fox Chapel	5,297	0	0	0	0	0	13	1	12	0	0
Frackville	3,624	9	0	0	0	9	12	0	12	0	0
Franconia Township	13,343	3	0	0	0	3	47	3	40	4	0
Franklin	6,081	12	0	4	0	8	100	11	83	6	1
Franklin Park	14,706	3	0	0	1	2	43	5	38	0	1
Franklin Township, Beaver County	3,893	7	0	0	0	7	22	4	18	0	0
Franklin Township, Carbon County	4,132	21	0	0	1	20	44	7	33	4	0
Franklin Township, Columbia County	585	0	0	0	0	0	2	0	2	0	0
Frazer Township	1,130	0	0	0	0	0	163	1	162	0	0
Freedom	1,488	4	0	1	0	3	18	3	12	3	0
Freedom Township	3,352	1	0	0	0	1	60	3	57	0	0
Freeland	3,441	5	0	0	0	5	47	8	38	1	0
Freemansburg	2,620	0	0	0	0	0	11	2	8	1	0
Freeport	1,693	1	0	1	0	0	13	6	7	0	0
Gaines Township	535	0	0	0	0	0	4	0	4	0	0
Galeton	1,095	9	0	1	0	8	17	2	15	0	0
Gallitzin	1,779	0	0	0	0	0	9	2	7	0	0
Gallitzin Township	1,256	0	0	0	0	0	0	0	0	0	0
Geistown	2,281	0	0	0	0	0	2	1	0	1	0
Gettysburg	7,637	30	0	6	2	22	89	19	70	0	0
Girard	2,959	12	0	2	1	9	32	3	28	1	0
Girardville	1,445	3	0	0	0	3	2	0	2	0	0
Glassport	4,351	9	0	0	3	6	106	16	83	7	1
Glenolden	7,163	11	0	0	3	8	147	21	122	4	0
Granville Township	5,000	0	0	0	0	0	79	3	75	1	0
Great Bend	673	0	0	0	0	0	7	2	3	2	0
Greene County Regional Police Department	4,492	1	0	1	0	0	43	5	37	1	0
Greenfield Township	2,004	0	0	0	0	0	0	0	0	0	0
Greenfield Township, Blair County	3,981	1	0	1	0	0	43	5	37	1	1
Greensburg	14,217	58	0	4	2	52	292	46	242	4	1
Green Tree	4,966	6	0	0	0	6	49	8	39	2	0
Greenville	5,472	30	0	4	5	21	100	14	81	5	1
Greenwood Township	1,902	1	0	0	0	1	3	0	3	0	0
Grove City	7,969	9	0	0	1	8	33	6	27	0	0
Halifax	834	0	0	0	0	0	2	0	2	0	0
Hamburg	4,427	13	1	0	1	11	35	2	29	4	0
Hampden Township	30,399	10	0	3	4	3	156	10	139	7	0
Hampton Township	18,318	14	0	3	2	9	67	6	60	1	0
Hanover	15,653	49	1	2	13	33	437	30	396	11	2
Hanover Township, Luzerne County	10,843	41	1	4	2	34	205	23	174	8	1
Harmar Township	3,046	5	0	1	1	3	63	3	59	1	0
Harmony Township	3,033	7	0	0	1	6	32	6	22	4	1
Harrisburg	49,147	531	15	72	190	254	1,252	259	806	187	22
Harrisville	865	0	0	0	0	0	0	0	0	0	0
Hartleton	280	0	0	0	0	0	0	0	0	0	0
Harveys Lake	2,782	4	0	2	0	2	17	2	15	0	0
Hastings	2,154	4	0	1	0	3	8	2	6	0	0
Hatboro	7,446	7	0	2	0	5	34	4	30	0	0
Hatfield Township	21,048	22	0	8	0	14	194	26	163	5	0
Haverford Township	49,422	24	0	1	7	16	563	57	493	13	0
Hawley	1,149	0	0	0	0	0	0	0	0	0	0
Hazleton	24,637	117	0	11	26	80	229	72	121	36	6
Hegins Township	3,391	10	0	1	1	8	32	8	23	1	0
Heidelberg	1,219	2	0	0	0	2	0	0	0	0	0
Hellam Township	8,645	12	1	4	0	7	58	9	48	1	0
Hellertown	5,840	17	0	0	4	13	49	2	43	4	0
Hemlock Township	2,242	3	0	1	1	1	87	3	82	2	0
Hempfield Township, Mercer County	3,614	21	0	3	0	18	90	15	74	1	0
Hermitage	15,531	19	1	1	2	15	497	40	443	14	1
Hickory Township	2,401	2	0	0	0	2	5	2	3	0	0
Highland Township	1,285	0	0	0	0	0	0	0	0	0	0
Highspire	2,369	16	0	0	3	13	40	3	37	0	0
Hilltown Township	15,467	10	0	2	1	7	156	16	135	5	0

Table 8. Offenses Known to Law Enforcement, by Selected State and City, 2018—Continued

(Number.)

State/city	Population	Violent crime	Murder and nonnegligent manslaughter	Rape[1]	Robbery	Aggravated assault	Property crime	Burglary	Larceny-theft	Motor vehicle theft	Arson[2]
Hollidaysburg	5,763	18	0	1	1	16	17	5	12	0	0
Homer City	1,597	0	0	0	0	0	0	0	0	0	0
Homestead	3,162	25	1	2	9	13	290	25	243	22	0
Honesdale	4,208	8	0	1	0	7	59	12	45	2	0
Honey Brook	1,752	1	0	0	0	1	1	0	0	1	0
Hooversville	601	2	0	0	0	2	2	1	1	0	0
Hopewell Township	12,711	22	0	2	3	17	98	22	72	4	0
Horsham Township	26,615	7	0	0	3	4	190	12	170	8	0
Houston	1,239	0	0	0	0	0	0	0	0	0	0
Hughestown	1,373	2	0	0	0	2	19	1	18	0	0
Hughesville	2,050	0	0	0	0	0	45	1	44	0	0
Hulmeville	995	0	0	0	0	0	5	4	1	0	0
Hummelstown	4,648	10	0	0	0	10	36	0	34	2	1
Huntingdon	6,946	22	0	0	0	22	81	16	64	1	0
Independence Township	1,507	0	0	0	0	0	3	0	3	0	0
Independence Township, Beaver County	2,409	2	0	0	0	2	8	1	7	0	0
Indiana	13,039	117	0	6	4	107	140	13	123	4	0
Indiana Township	7,195	3	0	0	0	3	15	1	13	1	0
Indian Lake	380	0	0	0	0	0	0	0	0	0	0
Ingram	3,236	3	0	0	2	1	28	3	25	0	1
Irwin	3,758	18	0	1	0	17	19	1	17	1	0
Ivyland	1,054	0	0	0	0	0	2	0	1	1	0
Jackson Township, Butler County	3,953	0	0	0	0	0	5	1	4	0	0
Jackson Township, Cambria County	4,083	1	0	0	0	1	1	0	1	0	0
Jackson Township, Luzerne County	4,631	1	0	1	0	0	7	0	7	0	0
Jamestown	577	1	0	0	0	1	4	0	4	0	0
Jeannette	9,127	10	0	0	5	5	51	12	39	0	1
Jefferson Hills Borough	11,309	20	0	0	0	20	60	9	48	3	0
Jefferson Township, Lackawanna County	3,661	0	0	0	0	0	3	1	0	2	0
Jefferson Township, Mercer County	1,829	0	0	0	0	0	8	5	3	0	0
Jefferson Township, Washington County	1,134	1	0	0	0	1	0	0	0	0	0
Jenkins Township	4,475	4	0	0	0	4	42	4	37	1	0
Jenkintown	4,442	10	0	1	1	8	70	6	64	0	1
Jennerstown	652	0	0	0	0	0	1	1	0	0	0
Jermyn	2,053	10	0	1	0	9	27	8	19	0	0
Jessup	4,397	5	0	1	0	4	17	1	13	3	0
Jim Thorpe	4,613	19	0	3	1	15	68	8	57	3	1
Johnsonburg	2,291	10	1	0	0	9	31	10	20	1	1
Johnstown	20,877	240	5	26	32	177	620	190	406	24	1
Kane	3,489	2	0	0	0	2	61	17	42	2	1
Kenhorst	2,874	8	0	1	2	5	54	9	44	1	0
Kennedy Township	8,183	21	1	2	5	13	134	16	113	5	1
Kennett Square	6,192	10	0	0	2	8	77	14	59	4	0
Kennett Township	8,317	2	0	1	0	1	46	14	31	1	3
Kidder Township	1,919	14	0	0	0	14	51	14	34	3	0
Kilbuck Township	721	0	0	0	0	0	4	0	4	0	0
Kingston	12,836	23	1	2	9	11	201	22	169	10	0
Kingston Township	6,898	9	0	0	0	9	20	2	16	2	0
Kiskiminetas Township	4,496	1	0	0	0	1	11	1	10	0	0
Kline Township	1,366	0	0	0	0	0	27	5	21	1	0
Knox	1,074	0	0	0	0	0	1	0	1	0	0
Koppel	723	4	0	1	0	3	3	0	3	0	0
Kulpmont	2,787	6	0	0	0	6	7	2	5	0	0
Kutztown	5,066	8	0	2	2	4	49	7	40	2	0
Lake City	2,906	0	0	0	0	0	9	1	8	0	0
Lamar Township	2,552	0	0	0	0	0	1	0	1	0	0
Lancaster	59,761	419	2	96	92	229	1,580	164	1,332	84	15
Lancaster Township, Butler County	2,577	0	0	0	0	0	8	0	8	0	0
Lancaster Township, Lancaster County	17,272	36	0	3	4	29	319	14	288	17	1
Lanesboro	465	4	0	0	0	4	1	1	0	0	0
Langhorne Borough	1,592	3	0	0	0	3	8	1	7	0	0
Langhorne Manor	1,431	0	0	0	0	0	4	0	4	0	0
Lansdale	16,633	15	1	5	4	5	176	10	153	13	0
Lansdowne	10,650	26	0	3	11	12	237	42	184	11	3
Lansford	3,778	16	0	1	1	14	105	29	75	1	0
Latimore Township	2,613	1	0	0	0	1	17	3	13	1	0
Latrobe	7,896	24	0	1	0	23	154	17	134	3	0
Laureldale	3,899	5	0	0	1	4	49	7	41	1	0
Lawrence Park Township	3,794	7	0	0	0	7	7	1	6	0	0
Lawrence Township, Clearfield County	7,581	31	0	4	1	26	164	16	144	4	3
Lawrence Township, Tioga County	1,650	3	0	0	0	3	0	0	0	0	0
Lawrenceville	611	1	0	0	0	1	0	0	0	0	0

Table 8. Offenses Known to Law Enforcement, by Selected State and City, 2018—Continued

(Number.)

State/city	Population	Violent crime	Murder and nonnegligent manslaughter	Rape[1]	Robbery	Aggravated assault	Property crime	Burglary	Larceny-theft	Motor vehicle theft	Arson[2]
Lebanon	25,816	83	2	12	12	57	469	75	372	22	3
Leechburg	2,002	4	0	0	0	4	13	7	6	0	0
Leetsdale	1,183	1	0	0	0	1	23	2	20	1	0
Leet Township	1,585	5	0	0	0	5	4	0	3	1	0
Lehighton	5,277	9	0	0	1	8	104	14	84	6	2
Lehigh Township	1,786	3	0	0	0	3	4	0	3	1	0
Lehigh Township, Northampton County	10,479	18	0	1	0	17	87	27	56	4	0
Lehman Township	3,470	12	0	0	0	12	14	2	10	2	0
Lewistown	8,188	36	0	5	3	28	193	38	144	11	1
Liberty	2,477	1	0	0	0	1	0	0	0	0	0
Liberty Township, Adams County	1,252	0	0	0	0	0	8	1	6	1	0
Ligonier	1,525	4	0	0	0	4	5	0	5	0	0
Ligonier Township	6,400	8	0	1	0	7	5	1	4	0	2
Limerick Township	19,144	8	0	1	0	7	309	10	296	3	0
Lincoln	1,038	0	0	0	0	0	0	0	0	0	0
Linesville	992	1	0	0	0	1	23	3	20	0	0
Lititz	9,448	8	2	1	1	4	25	3	21	1	0
Little Beaver Township	1,351	0	0	0	0	0	0	0	0	0	0
Littlestown	4,489	8	1	2	0	5	27	4	21	2	0
Lock Haven	9,218	20	0	6	2	12	118	12	104	2	3
Locust Township	1,399	9	0	0	0	9	8	3	5	0	0
Logan Township	12,364	16	0	3	3	10	137	18	115	4	0
Lower Allen Township	19,539	14	1	2	2	9	231	18	212	1	0
Lower Burrell	11,155	9	0	3	0	6	84	10	74	0	0
Lower Frederick Township	4,884	3	0	2	0	1	29	3	25	1	1
Lower Gwynedd Township	11,543	3	0	0	0	3	145	11	124	10	0
Lower Heidelberg Township	6,071	11	0	0	1	10	22	2	17	3	0
Lower Mahanoy Township	1,653	0	0	0	0	0	0	0	0	0	0
Lower Makefield Township	32,768	10	0	2	2	6	219	30	182	7	0
Lower Merion Township	59,262	32	1	2	18	11	973	110	815	48	3
Lower Moreland Township	13,204	4	0	0	1	3	122	20	97	5	0
Lower Paxton Township	49,296	87	0	25	10	52	665	70	573	22	2
Lower Pottsgrove Township	12,128	39	0	1	8	30	136	15	119	2	0
Lower Providence Township	27,051	33	0	1	0	32	154	20	130	4	1
Lower Salford Township	15,440	7	0	0	0	7	60	5	51	4	0
Lower Saucon Township	10,824	10	0	0	0	10	76	13	57	6	0
Lower Southampton Township	19,230	68	0	4	4	60	278	31	227	20	1
Lower Swatara Township	8,904	16	0	0	1	15	72	15	57	0	3
Lower Windsor Township	7,574	6	0	1	0	5	33	8	20	5	0
Luzerne	2,806	2	0	0	0	2	21	3	18	0	0
Luzerne Township	5,940	0	0	0	0	0	0	0	0	0	0
Lykens	1,770	0	0	0	0	0	1	1	0	0	0
Macungie	3,179	0	0	0	0	0	2	1	1	0	0
Mahanoy City	3,958	4	0	0	0	4	19	6	11	2	0
Mahanoy Township	3,186	1	0	1	0	0	3	0	3	0	0
Mahoning Township, Carbon County	4,209	13	0	3	1	9	146	16	127	3	0
Mahoning Township, Lawrence County	2,911	1	0	0	0	1	0	0	0	0	0
Mahoning Township, Montour County	4,163	15	0	1	0	14	40	6	32	2	0
Main Township	1,278	0	0	0	0	0	0	0	0	0	0
Malvern	3,510	2	0	0	0	2	22	0	21	1	0
Manheim	4,890	16	0	0	3	13	113	28	79	6	1
Manheim Township	40,395	50	0	4	8	38	556	42	500	14	3
Manor	3,369	1	0	1	0	0	4	2	2	0	0
Manor Township, Armstrong County	4,074	4	0	0	0	4	16	0	16	0	0
Manor Township, Lancaster County	21,090	24	0	2	1	21	129	15	110	4	0
Mansfield	3,034	2	0	0	0	2	6	0	6	0	1
Marcus Hook	2,402	29	0	1	2	26	37	4	31	2	0
Marietta	2,627	9	0	0	1	8	28	4	22	2	0
Marion Township, Beaver County	878	0	0	0	0	0	2	0	2	0	0
Marion Township, Berks County	1,915	1	0	0	0	1	1	0	1	0	0
Marlborough Township	3,366	1	0	0	0	1	9	3	6	0	0
Marple Township	23,872	4	0	0	2	2	355	13	335	7	0
Mars	1,628	1	0	0	1	0	5	0	5	0	0
Martinsburg	1,873	0	0	0	0	0	9	0	9	0	0
Marysville	2,553	0	0	0	0	0	22	1	21	0	0
Masontown	3,305	8	1	1	2	4	61	4	53	4	0
Mayfield	1,697	0	0	0	0	0	0	0	0	0	0
McAdoo	2,166	2	0	0	1	1	29	2	26	1	0
McCandless	28,475	5	0	0	2	3	140	3	133	4	0
McDonald Borough	2,066	3	0	0	0	3	29	2	26	1	0
McKeesport	20,915	320	4	9	24	283	506	117	349	40	16
McKees Rocks	5,929	100	5	8	27	60	280	60	206	14	3
McSherrystown	3,076	3	0	1	0	2	5	1	4	0	1
Meadville	12,917	21	1	3	9	8	157	21	127	9	2

Table 8. Offenses Known to Law Enforcement, by Selected State and City, 2018—Continued

(Number.)

State/city	Population	Violent crime	Murder and nonnegligent manslaughter	Rape[1]	Robbery	Aggravated assault	Property crime	Burglary	Larceny-theft	Motor vehicle theft	Arson[2]
Mechanicsburg	9,021	8	0	4	3	1	155	10	144	1	5
Media	5,367	32	0	0	2	30	57	6	50	1	0
Mercer	1,876	3	0	0	0	3	1	1	0	0	0
Meshoppen	1,442	7	0	0	0	7	23	4	16	3	0
Meyersdale	2,038	0	0	0	0	0	0	0	0	0	0
Middleburg	1,308	8	0	0	2	6	11	5	6	0	1
Middlesex Township, Butler County	5,636	2	0	0	0	2	19	0	19	0	0
Middlesex Township, Cumberland County	7,499	10	0	2	5	3	96	8	82	6	0
Middletown	9,319	42	0	8	5	29	56	9	47	0	1
Middletown Township	45,185	33	0	6	12	15	610	44	530	36	1
Midland	2,495	7	0	0	1	6	29	3	24	2	0
Midway	876	0	0	0	0	0	5	2	3	0	0
Mifflinburg	3,512	3	0	0	0	3	27	0	27	0	1
Mifflin County Regional	16,941	22	0	2	1	19	129	18	109	2	0
Milford	973	2	0	1	0	1	19	4	14	1	0
Millbourne	1,159	7	0	0	5	2	37	8	28	1	0
Millcreek Township, Erie County	53,422	137	2	14	11	110	564	88	464	12	3
Millcreek Township, Lebanon County	5,714	0	0	0	0	0	25	5	20	0	0
Millersburg	2,541	6	0	0	1	5	33	10	23	0	0
Millersville	8,380	10	0	5	1	4	75	13	58	4	0
Mill Hall	1,611	0	0	0	0	0	0	0	0	0	0
Millvale	3,635	4	0	0	0	4	90	5	84	1	0
Milton	6,819	66	0	3	2	61	87	18	69	0	2
Minersville	4,160	9	0	1	0	8	22	0	22	0	0
Mohnton	3,064	2	0	0	2	0	18	6	10	2	0
Monaca	5,492	8	0	0	3	5	62	7	47	8	0
Monessen	7,287	75	1	2	14	58	138	22	110	6	1
Monongahela	4,125	16	0	1	1	14	105	19	80	6	0
Monroeville	27,628	63	0	7	5	51	481	21	434	26	0
Montgomery	1,518	1	0	0	0	1	5	0	5	0	0
Montgomery Township	26,299	7	0	0	0	7	338	12	320	6	0
Montoursville	4,420	4	0	0	0	4	68	4	62	2	0
Montour Township	1,299	1	0	0	0	1	7	2	5	0	0
Montrose	1,484	0	0	0	0	0	0	0	0	0	0
Moon Township	25,758	20	0	4	7	9	233	22	209	2	0
Moore Township	9,343	4	0	0	0	4	59	12	41	6	0
Moosic	5,745	25	0	2	1	22	74	7	64	3	1
Morrisville	8,557	10	0	0	4	6	188	17	143	28	0
Morton	2,686	5	0	0	1	4	91	6	85	0	0
Moscow	1,927	4	0	1	0	3	20	2	17	1	0
Mount Carmel	5,618	60	0	3	0	57	74	21	53	0	0
Mount Carmel Township	3,007	25	0	0	1	24	21	4	17	0	0
Mount Gretna Borough	206	0	0	0	0	0	0	0	0	0	0
Mount Holly Springs	2,049	3	0	2	0	1	22	5	17	0	0
Mount Joy	8,332	26	0	4	2	20	90	8	80	2	0
Mount Lebanon	32,239	23	0	2	3	18	241	18	213	10	0
Mount Oliver	3,303	36	0	2	7	27	98	14	80	4	1
Mount Pleasant	4,273	17	0	0	0	17	34	4	30	0	0
Mount Pleasant Township	3,503	1	0	0	0	1	14	1	12	1	0
Mount Union	2,367	2	0	0	1	1	7	1	6	0	0
Mountville	2,874	3	0	0	0	3	17	3	14	0	0
Muhlenberg Township	20,303	22	0	2	10	10	503	30	454	19	0
Muncy	2,419	0	0	0	0	0	5	0	5	0	0
Muncy Township	1,063	2	0	0	0	2	69	0	69	0	0
Murrysville	19,759	4	0	0	1	3	92	11	81	0	0
Nanticoke	10,253	15	0	2	7	6	154	18	124	12	1
Nanty Glo	2,512	1	0	1	0	0	8	1	7	0	0
Nazareth	5,706	4	0	1	1	2	50	4	46	0	0
Nescopeck	1,540	0	0	0	0	0	9	2	7	0	0
Neshannock Township	9,223	5	0	0	2	3	47	11	33	3	0
Nesquehoning	3,231	13	0	0	1	12	43	6	35	2	0
Nether Providence Township	13,770	12	0	2	0	10	135	9	124	2	0
Neville Township	1,057	2	0	0	0	2	22	1	21	0	0
New Beaver	1,425	0	0	0	0	0	1	0	0	1	0
New Berlin	859	1	0	0	0	1	1	1	0	0	0
Newberry Township	15,749	22	0	1	1	20	200	28	169	3	2
New Brighton	8,807	38	0	3	8	27	233	24	205	4	0
New Britain Township	11,252	3	1	1	0	1	56	4	51	1	0
New Castle	21,910	123	4	14	43	62	596	179	387	30	17
New Castle Township	391	0	0	0	0	0	0	0	0	0	0
New Cumberland	7,323	4	0	1	1	2	57	3	53	1	0
New Florence	653	0	0	0	0	0	0	0	0	0	0
New Hanover Township	13,201	2	0	0	0	2	69	7	55	7	0
New Holland	5,507	7	0	0	1	6	64	2	59	3	0
New Hope	2,515	8	0	0	1	7	35	2	28	5	1
New Kensington	12,377	70	1	9	36	24	382	68	292	22	0
Newport Township	5,386	3	0	0	0	3	40	13	27	0	0
New Sewickley Township	7,249	5	0	2	0	3	54	11	39	4	0
Newtown	2,251	1	0	0	0	1	19	6	13	0	0

Table 8. Offenses Known to Law Enforcement, by Selected State and City, 2018—Continued

(Number.)

State/city	Population	Violent crime	Murder and nonnegligent manslaughter	Rape[1]	Robbery	Aggravated assault	Property crime	Burglary	Larceny-theft	Motor vehicle theft	Arson[2]
Newtown Township, Bucks County	22,880	5	0	0	1	4	128	8	115	5	1
Newtown Township, Delaware County	13,571	5	0	0	2	3	100	5	85	10	0
Newville	1,345	0	0	0	0	0	0	0	0	0	0
New Wilmington	2,188	4	0	1	0	3	21	1	20	0	0
Norristown	34,531	139	5	10	68	56	511	86	376	49	2
Northampton	9,884	2	1	0	0	1	79	8	68	3	0
Northampton Township	39,289	12	2	1	0	9	144	20	121	3	0
North Beaver	3,967	0	0	0	0	0	3	1	2	0	0
North Belle Vernon	1,861	5	0	0	1	4	36	1	35	0	0
North Buffalo	2,933	0	0	0	0	0	0	0	0	0	0
North Catasauqua	2,837	2	0	0	0	2	41	4	33	4	0
North Cornwall Township	7,868	11	0	0	1	10	112	3	106	3	0
North Coventry Township	8,012	2	0	0	1	1	156	14	140	2	0
North East, Erie County	4,105	4	0	2	0	2	77	3	73	1	0
Northeastern Regional	11,878	7	0	3	0	4	127	13	113	1	0
Northeast Police Department	409	0	0	0	0	0	0	0	0	0	0
Northern Berks Regional	13,366	8	0	2	1	5	118	16	93	9	1
Northern Cambria Borough	3,546	27	0	0	0	27	36	12	23	1	0
Northern Lancaster County Regional	36,089	20	1	2	3	14	136	25	97	14	0
Northern Regional	35,447	6	0	1	0	5	201	0	198	3	0
Northern York County Regional	69,814	36	0	4	10	22	623	83	506	34	4
North Fayette Township	14,935	6	0	0	0	6	214	9	205	0	2
North Hopewell Township	2,804	3	0	1	0	2	8	2	5	1	0
North Huntingdon Township	30,414	15	0	1	1	13	291	31	245	15	1
North Lebanon Township	12,042	29	0	1	0	28	176	14	158	4	0
North Londonderry Township	8,523	1	0	0	0	1	120	5	115	0	0
North Middleton Township	11,682	6	0	1	0	5	67	6	60	1	0
North Sewickley Township	5,406	4	0	0	0	4	47	9	33	5	0
North Strabane Township	14,703	27	0	2	0	25	86	4	80	2	1
Northumberland	3,655	4	0	0	1	3	6	6	0	0	0
North Union Township	1,409	0	0	0	0	0	0	0	0	0	0
North Versailles Township	12,127	35	0	2	4	29	85	10	70	5	1
North Wales	3,271	5	0	0	0	5	27	1	26	0	0
Northwest Lancaster County Regional	20,029	4	0	2	0	2	100	0	93	7	0
North Woodbury	2,614	0	0	0	0	0	12	2	10	0	0
Norwood	5,896	4	0	1	1	2	58	5	52	1	1
Oakdale	1,456	0	0	0	0	0	1	1	0	0	0
Oakland	566	1	0	0	0	1	2	0	2	0	0
Oakmont	6,466	9	0	0	2	7	82	5	71	6	0
O'Hara Township	8,724	13	0	0	0	13	47	2	43	2	0
Ohio Township	6,874	3	1	0	0	2	94	1	93	0	0
Ohioville	3,382	4	0	1	0	3	12	2	10	0	0
Oil City	9,769	18	1	1	0	16	126	10	103	13	0
Old Forge	7,885	9	0	1	1	7	72	12	55	5	0
Old Lycoming Township	4,927	2	0	1	0	1	100	5	89	6	6
Olyphant	5,026	10	0	0	1	9	13	1	11	1	0
Orangeville Area	1,731	0	0	0	0	0	1	0	1	0	0
Orwigsburg	2,956	3	0	0	0	3	25	0	25	0	0
Osceola Township	629	0	0	0	0	0	0	0	0	0	0
Otto Eldred Regional	2,260	0	0	0	0	0	5	1	4	0	0
Overfield Township	2,751	0	0	0	0	0	0	0	0	0	0
Oxford	5,648	14	0	2	1	11	63	8	54	1	0
Palmerton	5,289	13	0	0	2	11	89	8	80	1	0
Palmer Township	21,512	13	0	2	3	8	264	29	231	4	0
Palmyra	7,556	19	0	0	1	18	88	16	67	5	2
Palo Alto	982	0	0	0	0	0	0	0	0	0	0
Parker	806	0	0	0	0	0	0	0	0	0	0
Parkesburg	3,876	7	1	0	1	5	31	6	22	3	0
Parkside	2,331	19	2	1	1	15	59	10	46	3	0
Parks Township	2,571	0	0	0	0	0	0	0	0	0	0
Patterson Township	4,218	1	0	0	0	1	43	4	30	9	0
Patton	1,627	1	0	1	0	0	5	0	5	0	0
Patton Township	16,142	5	0	1	1	3	125	5	119	1	0
Penbrook	2,985	7	0	3	1	3	44	8	30	6	0
Penn	470	1	0	0	0	1	0	0	0	0	0
Penndel	2,185	7	0	0	3	4	10	1	6	3	0
Penn Hills	41,143	169	2	8	37	122	674	114	502	58	3
Pennridge Regional	11,013	5	0	0	0	5	53	13	39	1	0
Penn Township, Butler County	4,916	1	0	0	0	1	39	7	30	2	0
Penn Township, Westmoreland County	19,297	30	0	0	0	30	1	1	0	0	0
Penn Township, York County	16,511	22	0	0	3	19	143	11	132	0	0
Pequea Township	5,022	7	0	0	1	6	42	9	29	4	0
Perkasie	8,561	14	0	0	5	9	128	10	114	4	0
Perryopolis	1,690	5	0	0	1	4	2	0	2	0	1
Peters Township	22,136	12	1	1	3	7	135	14	119	2	1
Philadelphia	1,586,916	14,420	351	1,095	5,262	7,712	49,145	6,497	36,968	5,680	430
Phoenixville	17,012	32	1	2	1	28	192	8	181	3	0
Pine Creek Township	3,271	0	0	0	0	0	5	1	4	0	0

Table 8. Offenses Known to Law Enforcement, by Selected State and City, 2018—Continued

(Number.)

State/city	Population	Violent crime	Murder and nonnegligent manslaughter	Rape[1]	Robbery	Aggravated assault	Property crime	Burglary	Larceny-theft	Motor vehicle theft	Arson[2]
Pine Grove	2,079	0	0	0	0	0	0	0	0	0	0
Pitcairn	3,197	47	0	3	9	35	81	18	60	3	2
Pittsburgh	302,544	1,751	57	121	696	877	9,125	1,341	7,055	729	102
Pittston	7,689	16	0	3	1	12	133	15	113	5	0
Pittston Township	3,389	3	0	0	0	3	42	2	34	6	0
Plains Township	9,725	19	0	0	3	16	168	18	137	13	0
Pleasant Hills	8,113	0	0	0	0	0	55	6	47	2	0
Plum	27,274	65	0	3	5	57	150	19	116	15	0
Plumstead Township	14,244	11	0	4	0	7	66	7	57	2	1
Plymouth	5,789	42	1	2	7	32	115	22	88	5	0
Plymouth Township, Mont-gomery County	17,756	26	0	6	8	12	448	34	399	15	3
Pocono Mountain Regional	42,712	83	2	28	10	43	630	177	423	30	4
Pocono Township	10,855	29	0	3	3	23	241	23	215	3	1
Point Township	3,633	9	0	0	0	9	22	1	19	2	1
Polk	778	1	0	0	0	1	1	1	0	0	0
Portage	2,419	1	0	0	0	1	15	2	13	0	0
Port Allegany	2,021	0	0	0	0	0	7	0	7	0	0
Portersville	229	0	0	0	0	0	0	0	0	0	0
Portland	516	1	0	0	0	1	2	0	2	0	0
Port Vue	3,686	7	0	0	0	7	25	4	18	3	0
Pottstown	22,792	196	2	35	36	123	753	113	606	34	2
Pottsville	13,529	44	0	8	4	32	227	29	188	10	2
Pringle	957	1	0	0	0	1	31	2	28	1	0
Prospect	1,117	0	0	0	0	0	0	0	0	0	0
Prospect Park	6,496	20	0	1	1	18	65	5	57	3	1
Pulaski Township, Lawrence County	3,290	9	0	1	0	8	29	6	19	4	0
Punxsutawney	5,764	5	0	0	0	5	18	1	17	0	0
Pymatuning Township	3,090	5	0	0	0	5	50	9	40	1	0
Quakertown	8,824	38	0	3	2	33	147	15	127	5	4
Quarryville	2,787	3	0	0	0	3	52	5	46	1	0
Raccoon Township	2,925	0	0	0	0	0	18	1	17	0	0
Radnor Township	31,935	31	4	0	1	26	223	20	192	11	0
Ralpho Township	4,242	9	0	0	0	9	9	3	5	1	0
Rankin	2,059	26	0	1	3	22	26	9	16	1	1
Reading	88,466	621	19	53	221	328	1,984	603	1,192	189	17
Reading Township	5,837	2	0	0	0	2	6	1	5	0	0
Redstone Township	4,225	1	1	0	0	0	4	1	3	0	0
Reilly Township	688	0	0	0	0	0	1	0	1	0	0
Renovo	1,219	2	0	1	0	1	13	0	12	1	0
Resa Regional	2,490	1	0	0	0	1	11	2	9	0	0
Reserve Township	3,238	2	0	0	2	0	25	3	22	0	0
Reynoldsville	2,660	4	0	1	0	3	7	0	7	0	1
Rice Township	3,559	2	0	1	0	1	18	4	14	0	0
Richland Township, Bucks County	13,388	18	0	9	5	4	180	28	150	2	0
Richland Township, Cambria County	11,940	7	0	5	1	1	420	17	402	1	0
Ridgway	3,764	2	0	1	0	1	90	9	78	3	0
Ridley Park	7,045	14	0	1	3	10	68	7	55	6	0
Ridley Township	31,190	27	0	0	9	18	323	39	270	14	1
Ringtown	784	0	0	0	0	0	1	0	1	0	0
Riverside	1,873	3	0	0	0	3	11	2	9	0	0
Roaring Brook Township	1,941	0	0	0	0	0	9	2	7	0	0
Roaring Creek Township	534	1	0	0	0	1	0	0	0	0	0
Roaring Spring	2,467	0	0	0	0	0	21	2	18	1	0
Robeson Township	7,432	9	0	0	0	9	42	16	23	3	0
Robinson Township, Allegheny County	13,673	20	0	2	3	15	272	12	252	8	0
Robinson Township, Washington County	1,900	5	0	0	0	5	13	1	12	0	0
Rochester	3,477	22	0	9	3	10	142	22	111	9	1
Rochester Township	2,667	4	0	0	2	2	15	1	14	0	0
Rockledge	2,542	3	0	0	1	2	52	4	45	3	0
Rockwood	830	0	0	0	0	0	0	0	0	0	0
Roseto	1,554	2	0	0	0	2	12	1	9	2	0
Rosslyn Farms	413	0	0	0	0	0	0	0	0	0	0
Ross Township	30,541	20	1	1	5	13	582	30	536	16	1
Rostraver Township	11,023	8	0	2	3	3	260	13	244	3	2
Royalton	1,041	0	0	0	0	0	0	0	0	0	0
Royersford	4,777	3	0	1	2	0	43	2	41	0	0
Rural Valley	820	0	0	0	0	0	1	0	1	0	0
Rush Township	3,260	5	0	2	0	3	57	3	54	0	1
Ryan Township	2,510	0	0	0	0	0	1	1	0	0	0
Sadsbury Township, Chester County	4,017	3	0	0	0	3	19	5	13	1	0
Salem Township, Luzerne County	4,192	2	0	1	0	1	20	7	12	1	0
Salisbury Township	13,977	8	0	1	3	4	154	15	133	6	1
Saltsburg	811	0	0	0	0	0	6	1	5	0	0
Sandy Lake	635	0	0	0	0	0	5	1	4	0	0
Sandy Township	10,475	31	0	2	0	29	134	17	117	0	10

Table 8. Offenses Known to Law Enforcement, by Selected State and City, 2018—Continued

(Number.)

State/city	Population	Violent crime	Murder and nonnegligent manslaughter	Rape[1]	Robbery	Aggravated assault	Property crime	Burglary	Larceny-theft	Motor vehicle theft	Arson[2]
Sankertown	627	0	0	0	0	0	0	0	0	0	0
Saxonburg	1,456	0	0	0	0	0	0	0	0	0	0
Sayre	6,410	16	0	3	0	13	42	4	37	1	0
Schuylkill Haven	5,116	9	4	1	0	4	79	5	74	0	0
Schuylkill Township, Chester County	8,658	2	0	0	0	2	33	1	32	0	0
Scottdale	4,151	19	0	0	5	14	87	8	76	3	0
Scott Township, Allegheny County	16,567	18	0	0	3	15	157	17	139	1	0
Scott Township, Columbia County	5,016	1	0	0	0	1	66	1	65	0	0
Scott Township, Lackawanna County	4,753	1	1	0	0	0	0	0	0	0	1
Scranton	77,827	811	2	43	62	704	1,505	340	1,080	85	18
Selinsgrove	5,962	49	0	5	2	42	79	11	66	2	0
Seward	469	1	0	0	0	1	0	0	0	0	0
Sewickley	4,381	6	0	0	2	4	41	1	40	0	0
Sewickley Heights	810	0	0	0	0	0	11	0	11	0	0
Shade Township	2,602	0	0	0	0	0	1	1	0	0	0
Shaler Township	28,039	20	0	1	2	17	211	35	169	7	3
Shamokin	7,020	57	1	4	4	48	221	40	165	16	1
Shamokin Dam	1,751	11	0	0	0	11	2	0	2	0	0
Sharon	13,154	65	3	14	14	34	414	117	279	18	7
Sharon Hill	5,705	39	0	2	7	30	180	13	151	16	0
Sharpsburg	3,344	18	0	0	0	18	27	4	18	5	0
Sharpsville	4,131	8	0	1	1	6	66	14	52	0	0
Shenandoah	4,779	46	0	2	4	40	56	20	35	1	1
Shenango Township, Lawrence County	7,253	6	0	0	2	4	68	17	49	2	0
Shenango Township, Mercer County	3,720	12	0	3	1	8	28	5	23	0	0
Shillington	5,289	4	0	1	0	3	72	11	58	3	0
Shinglehouse	1,068	5	0	0	0	5	0	0	0	0	0
Shippensburg	5,584	1	0	0	1	0	46	5	37	4	1
Shippingport	199	0	0	0	0	0	0	0	0	0	0
Shiremanstown	1,576	1	0	0	0	1	1	1	0	0	0
Shohola Township	2,399	0	0	0	0	0	12	4	8	0	0
Silver Lake Township	1,600	0	0	0	0	0	5	0	4	1	0
Silver Spring Township	18,078	3	0	2	1	0	67	2	64	1	0
Sinking Spring	4,128	3	0	0	2	1	45	8	33	4	0
Slate Belt Regional	12,451	35	0	8	0	27	99	9	86	4	1
Slatington	4,322	2	0	0	2	0	56	7	49	0	0
Slippery Rock	3,537	2	0	0	0	2	33	3	30	0	0
Smethport	1,541	3	0	1	0	2	7	0	7	0	0
Smithton Borough	949	0	0	0	0	0	2	1	1	0	0
Smith Township	4,367	14	0	0	0	14	25	7	13	5	0
Solebury Township	8,585	3	0	0	0	3	30	2	26	2	1
Somerset	5,899	16	0	2	2	12	99	15	80	4	13
Souderton	7,063	17	0	2	1	14	51	13	35	3	0
South Abington Township	8,904	9	0	0	0	9	67	9	55	3	0
South Annville Township	2,992	0	0	0	0	0	20	2	18	0	0
South Beaver Township	2,613	4	0	0	0	4	5	1	4	0	0
South Buffalo Township	2,533	0	0	0	0	0	5	1	3	1	0
South Centre Township	4,191	5	0	0	0	5	6	0	6	0	0
South Coatesville	1,467	18	0	0	0	18	29	7	21	1	0
South Connellsville Borough	1,884	0	0	0	0	0	0	0	0	0	0
Southern Chester County Regional	14,974	16	0	3	3	10	71	17	47	7	0
Southern Regional York County	11,515	15	0	4	2	9	93	13	79	1	2
South Fayette Township	15,788	2	0	0	1	1	59	6	52	1	0
South Fork	851	0	0	0	0	0	0	0	0	0	0
South Greensburg	2,003	1	0	0	0	1	34	4	30	0	0
South Heidelberg Township	7,378	2	0	0	0	2	14	0	13	1	0
South Heights	450	0	0	0	0	0	0	0	0	0	0
South Lebanon Township	9,935	3	0	0	0	3	62	5	57	0	1
South Londonderry Township	8,427	1	0	0	1	0	36	7	29	0	1
South Park Township	13,332	3	0	0	0	3	23	5	17	1	1
South Strabane Township	9,467	19	0	2	7	10	355	5	342	8	0
Southwestern Regional	17,789	23	0	9	0	14	90	11	72	7	0
Southwest Greensburg	2,033	6	0	0	1	5	18	2	14	2	0
Southwest Regional, Washington County	132	2	0	0	0	2	7	2	3	2	0
South Whitehall Township	19,918	13	1	1	8	3	483	46	417	20	0
South Williamsport	6,109	8	0	2	2	4	40	8	32	0	0
Spring City	3,329	5	0	2	1	2	48	7	33	8	2
Springdale	3,318	8	0	4	0	4	30	2	27	1	0
Springdale Township	1,590	1	1	0	0	0	6	0	6	0	0
Springettsbury Township	26,833	43	0	5	9	29	845	29	795	21	1
Springfield Township, Bucks County	5,045	6	0	0	0	6	35	9	26	0	0
Springfield Township, Delaware County	24,259	13	0	4	3	6	507	27	469	11	0

Table 8. Offenses Known to Law Enforcement, by Selected State and City, 2018—Continued

(Number.)

State/city	Population	Violent crime	Murder and nonnegligent manslaughter	Rape[1]	Robbery	Aggravated assault	Property crime	Burglary	Larceny-theft	Motor vehicle theft	Arson[2]
Springfield Township, Montgomery County	19,751	24	0	0	5	19	193	11	174	8	0
Spring Garden Township	13,120	51	0	2	6	43	339	40	284	15	0
Spring Township, Berks County	27,528	21	1	0	6	14	273	19	249	5	0
Spring Township, Centre County	7,905	3	0	0	0	3	16	2	14	0	0
State College	58,781	20	0	1	5	14	448	32	411	5	5
St. Clair Boro	2,835	3	0	0	1	2	55	0	55	0	0
St. Clair Township	1,439	0	0	0	0	0	1	1	0	0	0
Steelton	5,944	39	1	5	5	28	133	11	101	21	2
St. Marys City	12,279	13	0	3	2	8	138	14	121	3	1
Stockertown	917	2	0	0	0	2	1	0	1	0	0
Stoneboro	990	0	0	0	0	0	2	1	1	0	2
Stowe Township	6,179	27	4	0	0	23	124	22	93	9	0
Strasburg	2,988	4	0	2	1	1	25	7	16	2	0
Stroud Area Regional	34,887	66	3	13	12	38	944	66	851	27	0
Sugarcreek	4,969	3	0	1	0	2	27	6	20	1	0
Sugarloaf Township, Luzerne County	3,982	1	0	0	0	1	41	3	37	1	0
Sugar Notch	960	5	0	0	0	5	6	3	3	0	0
Summerhill Township	2,281	1	0	0	0	1	18	3	15	0	0
Summit Hill	2,934	5	0	0	0	5	3	1	0	2	0
Summit Township	2,141	0	0	0	0	0	0	0	0	0	0
Sunbury	9,469	90	0	1	8	81	87	16	67	4	0
Susquehanna	1,514	3	0	0	0	3	17	2	13	2	0
Susquehanna Regional	8,455	18	0	4	1	13	58	10	45	3	0
Susquehanna Township, Dauphin County	25,197	46	0	6	9	31	296	39	236	21	0
Swarthmore	6,266	4	0	0	0	4	33	8	23	2	0
Swatara Township	26,532	94	3	9	21	61	866	46	808	12	2
Sweden Township	828	0	0	0	0	0	0	0	0	0	0
Swissvale	8,713	21	0	0	9	12	143	22	111	10	2
Swoyersville	4,949	3	1	0	0	2	14	2	12	0	0
Sykesville	1,116	0	0	0	0	0	0	0	0	0	0
Tamaqua	6,698	12	0	1	4	7	120	5	112	3	1
Tarentum	4,401	13	0	0	0	13	46	10	33	3	0
Tatamy	1,135	0	0	0	0	0	1	0	1	0	0
Taylor	5,889	38	1	1	4	32	135	20	105	10	0
Telford	4,849	9	0	1	1	7	40	4	32	4	0
Terre Hill	1,440	1	0	1	0	0	13	2	11	0	0
Throop	3,892	15	0	0	1	14	33	8	21	4	0
Tiadaghton Valley Regional	7,586	15	0	2	0	13	31	2	29	0	0
Tilden Township	3,607	1	0	1	0	0	42	0	42	0	0
Tinicum Township, Bucks County	3,970	4	0	1	0	3	15	4	11	0	0
Tinicum Township, Delaware County	4,108	21	2	3	0	16	98	2	84	12	0
Tioga	645	3	0	0	0	3	1	0	1	0	0
Titusville	5,286	7	0	2	1	4	107	6	94	7	0
Towamencin Township	18,443	12	0	1	1	10	45	3	42	0	12
Towanda	2,828	14	0	0	0	14	82	8	70	4	1
Tower City	1,281	0	0	0	0	0	2	0	1	1	0
Trafford	3,065	14	0	0	0	14	37	5	30	2	0
Trainer	1,847	10	1	0	2	7	52	8	38	6	0
Tredyffrin Township	29,575	12	0	1	2	9	238	14	220	4	0
Tremont	1,675	5	0	0	0	5	11	2	6	3	0
Troy	1,246	1	0	1	0	0	22	1	21	0	0
Tullytown	1,839	8	0	0	1	7	110	3	107	0	0
Tulpehocken Township	3,368	0	0	0	0	0	9	1	6	2	0
Tunkhannock	1,730	2	0	1	0	1	5	3	2	0	0
Tunkhannock Township, Wyoming County	6,147	3	0	1	0	2	45	7	34	4	1
Turtle Creek	5,192	2	0	0	1	1	12	2	10	0	1
Tyrone	5,210	18	0	2	0	16	74	8	66	0	0
Union City	3,162	1	0	1	0	0	42	4	38	0	0
Uniontown	9,751	136	1	2	22	111	455	72	369	14	18
Union Township, Lawrence County	4,921	16	0	1	5	10	289	33	256	0	0
Union Township, Schuylkill County	1,209	0	0	0	0	0	0	0	0	0	0
Upland	3,250	59	3	4	3	49	104	16	71	17	0
Upper Allen Township	20,123	7	0	5	1	1	68	10	58	0	0
Upper Burrell Township	2,231	0	0	0	0	0	11	3	8	0	0
Upper Chichester Township	17,002	43	0	2	13	28	303	23	267	13	0
Upper Darby Township	82,931	439	4	9	186	240	873	133	534	206	1
Upper Gwynedd Township	15,958	9	1	0	0	8	52	4	48	0	1
Upper Leacock Township	8,963	7	0	3	4	0	71	9	60	2	1
Upper Macungie Township	24,995	7	0	1	3	3	164	19	134	11	1
Upper Makefield Township	8,479	5	0	0	1	4	30	8	22	0	0
Upper Merion Township	30,673	23	0	4	10	9	1,105	30	1,056	19	5
Upper Moreland Township	24,182	22	0	3	9	10	419	29	373	17	1
Upper Nazareth Township	6,947	6	0	0	0	6	41	2	37	2	0

Table 8. Offenses Known to Law Enforcement, by Selected State and City, 2018—Continued

(Number.)

State/city	Population	Violent crime	Murder and nonnegligent manslaughter	Rape[1]	Robbery	Aggravated assault	Property crime	Burglary	Larceny-theft	Motor vehicle theft	Arson[2]
Upper Perkiomen	3,877	1	0	0	0	1	27	0	26	1	0
Upper Pottsgrove Township	5,617	13	0	0	2	11	46	5	39	2	0
Upper Providence Township, Delaware County	10,478	4	0	0	1	3	18	3	15	0	0
Upper Providence Township, Montgomery County	24,445	11	0	4	0	7	250	16	229	5	1
Upper Saucon Township	17,121	2	0	0	0	2	79	15	64	0	0
Upper Southampton Township	15,038	6	0	1	1	4	87	18	68	1	0
Upper St. Clair Township	19,758	8	0	0	1	7	119	4	114	1	0
Upper Uwchlan Township	11,506	0	0	0	0	0	56	1	53	2	0
Upper Yoder Township	5,093	2	0	0	0	2	4	1	3	0	0
Uwchlan Township	19,044	16	0	1	1	14	111	15	95	1	0
Valley Township	7,869	20	0	1	1	18	64	15	48	1	0
Vandergrift	4,917	16	1	0	1	14	5	2	3	0	1
Vandling	707	3	0	0	0	3	5	1	2	2	0
Vernon Township	5,432	2	0	0	0	2	64	1	63	0	0
Verona	2,402	5	0	0	2	3	83	3	78	2	0
Versailles	1,471	14	0	0	0	14	27	4	20	3	0
Vintondale	380	0	0	0	0	0	0	0	0	0	0
Walker Township	998	1	0	0	0	1	0	0	0	0	0
Walnutport	2,088	0	0	0	0	0	0	0	0	0	0
Wampum	674	0	0	0	0	0	3	3	0	0	0
Warminster Township	32,395	25	1	8	11	5	282	18	258	6	0
Warren	9,088	58	0	4	2	52	190	20	168	2	3
Warrington Township	24,582	18	0	0	5	13	158	7	147	4	0
Warwick Township, Bucks County	14,618	12	0	1	0	11	54	4	50	0	0
Washington Township, Fayette County	3,662	7	0	2	0	5	22	4	17	1	0
Washington Township, Franklin County	14,671	12	0	3	5	4	214	20	190	4	1
Washington Township, Northampton County	5,228	4	0	0	0	4	40	5	34	1	0
Washington Township, Westmoreland County	7,103	9	0	0	1	8	38	7	30	1	2
Washington, Washington County	13,505	101	1	17	32	51	418	70	298	50	0
Watsontown	2,275	9	0	2	0	7	30	6	24	0	0
Waverly Township	1,674	1	0	0	0	1	3	2	1	0	0
Waymart	1,264	0	0	0	0	0	5	0	5	0	0
Waynesboro	10,920	13	0	4	3	6	189	27	155	7	3
Waynesburg	3,960	14	0	3	3	8	79	7	67	5	0
Wayne Township	2,488	0	0	0	0	0	3	1	2	0	0
Weatherly	2,443	47	0	1	0	46	45	13	32	0	0
Weissport	394	0	0	0	0	0	1	1	0	0	0
Wellsboro	3,228	6	0	1	0	5	13	1	12	0	0
Wesleyville	3,157	4	0	2	1	1	87	10	73	4	1
West Brandywine Township	7,495	11	0	1	2	8	59	15	39	5	0
West Brownsville	965	1	0	0	1	0	41	0	41	0	0
West Caln Township	9,087	41	1	2	0	38	48	12	29	7	0
West Carroll Township	1,212	4	0	0	0	4	4	2	2	0	0
West Chester	20,299	37	1	7	11	18	309	46	244	19	0
West Cocalico Township	7,469	7	0	1	0	6	20	7	10	3	1
West Conshohocken	1,415	1	0	0	0	1	12	2	9	1	0
West Cornwall Township	2,038	2	0	0	0	2	0	0	0	0	0
West Deer Township	11,973	1	0	0	0	1	48	4	41	3	0
West Earl Township	8,503	3	0	0	3	0	56	11	40	5	0
Western Berks Regional	4,833	6	0	0	2	4	19	10	8	1	0
West Fallowfield Township	2,597	1	1	0	0	0	17	0	17	0	0
West Goshen Township	23,160	34	1	5	4	24	223	11	207	5	0
West Hazleton	4,466	21	0	1	1	19	90	13	70	7	0
West Hempfield Township	16,598	18	1	2	8	7	143	11	131	1	0
West Hills Regional	10,032	6	0	0	2	4	82	10	72	0	0
West Homestead	1,891	4	1	0	1	2	16	1	15	0	0
West Lampeter Township	16,092	9	0	0	1	8	93	13	73	7	0
West Lebanon Township	822	0	0	0	0	0	44	2	42	0	0
West Leechburg	1,230	0	0	0	0	0	0	0	0	0	0
West Mahanoy Township	2,723	2	0	0	0	2	8	1	6	1	0
West Manchester Township	18,833	27	0	4	3	20	551	39	489	23	0
West Manheim Township	8,497	3	0	0	0	3	73	8	62	3	0
West Mead Township	5,082	9	0	0	0	9	38	5	32	1	0
West Mifflin	19,773	29	0	1	2	26	93	4	88	1	0
West Newton	2,484	10	0	2	1	7	27	6	19	2	0
West Norriton Township	15,708	32	0	2	8	22	259	20	233	6	0
West Nottingham Township	2,707	0	0	0	0	0	0	0	0	0	0
West Penn Township	4,259	1	0	0	0	1	10	3	7	0	0
West Pikeland Township	4,085	6	0	0	0	6	14	3	10	1	0
West Pike Run	1,546	0	0	0	0	0	2	2	0	0	0
West Pittston	4,741	8	0	1	1	6	47	4	42	1	0
West Pottsgrove Township	3,885	5	0	1	2	2	118	16	97	5	0
West Reading	4,209	20	0	0	3	17	117	13	103	1	0
West Sadsbury Township	2,479	2	0	0	0	2	102	0	99	3	0
West Salem Township	3,404	10	0	1	0	9	26	5	20	1	1

Table 8. Offenses Known to Law Enforcement, by Selected State and City, 2018—Continued

(Number.)

State/city	Population	Violent crime	Murder and nonnegligent manslaughter	Rape[1]	Robbery	Aggravated assault	Property crime	Burglary	Larceny-theft	Motor vehicle theft	Arson[2]
West Shore Regional	7,745	12	0	0	7	5	45	10	31	4	0
Westtown-East Goshen Regional	32,253	40	2	4	2	32	192	9	174	9	0
West View	6,578	4	0	0	0	4	110	7	101	2	0
West Vincent Township	5,572	1	0	0	0	1	28	8	20	0	0
West Whiteland Township	18,393	12	0	3	7	2	431	23	405	3	0
West Wyoming	2,671	3	0	1	0	2	7	2	5	0	0
West York	4,578	14	0	4	0	10	145	23	112	10	0
Whitaker Borough	1,239	1	0	0	0	1	12	3	9	0	0
Whitehall	13,703	9	0	0	1	8	41	11	26	4	0
Whitehall Township	27,679	21	0	1	9	11	898	57	818	23	5
White Haven Borough	1,096	2	0	0	0	2	20	5	14	1	0
Whitemarsh Township	17,966	9	1	0	5	3	134	14	115	5	0
White Oak	7,646	7	0	0	3	4	47	6	36	5	0
Whitpain Township	19,326	6	0	0	0	6	165	6	155	4	1
Wiconisco Township	1,199	0	0	0	0	0	3	1	2	0	0
Wilkes-Barre	40,710	210	4	30	85	91	965	204	707	54	5
Wilkes-Barre Township	2,889	8	1	0	5	2	505	16	484	5	0
Wilkins Township	6,184	1	0	0	1	0	92	6	77	9	0
Williamsburg	1,193	4	0	0	0	4	7	0	7	0	0
Williamsport	28,331	71	1	11	12	47	646	84	543	19	6
Willistown Township	10,983	3	0	0	1	2	29	3	24	2	0
Windber	3,867	25	0	1	0	24	25	3	18	4	0
Womelsdorf	2,878	2	0	0	0	2	15	2	11	2	0
Woodward Township	2,378	0	0	0	0	0	0	0	0	0	0
Worthington	596	0	0	0	0	0	2	0	2	0	0
Wright Township	5,611	0	0	0	0	0	29	3	25	1	0
Wyoming	3,008	11	0	1	1	9	60	6	54	0	1
Wyomissing	10,454	13	0	1	3	9	259	14	242	3	0
Yardley	2,489	7	0	0	1	6	5	1	3	1	1
Yeadon	11,512	86	1	5	15	65	384	45	288	51	1
York	44,170	450	20	7	130	293	1,137	197	710	230	10
York Area Regional	55,386	113	0	13	5	95	441	58	355	28	1
Youngsville	1,617	9	0	0	0	9	5	1	3	1	0
Zelienople	3,639	4	0	1	0	3	70	8	62	0	0
Zerbe Township	1,795	1	0	1	0	0	8	0	8	0	0
RHODE ISLAND											
Barrington	16,112	8	0	6	1	1	113	15	94	4	1
Bristol	22,131	10	0	5	0	5	89	8	78	3	0
Burrillville	16,781	19	0	6	0	13	97	22	72	3	3
Central Falls	19,293	83	1	12	16	54	293	47	190	56	4
Charlestown	7,810	7	0	3	0	4	48	7	37	4	2
Coventry	34,814	35	0	16	0	19	452	70	346	36	2
Cranston	81,059	118	0	26	24	68	1,140	158	887	95	2
Cumberland	35,018	23	0	5	4	14	304	53	227	24	0
East Greenwich	13,051	10	0	2	1	7	115	21	89	5	0
East Providence	47,526	50	2	12	5	31	515	68	399	48	4
Foster	4,735	6	0	1	0	5	39	13	22	4	0
Glocester	10,158	5	0	2	0	3	30	6	18	6	0
Hopkinton	8,109	4	0	1	1	2	54	10	42	2	0
Jamestown	5,537	3	0	0	0	3	76	11	58	7	0
Johnston	29,317	40	0	9	3	28	344	58	246	40	1
Lincoln	21,900	17	0	3	6	8	386	52	312	22	1
Little Compton	3,511	2	0	0	0	2	22	3	17	2	1
Middletown	16,030	13	0	4	1	8	209	34	164	11	2
Narragansett	15,448	8	0	3	1	4	123	18	100	5	0
Newport	24,863	85	0	22	7	56	600	79	495	26	4
New Shoreham	1,034	4	0	0	0	4	19	1	16	2	0
North Kingstown	26,101	10	0	5	0	5	231	32	183	16	0
North Providence	32,475	38	0	11	4	23	316	59	219	38	4
North Smithfield	12,469	13	0	7	0	6	261	25	221	15	0
Pawtucket	71,892	321	0	47	59	215	1,882	334	1,318	230	9
Portsmouth	17,474	7	0	3	0	4	77	12	57	8	0
Providence	180,169	819	10	109	248	452	5,679	931	4,196	552	10
Richmond	7,627	4	0	2	1	1	43	10	26	7	0
Scituate	10,617	8	0	1	0	7	38	4	33	1	0
Smithfield	21,746	21	0	7	2	12	189	20	164	5	0
South Kingstown	30,816	16	0	7	2	7	203	34	161	8	0
Tiverton	15,835	16	0	3	1	12	167	25	133	9	0
Warren	10,393	18	0	3	1	14	114	27	81	6	1
Warwick	80,380	73	1	27	9	36	1,372	136	1,178	58	8
Westerly	22,537	17	1	7	3	6	288	46	232	10	0
West Greenwich	6,227	5	0	3	0	2	45	12	25	8	0
West Warwick	28,464	65	0	24	7	34	306	68	213	25	3
Woonsocket	41,707	246	1	45	43	157	898	255	572	71	15
SOUTH CAROLINA											
Abbeville	5,059	33	1	3	2	27	145	35	98	12	2
Aiken[6]	30,881	120	2	19	34	65		184		64	7
Allendale	2,970	35	2	0	8	25	117	71	40	6	1
Aynor	904	3	0	0	0	3	25	0	25	0	0
Bamberg	3,239	17	0	1	5	11	115	21	89	5	1

Table 8. Offenses Known to Law Enforcement, by Selected State and City, 2018—Continued

(Number.)

State/city	Population	Violent crime	Murder and nonnegligent manslaughter	Rape[1]	Robbery	Aggravated assault	Property crime	Burglary	Larceny-theft	Motor vehicle theft	Arson[2]
Barnwell	4,385	55	0	1	4	50	287	98	184	5	1
Batesburg-Leesville	5,380	92	0	4	7	81	255	63	184	8	1
Beaufort	13,920	81	1	5	18	57	581	78	484	19	1
Belton	4,402	3	0	0	1	2	137	20	100	17	0
Bennettsville	7,898	64	4	2	8	50	266	35	221	10	0
Bishopville	3,089	32	1	0	4	27	146	27	114	5	0
Blacksburg	1,899	12	0	0	1	11	111	22	74	15	0
Blackville	2,217	24	1	0	4	19	128	56	67	5	1
Bluffton	22,578	50	1	2	5	42	252	25	206	21	1
Branchville	956	3	0	1	1	1	33	3	28	2	0
Burnettown	2,824	0	0	0	0	0	39	4	33	2	0
Calhoun Falls	1,925	7	0	1	2	4	25	3	22	0	0
Camden	7,215	93	1	2	11	79	438	62	354	22	1
Cameron	403	1	0	0	0	1	2	0	2	0	0
Cayce	14,238	112	0	13	8	91	661	86	515	60	3
Central	5,180	5	0	1	0	4	135	8	120	7	0
Chapin	1,629	4	0	0	3	1	74	5	65	4	0
Charleston	137,092	415	10	57	89	259	2,848	360	2,163	325	8
Cheraw	5,611	58	0	3	9	46	386	54	322	10	1
Chesnee	929	4	0	1	0	3	36	6	25	5	2
Chester	5,394	65	2	1	3	59	227	37	179	11	1
Chesterfield	1,424	10	0	1	1	8	23	4	18	1	0
Clinton	8,498	86	0	3	6	77	340	73	236	31	2
Clover	6,234	12	0	2	1	9	131	14	106	11	1
Columbia	133,540	986	16	90	224	656	6,753	1,006	4,979	768	29
Conway	24,784	141	1	15	22	103	960	164	748	48	2
Coward	767	0	0	0	0	0	11	2	9	0	0
Cowpens	2,348	5	0	0	0	5	65	13	50	2	1
Darlington	5,960	67	1	5	5	56	413	69	317	27	0
Denmark	2,896	9	1	1	1	6	87	24	52	11	0
Due West	1,289	4	0	0	0	4	18	1	16	1	0
Duncan	3,480	3	0	0	2	1	64	7	44	13	1
Easley	21,203	105	1	6	8	90	1,254	102	1,078	74	1
Edgefield	4,756	10	0	2	0	8	59	24	29	6	0
Edisto Beach	405	2	0	0	0	2	10	1	8	1	0
Elgin	1,587	3	0	0	0	3	82	4	77	1	0
Elloree	652	1	0	0	0	1	16	4	12	0	0
Estill	1,807	62	0	0	7	55	78	36	40	2	1
Florence	37,819	362	8	18	72	264	2,462	375	1,935	152	9
Forest Acres	10,375	50	0	7	14	29	654	91	505	58	0
Fort Lawn	878	5	0	2	1	2	28	4	24	0	0
Fort Mill	18,618	31	2	1	4	24	328	51	269	8	3
Fountain Inn	8,846	38	0	10	4	24	176	20	133	23	0
Gaffney	12,816	104	2	8	19	75	908	128	692	88	0
Gaston	1,690	0	0	0	0	0	49	16	29	4	0
Georgetown	8,819	98	2	18	10	68	512	97	391	24	5
Goose Creek	43,545	105	0	17	11	77	955	152	739	64	1
Great Falls	1,888	6	0	1	1	4	74	13	59	2	0
Greenville	69,608	368	2	34	74	258	2,810	403	2,177	230	7
Greenwood	23,265	392	2	30	31	329	1,594	314	1,245	35	1
Greer	31,722	134	3	11	32	88	1,144	158	912	74	4
Hampton	2,527	21	0	2	1	18	152	34	116	2	0
Hanahan	26,060	60	1	13	9	37	346	54	258	34	3
Hardeeville	6,561	45	0	4	21	20	179	16	148	15	0
Hartsville	7,608	114	3	7	18	86	658	89	553	16	2
Hemingway	405	5	0	0	4	1	20	0	20	0	0
Holly Hill	1,190	8	0	0	2	6	65	12	53	0	0
Honea Path	3,782	8	0	1	0	7	164	25	124	15	0
Inman	2,341	12	0	1	4	7	97	18	73	6	1
Irmo	12,413	64	0	7	2	55	447	55	380	12	0
Isle of Palms	4,396	2	0	2	0	0	80	11	61	8	0
Iva	1,302	10	1	0	1	8	71	10	56	5	0
Jackson	1,781	3	0	0	0	3	26	11	12	3	1
Jamestown	81	2	0	0	0	2	4	1	3	0	0
Johnsonville	1,493	2	0	0	0	2	19	9	8	2	0
Johnston	2,327	6	0	0	2	4	13	5	6	2	0
Jonesville	841	5	1	1	0	3	18	4	14	0	0
Kingstree	3,065	32	0	3	12	17	227	27	178	22	0
Lake City	6,668	75	0	9	14	52	384	77	286	21	0
Landrum	2,586	10	0	1	0	9	47	8	36	3	0
Latta	1,296	20	0	1	5	14	90	16	68	6	0
Laurens	8,868	86	0	9	5	72	554	87	447	20	2
Lexington	21,680	79	0	9	12	58	662	63	561	38	2
Liberty	3,161	7	0	0	0	7	115	18	94	3	0
Loris	2,722	21	1	2	3	15	129	24	91	14	0
Lyman	3,557	30	0	1	2	27	100	28	61	11	1
Manning	3,958	33	0	2	4	27	366	43	304	19	5
Marion	6,416	98	9	4	14	71	524	115	378	31	1
Mauldin	25,418	42	1	8	6	27	439	56	341	42	1
McColl	2,014	21	0	1	1	19	85	26	54	5	0
McCormick	2,446	10	0	0	1	9	54	12	39	3	0
Moncks Corner	11,484	68	3	4	9	52	409	37	349	23	3
Mount Pleasant	89,733	138	0	10	15	113	1,221	126	1,002	93	1

Table 8. Offenses Known to Law Enforcement, by Selected State and City, 2018—Continued

(Number.)

State/city	Population	Violent crime	Murder and nonnegligent manslaughter	Rape[1]	Robbery	Aggravated assault	Property crime	Burglary	Larceny-theft	Motor vehicle theft	Arson[2]
Mullins	4,350	26	0	2	5	19	247	116	120	11	3
Myrtle Beach	33,687	473	4	64	129	276	3,553	410	2,883	260	8
Newberry	10,293	91	1	9	18	63	457	82	366	9	1
New Ellenton	2,164	9	0	1	3	5	29	3	24	2	0
Ninety Six	2,037	5	0	2	0	3	39	6	31	2	0
North	719	10	0	2	2	6	60	9	48	3	1
North Augusta	23,161	43	2	8	20	13	893	104	743	46	3
North Charleston	112,840	1,039	25	77	302	635	6,567	880	4,985	702	20
North Myrtle Beach[5]	16,688	105	1	28	16	60		192	782		1
Olanta	565	4	0	0	0	4	11	2	9	0	0
Orangeburg	12,820	170	1	3	29	137	750	139	550	61	5
Pawleys Island	106	1	0	0	1	0	4	0	4	0	0
Pelion	701	1	0	1	0	0	18	1	16	1	0
Pickens	3,170	26	0	1	0	25	234	17	198	19	1
Port Royal	13,227	16	0	5	7	4	198	38	146	14	1
Prosperity	1,222	6	0	1	2	3	23	8	15	0	0
Quinby	931	0	0	0	0	0	0	0	0	0	0
Ridgeland	4,072	9	0	1	6	2	89	13	71	5	1
Ridge Spring	755	2	1	0	1	0	23	7	15	1	0
Rock Hill	74,049	361	3	51	61	246	2,794	325	2,263	206	13
Salem	154	0	0	0	0	0	0	0	0	0	0
Salley	420	0	0	0	0	0	1	0	0	1	0
Saluda	3,636	16	0	0	0	16	62	10	51	1	0
Seneca	8,371	40	1	5	7	27	215	39	163	13	0
Simpsonville	22,641	41	1	5	5	30	694	74	565	55	4
South Congaree	2,466	12	0	3	2	7	101	12	76	13	0
Springdale	2,760	18	0	1	6	11	104	13	74	17	0
St. George	2,163	12	0	2	1	9	82	20	58	4	0
St. Matthews	1,934	13	0	0	2	11	88	27	54	7	1
St. Stephen	1,828	10	0	0	2	8	57	16	39	2	0
Sullivans Island	1,942	1	0	0	0	1	26	0	21	5	0
Summerton	954	7	0	0	3	4	57	11	44	2	0
Summerville	51,565	140	2	25	19	94	1,740	217	1,403	120	4
Sumter	39,898	366	4	12	53	297	1,873	376	1,411	86	8
Surfside Beach	4,511	7	0	4	1	2	177	32	130	15	1
Swansea	941	14	0	0	6	8	64	7	44	13	0
Tega Cay	10,763	7	0	1	1	5	219	8	206	5	0
Travelers Rest	5,183	3	0	0	0	3	246	8	228	10	1
Turbeville	792	1	0	0	0	1	11	2	8	1	0
Union	7,748	73	1	6	4	62	461	71	371	19	1
Walhalla	4,327	9	0	3	0	6	90	31	55	4	1
Walterboro[5]	5,083	38	1	3	7	27			317	15	1
Ware Shoals	2,153	35	0	2	6	27	105	19	79	7	0
Wellford	2,629	1	0	0	0	1	24	4	20	0	0
West Columbia	17,368	181	3	30	35	113	1,292	107	1,063	122	5
Westminster	2,536	13	0	2	0	11	51	4	41	6	0
West Pelzer	939	1	0	0	0	1	14	1	10	3	0
West Union	319	0	0	0	0	0	14	1	12	1	0
Whitmire	1,473	6	0	0	0	6	53	7	45	1	0
Williamston	4,216	16	0	1	2	13	130	23	99	8	1
Williston	2,941	24	0	2	6	16	94	19	71	4	1
Winnsboro	3,197	19	1	0	1	17	58	12	44	2	0
Woodruff	4,253	15	0	0	3	12	149	28	107	14	0
Yemassee	958	15	0	0	2	13	52	14	34	4	2
York	8,203	71	0	5	7	59	367	38	303	26	2
SOUTH DAKOTA											
Aberdeen	28,713	124	1	33	4	86	602	101	466	35	4
Alcester	727	0	0	0	0	0	0	0	0	0	0
Avon	597	0	0	0	0	0	0	0	0	0	0
Belle Fourche	5,544	13	0	3	1	9	124	15	107	2	0
Beresford	1,944	2	0	1	1	0	26	2	22	2	0
Box Elder	9,761	43	0	5	1	37	175	41	116	18	2
Brandon	10,107	11	0	5	0	6	54	5	46	3	0
Brookings	24,206	46	0	13	2	31	324	36	274	14	0
Burke	586	0	0	0	0	0	0	0	0	0	0
Canton	3,481	8	0	2	0	6	59	19	36	4	0
Centerville	868	0	0	0	0	0	10	1	9	0	0
Chamberlain	2,388	19	1	3	1	14	61	11	46	4	0
Clark	1,035	2	0	1	0	1	6	1	4	1	0
Deadwood	1,305	1	0	0	0	1	0	0	0	0	0
Faith	417	0	0	0	0	0	3	0	1	2	0
Flandreau	2,332	9	0	2	2	5	57	9	41	7	0
Freeman	1,286	1	0	0	0	1	10	0	10	0	0
Hermosa	396	0	0	0	0	0	0	0	0	0	0
Hot Springs	3,426	11	0	1	0	10	37	5	25	7	0
Huron	13,193	56	0	9	1	46	221	40	170	11	0
Jefferson	495	1	0	0	0	1	5	1	4	0	0
Kadoka	711	2	0	0	0	2	4	1	2	1	0
Kimball	677	0	0	0	0	0	0	0	0	0	0
Lead	2,957	6	0	0	0	6	11	0	11	0	0
Madison	7,441	10	0	4	0	6	82	19	62	1	0
Martin	1,066	16	0	2	1	13	83	21	61	1	0

Table 8. Offenses Known to Law Enforcement, by Selected State and City, 2018—Continued

(Number.)

State/city	Population	Violent crime	Murder and nonnegligent manslaughter	Rape[1]	Robbery	Aggravated assault	Property crime	Burglary	Larceny-theft	Motor vehicle theft	Arson[2]
Menno	618	0	0	0	0	0	0	0	0	0	0
Miller	1,361	1	0	0	0	1	10	1	9	0	0
Mitchell	15,653	81	0	21	6	54	573	68	447	58	2
Murdo	447	2	0	0	0	2	0	0	0	0	0
North Sioux City	2,821	1	0	1	0	0	59	5	40	14	0
Parkston	1,495	0	0	0	0	0	0	0	0	0	0
Philip	785	0	0	0	0	0	1	1	0	0	0
Pierre	14,050	70	0	18	1	51	380	36	325	19	2
Platte	1,278	0	0	0	0	0	3	2	0	1	0
Rapid City	75,290	492	2	99	65	326	2,194	428	1,502	264	7
Rosholt	424	0	0	0	0	0	0	0	0	0	0
Scotland	814	0	0	0	0	0	0	0	0	0	0
Sioux Falls	180,335	788	5	121	107	555	5,288	652	4,092	544	36
Sisseton	2,395	2	0	1	0	1	31	5	20	6	1
Spearfish	11,763	25	0	8	3	14	375	40	318	17	0
Springfield	1,936	0	0	0	0	0	0	0	0	0	0
Sturgis	6,949	21	0	1	1	19	164	19	141	4	0
Summerset	2,690	1	0	0	0	1	38	5	31	2	0
Tea	5,725	8	0	3	0	5	75	13	58	4	0
Tripp	630	0	0	0	0	0	0	0	0	0	0
Tyndall	1,041	0	0	0	0	0	0	0	0	0	0
Vermillion	10,804	26	0	3	1	22	216	30	167	19	1
Viborg	768	0	0	0	0	0	9	7	2	0	0
Wagner	1,589	6	0	1	0	5	22	1	21	0	0
Watertown	22,323	67	0	18	4	45	382	54	309	19	0
Webster	1,757	0	0	0	0	0	0	0	0	0	0
Whitewood	949	0	0	0	0	0	2	0	2	0	0
Winner	2,832	13	0	7	0	6	24	3	20	1	0
Yankton	14,523	75	0	16	1	58	379	31	322	26	0
TENNESSEE											
Adamsville	2,199	4	0	0	0	4	38	7	27	4	0
Alamo	2,324	9	0	2	0	7	44	6	33	5	0
Alcoa	10,506	82	1	4	9	68	516	39	444	33	3
Alexandria	1,000	4	0	2	0	2	11	3	5	3	0
Algood	4,517	13	0	3	1	9	153	5	135	13	0
Ardmore	1,236	0	0	0	0	0	31	2	26	3	10
Ashland City	4,641	13	0	0	0	13	254	17	222	15	2
Athens	13,627	119	0	7	12	100	1,043	187	792	64	5
Atoka	9,305	9	0	2	1	6	81	10	66	5	1
Baileyton	441	1	0	0	0	1	15	2	13	0	0
Bartlett	59,407	190	2	16	29	143	1,119	126	920	73	0
Baxter	1,453	1	0	0	0	1	29	5	21	3	0
Bean Station	3,094	2	1	0	1	0	22	3	16	3	1
Belle Meade	2,917	1	0	0	0	1	25	3	20	2	0
Bells	2,477	13	0	1	0	12	31	9	20	2	0
Benton	1,277	3	0	0	0	3	29	1	26	2	1
Berry Hill	524	8	0	0	3	5	101	13	81	7	0
Big Sandy	517	1	0	0	0	1	10	1	8	1	1
Blaine	1,880	0	0	0	0	0	18	1	13	4	0
Bluff City	1,660	8	0	0	0	8	28	7	19	2	0
Bolivar	4,954	51	1	1	8	41	140	50	76	14	1
Bradford	974	2	0	0	1	1	5	2	3	0	0
Brentwood	43,507	35	4	3	9	19	403	35	345	23	0
Brighton	2,910	0	0	0	0	0	14	5	8	1	0
Bristol	26,863	151	0	18	16	117	857	117	656	84	3
Brownsville	9,490	106	2	12	7	85	385	107	265	13	4
Bruceton	1,403	2	0	0	0	2	18	6	12	0	0
Burns	1,509	0	0	0	0	0	8	2	3	3	0
Calhoun	492	1	0	0	1	0	1	1	0	0	0
Camden	3,500	5	0	0	0	5	108	15	86	7	0
Carthage	2,258	6	0	2	1	3	70	4	65	1	0
Caryville	2,146	9	0	1	1	7	41	2	26	13	0
Celina	1,458	4	0	0	0	4	35	2	29	4	0
Centerville	3,557	14	0	0	1	13	70	20	42	8	0
Chapel Hill	1,511	10	0	2	0	8	33	5	26	2	0
Charleston	686	2	0	0	0	2	2	0	2	0	0
Chattanooga	180,397	1,891	19	149	310	1,413	10,930	1,441	8,065	1,424	18
Church Hill	6,664	3	0	0	0	3	18	2	15	1	0
Clarksburg	377	0	0	0	0	0	2	0	2	0	0
Clarksville	156,264	1,041	15	81	130	815	4,514	598	3,572	344	17
Cleveland	44,954	412	0	22	32	358	2,512	384	1,908	220	1
Clifton	2,676	0	0	0	0	0	8	1	6	1	0
Clinton	10,137	56	0	7	5	44	431	44	360	27	2
Collegedale	12,189	5	0	0	2	3	181	16	154	11	1
Collierville	50,985	83	1	7	21	54	868	92	739	37	0
Collinwood	944	1	0	0	0	1	19	5	10	4	0
Columbia	38,802	246	7	26	22	191	1,246	203	946	97	2
Cookeville	33,785	143	0	19	13	111	1,418	194	1,067	157	2
Coopertown	4,552	1	0	0	0	1	24	5	15	4	1
Cornersville	1,243	3	0	0	0	3	8	2	6	0	0
Cross Plains	1,810	0	0	0	0	0	0	0	0	0	0
Crossville	11,535	95	2	8	9	76	538	87	399	52	2

Table 8. Offenses Known to Law Enforcement, by Selected State and City, 2018—Continued

(Number.)

State/city	Population	Violent crime	Murder and nonnegligent manslaughter	Rape[1]	Robbery	Aggravated assault	Property crime	Burglary	Larceny-theft	Motor vehicle theft	Arson[2]
Crump	1,463	3	0	1	0	2	10	3	7	0	0
Cumberland City	303	0	0	0	0	0	3	1	2	0	0
Dandridge	2,981	3	0	0	2	1	73	17	50	6	0
Dayton	7,365	13	0	0	2	11	175	27	141	7	1
Decatur	1,629	4	0	0	0	4	37	6	26	5	0
Decaturville	865	0	0	0	0	0	5	2	2	1	0
Decherd	2,388	8	0	0	0	8	92	19	70	3	1
Dickson	15,637	133	0	12	5	116	757	82	624	51	2
Dover	1,461	1	0	0	0	1	17	5	10	2	0
Dresden	2,902	4	0	0	0	4	32	7	24	1	0
Dunlap	5,111	34	0	5	5	24	239	20	175	44	1
Dyer	2,193	10	0	0	1	9	44	6	35	3	1
Dyersburg	16,382	204	0	7	16	181	943	216	663	64	0
Eagleville	687	0	0	0	0	0	2	0	2	0	0
East Ridge	21,135	100	2	9	19	70	749	140	515	94	2
Elizabethton	13,657	62	0	0	8	54	680	121	510	49	1
Elkton	541	2	0	0	0	2	9	4	5	0	0
Englewood	1,518	14	0	0	0	14	40	8	27	5	0
Erin	1,274	0	0	0	0	0	15	3	12	0	0
Erwin	5,840	17	0	2	1	14	72	7	52	13	1
Estill Springs	2,012	16	0	0	1	15	32	3	26	3	0
Ethridge	482	2	0	0	0	2	12	4	6	2	0
Etowah	3,461	17	0	1	0	16	51	6	35	10	1
Fairview	8,898	15	0	2	0	13	140	52	73	15	0
Fayetteville	7,024	58	0	2	6	50	254	45	195	14	0
Franklin	80,825	119	0	19	9	91	982	77	850	55	2
Friendship	679	0	0	0	0	0	5	0	5	0	0
Gadsden	467	0	0	0	0	0	4	1	3	0	0
Gainesboro	940	0	0	0	0	0	5	1	3	1	0
Gallatin	38,450	121	4	10	10	97	538	45	462	31	3
Gallaway	652	4	0	0	1	3	8	4	3	1	0
Gates	630	1	0	0	1	0	10	5	4	1	0
Gatlinburg	4,192	16	0	3	1	12	233	39	182	12	2
Germantown	39,179	30	0	4	4	22	605	58	513	34	2
Gibson	385	1	0	0	0	1	2	2	0	0	0
Gleason	1,365	2	0	0	0	2	12	7	4	1	0
Goodlettsville	17,000	78	0	4	21	53	534	33	452	49	0
Gordonsville	1,210	1	0	0	0	1	5	0	4	1	0
Grand Junction	269	2	0	0	1	1	4	0	4	0	0
Graysville	1,553	7	0	0	0	7	31	3	24	4	0
Greenbrier	6,899	24	0	2	1	21	67	13	44	10	0
Greeneville	14,867	65	1	5	1	58	636	73	493	70	1
Greenfield	2,067	4	0	0	0	4	30	4	24	2	0
Halls	2,118	5	0	0	0	5	15	6	8	1	0
Harriman	6,132	14	0	4	3	7	165	37	104	24	2
Henderson	6,234	27	0	1	0	26	112	16	86	10	1
Hendersonville	58,437	113	2	11	16	84	914	61	807	46	1
Henry	474	0	0	0	0	0	9	4	4	1	0
Hohenwald	3,671	25	0	0	0	25	113	11	86	16	1
Hollow Rock	674	0	0	0	0	0	9	4	5	0	0
Hornbeak	385	0	0	0	0	0	1	0	1	0	0
Humboldt	8,110	46	1	4	7	34	287	53	219	15	2
Huntingdon	3,807	1	0	0	0	1	64	3	58	3	0
Jacksboro	1,918	3	0	0	0	3	70	1	69	0	0
Jackson	66,848	670	9	29	102	530	2,866	447	2,197	222	18
Jamestown	1,956	3	0	0	0	3	94	4	88	2	0
Jasper	3,317	17	0	1	1	15	52	6	39	7	0
Jellico	2,198	5	0	0	1	4	41	8	26	7	0
Johnson City	66,795	274	1	24	38	211	2,622	290	2,143	189	7
Jonesborough	5,446	12	0	2	1	9	57	12	36	9	0
Kenton	1,201	2	0	0	0	2	29	4	25	0	0
Kimball	1,398	9	0	0	0	9	105	6	90	9	0
Kingsport	53,465	404	4	21	43	336	2,801	348	2,164	289	8
Kingston	5,794	17	0	4	3	10	62	13	40	9	1
Kingston Springs	2,776	0	0	0	0	0	2	0	2	0	0
Knoxville	188,653	1,508	20	132	249	1,107	8,827	1,374	6,379	1,074	7
Lafayette	5,318	10	0	1	1	8	109	9	84	16	1
La Follette	6,722	26	1	4	1	20	285	54	208	23	1
La Vergne	36,167	157	1	7	26	123	820	90	655	75	2
Lawrenceburg	10,807	67	0	4	6	57	556	98	441	17	1
Lebanon	33,181	185	3	26	20	136	940	142	719	79	0
Lenoir City	9,284	26	0	7	2	17	228	22	182	24	2
Lewisburg	11,967	80	0	6	1	73	216	39	158	19	0
Lexington	7,673	43	0	3	3	37	307	38	250	19	1
Livingston	4,016	11	0	0	0	11	72	16	49	7	0
Lookout Mountain	1,873	0	0	0	0	0	8	0	7	1	0
Loretto	1,769	5	0	0	0	5	49	19	29	1	0
Loudon	5,815	4	0	1	0	3	47	3	41	3	0
Madisonville	4,754	22	0	1	0	21	218	28	161	29	1
Manchester	10,719	62	1	4	7	50	401	60	322	19	2
Martin	10,418	27	0	1	1	25	245	24	217	4	0
Maryville	28,961	47	0	7	2	38	480	50	399	31	2
Mason	1,571	3	0	1	0	2	7	3	4	0	0

Table 8. Offenses Known to Law Enforcement, by Selected State and City, 2018—Continued

(Number.)

State/city	Population	Violent crime	Murder and nonnegligent manslaughter	Rape[1]	Robbery	Aggravated assault	Property crime	Burglary	Larceny-theft	Motor vehicle theft	Arson[2]
Maury City	669	5	0	0	0	5	13	2	11	0	0
Maynardville	2,351	8	0	0	0	8	48	4	39	5	0
McEwen	1,723	3	0	0	0	3	36	10	22	4	0
McKenzie	5,392	8	0	1	0	7	76	19	56	1	0
McMinnville	13,668	86	1	12	8	65	489	113	334	42	3
Medina	4,313	11	0	3	0	8	28	10	16	2	0
Memphis	652,226	12,674	186	491	3,050	8,947	41,779	8,494	28,835	4,450	288
Metropolitan Nashville Police Department	686,492	7,641	91	480	2,116	4,954	27,537	3,627	20,828	3,082	63
Middleton	636	0	0	0	0	0	4	0	3	1	0
Milan	7,640	49	2	2	3	42	191	63	123	5	1
Millersville	6,914	22	0	2	2	18	74	19	43	12	1
Millington	11,016	101	1	7	12	81	586	90	456	40	4
Minor Hill	520	1	0	0	0	1	2	0	1	1	0
Monteagle	1,173	6	0	1	0	5	18	7	9	2	1
Monterey	2,875	11	0	0	1	10	64	19	36	9	0
Morristown	29,884	242	0	22	14	206	1,388	164	1,131	93	3
Moscow	522	5	0	0	0	5	2	0	2	0	0
Mountain City	2,395	4	0	0	1	3	39	7	29	3	0
Mount Carmel	5,345	8	0	0	0	8	59	21	31	7	0
Mount Juliet	36,397	72	0	19	9	44	630	43	535	52	0
Mount Pleasant	4,924	19	0	3	0	16	69	10	46	13	0
Munford	6,090	27	0	6	1	20	113	30	76	7	0
Murfreesboro	140,702	613	11	77	107	418	4,417	649	3,458	310	6
Newbern	3,334	13	0	1	3	9	74	5	63	6	0
New Johnsonville	1,905	1	0	0	0	1	32	18	13	1	0
New Market	1,353	1	0	0	0	1	11	5	5	1	0
Newport	6,770	60	0	4	3	53	534	34	454	46	0
New Tazewell	2,709	8	0	0	4	4	109	14	87	8	0
Niota	723	1	0	0	0	1	6	0	5	1	0
Nolensville	8,545	16	0	1	1	14	125	47	74	4	0
Norris	1,640	6	0	2	0	4	15	0	12	3	1
Oakland	8,107	3	0	2	0	1	86	9	77	0	0
Oak Ridge	29,067	164	0	16	18	130	734	102	578	54	4
Obion	1,049	1	0	0	0	1	3	0	2	1	0
Oliver Springs	3,256	5	0	0	1	4	72	6	62	4	0
Oneida	3,673	18	0	0	1	17	145	16	123	6	0
Paris	10,088	45	1	1	4	39	283	45	227	11	0
Parsons	2,316	8	0	1	0	7	35	8	24	3	0
Petersburg	552	0	0	0	0	0	3	0	2	1	0
Pigeon Forge	6,291	55	0	10	8	37	486	92	331	63	0
Pikeville	1,626	6	0	0	0	6	44	12	23	9	0
Piperton	1,757	6	0	0	0	6	12	4	6	2	0
Pittman Center	583	0	0	0	0	0	0	0	0	0	0
Plainview	2,091	1	0	0	0	1	16	4	12	0	0
Pleasant View	4,449	3	0	0	0	3	49	6	38	5	1
Portland	12,887	36	1	5	7	23	227	51	166	10	1
Pulaski	7,650	59	0	6	3	50	403	53	331	19	2
Puryear	667	1	0	0	0	1	6	2	4	0	0
Red Bank	11,768	52	0	3	9	40	296	72	195	29	3
Red Boiling Springs	1,148	9	0	1	0	8	13	3	10	0	0
Ridgely	1,662	6	1	0	0	5	30	11	18	1	2
Ridgetop	2,071	2	0	1	1	0	10	0	8	2	0
Ripley	7,977	70	0	2	3	65	309	94	200	15	3
Rockwood	5,417	36	0	1	4	31	318	28	268	22	0
Rocky Top	1,774	12	0	0	2	10	84	13	52	19	2
Rogersville	4,264	23	0	0	3	20	224	33	177	14	0
Rossville	890	1	0	0	0	1	14	7	7	0	0
Rutherford	1,077	9	0	0	0	9	9	0	8	1	0
Rutledge	1,358	1	0	0	0	1	19	8	9	2	0
Saltillo	531	1	0	0	0	1	5	0	1	4	0
Savannah	6,968	81	2	6	5	68	495	76	382	37	2
Scotts Hill	974	2	0	0	0	2	5	3	1	1	0
Selmer	4,445	40	0	2	3	35	149	27	114	8	0
Sevierville	16,999	92	0	5	10	77	833	50	701	82	0
Sharon	914	1	0	0	0	1	6	4	1	1	0
Shelbyville	21,708	153	1	12	14	126	657	96	498	63	2
Signal Mountain	8,602	6	0	0	0	6	37	6	25	6	0
Smithville	4,783	18	0	2	0	16	131	18	99	14	1
Soddy-Daisy	13,804	20	1	1	4	14	316	45	232	39	2
Somerville	3,213	24	0	2	2	20	55	6	41	8	0
South Carthage	1,356	7	0	0	0	7	31	7	18	6	0
South Fulton	2,200	20	0	1	0	19	41	6	32	3	0
South Pittsburg	3,031	5	0	0	2	3	39	11	24	4	1
Sparta	4,951	13	0	2	0	11	205	39	156	10	3
Spencer	1,641	0	0	0	0	0	14	2	11	1	0
Spring City	1,856	7	0	0	0	7	40	4	34	2	0
Springfield	16,896	145	1	15	12	117	530	45	451	34	0
Spring Hill	41,354	43	0	5	0	38	446	40	392	14	0
St. Joseph	811	0	0	0	0	0	0	0	0	0	0
Surgoinsville	1,770	0	0	0	0	0	16	3	12	1	0
Sweetwater	5,873	51	0	0	1	50	307	48	232	27	0
Tazewell	2,278	10	0	0	1	9	68	10	51	7	2

Table 8. Offenses Known to Law Enforcement, by Selected State and City, 2018—Continued

(Number.)

State/city	Population	Violent crime	Murder and nonnegligent manslaughter	Rape[1]	Robbery	Aggravated assault	Property crime	Burglary	Larceny-theft	Motor vehicle theft	Arson[2]
Tellico Plains	945	15	0	0	0	15	26	4	16	6	0
Tiptonville	4,304	8	0	0	0	8	32	8	22	2	0
Toone	338	2	0	0	0	2	2	0	2	0	0
Townsend	446	6	0	0	0	6	17	2	15	0	0
Tracy City	1,394	3	0	0	0	3	39	4	28	7	2
Trenton	4,043	20	1	2	0	17	91	8	79	4	0
Trezevant	839	1	0	0	0	1	9	7	0	2	1
Trimble	615	4	0	0	0	4	6	1	4	1	0
Troy	1,269	2	0	1	1	0	13	5	5	3	0
Tullahoma	19,321	106	0	9	5	92	618	78	498	42	1
Tusculum	2,695	0	0	0	0	0	1	0	1	0	0
Vonore	1,517	10	0	1	2	7	59	12	41	6	1
Wartburg	898	7	0	0	0	7	13	3	8	2	0
Wartrace	679	0	0	0	0	0	0	0	0	0	0
Watertown	1,537	1	0	0	0	1	10	3	6	1	0
Waverly	4,093	9	0	1	2	6	79	11	65	3	0
Waynesboro	2,322	5	0	0	0	5	14	1	11	2	0
Westmoreland	2,325	15	0	0	1	14	11	2	5	4	1
White Bluff	3,535	15	0	0	3	12	40	6	29	5	0
White House	11,818	36	0	7	1	28	201	7	175	19	0
White Pine	2,288	6	0	0	0	6	50	9	35	6	0
Whiteville	4,500	14	0	0	0	14	19	0	17	2	0
Whitwell	1,706	8	0	0	0	8	28	9	13	6	1
Winchester	8,504	54	1	2	4	47	290	46	228	16	0
Woodbury	2,815	13	0	0	1	12	30	8	19	3	0
TEXAS											
Abernathy	2,743	3	0	0	1	2	17	4	11	2	0
Abilene	122,480	591	8	97	104	382	3,528	734	2,561	233	3
Addison	15,839	72	0	13	19	40	872	78	706	88	2
Alamo[4]	19,840	130	0	18	10	102	953	97	816	40	3
Alamo Heights	8,629	11	0	2	3	6	131	12	116	3	0
Alice	18,925	91	0	11	4	76	939	246	659	34	5
Allen	103,168	111	0	31	22	58	1,277	115	1,095	67	0
Alpine	6,073	17	1	1	0	15	60	34	25	1	1
Alton	17,805	57	0	4	7	46	217	31	174	12	1
Alvarado	4,179	6	0	2	2	2	81	21	50	10	1
Alvin	26,798	57	1	17	11	28	467	48	370	49	1
Amarillo	201,082	1,622	12	199	305	1,106	8,433	1,527	5,996	910	36
Andrews	13,845	55	0	8	1	46	200	42	137	21	0
Angleton	19,650	32	0	6	2	24	241	45	173	23	0
Anna	13,579	16	0	3	2	11	174	22	140	12	0
Anson	2,293	11	0	0	1	10	9	3	6	0	0
Anthony	5,761	14	0	0	2	12	102	13	81	8	0
Aransas Pass	8,280	48	2	0	4	42	443	101	309	33	1
Argyle	4,236	0	0	0	0	0	17	7	9	1	0
Arlington	400,920	1,784	7	203	360	1,214	11,780	1,509	9,033	1,238	13
Arp[4]	1,009	4	0	1	0	3	3	1	2	0	0
Athens[4]	12,704	55	1	8	12	34	286	80	179	27	0
Atlanta	5,462	36	0	7	3	26	173	45	122	6	0
Aubrey	3,523	13	0	0	0	13	30	16	11	3	0
Austin	973,344	3,720	32	787	1,021	1,880	33,655	4,549	26,568	2,538	56
Azle	12,741	25	0	1	6	18	254	28	198	28	0
Baird[4]	1,506	0	0	0	0	0	26	11	13	2	1
Balch Springs	25,565	179	2	11	54	112	883	114	574	195	3
Balcones Heights[4]	3,361	25	0	0	9	16	341	18	300	23	0
Ballinger	3,640	14	0	0	0	14	65	18	44	3	0
Bangs	1,561	0	0	0	0	0	5	2	3	0	0
Bartonville	1,756	0	0	0	0	0	20	1	18	1	0
Bastrop	9,050	94	0	6	8	80	389	36	327	26	0
Bay City	17,517	73	3	12	18	40	686	124	544	18	4
Baytown	77,539	302	2	35	94	171	2,911	384	2,028	499	2
Beaumont	119,368	1,265	13	96	358	798	4,516	961	3,145	410	35
Bedford	49,841	90	0	20	17	53	1,057	142	831	84	2
Bee Cave	7,253	16	0	2	2	12	186	19	149	18	0
Beeville	12,951	40	1	0	7	32	390	91	297	2	1
Bellaire	19,076	26	0	4	13	9	265	58	191	16	0
Bellmead	10,587	137	0	13	11	113	656	77	539	40	1
Bellville	4,257	13	0	3	0	10	52	5	42	5	2
Belton	22,248	57	1	5	12	39	511	80	412	19	5
Benbrook	23,924	29	0	9	6	14	411	64	323	24	2
Beverly Hills	1,982	4	0	1	1	2	61	14	31	16	0
Big Sandy	1,390	0	0	0	0	0	0	0	0	0	0
Big Spring[4]	28,001	152	2	7	14	129	795	166	552	77	3
Bishop	3,079	3	0	0	0	3	27	11	16	0	0
Blanco[4]	2,062	4	0	0	0	4	13	1	11	1	0
Blue Mound	2,494	3	0	0	1	2	18	2	10	6	0
Boerne	17,008	27	0	12	2	13	341	29	279	33	0
Bogata	1,066	11	0	0	0	11	36	21	14	1	0
Bonham	10,203	17	0	9	2	6	174	43	128	3	1
Borger	12,675	40	0	10	4	26	499	88	376	35	1
Bovina[4]	1,799	2	0	0	0	2	14	5	4	5	0
Bowie	5,067	10	0	0	3	7	136	43	82	11	1

Table 8. Offenses Known to Law Enforcement, by Selected State and City, 2018—Continued

(Number.)

State/city	Population	Violent crime	Murder and nonnegligent manslaughter	Rape[1]	Robbery	Aggravated assault	Property crime	Burglary	Larceny-theft	Motor vehicle theft	Arson[2]
Boyd	1,443	0	0	0	0	0	7	1	6	0	0
Brady	5,272	5	0	0	1	4	78	12	58	8	0
Brazoria	3,109	8	0	1	3	4	75	11	58	6	0
Breckenridge[4]	5,396	14	2	4	2	6	131	37	90	4	0
Bremond	956	2	1	0	0	1	6	2	3	1	0
Brenham[4]	17,116	65	0	14	11	40	367	49	298	20	2
Bridge City	8,208	11	0	5	0	6	107	12	82	13	1
Bridgeport	6,691	22	1	0	0	21	51	14	34	3	0
Brookshire	5,346	24	0	2	7	15	70	10	51	9	1
Brownfield[4]	9,698	41	1	5	1	34	157	46	96	15	0
Brownsboro	1,259	1	0	0	0	1	6	2	2	2	0
Brownsville[4]	184,461	694	2	12	141	539	4,834	553	4,142	139	8
Brownwood[4]	18,772	79	1	19	4	55	550	85	437	28	1
Bryan	85,152	332	2	55	53	222	2,073	373	1,561	139	15
Buda	18,028	20	0	4	8	8	277	17	250	10	0
Bullard[4]	3,421	13	1	4	0	8	16	4	12	0	0
Bulverde[4]	5,257	8	0	0	2	6	87	7	78	2	0
Burkburnett	11,221	33	0	7	1	25	267	50	201	16	3
Burleson	47,612	133	2	42	13	76	776	72	652	52	1
Burnet	6,410	23	0	2	0	21	54	16	35	3	3
Cactus[4]	3,268	10	0	0	0	10	21	7	13	1	0
Caddo Mills	1,596	0	0	0	0	0	1	1	0	0	0
Caldwell	4,361	3	0	0	1	2	45	0	45	0	0
Calvert[4]	1,149	6	0	0	1	5	29	18	8	3	1
Cameron[4]	5,524	19	0	3	0	16	66	32	30	4	0
Canton	3,924	4	0	0	2	2	99	12	77	10	0
Canyon	15,608	14	0	2	1	11	120	14	100	6	2
Carrollton	138,216	191	5	46	57	83	2,364	329	1,755	280	0
Carthage[4]	6,555	26	0	0	2	24	179	31	141	7	0
Castle Hills	4,508	15	1	2	6	6	309	47	240	22	0
Castroville[4]	3,064	3	0	1	0	2	47	16	27	4	5
Cedar Hill	49,253	85	1	18	27	39	1,379	118	1,162	99	2
Cedar Park	79,087	97	2	36	12	47	966	103	811	52	4
Celina[4]	10,559	15	0	3	1	11	88	19	68	1	0
Center	5,324	23	1	2	1	19	234	58	171	5	3
Chandler	3,055	1	0	0	0	1	33	6	20	7	0
Cibolo	30,768	37	0	10	1	26	271	35	226	10	1
Cisco[4]	3,789	10	0	0	0	10	30	8	20	2	0
Cleburne	30,317	77	2	8	13	54	543	80	431	32	0
Cleveland	8,171	38	0	1	5	32	347	43	275	29	4
Clifton	3,390	2	0	0	0	2	25	4	20	1	0
Clute	11,695	39	0	20	8	11	290	41	226	23	1
Clyde	3,890	1	0	0	0	1	78	41	31	6	0
Cockrell Hill	4,259	18	0	3	8	7	106	17	71	18	0
Coleman	4,366	17	0	3	1	13	40	31	6	3	0
College Station	116,565	237	1	76	30	130	2,422	285	1,988	149	0
Colleyville	27,262	8	0	3	2	3	149	13	136	0	0
Collinsville	1,816	2	0	1	0	1	14	4	9	1	0
Colorado City	3,915	7	0	0	1	6	122	33	86	3	0
Columbus[4]	3,654	9	0	1	2	6	69	12	52	5	1
Comanche	4,188	19	0	0	1	18	81	28	51	2	1
Combes	3,090	4	0	0	0	4	53	14	39	0	0
Commerce	9,307	32	2	3	0	27	168	35	121	12	0
Conroe	87,544	219	3	50	49	117	2,183	284	1,763	136	0
Converse	24,185	172	1	1	11	159	482	95	334	53	2
Coppell	42,415	30	0	6	11	13	532	54	436	42	0
Copperas Cove	32,754	143	0	6	11	126	629	123	486	20	5
Corinth	21,352	12	0	1	2	9	190	31	150	9	0
Corpus Christi	328,614	2,488	24	295	515	1,654	11,975	2,146	8,913	916	70
Corrigan	1,581	2	0	0	0	2	27	5	20	2	0
Corsicana	23,660	135	2	26	13	94	764	149	579	36	3
Crandall	3,721	6	0	1	1	4	31	6	20	5	0
Crane	3,692	1	0	1	0	0	11	2	8	1	1
Crockett[5]	6,470	33	0	1	0	32			129	5	0
Crowley	15,777	18	0	0	5	13	378	33	331	14	0
Crystal City	7,279	9	0	0	2	7	59	35	24	0	0
Cumby	792	0	0	0	0	0	0	0	0	0	0
Daingerfield	2,394	10	0	1	1	8	43	10	32	1	2
Dalhart	8,401	23	1	7	0	15	181	57	109	15	0
Dallas[4]	1,362,465	10,422	155	828	3,987	5,452	44,266	9,065	25,541	9,660	197
Dalworthington Gardens	2,405	1	0	0	0	1	39	4	34	1	1
Dayton	8,070	24	0	2	11	11	231	31	170	30	0
Decatur	6,826	17	0	2	0	15	172	54	109	9	2
Deer Park	34,155	30	0	7	5	18	492	63	384	45	2
De Kalb	1,623	3	0	0	2	1	13	6	6	1	0
De Leon	2,169	4	1	1	0	2	39	9	28	2	0
Del Rio	36,007	22	1	12	3	6	742	159	565	18	4
Denison	24,623	92	2	17	12	61	467	101	312	54	0
Denton	139,262	439	2	124	97	216	3,228	404	2,600	224	1
Denver City	4,933	2	0	1	0	1	35	11	19	5	0
DeSoto	54,201	183	0	29	59	95	1,235	206	844	185	4
Devine	4,876	7	0	2	2	3	79	8	57	14	0
Diboll	5,289	8	0	0	1	7	42	6	35	1	0

Table 8. Offenses Known to Law Enforcement, by Selected State and City, 2018—Continued

(Number.)

State/city	Population	Violent crime	Murder and nonnegligent manslaughter	Rape[1]	Robbery	Aggravated assault	Property crime	Burglary	Larceny-theft	Motor vehicle theft	Arson[2]
Dickinson	20,600	44	0	17	10	17	410	77	298	35	0
Dilley	4,427	11	0	0	2	9	53	24	27	2	0
Dimmitt	4,255	13	0	3	0	10	68	18	40	10	0
Double Oak	3,108	2	0	1	0	1	12	0	12	0	0
Driscoll	747	2	0	0	0	2	2	0	2	0	0
Dublin	3,604	2	0	1	0	1	16	6	8	2	1
Dumas[4]	14,790	22	0	2	1	19	259	29	199	31	0
Duncanville	39,618	215	1	17	100	97	1,253	183	917	153	5
Eagle Lake	3,731	0	0	0	0	0	5	4	1	0	0
Eagle Pass	29,329	55	0	2	13	40	600	133	451	16	0
Early	3,009	21	0	7	1	13	49	10	36	3	0
Eastland	3,929	10	0	6	1	3	90	28	57	5	0
Edcouch	3,393	6	0	1	1	4	25	6	19	0	1
Edinburg	92,391	304	2	78	50	174	3,248	418	2,756	74	13
Edna	5,811	14	0	5	2	7	80	20	57	3	0
El Campo	11,764	43	0	2	1	40	241	37	192	12	1
Electra	2,699	5	0	1	0	4	49	19	26	4	0
Elgin[4]	9,918	12	1	0	2	9	94	18	72	4	0
El Paso	688,442	2,554	23	405	376	1,750	10,365	1,107	8,441	817	26
Encinal	591	1	0	1	0	0	2	0	2	0	0
Ennis[4]	19,367	44	0	9	11	24	343	43	272	28	1
Euless	55,731	91	0	6	30	55	1,187	154	922	111	1
Everman	6,382	35	1	7	9	18	101	13	72	16	2
Fairfield	2,913	6	0	0	2	4	31	10	21	0	0
Fair Oaks Ranch	9,516	4	0	2	0	2	44	11	31	2	0
Fairview	9,220	2	0	2	0	0	53	5	47	1	0
Falfurrias	4,921	12	0	0	0	12	143	79	64	0	0
Farmers Branch	38,495	65	2	11	27	25	929	110	687	132	4
Farmersville	3,489	16	0	3	2	11	53	13	39	1	0
Farwell[4]	1,312	3	0	0	1	2	6	1	4	1	0
Fate	13,003	9	0	3	0	6	63	6	50	7	0
Ferris	2,651	3	0	0	1	2	51	9	34	8	0
Flatonia	1,449	3	1	1	1	0	9	3	5	1	2
Floresville[4]	7,750	14	0	0	4	10	55	24	25	6	1
Flower Mound	78,542	45	0	13	10	22	663	44	585	34	0
Floydada	2,717	17	0	3	2	12	36	10	22	4	1
Forest Hill	13,037	54	2	5	23	24	403	67	261	75	1
Forney	21,464	18	0	7	5	6	267	22	218	27	0
Fort Stockton	8,365	65	1	3	2	59	108	49	55	4	2
Fort Worth	893,756	4,482	58	482	1,116	2,826	25,433	4,504	17,957	2,972	138
Frankston	1,183	4	1	0	0	3	18	6	11	1	0
Fredericksburg	11,490	13	2	1	1	9	120	18	96	6	0
Freeport[4]	12,185	50	0	5	1	44	160	24	136	0	2
Friendswood	40,419	34	0	16	9	9	332	62	252	18	8
Friona[4]	3,881	5	0	1	1	3	20	8	11	1	0
Frisco	187,889	163	2	44	21	96	2,562	245	2,179	138	3
Fulshear[4]	13,790	2	0	0	0	2	61	2	59	0	0
Gainesville	16,478	95	0	20	11	64	363	75	270	18	7
Galena Park	11,000	29	2	4	6	17	156	37	102	17	1
Galveston	50,896	265	7	82	70	106	1,539	176	1,110	253	2
Garden Ridge[4]	4,055	3	0	1	0	2	50	12	36	2	0
Garland	239,577	659	9	114	246	290	6,454	1,113	4,514	827	14
Gatesville	12,377	24	0	9	1	14	209	60	137	12	0
Georgetown	74,709	78	0	22	10	46	731	92	595	44	0
Giddings	5,141	17	0	6	2	9	83	0	78	5	0
Gilmer	5,226	41	0	4	4	33	136	27	101	8	2
Gladewater[4]	6,402	24	1	1	2	20	156	42	103	11	2
Glenn Heights[4]	13,375	35	0	7	8	20	209	60	130	19	6
Godley	1,150	3	0	1	0	2	15	1	13	1	0
Gonzales[5]	7,687		0	14	1		124	27	92	5	1
Gorman	1,038	1	0	1	0	0	7	4	2	1	0
Graham	8,656	20	0	8	1	11	58	12	44	2	0
Granbury	10,228	25	0	10	5	10	494	25	454	15	0
Grand Prairie[4]	196,535	496	10	77	129	280	3,886	497	2,905	484	9
Grand Saline[4]	3,120	9	0	1	0	8	24	8	13	3	0
Granger	1,531	0	0	0	0	0	11	3	7	1	0
Granite Shoals	5,144	6	0	1	0	5	25	3	20	2	0
Grapeland[4]	1,418	1	0	0	0	1	16	5	9	2	0
Grapevine	55,130	87	0	7	16	64	1,288	91	1,061	136	0
Greenville	27,713	83	0	24	11	48	579	87	446	46	8
Gregory	1,949	3	0	0	1	2	13	4	8	1	0
Groesbeck[4]	4,316	10	0	5	0	5	101	36	58	7	1
Groves	15,722	71	0	8	13	50	307	56	231	20	0
Gun Barrel City[4]	6,165	11	0	0	2	9	83	11	55	17	0
Hallettsville	2,626	14	0	0	0	14	48	8	37	3	0
Hallsville[5]	4,344	6	0	2	0	4		14		2	0
Haltom City	44,708	140	0	49	35	56	1,154	193	758	203	6
Hamilton[4]	2,994	6	0	1	0	5	57	7	45	5	1
Hamlin[4]	2,003	7	0	0	3	4	12	5	6	1	0
Harker Heights	31,710	63	2	12	22	27	749	86	620	43	2
Harlingen[4]	65,525	272	2	49	50	171	2,792	455	2,262	75	12
Haskell	3,204	2	0	0	1	1	13	9	4	0	0
Hawkins	1,311	3	0	0	0	3	7	1	3	3	0

Table 8. Offenses Known to Law Enforcement, by Selected State and City, 2018—Continued

(Number.)

State/city	Population	Violent crime	Murder and nonnegligent manslaughter	Rape[1]	Robbery	Aggravated assault	Property crime	Burglary	Larceny-theft	Motor vehicle theft	Arson[2]
Hearne	4,536	30	0	7	6	17	115	32	75	8	0
Heath	8,938	7	0	3	1	3	54	16	35	3	0
Hedwig Village[4]	2,685	5	0	0	1	4	141	7	126	8	0
Helotes	9,456	6	1	2	1	2	154	17	133	4	0
Hempstead	7,969	87	0	2	10	75	202	44	151	7	2
Henderson	13,241	86	0	4	10	72	516	62	426	28	3
Hereford	14,812	97	0	6	15	76	348	83	240	25	3
Hewitt	14,556	18	1	7	1	9	204	31	171	2	0
Hickory Creek	4,795	11	0	2	0	9	101	8	89	4	0
Hidalgo	14,133	44	0	8	1	35	147	18	118	11	0
Highland Park	9,302	4	0	1	2	1	215	28	163	24	0
Highland Village[4]	16,805	8	0	1	1	6	132	9	116	7	0
Hill Country Village	1,098	0	0	0	0	0	35	7	24	4	0
Hillsboro[4]	8,422	20	1	5	4	10	310	29	270	11	0
Hitchcock	8,038	26	0	0	8	18	159	51	97	11	0
Hollywood Park	3,400	2	0	1	1	0	73	5	63	5	0
Hondo	9,375	27	0	7	1	19	275	34	237	4	0
Hooks	2,740	0	0	0	0	0	20	5	14	1	0
Horizon City	19,978	12	0	0	4	8	111	24	83	4	0
Horseshoe Bay[4]	3,936	10	0	0	1	9	50	5	41	4	0
Houston[4,6]	2,344,966	24,062	276	1,261	8,761	13,764	94,033	16,317	65,767	11,949	
Howe	3,163	5	0	1	0	4	25	8	15	2	0
Hudson	4,910	13	0	0	0	13	61	42	19	0	0
Humble	16,122	145	2	44	55	44	1,562	155	1,202	205	1
Huntington[4]	2,127	2	0	1	0	1	42	13	22	7	0
Huntsville	41,651	134	0	14	16	104	666	103	510	53	2
Hurst	39,292	95	1	30	32	32	1,422	100	1,275	47	1
Hutchins	5,671	13	0	1	7	5	268	93	145	30	0
Hutto	26,924	11	0	3	0	8	87	10	76	1	0
Idalou	2,311	4	0	3	0	1	16	1	9	6	0
Ingleside	10,453	14	1	5	1	7	206	60	131	15	2
Ingram[4]	1,863	3	0	0	0	3	36	10	25	1	0
Iowa Park	6,352	9	0	3	0	6	38	6	27	5	1
Irving	243,940	510	10	55	218	227	5,759	712	4,327	720	15
Itasca	1,692	1	0	0	0	1	17	6	9	2	0
Jacinto City	10,675	17	0	0	9	8	232	38	152	42	1
Jacksboro	4,338	7	0	1	0	6	46	12	31	3	1
Jacksonville	14,960	77	1	10	4	62	375	98	258	19	0
Jarrell[4]	1,643	1	0	0	0	1	13	0	13	0	0
Jasper[4]	7,602	21	1	0	2	18	331	49	268	14	2
Jersey Village	7,974	7	0	0	3	4	167	32	109	26	1
Jones Creek	2,099	1	0	0	1	0	27	9	17	1	0
Jonestown	2,109	5	0	1	0	4	39	8	30	1	0
Joshua	8,019	13	0	3	0	10	123	25	91	7	0
Jourdanton	4,403	0	0	0	0	0	2	0	2	0	0
Junction	2,431	5	0	0	0	5	17	5	10	2	1
Karnes City	3,333	11	0	1	2	8	40	13	23	4	0
Katy	18,965	49	0	17	14	18	560	38	493	29	1
Kaufman	7,428	16	0	4	1	11	178	32	129	17	0
Keene	6,487	27	0	2	0	25	55	11	38	6	0
Keller	48,439	25	0	10	3	12	321	20	287	14	0
Kemah	2,060	5	0	2	1	2	139	15	109	15	0
Kenedy	3,340	20	0	0	1	19	186	34	147	5	0
Kennedale	8,587	10	0	4	4	2	133	39	77	17	0
Kermit	6,131	28	0	2	1	25	56	14	30	12	2
Kerrville	23,532	68	1	6	6	55	400	41	343	16	1
Kilgore[4]	14,978	42	0	6	4	32	409	80	292	37	0
Killeen	148,007	577	7	117	146	307	3,336	854	2,233	249	30
Kingsville	25,383	81	0	0	8	73	754	162	571	21	1
Kirby[4]	8,807	29	0	2	9	18	194	48	111	35	1
Knox City[4]	1,137	1	0	0	1	0	17	13	4	0	0
Kountze	2,111	6	0	1	2	3	52	22	28	2	1
Kress	689	1	0	0	0	1	1	0	1	0	0
Kyle[4]	46,155	80	1	20	7	52	538	42	452	44	2
La Feria	7,384	31	0	0	0	31	138	41	92	5	0
Lago Vista	6,923	12	0	2	1	9	69	18	45	6	0
La Grange[4]	4,686	21	0	2	3	16	115	25	86	4	0
La Grulla[4]	1,711	4	0	0	0	4	8	0	6	2	0
Laguna Vista[4]	3,206	6	0	0	0	6	21	14	6	1	0
La Joya	4,328	40	0	5	2	33	61	10	51	0	0
Lake Dallas	8,084	37	0	8	1	28	102	25	65	12	1
Lake Jackson	27,568	50	0	21	7	22	553	61	459	33	2
Lakeside	1,404	2	0	2	0	0	18	0	13	5	0
Lakeview, Harrison County	6,388	6	0	2	1	3	54	8	41	5	0
Lakeway	15,722	22	0	10	1	11	154	14	131	9	1
Lake Worth	5,002	15	0	0	9	6	356	65	279	12	0
La Marque	17,107	73	1	6	24	42	904	129	729	46	1
Lamesa	9,183	43	1	10	3	29	374	98	257	19	1
Lampasas	7,992	21	0	10	1	10	183	24	155	4	1
Lancaster	39,772	171	4	12	64	91	983	149	652	182	1
La Porte	35,591	65	2	21	10	32	457	71	334	52	2
Laredo	264,214	890	10	145	141	594	6,367	692	5,506	169	37
La Vernia	1,464	2	0	0	0	2	28	2	26	0	0

Table 8. Offenses Known to Law Enforcement, by Selected State and City, 2018—Continued

(Number.)

State/city	Population	Violent crime	Murder and nonnegligent manslaughter	Rape[1]	Robbery	Aggravated assault	Property crime	Burglary	Larceny-theft	Motor vehicle theft	Arson[2]
Lavon	3,299	3	0	1	0	2	27	1	26	0	0
League City	108,275	109	1	41	20	47	1,814	215	1,485	114	12
Leander	53,637	48	0	27	3	18	501	44	443	14	3
Leon Valley[4]	11,598	34	0	2	6	26	489	55	388	46	1
Levelland[4]	13,646	124	1	23	3	97	426	120	275	31	3
Lewisville	107,560	275	4	57	71	143	2,396	354	1,807	235	6
Liberty	9,334	33	0	5	4	24	184	21	145	18	0
Liberty Hill	2,119	2	0	0	0	2	33	10	19	4	0
Lindale	6,268	12	0	2	1	9	142	35	102	5	0
Linden	1,927	3	0	0	0	3	37	6	28	3	0
Little Elm	50,547	88	1	37	7	43	275	39	216	20	1
Littlefield	5,934	36	0	7	2	27	142	30	104	8	2
Live Oak	16,230	42	0	10	7	25	505	38	428	39	3
Livingston	5,128	36	0	7	8	21	259	34	209	16	1
Lockhart[4]	13,944	12	1	1	0	10	171	44	120	7	0
Log Cabin	752	2	0	0	0	2	12	8	4	0	0
Lone Star	1,497	15	0	1	0	14	16	3	13	0	0
Longview	81,660	326	8	53	46	219	2,506	584	1,722	200	6
Lorena[4]	1,771	8	0	1	2	5	34	6	28	0	0
Los Fresnos	7,947	42	0	2	0	40	132	10	115	7	1
Lubbock	257,372	2,565	13	239	443	1,870	11,743	2,312	8,228	1,203	57
Lufkin	35,937	134	1	20	16	97	1,403	260	1,067	76	5
Luling	5,979	35	0	5	4	26	97	17	75	5	0
Lumberton	12,948	18	0	5	2	11	153	15	118	20	0
Lyford	2,546	11	0	0	1	10	35	7	25	3	0
Lytle[4]	2,992	3	0	2	0	1	93	5	73	15	0
Madisonville	4,709	16	0	0	4	12	118	31	80	7	0
Magnolia	2,143	3	0	0	1	2	18	4	13	1	0
Manor[4]	10,102	41	0	4	3	34	220	27	182	11	2
Mansfield	70,851	73	0	31	15	27	766	93	624	49	1
Manvel[4]	11,097	13	0	3	0	10	72	30	36	6	0
Marble Falls	6,579	9	0	2	1	6	236	45	184	7	0
Marfa	1,742	6	0	0	0	6	2	1	1	0	0
Marshall	23,146	136	2	6	17	111	687	143	493	51	10
Mathis	4,797	53	0	3	2	48	89	32	47	10	6
McAllen	144,363	122	0	39	26	57	3,856	203	3,598	55	7
McGregor	5,134	18	0	11	0	7	45	11	29	5	2
McKinney	189,555	288	0	63	77	148	1,980	251	1,573	156	15
Meadows Place	4,621	12	0	1	7	4	111	16	85	10	0
Melissa[4]	10,107	9	0	3	0	6	58	16	41	1	0
Memorial Villages	12,402	4	0	0	2	2	72	15	54	3	0
Memphis[4]	2,062	7	0	0	0	7	33	17	11	5	0
Mercedes	16,869	81	1	17	9	54	646	92	510	44	1
Merkel	2,601	9	0	4	0	5	23	12	10	1	0
Mesquite[4]	144,558	573	6	54	210	303	5,238	811	3,603	824	10
Midland	140,072	403	5	60	59	279	2,764	378	2,108	278	16
Midlothian	26,346	22	0	6	4	12	336	34	290	12	1
Mineola	4,713	9	0	0	0	9	96	10	82	4	0
Mineral Wells	14,729	52	0	5	10	37	396	121	246	29	2
Mission	85,368	94	0	35	27	32	1,594	150	1,380	64	22
Missouri City	75,628	102	5	21	27	49	815	96	674	45	5
Monahans	7,611	10	1	3	1	5	84	23	59	2	0
Mont Belvieu	6,301	6	0	2	0	4	102	15	74	13	0
Montgomery	1,034	4	0	0	0	4	8	2	6	0	0
Morgans Point Resort	4,499	0	0	0	0	0	0	0	0	0	0
Mount Pleasant	16,291	63	1	14	8	40	555	72	460	23	3
Muleshoe[4]	5,073	7	0	0	0	7	44	6	34	4	0
Murphy	21,084	10	0	1	2	7	113	6	102	5	1
Nacogdoches	33,703	102	3	13	29	57	979	199	749	31	1
Nash	3,483	9	0	1	0	8	97	18	66	13	0
Nassau Bay	4,058	16	0	4	5	7	102	10	84	8	0
Natalia	1,567	5	0	0	0	5	19	10	7	2	1
Navasota[4]	7,677	34	0	5	3	26	162	64	65	33	0
Nederland[4]	17,563	47	1	11	1	34	309	50	234	25	0
Needville	3,083	4	0	1	0	3	18	2	14	2	0
New Boston	4,642	39	0	0	0	39	182	16	164	2	0
New Braunfels[4]	82,739	241	2	43	22	174	1,197	215	892	90	0
Nixon	2,506	21	0	1	1	19	13	3	10	0	0
Nocona	2,966	8	0	2	0	6	16	11	5	0	0
Nolanville	5,380	8	0	6	0	2	70	17	53	0	0
Northeast	3,106	2	0	0	1	1	67	4	60	3	0
Northlake[4]	2,946	14	2	2	3	7	63	4	51	8	0
North Richland Hills[4]	71,498	104	1	13	26	64	1,387	151	1,113	123	0
Oak Ridge North	3,143	2	0	0	1	1	33	5	23	5	0
Odessa	119,545	1,049	8	118	104	819	2,996	504	2,123	369	8
Olmos Park	2,434	1	0	0	0	1	24	5	17	2	0
Olney[4]	3,078	4	0	1	1	2	60	15	42	3	0
Olton	2,097	6	0	1	0	5	28	16	12	0	5
Omaha	980	1	0	0	0	1	4	2	1	1	0
Onalaska[4]	2,771	8	0	0	0	8	22	13	5	4	0
Overton	2,490	12	0	1	1	10	22	9	12	1	0
Ovilla	4,207	2	0	0	0	2	21	1	17	3	0
Oyster Creek	1,163	16	0	0	1	15	27	6	16	5	0

Table 8. Offenses Known to Law Enforcement, by Selected State and City, 2018—Continued

(Number.)

State/city	Population	Violent crime	Murder and nonnegligent manslaughter	Rape[1]	Robbery	Aggravated assault	Property crime	Burglary	Larceny-theft	Motor vehicle theft	Arson[2]
Palacios[4]	4,634	12	0	1	2	9	94	40	51	3	1
Palmer	2,083	3	0	0	1	2	15	5	9	1	0
Palmhurst	2,765	6	0	0	0	6	158	0	158	0	0
Palmview[4]	5,842	48	0	1	9	38	262	43	201	18	2
Pampa	17,412	103	1	8	8	86	653	157	453	43	0
Panhandle	2,337	11	0	1	0	10	15	7	6	2	0
Pantego	2,564	11	0	0	2	9	83	9	71	3	1
Paris	24,736	218	1	4	23	190	725	173	507	45	0
Parker[4]	4,746	2	0	1	0	1	27	4	22	1	0
Pasadena	154,101	679	7	109	159	404	3,467	519	2,603	345	9
Patton Village	2,016	3	0	1	0	2	14	5	7	2	0
Pearland	124,179	118	2	19	32	65	1,841	215	1,532	94	3
Pearsall[4]	10,525	14	0	1	1	12	209	69	129	11	1
Pecos	10,094	124	0	17	5	102	164	26	135	3	1
Pelican Bay	1,780	1	0	0	0	1	25	14	10	1	0
Penitas	4,961	16	0	3	1	12	64	12	48	4	0
Perryton	8,675	30	0	6	0	24	164	47	109	8	0
Petersburg	1,128	3	0	0	1	2	6	4	2	0	0
Pharr	80,814	238	2	58	26	152	1,585	244	1,280	61	12
Pilot Point	4,387	0	0	0	0	0	11	3	7	1	0
Pinehurst	2,070	9	0	0	1	8	56	2	49	5	0
Pittsburg[4]	4,668	22	0	3	0	19	90	27	54	9	0
Plainview[4]	20,569	59	0	8	5	46	503	108	376	19	0
Plano	289,897	402	5	77	112	208	4,955	671	3,911	373	16
Pleasanton	10,627	30	0	9	1	20	406	70	315	21	0
Ponder	2,049	12	4	2	0	6	19	3	14	2	0
Port Aransas	4,245	15	0	3	1	11	279	38	216	25	0
Port Arthur	55,643	390	13	20	96	261	1,445	504	807	134	7
Port Isabel[4]	5,064	18	0	1	0	17	168	17	142	9	0
Portland	17,547	25	0	8	5	12	376	33	323	20	1
Port Neches	12,881	56	0	11	2	43	178	49	114	15	0
Poteet	3,436	11	0	1	0	10	99	25	65	9	0
Pottsboro	2,381	1	0	0	0	1	6	1	4	1	0
Prairie View	6,526	6	1	3	1	1	22	3	18	1	0
Primera	4,954	3	0	2	0	1	30	7	21	2	0
Princeton	10,749	19	0	8	3	8	183	14	157	12	0
Prosper	22,570	63	0	7	0	56	188	31	154	3	0
Queen City	1,449	10	0	1	0	9	18	2	15	1	0
Quitman	1,826	9	0	5	0	4	25	10	14	1	0
Ralls[4]	1,852	6	0	0	1	5	11	4	3	4	0
Rancho Viejo	2,483	2	0	0	0	2	14	6	8	0	2
Ranger	2,454	22	0	1	0	21	37	19	16	2	0
Raymondville	10,959	106	0	9	7	90	318	91	216	11	6
Red Oak	13,095	22	0	0	9	13	336	59	257	20	1
Refugio	2,826	3	0	0	0	3	12	3	7	2	0
Reno, Lamar County	3,318	2	0	0	0	2	72	8	54	10	0
Reno, Parker County	2,971	27	0	0	0	27	31	10	18	3	0
Richardson	119,480	135	2	18	52	63	2,522	364	1,944	214	3
Richland Hills	8,089	38	0	8	15	15	283	38	207	38	0
Richmond	12,130	46	1	9	7	29	255	58	187	10	1
Richwood	3,967	4	0	2	2	0	35	7	24	4	0
Riesel	1,026	0	0	0	0	0	4	3	0	1	0
Rio Bravo	4,755	0	0	0	0	0	0	0	0	0	0
Rio Grande City	14,617	59	0	1	3	55	194	29	151	14	1
Rio Hondo	2,835	4	0	0	0	4	30	10	20	0	0
River Oaks	7,743	5	0	0	0	5	101	11	85	5	0
Roanoke	8,489	21	0	0	3	18	99	15	78	6	0
Robinson	11,774	25	0	0	1	24	156	23	125	8	0
Rockdale	5,663	12	1	2	3	6	146	28	108	10	0
Rockport	10,734	22	0	5	1	16	443	114	309	20	2
Rockwall	45,183	42	1	15	6	20	750	34	653	63	0
Rollingwood	1,585	0	0	0	0	0	17	1	14	2	0
Roma	11,506	25	0	4	2	19	82	16	48	18	0
Roman Forest	1,968	1	0	1	0	0	1	0	0	1	0
Rosenberg[4]	38,541	157	1	26	29	101	615	97	433	85	0
Round Rock	127,354	154	1	34	29	90	2,494	288	2,148	58	5
Rowlett	63,863	114	1	18	16	79	912	94	744	74	0
Royse City	13,104	20	0	3	1	16	129	17	101	11	1
Runaway Bay[4]	1,524	0	0	0	0	0	8	3	4	1	0
Rusk	5,539	18	0	3	4	11	84	27	51	6	1
Sabinal	1,696	0	0	0	0	0	10	2	7	1	0
Sachse	26,839	15	0	8	2	5	208	26	167	15	0
Salado[4]	2,308	5	0	1	1	3	15	5	9	1	0
San Angelo	101,084	373	2	82	52	237	3,383	583	2,567	233	3
San Antonio	1,539,328	9,647	107	1,346	1,767	6,427	61,478	9,118	46,271	6,089	186
San Augustine	1,856	0	0	0	0	0	6	4	2	0	0
San Benito	24,559	65	0	33	9	23	1,018	193	798	27	3
San Diego	4,261	13	0	0	1	12	3	3	0	0	0
San Elizario	9,161	4	0	0	1	3	28	11	10	7	0
Sanger[5]	8,457	27	0	6	0	21		23		12	0
San Juan	37,398	155	1	19	14	121	858	98	715	45	1
San Marcos[4]	66,157	263	1	83	42	137	1,415	270	1,044	101	3
San Saba	3,059	8	0	0	0	8	46	15	28	3	2

Table 8. Offenses Known to Law Enforcement, by Selected State and City, 2018—Continued

(Number.)

State/city	Population	Violent crime	Murder and nonnegligent manslaughter	Rape[1]	Robbery	Aggravated assault	Property crime	Burglary	Larceny-theft	Motor vehicle theft	Arson[2]
Sansom Park Village	6,034	12	0	0	4	8	120	43	58	19	0
Santa Fe	13,600	17	0	7	4	6	171	45	108	18	1
Santa Rosa	2,797	0	0	0	0	0	8	4	4	0	0
Schertz	41,383	95	1	23	13	58	670	117	517	36	1
Schulenburg[4]	2,915	18	0	0	0	18	52	12	37	3	1
Seabrook	13,958	25	0	12	2	11	144	34	98	12	0
Seagoville	16,981	12	0	0	4	8	384	72	210	102	0
Seagraves	2,875	5	0	1	0	4	13	2	10	1	0
Sealy[4]	6,544	14	0	2	3	9	91	28	55	8	0
Seguin[4]	29,487	88	1	6	18	63	745	78	633	34	1
Selma	11,742	24	0	8	5	11	240	33	178	29	1
Seminole	7,725	52	0	2	2	48	112	26	80	6	2
Seven Points	1,504	5	0	2	0	3	28	3	21	4	0
Seymour	2,606	7	0	0	0	7	30	3	25	2	0
Shavano Park	3,913	2	0	0	0	2	22	6	16	0	0
Shenandoah	3,008	9	0	1	4	4	229	12	197	20	1
Sherman	42,448	147	0	29	28	90	1,068	224	778	66	5
Shiner	2,173	1	0	0	0	1	14	3	10	1	0
Silsbee	6,734	18	0	2	2	14	129	27	88	14	0
Sinton	5,424	46	0	11	0	35	190	41	144	5	2
Smithville	4,322	15	1	3	1	10	87	18	63	6	0
Snyder	11,337	34	0	3	2	29	198	55	140	3	0
Socorro	34,327	45	0	6	8	31	251	24	202	25	0
Somerset	1,893	2	0	0	0	2	6	1	3	2	0
Somerville	1,445	6	0	1	1	4	23	6	14	3	0
Sonora	2,737	7	0	2	1	4	25	0	23	2	0
Sour Lake	1,860	0	0	0	0	0	23	2	17	4	0
South Houston	17,619	73	1	6	35	31	422	71	245	106	2
Southlake	32,639	11	0	3	4	4	450	21	414	15	0
South Padre Island[4]	2,830	55	0	21	1	33	457	33	394	30	0
Southside Place[4]	1,874	0	0	0	0	0	16	2	13	1	0
Spearman[4]	3,267	4	0	0	0	4	11	9	1	1	0
Splendora	2,109	4	0	0	2	2	44	21	16	7	0
Springtown	2,950	7	0	1	0	6	78	12	66	0	0
Spring Valley[4]	4,363	3	0	0	1	2	73	11	57	5	0
Spur	1,187	0	0	0	0	0	3	3	0	0	0
Stagecoach	600	0	0	0	0	0	0	0	0	0	0
Stamford	2,933	4	0	0	2	2	50	10	37	3	0
Stanton	3,016	9	0	3	1	5	32	5	17	10	1
Stephenville	21,400	30	0	8	3	19	404	64	316	24	1
Sugar Land	89,919	82	0	15	45	22	1,537	186	1,288	63	0
Sullivan City	4,172	29	0	5	1	23	91	25	62	4	0
Sulphur Springs	16,111	37	2	6	9	20	157	33	98	26	2
Sunset Valley	693	6	0	0	3	3	138	11	122	5	0
Surfside Beach[4]	582	6	0	2	1	3	32	7	24	1	0
Sweeny[4]	3,753	13	0	5	1	7	82	10	68	4	1
Sweetwater	10,530	50	0	4	5	41	307	139	152	16	1
Taft[4]	2,924	5	0	0	0	5	60	24	32	4	0
Tahoka[4]	2,617	1	0	0	0	1	26	7	15	4	0
Tatum	1,386	4	0	0	0	4	25	14	9	2	0
Taylor	17,225	50	0	8	5	37	387	92	281	14	7
Teague[4]	3,498	4	0	0	2	2	45	15	26	4	0
Temple	75,706	236	12	70	51	103	1,940	342	1,408	190	9
Terrell	18,104	73	3	9	14	47	581	97	424	60	2
Terrell Hills	5,473	4	0	1	0	3	43	15	28	0	0
Texarkana	37,460	171	3	28	45	95	1,914	348	1,427	139	16
Texas City	49,044	236	5	46	62	123	1,489	278	1,100	111	2
The Colony	43,697	100	0	61	5	34	477	60	382	35	5
Thorndale	1,302	7	0	3	0	4	21	6	13	2	0
Tioga[4]	1,009	2	0	0	0	2	4	3	1	0	0
Tool[4]	2,299	0	0	0	0	0	9	4	3	2	0
Trophy Club	13,090	2	0	1	1	0	69	5	58	6	1
Troup	2,019	9	0	2	2	5	66	28	38	0	0
Troy	2,030	6	0	0	2	4	35	4	29	2	0
Tulia[4]	4,690	34	0	2	1	31	132	34	89	9	1
Tye[4]	1,300	3	0	1	0	2	30	5	23	2	0
Tyler	106,159	412	7	71	82	252	3,133	386	2,596	151	1
Universal City	20,825	63	0	15	20	28	546	120	391	35	3
University Park[4]	25,516	5	0	1	4	0	302	33	232	37	0
Uvalde	16,375	36	0	11	7	18	621	109	499	13	4
Van	2,742	5	0	4	0	1	48	8	36	4	0
Van Alstyne	4,115	10	0	0	3	7	59	17	40	2	0
Venus	3,683	3	0	0	0	3	30	2	27	1	0
Vernon	10,259	46	0	5	3	38	269	64	195	10	1
Victoria	67,766	280	4	51	46	179	1,885	358	1,440	87	4
Waco[4]	138,091	878	3	129	122	624	4,851	1,194	3,329	328	20
Waelder	1,129	4	0	1	2	1	2	1	1	0	0
Wake Village	5,416	9	2	0	2	5	99	17	71	11	0
Waller[4]	3,546	2	0	1	0	1	43	10	31	2	0
Wallis	1,304	5	0	0	0	5	5	1	4	0	0
Watauga[4]	24,757	48	0	13	10	25	319	40	244	35	0
Waxahachie	36,225	73	1	4	17	51	527	65	417	45	2
Weatherford	31,389	58	0	15	10	33	508	67	407	34	0

Table 8. Offenses Known to Law Enforcement, by Selected State and City, 2018—Continued

(Number.)

State/city	Population	Violent crime	Murder and nonnegligent manslaughter	Rape[1]	Robbery	Aggravated assault	Property crime	Burglary	Larceny-theft	Motor vehicle theft	Arson[2]
Webster	11,194	47	0	12	16	19	774	84	594	96	0
Weimar	2,189	3	0	2	0	1	23	5	17	1	0
Weslaco	40,856	162	0	29	42	91	1,595	162	1,404	29	3
West[4]	2,990	5	0	2	0	3	40	8	30	2	0
West Columbia	3,899	3	0	2	0	1	97	24	69	4	0
West Lake Hills	3,444	7	0	0	0	7	89	9	79	1	0
West Orange	3,414	9	0	1	2	6	97	10	80	7	0
Westover Hills[4]	701	1	0	0	0	1	12	6	6	0	0
West University Place	15,759	2	0	1	1	0	111	35	71	5	0
Westworth	2,763	1	0	0	0	1	239	31	208	0	0
Wharton[4]	8,754	31	0	0	4	27	256	60	187	9	5
Whitehouse	8,406	9	0	1	0	8	53	10	40	3	0
White Oak	6,332	3	0	0	0	3	72	21	47	4	0
Whitesboro	4,039	3	0	0	1	2	44	6	34	4	0
White Settlement	18,082	33	0	0	14	19	338	56	231	51	0
Whitewright	1,689	1	0	0	0	1	8	3	5	0	0
Whitney	2,146	6	0	0	0	6	27	8	18	1	0
Wichita Falls	104,738	387	5	78	139	165	3,234	602	2,381	251	1
Willis	6,515	40	0	7	6	27	141	25	101	15	5
Willow Park	5,569	9	0	3	0	6	49	6	36	7	0
Wills Point[4]	3,639	9	0	3	0	6	22	8	13	1	0
Wilmer	4,199	9	0	0	2	7	93	16	68	9	0
Windcrest	5,936	11	0	1	8	2	252	19	206	27	1
Winnsboro[4]	3,337	6	0	1	0	5	36	8	28	0	0
Winters[4]	2,461	9	0	0	1	8	28	20	8	0	0
Wolfforth	5,131	0	0	0	0	0	32	10	22	0	0
Woodville	2,488	4	0	1	2	1	10	5	5	0	0
Woodway	8,878	5	0	1	1	3	109	5	100	4	1
Wortham[4]	994	1	0	0	0	1	12	2	9	1	0
Wylie	51,051	52	0	16	9	27	398	31	347	20	4
Yoakum	5,983	14	0	3	0	11	51	18	30	3	0
UTAH											
Alta	385	0	0	0	0	0	15	1	14	0	0
American Fork/Cedar Hills	40,366	22	0	8	1	13	702	36	641	25	2
Aurora	1,047	0	0	0	0	0	0	0	0	0	0
Big Water	500	1	0	0	0	1	0	0	0	0	0
Bluffdale	14,648	13	0	3	0	10	177	51	100	26	0
Bountiful	44,317	43	1	25	7	10	642	87	500	55	1
Brigham City	19,362	28	0	7	2	19	362	72	261	29	
Cedar City	32,242	70	1	8	2	59	751	119	571	61	4
Centerville	18,013	23	0	18	1	4	380	32	317	31	0
Clearfield	31,558	59	0	15	8	36	462	68	341	53	2
Clinton	22,179	13	1	2	2	8	301	17	265	19	0
Cottonwood Heights	34,054	43	0	7	12	24	787	103	638	46	2
Draper	48,518	84	0	35	6	43	976	114	729	133	4
Enoch	6,892	31	0	2	0	29	38	8	24	6	0
Ephraim	7,302	16	0	7	1	8	90	6	83	1	0
Farmington	25,006	15	0	6	1	8	306	38	245	23	4
Garland	2,541	5	0	2	1	2	51	14	35	2	
Grantsville	11,326	29	0	9	2	18	192	34	142	16	4
Harrisville	6,678	7	0	5	1	1	224	21	184	19	2
Heber	16,527	26	0	4	2	20	228	17	194	17	
Helper	2,075	4	0	0	0	4	47	12	33	2	0
Hurricane	17,676	22	0	8	0	14	283	60	201	22	0
Kanab	4,729	3	0	0	0	3	32	5	26	1	0
Kaysville	32,404	24	0	13	2	9	246	41	190	15	2
La Verkin[4]	4,387	9	0	6	0	3	61	11	42	8	0
Layton	78,052	134	1	58	17	58	1,561	249	1,238	74	5
Lehi	65,125	59	0	28	1	30	694	97	563	34	4
Logan	51,508	70	1	35	3	31	852	145	675	32	4
Lone Peak	29,969	7	0	6	0	1	151	28	112	11	
Mapleton	10,041	1	0	0	0	1	56	11	42	3	0
Moab	5,274	33	1	7	2	23	175	15	138	22	2
Monticello	1,995	0	0	0	0	0	18	3	13	2	0
Mount Pleasant	3,440	4	0	2	0	2	49	4	43	2	0
Murray	49,675	216	1	56	41	118	3,027	431	2,188	408	4
Nephi	6,037	9	0	5	1	3	100	21	72	7	
North Ogden	19,771	6	0	3	1	2	232	34	173	25	0
North Park	15,713	6	0	3	1	2	169	12	150	7	
North Salt Lake	21,190	27	1	8	7	11	405	49	314	42	1
Ogden	87,616	417	5	74	81	257	3,218	500	2,319	399	10
Orem	99,221	69	1	20	12	36	1,827	152	1,576	99	0
Park City	8,491	51	0	2	2	47	225	14	193	18	0
Parowan	3,073	14	0	12	0	2	50	7	36	7	
Payson	20,079	10	0	3	1	6	318	54	254	10	
Pleasant Grove	39,641	29	1	6	0	22	424	62	335	27	0
Pleasant View	10,663	11	0	3	1	7	108	21	74	13	1
Price	8,201	34	0	4	2	28	486	57	420	9	0
Provo	117,986	207	2	70	22	113	2,090	209	1,747	134	3
Richfield	7,777	4	0	2	0	2	247	27	205	15	
Riverdale	8,795	23	0	1	6	16	530	38	476	16	0
Roosevelt	6,962	22	0	14	2	6	201	28	150	23	0

Table 8. Offenses Known to Law Enforcement, by Selected State and City, 2018—Continued

(Number.)

State/city	Population	Violent crime	Murder and nonnegligent manslaughter	Rape[1]	Robbery	Aggravated assault	Property crime	Burglary	Larceny-theft	Motor vehicle theft	Arson[2]
Roy	38,834	53	0	19	6	28	514	90	369	55	0
Salem	8,496	1	0	0	0	1	69	10	57	2	0
Salina	2,560	4	0	1	1	2	91	21	59	11	0
Salt Lake City	202,633	1,480	10	245	414	811	12,516	1,601	9,422	1,493	32
Sandy	97,057	159	0	54	21	84	2,613	405	1,940	268	5
Santa Clara/Ivins	16,671	9	0	0	0	9	126	28	87	11	0
Santaquin/Genola	13,584	4	0	3	0	1	114	21	78	15	0
Saratoga Springs	31,786	32	0	14	0	18	226	47	169	10	0
South Jordan	74,321	77	1	17	16	43	1,453	160	1,165	128	3
South Ogden	17,174	25	1	12	3	9	329	80	226	23	1
South Salt Lake	25,160	242	6	50	57	129	1,796	237	1,246	313	2
Spanish Fork	40,095	12	0	4	2	6	352	29	294	29	0
Spring City	1,053	0	0	0	0	0	20	6	14	0	0
Springdale	601	1	0	0	0	1	21	4	16	1	0
Springville	33,824	23	0	9	3	11	627	52	538	37	
St. George	86,202	196	3	48	19	126	1,388	228	1,049	111	7
Sunset	5,304	15	0	3	0	12	83	14	64	5	1
Syracuse	30,301	23	0	13	2	8	235	39	180	16	0
Tooele	35,065	104	1	35	17	51	1,143	110	939	94	6
Tremonton	8,764	9	1	3	0	5	151	30	107	14	
Vernal	10,484	32	2	8	1	21	261	28	221	12	0
Washington	27,705	35	0	16	2	17	477	51	410	16	0
West Bountiful	5,705	18	0	13	1	4	147	10	115	22	0
West Jordan	115,392	298	1	39	50	208	3,036	352	2,374	310	3
West Valley	137,132	945	8	183	148	606	4,915	741	3,353	821	15
Willard	1,872	6	0	0	0	6	35	10	21	4	0
Woods Cross	11,600	11	0	1	7	3	176	27	129	20	2
VERMONT											
Barre	8,605	72	1	28	3	40	237	24	212	1	2
Barre Town	7,693	8	0	3	2	3	44	8	36	0	0
Bellows Falls	2,993	3	0	0	0	3	56	9	44	3	0
Bennington	14,900	31	0	5	4	22	415	51	351	13	0
Berlin	2,796	4	0	0	1	3	120	6	113	1	0
Bradford	2,697	0	0	0	0	0	22	7	14	1	0
Brandon	3,766	9	0	1	0	8	41	7	34	0	0
Brattleboro	11,410	40	0	2	9	29	457	67	368	22	2
Bristol	3,891	4	0	0	1	3	17	4	10	3	0
Burlington	42,212	115	1	22	10	82	837	120	704	13	3
Castleton	4,595	0	0	0	0	0	0	0	0	0	0
Chester	3,006	3	0	1	0	2	28	8	19	1	0
Colchester	17,313	16	0	6	1	9	196	21	175	0	1
Dover	1,057	5	0	1	0	4	52	6	46	0	0
Essex	21,803	13	0	0	3	10	297	59	227	11	2
Hardwick	2,849	7	0	2	1	4	33	6	27	0	0
Hartford	9,567	25	0	12	0	13	127	25	92	10	0
Hinesburg	4,577	3	0	1	0	2	18	2	14	2	0
Ludlow	1,870	3	0	1	0	2	12	1	11	0	0
Lyndonville	1,157	4	0	0	1	3	23	1	22	0	0
Manchester	4,230	5	0	0	0	5	46	8	38	0	1
Middlebury	8,613	5	0	1	0	4	96	11	82	3	0
Milton	11,024	16	0	8	1	7	104	20	84	0	0
Montpelier	7,434	7	0	4	1	2	161	28	132	1	1
Morristown	5,450	6	0	3	1	2	73	5	68	0	0
Newport	4,248	22	0	5	1	16	104	13	88	3	1
Northfield	6,006	16	0	4	2	10	46	8	35	3	0
Norwich	3,304	2	0	1	0	1	13	5	7	1	0
Pittsford	2,806	1	0	0	0	1	6	2	4	0	0
Royalton	2,835	0	0	0	0	0	9	1	7	1	0
Rutland	15,300	60	0	3	5	52	383	56	312	15	2
Rutland Town	4,078	5	0	3	0	2	48	4	44	0	0
Shelburne	7,817	3	0	1	0	2	48	8	36	4	0
South Burlington	19,318	32	1	17	1	13	572	51	520	1	1
Springfield	8,864	16	0	5	2	9	185	42	142	1	1
St. Albans	6,777	39	0	6	0	33	431	36	393	2	1
St. Johnsbury	7,158	15	0	3	0	12	98	12	85	1	1
Stowe	4,495	3	0	2	0	1	51	4	47	0	0
Swanton	6,560	8	0	0	0	8	55	12	40	3	0
Thetford	2,557	0	0	0	0	0	5	0	5	0	0
Vergennes	2,547	2	0	1	0	1	37	2	34	1	0
Weathersfield	2,745	4	0	1	0	3	15	4	11	0	0
Williston	9,778	7	0	2	0	5	193	17	174	2	0
Wilmington	1,796	2	0	2	0	0	11	2	7	2	0
Windsor	3,377	8	0	0	0	8	34	5	26	3	0
Winhall	730	1	0	0	0	1	9	0	9	0	0
Winooski	7,233	28	0	5	2	21	121	26	95	0	2
Woodstock	2,917	3	0	1	0	2	23	2	20	1	0
VIRGINIA											
Abingdon	7,949	6	0	2	2	2	129	7	112	10	0
Alexandria	162,588	260	4	24	78	154	2,482	128	1,967	387	5
Altavista	3,417	7	0	1	1	5	86	5	77	4	0
Amherst	2,194	4	0	0	0	4	8	1	7	0	0

Table 8. Offenses Known to Law Enforcement, by Selected State and City, 2018—Continued

(Number.)

State/city	Population	Violent crime	Murder and nonnegligent manslaughter	Rape[1]	Robbery	Aggravated assault	Property crime	Burglary	Larceny-theft	Motor vehicle theft	Arson[2]
Appalachia	1,568	2	0	0	0	2	18	10	5	3	3
Ashland	7,876	37	1	3	6	27	199	13	177	9	0
Bedford	6,532	20	0	9	1	10	199	14	178	7	2
Berryville	4,361	1	0	0	0	1	36	4	32	0	1
Big Stone Gap	5,215	3	0	2	0	1	110	12	94	4	3
Blacksburg	44,853	41	0	20	4	17	322	28	285	9	0
Blackstone	3,367	14	0	4	3	7	83	16	64	3	0
Bluefield	4,624	6	1	3	1	1	218	16	198	4	0
Bridgewater	6,125	3	0	1	0	2	25	2	23	0	0
Bristol	16,613	42	2	9	3	28	513	68	395	50	2
Broadway	3,908	1	0	0	1	0	9	2	6	1	0
Buena Vista	6,272	5	0	1	0	4	54	10	39	5	0
Burkeville	402	0	0	0	0	0	10	0	10	0	0
Cape Charles	1,009	1	0	0	0	1	4	0	3	1	0
Cedar Bluff	1,011	1	0	1	0	0	5	1	4	0	1
Charlottesville	48,585	174	1	36	30	107	1,161	116	961	84	0
Chase City	2,219	4	1	0	0	3	46	12	29	5	0
Chatham	1,434	0	0	0	0	0	4	0	4	0	0
Chesapeake	242,310	979	7	99	143	730	5,191	596	4,285	310	11
Chilhowie	1,718	1	0	1	0	0	17	3	13	1	0
Chincoteague	2,881	11	0	2	2	7	73	8	64	1	0
Christiansburg	22,444	43	0	15	2	26	532	34	485	13	1
Clarksville	1,175	0	0	0	0	0	12	1	11	0	0
Clifton Forge	3,524	7	0	0	0	7	48	6	35	7	0
Clintwood	1,311	2	0	0	0	2	15	2	13	0	0
Coeburn	1,881	9	0	2	0	7	38	5	32	1	0
Colonial Heights	17,857	50	0	17	8	25	676	29	620	27	2
Covington	5,462	4	0	1	0	3	107	10	93	4	2
Crewe	2,151	8	0	0	2	6	52	5	36	11	1
Culpeper	18,671	31	0	6	9	16	296	17	266	13	0
Damascus	788	0	0	0	0	0	16	3	13	0	0
Danville	40,781	216	11	26	61	118	1,632	222	1,326	84	14
Dayton	1,615	3	0	0	0	3	6	0	6	0	0
Dublin	2,667	3	0	2	0	1	23	4	19	0	0
Dumfries	5,265	9	0	0	5	4	74	14	45	15	0
Elkton	2,860	2	0	0	0	2	29	5	21	3	0
Emporia	5,184	26	0	2	8	16	192	14	176	2	0
Exmore	1,386	1	0	0	0	1	24	5	18	1	0
Fairfax City	24,259	24	0	5	13	6	405	13	366	26	1
Falls Church	14,884	12	0	1	3	8	176	15	148	13	1
Farmville	7,778	10	1	3	0	6	162	16	135	11	0
Franklin	8,100	25	1	6	7	11	348	38	290	20	2
Fredericksburg	28,919	108	2	13	16	77	999	58	905	36	4
Front Royal	15,356	33	0	16	6	11	279	25	239	15	1
Galax	6,559	27	0	5	3	19	292	20	259	13	1
Gate City	1,888	0	0	0	0	0	41	3	33	5	0
Glade Spring	1,424	0	0	0	0	0	2	0	2	0	0
Glasgow	1,106	0	0	0	0	0	2	0	2	0	0
Gordonsville	1,606	3	0	0	2	1	16	2	14	0	0
Gretna	1,205	0	0	0	0	0	3	0	3	0	0
Grottoes	2,813	1	0	0	0	1	29	1	27	1	0
Grundy	917	1	0	0	0	1	36	0	35	1	0
Halifax	1,219	1	0	0	0	1	14	2	11	1	0
Hampton[6]	133,965	316	16	24	120	156		491		231	21
Harrisonburg	54,869	110	4	17	12	77	834	98	711	25	3
Haymarket	1,744	5	0	1	0	4	11	0	9	2	0
Haysi	480	0	0	0	0	0	7	1	6	0	0
Herndon	24,697	32	1	10	18	3	259	28	226	5	0
Hillsville	2,644	3	0	2	0	1	63	10	50	3	0
Hopewell	22,562	99	6	7	25	61	553	119	403	31	2
Hurt	1,235	0	0	0	0	0	14	1	11	2	0
Independence	895	1	0	0	0	1	9	1	6	2	0
Jonesville	938	1	0	1	0	0	5	0	5	0	0
Kenbridge	1,198	0	0	0	0	0	0	0	0	0	0
Kilmarnock	1,407	1	0	0	0	1	25	7	18	0	0
La Crosse	574	2	0	0	2	0	5	4	1	0	0
Lawrenceville	1,004	2	0	0	1	1	4	1	3	0	0
Lebanon	3,184	8	0	6	1	1	154	30	120	4	0
Leesburg	56,030	100	0	18	16	66	626	24	571	31	0
Lexington	7,098	3	0	0	1	2	36	2	33	1	0
Louisa	1,678	2	0	0	0	2	53	2	51	0	0
Luray	4,806	7	0	2	1	4	137	14	112	11	1
Lynchburg	81,603	275	8	33	41	193	1,627	181	1,278	168	11
Manassas	41,888	105	1	23	16	65	636	72	525	39	4
Manassas Park	16,882	25	0	9	6	10	111	10	90	11	0
Marion	5,615	29	0	2	5	22	183	27	147	9	1
Martinsville	13,025	54	2	3	8	41	471	72	366	33	0
Middleburg	879	0	0	0	0	0	9	0	9	0	0
Middletown	1,365	1	0	1	0	0	15	3	12	0	0
Mount Jackson	2,100	1	0	0	0	1	50	3	44	3	0
Narrows	1,950	1	0	0	0	1	7	1	6	0	0
New Market	2,245	3	0	0	1	2	8	1	6	1	1
Newport News	178,734	942	24	89	187	642	5,148	693	3,961	494	31

Table 8. Offenses Known to Law Enforcement, by Selected State and City, 2018—Continued

(Number.)

State/city	Population	Violent crime	Murder and nonnegligent manslaughter	Rape[1]	Robbery	Aggravated assault	Property crime	Burglary	Larceny-theft	Motor vehicle theft	Arson[2]
Norfolk	244,347	1,134	36	117	321	660	8,463	703	6,972	788	14
Norton	3,914	9	0	3	1	5	138	6	127	5	0
Occoquan	1,097	0	0	0	0	0	2	0	2	0	0
Onancock	1,218	3	0	0	2	1	31	4	26	1	0
Onley	502	0	0	0	0	0	20	3	15	2	0
Orange	5,016	9	0	2	0	7	49	9	36	4	0
Parksley	817	1	0	0	0	1	6	0	4	2	0
Pearisburg	2,643	3	0	2	0	1	49	5	38	6	0
Pennington Gap	1,732	3	1	1	0	1	47	2	44	1	1
Petersburg	31,568	224	14	13	53	144	916	141	681	94	7
Pocahontas	357	0	0	0	0	0	0	0	0	0	0
Poquoson	12,011	19	0	6	1	12	101	18	80	3	1
Portsmouth	94,218	749	20	44	203	482	4,977	958	3,651	368	11
Pound	939	3	0	1	0	2	3	0	3	0	0
Pulaski	8,720	27	1	11	8	7	258	32	213	13	1
Purcellville	10,090	13	0	3	1	9	46	2	38	6	0
Radford	17,797	52	0	20	4	28	237	38	192	7	2
Rich Creek	744	2	0	2	0	0	16	2	13	1	0
Richlands	5,256	16	0	3	0	13	136	29	99	8	2
Richmond	229,927	1,190	52	77	428	633	8,807	1,121	6,518	1,168	50
Roanoke	100,042	427	12	48	103	264	4,434	488	3,579	367	26
Rocky Mount	4,762	12	0	1	4	7	143	4	137	2	0
Rural Retreat	1,459	0	0	0	0	0	15	1	14	0	0
Salem	25,942	24	1	8	8	7	503	29	438	36	2
Saltville	1,927	1	0	1	0	0	11	3	8	0	0
Shenandoah	2,316	2	0	0	1	1	22	1	19	2	0
Smithfield	8,392	7	0	0	0	7	127	14	98	15	2
South Boston	7,721	28	0	2	8	18	335	40	291	4	1
South Hill	4,345	12	0	2	3	7	121	9	105	7	0
Stanley	1,651	1	0	0	0	1	19	4	15	0	0
Staunton	24,584	46	1	7	11	27	608	63	523	22	3
Stephens City	2,024	1	0	0	0	1	49	2	46	1	0
St. Paul	877	1	0	1	0	0	16	1	12	3	0
Strasburg	6,643	15	0	2	1	12	82	14	64	4	1
Suffolk	90,817	251	2	30	69	150	2,340	296	1,892	152	10
Tappahannock	2,417	17	0	1	0	16	46	7	37	2	0
Tazewell	4,185	6	0	1	0	5	35	10	21	4	0
Timberville	2,662	2	0	0	1	1	22	1	19	2	0
Victoria	1,631	1	0	0	0	1	30	4	25	1	0
Vienna	16,660	8	0	2	2	4	149	15	125	9	0
Vinton	8,077	9	0	0	0	9	180	15	146	19	0
Virginia Beach	451,001	528	7	81	174	266	7,772	584	6,611	577	39
Warrenton	9,912	12	0	4	2	6	215	8	204	3	1
Warsaw	1,484	0	0	0	0	0	13	2	11	0	0
Waverly	1,976	9	0	1	0	8	32	8	22	2	1
Waynesboro	22,470	50	1	10	12	27	477	53	382	42	0
Weber City	1,224	2	0	0	0	2	15	1	12	2	0
West Point	3,311	3	0	0	0	3	28	1	26	1	0
White Stone	332	0	0	0	0	0	2	0	2	0	0
Williamsburg	15,191	20	0	3	7	10	193	5	180	8	0
Winchester	28,128	93	0	38	15	40	692	86	567	39	2
Windsor	2,731	4	0	0	0	4	15	3	12	0	0
Wise	2,965	1	0	0	0	1	36	10	23	3	1
Woodstock	5,232	9	0	0	1	8	97	4	91	2	0
Wytheville	7,969	5	0	1	1	3	194	12	168	14	0
WASHINGTON											
Aberdeen	16,404	85	0	15	16	54	834	159	614	61	3
Airway Heights	9,085	33	0	8	4	21	480	72	347	61	2
Algona	3,207	2	0	0	1	1	31	11	18	2	0
Anacortes	17,130	30	0	8	3	19	380	64	308	8	1
Arlington	19,394	60	0	15	8	37	662	118	473	71	1
Auburn	82,381	360	1	59	120	180	3,334	605	2,116	613	21
Bainbridge Island	24,739	25	1	10	2	12	242	48	188	6	2
Battle Ground	21,002	32	2	9	4	17	404	56	314	34	3
Bellevue	146,913	194	0	27	82	85	4,294	519	3,395	380	16
Bellingham	90,208	204	0	34	53	117	3,346	459	2,722	165	5
Black Diamond	4,476	0	0	0	0	0	16	3	12	1	0
Bonney Lake	21,192	33	0	10	2	21	451	77	330	44	3
Bothell	46,387	65	0	17	19	29	1,017	165	774	78	6
Brier	6,975	3	0	0	0	3	47	9	34	4	1
Buckley	5,402	6	0	2	1	3	66	21	36	9	2
Burien[4,8]	52,189		4		66	113	1,900	332	1,005	563	17
Burlington	8,839	17	0	4	5	8	705	82	584	39	0
Camas	23,865	19	1	10	2	6	219	35	169	15	1
Carnation[4,8]	2,224		0		0	0	17	1	12	4	2
Castle Rock	2,251	3	0	1	0	2	70	10	51	9	0
Centralia	17,299	88	0	19	23	46	794	145	590	59	1
Chehalis	7,573	17	0	1	2	14	454	68	365	21	0
Cheney	12,715	43	0	18	0	25	203	55	135	13	0
Chewelah	2,643	5	0	0	0	5	33	5	26	2	0
Clarkston	7,417	17	0	5	4	8	342	70	264	8	2
Cle Elum	2,966	4	0	0	0	4	78	18	56	4	0

Table 8. Offenses Known to Law Enforcement, by Selected State and City, 2018—Continued

(Number.)

State/city	Population	Violent crime	Murder and nonnegligent manslaughter	Rape[1]	Robbery	Aggravated assault	Property crime	Burglary	Larceny-theft	Motor vehicle theft	Arson[2]
Colville	4,777	4	0	2	0	2	55	5	48	2	0
Connell	5,765	3	0	0	0	3	25	7	16	2	0
Coulee Dam	1,076	0	0	0	0	0	18	7	11	0	0
Covington[4,8]	21,436		1		13	10	584	111	433	40	3
Darrington	1,414	9	0	2	0	7	28	9	13	6	1
Des Moines	31,460	111	2	11	55	43	1,092	197	652	243	9
Dupont	9,678	31	0	4	0	27	113	15	91	7	1
Duvall	7,980	5	1	0	2	2	39	7	28	4	1
East Wenatchee	14,097	14	0	4	2	8	377	33	328	16	1
Eatonville	3,027	4	0	1	1	2	44	13	23	8	1
Edgewood	11,510	15	0	2	2	11	231	60	140	31	1
Edmonds	42,565	65	3	15	16	31	842	140	632	70	2
Ellensburg	20,616	42	0	14	5	23	601	84	489	28	5
Elma	3,089	6	0	1	0	5	82	17	58	7	1
Enumclaw	11,882	9	0	5	3	1	229	38	170	21	0
Ephrata	8,062	12	0	1	3	8	407	90	289	28	2
Everett	111,091	373	5	55	110	203	4,683	650	3,077	956	13
Federal Way	97,762	458	0	51	210	197	4,480	668	3,042	770	14
Ferndale	14,439	16	0	2	1	13	308	50	240	18	2
Fircrest	6,839	16	0	1	4	11	105	24	74	7	1
Forks	3,874	11	0	3	0	8	71	11	52	8	0
Gig Harbor	9,909	22	0	4	4	14	511	47	441	23	2
Gold Bar	2,323	2	0	0	0	2	44	20	22	2	1
Goldendale	3,496	2	0	1	0	1	57	7	47	3	0
Grand Coulee	2,047	1	0	0	0	1	79	31	38	10	0
Grandview	11,163	7	0	1	2	4	205	43	142	20	3
Granite Falls	3,634	3	0	0	0	3	73	22	45	6	0
Hoquiam	8,469	13	0	2	3	8	268	55	201	12	2
Index	210	0	0	0	0	0	1	0	1	0	0
Issaquah	38,606	30	0	16	7	7	1,357	133	1,134	90	2
Kalama	2,737	2	0	1	1	0	40	11	28	1	0
Kelso	12,164	52	0	13	4	35	486	76	365	45	6
Kenmore[4,8]	23,219		1		4	5	259	58	161	40	1
Kennewick	82,687	158	3	36	35	84	2,126	293	1,680	153	21
Kent	129,870	452	5	92	196	159	5,953	854	3,949	1,150	13
Kettle Falls	1,616	4	0	0	1	3	23	12	11	0	0
Kirkland	89,805	101	0	26	17	58	2,004	288	1,538	178	12
La Center	3,258	2	0	0	0	2	17	2	9	6	0
Lacey	50,844	96	4	15	17	60	1,374	190	1,087	97	3
Lake Forest Park	13,504	14	0	5	6	3	262	37	205	20	3
Lake Stevens	33,491	63	0	20	9	34	356	76	239	41	5
Lakewood	60,694	393	9	34	80	270	2,818	486	1,939	393	13
Liberty Lake	10,272	10	0	3	0	7	125	13	99	13	0
Long Beach	1,416	2	0	1	0	1	29	4	22	3	0
Longview	37,720	110	2	36	21	51	1,350	230	948	172	14
Lynden	14,612	18	0	7	3	8	205	32	163	10	4
Lynnwood	38,620	101	0	17	36	48	1,646	159	1,286	201	3
Maple Valley[4,8]	26,212		0		7	8	354	86	221	47	1
Marysville	70,204	170	1	21	38	110	1,549	235	1,061	253	9
Medina	3,311	1	0	0	0	1	51	6	41	4	1
Mercer Island	25,641	10	0	4	4	2	452	63	366	23	1
Mill Creek	21,234	19	0	6	8	5	333	52	254	27	3
Milton	8,366	27	0	1	5	21	257	36	192	29	0
Monroe	19,003	69	0	17	6	46	458	50	377	31	1
Montesano	3,959	10	0	1	0	9	77	16	58	3	0
Morton	1,164	0	0	0	0	0	13	2	11	0	0
Moses Lake	23,763	80	1	11	9	59	1,049	174	804	71	3
Mossyrock	794	0	0	0	0	0	9	1	7	1	0
Mountlake Terrace	21,549	39	1	12	9	17	538	121	365	52	1
Mount Vernon	35,550	99	2	16	26	55	1,308	233	964	111	6
Moxee	4,114	8	0	1	0	7	20	4	12	4	0
Mukilteo	21,638	37	2	11	3	21	433	87	308	38	1
Napavine	1,908	0	0	0	0	0	41	2	36	3	0
Newcastle[4,8]	11,878		0		2	4	243	54	150	39	0
North Bend	6,971	2	0	0	1	1	181	11	162	8	1
Oak Harbor	23,330	24	0	8	1	15	162	19	122	21	0
Oakville	683	1	0	1	0	0	14	7	6	1	0
Ocean Shores	5,977	9	0	1	1	7	120	42	74	4	0
Olympia	52,312	246	1	38	50	157	2,020	320	1,473	227	12
Oroville	1,669	3	0	1	0	2	48	5	39	4	0
Orting	8,179	11	0	0	4	7	132	23	90	19	3
Othello	8,247	9	0	1	0	8	177	32	106	39	0
Pacific	7,269	11	0	1	8	2	107	13	57	37	3
Pasco	74,582	166	5	33	34	94	1,328	252	936	140	15
Port Angeles	19,992	106	0	20	11	75	823	162	612	49	1
Port Orchard	14,269	67	1	8	7	51	633	100	489	44	1
Port Townsend	9,615	29	3	5	2	19	179	33	133	13	7
Poulsbo	10,886	19	0	7	1	11	227	34	182	11	1
Prosser	6,342	12	0	1	0	11	176	49	110	17	0
Pullman	33,896	41	0	16	5	20	371	65	292	14	5
Puyallup	41,572	108	1	17	33	57	2,337	336	1,770	231	25
Quincy	7,598	16	0	5	2	9	376	80	258	38	3
Raymond	2,928	7	0	1	1	5	30	9	20	1	0

Table 8. Offenses Known to Law Enforcement, by Selected State and City, 2018—Continued

(Number.)

State/city	Population	Violent crime	Murder and nonnegligent manslaughter	Rape[1]	Robbery	Aggravated assault	Property crime	Burglary	Larceny-theft	Motor vehicle theft	Arson[2]
Redmond	65,827	89	1	6	32	50	1,854	186	1,577	91	14
Renton	102,749	331	5	53	110	163	4,915	542	3,447	926	14
Richland	57,450	127	0	17	18	92	1,281	177	1,039	65	7
Ridgefield	8,552	8	0	2	1	5	90	15	72	3	2
Ritzville	1,631	3	0	0	0	3	82	32	46	4	1
Roy	826	9	0	2	0	7	24	6	16	2	0
Royal City	2,212	4	0	0	2	2	20	2	13	5	0
Ruston	840	1	0	0	0	1	34	12	20	2	0
Sammamish[4,8]	65,604		1		6	6	371	86	260	25	5
SeaTac[4,8]	29,463		4		55	71	1,402	227	785	390	5
Seattle	742,759	5,052	32	292	1,649	3,079	38,246	7,985	26,219	4,042	109
Sedro Woolley	11,953	10	0	1	0	9	309	57	233	19	0
Selah	7,932	8	0	2	1	5	196	29	148	19	0
Sequim	7,183	18	0	7	2	9	295	29	258	8	1
Shelton	10,188	52	0	13	3	36	657	103	504	50	3
Shoreline[4,8]	56,637		1		22	45	1,100	230	715	155	8
Snohomish	10,227	25	0	2	4	19	265	42	193	30	0
Snoqualmie	13,947	3	0	1	1	1	169	10	148	11	2
Soap Lake	1,583	1	0	0	0	1	35	0	30	5	0
Spokane	218,222	1,742	8	351	297	1,086	15,439	2,130	11,631	1,678	45
Spokane Valley	99,020	346	1	79	59	207	4,165	484	3,328	353	3
Stanwood	7,225	13	0	3	3	7	132	21	97	14	0
Steilacoom	6,389	6	1	0	1	4	95	18	74	3	0
Sultan	5,204	7	0	1	3	3	60	20	36	4	1
Sumas	1,488	0	0	0	0	0	14	5	8	1	0
Sumner	10,191	26	0	2	8	16	532	101	362	69	2
Sunnyside	16,468	37	2	4	6	25	422	74	282	66	0
Tacoma	215,687	1,869	17	198	503	1,151	11,362	1,912	7,573	1,877	90
Toppenish	8,898	33	1	8	5	19	491	89	282	120	0
Tukwila	20,288	148	3	20	72	53	3,401	273	2,556	572	4
Tumwater	23,405	84	1	15	9	59	703	155	481	67	2
Union Gap	6,163	19	1	4	9	5	661	61	553	47	0
University Place	33,743	72	3	10	23	36	719	137	524	58	5
Vancouver	177,580	819	3	150	155	511	5,852	789	3,987	1,076	52
Walla Walla	32,906	128	0	25	12	91	1,194	162	972	60	15
Warden	2,733	4	0	0	0	4	79	19	34	26	0
Washougal	15,949	25	0	10	0	15	251	35	193	23	2
Wenatchee	34,169	100	0	20	17	63	851	97	698	56	5
Westport	2,047	3	0	1	0	2	40	13	26	1	0
West Richland	15,012	11	1	3	1	6	125	21	95	9	1
White Salmon	2,583	1	0	0	0	1	14	0	12	2	0
Winthrop	444	0	0	0	0	0	7	0	7	0	0
Woodinville[4,8]	12,153		0		2	7	308	42	241	25	1
Woodland	6,228	6	0	3	2	1	234	41	176	17	3
Woodway	1,390	0	0	0	0	0	8	5	3	0	0
Yakima	93,959	421	16	49	121	235	3,343	625	2,212	506	23
Yarrow Point	1,144	1	0	0	0	1	3	0	2	1	0
Zillah	3,139	2	0	2	0	0	68	11	53	4	0
WEST VIRGINIA											
Alderson	1,151	3	0	0	0	3	32	5	25	2	0
Barboursville	4,256	3	0	1	2	0	208	11	193	4	0
Beckley	16,234	147	3	24	11	109	836	136	669	31	2
Bluefield	9,789	92	0	3	1	88	103	32	66	5	1
Bridgeport	8,708	9	0	1	2	6	204	7	192	5	0
Buckhannon	5,516	4	0	2	0	2	176	7	165	4	0
Ceredo	1,339	1	0	0	0	1	4	0	3	1	0
Charleston	47,470	331	10	50	48	223	2,853	660	1,947	246	25
Charles Town	6,060	10	0	2	2	6	37	13	22	2	0
Dunbar	7,262	44	1	3	0	40	299	67	190	42	2
Fairmont	18,430	63	2	11	9	41	261	48	182	31	8
Glen Dale	1,398	6	0	0	0	6	5	3	2	0	0
Hinton	2,417	1	0	0	1	0	38	14	20	4	1
Kenova	2,979	6	0	4	2	0	38	5	28	5	0
Lewisburg	3,917	3	0	0	0	3	93	0	93	0	0
Madison	2,764	0	0	0	0	0	48	19	25	4	1
Marmet	1,397	2	0	0	0	2	23	4	18	1	0
Martinsburg	17,428	55	0	10	6	39	540	69	456	15	3
Mason	941	0	0	0	0	0	83	2	79	2	1
Moorefield	2,417	20	0	1	0	19	69	2	66	1	0
Morgantown	30,855	82	0	11	6	65	500	85	386	29	4
Moundsville	8,417	17	0	4	1	12	212	31	173	8	2
Mount Hope	1,297	0	0	0	0	0	10	2	8	0	0
Nitro	6,509	25	0	3	0	22	259	25	218	16	1
Oak Hill	8,264	13	1	1	1	10	147	40	97	10	0
Point Pleasant	4,126	4	0	3	0	1	61	7	45	9	0
Ranson	5,292	15	1	1	1	12	27	2	22	3	1
Ravenswood	3,720	16	0	0	1	15	34	6	26	2	0
Shepherdstown	1,757	2	0	0	0	2	6	2	4	0	0
South Charleston	12,357	47	0	10	4	33	577	52	503	22	4
St. Albans	10,161	19	0	4	4	11	187	41	126	20	0
Summersville	3,332	4	0	0	0	4	78	3	73	2	0
Vienna	10,306	23	0	4	0	19	351	17	329	5	1

Table 8. Offenses Known to Law Enforcement, by Selected State and City, 2018—Continued

(Number.)

State/city	Population	Violent crime	Murder and nonnegligent manslaughter	Rape[1]	Robbery	Aggravated assault	Property crime	Burglary	Larceny-theft	Motor vehicle theft	Arson[2]
Weirton	18,542	9	0	2	0	7	166	21	137	8	4
Wellsburg	2,560	1	0	0	1	0	22	2	17	3	1
Weston	3,953	11	0	0	0	11	6	1	2	3	0
Wheeling	26,855	229	1	16	12	200	321	81	219	21	1
Williamson	2,745	16	0	0	1	15	34	8	24	2	0
WISCONSIN											
Adams	1,852	7	0	4	1	2	77	6	69	2	1
Albany	999	2	0	0	0	2	6	2	4	0	0
Algoma	3,071	1	0	1	0	0	23	4	19	0	0
Altoona[4]	7,827	12	0	8	1	3	105	23	78	4	0
Amery	2,809	26	0	4	0	22	34	4	29	1	0
Antigo	7,720	25	0	1	0	24	351	29	307	15	0
Appleton	74,931	165	0	26	23	116	1,151	131	973	47	5
Arcadia	3,065	0	0	0	0	0	6	1	5	0	0
Ashland	7,770	31	1	3	1	26	254	23	214	17	4
Ashwaubenon	17,316	13	0	6	2	5	528	36	474	18	2
Athens	1,086	0	0	0	0	0	3	0	3	0	0
Avoca	627	0	0	0	0	0	0	0	0	0	0
Bangor	1,472	1	0	0	0	1	5	0	5	0	0
Baraboo	12,178	24	0	15	0	9	358	35	317	6	1
Barneveld	1,240	0	0	0	0	0	11	6	5	0	0
Barron	3,300	0	0	0	0	0	1	1	0	0	0
Bayfield	471	2	0	0	0	2	24	11	10	3	0
Bayside	4,375	0	0	0	0	0	19	2	14	3	0
Beaver Dam[4]	16,394	25	0	11	4	10	239	21	210	8	0
Beaver Dam Township	3,912	0	0	0	0	0	2	0	2	0	0
Belleville	2,432	0	0	0	0	0	13	2	10	1	0
Beloit	36,746	171	1	38	41	91	979	125	815	39	9
Beloit Town	7,688	7	0	1	1	5	103	25	70	8	0
Berlin	5,365	3	0	0	0	3	72	7	61	4	0
Big Bend	1,395	3	0	1	0	2	22	2	19	1	0
Birchwood	428	1	0	0	0	1	10	1	9	0	0
Black River Falls	3,488	6	0	3	1	2	115	11	97	7	0
Blair	1,365	0	0	0	0	0	6	1	5	0	0
Blanchardville	795	0	0	0	0	0	3	0	2	1	0
Bloomer	3,491	2	0	0	0	2	27	3	21	3	0
Bloomfield	6,323	11	0	3	0	8	50	11	37	2	1
Boscobel	3,104	10	0	2	0	8	17	4	13	0	0
Boyceville	1,098	4	0	2	0	2	6	1	5	0	0
Brandon-Fairwater	1,208	0	0	0	0	0	1	0	1	0	0
Brillion	3,116	4	0	0	1	3	11	0	11	0	0
Brodhead	3,247	3	0	0	0	3	58	3	52	3	0
Brookfield	38,065	28	1	1	20	6	815	62	734	19	0
Brookfield Township	6,295	10	1	1	4	4	110	6	102	2	0
Brooklyn[4]	1,464	0	0	0	0	0	20	1	19	0	0
Brown Deer	11,963	51	0	2	6	43	548	34	440	74	2
Brownsville	573	0	0	0	0	0	9	3	6	0	0
Burlington[4]	11,039	15	0	2	0	13	108	13	92	3	2
Butler	1,812	9	0	2	1	6	82	1	70	11	0
Caledonia	25,047	21	0	0	3	18	151	37	110	4	1
Campbellsport	1,963	0	0	0	0	0	12	2	10	0	0
Campbell Township	4,366	3	0	0	0	3	37	2	34	1	0
Cascade	697	0	0	0	0	0	1	0	1	0	0
Cashton	1,103	0	0	0	0	0	1	0	1	0	0
Cedarburg	11,469	3	0	0	0	3	54	1	53	0	0
Chenequa	597	0	0	0	0	0	3	0	3	0	0
Chetek	2,141	2	0	1	0	1	26	2	18	6	0
Chilton	3,798	4	0	1	0	3	11	0	10	1	0
Chippewa Falls	14,084	26	0	11	1	14	175	20	144	11	1
Cleveland	1,457	0	0	0	0	0	2	0	2	0	0
Clinton	2,124	0	0	0	0	0	21	7	12	2	1
Clintonville	4,332	7	0	3	1	3	154	15	134	5	2
Colby-Abbotsford	4,085	6	2	0	0	4	18	2	15	1	0
Colfax	1,142	1	0	1	0	0	11	3	7	1	0
Columbus	5,037	19	0	7	0	12	21	1	19	1	0
Cornell	1,412	0	0	0	0	0	35	3	30	2	1
Cottage Grove	7,024	6	0	2	0	4	21	0	21	0	0
Crandon	1,833	1	0	0	0	1	16	1	15	0	0
Cross Plains	4,331	2	0	0	0	2	25	2	23	0	0
Cuba City	2,037	0	0	0	0	0	2	0	2	0	0
Cudahy	18,290	24	1	3	6	14	221	30	174	17	0
Cumberland	2,112	0	0	0	0	0	0	0	0	0	0
Darlington	2,351	10	0	0	0	10	26	2	24	0	0
Deforest	10,557	9	0	3	0	6	98	8	85	5	0
Delafield	7,588	3	0	0	1	2	96	6	87	3	0
Delavan[4]	9,938	21	0	6	1	14	251	19	222	10	2
Delavan Town	5,322	1	0	0	0	1	37	9	24	4	5
De Pere	25,199	38	0	10	0	28	205	16	182	7	0
Dodgeville	4,734	6	0	2	1	3	88	3	83	2	0
Durand	1,805	2	0	1	0	1	2	2	0	0	0
Eagle River	1,514	1	0	1	0	0	57	5	48	4	0
Eagle Village	2,086	0	0	0	0	0	8	1	7	0	0

Table 8. Offenses Known to Law Enforcement, by Selected State and City, 2018—Continued

(Number.)

State/city	Population	Violent crime	Murder and nonnegligent manslaughter	Rape[1]	Robbery	Aggravated assault	Property crime	Burglary	Larceny-theft	Motor vehicle theft	Arson[2]
East Troy	4,333	4	0	0	1	3	43	2	41	0	0
Eau Claire[4]	68,923	199	0	58	23	118	1,688	292	1,332	64	7
Edgar	1,452	0	0	0	0	0	2	1	1	0	0
Edgerton[4]	5,602	2	0	0	1	1	51	7	44	0	0
Elkhart Lake	1,022	0	0	0	0	0	9	1	8	0	0
Elkhorn	9,934	13	0	3	1	9	113	16	93	4	0
Elk Mound	875	1	0	1	0	0	9	3	4	2	0
Ellsworth	3,287	5	0	4	0	1	33	3	29	1	0
Elm Grove[4]	6,205	3	0	2	0	1	58	1	53	4	1
Elroy	1,355	0	0	0	0	0	6	1	5	0	0
Endeavor	460	2	0	2	0	0	1	0	1	0	0
Evansville[4]	5,379	2	0	0	0	2	40	1	37	2	0
Everest Metropolitan	17,392	19	0	7	0	12	198	20	173	5	1
Fall Creek	1,309	0	0	0	0	0	7	0	7	0	0
Fall River	1,703	2	0	0	0	2	0	0	0	0	0
Fennimore	2,478	5	0	3	0	2	7	1	6	0	0
Fitchburg	30,151	86	1	10	19	56	581	66	461	54	0
Fond du Lac	42,777	101	4	29	14	54	1,012	78	887	47	3
Fontana	1,719	0	0	0	0	0	14	4	10	0	0
Fort Atkinson	12,495	25	1	7	3	14	169	17	152	0	0
Fox Crossing	19,323	20	0	8	1	11	189	31	138	20	0
Fox Lake[4]	1,452	1	0	1	0	0	2	0	0	2	0
Fox Point	6,671	8	0	0	1	7	68	5	50	13	0
Fox Valley Metro	22,006	16	0	2	1	13	82	3	76	3	0
Franklin	36,251	13	0	3	5	5	527	30	472	25	0
Frederic	1,098	0	0	0	0	0	5	3	2	0	1
Fulton	3,379	0	0	0	0	0	1	0	1	0	0
Galesville	1,585	2	0	1	0	1	6	0	6	0	0
Geneva Town	5,032	0	0	0	0	0	23	4	18	1	0
Genoa City	3,005	2	0	0	2	0	18	2	15	1	0
Germantown	20,014	8	0	1	2	5	422	25	391	6	1
Gillett	1,313	4	0	0	0	4	22	2	20	0	0
Gilman	392	0	0	0	0	0	2	0	2	0	0
Glendale	12,710	53	1	7	20	25	965	41	844	80	0
Grafton	11,662	7	0	3	1	3	136	2	131	3	0
Grand Chute	22,865	52	0	16	2	34	683	24	633	26	0
Grand Rapids	7,385	2	0	1	0	1	49	12	37	0	0
Grantsburg	1,287	0	0	0	0	0	37	1	36	0	0
Green Bay	105,281	483	1	78	56	348	1,798	250	1,448	100	7
Greendale	14,181	12	0	2	2	8	251	15	231	5	0
Greenfield	36,850	64	0	6	16	42	898	80	772	46	1
Green Lake	925	0	0	0	0	0	13	0	13	0	0
Hales Corners	7,640	8	0	2	0	6	97	7	87	3	0
Hammond	1,887	1	0	1	0	0	7	0	7	0	0
Hancock	404	0	0	0	0	0	0	0	0	0	0
Hartford	15,183	17	0	12	4	1	204	10	191	3	0
Hartford Township	3,561	0	0	0	0	0	0	0	0	0	0
Hartland	9,302	3	0	1	1	1	61	8	52	1	0
Hayward	2,296	5	0	0	0	5	62	13	46	3	1
Hazel Green	1,230	1	0	0	0	1	4	1	2	1	0
Highland	834	0	0	0	0	0	3	1	2	0	0
Hobart-Lawrence[4]	14,667	7	0	4	1	2	69	31	36	2	1
Holmen	9,993	7	0	1	0	6	69	18	50	1	0
Horicon[4]	3,605	11	0	7	0	4	28	1	24	3	0
Hortonville	2,776	1	0	0	0	1	22	1	21	0	0
Hudson	13,848	19	0	2	1	16	383	20	349	14	0
Hurley	1,426	1	0	0	0	1	11	0	9	2	0
Independence	1,305	0	0	0	0	0	6	3	3	0	0
Iron Ridge	895	0	0	0	0	0	9	1	8	0	0
Iron River	1,133	1	0	0	0	1	4	1	3	0	1
Jackson	7,156	7	0	3	4	0	74	1	73	0	0
Janesville[4]	64,471	167	1	41	28	97	1,800	282	1,454	64	4
Jefferson	8,021	13	0	7	0	6	141	4	132	5	2
Juneau[4]	2,662	4	0	1	0	3	28	1	27	0	0
Kaukauna	16,172	25	0	6	0	19	135	24	104	7	0
Kenosha	99,948	338	4	48	80	206	1,495	248	1,196	51	3
Kewaskum	4,139	1	0	1	0	0	29	1	27	1	0
Kewaunee	2,856	2	0	2	0	0	12	0	11	1	0
Kiel	3,780	12	0	1	0	11	18	2	15	1	0
Kohler	2,077	0	0	0	0	0	36	0	35	1	0
Kronenwetter	7,813	10	0	4	0	6	36	12	24	0	1
La Crosse	51,901	145	1	41	22	81	1,924	260	1,600	64	3
Ladysmith	3,120	6	0	1	0	5	24	3	21	0	1
La Farge	766	1	0	0	0	1	5	1	3	1	1
Lake Delton	3,005	17	0	5	2	10	421	8	408	5	2
Lake Geneva	7,907	13	0	7	1	5	177	5	172	0	0
Lake Hallie	6,742	0	0	0	0	0	260	6	245	9	0
Lake Mills	5,925	9	0	0	0	9	14	1	13	0	0
Lancaster	3,717	14	0	3	0	11	39	4	34	1	0
Lena	539	0	0	0	0	0	7	0	7	0	0
Linden	532	0	0	0	0	0	0	0	0	0	0
Linn Township	2,403	1	0	0	0	1	6	0	3	3	0
Lodi	3,058	2	0	0	0	2	7	1	5	1	0

Table 8. Offenses Known to Law Enforcement, by Selected State and City, 2018—Continued

(Number.)

State/city	Population	Violent crime	Murder and nonnegligent manslaughter	Rape[1]	Robbery	Aggravated assault	Property crime	Burglary	Larceny-theft	Motor vehicle theft	Arson[2]
Lomira	2,366	3	0	1	0	2	9	0	9	0	0
Luxemburg	2,562	0	0	0	0	0	8	0	8	0	0
Madison	258,455	1,043	5	116	240	682	6,722	1,061	5,129	532	16
Manawa	1,284	8	0	4	0	4	14	2	12	0	1
Manitowoc	32,557	71	3	6	5	57	661	103	532	26	0
Maple Bluff	1,333	0	0	0	0	0	11	3	7	1	0
Marathon City	1,506	1	0	0	0	1	14	3	11	0	0
Marinette	10,561	9	0	3	2	4	182	17	160	5	0
Marion	1,191	1	0	0	0	1	6	2	4	0	0
Markesan	1,399	0	0	0	0	0	14	0	12	2	0
Marshall Village	3,988	10	0	2	0	8	9	0	8	1	0
Marshfield	18,309	12	0	9	0	3	382	31	343	8	0
Mauston	4,390	16	0	0	0	16	34	2	29	3	0
Mayville	4,862	3	0	1	1	1	50	4	42	4	1
McFarland	8,544	9	0	0	1	8	82	17	59	6	0
Medford	4,294	6	0	0	0	6	103	6	91	6	1
Menasha	17,788	45	0	9	5	31	367	44	297	26	1
Menomonee Falls	37,712	21	1	1	9	10	408	24	355	29	0
Menomonie	16,450	28	1	6	1	20	306	27	263	16	1
Mequon	24,311	5	0	0	1	4	241	34	192	15	0
Merrill	9,091	19	0	3	1	15	139	15	120	4	2
Middleton	19,970	52	0	2	9	41	276	39	218	19	0
Milton[4]	5,585	6	0	0	0	6	58	4	52	2	0
Milton Town	3,114	0	0	0	0	0	6	1	4	1	0
Milwaukee	595,619	8,416	99	489	2,279	5,549	17,699	4,259	8,851	4,589	251
Mineral Point	2,478	2	0	0	0	2	28	6	22	0	0
Minocqua	4,380	7	0	0	0	7	33	2	31	0	0
Mishicot	1,381	5	0	0	0	5	4	2	2	0	0
Mondovi	2,613	1	0	1	0	0	16	3	12	1	0
Monona	8,183	9	0	0	6	3	495	9	478	8	0
Monroe	10,575	11	0	3	0	8	127	9	110	8	0
Montello	1,439	1	0	0	0	1	19	2	16	1	0
Monticello	1,204	0	0	0	0	0	1	0	1	0	0
Mosinee	4,003	5	0	4	0	1	46	7	34	5	0
Mount Horeb	7,462	8	0	2	0	6	71	14	57	0	1
Mount Pleasant	26,571	23	0	3	5	15	569	70	474	25	1
Mukwonago	8,034	6	0	2	1	3	114	9	103	2	0
Mukwonago Town	8,146	3	0	0	0	3	7	4	3	0	0
Muscoda	1,253	2	0	0	0	2	20	2	18	0	0
Muskego	25,118	9	1	1	0	7	143	14	124	5	0
Neillsville	2,410	2	0	1	0	1	35	3	26	6	0
Nekoosa	2,408	0	0	0	0	0	49	1	47	1	0
Neshkoro	426	0	0	0	0	0	2	0	2	0	0
New Berlin	39,763	15	0	1	3	11	432	54	365	13	0
New Glarus	2,148	1	0	0	0	1	21	1	19	1	1
New Holstein	3,098	2	0	0	0	2	16	1	14	1	0
New Lisbon	2,500	8	0	0	0	8	8	0	8	0	0
New London	7,083	18	0	2	0	16	62	3	58	1	0
New Richmond	9,052	18	0	0	1	17	153	9	135	9	0
Niagara	1,543	0	0	0	0	0	14	4	9	1	0
North Fond du Lac	5,079	9	0	1	1	7	66	8	55	3	0
North Hudson	3,801	0	0	0	0	0	26	0	24	2	0
North Prairie	2,236	0	0	0	0	0	4	1	3	0	0
Norwalk	628	0	0	0	0	0	1	0	1	0	0
Oak Creek	36,643	46	0	10	11	25	739	52	662	25	0
Oconomowoc	16,850	7	0	1	0	6	133	12	118	3	0
Oconomowoc Lake	600	0	0	0	0	0	8	0	8	0	0
Oconomowoc Town	8,692	1	0	0	0	1	10	2	6	2	0
Oconto	4,421	2	0	0	0	2	71	6	61	4	0
Oconto Falls	2,810	1	0	0	0	1	34	1	30	3	0
Omro	3,590	4	0	1	0	3	27	8	18	1	0
Onalaska	18,841	6	0	0	0	6	415	22	386	7	0
Oregon	10,549	4	0	1	0	3	97	14	82	1	0
Osceola	2,500	7	0	0	1	6	19	4	15	0	0
Oshkosh	66,736	115	1	5	17	92	1,107	126	913	68	3
Osseo	1,671	2	0	0	1	1	30	5	23	2	0
Oxford	599	1	0	0	0	1	9	1	8	0	0
Palmyra	1,766	2	0	0	0	2	15	3	12	0	0
Park Falls	2,227	7	0	0	0	7	1	0	1	0	0
Pepin	775	1	0	0	0	1	12	0	10	2	0
Peshtigo	3,355	2	0	1	0	1	29	4	24	1	0
Pewaukee Village	8,172	8	1	5	0	2	103	8	89	6	0
Phillips	1,345	1	0	0	0	1	19	2	16	1	0
Pittsville	833	0	0	0	0	0	31	0	30	1	0
Platteville	12,642	31	0	8	0	23	208	11	194	3	0
Pleasant Prairie	20,911	36	0	22	5	9	390	29	358	3	3
Plover	12,853	14	0	3	0	11	175	13	156	6	3
Plymouth	8,554	10	0	5	2	3	96	8	85	3	0
Portage	10,496	25	1	4	3	17	156	26	127	3	1
Port Edwards	1,772	1	0	0	0	1	14	4	10	0	0
Port Washington	11,831	19	0	6	1	12	73	5	64	4	0
Poynette	2,489	4	0	2	0	2	8	0	8	0	0
Prairie du Chien	5,618	9	0	4	0	5	117	7	110	0	1

Table 8. Offenses Known to Law Enforcement, by Selected State and City, 2018—Continued

(Number.)

State/city	Population	Violent crime	Murder and nonnegligent manslaughter	Rape[1]	Robbery	Aggravated assault	Property crime	Burglary	Larceny-theft	Motor vehicle theft	Arson[2]
Prescott	4,273	9	0	2	0	7	24	5	11	8	0
Princeton	1,165	1	0	1	0	0	16	1	15	0	0
Pulaski	3,581	3	0	0	0	3	21	1	19	1	0
Racine	77,373	435	8	54	81	292	1,662	347	1,196	119	16
Reedsburg	9,518	8	0	5	0	3	125	4	118	3	0
Rhinelander	7,535	21	0	6	0	15	192	22	168	2	0
Rib Lake	875	0	0	0	0	0	0	0	0	0	0
Rice Lake	8,332	25	0	13	0	12	239	17	215	7	0
Richland Center	4,968	7	0	2	0	5	58	10	46	2	0
Rio	1,040	0	0	0	0	0	3	0	3	0	0
Ripon	7,823	9	0	0	1	8	83	7	74	2	0
Ripon Town	1,381	0	0	0	0	0	1	1	0	0	0
River Falls	15,578	16	0	6	1	9	259	43	203	13	1
River Hills	1,590	0	0	0	0	0	15	3	10	2	0
Rome Town	2,670	2	0	0	0	2	5	0	5	0	1
Rosendale	1,032	0	0	0	0	0	0	0	0	0	0
Rothschild	5,334	9	0	6	0	3	44	4	40	0	0
Sauk Prairie	4,611	1	0	0	0	1	78	1	74	3	0
Saukville	4,415	2	0	1	0	1	50	0	50	0	0
Seymour	3,460	5	0	0	0	5	29	1	26	2	0
Sharon	1,572	0	0	0	0	0	3	0	3	0	0
Shawano	8,936	34	0	2	2	30	300	31	256	13	1
Sheboygan	48,195	183	0	27	10	146	826	89	715	22	8
Sheboygan Falls	7,945	2	0	1	0	1	77	8	67	2	0
Shiocton	920	0	0	0	0	0	15	0	15	0	0
Shorewood	13,368	18	0	0	6	12	374	12	331	31	0
Shorewood Hills	2,101	2	0	0	1	1	42	2	36	4	0
Shullsburg	1,203	1	0	1	0	0	19	2	17	0	0
Siren	773	2	0	0	0	2	45	10	34	1	1
Slinger	5,476	10	0	3	3	4	52	5	43	4	0
South Milwaukee	20,972	35	0	5	8	22	366	28	320	18	1
Sparta	9,681	20	0	9	2	9	100	16	81	3	0
Spencer	1,908	4	0	2	0	2	3	1	2	0	0
Spooner	2,583	13	0	3	0	10	30	3	27	0	0
Spring Green	1,641	0	0	0	0	0	4	1	3	0	0
Spring Valley	1,374	0	0	0	0	0	0	0	0	0	0
St. Croix Falls	2,036	4	0	0	0	4	112	6	97	9	0
Stevens Point	26,233	40	0	4	4	32	392	41	341	10	3
St. Francis	9,459	14	0	1	3	10	115	15	94	6	0
Stoughton	13,149	22	0	1	2	19	238	16	216	6	0
Strum	1,094	0	0	0	0	0	4	2	2	0	0
Sturgeon Bay	8,889	6	1	2	0	3	78	7	70	1	1
Sturtevant	6,966	3	0	0	0	3	42	8	31	3	0
Summit	4,947	6	0	1	0	5	35	5	28	2	0
Sun Prairie	33,390	27	0	4	7	16	676	62	570	44	4
Superior	26,054	76	0	11	16	49	1,114	150	882	82	0
Theresa	1,206	2	0	0	0	2	12	0	12	0	0
Thiensville	3,137	0	0	0	0	0	14	1	12	1	0
Three Lakes	2,088	3	0	0	0	3	26	9	17	0	0
Tomah	9,394	13	0	1	0	12	213	10	199	4	1
Tomahawk	3,147	1	0	1	0	0	62	11	50	1	0
Town of East Troy	4,058	2	0	1	0	1	11	4	7	0	0
Town of Madison	6,942	50	0	4	9	37	148	29	93	26	0
Trempealeau	1,645	0	0	0	0	0	7	4	3	0	0
Twin Lakes	6,077	6	0	1	0	5	25	6	17	2	0
Two Rivers	11,077	36	0	1	1	34	136	19	110	7	2
Verona	13,490	19	0	7	1	11	207	30	166	11	1
Viroqua	4,461	6	0	2	0	4	63	13	48	2	0
Walworth	2,849	1	0	0	0	1	19	2	17	0	0
Washburn	2,039	6	0	1	0	5	16	1	12	3	0
Waterloo	3,337	8	0	3	0	5	24	1	23	0	0
Watertown	23,628	46	0	11	4	31	220	30	185	5	0
Waukesha	72,672	92	2	37	13	40	750	83	618	49	1
Waunakee	14,000	20	1	4	0	15	92	28	55	9	0
Waupaca	5,859	14	0	4	1	9	189	12	174	3	0
Waupun	11,260	12	0	7	0	5	92	13	75	4	0
Wausau	38,682	119	1	21	11	86	626	94	491	41	1
Wautoma	2,130	3	0	1	0	2	127	5	121	1	0
Wauwatosa[4]	48,562	55	3	6	34	12	1,249	123	1,008	118	2
Webster	619	1	0	1	0	0	9	1	8	0	0
West Allis	59,887	195	1	31	84	79	1,673	258	1,292	123	6
West Bend[4]	31,651	56	0	7	4	45	528	29	485	14	0
Westby	2,255	4	0	0	0	4	34	2	31	1	0
Westfield	1,244	0	0	0	0	0	12	1	11	0	0
West Milwaukee	4,152	51	0	2	25	24	434	22	376	36	0
West Salem	5,055	5	0	1	0	4	21	3	17	1	0
Whitefish Bay	13,933	10	0	3	3	4	191	24	139	28	0
Whitehall	1,582	1	0	1	0	0	15	1	14	0	0
Whitewater	14,561	24	0	8	3	13	104	20	74	10	0
Wild Rose	700	0	0	0	0	0	1	0	1	0	0
Williams Bay	2,600	0	0	0	0	0	11	1	10	0	0
Wilton	498	0	0	0	0	0	2	0	2	0	0
Wind Point	1,705	0	0	0	0	0	4	2	2	0	0

Table 8. Offenses Known to Law Enforcement, by Selected State and City, 2018—Continued

(Number.)

State/city	Population	Violent crime	Murder and nonnegligent manslaughter	Rape[1]	Robbery	Aggravated assault	Property crime	Burglary	Larceny-theft	Motor vehicle theft	Arson[2]
Winneconne	2,429	1	0	0	0	1	20	0	20	0	0
Wisconsin Dells	3,018	10	0	4	0	6	146	9	131	6	0
Wisconsin Rapids	17,725	27	2	12	2	11	599	54	518	27	4
Woodruff	1,952	1	0	0	0	1	8	0	8	0	0
WYOMING											
Afton	2,018	0	0	0	0	0	28	2	26	0	0
Buffalo	4,583	10	0	2	0	8	65	8	52	5	0
Casper	58,200	117	2	60	4	51	1,630	327	1,165	138	5
Cheyenne	64,178	207	2	30	23	152	2,559	280	2,063	216	10
Cody	9,935	23	0	4	0	19	146	15	125	6	0
Diamondville	761	0	0	0	0	0	0	0	0	0	0
Douglas	6,386	11	1	0	0	10	73	5	63	5	0
Evanston	11,797	11	0	3	1	7	212	11	193	8	0
Evansville	3,001	17	0	1	0	16	57	8	41	8	0
Gillette	30,659	56	0	13	3	40	667	83	561	23	2
Glenrock	2,584	2	0	0	0	2	17	2	15	0	0
Green River	12,025	14	0	0	0	14	102	22	78	2	0
Greybull	1,864	9	0	1	0	8	10	5	4	1	0
Hanna	787	0	0	0	0	0	6	2	4	0	0
Kemmerer	2,761	2	0	0	0	2	17	1	15	1	0
Lander	7,542	0	0	0	0	0	257	12	234	11	0
Laramie	32,509	32	1	8	1	22	395	44	332	19	6
Lusk	1,539	10	0	1	0	9	7	3	4	0	0
Mills	3,966	2	1	0	0	1	89	28	50	11	0
Moorcroft	1,060	1	0	0	0	1	9	0	9	0	0
Newcastle	3,370	14	0	4	0	10	39	6	27	6	0
Pine Bluffs	1,143	1	0	0	0	1	17	5	11	1	0
Powell	6,458	17	0	10	0	7	113	20	89	4	0
Rawlins	8,806	37	0	8	0	29	171	19	135	17	3
Riverton	11,076	26	0	5	7	14	332	29	278	25	1
Rock Springs	23,405	43	0	21	0	22	314	53	257	4	0
Saratoga	1,651	1	0	0	0	1	8	0	8	0	0
Sheridan	17,919	17	1	2	0	14	313	39	261	13	1
Thermopolis	2,919	13	0	0	0	13	64	10	48	6	0
Torrington	6,699	35	0	0	0	35	73	12	57	4	0
Wheatland	3,557	3	0	0	0	3	56	19	33	4	0
Worland	5,148	2	0	2	0	0	69	18	46	5	1

1 The figures shown in this column for the offense of rape were reported using only the revised Uniform Crime Reporting (UCR) definition of rape. See the chapter notes for further explanation.   2 The FBI does not publish arson data unless it receives data from either the agency or the state for all 12 months of the calendar year.   3 The population for the city of Mobile, Alabama, includes 55,819 inhabitants from the jurisdiction of the Mobile County Sheriff's Department.   4 Because of changes in the state/local agency's reporting practices, figures are not comparable to previous years' data.   5 The FBI determined that the agency's data were overreported. Consequently, those data are not included in this table.   6 The FBI determined that the agency's data were underreported. Consequently, those data are not included in this table.   7 Limited data for 2018 were available for Iowa.   8 This agency/state submits rape data classified according to the legacy UCR definition; therefore the rape offense and violent crime total, which rape is a part of, is not included in this table.   8 The FBI determined that the agency's data were underreported. Consequently, those data are not included in this table.   9 The FBI determined that the agency did not follow national UCR Program guidelines for reporting an offense. Consequently, this figure is not included in this table.   10 Arson offenses are reported by the Toledo Fire Department; therefore, those figures are not included in this report.

Table 9. Offenses Known to Law Enforcement, by Selected State and University and College, 2018

(Number.)

State and university/college	Student enrollment[1]	Violent crime	Murder and nonnegligent manslaughter	Rape[2]	Robbery	Aggravated assault	Property crime	Burglary	Larceny-theft	Motor vehicle theft	Arson[3]
ALABAMA											
Jacksonville State University	10,166	3	0	0	0	3	45	9	36	0	
University of Alabama											
Birmingham	23,196	31	0	0	1	30	432	8	414	10	
Huntsville	9,897	13	0	4	0	9	59	10	49	0	
Tuscaloosa	41,834	21	0	8	4	9	243	38	203	2	
University of South Alabama	18,481	21	0	3	0	18	153	10	137	6	
	16,443	22	0	0	0	22	168	14	148	6	
ALASKA											
University of Alaska											
Anchorage	25,009	2	0	2	0	0	72	2	60	10	0
Fairbanks	13,263	5	0	3	0	2	41	1	40	0	0
ARIZONA											
Arizona State University, Main Campus	118,390	29	0	10	5	14	875	56	794	25	6
Arizona Western College	11,653	0	0	0	0	0	28	0	28	0	0
Central Arizona College	9,741	4	0	0	0	4	26	3	21	2	1
Northern Arizona University	34,554	10	0	6	2	2	265	28	236	1	0
University of Arizona	47,648	26	0	9	2	15	613	53	532	28	1
ARKANSAS											
Arkansas State University											
Beebe	5,491	2	0	2	0	0	10	0	9	1	0
Jonesboro	19,148	7	0	4	0	3	51	5	46	0	0
Arkansas Tech University	13,677	4	0	1	0	3	56	6	50	0	0
Henderson State University	4,043	2	0	2	0	0	29	5	23	1	0
Southern Arkansas University	5,683	2	0	1	1	0	37	4	32	1	0
University of Arkansas											
Fayetteville	29,958	19	1	3	2	13	170	17	92	61	1
Little Rock	14,292	4	0	1	0	3	73	3	66	4	0
Medical Sciences	3,147	4	0	0	0	4	107	4	99	4	0
Monticello	4,702	1	0	1	0	0	17	0	17	0	0
University of Arkansas Community College, Morrilton	2,684	0	0	0	0	0	4	1	3	0	0
University of Central Arkansas	13,347	5	0	3	0	2	87	2	80	5	0
CALIFORNIA											
Allan Hancock College	17,716	0	0	0	0	0	27	3	24	0	0
California State Polytechnic University											
Pomona	26,669	7	1	2	2	2	183	13	154	16	0
San Luis Obispo	22,168	4	0	1	0	3	164	16	143	5	2
California State University											
Bakersfield	11,152	1	0	0	0	1	62	6	53	3	0
Channel Islands	7,161	4	0	2	0	2	40	1	39	0	0
Chico	19,004	9	1	4	1	3	136	5	130	1	2
Dominguez Hills	15,580	6	0	3	1	2	38	2	32	4	1
East Bay	17,600	3	0	2	1	0	82	16	64	2	0
Fresno	26,380	11	0	3	3	5	147	18	118	11	0
Fullerton	44,790	6	0	4	0	2	191	7	175	9	1
Long Beach	40,641	5	0	1	2	2	140	7	120	13	0
Los Angeles	29,181	7	0	5	1	1	109	8	92	9	1
Monterey Bay	7,801	9	0	4	0	5	34	4	29	1	0
Northridge	41,909	11	0	5	1	5	221	4	212	5	0
Sacramento	33,379	10	0	5	3	2	148	16	130	2	0
San Bernardino	21,914	4	0	3	1	0	110	8	89	13	0
San Jose	34,035	18	0	5	7	6	325	30	271	24	5
San Marcos	13,615	2	0	1	1	0	30	2	27	1	0
Stanislaus	10,627	2	0	2	0	0	35	0	34	1	0
Chaffey College	28,430	0	0	0	0	0	28	1	27	0	0
College of the Sequoias	15,236	1	0	1	0	0	64	10	51	3	11
Contra Costa Community College	52,597	9	0	0	1	8	123	12	108	3	0
Cuesta College	14,878	1	0	0	0	1	11	3	8	0	0
El Camino College	33,150	3	0	0	3	0	51	2	44	5	0
Foothill-De Anza College	63,210	1	0	0	1	0	14	1	13	0	0
Humboldt State University	9,171	7	0	2	1	4	93	13	80	0	0
Irvine Valley College	21,294	0	0	0	0	0	17	0	17	0	0
Marin Community College	7,905	4	0	0	0	4	20	0	20	0	0
Mt. San Jacinto College	20,697	1	0	0	1	0	25	7	17	1	0
Pasadena Community College	38,096	1	0	0	1	0	78	5	70	3	0
Riverside Community College	58,507	0	0	0	0	0	37	1	31	5	0
San Bernardino Community College	26,697	1	0	0	0	1	73	3	64	6	0
San Diego State University	36,908	17	0	6	5	6	457	36	415	6	0
San Francisco State University	33,036	9	0	4	3	2	208	26	170	12	0
San Jose/Evergreen Community College	26,585	1	0	0	0	1	60	13	45	2	0
Sonoma County Junior College	30,921	13	0	0	2	11	65	4	60	1	0
Sonoma State University	10,041	5	1	4	0	0	69	12	57	0	0
State Center Community College District	60,065	1	0	0	1	0	136	20	110	6	0
University of California											
Berkeley	42,684	37	0	11	10	16	779	40	702	37	1
Davis	38,778	22	0	8	3	11	640	37	591	12	0
Irvine	34,754	20	0	12	1	7	447	42	395	10	2
Los Angeles	46,298	72	0	28	11	33	691	143	536	12	4

Table 9. Offenses Known to Law Enforcement, by Selected State and University and College, 2018—Continued

(Number.)

State and university/college	Student enrollment[1]	Violent crime	Murder and nonnegligent manslaughter	Rape[2]	Robbery	Aggravated assault	Property crime	Burglary	Larceny-theft	Motor vehicle theft	Arson[3]
Medical Center, Sacramento[4]		3	0	0	0	3	129	3	122	4	1
Merced	7,703	2	0	0	0	2	57	4	51	2	2
Riverside	24,371	14	0	4	2	8	258	16	221	21	0
San Diego	36,785	16	0	5	2	9	471	36	426	9	1
San Francisco	3,176	17	0	0	2	15	419	35	378	6	0
Santa Barbara	25,833	47	0	35	4	8	321	19	297	5	0
Santa Cruz	19,912	10	0	4	0	6	182	28	153	1	1
Ventura County Community College District	49,927	2	0	1	0	1	59	8	50	1	0
West Valley-Mission College	25,905	5	0	3	1	1	29	11	17	1	1
COLORADO											
Adams State University	4,343	0	0	0	0	0	32	5	23	4	0
Aims Community College	7,966	0	0	0	0	0	4	0	4	0	0
Auraria Higher Education Center[4]		8	0	2	2	4	150	15	126	9	0
Colorado School of Mines	6,910	2	0	2	0	0	65	2	63	0	0
Colorado State University, Fort Collins	36,966	9	0	3	1	5	418	16	397	5	4
Fort Lewis College	3,936	3	0	1	0	2	24	5	18	1	1
Pikes Peak Community College	18,666	0	0	0	0	0	14	2	12	0	0
Red Rocks Community College	13,644	0	0	0	0	0	13	0	13	0	0
University of Colorado											
Boulder	37,921	11	0	10	1	0	605	24	575	6	10
Colorado Springs	16,743	6	0	6	0	0	68	1	64	3	0
Denver	31,281	3	0	1	1	1	115	0	101	14	1
University of Northern Colorado	15,365	6	0	6	0	0	84	6	77	1	0
CONNECTICUT											
Central Connecticut State University	13,930	1	0	0	0	1	24	1	22	1	0
Eastern Connecticut State University	6,068	0	0	0	0	0	15	0	15	0	0
Southern Connecticut State University	11,978	0	0	0	0	0	20	2	17	1	2
University of Connecticut, Storrs, Avery Point, and Hartford[4]		8	0	6	1	1	146	14	104	28	2
Western Connecticut State University	6,853	2	0	2	0	0	26	3	23	0	0
Yale University	13,613	4	0	1	1	2	252	31	217	4	0
DELAWARE											
Delaware State University	5,162	6	0	3	1	2	75	9	65	1	1
University of Delaware	24,855	10	0	4	2	4	125	2	122	1	1
FLORIDA											
Florida A&M University	10,797	1	0	0	0	1	64	32	30	2	0
Florida Atlantic University	37,793	7	0	3	2	2	104	18	80	6	0
Florida Gulf Coast University	16,732	2	0	2	0	0	38	2	36	0	0
Florida International University	68,005	6	0	0	1	5	258	20	230	8	0
Florida Polytechnic University	1,370	1	0	1	0	0	1	0	1	0	0
Florida SouthWestern State College	21,624	0	0	0	0	0	6	0	6	0	0
Florida State University											
Panama City[4]		0	0	0	0	0	5	0	5	0	0
Tallahassee	46,686	12	0	5	3	4	453	44	372	37	1
New College of Florida	899	2	0	2	0	0	17	0	17	0	0
Northwest Florida State College	8,079	0	0	0	0	0	4	3	1	0	0
Pensacola State College	13,602	0	0	0	0	0	25	4	19	2	0
Santa Fe College	20,335	1	0	0	1	0	17	2	15	0	0
Tallahassee Community College	16,979	4	0	0	1	3	47	6	39	2	0
University of Central Florida	75,824	15	0	7	3	5	211	14	190	7	0
University of Florida	58,993	16	0	7	2	7	384	31	331	22	0
University of North Florida	19,013	1	0	1	0	0	60	3	57	0	0
University of South Florida											
St. Petersburg	5,731	0	0	0	0	0	25	2	22	1	0
Tampa	50,961	7	0	4	1	2	236	12	216	8	0
University of West Florida	16,517	1	0	1	0	0	23	2	19	2	0
GEORGIA											
Abraham Baldwin Agricultural College	4,012	1	0	1	0	0	13	0	12	1	0
Agnes Scott College	981	0	0	0	0	0	14	1	13	0	0
Albany State University	9,171	0	0	0	0	0	5	1	4	0	0
Albany Technical College	4,798	0	0	0	0	0	1	0	1	0	0
Andrew College	320	0	0	0	0	0	16	2	13	1	0
Athens Technical College	5,859	0	0	0	0	0	0	0	0	0	0
Atlanta Metropolitan State College	4,068	2	0	0	0	2	19	0	19	0	0
Augusta Technical College	6,284	0	0	0	0	0	3	0	3	0	0
Augusta University	8,998	4	0	2	2	0	161	7	153	1	0
Bainbridge State College	3,193	0	0	0	0	0	0	0	0	0	0
Berry College	2,339	0	0	0	0	0	31	4	27	0	0
Chattahoochee Technical College	14,643	0	0	0	0	0	7	0	7	0	0
Clark Atlanta University	4,263	4	0	0	1	3	69	10	57	2	0
College of Coastal Georgia	4,372	1	0	1	0	0	23	3	20	0	0
Columbus State University	10,295	3	0	2	1	0	56	2	53	1	0
Dalton State College	6,043	1	0	0	0	1	3	0	3	0	0
East Georgia State College	3,777	0	0	0	0	0	5	0	5	0	0
Emory University	15,653	17	0	15	2	0	380	33	340	7	0
Fort Valley State University	3,044	1	0	1	0	0	16	2	14	0	0
Georgia College and State University	7,989	2	0	2	0	0	39	5	31	3	0
Georgia Gwinnett College	14,770	7	0	1	0	6	56	1	54	1	0

Table 9. Offenses Known to Law Enforcement, by Selected State and University and College, 2018—Continued

(Number.)

State and university/college	Student enrollment[1]	Violent crime	Murder and nonnegligent manslaughter	Rape[2]	Robbery	Aggravated assault	Property crime	Burglary	Larceny-theft	Motor vehicle theft	Arson[3]
Georgia Institute of Technology	31,513	3	0	2	0	1	305	65	231	9	0
Georgia Military College	14,343	0	0	0	0	0	0	0	0	0	0
Georgia Southern University	23,596	12	0	9	2	1	147	1	146	0	0
Georgia Southwestern State University[5]	3,646	6	0	1	0	5	17	0	16	1	0
Georgia State University	38,370	20	0	6	9	5	178	10	164	4	0
Gordon State College	4,523	0	0	0	0	0	20	3	17	0	0
Gwinnett Technical College	11,152	0	0	0	0	0	1	0	1	0	0
Kennesaw State University	40,676	9	0	6	1	2	143	22	118	3	0
Mercer University	9,597	7	0	2	0	5	67	4	60	3	0
Middle Georgia State University	9,429	3	0	1	1	1	16	8	8	0	0
Morehouse College	2,219	2	0	0	1	1	90	27	60	3	0
Piedmont College	3,088	0	0	0	0	0	0	0	0	0	0
Savannah Technical College	6,050	0	0	0	0	0	4	0	4	0	0
Southern Crescent Technical College	6,558	0	0	0	0	0	14	0	14	0	0
Southern Regional Technical College	4,957	0	0	0	0	0	0	0	0	0	0
Spelman College	2,166	2	0	0	0	2	8	1	7	0	0
University of Georgia	40,462	14	0	8	1	5	252	40	208	4	0
University of North Georgia	21,419	0	0	0	0	0	26	0	26	0	0
University of West Georgia	15,672	3	0	1	1	1	61	4	54	3	0
Valdosta State University	13,710	1	0	0	0	1	139	4	131	4	0
Wesleyan College	848	0	0	0	0	0	2	1	1	0	0
West Georgia Technical College	9,696	0	0	0	0	0	14	0	14	0	0
ILLINOIS											
Chicago State University	4,210	0	0	0	0	0	13	2	11	0	0
College of DuPage	45,144	3	0	3	0	0	22	1	21	0	0
College of Lake County	24,345	0	0	0	0	0	49	0	49	0	0
Eastern Illinois University	8,590	8	0	3	0	5	32	4	27	1	0
Elgin Community College	15,211	0	0	0	0	0	13	0	13	0	0
Illinois Central College	13,461	0	0	0	0	0	17	0	17	0	0
Illinois State University	23,330	10	0	7	0	3	77	7	70	0	0
John Wood Community College	2,925	0	0	0	0	0	5	0	5	0	0
Joliet Junior College	22,351	1	0	0	0	1	4	0	4	0	0
Lake Land College	20,207	0	0	0	0	0	0	0	0	0	0
Lewis University	8,101	2	0	2	0	0	22	1	21	0	0
Lincoln Land Community College	11,353	0	0	0	0	0	3	0	3	0	0
Millikin University	2,258	0	0	0	0	0	39	2	37	0	0
Morton College	6,647	0	0	0	0	0	8	0	8	0	0
Northeastern Illinois University	11,873	4	0	1	1	2	10	0	10	0	0
Northern Illinois University	21,615	17	0	10	1	6	124	10	112	2	1
Oakton Community College	18,527	0	0	0	0	0	7	0	7	0	0
Parkland College	12,686	1	0	0	0	1	11	0	11	0	0
Rend Lake College	5,773	0	0	0	0	0	1	0	1	0	0
Southern Illinois University											
Carbondale	17,873	3	0	0	0	3	96	7	86	3	1
School of Medicine[4]		0	0	0	0	0	0	0	0	0	0
South Suburban College	9,610	1	0	0	0	1	8	1	7	0	0
Southwestern Illinois College	17,176	4	0	0	2	2	36	3	33	0	0
Triton College	18,537	1	0	0	1	0	18	0	18	0	0
University of Chicago, Cook County	18,141	25	0	0	15	10	263	20	242	1	0
University of Illinois											
Springfield	6,590	1	0	0	1	0	27	2	25	0	0
Urbana	50,885	15	0	8	2	5	248	8	238	2	0
Waubonsee Community College	18,016	0	0	0	0	0	9	0	9	0	0
Western Illinois University	11,951	10	0	9	1	0	68	4	63	1	0
INDIANA											
Ball State University	26,419	13	0	9	3	1	181	33	141	7	0
Indiana University											
Bloomington	53,254	28	0	18	0	10	386	77	307	2	
Indianapolis	34,984	15	0	9	3	3	263	12	245	6	0
Southeast	7,159	1	0	1	0	0	4	1	3	0	0
Marian University	4,042	3	0	2	0	1	19	2	16	1	0
Purdue University	44,190	2	0	0	0	2	278	24	252	2	0
IOWA[6]											
KANSAS											
Kansas State University	25,775	0	0	0	0	0	128	9	118	1	0
Pittsburg State University	8,480	1	0	1	0	0	39	0	39	0	0
University of Kansas											
Main Campus	31,201	7	0	3	1	3	155	13	139	3	0
Medical Center[4]		20	0	0	2	18	187	1	184	2	0
Washburn University	7,702	3	0	0	0	3	64	2	60	2	1
KENTUCKY											
Eastern Kentucky University	19,517	6	0	5	1	0	136	27	104	5	2
Murray State University	11,950	4	0	3	0	1	50	8	42	0	0
Northern Kentucky University	16,475	0	0	0	0	0	34	3	31	0	0
University of Kentucky	31,564	12	0	7	0	5	519	15	485	19	0
University of Louisville	25,091	9	0	3	4	2	345	24	293	28	0
Western Kentucky University	25,038	3	0	2	1	0	47	11	36	0	0

Table 9. Offenses Known to Law Enforcement, by Selected State and University and College, 2018—Continued

(Number.)

State and university/college	Student enrollment[1]	Violent crime	Murder and nonnegligent manslaughter	Rape[2]	Robbery	Aggravated assault	Property crime	Burglary	Larceny-theft	Motor vehicle theft	Arson[3]
LOUISIANA											
Delgado Community College	21,530	5	0	0	0	5	17	2	15	0	0
Grambling State University	6,941	6	0	3	0	3	62	15	45	2	0
Louisiana State University											
Baton Rouge	33,801	18	0	9	5	4	359	40	306	13	0
Health Sciences Center, New Orleans	3,116	0	0	0	0	0	0	0	0	0	0
Health Sciences Center, Shreveport	1,011	5	0	0	0	5	27	0	25	2	0
Shreveport	6,375	2	0	0	2	0	20	2	17	1	5
Louisiana Tech University	14,489	1	0	1	0	0	64	6	56	2	0
McNeese State University	8,689	0	0	0	0	0	26	4	21	1	0
Nicholls State University	7,333	1	0	0	0	1	29	3	26	0	0
Southern University and A&M College											
Baton Rouge	7,415	8	0	0	4	4	112	8	103	1	0
New Orleans	3,113	0	0	0	0	0	0	0	0	0	0
Shreveport	4,654	0	0	0	0	0	0	0	0	0	0
Tulane University	14,066	4	0	0	1	3	174	22	146	6	0
University of Louisiana											
Lafayette	19,297	11	0	0	1	10	169	21	144	4	0
Monroe	10,087	2	0	1	1	0	34	3	30	1	0
University of New Orleans[7]	10,011	6	0	0	0	6		5		4	0
MAINE											
University of Maine											
Farmington	2,351	2	0	2	0	0	16	0	15	1	0
Orono	12,693	4	0	3	0	1	95	1	94	0	0
University of Southern Maine	10,156	1	0	1	0	0	8	1	7	0	0
MARYLAND											
Bowie State University	6,570	7	0	2	2	3	37	9	27	1	0
Coppin State University	3,442	4	0	2	0	2	41	12	29	0	0
Frostburg State University	6,455	4	0	2	2	0	17	3	14	0	0
Hagerstown Community College	5,827	0	0	0	0	0	0	0	0	0	0
Morgan State University	8,522	18	0	4	12	2	98	8	88	2	0
Prince George's County Community College	17,365	4	0	0	1	3	23	0	23	0	0
Salisbury University	9,800	4	0	0	1	3	66	1	65	0	0
St. Mary's College	1,779	4	0	3	1	0	55	8	47	0	1
Towson University	25,467	10	0	5	2	3	58	6	51	1	0
University of Baltimore	7,008	1	0	0	0	1	17	1	16	0	0
University of Maryland											
Baltimore City	7,158	20	0	0	12	8	50	3	43	4	0
Baltimore County	15,700	5	0	1	3	1	49	1	48	0	0
College Park	43,691	5	0	1	1	3	203	11	170	22	0
Eastern Shore	4,258	2	0	0	2	0	32	11	21	0	0
MASSACHUSETTS											
Amherst College	1,945	29	0	28	0	1	36	11	25	0	
Assumption College	2,913	10	0	6	0	4	22	1	21	0	0
Babson College	3,726	15	0	11	0	4	25	3	22	0	
Becker College	2,675	1	0	0	0	1	11	1	9	1	0
Bentley University	5,771	7	0	5	0	2	32	1	31	0	1
Boston University	40,807	23	0	10	2	11	425	22	403	0	2
Brandeis University	6,325	1	0	0	0	1	22	2	20	0	
Bridgewater State University	13,289	19	0	9	1	9	30	3	26	1	0
Bunker Hill Community College	18,428	2	0	0	0	2	21	0	21	0	
Clark University	3,524	2	0	0	1	1	29	1	28	0	
College of the Holy Cross	2,806	2	0	0	0	2	24	0	24	0	
Dean College	1,568	1	0	0	1	0	27	13	14	0	0
Emerson College	4,774	2	0	1	0	1	28	2	26	0	
Endicott College	7,103	4	0	4	0	0	25	2	23	0	
Fitchburg State University	11,434	6	0	5	0	1	15	0	14	1	
Gordon College	2,465	2	0	2	0	0	39	0	39	0	
Greenfield Community College	2,582	0	0	0	0	0	11	11	0	0	0
Hampshire College	1,382	1	0	1	0	0	25	5	20	0	0
Harvard University	38,934	11	0	7	2	2	413	44	360	9	
Massachusetts Bay Community College	7,695	0	0	0	0	0	4	0	4	0	
Massachusetts College of Liberal Arts	2,249	1	0	0	0	1	5	0	5	0	0
Massachusetts Institute of Technology	12,144	4	0	2	0	2	318	23	292	3	0
Massasoit Community College	10,613	2	0	0	0	2	5	1	4	0	0
Merrimack College	4,683	17	0	6	0	11	31	3	28	0	
Mount Holyoke College	2,599	0	0	0	0	0	25	5	20	0	0
Northeastern University	27,486	14	0	7	1	6	220	8	208	4	
North Shore Community College	8,852	0	0	0	0	0	9	2	7	0	
Quinsigamond Community College	10,602	2	0	0	0	2	11	1	10	0	0
Regis College	2,192	5	0	0	1	4	8	0	7	1	
Salem State University	11,057	4	0	3	0	1	38	6	32	0	0
Smith College	3,221	2	0	1	0	1	29	3	26	0	
Springfield College	3,290	1	0	0	0	1	48	9	38	1	
Springfield Technical Community College	7,713	0	0	0	0	0	21	0	21	0	0
Stonehill College	2,536	14	0	3	0	11	9	0	9	0	
Tufts University											
Medford	12,802	2	0	1	1	0	41	6	35	0	0
Suffolk[4]		0	0	0	0	0	17	1	16	0	0
Worcester[4]		0	0	0	0	0	1	0	1	0	0

Table 9. Offenses Known to Law Enforcement, by Selected State and University and College, 2018—Continued

(Number.)

State and university/college	Student enrollment[1]	Violent crime	Murder and nonnegligent manslaughter	Rape[2]	Robbery	Aggravated assault	Property crime	Burglary	Larceny-theft	Motor vehicle theft	Arson[3]
University of Massachusetts											
Amherst	34,778	3	0	1	1	1	175	10	164	1	2
Harbor Campus, Boston	20,882	0	0	0	0	0	36	0	36	0	0
Medical Center, Worcester	1,171	18	0	0	0	18	46	0	45	1	0
Wellesley College	2,688	1	0	1	0	0	32	2	30	0	
Wentworth Institute of Technology	4,778	0	0	0	0	0	44	1	43	0	
Western New England University	4,201	3	0	1	1	1	25	0	25	0	
Westfield State University	8,017	0	0	0	0	0	15	4	11	0	2
Worcester Polytechnic Institute	7,288	3	0	1	1	1	41	6	35	0	0
MICHIGAN											
Central Michigan University	28,486	5	2	1	0	2	48	1	47	0	0
Delta College	12,428	0	0	0	0	0	16	3	13	0	0
Eastern Michigan University	24,545	10	0	6	1	3	94	6	85	3	4
Ferris State University	16,828	12	0	8	1	3	28	2	25	1	0
Grand Rapids Community College	20,473	1	0	0	1	0	51	1	50	0	0
Grand Valley State University	28,875	14	0	11	0	3	107	4	103	0	0
Kalamazoo Valley Community College	12,245	0	0	0	0	0	17	0	17	0	0
Kellogg Community College	5,672	0	0	0	0	0	7	0	7	0	0
Kirtland Community College	2,014	0	0	0	0	0	0	0	0	0	0
Lansing Community College	19,206	3	0	1	1	1	45	0	45	0	0
Macomb Community College	30,719	1	0	0	1	0	25	0	24	1	0
Michigan State University	55,545	45	0	27	2	16	473	42	381	50	0
Michigan Technological University	7,784	0	0	0	0	0	31	1	30	0	0
Mott Community College	10,769	0	0	0	0	0	13	0	13	0	0
Northern Michigan University	9,235	0	0	0	0	0	22	1	21	0	0
Oakland Community College	29,644	0	0	0	0	0	11	0	11	0	0
Oakland University	23,532	3	0	1	0	2	31	1	30	0	1
Saginaw Valley State University	10,320	7	0	1	0	6	44	4	39	1	0
Schoolcraft College	17,861	0	0	0	0	0	19	0	19	0	0
University of Michigan											
Ann Arbor	46,316	30	0	12	3	15	567	18	541	8	4
Dearborn	10,714	0	0	0	0	0	15	0	15	0	0
Flint	9,455	2	0	0	0	2	60	1	58	1	0
Western Michigan University	26,096	1	0	0	0	1	94	1	92	1	0
MINNESOTA											
University of Minnesota											
Duluth	11,613	1	0	0	1	0	36	1	34	1	2
Morris	1,912	0	0	0	0	0	0	0	0	0	0
Twin Cities	64,860	14	0	1	7	6	632	49	568	15	0
MISSISSIPPI											
Coahoma Community College	2,940	1	0	1	0	0	12	11	0	1	0
Jackson State University	11,185	28	0	2	1	25	98	20	76	2	0
Mississippi State University	23,820	3	0	2	0	1	139	17	117	5	0
University of Mississippi, Oxford[8]	25,877		0	2		1	48	0	45	3	0
MISSOURI											
Jefferson College	6,046	1	0	0	0	1	7	1	6	0	0
Lincoln University	3,289	6	0	4	0	2	67	9	56	2	1
Metropolitan Community College	22,584	2	0	0	0	2	32	2	30	0	0
Mineral Area College	4,858	1	0	1	0	0	2	0	2	0	0
Missouri Southern State University	7,031	1	0	0	0	1	22	4	18	0	0
Missouri University of Science and Technology	9,547	1	0	0	0	1	30	0	30	0	0
Southeast Missouri State University	13,984	7	0	2	0	5	45	8	34	3	0
St. Charles Community College	9,689	0	0	0	0	0	3	0	3	0	0
St. Louis Community College, Meramec	29,716	3	0	2	1	0	58	1	56	1	0
Truman State University	6,918	1	0	1	0	0	42	0	42	0	0
University of Central Missouri	18,509	3	0	3	0	0	71	8	59	4	0
University of Missouri											
Columbia	36,780	7	0	6	0	1	255	7	233	15	0
Kansas City	19,796	2	0	0	0	2	67	12	54	1	
St. Louis	20,987	2	0	1	1	0	63	9	54	0	0
Washington University	16,703	1	0	0	0	1	49	4	45	0	0
MONTANA											
Montana State University	18,420	7	0	0	0	7	132	4	128	0	1
University of Montana	14,683	2	0	1	1	0	111	4	106	1	0
NEBRASKA											
University of Nebraska											
Kearney	8,264	1	0	1	0	0	24	4	20	0	
Lincoln	28,550	18	0	16	1	1	164	7	155	2	0
NEVADA											
College of Southern Nevada	47,602	0	0	0	0	0	31	0	26	5	0
University of Nevada											
Las Vegas	34,647	17	0	2	4	11	357	44	266	47	1
Reno	24,118	5	0	3	0	2	195	19	167	9	0

Table 9. Offenses Known to Law Enforcement, by Selected State and University and College, 2018—Continued

(Number.)

State and university/colleige	Student enrollment[1]	Violent crime	Murder and nonnegligent manslaughter	Rape[2]	Robbery	Aggravated assault	Property crime	Burglary	Larceny-theft	Motor vehicle theft	Arson[3]
NEW HAMPSHIRE											
University of New Hampshire	16,599	8	0	6	1	1	96	11	83	2	1
NEW JERSEY											
Brookdale Community College	18,974	0	0	0	0	0	12	0	11	1	0
Essex County College	12,638	3	0	0	1	2	47	2	45	0	0
Kean University	16,633	5	0	4	1	0	57	2	54	1	0
Middlesex County College	17,304	0	0	0	0	0	8	0	8	0	0
Monmouth University	7,049	1	0	1	0	0	24	2	22	0	0
Montclair State University	23,989	9	0	5	0	4	85	1	83	1	0
New Jersey Institute of Technology	13,130	4	0	1	1	2	70	5	65	0	0
Princeton University	8,483	2	0	2	0	0	190	12	162	16	0
Rowan University	19,833	6	0	3	2	1	104	31	73	0	1
Rutgers University											
Camden	7,675	1	0	0	1	0	77	2	75	0	0
Newark	15,098	23	0	4	3	16	269	11	252	6	0
New Brunswick	56,027	27	0	6	4	17	388	24	360	4	0
Stevens Institute of Technology	7,723	0	0	0	0	0	16	0	16	0	0
Stockton University	10,221	1	0	1	0	0	29	1	27	1	0
The College of New Jersey	8,792	2	0	2	0	0	67	3	64	0	0
William Paterson University	12,687	1	0	1	0	0	57	8	48	1	0
NEW MEXICO											
Eastern New Mexico University	7,440	6	0	4	0	2	56	13	42	1	
New Mexico Institute of Mining and Technology	2,471	0	0	0	0	0	48	5	43	0	
New Mexico Military Institute	457	3	0	1	0	2	24	3	20	1	
New Mexico State University	16,895	16	0	12	0	4	172	22	141	9	
University of New Mexico	31,224	40	0	9	4	27	631	35	522	74	
Western New Mexico University	4,454	3	0	1	0	2	33	12	21	0	
NEW YORK											
Cornell University	22,820	2	0	2	0	0	227	26	199	2	0
Ithaca College	7,184	12	0	11	0	1	91	11	79	1	0
State University of New York Police											
Albany	19,834	7	0	4	1	2	142	20	122	0	0
Alfred	4,198	2	0	1	1	0	35	2	33	0	0
Binghamton	18,758	2	1	1	0	0	134	6	128	0	2
Brockport	9,340	1	0	0	1	0	51	12	38	1	0
Buffalo	33,647	8	0	5	0	3	198	23	173	2	0
Buffalo State College	10,918	13	0	5	6	2	131	4	127	0	0
Canton	5,183	3	0	3	0	0	30	1	29	0	0
Cortland	7,827	3	0	2	0	1	34	10	23	1	0
Delhi	4,093	4	0	2	0	2	42	2	40	0	0
Downstate Medical	2,071	0	0	0	0	0	57	0	56	1	0
Environmental Science	2,295	0	0	0	0	0	21	0	20	1	0
Farmingdale	12,307	2	0	1	0	1	28	2	25	1	0
Fredonia	4,935	2	0	2	0	0	56	10	46	0	0
Maritime	2,007	0	0	0	0	0	24	8	16	0	1
Morrisville	3,713	6	0	6	0	0	27	3	24	0	2
New Paltz	8,940	1	0	1	0	0	29	2	27	0	0
Oneonta	6,593	0	0	0	0	0	47	11	34	2	0
Optometry	402	0	0	0	0	0	3	0	3	0	0
Oswego	9,566	3	0	3	0	0	64	3	61	0	0
Plattsburgh	6,271	3	0	2	0	1	54	2	52	0	0
Polytechnic Institute	3,060	1	0	1	0	0	9	0	9	0	0
Potsdam	4,119	0	0	0	0	0	52	3	47	2	0
Stony Brook	29,798	7	0	2	3	2	216	33	183	0	2
Upstate Medical	1,581	7	0	0	0	7	110	2	105	3	0
NORTH CAROLINA[8]											
Appalachian State University	19,974		0		0	1	51	9	42	0	0
Duke University	16,599		0		2	2	392	18	348	26	0
East Carolina University	32,388		0		2	3	128	11	117	0	0
Fayetteville State University	7,618		0		5	0	52	9	40	3	0
Meredith College	2,143		0		0	0	9	1	8	0	0
North Carolina State University, Raleigh	38,431		0		1	8	167	13	152	2	1
University of North Carolina											
Asheville	4,461		0		0	3	23	2	21	0	0
Chapel Hill	31,720		0		4	0	154	18	133	3	1
Charlotte	33,351		0		2	1	109	3	104	2	1
Greensboro	22,138		0		3	0	91	6	84	1	0
Wilmington	18,287		0		0	0	0	0	0	0	0
Western Carolina University	12,280		0		1	0	50	5	45	0	0
NORTH DAKOTA											
Bismarck State College	5,067	0	0	0	0	0	2	0	0	2	0
North Dakota State College of Science	3,683	0	0	0	0	0	8	1	7	0	0
North Dakota State University	15,816	1	0	0	1	0	77	1	74	2	0
University of North Dakota	18,104	3	0	2	0	1	84	5	79	0	0

Table 9. Offenses Known to Law Enforcement, by Selected State and University and College, 2018—Continued

(Number.)

State and university/college	Student enrollment[1]	Violent crime	Murder and nonnegligent manslaughter	Rape[2]	Robbery	Aggravated assault	Property crime	Burglary	Larceny-theft	Motor vehicle theft	Arson[3]
OHIO											
Bowling Green State University	20,395	3	0	3	0	0	92	4	88	0	0
Capital University	3,974	0	0	0	0	0	36	13	23	0	0
Kent State University	35,611	10	0	4	0	6	96	3	92	1	0
Lakeland Community College	10,630	0	0	0	0	0	13	0	13	0	0
Miami University	21,717	19	0	17	0	2	141	8	132	1	6
Ohio State University, Columbus	64,723	31	0	17	2	12	505	35	465	5	4
Ohio University	33,991	2	0	1	0	1	96	5	86	5	0
Shawnee State University	3,972	0	0	0	0	0	32	4	28	0	0
Sinclair Community College	30,680	0	0	0	0	0	42	8	34	0	0
University of Akron	24,339	10	0	2	5	3	121	9	105	7	2
University of Cincinnati	42,252	14	0	7	0	7	209	6	197	6	0
University of Toledo	23,248	8	0	4	0	4	168	16	146	6	0
Wright State University	19,277	4	0	3	1	0	67	8	58	1	0
OKLAHOMA											
Bacone College	1,094	0	0	0	0	0	22	7	14	1	0
Cameron University	5,918	0	0	0	0	0	16	5	11	0	0
East Central University	4,962	0	0	0	0	0	19	5	14	0	0
Eastern Oklahoma State College	2,104	1	0	1	0	0	8	2	6	0	0
Langston University	2,879	11	0	3	2	6	56	27	27	2	0
Mid-America Christian University	2,936	0	0	0	0	0	1	0	1	0	0
Northeastern Oklahoma A&M College	2,649	0	0	0	0	0	24	14	10	0	1
Northeastern State University, Tahlequah	9,556	1	0	0	0	1	9	0	9	0	0
Oklahoma City Community College	18,552	1	0	1	0	0	13	0	11	2	0
Oklahoma City University	3,420	1	0	1	0	0	27	5	20	2	0
Main Campus[5]	28,608	8	0	7	0	1	151	31	119	1	0
Okmulgee	3,268	1	0	0	1	0	6	0	6	0	0
Tulsa	1,037	0	0	0	0	0	5	1	4	0	0
Rogers State University	4,795	1	0	0	0	1	4	2	2	0	0
Seminole State College	2,275	0	0	0	0	0	8	1	7	0	0
Southeastern Oklahoma State University	4,631	1	0	1	0	0	20	4	14	2	0
Southwestern Oklahoma State University	6,247	5	0	1	0	4	19	1	18	0	0
Tulsa Community College	24,245	0	0	0	0	0	41	1	38	2	1
University of Central Oklahoma	19,428	2	0	2	0	0	54	16	37	1	0
University of Oklahoma											
Health Sciences Center	3,872	4	0	0	0	4	130	3	123	4	0
Norman	32,274	20	0	16	1	3	298	7	283	8	0
OREGON											
Portland State University	36,762	9	0	3	5	1	324	43	281	0	4
PENNSYLVANIA											
Bloomsburg University	10,656	1	0	0	0	1	12	0	12	0	0
California University	9,869	1	0	0	1	0	16	2	14	0	0
Cheyney University	846	1	0	1	0	0	7	2	5	0	0
Clarion University	6,240	2	0	2	0	0	20	2	18	0	0
Dickinson College	2,422	3	0	2	0	1	52	5	46	1	1
East Stroudsburg University	7,899	4	0	0	0	4	43	5	38	0	0
Edinboro University	7,245	7	0	3	0	4	16	3	13	0	0
Elizabethtown College	1,825	4	0	1	0	3	10	3	7	0	0
Indiana University	14,728	4	0	1	1	2	24	0	23	1	0
Kutztown University	9,467	10	0	8	0	2	38	2	36	0	0
Lehigh University	7,586	4	0	2	0	2	32	1	31	0	0
Lock Haven University	4,701	3	0	2	0	1	16	4	12	0	0
Mansfield University	2,403	0	0	0	0	0	13	0	13	0	0
Millersville University	9,502	0	0	0	0	0	20	0	20	0	0
Moravian College	2,781	0	0	0	0	0	24	10	14	0	0
Pennsylvania State University											
Abington	4,599	4	0	3	1	0	16	0	16	0	1
Altoona	3,607	3	0	3	0	0	15	1	14	0	0
Beaver	800	3	0	0	0	3	7	0	7	0	1
Behrend	4,832	3	0	3	0	0	18	1	17	0	0
Berks	3,163	0	0	0	0	0	10	0	10	0	0
Brandywine	1,533	2	0	0	0	2	10	0	10	0	0
Fayette	693	0	0	0	0	0	0	0	0	0	0
Greater Allegheny	612	0	0	0	0	0	6	0	6	0	0
Harrisburg	5,645	3	0	3	0	0	13	0	13	0	0
Hazleton	959	3	0	3	0	0	0	0	0	0	0
Mont Alto	999	0	0	0	0	0	1	0	1	0	0
New Kensington	833	0	0	0	0	0	0	0	0	0	0
Schuylkill	884	0	0	0	0	0	5	2	3	0	0
University Park	50,920	60	0	47	3	10	327	26	295	6	2
Wilkes-Barre	576	0	0	0	0	0	1	0	1	0	0
Shippensburg University	7,812	3	0	3	0	0	27	7	20	0	0
Slippery Rock University	10,516	1	0	1	0	0	14	0	14	0	0
University of Pittsburgh											
Bradford	1,575	2	0	1	0	1	9	0	9	0	0
Greensburg	1,589	1	0	1	0	0	2	0	2	0	0
Johnstown	2,883	0	0	0	0	0	21	1	18	2	0
Pittsburgh	31,947	3	0	2	0	1	155	4	150	1	0
Titusville	358	0	0	0	0	0	1	1	0	0	0
West Chester University	19,348	0	0	0	0	0	15	1	14	0	0

Table 9. Offenses Known to Law Enforcement, by Selected State and University and College, 2018—Continued

(Number.)

State and university/college	Student enrollment[1]	Violent crime	Murder and nonnegligent manslaughter	Rape[2]	Robbery	Aggravated assault	Property crime	Burglary	Larceny-theft	Motor vehicle theft	Arson[3]
RHODE ISLAND										
Brown University	10,335	0	0	0	0	0	64	12	52	0	0
University of Rhode Island	19,699	4	0	2	0	2	61	2	59	0	1
SOUTH CAROLINA										
Benedict College	2,552	11	0	3	3	5	57	10	47	0	0
Bob Jones University	3,375	0	0	0	0	0	13	0	13	0	0
Clemson University	24,758	6	0	4	1	1	148	10	110	28	2
Coastal Carolina University	11,988	17	0	6	0	11	116	4	107	5	0
College of Charleston	13,539	0	0	0	0	0	64	0	62	2	0
Denmark Technical College	996	0	0	0	0	0	2	0	2	0	0
Erskine College	911	0	0	0	0	0	1	0	1	0	0
Francis Marion University	4,476	3	0	3	0	0	11	1	9	1	0
Greenville Technical College	15,978	1	0	0	0	1	22	2	20	0	0
Lander University	3,017	3	0	2	0	1	35	0	35	0	0
Medical University of South Carolina	3,454	6	0	0	1	5	98	3	92	3	0
Orangeburg-Calhoun Technical College	3,533	0	0	0	0	0	0	0	0	0	0
Presbyterian College	1,434	1	0	1	0	0	55	7	47	1	0
South Carolina State University	3,208	11	0	0	8	3	48	17	30	1	1
Spartanburg Methodist College	778	0	0	0	0	0	9	1	7	1	0
The Citadel	4,212	0	0	0	0	0	43	9	33	1	0
University of South Carolina											
Beaufort	2,270	3	0	3	0	0	10	0	10	0	0
Columbia	36,813	6	0	2	0	4	268	15	230	23	1
Upstate	7,040	0	0	0	0	0	27	1	26	0	0
Winthrop University	7,223	1	0	0	0	1	26	2	24	0	0
SOUTH DAKOTA										
South Dakota State University	15,209	3	0	3	0	0	41	0	39	2	1
TENNESSEE										
Austin Peay State University	12,144	3	0	1	1	1	54	7	44	3	0
Chattanooga State Community College	11,237	0	0	0	0	0	18	0	18	0	0
Christian Brothers University	2,597	0	0	0	0	0	33	2	27	4	0
Cleveland State Community College	4,270	0	0	0	0	0	6	0	6	0	0
East Tennessee State University	16,026	4	0	2	0	2	77	6	70	1	0
Jackson State Community College	6,331	0	0	0	0	0	5	1	4	0	0
Lincoln Memorial University	4,847	0	0	0	0	0	5	0	4	1	0
Middle Tennessee State University	26,214	5	0	4	0	1	116	5	106	5	0
Motlow State Community College	7,198	0	0	0	0	0	2	0	2	0	0
Northeast State Community College	7,608	0	0	0	0	0	8	0	8	0	0
Pellissippi State Community College	14,241	0	0	0	0	0	17	0	17	0	0
Roane State Community College	7,227	0	0	0	0	0	1	0	1	0	0
Southwest Tennessee Community College	12,453	2	0	1	0	1	16	1	13	2	0
Tennessee State University	9,820	5	0	2	0	3	50	7	43	0	0
Tennessee Technological University	11,507	2	0	1	0	1	63	3	57	3	0
University of Memphis	24,809	8	0	1	2	5	135	17	105	13	0
University of Tennessee											
Chattanooga	12,844	8	0	3	0	5	118	28	82	8	0
Health Science Center	3,250	0	0	0	0	0	29	3	26	0	0
Knoxville	30,680	7	0	4	2	1	209	12	177	20	0
Martin	7,789	2	0	2	0	0	28	1	27	0	0
University of the South	2,035	6	0	5	0	1	50	9	40	1	2
Vanderbilt University	13,397	22	1	7	1	13	376	13	354	9	0
Volunteer State Community College	11,544	0	0	0	0	0	13	0	13	0	0
Walters State Community College	7,285	2	0	0	0	2	4	1	3	0	0
TEXAS										
Abilene Christian University	5,566	0	0	0	0	0	54	4	50	0	0
Alamo Colleges District	107,934	8	0	1	0	7	111	4	100	7	0
Alvin Community College	8,818	0	0	0	0	0	5	0	5	0	0
Amarillo College	13,023	0	0	0	0	0	17	1	16	0	0
Angelo State University[5]	11,025	3	0	1	0	2	41	6	33	2	0
Austin College	1,304	0	0	0	0	0	44	7	36	1	0
Baylor Health Care System[4]		7	0	0	1	6	392	2	375	15	0
Baylor University, Waco	18,094	3	0	3	0	0	216	9	202	5	0
Central Texas College	32,309	1	0	0	0	1	8	0	8	0	0
College of the Mainland	5,575	0	0	0	0	0	5	1	4	0	0
El Paso Community College	39,117	1	0	0	0	1	13	0	13	0	0
Hardin-Simmons University	2,441	0	0	0	0	0	22	3	18	1	0
Houston Baptist University	3,885	1	0	0	1	0	40	23	16	1	0
Houston Community College	84,374	8	0	0	6	2	149	8	125	16	0
Lamar University, Beaumont	20,864	4	0	3	1	0	48	1	47	0	0
Lubbock Christian University	2,239	0	0	0	0	0	2	2	0	0	0
Midwestern State University	7,024	4	0	4	0	0	32	5	27	0	0
Paris Junior College	6,895	2	0	1	1	0	7	0	7	0	0
Prairie View A&M University	9,861	12	0	9	0	3	93	15	75	3	0
Rice University	7,251	1	0	0	0	1	143	6	134	3	0
San Jacinto College, Central Campus[4]		0	0	0	0	0	56	4	45	7	0
Southern Methodist University	13,012	4	0	2	0	2	172	15	154	3	1
South Plains College	13,022	0	0	0	0	0	25	1	23	1	0
Southwestern University	1,536	0	0	0	0	0	16	2	14	0	0
Stephen F. Austin State University[5]	14,493	5	0	5	0	0	39	4	35	0	0

Table 9. Offenses Known to Law Enforcement, by Selected State and University and College, 2018—Continued

(Number.)

State and university/college	Student enrollment[1]	Violent crime	Murder and nonnegligent manslaughter	Rape[2]	Robbery	Aggravated assault	Property crime	Burglary	Larceny-theft	Motor vehicle theft	Arson[3]
St. Mary's University[5]	3,832	8	0	3	1	4	44	2	39	3	0
St. Thomas University	3,799	0	0	0	0	0	17	3	14	0	0
Sul Ross State University[5]	3,760	0	0	0	0	0	8	4	4	0	0
Tarleton State University	14,978	9	0	8	0	1	40	3	37	0	0
Texas A&M International University	8,459	4	0	0	0	4	27	4	23	0	0
Texas A&M University											
College Station	70,245	16	0	10	0	6	401	51	339	11	0
Commerce	16,132	2	0	1	0	1	52	5	45	2	0
Corpus Christi	13,649	2	0	1	0	1	88	9	77	2	0
Galveston[4]		2	0	2	0	0	19	1	18	0	0
Kingsville	10,692	1	0	1	0	0	41	4	37	0	0
San Antonio	6,968	1	0	1	0	0	13	0	13	0	0
Texas Christian University	10,955	1	0	0	0	1	72	11	59	2	0
Texas Southern University	10,674	16	0	4	9	3	131	9	120	2	0
Texas State Technical College											
Harlingen[4]		1	0	0	0	1	15	0	15	0	0
Waco[4]		5	0	4	1	0	44	11	30	3	0
Texas State University, San Marcos	43,018	13	0	6	2	5	125	15	109	1	0
Texas Tech University, Lubbock	40,105	13	0	9	1	3	291	9	277	5	0
Texas Woman's University[5]	18,819	3	0	1	0	2	38	0	38	0	1
Tyler Junior College	10,261	2	0	1	0	1	6	2	3	1	0
University of Houston	16,046	1	0	0	0	1	35	3	31	1	0
Central Campus	50,293	26	0	9	10	7	481	43	419	19	1
Clearlake	10,640	0	0	0	0	0	21	1	20	0	0
University of North Texas, Denton	43,725	5	0	3	1	1	172	12	157	3	1
University of Texas											
Arlington	59,019	8	0	4	0	4	118	18	98	2	0
Austin	55,008	12	0	6	0	6	319	7	302	10	0
Dallas	29,645	2	0	1	0	1	139	10	125	4	0
El Paso	28,878	6	0	1	0	5	97	12	82	3	0
Health Science Center, San Antonio	3,848	0	0	0	0	0	35	1	32	2	0
Health Science Center, Tyler	42	4	0	0	0	4	6	0	6	0	0
Houston[5]	6,634	17	0	5	5	7	304	12	290	2	0
Medical Branch	3,808	0	0	0	0	0	79	2	76	1	0
Permian Basin	9,148	2	0	1	0	1	20	13	7	0	0
Rio Grande Valley	32,508	2	0	2	0	0	56	0	56	0	0
San Antonio	32,871	5	0	4	1	0	93	5	87	1	0
Southwestern Medical School	2,456	3	0	0	2	1	155	0	143	12	0
Tyler	12,052	0	0	0	0	0	31	0	30	1	0
West Texas A&M University[5]	11,757	0	0	0	0	0	27	3	24	0	0
UTAH											
Brigham Young University	39,582	6	0	1	0	5	169	0	165	4	0
Dixie State University	11,441	3	0	1	1	1	28	3	21	4	0
Southern Utah University	15,098	0	0	0	0	0	27	3	22	2	0
University of Utah	37,585	11	1	0	3	7	409	31	360	18	0
Utah State University, Logan	34,904	1	0	0	1	0	45	8	37	0	0
Utah Valley University	45,411	0	0	0	0	0	40	2	38	0	
Weber State University	33,339	5	0	5	0	0	31	1	29	1	0
VERMONT											
University of Vermont	15,069	6	0	5	0	1	102	10	91	1	0
VIRGINIA											
Bridgewater College	1,959	0	0	0	0	0	15	2	12	1	0
Christopher Newport University	5,215	3	0	2	0	1	62	0	60	2	1
College of William and Mary	9,767	1	0	0	1	0	101	5	96	0	0
Eastern Virginia Medical School	1,334	0	0	0	0	0	38	0	37	1	0
Emory and Henry College	1,257	0	0	0	0	0	1	0	1	0	0
Ferrum College	1,338	2	0	2	0	0	10	0	10	0	0
George Mason University	46,266	4	0	4	0	0	86	0	86	0	0
Hampton University	4,874	5	0	3	0	2	42	6	33	3	0
James Madison University	23,354	7	0	2	0	5	81	5	75	1	0
J. Sargeant Reynolds Community College	15,028	0	0	0	0	0	14	0	14	0	0
Lord Fairfax Community College	9,129	0	0	0	0	0	3	0	3	0	0
Norfolk State University	6,168	12	0	9	2	1	80	24	53	3	0
Northern Virginia Community College	74,283	1	0	0	1	0	30	0	30	0	0
Old Dominion University	28,758	21	0	4	6	11	242	19	218	5	1
Radford University	10,254	8	0	6	0	2	64	4	59	1	2
Richard Bland College	2,808	2	0	1	0	1	12	0	12	0	0
University of Mary Washington	5,276	3	0	2	0	1	47	3	43	1	1
University of Richmond	4,811	5	0	4	1	0	99	10	87	2	0
University of Virginia	27,960	18	0	15	1	2	137	4	132	1	0
University of Virginia's College at Wise	3,474	1	0	1	0	0	8	0	8	0	0
Virginia Commonwealth University	34,271	19	0	3	3	13	486	12	467	7	2
Virginia Military Institute	1,766	0	0	0	0	0	16	1	15	0	0
Virginia Polytechnic Institute and State University	34,947	6	0	4	0	2	186	22	159	5	0
Virginia State University	5,137	3	0	1	1	1	45	5	37	3	0
Virginia Western Community College	10,802	0	0	0	0	0	1	0	1	0	0
WASHINGTON											
Central Washington University	17,163	0	0	0	0	0	95	7	85	3	0
Eastern Washington University	15,602	3	0	2	0	1	33	1	32	0	0

Table 9. Offenses Known to Law Enforcement, by Selected State and University and College, 2018—Continued

(Number.)

State and university/college	Student enrollment[1]	Violent crime	Murder and nonnegligent manslaughter	Rape[2]	Robbery	Aggravated assault	Property crime	Burglary	Larceny-theft	Motor vehicle theft	Arson[3]
Evergreen State College	4,996	3	0	1	0	2	39	2	35	2	0
University of Washington	55,073	24	0	5	6	13	616	50	559	7	0
Washington State University											
Pullman	33,974	6	0	5	0	1	56	7	48	1	0
Vancouver[4]		1	0	1	0	0	2	0	2	0	0
Western Washington University	17,475	2	0	2	0	0	99	6	92	1	0
WEST VIRGINIA											
West Virginia University	31,900	8	0	3	2	3	234	28	201	5	0
WISCONSIN											
Marquette University	11,967	34	0	6	11	17	220	20	173	27	0
University of Wisconsin											
Eau Claire	11,836	2	0	1	0	1	51	1	50	0	0
Green Bay	8,412	0	0	0	0	0	8	0	8	0	0
La Crosse	11,943	2	0	2	0	0	50	0	50	0	0
Madison	46,350	18	0	7	5	6	219	48	166	5	1
Milwaukee	30,031	4	0	3	1	0	121	8	110	3	1
Oshkosh	16,213	7	0	1	1	5	10	1	9	0	0
Parkside	5,217	1	0	1	0	0	18	0	18	0	0
Platteville	9,916	3	0	3	0	0	39	1	37	1	0
River Falls	6,633	5	0	2	0	3	32	4	27	1	0
Stevens Point	9,703	1	0	1	0	0	33	0	33	0	0
Stout	11,232	0	0	0	0	0	44	0	43	1	0
Superior	3,040	0	0	0	0	0	16	1	15	0	0
Whitewater	14,456	1	0	1	0	0	23	1	22	0	0
WYOMING											
University of Wyoming	13,975	0	0	0	0	0	99	8	91	0	0

Note: Caution should be exercised in making any intercampus comparisons or ranking schools because university/college crime statistics are affected by a variety of factors. These include demographic characteristics of the surrounding community, ratio of male to female students, number of on-campus residents, accessibility of the campus to outside visitors, size of enrollment, etc.
1 The student enrollment figures provided by the United States Department of Education are for the 2017 school year, the most recent available. The enrollment figures include full-time and part-time students. 2 The figures shown in this column for the offense of rape were reported using only the revised Uniform Crime Reporting (UCR) definition of rape. See chapter notes for more detail. 3 The FBI does not publish arson data unless it receives data from either the agency or the state for all 12 months of the calendar year. 4 Student enrollment figures were not available. 5 Because of changes in the state/local agency's reporting practices, figures are not comparable to previous years' data. 6 Limited data for 2018 were available for Iowa. 7 The FBI determined that the agency's data were underreported. Consequently, those data are not included in this table. 8 This agency/state submits rape data classified according to the legacy UCR definition; therefore the rape offense and violent crime total, which rape is a part of, is not included in this table. See chapter notes for more detail.

Table 10. Offenses Known to Law Enforcement, by Selected State Metropolitan and Nonmetropolitan Counties, 2018

(Number.)

State/county	Violent crime	Murder and nonnegligent manslaughter	Rape[1]	Robbery	Aggravated assault	Property crime	Burglary	Larceny-theft	Motor vehicle theft	Arson[2]
ALABAMA										
Metropolitan Counties										
Autauga	51	0	6	5	40	372	92	240	40	
Baldwin	223	0	9	37	177	615	173	397	45	
Blount	375	1	19	5	350	796	191	492	113	
Calhoun	14	0	5	7	2	144	49	95	0	
Elmore	68	4	30	12	22	669	178	427	64	
Etowah	99	2	32	1	64	444	152	233	59	
Geneva	40	1	7	2	30	202	74	112	16	
Greene	31	0	2	1	28	123	45	60	18	
Houston	121	1	9	19	92	657	187	400	70	
Jefferson	729	10	45	128	546	2,255	1,181	888	186	
Lawrence	48	0	8	3	37	351	112	195	44	
Lee	417	2	23	10	382	1,015	263	620	132	
Madison	390	2	46	42	300	2,007	486	1,306	215	
Mobile	147	1	9	23	114	2,008	564	1,130	314	
Montgomery	111	0	8	10	93	404	136	230	38	
Russell	40	2	9	6	23	268	70	158	40	
St. Clair	221	1	11	1	208	416	130	255	31	
Tuscaloosa	197	3	6	22	166	1,371	361	831	179	
Nonmetropolitan Counties										
Bullock	7	0	0	3	4	42	23	17	2	
Chambers	0	0	0	0	0	70	29	39	2	
Cherokee	65	0	11	1	53	295	101	160	34	
Clarke	18	0	8	1	9	49	25	16	8	
Clay	1	0	0	0	1	65	32	32	1	
Cleburne	8	0	2	1	5	144	43	90	11	
Coffee	18	1	3	0	14	132	55	65	12	
Coosa	41	0	3	0	38	171	64	100	7	
Covington	4	0	0	0	4	37	14	19	4	
Cullman	52	1	23	2	26	911	235	553	123	
Dale	31	0	9	1	21	147	39	99	9	
Dallas	76	1	11	10	54	427	131	255	41	
DeKalb	113	2	35	2	74	624	198	318	108	
Fayette	2	0	1	0	1	72	32	27	13	
Lamar	6	0	1	0	5	64	27	33	4	
Macon	19	1	4	2	12	68	29	21	18	
Marengo	30	0	3	3	24	149	53	77	19	
Marshall	89	0	14	4	71	370	134	193	43	
Monroe	27	2	0	0	25	56	19	29	8	
Pike	27	0	3	3	21	124	45	69	10	
Sumter	10	0	1	1	8	39	21	15	3	
Talladega	92	0	8	13	71	701	182	444	75	
Tallapoosa	15	0	4	1	10	115	28	78	9	
ARIZONA										
Metropolitan Counties										
Cochise	50	0	3	5	42	539	180	284	75	2
Coconino	110	2	15	1	92	295	86	194	15	19
Mohave	149	4	6	17	122	2,058	693	1,184	181	11
Pima	619	10	76	163	370	8,574	1,429	6,480	665	62
Pinal	212	3	5	18	186	1,807	432	1,154	221	11
Yavapai	238	3	21	5	209	952	225	641	86	13
Yuma	144	11	17	7	109	856	317	440	99	5
Nonmetropolitan Counties										
Gila	168	1	5	7	155	402	79	251	72	0
Graham	15	0	1	3	11	111	27	72	12	15
Greenlee	2	0	0	0	2	29	12	10	7	0
La Paz[3]		2	0		19	294	76	205	13	
Navajo	49	0	2	5	42	347	129	166	52	1
Santa Cruz	5	2	2	0	1	145	34	80	31	0
ARKANSAS										
Metropolitan Counties										
Benton	136	2	33	4	97	413	136	234	43	2
Cleveland	16	2	4	0	10	83	45	37	1	1
Craighead	56	0	14	3	39	351	138	178	35	2
Crawford	37	0	9	1	27	264	46	189	29	0
Crittenden	120	5	11	8	96	306	75	194	37	5
Faulkner	81	2	10	3	66	794	202	492	100	12
Garland	352	0	35	14	303	1,591	666	785	140	0
Grant	31	0	6	0	25	140	30	94	16	2
Jefferson	67	3	15	4	45	412	151	212	49	12
Lincoln	9	0	4	0	5	61	15	40	6	0
Little River	21	0	3	0	18	89	23	48	18	3
Lonoke	78	0	16	4	58	385	69	232	84	2
Miller[3]	35	0	8	0	27			149	22	1
Perry	16	0	5	0	11	137	16	121	0	0
Pulaski	345	1	18	26	300	1,688	404	1,088	196	13

Table 10. Offenses Known to Law Enforcement, by Selected State Metropolitan and Nonmetropolitan Counties, 2018—Continued

(Number.)

State/county	Violent crime	Murder and nonnegligent manslaughter	Rape[1]	Robbery	Aggravated assault	Property crime	Burglary	Larceny-theft	Motor vehicle theft	Arson[2]
Saline	193	0	40	12	141	843	326	395	122	7
Sebastian	53	0	9	1	43	212	80	122	10	2
Washington[3]			21	1	149	509	167	272	70	2
Nonmetropolitan Counties										
Arkansas	11	1	0	0	10	78	22	43	13	1
Ashley	17	2	5	2	8	212	56	128	28	5
Baxter	64	0	14	1	49	606	60	502	44	3
Boone	207	0	66	1	140	244	65	144	35	2
Bradley	14	0	4	0	10	37	15	15	7	1
Calhoun	3	0	0	0	3	50	7	38	5	0
Carroll	41	1	1	0	39	213	64	116	33	4
Chicot	4	0	0	0	4	96	34	62	0	0
Clark	39	0	4	0	35	46	17	26	3	0
Clay	7	0	3	0	4	53	16	34	3	0
Cleburne	122	3	8	2	109	302	94	189	19	5
Columbia	20	1	0	2	17	71	22	41	8	1
Conway	53	0	14	3	36	274	48	200	26	6
Cross	33	0	3	0	30	131	23	97	11	0
Drew	19	0	4	2	13	88	28	47	13	1
Fulton	28	0	4	0	24	57	0	48	9	6
Greene	26	0	3	0	23	180	49	107	24	2
Hempstead	54	0	5	0	49	121	32	74	15	0
Howard	23	0	4	3	16	45	24	19	2	0
Independence	195	3	38	4	150	439	149	235	55	18
Izard	48	1	18	0	29	282	76	191	15	11
Jackson	26	0	6	0	20	128	3	97	28	3
Johnson	36	2	1	2	31	165	60	77	28	0
Lee	10	0	2	0	8	106	17	74	15	0
Logan	11	0	2	0	9	138	22	98	18	1
Marion	87	2	18	0	67	292	100	182	10	1
Mississippi	31	1	5	1	24	249	74	132	43	0
Montgomery	9	0	4	0	5	92	41	49	2	0
Newton	27	0	3	0	24	32	17	13	2	3
Pike	1	0	0	0	1	60	26	32	2	1
Polk	41	0	7	0	34	69	22	44	3	0
Pope	50	2	12	0	36	287	87	173	27	2
Prairie	3	0	0	0	3	58	18	33	7	0
Scott	24	0	4	0	20	67	31	33	3	0
Searcy	23	1	6	0	16	30	9	17	4	1
Sevier	19	0	5	0	14	103	32	64	7	3
St. Francis	22	0	4	2	16	277	67	210	0	1
Union	51	1	4	4	42	278	43	197	38	3
White	190	2	54	3	131	668	193	383	92	14
Woodruff	11	0	2	0	9	50	15	21	14	2
Yell	44	1	9	3	31	178	53	101	24	2
CALIFORNIA										
Metropolitan Counties										
Alameda	670	7	35	223	405	2,064	385	1,192	487	23
Butte	327	3	32	31	261	1,394	588	757	49	2
Contra Costa	300	4	25	111	160	1,462	376	1,062	24	10
El Dorado	239	2	55	27	155	1,991	526	1,432	33	5
Fresno	1,534	7	39	101	1,387	3,395	1,546	1,245	604	136
Imperial	241	3	13	15	210	721	174	456	91	21
Kern	2,423	50	177	420	1,776	9,472	2,781	4,622	2,069	300
Kings	133	2	19	12	100	462	158	281	23	7
Los Angeles	5,790	73	291	1,457	3,969	15,912	3,397	8,676	3,839	232
Madera	453	3	32	16	402	1,138	469	640	29	7
Marin	96	2	9	15	70	685	128	548	9	5
Merced	608	5	25	44	534	1,434	439	950	45	5
Monterey	253	2	32	51	168	1,331	354	935	42	9
Napa	72	1	9	3	59	222	62	152	8	0
Orange	310	1	36	17	256	1,089	197	747	145	16
Placer	223	1	27	31	164	1,284	353	878	53	4
Riverside	829	16	45	167	601	7,529	1,507	4,578	1,444	17
Sacramento	2,351	28	195	617	1,511	7,909	2,119	5,586	204	75
San Benito	51	0	4	8	39	152	62	83	7	0
San Bernardino	1,054	13	139	179	723	4,809	1,357	2,329	1,123	65
San Diego	1,523	13	114	225	1,171	4,533	950	2,768	815	48
San Joaquin	757	6	29	179	543	2,729	779	1,823	127	19
San Luis Obispo	115	1	23	7	84	1,083	394	670	19	4
San Mateo	310	3	77	78	152	2,840	335	2,124	381	11
Santa Barbara	229	3	25	22	179	1,208	336	848	24	3
Santa Clara	321	1	41	31	248	1,421	213	974	234	0
Santa Cruz	297	3	34	45	215	1,807	432	1,354	21	10
Shasta	477	10	44	19	404	972	477	446	49	40
Solano	147	2	11	14	120	396	153	140	103	14
Sonoma	516	4	64	42	406	1,080	340	734	6	13
Stanislaus	435	13	31	133	258	1,735	614	1,053	68	18
Sutter	64	0	8	2	54	591	184	367	40	1

Table 10. Offenses Known to Law Enforcement, by Selected State Metropolitan and Nonmetropolitan Counties, 2018—Continued

(Number.)

State/county	Violent crime	Murder and nonnegligent manslaughter	Rape[1]	Robbery	Aggravated assault	Property crime	Burglary	Larceny-theft	Motor vehicle theft	Arson[2]
Tulare[4]	372	13	40	60	259	1,976	627	1,349	0	0
Ventura	141	3	19	21	98	697	154	473	70	7
Yolo	81	2	7	7	65	287	82	194	11	2
Yuba	225	7	28	45	145	912	338	560	14	21
Nonmetropolitan Counties										
Alpine	12	0	2	1	9	27	11	16	0	0
Amador	83	3	8	5	67	338	78	258	2	4
Calaveras	187	2	27	14	144	615	217	376	22	0
Colusa	24	2	7	5	10	185	68	114	3	1
Del Norte	102	1	20	12	69	299	130	163	6	4
Glenn	55	1	9	7	38	444	132	276	36	3
Humboldt	240	7	17	52	164	899	338	538	23	16
Inyo	80	0	6	4	70	139	58	80	1	3
Lake	201	4	13	20	164	490	278	206	6	10
Lassen	57	0	6	3	48	224	109	113	2	7
Mariposa	67	0	7	1	59	192	41	147	4	0
Mendocino	213	5	21	28	159	383	199	178	6	13
Modoc	27	0	3	1	23	41	15	24	2	1
Mono	22	0	6	0	16	45	8	36	1	1
Nevada	150	2	16	5	127	423	211	205	7	1
Plumas	130	0	14	4	112	312	139	165	8	3
Sierra	5	0	1	0	4	22	9	11	2	0
Siskiyou	73	2	6	0	65	172	101	56	15	0
Tehama	62	1	12	6	43	452	197	244	11	5
Trinity	77	2	11	7	57	194	89	102	3	6
Tuolumne	169	2	52	11	104	555	272	271	12	3
COLORADO										
Metropolitan Counties										
Arapahoe	350	2	66	33	249	1,865	322	1,252	291	28
Boulder	78	1	16	6	55	672	149	462	61	4
Clear Creek	24	0	4	0	20	56	11	37	8	8
Douglas	366	1	131	20	214	2,489	373	1,829	287	26
Elbert	19	0	1	0	18	3	0	1	2	0
El Paso	588	10	147	41	390	2,368	431	1,590	347	25
Gilpin	36	0	5	2	29	86	18	62	6	2
Larimer	153	1	33	6	113	903	195	626	82	9
Mesa	146	1	27	7	111	1,017	206	717	94	20
Pueblo	52	1	1	14	36	1,116	227	727	162	4
Teller	31	1	9	1	20	104	37	61	6	5
Weld	155	1	26	4	124	716	208	386	122	6
Nonmetropolitan Counties										
Archuleta	49	1	2	2	44	94	25	63	6	6
Baca	3	0	0	0	3	2	2	0	0	0
Bent	32	1	2	0	29	187	76	102	9	1
Chaffee	11	0	2	0	9	60	18	35	7	0
Cheyenne	0	0	0	0	0	1	0	1	0	0
Conejos	5	0	0	1	4	31	28	0	3	0
Crowley	11	0	0	1	10	42	14	23	5	0
Custer	19	0	0	0	19	69	9	57	3	2
Delta	34	3	14	0	17	193	65	106	22	2
Dolores	1	0	1	0	0	24	17	6	1	1
Fremont	44	0	9	2	33	265	72	150	43	3
Garfield	63	3	19	0	41	209	41	142	26	8
Grand	9	0	0	0	9	47	13	32	2	2
Gunnison	8	0	0	0	8	25	2	21	2	0
Hinsdale	1	0	1	0	0	4	0	4	0	0
Huerfano	20	3	1	2	14	119	35	75	9	5
Jackson	1	0	0	0	1	5	1	3	1	0
Kit Carson	7	0	2	1	4	41	11	27	3	0
Lake	11	0	0	1	10	36	4	29	3	0
La Plata	76	1	25	0	50	202	57	119	26	2
Logan	13	0	6	0	7	91	24	49	18	2
Mineral	1	0	0	0	1	0	0	0	0	0
Moffat	4	0	0	0	4	28	6	22	0	0
Montezuma	29	0	5	1	23	130	36	80	14	3
Montrose	24	0	5	0	19	215	64	129	22	1
Morgan	42	1	1	0	40	83	18	50	15	0
Otero	4	0	0	0	4	104	47	43	14	0
Pitkin	4	0	2	0	2	39	2	36	1	0
Prowers	5	0	1	2	2	7	1	3	3	0
Routt	13	0	4	0	9	45	14	28	3	1
San Juan	1	0	0	0	1	3	0	2	1	0
San Miguel	3	0	0	0	3	3	1	0	2	1
Sedgwick	0	0	0	0	0	5	2	2	1	0
Washington	2	0	2	0	0	56	4	47	5	0
DELAWARE										
Metropolitan Counties										
New Castle County Police Department	851	8	78	130	635	4,464	775	3,256	433	0

Table 10. Offenses Known to Law Enforcement, by Selected State Metropolitan and Nonmetropolitan Counties, 2018—Continued

(Number.)

State/county	Violent crime	Murder and nonnegligent manslaughter	Rape[1]	Robbery	Aggravated assault	Property crime	Burglary	Larceny-theft	Motor vehicle theft	Arson[2]
FLORIDA										
Metropolitan Counties										
Alachua	734	7	106	105	516	1,938	545	1,257	136	18
Baker	94	2	5	7	80	287	49	214	24	1
Bay	327	2	36	24	265	2,124	517	1,430	177	4
Brevard	642	4	46	74	518	3,691	754	2,636	301	14
Broward	300	5	18	66	211	722	113	528	81	1
Charlotte	350	2	31	17	300	1,763	227	1,434	102	6
Citrus	345	2	19	42	282	2,102	369	1,504	229	8
Clay	574	2	94	87	391	3,115	594	2,295	226	14
Collier	898	9	109	138	642	3,762	505	3,042	215	4
Escambia	1,419	11	187	237	984	7,580	1,502	5,508	570	6
Flagler	195	3	28	9	155	1,244	164	1,021	59	2
Gadsden	104	0	14	5	85	247	112	121	14	3
Gilchrist	22	0	3	1	18	115	56	53	6	1
Hernando	466	6	77	50	333	2,855	490	2,169	196	23
Highlands	220	2	37	30	151	1,854	456	1,319	79	8
Hillsborough	1,849	35	245	298	1,271	12,516	1,889	9,520	1,107	47
Indian River	250	9	27	36	178	1,622	277	1,260	85	2
Jefferson	78	1	4	4	69	219	91	109	19	1
Lake	504	3	83	52	366	2,603	660	1,662	281	9
Lee	1,272	26	202	257	787	5,647	1,000	4,023	624	42
Leon	367	4	33	40	290	1,926	331	1,483	112	10
Levy	472	1	22	2	447	592	274	243	75	0
Manatee	1,335	18	132	203	982	5,156	821	3,969	366	10
Marion	1,040	21	182	85	752	4,185	1,113	2,623	449	6
Martin	346	3	74	69	200	1,632	206	1,371	55	5
Miami-Dade	5,362	80	453	1,207	3,622	32,805	3,322	25,946	3,537	46
Nassau	182	2	17	6	157	1,004	380	530	94	8
Okaloosa	532	7	77	29	419	2,718	375	2,155	188	0
Orange	4,803	51	467	1,084	3,201	21,318	3,588	15,801	1,929	0
Osceola	706	12	102	86	506	4,385	990	3,180	215	3
Palm Beach	1,691	23	233	354	1,081	10,754	1,420	8,244	1,090	38
Pasco	1,468	9	223	219	1,017	6,768	1,134	5,069	565	29
Pinellas	525	6	111	94	314	4,414	553	3,566	295	17
Polk	1,205	15	83	100	1,007	5,437	1,196	3,677	564	4
Santa Rosa	235	1	54	13	167	1,513	336	1,079	98	5
Sarasota	466	3	20	53	390	4,182	605	3,381	196	9
Seminole	538	8	99	50	381	2,573	491	1,922	160	3
St. Johns	257	4	27	24	202	2,249	304	1,767	178	2
St. Lucie	282	9	48	35	190	1,312	249	976	87	1
Sumter	191	7	18	13	153	861	184	580	97	3
Volusia	570	9	88	94	379	2,801	613	1,933	255	21
Wakulla	57	1	5	5	46	526	127	372	27	1
Walton	117	3	18	2	94	935	225	633	77	1
Nonmetropolitan Counties										
Bradford	50	1	6	4	39	231	81	123	27	0
Calhoun	17	2	0	0	15	71	26	39	6	0
Columbia	134	4	17	11	102	858	356	468	34	3
DeSoto	96	0	7	16	73	586	204	340	42	2
Dixie	72	1	8	1	62	169	106	48	15	4
Franklin	52	1	3	1	47	209	42	166	1	0
Glades	26	0	2	1	23	126	33	84	9	0
Gulf	37	0	2	0	35	121	42	72	7	0
Hamilton	39	1	2	2	34	183	56	120	7	0
Hardee	49	0	6	6	37	300	97	170	33	0
Hendry	153	1	11	23	118	655	203	414	38	3
Holmes	48	0	3	0	45	170	50	108	12	0
Jackson	91	1	19	3	68	717	146	527	44	0
Lafayette	22	0	0	0	22	39	17	19	3	3
Liberty	9	0	3	0	6	47	13	28	6	0
Madison	137	0	13	3	121	173	71	99	3	0
Monroe	163	2	11	13	137	840	110	688	42	3
Okeechobee	181	1	18	15	147	928	188	661	79	0
Putnam	136	4	20	20	92	1,033	263	716	54	3
Suwannee	112	1	14	6	91	443	154	266	23	0
Taylor	151	0	10	2	139	221	115	86	20	1
Union	33	0	2	3	28	67	29	36	2	1
Washington	33	1	2	3	27	185	78	94	13	0
GEORGIA										
Metropolitan Counties										
Brooks	36	0	3	0	33	155	43	100	12	0
Bryan	37	1	3	1	32	330	62	253	15	0
Burke	22	0	2	6	14	289	65	202	22	0
Butts	65	2	2	10	51	267	32	217	18	1
Carroll	167	0	24	9	134	1,289	390	755	144	4
Cherokee	97	0	12	13	72	1,307	201	1,006	100	0
Clayton	14	0	0	0	14	5	0	4	1	0
Clayton County Police Department	1,388	37	182	465	704	8,263	1,979	5,064	1,220	24

Table 10. Offenses Known to Law Enforcement, by Selected State Metropolitan and Nonmetropolitan Counties, 2018—Continued

(Number.)

State/county	Violent crime	Murder and nonnegligent manslaughter	Rape[1]	Robbery	Aggravated assault	Property crime	Burglary	Larceny-theft	Motor vehicle theft	Arson[2]
Cobb	2	0	0	0	2	25	0	25	0	0
Cobb County Police Department	1,136	8	126	372	630	9,693	1,387	7,442	864	29
Columbia	53	1	7	9	36	1,816	164	1,551	101	1
Coweta[5]	91	1	12	19	59	1,052	234	735	83	2
Crawford	22	0	2	2	18	210	56	137	17	0
Dawson	32	0	5	1	26	433	71	336	26	1
DeKalb	0	0	0	0	0	0	0	0	0	0
DeKalb County Police Department	3,085	82	170	1,234	1,599	21,426	4,407	13,825	3,194	107
Dougherty	0	0	0	0	0	119	0	119	0	0
Dougherty County Police Department	29	1	2	8	18	327	103	209	15	0
Echols[5]	1	0	0	0	1	43	15	26	2	0
Effingham	40	0	3	2	35	351	157	140	54	0
Fayette	37	0	9	5	23	503	88	379	36	3
Forsyth	106	1	25	9	71	1,840	266	1,494	80	1
Fulton	9	0	0	0	9	4	0	4	0	0
Fulton County Police Department[5]	256	5	10	77	164	1,510	182	1,040	288	1
Glynn	0	0	0	0	0	0	0	0	0	0
Glynn County Police Department	192	3	22	46	121	1,635	331	1,184	120	4
Gwinnett County Police Department	1,605	30	173	583	819	14,551	2,450	10,631	1,470	38
Hall	240	3	54	26	157	1,561	327	1,015	219	29
Haralson	145	0	7	1	137	477	154	272	51	
Heard	18	0	1	1	16	107	22	63	22	0
Henry	0	0	0	0	0	78	0	78	0	
Henry County Police Department	300	4	44	87	165	3,589	572	2,608	409	3
Houston	117	0	10	9	98	1,002	161	792	49	3
Jasper	63	0	0	2	61	174	26	141	7	0
Jones	22	0	2	3	17	262	62	179	21	3
Lamar	22	0	2	0	20	114	25	71	18	0
Lanier	36	0	2	1	33	164	31	120	13	0
Lee	56	0	5	4	47	516	76	419	21	0
Liberty	164	3	1	5	155	232	60	147	25	0
Long	16	1	5	1	9	151	61	76	14	0
Madison	90	0	3	3	84	405	60	311	34	0
Marion	4	0	0	0	4	39	8	31	0	0
McDuffie	50	3	4	3	40	196	80	100	16	
McIntosh	35	2	3	4	26	247	53	176	18	1
Meriwether	51	3	0	1	47	287	56	214	17	0
Monroe	22	0	2	2	18	314	64	231	19	0
Murray	36	0	0	1	35	56	10	38	8	1
Muscogee	56	0	0	1	55	33	1	30	2	0
Newton	305	4	14	36	251	1,565	327	974	264	13
Oconee	21	0	0	1	20	442	35	386	21	0
Oglethorpe	40	0	1	3	36	165	35	120	10	1
Paulding	185	1	8	21	155	2,083	347	1,456	280	9
Peach	23	0	3	2	18	214	47	147	20	0
Pickens	76	0	8	1	67	383	91	253	39	0
Pike	19	0	1	4	14	218	32	178	8	0
Rockdale	167	5	20	31	111	1,319	175	1,041	103	
Spalding	134	0	3	16	115	810	180	538	92	
Talbot	13	0	1	1	11	47	14	28	5	0
Twiggs	15	0	2	1	12	99	28	59	12	2
Walton	69	1	12	14	42	599	116	408	75	1
Whitfield	159	1	11	11	136	1,327	358	852	117	
Nonmetropolitan Counties										
Bacon	15	0	1	0	14	163	62	98	3	0
Baldwin	259	1	8	6	244	646	123	481	42	1
Banks	52	0	8	1	43	395	95	279	21	0
Ben Hill	22	0	0	2	20	167	51	99	17	0
Berrien	32	0	2	2	28	229	58	161	10	0
Bleckley	9	0	3	1	5	109	24	82	3	0
Bulloch	38	1	4	7	26	550	107	400	43	0
Calhoun	1	0	0	0	1	5	3	2	0	0
Candler	9	0	3	1	5	100	28	70	2	0
Charlton	21	4	0	0	17	119	52	51	16	0
Chattooga	5	0	1	0	4	86	14	70	2	0
Clay	10	0	1	0	9	16	1	14	1	0
Clinch	10	1	1	0	8	63	29	27	7	0
Coffee	93	1	10	4	78	563	165	320	78	3
Cook	43	0	0	1	42	133	43	77	13	0
Crisp	9	0	2	1	6	370	49	302	19	0
Decatur	48	0	5	2	41	246	66	165	15	0
Dodge	32	2	2	6	22	178	68	92	18	0
Dooly	2	0	0	0	2	94	22	64	8	0
Early	12	0	0	0	12	98	39	58	1	0
Elbert	19	0	5	3	11	266	68	187	11	0
Emanuel	1	1	0	0	0	216	48	145	23	0
Evans	8	0	0	0	8	33	8	15	10	0
Fannin	23	1	4	2	16	204	56	125	23	5
Gilmer	66	0	8	1	57	382	110	239	33	0
Glascock	3	0	0	1	2	28	6	20	2	0

Table 10. Offenses Known to Law Enforcement, by Selected State Metropolitan and Nonmetropolitan Counties, 2018—Continued

(Number.)

State/county	Violent crime	Murder and nonnegligent manslaughter	Rape[1]	Robbery	Aggravated assault	Property crime	Burglary	Larceny-theft	Motor vehicle theft	Arson[2]
Grady	40	0	2	0	38	180	48	111	21	0
Greene	10	1	2	0	7	112	21	85	6	0
Habersham	27	0	7	1	19	324	134	164	26	0
Hancock	12	0	0	2	10	88	31	53	4	0
Irwin	8	0	1	1	6	119	22	84	13	
Jeff Davis	16	0	0	0	16	115	28	77	10	0
Jefferson	32	0	3	0	29	80	26	49	5	0
Laurens	92	1	11	10	70	547	146	339	62	0
Mitchell	35	0	1	1	33	246	46	179	21	0
Pierce	37	1	3	1	32	247	68	175	4	0
Polk	0	0	0	0	0	0	0	0	0	0
Polk County Police Department	52	0	4	2	46	543	167	319	57	0
Pulaski	61	2	0	4	55	226	68	147	11	0
Rabun	14	0	1	2	11	210	51	154	5	0
Randolph	3	0	0	0	3	29	11	16	2	0
Schley	4	1	0	0	3	11	2	8	1	2
Seminole	10	1	1	0	8	64	13	48	3	1
Stephens	15	0	4	2	9	280	84	188	8	
Sumter	30	1	4	1	24	179	55	111	13	0
Taylor	7	0	0	0	7	47	21	24	2	0
Thomas	45	0	6	9	30	463	117	305	41	4
Toombs	12	0	0	1	11	140	44	77	19	0
Towns	35	0	2	0	33	148	33	108	7	0
Treutlen	8	0	1	4	3	42	20	22	0	
Troup	65	0	6	11	48	602	115	409	78	
Turner	1	0	0	0	1	46	23	17	6	
Union	14	0	3	0	11	239	49	161	29	1
Upson	22	0	1	2	19	303	48	223	32	
Ware	93	0	2	3	88	625	133	462	30	
Warren	2	0	1	1	0	32	6	18	8	
Wayne	135	1	10	9	115	730	171	531	28	0
Webster	2	0	0	0	2	1	1	0	0	0
White	28	1	2	0	25	118	32	81	5	0
Wilkes	23	1	0	1	21	18	10	5	3	0
Wilkinson	9	0	0	1	8	40	17	20	3	2
HAWAII										
Metropolitan Counties										
Maui Police Department	435	5	114	53	263	5,084	751	3,640	693	124
IDAHO										
Metropolitan Counties										
Ada	220	0	40	5	175	659	125	491	43	6
Bannock	3	0	1	0	2	48	9	30	9	0
Boise	22	0	6	0	16	67	24	38	5	0
Bonneville	99	2	14	2	81	532	146	350	36	2
Butte	1	0	0	0	1	6	0	6	0	0
Canyon	116	1	26	3	86	511	176	251	84	4
Franklin	4	0	0	0	4	28	3	24	1	0
Gem	16	0	1	1	14	42	14	23	5	0
Jefferson	6	0	1	0	5	101	18	68	15	1
Jerome	11	0	0	0	11	97	26	62	9	1
Kootenai	103	3	18	2	80	835	157	623	55	7
Nez Perce	15	1	3	0	11	62	15	40	7	0
Power	4	0	0	0	4	30	5	22	3	0
Twin Falls	40	0	10	0	30	213	102	99	12	1
Nonmetropolitan Counties										
Bingham	37	1	5	2	29	166	38	110	18	2
Blaine	16	0	4	0	12	25	7	18	0	1
Camas	1	0	0	0	1	8	0	8	0	0
Caribou	2	0	0	0	2	4	1	3	0	0
Elmore	27	0	4	0	23	59	19	35	5	2
Gooding	6	0	1	0	5	63	20	33	10	1
Idaho	20	0	2	1	17	82	26	49	7	0
Latah	14	0	4	0	10	131	39	82	10	0
Madison	16	1	9	0	6	45	11	29	5	0
Minidoka	32	2	3	0	27	129	41	77	11	2
Oneida	5	0	0	1	4	43	18	20	5	0
Payette	21	0	2	0	19	98	17	70	11	0
Shoshone	18	0	3	0	15	146	41	99	6	0
Teton	10	0	3	0	7	64	6	53	5	0
Valley	15	0	7	0	8	70	22	47	1	1
ILLINOIS										
Metropolitan Counties										
Alexander	7	0	0	1	6	38	10	24	4	0
Bond	2	0	0	0	2	80	20	58	2	0
Boone	43	1	17	1	24	160	39	112	9	1
Champaign	106	0	29	3	74	370	105	239	26	4
Clinton	10	0	1	0	9	38	12	15	11	0

Table 10. Offenses Known to Law Enforcement, by Selected State Metropolitan and Nonmetropolitan Counties, 2018—Continued

(Number.)

State/county	Violent crime	Murder and nonnegligent manslaughter	Rape[1]	Robbery	Aggravated assault	Property crime	Burglary	Larceny-theft	Motor vehicle theft	Arson[2]
Cook	216	1	73	27	115	1,068	162	773	133	12
DeKalb	16	1	5	1	9	51	28	20	3	2
DuPage	82	3	18	12	49	566	129	380	57	2
Fulton	13	0	5	0	8	141	40	90	11	1
Grundy	17	0	5	1	11	111	30	75	6	0
Henry	3	0	0	0	3	62	12	46	4	0
Jackson	23	0	7	0	16	291	94	174	23	0
Jersey	23	0	9	0	14	105	38	57	10	0
Kane	75	0	29	3	43	224	74	123	27	2
Kankakee	47	2	12	2	31	295	111	149	35	4
Kendall	47	1	9	5	32	140	60	73	7	2
Macon	39	0	5	1	33	355	71	275	9	2
Macoupin	25	3	2	1	19	255	59	177	19	0
Madison	145	2	29	12	102	953	234	639	80	4
Marshall	4	0	1	1	2	36	19	13	4	1
McHenry	91	0	20	2	69	345	80	235	30	0
McLean	31	0	9	1	21	103	18	71	14	0
Menard	8	0	2	0	6	27	10	14	3	7
Monroe	7	0	2	1	4	58	17	35	6	0
Peoria	103	2	23	10	68	794	182	557	55	11
Piatt	21	0	3	1	17	27	14	10	3	1
Rock Island	58	0	9	4	45	309	72	209	28	1
Sangamon	181	1	19	13	148	724	217	427	80	2
Stark	9	0	1	0	8	44	10	31	3	1
St. Clair	111	2	19	9	81	844	213	563	68	7
Vermilion	87	3	20	5	59	414	139	256	19	0
Will	118	5	28	18	67	623	152	394	77	6
Winnebago	142	7	38	12	85	536	175	313	48	3
Woodford	6	0	2	1	3	84	14	66	4	3
Nonmetropolitan Counties										
Adams	30	0	15	0	15	165	64	93	8	0
Brown	4	0	0	0	4	10	5	5	0	0
Bureau	19	0	5	2	12	128	42	79	7	0
Carroll	7	0	0	0	7	27	13	14	0	0
Cass	4	0	0	2	2	4	1	3	0	0
Clark	6	0	1	0	5	37	19	16	2	0
Clay	3	1	0	0	2	52	21	26	5	0
Coles	19	0	7	1	11	98	45	44	9	2
Crawford	8	0	0	1	7	53	24	28	1	0
Cumberland	1	0	0	0	1	27	11	13	3	0
DeWitt	1	0	1	0	0	77	33	44	0	0
Edgar	11	0	5	0	6	52	28	20	4	1
Effingham	14	0	1	2	11	108	16	81	11	1
Fayette	5	0	1	1	3	89	22	57	10	0
Ford	13	1	1	0	11	39	15	24	0	2
Franklin	7	0	0	0	7	280	73	182	25	0
Gallatin	4	0	0	0	4	52	14	37	1	0
Greene	13	0	0	0	13	14	4	10	0	0
Hancock	7	0	1	0	6	118	29	87	2	1
Iroquois	11	0	0	2	9	151	59	80	12	1
Jasper	1	0	0	0	1	8	5	1	2	0
Jefferson	57	1	3	5	48	236	84	135	17	2
Jo Daviess	12	0	5	1	6	86	16	64	6	1
Knox	51	1	11	1	38	155	55	87	13	0
Lee	29	0	0	0	29	126	48	72	6	1
Livingston	28	0	5	0	23	89	25	53	11	1
Logan	9	0	2	0	7	47	21	21	5	0
Marion	30	0	13	0	17	190	81	84	25	0
Mason	13	0	7	0	6	87	24	59	4	0
Massac	10	0	0	0	10	116	43	67	6	9
McDonough	11	0	1	0	10	31	12	18	1	0
Montgomery	21	0	1	0	20	174	63	109	2	2
Morgan	28	0	16	0	12	101	36	65	0	0
Ogle	17	0	3	2	12	102	23	69	10	1
Perry	11	0	0	0	11	78	24	44	10	0
Pike	10	0	2	0	8	41	15	25	1	0
Putnam	1	1	0	0	0	13	2	10	1	0
Randolph	1	0	0	0	1	19	6	13	0	0
Richland	15	0	3	0	12	87	46	36	5	0
Saline	31	0	0	1	30	127	30	83	14	3
Schuyler	3	0	1	0	2	2	0	2	0	0
Scott	1	0	1	0	0	15	7	7	1	0
Shelby	5	0	5	0	0	41	20	20	1	1
Stephenson	13	0	9	0	4	125	23	94	8	0
Union	17	0	5	0	12	85	23	49	13	0
Wabash	0	0	0	0	0	7	0	5	2	1
White	22	0	4	0	18	161	37	120	4	0
INDIANA										
Metropolitan Counties										
Allen	146	0	21	26	99	643	155	425	63	2
Brown	41	0	3	0	38	213	56	143	14	0

Table 10. Offenses Known to Law Enforcement, by Selected State Metropolitan and Nonmetropolitan Counties, 2018—Continued

(Number.)

State/county	Violent crime	Murder and nonnegligent manslaughter	Rape[1]	Robbery	Aggravated assault	Property crime	Burglary	Larceny-theft	Motor vehicle theft	Arson[2]
Clark	105	0	6	13	86	386	103	231	52	
Delaware	48	0	10	0	38	294	73	177	44	3
Floyd	13	0	0	1	12	295	38	227	30	
Franklin	2	0	0	1	1	168	58	83	27	0
Hancock	46	0	4	8	34	233	52	143	38	0
Johnson	46	0	0	6	40	471	62	407	2	0
Lake	44	3	2	11	28	529	57	405	67	2
La Porte	65	0	4	6	55	354	112	211	31	0
Madison	32	2	14	2	14	449	109	321	19	2
Monroe	65	0	17	2	46	638	90	472	76	1
Porter	29	0	8	1	20	271	58	185	28	
Shelby	51	0	7	1	43	181	53	97	31	1
Tippecanoe	34	0	12	6	16	475	142	306	27	3
Vanderburgh	43	0	9	6	28	614	87	485	42	3
Vigo	90	2	9	8	71	906	316	462	128	18
Warrick	120	1	9	9	101	576	87	443	46	0
Nonmetropolitan Counties										
Clinton	9	0	4	3	2	163	43	105	15	1
DeKalb	6	0	5	0	1	127	28	78	21	
Gibson	28	1	4	3	20	123	28	75	20	0
Grant	27	1	1	6	19	206	88	110	8	0
Jackson	17	1	4	1	11	341	78	245	18	
Jay	16	0	0	2	14	65	3	59	3	
Jennings	3	0	2	0	1	116	70	46	0	
Scott	9	0	7	1	1	192	45	137	10	
Starke	15	0	1	2	12	191	17	157	17	0
Steuben	11	0	7	1	3	383	102	249	32	2
Wayne	12	0	7	0	5	118	35	73	10	
White	0	0	0	0	0	21	19	1	1	
IOWA[6]										
KANSAS										
Metropolitan Counties										
Butler	43	0	6	3	34	431	127	263	41	2
Geary	21	0	2	0	19	27	9	18	0	0
Harvey	7	0	1	0	6	68	33	30	5	2
Jackson	33	1	6	0	26	129	25	90	14	3
Jefferson	29	1	6	1	21	189	38	134	17	2
Johnson	61	0	6	1	54	203	33	146	24	4
Leavenworth	52	2	5	2	43	201	75	90	36	5
Miami	43	0	6	0	37	177	51	100	26	2
Osage	10	0	5	0	5	59	20	34	5	1
Pottawatomie	33	1	0	0	32	199	45	134	20	2
Riley County Police Department	251	1	57	28	165	1,283	165	1,029	89	16
Sedgwick	134	4	11	9	110	528	169	275	84	6
Shawnee	93	0	7	6	80	956	230	607	119	10
Sumner	22	1	1	4	16	176	68	90	18	1
Nonmetropolitan Counties										
Allen	9	0	2	0	7	53	18	34	1	2
Anderson	8	0	0	0	8	40	8	27	5	1
Atchison	3	0	0	0	3	22	2	16	4	0
Bourbon	26	0	2	1	23	54	19	30	5	5
Brown	4	0	0	0	4	8	3	4	1	1
Cherokee	29	0	6	0	23	153	63	73	17	5
Cheyenne	4	0	2	0	2	26	7	17	2	0
Clark	3	0	0	0	3	11	2	7	2	1
Clay	3	0	1	0	2	14	6	8	0	0
Cloud	3	0	2	0	1	49	20	21	8	2
Comanche	1	0	1	0	0	10	2	6	2	0
Cowley	33	0	9	2	22	123	42	69	12	1
Dickinson	19	1	4	0	14	108	31	58	19	4
Edwards	3	0	0	0	3	22	9	12	1	0
Ellis	10	0	2	0	8	48	15	31	2	2
Ellsworth	6	0	3	0	3	34	9	22	3	1
Finney	33	1	7	2	23	150	49	94	7	0
Ford	13	0	0	0	13	65	27	28	10	0
Franklin	40	0	3	0	37	154	43	95	16	2
Grant	2	0	0	1	1	20	5	11	4	0
Gray	4	0	3	0	1	59	12	43	4	0
Greenwood	14	0	4	0	10	72	13	51	8	0
Hamilton	3	0	1	0	2	27	8	17	2	0
Haskell	6	0	0	0	6	30	8	20	2	0
Kearny[3]	19	0	3	0	16			70	10	0
Kingman	2	0	0	0	2	70	21	43	6	0
Kiowa	2	0	1	0	1	27	8	19	0	0
Labette	19	0	1	0	18	48	12	35	1	0
Logan	3	0	0	0	3	15	6	9	0	0
Lyon	16	0	2	1	13	61	14	41	6	1
Marion	27	0	1	1	25	43	18	17	8	1
Marshall	2	0	0	0	2	16	8	4	4	0

Table 10. Offenses Known to Law Enforcement, by Selected State Metropolitan and Nonmetropolitan Counties, 2018—Continued

(Number.)

State/county	Violent crime	Murder and nonnegligent manslaughter	Rape[1]	Robbery	Aggravated assault	Property crime	Burglary	Larceny-theft	Motor vehicle theft	Arson[2]
Mitchell	3	0	0	0	3	12	6	5	1	0
Montgomery	17	0	3	0	14	132	52	70	10	1
Morton	1	0	0	0	1	24	10	12	2	0
Nemaha	1	0	0	0	1	34	11	21	2	2
Neosho	21	0	4	0	17	66	27	27	12	2
Ness	4	0	0	0	4	33	7	22	4	0
Norton	1	0	0	0	1	18	3	10	5	1
Ottawa	2	1	0	0	1	42	14	26	2	2
Pawnee	2	0	0	0	2	18	12	6	0	0
Phillips	4	0	0	0	4	0	0	0	0	1
Pratt	4	0	2	0	2	28	12	14	2	0
Reno	26	0	5	0	21	235	67	133	35	3
Republic	1	0	0	0	1	36	8	24	4	0
Rice	6	0	0	1	5	37	17	17	3	0
Rooks	6	0	0	0	6	16	7	8	1	8
Rush	3	0	0	0	3	54	17	31	6	0
Russell	29	0	2	1	26	45	14	25	6	0
Saline	26	1	3	0	22	106	31	65	10	3
Seward	3	0	1	0	2	12	3	6	3	0
Sherman	0	0	0	0	0	1	0	1	0	0
Smith	2	1	0	0	1	5	1	2	2	0
Stafford	5	0	0	0	5	32	15	13	4	0
Thomas	8	0	0	0	8	50	14	32	4	1
Trego	0	0	0	0	0	16	5	10	1	1
Washington	4	0	0	0	4	5	1	3	1	0
Wilson	19	0	3	0	16	50	13	28	9	0
Woodson	2	0	0	0	2	49	21	26	2	0
KENTUCKY										
Metropolitan Counties										
Allen	6	0	2	1	3	137	55	64	18	1
Boone	56	0	23	12	21	824	142	579	103	1
Bourbon	2	0	0	0	2	45	16	25	4	0
Boyd	13	0	3	3	7	184	62	91	31	0
Bracken	3	0	0	0	3	46	20	18	8	0
Bullitt	29	1	8	3	17	371	100	203	68	0
Butler	1	0	0	0	1	56	19	30	7	0
Campbell	1	0	0	0	1	0	0	0	0	0
Campbell County Police Department	20	0	11	1	8	141	35	93	13	0
Carter	6	0	1	1	4	71	25	24	22	0
Christian	23	1	5	2	15	325	114	172	39	1
Clark	10	0	3	2	5	158	68	73	17	0
Daviess	14	2	4	4	4	395	104	249	42	0
Edmonson	5	0	1	1	3	28	7	13	8	1
Fayette	0	0	0	0	0	0	0	0	0	0
Gallatin	5	0	1	0	4	43	12	21	10	0
Grant	12	0	3	0	9	115	37	65	13	1
Greenup	5	0	0	0	5	33	14	13	6	1
Hancock	0	0	0	0	0	9	3	5	1	0
Hardin	5	3	0	0	2	160	56	86	18	0
Henderson	20	0	8	1	11	148	41	93	14	0
Henry	1	0	0	0	1	7	3	3	1	0
Jefferson	0	0	0	0	0	1	1	0	0	0
Jessamine	13	1	5	1	6	231	84	133	14	1
Kenton	0	0	0	0	0	3	0	3	0	0
Kenton County Police Department	12	0	9	1	2	113	28	80	5	1
Larue	5	0	1	1	3	45	20	18	7	0
McLean	6	0	3	0	3	45	20	22	3	0
Meade	5	0	0	2	3	144	49	54	41	1
Oldham	0	0	0	0	0	4	0	4	0	0
Oldham County Police Department	25	0	10	5	10	332	90	212	30	3
Pendleton	7	0	0	0	7	62	17	36	9	0
Scott	10	0	1	5	4	157	37	99	21	0
Shelby	17	0	1	4	12	253	46	189	18	0
Spencer	0	0	0	0	0	70	27	39	4	0
Trigg	4	0	2	0	2	92	49	36	7	1
Warren	44	1	14	4	25	421	156	229	36	2
Woodford	2	0	0	1	1	26	5	20	1	0
Nonmetropolitan Counties										
Adair	4	0	1	0	3	11	2	4	5	0
Anderson	4	0	0	0	4	53	22	24	7	1
Ballard	4	0	1	0	3	78	34	37	7	2
Barren	18	1	1	4	12	120	61	42	17	1
Bath	0	0	0	0	0	11	2	4	5	0
Bell	12	0	2	1	9	136	43	74	19	4
Boyle	5	0	2	0	3	38	19	10	9	0
Breathitt	0	0	0	0	0	2	0	1	1	0
Breckinridge	3	0	1	0	2	13	0	8	5	0
Caldwell	2	0	0	0	2	38	15	19	4	1
Calloway	14	1	8	0	5	245	105	114	26	1

Table 10. Offenses Known to Law Enforcement, by Selected State Metropolitan and Nonmetropolitan Counties, 2018—Continued

(Number.)

State/county	Violent crime	Murder and nonnegligent manslaughter	Rape[1]	Robbery	Aggravated assault	Property crime	Burglary	Larceny-theft	Motor vehicle theft	Arson[2]
Carlisle	1	0	0	0	1	15	8	5	2	0
Carroll	2	0	0	0	2	6	2	3	1	0
Casey	3	0	0	2	1	23	9	10	4	0
Clay	4	0	0	0	4	81	22	26	33	2
Clinton	3	0	0	0	3	17	3	6	8	0
Crittenden	2	0	0	0	2	19	6	7	6	0
Cumberland	0	0	0	0	0	7	5	2	0	0
Fleming	2	0	0	0	2	19	2	12	5	0
Floyd	4	0	0	0	4	47	17	22	8	0
Franklin	30	1	8	5	16	260	81	149	30	0
Fulton	0	0	0	0	0	5	1	3	1	0
Garrard County Police Department	4	0	0	0	4	73	22	41	10	0
Graves	24	1	7	3	13	281	108	146	27	4
Grayson	12	0	2	0	10	65	14	41	10	0
Green	1	0	0	0	1	5	2	2	1	0
Harlan	7	0	0	0	7	27	12	13	2	0
Harrison	1	0	0	0	1	86	38	38	10	0
Hart	3	0	0	0	3	40	12	22	6	0
Hickman	1	0	0	0	1	8	2	3	3	1
Hopkins	16	0	4	1	11	267	90	133	44	5
Jackson	2	0	1	0	1	61	26	18	17	0
Johnson	9	0	3	0	6	45	12	13	20	0
Knott	0	0	0	0	0	16	3	8	5	0
Knox	19	0	0	3	16	142	70	34	38	2
Laurel	36	2	8	5	21	503	142	255	106	1
Lawrence	2	0	0	0	2	34	18	6	10	0
Lee	0	0	0	0	0	7	2	3	2	0
Letcher	3	0	2	0	1	9	5	0	4	0
Lewis	3	0	0	0	3	17	8	3	6	0
Lincoln	6	0	0	1	5	77	33	23	21	0
Livingston	3	0	0	0	3	73	41	26	6	0
Logan	19	0	8	3	8	117	43	67	7	4
Lyon	0	0	0	0	0	41	22	17	2	0
Madison[3]	29	0	3	3	23			177	34	0
Magoffin	0	0	0	0	0	12	2	5	5	1
Marion	3	0	0	0	3	69	24	27	18	0
Marshall	11	1	5	0	5	204	86	94	24	2
Martin	3	0	0	0	3	20	6	8	6	0
Mason	7	0	0	3	4	72	27	40	5	0
McCracken	38	0	12	10	16	508	138	317	53	5
McCreary	2	0	0	0	2	55	10	30	15	0
Menifee	0	0	0	0	0	27	12	12	3	1
Mercer	4	0	2	0	2	30	12	11	7	0
Metcalfe	0	0	0	0	0	82	35	40	7	0
Monroe	2	0	0	0	2	13	8	2	3	0
Montgomery	7	1	1	1	4	195	69	100	26	0
Morgan	1	0	0	0	1	10	3	5	2	0
Muhlenberg	8	0	1	1	6	66	28	21	17	0
Nelson	16	4	6	3	3	177	55	96	26	1
Ohio	25	0	12	4	9	103	40	43	20	1
Owen	1	0	0	0	1	42	19	15	8	0
Perry	6	0	0	1	5	40	12	14	14	1
Pike	1	0	0	0	1	36	8	21	7	0
Powell	1	0	0	0	1	15	2	6	7	0
Pulaski[3]	39	2	16	6	15			152	76	0
Robertson	0	0	0	0	0	5	3	1	1	0
Rockcastle	4	0	1	0	3	44	22	10	12	0
Rowan	7	0	0	1	6	72	26	35	11	1
Russell	9	0	0	0	9	13	4	8	1	0
Simpson	7	0	1	2	4	48	24	19	5	0
Taylor	11	0	2	5	4	188	74	93	21	1
Todd	4	0	0	0	4	51	20	22	9	0
Trimble	1	0	0	0	1	13	5	5	3	1
Union	4	0	1	0	3	43	26	13	4	0
Washington	3	0	0	0	3	31	8	14	9	0
Wayne	0	0	0	0	0	42	14	16	12	1
Webster	1	0	0	0	1	11	2	8	1	0
Whitley	6	0	0	0	6	118	42	52	24	0
Wolfe	0	0	0	0	0	13	4	5	4	0
LOUISIANA										
Metropolitan Counties										
Acadia	111	3	8	16	84	618	257	315	46	0
Ascension	321	2	14	31	274	2,882	541	2,170	171	4
Assumption	76	0	6	0	70	263	79	171	13	0
Bossier	56	2	6	5	43	586	107	427	52	3
Caddo	50	1	0	9	40	609	158	386	65	0
Calcasieu	434	3	65	26	340	4,838	1,216	3,250	372	3
De Soto	57	1	9	0	47	370	111	234	25	1
East Baton Rouge	563	11	52	201	299	6,724	891	5,467	366	7
East Feliciana	60	4	4	3	49	160	41	94	25	0

Table 10. Offenses Known to Law Enforcement, by Selected State Metropolitan and Nonmetropolitan Counties, 2018—Continued

(Number.)

State/county	Violent crime	Murder and nonnegligent manslaughter	Rape[1]	Robbery	Aggravated assault	Property crime	Burglary	Larceny-theft	Motor vehicle theft	Arson[2]
Iberville	228	4	10	18	196	390	94	291	5	0
Jefferson	1,448	24	94	286	1,044	9,520	1,297	7,595	628	42
Lafayette	299	3	28	26	242	1,419	332	919	168	14
Lafourche	211	6	26	11	168	1,685	312	1,281	92	7
Livingston	403	10	42	13	338	3,231	877	2,332	22	3
Morehouse	39	1	2	1	35	273	74	192	7	0
Ouachita[5]	404	2	37	47	318	2,850	917	1,734	199	11
Plaquemines	39	1	2	1	35	130	25	93	12	1
Pointe Coupee	139	2	8	11	118	335	72	234	29	0
St. Bernard	116	3	5	36	72	1,514	215	1,218	81	11
St. Charles	151	2	5	22	122	838	185	598	55	3
St. Helena	43	5	1	2	35	106	46	51	9	0
St. James	43	0	3	2	38	295	51	216	28	0
St. John the Baptist	101	4	4	32	61	951	221	672	58	2
St. Martin	116	4	18	7	87	652	141	467	44	0
St. Tammany	210	8	30	25	147	1,455	262	1,078	115	3
Tangipahoa	689	8	47	89	545	2,357	764	1,345	248	14
Terrebonne	251	1	19	31	200	2,208	328	1,777	103	7
Union	67	1	8	3	55	209	49	143	17	0
Vermilion	74	1	1	2	70	754	289	276	189	0
West Baton Rouge	34	0	4	3	27	475	45	380	50	0
West Feliciana	39	2	6	0	31	96	25	68	3	0
Nonmetropolitan Counties										
Allen	24	0	5	1	18	130	27	93	10	1
Avoyelles	197	1	7	0	189	395	135	231	29	0
Beauregard	18	0	7	0	11	156	17	127	12	4
Bienville	57	0	3	10	44	172	62	99	11	0
Caldwell	36	0	0	0	36	250	76	164	10	2
Catahoula	40	0	3	0	37	108	43	63	2	0
Claiborne	8	0	1	2	5	102	25	71	6	0
Concordia	66	2	1	7	56	340	112	220	8	1
Evangeline	34	1	4	2	27	305	71	202	32	0
Franklin	38	1	1	0	36	128	35	80	13	0
Jackson	11	1	2	4	4	105	19	84	2	0
La Salle	78	1	3	2	72	48	14	30	4	0
Lincoln	52	0	2	1	49	158	48	106	4	0
Madison	20	2	1	1	16	27	8	16	3	0
Natchitoches	50	2	5	3	40	355	79	240	36	0
Red River	27	0	0	0	27	112	26	77	9	0
Richland	28	0	2	1	25	47	30	16	1	1
Sabine	16	2	3	0	11	229	12	214	3	0
St. Landry	146	1	9	7	129	996	541	383	72	0
St. Mary	131	1	13	18	99	706	151	510	45	3
Vernon	55	0	18	1	36	507	84	380	43	3
Washington	182	0	24	7	151	612	183	373	56	2
Webster	17	0	1	6	10	155	73	62	20	2
West Carroll	40	0	1	0	39	118	32	75	11	0
Winn	24	0	0	0	24	69	26	36	7	0
MAINE										
Metropolitan Counties										
Androscoggin	7	0	2	1	4	113	32	72	9	1
Cumberland	24	0	3	3	18	412	110	283	19	1
Penobscot	8	0	0	4	4	248	54	182	12	0
Sagadahoc	4	0	1	0	3	112	26	83	3	0
York	20	0	4	1	15	272	69	189	14	1
Nonmetropolitan Counties										
Aroostook	6	0	0	1	5	55	17	36	2	0
Franklin	8	0	5	1	2	49	9	34	6	0
Hancock	4	0	0	0	4	127	32	92	3	0
Kennebec	24	0	5	1	18	159	41	103	15	0
Knox	16	0	0	2	14	168	23	134	11	0
Lincoln	26	0	16	2	8	189	33	147	9	0
Oxford	28	0	15	2	11	279	73	186	20	0
Piscataquis	3	0	1	0	2	53	14	35	4	0
Somerset	31	3	14	1	13	366	95	247	24	1
Waldo	13	0	4	1	8	157	39	113	5	0
Washington	7	0	1	4	2	113	42	65	6	0
MARYLAND										
Metropolitan Counties										
Allegany	40	1	5	6	28	263	51	203	9	2
Anne Arundel	0	0	0	0	0	0	0	0	0	0
Anne Arundel County Police Department	1,825	22	141	425	1,237	9,557	1,226	7,703	628	29
Baltimore County	0	0	0	0	0	0	0	0	0	0
Baltimore County Police Department	4,823	27	346	1,332	3,118	21,223	2,605	16,776	1,842	120
Calvert	94	1	12	16	65	830	135	651	44	1
Carroll	119	1	33	11	74	708	99	565	44	0
Cecil	74	2	15	22	35	439	117	292	30	4

Table 10. Offenses Known to Law Enforcement, by Selected State Metropolitan and Nonmetropolitan Counties, 2018—Continued

(Number.)

State/county	Violent crime	Murder and nonnegligent manslaughter	Rape[1]	Robbery	Aggravated assault	Property crime	Burglary	Larceny-theft	Motor vehicle theft	Arson[2]
Charles	610	11	48	111	440	2,191	223	1,808	160	22
Frederick	170	0	23	22	125	1,233	178	1,013	42	3
Harford	348	8	53	62	225	1,894	287	1,506	101	0
Howard	0	0	0	0	0	0	0	0	0	0
Howard County Police Department	643	1	73	130	439	4,548	442	3,852	254	62
Montgomery	0	0	0	0	0	0	0	0	0	0
Montgomery County Police Department	1,458	19	287	521	631	13,080	1,342	10,988	750	11
Prince George's County Police Department	2,001	50	214	825	912	12,702	1,752	8,620	2,330	104
Queen Anne's	33	1	7	7	18	354	74	272	8	0
Somerset	31	0	1	0	30	42	10	32	0	0
St. Mary's	221	2	26	53	140	1,698	418	1,217	63	6
Washington	313	3	16	32	262	1,469	311	1,100	58	0
Wicomico	97	0	11	11	75	583	160	388	35	4
Worcester	8	0	2	2	4	198	32	159	7	0
Nonmetropolitan Counties										
Caroline	14	0	6	5	3	171	37	126	8	
Dorchester	20	0	2	4	14	146	35	99	12	0
Garrett	50	0	7	1	42	193	65	119	9	0
Kent	5	0	3	0	2	54	17	37	0	0
Talbot	27	0	4	2	21	140	47	88	5	0
MICHIGAN										
Metropolitan Counties										
Bay	59	4	14	8	33	443	63	353	27	8
Berrien	128	1	38	5	84	606	177	398	31	2
Calhoun	122	0	30	3	89	636	188	417	31	3
Clinton	21	0	9	1	11	117	42	65	10	0
Eaton	151	1	44	29	77	1,010	166	783	61	4
Genesee	99	0	16	3	80	363	62	274	27	2
Ingham	160	0	46	8	106	546	131	382	33	1
Ionia	72	1	37	1	33	242	58	167	17	2
Jackson	179	2	39	3	135	466	69	351	46	1
Kalamazoo	275	2	45	43	185	2,756	564	2,004	188	16
Kent	415	8	157	43	207	2,419	361	1,926	132	15
Lapeer	51	0	22	0	29	286	89	178	19	4
Livingston	82	0	36	8	38	483	113	347	23	3
Macomb	321	2	62	21	236	1,081	152	826	103	7
Midland	54	0	27	0	27	252	64	174	14	0
Monroe	192	1	69	16	106	1,287	291	889	107	13
Montcalm	21	0	13	0	8	130	21	99	10	2
Muskegon	83	0	34	6	43	591	97	458	36	2
Oakland	25	0	12	0	13	30	3	23	4	2
Ottawa	550	3	227	23	297	2,242	433	1,718	91	19
Saginaw	115	4	30	6	75	504	77	406	21	2
Shiawassee	18	0	5	0	13	167	35	112	20	0
St. Clair	242	1	40	4	197	684	165	467	52	10
Washtenaw	524	6	70	47	401	1,359	287	941	131	17
Wayne	1	0	0	0	1	4	0	4	0	0
Nonmetropolitan Counties										
Alcona	10	0	5	1	4	52	14	36	2	0
Alger	0	0	0	0	0	2	0	2	0	0
Allegan	90	0	9	2	79	535	109	364	62	3
Alpena	14	0	4	0	10	73	15	58	0	0
Antrim	27	1	9	0	17	129	52	68	9	1
Arenac	35	0	6	1	28	65	20	37	8	1
Baraga	4	0	0	0	4	22	6	12	4	0
Barry	63	0	31	3	29	295	76	203	16	2
Benzie	21	0	6	0	15	61	11	46	4	1
Branch	9	0	5	1	3	105	56	46	3	0
Charlevoix	18	0	6	0	12	78	22	52	4	0
Cheboygan	20	0	13	0	7	37	10	26	1	1
Chippewa	7	0	1	0	6	29	11	17	1	0
Clare	71	0	21	0	50	256	93	146	17	1
Crawford	11	0	5	0	6	70	22	34	14	0
Delta	7	0	4	0	3	58	7	44	7	0
Emmet	47	0	12	1	34	107	12	90	5	1
Gladwin	27	0	6	1	20	124	38	77	9	0
Gogebic	4	0	0	1	3	105	91	13	1	0
Grand Traverse	133	1	35	3	94	487	50	419	18	9
Gratiot	38	0	20	1	17	252	35	213	4	1
Hillsdale	37	3	7	0	27	111	36	64	11	0
Houghton	3	0	1	0	2	59	15	40	4	0
Huron	17	0	5	0	12	81	24	56	1	1
Iosco	4	0	0	0	4	5	2	3	0	0
Iron	12	0	4	0	8	18	4	14	0	0
Isabella	39	1	10	1	27	262	68	180	14	3
Kalkaska	46	0	0	0	46	156	30	122	4	0
Keweenaw	3	0	0	0	3	8	2	6	0	0

Table 10. Offenses Known to Law Enforcement, by Selected State Metropolitan and Nonmetropolitan Counties, 2018—Continued

(Number.)

State/county	Violent crime	Murder and nonnegligent manslaughter	Rape[1]	Robbery	Aggravated assault	Property crime	Burglary	Larceny-theft	Motor vehicle theft	Arson[2]
Lake	44	0	13	2	29	201	65	128	8	6
Leelanau	5	0	1	0	4	40	12	26	2	0
Lenawee	24	0	10	0	14	212	60	141	11	1
Luce	22	0	5	0	17	69	24	44	1	1
Mackinac	11	1	4	0	6	121	22	96	3	0
Manistee	39	0	14	0	25	150	19	128	3	0
Marquette	14	0	2	0	12	165	12	151	2	1
Mason	17	0	5	3	9	119	30	80	9	0
Mecosta	208	1	23	2	182	326	61	253	12	9
Menominee	20	0	9	0	11	80	28	44	8	0
Missaukee	39	0	16	0	23	99	21	78	0	1
Newaygo	55	0	18	0	37	241	57	158	26	5
Oceana	45	0	6	0	39	154	25	124	5	0
Ogemaw	17	0	3	0	14	107	17	85	5	0
Ontonagon	14	0	0	0	14	8	2	6	0	0
Osceola	22	0	2	2	18	101	27	65	9	2
Oscoda	25	0	3	1	21	80	13	59	8	0
Otsego	15	1	5	0	9	49	17	32	0	0
Presque Isle	13	0	7	0	6	36	11	24	1	0
Roscommon	15	0	7	1	7	98	14	80	4	1
Sanilac	52	2	11	1	38	122	47	58	17	4
Schoolcraft	0	0	0	0	0	2	1	1	0	0
St. Joseph	84	1	11	0	72	225	72	133	20	5
Tuscola	51	1	21	0	29	153	46	94	13	0
Van Buren	110	2	30	2	76	460	155	268	37	8
Wexford	39	0	11	2	26	188	33	147	8	2
MINNESOTA										
Metropolitan Counties										
Anoka	39	0	13	2	24	791	92	643	56	3
Benton	17	1	6	0	10	164	40	102	22	1
Blue Earth[5]	21	1	6	2	12	117	44	58	15	0
Carlton	15	1	6	0	8	147	46	89	12	0
Carver	50	0	26	6	18	515	75	411	29	5
Chisago	3	0	0	1	2	82	11	64	7	0
Clay	8	1	1	1	5	57	25	23	9	0
Dakota	38	0	7	0	31	102	22	72	8	0
Dodge	9	1	0	0	8	110	17	85	8	0
Fillmore	10	0	2	0	8	46	6	37	3	1
Hennepin	20	0	0	2	18	59	3	54	2	0
Houston	3	0	1	0	2	29	7	18	4	0
Isanti	17	0	4	1	12	207	46	139	22	0
Lake	1	0	0	0	1	4	2	2	0	0
Le Sueur	8	0	2	0	6	101	21	78	2	0
Mille Lacs	33	3	6	3	21	481	104	326	51	1
Nicollet	7	0	2	1	4	76	27	45	4	0
Olmsted	41	0	20	7	14	324	99	205	20	1
Polk	20	0	8	1	11	127	27	82	18	2
Ramsey[5]	96	0	19	14	63	1,038	150	795	93	5
Scott	9	1	2	0	6	139	21	112	6	0
Sherburne	28	0	12	2	14	290	37	232	21	0
Stearns	31	0	15	0	16	250	59	165	26	3
St. Louis	38	1	14	4	19	674	231	376	67	6
Wabasha[5]	7	0	2	0	5	46	8	32	6	0
Washington	53	0	23	5	25	643	109	483	51	0
Wright	112	0	41	4	67	1,480	124	1,289	67	1
Nonmetropolitan Counties										
Aitkin	10	1	2	1	6	166	63	91	12	1
Becker	38	1	14	1	22	210	87	97	26	1
Beltrami	43	0	7	4	32	347	103	205	39	4
Big Stone	2	0	0	0	2	34	9	24	1	0
Brown	2	0	2	0	0	25	12	8	5	1
Cass	55	3	30	0	22	632	112	456	64	2
Chippewa	0	0	0	0	0	0	0	0	0	0
Clearwater	15	0	7	0	8	66	22	31	13	2
Cook	7	0	4	0	3	32	3	29	0	0
Cottonwood	6	0	0	0	6	20	8	11	1	0
Crow Wing	34	0	9	1	24	329	119	194	16	0
Douglas[5]	13	1	5	0	7	197	46	130	21	1
Faribault[5]	16	0	0	0	16	79	46	22	11	0
Freeborn	7	0	2	1	4	124	47	63	14	0
Goodhue	16	0	2	1	13	183	56	114	13	3
Grant	2	0	0	0	2	10	3	6	1	0
Hubbard	25	0	7	0	18	223	76	125	22	1
Itasca	19	0	6	1	12	217	71	134	12	0
Jackson	4	0	1	0	3	30	6	21	3	0
Kanabec	29	0	0	0	29	46	8	26	12	0
Kandiyohi	22	1	6	1	14	215	50	143	22	0
Kittson	0	0	0	0	0	4	1	2	1	0
Koochiching	2	0	1	0	1	19	1	15	3	0

Table 10. Offenses Known to Law Enforcement, by Selected State Metropolitan and Nonmetropolitan Counties, 2018—Continued

(Number.)

State/county	Violent crime	Murder and nonnegligent manslaughter	Rape[1]	Robbery	Aggravated assault	Property crime	Burglary	Larceny-theft	Motor vehicle theft	Arson[2]
Lac qui Parle	1	0	0	0	1	10	3	4	3	0
Lake of the Woods	1	0	0	0	1	11	3	7	1	0
Lincoln	2	0	1	0	1	21	6	12	3	0
Lyon	5	0	1	0	4	11	6	4	1	0
Mahnomen	12	0	4	0	8	63	16	36	11	1
Marshall	4	0	1	0	3	41	7	30	4	0
Martin[5]	4	0	1	0	3	17	8	7	2	0
McLeod	8	0	3	0	5	71	23	46	2	0
Meeker	11	0	1	0	10	83	27	48	8	0
Morrison	8	0	0	2	6	267	65	184	18	0
Mower	10	0	3	0	7	76	23	37	16	1
Murray	2	0	1	0	1	12	1	10	1	0
Nobles	11	0	6	0	5	26	8	18	0	2
Norman	1	0	1	0	0	0	0	0	0	0
Otter Tail	25	1	8	0	16	241	81	132	28	0
Pennington	2	0	1	0	1	68	18	42	8	1
Pine	43	0	12	0	31	412	105	240	67	3
Pipestone	5	0	0	1	4	109	13	95	1	0
Pope	0	0	0	0	0	33	16	14	3	0
Red Lake	0	0	0	0	0	10	4	5	1	0
Redwood	6	0	1	0	5	42	8	30	4	0
Renville	3	0	1	0	2	67	12	46	9	0
Rice	16	0	6	1	9	209	47	143	19	1
Rock	1	0	0	1	0	38	4	29	5	0
Roseau	4	0	1	0	3	63	14	41	8	0
Sibley	1	0	0	0	1	3	0	3	0	0
Steele	8	0	2	0	6	88	25	51	12	0
Stevens	6	1	1	0	4	40	4	36	0	0
Swift	4	0	1	0	3	18	5	13	0	0
Todd	15	0	5	1	9	146	41	98	7	1
Traverse	0	0	0	0	0	28	5	21	2	0
Wadena[5]	8	0	1	0	7	12	7	5	0	0
Waseca[5]	9	0	3	0	6	72	28	42	2	0
Watonwan	6	0	3	0	3	39	15	21	3	0
Wilkin	4	0	2	0	2	20	0	16	4	0
Winona	7	0	4	0	3	78	17	54	7	0
Yellow Medicine	3	0	0	0	3	30	5	22	3	0
MISSISSIPPI										
Metropolitan Counties										
Hancock	32	2	0	6	24	493	94	351	48	0
Harrison	41	1	9	10	21	867	233	511	123	8
Hinds	101	4	5	5	87	454	198	198	58	0
Lamar	108	2	10	9	87	789	267	473	49	4
Rankin	49	4	2	6	37	422	78	301	43	5
Stone	47	2	7	1	37	194	70	100	24	3
Tunica[7]			3		15	32	444	83	322	39	1
Nonmetropolitan Counties										
Claiborne	19	1	1	6	11	75	43	21	11	0
Greene	7	0	0	0	7	41	18	16	7	1
Kemper	8	0	2	0	6	30	18	12	0	0
Lauderdale	33	2	7	6	18	437	253	144	40	6
Lincoln	19	0	0	4	15	248	55	179	14	0
Oktibbeha[7]		0		9	37	472	324	133	15	0
Panola	109	0	14	16	79	643	317	309	17	2
MISSOURI										
Metropolitan Counties										
Andrew	7	0	1	2	4	94	26	60	8	1
Bollinger	30	1	7	1	21	47	20	27	0	2
Boone	105	4	12	7	82	700	94	522	84	2
Buchanan[5]	38	0	15	3	20	229	58	128	43	4
Caldwell[8]		0	4	0		87	23	48	16	2
Callaway	68	1	17	4	46	381	100	241	40	
Cape Girardeau	30	2	2	3	23	248	83	139	26	1
Cass	35	2	5	0	28	376	128	209	39	0
Christian	64	0	6	5	53	230	72	146	12	1
Clay	41	0	3	5	33	212	59	123	30	1
Clinton	16	0	0	2	14	77	29	45	3	3
Cole	55	0	0	0	55	268	50	198	20	2
Cooper	3	0	1	1	1	78	19	50	9	0
Dallas	7	2	0	1	4	40	12	25	3	0
DeKalb	2	0	0	0	2	35	12	14	9	1
Franklin[5]	61	1	6	1	53	439	169	219	51	1
Greene	74	4	35	10	25	1,045	259	663	123	12
Howard	8	0	0	0	8	47	28	12	7	0
Jackson	45	0	5	7	33	484	152	278	54	5
Jasper	84	0	10	10	64	505	126	302	77	
Jefferson	335	5	31	20	279	2,415	551	1,471	393	13
Lafayette	14	0	0	1	13	59	23	32	4	0

Table 10. Offenses Known to Law Enforcement, by Selected State Metropolitan and Nonmetropolitan Counties, 2018—Continued

(Number.)

State/county	Violent crime	Murder and nonnegligent manslaughter	Rape[1]	Robbery	Aggravated assault	Property crime	Burglary	Larceny-theft	Motor vehicle theft	Arson[2]
Lincoln[3]	131	2	18	1	110			155	3	2
Newton	134	0	8	10	116	667	126	442	99	5
Osage	2	0	0	0	2	68	19	38	11	1
Platte	46	4	10	5	27	244	52	164	28	0
Polk	37	0	4	2	31	349	97	223	29	0
St. Charles	0	0	0	0	0	0	0	0	0	0
St. Charles County Police Department	119	2	11	10	96	729	150	517	62	4
St. Louis County Police Department	1,834	37	174	342	1,281	7,508	1,305	5,211	992	75
Warren	41	0	6	2	33	176	45	106	25	1
Webster	13	3	3	3	4	170	52	89	29	0
Nonmetropolitan Counties										
Adair	23	0	1	1	21	118	44	71	3	0
Atchison	3	0	0	1	2	8	0	7	1	0
Audrain	14	0	0	0	14	86	34	48	4	0
Barry	38	0	1	3	34	403	111	228	64	1
Benton	26	0	1	0	25	140	61	69	10	0
Butler	153	2	2	2	147	691	244	408	39	1
Camden	87	1	33	0	53	487	156	292	39	2
Carroll	4	0	1	0	3	32	22	8	2	0
Carter	22	1	1	0	20	101	36	56	9	
Cedar	24	1	6	0	17	78	20	58	0	1
Clark	6	0	1	1	4	67	23	38	6	0
Crawford	13	0	2	0	11	227	88	110	29	1
Daviess	8	0	1	0	7	38	16	15	7	2
Dent	2	0	0	1	1	68	34	29	5	0
Douglas	16	1	2	0	13	24	11	7	6	1
Dunklin	15	1	1	2	11	132	43	67	22	1
Gasconade	56	0	2	2	52	116	39	64	13	0
Gentry	1	0	0	0	1	24	11	10	3	1
Grundy	5	0	0	0	5	13	7	3	3	1
Harrison	10	0	0	1	9	42	28	12	2	0
Henry[6]	60	0	8	0	52	345	174	138	33	4
Hickory	3	0	0	0	3	89	30	54	5	0
Holt	6	0	0	0	6	57	16	28	13	0
Howell	55	1	1	0	53	308	101	172	35	0
Iron	11	0	2	0	9	63	26	30	7	
Johnson	27	1	3	2	21	289	73	180	36	0
Laclede	30	0	8	1	21	359	79	219	61	4
Lawrence	19	0	7	4	8	213	73	118	22	0
Lewis	4	0	0	0	4	42	15	26	1	1
Linn	9	1	0	0	8	42	18	22	2	1
Livingston	1	0	0	0	1	38	8	26	4	1
Macon	6	1	0	0	5	72	27	44	1	0
Madison	10	0	1	0	9	31	5	25	1	0
Marion	6	0	0	0	6	203	11	189	3	0
McDonald	77	0	10	0	67	234	32	202	0	1
Mercer	0	0	0	0	0	19	14	4	1	0
Miller	44	1	4	1	38	204	87	94	23	0
Mississippi	7	0	1	1	5	59	24	31	4	2
Monroe	22	0	2	0	20	35	7	27	1	1
Montgomery	4	0	0	0	4	47	21	26	0	0
Morgan	48	0	13	0	35	150	81	63	6	0
Nodaway	6	0	1	0	5	86	36	43	7	0
Oregon	30	1	2	1	26	47	20	23	4	0
Ozark	13	1	2	0	10	62	26	30	6	6
Pemiscot	26	1	1	1	23	91	28	49	14	2
Perry	18	0	1	0	17	38	11	23	4	0
Pettis	38	1	0	2	35	171	61	97	13	1
Phelps	40	0	2	1	37	202	36	144	22	1
Pulaski	129	2	12	3	112	336	76	213	47	0
Putnam	9	0	2	0	7	15	5	5	5	0
Ralls	8	0	0	0	8	72	14	51	7	0
Randolph	22	0	2	1	19	72	29	33	10	0
Ripley	17	1	2	0	14	102	39	51	12	1
Saline	7	0	0	0	7	66	20	40	6	1
Schuyler	3	0	2	0	1	52	10	33	9	1
Scotland	2	0	1	0	1	20	2	17	1	1
Shannon	10	0	0	0	10	24	8	13	3	2
Shelby	0	0	0	0	0	15	1	10	4	0
Ste. Genevieve	39	0	8	0	30	113	22	73	18	1
St. Francois	62	1	1	1	59	261	42	149	70	3
Stone	73	0	6	0	67	246	65	179	2	1
Sullivan	5	0	1	0	4	42	19	16	7	0
Taney	113	0	3	1	109	221	46	134	41	0
Texas	39	1	4	0	34	158	52	87	19	5
Vernon	78	0	4	5	69	272	91	133	48	2
Washington	64	0	8	1	55	466	140	252	74	0
Wayne	29	3	2	0	24	198	65	110	23	0
Worth	1	0	0	0	1	12	0	11	1	0
Wright	15	0	0	0	15	76	28	41	7	1

Table 10. Offenses Known to Law Enforcement, by Selected State Metropolitan and Nonmetropolitan Counties, 2018—Continued

(Number.)

State/county	Violent crime	Murder and nonnegligent manslaughter	Rape[1]	Robbery	Aggravated assault	Property crime	Burglary	Larceny-theft	Motor vehicle theft	Arson[2]
MONTANA										
Metropolitan Counties										
Carbon	24	1	5	1	17	56	7	43	6	0
Cascade	51	0	4	0	47	293	60	196	37	2
Missoula	78	0	17	4	57	499	114	330	55	0
Stillwater	16	0	2	0	14	59	19	36	4	0
Yellowstone	112	1	9	7	95	740	111	528	101	4
Nonmetropolitan Counties										
Beaverhead	1	0	1	0	0	2	0	2	0	0
Big Horn	40	1	3	0	36	257	27	179	51	0
Blaine	31	0	4	0	27	9	1	5	3	0
Broadwater	24	0	2	0	22	37	1	26	10	1
Carter	0	0	0	0	0	0	0	0	0	0
Chouteau	1	0	1	0	0	3	2	1	0	1
Custer	5	1	0	0	4	24	6	18	0	0
Daniels	0	0	0	0	0	0	0	0	0	0
Dawson	9	0	2	0	7	29	13	15	1	3
Deer Lodge	40	1	2	0	37	252	58	163	31	1
Fallon	0	0	0	0	0	5	0	4	1	0
Fergus	11	0	4	0	7	52	9	34	9	0
Flathead	190	2	26	0	162	893	134	632	127	7
Gallatin	86	0	20	2	64	415	32	351	32	3
Garfield	0	0	0	0	0	0	0	0	0	0
Glacier	3	0	0	0	3	23	2	19	2	0
Golden Valley	2	0	0	0	2	15	1	12	2	0
Granite	1	0	0	0	1	20	3	16	1	0
Hill	22	1	2	0	19	178	11	155	12	2
Jefferson	36	0	2	0	34	108	15	80	13	0
Lake	76	1	17	3	55	229	67	122	40	6
Lewis and Clark	84	2	18	0	64	438	112	290	36	3
Liberty	1	0	0	1	0	0	0	0	0	0
Lincoln	15	0	3	0	12	55	4	44	7	0
Madison	7	0	2	0	5	67	17	49	1	0
McCone	1	0	0	0	1	2	1	0	1	0
Meagher	3	0	0	0	3	14	4	10	0	0
Mineral	2	0	1	0	1	11	1	9	1	0
Musselshell	7	0	2	0	5	98	10	84	4	0
Park	25	0	3	0	22	43	7	31	5	1
Phillips	17	0	3	0	14	49	8	32	9	1
Pondera	1	0	0	0	1	3	2	0	1	0
Powell	3	0	1	0	2	8	3	5	0	1
Prairie	12	0	0	0	12	3	0	3	0	0
Ravalli	44	0	3	1	40	261	23	229	9	1
Richland	7	0	0	0	7	39	7	26	6	0
Roosevelt	88	1	1	1	85	101	37	39	25	3
Rosebud	14	0	1	1	12	23	3	17	3	1
Sanders	14	1	7	2	4	32	2	21	9	1
Sheridan	8	0	1	0	7	36	6	28	2	0
Silver Bow	173	0	11	9	153	1,847	235	1,399	213	9
Sweet Grass	14	0	4	0	10	41	2	35	4	0
Teton	4	0	1	0	3	47	8	33	6	1
Toole	26	0	3	0	23	51	2	44	5	0
Valley	9	1	6	0	2	21	7	12	2	0
Wheatland	5	0	1	0	4	3	2	0	1	0
Wibaux	0	0	0	0	0	1	0	1	0	0
NEBRASKA										
Metropolitan Counties										
Cass	17	2	7	0	8	159	20	124	15	0
Dakota	16	0	1	0	15	75	13	44	18	
Dixon	2	0	1	0	1	27	15	12	0	0
Douglas[5]	83	2	19	5	57	669	135	440	94	1
Hall	25	0	4	1	20	123	23	94	6	1
Howard	7	0	0	0	7	9	3	2	4	0
Lancaster	24	0	17	0	7	178	40	123	15	
Merrick	1	0	0	0	1	11	1	6	4	0
Sarpy	51	0	13	6	32	703	83	546	74	1
Saunders	6	0	4	0	2	66	33	27	6	1
Seward	8	0	3	0	5	36	7	20	9	1
Washington	1	0	0	0	1	91	8	72	11	0
Nonmetropolitan Counties										
Adams	5	0	2	0	3	62	18	42	2	0
Antelope	3	0	1	0	2	23	1	19	3	
Arthur	0	0	0	0	0	1	0	1	0	
Box Butte	4	0	0	0	4	12	6	6	0	
Brown	0	0	0	0	0	14	1	11	2	
Buffalo	15	0	4	0	11	122	20	94	8	0
Burt	8	1	2	1	4	30	8	20	2	
Butler	5	0	1	0	4	22	0	21	1	0

Table 10. Offenses Known to Law Enforcement, by Selected State Metropolitan and Nonmetropolitan Counties, 2018—Continued

(Number.)

State/county	Violent crime	Murder and nonnegligent manslaughter	Rape[1]	Robbery	Aggravated assault	Property crime	Burglary	Larceny-theft	Motor vehicle theft	Arson[2]
Cedar	1	0	0	0	1	6	0	6	0	
Chase	0	0	0	0	0	8	0	5	3	
Cherry	5	0	0	0	5	7	0	5	2	
Cheyenne	2	1	0	0	1	16	3	9	4	0
Colfax	1	0	0	0	1	27	5	19	3	0
Custer	9	0	2	0	7	50	15	29	6	2
Dawes	1	0	0	0	1	4	0	4	0	
Dawson	8	0	5	0	3	49	13	27	9	0
Deuel	1	0	0	0	1	5	0	4	1	0
Dodge	7	0	2	0	5	103	24	69	10	
Franklin	0	0	0	0	0	8	4	3	1	
Frontier	0	0	0	0	0	1	0	0	1	0
Furnas	10	0	0	0	10	32	7	23	2	0
Gage	16	0	6	0	10	68	26	38	4	0
Garfield	0	0	0	0	0	1	0	1	0	0
Gosper	0	0	0	0	0	10	2	7	1	0
Hayes	0	0	0	0	0	1	0	1	0	
Hitchcock	2	0	1	0	1	12	4	6	2	
Hooker	0	0	0	0	0	2	0	2	0	
Jefferson	2	0	1	0	1	19	6	12	1	0
Johnson	7	0	6	0	1	18	8	9	1	0
Kearney	1	0	0	0	1	28	6	18	4	0
Keith	5	0	3	0	2	13	2	8	3	0
Keya Paha	0	0	0	0	0	0	0	0	0	
Knox	4	0	0	0	4	30	4	16	10	
Lincoln	8	0	1	0	7	117	30	78	9	0
Madison	10	0	4	0	6	47	10	35	2	2
Morrill	1	0	0	0	1	26	2	24	0	
Nemaha	7	0	5	0	2	49	12	27	10	0
Perkins	5	0	1	0	4	31	6	22	3	0
Phelps	2	0	1	0	1	23	4	16	3	0
Platte	8	0	2	0	6	95	15	71	9	2
Polk	1	0	0	0	1	31	0	25	6	0
Red Willow	0	0	0	0	0	1	0	0	1	0
Saline	13	0	3	0	10	34	7	22	5	0
Scotts Bluff	14	0	4	0	10	74	10	56	8	0
Sheridan	8	0	0	0	8	54	10	30	14	
Sherman	0	0	0	0	0	8	0	6	2	0
Stanton	9	0	0	0	9	32	4	26	2	
Thayer	4	0	0	0	4	30	2	27	1	
Thurston	7	0	1	0	6	13	5	4	4	0
Valley	2	0	0	0	2	11	0	11	0	0
Wayne	2	0	0	0	2	15	5	7	3	0
Webster	0	0	0	0	0	16	11	4	1	
Wheeler[5]	1	0	0	0	1	0	0	0	0	
York	6	0	4	0	2	37	2	30	5	1
NEVADA										
Metropolitan Counties										
Carson City	198	1	43	13	141	737	157	507	73	8
Storey	44	0	5	1	38	86	29	53	4	1
Washoe	168	6	45	12	105	637	162	404	71	6
Nonmetropolitan Counties										
Churchill	30	0	7	1	22	160	53	91	16	4
Douglas	64	1	13	13	37	594	107	446	41	9
Elko	55	2	9	0	44	175	35	112	28	3
Esmeralda	1	0	0	0	1	11	2	7	2	0
Eureka	5	0	1	0	4	50	17	31	2	0
Humboldt	26	1	10	0	15	79	53	18	8	2
Lander	52	3	10	0	39	97	44	50	3	4
Lincoln	13	0	5	0	8	31	6	18	7	0
Lyon	159	1	10	8	140	569	140	389	40	8
Mineral	2	0	0	0	2	30	9	15	6	0
Nye	60	1	9	10	40	774	239	396	139	2
Pershing	36	0	6	0	30	27	9	17	1	0
White Pine	28	1	6	2	19	117	41	61	15	1
NEW HAMPSHIRE										
Metropolitan Counties										
Rockingham	2	0	1	0	1	4	0	4	0	0
Strafford	9	0	0	0	9	3	0	3	0	0
Nonmetropolitan Counties										
Carroll	3	0	0	0	3	32	7	24	1	0
Cheshire	0	0	0	0	0	9	1	8	0	0
Grafton	5	0	3	0	2	2	0	2	0	0
Merrimack	1	0	1	0	0	5	1	4	0	0
NEW JERSEY										
Metropolitan Counties										
Atlantic	0	0	0	0	0	0	0	0	0	0
Bergen	0	0	0	0	0	0	0	0	0	0

Table 10. Offenses Known to Law Enforcement, by Selected State Metropolitan and Nonmetropolitan Counties, 2018—Continued

(Number.)

State/county	Violent crime	Murder and nonnegligent manslaughter	Rape[1]	Robbery	Aggravated assault	Property crime	Burglary	Larceny-theft	Motor vehicle theft	Arson[2]
Burlington	0	0	0	0	0	0	0	0	0	0
Camden	6	0	0	0	6	37	0	35	2	0
Cape May	1	0	0	0	1	1	0	1	0	0
Cumberland	1	0	0	0	1	0	0	0	0	0
Essex	107	0	4	29	74	111	20	84	7	0
Gloucester	1	0	0	0	1	1	0	1	0	0
Hudson	0	0	0	0	0	0	0	0	0	0
Hunterdon	0	0	0	0	0	0	0	0	0	0
Mercer	1	0	0	0	1	13	7	4	2	0
Middlesex	0	0	0	0	0	0	0	0	0	0
Monmouth	8	0	0	0	8	0	0	0	0	0
Morris	0	0	0	0	0	0	0	0	0	0
Ocean	1	0	0	0	1	7	0	7	0	0
Passaic	0	0	0	0	0	0	0	0	0	0
Salem	0	0	0	0	0	0	0	0	0	0
Somerset	0	0	0	0	0	0	0	0	0	0
Sussex	0	0	0	0	0	0	0	0	0	0
Union	0	0	0	0	0	0	0	0	0	0
Warren	0	0	0	0	0	0	0	0	0	0
NEW MEXICO										
Metropolitan Counties										
Sandoval	110	0	1	2	107	113	45	64	4	
San Juan	764	0	55	12	697	774	217	481	76	
Santa Fe	108	0	8	9	91	430	229	201	0	
Torrance	100	0	3	1	96	123	58	44	21	
Valencia	391	0	31	14	346	966	367	457	142	
Nonmetropolitan Counties										
Catron	5	0	1	0	4	14	7	6	1	
Chaves	45	4	10	3	28	209	102	73	34	
Cibola	18	1	3	0	14	41	10	21	10	
Colfax	12	0	0	0	12	23	10	12	1	
De Baca	8	0	1	1	6	40	23	11	6	
Eddy	80	0	10	0	70	287	79	140	68	
Grant	20	0	4	0	16	114	54	60	0	
Hidalgo	9	0	0	0	9	12	5	5	2	
Lincoln	48	0	5	0	43	111	48	52	11	
Luna	70	1	0	1	68	272	105	130	37	
McKinley	192	2	4	8	178	259	70	138	51	
Mora	14	0	0	0	14	12	2	6	4	
Otero	158	0	13	0	145	264	110	128	26	
Quay	6	0	0	0	6	26	13	9	4	
Rio Arriba	63	0	6	7	50	197	72	114	11	
San Miguel	0	0	0	0	0	0	0	0	0	
Sierra	23	0	2	1	20	64	29	31	4	
Socorro	19	1	4	1	13	70	18	42	10	
Taos	31	1	1	1	28	138	75	34	29	
Union	7	1	3	0	3	9	2	6	1	
NEW YORK										
Metropolitan Counties										
Albany	16	0	6	0	10	114	19	82	13	1
Broome	44	0	17	5	22	513	72	418	23	0
Chemung	10	0	3	3	4	244	31	211	2	1
Erie	45	0	0	9	36	576	79	475	22	1
Herkimer	0	0	0	0	0	0	0	0	0	0
Jefferson	17	0	5	1	11	253	23	226	4	0
Livingston	23	0	10	2	11	260	30	215	15	0
Madison	21	1	8	0	12	127	25	98	4	0
Nassau	1,000	11	13	337	639	9,650	786	8,406	458	39
Niagara	59	0	16	10	33	597	102	457	38	3
Oneida	107	0	91	1	15	290	47	225	18	1
Ontario	41	0	17	2	22	651	93	549	9	3
Orleans	14	0	2	3	9	170	37	130	3	2
Oswego	57	2	18	7	30	307	48	240	19	2
Putnam	14	0	2	0	12	154	16	135	3	2
Rensselaer	13	0	3	1	9	184	27	144	13	3
Rockland	10	0	1	0	9	24	1	23	0	0
Saratoga	79	0	13	4	62	1,095	136	935	24	3
Schenectady	1	0	0	0	1	18	1	15	2	0
Schoharie	5	0	1	1	3	27	3	24	0	0
Suffolk	55	0	0	0	55	0	0	0	0	0
Suffolk County Police Department	1,134	22	39	375	698	15,235	955	13,396	884	81
Tioga	9	0	4	1	4	112	25	82	5	0
Tompkins	21	0	11	2	8	256	43	207	6	0
Ulster	26	0	10	1	15	139	22	115	2	1
Warren	47	0	23	5	19	472	34	431	7	3
Washington	25	0	14	3	8	156	26	126	4	1
Wayne	54	4	19	4	27	393	82	299	12	1
Westchester Public Safety	67	1	1	8	57	208	9	194	5	1
Yates	11	1	1	0	9	127	42	81	4	1

Table 10. Offenses Known to Law Enforcement, by Selected State Metropolitan and Nonmetropolitan Counties, 2018—Continued

(Number.)

State/county	Violent crime	Murder and nonnegligent manslaughter	Rape[1]	Robbery	Aggravated assault	Property crime	Burglary	Larceny-theft	Motor vehicle theft	Arson[2]
Nonmetropolitan Counties										
Allegany	5	0	0	0	5	0	0	0	0	0
Cattaraugus	33	2	10	1	20	254	55	184	15	7
Cayuga	11	0	2	1	8	168	30	135	3	1
Chenango	15	0	6	1	8	269	56	208	5	0
Clinton	13	0	0	0	13	27	1	25	1	0
Columbia	27	0	12	0	15	290	55	226	9	1
Cortland	14	1	5	4	4	234	58	167	9	0
Delaware	31	0	15	1	15	145	39	97	9	0
Essex	1	0	0	0	1	3	0	2	1	0
Franklin	0	0	0	0	0	0	0	0	0	0
Fulton	25	0	6	1	18	204	20	176	8	0
Genesee	48	1	18	1	28	284	35	231	18	3
Greene	6	1	0	0	6	20	12	7	1	0
Hamilton	0	0	0	0	0	6	2	4	0	0
Montgomery	7	0	2	0	5	189	19	163	7	0
Schuyler	8	0	1	0	7	15	1	11	3	0
Seneca	8	0	0	1	7	50	3	45	2	0
St. Lawrence	12	0	1	1	10	39	8	28	3	1
Sullivan	30	0	6	4	20	295	40	247	8	1
Wyoming	14	1	6	1	6	117	18	95	4	0
NORTH CAROLINA[7]										
Metropolitan Counties										
Alamance		0		6	90	677	296	342	39	3
Buncombe		1		29	115	1,450	500	774	176	12
Cabarrus		1		18	27	595	171	406	18	5
Catawba		2		15	81	1,112	362	645	105	7
Chatham		1		5	61	552	239	288	25	2
Craven		0		7	107	791	309	423	59	4
Cumberland		2		66	338	2,512	797	1,555	160	41
Currituck		1		3	36	312	73	231	8	0
Davidson		6		30	76	1,563	808	601	154	8
Davie		1		6	65	471	169	286	16	1
Gaston		0		0	14	1	0	0	1	0
Granville		0		7	45	467	197	239	31	4
Guilford		3		29	160	969	336	560	73	11
Haywood		0		4	113	927	402	440	85	2
Hoke		1		8	12	943	331	531	81	0
Johnston		6		21	169	1,564	465	986	113	3
Madison		0		0	17	163	66	84	13	2
New Hanover		1		20	85	1,320	278	983	59	13
Orange		1		7	52	510	178	304	28	2
Pamlico		1		3	14	191	39	134	18	1
Person		0		2	45	295	122	154	19	1
Pitt		2		24	169	890	276	562	52	5
Rockingham		2		7	26	720	280	395	45	0
Stokes		0		0	61	685	180	437	68	2
Yadkin		1		4	92	555	231	285	39	3
Nonmetropolitan Counties										
Beaufort		1		8	29	470	186	264	20	6
Bertie		0		4	14	123	40	67	16	0
Chowan		1		0	16	131	52	72	7	0
Clay		0		1	15	258	101	142	15	2
Graham		1		2	21	235	64	149	22	0
Greene		3		8	23	328	169	145	14	0
Halifax		11		22	59	539	297	210	32	7
Hertford		4		9	25	201	87	105	9	6
Jackson		0		8	43	813	443	310	60	2
Martin		2		7	42	282	121	136	25	3
McDowell		4		7	23	836	229	493	114	8
Montgomery		0		3	38	254	109	126	19	5
Moore		2		4	67	631	286	323	22	
Pasquotank		2		2	42	250	103	142	5	0
Perquimans		0		1	8	82	38	41	3	1
Polk		1		0	6	207	69	123	15	2
Rutherford		2		4	108	915	492	322	101	10
Sampson		3		17	96	854	424	344	86	6
Transylvania		1		2	15	236	87	143	6	2
Tyrrell		0		1	5	30	11	18	1	0
Watauga		0		1	10	253	38	204	11	1
Wilkes		3		7	143	694	287	356	51	12
Yancey		0		3	10	71	29	32	10	2
NORTH DAKOTA										
Metropolitan Counties										
Burleigh	21	0	6	0	15	170	64	84	22	0
Cass	18	0	8	1	9	138	53	69	16	0
Grand Forks	13	0	5	3	5	86	13	64	9	0
Morton	6	0	3	0	3	118	15	93	10	0
Oliver	1	0	1	0	0	1	0	1	0	0

Table 10. Offenses Known to Law Enforcement, by Selected State Metropolitan and Nonmetropolitan Counties, 2018—Continued

(Number.)

State/county	Violent crime	Murder and nonnegligent manslaughter	Rape[1]	Robbery	Aggravated assault	Property crime	Burglary	Larceny-theft	Motor vehicle theft	Arson[2]
Nonmetropolitan Counties										
Adams	2	0	0	0	2	19	4	14	1	0
Barnes	4	0	1	0	3	12	5	4	3	0
Benson	0	0	0	0	0	12	1	5	6	0
Billings	0	0	0	0	0	13	0	11	2	0
Bottineau	5	0	2	0	3	67	27	27	13	0
Bowman	2	0	0	0	2	2	0	1	1	0
Burke	0	0	0	0	0	4	0	2	2	0
Cavalier	2	0	1	0	1	21	5	8	8	2
Dickey	5	0	1	0	4	9	2	7	0	0
Divide	0	0	0	0	0	8	2	5	1	0
Dunn	8	0	0	0	8	20	2	10	8	0
Eddy	1	0	0	0	1	21	0	17	4	0
Emmons	1	0	1	0	0	38	10	27	1	0
Foster	0	0	0	0	0	9	3	5	1	0
Golden Valley	1	0	1	0	0	1	0	1	0	0
Grant	0	0	0	0	0	8	5	3	0	1
Griggs	0	0	0	0	0	9	2	5	2	0
Hettinger	6	0	2	0	4	24	6	17	1	0
Kidder	1	0	1	0	0	4	3	1	0	0
Lamoure	2	0	0	0	2	9	0	9	0	0
Logan	0	0	0	0	0	0	0	0	0	0
McHenry	4	0	0	0	4	33	17	12	4	0
McIntosh	0	0	0	0	0	1	0	1	0	0
McKenzie	30	0	11	0	19	179	24	127	28	1
McLean	4	0	1	0	3	70	12	50	8	0
Mercer	4	0	1	0	3	25	5	17	3	0
Mountrail	7	0	3	1	3	62	7	47	8	0
Nelson	2	0	0	0	2	28	6	19	3	0
Pembina	5	0	1	0	4	36	11	20	5	0
Pierce	5	0	3	0	2	20	4	12	4	0
Ramsey	4	0	2	0	2	26	3	17	6	1
Ransom	1	0	0	0	1	25	3	14	8	0
Renville	3	0	0	0	3	11	2	8	1	0
Richland	2	0	0	0	2	82	23	54	5	0
Rolette	8	0	2	0	6	39	10	23	6	1
Sargent	2	0	0	0	2	17	1	14	2	0
Sheridan	0	0	0	0	0	11	2	9	0	0
Sioux	0	0	0	0	0	1	0	1	0	0
Slope	0	0	0	0	0	0	0	0	0	0
Stark	3	0	0	0	3	36	7	24	5	0
Steele	3	0	0	0	3	2	2	0	0	0
Stutsman	2	0	1	0	1	29	11	16	2	0
Towner	2	0	1	0	1	24	6	11	7	0
Traill	7	0	4	1	2	85	23	46	16	1
Walsh	9	0	1	0	8	82	23	43	16	2
Ward	32	0	1	2	29	192	70	72	50	2
Wells	2	0	1	1	0	16	6	9	1	0
Williams	16	0	1	0	15	132	23	96	13	0
OHIO										
Metropolitan Counties										
Allen[7]		1		15	9	803	139	637	27	2
Belmont	52	2	19	3	28	217	41	165	11	2
Clark	38	0	4	9	25	630	148	470	12	1
Clermont	103	0	25	8	70	948	214	671	63	2
Delaware	60	0	25	6	29	1,096	174	884	38	1
Fairfield	46	0	13	6	27	1,071	149	881	41	3
Fulton	15	0	4	3	8	222	59	163	0	0
Geauga	21	0	3	1	17	117	23	91	3	2
Greene	43	0	10	2	31	306	60	230	16	1
Hamilton	168	3	50	31	84	1,933	232	1,535	166	14
Hocking	19	4	2	1	12	495	112	246	137	3
Jefferson	12	0	1	0	11	75	25	43	7	1
Lake[7]		3		5	182	305	82	218	5	0
Lawrence	56	1	13	4	38	510	145	315	50	2
Lorain	76	2	18	12	44	460	164	274	22	5
Lucas	104	0	31	30	43	950	155	729	66	4
Madison	13	0	1	4	8	334	83	234	17	2
Mahoning	4	0	1	1	2	81	5	72	4	0
Medina	5	0	0	1	4	86	23	63	0	0
Miami	35	0	11	0	24	321	78	212	31	8
Montgomery	269	7	42	67	153	1,266	282	663	321	9
Perry	6	0	2	0	4	85	32	50	3	0
Pickaway	31	1	9	2	19	619	145	443	31	4
Portage[7]		1		13	337	991	217	731	43	3
Richland	65	0	35	9	21	748	185	507	56	4
Stark	116	1	32	26	57	1,578	422	1,057	99	11
Summit	70	0	26	12	32	889	129	712	48	3
Trumbull	17	0	4	2	11	201	76	119	6	0
Union	39	0	21	1	17	181	33	133	15	0
Warren	51	0	10	4	37	741	96	586	59	1
Wood	25	0	9	2	14	362	86	261	15	2

Table 10. Offenses Known to Law Enforcement, by Selected State Metropolitan and Nonmetropolitan Counties, 2018—Continued

(Number.)

State/county	Violent crime	Murder and nonnegligent manslaughter	Rape[1]	Robbery	Aggravated assault	Property crime	Burglary	Larceny-theft	Motor vehicle theft	Arson[2]
Nonmetropolitan Counties										
Adams	11	0	5	0	6	196	79	100	17	2
Ashland	18	0	13	0	5	144	47	93	4	3
Ashtabula	45	0	6	8	31	479	113	327	39	1
Athens	18	0	6	3	9	308	96	186	26	0
Champaign	21	0	6	0	15	167	48	112	7	2
Clinton	14	0	5	0	9	112	37	63	12	1
Columbiana	28	0	4	4	20	326	90	208	28	4
Coshocton	42	0	13	2	27	389	92	263	34	3
Crawford	3	0	1	0	2	102	36	59	7	0
Defiance	13	0	6	0	7	122	34	85	3	2
Erie	5	0	0	0	5	202	45	151	6	0
Fayette	39	2	11	7	19	388	117	252	19	2
Gallia	30	0	3	2	25	369	105	238	26	4
Hancock	20	0	7	3	10	156	35	113	8	1
Hardin	10	0	0	3	7	89	19	67	3	4
Henry	15	1	3	0	11	122	40	75	7	1
Highland	20	2	12	2	4	271	95	157	19	1
Jackson	29	0	7	3	19	230	67	143	20	0
Knox	51	0	21	2	28	333	94	239	0	1
Logan	19	0	3	1	15	176	43	119	14	1
Marion	36	0	16	7	13	888	122	742	24	2
Meigs	17	1	3	1	12	217	51	133	33	4
Mercer	10	0	4	0	6	82	8	73	1	0
Monroe	15	0	7	0	8	44	14	23	7	1
Morgan	24	0	4	0	20	138	51	77	10	2
Noble	1	0	1	0	0	38	12	25	1	0
Pike	37	0	12	2	23	380	101	231	48	5
Preble	14	0	2	0	12	207	38	135	34	1
Putnam	10	0	1	0	9	75	10	65	0	0
Ross	114	0	31	3	80	1,071	270	676	125	17
Scioto	58	0	12	13	33	882	240	539	103	14
Shelby	14	0	6	1	7	120	14	96	10	0
Tuscarawas	18	0	7	1	10	284	68	193	23	2
Van Wert	25	1	7	0	17	105	36	61	8	1
Vinton	20	0	1	2	17	192	72	101	19	0
Washington	31	0	15	1	15	273	89	165	19	2
Wayne	46	1	13	2	30	478	149	281	48	3
Wyandot	3	1	0	0	2	1	0	1	0	1
OKLAHOMA										
Metropolitan Counties										
Canadian	8	0	3	1	4	164	32	108	24	2
Cleveland	44	0	12	2	30	259	92	126	41	2
Comanche	23	0	6	0	17	237	95	113	29	2
Cotton	0	0	0	0	0	17	4	9	4	0
Creek	44	0	13	4	27	370	120	172	78	1
Garfield	14	0	4	0	10	124	40	72	12	3
Grady	41	0	3	0	38	394	127	211	56	3
Lincoln	26	1	5	1	19	275	91	142	42	6
Logan	42	0	8	3	31	371	122	215	34	0
McClain	19	1	8	1	9	272	101	136	35	1
Oklahoma	37	1	1	1	34	247	61	141	45	1
Okmulgee	44	2	5	2	35	182	72	79	31	9
Osage	62	3	9	3	47	395	167	175	53	4
Pawnee	52	1	2	1	48	115	35	56	24	0
Rogers	102	3	19	1	79	470	183	249	38	12
Sequoyah	82	0	10	1	71	312	129	157	26	4
Tulsa	239	5	33	21	180	885	267	417	201	8
Wagoner	53	0	6	4	43	382	133	192	57	4
Nonmetropolitan Counties										
Adair	63	0	12	2	49	179	61	81	37	1
Alfalfa	5	0	1	1	3	40	7	28	5	2
Atoka	1	0	1	0	0	61	20	31	10	0
Beaver	2	0	2	0	0	19	11	7	1	1
Beckham	14	0	5	0	9	61	21	31	9	1
Blaine	9	0	2	0	7	82	26	46	10	0
Bryan	19	0	2	0	17	194	68	92	34	1
Caddo	30	0	0	3	27	170	54	102	14	1
Carter	10	0	2	0	8	146	35	101	10	0
Cherokee	70	2	11	5	52	475	151	241	83	7
Choctaw	50	0	0	0	50	106	46	44	16	6
Coal	3	0	1	0	2	41	12	27	2	0
Craig	12	0	4	0	8	117	53	51	13	4
Custer	10	0	2	2	6	76	32	29	15	4
Delaware	49	2	11	1	35	230	89	111	30	10
Dewey	2	0	0	0	2	46	14	28	4	2
Ellis	2	0	0	0	2	38	11	26	1	1
Garvin	26	0	3	1	22	262	77	160	25	4
Grant	3	0	0	1	2	42	14	27	1	0

Table 10. Offenses Known to Law Enforcement, by Selected State Metropolitan and Nonmetropolitan Counties, 2018—Continued

(Number.)

State/county	Violent crime	Murder and nonnegligent manslaughter	Rape[1]	Robbery	Aggravated assault	Property crime	Burglary	Larceny-theft	Motor vehicle theft	Arson[2]
Harmon	1	0	1	0	0	8	1	7	0	0
Harper	1	0	1	0	0	4	2	2	0	0
Haskell	4	0	1	0	3	53	11	35	7	1
Hughes	18	3	0	0	15	143	40	82	21	4
Jackson	9	0	1	1	7	43	15	23	5	2
Jefferson	2	0	0	1	1	27	5	18	4	1
Johnston	7	0	1	0	6	49	20	23	6	2
Kay	21	0	0	1	20	77	42	34	1	0
Kingfisher	5	0	1	0	4	54	9	37	8	0
Kiowa	10	1	2	0	7	23	11	8	4	1
Latimer	14	0	1	0	13	53	24	27	2	2
Le Flore	46	1	4	3	38	284	117	143	24	1
Love	9	0	2	0	7	116	33	70	13	1
Major	3	0	0	0	3	23	7	12	4	0
Marshall	19	0	5	2	12	201	83	83	35	2
Mayes	31	0	9	0	22	297	108	137	52	7
McCurtain	20	0	2	3	15	350	128	189	33	18
McIntosh	29	0	4	4	21	203	80	96	27	2
Murray	6	0	0	0	6	24	13	8	3	0
Muskogee[5]	79	0	13	1	65	319	119	171	29	3
Noble	4	0	0	2	2	107	34	62	11	2
Nowata	6	0	1	0	5	41	15	22	4	2
Okfuskee	14	0	5	0	9	126	49	60	17	4
Ottawa	10	0	2	0	8	165	61	79	25	4
Payne	34	0	11	0	23	291	88	163	40	1
Pittsburg	75	1	10	3	61	459	195	215	49	8
Pontotoc	28	1	0	1	26	177	88	76	13	2
Pottawatomie	60	1	12	1	46	457	145	254	58	4
Pushmataha	8	0	1	0	7	70	34	29	7	3
Roger Mills	5	0	2	0	3	27	6	21	0	0
Seminole	38	0	3	1	34	274	104	130	40	0
Stephens	18	0	5	2	11	197	55	115	27	1
Texas	8	0	3	0	5	46	17	26	3	0
Tillman	1	0	0	0	1	49	24	22	3	0
Washita	13	1	3	0	9	67	18	40	9	0
Woods	3	0	1	0	2	39	17	19	3	0
Woodward	14	0	3	0	11	54	18	27	9	1
OREGON										
Metropolitan Counties										
Benton	20	1	4	1	14	189	64	114	11	2
Clackamas	423	4	127	86	206	5,423	735	3,949	739	20
Deschutes	93	0	17	8	68	604	143	411	50	7
Jackson	195	1	24	17	153	1,633	383	1,089	161	11
Josephine	52	1	5	4	42	392	107	140	145	3
Linn	66	1	16	3	46	825	230	496	99	14
Marion[7]		3		25	23	2,521	397	1,754	370	9
Multnomah	157	1	32	24	100	1,493	161	981	351	9
Polk	63	2	2	4	55	281	86	174	21	6
Washington	405	3	131	39	232	2,280	358	1,627	295	28
Yamhill	36	1	16	3	16	555	139	362	54	9
Nonmetropolitan Counties										
Baker	2	0	0	0	2	38	12	21	5	1
Clatsop	33	1	11	0	21	165	38	114	13	1
Crook	15	0	4	0	11	163	41	106	16	1
Curry	41	0	10	1	30	270	81	165	24	4
Douglas	160	1	31	7	121	952	222	535	195	7
Harney	0	0	0	0	0	41	15	20	6	0
Hood River	11	0	3	0	8	111	25	75	11	0
Jefferson	20	1	1	3	15	157	38	88	31	6
Lake	5	0	0	0	5	56	16	28	12	1
Lincoln	48	0	8	3	37	343	123	201	19	4
Malheur[5]	15	1	4	1	9	189	59	95	35	0
Morrow	16	0	3	0	13	186	38	118	30	3
Sherman	1	0	0	0	1	50	7	36	7	2
Tillamook	34	0	4	2	28	251	75	147	29	2
Umatilla	33	1	4	8	20	405	133	210	62	4
Union	14	1	1	1	11	114	18	86	10	0
Wasco	27	1	1	1	24	120	31	68	21	1
PENNSYLVANIA										
Metropolitan Counties										
Adams	1	0	0	0	1	0	0	0	0	0
Allegheny	1	0	0	0	1	3	0	3	0	0
Beaver	2	0	0	0	2	1	0	1	0	0
Berks	1	0	0	0	1	0	0	0	0	0
Blair	0	0	0	0	0	0	0	0	0	0
Bucks	1	0	0	0	1	0	0	0	0	0
Butler	0	0	0	0	0	0	0	0	0	0
Centre	0	0	0	0	0	0	0	0	0	0

Table 10. Offenses Known to Law Enforcement, by Selected State Metropolitan and Nonmetropolitan Counties, 2018—Continued

(Number.)

State/county	Violent crime	Murder and nonnegligent manslaughter	Rape[1]	Robbery	Aggravated assault	Property crime	Burglary	Larceny-theft	Motor vehicle theft	Arson[2]
Chester	0	0	0	0	0	3	0	3	0	0
Cumberland	0	0	0	0	0	0	0	0	0	0
Erie	10	0	1	0	9	2	0	2	0	0
Lancaster	1	0	0	0	1	0	0	0	0	0
Lycoming	0	0	0	0	0	0	0	0	0	0
Mercer	2	0	0	0	2	0	0	0	0	0
Monroe	0	0	0	0	0	0	0	0	0	0
Montgomery	0	0	0	0	0	0	0	0	0	0
Northampton	6	0	0	0	6	0	0	0	0	0
Pike	0	0	0	0	0	0	0	0	0	0
Washington	2	0	0	0	2	1	0	1	0	0
Westmoreland	0	0	0	0	0	0	0	0	0	0
Wyoming	0	0	0	0	0	0	0	0	0	0
York	1	0	0	0	1	0	0	0	0	0
Nonmetropolitan Counties										
Bedford	0	0	0	0	0	0	0	0	0	0
Bradford	0	0	0	0	0	0	0	0	0	0
Clarion	0	0	0	0	0	1	0	1	0	0
Elk	0	0	0	0	0	0	0	0	0	0
Greene	0	0	0	0	0	0	0	0	0	0
Indiana	0	0	0	0	0	0	0	0	0	0
Jefferson	0	0	0	0	0	0	0	0	0	0
Lawrence	0	0	0	0	0	0	0	0	0	0
Northumberland	0	0	0	0	0	0	0	0	0	0
Schuylkill	0	0	0	0	0	0	0	0	0	0
Snyder	0	0	0	0	0	0	0	0	0	0
Tioga	0	0	0	0	0	0	0	0	0	0
Union	0	0	0	0	0	0	0	0	0	0
Warren	0	0	0	0	0	0	0	0	0	0
Wayne	0	0	0	0	0	0	0	0	0	0
SOUTH CAROLINA										
Metropolitan Counties										
Aiken	478	10	97	42	329	2,881	860	1,654	367	6
Anderson	740	13	68	87	572	5,402	1,120	3,575	707	31
Beaufort	645	8	52	48	537	2,199	425	1,585	189	7
Berkeley	384	4	41	48	291	2,516	539	1,655	322	14
Calhoun	59	1	14	4	40	297	76	180	41	1
Chester	111	1	5	10	95	574	140	397	37	1
Clarendon	122	3	12	8	99	743	209	472	62	2
Darlington	372	4	23	40	305	1,714	608	947	159	11
Fairfield	130	0	7	8	115	455	129	279	47	5
Florence	527	16	70	65	376	2,270	549	1,518	203	15
Greenville	1,621	19	220	271	1,111	8,677	1,808	5,864	1,005	39
Horry	3	0	1	0	2	3	0	3	0	1
Horry County Police Department	889	21	172	118	578	5,991	1,105	4,282	604	44
Kershaw	120	2	18	13	87	1,016	207	710	99	5
Lancaster	260	3	44	28	185	1,798	442	1,264	92	7
Lexington	549	9	70	75	395	5,064	947	3,446	671	11
Pickens	286	4	34	21	227	1,571	466	899	206	6
Richland	2,050	27	134	283	1,606	9,865	1,715	6,805	1,345	31
Saluda	39	0	2	4	33	193	64	110	19	1
Spartanburg	986	20	54	95	817	4,149	1,217	2,619	313	33
Sumter	426	3	14	35	374	1,740	503	1,067	170	14
York	375	5	42	30	298	2,482	567	1,696	219	15
Nonmetropolitan Counties										
Bamberg	13	0	8	0	5	127	52	58	17	1
Barnwell	56	2	1	4	49	228	70	137	21	4
Dillon	147	5	8	25	109	556	195	296	65	0
Georgetown	153	4	33	10	106	1,077	308	657	112	7
Greenwood	231	5	26	16	184	1,087	220	792	75	2
Hampton	44	3	8	3	30	242	83	139	20	6
Lee	43	0	5	2	36	296	112	154	30	1
Marion	101	1	3	7	90	481	166	269	46	2
Marlboro	67	0	8	4	55	326	89	207	30	3
McCormick	19	1	5	1	12	70	12	51	7	1
Newberry	56	0	4	6	46	301	85	197	19	0
Oconee	137	4	25	7	101	1,785	414	1,185	186	9
Orangeburg	351	5	30	50	266	2,680	901	1,511	268	9
Union	73	1	8	3	61	496	120	348	28	2
SOUTH DAKOTA										
Metropolitan Counties										
Lincoln	16	0	4	0	12	240	95	135	10	0
McCook	6	0	3	0	3	44	17	23	4	0
Meade	22	0	2	0	20	140	38	91	11	0
Minnehaha	52	0	8	0	44	307	94	181	32	1
Pennington	134	0	77	1	56	409	95	269	45	0
Turner	7	0	4	0	3	31	14	14	3	1
Union	10	0	3	0	7	48	5	36	7	0

Table 10. Offenses Known to Law Enforcement, by Selected State Metropolitan and Nonmetropolitan Counties, 2018—Continued

(Number.)

State/county	Violent crime	Murder and nonnegligent manslaughter	Rape[1]	Robbery	Aggravated assault	Property crime	Burglary	Larceny-theft	Motor vehicle theft	Arson[2]
Nonmetropolitan Counties										
Aurora	3	0	2	0	1	4	3	1	0	0
Beadle	3	0	0	0	3	14	4	5	5	0
Bennett	0	0	0	0	0	3	0	1	2	0
Bon Homme	0	0	0	0	0	0	0	0	0	0
Brookings	7	0	0	0	7	52	14	37	1	2
Brown	17	0	2	0	15	26	9	15	2	0
Brule	4	0	0	0	4	2	1	1	0	0
Butte	9	0	0	0	9	40	3	35	2	0
Campbell	1	0	0	0	1	2	1	0	1	0
Charles Mix	14	0	0	0	14	39	12	22	5	0
Clark	1	0	0	0	1	2	0	2	0	0
Clay	6	0	4	0	2	39	6	29	4	0
Codington	16	1	4	0	11	25	4	17	4	0
Corson	4	0	0	0	4	40	13	22	5	4
Custer	11	0	5	1	5	72	11	53	8	0
Davison	4	0	1	0	3	15	5	8	2	0
Day	0	0	0	0	0	0	0	0	0	0
Deuel	1	0	0	0	1	10	3	7	0	0
Dewey	5	0	0	0	5	2	0	1	1	0
Edmunds	1	0	0	0	1	0	0	0	0	0
Gregory	3	0	1	0	2	2	0	2	0	0
Hamlin	8	0	1	0	7	37	6	28	3	0
Hanson	0	0	0	0	0	8	2	4	2	0
Harding	0	0	0	0	0	2	1	1	0	0
Hughes	4	0	0	0	4	13	5	8	0	0
Hutchinson	0	0	0	0	0	6	3	2	1	0
Hyde	0	0	0	0	0	0	0	0	0	0
Jackson	1	0	0	0	1	0	0	0	0	0
Jerauld	1	0	0	0	1	3	2	1	0	0
Jones	0	0	0	0	0	4	0	3	1	0
Kingsbury	0	0	0	0	0	2	2	0	0	0
Lake	7	0	2	1	4	35	8	24	3	0
Lawrence	6	0	4	0	2	96	18	78	0	0
Lyman	1	0	0	0	1	11	5	6	0	0
Marshall	7	0	0	0	7	31	17	14	0	0
McPherson	0	0	0	0	0	11	1	7	3	0
Mellette	0	0	0	0	0	0	0	0	0	0
Miner	1	0	0	0	1	8	7	1	0	0
Moody	2	0	0	0	2	8	3	5	0	0
Perkins	1	0	0	1	0	13	3	9	1	0
Potter	0	0	0	0	0	0	0	0	0	0
Roberts	3	0	0	0	3	9	2	2	5	1
Sanborn	1	0	0	0	1	9	5	4	0	1
Stanley	2	0	1	0	1	12	5	4	3	0
Sully	6	0	0	0	6	7	3	2	2	0
Tripp	0	0	0	0	0	19	2	16	1	0
Walworth	3	0	2	0	1	4	1	2	1	0
Yankton	11	0	0	0	11	64	22	35	7	0
Ziebach	0	0	0	0	0	0	0	0	0	0
TENNESSEE										
Metropolitan Counties										
Anderson	140	1	14	4	121	534	149	301	84	3
Blount	363	1	42	10	310	956	281	567	108	5
Bradley	195	0	9	10	176	898	212	563	123	1
Campbell	48	0	13	1	34	367	178	153	36	5
Cannon	20	0	0	0	20	85	38	29	18	1
Carter	62	1	2	3	56	519	109	375	35	3
Cheatham	108	0	5	4	99	332	52	230	50	5
Chester	11	0	4	0	7	44	12	30	2	0
Crockett	18	0	2	1	15	77	21	38	18	0
Dickson	111	0	18	0	93	421	105	253	63	5
Fayette	59	1	2	9	47	251	62	145	44	1
Gibson	75	0	4	26	45	227	93	101	33	2
Grainger	38	0	6	0	32	191	28	131	32	2
Hamblen	125	0	9	10	106	518	130	301	87	3
Hamilton	270	4	18	10	238	1,472	315	980	177	4
Hartsville/Trousdale	37	0	4	3	30	149	52	84	13	1
Hawkins	61	0	6	1	54	640	191	361	88	3
Jefferson	90	0	12	9	69	416	122	247	47	3
Knox	680	7	66	43	564	3,499	566	2,452	481	18
Loudon	109	0	4	1	104	382	86	257	39	0
Macon	51	0	0	0	51	128	38	65	25	0
Madison	107	2	4	8	93	465	133	268	64	1
Marion	56	0	2	1	53	231	43	132	56	0
Maury	167	4	22	5	136	489	79	310	100	2
Montgomery	117	1	5	3	108	641	173	408	60	0
Morgan	72	1	7	2	62	297	79	153	65	3
Polk	52	1	2	2	47	379	77	243	59	2
Roane	49	0	6	2	41	341	101	186	54	1

Table 10. Offenses Known to Law Enforcement, by Selected State Metropolitan and Nonmetropolitan Counties, 2018—Continued

(Number.)

State/county	Violent crime	Murder and nonnegligent manslaughter	Rape[1]	Robbery	Aggravated assault	Property crime	Burglary	Larceny-theft	Motor vehicle theft	Arson[2]
Robertson	76	2	5	6	63	246	60	160	26	2
Rutherford[8]	191	6	17	7	161		99	451		7
Sequatchie	33	0	2	0	31	136	24	75	37	3
Shelby	706	2	34	74	596	2,700	637	1,759	304	9
Smith	25	0	4	0	21	174	48	103	23	2
Stewart	25	0	1	0	24	111	46	51	14	1
Sullivan	305	3	28	16	258	1,262	281	801	180	14
Sumner	150	0	16	5	129	433	105	275	53	2
Tipton	126	4	11	8	103	448	115	273	60	1
Unicoi	27	1	1	4	21	106	29	65	12	1
Union	35	0	6	1	28	218	57	139	22	2
Washington	208	2	18	5	183	716	196	425	95	0
Williamson	77	2	10	5	60	323	80	221	22	1
Wilson	111	3	0	3	105	631	143	416	72	2
Nonmetropolitan Counties										
Bedford	51	0	7	0	44	265	79	163	23	2
Benton	31	0	4	1	26	223	83	107	33	1
Carroll	27	1	1	1	24	188	77	85	26	1
Claiborne	49	0	5	3	41	321	97	171	53	1
Clay	13	0	2	0	11	27	10	13	4	0
Cocke	81	0	7	0	74	436	146	201	89	3
Coffee	48	0	4	4	40	203	45	127	31	0
Cumberland	38	0	2	1	35	710	197	423	90	4
Decatur	13	1	0	0	12	124	45	57	22	0
DeKalb	10	0	2	0	8	116	20	81	15	3
Dyer	26	1	3	1	21	231	47	147	37	4
Fentress	29	0	1	3	25	200	61	120	19	0
Franklin	104	0	3	1	100	297	43	200	54	3
Giles	53	2	9	2	40	230	54	143	33	4
Greene	165	1	18	9	137	938	249	531	158	8
Grundy	92	1	8	0	83	235	48	143	44	5
Hancock	1	0	0	0	1	74	1	66	7	0
Hardeman	62	0	4	8	50	209	88	96	25	3
Hardin	27	1	1	4	21	372	118	190	64	1
Haywood	30	0	6	1	23	145	61	63	21	1
Henderson	116	0	12	1	103	308	116	137	55	4
Henry	55	0	6	1	48	364	102	221	41	5
Hickman	91	3	13	3	72	314	62	192	60	3
Houston	15	0	0	0	15	85	22	52	11	0
Humphreys	46	1	5	0	40	155	60	73	22	2
Jackson	34	4	3	0	27	102	23	58	21	1
Johnson	52	1	8	1	42	201	48	119	34	0
Lake	5	0	1	0	4	34	7	24	3	0
Lauderdale	55	1	5	2	47	249	101	131	17	2
Lewis	27	0	2	0	25	91	36	40	15	1
Lincoln	87	1	8	3	75	320	114	171	35	3
Marshall	31	0	3	2	26	94	5	76	13	0
McMinn	80	2	3	6	69	543	113	310	120	6
McNairy	70	0	3	4	63	266	66	147	53	7
Meigs	58	1	7	0	50	294	87	161	46	8
Monroe	170	1	9	2	158	867	306	422	139	11
Moore	15	0	4	0	11	59	11	43	5	0
Obion	18	1	0	0	17	163	26	121	16	0
Overton	13	0	1	0	12	70	15	46	9	0
Perry	7	0	1	0	6	72	15	51	6	2
Pickett	5	0	3	0	2	45	12	27	6	0
Putnam	127	0	20	3	104	625	159	377	89	7
Rhea	70	0	3	6	61	234	51	154	29	1
Scott	40	0	0	0	40	157	46	92	19	0
Sevier	208	1	23	4	180	893	225	525	143	2
Van Buren	6	0	0	0	6	57	7	42	8	0
Warren	88	1	4	0	83	313	81	187	45	6
Wayne	12	0	3	0	9	65	7	47	11	0
Weakley	36	1	1	2	32	89	33	48	8	1
White	59	3	9	2	45	269	51	180	38	0
TEXAS										
Metropolitan Counties										
Atascosa	83	4	3	8	68	520	136	317	67	0
Austin	14	0	6	0	8	100	48	36	16	3
Bandera	34	1	24	2	7	284	108	134	42	0
Bastrop	162	3	45	15	99	646	234	348	64	0
Bell[8]	83	2	28	6	47	683	157	495	31	
Bexar	627	10	166	79	372	5,166	975	3,770	421	49
Bowie	80	0	20	5	55	349	113	191	45	11
Brazoria	171	0	20	35	116	1,226	251	838	137	2
Brazos	49	1	11	0	37	305	75	199	31	2
Burleson	26	0	5	0	21	112	54	50	8	2
Caldwell	33	0	0	5	28	114	39	59	16	1
Callahan	8	0	1	1	6	37	15	16	6	0

Table 10. Offenses Known to Law Enforcement, by Selected State Metropolitan and Nonmetropolitan Counties, 2018—Continued

(Number.)

State/county	Violent crime	Murder and nonnegligent manslaughter	Rape[1]	Robbery	Aggravated assault	Property crime	Burglary	Larceny-theft	Motor vehicle theft	Arson[2]
Cameron	164	1	51	15	97	937	324	564	49	2
Carson	11	0	2	0	9	36	11	20	5	0
Clay	25	0	9	5	11	124	65	40	19	3
Collin	76	3	35	3	35	346	93	204	49	0
Comal[8]		0	44	2		517	161	320	36	0
Coryell	7	0	0	0	7	75	10	61	4	0
Crosby[5]	4	0	0	0	4	19	11	5	3	0
Dallas	50	1	20	2	27	236	44	155	37	0
Denton	75	0	29	1	45	486	125	326	35	0
Ector	109	4	6	22	77	1,554	271	1,020	263	1
Ellis	118	0	27	5	86	412	92	280	40	0
El Paso	243	8	44	10	181	668	141	470	57	3
Falls	17	1	4	0	12	53	14	33	6	0
Fort Bend[5]	836	6	126	145	559	3,969	595	3,166	208	20
Galveston	128	1	14	16	97	693	196	428	69	6
Goliad	13	0	4	0	9	95	27	54	14	0
Grayson	91	1	27	4	59	398	127	209	62	1
Gregg	67	0	15	3	49	417	107	244	66	0
Guadalupe	71	3	30	5	33	448	126	283	39	20
Hardin	45	3	5	6	31	301	100	144	57	5
Harris[3]		86	591	2,271		41,708	7,640	28,113	5,955	176
Harrison[5]	61	4	6	6	45	494	135	307	52	0
Hays	135	2	17	8	108	656	175	449	32	0
Hidalgo	522	4	121	101	296	3,489	1,022	2,286	181	19
Hudspeth[5]	3	0	0	0	3	32	20	4	8	0
Irion[5]	4	0	1	0	3	30	7	20	3	0
Jefferson	51	0	1	6	44	381	97	233	51	5
Johnson	213	1	35	7	170	675	164	420	91	4
Jones	1	1	0	0	0	49	21	23	5	0
Kaufman	143	2	58	8	75	571	162	330	79	0
Kendall	14	0	7	0	7	111	29	68	14	1
Lampasas	11	0	0	0	11	70	31	38	1	0
Liberty	177	2	46	4	125	666	237	331	98	5
Lubbock	25	1	9	0	15	366	79	254	33	1
Lynn	0	0	0	0	0	25	7	11	7	0
Martin	3	0	1	0	2	39	4	34	1	0
McLennan	68	0	23	2	43	424	137	225	62	6
Medina	75	1	20	4	50	336	96	200	40	2
Midland	100	4	3	7	86	559	86	362	111	5
Montgomery	847	10	107	132	598	4,918	979	3,421	518	23
Nueces	71	2	13	5	51	258	49	198	11	1
Oldham	2	0	0	0	2	6	2	3	1	0
Orange	70	0	20	7	43	541	178	268	95	1
Parker	136	2	40	6	88	825	224	523	78	3
Potter[5]	34	0	3	0	31	194	43	126	25	0
Randall	54	0	24	6	24	248	70	156	22	2
Robertson	6	0	1	1	4	86	20	55	11	1
Rockwall	13	0	4	0	9	110	20	66	24	0
Rusk	65	0	7	2	56	536	207	279	50	10
San Patricio	41	3	0	1	37	258	71	167	20	0
Smith	272	8	55	7	202	1,345	409	747	189	3
Sterling[5]	1	0	0	0	1	4	1	3	0	0
Tarrant	109	4	34	11	60	728	213	458	57	6
Taylor	35	0	6	1	28	107	46	52	9	0
Tom Green	20	1	17	0	2	260	104	133	23	2
Travis	837	6	123	50	658	3,090	701	2,158	231	22
Upshur	74	4	6	2	62	235	121	92	22	0
Victoria	77	3	19	1	54	372	118	221	33	0
Waller	71	0	35	3	33	349	93	238	18	0
Webb	71	0	10	4	57	250	95	155	0	1
Wichita	32	1	1	0	30	139	60	59	20	1
Williamson[5]	195	2	52	17	124	1,394	304	1,010	80	8
Wilson	15	0	2	0	13	188	80	97	11	1
Wise[5]	110	3	23	6	78	351	101	209	41	7
Nonmetropolitan Counties										
Anderson	54	0	2	6	46	350	121	188	41	0
Andrews	17	0	2	0	15	80	18	50	12	0
Angelina	96	0	24	3	69	492	152	274	66	1
Aransas	76	0	18	3	55	264	94	152	18	0
Bailey	10	1	0	0	9	28	8	19	1	0
Bee[5]	31	1	6	1	23	145	40	88	17	5
Blanco	9	0	1	0	8	36	13	22	1	1
Bosque	2	0	0	0	2	51	22	25	4	1
Brewster	8	0	3	1	4	13	6	7	0	1
Briscoe[5]	1	0	0	0	1	7	1	6	0	0
Brooks	0	0	0	0	0	0	0	0	0	0
Brown	21	0	0	0	21	153	65	82	6	1
Burnet[5]	55	0	20	1	34	175	42	99	34	0
Calhoun	34	0	9	0	25	93	26	51	16	0
Camp	2	0	0	0	2	74	28	35	11	0

Table 10. Offenses Known to Law Enforcement, by Selected State Metropolitan and Nonmetropolitan Counties, 2018—Continued

(Number.)

State/county	Violent crime	Murder and nonnegligent manslaughter	Rape[1]	Robbery	Aggravated assault	Property crime	Burglary	Larceny-theft	Motor vehicle theft	Arson[2]
Cass[5]	39	0	4	3	32	208	93	85	30	3
Castro[5]	2	1	0	0	1	20	7	11	2	0
Cherokee[5]	85	1	10	2	72	418	143	229	46	1
Childress	0	0	0	0	0	10	6	3	1	0
Colorado[5]	12	0	2	0	10	102	16	65	21	0
Comanche	2	0	0	0	2	61	19	36	6	2
Concho	11	0	0	0	11	9	2	7	0	0
Cooke	16	0	4	1	11	116	49	59	8	1
Crockett[3,5]	3	0	0	1	2			11	0	0
Culberson	0	0	0	0	0	0	0	0	0	0
Dallam	1	0	0	0	1	3	3	0	0	0
Dawson	4	0	0	1	3	51	19	30	2	0
Deaf Smith[5]	6	0	1	0	5	53	14	35	4	0
Delta	2	0	0	0	2	29	10	18	1	0
DeWitt[3]	32	2	7	0	23			75	7	0
Dimmit	9	0	1	0	8	116	21	88	7	0
Donley	5	0	0	2	3	37	10	22	5	2
Duval	17	0	1	0	16	122	36	56	30	2
Eastland	2	0	2	0	0	32	12	12	8	0
Edwards	3	0	1	0	2	21	11	10	0	0
Erath	34	1	2	0	31	123	66	47	10	2
Fannin	35	0	10	1	24	172	94	63	15	0
Fayette	19	0	3	2	14	111	35	73	3	0
Floyd	23	0	5	1	17	36	11	23	2	0
Foard	0	0	0	0	0	0	0	0	0	0
Franklin	17	1	0	1	15	51	21	26	4	0
Freestone	17	0	0	1	16	109	39	63	7	2
Frio	28	2	0	0	26	57	22	32	3	0
Gaines	10	0	4	0	6	82	27	43	12	0
Garza	7	0	0	0	7	35	15	17	3	0
Gillespie	5	1	2	0	2	47	9	35	3	2
Glasscock[5]	0	0	0	0	0	19	2	16	1	0
Gonzales	11	0	2	1	8	100	31	66	3	1
Gray	7	0	1	1	5	97	35	51	11	1
Grimes	8	0	0	0	8	122	39	73	10	4
Hale	26	0	0	0	26	66	22	42	2	0
Hall[5]	1	0	0	0	1	12	7	3	2	0
Hansford	5	0	1	0	4	9	3	2	4	0
Hartley	1	0	0	0	1	7	5	2	0	0
Haskell	0	0	0	0	0	13	5	7	1	0
Hemphill	1	0	0	0	1	28	7	18	3	0
Henderson	153	3	40	6	104	611	234	329	48	0
Hill[5]	50	0	13	3	34	280	96	150	34	5
Hockley	7	0	2	1	4	97	46	45	6	1
Hood	71	2	13	3	53	391	111	244	36	2
Hopkins	16	2	8	0	6	70	26	33	11	2
Houston[5]	10	0	1	1	8	101	33	58	10	0
Howard	33	1	2	0	30	185	38	117	30	1
Hutchinson	15	0	5	0	10	70	14	44	12	0
Jack	5	1	0	0	4	58	10	27	21	0
Jackson	4	0	1	0	3	52	12	32	8	0
Jasper	69	1	20	3	45	317	111	168	38	6
Jim Wells	109	2	12	1	94	344	178	141	25	6
Karnes	2	0	0	0	2	92	39	42	11	1
Kenedy[5]	2	0	0	0	2	5	1	2	2	0
Kent	2	0	1	0	1	9	0	8	1	0
Kerr	30	0	14	0	16	155	45	106	4	0
Kimble	0	0	0	0	0	11	2	7	2	0
Kinney	0	0	0	0	0	1	1	0	0	0
Kleberg	31	0	0	0	31	56	15	37	4	1
Knox	1	0	1	0	0	12	3	9	0	0
Lamar	34	2	12	1	19	144	31	103	10	0
Lamb	5	0	3	0	2	42	9	26	7	3
La Salle	2	0	0	0	2	37	6	31	0	0
Lavaca	16	1	10	0	5	47	20	24	3	0
Lee	19	1	6	0	12	76	24	45	7	0
Leon[5]	16	1	0	0	15	129	38	84	7	2
Limestone	26	0	2	0	24	106	49	48	9	1
Lipscomb	4	0	2	0	2	30	2	17	11	0
Llano	11	0	0	2	9	79	32	43	4	0
Madison	7	0	2	0	5	64	21	38	5	0
Marion	38	1	4	1	32	124	52	67	5	0
Mason	1	0	0	0	1	17	7	9	1	0
Matagorda	57	2	7	2	46	306	96	184	26	0
McCulloch	0	0	0	0	0	14	6	6	2	0
McMullen	1	0	0	0	1	18	5	12	1	0
Menard	1	0	0	0	1	13	13	0	0	0
Milam	18	0	0	1	17	74	20	47	7	0
Mills	2	0	0	0	2	14	6	7	1	0
Mitchell	0	0	0	0	0	29	12	12	5	0
Montague	28	0	2	3	23	87	31	45	11	0

Table 10. Offenses Known to Law Enforcement, by Selected State Metropolitan and Nonmetropolitan Counties, 2018—Continued

(Number.)

State/county	Violent crime	Murder and nonnegligent manslaughter	Rape[1]	Robbery	Aggravated assault	Property crime	Burglary	Larceny-theft	Motor vehicle theft	Arson[2]
Moore	3	0	1	0	2	36	13	19	4	0
Morris	6	0	3	0	3	70	26	39	5	0
Motley	1	0	0	0	1	4	1	3	0	0
Nacogdoches	60	1	7	0	52	309	100	179	30	0
Navarro	53	2	14	2	35	281	110	143	28	4
Newton	22	1	0	0	21	109	39	52	18	1
Nolan	5	0	0	0	5	20	6	12	2	0
Ochiltree	3	0	0	0	3	29	13	15	1	0
Palo Pinto	4	0	0	1	3	98	32	49	17	0
Parmer	5	0	1	0	4	11	2	7	2	0
Pecos	0	0	0	0	0	91	18	64	9	1
Polk	70	1	12	1	56	521	178	298	45	4
Presidio[5]	0	0	0	0	0	3	0	2	1	0
Rains	18	0	1	0	17	102	28	63	11	0
Reagan[5]	8	0	0	0	8	58	12	40	6	0
Real[5]	4	0	0	0	4	46	18	25	3	0
Red River	12	0	4	0	8	46	20	23	3	0
Reeves	4	0	0	1	3	107	0	105	2	0
Refugio	8	0	0	0	8	48	12	32	4	0
Roberts	0	0	0	0	0	7	0	7	0	0
Runnels[5]	1	0	0	0	1	15	7	8	0	0
Sabine	36	0	5	0	31	126	61	51	14	1
San Augustine	21	0	3	1	17	52	22	23	7	1
San Jacinto	42	0	16	2	24	360	144	168	48	0
San Saba	8	0	0	0	8	34	25	7	2	0
Schleicher	0	0	0	0	0	27	3	21	3	0
Scurry	7	0	2	0	5	27	10	15	2	0
Sherman	1	0	1	0	0	4	4	0	0	0
Somervell	5	1	1	1	2	35	6	28	1	0
Starr	61	0	10	2	49	160	62	85	13	9
Stephens[5]	2	0	0	0	2	45	17	25	3	0
Stonewall	4	0	0	0	4	3	1	2	0	0
Sutton	0	0	0	0	0	2	1	1	0	0
Swisher	1	0	1	0	0	7	4	2	1	0
Throckmorton	4	0	1	0	3	5	5	0	0	0
Titus	53	1	8	3	41	176	58	99	19	0
Trinity	18	0	2	0	16	167	52	92	23	1
Tyler	67	1	9	3	54	254	145	76	33	9
Upton	1	0	0	0	1	18	0	16	2	1
Uvalde	20	1	0	0	19	82	33	38	11	0
Val Verde	27	0	2	0	25	102	40	57	5	10
Van Zandt	1	0	0	1	0	156	70	67	19	0
Walker	66	1	21	4	40	210	79	113	18	0
Ward[5]	29	0	1	0	28	160	44	112	4	0
Washington[5]	39	0	14	4	21	90	29	53	8	1
Wharton	69	3	15	4	47	229	65	146	18	1
Wheeler	0	0	0	0	0	31	6	21	4	0
Wilbarger	1	0	0	0	1	18	9	9	0	0
Willacy	64	2	2	2	58	194	70	120	4	2
Winkler	10	0	4	0	6	61	15	41	5	0
Wood	73	0	30	0	43	201	60	117	24	0
Yoakum	5	0	4	0	1	30	5	21	4	0
Young	8	0	0	2	6	39	21	12	6	1
Zapata	7	0	1	1	5	202	91	102	9	0
Zavala	6	0	5	0	1	38	19	17	2	0
UTAH										
Metropolitan Counties										
Box Elder	15	0	6	0	9	196	45	131	20	0
Cache	38	0	30	0	8	142	31	92	19	1
Davis	41	0	13	2	26	195	17	166	12	0
Juab	1	0	1	0	0	41	7	26	8	0
Tooele	28	0	14	0	14	288	39	225	24	0
Utah	51	1	22	2	26	386	34	326	26	0
Washington	36	0	6	1	29	119	31	72	16	1
Weber	66	0	23	8	35	874	225	584	65	4
Nonmetropolitan Counties										
Beaver	1	0	0	0	1	133	22	105	6	0
Carbon	5	0	3	1	1	103	29	69	5	0
Duchesne	52	1	14	0	37	252	51	163	38	3
Iron	37	0	7	0	30	130	38	75	17	2
Kane	5	0	0	0	5	20	4	13	3	0
Millard	27	0	9	1	17	191	34	138	19	3
Rich	0	0	0	0	0	37	6	30	1	0
Sanpete	15	0	5	0	10	142	27	102	13	1
Sevier	12	0	4	1	7	124	29	84	11	0
Summit	36	0	0	2	34	404	44	322	38	
Uintah	32	1	8	0	23	212	80	116	16	2
Wasatch	9	0	0	0	9	60	13	41	6	0

Table 10. Offenses Known to Law Enforcement, by Selected State Metropolitan and Nonmetropolitan Counties, 2018—Continued

(Number.)

State/county	Violent crime	Murder and nonnegligent manslaughter	Rape[1]	Robbery	Aggravated assault	Property crime	Burglary	Larceny-theft	Motor vehicle theft	Arson[2]
VERMONT										
Metropolitan Counties										
Franklin	18	0	8	2	8	47	18	27	2	0
Grand Isle	1	0	0	0	1	42	11	29	2	0
Nonmetropolitan Counties										
Bennington	0	0	0	0	0	8	1	7	0	0
Essex	2	0	2	0	0	14	5	8	1	0
Lamoille	5	0	2	0	3	43	6	37	0	1
Orange	3	0	2	0	1	4	0	4	0	0
Orleans	2	0	0	0	2	22	4	18	0	0
Rutland	2	0	0	0	2	8	1	7	0	0
Washington	0	0	0	0	0	0	0	0	0	0
Windham	2	0	0	0	2	13	2	11	0	1
VIRGINIA										
Metropolitan Counties										
Albemarle County Police Department	144	1	46	20	77	1,290	118	1,106	66	1
Amelia	17	1	7	0	9	116	19	88	9	1
Amherst	58	1	14	4	39	336	44	262	30	3
Appomattox	14	0	5	0	9	96	6	81	9	1
Arlington County Police Department	323	4	69	75	175	2,630	127	2,336	167	10
Augusta	102	3	33	8	58	794	195	527	72	2
Bedford	56	2	11	2	41	442	117	297	28	3
Botetourt	20	0	5	2	13	236	30	196	10	0
Campbell	77	3	18	7	49	715	127	504	84	8
Charles City	9	0	4	0	5	41	6	23	12	2
Chesterfield County Police Department	437	4	106	140	187	5,645	792	4,509	344	33
Clarke	9	0	2	5	2	57	8	48	1	0
Craig	2	0	0	0	2	3	0	2	1	0
Culpeper	18	1	3	0	14	153	19	116	18	0
Dinwiddie	71	2	7	4	58	292	46	233	13	5
Fairfax County Police Department	911	14	174	351	372	13,165	752	11,601	812	24
Fauquier	52	4	19	4	25	272	35	227	10	6
Fluvanna	19	0	9	1	9	141	22	107	12	3
Franklin	64	2	22	1	39	536	127	347	62	4
Frederick	70	0	19	7	44	1,059	87	910	62	1
Giles	28	0	10	2	16	79	17	55	7	0
Gloucester	19	0	4	2	13	228	8	195	25	3
Goochland	23	2	4	1	16	159	19	128	12	1
Greene	21	0	10	3	8	241	16	210	15	0
Hanover	137	2	26	9	100	882	48	803	31	3
Henrico County Police Department	506	12	38	114	342	7,507	655	6,302	550	29
Isle of Wight	32	1	4	5	22	205	31	154	20	1
James City County Police Department	105	1	18	13	73	870	61	778	31	4
King and Queen	13	2	4	0	7	44	13	29	2	1
King William	6	0	1	0	5	62	11	46	5	1
Loudoun	376	5	179	48	144	2,384	132	2,101	151	18
Madison	11	0	6	1	4	87	5	75	7	0
Mathews	11	0	4	0	7	53	11	38	4	1
Montgomery	52	0	10	1	41	294	59	208	27	1
Nelson	30	0	9	1	20	213	74	125	14	1
New Kent	47	0	6	2	39	187	18	161	8	0
Prince George County Police Department	49	1	11	6	31	327	45	261	21	0
Prince William County Police Department	815	11	127	180	497	5,143	455	4,151	537	24
Rappahannock	6	0	1	0	5	25	2	21	2	1
Roanoke County Police Department	170	6	40	30	94	1,401	147	1,172	82	1
Rockingham	52	1	19	0	32	471	129	332	10	3
Scott	21	1	6	3	11	183	44	121	18	5
Southampton	19	2	9	5	3	171	35	121	15	0
Spotsylvania	221	1	37	35	148	1,458	169	1,202	87	1
Stafford	302	5	72	31	194	1,558	110	1,379	69	6
Sussex	18	1	5	2	10	64	19	39	6	2
Warren	36	0	23	2	11	190	22	166	2	2
Washington	52	3	9	3	37	730	100	578	52	0
York	95	3	16	16	60	1,010	104	875	31	6
Nonmetropolitan Counties										
Accomack	57	1	14	9	33	265	62	196	7	1
Alleghany	16	0	3	0	13	100	33	63	4	1
Bath	1	0	0	0	1	10	1	9	0	0
Bland	2	0	0	1	1	37	15	21	1	1
Brunswick	18	1	3	3	11	88	19	62	7	1
Buchanan	45	0	20	1	24	262	70	175	17	3
Buckingham	16	1	6	2	7	103	14	76	13	1
Caroline	18	0	12	2	4	233	38	195	0	1
Carroll	21	0	4	1	16	227	62	143	22	0
Charlotte	18	1	4	0	13	116	30	76	10	0
Cumberland	12	0	2	2	8	40	9	23	8	0

Table 10. Offenses Known to Law Enforcement, by Selected State Metropolitan and Nonmetropolitan Counties, 2018—Continued

(Number.)

State/county	Violent crime	Murder and nonnegligent manslaughter	Rape[1]	Robbery	Aggravated assault	Property crime	Burglary	Larceny-theft	Motor vehicle theft	Arson[2]
Dickenson	22	0	13	0	9	74	11	59	4	3
Essex	22	0	4	1	17	47	13	27	7	1
Floyd	17	0	4	1	12	106	30	66	10	1
Grayson	15	0	8	1	6	155	38	87	30	7
Greensville	17	1	4	2	10	93	18	68	7	1
Halifax	48	4	12	7	25	223	57	144	22	3
Henry	129	4	19	20	86	1,191	320	776	95	10
Highland	2	0	1	0	1	14	2	11	1	1
King George	26	0	5	4	17	219	24	173	22	0
Lancaster	14	0	2	2	10	76	13	54	9	0
Louisa	42	0	9	3	30	358	25	293	40	2
Lunenburg	8	2	3	0	3	40	13	22	5	0
Mecklenburg	60	1	33	5	21	205	69	116	20	1
Middlesex	10	1	4	0	5	141	38	91	12	5
Northampton	5	0	1	3	1	82	24	56	2	1
Northumberland	10	0	2	0	8	77	14	57	6	0
Nottoway	14	2	1	0	11	89	16	70	3	1
Orange	18	1	6	1	10	141	25	109	7	1
Page	15	1	4	1	9	120	26	87	7	3
Patrick	53	3	10	1	39	202	33	152	17	3
Pittsylvania	75	3	23	7	42	457	124	298	35	5
Prince Edward	15	0	10	0	5	93	25	58	10	0
Richmond	5	1	1	2	1	27	8	15	4	0
Rockbridge	25	1	5	0	19	209	32	162	15	1
Russell	44	1	19	1	23	209	58	142	9	3
Shenandoah	49	0	23	1	25	210	37	161	12	0
Smyth	26	0	10	2	14	205	21	163	21	3
Surry	7	0	3	0	4	61	11	47	3	1
Tazewell	47	0	21	2	24	285	75	189	21	4
Westmoreland	11	1	3	2	5	113	18	87	8	2
Wise	46	0	29	1	16	212	41	144	27	2
Wythe	25	2	12	1	10	147	17	112	18	0
WASHINGTON										
Metropolitan Counties										
Asotin	8	0	2	2	4	131	28	88	15	0
Benton	80	2	13	5	60	464	113	309	42	5
Chelan	44	0	6	1	37	438	132	266	40	1
Cowlitz	83	0	26	7	50	377	115	198	64	2
Douglas	18	3	5	1	9	343	110	198	35	2
Franklin	40	0	5	5	30	100	24	59	17	4
King[5,7]		7		111	294	3,673	1,012	1,850	811	59
Kitsap	451	3	107	39	302	2,839	633	1,978	228	21
Pierce	1,167	16	131	180	840	7,758	1,899	4,660	1,199	39
Skagit	70	2	10	12	46	886	257	545	84	6
Skamania	14	0	5	0	9	108	29	60	19	0
Snohomish	606	2	97	106	401	4,807	1,066	2,917	824	36
Spokane	220	3	63	22	132	3,488	722	2,508	258	8
Stevens	25	1	4	0	20	259	96	141	22	3
Thurston	290	2	40	22	226	1,744	703	842	199	17
Walla Walla	40	1	5	1	33	280	74	186	20	5
Whatcom	126	0	28	14	84	1,295	339	844	112	10
Nonmetropolitan Counties										
Adams	17	0	2	2	13	128	57	49	22	0
Clallam	72	3	19	7	43	573	194	351	28	2
Columbia	9	0	1	0	8	63	25	37	1	0
Ferry	7	0	3	0	4	27	7	16	4	1
Garfield	11	0	3	0	8	52	9	40	3	0
Grays Harbor	42	1	11	2	28	397	135	233	29	4
Island	30	0	4	1	25	508	186	289	33	1
Jefferson	24	0	4	1	19	244	100	123	21	1
Kittitas	14	1	3	1	9	253	91	149	13	3
Klickitat	3	1	0	1	1	65	38	16	11	0
Lewis	60	2	7	4	47	549	207	299	43	2
Lincoln	8	0	1	1	6	136	28	97	11	0
Mason	72	4	9	13	46	979	379	495	105	5
Pacific	17	0	5	2	10	158	56	92	10	2
Pend Oreille	10	1	0	0	9	190	68	107	15	0
Wahkiakum	7	0	0	0	7	47	12	35	0	0
Whitman	9	1	1	0	7	47	13	28	6	0
WEST VIRGINIA										
Metropolitan Counties										
Berkeley	65	0	10	7	48	434	110	301	23	2
Brooke	2	0	0	0	2	34	12	19	3	2
Cabell	0	0	0	0	0	298	39	259	0	0
Fayette	64	0	8	2	54	176	57	99	20	4
Hampshire	14	0	0	1	13	112	50	60	2	1
Hancock	10	0	2	0	8	20	6	13	1	0
Jefferson	24	0	5	1	18	169	20	133	16	1

Table 10. Offenses Known to Law Enforcement, by Selected State Metropolitan and Nonmetropolitan Counties, 2018—Continued

(Number.)

State/county	Violent crime	Murder and nonnegligent manslaughter	Rape[1]	Robbery	Aggravated assault	Property crime	Burglary	Larceny-theft	Motor vehicle theft	Arson[2]
Marshall	19	0	2	0	17	32	12	16	4	1
Mineral	16	0	1	0	15	21	5	13	3	0
Morgan	33	0	1	0	32	62	17	42	3	0
Preston	21	1	4	0	16	90	3	75	12	1
Putnam	193	1	6	0	186	236	43	154	39	2
Raleigh	112	2	21	3	86	578	180	361	37	4
Wirt	8	0	0	0	8	19	4	14	1	2
Wood	95	1	15	0	79	274	80	156	38	4
Nonmetropolitan Counties										
Calhoun	0	0	0	0	0	10	2	7	1	1
Doddridge	6	0	1	1	4	28	9	18	1	0
Grant	2	0	1	0	1	10	5	5	0	0
Greenbrier	8	2	0	2	4	70	27	38	5	0
Hardy	16	0	0	0	16	19	16	2	1	0
Harrison	45	1	16	3	25	201	61	111	29	1
Lewis	7	0	1	0	6	48	13	25	10	0
Logan	89	2	1	1	85	22	9	12	1	0
Mason	7	0	0	0	7	72	23	37	12	0
McDowell	2	0	0	0	2	19	13	2	4	0
Monroe	2	0	0	0	2	36	15	19	2	2
Nicholas	174	0	18	1	155	69	19	49	1	0
Randolph	57	1	0	0	56	122	58	63	1	1
Roane	10	1	0	0	9	29	2	24	3	0
Summers	13	0	0	0	13	40	16	21	3	0
Tyler	11	0	0	0	11	7	4	3	0	0
Upshur	13	1	5	2	5	41	7	29	5	0
Wetzel	11	0	1	0	10	13	2	9	2	0
Wyoming	55	0	1	0	54	43	16	25	2	3
WISCONSIN										
Metropolitan Counties										
Brown	103	0	44	4	55	639	71	538	30	4
Calumet	9	2	4	0	3	49	9	35	5	1
Chippewa	30	1	14	0	15	263	46	196	21	1
Columbia	21	0	8	1	12	184	43	128	13	1
Dane	82	1	22	6	53	605	141	414	50	1
Douglas	20	0	7	1	12	204	79	105	20	2
Eau Claire[5]	30	1	14	3	12	223	65	147	11	0
Fond du Lac	22	0	8	1	13	155	40	101	14	0
Green	7	0	0	2	5	50	11	37	2	0
Iowa	12	1	1	0	10	43	6	33	4	1
Kenosha	42	1	11	3	27	365	75	271	19	0
Kewaunee	3	0	1	1	1	47	4	36	7	0
La Crosse	15	0	2	1	12	133	33	93	7	0
Lincoln	21	0	8	0	13	67	18	46	3	1
Marathon	19	0	3	0	16	254	54	191	9	1
Milwaukee	82	1	5	7	69	144	3	59	82	3
Oconto	15	0	6	1	8	224	57	151	16	0
Outagamie	52	0	12	1	39	233	72	149	12	2
Ozaukee	12	0	6	1	5	102	26	71	5	0
Pierce	15	1	0	1	13	123	45	72	6	0
Racine	21	0	0	4	17	208	44	149	15	0
Rock[5]	34	0	14	3	17	380	122	238	20	1
Sheboygan	42	0	16	1	25	310	40	256	14	1
St. Croix	25	1	3	1	20	259	58	188	13	2
Washington	6	0	4	1	1	205	37	143	25	8
Waukesha	56	0	0	3	53	320	59	237	24	2
Winnebago	21	0	1	1	19	167	35	124	8	0
Nonmetropolitan Counties										
Adams	27	0	0	1	26	187	94	85	8	1
Ashland	5	0	0	0	5	24	4	19	1	0
Barron	2	2	0	0	0	113	38	62	13	0
Bayfield	16	0	0	0	16	81	38	39	4	1
Buffalo	3	0	2	0	1	10	2	4	4	0
Burnett	30	0	5	1	24	341	124	193	24	2
Clark	6	3	0	0	3	99	23	60	16	1
Crawford	17	0	4	0	13	105	13	90	2	0
Dodge	67	1	26	2	38	168	45	105	18	1
Door	16	0	10	0	6	59	1	56	2	0
Dunn	15	1	1	0	13	131	33	95	3	0
Florence	8	0	0	0	8	45	14	29	2	0
Forest	21	0	9	1	11	96	18	68	10	0
Grant	32	1	11	0	20	121	21	92	8	1
Green Lake	5	0	1	0	4	42	16	23	3	0
Iron	6	0	1	0	5	65	16	43	6	0
Jackson	11	0	2	1	8	170	56	85	29	0
Jefferson	34	0	1	0	33	266	40	207	19	2
Lafayette	14	0	3	0	11	72	12	54	6	1
Langlade	4	0	2	0	2	107	16	85	6	0

Table 10. Offenses Known to Law Enforcement, by Selected State Metropolitan and Nonmetropolitan Counties, 2018—Continued

(Number.)

State/county	Violent crime	Murder and nonnegligent manslaughter	Rape[1]	Robbery	Aggravated assault	Property crime	Burglary	Larceny-theft	Motor vehicle theft	Arson[2]
Manitowoc	23	0	4	1	18	183	60	118	5	0
Marinette	6	0	5	0	1	136	39	90	7	0
Marquette	3	0	1	0	2	69	14	52	3	0
Menominee	1	0	0	0	1	26	4	21	1	0
Monroe	7	2	1	0	4	100	31	61	8	0
Oneida	44	0	10	0	34	168	52	99	17	0
Pepin	10	0	1	0	9	23	6	16	1	1
Polk	35	0	9	0	26	245	85	141	19	2
Portage	35	2	6	0	27	166	45	104	17	1
Price	9	0	3	0	6	73	16	53	4	1
Richland	0	0	0	0	0	11	4	3	4	0
Rusk	16	1	7	1	7	36	13	19	4	1
Sauk	26	0	12	2	12	282	53	219	10	0
Sawyer	13	0	0	1	12	135	28	90	17	2
Shawano	42	0	21	1	20	308	88	199	21	0
Taylor	14	0	3	0	11	51	4	45	2	1
Trempealeau	18	0	3	1	14	82	25	53	4	0
Vernon	10	0	0	0	10	66	11	51	4	3
Vilas	8	0	1	1	6	120	24	93	3	0
Walworth	9	0	8	0	1	131	26	91	14	4
Washburn	31	0	4	0	27	86	28	49	9	0
Waupaca	65	0	18	0	47	346	62	264	20	0
Waushara	18	0	4	0	14	151	23	123	5	1
Wood	17	0	13	2	2	154	54	92	8	1
WYOMING										
Metropolitan Counties										
Natrona	40	0	11	0	29	230	64	133	33	1
Nonmetropolitan Counties										
Albany	6	0	0	1	5	57	16	38	3	1
Big Horn	6	0	0	0	6	24	4	19	1	1
Campbell	90	0	13	0	77	99	26	62	11	1
Carbon	6	0	1	0	5	17	1	15	1	0
Crook	2	0	2	0	0	15	6	5	4	0
Fremont	24	0	1	0	23	254	16	225	13	1
Goshen	9	1	1	0	7	42	20	20	2	0
Hot Springs	1	0	0	0	1	18	1	15	2	0
Johnson	4	0	1	0	3	41	8	31	2	0
Lincoln	13	0	5	0	8	73	12	53	8	0
Niobrara	6	0	1	1	4	6	1	4	1	0
Park	8	1	0	0	7	42	10	30	2	1
Platte	4	0	2	0	2	43	5	31	7	0
Sheridan	3	0	1	0	2	31	4	25	2	0
Sublette	4	0	0	0	4	49	11	35	3	0
Sweetwater	22	0	8	0	14	77	17	52	8	0
Uinta	7	1	1	1	4	53	12	35	6	0
Washakie	0	0	0	0	0	17	4	13	0	0
Weston	5	0	1	0	4	0	0	0	0	0

NOTE: The data shown in this table do not reflect county totals but are the number of offenses reported by the sheriff's office or county police department.
1 The figures shown in this column for the offense of rape were reported using only the revised Uniform Crime Reporting (UCR) definition of rape. See chapter notes for more detail.   2 The FBI does not publish arson data unless it receives data from either the agency or the state for all 12 months of the calendar year.   3 The FBI determined that the agency's data were overreported. Consequently, those data are not included in this table.   4 The Tulare County Highway Patrol collects the motor vehicle thefts for this county. These data can be found in Table 11.   5 Because of changes in the state/local agency's reporting practices, figures are not comparable to previous years' data.   6 Limited data for 2018 were available for Iowa.   7 This agency/state submits rape data classified according to the legacy UCR definition; therefore the rape offense and violent crime total, which rape is a part of, is not included in this table. See the chapter notes for more detail.   8 The FBI determined that the agency's data were underreported. Consequently, those data are not included in this table.

Table 11. Offenses Known to Law Enforcement, by Selected State, Tribal, and Other Agencies, 2018

(Number.)

State/other agency unit/office	Violent crime	Murder and nonnegligent manslaughter	Rape[1]	Robbery	Aggravated assault	Property crime	Burglary	Larceny-theft	Motor vehicle theft	Arson[2]
ALASKA										
State Agencies										
Alaska state troopers	1,387	12	344	47	984	3,154	1,040	1,639	475	44
Other Agencies										
Fairbanks International Airport	2	0	0	0	2	16	0	13	3	0
Ted Stevens Anchorage International Airport	3	0	1	0	2	206	6	116	84	0
ARIZONA										
Tribal Agencies										
Fort McDowell Tribal	15	0	0	0	15	29	3	25	1	1
Fort Mojave Tribal	19	0	0	0	19	19	0	19	0	0
Hopi Tribal	44	1	1	0	42	120	38	78	4	0
Hualapai Tribal	25	1	0	0	24	89	21	61	7	0
Navajo Nation	2,436	23	205	15	2,193	905	238	339	328	49
Pascua Yaqui Tribal	31	0	3	6	22	273	43	211	19	0
Salt River Tribal	377	2	0	5	370	612	88	472	52	7
Tonto Apache Tribal	1	0	0	1	0	14	2	10	2	0
Yavapai-Apache Nation	7	0	0	0	7	13	3	8	2	0
Other Agencies										
Tucson Airport Authority	0	0	0	0	0	60	4	40	16	0
ARKANSAS										
State Agencies										
State Capitol Police	1	0	0	0	1	35	0	35	0	0
Other Agencies										
Northwest Arkansas Regional Airport	0	0	0	0	0	13	0	12	1	0
CALIFORNIA										
State Agencies										
Atascadero State Hospital	165	0	0	1	164	2	0	1	1	0
California State Fair	6	0	0	2	4	71	38	28	5	0
Department of Parks and Recreation										
Angeles	1	0	0	0	1	26	1	25	0	0
Bay Area	0	0	0	0	0	2	0	2	0	0
Calaveras County	0	0	0	0	0	1	0	0	1	0
Capital	1	0	0	0	1	4	1	3	0	0
Channel Coast	1	0	0	0	1	99	6	92	1	0
Colorado	0	0	0	0	0	0	0	0	0	0
Four Rivers District	0	0	0	0	0	0	0	0	0	0
Gold Fields District	0	0	0	0	0	49	0	49	0	1
Hollister Hills	0	0	0	0	0	0	0	0	0	0
Hungry Valley	1	0	0	0	1	2	2	0	0	0
Inland Empire	0	0	0	0	0	2	1	0	1	0
Marin County	0	0	0	0	0	8	2	6	0	0
Monterey County	0	0	0	0	0	41	15	26	0	0
North Coast Redwoods	0	0	0	0	0	26	2	23	1	3
Northern Buttes	0	0	0	0	0	12	0	12	0	0
Oceano Dunes	8	0	1	1	6	51	0	50	1	3
Ocotillo Wells	0	0	0	0	0	0	0	0	0	0
Orange Coast	0	0	0	0	0	115	82	31	2	0
San Diego Coast	4	0	0	0	4	69	9	59	1	0
San Joaquin	1	0	0	0	1	0	0	0	0	0
San Luis Obispo Coast	0	0	0	0	0	20	1	19	0	0
Santa Cruz Mountains	6	0	2	1	3	95	0	94	1	0
Sierra	0	0	0	0	0	33	1	32	0	0
Sonoma	0	0	0	0	0	0	0	0	0	0
Sonoma-Mendocino Coast	0	0	0	0	0	19	0	19	0	0
Tehachapi District	1	0	0	0	1	10	8	2	0	0
Twin Cities	0	0	0	0	0	0	0	0	0	0
Fairview Developmental Center	0	0	0	0	0	0	0	0	0	0
Highway Patrol										
Alameda County	8	0	0	1	7	185	1	57	127	0
Alpine County	0	0	0	0	0	2	0	1	1	0
Amador County	0	0	0	0	0	35	0	8	27	0
Butte County	0	0	0	0	0	329	1	140	188	0
Calaveras County	0	0	0	0	0	164	0	63	101	0
Colusa County	0	0	0	0	0	19	1	6	12	0
Contra Costa County	1	0	0	0	1	358	0	40	318	0
Del Norte County	0	0	0	0	0	76	0	39	37	0
El Dorado County	0	0	0	0	0	141	0	75	66	0
Fresno County	1	0	0	0	1	226	0	41	185	0
Glenn County	0	0	0	0	0	38	0	13	25	0
Humboldt County	3	0	0	0	3	350	1	82	267	1
Imperial County	1	0	0	0	1	34	0	11	23	0
Inyo County	1	0	0	0	1	23	0	5	18	0
Kern County	1	0	0	0	1	246	0	38	208	0
Kings County	0	0	0	0	0	87	0	13	74	0
Lake County	1	0	0	0	1	170	1	32	137	0
Lassen County	0	0	0	0	0	32	0	7	25	0
Los Angeles County	51	0	0	0	51	647	8	169	470	0
Madera County	2	0	0	1	1	192	3	46	143	0
Marin County	2	0	0	0	2	165	0	134	31	0

Table 11. Offenses Known to Law Enforcement, by Selected State, Tribal, and Other Agencies, 2018—Continued

(Number.)

State/other agency unit/office	Violent crime	Murder and nonnegligent manslaughter	Rape[1]	Robbery	Aggravated assault	Property crime	Burglary	Larceny-theft	Motor vehicle theft	Arson[2]
Mariposa County	0	0	0	0	0	19	0	11	8	0
Mendocino County	9	7	0	0	2	146	1	43	102	0
Merced County	0	0	0	0	0	466	0	97	369	0
Modoc County	0	0	0	0	0	15	0	7	8	0
Mono County	0	0	0	0	0	6	0	5	1	0
Monterey County	0	0	0	0	0	289	0	66	223	0
Napa County	0	0	0	0	0	17	0	6	11	0
Nevada County	0	0	0	0	0	94	2	13	79	0
Orange County	7	0	0	0	7	115	1	47	67	0
Placer County	7	0	0	0	7	186	1	65	120	0
Plumas County	0	0	0	0	0	28	0	11	17	0
Riverside County	11	0	0	0	11	91	3	39	49	0
Sacramento County	9	1	0	1	7	3,662	6	1,344	2,312	1
San Benito County	0	0	0	0	0	19	0	5	14	0
San Bernardino County	44	0	0	2	42	169	6	70	93	0
San Diego County	31	0	0	0	31	157	2	52	103	0
San Francisco County	5	1	0	0	4	35	0	19	16	0
San Joaquin County	2	0	0	0	2	689	0	194	495	0
San Luis Obispo County	1	0	0	0	1	94	0	31	63	0
San Mateo County	4	0	0	0	4	22	0	10	12	1
Santa Barbara County	2	0	0	0	2	140	5	49	86	0
Santa Clara County	3	0	0	0	3	115	0	19	96	0
Santa Cruz County	0	0	0	0	0	513	2	220	291	0
Shasta County	1	0	0	0	1	331	2	86	243	0
Sierra County	0	0	0	0	0	0	0	0	0	0
Siskiyou County	0	0	0	0	0	49	1	19	29	0
Solano County	3	0	0	0	3	57	0	13	44	0
Sonoma County	0	0	0	0	0	143	0	85	58	0
Stanislaus County	0	0	0	0	0	390	5	162	223	0
Sutter County	0	0	0	0	0	58	0	20	38	0
Tehama County	0	0	0	0	0	157	2	59	96	0
Trinity County	2	0	0	0	2	63	0	15	48	0
Tulare County	0	0	0	0	0	897	0	106	791	55
Tuolumne County	1	0	0	0	1	144	1	65	78	0
Ventura County	5	0	0	0	5	43	0	21	22	0
Yolo County	0	0	0	0	0	43	1	17	25	0
Yuba County	1	0	0	1	0	359	0	82	277	0
Metropolitan State Hospital	1,134	0	10	0	1,124	6	2	4	0	0
Napa State Hospital	265	0	7	2	256	6	0	6	0	0
Patton State Hospital	360	0	2	0	358	3	2	1	0	0
Porterville Developmental Center	70	0	2	1	67	5	2	3	0	0
Sonoma Developmental Center	1	0	0	0	1	0	0	0	0	0
Tribal Agencies										
Blue Lake Tribal	4	0	1	1	2	75	0	71	4	
Hoopa Valley Tribal	40	0	0	1	39	40	15	24	1	1
La Jolla Tribal	4	0	0	0	4	2	2	0	0	0
Los Coyotes Tribal	3	0	0	0	3	2	1	1	0	
Sycuan Tribal	16	0	1	3	12	62	23	25	14	
Table Mountain Rancheria	4	0	0	3	1	113	4	97	12	0
Yurok Tribal	7	0	0	1	6	23	6	14	3	0
Other Agencies										
East Bay Regional Park District	43	1	3	12	27	398	103	283	12	13
Fontana Unified School District	27	0	1	3	23	51	23	28	0	1
Kern High School District	40	0	1	8	31	141	54	84	3	10
Los Angeles County Metropolitan Transportation Authority	2	0	0	1	1	6	0	6	0	0
Los Angeles Transportation Services Bureau	185	1	3	97	84	217	4	186	27	0
Monterey Peninsula Airport	0	0	0	0	0	4	1	2	1	0
San Bernardino Unified School District	42	0	1	39	2	237	103	122	12	6
San Francisco Bay Area Rapid Transit										
Alameda County	303	2	3	211	87	1,484	11	1,272	201	2
Contra Costa County	50	1	0	29	20	805	1	669	135	1
San Francisco County	115	0	0	97	18	480	6	473	1	0
San Mateo County	13	0	0	8	5	179	0	161	18	0
Santa Clara Transit District	79	0	4	39	36	122	0	86	36	0
Shasta County Marshal	0	0	0	0	0	1	1	0	0	0
Stockton Unified School District	45	0	0	18	27	180	48	125	7	1
Twin Rivers Unified School District	17	0	0	3	14	82	53	21	8	0
Union Pacific Railroad										
Alameda County	0	0	0	0	0	12	6	6	0	0
Amador County	0	0	0	0	0	0	0	0	0	0
Butte County	0	0	0	0	0	5	2	3	0	0
Calaveras County	0	0	0	0	0	0	0	0	0	0
Colusa County	0	0	0	0	0	0	0	0	0	0
Contra Costa County	0	0	0	0	0	2	2	0	0	0
El Dorado County	0	0	0	0	0	0	0	0	0	0
Fresno County	0	0	0	0	0	3	0	3	0	0
Glenn County	0	0	0	0	0	0	0	0	0	0
Humboldt County	0	0	0	0	0	0	0	0	0	0
Imperial County	0	0	0	0	0	3	2	1	0	0
Inyo County	0	0	0	0	0	0	0	0	0	0
Kern County	1	0	0	0	1	33	10	23	0	1

Table 11. Offenses Known to Law Enforcement, by Selected State, Tribal, and Other Agencies, 2018—Continued

(Number.)

State/other agency unit/office	Violent crime	Murder and nonnegligent manslaughter	Rape[1]	Robbery	Aggravated assault	Property crime	Burglary	Larceny-theft	Motor vehicle theft	Arson[2]
Kings County	0	0	0	0	0	0	0	0	0	0
Lassen County	0	0	0	0	0	1	0	1	0	0
Los Angeles County	0	0	0	0	0	611	376	235	0	1
Madera County	0	0	0	0	0	0	0	0	0	0
Marin County	0	0	0	0	0	0	0	0	0	0
Mendocino County	0	0	0	0	0	0	0	0	0	0
Merced County	0	0	0	0	0	0	0	0	0	0
Modoc County	0	0	0	0	0	0	0	0	0	0
Monterey County	0	0	0	0	0	1	0	1	0	0
Napa County	0	0	0	0	0	0	0	0	0	0
Nevada County	0	0	0	0	0	0	0	0	0	0
Orange County	1	0	0	0	1	2	1	1	0	0
Placer County	0	0	0	0	0	7	1	6	0	0
Plumas County	0	0	0	0	0	1	0	1	0	0
Riverside County	0	0	0	0	0	18	6	12	0	0
Sacramento County	0	0	0	0	0	3	0	3	0	0
San Benito County	0	0	0	0	0	0	0	0	0	0
San Bernardino County	0	0	0	0	0	28	18	10	0	0
San Francisco County	0	0	0	0	0	0	0	0	0	0
San Joaquin County	0	0	0	0	0	56	17	39	0	0
San Luis Obispo County	0	0	0	0	0	1	0	1	0	0
San Mateo County	0	0	0	0	0	0	0	0	0	0
Santa Barbara County	1	0	0	0	1	3	0	3	0	1
Santa Clara County	0	0	0	0	0	4	0	4	0	0
Santa Cruz County	0	0	0	0	0	0	0	0	0	0
Shasta County	1	0	0	0	1	6	0	6	0	0
Sierra County	0	0	0	0	0	0	0	0	0	0
Siskiyou County	0	0	0	0	0	1	1	0	0	0
Solano County	0	0	0	0	0	0	0	0	0	0
Sonoma County	0	0	0	0	0	0	0	0	0	0
Stanislaus County	0	0	0	0	0	3	2	1	0	0
Sutter County	0	0	0	0	0	0	0	0	0	0
Tehama County	0	0	0	0	0	1	0	1	0	0
Trinity County	0	0	0	0	0	0	0	0	0	0
Tulare County	0	0	0	0	0	1	0	1	0	0
Ventura County	0	0	0	0	0	1	0	1	0	0
Yolo County	0	0	0	0	0	1	0	1	0	0
Yuba County	0	0	0	0	0	3	1	2	0	0
COLORADO										
State Agencies										
Colorado Mental Health Institute	0	0	0	0	0	5	0	5	0	0
State Patrol	12	0	0	0	12	19	0	6	13	0
Tribal Agencies										
Southern Ute Tribal	14	0	1	0	13	33	6	23	4	1
Other Agencies										
All Crimes Enforcement Team	0	0	0	0	0	1	0	1	0	0
Delta Montrose Drug Task Force	0	0	0	0	0	1	0	1	0	0
Southwest Drug Task Force	0	0	0	0	0	0	0	0	0	0
CONNECTICUT										
State Agencies										
Connecticut State Police	299	8	86	40	165	2,161	506	1,281	374	11
Department of Motor Vehicles	0	0	0	0	0	1	0	0	1	0
State Capitol Police	0	0	0	0	0	2	0	2	0	0
Tribal Agencies										
Mashantucket Pequot Tribal	23	0	3	3	17	212	6	200	6	1
Mohegan Tribal	12	0	1	2	9	257	0	252	5	0
Other Agencies										
Metropolitan Transportation Authority	4	0	0	2	2	57	0	57	0	0
DELAWARE										
State Agencies										
Alcohol and Tobacco Enforcement	2	0	0	0	2	1	0	1	0	0
Animal Welfare										
Kent County	0	0	0	0	0	0	0	0	0	0
New Castle County	0	0	0	0	0	0	0	0	0	0
Sussex County	0	0	0	0	0	0	0	0	0	0
Attorney General, New Castle County	0	0	0	0	0	0	0	0	0	0
Environmental Control	0	0	0	0	0	6	0	6	0	0
Fish and Wildlife	1	0	0	0	1	12	0	12	0	1
Park Rangers	2	0	0	0	2	75	23	51	1	0
River and Bay Authority	3	0	0	0	3	5	1	4	0	0
State Capitol Police	2	0	0	0	2	13	1	11	1	0
State Fire Marshal	20	0	0	0	20	4	4	0	0	113
State Police										
Headquarters	0	0	0	0	0	3	0	3	0	0
Kent County	260	2	45	21	192	962	211	694	57	1
New Castle County	423	4	35	141	243	4,416	297	3,944	175	1
Sussex County	469	6	67	38	358	2,586	648	1,835	103	3
Other Agencies										
Amtrak Police	1	0	0	0	1	3	0	3	0	0

Table 11. Offenses Known to Law Enforcement, by Selected State, Tribal, and Other Agencies, 2018—Continued

(Number.)

State/other agency unit/office	Violent crime	Murder and nonnegligent manslaughter	Rape[1]	Robbery	Aggravated assault	Property crime	Burglary	Larceny-theft	Motor vehicle theft	Arson[2]
DISTRICT OF COLUMBIA										
Other Agencies										
District of Columbia Fire and Emergency Medical Services, Arson Investigation Unit	0	0	0	0	0	0	0	0	0	190
Metro Transit Police	383	0	5	258	120	731	2	685	44	4
FLORIDA										
State Agencies										
Capitol Police	0	0	0	0	0	14	1	13	0	0
Department of Corrections, Office of the Inspector General										
Alachua County	0	0	0	0	0	0	0	0	0	0
Baker County	0	0	0	0	0	0	0	0	0	0
Bay County	0	0	0	0	0	0	0	0	0	0
Bradford County	0	0	0	0	0	0	0	0	0	0
Brevard County	0	0	0	0	0	0	0	0	0	0
Broward County	0	0	0	0	0	0	0	0	0	0
Calhoun County	0	0	0	0	0	0	0	0	0	0
Charlotte County	0	0	0	0	0	0	0	0	0	0
Citrus County	0	0	0	0	0	0	0	0	0	0
Clay County	0	0	0	0	0	0	0	0	0	0
Collier County	0	0	0	0	0	0	0	0	0	0
Columbia County	0	0	0	0	0	0	0	0	0	0
DeSoto County	0	0	0	0	0	0	0	0	0	0
Dixie County	0	0	0	0	0	0	0	0	0	0
Duval County	0	0	0	0	0	0	0	0	0	0
Escambia County	0	0	0	0	0	0	0	0	0	0
Flagler County	0	0	0	0	0	0	0	0	0	0
Franklin County	0	0	0	0	0	0	0	0	0	0
Gadsden County	0	0	0	0	0	0	0	0	0	0
Gilchrist County	0	0	0	0	0	0	0	0	0	0
Glades County	0	0	0	0	0	0	0	0	0	0
Gulf County	0	0	0	0	0	0	0	0	0	0
Hamilton County	0	0	0	0	0	0	0	0	0	0
Hardee County	0	0	0	0	0	0	0	0	0	0
Hendry County	0	0	0	0	0	0	0	0	0	0
Hernando County	0	0	0	0	0	0	0	0	0	0
Highlands County	0	0	0	0	0	0	0	0	0	0
Hillsborough County	0	0	0	0	0	0	0	0	0	0
Holmes County	0	0	0	0	0	0	0	0	0	0
Indian River County	0	0	0	0	0	0	0	0	0	0
Jackson County	0	0	0	0	0	0	0	0	0	0
Jefferson County	0	0	0	0	0	0	0	0	0	0
Lafayette County	0	0	0	0	0	0	0	0	0	0
Lake County	0	0	0	0	0	0	0	0	0	0
Lee County	0	0	0	0	0	0	0	0	0	0
Leon County	0	0	0	0	0	0	0	0	0	0
Levy County	0	0	0	0	0	0	0	0	0	0
Liberty County	0	0	0	0	0	0	0	0	0	0
Madison County	0	0	0	0	0	0	0	0	0	0
Manatee County	0	0	0	0	0	0	0	0	0	0
Marion County	0	0	0	0	0	0	0	0	0	0
Martin County	0	0	0	0	0	0	0	0	0	0
Miami-Dade County	0	0	0	0	0	0	0	0	0	0
Monroe County	0	0	0	0	0	0	0	0	0	0
Nassau County	0	0	0	0	0	0	0	0	0	0
Okaloosa County	0	0	0	0	0	0	0	0	0	0
Okeechobee County	0	0	0	0	0	0	0	0	0	0
Orange County	0	0	0	0	0	0	0	0	0	0
Osceola County	0	0	0	0	0	0	0	0	0	0
Palm Beach County	0	0	0	0	0	0	0	0	0	0
Pasco County	0	0	0	0	0	0	0	0	0	0
Pinellas County	0	0	0	0	0	0	0	0	0	0
Polk County	0	0	0	0	0	0	0	0	0	0
Putnam County	0	0	0	0	0	0	0	0	0	0
Santa Rosa County	0	0	0	0	0	0	0	0	0	0
Sarasota County	0	0	0	0	0	0	0	0	0	0
Seminole County	0	0	0	0	0	0	0	0	0	0
St. Johns County	0	0	0	0	0	0	0	0	0	0
St. Lucie County	0	0	0	0	0	0	0	0	0	0
Sumter County	0	0	0	0	0	0	0	0	0	0
Suwannee County	0	0	0	0	0	0	0	0	0	0
Taylor County	0	0	0	0	0	0	0	0	0	0
Union County	0	0	0	0	0	0	0	0	0	0
Volusia County	0	0	0	0	0	0	0	0	0	0
Wakulla County	0	0	0	0	0	0	0	0	0	0
Walton County	0	0	0	0	0	0	0	0	0	0
Washington County	0	0	0	0	0	0	0	0	0	0
Department of Law Enforcement										
Duval County, Jacksonville	0	0	0	0	0	0	0	0	0	0
Escambia County, Pensacola	1	0	0	0	1	0	0	0	0	0

Table 11. Offenses Known to Law Enforcement, by Selected State, Tribal, and Other Agencies, 2018—Continued

(Number.)

State/other agency unit/office	Violent crime	Murder and nonnegligent manslaughter	Rape[1]	Robbery	Aggravated assault	Property crime	Burglary	Larceny-theft	Motor vehicle theft	Arson[2]
Hillsborough County, Tampa	1	0	1	0	0	2	0	2	0	0
Lee County, Fort Myers	0	0	0	0	0	0	0	0	0	0
Leon County, Tallahassee	0	0	0	0	0	3	0	3	0	0
Miami-Dade County, Miami	0	0	0	0	0	0	0	0	0	0
Orange County, Orlando	1	1	0	0	0	10	0	10	0	0
Division of Alcoholic Beverages and Tobacco										
Alachua County	0	0	0	0	0	0	0	0	0	0
Baker County	0	0	0	0	0	0	0	0	0	0
Bay County	0	0	0	0	0	0	0	0	0	0
Bradford County	0	0	0	0	0	0	0	0	0	0
Brevard County	0	0	0	0	0	0	0	0	0	0
Broward County	0	0	0	0	0	0	0	0	0	0
Calhoun County	0	0	0	0	0	0	0	0	0	0
Charlotte County	0	0	0	0	0	0	0	0	0	0
Citrus County	0	0	0	0	0	0	0	0	0	0
Clay County	0	0	0	0	0	0	0	0	0	0
Collier County	0	0	0	0	0	0	0	0	0	0
Columbia County	0	0	0	0	0	0	0	0	0	0
DeSoto County	0	0	0	0	0	0	0	0	0	0
Dixie County	0	0	0	0	0	0	0	0	0	0
Duval County	0	0	0	0	0	0	0	0	0	0
Escambia County	0	0	0	0	0	0	0	0	0	0
Flagler County	0	0	0	0	0	0	0	0	0	0
Franklin County	0	0	0	0	0	0	0	0	0	0
Gadsden County	0	0	0	0	0	0	0	0	0	0
Gilchrist County	0	0	0	0	0	0	0	0	0	0
Glades County	0	0	0	0	0	0	0	0	0	0
Gulf County	0	0	0	0	0	0	0	0	0	0
Hamilton County	0	0	0	0	0	0	0	0	0	0
Hardee County	0	0	0	0	0	0	0	0	0	0
Hendry County	0	0	0	0	0	0	0	0	0	0
Hernando County	0	0	0	0	0	0	0	0	0	0
Highlands County	0	0	0	0	0	0	0	0	0	0
Hillsborough County	0	0	0	0	0	0	0	0	0	0
Holmes County	0	0	0	0	0	0	0	0	0	0
Indian River County	0	0	0	0	0	0	0	0	0	0
Jackson County	0	0	0	0	0	0	0	0	0	0
Jefferson County	0	0	0	0	0	0	0	0	0	0
Lafayette County	0	0	0	0	0	0	0	0	0	0
Lake County	0	0	0	0	0	0	0	0	0	0
Lee County	0	0	0	0	0	0	0	0	0	0
Leon County	0	0	0	0	0	0	0	0	0	0
Levy County	0	0	0	0	0	0	0	0	0	0
Liberty County	0	0	0	0	0	0	0	0	0	0
Madison County	0	0	0	0	0	0	0	0	0	0
Manatee County	0	0	0	0	0	0	0	0	0	0
Marion County	0	0	0	0	0	0	0	0	0	0
Martin County	0	0	0	0	0	0	0	0	0	0
Miami-Dade County	0	0	0	0	0	0	0	0	0	0
Monroe County	0	0	0	0	0	0	0	0	0	0
Nassau County	0	0	0	0	0	0	0	0	0	0
Okaloosa County	0	0	0	0	0	0	0	0	0	0
Okeechobee County	0	0	0	0	0	0	0	0	0	0
Orange County	0	0	0	0	0	0	0	0	0	0
Osceola County	0	0	0	0	0	0	0	0	0	0
Palm Beach County	0	0	0	0	0	0	0	0	0	0
Pasco County	0	0	0	0	0	0	0	0	0	0
Pinellas County	0	0	0	0	0	0	0	0	0	0
Polk County	0	0	0	0	0	0	0	0	0	0
Putnam County	0	0	0	0	0	0	0	0	0	0
Santa Rosa County	0	0	0	0	0	0	0	0	0	0
Sarasota County	0	0	0	0	0	0	0	0	0	0
Seminole County	0	0	0	0	0	0	0	0	0	0
St. Johns County	0	0	0	0	0	0	0	0	0	0
St. Lucie County	0	0	0	0	0	0	0	0	0	0
Sumter County	0	0	0	0	0	0	0	0	0	0
Suwannee County	0	0	0	0	0	0	0	0	0	0
Taylor County	0	0	0	0	0	0	0	0	0	0
Union County	0	0	0	0	0	0	0	0	0	0
Volusia County	0	0	0	0	0	0	0	0	0	0
Wakulla County	0	0	0	0	0	0	0	0	0	0
Walton County	0	0	0	0	0	0	0	0	0	0
Washington County	0	0	0	0	0	0	0	0	0	0
Broward County	0	0	0	0	0	0	0	0	0	0
Duval County	0	0	0	0	0	0	0	0	0	0
Escambia County	0	0	0	0	0	0	0	0	0	0
Hillsborough County	0	0	0	0	0	0	0	0	0	0
Lee County	0	0	0	0	0	0	0	0	0	0
Leon County	0	0	0	0	0	0	0	0	0	0
Miami-Dade County	0	0	0	0	0	0	0	0	0	0
Orange County	0	0	0	0	0	0	0	0	0	0
Palm Beach County	0	0	0	0	0	0	0	0	0	0

Table 11. Offenses Known to Law Enforcement, by Selected State, Tribal, and Other Agencies, 2018—Continued

(Number.)

State/other agency unit/office	Violent crime	Murder and nonnegligent manslaughter	Rape[1]	Robbery	Aggravated assault	Property crime	Burglary	Larceny-theft	Motor vehicle theft	Arson[2]
Pinellas County	0	0	0	0	0	0	0	0	0	0
Alachua County	0	0	0	0	0	0	0	0	0	0
Baker County	0	0	0	0	0	0	0	0	0	0
Bay County	0	0	0	0	0	0	0	0	0	0
Bradford County	0	0	0	0	0	0	0	0	0	0
Brevard County	0	0	0	0	0	0	0	0	0	0
Broward County	0	0	0	0	0	0	0	0	0	0
Calhoun County	0	0	0	0	0	0	0	0	0	0
Charlotte County	0	0	0	0	0	0	0	0	0	0
Citrus County	0	0	0	0	0	0	0	0	0	0
Clay County	0	0	0	0	0	0	0	0	0	0
Collier County	0	0	0	0	0	0	0	0	0	0
Columbia County	0	0	0	0	0	0	0	0	0	0
DeSoto County	0	0	0	0	0	0	0	0	0	0
Dixie County	0	0	0	0	0	0	0	0	0	0
Duval County	0	0	0	0	0	0	0	0	0	0
Escambia County	0	0	0	0	0	0	0	0	0	0
Flagler County	0	0	0	0	0	0	0	0	0	0
Franklin County	0	0	0	0	0	0	0	0	0	0
Gadsden County	0	0	0	0	0	0	0	0	0	0
Gilchrist County	0	0	0	0	0	0	0	0	0	0
Glades County	0	0	0	0	0	0	0	0	0	0
Gulf County	0	0	0	0	0	0	0	0	0	0
Hamilton County	0	0	0	0	0	0	0	0	0	0
Hardee County	0	0	0	0	0	0	0	0	0	0
Hendry County	0	0	0	0	0	0	0	0	0	0
Hernando County	0	0	0	0	0	0	0	0	0	0
Highlands County	0	0	0	0	0	0	0	0	0	0
Hillsborough County	0	0	0	0	0	0	0	0	0	0
Holmes County	0	0	0	0	0	0	0	0	0	0
Indian River County	0	0	0	0	0	0	0	0	0	0
Jackson County	0	0	0	0	0	0	0	0	0	0
Jefferson County	0	0	0	0	0	0	0	0	0	0
Lafayette County	0	0	0	0	0	0	0	0	0	0
Lake County	0	0	0	0	0	0	0	0	0	0
Lee County	0	0	0	0	0	0	0	0	0	0
Leon County	0	0	0	0	0	0	0	0	0	0
Levy County	0	0	0	0	0	0	0	0	0	0
Liberty County	0	0	0	0	0	0	0	0	0	0
Madison County	0	0	0	0	0	0	0	0	0	0
Manatee County	0	0	0	0	0	0	0	0	0	0
Marion County	0	0	0	0	0	0	0	0	0	0
Martin County	0	0	0	0	0	0	0	0	0	0
Miami-Dade County	0	0	0	0	0	0	0	0	0	0
Monroe County	0	0	0	0	0	0	0	0	0	0
Nassau County	0	0	0	0	0	0	0	0	0	0
Okaloosa County	0	0	0	0	0	0	0	0	0	0
Okeechobee County	0	0	0	0	0	0	0	0	0	0
Orange County	0	0	0	0	0	0	0	0	0	0
Osceola County	0	0	0	0	0	0	0	0	0	0
Palm Beach County	0	0	0	0	0	0	0	0	0	0
Pasco County	0	0	0	0	0	0	0	0	0	0
Pinellas County	0	0	0	0	0	0	0	0	0	0
Polk County	0	0	0	0	0	0	0	0	0	0
Putnam County	0	0	0	0	0	0	0	0	0	0
Santa Rosa County	0	0	0	0	0	0	0	0	0	0
Sarasota County	0	0	0	0	0	0	0	0	0	0
Seminole County	0	0	0	0	0	0	0	0	0	0
St. Johns County	0	0	0	0	0	0	0	0	0	0
St. Lucie County	0	0	0	0	0	0	0	0	0	0
Sumter County	0	0	0	0	0	0	0	0	0	0
Suwannee County	0	0	0	0	0	0	0	0	0	0
Taylor County	0	0	0	0	0	0	0	0	0	0
Union County	0	0	0	0	0	0	0	0	0	0
Volusia County	0	0	0	0	0	0	0	0	0	0
Wakulla County	0	0	0	0	0	0	0	0	0	0
Walton County	0	0	0	0	0	0	0	0	0	0
Washington County	0	0	0	0	0	0	0	0	0	0
Division of Investigative and Forensic Services										
Broward County	0	0	0	0	0	0	0	0	0	0
Duval County	0	0	0	0	0	0	0	0	0	0
Escambia County	0	0	0	0	0	0	0	0	0	0
Hillsborough County	0	0	0	0	0	0	0	0	0	0
Lee County	0	0	0	0	0	0	0	0	0	0
Leon County	0	0	0	0	0	0	0	0	0	0
Miami-Dade County	0	0	0	0	0	0	0	0	0	0
Orange County	0	0	0	0	0	0	0	0	0	0
Palm Beach County	0	0	0	0	0	0	0	0	0	0
Pinellas County	0	0	0	0	0	0	0	0	0	0
Fish and Wildlife Conservation Commission										
Alachua County	0	0	0	0	0	0	0	0	0	0

Table 11. Offenses Known to Law Enforcement, by Selected State, Tribal, and Other Agencies, 2018—Continued

(Number.)

State/other agency unit/office	Violent crime	Murder and nonnegligent manslaughter	Rape[1]	Robbery	Aggravated assault	Property crime	Burglary	Larceny-theft	Motor vehicle theft	Arson[2]
Baker County	0	0	0	0	0	0	0	0	0	0
Bay County	0	0	0	0	0	0	0	0	0	0
Bradford County	0	0	0	0	0	0	0	0	0	0
Brevard County	0	0	0	0	0	0	0	0	0	0
Broward County	0	0	0	0	0	0	0	0	0	0
Calhoun County	0	0	0	0	0	0	0	0	0	0
Charlotte County	0	0	0	0	0	0	0	0	0	0
Citrus County	0	0	0	0	0	0	0	0	0	0
Clay County	0	0	0	0	0	0	0	0	0	0
Collier County	0	0	0	0	0	0	0	0	0	0
Columbia County	0	0	0	0	0	0	0	0	0	0
DeSoto County	0	0	0	0	0	0	0	0	0	0
Dixie County	0	0	0	0	0	0	0	0	0	0
Duval County	0	0	0	0	0	0	0	0	0	0
Escambia County	0	0	0	0	0	0	0	0	0	0
Flagler County	0	0	0	0	0	0	0	0	0	0
Franklin County	0	0	0	0	0	0	0	0	0	0
Gadsden County	0	0	0	0	0	0	0	0	0	0
Gilchrist County	0	0	0	0	0	0	0	0	0	0
Glades County	0	0	0	0	0	0	0	0	0	0
Gulf County	0	0	0	0	0	0	0	0	0	0
Hamilton County	0	0	0	0	0	0	0	0	0	0
Hardee County	0	0	0	0	0	0	0	0	0	0
Hendry County	0	0	0	0	0	0	0	0	0	0
Hernando County	0	0	0	0	0	0	0	0	0	0
Highlands County	0	0	0	0	0	0	0	0	0	0
Hillsborough County	0	0	0	0	0	0	0	0	0	0
Holmes County	0	0	0	0	0	0	0	0	0	0
Indian River County	0	0	0	0	0	0	0	0	0	0
Jackson County	0	0	0	0	0	0	0	0	0	0
Jefferson County	0	0	0	0	0	0	0	0	0	0
Lafayette County	0	0	0	0	0	0	0	0	0	0
Lake County	0	0	0	0	0	0	0	0	0	0
Lee County	0	0	0	0	0	0	0	0	0	0
Leon County	0	0	0	0	0	0	0	0	0	0
Levy County	0	0	0	0	0	0	0	0	0	0
Liberty County	0	0	0	0	0	0	0	0	0	0
Madison County	0	0	0	0	0	0	0	0	0	0
Manatee County	0	0	0	0	0	0	0	0	0	0
Marion County	0	0	0	0	0	0	0	0	0	0
Martin County	0	0	0	0	0	0	0	0	0	0
Miami-Dade County	0	0	0	0	0	0	0	0	0	0
Monroe County	0	0	0	0	0	0	0	0	0	0
Nassau County	0	0	0	0	0	0	0	0	0	0
Okaloosa County	0	0	0	0	0	0	0	0	0	0
Okeechobee County	0	0	0	0	0	0	0	0	0	0
Orange County	0	0	0	0	0	0	0	0	0	0
Osceola County	0	0	0	0	0	0	0	0	0	0
Palm Beach County	0	0	0	0	0	0	0	0	0	0
Pasco County	0	0	0	0	0	0	0	0	0	0
Pinellas County	0	0	0	0	0	0	0	0	0	0
Polk County	0	0	0	0	0	0	0	0	0	0
Putnam County	0	0	0	0	0	0	0	0	0	0
Santa Rosa County	0	0	0	0	0	0	0	0	0	0
Sarasota County	0	0	0	0	0	0	0	0	0	0
Seminole County	0	0	0	0	0	0	0	0	0	0
St. Johns County	0	0	0	0	0	0	0	0	0	0
St. Lucie County	0	0	0	0	0	0	0	0	0	0
Sumter County	0	0	0	0	0	0	0	0	0	0
Suwannee County	0	0	0	0	0	0	0	0	0	0
Taylor County	0	0	0	0	0	0	0	0	0	0
Union County	0	0	0	0	0	0	0	0	0	0
Volusia County	0	0	0	0	0	0	0	0	0	0
Wakulla County	0	0	0	0	0	0	0	0	0	0
Walton County	0	0	0	0	0	0	0	0	0	0
Washington County	0	0	0	0	0	0	0	0	0	0
Highway Patrol										
Alachua County	4	0	0	0	4	34	0	14	20	0
Baker County	1	0	0	0	1	1	0	1	0	0
Bay County	5	0	0	0	5	75	0	72	3	0
Bradford County	0	0	0	0	0	8	0	7	1	0
Brevard County	0	0	0	0	0	2	0	2	0	0
Broward County	4	0	0	0	4	11	0	9	2	0
Calhoun County	0	0	0	0	0	0	0	0	0	0
Charlotte County	0	0	0	0	0	0	0	0	0	0
Citrus County	0	0	0	0	0	2	0	1	1	0
Clay County	9	0	0	9	0	1	0	1	0	0
Collier County	0	0	0	0	0	48	0	48	0	0
Columbia County	53	0	0	0	53	56	0	1	55	0
DeSoto County	0	0	0	0	0	0	0	0	0	0
Dixie County	0	0	0	0	0	8	0	4	4	0
Duval County	6	0	0	0	6	172	0	118	54	0
Escambia County	4	0	0	0	4	11	0	11	0	0
Flagler County	0	0	0	0	0	3	0	3	0	0

Table 11. Offenses Known to Law Enforcement, by Selected State, Tribal, and Other Agencies, 2018—Continued

(Number.)

State/other agency unit/office	Violent crime	Murder and nonnegligent manslaughter	Rape[1]	Robbery	Aggravated assault	Property crime	Burglary	Larceny-theft	Motor vehicle theft	Arson[2]
Franklin County	0	0	0	0	0	0	0	0	0	0
Gadsden County	13	0	0	0	13	6	0	6	0	0
Gilchrist County	0	0	0	0	0	0	0	0	0	0
Glades County	0	0	0	0	0	0	0	0	0	0
Gulf County	0	0	0	0	0	0	0	0	0	0
Hamilton County	0	0	0	0	0	1	0	0	1	0
Hardee County	0	0	0	0	0	0	0	0	0	0
Hendry County	0	0	0	0	0	0	0	0	0	0
Hernando County	2	0	0	0	2	8	0	1	7	0
Highlands County	0	0	0	0	0	0	0	0	0	0
Hillsborough County	106	0	0	0	106	116	0	68	48	0
Holmes County	0	0	0	0	0	0	0	0	0	0
Indian River County	0	0	0	0	0	1	0	1	0	0
Jackson County	0	0	0	0	0	39	0	3	36	0
Jefferson County	0	0	0	0	0	2	0	1	1	0
Lafayette County	0	0	0	0	0	0	0	0	0	0
Lake County	3	0	0	0	3	0	0	0	0	0
Lee County	1	0	0	0	1	21	0	17	4	0
Leon County	1	0	0	0	1	35	0	29	6	0
Levy County	0	0	0	0	0	0	0	0	0	0
Liberty County	0	0	0	0	0	0	0	0	0	0
Madison County	0	0	0	0	0	4	0	4	0	0
Manatee County	2	0	0	0	2	7	0	7	0	0
Marion County	1	0	0	0	1	37	0	37	0	0
Martin County	0	0	0	0	0	0	0	0	0	0
Miami-Dade County	8	0	0	1	7	70	0	70	0	1
Monroe County	1	0	0	0	1	0	0	0	0	0
Nassau County	0	0	0	0	0	1	0	1	0	0
Okaloosa County	0	0	0	0	0	0	0	0	0	0
Okeechobee County	0	0	0	0	0	7	0	0	7	0
Orange County	4	0	0	0	4	33	0	33	0	3
Osceola County	10	0	0	0	10	3	0	3	0	0
Palm Beach County	22	0	0	0	22	19	0	15	4	1
Pasco County	34	0	0	0	34	117	0	116	1	1
Pinellas County	7	0	0	0	7	1	0	1	0	0
Polk County	1	0	0	0	1	4	0	4	0	0
Putnam County	0	0	0	0	0	0	0	0	0	0
Santa Rosa County	0	0	0	0	0	1	0	1	0	0
Sarasota County	0	0	0	0	0	0	0	0	0	0
Seminole County	3	0	0	0	3	2	0	2	0	0
St. Johns County	3	0	0	0	3	57	0	51	6	0
St. Lucie County	20	0	0	0	20	114	0	94	20	0
Sumter County	0	0	0	0	0	59	0	14	45	0
Suwannee County	14	0	0	0	14	2	0	2	0	0
Taylor County	1	0	0	0	1	1	0	1	0	0
Union County	0	0	0	0	0	0	0	0	0	0
Volusia County	0	0	0	0	0	5	0	1	4	0
Wakulla County	1	0	0	0	1	0	0	0	0	0
Walton County	20	0	0	0	20	0	0	0	0	0
Washington County	0	0	0	0	0	0	0	0	0	0
Tribal Agencies										
Miccosukee Tribal	9	0	1	1	7	211	7	196	8	0
Seminole Tribal	71	0	5	30	36	687	34	617	36	0
Other Agencies										
Duval County Schools	35	1	4	1	29	296	107	181	8	1
Florida School for the Deaf and Blind	0	0	0	0	0	0	0	0	0	0
Fort Lauderdale Airport	6	0	0	4	2	419	3	339	77	0
Jacksonville Aviation Authority	2	0	0	0	2	101	1	36	64	0
Lee County Port Authority	0	0	0	0	0	36	0	36	0	0
Melbourne International Airport	0	0	0	0	0	17	2	8	7	0
Miami-Dade County Public Schools	129	0	7	27	95	507	147	348	12	2
Northwest Florida Beaches International Airport	0	0	0	0	0	2	0	2	0	0
Palm Beach County School District	57	0	6	13	38	436	10	420	6	1
Port Everglades	15	0	7	0	8	72	4	68	0	0
Sarasota-Manatee Airport Authority	0	0	0	0	0	39	0	6	33	0
St. Petersburg-Clearwater International Airport	0	0	0	0	0	9	0	6	3	0
Tampa International Airport	7	0	1	0	6	188	10	122	56	0
Volusia County Beach Safety	15	0	3	2	10	85	3	80	2	0
GEORGIA										
State Agencies										
Georgia Department of Public Safety	25	2	0	1	22	0	0	0	0	0
Georgia Department of Transportation, Office of Investigations	0	0	0	0	0	0	0	0	0	0
Georgia Forestry Commission	0	0	0	0	0	0	0	0	0	19
Georgia Public Safety Training Center	0	0	0	0	0	0	0	0	0	0
Georgia World Congress	6	0	0	4	2	198	1	195	2	0
Ports Authority, Savannah[3]	1	0	0	0	1	18	2	15	1	0
State Board of Workers Compensation, Fraud Investigation Division	0	0	0	0	0	0	0	0	0	0
State Patrol, Jekyll Island	0	0	0	0	0	4	0	4	0	0

Table 11. Offenses Known to Law Enforcement, by Selected State, Tribal, and Other Agencies, 2018—Continued

(Number.)

State/other agency unit/office	Violent crime	Murder and nonnegligent manslaughter	Rape[1]	Robbery	Aggravated assault	Property crime	Burglary	Larceny-theft	Motor vehicle theft	Arson[2]
Other Agencies										
Appling County Board of Education	0	0	0	0	0	2	0	2	0	0
Atlanta Public Schools	31	0	13	5	13	242	28	199	15	2
Augusta Board of Education	1	0	0	1	0	59	1	58	0	
Cherokee County Board of Education	2	0	1	0	1	67	0	67	0	0
Cherokee County Marshal	0	0	0	0	0	0	0	0	0	0
Cobb County Board of Education	65	0	0	2	63	284	8	276	0	1
Decatur County Schools	1	0	0	0	1	1	1	0	0	0
DeKalb County School System	32	0	5	5	22	392	38	345	9	0
Dougherty County Board of Education	17	0	2	2	13	47	4	42	1	0
Fayette County Marshal	0	0	0	0	0	1	1	0	0	0
Forsyth County Fire Investigation Unit	0	0	0	0	0	0	0	0	0	4
Fulton County Marshal	0	0	0	0	0	21	0	16	5	0
Fulton County School System	5	0	3	0	2	136	28	101	7	0
Glynn County School System	1	0	0	0	1	21	1	18	2	0
Gwinnett County Public Schools	6	0	1	0	5	163	4	158	1	0
Hall County Marshal[3]	0	0	0	0	0	0	0	0	0	0
Hartsfield-Jackson Atlanta International Airport	9	0	0	2	7	335	1	240	94	0
Metropolitan Atlanta Rapid Transit Authority	162	0	0	60	102	276	4	248	24	5
Stone Mountain Park	0	0	0	0	0	40	0	37	3	0
Twiggs County Board of Education	0	0	0	0	0	2	0	2	0	
IDAHO										
State Agencies										
Idaho State Police	26	5	3	0	18	10	3	5	2	0
Tribal Agencies										
Coeur d'Alene Tribal	16	1	0	2	13	53	19	29	5	0
ILLINOIS										
State Agencies										
Illinois Department of Natural Resources	0	0	0	0	0	0	0	0	0	0
Secretary of State Police	0	0	0	0	0	7	0	5	2	0
Other Agencies	0	0	0	0	0	0	0	0	0	340
Alton & Southern Railway	3	0	0	0	3	3	2	1	0	0
Belt Railway	0	0	0	0	0	1	1	0	0	0
Canton Park District	0	0	0	0	0	0	0	0	0	0
Capitol Airport Authority	0	0	0	0	0	0	0	0	0	0
Cook County Forest Preserve	15	0	9	3	3	116	5	110	1	0
Crystal Lake Park District	2	0	0	0	2	12	0	12	0	0
Decatur Park District	2	0	0	0	2	7	2	5	0	0
DuPage County Forest Preserve	1	0	0	0	1	40	2	38	0	1
Fon du Lac Park District	4	0	0	0	4	0	0	0	0	0
Fox Valley Park District	3	0	0	2	1	33	0	33	0	0
Indiana Harbor Belt Railroad	0	0	0	0	0	2	1	1	0	0
Kane County Forest Preserve	1	0	0	1	0	7	0	7	0	0
Lake County Forest Preserve	0	0	0	0	0	35	0	35	0	0
McHenry County Conservation District	0	0	0	0	0	4	1	3	0	0
Norfolk Southern Railway										
Cook County	0	0	0	0	0	495	375	120	0	0
Macon County	0	0	0	0	0	1	1	0	0	0
Madison County	0	0	0	0	0	4	1	3	0	0
Pekin Park District	1	0	1	0	0	6	2	4	0	0
Rockford Park District	28	0	1	8	19	88	57	28	3	3
Springfield Park District	30	0	2	1	27	33	17	14	2	0
Terminal Railroad Association	0	0	0	0	0	2	0	2	0	0
Tri-County Drug Enforcement Narcotics Team	1	0	0	0	1	0	0	0	0	0
Union Pacific Railroad, Cook County	0	0	0	0	0	985	159	826	0	0
INDIANA										
State Agencies										
Indiana State Excise Police	0	0	0	0	0	9	0	9	0	0
Northern Indiana Commuter Transportation District	0	0	0	0	0	0	0	0	0	0
State Police										
Adams County	3	0	3	0	0	2	0	1	1	0
Allen County	0	0	0	0	0	30	2	22	6	0
Bartholomew County	3	0	0	0	3	11	0	6	5	0
Benton County	1	0	1	0	0	1	0	0	1	0
Blackford County	1	0	1	0	0	1	1	0	0	0
Boone County	4	1	0	1	2	3	0	1	2	0
Brown County	0	0	0	0	0	8	1	6	1	0
Carroll County	1	0	0	0	1	1	0	1	0	0
Cass County	2	0	0	0	2	7	0	4	3	0
Clark County	5	0	2	0	3	33	4	20	9	0
Clay County	4	0	2	0	2	1	0	1	0	0
Clinton County	3	0	1	0	2	2	0	2	0	0
Crawford County	4	0	0	0	4	15	3	8	4	0
Daviess County	4	0	1	0	3	14	3	7	4	0
Dearborn County	9	3	2	0	4	11	2	5	4	0
Decatur County	2	0	2	0	0	4	1	2	1	0

Table 11. Offenses Known to Law Enforcement, by Selected State, Tribal, and Other Agencies, 2018—Continued

(Number.)

State/other agency unit/office	Violent crime	Murder and nonnegligent manslaughter	Rape[1]	Robbery	Aggravated assault	Property crime	Burglary	Larceny-theft	Motor vehicle theft	Arson[2]
DeKalb County	11	0	5	0	6	5	2	1	2	1
Delaware County	1	0	0	0	1	4	0	4	0	1
Dubois County	12	0	2	0	10	24	4	16	4	0
Elkhart County	4	0	0	0	4	19	2	11	6	0
Fayette County	0	0	0	0	0	5	0	5	0	0
Floyd County	3	0	1	0	2	25	2	10	13	0
Fountain County	1	0	1	0	0	2	0	2	0	0
Franklin County	5	0	1	0	4	1	0	0	1	0
Fulton County	1	0	0	0	1	2	1	0	1	0
Gibson County	6	0	1	0	5	7	2	3	2	0
Grant County	1	0	0	0	1	6	2	3	1	0
Greene County	17	0	2	0	15	21	4	15	2	0
Hamilton County	1	0	0	0	1	10	0	7	3	0
Hancock County	1	0	1	0	0	6	0	4	2	0
Harrison County	2	0	0	0	2	17	4	9	4	0
Hendricks County	2	0	2	0	0	10	1	6	3	0
Henry County	3	0	0	0	3	5	2	2	1	0
Howard County	4	0	2	0	2	5	0	4	1	0
Huntington County	2	0	2	0	0	1	0	0	1	0
Jackson County	14	0	2	0	12	11	0	6	5	0
Jasper County	1	0	0	1	0	6	0	2	4	0
Jay County	1	0	0	0	1	4	0	3	1	0
Jefferson County	6	0	1	0	5	6	0	5	1	0
Jennings County	5	0	0	0	5	12	2	7	3	0
Johnson County	0	0	0	0	0	9	0	4	5	0
Knox County	9	2	2	0	5	18	2	13	3	0
Kosciusko County	4	0	3	0	1	7	0	6	1	0
LaGrange County	9	0	1	0	8	15	2	12	1	0
Lake County	6	0	1	0	5	41	0	14	27	0
La Porte County	6	0	1	0	5	13	2	8	3	0
Lawrence County	9	0	2	0	7	10	2	8	0	0
Madison County	10	1	3	0	6	16	0	11	5	1
Marion County	34	3	5	2	24	302	3	145	154	0
Marshall County	7	0	0	0	7	5	0	4	1	1
Martin County	10	0	2	0	8	5	2	2	1	0
Miami County	26	1	4	2	19	23	5	15	3	0
Monroe County	7	1	2	0	4	39	4	26	9	0
Montgomery County	4	0	3	0	1	2	0	0	2	0
Morgan County	4	0	0	0	4	22	1	5	16	0
Newton County	1	0	1	0	0	0	0	0	0	0
Noble County	6	0	1	0	5	18	3	14	1	0
Ohio County	2	0	0	0	2	0	0	0	0	0
Orange County	7	0	1	0	6	6	0	5	1	0
Owen County	6	0	1	0	5	6	1	4	1	0
Parke County	3	0	1	0	2	2	0	0	2	0
Perry County	5	0	1	0	4	12	6	4	2	0
Pike County	8	1	2	0	5	11	3	6	2	0
Porter County	1	0	1	0	0	13	0	9	4	0
Posey County	5	0	2	0	3	9	2	6	1	0
Putnam County	1	0	0	0	1	18	1	11	6	0
Randolph County	1	0	0	0	1	3	0	2	1	0
Ripley County	28	0	4	1	23	32	6	21	5	1
Rush County	1	0	0	0	1	0	0	0	0	0
Scott County	10	0	0	0	10	14	5	8	1	0
Shelby County	1	0	1	0	0	4	0	3	1	0
Spencer County	7	0	3	0	4	15	4	8	3	0
Starke County	0	0	0	0	0	0	0	0	0	0
Steuben County	0	0	0	0	0	8	1	3	4	0
St. Joseph County	3	0	0	0	3	19	1	14	4	0
Sullivan County	4	0	0	0	4	8	0	7	1	0
Switzerland County	2	0	0	0	2	1	0	1	0	0
Tippecanoe County	10	0	2	0	8	14	0	10	4	0
Tipton County	0	0	0	0	0	0	0	0	0	0
Union County	0	0	0	0	0	1	0	1	0	0
Vanderburgh County	5	0	3	0	2	23	2	18	3	1
Vermillion County	5	0	3	0	2	1	0	1	0	0
Vigo County	12	1	1	1	9	42	3	25	14	0
Wabash County	5	3	0	1	1	3	0	2	1	0
Warren County	2	0	0	0	2	3	0	2	1	0
Warrick County	6	0	0	0	6	8	1	6	1	0
Washington County	8	1	0	0	7	8	1	6	1	1
Wayne County	4	0	0	0	4	9	0	8	1	1
Wells County	7	0	1	0	6	7	2	4	1	0
White County	2	0	1	0	1	8	0	6	2	0
Whitley County	10	0	4	0	6	11	3	5	3	0
IOWA[4]										
KANSAS										
State Agencies										
Highway Patrol										
Troop A	15	0	0	0	15	1	0	0	1	0
Troop B	5	0	0	0	5	2	0	0	2	0

Table 11. Offenses Known to Law Enforcement, by Selected State, Tribal, and Other Agencies, 2018—Continued

(Number.)

State/other agency unit/office	Violent crime	Murder and nonnegligent manslaughter	Rape[1]	Robbery	Aggravated assault	Property crime	Burglary	Larceny-theft	Motor vehicle theft	Arson[2]
Troop C	5	0	1	0	4	2	0	2	0	0
Troop D	0	0	0	0	0	4	0	3	1	0
Troop E	0	0	0	0	0	0	0	0	0	0
Troop F	10	0	0	0	10	3	0	2	1	0
Troop G	10	0	0	0	10	27	2	19	6	0
Troop H	3	0	0	0	3	0	0	0	0	0
Kansas Alcoholic Beverage Control	0	0	0	0	0	0	0	0	0	0
Kansas Bureau of Investigation	18	2	0	0	16	2	0	1	1	0
Kansas Department of Wildlife and Parks	3	0	0	0	3	19	0	19	0	0
Kansas Lottery Security Division	0	0	0	0	0	0	0	0	0	0
Securities Office, Investigation Section	0	0	0	0	0	0	0	0	0	0
Tribal Agencies										
Iowa Tribal	0	0	0	0	0	0	0	0	0	0
Kickapoo Tribal	13	0	1	0	12	14	7	3	4	1
Potawatomi Tribal	5	0	0	0	5	23	2	21	0	0
Sac and Fox Tribal	0	0	0	0	0	8	0	6	2	0
Other Agencies										
El Dorado School District	0	0	0	0	0	3	0	3	0	0
Johnson County Park	4	0	1	0	3	44	1	43	0	0
Kansas City Fire Department, Fire Investigation Division	0	0	0	0	0	0	0	0	0	48
Metropolitan Topeka Airport Authority	0	0	0	0	0	8	1	3	4	0
Shawnee Mission Public Schools	0	0	0	0	0	8	0	8	0	0
Topeka Fire Department Arson Investigation	0	0	0	0	0	4	4	0	0	50
Unified School District, Kansas City[5]	0	0	0	0	0		2		0	0
KENTUCKY										
State Agencies										
Fish and Wildlife Enforcement	0	0	0	0	0	2	0	2	0	0
Kentucky Horse Park	1	0	0	1	0	26	0	26	0	0
Motor Vehicle Enforcement	0	0	0	0	0	6	0	4	2	0
Park Security	0	0	0	0	0	9	1	8	0	0
State Police										
Ashland	44	2	20	1	21	153	46	81	26	3
Bowling Green	37	7	19	0	11	133	47	56	30	3
Campbellsburg	41	2	22	1	16	170	69	87	14	1
Cannabis Suppression Section	0	0	0	0	0	0	0	0	0	0
Columbia	53	1	37	2	13	112	38	50	24	6
Drug Enforcement Area [2]	0	0	0	0	0	5	1	4	0	0
Dry Ridge	50	3	27	2	18	117	44	56	17	2
Electronic Crimes	2	0	2	0	0	0	0	0	0	0
Elizabethtown	60	4	28	5	23	179	71	71	37	0
Frankfort	34	2	13	0	19	77	18	38	21	10
Harlan	59	3	27	5	24	184	67	73	44	7
Hazard	66	6	22	2	36	216	83	60	73	3
Henderson	22	0	18	0	4	104	38	60	6	2
London	68	2	35	3	28	249	80	95	74	12
Madisonville	46	3	26	0	17	100	36	49	15	3
Mayfield	71	8	27	3	33	168	55	95	18	2
Morehead	65	4	28	4	29	207	67	106	34	2
Pikeville	82	12	25	10	35	241	92	85	64	7
Richmond	67	10	28	7	22	203	67	91	45	9
Vehicle Investigations	0	0	0	0	0	5	0	4	1	0
West Drug Enforcement Branch	0	0	0	0	0	7	0	7	0	0
Other Agencies										
Barren County Drug Task Force	0	0	0	0	0	0	0	0	0	0
Cincinnati-Northern Kentucky International Airport	0	0	0	0	0	81	2	44	35	0
Clark County School System	0	0	0	0	0	0	0	0	0	0
Fayette County Schools	6	0	0	0	6	75	4	69	2	0
Greater Hardin County Narcotics Task Force	1	0	0	1	0	0	0	0	0	0
Jefferson County School District	7	0	0	0	7	53	19	34	0	2
Lexington Bluegrass Airport	0	0	0	0	0	11	0	6	5	0
Louisville Fire Department Arson Division	0	0	0	0	0	0	0	0	0	117
Louisville Regional Airport Authority	0	0	0	0	0	64	0	22	42	0
Northern Kentucky Drug Strike Force	0	0	0	0	0	0	0	0	0	0
Pennyrile Narcotics Task Force	0	0	0	0	0	1	0	1	0	0
Pulaski County Constable District [5]	3	0	0	0	3	2	1	1	0	0
South Central Kentucky Drug Task Force	0	0	0	0	0	0	0	0	0	0
LOUISIANA										
State Agencies										
Tensas Basin Levee District	0	0	0	0	0	0	0	0	0	0
MAINE										
State Agencies										
Bureau of Capitol Police	1	0	0	0	1	8	0	6	2	0
Drug Enforcement Agency	1	0	0	1	0	2	0	2	0	0
State Fire Marshal	1	0	0	0	1	1	1	0	0	42
State Police	152	9	51	8	84	975	260	639	76	0

Table 11. Offenses Known to Law Enforcement, by Selected State, Tribal, and Other Agencies, 2018—Continued

(Number.)

State/other agency unit/office	Violent crime	Murder and nonnegligent manslaughter	Rape[1]	Robbery	Aggravated assault	Property crime	Burglary	Larceny-theft	Motor vehicle theft	Arson[2]
Tribal Agencies										
Passamaquoddy Pleasant Point Tribal	1	0	0	1	0	5	3	1	1	0
Penobscot Nation	0	0	0	0	0	6	1	5	0	0
MARYLAND										
State Agencies										
Comptroller of the Treasury Field Enforcement Division	0	0	0	0	0	0	0	0	0	0
Department of Public Safety and Correctional Services, Internal Investigation Division	475	0	0	0	475	0	0	0	0	0
General Services										
Annapolis, Anne Arundel County	0	0	0	0	0	2	0	2	0	0
Baltimore City	1	0	0	0	1	19	0	18	1	0
Maryland State Police Statewide	0	0	0	0	0	0	0	0	0	0
Natural Resources Police	8	0	1	1	6	105	8	94	3	0
Springfield Hospital	0	0	0	0	0	5	0	5	0	0
State Fire Marshal	0	0	0	0	0	3	3	0	0	13
State Police										
Allegany County	45	1	2	2	40	344	80	241	23	4
Anne Arundel County	8	2	0	1	5	23	0	18	5	0
Baltimore City	3	0	0	0	3	0	0	0	0	0
Baltimore County	13	0	0	0	13	11	0	7	4	1
Calvert County	17	0	3	3	11	92	13	75	4	4
Caroline County	6	0	1	2	3	11	3	7	1	1
Carroll County	20	0	0	9	11	167	15	135	17	6
Cecil County	58	1	2	2	53	524	108	366	50	3
Charles County	0	0	0	0	0	4	0	4	0	0
Dorchester County	7	0	0	0	7	7	1	3	3	0
Frederick County	55	0	4	3	48	143	26	106	11	0
Garrett County	16	0	6	1	9	77	32	41	4	2
Harford County	38	0	2	7	29	188	7	169	12	8
Howard County	2	0	0	0	2	4	0	3	1	0
Kent County	1	0	1	0	0	7	4	3	0	1
Montgomery County	2	0	0	0	2	3	2	1	0	0
Prince George's County	3	0	0	1	2	19	0	8	11	0
Queen Anne's County	29	0	0	2	27	81	15	55	11	3
Somerset County	26	1	4	3	18	117	46	66	5	0
St. Mary's County	25	0	7	3	15	160	20	127	13	8
Talbot County	1	0	0	0	1	6	2	4	0	0
Washington County	14	0	1	2	11	214	29	176	9	14
Wicomico County	50	0	1	7	42	198	63	109	26	6
Worcester County	8	0	0	1	7	87	14	71	2	0
Transit Administraion	73	0	0	40	33	125	3	115	7	0
Transportation Authority	31	0	0	0	31	163	2	135	26	0
Other Agencies										
Maryland-National Capital Park Police										
Montgomery County	20	0	5	4	11	120	6	110	4	0
Prince George's County	43	2	2	20	19	126	12	111	3	0
MASSACHUSETTS										
State Agencies										
Division of Law Enforcement, Environmental Police	5	0	0	0	5	20	7	9	4	0
Massachusetts Bay Transportation Authority										
Bristol County	0	0	0	0	0	8	0	7	1	
Middlesex County	26	0	0	11	15	162	4	158	0	
Norfolk County	10	0	0	3	7	72	0	71	1	
Plymouth County	0	0	0	0	0	13	0	13	0	
Suffolk County	210	0	1	85	124	269	6	251	12	
Worcester County	1	0	0	0	1	2	0	1	1	
State Police										
Berkshire County	3	0	0	0	3	63	35	24	4	
Franklin County	3	0	0	0	3	0	0	0	0	
Hampden County	33	0	0	0	33	11	2	1	8	
Hampshire County	8	0	1	0	7	0	0	0	0	
Worcester County	4	0	0	0	4	0	0	0	0	
Tribal Agencies										
Wampanoag Tribe of Gay Head	0	0	0	0	0	0	0	0	0	0
Other Agencies										
Massachusetts General Hospital	1	0	0	1	0	163	2	161	0	
MICHIGAN										
State Agencies										
State Police										
Alcona County	5	0	2	0	3	8	3	3	2	0
Alger County	18	0	2	0	16	19	6	12	1	1
Allegan County	80	0	38	1	41	275	99	150	26	3
Alpena County	21	0	14	1	6	122	19	99	4	1
Antrim County	6	0	3	0	3	17	5	9	3	0
Arenac County	8	0	6	0	2	2	0	1	1	0
Baraga County	11	0	1	0	10	18	4	14	0	0

Table 11. Offenses Known to Law Enforcement, by Selected State, Tribal, and Other Agencies, 2018—Continued

(Number.)

State/other agency unit/office	Violent crime	Murder and nonnegligent manslaughter	Rape[1]	Robbery	Aggravated assault	Property crime	Burglary	Larceny-theft	Motor vehicle theft	Arson[2]
Barry County	44	0	20	0	24	188	92	88	8	0
Bay County	57	2	34	0	21	90	29	55	6	1
Benzie County	11	0	7	0	4	6	2	3	1	0
Berrien County	55	0	21	2	32	122	55	58	9	1
Branch County	50	0	20	1	29	159	96	48	15	3
Calhoun County	47	1	20	1	25	109	43	49	17	1
Cass County	11	0	7	0	4	35	28	6	1	0
Charlevoix County	6	0	5	0	1	8	0	7	1	0
Cheboygan County	12	0	7	0	5	24	8	16	0	0
Chippewa County	60	1	12	0	47	55	21	28	6	1
Clare County	21	0	16	0	5	28	13	15	0	0
Clinton County	13	0	11	0	2	14	6	5	3	0
Crawford County	13	0	13	0	0	11	1	9	1	0
Delta County	17	0	4	0	13	48	14	29	5	0
Dickinson County	7	0	3	0	4	28	9	17	2	0
Eaton County	15	0	12	0	3	71	25	43	3	1
Emmet County	19	0	7	0	12	37	3	33	1	0
Genesee County	77	0	21	6	50	127	49	59	19	3
Gladwin County	19	0	18	0	1	6	0	5	1	0
Gogebic County	13	0	8	0	5	11	5	4	2	1
Grand Traverse County	17	1	15	0	1	35	4	31	0	0
Gratiot County	21	0	9	0	12	7	0	7	0	0
Hillsdale County	66	0	28	2	36	108	43	52	13	4
Houghton County	12	0	7	0	5	63	11	50	2	1
Huron County	1	0	1	0	0	2	2	0	0	0
Ingham County	38	1	18	2	17	45	10	24	11	0
Ionia County	72	0	27	1	44	100	20	62	18	0
Iosco County	35	1	13	0	21	78	33	41	4	1
Iron County	10	0	5	0	5	27	9	13	5	0
Isabella County	41	0	26	1	14	143	25	107	11	0
Jackson County	108	2	54	1	51	173	58	97	18	1
Kalamazoo County	50	0	18	0	32	51	10	37	4	0
Kalkaska County	23	0	17	0	6	14	3	10	1	0
Kent County	27	1	15	0	11	25	0	20	5	0
Lake County	20	1	7	0	12	5	2	3	0	0
Lapeer County	21	0	12	0	9	55	24	22	9	1
Leelanau County	1	0	1	0	0	2	0	2	0	0
Lenawee County	48	0	19	1	28	58	21	35	2	1
Livingston County	46	0	23	2	21	120	30	84	6	0
Luce County	12	1	4	0	7	22	12	7	3	0
Mackinac County	15	0	8	0	7	17	4	13	0	0
Macomb County	48	0	19	1	28	43	13	26	4	0
Manistee County	26	0	15	0	11	48	8	37	3	0
Marquette County	57	0	13	0	44	142	38	97	7	1
Mason County	8	0	2	0	6	63	40	23	0	0
Mecosta County	32	0	12	0	20	59	20	35	4	0
Menominee County	5	0	2	0	3	24	8	14	2	0
Midland County	10	0	9	0	1	11	1	9	1	0
Missaukee County	4	0	1	0	3	3	1	2	0	0
Monroe County	60	1	16	5	38	112	27	75	10	0
Montcalm County	131	2	49	2	78	283	99	142	42	3
Montmorency County	7	1	2	0	4	15	5	10	0	0
Muskegon County	79	1	39	1	38	229	47	167	15	4
Newaygo County	58	0	26	0	32	96	40	51	5	0
Oakland County	83	1	20	5	57	191	38	134	19	1
Oceana County	31	0	11	0	20	79	16	59	4	1
Ogemaw County	47	0	21	1	25	88	29	51	8	0
Ontonagon County	6	0	5	0	1	8	2	6	0	0
Osceola County	28	0	12	0	16	31	10	15	6	1
Oscoda County	4	0	3	0	1	1	1	0	0	0
Otsego County	32	1	23	0	8	92	46	42	4	4
Ottawa County	4	0	4	0	0	1	0	1	0	0
Presque Isle County	10	0	8	0	2	3	0	2	1	0
Roscommon County	19	0	11	0	8	42	11	28	3	0
Saginaw County	97	2	37	1	57	103	38	57	8	7
Sanilac County	17	0	9	0	8	24	9	12	3	1
Schoolcraft County	4	0	2	0	2	29	11	16	2	0
Shiawassee County	51	2	21	0	28	133	20	103	10	1
St. Clair County	22	0	6	1	15	35	11	17	7	0
St. Joseph County	21	0	8	1	12	110	41	45	24	1
Tuscola County	34	2	16	1	15	56	30	23	3	0
Van Buren County	60	3	16	2	39	144	49	80	15	1
Washtenaw County	69	0	35	2	32	150	58	67	25	2
Wayne County	83	4	22	1	56	114	4	85	25	0
Wexford County	31	0	17	2	12	115	16	90	9	0
Tribal Agencies										
Little River Band of Ottawa Indians	8	0	5	1	2	31	3	28	0	0
Nottawaseppi Huron Band of Potawatomi	3	0	1	1	1	118	4	109	5	0
Other Agencies										
Bishop International Airport	0	0	0	0	0	3	0	1	2	0
Capitol Region Airport Authority	0	0	0	0	0	3	0	0	3	0
Genesee County Parks and Recreation	2	0	0	0	2	5	0	4	1	0
Gerald R. Ford International Airport	0	0	0	0	0	1	0	1	0	0

Table 11. Offenses Known to Law Enforcement, by Selected State, Tribal, and Other Agencies, 2018—Continued

(Number.)

State/other agency unit/office	Violent crime	Murder and nonnegligent manslaughter	Rape[1]	Robbery	Aggravated assault	Property crime	Burglary	Larceny-theft	Motor vehicle theft	Arson[2]
Huron-Clinton Metropolitan Authority										
Hudson Mills Metropark	0	0	0	0	0	1	0	1	0	0
Kensington Metropark	1	0	0	0	1	7	0	7	0	0
Lower Huron Metropark	0	0	0	0	0	4	0	4	0	0
Stony Creek Metropark	3	0	1	0	2	9	0	9	0	0
Wayne County Airport	4	0	0	0	4	213	3	122	88	0
MINNESOTA										
State Agencies										
Bureau of Criminal Apprehension	0	0	0	0	0	0	0	0	0	0
Capitol Security, St. Paul	0	0	0	0	0	28	0	28	0	0
Department of Natural Resources										
Enforcement Division	0	0	0	0	0	0	0	0	0	0
Minnesota State Patrol	0	0	0	0	0	0	0	0	0	0
State Patrol										
Brainerd	0	0	0	0	0	0	0	0	0	0
Detroit Lakes	0	0	0	0	0	0	0	0	0	0
Duluth	0	0	0	0	0	0	0	0	0	0
Golden Valley	0	0	0	0	0	0	0	0	0	0
Mankato	0	0	0	0	0	0	0	0	0	0
Marshall	0	0	0	0	0	0	0	0	0	0
Oakdale	0	0	0	0	0	0	0	0	0	0
Rochester	0	0	0	0	0	0	0	0	0	0
St. Cloud	0	0	0	0	0	0	0	0	0	0
Thief River Falls	0	0	0	0	0	0	0	0	0	0
Virginia	0	0	0	0	0	0	0	0	0	0
Tribal Agencies										
Fond du Lac Tribal	7	0	1	0	6	112	19	81	12	0
Mille Lacs Tribal	23	0	1	4	18	229	43	167	19	3
Upper Sioux Community	2	0	0	0	2	13	0	12	1	0
White Earth Tribal	34	0	5	0	29	244	46	176	22	1
Other Agencies										
Metropolitan Transit Commission	247	0	2	161	84	486	2	480	4	0
Minneapolis-St. Paul International Airport	5	0	0	1	4	285	0	225	60	0
Three Rivers Park District	1	0	0	0	1	55	1	53	1	0
MISSISSIPPI										
State Agencies										
Department of Marine Resources[6]		0		0	0	0	0	0	0	0
State Capitol Police	0	0	0	0	0	24	13	10	1	0
Tribal Agencies										
Choctaw Tribal	139	0	5	1	133	233	10	223	0	1
MISSOURI										
State Agencies										
Department of Conservation	0	0	0	0	0	0	0	0	0	0
Department of Revenue, Compliance and										
Investigation Bureau	0	0	0	0	0	0	0	0	0	0
Department of Social Services, State										
Technical Assistance Team	0	0	0	0	0	0	0	0	0	0
Division of Alcohol and Tobacco Control	0	0	0	0	0	0	0	0	0	0
Gaming Commission, Enforcement										
Division[3]	2	0	0	0	2	128	0	126	2	0
State Fire Marshal	0	0	0	0	0	0	0	0	0	130
State Park Rangers	1	0	0	0	1	56	4	51	1	
Other Agencies										
Clay County Drug Task Force	0	0	0	0	0	0	0	0	0	0
Clay County Park Authority	1	0	0	0	1	15	0	15	0	0
Jackson County Drug Task Force	0	0	0	0	0	0	0	0	0	0
Jackson County Park Rangers	0	0	0	0	0	0	0	0	0	0
Kansas City International Airport	6	0	1	0	5	97	3	47	47	0
Lambert-St. Louis International Airport	1	0	0	0	1	107	0	96	11	0
Platte County Multi-Jurisdictional										
Enforcement Group	0	0	0	0	0	0	0	0	0	0
Springfield-Branson Airport	0	0	0	0	0	10	0	7	3	0
Springfield-Greene County Park Rangers	0	0	0	0	0	14	5	9	0	0
St. Charles County Park Rangers	0	0	0	0	0	26	0	26	0	0
Terminal Railroad	0	0	0	0	0	1	0	1	0	0
Western Missouri Cyber Crimes Task										
Force	0	0	0	0	0	0	0	0	0	0
MONTANA										
Tribal Agencies										
Crow Agency	51	0	5	1	45	144	31	72	41	6
Fort Belknap Tribal	7	0	0	0	7	40	8	26	6	0
Northern Cheyenne Agency	85	1	10	2	72	116	21	63	32	1
NEBRASKA										
State Agencies										
Nebraska State Patrol	2	0	0	0	2	6	1	5	0	
State Police										
Adams County	0	0	0	0	0	2	0	2	0	
Antelope County	0	0	0	0	0	0	0	0	0	

Table 11. Offenses Known to Law Enforcement, by Selected State, Tribal, and Other Agencies, 2018—Continued

(Number.)

State/other agency unit/office	Violent crime	Murder and nonnegligent manslaughter	Rape[1]	Robbery	Aggravated assault	Property crime	Burglary	Larceny-theft	Motor vehicle theft	Arson[2]
Arthur County	0	0	0	0	0	0	0	0	0	
Banner County	0	0	0	0	0	0	0	0	0	
Blaine County	0	0	0	0	0	0	0	0	0	
Boone County	0	0	0	0	0	0	0	0	0	
Box Butte County	0	0	0	0	0	0	0	0	0	
Boyd County	0	0	0	0	0	1	0	1	0	
Brown County	0	0	0	0	0	1	0	0	1	
Buffalo County	0	0	0	0	0	1	0	1	0	
Burt County	0	0	0	0	0	0	0	0	0	
Butler County	0	0	0	0	0	0	0	0	0	
Cass County	1	0	0	0	1	1	0	0	1	
Cedar County	0	0	0	0	0	0	0	0	0	
Chase County	1	0	0	0	1	0	0	0	0	
Cherry County	0	0	0	0	0	0	0	0	0	
Cheyenne County	0	0	0	0	0	0	0	0	0	
Colfax County	0	0	0	0	0	0	0	0	0	
Cuming County	0	0	0	0	0	0	0	0	0	
Custer County	0	0	0	0	0	0	0	0	0	
Dawes County	0	0	0	0	0	0	0	0	0	
Dawson County	0	0	0	0	0	4	2	1	1	
Deuel County	0	0	0	0	0	0	0	0	0	
Dixon County	0	0	0	0	0	0	0	0	0	
Dodge County	0	0	0	0	0	0	0	0	0	
Douglas County	0	0	0	0	0	1	0	0	1	
Dundy County	0	0	0	0	0	0	0	0	0	
Fillmore County	0	0	0	0	0	0	0	0	0	
Franklin County	0	0	0	0	0	0	0	0	0	
Frontier County	0	0	0	0	0	1	0	0	1	
Furnas County	0	0	0	0	0	0	0	0	0	
Gage County	0	0	0	0	0	0	0	0	0	
Garden County	0	0	0	0	0	0	0	0	0	
Garfield County	0	0	0	0	0	0	0	0	0	
Gosper County	0	0	0	0	0	0	0	0	0	
Grant County	0	0	0	0	0	0	0	0	0	
Greeley County	0	0	0	0	0	0	0	0	0	
Hall County	0	0	0	0	0	4	0	3	1	
Hamilton County	0	0	0	0	0	0	0	0	0	
Harlan County	0	0	0	0	0	0	0	0	0	
Hayes County	0	0	0	0	0	0	0	0	0	
Hitchcock County	0	0	0	0	0	0	0	0	0	
Holt County	0	0	0	0	0	0	0	0	0	
Hooker County	0	0	0	0	0	0	0	0	0	
Howard County	0	0	0	0	0	0	0	0	0	
Jefferson County	0	0	0	0	0	0	0	0	0	
Johnson County	0	0	0	0	0	0	0	0	0	
Kearney County	0	0	0	0	0	0	0	0	0	
Keya Paha County	0	0	0	0	0	0	0	0	0	
Kimball County	0	0	0	0	0	0	0	0	0	
Knox County	0	0	0	0	0	0	0	0	0	
Lancaster County	1	0	0	0	1	1	0	1	0	
Lincoln County	1	0	0	0	1	0	0	0	0	
Logan County	0	0	0	0	0	0	0	0	0	
Loup County	0	0	0	0	0	0	0	0	0	
Madison County	0	0	0	0	0	2	0	2	0	
McPherson County	0	0	0	0	0	0	0	0	0	
Merrick County	0	0	0	0	0	1	1	0	0	
Morrill County	1	0	0	0	1	1	0	1	0	
Nance County	0	0	0	0	0	0	0	0	0	
Nemaha County	0	0	0	0	0	0	0	0	0	
Nuckolls County	0	0	0	0	0	0	0	0	0	
Otoe County	0	0	0	0	0	0	0	0	0	
Pawnee County	0	0	0	0	0	0	0	0	0	
Perkins County	0	0	0	0	0	0	0	0	0	
Phelps County	0	0	0	0	0	1	1	0	0	
Pierce County	2	0	0	0	2	1	1	0	0	
Platte County	0	0	0	0	0	0	0	0	0	
Polk County	0	0	0	0	0	0	0	0	0	
Red Willow County	1	0	0	0	1	0	0	0	0	
Richardson County	0	0	0	0	0	0	0	0	0	
Rock County	0	0	0	0	0	0	0	0	0	
Saline County	0	0	0	0	0	0	0	0	0	
Sarpy County	0	0	0	0	0	2	1	1	0	
Saunders County	0	0	0	0	0	0	0	0	0	
Scotts Bluff County	2	0	1	0	1	1	1	0	0	
Seward County	1	0	0	0	1	1	0	1	0	
Sheridan County	0	0	0	0	0	0	0	0	0	
Sherman County	0	0	0	0	0	1	0	1	0	
Sioux County	0	0	0	0	0	1	0	1	0	
Stanton County	0	0	0	0	0	0	0	0	0	
Thayer County	1	1	0	0	0	0	0	0	0	
Thomas County	0	0	0	0	0	0	0	0	0	
Thurston County	0	0	0	0	0	0	0	0	0	
Valley County	0	0	0	0	0	0	0	0	0	

Table 11. Offenses Known to Law Enforcement, by Selected State, Tribal, and Other Agencies, 2018—Continued

(Number.)

State/other agency unit/office	Violent crime	Murder and nonnegligent manslaughter	Rape[1]	Robbery	Aggravated assault	Property crime	Burglary	Larceny-theft	Motor vehicle theft	Arson[2]
Washington County	0	0	0	0	0	0	0	0	0	
Wayne County	0	0	0	0	0	0	0	0	0	
Webster County	0	0	0	0	0	0	0	0	0	
Wheeler County	0	0	0	0	0	0	0	0	0	
York County	0	0	0	0	0	0	0	0	0	
NEVADA										
State Agencies										
Capitol Police	1	0	0	0	1	48	16	26	6	0
Department of Public Safety, Investigative Division	0	0	0	0	0	0	0	0	0	0
Department of Wildlife, Law Enforcement Division	0	0	0	0	0	0	0	0	0	0
Highway Patrol										
Northeastern Division	0	0	0	0	0	3	0	1	2	0
Northwestern Division	1	0	0	0	1	5	0	0	5	0
Southern Division	3	0	0	1	2	2	0	2	0	0
Secretary of State Securities Division, Enforcement Section	0	0	0	0	0	0	0	0	0	0
State Fire Marshal	0	0	0	0	0	0	0	0	0	1
Tribal Agencies										
Eastern Nevada Agency	2	0	0	0	2	0	0	0	0	0
Ely Shoshone Tribal	0	0	0	0	0	0	0	0	0	0
Pyramid Lake Tribal	17	0	5	0	12	27	9	14	4	0
Other Agencies										
Clark County School District[7]		0	11	28		845	213	617	15	16
Las Vegas Fire and Rescue, Arson Bomb Unit	0	0	0	0	0	0	0	0	0	60
North Las Vegas Fire Department Arson Investigations	0	0	0	0	0	0	0	0	0	78
Reno Municipal Court Marshal	0	0	0	0	0	0	0	0	0	0
Reno Tahoe Airport Authority	2	0	0	0	2	35	3	24	8	0
Washoe County School District	27	0	0	3	24	91	13	77	1	3
NEW HAMPSHIRE										
State Agencies										
Liquor Commission	0	0	0	0	0	60	0	60	0	0
State Police										
Belknap County	0	0	0	0	0	3	1	2	0	0
Carroll County	3	0	0	1	2	3	0	2	1	0
Cheshire County	2	0	0	0	2	15	4	9	2	0
Coos County	7	0	3	0	4	34	11	20	3	0
Grafton County	12	0	5	1	6	33	14	16	3	0
Hillsborough County	1	0	0	0	1	2	0	1	1	0
Merrimack County	4	1	1	0	2	25	6	15	4	0
Rockingham County	7	0	1	1	5	3	1	0	2	0
Strafford County	2	0	0	0	2	0	0	0	0	0
Sullivan County	2	0	0	0	2	16	7	9	0	0
NEW JERSEY										
State Agencies										
Department of Human Services	59	0	0	0	59	34	1	33	0	0
Division of Fish and Wildlife	0	0	0	0	0	7	0	7	0	0
New Jersey Transit Police	21	0	0	8	13	288	1	283	4	0
Palisades Interstate Parkway	4	0	0	0	4	8	3	5	0	0
Port Authority of New York and New Jersey	33	0	0	9	24	649	25	585	39	0
State Park Police	7	0	1	1	5	52	8	42	2	6
State Police										
Atlantic County	32	0	1	7	24	721	48	663	10	2
Bergen County	6	0	0	1	5	46	1	40	5	1
Burlington County	35	1	7	3	24	282	75	186	21	2
Camden County	10	0	0	2	8	34	1	24	9	0
Cape May County	23	0	4	4	15	139	39	92	8	0
Cumberland County	74	1	9	8	56	613	188	407	18	4
Essex County	12	0	1	3	8	25	0	13	12	0
Gloucester County	2	0	0	0	2	13	2	10	1	0
Hudson County	3	0	0	0	3	9	0	5	4	0
Hunterdon County	11	0	1	3	7	102	17	76	9	2
Mercer County	14	1	3	0	10	62	3	57	2	1
Middlesex County	10	0	0	3	7	39	2	34	3	0
Monmouth County	18	0	1	1	16	104	23	71	10	3
Morris County	10	0	4	1	5	9	0	7	2	0
Ocean County	2	0	0	0	2	22	4	16	2	0
Passaic County	0	0	0	0	0	10	0	8	2	0
Salem County	20	0	2	6	12	289	81	191	17	1
Somerset County	0	0	0	0	0	4	1	3	0	0
Sussex County	25	0	6	1	18	258	52	200	6	0
Union County	4	0	0	2	2	9	1	8	0	0
Warren County	8	0	2	1	5	138	37	86	15	1
Other Agencies										
Park Police										
Morris County	1	0	0	1	0	9	0	9	0	0

Table 11. Offenses Known to Law Enforcement, by Selected State, Tribal, and Other Agencies, 2018—Continued

(Number.)

State/other agency unit/office	Violent crime	Murder and nonnegligent manslaughter	Rape[1]	Robbery	Aggravated assault	Property crime	Burglary	Larceny-theft	Motor vehicle theft	Arson[2]
Union County	20	0	0	3	17	30	1	29	0	0
Prosecutor										
Atlantic County	0	0	0	0	0	0	0	0	0	0
Bergen County	0	0	0	0	0	0	0	0	0	0
Burlington County	1	1	0	0	0	0	0	0	0	0
Camden County	0	0	0	0	0	0	0	0	0	0
Cape May County	0	0	0	0	0	0	0	0	0	0
Cumberland County	0	0	0	0	0	0	0	0	0	0
Essex County	0	0	0	0	0	0	0	0	0	0
Gloucester County	0	0	0	0	0	0	0	0	0	0
Hudson County	0	0	0	0	0	0	0	0	0	0
Hunterdon County	0	0	0	0	0	0	0	0	0	0
Mercer County	0	0	0	0	0	0	0	0	0	0
Middlesex County	0	0	0	0	0	0	0	0	0	0
Monmouth County	0	0	0	0	0	0	0	0	0	0
Morris County	0	0	0	0	0	0	0	0	0	0
Ocean County	0	0	0	0	0	0	0	0	0	0
Passaic County	0	0	0	0	0	0	0	0	0	0
Salem County	0	0	0	0	0	0	0	0	0	0
Somerset County	0	0	0	0	0	0	0	0	0	0
Sussex County	0	0	0	0	0	0	0	0	0	0
Union County	0	0	0	0	0	0	0	0	0	0
Warren County	0	0	0	0	0	0	0	0	0	0
NEW MEXICO										
State Agencies										
New Mexico State Police	831	9	119	16	687	798	214	434	150	
Tribal Agencies										
Isleta Tribal	7	2	0	0	5	2	1	1	0	1
Laguna Tribal	46	0	7	7	32	72	8	53	11	0
Mescalero Tribal	12	1	1	0	10	6	0	6	0	0
Northern Pueblos Agency	5	0	0	0	5	6	2	4	0	0
Ohkay Owingeh Tribal	19	1	1	1	16	25	6	15	4	0
Pojoaque Tribal	18	0	1	2	15	64	13	45	6	0
Ramah Navajo Tribal	24	0	2	0	22	21	8	11	2	0
Santa Ana Tribal	10	0	0	0	10	20	2	17	1	0
Santa Clara Pueblo	1	0	1	0	0	26	6	16	4	0
Southern Pueblos Agency	31	1	3	0	27	35	10	20	5	0
NEW YORK										
State Agencies										
State Park										
Allegany Region	1	0	1	0	0	7	1	6	0	0
Central Region	0	0	0	0	0	8	0	7	1	0
Finger Lakes Region	1	0	0	1	0	10	1	9	0	0
Genesee Region	0	0	0	0	0	10	1	9	0	0
Long Island Region	8	0	1	1	6	65	0	64	1	0
New York City Region	7	0	0	2	5	49	0	46	3	0
Niagara Region	2	0	0	1	1	19	2	17	0	0
Thousand Island Region	0	0	0	0	0	12	0	11	1	0
State Police										
Albany County	30	0	25	0	5	128	5	121	2	1
Allegany County	43	1	24	1	17	219	70	138	11	5
Broome County	77	0	36	2	39	451	72	355	24	6
Cattaraugus County	28	0	16	1	11	203	30	158	15	2
Cayuga County	47	0	24	2	21	134	18	106	10	3
Chautauqua County	27	1	18	1	7	152	25	119	8	0
Chemung County	50	0	16	0	34	204	19	177	8	1
Chenango County	39	0	30	0	9	146	35	103	8	1
Clinton County	123	2	76	4	41	576	104	450	22	0
Columbia County	42	0	25	0	17	148	22	121	5	3
Cortland County	13	0	11	0	2	127	20	103	4	1
Delaware County	28	1	11	2	14	151	26	120	5	3
Dutchess County	174	1	55	4	114	466	58	380	28	4
Erie County	35	1	16	0	18	226	24	189	13	0
Essex County	33	1	21	0	11	185	43	139	3	2
Franklin County	50	0	35	0	15	246	65	162	19	2
Fulton County	23	0	12	1	10	78	24	52	2	0
Genesee County	12	0	6	0	6	104	7	89	8	1
Greene County	92	1	38	1	52	290	74	212	4	6
Hamilton County	3	0	0	1	2	36	17	19	0	1
Herkimer County	25	0	16	0	9	188	65	113	10	3
Jefferson County	55	0	32	1	22	499	76	408	15	6
Lewis County	13	0	10	1	2	85	20	61	4	0
Livingston County	22	0	9	0	13	26	0	23	3	0
Madison County	41	0	30	0	11	159	32	115	12	5
Monroe County	26	0	24	0	2	73	3	62	8	0
Montgomery County	18	0	13	1	4	110	14	90	6	0
Nassau County	8	0	1	0	7	8	0	7	1	0
New York County	6	0	6	0	0	24	0	10	14	0
Niagara County	35	0	24	0	11	214	30	179	5	1
Oneida County	90	1	42	1	46	378	59	303	16	0
Onondaga County	71	0	42	5	24	523	62	429	32	2

Table 11. Offenses Known to Law Enforcement, by Selected State, Tribal, and Other Agencies, 2018—Continued

(Number.)

State/other agency unit/office	Violent crime	Murder and nonnegligent manslaughter	Rape[1]	Robbery	Aggravated assault	Property crime	Burglary	Larceny-theft	Motor vehicle theft	Arson[2]
Ontario County	33	0	22	1	10	253	34	210	9	3
Orange County	108	3	67	5	33	694	56	623	15	
Orleans County	12	0	5	0	7	80	11	65	4	1
Oswego County	83	0	50	2	31	528	102	397	29	3
Otsego County	48	0	29	1	18	352	50	292	10	4
Putnam County	19	0	13	1	5	92	8	80	4	0
Rensselaer County	40	0	30	3	7	359	61	284	14	1
Rockland County	5	0	5	0	0	13	1	12	0	1
Saratoga County	68	0	45	3	20	618	53	551	14	
Schenectady County	6	0	3	0	3	67	4	59	4	0
Schoharie County	18	1	10	0	7	109	30	75	4	1
Schuyler County	7	0	4	0	3	10	3	7	0	
Seneca County	28	2	16	1	9	101	8	91	2	0
St. Lawrence County	71	0	48	0	23	317	101	204	12	3
Steuben County	64	1	35	0	28	335	74	251	10	2
Suffolk County	19	0	9	1	9	23	2	16	5	0
Sullivan County	90	0	47	5	38	272	76	179	17	4
Tioga County	14	0	7	0	7	78	12	60	6	0
Tompkins County	34	0	23	2	9	257	38	215	4	2
Ulster County	91	1	45	4	41	372	70	287	15	2
Warren County	25	0	21	0	4	229	20	205	4	0
Washington County	27	1	13	1	12	99	24	68	7	1
Wayne County	77	1	41	4	31	489	125	346	18	
Westchester County	71	0	26	3	42	344	34	294	16	
Wyoming County	21	0	2	0	19	17	4	13	0	0
Yates County	3	0	3	0	0	32	4	27	1	0
Tribal Agencies										
Oneida Indian Nation	15	0	2	0	13	145	2	142	1	0
St. Regis Tribal	8	0	2	1	5	35	11	18	6	0
Other Agencies										
New York City Department of Environmental Protection Police										
Ashokan Precinct	0	0	0	0	0	0	0	0	0	0
Beerston Precinct	0	0	0	0	0	6	0	6	0	0
Eastview Precinct	0	0	0	0	0	8	1	7	0	0
Gilboa Precinct	0	0	0	0	0	0	0	0	0	0
Grahamsville Precinct	0	0	0	0	0	0	0	0	0	0
Hillview Precinct	0	0	0	0	0	0	0	0	0	0
New York City Metropolitan Transportation Authority	77	0	0	21	56	422	19	399	4	0
Onondaga County Parks	0	0	0	0	0	13	1	12	0	0
NORTH CAROLINA										
State Agencies[6]										
North Carolina Highway Patrol		0		0	0	0	0	0	0	0
Tribal Agencies										
Cherokee Tribal	103	2	1	6	94	926	168	677	81	0
Other Agencies[6]										
Raleigh-Durham International Airport		0		0	0	97	0	85	12	0
NORTH DAKOTA										
State Agencies										
North Dakota Highway Patrol	6	0	0	0	6	20	0	2	18	0
OHIO										
State Agencies										
Ohio Department of Natural Resources	23	0	3	0	20	310	22	283	5	4
Ohio State Highway Patrol	243	0	32	3	208	174	5	113	56	0
Other Agencies										
Cleveland Metropolitan Park District	19	0	2	1	16	59	2	55	2	0
Greater Cleveland Regional Transit Authority	18	0	1	7	10	67	0	67	0	0
Hamilton County Park District	1	0	1	0	0	45	2	43	0	1
Lake Metroparks	0	0	0	0	0	0	0	0	0	0
Toledo Fire Department Fire Investigation Unit	0	0	0	0	0	0	0	0	0	121
University Hospitals Portage Medical Center	0	0	0	0	0	2	0	1	1	0
OKLAHOMA										
State Agencies										
Capitol Park Police	0	0	0	0	0	1	0	1	0	0
Oklahoma Highway Patrol	0	0	0	0	0	0	0	0	0	0
State Park Rangers	10	0	3	1	6	136	22	108	6	4
Tribal Agencies										
Absentee Shawnee Tribal	7	0	0	0	7	13	4	9	0	0
Anadarko Agency	10	1	0	1	8	64	6	51	7	2
Cherokee Nation	28	0	0	3	25	39	5	29	5	0
Chickasaw Nation	28	0	1	6	21	1,004	73	891	40	0
Choctaw Nation	46	0	0	3	43	291	27	236	28	0
Citizen Potawatomi Nation	8	0	2	3	3	198	8	176	14	0
Comanche Nation	2	0	0	1	1	123	4	110	9	2
Concho Agency	6	0	2	0	4	31	2	27	2	1

Table 11. Offenses Known to Law Enforcement, by Selected State, Tribal, and Other Agencies, 2018—Continued

(Number.)

State/other agency unit/office	Violent crime	Murder and nonnegligent manslaughter	Rape[1]	Robbery	Aggravated assault	Property crime	Burglary	Larceny-theft	Motor vehicle theft	Arson[2]
Eastern Shawnee Tribal	3	0	0	0	3	88	0	84	4	2
Iowa Tribal	1	0	0	0	1	19	2	15	2	0
Kaw Tribal	0	0	0	0	0	12	0	12	0	0
Kickapoo Tribal	1	1	0	0	0	20	6	10	4	1
Miami Agency	3	0	0	0	3	50	1	40	9	0
Miami Tribal	0	0	0	0	0	20	7	12	1	0
Muscogee Nation Tribal	29	0	1	3	25	202	10	140	52	0
Osage Nation	9	1	0	4	4	150	37	83	30	0
Otoe-Missouria Tribal	2	0	0	0	2	23	7	13	3	0
Pawnee Tribal	1	0	0	0	1	6	0	5	1	0
Ponca Tribal	4	1	0	0	3	25	5	19	1	4
Quapaw Tribal	7	0	0	1	6	129	8	116	5	3
Sac and Fox Tribal	6	0	0	1	5	17	3	11	3	2
Seminole Nation Lighthorse	1	0	1	0	0	17	2	12	3	0
Tonkawa Tribal	4	0	0	0	4	20	0	17	3	0
Wyandotte Nation	8	0	0	0	8	16	3	13	0	0
Other Agencies										
Jenks Public Schools	0	0	0	0	0	2	1	1	0	0
Lawton Public Schools	3	0	2	0	1	24	3	20	1	0
Muskogee City Schools	5	0	0	0	5	5	2	2	1	1
Putnam City Campus	6	0	0	0	6	4	0	4	0	0
OREGON										
State Agencies										
Liquor Commission										
Baker County	0	0	0	0	0	0	0	0	0	0
Benton County	0	0	0	0	0	0	0	0	0	0
Clackamas County	0	0	0	0	0	0	0	0	0	0
Clatsop County	0	0	0	0	0	0	0	0	0	0
Columbia County	0	0	0	0	0	0	0	0	0	0
Coos County	0	0	0	0	0	0	0	0	0	0
Crook County	0	0	0	0	0	0	0	0	0	0
Curry County	0	0	0	0	0	0	0	0	0	0
Deschutes County	0	0	0	0	0	0	0	0	0	0
Douglas County	0	0	0	0	0	0	0	0	0	0
Gilliam County	0	0	0	0	0	0	0	0	0	0
Grant County	0	0	0	0	0	0	0	0	0	0
Harney County	0	0	0	0	0	0	0	0	0	0
Headquarters	0	0	0	0	0	0	0	0	0	0
Hood River County	0	0	0	0	0	0	0	0	0	0
Jackson County	0	0	0	0	0	0	0	0	0	0
Jefferson County	0	0	0	0	0	0	0	0	0	0
Josephine County	0	0	0	0	0	0	0	0	0	0
Klamath County	0	0	0	0	0	0	0	0	0	0
Lake County	0	0	0	0	0	0	0	0	0	0
Lane County	0	0	0	0	0	0	0	0	0	0
Lincoln County	0	0	0	0	0	0	0	0	0	0
Linn County	0	0	0	0	0	0	0	0	0	0
Malheur County	0	0	0	0	0	0	0	0	0	0
Marion County	0	0	0	0	0	0	0	0	0	0
Morrow County	0	0	0	0	0	0	0	0	0	0
Multnomah County	0	0	0	0	0	0	0	0	0	0
Polk County	0	0	0	0	0	0	0	0	0	0
Sherman County	0	0	0	0	0	0	0	0	0	0
Tillamook County	0	0	0	0	0	0	0	0	0	0
Umatilla County	0	0	0	0	0	0	0	0	0	0
Union County	0	0	0	0	0	0	0	0	0	0
Wallowa County	0	0	0	0	0	0	0	0	0	0
Wasco County	0	0	0	0	0	0	0	0	0	0
Washington County	0	0	0	0	0	0	0	0	0	0
Wheeler County	0	0	0	0	0	0	0	0	0	0
Yamhill County	0	0	0	0	0	0	0	0	0	0
State Police										
Baker County	2	0	1	0	2	10	0	8	2	1
Benton County	3	0	1	0	2	279	4	274	1	2
Clackamas County	17	0	0	0	17	37	2	20	15	1
Clatsop County	0	0	0	0	0	7	0	6	1	1
Columbia County	7	0	0	0	7	7	0	7	0	1
Coos County	7	0	0	1	6	39	1	28	10	1
Crook County	0	0	0	0	0	1	0	1	0	1
Curry County	3	0	0	0	3	15	0	12	3	0
Deschutes County	13	0	1	2	10	11	0	7	4	0
Douglas County	9	0	1	0	8	19	0	10	9	0
Gilliam County	1	0	0	0	1	0	0	0	0	1
Grant County	1	0	0	0	1	5	3	2	0	0
Harney County	2	0	0	1	1	1	0	1	0	0
Hood River County	5	0	0	0	5	2	0	2	0	0
Jackson County	16	0	3	1	12	24	1	15	8	0
Jefferson County	2	1	1	0	0	0	0	0	0	0
Josephine County	49	1	7	4	37	19	1	9	9	9
Klamath County	18	0	0	0	18	27	3	16	8	4
Lake County	1	0	0	0	1	1	0	0	1	0
Lane County	27	0	2	2	23	43	3	30	10	1

Table 11. Offenses Known to Law Enforcement, by Selected State, Tribal, and Other Agencies, 2018—Continued

(Number.)

State/other agency unit/office	Violent crime	Murder and nonnegligent manslaughter	Rape[1]	Robbery	Aggravated assault	Property crime	Burglary	Larceny-theft	Motor vehicle theft	Arson[2]
Lincoln County	1	0	0	0	1	22	0	21	1	0
Linn County	13	0	0	0	13	15	0	12	3	0
Malheur County	12	0	0	0	12	4	0	2	2	0
Marion County	35	0	4	1	30	63	6	38	19	2
Morrow County	1	0	1	0	0	4	0	3	1	0
Multnomah County	6	0	0	0	6	8	0	3	5	1
Polk County	7	0	0	0	7	7	0	4	3	1
Sherman County	1	0	0	0	1	4	0	4	0	0
Tillamook County	5	0	1	0	4	12	0	9	3	0
Umatilla County	8	0	0	0	8	15	0	11	4	0
Union County	1	0	1	0	0	6	0	3	3	0
Wallowa County	0	0	0	0	0	1	0	1	0	0
Wasco County	3	0	0	1	2	15	0	12	3	2
Washington County	0	0	0	0	0	7	0	4	3	1
Wheeler County	0	0	0	0	0	1	0	1	0	0
Yamhill County	6	0	2	0	4	3	0	3	0	2
Tribal Agencies										
Coos, Lower Umpqua, and Siuslaw Tribal	0	0	0	0	0	12	1	11	0	
Grand Ronde Tribal	4	0	1	1	2	90	6	82	2	0
Siletz Tribal	1	0	0	1	0	4	2	2	0	0
Other Agencies										
Port of Portland	8	0	3	0	5	601	4	535	62	0
PENNSYLVANIA										
State Agencies										
Bureau of Forestry										
Adams County	0	0	0	0	0	0	0	0	0	0
Allegheny County	0	0	0	0	0	0	0	0	0	0
Armstrong County	0	0	0	0	0	0	0	0	0	0
Beaver County	0	0	0	0	0	0	0	0	0	0
Bedford County	0	0	0	0	0	0	0	0	0	0
Berks County	0	0	0	0	0	0	0	0	0	6
Blair County	0	0	0	0	0	0	0	0	0	0
Bradford County	0	0	0	0	0	0	0	0	0	0
Bucks County	0	0	0	0	0	0	0	0	0	0
Butler County	0	0	0	0	0	0	0	0	0	2
Cambria County	0	0	0	0	0	0	0	0	0	1
Cameron County	0	0	0	0	0	0	0	0	0	0
Carbon County	0	0	0	0	0	0	0	0	0	1
Centre County	0	0	0	0	0	0	0	0	0	4
Chester County	0	0	0	0	0	0	0	0	0	0
Clarion County	0	0	0	0	0	0	0	0	0	0
Clearfield County	0	0	0	0	0	0	0	0	0	4
Clinton County	0	0	0	0	0	0	0	0	0	1
Columbia County	0	0	0	0	0	0	0	0	0	0
Crawford County	0	0	0	0	0	0	0	0	0	0
Cumberland County	1	0	0	0	1	2	0	1	1	0
Dauphin County	0	0	0	0	0	0	0	0	0	0
Delaware County	0	0	0	0	0	0	0	0	0	1
Elk County	0	0	0	0	0	0	0	0	0	0
Erie County	0	0	0	0	0	0	0	0	0	1
Fayette County	0	0	0	0	0	0	0	0	0	0
Forest County	0	0	0	0	0	0	0	0	0	0
Franklin County	0	0	0	0	0	0	0	0	0	0
Fulton County	0	0	0	0	0	0	0	0	0	1
Greene County	0	0	0	0	0	0	0	0	0	1
Huntingdon County	0	0	0	0	0	0	0	0	0	0
Indiana County	0	0	0	0	0	0	0	0	0	0
Jefferson County	0	0	0	0	0	0	0	0	0	1
Juniata County	0	0	0	0	0	0	0	0	0	0
Lackawanna County	0	0	0	0	0	0	0	0	0	5
Lancaster County	0	0	0	0	0	0	0	0	0	1
Lawrence County	0	0	0	0	0	0	0	0	0	0
Lebanon County	0	0	0	0	0	0	0	0	0	0
Lehigh County	0	0	0	0	0	0	0	0	0	2
Luzerne County	0	0	0	0	0	0	0	0	0	7
Lycoming County	0	0	0	0	0	0	0	0	0	0
McKean County	0	0	0	0	0	0	0	0	0	1
Mercer County	0	0	0	0	0	0	0	0	0	0
Mifflin County	0	0	0	0	0	0	0	0	0	0
Monroe County	0	0	0	0	0	0	0	0	0	0
Montgomery County	0	0	0	0	0	0	0	0	0	0
Montour County	0	0	0	0	0	0	0	0	0	0
Northampton County	0	0	0	0	0	0	0	0	0	0
Northumberland County	0	0	0	0	0	0	0	0	0	0
Perry County	0	0	0	0	0	0	0	0	0	0
Philadelphia County	0	0	0	0	0	0	0	0	0	0
Pike County	0	0	0	0	0	0	0	0	0	0
Potter County	0	0	0	0	0	0	0	0	0	0
Schuylkill County	0	0	0	0	0	0	0	0	0	9
Snyder County	0	0	0	0	0	0	0	0	0	0
Somerset County	0	0	0	0	0	0	0	0	0	0
Sullivan County	0	0	0	0	0	0	0	0	0	0

Table 11. Offenses Known to Law Enforcement, by Selected State, Tribal, and Other Agencies, 2018—Continued

(Number.)

State/other agency unit/office	Violent crime	Murder and nonnegligent manslaughter	Rape[1]	Robbery	Aggravated assault	Property crime	Burglary	Larceny-theft	Motor vehicle theft	Arson[2]
Susquehanna County	0	0	0	0	0	0	0	0	0	0
Tioga County	0	0	0	0	0	0	0	0	0	0
Union County	0	0	0	0	0	0	0	0	0	0
Venango County	0	0	0	0	0	0	0	0	0	0
Warren County	0	0	0	0	0	0	0	0	0	1
Washington County	0	0	0	0	0	0	0	0	0	0
Wayne County	0	0	0	0	0	0	0	0	0	0
Westmoreland County	0	0	0	0	0	0	0	0	0	4
Wyoming County	0	0	0	0	0	0	0	0	0	1
York County	0	0	0	0	0	0	0	0	0	0
Bureau of Narcotics										
Adams County	0	0	0	0	0	0	0	0	0	0
Allegheny County	0	0	0	0	0	0	0	0	0	0
Armstrong County	0	0	0	0	0	0	0	0	0	0
Beaver County	0	0	0	0	0	0	0	0	0	0
Bedford County	0	0	0	0	0	0	0	0	0	0
Berks County	0	0	0	0	0	0	0	0	0	0
Blair County	0	0	0	0	0	0	0	0	0	0
Bradford County	0	0	0	0	0	0	0	0	0	0
Bucks County	0	0	0	0	0	0	0	0	0	0
Butler County	0	0	0	0	0	0	0	0	0	0
Cambria County	0	0	0	0	0	0	0	0	0	0
Cameron County	0	0	0	0	0	0	0	0	0	0
Carbon County	0	0	0	0	0	0	0	0	0	0
Centre County	0	0	0	0	0	0	0	0	0	0
Chester County	0	0	0	0	0	0	0	0	0	0
Clarion County	0	0	0	0	0	0	0	0	0	0
Clearfield County	0	0	0	0	0	0	0	0	0	0
Clinton County	0	0	0	0	0	0	0	0	0	0
Columbia County	0	0	0	0	0	0	0	0	0	0
Crawford County	0	0	0	0	0	0	0	0	0	0
Cumberland County	0	0	0	0	0	0	0	0	0	0
Dauphin County	0	0	0	0	0	0	0	0	0	0
Delaware County	0	0	0	0	0	0	0	0	0	0
Elk County	0	0	0	0	0	0	0	0	0	0
Erie County	0	0	0	0	0	0	0	0	0	0
Fayette County	0	0	0	0	0	0	0	0	0	0
Forest County	0	0	0	0	0	0	0	0	0	0
Franklin County	0	0	0	0	0	0	0	0	0	0
Fulton County	0	0	0	0	0	0	0	0	0	0
Greene County	0	0	0	0	0	0	0	0	0	0
Huntingdon County	0	0	0	0	0	0	0	0	0	0
Indiana County	0	0	0	0	0	0	0	0	0	0
Jefferson County	0	0	0	0	0	0	0	0	0	0
Juniata County	0	0	0	0	0	0	0	0	0	0
Lackawanna County	0	0	0	0	0	0	0	0	0	0
Lancaster County	0	0	0	0	0	0	0	0	0	0
Lawrence County	0	0	0	0	0	0	0	0	0	0
Lebanon County	0	0	0	0	0	0	0	0	0	0
Lehigh County	0	0	0	0	0	0	0	0	0	0
Luzerne County	0	0	0	0	0	0	0	0	0	0
Lycoming County	0	0	0	0	0	0	0	0	0	0
McKean County	0	0	0	0	0	0	0	0	0	0
Mercer County	0	0	0	0	0	0	0	0	0	0
Mifflin County	0	0	0	0	0	0	0	0	0	0
Monroe County	0	0	0	0	0	0	0	0	0	0
Montgomery County	0	0	0	0	0	0	0	0	0	0
Montour County	0	0	0	0	0	0	0	0	0	0
Northampton County	0	0	0	0	0	0	0	0	0	0
Northumberland County	0	0	0	0	0	0	0	0	0	0
Perry County	0	0	0	0	0	0	0	0	0	0
Philadelphia County	0	0	0	0	0	0	0	0	0	0
Pike County	0	0	0	0	0	0	0	0	0	0
Potter County	0	0	0	0	0	0	0	0	0	0
Schuylkill County	0	0	0	0	0	0	0	0	0	0
Snyder County	0	0	0	0	0	0	0	0	0	0
Somerset County	0	0	0	0	0	0	0	0	0	0
Sullivan County	0	0	0	0	0	0	0	0	0	0
Susquehanna County	0	0	0	0	0	0	0	0	0	0
Tioga County	0	0	0	0	0	0	0	0	0	0
Union County	0	0	0	0	0	0	0	0	0	0
Venango County	0	0	0	0	0	0	0	0	0	0
Warren County	0	0	0	0	0	0	0	0	0	0
Washington County	0	0	0	0	0	0	0	0	0	0
Wayne County	0	0	0	0	0	0	0	0	0	0
Westmoreland County	0	0	0	0	0	0	0	0	0	0
Wyoming County	0	0	0	0	0	0	0	0	0	0
York County	0	0	0	0	0	0	0	0	0	0
Pennsylvania Fish and Boat Commission	0	0	0	0	0	0	0	0	0	0
State Capitol Police	1	0	0	0	1	11	0	11	0	0
State Park Rangers										
Bald Eagle	0	0	0	0	0	1	0	1	0	0
Beltzville	0	0	0	0	0	9	0	9	0	0

Table 11. Offenses Known to Law Enforcement, by Selected State, Tribal, and Other Agencies, 2018—Continued

(Number.)

State/other agency unit/office	Violent crime	Murder and nonnegligent manslaughter	Rape[1]	Robbery	Aggravated assault	Property crime	Burglary	Larceny-theft	Motor vehicle theft	Arson[2]
Ben Rush	0	0	0	0	0	0	0	0	0	0
Bendigo	0	0	0	0	0	0	0	0	0	0
Black Moshannon	0	0	0	0	0	0	0	0	0	0
Blue Knob	0	0	0	0	0	0	0	0	0	0
Caledonia	0	0	0	0	0	1	0	1	0	0
Canoe Creek	0	0	0	0	0	1	0	1	0	0
Chapman	0	0	0	0	0	0	0	0	0	0
Clear Creek	0	0	0	0	0	0	0	0	0	0
Codorus	0	0	0	0	0	7	0	7	0	0
Colonel Denning	0	0	0	0	0	0	0	0	0	0
Cook Forest	0	0	0	0	0	0	0	0	0	0
Cowans Gap	0	0	0	0	0	0	0	0	0	0
Delaware Canal	0	0	0	0	0	5	0	5	0	0
Evansburg	0	0	0	0	0	0	0	0	0	0
Fort Washington	0	0	0	0	0	0	0	0	0	0
Frances Slocum	0	0	0	0	0	0	0	0	0	0
French Creek	0	0	0	0	0	0	0	0	0	0
Gifford Pinchot	0	0	0	0	0	2	0	2	0	0
Greenwood Furnace	0	0	0	0	0	0	0	0	0	0
Hickory Run	1	0	0	0	1	13	0	12	1	0
Hills Creek	0	0	0	0	0	5	4	1	0	0
Jacobsburg Environmental Education Center	0	0	0	0	0	0	0	0	0	0
Jennings Environmental Education Center	0	0	0	0	0	0	0	0	0	0
Kettle Creek	0	0	0	0	0	0	0	0	0	0
Keystone	0	0	0	0	0	3	0	3	0	0
Kings Gap Environmental Education Center	0	0	0	0	0	0	0	0	0	0
Kooser	0	0	0	0	0	0	0	0	0	0
Lackawanna	0	0	0	0	0	0	0	0	0	0
Laurel Hill	0	0	0	0	0	3	0	3	0	0
Laurel Ridge	0	0	0	0	0	0	0	0	0	0
Leonard Harrison	0	0	0	0	0	1	0	1	0	0
Linn Run	0	0	0	0	0	1	0	1	0	0
Little Buffalo	0	0	0	0	0	0	0	0	0	0
Little Pine	0	0	0	0	0	1	0	1	0	0
Lyman Run	0	0	0	0	0	0	0	0	0	0
Marsh Creek	0	0	0	0	0	0	0	0	0	0
Maurice K. Goddard	0	0	0	0	0	0	0	0	0	0
Moraine	0	0	0	0	0	0	0	0	0	0
Mount Pisgah	0	0	0	0	0	0	0	0	0	0
Neshaminy	0	0	0	0	0	0	0	0	0	0
Nockamixon	0	0	0	0	0	3	0	3	0	0
Ohiopyle	0	0	0	0	0	8	1	7	0	0
Oil Creek	0	0	0	0	0	1	0	1	0	0
Ole Bull	0	0	0	0	0	0	0	0	0	0
Parker Dam	0	0	0	0	0	0	0	0	0	0
Pine Grove Furnace	0	0	0	0	0	1	0	1	0	0
Point	0	0	0	0	0	0	0	0	0	0
Presque Isle	1	0	1	0	0	10	0	10	0	0
Prince Gallitzin	1	0	0	0	1	5	1	4	0	0
Promised Land	0	0	0	0	0	3	1	2	0	0
Pymatuning	0	0	0	0	0	0	0	0	0	0
Raccoon Creek	1	0	0	0	1	6	0	6	0	0
Raymond B. Winter	0	0	0	0	0	0	0	0	0	0
Reeds Gap	0	0	0	0	0	0	0	0	0	0
Ricketts Glen	0	0	0	0	0	0	0	0	0	0
Ridley Creek	0	0	0	0	0	0	0	0	0	0
Ryerson Station	0	0	0	0	0	1	0	1	0	0
Samuel S. Lewis	0	0	0	0	0	0	0	0	0	0
Shawnee	0	0	0	0	0	0	0	0	0	0
Shikellamy	0	0	0	0	0	0	0	0	0	0
Sinnemahoning	0	0	0	0	0	0	0	0	0	0
Sizerville	0	0	0	0	0	0	0	0	0	0
Susquehannock	0	0	0	0	0	0	0	0	0	0
Tobyhanna	0	0	0	0	0	1	0	1	0	0
Trough Creek	0	0	0	0	0	0	0	0	0	0
Tuscarora	0	0	0	0	0	3	0	3	0	0
Tyler	0	0	0	0	0	1	0	1	0	0
White Clay	0	0	0	0	0	0	0	0	0	0
Worlds End	0	0	0	0	0	0	0	0	0	0
Yellow Creek	0	0	0	0	0	1	0	1	0	0
State Police, Bureau of Criminal Investigation										
Adams County	0	0	0	0	0	0	0	0	0	0
Allegheny County	0	0	0	0	0	0	0	0	0	0
Armstrong County	0	0	0	0	0	0	0	0	0	0
Beaver County	0	0	0	0	0	0	0	0	0	0
Bedford County	0	0	0	0	0	0	0	0	0	0
Berks County	0	0	0	0	0	2	0	2	0	0
Blair County	0	0	0	0	0	0	0	0	0	0
Bradford County	0	0	0	0	0	0	0	0	0	0

Table 11. Offenses Known to Law Enforcement, by Selected State, Tribal, and Other Agencies, 2018—Continued

(Number.)

State/other agency unit/office	Violent crime	Murder and nonnegligent manslaughter	Rape[1]	Robbery	Aggravated assault	Property crime	Burglary	Larceny-theft	Motor vehicle theft	Arson[2]
Bucks County	0	0	0	0	0	0	0	0	0	0
Butler County	0	0	0	0	0	0	0	0	0	0
Cambria County	0	0	0	0	0	3	0	3	0	0
Cameron County	0	0	0	0	0	0	0	0	0	0
Carbon County	0	0	0	0	0	0	0	0	0	0
Centre County	0	0	0	0	0	0	0	0	0	0
Chester County	1	0	1	0	0	0	0	0	0	0
Clarion County	0	0	0	0	0	0	0	0	0	0
Clearfield County	0	0	0	0	0	1	0	1	0	0
Clinton County	0	0	0	0	0	0	0	0	0	0
Columbia County	0	0	0	0	0	0	0	0	0	0
Crawford County	0	0	0	0	0	0	0	0	0	0
Cumberland County	0	0	0	0	0	2	0	2	0	0
Dauphin County	0	0	0	0	0	2	0	2	0	0
Delaware County	0	0	0	0	0	2	0	2	0	0
Elk County	0	0	0	0	0	0	0	0	0	0
Erie County	0	0	0	0	0	1	0	1	0	0
Fayette County	0	0	0	0	0	1	0	1	0	0
Forest County	0	0	0	0	0	0	0	0	0	0
Franklin County	0	0	0	0	0	2	0	2	0	0
Fulton County	0	0	0	0	0	0	0	0	0	0
Greene County	0	0	0	0	0	1	0	1	0	0
Huntingdon County	0	0	0	0	0	0	0	0	0	0
Indiana County	0	0	0	0	0	0	0	0	0	0
Jefferson County	0	0	0	0	0	0	0	0	0	0
Juniata County	0	0	0	0	0	0	0	0	0	0
Lackawanna County	3	0	3	0	0	1	0	1	0	0
Lancaster County	0	0	0	0	0	0	0	0	0	0
Lawrence County	0	0	0	0	0	0	0	0	0	0
Lebanon County	0	0	0	0	0	0	0	0	0	0
Lehigh County	0	0	0	0	0	0	0	0	0	0
Luzerne County	0	0	0	0	0	1	0	1	0	0
Lycoming County	0	0	0	0	0	0	0	0	0	0
McKean County	0	0	0	0	0	0	0	0	0	0
Mercer County	0	0	0	0	0	1	0	1	0	0
Mifflin County	0	0	0	0	0	0	0	0	0	0
Monroe County	0	0	0	0	0	0	0	0	0	0
Montgomery County	0	0	0	0	0	1	0	1	0	0
Montour County	0	0	0	0	0	0	0	0	0	0
Northampton County	0	0	0	0	0	0	0	0	0	0
Northumberland County	0	0	0	0	0	0	0	0	0	0
Perry County	0	0	0	0	0	0	0	0	0	0
Philadelphia County	0	0	0	0	0	0	0	0	0	0
Pike County	0	0	0	0	0	0	0	0	0	0
Potter County	0	0	0	0	0	0	0	0	0	0
Schuylkill County	0	0	0	0	0	0	0	0	0	0
Snyder County	0	0	0	0	0	0	0	0	0	0
Somerset County	0	0	0	0	0	0	0	0	0	0
Sullivan County	0	0	0	0	0	0	0	0	0	0
Susquehanna County	0	0	0	0	0	0	0	0	0	0
Tioga County	0	0	0	0	0	0	0	0	0	0
Union County	0	0	0	0	0	0	0	0	0	0
Venango County	0	0	0	0	0	0	0	0	0	0
Warren County	0	0	0	0	0	0	0	0	0	0
Washington County	0	0	0	0	0	1	0	1	0	0
Wayne County	0	0	0	0	0	0	0	0	0	0
Westmoreland County	0	0	0	0	0	2	0	2	0	0
Wyoming County	0	0	0	0	0	0	0	0	0	0
York County	1	0	0	1	0	0	0	0	0	0
State Police										
Adams County	55	2	20	8	25	327	69	250	8	3
Allegheny County	14	0	1	0	13	120	2	108	10	0
Armstrong County	48	0	24	1	23	266	63	194	9	3
Beaver County	28	1	8	6	13	89	25	55	9	1
Bedford County	69	2	27	13	27	308	58	244	6	4
Berks County	47	2	16	4	25	485	136	316	33	15
Blair County	15	0	8	1	6	133	38	91	4	1
Bradford County	70	1	33	2	34	342	80	230	32	5
Bucks County	19	0	5	3	11	289	52	228	9	2
Butler County	160	0	18	7	135	386	108	264	14	2
Cambria County	23	0	7	3	13	146	53	77	16	1
Cameron County	7	0	4	0	3	24	6	18	0	0
Carbon County	61	0	43	1	17	300	86	193	21	1
Centre County	64	2	20	0	42	309	58	245	6	4
Chester County	145	1	65	13	66	791	139	614	38	4
Clarion County	54	0	15	2	37	202	69	121	12	1
Clearfield County	53	0	47	1	5	488	111	348	29	4
Clinton County	27	0	10	3	14	169	29	135	5	0
Columbia County	9	0	5	0	4	122	23	99	0	0
Crawford County	79	1	18	7	53	473	185	257	31	2
Cumberland County	81	0	40	9	32	558	105	428	25	3
Delaware County	46	0	9	12	25	566	47	498	21	1
Elizabethville	253	0	50	27	176	687	114	536	37	1
Elk County	10	0	2	1	7	170	22	146	2	2

Table 11. Offenses Known to Law Enforcement, by Selected State, Tribal, and Other Agencies, 2018—Continued

(Number.)

State/other agency unit/office	Violent crime	Murder and nonnegligent manslaughter	Rape[1]	Robbery	Aggravated assault	Property crime	Burglary	Larceny-theft	Motor vehicle theft	Arson[2]
Erie County	96	4	38	9	45	1,367	154	1,179	34	6
Fayette County	264	10	72	36	146	1,563	353	1,148	62	21
Franklin County	172	3	51	8	110	867	218	614	35	8
Fulton County	23	0	9	0	14	147	56	85	6	1
Greene County	37	0	9	15	13	197	54	137	6	0
Huntingdon County	88	4	47	4	33	313	87	218	8	2
Indiana County	69	1	22	7	39	535	121	395	19	3
Jefferson County	28	3	16	1	8	179	55	112	12	1
Juniata County	25	0	13	0	12	178	41	137	0	1
Lackawanna County	37	0	7	5	25	125	44	69	12	22
Lancaster County	99	0	39	8	52	678	193	447	38	5
Lawrence County	27	0	2	2	23	148	39	99	10	3
Lebanon County	63	0	18	4	41	306	90	203	13	6
Lehigh County	37	1	6	6	24	709	99	591	19	1
Luzerne County	118	6	41	12	59	587	140	423	24	13
Lycoming County	91	2	17	1	71	300	75	209	16	0
McKean County	26	0	6	0	20	100	33	61	6	3
Mercer County	57	1	13	6	37	280	68	201	11	0
Mifflin County	18	1	9	1	7	81	11	67	3	1
Monroe County	112	1	43	14	54	1,030	214	754	62	3
Montour County	9	0	4	0	5	83	24	52	7	0
Northampton County	20	1	2	3	14	266	43	207	16	1
Northumberland County	57	0	16	4	37	232	72	140	20	2
Perry County	98	0	15	10	73	380	93	264	23	2
Philadelphia County	24	4	2	0	18	8	2	4	2	0
Pike County	57	1	13	8	35	278	107	161	10	1
Potter County	20	0	7	1	12	73	25	43	5	0
Schuylkill County	136	1	27	11	97	650	163	431	56	8
Skippack	51	0	14	4	33	329	49	261	19	6
Snyder County	36	0	7	1	28	226	54	167	5	1
Somerset County	42	3	19	2	18	310	86	210	14	12
Sullivan County	10	1	5	0	4	62	29	29	4	0
Susquehanna County	44	1	17	7	19	351	114	202	35	2
Tioga County	39	0	19	3	17	281	110	151	20	0
Tionesta	21	0	11	0	10	50	14	34	2	2
Union County	37	1	21	3	12	286	28	252	6	0
Venango County	25	0	11	2	12	156	42	103	11	2
Warren County	31	1	11	2	17	189	66	114	9	1
Washington County	76	2	17	9	48	377	73	262	42	10
Wayne County	59	5	28	4	22	360	76	263	21	3
Westmoreland County	144	4	45	19	76	979	206	717	56	5
Wyoming County	14	0	9	0	5	219	59	144	16	4
York County	174	2	28	11	133	475	94	358	23	8
Other Agencies										
Allegheny County District Attorney, Criminal Investigation Division	2	1	0	0	1	41	0	41	0	0
Allegheny County Housing Authority	9	2	0	0	7	25	6	18	1	1
Allegheny County Port Authority	98	0	1	14	83	72	0	71	1	0
County Detective										
Adams County	0	0	0	0	0	1	0	1	0	0
Beaver County	5	1	0	0	4	1	0	1	0	0
Berks County	39	0	1	0	38	3	0	1	2	0
Bucks County	3	1	1	0	1	3	1	2	0	0
Butler County	0	0	0	0	0	0	0	0	0	0
Chester County	13	2	3	1	7	9	0	8	1	0
Clarion County	7	0	0	1	6	4	0	4	0	0
Cumberland County	3	0	2	0	1	1	0	1	0	0
Dauphin County	3	0	0	1	2	15	0	15	0	0
Erie County	12	0	0	0	12	0	0	0	0	0
Lackawanna County	13	0	5	0	8	0	0	0	0	0
Lancaster County	2	0	0	0	2	4	0	4	0	0
Lawrence County	0	0	0	0	0	0	0	0	0	0
Lebanon County	1	0	1	0	0	1	0	1	0	0
Lehigh County	2	0	0	2	0	58	4	0	54	0
Luzerne County	1	0	0	0	1	0	0	0	0	0
McKean County	0	0	0	0	0	0	0	0	0	0
Monroe County	58	0	0	0	58	3	0	3	0	0
Montgomery County	5	0	0	2	3	4	0	4	0	0
Montour County	0	0	0	0	0	0	0	0	0	0
Pike County	19	0	1	0	18	0	0	0	0	0
Schuylkill County	0	0	0	0	0	1	0	1	0	0
Wayne County	1	0	1	0	0	5	1	4	0	0
Westmoreland County	11	1	0	0	10	33	0	33	0	0
Wyoming County	2	0	0	0	2	0	0	0	0	0
York County	4	0	0	0	4	5	0	3	2	0
Delaware County District Attorney, Criminal Investigation Division	11	0	1	0	10	3	0	2	1	0
Delaware County Park	20	0	0	0	20	83	0	83	0	0
Fort Indiantown Gap	0	0	0	0	0	2	1	1	0	0
Franklin County Drug Task Force	0	0	0	0	0	0	0	0	0	0
Harrisburg International Airport	1	0	0	1	0	19	0	11	8	0
Lehigh Valley International Airport	0	0	0	0	0	28	0	16	12	0
Westmoreland County Park	11	0	0	1	10	18	0	18	0	0
Wyoming Area School District	0	0	0	0	0	0	0	0	0	0

Table 11. Offenses Known to Law Enforcement, by Selected State, Tribal, and Other Agencies, 2018—Continued

(Number.)

State/other agency unit/office	Violent crime	Murder and nonnegligent manslaughter	Rape[1]	Robbery	Aggravated assault	Property crime	Burglary	Larceny-theft	Motor vehicle theft	Arson[2]
RHODE ISLAND										
State Agencies										
Department of Environmental Management	1	0	0	0	1	22	1	21	0	2
Rhode Island State Police Headquarters	27	0	15	0	12	74	0	64	10	0
State Police										
Chepachet/Scituate	10	0	4	1	5	18	0	10	8	0
Hope Valley	7	0	4	0	3	35	5	23	7	0
Lincoln	11	0	3	2	6	44	1	18	25	0
Portsmouth	0	0	0	0	0	4	0	4	0	0
Wickford	10	0	4	1	5	39	4	28	7	0
T.F. Green Airport	0	0	0	0	0	23	1	20	2	0
SOUTH CAROLINA										
State Agencies										
Bureau of Protective Services										
Department of Mental Health	3	0	0	0	3	1	0	1	0	0
Department of Natural Resources										
Abbeville County	0	0	0	0	0	0	0	0	0	0
Aiken County	0	0	0	0	0	0	0	0	0	0
Allendale County	0	0	0	0	0	0	0	0	0	0
Anderson County	0	0	0	0	0	0	0	0	0	0
Bamberg County	0	0	0	0	0	0	0	0	0	0
Barnwell County	0	0	0	0	0	0	0	0	0	0
Beaufort County	0	0	0	0	0	0	0	0	0	0
Berkeley County	0	0	0	0	0	0	0	0	0	0
Calhoun County	0	0	0	0	0	0	0	0	0	0
Charleston County	0	0	0	0	0	0	0	0	0	0
Cherokee County	0	0	0	0	0	0	0	0	0	0
Chester County	0	0	0	0	0	0	0	0	0	0
Chesterfield County	0	0	0	0	0	0	0	0	0	0
Clarendon County	0	0	0	0	0	0	0	0	0	0
Colleton County	0	0	0	0	0	0	0	0	0	0
Darlington County	0	0	0	0	0	0	0	0	0	0
Dillon County	0	0	0	0	0	0	0	0	0	0
Dorchester County	0	0	0	0	0	0	0	0	0	0
Edgefield County	0	0	0	0	0	0	0	0	0	0
Fairfield County	0	0	0	0	0	0	0	0	0	0
Florence County	0	0	0	0	0	0	0	0	0	0
Georgetown County	0	0	0	0	0	0	0	0	0	0
Greenville County	0	0	0	0	0	0	0	0	0	0
Greenwood County	0	0	0	0	0	0	0	0	0	0
Hampton County	0	0	0	0	0	0	0	0	0	0
Horry County	0	0	0	0	0	0	0	0	0	0
Jasper County	0	0	0	0	0	0	0	0	0	0
Kershaw County	0	0	0	0	0	0	0	0	0	0
Lancaster County	0	0	0	0	0	0	0	0	0	0
Laurens County	0	0	0	0	0	0	0	0	0	0
Lee County	0	0	0	0	0	0	0	0	0	0
Lexington County	0	0	0	0	0	0	0	0	0	0
Marion County	0	0	0	0	0	0	0	0	0	0
Marlboro County	0	0	0	0	0	0	0	0	0	0
McCormick County	0	0	0	0	0	0	0	0	0	0
Newberry County	0	0	0	0	0	0	0	0	0	0
Oconee County	0	0	0	0	0	0	0	0	0	0
Orangeburg County	0	0	0	0	0	0	0	0	0	0
Pickens County	0	0	0	0	0	0	0	0	0	0
Richland County	0	0	0	0	0	0	0	0	0	0
Saluda County	0	0	0	0	0	0	0	0	0	0
Spartanburg County	0	0	0	0	0	0	0	0	0	0
Sumter County	0	0	0	0	0	0	0	0	0	0
Union County	0	0	0	0	0	0	0	0	0	0
Williamsburg County	0	0	0	0	0	0	0	0	0	0
York County	0	0	0	0	0	0	0	0	0	0
Forestry Commission										
Abbeville County	0	0	0	0	0	0	0	0	0	0
Aiken County	0	0	0	0	0	0	0	0	0	0
Allendale County	0	0	0	0	0	0	0	0	0	0
Anderson County	0	0	0	0	0	0	0	0	0	0
Barnwell County	0	0	0	0	0	0	0	0	0	0
Beaufort County	0	0	0	0	0	0	0	0	0	0
Berkeley County	0	0	0	0	0	0	0	0	0	0
Calhoun County	0	0	0	0	0	0	0	0	0	0
Charleston County	0	0	0	0	0	0	0	0	0	0
Cherokee County	0	0	0	0	0	0	0	0	0	0
Chester County	0	0	0	0	0	0	0	0	0	0
Colleton County	0	0	0	0	0	0	0	0	0	0
Dillon County	0	0	0	0	0	0	0	0	0	0
Dorchester County	0	0	0	0	0	0	0	0	0	0
Edgefield County	0	0	0	0	0	0	0	0	0	0
Fairfield County	0	0	0	0	0	0	0	0	0	0
Florence County	0	0	0	0	0	0	0	0	0	0
Georgetown County	0	0	0	0	0	0	0	0	0	0

Table 11. Offenses Known to Law Enforcement, by Selected State, Tribal, and Other Agencies, 2018—Continued

(Number.)

State/other agency unit/office	Violent crime	Murder and nonnegligent manslaughter	Rape[1]	Robbery	Aggravated assault	Property crime	Burglary	Larceny-theft	Motor vehicle theft	Arson[2]
Greenville County	0	0	0	0	0	0	0	0	0	0
Greenwood County	0	0	0	0	0	0	0	0	0	0
Horry County	0	0	0	0	0	0	0	0	0	0
Lancaster County	0	0	0	0	0	0	0	0	0	0
Lexington County	0	0	0	0	0	0	0	0	0	0
Marion County	0	0	0	0	0	0	0	0	0	0
McCormick County	0	0	0	0	0	0	0	0	0	0
Newberry County	0	0	0	0	0	0	0	0	0	0
Oconee County	0	0	0	0	0	0	0	0	0	0
Pickens County	0	0	0	0	0	0	0	0	0	0
Saluda County	0	0	0	0	0	0	0	0	0	0
Spartanburg County	0	0	0	0	0	0	0	0	0	0
Union County	0	0	0	0	0	0	0	0	0	0
Highway Patrol	2	0	1	1	0	46	1	44	1	0
Abbeville County	0	0	0	0	0	1	0	1	0	0
Aiken County	0	0	0	0	0	1	0	0	1	0
Allendale County	0	0	0	0	0	0	0	0	0	0
Anderson County	0	0	0	0	0	0	0	0	0	0
Bamberg County	0	0	0	0	0	0	0	0	0	0
Barnwell County	0	0	0	0	0	1	0	0	1	0
Beaufort County	0	0	0	0	0	0	0	0	0	0
Berkeley County	0	0	0	0	0	1	0	1	0	0
Calhoun County	0	0	0	0	0	0	0	0	0	0
Charleston County	0	0	0	0	0	0	0	0	0	0
Cherokee County	0	0	0	0	0	1	0	0	1	0
Chester County	0	0	0	0	0	0	0	0	0	0
Chesterfield County	0	0	0	0	0	0	0	0	0	0
Clarendon County	0	0	0	0	0	0	0	0	0	0
Colleton County	1	1	0	0	0	1	0	0	1	0
Darlington County	1	1	0	0	0	0	0	0	0	0
Dillon County	0	0	0	0	0	0	0	0	0	0
Dorchester County	0	0	0	0	0	0	0	0	0	0
Edgefield County	0	0	0	0	0	0	0	0	0	0
Fairfield County	0	0	0	0	0	0	0	0	0	0
Florence County	0	0	0	0	0	0	0	0	0	0
Georgetown County	0	0	0	0	0	0	0	0	0	0
Greenville County	0	0	0	0	0	1	0	0	1	0
Greenwood County	0	0	0	0	0	1	0	1	0	0
Hampton County	0	0	0	0	0	0	0	0	0	0
Horry County	0	0	0	0	0	0	0	0	0	0
Jasper County	0	0	0	0	0	0	0	0	0	0
Kershaw County	0	0	0	0	0	0	0	0	0	0
Lancaster County	0	0	0	0	0	0	0	0	0	0
Laurens County	0	0	0	0	0	1	0	0	1	0
Lee County	0	0	0	0	0	0	0	0	0	0
Lexington County	0	0	0	0	0	1	0	1	0	0
Marion County	0	0	0	0	0	0	0	0	0	0
Marlboro County	0	0	0	0	0	0	0	0	0	0
McCormick County	0	0	0	0	0	0	0	0	0	0
Newberry County	0	0	0	0	0	0	0	0	0	0
Oconee County	0	0	0	0	0	0	0	0	0	0
Orangeburg County	0	0	0	0	0	0	0	0	0	0
Pickens County	0	0	0	0	0	0	0	0	0	0
Richland County	0	0	0	0	0	0	0	0	0	0
Saluda County	0	0	0	0	0	0	0	0	0	0
Spartanburg County	0	0	0	0	0	0	0	0	0	0
Sumter County	0	0	0	0	0	0	0	0	0	0
Union County	0	0	0	0	0	0	0	0	0	0
Williamsburg County	0	0	0	0	0	0	0	0	0	0
York County	0	0	0	0	0	2	0	1	1	0
South Carolina School for the Deaf and Blind	0	0	0	0	0	0	0	0	0	0
State Museum	0	0	0	0	0	0	0	0	0	0
State Ports Authority	0	0	0	0	0	1	0	1	0	0
State Transport Police										
Abbeville County	0	0	0	0	0	0	0	0	0	0
Aiken County	0	0	0	0	0	0	0	0	0	0
Allendale County	0	0	0	0	0	0	0	0	0	0
Anderson County	0	0	0	0	0	0	0	0	0	0
Bamberg County	0	0	0	0	0	0	0	0	0	0
Barnwell County	0	0	0	0	0	0	0	0	0	0
Beaufort County	0	0	0	0	0	0	0	0	0	0
Berkeley County	0	0	0	0	0	0	0	0	0	0
Calhoun County	0	0	0	0	0	0	0	0	0	0
Charleston County	0	0	0	0	0	0	0	0	0	0
Cherokee County	0	0	0	0	0	0	0	0	0	0
Chester County	0	0	0	0	0	0	0	0	0	0
Chesterfield County	0	0	0	0	0	0	0	0	0	0
Clarendon County	0	0	0	0	0	0	0	0	0	0
Colleton County	0	0	0	0	0	0	0	0	0	0
Darlington County	0	0	0	0	0	0	0	0	0	0
Dillon County	0	0	0	0	0	0	0	0	0	0
Dorchester County	0	0	0	0	0	0	0	0	0	0

Table 11. Offenses Known to Law Enforcement, by Selected State, Tribal, and Other Agencies, 2018—Continued

(Number.)

State/other agency unit/office	Violent crime	Murder and nonnegligent manslaughter	Rape[1]	Robbery	Aggravated assault	Property crime	Burglary	Larceny-theft	Motor vehicle theft	Arson[2]
Edgefield County	0	0	0	0	0	0	0	0	0	0
Fairfield County	0	0	0	0	0	0	0	0	0	0
Florence County	0	0	0	0	0	0	0	0	0	0
Georgetown County	0	0	0	0	0	0	0	0	0	0
Greenwood County	0	0	0	0	0	0	0	0	0	0
Hampton County	0	0	0	0	0	0	0	0	0	0
Horry County	0	0	0	0	0	0	0	0	0	0
Jasper County	0	0	0	0	0	0	0	0	0	0
Kershaw County	0	0	0	0	0	0	0	0	0	0
Lancaster County	0	0	0	0	0	0	0	0	0	0
Laurens County	0	0	0	0	0	0	0	0	0	0
Lee County	0	0	0	0	0	0	0	0	0	0
Lexington County	0	0	0	0	0	0	0	0	0	0
Marion County	0	0	0	0	0	0	0	0	0	0
Marlboro County	0	0	0	0	0	0	0	0	0	0
McCormick County	0	0	0	0	0	0	0	0	0	0
Newberry County	0	0	0	0	0	0	0	0	0	0
Oconee County	0	0	0	0	0	0	0	0	0	0
Orangeburg County	0	0	0	0	0	0	0	0	0	0
Pickens County	0	0	0	0	0	0	0	0	0	0
Richland County	0	0	0	0	0	0	0	0	0	0
Saluda County	0	0	0	0	0	0	0	0	0	0
Sumter County	0	0	0	0	0	0	0	0	0	0
Union County	0	0	0	0	0	0	0	0	0	0
Williamsburg County	0	0	0	0	0	0	0	0	0	0
York County	0	0	0	0	0	0	0	0	0	0
United States Department of Energy										
Savannah River Plant	0	0	0	0	0	15	0	15	0	0
Other Agencies										
Charleston County Aviation Authority	0	0	0	0	0	46	0	27	19	0
Columbia Metropolitan Airport	0	0	0	0	0	24	0	8	16	0
Greenville Hospital										
Greenville	11	0	1	0	10	114	0	111	3	0
Laurens	0	0	0	0	0	3	0	3	0	0
Oconee	1	0	0	0	1	21	0	21	0	0
Greenville-Spartanburg International										
Airport	0	0	0	0	0	17	0	2	15	0
Lexington County Medical Center	2	0	0	0	2	44	2	41	1	0
SOUTH DAKOTA										
State Agencies										
Division of Criminal Investigation	2	2	0	0	0	0	0	0	0	0
Highway Patrol	4	0	0	0	4	11	0	4	7	0
TENNESSEE										
State Agencies										
Alcoholic Beverage Commission	0	0	0	0	0	0	0	0	0	0
Department of Agriculture, Agricultural										
Crime Unit	0	0	0	0	0	2	2	0	0	6
Department of Correction, Internal Affairs	6	0	0	0	6	0	0	0	0	0
Department of Safety	99	0	0	0	99	177	0	24	153	0
State Fire Marshal	0	0	0	0	0	0	0	0	0	2
State Park Rangers										
Bicentennial Capitol Mall	0	0	0	0	0	0	0	0	0	0
Big Hill Pond	0	0	0	0	0	0	0	0	0	0
Big Ridge	0	0	0	0	0	1	0	1	0	0
Bledsoe Creek	0	0	0	0	0	2	0	2	0	0
Booker T. Washington	0	0	0	0	0	1	0	1	0	0
Burgess Falls Natural Area	0	0	0	0	0	0	0	0	0	0
Cedars of Lebanon	0	0	0	0	0	3	0	3	0	0
Chickasaw	0	0	0	0	0	0	0	0	0	0
Cordell Hull Birthplace	0	0	0	0	0	0	0	0	0	0
Cove Lake	0	0	0	0	0	0	0	0	0	0
Cumberland Mountain	0	0	0	0	0	0	0	0	0	0
Cumberland Trail	0	0	0	0	0	4	0	2	2	0
Cummins Falls	0	0	0	0	0	1	0	1	0	0
David Crockett	0	0	0	0	0	1	0	1	0	0
Davy Crockett Birthplace	0	0	0	0	0	0	0	0	0	0
Dunbar Cave Natural Area	0	0	0	0	0	0	0	0	0	0
Edgar Evins	0	0	0	0	0	9	0	9	0	0
Fall Creek Falls	1	0	0	0	1	3	0	3	0	0
Fort Loudon State Historic Park	0	0	0	0	0	0	0	0	0	0
Fort Pillow State Historic Park	0	0	0	0	0	0	0	0	0	0
Frozen Head Natural Area	0	0	0	0	0	1	0	1	0	0
Harpeth Scenic Rivers	0	0	0	0	0	2	0	2	0	0
Harrison Bay	0	0	0	0	0	5	0	5	0	0
Henry Horton	0	0	0	0	0	6	0	5	1	0
Indian Mountain	0	0	0	0	0	0	0	0	0	0
Johnsonville State Historic Park	0	0	0	0	0	0	0	0	0	0
Long Hunter	0	0	0	0	0	3	0	3	0	0
Meeman-Shelby Forest	0	0	0	0	0	1	0	1	0	0
Montgomery Bell	0	0	0	0	0	2	0	2	0	0
Mousetail Landing	1	0	0	0	1	0	0	0	0	0
Natchez Trace	0	0	0	0	0	1	0	1	0	0

Table 11. Offenses Known to Law Enforcement, by Selected State, Tribal, and Other Agencies, 2018—Continued

(Number.)

State/other agency unit/office	Violent crime	Murder and nonnegligent manslaughter	Rape[1]	Robbery	Aggravated assault	Property crime	Burglary	Larceny-theft	Motor vehicle theft	Arson[2]
Nathan Bedford Forrest	0	0	0	0	0	0	0	0	0	1
Norris Dam	0	0	0	0	0	1	0	1	0	1
Old Stone Fort State Archaeological Park	0	0	0	0	0	0	0	0	0	0
Panther Creek	0	0	0	0	0	2	0	2	0	0
Paris Landing	0	0	0	0	0	1	0	1	0	0
Pickett	0	0	0	0	0	0	0	0	0	0
Pickwick Landing	0	0	0	0	0	4	0	4	0	0
Pinson Mounds State Archaeological Park	0	0	0	0	0	0	0	0	0	0
Radnor Lake Natural Area	0	0	0	0	0	5	0	5	0	0
Red Clay State Historic Park	0	0	0	0	0	0	0	0	0	0
Reelfoot Lake	0	0	0	0	0	0	0	0	0	0
Roan Mountain	0	0	0	0	0	1	0	1	0	0
Rock Island	0	0	0	0	0	7	0	7	0	0
Rocky Fork	0	0	0	0	0	0	0	0	0	0
Seven Islands Birding Park	0	0	0	0	0	1	0	1	0	0
Sgt. Alvin C. York	0	0	0	0	0	0	0	0	0	0
South Cumberland Recreation Area	1	0	0	0	1	5	0	5	0	0
Standing Stone	0	0	0	0	0	1	0	1	0	0
Sycamore Shoals State Historic Park	0	0	0	0	0	0	0	0	0	0
Tim's Ford	0	0	0	0	0	0	0	0	0	0
T.O. Fuller	0	0	0	0	0	1	0	1	0	0
Warrior's Path	0	0	0	0	0	1	0	1	0	0
TennCare Office of Inspector General	0	0	0	0	0	0	0	0	0	0
Tennessee Bureau of Investigation	6	4	1	0	1	7	0	7	0	0
Tennessee Department of Revenue, Special Investigations Unit	0	0	0	0	0	0	0	0	0	0
Wildlife Resources Agency										
Region 1	0	0	0	0	0	0	0	0	0	0
Region 2	0	0	0	0	0	0	0	0	0	0
Region 3	0	0	0	0	0	0	0	0	0	0
Region 4	0	0	0	0	0	0	0	0	0	0
Other Agencies										
7th Judicial District Crime Task Force	0	0	0	0	0	5	0	5	0	0
Chattanooga Housing Authority	0	0	0	0	0	0	0	0	0	0
Chattanooga Metropolitan Airport	0	0	0	0	0	2	0	2	0	0
Dickson City Park Ranger Division	0	0	0	0	0	1	1	0	0	0
Drug Task Force										
2nd Judicial District	0	0	0	0	0	2	0	2	0	0
3rd Judicial District	0	0	0	0	0	0	0	0	0	0
4th Judicial District	0	0	0	0	0	1	0	1	0	0
5th Judicial District	0	0	0	0	0	0	0	0	0	0
8th Judicial District	0	0	0	0	0	0	0	0	0	0
9th Judicial District	0	0	0	0	0	5	0	5	0	0
10th Judicial District	0	0	0	0	0	0	0	0	0	0
12th Judicial District	0	0	0	0	0	0	0	0	0	0
14th Judicial District	0	0	0	0	0	0	0	0	0	0
15th Judicial District	2	0	0	0	2	0	0	0	0	0
17th Judicial District	0	0	0	0	0	0	0	0	0	0
18th Judicial District	0	0	0	0	0	0	0	0	0	0
19th Judicial District	0	0	0	0	0	1	0	1	0	0
21st Judicial District	0	0	0	0	0	0	0	0	0	0
22nd Judicial District	0	0	0	0	0	0	0	0	0	0
23rd Judicial District	1	0	0	0	1	2	0	0	2	0
24th Judicial District	0	0	0	0	0	0	0	0	0	0
27th Judicial District	0	0	0	0	0	0	0	0	0	0
31st Judicial District	0	0	0	0	0	0	0	0	0	0
Knoxville Metropolitan Airport	0	0	0	0	0	9	0	9	0	0
Memphis-Shelby County Airport Authority	4	0	1	0	3	220	0	131	89	0
Metropolitan Nashville Park Police	5	0	0	0	5	131	2	122	7	0
Nashville International Airport	2	0	0	1	1	82	0	56	26	0
Tri-Cities Regional Airport	0	0	0	0	0	3	0	0	3	0
West Tennessee Violent Crime Task Force	0	0	0	0	0	0	0	0	0	0
TEXAS										
State Agencies										
Texas Comptroller of Public Accounts Criminal Investigation Division	0	0	0	0	0	39	7	32	0	0
Tribal Agencies										
Ysleta del Sur Pueblo Tribal	5	1	0	1	3	49	4	35	10	1
Other Agencies										
Dallas-Fort Worth International Airport	14	0	0	5	9	483	8	387	88	0
Hospital District										
Dallas County	12	0	1	2	9	348	9	329	10	0
Tarrant County	7	0	1	1	5	122	0	118	4	0
Houston Metropolitan Transit Authority	4	0	1	1	2	55	0	39	16	0
Independent School District										
Aldine	11	0	0	4	7	81	15	63	3	0
Alief	45	0	0	6	39	55	4	44	7	0
Alvin	12	0	3	2	7	154	6	148	0	0
Angleton	9	0	2	0	7	22	4	18	0	0
Austin	10	0	0	4	6	292	14	271	7	4
Barbers Hill	0	0	0	0	0	2	0	2	0	0

Table 11. Offenses Known to Law Enforcement, by Selected State, Tribal, and Other Agencies, 2018—Continued

(Number.)

State/other agency unit/office	Violent crime	Murder and nonnegligent manslaughter	Rape[1]	Robbery	Aggravated assault	Property crime	Burglary	Larceny-theft	Motor vehicle theft	Arson[2]
Bastrop	1	0	0	0	1	4	0	4	0	0
Bay City[3]	9	0	0	0	9	2	0	2	0	0
Brazosport	14	0	1	0	13	18	0	18	0	0
Brownsville	43	0	1	1	41	192	7	184	1	0
Calhoun County	1	0	0	0	1	0	0	0	0	0
Conroe	26	0	18	2	6	98	5	93	0	0
Corpus Christi	179	0	0	3	176	68	19	46	3	1
Corsicana	3	0	0	0	3	11	4	6	1	0
East Central	31	0	0	0	31	9	2	7	0	0
Ector County	73	0	0	1	72	55	15	39	1	1
Edinburg	2	0	0	0	2	46	2	44	0	2
El Paso	24	0	8	2	14	253	31	221	1	2
Farmersville	0	0	0	0	0	1	0	1	0	0
Floresville	0	0	0	0	0	19	1	18	0	0
Fort Bend	112	0	0	0	112	234	1	233	0	0
Galveston	10	0	0	0	10	14	0	14	0	0
Houston	83	0	40	16	27	344	59	265	20	4
Humble	7	0	1	1	5	48	0	47	1	1
Judson	2	0	0	0	2	64	0	62	2	0
Katy	19	0	10	5	4	229	1	228	0	1
Killeen	2	0	0	1	1	55	1	54	0	0
Klein	9	0	5	0	4	118	2	113	3	4
Pasadena	5	0	0	3	2	60	7	50	3	0
Pflugerville	39	0	2	0	37	35	1	34	0	0
Raymondville	2	0	0	0	2	9	2	7	0	0
Rio Grande City	5	0	0	0	5	42	1	41	0	0
Santa Fe	38	10	1	0	27	11	0	11	0	0
Socorro	14	0	0	0	14	47	5	41	1	0
Spring[3]	54	0	3	1	50	49	2	42	5	0
Spring Branch	4	0	1	1	2	51	8	40	3	0
United	4	0	1	0	3	11	4	7	0	0
Port of Houston Authority	0	0	0	0	0	25	3	21	1	0
UTAH										
State Agencies										
Parks And Recreation	4	0	1	0	3	23	3	18	2	2
Utah Highway Patrol	57	0	5	2	50	184	8	158	18	2
Wildlife Resources	0	0	0	0	0	9	0	9	0	0
Other Agencies										
Cache-Rich Drug Task Force	0	0	0	0	0	3	0	3	0	0
Davis Metropolitan Narcotics Strike Force	0	0	0	0	0	0	0	0	0	0
Granite School District	25	0	2	5	18	143	3	135	5	10
Utah County Attorney, Investigations Division	0	0	0	0	0	0	0	0	0	
Utah County Major Crimes Task Force	0	0	0	0	0	2	0	1	1	0
Utah Transit Authority	23	0	0	10	13	1,598	1	1,547	50	2
Weber Morgan Narcotics Strike Force	2	0	0	0	2	4	0	2	2	0
VERMONT										
State Agencies										
Capitol Police	0	0	0	0	0	0	0	0	0	0
Fish and Wildlife Department, Law Enforcement Division	0	0	0	0	0	1	0	1	0	0
State Police										
Derby	41	0	7	1	33	229	81	124	24	0
Middlesex	33	0	11	2	20	210	69	128	13	0
New Haven	19	0	6	0	13	115	34	74	7	0
Royalton	33	0	9	0	24	98	33	60	5	0
Rutland	33	0	4	3	26	120	43	63	14	0
Shaftsbury	37	0	15	1	21	71	23	41	7	2
St. Albans	32	0	10	4	18	226	55	154	17	4
St. Johnsbury	35	2	3	1	29	275	127	131	17	1
Westminster	34	1	12	2	19	205	91	109	5	1
Williston	24	2	4	1	17	100	24	71	5	8
Vermont State Police Headquarters, Bureau of Criminal Investigations	0	0	0	0	0	0	0	0	0	0
VIRGINIA										
State Agencies										
Alcoholic Beverage Control Commission	5	0	0	0	5	50	3	47	0	0
Department of Conservation and Recreation	0	0	0	0	0	34	0	34	0	0
Department of Game and Inland Fisheries, Enforcement Division	2	0	0	0	2	22	0	20	2	0
Department of Motor Vehicles	0	0	0	0	0	74	0	11	63	0
State Police										
Accomack County	27	0	1	0	26	17	1	14	2	1
Albemarle County	3	0	0	0	3	6	0	5	1	0
Alexandria	1	0	0	0	1	0	0	0	0	0
Alleghany County	10	0	0	0	10	5	1	4	0	1
Amelia County	1	0	0	0	1	1	0	0	1	0
Amherst County	3	0	0	0	3	6	1	4	1	1
Appomattox County	1	0	0	1	0	4	0	4	0	0

Table 11. Offenses Known to Law Enforcement, by Selected State, Tribal, and Other Agencies, 2018—Continued

(Number.)

State/other agency unit/office	Violent crime	Murder and nonnegligent manslaughter	Rape[1]	Robbery	Aggravated assault	Property crime	Burglary	Larceny-theft	Motor vehicle theft	Arson[2]
Arlington County	4	0	0	1	3	1	0	1	0	0
Augusta County	9	0	0	0	9	15	1	8	6	0
Bath County	2	0	2	0	0	1	0	1	0	0
Bedford County	4	0	0	0	4	0	0	0	0	0
Bland County	4	0	1	0	3	6	4	1	1	0
Botetourt County	3	0	0	0	3	6	0	4	2	0
Bristol	4	0	0	0	4	1	0	1	0	0
Brunswick County	2	0	0	0	2	2	1	0	1	0
Buchanan County	2	0	1	0	1	8	1	6	1	5
Buckingham County	4	0	1	0	3	2	0	1	1	0
Buena Vista	1	0	0	0	1	0	0	0	0	0
Campbell County	4	0	0	0	4	3	1	2	0	2
Caroline County	13	0	0	0	13	18	0	12	6	1
Carroll County	1	0	0	0	1	13	1	8	4	1
Charles City County	1	0	0	0	1	3	1	2	0	0
Charlotte County	1	0	1	0	0	0	0	0	0	1
Charlottesville	1	0	0	0	1	0	0	0	0	0
Chesapeake	6	0	0	0	6	16	0	2	14	0
Chesterfield County	12	0	0	1	11	8	0	6	2	0
Clarke County	3	0	0	0	3	0	0	0	0	0
Clifton Forge	0	0	0	0	0	0	0	0	0	0
Colonial Heights	0	0	0	0	0	0	0	0	0	0
Covington	5	0	0	0	5	2	0	2	0	0
Craig County	2	1	0	0	1	2	1	1	0	0
Culpeper County	4	1	2	0	1	5	0	4	1	0
Cumberland County	1	0	0	0	1	1	1	0	0	1
Danville	1	1	0	0	0	0	0	0	0	0
Dickenson County	1	0	0	0	1	0	0	0	0	2
Dinwiddie County	12	0	2	0	10	1	0	1	0	0
Emporia	0	0	0	0	0	0	0	0	0	0
Essex County	1	0	0	0	1	1	0	0	1	0
Fairfax County	16	0	0	0	16	11	2	5	4	0
Falls Church	0	0	0	0	0	0	0	0	0	0
Fauquier County	5	1	0	0	4	8	0	4	4	0
Floyd County	1	0	0	0	1	1	0	1	0	0
Fluvanna County	0	0	0	0	0	0	0	0	0	0
Franklin	0	0	0	0	0	0	0	0	0	1
Franklin County	1	0	0	1	0	3	1	1	1	0
Frederick County	2	0	0	0	2	9	0	6	3	0
Fredericksburg	1	0	0	0	1	1	0	1	0	0
Galax	0	0	0	0	0	0	0	0	0	0
Giles County	3	0	3	0	0	4	0	4	0	0
Gloucester County	0	0	0	0	0	0	0	0	0	1
Goochland County	2	0	1	0	1	0	0	0	0	0
Grayson County	1	0	0	0	1	2	0	1	1	1
Greene County	1	0	0	1	0	0	0	0	0	0
Greensville County	2	0	0	0	2	4	0	4	0	0
Halifax County	2	0	1	0	1	7	1	6	0	0
Hampton	17	0	0	0	17	8	0	2	6	0
Hanover County	7	0	0	0	7	5	0	4	1	1
Harrisonburg	0	0	0	0	0	1	1	0	0	0
Henrico County	3	0	0	0	3	6	0	5	1	0
Henry County	3	0	1	1	1	1	0	0	1	0
Highland County	0	0	0	0	0	0	0	0	0	0
Hopewell	0	0	0	0	0	0	0	0	0	0
Isle of Wight County	0	0	0	0	0	3	0	2	1	0
James City County	0	0	0	0	0	0	0	0	0	0
King and Queen County	0	0	0	0	0	1	1	0	0	0
King George County	1	0	0	0	1	3	0	3	0	0
King William County	1	0	1	0	0	0	0	0	0	0
Lancaster County	0	0	0	0	0	0	0	0	0	0
Lee County	5	2	0	0	3	9	0	5	4	1
Loudoun County	1	0	1	0	0	1	0	1	0	1
Louisa County	0	0	0	0	0	3	0	3	0	0
Lunenburg County	5	0	0	0	5	0	0	0	0	0
Lynchburg	3	0	0	0	3	2	0	2	0	0
Madison County	4	0	0	0	4	0	0	0	0	0
Martinsville	1	0	0	1	0	0	0	0	0	0
Mathews County	1	0	1	0	0	0	0	0	0	1
Mecklenburg County	7	0	0	0	7	4	1	3	0	0
Middlesex County	2	0	0	0	2	1	0	1	0	0
Montgomery County	2	0	0	0	2	1	1	0	0	0
Nelson County	3	1	0	0	2	3	0	3	0	0
New Kent County	11	0	1	1	9	7	0	5	2	0
Newport News	3	1	0	1	1	6	0	1	5	0
Norfolk	8	0	0	0	8	4	0	1	3	0
Northampton County	1	0	0	0	1	1	0	1	0	0
Northumberland County	0	0	0	0	0	0	0	0	0	0
Norton	0	0	0	0	0	0	0	0	0	0
Nottoway County	2	0	0	0	2	7	0	5	2	0
Orange County	6	0	0	0	6	2	0	2	0	0
Page County	2	0	2	0	0	1	0	1	0	1
Patrick County	1	0	0	0	1	3	0	3	0	1

Table 11. Offenses Known to Law Enforcement, by Selected State, Tribal, and Other Agencies, 2018—Continued

(Number.)

State/other agency unit/office	Violent crime	Murder and nonnegligent manslaughter	Rape[1]	Robbery	Aggravated assault	Property crime	Burglary	Larceny-theft	Motor vehicle theft	Arson[2]
Petersburg	5	0	0	0	5	0	0	0	0	0
Pittsylvania County	3	0	0	0	3	25	1	14	10	0
Portsmouth	1	0	0	1	0	3	0	0	3	1
Powhatan County	3	0	0	0	3	0	0	0	0	0
Prince Edward County	4	1	2	0	1	3	1	2	0	0
Prince George County	1	0	0	0	1	1	0	0	1	0
Prince William County	13	0	0	0	13	8	0	5	3	0
Pulaski County	3	0	1	0	2	12	1	10	1	0
Radford	0	0	0	0	0	1	0	1	0	0
Rappahannock County	0	0	0	0	0	0	0	0	0	0
Richmond	7	0	0	1	6	9	0	7	2	0
Richmond County	1	0	0	0	1	1	0	1	0	0
Roanoke	0	0	0	0	0	7	0	4	3	0
Roanoke County	2	0	0	0	2	4	0	3	1	0
Rockbridge County	3	0	1	0	2	4	0	4	0	0
Rockingham County	4	0	0	0	4	18	0	9	9	1
Russell County	2	0	1	0	1	3	0	1	2	2
Salem	1	0	0	0	1	3	0	3	0	0
Scott County	5	1	2	0	2	6	1	3	2	3
Shenandoah County	4	0	1	0	3	6	1	5	0	0
Smyth County	4	1	0	0	3	12	1	10	1	1
South Boston	0	0	0	0	0	0	0	0	0	0
Southampton County	0	0	0	0	0	0	0	0	0	0
Spotsylvania County	7	1	0	0	6	6	0	6	0	0
Stafford County	4	0	1	0	3	3	0	2	1	0
Staunton	3	0	1	0	2	1	0	1	0	0
Suffolk	0	0	0	0	0	3	0	2	1	1
Surry County	0	0	0	0	0	1	0	1	0	0
Sussex County	1	0	0	0	1	2	0	2	0	0
Tazewell County	7	0	1	0	6	15	3	11	1	0
Virginia Beach	9	0	0	0	9	10	1	1	8	0
Warren County	0	0	0	0	0	0	0	0	0	0
Washington County	3	0	0	0	3	8	0	5	3	2
Waynesboro	1	0	0	1	0	1	0	1	0	0
Westmoreland County	3	0	0	0	3	1	0	0	1	1
Winchester	0	0	0	0	0	3	0	3	0	0
Wise County	9	1	2	1	5	5	0	5	0	0
Wythe County	10	0	1	1	8	11	1	10	0	3
York County	3	0	0	0	3	3	2	0	1	0
Virginia State Capitol	0	0	0	0	0	23	0	23	0	0
Other Agencies										
Norfolk Airport Authority	0	0	0	0	0	72	0	52	20	0
Port Authority, Norfolk	0	0	0	0	0	1	0	1	0	0
Reagan National Airport	1	0	0	0	1	444	3	376	65	0
Richmond International Airport	0	0	0	0	0	27	0	17	10	0
WASHINGTON										
State Agencies										
State Gambling Commission, Enforcement Unit	0	0	0	0	0	11	2	9	0	0
Washington State Patrol	0	0	0	0	0	0	0	0	0	0
Tribal Agencies										
Colville Tribal	41	0	6	0	35	250	58	157	35	3
Kalispel Tribal	0	0	0	0	0	125	3	105	17	0
La Push Tribal	1	0	1	0	0	24	6	18	0	0
Makah Tribal	4	0	2	1	1	16	6	9	1	0
Port Gamble S'Klallam Tribal	1	0	0	0	1	11	1	7	3	0
Quinault Indian Nation	6	0	1	1	4	9	6	2	1	0
Squaxin Island Tribal	20	0	0	1	19	152	6	128	18	0
Other Agencies										
Law Enforcement Against Drugs Task Force	0	0	0	0	0	0	0	0	0	0
Port of Seattle	15	0	4	2	9	954	29	790	135	0
WEST VIRGINIA										
State Agencies										
Capitol Protective Services	0	0	0	0	0	10	2	7	1	0
Department of Natural Resources										
Cabell County	0	0	0	0	0	0	0	0	0	0
Hardy County	0	0	0	0	0	0	0	0	0	0
Harrison County	0	0	0	0	0	0	0	0	0	0
Mason County	0	0	0	0	0	0	0	0	0	0
Mineral County	0	0	0	0	0	0	0	0	0	0
Mon Metro Drug Task Force	0	0	0	0	0	0	0	0	0	0
State Police, Bureau of Criminal Investigations	0	0	0	0	0	0	0	0	0	0
Beckley	19	0	5	0	14	219	29	179	11	0
Berkeley Springs	6	0	1	0	5	21	3	15	3	0
Bridgeport	5	1	1	0	3	128	24	80	24	0
Clay	8	0	0	0	8	53	14	22	17	2
Elkins	15	1	5	1	8	59	12	43	4	0
Fairmont	5	0	2	0	3	82	47	23	12	0
Franklin	5	0	0	0	5	31	20	9	2	1

Table 11. Offenses Known to Law Enforcement, by Selected State, Tribal, and Other Agencies, 2018—Continued

(Number.)

State/other agency unit/office	Violent crime	Murder and nonnegligent manslaughter	Rape[1]	Robbery	Aggravated assault	Property crime	Burglary	Larceny-theft	Motor vehicle theft	Arson[2]
Glenville	11	0	1	0	10	15	9	3	3	1
Grantsville	2	0	0	0	2	10	2	8	0	1
Hamlin	47	0	10	2	35	169	35	108	26	0
Harrisville	7	1	2	0	4	22	7	14	1	2
Hinton	2	0	0	0	2	27	12	9	6	1
Huntington	26	0	17	1	8	226	57	158	11	0
Jesse	5	0	3	0	2	5	2	3	0	0
Kearneysville	13	1	1	1	10	85	15	69	1	0
Keyser	9	0	0	1	8	68	13	42	13	1
Kingwood	6	0	1	0	5	57	19	28	10	0
Lewisburg	9	0	0	2	7	36	4	29	3	0
Logan	37	0	6	5	26	83	23	50	10	0
Madison	10	0	1	0	9	75	8	53	14	1
Marlinton	11	0	2	0	9	33	8	21	4	2
Martinsburg	36	2	8	3	23	217	32	160	25	4
Moorefield	3	0	1	0	2	23	8	13	2	0
Morgantown	15	0	4	0	11	113	16	85	12	1
Moundsville	5	0	2	0	3	3	0	3	0	0
New Cumberland	3	0	0	0	3	2	0	2	0	0
Paden City	12	0	7	0	5	25	7	15	3	1
Parkersburg	14	0	8	0	6	71	34	33	4	1
Parsons	6	0	2	0	4	18	6	10	2	0
Petersburg	10	0	1	0	9	42	17	23	2	0
Philippi	8	0	2	0	6	27	11	13	3	1
Point Pleasant	5	0	1	0	4	22	6	10	6	1
Princeton	9	0	0	1	8	131	19	103	9	0
Richwood	6	0	1	0	5	32	8	22	2	0
Ripley	4	0	1	0	3	31	7	22	2	0
Romney	6	0	0	0	6	20	2	15	3	0
South Charleston	24	2	15	0	7	358	24	316	18	1
Spencer	11	0	2	0	9	22	8	7	7	1
Summersville	2	0	0	0	2	29	6	21	2	0
Sutton	8	0	1	0	7	21	3	14	4	1
Union	4	0	0	0	4	18	3	11	4	0
Upperglade	13	0	1	1	11	33	8	22	3	0
Wayne	31	0	10	0	21	103	32	50	21	3
Welch	19	3	1	0	15	23	7	14	2	1
Wellsburg	10	0	2	0	8	6	0	6	0	0
West Union	3	0	2	0	1	17	3	10	4	1
Weston	11	0	1	0	10	54	8	41	5	0
Wheeling	2	0	0	0	2	1	1	0	0	0
Williamson	29	0	4	1	24	55	12	27	16	3
Winfield	17	0	1	3	13	76	4	64	8	0
Other Agencies										
Metropolitan Drug Enforcement Network Team	0	0	0	0	0	0	0	0	0	0
Ohio Valley Drug and Violent Crime Task Force	1	0	0	0	1	0	0	0	0	0
WISCONSIN										
State Agencies										
Capitol Police	0	0	0	0	0	16	0	15	1	0
Department of Natural Resources	0	0	0	0	0	0	0	0	0	0
State Fair Park Police	2	0	0	0	2	20	1	18	1	1
Wisconsin State Patrol	0	0	0	0	0	0	0	0	0	0
Tribal Agencies										
Bad River Tribal	27	0	0	0	27	25	3	16	6	0
Lac Courte Oreilles Tribal	27	0	5	1	21	77	9	62	6	2
Lac du Flambeau Tribal	21	0	5	1	15	169	11	152	6	0
Oneida Tribal	25	0	9	0	16	99	5	85	9	0
St. Croix Tribal	1	0	0	0	1	36	3	29	4	0
WYOMING										
Tribal Agencies										
Wind River Agency	68	1	8	2	57	133	17	80	36	2
PUERTO RICO AND OTHER OUTLYING AREAS										
Puerto Rico	6,417	639	198	2,271	3,309	24,851	5,486	15,658	3,707	
U.S. Virgin Islands, St. Thomas	309	12	1	34	262	646	218	339	89	5

1 The figures shown in this column for the offense of rape were reported using the revised Uniform Crime Reporting (UCR) definition of rape. See notes for further explanation.   2 The FBI does not publish arson data unless it receives data from either the agency or the state for all 12 months of the calendar year.   3 Because of changes in the local agency's reporting practices, figures are not comparable to previous years' data.   4 Limited data for 2018 were available for Iowa.   5 The FBI determined that the agency's data were underreported. Consequently, those data are not included in this table.   6 This agency/state submits rape data classified according to the legacy UCR definition; therefore the rape offense and violent crime total, which rape is a part of, is not included in this table. See the notes for further explanation.   7 The FBI determined that the agency's data were overreported. Consequently, those data are not included in this table.

Table 12. Crime Trends, by Population Group, 2017–2018

(Number, percent change.)

Population group	Violent crime	Murder and nonnegligent manslaughter	Rape[1]	Robbery	Aggravated assault	Property crime	Burglary	Larceny-theft	Motor vehicle theft	Arson	Number of agencies	Estimated population, 2018
Total, All Agencies												
2017	1,225,124	16,499	128,022	307,910	772,693	7,318,954	1,310,167	5,227,521	741,228	40,038		
2018	1,186,742	15,498	131,560	272,160	767,524	6,852,010	1,151,302	4,946,341	718,240	36,127	15,509	312,099,511
Percent change	-3.1	-6.1	+2.8	-11.6	-0.7	-6.4	-12.1	-5.4	-3.1	-9.8		
Total, Cities												
2017	989,698	13,108	96,224	272,864	607,502	5,873,222	977,896	4,264,860	599,574	30,892		
2018	955,635	12,230	98,807	241,196	603,402	5,517,706	865,153	4,044,331	580,261	27,961	11,285	213,864,890
Percent change	-3.4	-6.7	+2.7	-11.6	-0.7	-6.1	-11.5	-5.2	-3.2	-9.5		
Group I (250,000 and over)												
2017	478,004	6,795	36,994	154,479	279,736	2,078,037	356,734	1,435,156	274,192	11,955		
2018	461,961	6,310	38,134	136,958	280,559	2,004,896	322,482	1,405,363	266,041	11,010	85	62,903,034
Percent change	-3.4	-7.1	+3.1	-11.3	+0.3	-3.5	-9.6	-2.1	-3.0	-7.9		
1,000,000 and over (Group I subset)												
2017	200,257	2,453	14,809	68,685	114,310	739,196	119,624	518,657	97,404	3,511		
2018	194,004	2,314	15,586	61,584	114,520	725,865	110,246	517,071	95,010	3,538	11	27,887,008
Percent change	-3.1	-5.7	+5.2	-10.3	+0.2	-1.8	-7.8	-0.3	-2.5	+0.8		
500,000 to 999,999 (Group I subset)												
2017	158,078	2,412	11,584	49,355	94,727	756,710	134,646	520,199	97,212	4,653		
2018	153,668	2,225	11,565	44,288	95,590	727,565	120,868	507,805	94,884	4,008	26	18,736,687
Percent change	-2.8	-7.8	-0.2	-10.3	+0.9	-3.9	-10.2	-2.4	-2.4	-13.9		
250,000 to 499,999 (Group I subset)												
2017	119,669	1,930	10,601	36,439	70,699	582,131	102,464	396,300	79,576	3,791		
2018	114,289	1,771	10,983	31,086	70,449	551,466	91,368	380,487	76,147	3,464	48	16,279,339
Percent change	-4.5	-8.2	+3.6	-14.7	-0.4	-5.3	-10.8	-4.0	-4.3	-8.6		
Group II (100,000 to 249,999)												
2017	154,345	2,208	15,617	42,879	93,641	1,006,514	170,623	714,579	116,326	4,986		
2018	150,104	2,036	16,023	38,503	93,542	945,110	150,659	677,674	112,261	4,516	224	33,187,392
Percent change	-2.7	-7.8	+2.6	-10.2	-0.1	-6.1	-11.7	-5.2	-3.5	-9.4		
Group III (50,000 to 99,999)												
2017	118,693	1,376	12,884	31,094	73,339	869,568	141,508	641,611	82,011	4,438		
2018	115,334	1,318	13,286	27,804	72,926	805,960	124,483	599,991	77,470	4,016	499	34,785,719
Percent change	-2.8	-4.2	+3.1	-10.6	-0.6	-7.3	-12.0	-6.5	-5.5	-9.5		
Group IV (25,000 to 49,999)												
2017	89,860	1,084	11,287	20,676	56,813	707,572	112,290	539,543	52,544	3,195		
2018	83,297	1,006	11,627	17,450	53,214	650,246	96,891	499,823	50,745	2,787	892	30,904,313
Percent change	-7.3	-7.2	+3.0	-15.6	-6.3	-8.1	-13.7	-7.4	-3.4	-12.8		
Group V (10,000 to 24,999)												
2017	77,094	882	9,930	14,722	51,560	651,163	106,440	499,635	42,300	2,788		
2018	75,416	869	10,257	12,548	51,742	604,372	93,512	466,574	41,853	2,433	1,816	28,985,640
Percent change	-2.2	-1.5	+3.3	-14.8	+0.4	-7.2	-12.1	-6.6	-1.1	-12.7		
Group VI (under 10,000)												
2017	71,702	763	9,512	9,014	52,413	560,368	90,301	434,336	32,201	3,530		
2018	69,523	691	9,480	7,933	51,419	507,122	77,126	394,906	31,891	3,199	7,769	23,098,792
Percent change	-3.0	-9.4	-0.3	-12.0	-1.9	-9.5	-14.6	-9.1	-1.0	-9.4		
Metropolitan Counties												
2017	188,087	2,581	23,058	32,660	129,788	1,170,375	247,606	799,154	116,665	6,950		
2018	184,616	2,474	23,998	28,685	129,459	1,084,351	213,129	751,870	113,164	6,188	1,941	74,367,434
Percent change	-1.8	-4.1	+4.1	-12.2	-0.3	-7.4	-13.9	-5.9	-3.0	-11.0		
Nonmetropolitan Counties[2]												
2017	47,339	810	8,740	2,386	35,403	275,357	84,665	163,507	24,989	2,196		
2018	46,491	794	8,755	2,279	34,663	249,953	73,020	150,140	24,815	1,978	2,283	23,867,187
Percent change	-1.8	-2.0	+0.2	-4.5	-2.1	-9.2	-13.8	-8.2	-0.7	-9.9		
Suburban Areas[3]												
2017	333,191	4,166	41,933	64,036	223,056	2,432,539	435,749	1,778,053	205,911	12,826		
2018	322,582	4,023	43,220	55,423	219,916	2,239,385	373,609	1,654,993	199,514	11,269	8,593	135,384,349
Percent change	-3.2	-3.4	+3.1	-13.5	-1.4	-7.9	-14.3	-6.9	-3.1	-12.1		

1 The figures shown in the rape (revised definition) column include only those reported by law enforcement agencies that used the revised Uniform Crime Reporting (UCR) definition of rape. See chapter notes for more detail.   2 Includes state police agencies that report aggregately for the entire state.   3 Suburban areas include law enforcement agencies in cities with less than 50,000 inhabitants and county law enforcement agencies that are within a Metropolitan Statistical Area. Suburban areas exclude all metropolitan agencies associated with a principal city. The agencies associated with suburban areas also appear in other groups within this table.

Table 13. Crime Trends, by Suburban and Nonsuburban Cities,[1] by Population Group, 2017–2018

(Number, percent change.)

Population group	Violent crime	Murder and nonnegligent manslaughter	Rape[2]	Robbery	Aggravated assault	Property crime	Burglary	Larceny-theft	Motor vehicle theft	Arson	Number of agencies	Estimated population, 2018
Suburban Cities												
2017	145,104	1,585	18,875	31,376	93,268	1,262,164	188,143	978,899	89,246	5,876		
2018	137,966	1,549	19,222	26,738	90,457	1,155,034	160,480	903,123	86,350	5,081	6,652	61,016,915
Percent change	-4.9	-2.3	+1.8	-14.8	-3.0	-8.5	-14.7	-7.7	-3.2	-13.5		
Group IV (25,000 to 49,999)												
2017	55,697	587	7,316	14,018	33,776	479,991	70,980	369,126	37,927	1,958		
2018	52,095	605	7,476	11,876	32,138	439,670	60,560	341,514	35,948	1,648	704	24,161,235
Percent change	-6.5	+3.1	+2.2	-15.3	-4.8	-8.4	-14.7	-7.5	-5.2	-15.8		
Group V (10,000 to 24,999)												
2017	49,767	573	6,233	10,891	32,070	432,811	66,478	333,684	30,884	1,765		
2018	47,978	557	6,558	9,111	31,752	400,423	57,341	311,235	30,300	1,547	1,389	22,300,043
Percent change	-3.6	-2.8	+5.2	-16.3	-1.0	-7.5	-13.7	-6.7	-1.9	-12.4		
Group VI (under 10,000)												
2017	39,640	425	5,326	6,467	27,422	349,362	50,685	276,089	20,435	2,153		
2018	37,893	387	5,188	5,751	26,567	314,941	42,579	250,374	20,102	1,886	4,559	14,555,637
Percent change	-4.4	-8.9	-2.6	-11.1	-3.1	-9.9	-16.0	-9.3	-1.6	-12.4		
Nonsuburban Cities												
2017	63,602	686	8,632	6,921	47,363	461,093	85,962	346,645	25,824	2,662		
2018	63,109	664	8,772	6,020	47,653	427,029	76,427	322,048	26,156	2,398	3,648	16,399,697
Percent change	-0.8	-3.2	+1.6	-13.0	+0.6	-7.4	-11.1	-7.1	+1.3	-9.9		
Group IV (25,000 to 49,999)												
2017	8,613	108	1,265	1,340	5,900	65,587	12,170	48,809	4,226	382		
2018	8,329	95	1,323	1,100	5,811	62,263	10,832	46,750	4,390	291	68	2,207,420
Percent change	-3.3	-12.0	+4.6	-17.9	-1.5	-5.1	-11.0	-4.2	+3.9	-23.8		
Group V (10,000 to 24,999)												
2017	22,964	240	3,185	3,041	16,498	184,636	34,191	139,709	9,833	903		
2018	23,180	265	3,163	2,740	17,012	172,674	31,067	130,836	9,977	794	371	5,656,759
Percent change	+0.9	+10.4	-0.7	-9.9	+3.1	-6.5	-9.1	-6.4	+1.5	-12.1		
Group VI (under 10,000)												
2017	32,025	338	4,182	2,540	24,965	210,870	39,601	158,127	11,765	1,377		
2018	31,600	304	4,286	2,180	24,830	192,092	34,528	144,462	11,789	1,313	3,209	8,535,518
Percent change	-1.3	-10.1	+2.5	-14.2	-0.5	-8.9	-12.8	-8.6	+0.2	-4.6		

1 Suburban cities include law enforcement agencies in cities with less than 50,000 inhabitants that are within a Metropolitan Statistical Area. Suburban cities exclude all metropolitan agencies associated with a principal city. Nonsuburban cities include law enforcement agencies in cities with less than 50,000 inhabitants that are not associated with a Metropolitan Statistical Area.   2 The figures shown in the rape column include only those reported by law enforcement agencies that used the revised Uniform Crime Reporting (UCR) definition of rape. See chapter notes for more detail.

Table 14. Crime Trends, by Metropolitan and Nonmetropolitan Counties,[1] by Population Group, 2017–2018

(Number, percent change.)

Population group and range	Violent crime	Murder and nonnegligent manslaughter	Rape[2]	Robbery	Aggravated assault	Property crime	Burglary	Larceny-theft	Motor vehicle theft	Arson	Number of agencies	Estimated population, 2018
Metropolitan Counties												
100,000 and over												
2017	122,314	1,694	13,081	26,703	80,836	770,468	147,120	543,565	75,461	4,322		
2018	119,595	1,601	13,970	23,766	80,258	715,195	126,708	511,555	73,078	3,854	173	45,723,713
Percent change	-2.2	-5.5	+6.8	-11.0	-0.7	-7.2	-13.9	-5.9	-3.2	-10.8		
25,000 to 99,999												
2017	45,993	644	6,588	4,213	34,548	296,794	78,926	191,773	24,396	1,699		
2018	45,830	626	6,711	3,646	34,847	272,409	67,433	179,007	24,442	1,527	453	23,682,240
Percent change	-0.4	-2.8	+1.9	-13.5	+0.9	-8.2	-14.6	-6.7	+0.2	-10.1		
Under 25,000												
2017	19,780	243	3,389	1,744	14,404	103,113	21,560	63,816	16,808	929		
2018	19,191	247	3,317	1,273	14,354	96,747	18,988	61,308	15,644	807	1,315	4,961,481
Percent change	-3.0	+1.6	-2.1	-27.0	-0.3	-6.2	-11.9	-3.9	-6.9	-13.1		
Nonmetropolitan Counties												
25,000 and over												
2017	19,585	322	3,326	1,301	14,636	122,224	37,426	73,470	10,527	801		
2018	19,181	299	3,413	1,240	14,229	112,568	32,986	68,028	10,802	752	265	10,648,857
Percent change	-2.1	-7.1	+2.6	-4.7	-2.8	-7.9	-11.9	-7.4	+2.6	-6.1		
10,000 to 24,999												
2017	15,556	226	2,414	722	12,194	94,917	29,943	56,685	7,564	725		
2018	15,252	243	2,468	726	11,815	86,046	25,704	51,867	7,812	663	562	9,014,447
Percent change	-2.0	+7.5	+2.2	+0.6	-3.1	-9.3	-14.2	-8.5	+3.3	-8.6		
Under 10,000												
2017	12,198	262	3,000	363	8,573	58,216	17,296	33,352	6,898	670		
2018	12,058	252	2,874	313	8,619	51,339	14,330	30,245	6,201	563	1,456	4,203,883
Percent change	-1.1	-3.8	-4.2	-13.8	+0.5	-11.8	-17.1	-9.3	-10.1	-16.0		

1 Metropolitan counties include sheriffs and county law enforcement agencies associated with a Metropolitan Statistical Area. Nonmetropolitan counties include sheriffs and county law enforcement agencies that are not associated with a Metropolitan Statistical Area. The offenses from state police agencies are not included in this table.   2 The figures shown in the rape column include only those reported by law enforcement agencies that used the revised Uniform Crime Reporting (UCR) definition of rape. See notes for further detail.

Table 15. Crime Trends, Additional Information About Selected Offenses, by Population Group, 2017–2018

(Number, percent change.)

Population group	Rape[1] Rape by force	Rape[1] Assault to rape-attempts	Robbery Firearm	Robbery Knife or cutting instrument	Robbery Other weapon	Robbery Strong-arm	Aggravated assault Firearm	Aggravated assault Knife or cutting instrument	Aggravated assault Other weapon	Aggravated assault Hands, fists, feet, etc.
Total, All Agencies										
2017	117,367	5,635	118,382	23,678	28,591	120,502	195,812	128,154	233,817	186,234
2018	120,441	5,637	99,585	21,538	26,800	110,587	192,767	127,485	231,900	187,496
Percent change	+2.6	*	-15.9	-9.0	-6.3	-8.2	-1.6	-0.5	-0.8	+0.7
Total, Cities										
2017	87,379	4,404	102,555	21,114	25,202	107,478	157,502	104,596	180,836	137,630
2018	89,540	4,424	85,971	19,264	23,545	98,953	155,553	104,535	179,545	137,746
Percent change	+2.5	+0.5	-16.2	-8.8	-6.6	-7.9	-1.2	-0.1	-0.7	+0.1
Group I (250,000 and over)										
2017	33,278	1,954	58,959	11,350	13,340	58,943	83,996	49,108	84,518	46,679
2018	34,394	1,942	49,554	10,582	12,663	54,475	83,609	50,079	85,429	46,130
Percent change	+3.4	-0.6	-16.0	-6.8	-5.1	-7.6	-0.5	+2.0	+1.1	-1.2
1,000,000 and over (Group I subset)										
2017	12,203	844	20,893	5,186	5,351	25,368	23,696	21,247	31,344	22,588
2018	12,913	875	17,926	4,908	5,016	24,050	24,662	21,596	31,205	21,745
Percent change	+5.8	+3.7	-14.2	-5.4	-6.3	-5.2	+4.1	+1.6	-0.4	-3.7
500,000 to 999,999 (Group I subset)										
2017	10,981	603	22,708	3,845	5,279	17,523	33,237	16,209	32,341	12,940
2018	11,009	556	19,338	3,480	5,209	16,261	32,786	16,428	32,980	13,396
Percent change	+0.3	-7.8	-14.8	-9.5	-1.3	-7.2	-1.4	+1.4	+2.0	+3.5
250,000 to 499,999 (Group I subset)										
2017	10,094	507	15,358	2,319	2,710	16,052	27,063	11,652	20,833	11,151
2018	10,472	511	12,290	2,194	2,438	14,164	26,161	12,055	21,244	10,989
Percent change	+3.7	+0.8	-20.0	-5.4	-10.0	-11.8	-3.3	+3.5	+2.0	-1.5
Group II (100,000 to 249,999)										
2017	14,744	531	17,235	3,631	4,240	16,885	26,745	17,258	28,786	18,622
2018	15,039	634	14,490	3,347	4,009	15,946	26,244	17,280	28,441	19,508
Percent change	+2.0	+19.4	-15.9	-7.8	-5.4	-5.6	-1.9	+0.1	-1.2	+4.8
Group III (50,000 to 99,999)										
2017	11,934	478	10,521	2,693	3,177	13,685	16,832	13,105	22,752	18,690
2018	12,319	501	8,888	2,374	2,923	12,752	16,830	13,031	22,878	18,333
Percent change	+3.2	+4.8	-15.5	-11.8	-8.0	-6.8	*	-0.6	+0.6	-1.9
Group IV (25,000 to 49,999)										
2017	10,064	462	7,400	1,654	2,113	8,276	12,213	9,975	16,659	14,610
2018	10,280	426	5,923	1,387	1,856	7,207	11,325	9,107	15,428	14,384
Percent change	+2.1	-7.8	-20.0	-16.1	-12.2	-12.9	-7.3	-8.7	-7.4	-1.5
Group V (10,000 to 24,999)										
2017	8,885	348	5,285	1,102	1,487	5,688	10,333	8,155	15,058	15,805
2018	9,053	370	4,443	951	1,241	5,048	10,324	7,921	14,894	16,439
Percent change	+1.9	+6.3	-15.9	-13.7	-16.5	-11.3	-0.1	-2.9	-1.1	+4.0
Group VI (under 10,000)										
2017	8,474	631	3,155	684	845	4,001	7,383	6,995	13,063	23,224
2018	8,455	551	2,673	623	853	3,525	7,221	7,117	12,475	22,952
Percent change	-0.2	-12.7	-15.3	-8.9	+0.9	-11.9	-2.2	+1.7	-4.5	-1.2
Metropolitan Counties										
2017	21,768	859	14,775	2,380	3,073	12,210	31,117	19,210	42,516	35,726
2018	22,666	850	12,627	2,096	2,927	10,873	30,354	18,795	42,199	36,796
Percent change	+4.1	-1.0	-14.5	-11.9	-4.8	-11.0	-2.5	-2.2	-0.7	+3.0
Nonmetropolitan Counties										
2017	8,220	372	1,052	184	316	814	7,193	4,348	10,465	12,878
2018	8,235	363	987	178	328	761	6,860	4,155	10,156	12,954
Percent change	+0.2	-2.4	-6.2	-3.3	+3.8	-6.5	-4.6	-4.4	-3.0	+0.6
Suburban Areas[2]										
2017	38,449	1,708	25,806	4,713	6,125	24,916	47,957	33,700	68,711	66,646
2018	39,480	1,660	21,684	4,081	5,748	21,974	46,602	32,714	67,276	67,749
Percent change	+2.7	-2.8	-16.0	-13.4	-6.2	-11.8	-2.8	-2.9	-2.1	+1.7

Table 15. Crime Trends, Additional Information About Selected Offenses, by Population Group, 2017–2018 —Continued

(Number, percent change.)

Population group	Burglary			Motor vehicle theft			Arson			Number of agencies	Estimated population, 2018
	Forcible entry	Unlawful entry	Attempted forcible entry	Autos	Trucks and buses	Other vehicles	Structure	Mobile	Other		
Total, All Agencies											
2017	730,752	460,169	79,706	543,050	109,496	68,958	16,904	9,051	12,504		
2018	631,744	411,200	72,703	524,103	110,662	65,011	15,033	8,295	11,548	14,815	300,222,367
Percent change	-13.5	-10.6	-8.8	-3.5	+1.1	-5.7	-11.1	-8.4	-7.6		
Total, Cities											
2017	544,770	335,925	62,693	445,924	87,373	47,593	13,011	6,697	9,759		
2018	473,764	302,982	57,556	428,416	89,166	45,488	11,588	6,120	9,120	10,689	203,796,413
Percent change	-13.0	-9.8	-8.2	-3.9	+2.1	-4.4	-10.9	-8.6	-6.5		
Group I (250,000 and over)											
2017	219,389	102,117	22,316	195,875	48,374	18,365	4,659	3,001	3,781		
2018	191,952	96,793	22,051	187,180	50,762	17,967	4,196	2,677	3,699	84	60,183,883
Percent change	-12.5	-5.2	-1.2	-4.4	+4.9	-2.2	-9.9	-10.8	-2.2		
1,000,000 and over (Group I subset)											
2017	70,324	29,693	6,695	58,701	20,938	6,187	1,071	682	1,244		
2018	63,698	28,000	6,862	54,591	24,343	5,944	957	602	1,541	10	25,167,857
Percent change	-9.4	-5.7	+2.5	-7.0	+16.3	-3.9	-10.6	-11.7	+23.9		
500,000 to 999,999 (Group I subset)											
2017	86,457	39,409	8,780	73,487	16,699	7,026	1,950	1,268	1,435		
2018	74,092	37,870	8,906	72,890	15,291	6,703	1,601	1,139	1,268	26	18,736,687
Percent change	-14.3	-3.9	+1.4	-0.8	-8.4	-4.6	-17.9	-10.2	-11.6		
250,000 to 499,999 (Group I subset)											
2017	62,608	33,015	6,841	63,687	10,737	5,152	1,638	1,051	1,102		
2018	54,162	30,923	6,283	59,699	11,128	5,320	1,638	936	890	48	16,279,339
Percent change	-13.5	-6.3	-8.2	-6.3	+3.6	+3.3	0.0	-10.9	-19.2		
Group II (100,000 to 249,999)											
2017	97,016	58,084	12,058	90,069	15,910	9,238	2,093	1,134	1,550		
2018	84,196	52,609	10,666	86,792	16,065	8,350	1,836	1,061	1,464	218	32,348,740
Percent change	-13.2	-9.4	-11.5	-3.6	+1.0	-9.6	-12.3	-6.4	-5.5		
Group III (50,000 to 99,999)											
2017	74,874	53,315	9,257	63,286	10,421	7,093	1,934	890	1,490		
2018	65,135	47,952	7,972	59,532	10,340	6,571	1,623	856	1,438	478	33,394,344
Percent change	-13.0	-10.1	-13.9	-5.9	-0.8	-7.4	-16.1	-3.8	-3.5		
Group IV (25,000 to 49,999)											
2017	56,954	42,359	7,405	40,670	5,077	4,882	1,258	556	1,131		
2018	48,168	37,123	6,580	38,949	4,914	4,761	1,120	490	975	830	28,830,675
Percent change	-15.4	-12.4	-11.1	-4.2	-3.2	-2.5	-11.0	-11.9	-13.8		
Group V (10,000 to 24,999)											
2017	52,629	42,612	6,077	31,883	4,413	4,054	1,205	497	910		
2018	46,608	36,985	5,392	31,890	4,126	3,966	1,089	474	730	1,701	27,096,275
Percent change	-11.4	-13.2	-11.3	*	-6.5	-2.2	-9.6	-4.6	-19.8		
Group VI (under 10,000)											
2017	43,908	37,438	5,580	24,141	3,178	3,961	1,862	619	897		
2018	37,705	31,520	4,895	24,073	2,959	3,873	1,724	562	814	7,378	21,942,496
Percent change	-14.1	-15.8	-12.3	-0.3	-6.9	-2.2	-7.4	-9.2	-9.3		
Metropolitan Counties											
2017	137,772	92,446	13,832	80,622	18,282	16,961	2,817	1,913	2,123		
2018	116,912	80,452	12,402	79,054	17,693	15,441	2,464	1,764	1,877	1,895	73,115,822
Percent change	-15.1	-13.0	-10.3	-1.9	-3.2	-9.0	-12.5	-7.8	-11.6		
Nonmetropolitan Counties											
2017	48,210	31,798	3,181	16,504	3,841	4,404	1,076	441	622		
2018	41,068	27,766	2,745	16,633	3,803	4,082	981	411	551	2,231	23,310,132
Percent change	-14.8	-12.7	-13.7	+0.8	-1.0	-7.3	-8.8	-6.8	-11.4		
Suburban Areas[2]											
2017	230,502	164,814	27,001	148,376	27,145	25,627	5,373	3,003	3,965		
2018	195,900	141,506	23,958	144,694	26,023	23,741	4,732	2,763	3,416	8,128	129,869,133
Percent change	-15.0	-14.1	-11.3	-2.5	-4.1	-7.4	-11.9	-8.0	-13.8		

* = Less than one-tenth of one percent.
1 The figures shown in the rape column include only those reported by law enforcement agencies that used the revised Uniform Crime Reporting (UCR) definition of rape. See notes for more detail.   2 Suburban areas include law enforcement agencies in cities with less than 50,000 inhabitants and county law enforcement agencies that are within a Metropolitan Statistical Area. Suburban areas exclude all metropolitan agencies associated with a principal city. The agencies associated with suburban areas also appear in other groups within this table.

Table 16. Rate: Number of Crimes Per 100,000 Population, by Population Group, 2018

(Number, rate.)

Population group	Violent crime		Murder and nonnegligent manslaughter		Rape[1]		Robbery		Aggravated assault	
	Number of offenses known	Rate	Number of offenses known	Rate	Number of offenses known	Rate	Number of offenses known	Rate	Number of offenses known	Rate
Total, All Agencies	1,146,904	388.2	14,905	5.0	127,945	44.4	265,464	89.9	738,590	250.0
Total, Cities	930,407	451.5	11,890	5.8	96,818	48.0	236,682	114.9	585,017	283.9
Group I (250,000 and over)	458,601	737.1	6,243	10.0	38,051	62.7	136,047	218.7	278,260	447.2
1,000,000 and over (Group I subset)	194,010	695.7	2,320	8.3	15,586	55.9	61,584	220.8	114,520	410.7
500,000 to 999,999 (Group I subset)	149,910	830.3	2,151	11.9	11,414	66.7	43,297	239.8	93,048	515.4
250,000 to 499,999 (Group I subset)	114,681	704.5	1,772	10.9	11,051	70.3	31,166	191.4	70,692	434.2
Group II (100,000 to 249,999)	144,799	453.2	1,973	6.2	15,744	50.2	37,512	117.4	89,570	280.4
Group III (50,000 to 99,999)	113,321	337.9	1,285	3.8	13,097	40.1	27,067	80.7	71,872	214.3
Group IV (25,000 to 49,999)	79,394	268.8	944	3.2	11,241	38.7	16,703	56.5	50,506	171.0
Group V (10,000 to 24,999)	71,086	259.6	820	3.0	9,834	36.6	11,886	43.4	48,546	177.3
Group VI (under 10,000)	63,206	294.7	625	2.9	8,851	42.1	7,467	34.8	46,263	215.7
Metropolitan Counties	173,261	253.9	2,308	3.4	22,778	34.4	26,719	39.2	121,456	178.0
Nonmetropolitan Counties[2]	43,236	204.6	707	3.3	8,349	40.7	2,063	9.8	32,117	152.0
Suburban Areas[3]	305,031	241.0	3,745	3.0	41,333	33.5	52,300	41.3	207,653	164.0

Table 16. Rate: Number of Crimes Per 100,000 Population, by Population Group, 2018—Continued

(Number, rate.)

Population group	Property crime		Burglary		Larceny-theft		Motor vehicle theft		Number of agencies	Estimated population, 2018
	Number of offenses known	Rate	Number of offenses known	Rate	Number of offenses known	Rate	Number of offenses known	Rate		
Total, All Agencies	6,548,109	2,216.4	1,097,816	371.6	4,758,121	1,610.5	692,172	234.3	14,414	295,438,651
Total, Cities	5,316,335	2,579.9	834,355	404.9	3,916,991	1,900.8	564,989	274.2	10,369	206,071,411
Group I (250,000 and over)	1,971,670	3,168.8	318,588	512.0	1,390,362	2,234.6	262,720	422.2	84	62,221,029
1,000,000 and over (Group I subset)	722,327	2,590.2	110,246	395.3	517,071	1,854.2	95,010	340.7	11	27,887,008
500,000 to 999,999 (Group I subset)	698,786	3,870.4	116,567	645.6	490,826	2,718.6	91,393	506.2	25	18,054,682
250,000 to 499,999 (Group I subset)	550,557	3,381.9	91,775	563.8	382,465	2,349.4	76,317	468.8	48	16,279,339
Group II (100,000 to 249,999)	910,019	2,848.5	144,246	451.5	656,691	2,055.5	109,082	341.4	217	31,947,237
Group III (50,000 to 99,999)	775,424	2,312.5	120,324	358.8	579,324	1,727.7	75,776	226.0	479	33,532,131
Group IV (25,000 to 49,999)	619,682	2,097.7	92,425	312.9	478,688	1,620.4	48,569	164.4	853	29,541,212
Group V (10,000 to 24,999)	566,422	2,068.6	87,109	318.1	439,972	1,606.8	39,341	143.7	1,718	27,382,277
Group VI (under 10,000)	473,118	2,205.9	71,663	334.1	371,954	1,734.3	29,501	137.5	7,018	21,447,525
Metropolitan Counties	1,005,007	1,473.0	196,900	288.6	703,855	1,031.6	104,252	152.8	1,875	68,230,825
Nonmetropolitan Counties[2]	226,767	1,072.9	66,561	314.9	137,275	649.5	22,931	108.5	2,170	21,136,415
Suburban Areas[3]	2,108,438	1,665.6	350,294	276.7	1,571,340	1,241.3	186,804	147.6	8,093	126,589,134

1 The figures shown in this column for the offense of rape were reported using only the revised Uniform Crime Reporting definition of rape. See the chapter notes for further explanation.   2 Includes state police agencies that report aggregately for the entire state.   3 Suburban areas include law enforcement agencies in cities with less than 50,000 inhabitants and county law enforcement agencies that are within a Metropolitan Statistical Area. Suburban areas exclude all metropolitan agencies associated with a principal city. The agencies associated with suburban areas also appear in other groups within this table.

Table 17. Rate: Number of Crimes Per 100,000 Inhabitants, by Suburban and Nonsuburban Cities,[1] by Population Group, 2018

(Number, rate.)

Population group	Violent crime		Murder and nonnegligent manslaughter		Rape[2]		Robbery		Aggravated assault	
	Number of offenses known	Rate	Number of offenses known	Rate	Number of offenses known	Rate	Number of offenses known	Rate	Number of offenses known	Rate
Total, Suburban Cities	131,770	225.8	1,437	2.5	18,555	32.3	25,581	43.8	86,197	147.7
Group IV (25,000 to 49,999)	50,000	214.0	549	2.4	7,287	31.7	11,375	48.7	30,789	131.8
Group V (10,000 to 24,999)	45,959	215.8	531	2.5	6,322	30.2	8,722	40.9	30,384	142.7
Group VI (under 10,000)	35,811	261.4	357	2.6	4,946	36.8	5,484	40.0	25,024	182.7
Total, Nonsuburban Cities	55,887	377.2	611	4.1	8,104	56.3	5,540	37.4	41,632	281.0
Group IV (25,000 to 49,999)	7,520	378.6	100	5.0	1,195	62.7	1,075	54.1	5,150	259.3
Group V (10,000 to 24,999)	21,002	412.8	243	4.8	3,010	61.3	2,484	48.8	15,265	300.0
Group VI (under 10,000)	27,365	353.5	268	3.5	3,899	51.4	1,981	25.6	21,217	274.1

Population group	Property crime		Burglary		Larceny-theft		Motor vehicle theft		Number of agencies	Estimated population, 2018
	Number of offenses known	Rate	Number of offenses known	Rate	Number of offenses known	Rate	Number of offenses known	Rate		
Total, Suburban Cities	1,103,431	1,890.8	153,394	262.8	867,485	1,486.5	82,552	141.5	6,218	58,358,309
Group IV (25,000 to 49,999)	425,246	1,820.5	58,555	250.7	331,831	1,420.5	34,860	149.2	681	23,359,345
Group V (10,000 to 24,999)	379,928	1,783.8	54,680	256.7	296,607	1,392.6	28,641	134.5	1,328	21,299,192
Group VI (under 10,000)	298,257	2,177.1	40,159	293.1	239,047	1,744.9	19,051	139.1	4,209	13,699,772
Total, Nonsuburban Cities	387,921	2,618.6	68,982	465.6	295,434	1,994.2	23,505	158.7	3,202	14,814,315
Group IV (25,000 to 49,999)	56,703	2,854.9	9,968	501.9	42,783	2,154.0	3,952	199.0	61	1,986,184
Group V (10,000 to 24,999)	156,543	3,076.7	27,542	541.3	119,891	2,356.3	9,110	179.0	336	5,088,015
Group VI (under 10,000)	174,675	2,256.7	31,472	406.6	132,760	1,715.2	10,443	134.9	2,805	7,740,116

1 Suburban cities include law enforcement agencies in cities with less than 50,000 inhabitants that are within a Metropolitan Statistical Area. Suburban cities exclude all metropolitan agencies associated with a principal city. Nonsuburban cities include law enforcement agencies in cities with less than 50,000 inhabitants that are not associated with a Metropolitan Statistical Area.   2 The figures shown in this column for the offense of rape were reported using only the revised Uniform Crime Reporting definition of rape. See chapter notes for more detail.

Table 18. Rate: Number of Crimes Per 100,000 Inhabitants, by Metropolitan and Nonmetropolitan Counties,[1] by Population Group, 2018

(Number, rate.)

Population group	Violent crime		Murder and nonnegligent manslaughter		Rape[2]		Robbery		Aggravated assault	
	Number of offenses known	Rate	Number of offenses known	Rate	Number of offenses known	Rate	Number of offenses known	Rate	Number of offenses known	Rate
Metropolitan Counties										
100,000 and over	112,401	266.9	1,518	3.6	13,134	31.9	21,988	52.2	75,761	179.9
25,000 to 99,999	42,762	197.7	556	2.6	6,530	31.8	3,506	16.2	32,170	148.7
Under 25,000	18,098	402.8	234	5.2	3,114	70.3	1,225	27.3	13,525	301.0
Nonmetropolitan Counties										
25,000 and over	17,616	188.6	256	2.7	3,209	36.0	1,079	11.6	13,072	140.0
10,000 to 24,999	14,311	175.1	222	2.7	2,369	29.7	690	8.4	11,030	134.9
Under 10,000	11,309	312.1	229	6.3	2,771	76.9	294	8.1	8,015	221.2

Table 18. Rate: Number of Crimes Per 100,000 Inhabitants, by Metropolitan and Nonmetropolitan Counties,[1] by Population Group, 2018—Continued

(Number, rate.)

Population group	Property crime		Burglary		Larceny-theft		Motor vehicle theft		Number of agencies	Estimated population, 2018
	Number of offenses known	Rate	Number of offenses known	Rate	Number of offenses known	Rate	Number of offenses known	Rate		
Metropolitan Counties										
100,000 and over	660,372	1,568.2	116,868	277.5	477,030	1,132.8	66,474	157.9	158	42,108,975
25,000 to 99,999	252,594	1,167.8	62,181	287.5	167,956	776.5	22,457	103.8	416	21,629,132
Under 25,000	92,041	2,048.7	17,851	397.3	58,869	1,310.3	15,321	341.0	1,301	4,492,718
Nonmetropolitan Counties										
25,000 and over	99,175	1,061.9	28,988	310.4	60,638	649.2	9,549	102.2	233	9,339,811
10,000 to 24,999	79,833	976.7	24,139	295.3	48,240	590.2	7,454	91.2	505	8,173,547
Under 10,000	47,759	1,318.2	13,434	370.8	28,397	783.8	5,928	163.6	1,432	3,623,057

1 Metropolitan counties include sheriffs and county law enforcement agencies associated with a Metropolitan Statistical Area. Nonmetropolitan counties include sheriffs and county law enforcement agencies that are not associated with a Metropolitan Statistical Area.   2 The figures shown in this column for the offense of rape were reported using only the revised Uniform Crime Reporting definition of rape. See the chapter notes for further explanation.

Table 19. Rate: Number of Crimes Per 100,000 Inhabitants, Additional Information About Selected Offenses, by Population Group, 2018

(Number, rate.)

Population group	Rape[1] Rape by force	Rape[1] Assault to rape-attempts	Robbery Firearm	Robbery Knife or cutting instrument	Robbery Other weapon	Aggravated assault Strong-arm	Aggravated assault Firearm	Aggravated assault Knife or cutting instrument	Aggravated assault Other weapon
Total, All Agencies									
Number of offenses known	117,196	5,488	96,490	21,049	26,258	108,541	185,437	123,253	223,997
Rate	42.3	2.0	33.9	7.4	9.2	38.2	65.2	43.4	78.8
Total, Cities									
Number of offenses known	87,845	4,316	84,201	18,919	23,158	97,452	150,845	101,841	175,048
Rate	45.7	2.2	42.9	9.6	11.8	49.6	76.8	51.8	89.1
Group I (250,000 and over)									
Number of offenses known	34,311	1,942	49,085	10,523	12,562	54,193	82,451	49,869	84,699
Rate	59.2	3.3	82.5	17.7	21.1	91.1	138.6	83.8	142.3
1,000,000 and over (Group I subset)									
Number of offenses known	12,913	875	17,926	4,908	5,016	24,050	24,662	21,596	31,205
Rate	51.3	3.5	71.2	19.5	19.9	95.6	98.0	85.8	124.0
500,000 to 999,999 (Group I subset)									
Number of offenses known	10,862	552	18,836	3,414	5,104	15,943	31,542	16,179	32,164
Rate	63.4	3.2	104.3	18.9	28.3	88.3	174.7	89.6	178.1
250,000 to 499,999 (Group I subset)									
Number of offenses known	10,536	515	12,323	2,201	2,442	14,200	26,247	12,094	21,330
Rate	67.1	3.3	75.7	13.5	15.0	87.2	161.2	74.3	131.0
Group II (100,000 to 249,999)									
Number of offenses known	14,772	622	14,068	3,243	3,909	15,581	24,698	16,520	27,544
Rate	48.4	2.0	45.2	10.4	12.6	50.1	79.4	53.1	88.5
Group III (50,000 to 99,999)									
Number of offenses known	12,173	494	8,715	2,324	2,879	12,529	16,565	12,708	22,471
Rate	38.8	1.6	27.0	7.2	8.9	38.8	51.3	39.4	69.6
Group IV (25,000 to 49,999)									
Number of offenses known	10,011	423	5,698	1,336	1,793	6,989	10,734	8,801	14,640
Rate	36.9	1.6	20.6	4.8	6.5	25.3	38.9	31.9	53.0
Group V (10,000 to 24,999)									
Number of offenses known	8,690	338	4,177	911	1,171	4,820	9,775	7,480	14,313
Rate	34.7	1.3	16.3	3.6	4.6	18.8	38.2	29.2	55.9
Group VI (under 10,000)									
Number of offenses known	7,888	497	2,458	582	844	3,340	6,622	6,463	11,381
Rate	39.6	2.5	12.1	2.9	4.1	16.4	32.5	31.7	55.9
Metropolitan Counties									
Number of offenses known	21,499	819	11,397	1,970	2,809	10,391	28,258	17,535	39,459
Rate	33.0	1.3	17.0	2.9	4.2	15.5	42.1	26.1	58.8
Nonmetropolitan Counties									
Number of offenses known	7,852	353	892	160	291	698	6,334	3,877	9,490
Rate	39.2	1.8	4.3	0.8	1.4	3.4	30.7	18.8	46.0
Suburban Areas[2]									
Number of offenses known	37,824	1,599	19,988	3,894	5,573	21,173	43,896	30,939	63,532
Rate	31.9	1.3	16.4	3.2	4.6	17.4	36.1	25.5	52.3

Table 19. Rate: Number of Crimes Per 100,000 Inhabitants, Additional Information About Selected Offenses, by Population Group, 2018—Continued

(Number, rate.)

Population group	Burglary			Motor vehicle theft				Number of agencies	Estimated population, 2018
	Hands, fists, feet, etc.	Forcible entry	Unlawful entry	Attempted forcible entry	Autos	Trucks and buses	Other vehicles		
Total, All Agencies									
Number of offenses known	179,008	603,620	390,368	70,052	505,366	106,430	62,545	13,765	284,229,008
Rate	63.0	212.4	137.3	24.6	177.8	37.4	22.0		
Total, Cities									
Number of offenses known	132,162	459,366	290,342	55,411	416,900	87,294	44,167	9,812	196,464,641
Rate	67.3	233.8	147.8	28.2	212.2	44.4	22.5		
Group I (250,000 and over)									
Number of offenses known	45,929	189,997	95,076	21,829	184,989	49,860	17,739	83	59,501,878
Rate	77.2	319.3	159.8	36.7	310.9	83.8	29.8		
1,000,000 and over (Group I subset)									
Number of offenses known	21,745	63,698	28,000	6,862	54,591	24,343	5,944	10	25,167,857
Rate	86.4	253.1	111.3	27.3	216.9	96.7	23.6		
500,000 to 999,999 (Group I subset)									
Number of offenses known	13,163	71,889	36,038	8,640	70,594	14,345	6,454	25	18,054,682
Rate	72.9	398.2	199.6	47.9	391.0	79.5	35.7		
250,000 to 499,999 (Group I subset)									
Number of offenses known	11,021	54,410	31,038	6,327	59,804	11,172	5,341	48	16,279,339
Rate	67.7	334.2	190.7	38.9	367.4	68.6	32.8		
Group II (100,000 to 249,999)									
Number of offenses known	18,739	81,003	50,129	9,926	84,097	15,793	8,138	211	31,108,585
Rate	60.2	260.4	161.1	31.9	270.3	50.8	26.2		
Group III (50,000 to 99,999)									
Number of offenses known	18,472	63,546	46,166	7,805	58,294	10,204	6,367	460	32,280,599
Rate	57.2	196.9	143.0	24.2	180.6	31.6	19.7		
Group IV (25,000 to 49,999)									
Number of offenses known	13,877	46,613	35,075	6,370	37,390	4,734	4,600	796	27,627,138
Rate	50.2	168.7	127.0	23.1	135.3	17.1	16.7		
Group V (10,000 to 24,999)									
Number of offenses known	14,959	43,457	34,460	4,987	29,943	3,949	3,671	1,609	25,584,366
Rate	58.5	169.9	134.7	19.5	117.0	15.4	14.3		
Group VI (under 10,000)									
Number of offenses known	20,186	34,750	29,436	4,494	22,187	2,754	3,652	6,653	20,362,075
Rate	99.1	170.7	144.6	22.1	109.0	13.5	17.9		
Metropolitan Counties									
Number of offenses known	34,917	106,849	74,707	12,140	73,277	15,548	14,506	1,831	67,132,139
Rate	52.0	159.2	111.3	18.1	109.2	23.2	21.6		
Nonmetropolitan Counties									
Number of offenses known	11,929	37,405	25,319	2,501	15,189	3,588	3,872	2,122	20,632,228
Rate	57.8	181.3	122.7	12.1	73.6	17.4	18.8		
Suburban Areas[2]									
Number of offenses known	64,378	182,600	133,285	23,266	136,057	23,639	22,523	7,664	121,520,421
Rate	53.0	150.3	109.7	19.1	112.0	19.5	18.5		

1 The figures shown in this column for the offense of rape were reported using only the revised Uniform Crime Reporting definition of rape. See the chapter notes for further explanation.   2 Suburban areas include law enforcement agencies in cities with less than 50,000 inhabitants and county law enforcement agencies that are within a Metropolitan Statistical Area. Suburban areas exclude all metropolitan agencies associated with a principal city. The agencies associated with suburban areas also appear in other groups within this table.

Table 20. Murder, by Selected State, Territory, and Type of Weapon, 2018

(Number.)

State/territory	Total murders[1]	Total firearms	Handguns	Rifles	Shotguns	Firearms (type unknown)	Knives or cutting instruments	Other weapons	Hands, fists, feet, etc.[2]
Alabama[3]	2	2	2	0	0	0	0	0	0
Alaska	47	31	7	3	0	21	8	3	5
Arizona	339	203	139	12	6	46	45	87	4
Arkansas	218	156	66	6	5	79	17	38	7
California	1,739	1,177	834	24	27	292	252	223	87
Colorado	207	147	99	2	8	38	27	13	20
Connecticut	83	54	10	2	0	42	18	9	2
Delaware	48	40	14	1	2	23	4	3	1
District of Columbia	151	120	120	0	0	0	20	7	4
Georgia	568	460	410	11	10	29	44	62	2
Hawaii	33	11	6	1	0	4	10	6	6
Idaho	32	19	14	2	2	1	4	8	1
Illinois[3]	864	708	592	14	4	98	77	53	26
Indiana	371	294	136	10	7	141	33	29	15
Iowa[4]	43	20	6	2	2	10	8	9	6
Kansas	110	78	47	0	2	29	7	19	6
Kentucky	237	179	112	12	6	49	17	32	9
Louisiana	521	436	233	12	5	186	30	44	11
Maine	23	11	6	0	1	4	2	6	4
Maryland	470	388	345	1	10	32	39	30	13
Massachusetts	136	93	37	0	1	55	25	13	5
Michigan	550	394	166	17	11	200	31	99	26
Minnesota	104	49	36	4	0	9	16	28	11
Mississippi	142	118	99	3	2	14	7	15	2
Missouri	555	473	235	16	9	213	40	32	10
Montana	34	17	9	3	0	5	2	12	3
Nebraska	43	26	22	0	1	3	5	9	3
Nevada	201	134	46	1	1	86	23	24	20
New Hampshire	21	12	6	0	0	6	3	4	2
New Jersey	286	202	152	0	2	48	37	28	19
New Mexico	137	87	39	3	0	45	23	22	5
New York	546	313	254	6	10	43	124	63	46
North Carolina	479	346	231	15	16	84	44	52	37
North Dakota	16	9	8	0	0	1	1	1	5
Ohio	546	383	184	3	7	189	49	87	27
Oklahoma	202	134	95	7	3	29	28	29	11
Oregon	81	48	30	3	1	14	12	18	3
Pennsylvania	787	580	464	17	7	92	83	99	25
Rhode Island	16	12	1	1	1	9	2	1	1
South Carolina	386	296	188	8	6	94	29	42	19
South Dakota	13	8	5	0	0	3	4	1	0
Tennessee	496	397	245	26	8	118	28	49	22
Texas	1,301	956	522	33	37	364	128	133	84
Utah	59	28	17	1	0	10	12	10	9
Vermont	10	3	3	0	0	0	0	5	2
Virginia	391	297	141	8	5	143	30	49	15
Washington	232	138	76	2	5	55	45	35	14
West Virginia	57	34	21	1	1	11	5	14	4
Wisconsin	178	136	67	4	2	63	15	16	11
Wyoming	12	8	6	0	2	0	2	0	2

1 Total number of murders for which supplemental homicide data were received.   2 Pushed is included in hands, fists, feet, etc.   3 Limited supplemental homicide data were received.   4 Limited data for 2018 were available for Iowa.

Table 21. Robbery, by State and Type of Weapon, 2018

(Number.)

State	Total robberies[1]	Firearms	Knives or cutting instruments	Other weapons	Strong-arm	Agency count	Population
Alabama	3,311	2,145	111	324	731	203	3,625,366
Alaska	896	242	99	127	428	32	733,747
Arizona	6,331	2,530	774	734	2,293	92	6,572,138
Arkansas	1,457	724	110	144	479	237	2,593,420
California	54,311	13,503	5,031	6,535	29,242	736	39,549,496
Colorado	3,483	1,530	306	432	1,215	186	5,028,003
Connecticut	2,194	651	277	230	1,036	106	3,572,665
Delaware	866	349	59	73	385	52	964,106
District of Columbia	2,415	964	217	159	1,075	3	702,455
Florida	16,874	6,685	1,168	1,622	7,399	671	21,279,120
Georgia	6,766	3,873	251	589	2,053	447	8,454,996
Hawaii	857	115	90	158	494	2	1,148,121
Idaho	186	49	21	30	86	79	1,587,760
Illinois[2]	346	167	30	31	118	1	146,198
Indiana	5,192	2,562	273	457	1,900	214	4,430,415
Iowa[3]							
Kansas	1,181	563	91	119	408	212	2,159,192
Kentucky	1,195	459	120	150	466	331	3,382,683
Louisiana	4,462	2,311	217	355	1,579	179	4,364,269
Maine	228	58	30	25	115	134	1,338,404
Maryland	9,716	4,572	855	836	3,453	154	6,042,718
Massachusetts	4,011	965	697	827	1,522	338	6,667,870
Michigan	5,627	2,496	321	510	2,300	611	9,865,692
Minnesota	2,940	979	219	627	1,115	378	5,570,925
Mississippi	978	635	50	62	231	51	1,086,688
Missouri	5,061	2,812	260	387	1,602	498	5,720,610
Montana	223	52	30	36	105	99	995,183
Nebraska	732	349	59	56	268	216	1,822,672
Nevada	3,832	1,616	354	429	1,433	47	3,022,875
New Hampshire	333	47	54	43	189	184	1,317,257
New Jersey	6,364	1,955	602	413	3,394	576	8,908,520
New Mexico	2,530	1,160	309	353	708	102	1,760,050
New York	18,020	3,293	2,182	1,743	10,802	516	18,332,434
North Carolina	5,367	2,925	402	426	1,614	211	5,943,830
North Dakota	158	40	21	20	77	103	757,131
Ohio	8,386	2,662	360	667	4,697	425	9,409,029
Oklahoma	2,790	1,298	260	227	1,005	405	3,911,076
Oregon	2,405	482	300	382	1,241	196	3,792,813
Pennsylvania	9,742	3,816	740	604	4,582	1,442	12,629,530
Rhode Island	454	124	79	39	212	48	1,057,315
South Carolina	3,154	1,809	183	260	902	375	4,474,961
South Dakota	207	41	29	25	112	114	816,012
Tennessee	7,151	3,992	383	1,095	1,681	448	6,548,896
Texas	25,841	13,690	1,842	2,294	8,015	910	26,050,117
Utah	1,064	289	121	122	532	114	2,705,615
Vermont	69	22	13	9	25	72	615,720
Virginia	3,594	1,831	287	321	1,155	394	8,434,883
Washington	5,356	1,314	539	727	2,776	209	6,980,830
West Virginia	164	42	24	31	67	135	1,099,657
Wisconsin	3,474	1,689	197	387	1,201	423	5,747,929
Wyoming	44	13	2	6	23	54	507,616

1 The number of robberies from agencies that submitted 12 months of data in 2018 for which breakdowns by type of weapon were included.   2 Limited data were received.   3 Limited data for 2018 were available for Iowa.

Table 22. Aggravated Assault, by State and Type of Weapon, 2018

(Number.)

State	Total aggravated assaults[1]	Firearms	Knives or cutting instruments	Other weapons	Personal weapons	Agency count	Population
Alabama	14,986	3,619	1,216	9,169	982	203	3,625,366
Alaska	4,377	935	763	1,411	1,268	32	733,747
Arizona	20,471	5,353	2,885	4,645	7,588	92	6,572,138
Arkansas	11,150	3,817	1,414	2,316	3,603	237	2,593,420
California	105,343	17,907	16,934	36,486	34,016	736	39,549,496
Colorado	13,035	3,947	2,624	3,120	3,344	186	5,028,003
Connecticut	4,294	690	1,030	1,505	1,069	106	3,572,665
Delaware	2,837	856	630	1,060	291	52	964,106
District of Columbia	3,971	936	1,109	1,490	436	3	702,455
Florida	55,504	16,799	10,389	19,619	8,697	671	21,279,120
Georgia	17,481	6,268	2,387	4,550	4,276	447	8,454,996
Hawaii	1,545	133	397	639	376	2	1,148,121
Idaho	2,681	524	484	801	872	79	1,587,760
Illinois[2]	1,525	676	155	276	418	1	146,198
Indiana	13,761	3,567	1,379	3,875	4,940	214	4,430,415
Iowa[3]							
Kansas	7,512	2,749	1,120	1,856	1,787	212	2,159,192
Kentucky	2,039	372	382	972	313	331	3,382,683
Louisiana	16,901	5,200	2,447	5,229	4,025	179	4,364,269
Maine	801	72	132	250	347	134	1,338,404
Maryland	16,135	2,914	3,468	6,160	3,593	154	6,042,718
Massachusetts	16,265	1,692	3,453	7,395	3,725	338	6,667,870
Michigan	30,849	9,051	5,768	9,935	6,095	611	9,865,692
Minnesota	6,762	1,635	1,281	1,795	2,051	378	5,570,925
Mississippi	2,173	969	286	453	465	51	1,086,688
Missouri	20,677	8,285	2,254	5,100	5,038	498	5,720,610
Montana	2,613	448	309	916	940	99	995,183
Nebraska	3,368	749	662	1,167	790	216	1,822,672
Nevada	9,976	2,971	1,922	2,905	2,178	47	3,022,875
New Hampshire	1,417	296	288	362	471	184	1,317,257
New Jersey	10,463	1,729	2,064	3,349	3,321	576	8,908,520
New Mexico	11,324	2,681	1,602	2,711	4,330	102	1,760,050
New York	42,538	4,155	11,007	13,262	14,114	516	18,332,434
North Carolina	16,339	7,813	2,285	3,270	2,971	211	5,943,830
North Dakota	1,284	44	166	494	580	103	757,131
Ohio	16,456	6,328	3,208	4,668	2,252	425	9,409,029
Oklahoma	13,054	3,175	2,068	4,164	3,647	405	3,911,076
Oregon	6,814	940	1,306	2,487	2,081	196	3,792,813
Pennsylvania	23,576	4,664	3,300	4,849	10,763	1,442	12,629,530
Rhode Island	1,366	257	350	457	302	48	1,057,315
South Carolina	16,129	7,091	2,525	3,862	2,651	375	4,474,961
South Dakota	1,737	206	390	443	698	114	816,012
Tennessee	31,086	11,102	5,317	12,444	2,223	448	6,548,896
Texas	66,682	21,746	13,769	20,373	10,794	910	26,050,117
Utah	3,810	655	835	1,154	1,166	114	2,705,615
Vermont	703	77	103	96	427	72	615,720
Virginia	10,040	3,105	1,653	2,659	2,623	394	8,434,883
Washington	13,394	2,687	2,206	4,482	4,019	209	6,980,830
West Virginia	2,493	607	309	608	969	135	1,099,657
Wisconsin	11,185	2,858	1,099	2,558	4,670	423	5,747,929
Wyoming	773	87	123	150	413	54	507,616

1 The number of aggravated assaults from agencies that submitted 12 months of data in 2018 for which breakdowns by type of weapon were included.　2 Limited data were received.　3 Limited data for 2018 were available for Iowa.

Table 23. Offense Analysis, Number and Percent Change, 2017–2018

(Number, percent, dollars; 14,225 agencies; 2018 estimated population 278,869,698.)

Classification	Number of offenses, 2018	Percent change from 2017	Percent distribution[1]	Average value (dollars)
Murder	13,382	-6.3	NA	X
Rape[2]	119,653	+2.4	NA	X
Robbery	230,621	-11.3	100.0	$2,119
By location				
Street/highway	83,752	-15.0	36.3	1,739
Commercial house	37,017	-8.3	16.1	1,546
Gas or service station	7,267	-9.3	3.2	1,028
Convenience store	16,109	-7.4	7.0	961
Residence	37,230	-9.1	16.1	4,600
Bank	3,658	-18.2	1.6	4,303
Miscellaneous	45,588	-9.3	19.8	1,662
Burglary	1,047,388	-12.3	100.0	2,799
By location				
Residence (dwelling)	685,766	-45.0	65.5	8,407
Residence, night	218,028	-10.7	20.8	2,123
Residence, day	346,312	-14.2	33.1	2,401
Residence, unknown	121,426	-20.1	11.6	3,833
Nonresidence (store, office, etc.)	361,622	-27.9	34.5	10,183
Nonresidence, night	161,828	-7.3	15.5	2,833
Nonresidence, day	128,137	-4.4	12.2	3,199
Nonresidence, unknown	71,657	-16.2	6.8	4,151
Larceny-theft (except motor vehicle theft)	4,390,400	-5.7	100.0	1,153
By type				
Pocket-picking	22,930	-5.0	0.5	1,169
Purse-snatching	16,877	-8.7	0.4	718
Shoplifting	937,012	-2.1	21.3	304
From motor vehicles (except accessories)	1,183,631	-8.6	27.0	994
Motor vehicle accessories	272,124	-4.1	6.2	648
Bicycles	131,777	-10.9	3.0	546
From buildings	448,439	-8.0	10.2	1,610
From coin-operated machines	9,659	-8.8	0.2	851
All others	1,367,955	-4.6	31.2	1,890
By value				
Over $200	2,052,409	-4.7	46.7	2,407
$50 to $200	939,820	-5.6	21.4	107
Under $50	1,398,124	-7.3	31.8	15
Motor Vehicle Theft	660,346	-3.2	*	8,407

NA = Not available.
X = Not applicable.
* = Less than one-tenth of one percent.
1 Because of rounding, the percentages may not add to 100.0.   2 The rape figure in this table is an aggregate total of the data submitted using both the revised and legacy Uniform Crime Reporting definitions. See the chapter notes for further explanation.

Table 24. Property Stolen and Recovered, by Type and Value, 2018

(Dollars, percent; 14,236 agencies; 2018 estimated population 274,390,299.)

Type of property	Value of property (dollars)		Percent recovered
	Stolen	Recovered	
Total	$14,499,870,046	$4,122,148,212	28.4
Currency, notes, etc.	1,624,262,633	32,603,322	2.0
Jewelry and precious metals	1,165,108,482	45,683,077	3.9
Clothing and furs	388,553,438	30,887,599	7.9
Locally stolen motor vehicles	5,836,517,020	3,463,590,213	59.3
Office equipment	435,429,414	22,788,193	5.2
Televisions, radios, stereos, etc.	352,169,167	18,937,548	5.4
Firearms	142,154,108	15,755,404	11.1
Household goods	211,980,697	9,133,819	4.3
Consumable goods	226,586,895	14,388,138	6.3
Livestock	14,242,720	1,371,236	9.6
Miscellaneous	4,102,865,472	467,009,663	11.4

SECTION III

OFFENSES CLEARED

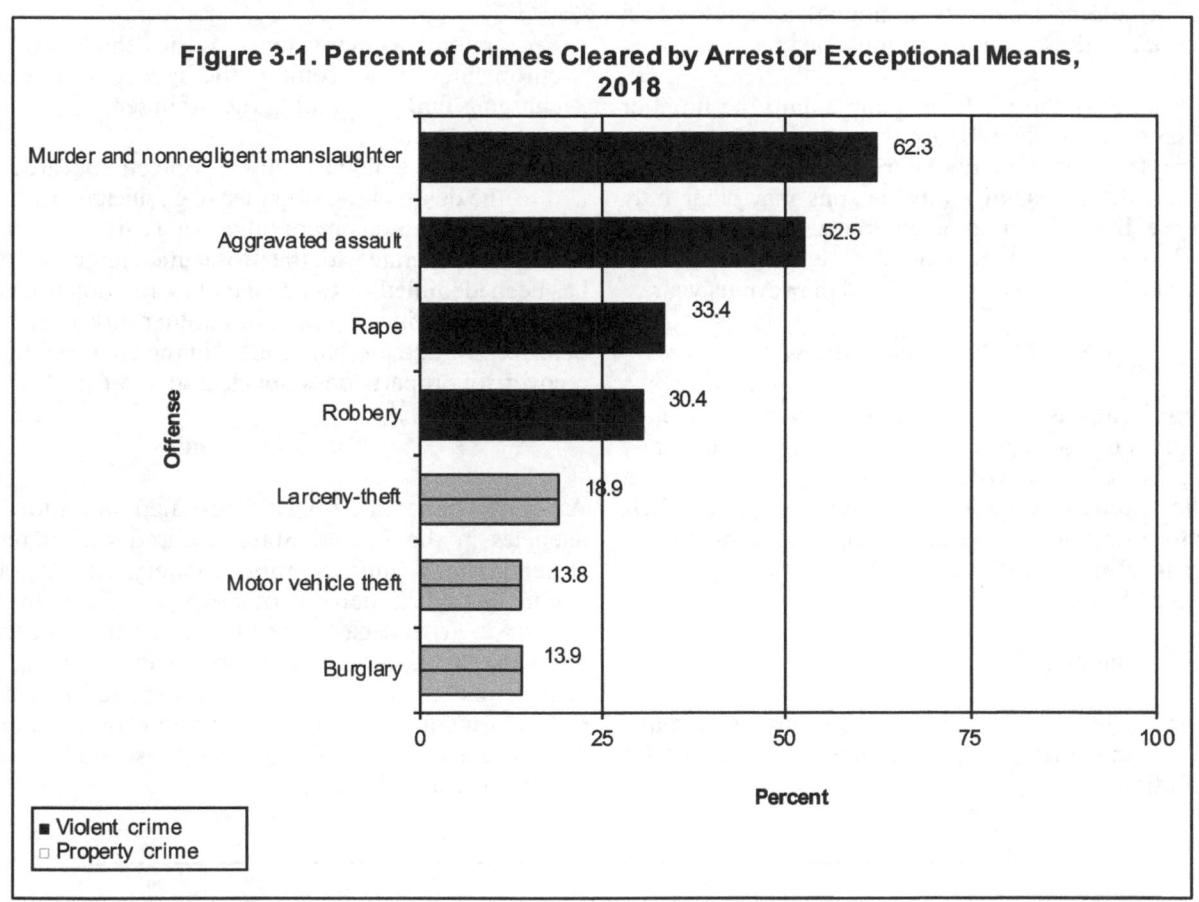

Figure 3-1. Percent of Crimes Cleared by Arrest or Exceptional Means, 2018

Law enforcement agencies that report crime to the Federal Bureau of Investigation (FBI) can clear, or "close," offenses in one of two ways: by arrest or by exceptional means. However, the administrative closing of a case by a local law enforcement agency does not necessarily mean that the agency can clear an offense for Uniform Crime Reporting (UCR) purposes. To clear an offense within the program's guidelines, the reporting agency must adhere to certain criteria, which are outlined in this section. (*Note:* The UCR program does not distinguish between offenses cleared by arrest and those cleared by exceptional means in its data presentations. The distinction is made solely for the purpose of a definition and not for data collection and publication.) See Appendix I for information on the UCR program's statistical methodology.

Important Note: Rape Data

In 2016, the FBI UCR Program initiated the collection of rape data within the Summary Reporting System under a revised definition. The changes bring uniformity to the offense in both the Summary Reporting System (SRS) and the National Incident-Based Reporting System

(NIBRS) by capturing data (1) without regard to gender, (2) including penetration of any bodily orifice by any object or body part, and (3) including offenses where physical force is not involved. The term "forcible" was removed, and the definition changed to the revised UCR definition below.

- Legacy UCR definition of rape: The carnal knowledge of a female forcibly and against her will. This definition ceased to be used as of January 1, 2018.

- Revised UCR definition of rape: Penetration, no matter how slight, of the vagina or anus with any body part or object, or oral penetration by a sex organ of another person, without the consent of the victim. This is the definition currently in use; unless specified otherwise, "rape" refers to this definition.

Cleared by Arrest

In the UCR program, a law enforcement agency reports that an offense is cleared by arrest, or solved for crime reporting purposes, when at least one person is arrested,

299

charged with the commission of the offense, and turned over to the court for prosecution (whether following arrest, court summons, or police notice). To qualify as a clearance, *all* of these conditions must be met.

In its calculations, the UCR program counts the number of offenses that are cleared, not the number of arrestees. Therefore, the arrest of one person may clear several crimes, and the arrest of many persons may clear only one offense. In addition, some clearances recorded by an agency during a particular calendar year, such as 2018, may pertain to offenses that occurred in previous years.

Cleared by Exceptional Means

In certain situations, elements beyond law enforcement's control prevent the agency from arresting and formally charging the offender. When this occurs, the agency can clear the offense *exceptionally*. There are four UCR program requirements that law enforcement must meet in order to clear an offense by exceptional means. The agency must have:

- Identified the offender

- Gathered enough evidence to support an arrest, make a charge, and turn over the offender to the court for prosecution

- Identified the offender's exact location so that the suspect could be taken into custody immediately

- Encountered a circumstance outside the control of law enforcement that prohibits the agency from arresting, charging, and prosecuting the offender

Examples of exceptional clearances include, but are not limited to, the death of the offender (e.g., suicide or justifiably killed by a law enforcement officer or a citizen), the victim's refusal to cooperate with the prosecution after the offender has been identified, or the denial of extradition because the offender committed a crime in another jurisdiction and is being prosecuted for that offense. In the UCR program, the recovery of property does not clear an offense.

National Clearances

A review of the data for 2018 revealed law enforcement agencies in the United States cleared 45.5 percent of violent crimes (murder, rape, robbery, and aggravated assault) and 17.6 percent of property crimes (burglary, larceny-theft, and motor vehicle theft) brought to their attention. In addition, law enforcement cleared 22.4 percent of arson offenses, which are reported in a slightly different manner than the other property crimes. (Table 25) More details concerning this offense are furnished in the arson text in this section.

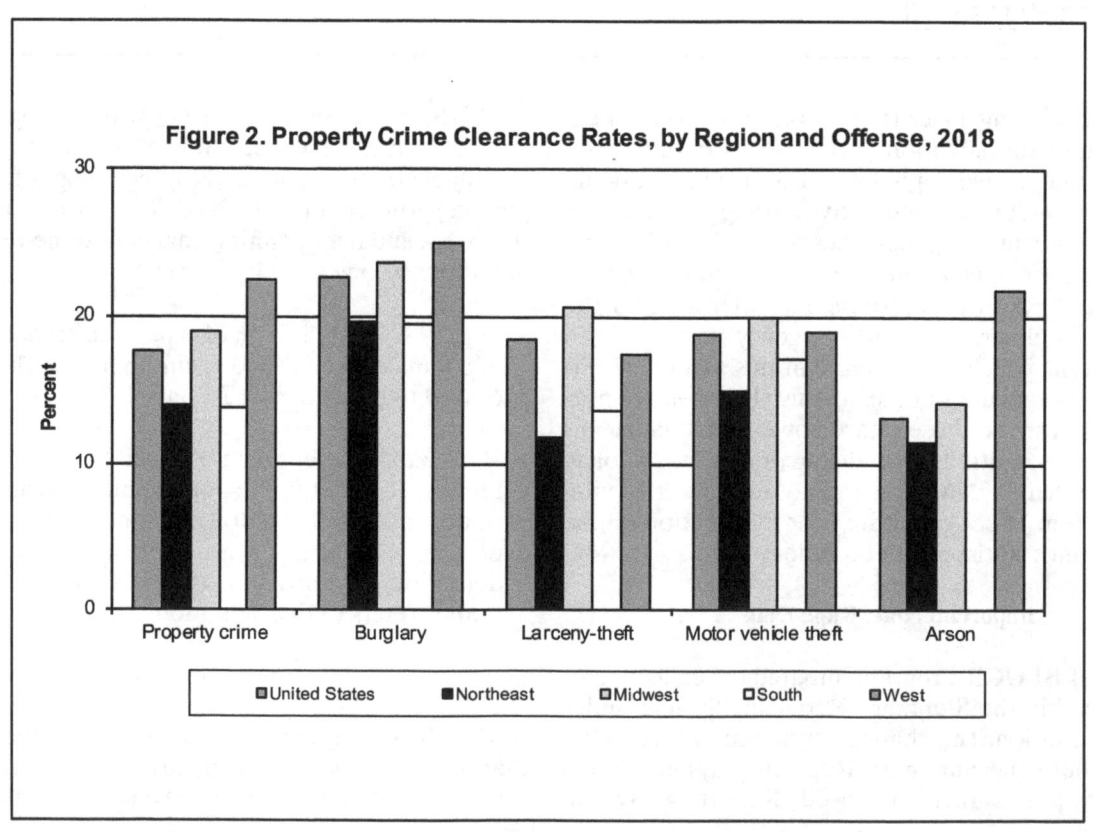

Figure 2. Property Crime Clearance Rates, by Region and Offense, 2018

As in most years, law enforcement agencies cleared a higher percentage of violent crimes than property crimes in 2018. As a rule, clearance rates generally rise due to the more vigorous investigative efforts put forth for violent crimes. In addition, violent crimes more often involve victims and/or witnesses who are able to identify the perpetrators.

A breakdown of the clearances for violent crimes for 2018 revealed that the nation's law enforcement agencies cleared 62.3 percent of murder offenses, 52.5 percent of aggravated assault offenses, 33.4 percent of rape offenses, and 30.4 percent of robbery offenses. (Table 25)

For property crime offenses in 2018, law enforcement agencies throughout the nation collectively 13.9 percent of burglary offenses, 18.9 percent of larceny-theft offenses, and 13.8 percent of motor vehicle theft offenses. (Table 25)

Regional Clearances

The UCR program divides the nation into four regions: the Northeast, the Midwest, the South, and the West. (See Appendix III for further details.) A review of clearance data for 2018 by region showed that agencies in the Northeast cleared the greatest proportion of their violent crime offenses (54.8 percent). Law enforcement agencies in the West cleared 45.0 percent of their violent crimes, while agencies in the South and Midwest cleared 44.2 percent and 41.7 percent of their violent crimes, respectively. (Table 26)

For murder and non-negligent manslaughter in 2018, the West cleared 65.5 percent of offenses, followed by the South (63.4 percent). The Northeast cleared 61.8 percent and the Midwest cleared 56.0 percent of these offenses. Rape offenses were cleared 36.6 percent of the time in the South, 36.3 percent of the time in the Northeast, 32.1 percent of the time in the Midwest, and 29.1 percent of the time in the West. For robbery, the Northeast had the highest clearance rate, at 38.6 percent. The Northeast also had the highest proportion of clearances for aggravated assault (64.5 percent). (Table 26)

Clearance data for 2018 showed that, among the regions, law enforcement agencies in the Northeast cleared the highest percentage of their property crimes (22.7 percent). Agencies in the South and Midwest cleared 18.8 percent and 18.4 percent, respectively. Agencies in the West cleared 13.2 percent of their property crimes. (Table 26)

Agencies in the Northeast cleared the highest percentage of burglary offenses at 19.7 percent, followed by the South at 14.9 percent, the Midwest at 11.8 percent, and the West at 11.5 percent. For larceny-theft, the Northeast (23.6 percent) was followed by the Midwest at 20.6 percent, the South at 19.9 percent, and the West at 14.2 percent. The Northeast and South cleared the highest proportion of motor vehicle thefts at 17.7 and 17.1 percent, respectively, followed by the Midwest at 13.7 percent and the West at 10.0 percent. The Northeast cleared the greatest percentage of arson offenses (29.7 percent), followed by the South (24.0 percent). (Table 26)

Clearances by Population Groups

The UCR program uses the following population group designations in its data presentations: cities (grouped according to population size) and counties (classified as either metropolitan or nonmetropolitan counties). A breakdown of these classifications is furnished in Appendix III.

CITIES

In 2018, the clearance data collected showed that law enforcement agencies in the nation's cities cleared 43.5 percent of their violent crime offenses. Among the city population groups and subsets, agencies in the smallest cities, those with fewer than 10,000 inhabitants, cleared the greatest proportion of their violent crime offenses (53.7 percent), and law enforcement in cities with 500,000 to 999,999 inhabitants cleared the smallest proportion of their violent crime offenses (34.9 percent). (Table 25)

The clearance data for murder showed that among the city population groups and subsets, cities with populations of 25,000 to 49,999 inhabitants cleared the greatest percentage of their murders (66.7 percent). Law enforcement agencies in cities with 250,000 to 499,999 inhabitants cleared the lowest percentage of their murders (55.5 percent). For rape, cities with 50,000 to 99,999 inhabitants cleared the largest percentage of offenses at 33.6 percent, while cities with 250,000 to 499,999 inhabitants cleared the lowest percentage of offenses at 29.2 percent. Cities with under 10,000 inhabitants cleared the greatest percentage of their robbery offenses at 37.6 percent, and cities with 500,000 to 999,999 inhabitants cleared the lowest proportion of their robbery offenses at 23.1 percent. For aggravated assault, cities with fewer than 10,000 inhabitants cleared the highest proportion of offenses (59.9 percent); cities with 500,000 to 999,999 inhabitants cleared the lowest percentage of offenses (40.4 percent). (Table 25)

In 2018, agencies in the nation's cities collectively cleared 17.3 percent of their property crime offenses. Law enforcement in cities with 10,000 to 24,999 inhabitants cleared the highest proportion of the property crimes (24.9 percent) brought to their attention; cities with 500,000 to 999,999 inhabitants cleared the smallest proportion of their property crimes (10.1 percent). (Table 25)

Law enforcement agencies in cities cleared 13.1 percent of burglaries, 18.8 percent of larceny-thefts, 12.6 percent of motor vehicle thefts, and 21.3 percent of arsons in 2018. For burglaries, cities with fewer than 10,000 inhabitants cleared the largest percentage of their offenses at 18.3 percent, while cities with 500,000 to 999,999 inhabitants cleared the smallest percentage of their offenses at 10.4 percent. Cities with 10,000 to 24,999 inhabitants cleared the greatest percentage of their larceny-theft offenses (27.2 percent), and cities with 500,000 to 999,999 inhabitants cleared the lowest proportion of larceny-theft offenses (10.4 percent). For motor vehicle theft, cities with fewer than 10,000 inhabitants cleared the highest percentages of their offenses at 23.6 percent, while cities with 250,000 to 499,999 inhabitants and 1,000,000 or more inhabitants cleared the lowest percentage (9.1 percent). Cities with 10,000 to 24,999 inhabitants cleared the greatest percentage of their arson offenses, at 28.1 percent, and cities with 1,000,000 or more inhabitants cleared the lowest percentage (12.5 percent). (Table 25)

METROPOLITAN AND NONMETROPOLITAN COUNTIES

In 2018, law enforcement agencies in metropolitan counties cleared 52.8 percent of their violent crime offenses. Of the violent crimes made known to law enforcement agencies in metropolitan counties, murder offenses had the highest proportion of clearance (66.0 percent), followed by aggravated assaults (59.1 percent), rapes (39.5 percent), and robberies (34.9 percent). Law enforcement agencies in metropolitan counties cleared 18.5 percent of their total property crimes, 15.8 percent of burglaries, 19.3 percent of larceny-thefts, 17.9 percent of motor vehicle thefts, and 25.0 percent of their arsons. (Table 25)

Like their counterparts in metropolitan counties, nonmetropolitan counties collectively cleared a greater proportion of their violent crimes than did the nation as a whole in 2018. Nonmetropolitan counties cleared 55.8 percent of their violent crime offenses and 19.7 percent of property crimes. Of the violent crimes known to them, law enforcement in nonmetropolitan counties had the highest number of clearances for murder (70.1 percent), with 38.1 percent of rapes, 44.0 percent of robberies, and 60.5 percent of aggravated assaults being cleared. Agencies in nonmetropolitan counties reported clearing 19.7 percent of property crimes, including 17.4 percent of their burglaries, 19.9 percent of their larceny-thefts, 24.8 percent of their motor vehicle thefts, and 30.0 percent of their arsons. In suburban areas, 52.8 percent of violent crimes (65.7 percent of murders, 37.2 percent of rapes, 35.5 percent of robberies, and 59.9 percent of aggravated assaults) and 20.8 percent of property crimes (16.0 percent of burglaries, 22.3 percent of larceny-thefts, 17.5 percent of motor vehicle thefts, and 25.7 percent of arsons) were cleared in 2018. (Table 25)

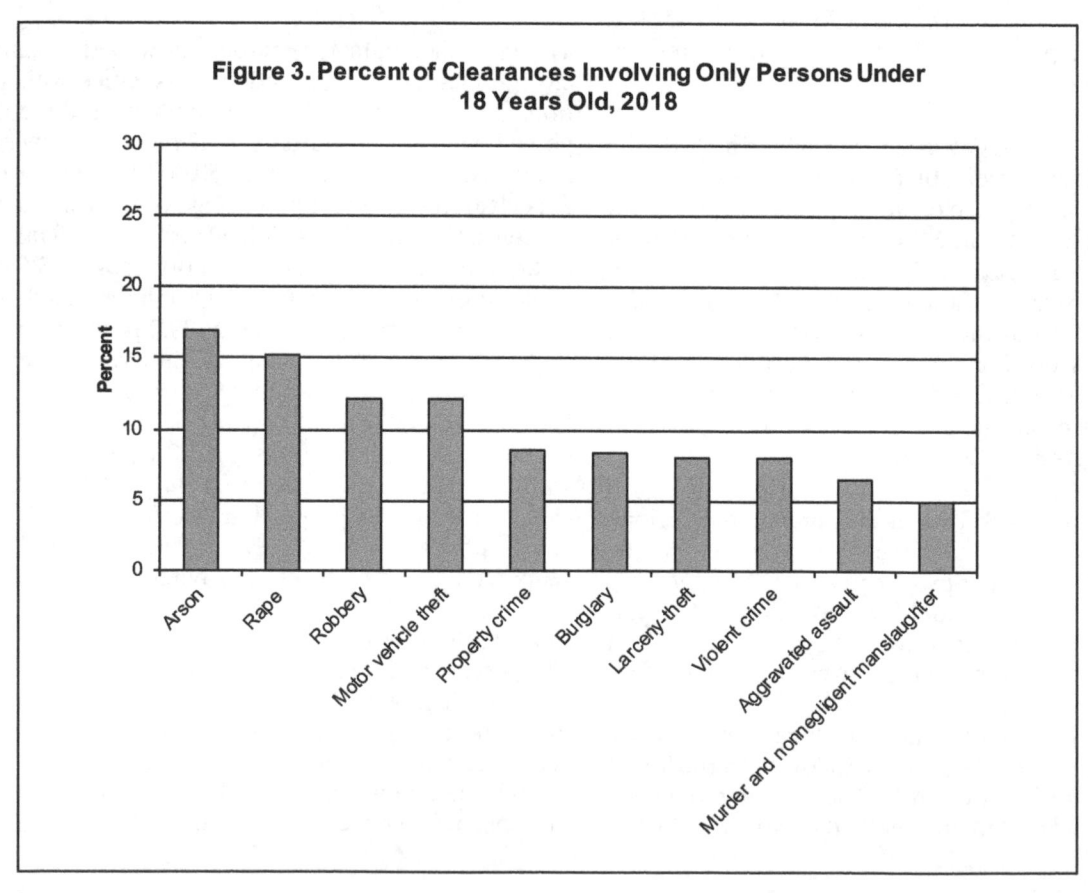

Figure 3. Percent of Clearances Involving Only Persons Under 18 Years Old, 2018

Clearances by Classification Group and Type

For rape, by classification group and type, law enforcement agencies cleared 37.5 percent of assault-to-rape attempts and 33.0 percent of rapes by force in 2018. Cleared robbery offenses included 31.3 percent of offenses involving strong-arm tactics, 32.7 percent of offenses involving knives or other cutting instruments, 29.4 percent of offenses involving other weapons, and 23.0 percent of offenses involving firearms. For aggravated assaults, agencies cleared 55.8 percent of offenses involving knives or other cutting instruments; 58.4 percent of offenses involving hands, feet, fists, etc.; 49.2 percent of offenses involving other weapons; and 32.4 percent of offenses involving firearms. (Table 27)

For property crime clearances grouped by classification and type, data showed that the highest percentage of burglary clearances in the nation in 2018 (15.6 percent) were of offenses that involved unlawful entry. Law enforcement agencies cleared 12.8 percent of burglaries involving forcible entry and 13.1 percent of burglaries involving attempted forcible entry. For motor vehicle theft, agencies cleared 14.6 percent of motor vehicle theft offenses involving automobiles and 11.5 percent of motor vehicle theft offenses involving trucks and buses. (Table 27)

In 2018, 26.1 percent of structural arson offenses were cleared by arrest or exceptional means, while 10.9 percent of mobile arson offenses and 25.9 percent of other arson crimes were cleared. (Table 27)

CLEARANCES AND JUVENILES

When an offender under 18 years of age is cited to appear in juvenile court or before other juvenile authorities, the UCR program considers the incident for which the juvenile is being held responsible to be cleared by arrest, although a physical arrest may not have occurred. In addition, according to program definitions, clearances that include both adult and juvenile offenders are classified as clearances for crimes committed by adults. Therefore, the juvenile clearance data are limited to those clearances involving juveniles only, and the figures in this publication should not be used to present a definitive picture of juvenile involvement in crime.

Of the clearances for violent crimes that were reported in the nation in 2018, 8.0 percent involved only juveniles. In the nation's cities, collectively, 8.0 percent of violent crime clearances also involved only juveniles, with juveniles in cities exclusively involved in 5.1 percent of murder clearances, 14.2 percent of rape clearances, 12.2 percent of robbery clearances, and 6.4 percent of aggravated assault clearances. Of the nation's city population groups and subsets, cities with under 10,000 inhabitants had the highest percentage of overall clearances for violent crime only involving juveniles (9.6 percent); cities with 1,000,000 or more inhabitants had the lowest percentage, 7.3 percent. (Table 28)

Law enforcement agencies in metropolitan counties reported that 8.6 percent of their violent crime clearances—including 4.3 percent of their murder clearances, 18.0 percent of their rape clearances, 12.6 percent of their robbery clearances, and 7.0 percent of their aggravated assault clearances—involved only juveniles. Agencies in nonmetropolitan counties reported that 6.8 percent of their clearances for violent crime involved only juveniles, including 2.8 percent of their murder clearances, 17.9 percent of their rape clearances, 4.3 percent of their robbery clearances, and 5.3 percent of their aggravated assault clearances. In suburban areas, 9.1 percent of violent crimes, 4.6 percent of murders, 17.3 percent of rapes, 12.3 percent of robberies, and 7.7 percent of aggravated assaults involved only juveniles. (Table 28)

In 2018, 8.5 percent of clearances for property crime involved only juveniles. In cities collectively, 8.4 percent of the clearances for property crime, 8.5 percent of clearances for burglary, 7.9 percent of clearances for larceny-theft, 12.6 percent of clearances for motor vehicle theft, and 17.3 percent of clearances for arson involved juveniles only. Among the population groups and subsets labeled *city*, the percentages of clearances involving only juveniles for overall property crime ranged from a low of 6.5 percent in cities with more than 1,000,000 inhabitants to a high of 9.7 percent in cities with populations of 250,000 to 499,999 inhabitants. (Table 28)

Metropolitan counties reported that 9.5 percent of all property crime clearances, 8.8 percent of burglary clearances, 9.2 percent of larceny-theft clearances, 11.9 percent of motor vehicle theft clearances, and 18.2 percent of arson clearances involved persons under 18 years of age. In nonmetropolitan counties, 6.2 percent of property crime clearances, 6.0 percent of burglary clearances, 5.8 percent of larceny-theft clearances, 8.0 percent of motor vehicle theft clearances, and 10.9 percent of arson clearances involved juveniles exclusively. In suburban areas, 20.2 percent of arson clearances involved only juveniles, as did 8.7 percent of property crimes, 9.0 percent of burglaries, 8.3 percent of larceny-thefts, and 11.9 percent of motor vehicle thefts. (Table 28)

Table 25. Number and Percent of Offenses Cleared by Arrest or Exceptional Means, by Population Group, 2018

(Number, percent.)

Population group	Violent crime	Murder and nonnegligent manslaughter	Rape[1]	Robbery	Aggravated assault	Property crime	Burglary	Larceny-theft	Motor vehicle theft	Arson[2]	Number of agencies	Estimated population, 2018
Total, All Agencies												
Offenses known	1,147,991	14,786	127,258	260,709	745,238	6,677,611	1,128,351	4,812,405	701,248	35,607	15,325	302,194,936
Percent cleared by arrest	45.5	62.3	33.4	30.4	52.5	17.6	13.9	18.9	13.8	22.4		
Total Cities												
Offenses known	915,256	11,463	94,822	228,461	580,510	5,333,263	839,903	3,901,143	564,974	27,243	10,971	204,451,288
Percent cleared by arrest	43.5	61.0	31.5	29.7	50.6	17.3	13.1	18.8	12.6	21.3		
Group I (250,000 and over)												
Offenses known	435,004	5,756	36,404	127,354	265,490	1,920,538	311,203	1,342,646	256,079	10,610	84	60,183,883
Percent cleared by arrest	38.1	57.7	29.8	26.9	44.3	11.6	10.3	12.3	9.5	15.8		
1,000,000 and over (Group I subset)												
Offenses known	166,653	1,757	13,788	51,900	99,208	638,914	98,560	452,376	84,878	3,100	10	25,167,857
Percent cleared by arrest	42.4	62.4	29.9	30.6	49.9	11.7	10.5	12.5	9.1	12.5		
500,000 to 999,999 (Group I subset)												
Offenses known	153,670	2,227	11,565	44,288	95,590	727,582	120,868	507,805	94,884	4,025	26	18,736,687
Percent cleared by arrest	34.9	55.7	30.4	23.1	40.4	10.1	9.6	10.4	9.1	16.5		
250,000 to 499,999 (Group I subset)												
Offenses known	114,681	1,772	11,051	31,166	70,692	554,042	91,775	382,465	76,317	3,485	48	16,279,339
Percent cleared by arrest	36.4	55.5	29.2	26.2	41.5	13.4	11.0	14.5	10.4	18.0		
Group II (100,000 to 249,999)												
Offenses known	149,163	2,029	15,833	38,327	92,974	942,037	149,522	675,531	112,518	4,466	219	32,568,127
Percent cleared by arrest	43.1	64.6	31.9	29.8	50.1	15.4	12.3	16.6	12.2	22.0		
Group III (50,000 to 99,999)												
Offenses known	112,621	1,226	13,088	26,767	71,540	781,305	121,205	579,839	76,291	3,970	477	33,353,799
Percent cleared by arrest	48.8	61.7	33.6	33.9	56.9	18.9	13.8	20.7	13.5	24.2		
Group IV (25,000 to 49,999)												
Offenses known	78,265	936	10,813	16,468	50,048	619,983	92,753	476,017	48,546	2,667	833	28,920,904
Percent cleared by arrest	49.5	66.7	31.7	34.7	57.9	22.8	15.1	25.0	15.6	26.2		
Group V (10,000 to 24,999)												
Offenses known	71,933	827	9,538	11,736	49,832	575,550	89,683	443,347	40,142	2,378	1,703	27,136,547
Percent cleared by arrest	52.2	65.7	33.4	37.0	59.2	24.9	16.4	27.2	19.3	28.1		
Group VI (under 10,000)												
Offenses known	68,270	689	9,146	7,809	50,626	493,850	75,537	383,763	31,398	3,152	7,655	22,288,028
Percent cleared by arrest	53.7	63.4	32.4	37.6	59.9	24.3	18.3	25.6	23.6	25.8		
Metropolitan Counties												
Offenses known	186,601	2,514	23,959	29,929	130,199	1,098,087	215,954	763,579	112,207	6,347	1,963	74,277,601
Percent cleared by arrest	52.8	66.0	39.5	34.9	59.1	18.5	15.8	19.3	17.9	25.0		
Nonmetropolitan Counties												
Offenses known	46,134	809	8,477	2,319	34,529	246,261	72,494	147,683	24,067	2,017	2,391	23,466,047
Percent cleared by arrest	55.8	70.1	38.1	44.0	60.5	19.7	17.4	19.9	24.8	30.0		
Suburban Areas[3]												
Offenses known	317,313	3,959	41,720	54,966	216,668	2,192,768	368,227	1,618,673	194,627	11,241	8,318	131,266,364
Percent cleared by arrest	52.8	65.7	37.2	35.5	59.9	20.8	16.0	22.3	17.5	25.7		

1 The figures shown in the rape column include only those reported by law enforcement agencies that used the revised Uniform Crime Reporting definition of rape. See chapter notes for more detail.   2 Not all agencies submit reports for arson to the FBI. As a result, the number of reports the FBI uses to compute the percent of offenses cleared for arson is less than the number it uses to compute the percent of offenses cleared for all other offenses.   3 Suburban area includes law enforcement agencies in cities with less than 50,000 inhabitants and county law enforcement agencies that are within a Metropolitan Statistical Area. Suburban area excludes all metropolitan agencies associated with a principal city. The agencies associated with suburban areas also appear in other groups within this table.

Table 26. Number and Percent of Offenses Cleared by Arrest or Exceptional Means, by Region and Geographic Division, 2018

(Number, percent.)

Geographic region/division	Violent crime	Murder and nonnegligent manslaughter	Rape[1]	Robbery	Aggravated assault	Property crime	Burglary	Larceny-theft	Motor vehicle theft	Arson[2]	Number of agencies	Estimated population, 2018
Total, All Agencies												
Offenses known	1,147,991	14,786	127,258	260,709	745,238	6,677,611	1,128,351	4,812,405	701,248	35,607	15,325	302,194,936
Percent cleared by arrest	45.5	62.3	33.4	30.4	52.5	17.6	13.9	18.9	13.8	22.4		
Northeast												
Offenses known	162,197	1,904	17,278	41,511	101,504	798,211	106,772	633,893	54,018	3,528	3,525	55,710,493
Percent cleared by arrest	54.8	61.8	36.3	38.6	64.5	22.7	19.7	23.6	17.7	29.7		
New England												
Offenses known	37,110	285	4,937	7,273	24,615	206,383	30,414	158,042	17,072	855	911	14,637,644
Percent cleared by arrest	50.7	56.1	26.2	30.4	61.6	18.6	16.6	19.5	13.2	29.9		
Middle Atlantic												
Offenses known	125,087	1,619	12,341	34,238	76,889	591,828	76,358	475,851	36,946	2,673	2,614	41,072,849
Percent cleared by arrest	56.0	62.8	40.3	40.3	65.4	24.1	21.0	24.9	19.8	29.6		
Midwest												
Offenses known	185,908	2,566	26,613	34,239	122,490	1,053,286	183,238	758,616	104,696	6,736	3,831	51,287,831
Percent cleared by arrest	41.7	56.0	32.1	25.1	48.1	18.4	11.8	20.6	13.7	17.5		
East North Central												
Offenses known	116,850	1,650	17,089	23,265	74,846	609,503	111,596	436,330	57,400	4,177	1,848	30,981,094
Percent cleared by arrest	39.9	50.5	30.9	23.4	46.8	17.2	11.3	19.4	11.8	17.6		
West North Central												
Offenses known	69,058	916	9,524	10,974	47,644	443,783	71,642	322,286	47,296	2,559	1,983	20,306,737
Percent cleared by arrest	44.8	66.0	34.2	28.7	50.2	20.1	12.7	22.3	16.0	17.2		
South												
Offenses known	477,475	7,146	46,886	102,775	320,668	2,878,560	508,546	2,092,984	265,835	11,195	5,893	118,755,909
Percent cleared by arrest	44.2	63.4	36.6	28.9	49.8	18.8	14.9	19.9	17.1	24.0		
South Atlantic												
Offenses known	226,961	3,689	19,464	51,508	152,300	1,425,437	234,817	1,064,646	120,587	5,387	2,772	62,414,752
Percent cleared by arrest	48.5	65.9	44.4	33.7	53.6	20.8	18.2	21.5	18.9	28.3		
East South Central												
Offenses known	78,143	1,225	6,597	14,327	55,994	440,256	84,736	308,497	45,118	1,905	1,259	17,273,677
Percent cleared by arrest	44.7	60.7	40.7	28.1	49.0	21.4	15.2	23.0	22.4	21.9		
West South Central												
Offenses known	172,371	2,232	20,825	36,940	112,374	1,012,867	188,993	719,841	100,130	3,903	1,862	39,067,480
Percent cleared by arrest	38.3	60.6	27.9	22.5	45.0	14.9	10.6	16.2	12.6	19.2		
West												
Offenses known	322,411	3,170	36,481	82,184	200,576	1,947,554	329,795	1,326,912	276,699	14,148	2,076	76,440,703
Percent cleared by arrest	45.0	65.5	29.1	30.3	53.6	13.2	11.5	14.2	10.0	21.8		
Mountain												
Offenses known	102,054	1,050	14,185	18,154	68,665	607,292	102,302	428,216	73,661	3,113	877	23,521,163
Percent cleared by arrest	43.8	66.3	25.6	27.4	51.5	17.0	11.9	19.1	11.1	25.0		
Pacific												
Offenses known	220,357	2,120	22,296	64,030	131,911	1,340,262	227,493	898,696	203,038	11,035	1,199	52,919,540
Percent cleared by arrest	45.5	65.1	31.3	31.1	54.6	11.5	11.4	11.8	9.6	20.9		

1 The figures shown in the rape column include only those reported by law enforcement agencies that used the revised Uniform Crime Reporting definition of rape. See chapter notes for more detail.   2 Not all agencies submit reports for arson to the FBI. As a result, the number of reports the FBI uses to compute the percent of offenses cleared for arson is less than the number it uses to compute the percent of offenses cleared for all other offenses.

Table 27. Number and Percent of Offenses Cleared by Arrest or Exceptional Means, Additional Information About Selected Offenses, by Population Group, 2018

(Number, percent.)

Population group	Rape[1]		Robbery				Aggravated assault			
	Rape by force	Assault to rape-attempts	Firearm	Knife or cutting instrument	Other weapon	Strong-arm	Firearm	Knife or cutting instrument	Other weapon	Hands, fists, feet, etc.
Total, All Agencies										
Offenses known	121,551	5,707	100,810	21,629	27,109	111,161	195,046	128,006	233,301	188,885
Percent cleared by arrest	33.0	37.5	23.0	32.7	29.4	31.3	32.4	55.8	49.2	58.4
Total Cities										
Offenses known	90,344	4,478	86,321	19,291	23,665	99,184	156,461	104,774	180,273	139,002
Percent cleared by arrest	31.1	37.0	22.9	32.7	29.3	31.2	30.6	55.9	49.3	59.2
Group I (250,000 and over)										
Offenses known	34,458	1,946	49,587	10,589	12,667	54,511	83,695	50,118	85,515	46,162
Percent cleared by arrest	29.3	37.2	20.8	30.6	26.8	29.9	26.3	53.4	45.4	55.4
1,000,000 and over (Group I subset)										
Offenses known	12,913	875	17,926	4,908	5,016	24,050	24,662	21,596	31,205	21,745
Percent cleared by arrest	29.2	40.8	21.3	36.2	31.4	36.3	28.2	58.9	52.5	61.9
500,000 to 999,999 (Group I subset)										
Offenses known	11,009	556	19,338	3,480	5,209	16,261	32,786	16,428	32,980	13,396
Percent cleared by arrest	29.6	36.5	18.4	25.6	22.4	26.2	25.3	50.6	41.3	51.4
250,000 to 499,999 (Group I subset)										
Offenses known	10,536	515	12,323	2,201	2,442	14,200	26,247	12,094	21,330	11,021
Percent cleared by arrest	29.0	31.7	23.9	26.2	27.0	23.3	25.7	47.2	41.5	47.5
Group II (100,000 to 249,999)										
Offenses known	15,194	639	14,857	3,365	4,026	16,079	26,745	17,385	29,118	19,726
Percent cleared by arrest	31.5	34.6	23.3	31.9	30.0	29.7	30.4	56.3	48.8	56.3
Group III (50,000 to 99,999)										
Offenses known	12,577	511	8,766	2,358	2,929	12,714	16,681	12,990	22,771	19,098
Percent cleared by arrest	33.2	37.4	26.0	36.4	32.4	32.2	33.7	57.6	54.5	61.8
Group IV (25,000 to 49,999)										
Offenses known	10,378	435	5,935	1,391	1,885	7,257	11,362	9,129	15,072	14,485
Percent cleared by arrest	31.2	38.4	27.1	34.1	30.5	34.5	37.0	57.8	55.3	61.2
Group V (10,000 to 24,999)										
Offenses known	9,164	374	4,470	959	1,247	5,060	10,659	7,941	15,033	16,199
Percent cleared by arrest	32.9	41.4	29.4	40.7	35.6	37.4	41.8	61.4	54.3	64.0
Group VI (under 10,000)										
Offenses known	8,573	573	2,706	629	911	3,563	7,319	7,211	12,764	23,332
Percent cleared by arrest	32.1	34.9	30.4	41.5	38.5	37.9	47.7	61.2	54.6	62.3
Metropolitan Counties										
Offenses known	23,084	875	13,459	2,156	3,103	11,211	31,384	19,046	42,846	36,923
Percent cleared by arrest	38.9	42.7	22.2	31.9	28.7	31.2	36.7	53.5	46.4	55.6
Nonmetropolitan Counties										
Offenses known	8,123	354	1,030	182	341	766	7,201	4,186	10,182	12,960
Percent cleared by arrest	37.8	30.5	35.8	42.9	43.1	45.2	51.8	64.4	57.5	57.7
Suburban Areas[3]										
Offenses known	40,024	1,696	22,510	4,137	5,992	22,327	47,850	33,023	67,950	67,845
Percent cleared by arrest	36.7	40.6	24.4	33.9	31.2	33.9	38.4	56.5	49.9	59.3

Table 27. Number and Percent of Offenses Cleared by Arrest or Exceptional Means, Additional Information About Selected Offenses, by Population Group, 2018—Continued

(Number, percent.)

Population group	Burglary			Motor vehicle theft			Arson[2]			Number of agencies	Estimated population, 2018
	Forcible entry	Unlawful entry	Attempted forcible entry	Autos	Trucks and buses	Other vehicles	Structure	Mobile	Other		
Total, All Agencies											
Offenses known	639,714	415,012	73,625	526,343	109,959	64,946	15,369	8,407	11,831	15,325	302,194,936
Percent cleared by arrest	12.8	15.6	13.1	14.6	11.5	11.2	26.1	10.9	25.9		
Total Cities											
Offenses known	476,647	305,385	57,871	429,858	89,406	45,710	11,758	6,202	9,283	10,971	204,451,288
Percent cleared by arrest	11.8	14.9	13.0	13.4	10.1	9.6	24.4	10.2	24.8		
Group I (250,000 and over)											
Offenses known	192,200	96,908	22,095	187,285	50,806	17,988	4,215	2,684	3,711	84	60,183,883
Percent cleared by arrest	9.2	12.2	11.4	10.1	8.1	7.6	19.3	7.0	18.2		
1,000,000 and over (Group I subset)											
Offenses known	63,698	28,000	6,862	54,591	24,343	5,944	957	602	1,541	10	25,167,857
Percent cleared by arrest	8.8	12.9	15.5	10.2	6.5	10.3	22.4	7.8	8.2		
500,000 to 999,999 (Group I subset)											
Offenses known	74,092	37,870	8,906	72,890	15,291	6,703	1,609	1,142	1,274	26	18,736,687
Percent cleared by arrest	8.5	11.8	8.9	9.2	9.6	6.2	16.5	6.9	25.0		
250,000 to 499,999 (Group I subset)											
Offenses known	54,410	31,038	6,327	59,804	11,172	5,341	1,649	940	896	48	16,279,339
Percent cleared by arrest	10.4	12.1	10.5	11.0	9.4	6.4	20.2	6.6	25.8		
Group II (100,000 to 249,999)											
Offenses known	85,352	53,430	10,740	87,932	16,105	8,481	1,892	1,074	1,500	219	32,568,127
Percent cleared by arrest	11.4	13.6	12.8	12.7	11.0	8.3	23.4	10.9	28.3		
Group III (50,000 to 99,999)											
Offenses known	64,891	48,337	7,977	59,334	10,378	6,579	1,631	875	1,464	477	33,353,799
Percent cleared by arrest	12.7	15.4	13.1	14.2	11.9	10.0	27.1	10.7	29.1		
Group IV (25,000 to 49,999)											
Offenses known	48,467	37,651	6,635	38,822	4,932	4,792	1,152	509	1,006	833	28,920,904
Percent cleared by arrest	14.4	16.3	13.5	16.5	14.1	10.0	28.5	14.5	29.4		
Group V (10,000 to 24,999)											
Offenses known	47,252	36,975	5,456	32,004	4,169	3,969	1,118	493	767	1,703	27,136,547
Percent cleared by arrest	15.3	17.7	16.9	20.7	15.4	11.9	31.4	15.2	31.6		
Group VI (under 10,000)											
Offenses known	38,485	32,084	4,968	24,481	3,016	3,901	1,750	567	835	7,655	22,288,028
Percent cleared by arrest	17.3	20.0	15.2	24.8	20.7	17.9	28.1	15.2	28.3		
Metropolitan Counties											
Offenses known	120,867	82,071	13,016	80,016	16,910	15,281	2,613	1,785	1,949	1,963	74,277,601
Percent cleared by arrest	14.9	17.5	13.7	18.7	17.1	14.2	30.8	10.5	30.5		
Nonmetropolitan Counties											
Offenses known	42,200	27,556	2,738	16,469	3,643	3,955	998	420	599	2,391	23,466,047
Percent cleared by arrest	17.4	17.5	13.9	27.4	18.9	19.0	34.0	22.1	28.9		
Suburban Areas[3]											
Offenses known	200,160	143,457	24,610	145,770	25,276	23,581	4,904	2,801	3,536	8,318	131,266,364
Percent cleared by arrest	15.1	17.7	13.9	18.4	16.1	13.4	30.5	11.8	30.1		

1 The figures shown in the rape column include only those reported by law enforcement agencies that used the revised Uniform Crime Reporting definition of rape. See chapter notes for more detail.   2 Not all agencies submit reports for arson to the FBI. As a result, the number of reports the FBI uses to compute the percent of offenses cleared for arson is less than the number it uses to compute the percent of offenses cleared for all other offenses. Agencies must report arson clearances by detailed property classification as specified on the *Monthly Return of Arson Offenses Known to Law Enforcement* to be included in this table; therefore, clearances in this table may differ from other clearance tables.   3 Suburban area includes law enforcement agencies in cities with less than 50,000 inhabitants and county law enforcement agencies that are within a Metropolitan Statistical Area. Suburban area excludes all metropolitan agencies associated with a principal city. The agencies associated with suburban areas also appear in other groups within this table.

Table 28. Number of Offenses Cleared by Arrest or Exceptional Means and Percent Involving Persons Under 18 Years of Age, by Population Group, 2018

(Number, percent.)

Population group	Violent crime	Murder and nonnegligent manslaughter	Rape[1]	Robbery	Aggravated assault	Property crime	Burglary	Larceny-theft	Motor vehicle theft	Arson[2]	Number of agencies	Estimated population, 2018
Total, All Agencies												
Offenses known	522,452	9,218	42,565	79,229	391,440	1,172,549	156,444	911,078	97,034	7,993	15,325	302,194,936
Percent under 18 years	8.0	4.9	15.3	12.2	6.5	8.5	8.3	8.0	12.2	17.0		
Total Cities												
Offenses known	398,221	6,991	29,881	67,755	293,594	920,820	109,653	734,342	71,025	5,800	10,971	204,451,288
Percent under 18 years	8.0	5.1	14.2	12.2	6.4	8.4	8.5	7.9	12.6	17.3		
Group I (250,000 and over)												
Offenses known	165,949	3,321	10,863	34,267	117,498	222,652	31,981	164,678	24,317	1,676	84	60,183,883
Percent under 18 years	7.6	5.1	12.6	13.4	5.5	8.1	7.4	7.5	12.6	12.0		
1,000,000 and over (Group I subset)												
Offenses known	70,661	1,097	4,127	15,898	49,539	74,994	10,311	56,555	7,741	387	10	25,167,857
Percent under 18 years	7.3	4.6	11.7	14.8	4.6	6.5	5.5	6.4	8.7	7.5		
500,000 to 999,999 (Group I subset)												
Offenses known	53,572	1,241	3,512	10,218	38,601	73,620	11,574	52,771	8,612	663	26	18,736,687
Percent under 18 years	7.4	5.0	13.6	11.9	5.8	8.0	8.0	7.0	14.0	12.4		
250,000 to 499,999 (Group I subset)												
Offenses known	41,716	983	3,224	8,151	29,358	74,038	10,096	55,352	7,964	626	48	16,279,339
Percent under 18 years	8.1	5.9	12.9	12.5	6.5	9.7	8.5	9.2	14.8	14.4		
Group II (100,000 to 249,999)												
Offenses known	64,357	1,310	5,053	11,415	46,579	145,486	18,362	112,467	13,674	983	219	32,568,127
Percent under 18 years	7.6	5.6	14.7	11.1	6.0	9.4	9.0	8.9	13.9	17.0		
Group III (50,000 to 99,999)												
Offenses known	54,931	756	4,395	9,078	40,702	147,815	16,756	119,784	10,313	962	477	33,353,799
Percent under 18 years	7.8	4.1	14.4	11.2	6.4	9.3	8.8	9.0	12.5	18.8		
Group IV (25,000 to 49,999)												
Offenses known	38,754	624	3,427	5,715	28,988	141,156	14,034	118,842	7,582	698	833	28,920,904
Percent under 18 years	8.6	4.6	16.3	10.8	7.4	8.3	8.7	7.9	14.0	21.3		
Group V (10,000 to 24,999)												
Offenses known	37,582	543	3,182	4,341	29,516	143,564	14,687	120,470	7,739	668	1,703	27,136,547
Percent under 18 years	8.4	4.6	15.9	9.3	7.6	7.5	8.2	7.1	11.0	19.2		
Group VI (under 10,000)												
Offenses known	36,648	437	2,961	2,939	30,311	120,147	13,833	98,101	7,400	813	7,655	22,288,028
Percent under 18 years	9.6	7.1	14.8	13.3	8.8	7.8	9.9	7.1	10.9	21.6		
Metropolitan Counties												
Offenses known	98,511	1,660	9,455	10,454	76,942	203,218	34,197	147,382	20,051	1,588	1,963	74,277,601
Percent under 18 years	8.6	4.3	18.0	12.6	7.0	9.5	8.8	9.2	11.9	18.2		
Nonmetropolitan Counties												
Offenses known	25,720	567	3,229	1,020	20,904	48,511	12,594	29,354	5,958	605	2,391	23,466,047
Percent under 18 years	6.8	2.8	17.9	4.3	5.3	6.2	6.0	5.8	8.0	10.9		
Suburban Areas[3]												
Offenses known	167,394	2,603	15,501	19,533	129,757	456,422	59,032	360,401	34,096	2,893	8,318	131,266,364
Percent under 18 years	9.1	4.6	17.3	12.3	7.7	8.7	9.0	8.3	11.9	20.2		

1 The figures shown in the rape column include only those reported by law enforcement agencies that used the revised Uniform Crime Reporting definition of rape. See chapter notes for more detail.   2 Not all agencies submit reports for arson to the FBI. As a result, the number of reports the FBI uses to compute the percent of offenses cleared for arson is less than the number it uses to compute the percent of offenses cleared for all other offenses.   3 Suburban area includes law enforcement agencies in cities with less than 50,000 inhabitants and county law enforcement agencies that are within a Metropolitan Statistical Area. Suburban area excludes all metropolitan agencies associated with a principal city. The agencies associated with suburban areas also appear in other groups within this table.

SECTION IV

PERSONS ARRESTED

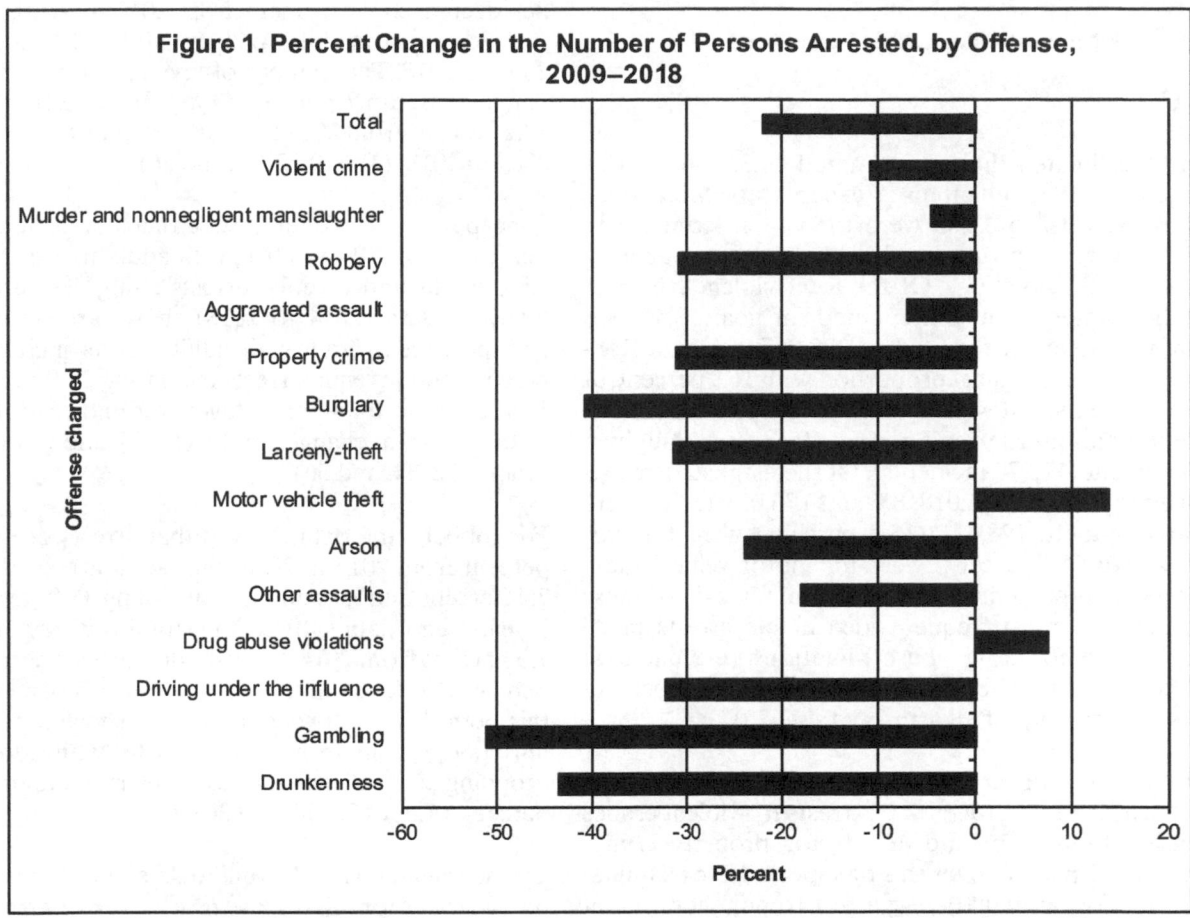

Figure 1. Percent Change in the Number of Persons Arrested, by Offense, 2009–2018

In the Uniform Crime Reporting (UCR) program, one arrest is counted for each separate instance in which an individual is arrested, cited, or summoned for criminal acts in Part I and Part II crimes. (See Appendix I for additional information concerning Part I and Part II crimes.) One person may be arrested multiple times during the year; as a result, the arrest figures in this section should not be taken as the total number of individuals arrested. Instead, it provides the number of *arrest occurrences* reported by law enforcement. Information regarding the UCR program's statistical methodology and table construction can be found in Appendix I.

Important Note: Rape Data

In 2014, the UCR Program initiated the collection of rape data under a revised definition and removed the term "forcible" from the offense name. The UCR Program now defines rape as follows:

Rape (revised definition): Penetration, no matter how slight, of the vagina or anus with any body part or object, or oral penetration by a sex organ of another person,

without the consent of the victim. (This includes the offenses of rape, sodomy, and sexual assault with an object as converted from data submitted via the National Incident-Based Reporting System.)

Rape (legacy definition): The carnal knowledge of a female forcibly and against her will. For tables within this publication that present data for 2018 only or provide a 2-year trend, the rape figures are an aggregate total of the data submitted based on both the legacy and revised UCR definitions. For 5- and 10-year trend tables, the rape figures for the previous year (2014 or 2009) are based on the legacy definition and the 2018 rape figures are an aggregate total based on both the legacy and revised definitions. For this reason, a percent change is not provided.

Data Collection: Juveniles

The UCR Program considers a juvenile to be an individual under 18 years of age regardless of state definition. The program does not collect data regarding police contact with a juvenile who has not committed an offense, nor does it collect data on situations in which police take a juvenile into custody for his or her protection, e.g., neglect cases.

National Volume, Trends, and Rates

VOLUME

The FBI estimated that an estimated 10,310,960 arrests occurred in 2018 for all offenses (except traffic violations). Of these arrests, 521,103 were for violent crimes, and 1,167,296 were for property crimes UCR does not collect data for traffic violations. Of the total violent crimes in 2018, aggravated assaults accounted for nearly 76.0 percent of the violent crime total, or 388,927 incidents. Robbery had the next highest proportion with 16.9 percent, or 88,128 incidents; followed by rape at 4.8 percent (25,205 incidents) and murder and non-negligent manslaughter, at 2.3 percent (11,970 incidents). Of the estimated arrests for property crimes in 2018, 887,622 (76.0 percent) were for larceny-theft, 178,611 (15.3 percent) were for burglary, 91,676 (7.9 percent) were for motor vehicle theft, and 9,387 (0.8 percent) were for arson. Outside of these categories, the most frequent identifiable arrests made in 2018 were for drug abuse violations (estimated at 1,654,282 arrests). These arrests comprised 16.0 percent of the total number of all arrests. (Table 29)

A comparison of arrest figures from 2017 to 2018 revealed a 2.8 percent decrease. Arrests for violent crimes increased 0.2 percent and arrests for property crimes decreased 7.1 percent over this time period. An examination of the 5-year and 10-year arrest trends showed that the total number of arrests in 2018 fell 6.7 percent from the 2014 total. Arrests for violent crimes showed a 3.4 percent increase from 2014 to 2018 and property crimes showed a 25.3 percent decrease. In the 10-year trend data (2009 to 2018), the number of arrests decreased 21.9 percent. For violent crimes, the number of arrests fell 11.0 percent, while arrests for property crimes decreased 31.2 percent. (Tables 32, 34, and 36)

TRENDS

The number of adults arrested for violent crime (arrestees age 18 years and over) increased 0.8 percent from 2017 to 2018, increased 3.3 percent from 2014 to 2018, and decreased 5.6 percent from 2009 to 2018. The number of juveniles arrested for violent crime (arrestees under 18 years of age) decreased 5.1 percent from 2017 to 2018, decreased 6.1 percent from 2014 to 2018, and decreased 44.6 percent from 2009 to 2018. (Tables 32, 34, and 36)

The trend data for murder and non-negligent manslaughter showed that the number of arrests for this offense decreased 3.7 percent from 2017 to 2018, increased 12.5 percent from 2014 to 2018, and decreased 4.6 percent from 2009 to 2018. The number of adults arrested for murder decreased 4.4 percent from 2017 to 2018, increased 11.1 percent from 2014 to 2018, and fell 3.1 percent from 2009 to 2018. The number of juveniles arrested for murder increased 5.7 percent from 2017 to 2018, increased 32.2 percent from 2014 to 2018, and fell 19.1 percent from 2009 to 2018. (Tables 32, 34, and 36)

For rape, the trend data showed that arrests increased 1.0 percent from 2017 to 2018, with adult arrests decreasing 4.8 percent and juvenile arrests rising 2.3 percent. The five-year data (2014 to 2018) shows arrests increasing 17.5 percent overall, with adult arrests increasing 16.3 percent and juvenile arrests increasing 23.9 percent. The 10-year trend data percentages were not calculated due to the program changes in the classification of rape data. (Tables 32, 34, and 36)

For robbery, the data showed that arrests decreased 8.3 percent from 2017 to 2018, with adult arrests decreasing 7.4 percent and juvenile arrests falling 11.9 percent. The 5-year trend data showed that total robbery arrests fell 7.0 percent from 2014 to 2018; adult arrests decreased 6.7 percent and juvenile arrests dropped 8.3 percent during this period. The 10-year trend data showed that arrests fell 30.9 percent from 2009 to 2018, with adult arrests dropping 26.2 percent and juvenile arrests falling by 45.3 percent. (Tables 32, 34, and 36)

The aggravated assault trend data showed that the number of arrests for this offense rose 2.4 percent from 2017 to 2018, increased 4.9 percent from 2014 to 2018, and fell 7.0 percent from 2009 to 2018. The number of adults arrested for aggravated assault increased 2.6 percent from 2017 to 2018, rose 6.0 percent from 2014 to 2018, and decreased 2.3 percent from 2009 to 2018. The number of juveniles arrested for aggravated assault decreased 0.8 percent from 2017 to 2018, fell 8.3 percent from 2014 to 2018, and dropped 42.5 percent from 2009 to 2018. (Tables 32, 34, and 36)

The 2-year, 5-year, and 10-year trend data showed that the number of arrests for property crime decreased 6.7 percent from 2017 to 2018, decreased 25.3 percent from 2014 to 2018, and decreased 31.2 percent from 2009 to 2018. The number of adults arrested for property crime offenses (arrestees age 18 years and over) decreased 4.8 percent from 2017 to 2018, decreased 22.2 percent from 2014 to 2018, and decreased 13.2 percent from 2009 to 2018. The number of juveniles arrested for property crime (arrestees under 18 years of age) decreased 21.6 percent from 2017 to 2018, decreased 43.0 percent from 2014 to 2018, and decreased 68.2 percent from 2009 to 2018. (Tables 32, 34, and 36)

The trend data for burglary showed that the number of arrests for this offense decreased 10.3 percent from 2017 to 2018, decreased 25.6 percent from 2014 to 2018, and decreased 40.9 percent from 2009 to 2018. The number of adults arrested for burglary fell 7.3 percent from 2017 to 2018, fell 21.9 percent from 2014 to 2018, and decreased 31.2 percent from 2009 to 2018. The number of juveniles arrested for burglary decreased 26.6 percent from 2017 to 2018, decreased 44.3 percent from 2014 to 2018, and fell 70.3 percent from 2009 to 2018. (Tables 32, 34, and 36)

For larceny-theft, the 2-year trend data showed that arrests fell 7.1 percent from 2017 to 2018, with adult arrests decreasing 4.9 percent and juvenile arrests decreasing 22.5 percent. The 5-year trend data showed that total larceny-theft arrests decreased 28.3 percent from 2014 to 2018; adult arrests fell 25.2 percent, while juvenile arrests dropped by 46.7 percent during this period. The 10-year trend data showed that larceny-theft arrests fell 31.6 percent from 2009 to 2018, with adult arrests decreasing by 19.1 percent and juvenile arrests falling by 70.1 percent. (Tables 32, 34, and 36)

For motor vehicle theft, the 2-year trend data showed that arrests fell 0.3 percent from 2017 to 2018, with adult arrests increasing 0.3 percent and juvenile arrests increasing 3.6 percent. The 5-year trend data showed that total motor vehicle theft arrests rose 29.1 percent from 2014 to 2018; juvenile arrests increased 20.3 percent and adult arrests increased 30.9 percent during this period. The 10-year trend data showed that arrests rose 13.8 percent from 2009 to 2018, with adult arrests rising 26.0 percent and juvenile arrests dropping 25.0 percent. (Tables 32, 34, and 36)

The arson trend data showed that the number of arrests for this offense decreased 0.7 percent from 2017 to 2018, fell 2.9 percent from 2014 to 2018, and fell 23.8 percent from 2009 to 2018. The number of adults arrested for arson rose 6.5 percent from 2017 to 2018, increased 18.2 percent from 2014 to 2018, and increased 12.4 percent from 2009 to 2018. The number of juveniles arrested for arson dropped 22.2 percent from 2017 to 2018, dropped 43.9 percent from 2014 to 2018, and dropped 66.8 percent from 2009 to 2018. (Tables 32, 34, and 36)

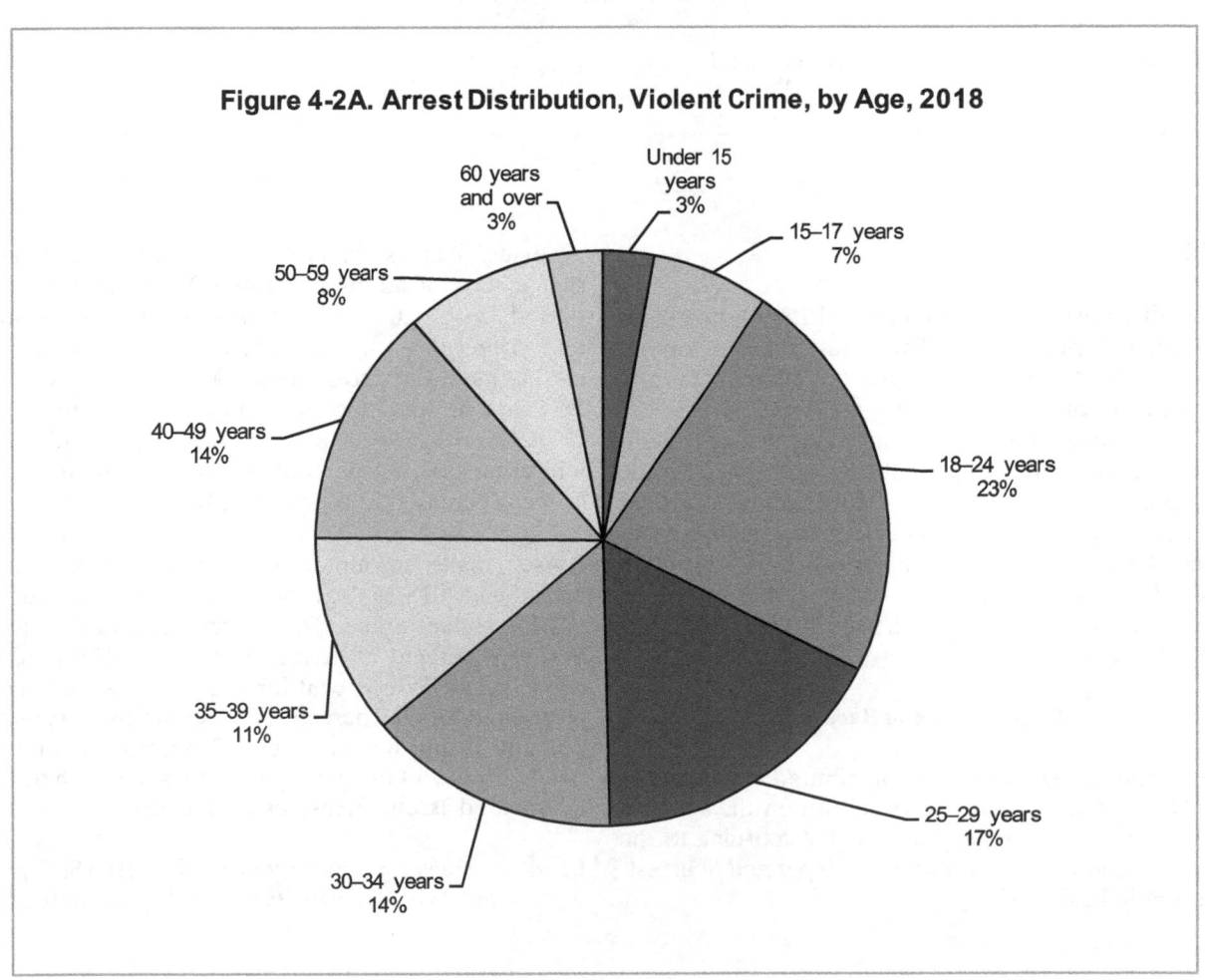

Figure 4-2A. Arrest Distribution, Violent Crime, by Age, 2018

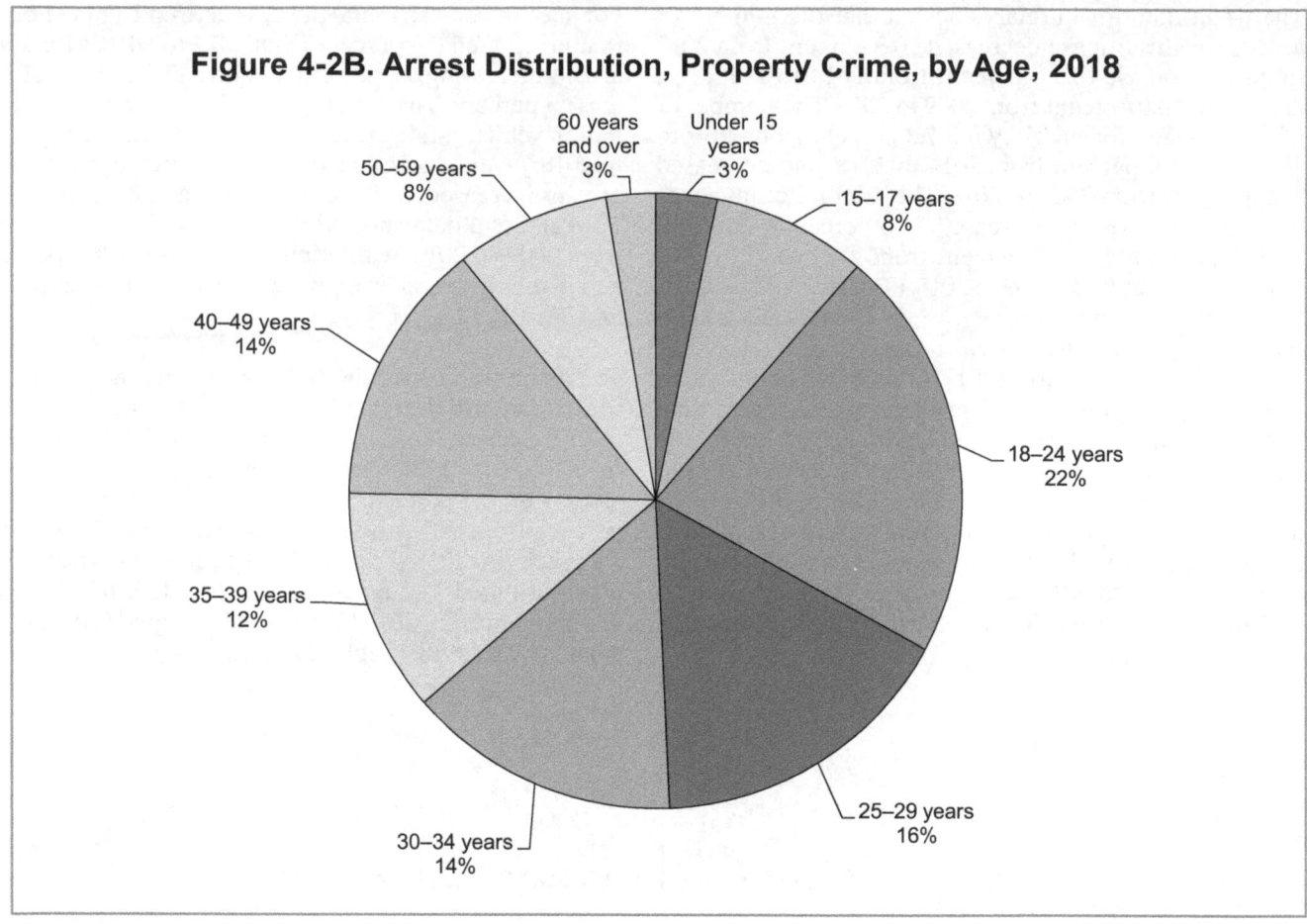

Figure 4-2B. Arrest Distribution, Property Crime, by Age, 2018

RATES

The rate of arrests was estimated at 3,152.6 arrests per 100,000 inhabitants in 2018. The arrest rate for violent crime was 159.9 arrests per 100,000 inhabitants, and the arrest rate for property crime was 361.2 arrests per 100,000 inhabitants. Law enforcement agencies throughout the nation reported 3.7 murder arrests, 7.7 rape arrests, 27.2 robbery arrests, and 121.4 aggravated assault arrests per 100,000 inhabitants in 2018. Law enforcement agencies throughout the nation reported 54.9 burglary arrests, 275.5 larceny-theft arrests, 28.1 motor vehicle theft arrests, and 2.8 arson arrests per 100,000 inhabitants in 2018. (Table 30)

By Age, Sex, and Race

Law enforcement agencies that contributed arrest data to the UCR program reported information on the age, sex, and race of the persons they arrested. According to the data for 2018, adults accounted for 92.9 percent of arrestees nationally. (Table 38)

A review of arrest data by age from 2017 to 2018 showed that arrests of adults decreased 2.1 percent during this period, with a 0.8 percent increase in arrests for violent crime and a 4.8 percent drop in arrests for property crimes. The arrest total for juveniles (those under 18 years of age) decreased 11.0 percent from 2017 to 2018. Over the 2-year period, arrests of juveniles for violent crimes fell 5.1 percent; juvenile arrests for property crimes decreased 21.6 percent. (Table 36)

By sex, males accounted for 72.8 percent of all persons arrested in 2018. Males represented 79.1 percent of arrestees for violent crime, 87.8 percent of arrestees for murder, 96.8 percent of arrestees for rape, 84.9 percent for robbery, and 76.4 percent for aggravated assault. Females accounted for 20.9 percent of violent crime arrestees, 12.2 percent of murder arrestees, 3.2 percent of rape arrestees, 15.1 percent of robbery arrestees, and 23.6 percent of aggravated assault arrestees. (Table 42)

Most arrestees for property crime in 2018 (88.7 percent) were over 18 years of age. By sex, males accounted for 63.1

percent of arrestees for property crime, 80.4 percent of arrestees for burglary, 58.0 percent of arrestees for larceny-theft, 77.2 percent of arrestees for motor vehicle theft, and 77.5 percent of arrestees for arson. Females accounted for 36.9 percent of property crime arrestees. Of the four property crimes, larceny-theft had the highest proportion of female arrestees at 42.0 percent. (Tables 38 and 42)

In 2018, 69.0 percent of all persons arrested were White, 27.4 percent were Black, and the remaining 3.5 percent were of other races (American Indian or Alaskan Native, Asian, and Native Hawaiian or Pacific Islander). Of all arrestees for violent crimes, 58.7 percent were White, 37.4 percent were Black, and 3.9 percent were of other races. For murder, 44.1 percent of arrestees were White, 53.3 percent were Black, and 2.5 percent were of other races. For rape, 68.1 percent of arrestees were White, 28.6 percent were Black, and 3.3 percent of arrestees were of other races. For robbery, 43.5 percent of arrestees were White, 54.2 percent of arrestees were Black, and 2.3 percent of arrestees were of other races. For aggravated assault, 61.9 percent of arrestees were White, 33.7 percent of arrestees were Black, and 4.4 percent were of other races. (Table 43)

Of all arrestees for property crimes in 2018, 66.9 percent were White, 30.1 percent were Black, and 3.0 percent were of other races. For burglary, 68.1 percent of arrestees were White, 29.4 percent were Black, and 2.5 percent were of other races. For larceny-theft, 66.9 percent of arrestees were White, 30.0 percent were Black, and 3.1 percent were of other races. For motor vehicle theft, 64.5 percent of arrestees were White, 32.3 percent of arrestees were Black, and 3.2 percent were of other races. For arson, 71.1 percent of arrestees were White, 25.1 percent of arrestees were Black, and 3.9 percent were of other races. (Table 43)

Outside of the scope of violent and property crimes, White adults were most commonly arrested for drug abuse violations (871,295 arrests) and driving under the influence (597,919 arrests). Black adults were most frequently arrested for drug abuse violations (333,113 arrests) and other assaults (254,360 arrests). (Table 43)

Regional Arrest Rates

The UCR program divides the United States into four regions: the Northeast, the Midwest, the South, and the West. (Appendix III provides more information about the regions.) Law enforcement agencies in the Northeast had an overall arrest rate of 2,610.6 arrests per 100,000 inhabitants, below the national rate (3,152.6 arrests per 100,000 inhabitants). In this region, the arrest rate for

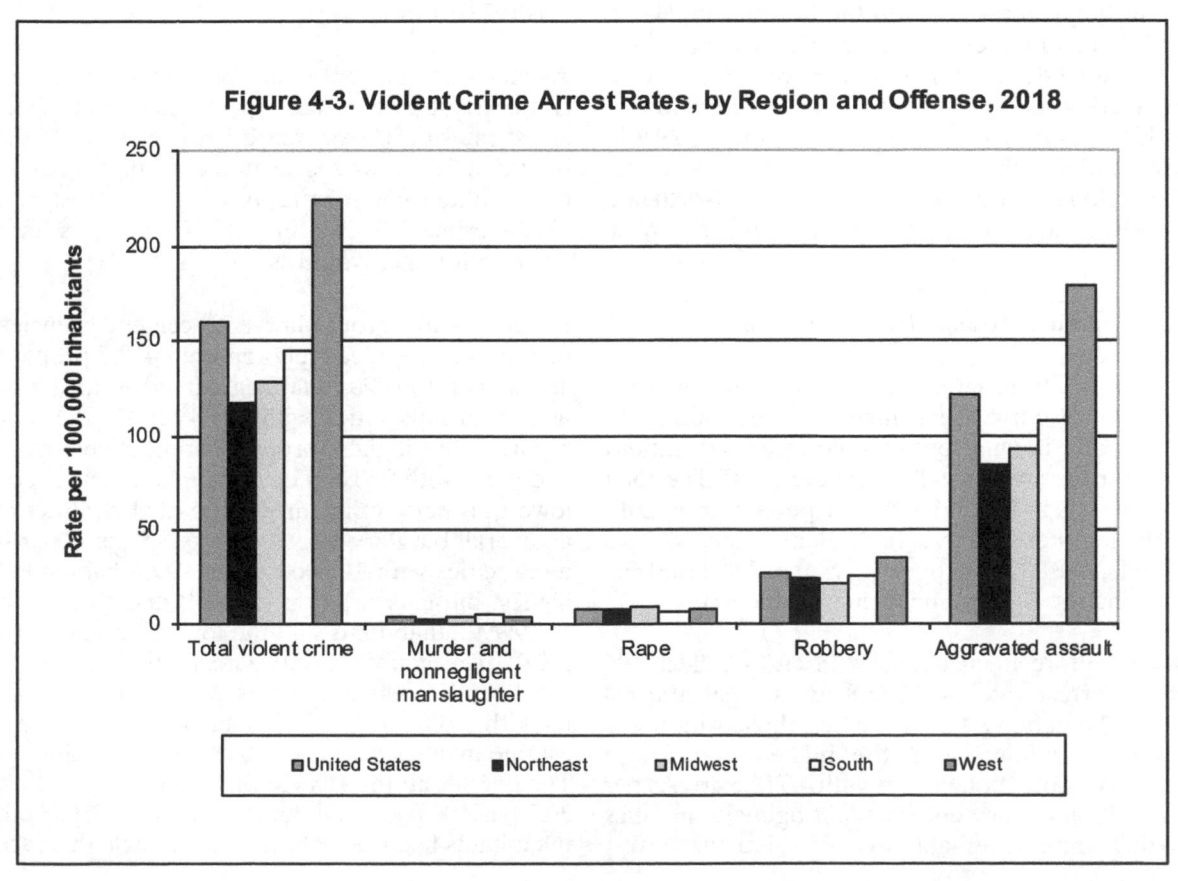

Figure 4-3. Violent Crime Arrest Rates, by Region and Offense, 2018

violent crimes was 117.5 arrests per 100,000 inhabitants, and for property crime, the arrest rate was 323.2 arrests per 100,000 inhabitants. In the Midwest, law enforcement agencies reported an arrest rate of 3,030.3 arrests per 100,000 inhabitants. The arrest rate for violent crimes was 127.8 and the arrest rate for property crime was 366.3. Law enforcement agencies in the South, the nation's most populous region, reported an arrest rate of 3,481.5 per 100,000 inhabitants. Arrests for violent crime occurred at a rate of 144.3 arrests per 100,000 residents, and for property crime, the arrest rate was 399.0 arrests per 100,000 inhabitants. In the West, law enforcement agencies reported an overall arrest rate of 3,177.1 arrests per 100,000 inhabitants. The region's violent crime arrest rate was 223.9, the highest of the regions, while its property crime arrest rate was 337.3. (Table 30)

The regional murder arrest rates were 2.2 in the Northeast, 3.9 in the Midwest, 4.5 in the South, and 3.4 in the West. For rape, the regional arrest rates were 7.3 in the Northeast, 9.5 in the Midwest, 7.1 in the South, and 7.5 in the West. Regional arrest rates for robbery were 23.6 in the Northeast, 21.9 in the Midwest, 25.5 in the South, and 34.7 in the West. For aggravated assault, the regional arrest rates were 84.5 in the Northeast, 92.5 in the Midwest, 107.2 in the South, and 178.3 in the West. (Table 30)

The regional burglary arrest rates were 39.2 in the Northeast, 37.3 in the Midwest, 55.6 in the South, and 74.6 in the West. For larceny-theft, the regional arrest rates were 266.4 in the Northeast, 296.8 in the Midwest, 317.1 in the South, and 219.4 in the West. Regional arrest rates for motor vehicle theft were 15.4 in the Northeast, 29.8 in the Midwest, 23.8 in the South, and 39.4 in the West. For arson, the regional arrest rates were 2.2 in the Northeast, 2.5 in the Midwest, 2.4 in the South, and 4.0 in the West. (Table 30)

Population Groups: Trends and Rates

The national UCR program aggregates data by various population groups, which include cities, metropolitan counties, and nonmetropolitan counties. Definitions of these groups can be found in Appendix III. The total number of arrests in U.S. cities fell 3.1 percent from 2017 to 2018. The number of arrests for violent crimes rose 0.6 percent and arrests for property crimes decreased 7.2 percent during the 2-year time frame. (Table 44)

In 2018, law enforcement agencies in cities collectively recorded an arrest rate of 3,275.8 arrests per 100,000 inhabitants. The nation's smallest cities, those with fewer than 10,000 inhabitants, had the highest arrest rate among the city population groups with 4,718.5 arrests per 100,000 inhabitants. Law enforcement agencies in cities with 250,000 or more inhabitants recorded the lowest

rate, 2,874.1. In the nation's metropolitan counties, law enforcement agencies reported an arrest rate of 2,751.2 per 100,000 inhabitants. Agencies in nonmetropolitan counties reported an arrest rate of 3,211.7. (Table 31)

By population group, law enforcement agencies in the nation's cities collectively reported 176.9 violent crime arrests per 100,000 inhabitants in 2018. In the city population groups, cities with 250,000 or more inhabitants reported the highest violent crime arrest rate (244.5) and cities with 10,000 to 24,999 inhabitants reported the lowest violent crime arrest rate (120.6). Cities reported an overall murder arrest rate of 3.9 per 100,000 inhabitants; cities with 250,000 or more inhabitants had the highest murder arrest rate (6.6) and cities with under 10,000 inhabitants had the lowest murder arrest rate (2.0). The collective city rape arrest rate was 8.0 per 100,000 inhabitants, with the highest rate in cities with 250,000 or more inhabitants (9.6) and the lowest rate in cities with 25,000 to 49,999 inhabitants (6.5). The overall robbery arrest rate for cities was 32.9 per 100,000 inhabitants; cities with 250,000 or more inhabitants had the highest robbery arrest rate (55.5) and cities with fewer than 10,000 inhabitants had the lowest robbery arrest rate (15.6). For aggravated assault, the collective city arrest rate was 132.1 per 100,000 inhabitants, with the greatest arrest rate in cities with 250,000 or more inhabitants (172.9) and the lowest arrest rate in cities with 25,000 to 49,999 inhabitants (92.6). (Table 31)

Agencies in metropolitan counties reported a violent crime arrest rate of 128.1 per 100,000 inhabitants, with arrest rates of 3.1 for murder, 6.7 for rape, 16.9 for robbery, and 101.3 for aggravated assault. Agencies in nonmetropolitan counties reported arrest rates of 99.9 for violent crime, 3.0 for murder, 8.4 for rape, 5.9 for robbery, and 82.6 for aggravated assault. (Table 31)

By population group, law enforcement agencies in the nation's cities collectively reported 418.7 property crime arrests per 100,000 inhabitants in 2018. In the city population groups, cities with 10,000 to 24,999 inhabitants reported the highest property crime arrest rate (487.3) and cities with 250,000 or more inhabitants reported the lowest property crime arrest rate (350.1). Cities reported an overall burglary arrest rate of 58.8 per 100,000 inhabitants; cities with 100,000 to 249,999 inhabitants had the highest burglary arrest rate (66.4) and cities with 25,000 to 49,999 inhabitants had the lowest burglary arrest rate (52.0). The collective city larceny-theft arrest rate was 326.7 per 100,000 inhabitants, with the highest rate in cities with 10,000 to 24,999 inhabitants (413.1) and the lowest rate in cities with 250,000 or more inhabitants (244.7). The overall motor vehicle theft arrest rate for cities was 30.3 per 100,000 inhabitants; cities with 250,000 or more inhabitants had the highest motor vehicle theft arrest rate

(43.2), and cities with 10,000 to 24,999 inhabitants had the lowest motor vehicle theft arrest rate (19.2). For arson, the collective city arrest rate was 2.9 per 100,000 inhabitants, with the greatest arrest rate in cities with less than 10,000 inhabitants (4.4) and the lowest arrest rate in cities with more than 10,000 to 24,999 inhabitants (2.5). (Table 31)

Agencies in metropolitan counties reported a property crime arrest rate of 245.2 per 100,000 inhabitants, with arrest rates of 44.4 for burglary, 174.8 for larceny-theft, 23.6 for motor vehicle theft, and 2.4 for arson. Agencies in nonmetropolitan counties reported arrest rates of 181.1 for property crime, 50.2 for burglary, 106.7 for larceny-theft, 20.6 for motor vehicle theft, and 3.6 for arson. (Table 31)

In suburban areas, the rates per 100,000 inhabitants for violent crime and property crime were 118.8 and 320.7, respectively. The rate for murder was 2.5; for rape, 6.4; for robbery, 17.0; and for aggravated assault, 93.0. Specific property crime rates included 45.2 for burglary, 252.1 for larceny-theft, 21.1 for motor vehicle theft, and 2.4 for arson. (Table 31)

Community Types

In 2018, law enforcement agencies in the nation's cities reported that 92.3 percent of arrests in their jurisdictions were of adults and 7.7 percent of arrests were of juveniles.

Adults accounted for 90.1 percent of arrestees for violent crimes, while juveniles accounted for 9.9 percent of these arrests. Adults made up 88.5 percent of the arrestees for property crimes, and juveniles accounted for the remaining 11.5 percent. Of all arrests in the nation's cities in 2018, 29.9 percent were of individuals under 25 years of age. In metropolitan counties, 26.8 percent of arrests were of individuals under 25 years of age. In nonmetropolitan counties, 23.7 percent of persons arrested were of individuals under 25 years of age. (Tables 46, 47, 53, and 59)

Males accounted for 72.5 percent and females accounted for 27.5 percent of arrestees in the nation's cities in 2018. In metropolitan counties, males comprised 73.7 percent of arrestees, and in nonmetropolitan counties, males represented 73.1 percent of all arrestees. (Tables 48, 54, and 60)

By race, 66.9 percent of arrestees in the nation's cities in 2018 were White, 29.2 percent were Black, and 3.9 percent were of other races (American Indian or Alaska Native and Asian or Pacific Islander). Whites accounted for 71.3 percent of arrestees in metropolitan counties in 2018, Blacks made up 26.3 percent of arrestees, and persons of other races made up 2.4 percent of the total. In nonmetropolitan counties, Whites made up 82.8 percent of arrestees, Blacks accounted for 13.5 percent of arrestees, and other races made up 3.8 percent of the total. (Tables 49, 55, and 61)

Table 29. Estimated Number of Arrests, 2018

(Number.)

Offense	Arrests
Total[1]	10,310,960
Violent crime[2]	521,103
Murder and nonnegligent manslaughter	11,970
Rape[3]	25,205
Robbery	88,128
Aggravated assault	395,800
Property crime[2]	1,167,296
Burglary	178,611
Larceny-theft	887,622
Motor vehicle theft	91,676
Arson	9,387
Other assaults	1,063,535
Forgery and counterfeiting	50,072
Fraud	119,951
Embezzlement	14,765
Stolen property; buying, receiving, possessing	93,161
Vandalism	179,828
Weapons; carrying, possessing, etc.	168,403
Prostitution and commercialized vice	31,147
Sex offenses (except forcible rape and prostitution)	46,937
Drug abuse violations	1,654,282
Gambling	3,323
Offenses against the family and children	87,475
Driving under the influence	1,001,329
Liquor laws	173,152
Drunkenness	328,772
Disorderly conduct	329,152
Vagrancy	23,546
All other offenses	3,231,700
Suspicion	564
Curfew and loitering law violations	22,031

1 Does not include suspicion.   2 Violent crimes are offenses of murder and nonnegligent manslaughter, rape, robbery, and aggravated assault. Property crimes are offenses of burglary, larceny-theft, motor vehicle theft, and arson.   3 The rape figures in this table are an aggregate total of the data submitted using both the revised and legacy Uniform Crime Reporting definitions.

Table 30. Number and Rate of Arrests, by Geographic Region, 2018

(Number, rate per 100,000 inhabitants.)

Offense charged	United States total (12,212 agencies; population 247,752,415)		Northeast (3,227 agencies; population 43,716,119)		Midwest (2,911 agencies; population 46,866,740)		South (4,237 agencies; population 84,035,509)		West (1,837 agencies; population 73,134,047)	
	Total	Rate	Total	Rate	Total	Rate	Total	Rate	Total	Rate
Total[1]	7,810,658	3,152.6	1,141,267	2,610.6	1,420,211	3,030.3	2,925,659	3,481.5	2,323,521	3,177.1
Violent crime[2]	396,265	159.9	51,388	117.5	59,917	127.8	121,247	144.3	163,713	223.9
Murder and nonnegligent manslaughter	9,049	3.7	944	2.2	1,839	3.9	3,766	4.5	2,500	3.4
Rape[3]	19,093	7.7	3,178	7.3	4,455	9.5	5,998	7.1	5,462	7.5
Robbery	67,397	27.2	10,334	23.6	10,278	21.9	21,405	25.5	25,380	34.7
Aggravated assault	300,726	121.4	36,932	84.5	43,345	92.5	90,078	107.2	130,371	178.3
Property crime[2]	894,987	361.2	141,305	323.2	171,689	366.3	335,276	399.0	246,717	337.3
Burglary	135,918	54.9	17,148	39.2	17,501	37.3	46,725	55.6	54,544	74.6
Larceny-theft	682,517	275.5	116,467	266.4	139,080	296.8	266,500	317.1	160,470	219.4
Motor vehicle theft	69,502	28.1	6,736	15.4	13,947	29.8	20,019	23.8	28,800	39.4
Arson	7,050	2.8	954	2.2	1,161	2.5	2,032	2.4	2,903	4.0
Other assaults	809,050	326.6	135,286	309.5	154,241	329.1	307,823	366.3	211,700	289.5
Forgery and counterfeiting	38,128	15.4	6,689	15.3	6,486	13.8	15,957	19.0	8,996	12.3
Fraud	90,886	36.7	19,536	44.7	17,795	38.0	36,019	42.9	17,536	24.0
Embezzlement	11,278	4.6	1,207	2.8	2,158	4.6	5,330	6.3	2,583	3.5
Stolen property; buying, receiving, possessing	70,996	28.7	9,302	21.3	12,282	26.2	22,977	27.3	26,435	36.1
Vandalism	137,108	55.3	28,619	65.5	24,394	52.0	35,264	42.0	48,831	66.8
Weapons; carrying, possessing, etc.	127,588	51.5	13,517	30.9	28,123	60.0	43,719	52.0	42,229	57.7
Prostitution and commercialized vice	23,699	9.6	2,951	6.8	2,319	4.9	7,291	8.7	11,138	15.2
Sex offenses (except forcible rape and prostitution)	35,549	14.3	5,967	13.6	6,048	12.9	9,348	11.1	14,186	19.4
Drug abuse violations	1,251,852	505.3	207,890	475.5	221,389	472.4	474,492	564.6	348,081	475.9
Gambling	2,475	1.0	150	0.3	851	1.8	877	1.0	597	0.8
Offenses against the family and children	64,872	26.2	12,720	29.1	11,956	25.5	28,977	34.5	11,219	15.3
Driving under the influence	746,575	301.3	117,749	269.3	131,207	280.0	244,559	291.0	253,060	346.0
Liquor laws	130,921	52.8	14,848	34.0	42,388	90.4	35,241	41.9	38,444	52.6
Drunkenness	252,727	102.0	28,881	66.1	10,102	21.6	136,644	162.6	77,100	105.4
Disorderly conduct	251,182	101.4	64,884	148.4	75,847	161.8	65,126	77.5	45,325	62.0
Vagrancy	18,121	7.3	1,155	2.6	2,355	5.0	2,606	3.1	12,005	16.4
All other offenses (except traffic)	2,439,500	984.7	272,047	622.3	435,153	928.5	992,362	1,180.9	739,938	1,011.8
Suspicion	427	0.2	7	*	34	0.1	298	0.4	88	0.1
Curfew and loitering law violations	16,899	6.8	5,176	11.8	3,511	7.5	4,524	5.4	3,688	5.0

* = Less than one-tenth of one percent.
1 Does not include suspicion.   2 Violent crimes are offenses of murder and nonnegligent manslaughter, rape, robbery, and aggravated assault. Property crimes are offenses of burglary, larceny-theft, motor vehicle theft, and arson.   3 The rape figures in this table are aggregate totals of the data submitted based on both the legacy and revised Uniform Crime Reporting definitions.

Table 31. Number and Rate of Arrests, by Population Group, 2018

(Number, rate per 100,000 inhabitants.)

Offense charged	Total (12,212 agencies; population 247,752,415)		Total cities (8,967 cities; population 172,802,238))		Group I (69 cities, 250,000 and over; population 47,674,339)		Group II (184 cities, 100,000 to 249,999; population 27,136,228)		Group III (409 cities, 50,000 to 99,999; population 28,755,433)	
	Total	Rate	Total	Rate	Total	Rate	Total	Rate	Total	Rate
Total[2]	7,810,658	3,152.6	5,660,586	3,275.8	1,370,185	2,874.1	852,057	3,139.9	896,269	3,116.9
Violent crime[3]	396,265	159.9	305,648	176.9	116,558	244.5	53,845	198.4	47,223	164.2
Murder and nonnegligent manslaughter	9,049	3.7	6,719	3.9	3,126	6.6	1,238	4.6	775	2.7
Rape[4]	19,093	7.7	13,740	8.0	4,581	9.6	2,126	7.8	2,019	7.0
Robbery	67,397	27.2	56,841	32.9	26,442	55.5	9,672	35.6	8,196	28.5
Aggravated assault	300,726	121.4	228,348	132.1	82,409	172.9	40,809	150.4	36,233	126.0
Property crime[3]	894,987	361.2	723,477	418.7	166,926	350.1	110,555	407.4	120,014	417.4
Burglary	135,918	54.9	101,535	58.8	28,344	59.5	18,030	66.4	17,649	61.4
Larceny-theft	682,517	275.5	564,524	326.7	116,637	244.7	81,848	301.6	94,337	328.1
Motor vehicle theft	69,502	28.1	52,376	30.3	20,576	43.2	9,920	36.6	7,270	25.3
Arson	7,050	2.8	5,042	2.9	1,369	2.9	757	2.8	758	2.6
Other assaults	809,050	326.6	616,990	357.0	183,831	385.6	98,155	361.7	96,386	335.2
Forgery and counterfeiting	38,128	15.4	28,226	16.3	4,926	10.3	4,462	16.4	4,773	16.6
Fraud	90,886	36.7	66,364	38.4	13,418	28.1	8,908	32.8	10,633	37.0
Embezzlement	11,278	4.6	9,067	5.2	2,318	4.9	1,586	5.8	1,572	5.5
Stolen property; buying, receiving, possessing	70,996	28.7	53,149	30.8	14,919	31.3	8,999	33.2	9,904	34.4
Vandalism	137,108	55.3	107,028	61.9	29,407	61.7	16,103	59.3	17,748	61.7
Weapons; carrying, possessing, etc.	127,588	51.5	97,680	56.5	39,725	83.3	14,780	54.5	13,099	45.6
Prostitution and commercialized vice	23,699	9.6	20,966	12.1	14,451	30.3	3,094	11.4	1,469	5.1
Sex offenses (except forcible rape and prostitution)	35,549	14.3	25,439	14.7	7,598	15.9	3,687	13.6	4,205	14.6
Drug abuse violations	1,251,852	505.3	888,318	514.1	199,611	418.7	141,740	522.3	148,178	515.3
Gambling	2,475	1.0	1,909	1.1	1,136	2.4	240	0.9	174	0.6
Offenses against the family and children	64,872	26.2	33,590	19.4	5,972	12.5	5,122	18.9	4,993	17.4
Driving under the influence	746,575	301.3	429,437	248.5	89,820	188.4	55,508	204.6	63,374	220.4
Liquor laws	130,921	52.8	103,908	60.1	16,190	34.0	9,987	36.8	13,804	48.0
Drunkenness	252,727	102.0	217,976	126.1	34,576	72.5	35,437	130.6	38,573	134.1
Disorderly conduct	251,182	101.4	206,822	119.7	32,178	67.5	23,951	88.3	31,454	109.4
Vagrancy	18,121	7.3	16,254	9.4	7,063	14.8	3,493	12.9	2,316	8.1
All other offenses (except traffic)	2,439,500	984.7	1,692,876	979.7	382,918	803.2	250,878	924.5	264,619	920.2
Suspicion	427	0.2	165	0.1	12	*	0	0.0	4	*
Curfew and loitering law violations	16,899	6.8	15,462	8.9	6,644	13.9	1,527	5.6	1,758	6.1

Table 31. Number and Rate of Arrests, by Population Group, 2018—Continued

(Number, rate per 100,000 inhabitants.)

Offense charged	Group IV (748 cities, 25,000 to 49,999; population 25,885,651)		Group V (1,525 cities, 10,000 to 24,999; population 24,273,410)		Group VI (6,032 cities, under 10,000; population 19,077,177)		Metropolitan counties (1,440 agencies; population 55,828,114)		Nonmetropolitan counties (1,805 agencies; population 19,122,063)		Suburban areas[1] (6,757 agencies; population 106,796,972)	
	Total	Rate	Total	Rate	Total	Rate	Total	Rate	Total	Rate	Total	Rate
Total[2]	807,357	3,118.9	834,564	3,438.2	900,154	4,718.5	1,535,929	2,751.2	614,143	3,211.7	3,099,959	2,902.7
Violent crime[3]	31,593	122.0	29,285	120.6	27,144	142.3	71,516	128.1	19,101	99.9	126,922	118.8
Murder and nonnegligent manslaughter	610	2.4	583	2.4	387	2.0	1,755	3.1	575	3.0	2,630	2.5
Rape[4]	1,680	6.5	1,730	7.1	1,604	8.4	3,753	6.7	1,600	8.4	6,816	6.4
Robbery	5,320	20.6	4,228	17.4	2,983	15.6	9,434	16.9	1,122	5.9	18,132	17.0
Aggravated assault	23,983	92.6	22,744	93.7	22,170	116.2	56,574	101.3	15,804	82.6	99,344	93.0
Property crime[3]	116,703	450.8	118,273	487.3	91,006	477.0	136,876	245.2	34,634	181.1	342,516	320.7
Burglary	13,468	52.0	12,750	52.5	11,294	59.2	24,780	44.4	9,603	50.2	48,234	45.2
Larceny-theft	97,456	376.5	100,262	413.1	73,984	387.8	97,589	174.8	20,404	106.7	269,196	252.1
Motor vehicle theft	5,056	19.5	4,665	19.2	4,889	25.6	13,191	23.6	3,935	20.6	22,555	21.1
Arson	723	2.8	596	2.5	839	4.4	1,316	2.4	692	3.6	2,531	2.4
Other assaults	82,761	319.7	80,999	333.7	74,858	392.4	141,785	254.0	50,275	262.9	286,906	268.6
Forgery and counterfeiting	4,541	17.5	4,674	19.3	4,850	25.4	7,550	13.5	2,352	12.3	16,328	15.3
Fraud	10,248	39.6	10,321	42.5	12,836	67.3	18,272	32.7	6,250	32.7	38,972	36.5
Embezzlement	1,499	5.8	1,084	4.5	1,008	5.3	1,766	3.2	445	2.3	4,072	3.8
Stolen property; buying, receiving, possessing	7,252	28.0	6,688	27.6	5,387	28.2	14,190	25.4	3,657	19.1	27,778	26.0
Vandalism	15,019	58.0	14,783	60.9	13,968	73.2	23,085	41.4	6,995	36.6	49,295	46.2
Weapons; carrying, possessing, etc.	10,050	38.8	9,589	39.5	10,437	54.7	23,014	41.2	6,894	36.1	42,873	40.1
Prostitution and commercialized vice	1,057	4.1	589	2.4	306	1.6	2,528	4.5	205	1.1	3,850	3.6
Sex offenses (except forcible rape and prostitution)	3,422	13.2	3,138	12.9	3,389	17.8	7,608	13.6	2,502	13.1	14,380	13.5
Drug abuse violations	127,034	490.8	124,261	511.9	147,494	773.1	265,238	475.1	98,296	514.0	526,907	493.4
Gambling	37	0.1	217	0.9	105	0.6	425	0.8	141	0.7	674	0.6
Offenses against the family and children	5,138	19.8	5,556	22.9	6,809	35.7	23,312	41.8	7,970	41.7	32,385	30.3
Driving under the influence	65,586	253.4	75,039	309.1	80,110	419.9	201,462	360.9	115,676	604.9	349,935	327.7
Liquor laws	14,068	54.3	18,310	75.4	31,549	165.4	17,026	30.5	9,987	52.2	53,293	49.9
Drunkenness	31,695	122.4	32,915	135.6	44,780	234.7	24,559	44.0	10,192	53.3	80,130	75.0
Disorderly conduct	33,374	128.9	37,097	152.8	48,768	255.6	30,511	54.7	13,849	72.4	100,631	94.2
Vagrancy	1,472	5.7	947	3.9	963	5.0	1,557	2.8	310	1.6	3,619	3.4
All other offenses (except traffic)	242,971	938.6	258,757	1,066.0	292,733	1,534.5	522,443	935.8	224,181	1,172.4	993,863	930.6
Suspicion	16	0.1	22	0.1	111	0.6	240	0.4	22	0.1	292	0.3
Curfew and loitering law violations	1,837	7.1	2,042	8.4	1,654	8.7	1,206	2.2	231	1.2	4,630	4.3

* = Less than one-tenth of one percent.
1 Suburban areas include law enforcement agencies in cities with less than 50,000 inhabitants and county law enforcement agencies that are within a Metropolitan Statistical Area. Suburban areas exclude all metropolitan agencies associated with a principal city. The agencies associated with suburban areas also appear in other groups within this table.   2 Does not include suspicion.   3 Violent crimes are offenses of murder and nonnegligent manslaughter, forcible rape, robbery, and aggravated assault. Property crimes are offenses of burglary, larceny-theft, motor vehicle theft, and arson.   4 The rape figures in this table are aggregate totals of the data submitted based on both the legacy and revised Uniform Crime Reporting definitions.

Table 32. Ten-Year Arrest Trends, 2009 and 2018

(Number, percent change; 10,141 agencies; 2018 estimated population 209,206,684; 2009 estimated population 196,617,314.)

Offense charged	Number of persons arrested								
	Total, all ages			Under 18 years of age			18 years of age and over		
	2009	2018	Percent change	2009	2018	Percent change	2009	2018	Percent change
Total[1]	8,420,343	6,576,654	-21.9	1,135,569	471,641	-58.5	7,284,774	6,105,013	-16.2
	7,090	6,764	-4.6	650	526	-19.1	6,440	6,238	-3.1
Violent crime[2]									
Murder and nonnegligent manslaughter	357,044	317,933	-11.0	51,187	30,531	-40.4	305,857	287,402	-6.0
Rape[3]	13,283	15,482	NA	2,010	2,600		11,273	12,882	NA
Robbery	72,891	50,348	-30.9	17,667	9,659	-45.3	55,224	40,689	-26.3
Aggravated assault	263,780	245,339	-7.0	30,860	17,746	-42.5	232,920	227,593	-2.3
Property crime[2]	1,100,772	757,587	-31.2	271,563	86,393	-68.2	829,209	671,194	-19.1
Burglary	190,903	112,742	-40.9	47,546	14,121	-70.3	143,357	98,621	-31.2
Larceny-theft	854,270	584,573	-31.6	208,987	62,521	-70.1	645,283	522,052	-19.1
Motor vehicle theft	47,668	54,231	+13.8	11,403	8,547	-25.0	36,265	45,684	+26.0
Arson	7,931	6,041	-23.8	3,627	1,204	-66.8	4,304	4,837	+12.4
Other assaults	813,030	667,143	-17.9	137,442	80,588	-41.4	675,588	586,555	-13.2
Forgery and counterfeiting	52,864	33,532	-36.6	1,404	730	-48.0	51,460	32,802	-36.3
Fraud	136,146	77,251	-43.3	4,238	2,457	-42.0	131,908	74,794	-43.3
Embezzlement	12,041	9,660	-19.8	406	391	-3.7	11,635	9,269	-20.3
Stolen property; buying, receiving, possessing	64,345	61,063	-5.1	11,572	5,971	-48.4	52,773	55,092	+4.4
Vandalism	170,327	115,493	-32.2	58,118	20,602	-64.6	112,209	94,891	-15.4
Weapons; carrying, possessing, etc.	99,142	97,287	-1.9	21,173	10,298	-51.4	77,969	86,989	+11.6
Prostitution and commercialized vice	29,952	14,236	-52.5	681	120	-82.4	29,271	14,116	-51.8
Sex offenses (except forcible rape and prostitution)	46,517	29,447	-36.7	8,669	4,992	-42.4	37,848	24,455	-35.4
Drug abuse violations	993,930	1,069,744	+7.6	105,523	59,598	-43.5	888,407	1,010,146	+13.7
Gambling	3,054	1,486	-51.3	312	79	-74.7	2,742	1,407	-48.7
Offenses against the family and children	71,110	55,726	-21.6	3,176	2,168	-31.7	67,934	53,558	-21.2
Driving under the influence	929,190	628,654	-32.3	9,071	3,468	-61.8	920,119	625,186	-32.1
Liquor laws	368,918	112,654	-69.5	76,006	18,263	-76.0	292,912	94,391	-67.8
Drunkenness	386,727	218,226	-43.6	9,578	2,263	-76.4	377,149	215,963	-42.7
Disorderly conduct	405,286	213,562	-47.3	106,528	38,148	-64.2	298,758	175,414	-41.3
Vagrancy	13,737	13,489	-1.8	901	468	-48.1	12,836	13,021	+1.4
All other offenses (except traffic)	2,315,382	2,071,036	-10.6	207,192	92,668	-55.3	2,108,190	1,978,368	-6.2
Suspicion	665	330	-50.4	86	29	-66.3	579	301	-48.0
Curfew and loitering law violations	50,829	11,445	-77.5	50,829	11,445	-77.5	NA	NA	NA

NA = Not available.

1 Does not include suspicion. 2 Violent crimes are offenses of murder and nonnegligent manslaughter, rape, robbery, and aggravated assault. Property crimes are offenses of burglary, larceny-theft, motor vehicle theft, and arson. 3 The 2009 rape figures are based on the legacy definition, and the 2018 rape figures are aggregate totals based on both the legacy and revised Uniform Crime Reporting definitions. For this reason, a percent change is not provided.

Table 33. Ten-Year Arrest Trends, by Age and Sex, 2009 and 2018

(Number, percent change; 10,141 agencies; 2018 estimated population 209,206,684; 2009 estimated population 196,617,314.)

Offense charged	Male						Female					
	Total			Under 18			Total			Under 18		
	2009	2018	Percent change	2009	2018	Percent change	2009	2018	Percent change	2009	2018	Percent change
Total[1]	6,284,503	4,763,534	-24.2	799,297	329,320	-58.8	2,135,840	1,813,120	-15.1	336,272	142,321	-57.7
Violent crime[2]	289,438	250,790	-13.4	41,718	24,341	-41.7	67,606	67,143	-0.7	9,469	6,190	-34.6
Murder and nonnegligent manslaughter	6,300	5,900	-6.3	597	469	-21.4	790	864	+9.4	53	57	+7.5
Rape[3]	13,091	14,969	NA	1,966	2,494		192	513		44	106	NA
Robbery	64,091	42,598	-33.5	15,866	8,561	-46.0	8,800	7,750	-11.9	1,801	1,098	-39.0
Aggravated assault	205,956	187,323	-9.0	23,289	12,817	-45.0	57,824	58,016	+0.3	7,571	4,929	-34.9
Property crime[2]	681,608	471,725	-30.8	167,419	58,051	-65.3	419,164	285,862	-31.8	104,144	28,342	-72.8
Burglary	160,887	90,292	-43.9	41,783	12,240	-70.7	30,016	22,450	-25.2	5,763	1,881	-67.4
Larceny-theft	475,041	334,964	-29.5	113,101	37,848	-66.5	379,229	249,609	-34.2	95,886	24,673	-74.3
Motor vehicle theft	39,067	41,766	+6.9	9,387	6,954	-25.9	8,601	12,465	+44.9	2,016	1,593	-21.0
Arson	6,613	4,703	-28.9	3,148	1,009	-67.9	1,318	1,338	+1.5	479	195	-59.3
Other assaults	599,675	473,643	-21.0	90,384	50,775	-43.8	213,355	193,500	-9.3	47,058	29,813	-36.6
Forgery and counterfeiting	32,995	22,118	-33.0	999	584	-41.5	19,869	11,414	-42.6	405	146	-64.0
Fraud	77,280	48,661	-37.0	2,750	1,645	-40.2	58,866	28,590	-51.4	1,488	812	-45.4
Embezzlement	5,908	4,767	-19.3	233	237	+1.7	6,133	4,893	-20.2	173	154	-11.0
Stolen property; buying, receiving, possessing	51,747	47,553	-8.1	9,642	4,995	-48.2	12,598	13,510	+7.2	1,930	976	-49.4
Vandalism	140,025	89,064	-36.4	50,186	16,752	-66.6	30,302	26,429	-12.8	7,932	3,850	-51.5
Weapons; carrying, possessing, etc.	91,038	87,684	-3.7	19,028	9,085	-52.3	8,104	9,603	+18.5	2,145	1,213	-43.4
Prostitution and commercialized vice	9,647	6,076	-37.0	166	69	-58.4	20,305	8,160	-59.8	515	51	-90.1
Sex offenses (except forcible rape and prostitution)	43,022	27,395	-36.3	7,730	4,467	-42.2	3,495	2,052	-41.3	939	525	-44.1
Drug abuse violations	801,150	800,512	-0.1	87,932	44,145	-49.8	192,780	269,232	+39.7	17,591	15,453	-12.2
Gambling	2,524	1,137	-55.0	303	70	-76.9	530	349	-34.2	9	9	+0.0
Offenses against the family and children	52,838	39,025	-26.1	2,027	1,327	-34.5	18,272	16,701	-8.6	1,149	841	-26.8
Driving under the influence	717,056	467,501	-34.8	6,807	2,589	-62.0	212,134	161,153	-24.0	2,264	879	-61.2
Liquor laws	260,650	77,771	-70.2	46,414	10,487	-77.4	108,268	34,883	-67.8	29,592	7,776	-73.7
Drunkenness	320,752	171,787	-46.4	7,128	1,555	-78.2	65,975	46,439	-29.6	2,450	708	-71.1
Disorderly conduct	294,293	150,010	-49.0	71,145	24,498	-65.6	110,993	63,552	-42.7	35,383	13,650	-61.4
Vagrancy	10,759	10,077	-6.3	699	358	-48.8	2,978	3,412	+14.6	202	110	-45.5
All other offenses (except traffic)	1,768,112	1,508,647	-14.7	152,601	65,699	-56.9	547,270	562,389	+2.8	54,591	26,969	-50.6
Suspicion	520	250	-51.9	71	20	-71.8	145	80	-44.8	15	9	-40.0
Curfew and loitering law violations	33,986	7,591	-77.7	33,986	7,591	-77.7	16,843	3,854	-77.1	16,843	3,854	-77.1

NA = Not available.
1 Does not include suspicion.   2 Violent crimes are offenses of murder and nonnegligent manslaughter, rape, robbery, and aggravated assault.   Property crimes are offenses of burglary, larceny-theft, motor vehicle theft, and arson.   3 The 2009 rape figures are based on the legacy definition, and the 2018 rape figures are aggregate totals based on both the legacy and revised Uniform Crime Reporting definitions. For this reason, a percent change is not provided.

Table 34. Five-Year Arrest Trends, by Age, 2014 and 2018

(Number, percent change; 10,559 agencies; 2018 estimated population 221,186,153; 2014 estimated population 215,903,409.)

Offense charged	Number of persons arrested								
	Total, all ages			Under 18 years of age			18 years of age and over		
	2014	2018	Percent change	2014	2018	Percent change	2014	2018	Percent change
Total[1]	7,478,854	6,980,786	-6.7	676,138	495,880	-26.7	6,802,716	6,484,906	-4.7
Violent crime[2]	329,113	340,372	+3.4	34,321	32,370	-5.7	294,792	308,002	+4.5
Murder and nonnegligent manslaughter	6,612	7,439	+12.5	451	596	+32.2	6,161	6,843	+11.1
Rape[3]	14,190	16,678	+17.5	2,255	2,795	+23.9	11,935	13,883	+16.3
Robbery	59,211	55,067	-7.0	11,488	10,540	-8.3	47,723	44,527	-6.7
Aggravated assault	249,100	261,188	+4.9	20,127	18,439	-8.4	228,973	242,749	+6.0
Property crime[2]	1,064,107	794,602	-25.3	157,889	89,924	-43.0	906,218	704,678	-22.2
Burglary	160,697	119,570	-25.6	26,782	14,924	-44.3	133,915	104,646	-21.9
Larceny-theft	852,299	611,087	-28.3	121,325	64,626	-46.7	730,974	546,461	-25.2
Motor vehicle theft	44,730	57,747	+29.1	7,615	9,158	+20.3	37,115	48,589	+30.9
Arson	6,381	6,198	-2.9	2,167	1,216	-43.9	4,214	4,982	+18.2
Other assaults	739,456	721,986	-2.4	95,369	85,511	-10.3	644,087	636,475	-1.2
Forgery and counterfeiting	37,938	34,999	-7.7	782	735	-6.0	37,156	34,264	-7.8
Fraud	93,507	81,288	-13.1	2,976	2,543	-14.5	90,531	78,745	-13.0
Embezzlement	11,009	10,566	-4.0	322	424	+31.7	10,687	10,142	-5.1
Stolen property; buying, receiving, possessing	61,466	64,640	+5.2	7,133	6,407	-10.2	54,333	58,233	+7.2
Vandalism	134,330	124,199	-7.5	30,743	21,611	-29.7	103,587	102,588	-1.0
Weapons; carrying, possessing, etc.	90,736	105,758	+16.6	13,252	10,855	-18.1	77,484	94,903	+22.5
Prostitution and commercialized vice	28,008	18,325	-34.6	461	173	-62.5	27,547	18,152	-34.1
Sex offenses (except forcible rape and prostitution)	36,640	31,632	-13.7	6,508	5,294	-18.7	30,132	26,338	-12.6
Drug abuse violations	1,021,125	1,131,434	+10.8	75,743	62,100	-18.0	945,382	1,069,334	+13.1
Gambling	2,018	1,524	-24.5	144	71	-50.7	1,874	1,453	-22.5
Offenses against the family and children	65,706	60,059	-8.6	2,171	2,313	+6.5	63,535	57,746	-9.1
Driving under the influence	757,178	672,113	-11.2	4,729	3,678	-22.2	752,449	668,435	-11.2
Liquor laws	217,713	120,149	-44.8	36,821	18,741	-49.1	180,892	101,408	-43.9
Drunkenness	298,720	228,891	-23.4	4,616	2,330	-49.5	294,104	226,561	-23.0
Disorderly conduct	290,175	226,166	-22.1	53,503	40,528	-24.3	236,672	185,638	-21.6
Vagrancy	19,717	17,540	-11.0	684	511	-25.3	19,033	17,029	-10.5
All other offenses (except traffic)	2,156,965	2,182,296	+1.2	124,744	97,514	-21.8	2,032,221	2,084,782	+2.6
Suspicion	840	284	-66.2	274	29	-89.4	566	255	-54.9
Curfew and loitering law violations	23,227	12,247	-47.3	23,227	12,247	-47.3	NA	NA	NA

NA = Not available.

1 Does not include suspicion.   2 Violent crimes are offenses of murder and nonnegligent manslaughter, rape, robbery, and aggravated assault.   Property crimes are offenses of burglary, larceny-theft, motor vehicle theft, and arson.   3 The rape figures in this table are aggregate totals of the data submitted based on both the legacy and revised Uniform Crime Reporting definitions.

Table 35. Five-Year Arrest Trends, by Age and Sex, 2014 and 2018

(Number, percent change; 10,559 agencies; 2018 estimated population 221,186,153; 2014 estimated population 215,903,409.)

Offense charged	Male						Female					
	Total			Under 18			Total			Under 18		
	2014	2018	Percent change	2014	2018	Percent change	2014	2018	Percent change	2014	2018	Percent change
Total[1]	5,461,833	5,062,465	-7.3	476,757	346,290	-27.4	2,017,021	1,918,321	-4.9	199,381	149,590	-25.0
Violent crime[2]	262,113	268,955	+2.6	27,985	25,868	-7.6	67,000	71,417	+6.6	6,336	6,502	+2.6
Murder and nonnegligent manslaughter	5,806	6,503	+12.0	414	528	+27.5	806	936	+16.1	37	68	+83.8
Rape[3]	13,778	16,134	+17.1	2,156	2,676	+24.1	412	544	+32.0	99	119	+20.2
Robbery	50,821	46,519	-8.5	10,309	9,318	-9.6	8,390	8,548	+1.9	1,179	1,222	+3.6
Aggravated assault	191,708	199,799	+4.2	15,106	13,346	-11.7	57,392	61,389	+7.0	5,021	5,093	+1.4
Property crime[2]	652,048	496,842	-23.8	103,433	60,383	-41.6	412,059	297,760	-27.7	54,456	29,541	-45.8
Burglary	131,302	95,776	-27.1	23,487	12,964	-44.8	29,395	23,794	-19.1	3,295	1,960	-40.5
Larceny-theft	480,037	351,830	-26.7	71,813	38,980	-45.7	372,262	259,257	-30.4	49,512	25,646	-48.2
Motor vehicle theft	35,532	44,407	+25.0	6,247	7,421	+18.8	9,198	13,340	+45.0	1,368	1,737	+27.0
Arson	5,177	4,829	-6.7	1,886	1,018	-46.0	1,204	1,369	+13.7	281	198	-29.5
Other assaults	531,106	512,245	-3.6	60,755	53,982	-11.1	208,350	209,741	+0.7	34,614	31,529	-8.9
Forgery and counterfeiting	24,100	23,110	-4.1	571	592	+3.7	13,838	11,889	-14.1	211	143	-32.2
Fraud	57,018	51,418	-9.8	1,972	1,681	-14.8	36,489	29,870	-18.1	1,004	862	-14.1
Embezzlement	5,585	5,306	-5.0	192	252	+31.3	5,424	5,260	-3.0	130	172	+32.3
Stolen property; buying, receiving, possessing	48,191	50,300	+4.4	5,959	5,348	-10.3	13,275	14,340	+8.0	1,174	1,059	-9.8
Vandalism	106,761	95,614	-10.4	25,867	17,519	-32.3	27,569	28,585	+3.7	4,876	4,092	-16.1
Weapons; carrying, possessing, etc.	82,770	95,444	+15.3	11,840	9,613	-18.8	7,966	10,314	+29.5	1,412	1,242	-12.0
Prostitution and commercialized vice	9,826	6,777	-31.0	92	68	-26.1	18,182	11,548	-36.5	369	105	-71.5
Sex offenses (except forcible rape and prostitution)	33,919	29,431	-13.2	5,803	4,750	-18.1	2,721	2,201	-19.1	705	544	-22.8
Drug abuse violations	792,985	847,591	+6.9	60,184	46,079	-23.4	228,140	283,843	+24.4	15,559	16,021	+3.0
Gambling	1,633	1,155	-29.3	125	63	-49.6	385	369	-4.2	19	8	-57.9
Offenses against the family and children	47,686	42,044	-11.8	1,323	1,404	+6.1	18,020	18,015	+0.0	848	909	+7.2
Driving under the influence	568,416	499,870	-12.1	3,507	2,758	-21.4	188,762	172,243	-8.8	1,222	920	-24.7
Liquor laws	155,590	83,256	-46.5	22,252	10,792	-51.5	62,123	36,893	-40.6	14,569	7,949	-45.4
Drunkenness	242,012	180,554	-25.4	3,284	1,603	-51.2	56,708	48,337	-14.8	1,332	727	-45.4
Disorderly conduct	208,491	158,780	-23.8	35,047	25,859	-26.2	81,684	67,386	-17.5	18,456	14,669	-20.5
Vagrancy	15,312	13,317	-13.0	541	387	-28.5	4,405	4,223	-4.1	143	124	-13.3
All other offenses (except traffic)	1,600,582	1,592,353	-0.5	90,336	69,186	-23.4	556,383	589,943	+6.0	34,408	28,328	-17.7
Suspicion	616	214	-65.3	203	20	-90.1	224	70	-68.8	71	9	-87.3
Curfew and loitering law violations	15,689	8,103	-48.4	15,689	8,103	-48.4	7,538	4,144	-45.0	7,538	4,144	-45.0

* = Less than one-tenth of one percent.
1 Does not include suspicion.   2 Violent crimes are offenses of murder and nonnegligent manslaughter, rape, robbery, and aggravated assault.   Property crimes are offenses of burglary, larceny-theft, motor vehicle theft, and arson.   3 The 2014 rape figures are based on the legacy definition, and the 2018 rape figures are aggregate totals based on both the legacy and revised Uniform Crime Reporting definitions.

Table 36. Current Year Over Previous Year Arrest Trends, 2017–2018

(Number, percent change; 11,266 agencies; 2018 estimated population 229,276,004; 2017 estimated population 228,289,680.)

Offense charged	Number of persons arrested											
	Total, all ages			Under 15 years of age			Under 18 years of age			18 years of age and over		
	2017	2018	Percent change	2017	2018	Percent change	2017	2018	Percent change	2017	2018	Percent change
Total[1]	7,427,239	7,220,062	-2.8	163,830	152,066	-7.2	571,974	508,863	-11.0	6,855,265	6,711,199	-2.1
Violent crime[2]	368,849	369,689	+0.2	10,479	10,545	+0.6	37,076	35,192	-5.1	331,773	334,497	+0.8
Murder and nonnegligent manslaughter	8,243	7,938	-3.7	59	62	+5.1	574	607	+5.7	7,669	7,331	-4.4
Rape[3]	17,504	17,685	+1.0	1,257	1,218	-3.1	3,100	2,952	-4.8	14,404	14,733	+2.3
Robbery	67,408	61,807	-8.3	2,653	2,413	-9.0	13,650	12,032	-11.9	53,758	49,775	-7.4
Aggravated assault	275,694	282,259	+2.4	6,510	6,852	+5.3	19,752	19,601	-0.8	255,942	262,658	+2.6
Property crime[2]	883,327	820,938	-7.1	33,851	26,335	-22.2	117,148	91,847	-21.6	766,179	729,091	-4.8
Burglary	141,240	126,738	-10.3	6,743	4,744	-29.6	21,444	15,731	-26.6	119,796	111,007	-7.3
Larceny-theft	673,239	625,591	-7.1	23,750	18,406	-22.5	83,888	65,027	-22.5	589,351	560,564	-4.9
Motor vehicle theft	62,303	62,107	-0.3	2,434	2,448	+0.6	10,188	9,823	-3.6	52,115	52,284	+0.3
Arson	6,545	6,502	-0.7	924	737	-20.2	1,628	1,266	-22.2	4,917	5,236	+6.5
Other assaults	750,294	741,767	-1.1	34,858	35,776	+2.6	87,979	86,788	-1.4	662,315	654,979	-1.1
Forgery and counterfeiting	39,060	35,454	-9.2	122	117	-4.1	856	697	-18.6	38,204	34,757	-9.0
Fraud	86,445	83,016	-4.0	681	787	+15.6	3,434	3,328	-3.1	83,011	79,688	-4.0
Embezzlement	11,624	10,641	-8.5	36	18	-50.0	466	418	-10.3	11,158	10,223	-8.4
Stolen property; buying, receiving, possessing	68,878	66,168	-3.9	1,549	1,415	-8.7	7,367	6,601	-10.4	61,511	59,567	-3.2
Vandalism	133,899	125,764	-6.1	10,633	8,167	-23.2	26,361	21,395	-18.8	107,538	104,369	-2.9
Weapons; carrying, possessing, etc.	113,645	113,457	-0.2	3,871	3,405	-12.0	12,618	11,572	-8.3	101,027	101,885	+0.8
Prostitution and commercialized vice	26,609	22,642	-14.9	30	40	+33.3	231	188	-18.6	26,378	22,454	-14.9
Sex offenses (except forcible rape and prostitution)	33,899	32,892	-3.0	2,872	2,510	-12.6	5,819	5,289	-9.1	28,080	27,603	-1.7
Drug abuse violations	1,155,123	1,158,206	+0.3	10,143	10,690	+5.4	67,060	62,645	-6.6	1,088,063	1,095,561	+0.7
Gambling	1,825	1,568	-14.1	23	13	-43.5	126	78	-38.1	1,699	1,490	-12.3
Offenses against the family and children	61,942	58,839	-5.0	915	803	-12.2	2,638	2,204	-16.5	59,304	56,635	-4.5
Driving under the influence	706,281	699,996	-0.9	69	85	+23.2	4,176	3,740	-10.4	702,105	696,256	-0.8
Liquor laws	145,918	120,100	-17.7	2,815	2,560	-9.1	24,014	18,601	-22.5	121,904	101,499	-16.7
Drunkenness	260,437	239,165	-8.2	367	366	-0.3	2,944	2,426	-17.6	257,493	236,739	-8.1
Disorderly conduct	248,063	231,647	-6.6	17,413	16,648	-4.4	44,159	40,995	-7.2	203,904	190,652	-6.5
Vagrancy	17,005	17,634	+3.7	130	133	+2.3	521	496	-4.8	16,484	17,138	+4.0
All other offenses (except traffic)	2,291,672	2,254,222	-1.6	26,302	26,657	+1.3	104,537	98,106	-6.2	2,187,135	2,156,116	-1.4
Suspicion	380	413	+8.7	14	13	-7.1	55	34	-38.2	325	379	+16.6
Curfew and loitering law violations	22,444	16,257	-27.6	6,671	4,996	-25.1	22,444	16,257	-27.6	NA	NA	NA

NA = Not available.

1 Does not include suspicion.   2 Violent crimes are offenses of murder and nonnegligent manslaughter, rape, robbery, and aggravated assault. Property crimes are offenses of burglary, larceny-theft, motor vehicle theft, and arson.   3 The rape figures in this table are aggregate totals of the data submitted based on both the legacy and revised Uniform Crime Reporting definitions.

Table 37. Current Year Over Previous Year Arrest Trends, by Age and Sex, 2017–2018

(Number, percent change; 11,266 agencies; 2018 estimated population 229,276,004; 2017 estimated population 228,289,680.)

| | Male | | | | | | Female | | | | | |
| | Total | | | Under 18 | | | Total | | | Under 18 | | |
Offense charged	2017	2018	Percent change	2017	2018	Percent change	2017	2018	Percent change	2017	2018	Percent change
Total[1]	5,421,829	5,249,271	-3.2	405,518	357,035	-12.0	2,005,410	1,970,791	-1.7	166,456	151,828	-8.8
Violent crime[2]	292,875	291,823	-0.4	30,231	28,178	-6.8	75,974	77,866	+2.5	6,845	7,014	+2.5
Murder and nonnegligent manslaughter	7,193	6,968	-3.1	529	538	+1.7	1,050	970	-7.6	45	69	+53.3
Rape[3]	16,959	17,114	+0.9	2,977	2,822	-5.2	545	571	+4.8	123	130	+5.7
Robbery	57,464	52,245	-9.1	12,183	10,626	-12.8	9,944	9,562	-3.8	1,467	1,406	-4.2
Aggravated assault	211,259	215,496	+2.0	14,542	14,192	-2.4	64,435	66,763	+3.6	5,210	5,409	+3.8
Property crime[2]	565,555	516,053	-8.8	81,253	62,125	-23.5	317,772	304,885	-4.1	35,895	29,722	-17.2
Burglary	114,290	101,504	-11.2	18,917	13,682	-27.7	26,950	25,234	-6.4	2,527	2,049	-18.9
Larceny-theft	397,699	361,649	-9.1	52,646	39,398	-25.2	275,540	263,942	-4.2	31,242	25,629	-18.0
Motor vehicle theft	48,330	47,871	-0.9	8,299	7,997	-3.6	13,973	14,236	+1.9	1,889	1,826	-3.3
Arson	5,236	5,029	-4.0	1,391	1,048	-24.7	1,309	1,473	+12.5	237	218	-8.0
Other assaults	534,487	527,380	-1.3	55,155	54,654	-0.9	215,807	214,387	-0.7	32,824	32,134	-2.1
Forgery and counterfeiting	25,744	23,489	-8.8	671	565	-15.8	13,316	11,965	-10.1	185	132	-28.6
Fraud	54,275	52,885	-2.6	2,303	2,281	-1.0	32,170	30,131	-6.3	1,131	1,047	-7.4
Embezzlement	5,938	5,353	-9.9	275	248	-9.8	5,686	5,288	-7.0	191	170	-11.0
Stolen property; buying, receiving, possessing	53,640	51,601	-3.8	6,194	5,522	-10.8	15,238	14,567	-4.4	1,173	1,079	-8.0
Vandalism	104,074	96,897	-6.9	21,670	17,333	-20.0	29,825	28,867	-3.2	4,691	4,062	-13.4
Weapons; carrying, possessing, etc.	103,121	102,591	-0.5	11,259	10,257	-8.9	10,524	10,866	+3.2	1,359	1,315	-3.2
Prostitution and commercialized vice	10,284	8,014	-22.1	75	74	-1.3	16,325	14,628	-10.4	156	114	-26.9
Sex offenses (except forcible rape and prostitution)	31,451	30,644	-2.6	5,135	4,745	-7.6	2,448	2,248	-8.2	684	544	-20.5
Drug abuse violations	875,150	870,743	-0.5	50,979	46,671	-8.5	279,973	287,463	+2.7	16,081	15,974	-0.7
Gambling	1,395	1,186	-15.0	106	71	-33.0	430	382	-11.2	20	7	-65.0
Offenses against the family and children	43,499	41,262	-5.1	1,652	1,349	-18.3	18,443	17,577	-4.7	986	855	-13.3
Driving under the influence	527,119	521,547	-1.1	3,167	2,804	-11.5	179,162	178,449	-0.4	1,009	936	-7.2
Liquor laws	101,155	83,209	-17.7	14,135	10,753	-23.9	44,763	36,891	-17.6	9,879	7,848	-20.6
Drunkenness	206,849	189,022	-8.6	2,072	1,667	-19.5	53,588	50,143	-6.4	872	759	-13.0
Disorderly conduct	174,381	162,615	-6.7	28,188	26,202	-7.0	73,682	69,032	-6.3	15,971	14,793	-7.4
Vagrancy	12,853	13,339	+3.8	408	380	-6.9	4,152	4,295	+3.4	113	116	+2.7
All other offenses (except traffic)	1,682,239	1,648,248	-2.0	74,845	69,786	-6.8	609,433	605,974	-0.6	29,692	28,320	-4.6
Suspicion	297	311	+4.7	41	23	-43.9	83	102	+22.9	14	11	-21.4
Curfew and loitering law violations	15,745	11,370	-27.8	15,745	11,370	-27.8	6,699	4,887	-27.0	6,699	4,887	-27.0

1 Does not include suspicion.   2 Violent crimes are offenses of murder and nonnegligent manslaughter, rape, robbery, and aggravated assault. Property crimes are offenses of burglary, larceny-theft, motor vehicle theft, and arson.   3 The rape figures in this table are aggregate totals of the data submitted based on both the legacy and revised Uniform Crime Reporting definitions.

Table 38. Arrests, Distribution by Age, 2018

(Number, percent; 12,212 agencies; 2018 estimated population 247,752,415.)

Offense charged	Total, all ages	Ages under 15	Ages under 18	Ages 18 and over	Under 10	10–12	13–14	15	16	17	18	19	20
Total	7,811,085	165,342	553,620	7,257,465	3,501	38,304	123,537	104,148	129,078	155,052	215,132	231,089	233,876
Total percent distribution[1]	100.0	2.1	7.1	92.9	*	0.5	1.6	1.3	1.7	2.0	2.8	3.0	3.0
Violent crime[2]	396,265	11,421	38,283	357,982	178	2,755	8,488	7,214	9,223	10,425	12,532	12,129	12,177
Violent crime percent distribution[1]	100.0	2.9	9.7	90.3	*	0.7	2.1	1.8	2.3	2.6	3.2	3.1	3.1
Murder and nonnegligent manslaughter	9,049	67	694	8,355	0	4	63	100	197	330	474	479	449
Rape[3]	19,093	1,324	3,144	15,949	22	412	890	552	613	655	764	694	653
Robbery	67,397	2,615	13,220	54,177	11	283	2,321	2,781	3,704	4,120	4,641	3,764	3,113
Aggravated assault	300,726	7,415	21,225	279,501	145	2,056	5,214	3,781	4,709	5,320	6,653	7,192	7,962
Property crime[2]	894,987	28,763	100,743	794,244	520	6,037	22,206	20,189	24,188	27,603	32,644	29,917	26,989
Property crime percent distribution[1]	100.0	3.2	11.3	88.7	0.1	0.7	2.5	2.3	2.7	3.1	3.6	3.3	3.0
Burglary	135,918	5,136	16,933	118,985	160	1,096	3,880	3,498	3,941	4,358	5,231	4,581	4,237
Larceny-theft	682,517	20,058	71,222	611,295	289	4,338	15,431	13,767	17,134	20,263	24,642	22,883	20,523
Motor vehicle theft	69,502	2,766	11,202	58,300	15	322	2,429	2,704	2,922	2,810	2,582	2,320	2,068
Arson	7,050	803	1,386	5,664	56	281	466	220	191	172	189	133	161
Other assaults	809,050	39,334	95,116	713,934	900	11,032	27,402	18,250	19,177	18,355	18,517	18,226	19,608
Forgery and counterfeiting	38,128	157	792	37,336	5	33	119	96	186	353	991	1,471	1,694
Fraud	90,886	840	3,567	87,319	9	146	685	685	834	1,208	1,843	2,231	2,632
Embezzlement	11,278	20	443	10,835	1	2	17	32	127	264	524	561	545
Stolen property; buying, receiving, possessing	70,996	1,524	7,100	63,896	14	172	1,338	1,474	1,939	2,163	2,734	2,703	2,433
Vandalism	137,108	8,939	23,329	113,779	362	2,572	6,005	4,490	4,972	4,928	4,971	4,472	4,179
Weapons; carrying, possessing, etc.	127,588	3,744	13,011	114,577	155	1,030	2,559	2,366	2,973	3,928	4,827	5,059	4,725
Prostitution and commercialized vice	23,699	41	199	23,500	1	7	33	27	43	88	707	763	883
Sex offenses (except forcible rape and prostitution)	35,549	2,698	5,719	29,830	88	708	1,902	1,052	966	1,003	1,028	947	820
Drug abuse violations	1,251,852	11,758	68,612	1,183,240	84	1,818	9,856	10,754	17,201	28,899	51,840	53,810	50,975
Gambling	2,475	23	134	2,341	1	3	19	19	33	59	73	88	78
Offenses against the family and children	64,872	893	2,477	62,395	35	215	643	524	529	531	778	818	930
Driving under the influence	746,575	102	4,064	742,511	8	12	82	173	931	2,858	8,738	12,302	15,201
Liquor laws	130,921	2,767	19,922	110,999	18	280	2,469	3,186	5,341	8,628	17,504	19,138	15,935
Drunkenness	252,727	378	2,512	250,215	7	32	339	390	597	1,147	3,405	4,315	4,679
Disorderly conduct	251,182	17,784	44,074	207,108	340	4,692	12,752	8,803	9,286	8,201	7,186	6,636	6,554
Vagrancy	18,121	145	527	17,594	3	18	124	126	137	119	300	253	281
All other offenses (except traffic)	2,439,500	28,812	106,060	2,333,440	669	5,697	22,446	20,521	25,871	30,856	43,979	55,238	62,544
Suspicion	427	14	37	390	0	3	11	3	7	13	11	12	14
Curfew and loitering law violations	16,899	5,185	16,899	NA	103	1,040	4,042	3,774	4,517	3,423	NA	NA	NA

Table 38. Arrests, Distribution by Age, 2018—Continued

(Number, percent; 12,212 agencies; 2018 estimated population 247,752,415.)

Offense charged	21	22	23	24	25–29	30–34	35–39	40–44	45–49	50–54	55–59	60–64	65 and over
Total	239,463	243,844	249,783	281,034	1,346,362	1,142,905	945,178	636,963	517,234	413,491	302,942	154,935	103,234
Total percent distribution[1]	3.1	3.1	3.2	3.6	17.2	14.6	12.1	8.2	6.6	5.3	3.9	2.0	1.3
Violent crime[2]	12,778	12,714	12,860	15,182	68,070	56,257	44,614	29,896	23,322	19,170	13,946	7,039	5,296
Violent crime percent distribution[1]	3.2	3.2	3.2	3.8	17.2	14.2	11.3	7.5	5.9	4.8	3.5	1.8	1.3
Murder and nonnegligent manslaughter	394	371	377	499	1,637	1,138	872	503	363	302	235	121	141
Rape[3]	648	556	481	551	2,357	2,282	1,997	1,443	1,116	888	707	385	427
Robbery	2,682	2,500	2,413	3,274	10,618	7,454	5,115	3,016	2,186	1,759	1,115	371	156
Aggravated assault	9,054	9,287	9,589	10,858	53,458	45,383	36,630	24,934	19,657	16,221	11,889	6,162	4,572
Property crime[2]	25,102	24,896	25,251	30,461	145,480	128,168	104,503	68,081	55,968	43,984	29,820	14,108	8,872
Property crime percent distribution[1]	2.8	2.8	2.8	3.4	16.3	14.3	11.7	7.6	6.3	4.9	3.3	1.6	1.0
Burglary	3,949	4,119	4,029	4,547	23,255	20,176	16,164	9,670	7,690	5,652	3,500	1,424	761
Larceny-theft	18,928	18,482	18,955	21,845	108,977	97,128	79,907	53,493	44,675	36,003	24,975	12,077	7,802
Motor vehicle theft	2,077	2,139	2,128	3,910	12,311	10,030	7,639	4,415	3,113	1,923	1,071	398	176
Arson	148	156	139	159	937	834	793	503	490	406	274	209	133
Other assaults	22,292	23,546	24,206	29,191	132,791	113,155	94,961	65,287	53,147	41,771	29,874	15,517	11,845
Forgery and counterfeiting	1,066	1,171	1,193	1,288	6,767	6,411	3,434	2,507	1,831	1,163	550	304	
Fraud	2,462	2,624	2,823	2,954	16,089	15,146	12,546	8,531	6,553	4,905	3,161	1,643	1,176
Embezzlement	482	423	455	401	1,962	1,557	1,218	955	704	482	304	150	112
Stolen property; buying, receiving, possessing	2,177	2,220	2,318	2,543	13,070	11,056	8,931	5,217	3,695	2,484	1,458	600	257
Vandalism	4,798	4,549	4,575	5,321	23,092	17,703	13,580	8,469	6,487	5,022	3,532	1,744	1,285
Weapons; carrying, possessing, etc.	5,164	5,256	5,108	7,469	23,818	17,055	12,885	7,853	5,537	4,178	2,917	1,563	1,163
Prostitution and commercialized vice	1,026	1,046	1,043	1,024	4,678	3,345	2,647	1,912	1,624	1,221	745	441	395
Sex offenses (except forcible rape and prostitution)	814	788	785	784	3,962	3,825	3,684	2,737	2,576	2,307	2,003	1,228	1,542
Drug abuse violations	47,929	47,154	47,147	51,871	232,737	184,653	145,439	91,452	69,736	51,784	34,958	15,250	6,505
Gambling	80	89	91	337	366	256	222	171	122	107	112	79	66
Offenses against the family and children	1,138	1,273	1,437	1,822	11,381	12,312	11,381	7,429	5,069	3,360	1,853	881	533
Driving under the influence	24,707	27,098	28,130	29,236	138,434	109,648	89,300	66,707	58,840	49,594	41,037	24,388	19,151
Liquor laws	3,108	2,218	1,816	1,806	8,098	6,877	6,796	5,682	5,686	5,951	5,593	3,066	1,725
Drunkenness	7,593	7,295	7,435	7,587	38,573	34,957	31,492	24,357	23,086	21,961	18,688	9,613	5,179
Disorderly conduct	8,119	7,425	7,183	8,335	35,323	29,704	25,033	17,405	15,066	13,110	10,291	5,533	4,205
Vagrancy	276	278	364	381	2,279	2,206	2,357	1,774	1,927	1,890	1,613	922	493
All other offenses (except traffic)	68,340	71,767	75,546	83,024	439,323	388,545	328,046	219,589	175,552	138,351	99,859	50,612	33,125
Suspicion	12	14	13	17	69	69	48	25	30	28	15	8	5
Curfew and loitering law violations	NA	NA	NA	NA	NA	NA	NA	NA	NA	NA	NA	NA	NA

NA = Not available.
* = Less than one-tenth of one percent.
1 Because of rounding, the percentages may not sum to 100 percent.   2 Violent crimes are offenses of murder and nonnegligent manslaughter, rape, robbery, and aggravated assault. Property crimes are offenses of burglary, larceny-theft, motor vehicle theft, and arson.   3 The rape figures in this table are aggregate totals of the data submitted based on both the legacy and revised Uniform Crime Reporting definitions.

Table 39. Male Arrests, Distribution by Age, 2018

(Number, percent; 12,212 agencies; 2018 estimated population 247,752,415.)

Offense charged	Total, all ages	Ages under 15	Ages under 18	Ages 18 and over	Under 10	10–12	13–14	15	16	17	18	19	20
Total	5,684,385	112,754	389,256	5,295,129	2,797	27,163	82,794	72,365	91,982	112,155	156,212	167,417	168,557
Total percent distribution[1]	100.0	2.0	6.8	93.2	*	0.5	1.5	1.3	1.6	2.0	2.7	2.9	3.0
Violent crime[2]	313,411	8,829	30,713	282,698	150	2,172	6,507	5,756	7,489	8,639	10,351	9,785	9,651
Violent crime percent distribution[1]	100.0	2.8	9.8	90.2	*	0.7	2.1	1.8	2.4	2.8	3.3	3.1	3.1
Murder and nonnegligent manslaughter	7,944	54	621	7,323	0	3	51	87	179	301	433	424	410
Rape[3]	18,487	1,258	3,011	15,476	19	387	852	527	584	642	741	669	644
Robbery	57,212	2,261	11,717	45,495	9	249	2,003	2,448	3,332	3,676	4,097	3,229	2,686
Aggravated assault	229,768	5,256	15,364	214,404	122	1,533	3,601	2,694	3,394	4,020	5,080	5,463	5,911
Property crime[2]	564,434	19,943	68,376	496,058	405	4,325	15,213	14,022	16,256	18,155	20,586	18,450	16,343
Property crime percent distribution[1]	100.0	3.5	12.1	87.9	0.1	0.8	2.7	2.5	2.9	3.2	3.6	3.3	2.9
Burglary	109,250	4,443	14,768	94,482	133	954	3,356	3,096	3,462	3,767	4,484	3,840	3,472
Larceny-theft	396,062	12,698	43,328	352,734	205	2,887	9,606	8,536	10,208	11,886	13,807	12,625	11,091
Motor vehicle theft	53,660	2,135	9,131	44,529	15	255	1,865	2,209	2,426	2,361	2,132	1,874	1,650
Arson	5,462	667	1,149	4,313	52	229	386	181	160	141	163	111	130
Other assaults	575,382	24,606	59,902	515,480	732	7,384	16,490	11,249	12,144	11,903	12,442	12,133	13,061
Forgery and counterfeiting	25,241	130	637	24,604	4	24	102	79	154	274	685	988	1,087
Fraud	57,971	585	2,450	55,521	8	102	475	476	572	817	1,192	1,471	1,654
Embezzlement	5,676	12	265	5,411	0	1	11	24	70	159	268	286	272
Stolen property; buying, receiving, possessing	55,411	1,223	5,942	49,469	14	148	1,061	1,245	1,628	1,846	2,310	2,198	1,961
Vandalism	105,557	7,289	18,915	86,642	316	2,149	4,824	3,627	4,077	3,922	3,912	3,476	3,160
Weapons; carrying, possessing, etc.	115,673	3,158	11,572	104,101	130	830	2,198	2,110	2,685	3,619	4,525	4,737	4,386
Prostitution and commercialized vice	8,456	21	78	8,378	0	4	17	8	14	35	97	98	157
Sex offenses (except forcible rape and prostitution)	33,082	2,405	5,124	27,958	73	631	1,701	927	876	916	951	901	751
Drug abuse violations	942,718	7,973	51,247	891,471	64	1,190	6,719	7,943	13,153	22,178	39,696	41,140	38,598
Gambling	2,050	20	124	1,926	1	2	17	17	32	55	66	78	65
Offenses against the family and children	45,203	527	1,526	43,677	23	143	361	304	344	351	548	556	610
Driving under the influence	556,231	65	3,039	553,192	4	9	52	121	677	2,176	6,653	9,350	11,540
Liquor laws	91,046	1,295	11,511	79,535	13	117	1,165	1,705	3,158	5,353	11,078	12,493	10,551
Drunkenness	199,755	219	1,727	198,028	7	26	186	261	408	839	2,563	3,310	3,607
Disorderly conduct	176,878	11,165	28,200	148,678	274	3,203	7,688	5,458	6,120	5,457	4,968	4,562	4,506
Vagrancy	13,714	113	400	13,314	1	13	99	90	108	89	210	173	197
All other offenses (except traffic)	1,784,377	19,672	75,686	1,708,691	504	3,924	15,244	14,312	18,796	22,906	33,101	41,223	46,387
Suspicion	323	7	26	297	0	3	4	2	6	11	10	9	13
Curfew and loitering law violations	11,796	3,497	11,796	NA	74	763	2,660	2,629	3,215	2,455	NA	NA	NA

Table 39. Male Arrests, Distribution by Age, 2018—Continued

(Number, percent; 12,212 agencies; 2018 estimated population 247,752,415.)

Offense charged	21	22	23	24	25–29	30–34	35–39	40–44	45–49	50–54	55–59	60–64	65 and over
Total	173,970	177,611	182,260	205,779	970,749	816,257	677,480	461,744	380,854	313,038	236,825	123,957	82,419
Total percent distribution[1]	3.1	3.1	3.2	3.6	17.1	14.4	11.9	8.1	6.7	5.5	4.2	2.2	1.4
Violent crime[2]	10,072	10,046	10,016	12,027	52,978	43,819	35,061	23,398	18,422	15,307	11,385	5,906	4,474
Violent crime percent distribution[1]	3.2	3.2	3.2	3.8	16.9	14.0	11.2	7.5	5.9	4.9	3.6	1.9	1.4
Murder and nonnegligent manslaughter	358	338	325	442	1,443	978	746	432	311	258	197	107	121
Rape[3]	623	542	468	537	2,286	2,206	1,916	1,387	1,087	873	694	381	422
Robbery	2,307	2,083	2,000	2,817	8,721	6,109	4,201	2,491	1,833	1,496	950	333	142
Aggravated assault	6,784	7,083	7,223	8,231	40,528	34,526	28,198	19,088	15,191	12,680	9,544	5,085	3,789
Property crime[2]	15,313	15,505	15,918	19,233	90,931	78,530	64,183	41,954	35,611	28,810	19,857	9,309	5,525
Property crime percent distribution[1]	2.7	2.7	2.8	3.4	16.1	13.9	11.4	7.4	6.3	5.1	3.5	1.6	1.0
Burglary	3,224	3,359	3,206	3,630	18,362	15,623	12,522	7,451	6,061	4,565	2,899	1,184	600
Larceny-theft	10,420	10,392	10,993	12,495	62,759	54,934	45,298	30,740	26,680	22,383	15,850	7,607	4,660
Motor vehicle theft	1,551	1,636	1,617	2,975	9,104	7,354	5,768	3,407	2,495	1,573	890	353	150
Arson	118	118	102	133	706	619	595	356	375	289	218	165	115
Other assaults	15,108	16,096	16,828	20,418	94,758	81,982	69,450	48,133	39,481	31,303	22,881	12,097	9,309
Forgery and counterfeiting	694	772	793	864	4,506	4,056	3,482	2,206	1,653	1,274	892	432	220
Fraud	1,620	1,704	1,844	1,838	10,121	9,480	7,571	5,299	4,243	3,257	2,231	1,192	804
Embezzlement	245	228	220	207	1,001	779	589	450	346	234	151	82	53
Stolen property; buying, receiving, possessing	1,701	1,695	1,825	1,945	9,859	8,104	6,816	4,065	2,967	2,038	1,222	523	240
Vandalism	3,659	3,467	3,462	3,968	17,480	13,402	10,286	6,466	4,948	3,794	2,760	1,407	995
Weapons; carrying, possessing, etc.	4,751	4,813	4,701	6,931	21,551	15,247	11,503	7,013	4,951	3,757	2,685	1,463	1,087
Prostitution and commercialized vice	172	205	232	246	1,347	1,244	1,183	906	756	626	431	324	354
Sex offenses (except forcible rape and prostitution)	758	722	717	718	3,640	3,558	3,419	2,567	2,422	2,194	1,924	1,200	1,516
Drug abuse violations	36,435	36,020	36,047	39,915	174,163	135,578	106,911	67,655	52,197	40,328	28,278	12,869	5,641
Gambling	70	77	81	323	306	204	178	124	86	83	79	58	48
Offenses against the family and children	693	821	882	1,130	7,270	8,197	8,096	5,647	3,974	2,682	1,483	689	399
Driving under the influence	18,143	19,840	20,602	21,418	102,690	81,947	66,464	49,456	43,209	36,618	31,094	18,953	15,215
Liquor laws	2,208	1,626	1,391	1,356	6,049	5,241	5,050	4,252	4,411	4,877	4,723	2,684	1,545
Drunkenness	5,876	5,738	5,812	5,967	30,226	27,160	24,427	18,741	18,160	17,916	15,725	8,263	4,537
Disorderly conduct	5,826	5,321	5,150	6,029	25,055	20,971	17,714	12,412	11,020	9,665	7,855	4,330	3,294
Vagrancy	203	198	283	301	1,719	1,655	1,741	1,310	1,369	1,491	1,332	715	417
All other offenses (except traffic)	50,416	52,705	55,447	60,932	315,051	275,055	233,318	159,671	130,602	106,761	79,825	41,456	26,741
Suspicion	7	12	9	13	48	48	38	19	26	23	12	5	5
Curfew and loitering law violations	NA	NA	NA	NA	NA	NA	NA	NA	NA	NA	NA	NA	NA

NA = Not available.
* = Less than one-tenth of one percent.
1 Because of rounding, the percentages may not sum to 100 percent.   2 Violent crimes are offenses of murder and nonnegligent manslaughter, rape, robbery, and aggravated assault. Property crimes are offenses of burglary, larceny-theft, motor vehicle theft, and arson.   3 The rape figures in this table are aggregate totals of the data submitted based on both the legacy and revised Uniform Crime Reporting definitions.

Table 40. Female Arrests, Distribution by Age, 2018

(Number, percent; 12,212 agencies; 2018 estimated population 247,752,415.)

Offense charged	Total, all ages	Ages under 15	Ages under 18	Ages 18 and over	Under 10	10–12	13–14	15	16	17	18	19
Total	2,126,700	52,588	164,364	1,962,336	704	11,141	40,743	31,783	37,096	42,897	58,920	63,672
Total percent distribution[1]	100.0	2.5	7.7	92.3	*	0.5	1.9	1.5	1.7	2.0	2.8	3.0
Violent crime[2]	82,854	2,592	7,570	75,284	28	583	1,981	1,458	1,734	1,786	2,181	2,344
Violent crime percent distribution[1]	100.0	3.1	9.1	90.9	*	0.7	2.4	1.8	2.1	2.2	2.6	2.8
Murder and nonnegligent manslaughter	1,105	13	73	1,032	0	1	12	13	18	29	41	55
Rape[3]	606	66	133	473	3	25	38	25	29	13	23	25
Robbery	10,185	354	1,503	8,682	2	34	318	333	372	444	544	535
Aggravated assault	70,958	2,159	5,861	65,097	23	523	1,613	1,087	1,315	1,300	1,573	1,729
Property crime[2]	330,553	8,820	32,367	298,186	115	1,712	6,993	6,167	7,932	9,448	12,058	11,467
Property crime percent distribution[1]	100.0	2.7	9.8	90.2	*	0.5	2.1	1.9	2.4	2.9	3.6	3.5
Burglary	26,668	693	2,165	24,503	27	142	524	402	479	591	747	741
Larceny-theft	286,455	7,360	27,894	258,561	84	1,451	5,825	5,231	6,926	8,377	10,835	10,258
Motor vehicle theft	15,842	631	2,071	13,771	0	67	564	495	496	449	450	446
Arson	1,588	136	237	1,351	4	52	80	39	31	31	26	22
Other assaults	233,668	14,728	35,214	198,454	168	3,648	10,912	7,001	7,033	6,452	6,075	6,093
Forgery and counterfeiting	12,887	27	155	12,732	1	9	17	17	32	79	306	483
Fraud	32,915	255	1,117	31,798	1	44	210	209	262	391	651	760
Embezzlement	5,602	8	178	5,424	1	1	6	8	57	105	256	275
Stolen property; buying, receiving, possessing	15,585	301	1,158	14,427	0	24	277	229	311	317	424	505
Vandalism	31,551	1,650	4,414	27,137	46	423	1,181	863	895	1,006	1,059	996
Weapons; carrying, possessing, etc.	11,915	586	1,439	10,476	25	200	361	256	288	309	302	322
Prostitution and commercialized vice	15,243	20	121	15,122	1	3	16	19	29	53	610	665
Sex offenses (except forcible rape and prostitution)	2,467	293	595	1,872	15	77	201	125	90	87	77	46
Drug abuse violations	309,134	3,785	17,365	291,769	20	628	3,137	2,811	4,048	6,721	12,144	12,670
Gambling	425	3	10	415	0	1	2	2	1	4	7	10
Offenses against the family and children	19,669	366	951	18,718	12	72	282	220	185	180	230	262
Driving under the influence	190,344	37	1,025	189,319	4	3	30	52	254	682	2,085	2,952
Liquor laws	39,875	1,472	8,411	31,464	5	163	1,304	1,481	2,183	3,275	6,426	6,645
Drunkenness	52,972	159	785	52,187	0	6	153	129	189	308	842	1,005
Disorderly conduct	74,304	6,619	15,874	58,430	66	1,489	5,064	3,345	3,166	2,744	2,218	2,074
Vagrancy	4,407	32	127	4,280	2	5	25	36	29	30	90	80
All other offenses (except traffic)	655,123	9,140	30,374	624,749	165	1,773	7,202	6,209	7,075	7,950	10,878	14,015
Suspicion	104	7	11	93	0	0	7	1	1	2	1	3
Curfew and loitering law violations	5,103	1,688	5,103	NA	29	277	1,382	1,145	1,302	968	NA	NA

Table 40. Female Arrests, Distribution by Age, 2018—Continued

(Number, percent; 12,212 agencies; 2018 estimated population 247,752,415.)

Offense charged	20	21	22	23	24	25–29	30–34	35–39	40–44	45–49	50–54	55–59	60–64	65 and over
Total	65,319	65,493	66,233	67,523	75,255	375,613	326,648	267,698	175,219	136,380	100,453	66,117	30,978	20,815
Total percent distribution[1]	3.1	3.1	3.1	3.2	3.5	17.7	15.4	12.6	8.2	6.4	4.7	3.1	1.5	1.0
Violent crime[2]	2,526	2,706	2,668	2,844	3,155	15,092	12,438	9,553	6,498	4,900	3,863	2,561	1,133	822
Violent crime percent distribution[1]	3.0	3.3	3.2	3.4	3.8	18.2	15.0	11.5	7.8	5.9	4.7	3.1	1.4	1.0
Murder and nonnegligent manslaughter	39	36	33	52	57	194	160	126	71	52	44	38	14	20
Rape[3]	9	25	14	13	14	71	76	81	56	29	15	13	4	5
Robbery	427	375	417	413	457	1,897	1,345	914	525	353	263	165	38	14
Aggravated assault	2,051	2,270	2,204	2,366	2,627	12,930	10,857	8,432	5,846	4,466	3,541	2,345	1,077	783
Property crime[2]	10,646	9,789	9,391	9,333	11,228	54,549	49,638	40,320	26,127	20,357	15,174	9,963	4,799	3,347
Property crime percent distribution[1]	3.2	3.0	2.8	2.8	3.4	16.5	15.0	12.2	7.9	6.2	4.6	3.0	1.5	1.0
Burglary	765	725	760	823	917	4,893	4,553	3,642	2,219	1,629	1,087	601	240	161
Larceny-theft	9,432	8,508	8,090	7,962	9,350	46,218	42,194	34,609	22,753	17,995	13,620	9,125	4,470	3,142
Motor vehicle theft	418	526	503	511	935	3,207	2,676	1,871	1,008	618	350	181	45	26
Arson	31	30	38	37	26	231	215	198	147	115	117	56	44	18
Other assaults	6,547	7,184	7,450	7,378	8,773	38,033	31,173	25,511	17,154	13,666	10,468	6,993	3,420	2,536
Forgery and counterfeiting	607	372	399	400	424	2,261	2,355	2,013	1,228	854	557	271	118	84
Fraud	978	842	920	979	1,116	5,968	5,666	4,975	3,232	2,310	1,648	930	451	372
Embezzlement	273	237	195	235	194	961	778	629	505	358	248	153	68	59
Stolen property; buying, receiving, possessing	472	476	525	493	598	3,211	2,952	2,115	1,152	728	446	236	77	17
Vandalism	1,019	1,139	1,082	1,113	1,353	5,612	4,301	3,294	2,003	1,539	1,228	772	337	290
Weapons; carrying, possessing, etc.	339	413	443	407	538	2,267	1,808	1,382	840	586	421	232	100	76
Prostitution and commercialized vice	726	854	841	811	778	3,331	2,101	1,464	1,006	868	595	314	117	41
Sex offenses (except forcible rape and prostitution)	69	56	66	68	66	322	267	265	170	154	113	79	28	26
Drug abuse violations	12,377	11,494	11,134	11,100	11,956	58,574	49,075	38,528	23,797	17,539	11,456	6,680	2,381	864
Gambling	13	10	12	14	14	60	52	44	47	36	24	33	21	18
Offenses against the family and children	320	445	452	555	692	4,111	4,115	3,285	1,782	1,095	678	370	192	134
Driving under the influence	3,661	6,564	7,258	7,528	7,818	35,744	27,701	22,836	17,251	15,631	12,976	9,943	5,435	3,936
Liquor laws	5,384	900	592	425	450	2,049	1,636	1,746	1,430	1,275	1,074	870	382	180
Drunkenness	1,072	1,717	1,557	1,623	1,620	8,347	7,797	7,065	5,616	4,926	4,045	2,963	1,350	642
Disorderly conduct	2,048	2,293	2,104	2,033	2,306	10,268	8,733	7,319	4,993	4,046	3,445	2,436	1,203	911
Vagrancy	84	73	80	81	80	560	551	616	464	558	399	281	207	76
All other offenses (except traffic)	16,157	17,924	19,062	20,099	22,092	124,272	113,490	94,728	59,918	44,950	31,590	20,034	9,156	6,384
Suspicion	1	5	2	4	4	21	21	10	6	4	5	3	3	0
Curfew and loitering law violations	NA	NA	NA	NA	NA	NA	NA	NA	NA	NA	NA	NA	NA	NA

NA = Not available.

* = Less than one-tenth of one percent.

1 Because of rounding, the percentages may not sum to 100 percent.   2 Violent crimes are offenses of murder and nonnegligent manslaughter, rape, robbery, and aggravated assault. Property crimes are offenses of burglary, larceny-theft, motor vehicle theft, and arson.   3 The rape figures in this table are aggregate totals of the data submitted based on both the legacy and revised Uniform Crime Reporting definitions.

Table 41. Arrests of Persons Under 15, 18, 21, and 25 Years of Age, 2018

(Number, percent; 12,212 agencies; 2018 estimated population 247,752,415.)

Offense charged	Total, all ages	Number of persons arrested				Percent of total all ages			
		Under 15	Under 18	Under 21	Under 25	Under 15	Under 18	Under 21	Under 25
Total	7,811,085	165,342	553,620	1,233,717	2,247,841	2.1	7.1	15.8	28.8
Violent crime[1]	396,265	11,421	38,283	75,121	128,655	2.9	9.7	19.0	32.5
Murder and nonnegligent manslaughter	9,049	67	694	2,096	3,737	0.7	7.7	23.2	41.3
Rape[2]	19,093	1,324	3,144	5,255	7,491	6.9	16.5	27.5	39.2
Robbery	67,397	2,615	13,220	24,738	35,607	3.9	19.6	36.7	52.8
Aggravated assault	300,726	7,415	21,225	43,032	81,820	2.5	7.1	14.3	27.2
Property crime[1]	894,987	28,763	100,743	190,293	296,003	3.2	11.3	21.3	33.1
Burglary	135,918	5,136	16,933	30,982	47,626	3.8	12.5	22.8	35.0
Larceny-theft	682,517	20,058	71,222	139,270	217,480	2.9	10.4	20.4	31.9
Motor vehicle theft	69,502	2,766	11,202	18,172	28,426	4.0	16.1	26.1	40.9
Arson	7,050	803	1,386	1,869	2,471	11.4	19.7	26.5	35.0
Other assaults	809,050	39,334	95,116	151,467	250,702	4.9	11.8	18.7	31.0
Forgery and counterfeiting	38,128	157	792	4,948	9,666	0.4	2.1	13.0	25.4
Fraud	90,886	840	3,567	10,273	21,136	0.9	3.9	11.3	23.3
Embezzlement	11,278	20	443	2,073	3,834	0.2	3.9	18.4	34.0
Stolen property; buying, receiving, possessing	70,996	1,524	7,100	14,970	24,228	2.1	10.0	21.1	34.1
Vandalism	137,108	8,939	23,329	36,951	56,194	6.5	17.0	27.0	41.0
Weapons; carrying, possessing, etc.	127,588	3,744	13,011	27,622	50,619	2.9	10.2	21.6	39.7
Prostitution and commercialized vice	23,699	41	199	2,552	6,691	0.2	0.8	10.8	28.2
Sex offenses (except forcible rape and prostitution)	35,549	2,698	5,719	8,514	11,685	7.6	16.1	24.0	32.9
Drug abuse violations	1,251,852	11,758	68,612	225,237	419,338	0.9	5.5	18.0	33.5
Gambling	2,475	23	134	373	974	0.9	5.4	15.1	39.4
Offenses against the family and children	64,872	893	2,477	5,003	10,673	1.4	3.8	7.7	16.5
Driving under the influence	746,575	102	4,064	40,305	149,476	*	0.5	5.4	20.0
Liquor laws	130,921	2,767	19,922	72,499	81,447	2.1	15.2	55.4	62.2
Drunkenness	252,727	378	2,512	14,911	44,821	0.1	1.0	5.9	17.7
Disorderly conduct	251,182	17,784	44,074	64,450	95,512	7.1	17.5	25.7	38.0
Vagrancy	18,121	145	527	1,361	2,660	0.8	2.9	7.5	14.7
All other offenses (except traffic)	2,439,500	28,812	106,060	267,821	566,498	1.2	4.3	11.0	23.2
Suspicion	427	14	37	74	130	3.3	8.7	17.3	30.4
Curfew and loitering law violations	16,899	5,185	16,899	16,899	16,899	30.7	100.0	100.0	100.0

* = Less than one-tenth of one percent.
1 Violent crimes in this table are offenses of murder and nonnegligent manslaughter, rape, robbery, and aggravated assault. Property crimes are offenses of burglary, larceny-theft, motor vehicle theft, and arson.   2 The rape figures in this table are aggregate totals of the data submitted based on both the legacy and revised Uniform Crime Reporting definitions.

Table 42. Arrests, Distribution by Sex, 2018

(Number, percent; 12,212 agencies; 2018 estimated population 247,752,415.)

Offense charged	Number of persons arrested			Percent male	Percent female	Percent distribution[1]		
	Total	Male	Female			Total	Male	Female
Total	7,811,085	5,684,385	2,126,700	72.8	27.2	100.0	100.0	100.0
Violent crime[2]	396,265	313,411	82,854	79.1	20.9	5.1	5.5	3.9
Murder and nonnegligent manslaughter	9,049	7,944	1,105	87.8	12.2	0.1	0.1	0.1
Rape[3]	19,093	18,487	606	96.8	3.2	0.2	0.3	*
Robbery	67,397	57,212	10,185	84.9	15.1	0.9	1.0	0.5
Aggravated assault	300,726	229,768	70,958	76.4	23.6	3.8	4.0	3.3
Property crime[2]	894,987	564,434	330,553	63.1	36.9	11.5	9.9	15.5
Burglary	135,918	109,250	26,668	80.4	19.6	1.7	1.9	1.3
Larceny-theft	682,517	396,062	286,455	58.0	42.0	8.7	7.0	13.5
Motor vehicle theft	69,502	53,660	15,842	77.2	22.8	0.9	0.9	0.7
Arson	7,050	5,462	1,588	77.5	22.5	0.1	0.1	0.1
Other assaults	809,050	575,382	233,668	71.1	28.9	10.4	10.1	11.0
Forgery and counterfeiting	38,128	25,241	12,887	66.2	33.8	0.5	0.4	0.6
Fraud	90,886	57,971	32,915	63.8	36.2	1.2	1.0	1.5
Embezzlement	11,278	5,676	5,602	50.3	49.7	0.1	0.1	0.3
Stolen property; buying, receiving, possessing	70,996	55,411	15,585	78.0	22.0	0.9	1.0	0.7
Vandalism	137,108	105,557	31,551	77.0	23.0	1.8	1.9	1.5
Weapons; carrying, possessing, etc.	127,588	115,673	11,915	90.7	9.3	1.6	2.0	0.6
Prostitution and commercialized vice	23,699	8,456	15,243	35.7	64.3	0.3	0.1	0.7
Sex offenses (except forcible rape and prostitution)	35,549	33,082	2,467	93.1	6.9	0.5	0.6	0.1
Drug abuse violations	1,251,852	942,718	309,134	75.3	24.7	16.0	16.6	14.5
Gambling	2,475	2,050	425	82.8	17.2	*	*	*
Offenses against the family and children	64,872	45,203	19,669	69.7	30.3	0.8	0.8	0.9
Driving under the influence	746,575	556,231	190,344	74.5	25.5	9.6	9.8	9.0
Liquor laws	130,921	91,046	39,875	69.5	30.5	1.7	1.6	1.9
Drunkenness	252,727	199,755	52,972	79.0	21.0	3.2	3.5	2.5
Disorderly conduct	251,182	176,878	74,304	70.4	29.6	3.2	3.1	3.5
Vagrancy	18,121	13,714	4,407	75.7	24.3	0.2	0.2	0.2
All other offenses (except traffic)	2,439,500	1,784,377	655,123	73.1	26.9	31.2	31.4	30.8
Suspicion	427	323	104	75.6	24.4	*	*	*
Curfew and loitering law violations	16,899	11,796	5,103	69.8	30.2	0.2	0.2	0.2

* = Less than one-tenth of 1 percent.
1 Because of rounding, the percentages may not sum to 100.   2 Violent crimes in this table are offenses of murder and nonnegligent manslaughter, rape, robbery, and aggravated assault. Property crimes are offenses of burglary, larceny-theft, motor vehicle theft, and arson.   3 The rape figures in this table are aggregate totals of the data submitted based on both the legacy and revised Uniform Crime Reporting definitions.

Table 43. Arrests, Distribution by Race, 2018

(Number, percent; 12,212 agencies; 2018 estimated population 247,752,415.)

Offense charged	Total arrests						Percent distribution[1]						Arrests under 18					
	Total	White	Black	American Indian or Alaskan Native	Asian	Native Hawaiian or Other Pacific Islander	Total	White	Black	American Indian or Alaskan Native	Asian	Native Hawaiian or Other Pacific Islander	Total	White	Black	American Indian or Alaskan Native	Asian	Native Hawaiian or Other Pacific Islander
Total	7,710,900	5,319,654	2,115,381	164,430	92,737	18,698	100.0	69.0	27.4	2.1	1.2	0.2	543,242	336,027	189,596	10,346	5,840	1,433
Violent crime[2]	392,562	230,299	146,734	7,784	6,102	1,643	100.0	58.7	37.4	2.0	1.6	0.4	37,788	18,447	18,290	479	426	146
Murder and nonnegligent manslaughter	8,957	3,953	4,778	105	94	27	100.0	44.1	53.3	1.2	1.0	0.3	693	280	401	6	3	3
Rape[3]	18,776	12,794	5,376	267	289	50	100.0	68.1	28.6	1.4	1.5	0.3	3,070	2,117	884	33	30	6
Robbery	66,789	29,025	36,187	676	641	260	100.0	43.5	54.2	1.0	1.0	0.4	13,082	4,423	8,398	72	125	64
Aggravated assault	298,040	184,527	100,393	6,736	5,078	1,306	100.0	61.9	33.7	2.3	1.7	0.4	20,943	11,627	8,607	368	268	73
Property crime[2]	880,473	589,224	264,748	14,865	9,665	1,971	100.0	66.9	30.1	1.7	1.1	0.2	98,701	54,259	41,224	1,661	1,257	300
Burglary	134,542	91,581	39,617	1,590	1,422	332	100.0	68.1	29.4	1.2	1.1	0.2	16,699	9,183	7,029	280	155	52
Larceny-theft	669,983	448,193	201,086	11,987	7,324	1,393	100.0	66.9	30.0	1.8	1.1	0.2	69,575	39,193	28,031	1,143	1,001	207
Motor vehicle theft	69,002	44,512	22,305	1,151	818	216	100.0	64.5	32.3	1.7	1.2	0.3	11,089	4,976	5,780	212	84	37
Arson	6,946	4,938	1,740	137	101	30	100.0	71.1	25.1	2.0	1.5	0.4	1,338	907	384	26	17	4
Other assaults	794,787	512,025	254,360	15,711	10,348	2,343	100.0	64.4	32.0	2.0	1.3	0.3	93,005	54,686	35,674	1,546	832	267
Forgery and counterfeiting	37,724	25,140	11,637	335	548	64	100.0	66.6	30.8	0.9	1.5	0.2	779	445	314	6	11	3
Fraud	89,610	58,572	28,387	1,419	1,088	144	100.0	65.4	31.7	1.6	1.2	0.2	3,499	1,447	1,944	67	36	5
Embezzlement	11,174	6,923	3,955	122	159	15	100.0	62.0	35.4	1.1	1.4	0.1	435	229	188	4	12	2
Stolen property; buying, receiving, possessing	69,874	44,179	23,661	881	819	334	100.0	63.2	33.9	1.3	1.2	0.5	6,936	2,598	4,123	76	95	44
Vandalism	134,794	91,176	38,887	2,949	1,552	230	100.0	67.6	28.8	2.2	1.2	0.2	22,753	15,418	6,612	496	197	30
Weapons; carrying, possessing, etc.	126,332	68,756	54,715	1,094	1,390	377	100.0	54.4	43.3	0.9	1.1	0.3	12,840	6,983	5,501	134	184	38
Prostitution and commercialized vice	23,502	12,928	9,109	95	1,309	61	100.0	55.0	38.8	0.4	5.6	0.3	199	118	75	3	2	1
Sex offenses (except forcible rape and prostitution)	35,157	25,338	8,403	587	751	78	100.0	72.1	23.9	1.7	2.1	0.2	5,585	4,062	1,361	61	84	17
Drug abuse violations	1,234,178	871,295	333,113	14,148	13,345	2,277	100.0	70.6	27.0	1.1	1.1	0.2	67,096	49,311	15,304	1,357	902	222
Gambling	2,465	1,000	1,198	11	205	51	100.0	40.6	48.6	0.4	8.3	2.1	134	30	103	1	0	0
Offenses against the family and children	64,357	43,371	18,530	1,895	510	51	100.0	67.4	28.8	2.9	0.8	0.1	2,447	1,674	573	181	18	1
Driving under the influence	736,644	597,919	108,703	13,150	14,323	2,549	100.0	81.2	14.8	1.8	1.9	0.3	3,998	3,512	278	133	64	11
Liquor laws	128,453	100,687	18,743	6,973	1,876	174	100.0	78.4	14.6	5.4	1.5	0.1	19,530	17,021	1,260	959	244	46
Drunkenness	251,490	193,042	37,781	17,412	2,825	430	100.0	76.8	15.0	6.9	1.1	0.2	2,479	1,989	316	138	32	4
Disorderly conduct	248,716	158,533	78,192	9,770	1,926	295	100.0	63.7	31.4	3.9	0.8	0.1	43,621	24,017	18,417	867	286	34
Vagrancy	18,048	12,823	4,458	482	261	24	100.0	71.0	24.7	2.7	1.4	0.1	525	265	246	8	4	2
All other offenses (except traffic)	2,413,408	1,666,825	663,086	54,410	23,550	5,537	100.0	69.1	27.5	2.3	1.0	0.2	104,133	70,131	30,929	1,893	970	210
Suspicion	432	237	129	65	1	0	100.0	54.9	29.9	15.0	0.2	0.0	39	23	12	4	0	0
Curfew and loitering law violations	16,720	9,362	6,852	272	184	50	100.0	56.0	41.0	1.6	1.1	0.3	16,720	9,362	6,852	272	184	50

Table 43. Arrests, Distribution by Race, 2018—Continued

(Number, percent; 12,212 agencies; 2018 estimated population 247,752,415.)

Offense charged	Percent distribution[1]						Arrests 18 and over						Percent distribution[1]					
	Total	White	Black	American Indian or Alaskan Native	Asian	Native Hawaiian or Other Pacific Islander	Total	White	Black	American Indian or Alaskan Native	Asian	Native Hawaiian or Other Pacific Islander	Total	White	Black	American Indian or Alaskan Native	Asian	Native Hawaiian or Other Pacific Islander
Total	100.0	61.9	34.9	1.9	1.1	0.3	7,167,658	4,983,627	1,925,785	154,084	86,897	17,265	100.0	69.5	26.9	2.1	1.2	0.2
Violent crime[2]	100.0	48.8	48.4	1.3	1.1	0.4	354,774	211,852	128,444	7,305	5,676	1,497	100.0	59.7	36.2	2.1	1.6	0.4
Murder and nonnegligent manslaughter	100.0	40.4	57.9	0.9	0.4	0.4	8,264	3,673	4,377	99	91	24	100.0	44.4	53.0	1.2	1.1	0.3
Rape[3]	100.0	69.0	28.8	1.1	1.0	0.2	15,706	10,677	4,492	234	259	44	100.0	68.0	28.6	1.5	1.6	0.3
Robbery	100.0	33.8	64.2	0.6	1.0	0.5	53,707	24,602	27,789	604	516	196	100.0	45.8	51.7	1.1	1.0	0.4
Aggravated assault	100.0	55.5	41.1	1.8	1.3	0.3	277,097	172,900	91,786	6,368	4,810	1,233	100.0	62.4	33.1	2.3	1.7	0.4
Property crime[2]	100.0	55.0	41.8	1.7	1.3	0.3	781,772	534,965	223,524	13,204	8,408	1,671	100.0	68.4	28.6	1.7	1.1	0.2
Burglary	100.0	55.0	42.1	1.7	0.9	0.3	117,843	82,398	32,588	1,310	1,267	280	100.0	69.9	27.7	1.1	1.1	0.2
Larceny-theft	100.0	56.3	40.3	1.6	1.4	0.3	600,408	409,000	173,055	10,844	6,323	1,186	100.0	68.1	28.8	1.8	1.1	0.2
Motor vehicle theft	100.0	44.9	52.1	1.9	0.8	0.3	57,913	39,536	16,525	939	734	179	100.0	68.3	28.5	1.6	1.3	0.3
Arson	100.0	67.8	28.7	1.9	1.3	0.3	5,608	4,031	1,356	111	84	26	100.0	71.9	24.2	2.0	1.5	0.5
Other assaults	100.0	58.8	38.4	1.7	0.9	0.3	701,782	457,339	218,686	14,165	9,516	2,076	100.0	65.2	31.2	2.0	1.4	0.3
Forgery and counterfeiting	100.0	57.1	40.3	0.8	1.4	0.4	36,945	24,695	11,323	329	537	61	100.0	66.8	30.6	0.9	1.5	0.2
Fraud	100.0	41.4	55.6	1.9	1.0	0.1	86,111	57,125	26,443	1,352	1,052	139	100.0	66.3	30.7	1.6	1.2	0.2
Embezzlement	100.0	52.6	43.2	0.9	2.8	0.5	10,739	6,694	3,767	118	147	13	100.0	62.3	35.1	1.1	1.4	0.1
Stolen property; buying, receiving, possessing	100.0	37.5	59.4	1.1	1.4	0.6	62,938	41,581	19,538	805	724	290	100.0	66.1	31.0	1.3	1.2	0.5
Vandalism	100.0	67.8	29.1	2.2	0.9	0.1	112,041	75,758	32,275	2,453	1,355	200	100.0	67.6	28.8	2.2	1.2	0.2
Weapons; carrying, possessing, etc.	100.0	54.4	42.8	1.0	1.4	0.3	113,492	61,773	49,214	960	1,206	339	100.0	54.4	43.4	0.8	1.1	0.3
Prostitution and commercialized vice	100.0	59.3	37.7	1.5	1.0	0.5	23,303	12,810	9,034	92	1,307	60	100.0	55.0	38.8	0.4	5.6	0.3
Sex offenses (except forcible rape and prostitution)	100.0	72.7	24.4	1.1	1.5	0.3	29,572	21,276	7,042	526	667	61	100.0	71.9	23.8	1.8	2.3	0.2
Drug abuse violations	100.0	73.5	22.8	2.0	1.3	0.3	1,167,082	821,984	317,809	12,791	12,443	2,055	100.0	70.4	27.2	1.1	1.1	0.2
Gambling	100.0	22.4	76.9	0.7	0.0	0.0	2,331	970	1,095	10	205	51	100.0	41.6	47.0	0.4	8.8	2.2
Offenses against the family and children	100.0	68.4	23.4	7.4	0.7	*	61,910	41,697	17,957	1,714	492	50	100.0	67.4	29.0	2.8	0.8	0.1
Driving under the influence	100.0	87.8	7.0	3.3	1.6	0.3	732,646	594,407	108,425	13,017	14,259	2,538	100.0	81.1	14.8	1.8	1.9	0.3
Liquor laws	100.0	87.2	6.5	4.9	1.2	0.2	108,923	83,666	17,483	6,014	1,632	128	100.0	76.8	16.1	5.5	1.5	0.1
Drunkenness	100.0	80.2	12.7	5.6	1.3	0.2	249,011	191,053	37,465	17,274	2,793	426	100.0	76.7	15.0	6.9	1.1	0.2
Disorderly conduct	100.0	55.1	42.2	2.0	0.7	0.1	205,095	134,516	59,775	8,903	1,640	261	100.0	65.6	29.1	4.3	0.8	0.1
Vagrancy	100.0	50.5	46.9	1.5	0.8	0.4	17,523	12,558	4,212	474	257	22	100.0	71.7	24.0	2.7	1.5	0.1
All other offenses (except traffic)	100.0	67.3	29.7	1.8	0.9	0.2	2,309,275	1,596,694	632,157	52,517	22,580	5,327	100.0	69.1	27.4	2.3	1.0	0.2
Suspicion	100.0	59.0	30.8	10.3	0.0	0.0	393	214	117	61	1	0	100.0	54.5	29.8	15.5	0.3	0.0
Curfew and loitering law violations	100.0	56.0	41.0	1.6	1.1	0.3	NA	NA	NA	NA	NA	NA	NA	NA	NA	NA	NA	NA

NA = Not available.
* = Less than one-tenth of one percent.
1 Because of rounding, the percentages may not sum to 100.   2 Violent crimes are offenses of murder and nonnegligent manslaughter, rape, robbery, and aggravated assault. Property crimes are offenses of burglary, larceny-theft, motor vehicle theft, and arson.   3 The rape figures in this table are aggregate totals of the data submitted based on both the legacy and revised Uniform Crime Reporting definitions.

Table 43A. Arrests, Distribution by Ethnicity, 2018

(Number, percent; 12,212 agencies; 2018 estimated population 247,752,415.)

Offense charged	Total arrests			Percent distribution[1]			Arrests under 18		
	Total[2]	Hispanic or Latino	Not Hispanic or Latino	Total[2]	Hispanic or Latino	Not Hispanic or Latino	Total[2]	Hispanic or Latino	Not Hispanic or Latino
Total	6,343,684	1,191,334	5,152,350	100.0	18.8	81.2	442,254	100,207	342,047
Violent crime[3]	334,028	83,441	250,587	100.0	25.0	75.0	31,906	8,381	23,525
Murder and nonnegligent manslaughter	7,050	1,472	5,578	100.0	20.9	79.1	535	149	386
Rape[4]	15,316	4,090	11,226	100.0	26.7	73.3	2,470	546	1,924
Robbery	57,048	12,823	44,225	100.0	22.5	77.5	11,262	2,802	8,460
Aggravated assault	254,614	65,056	189,558	100.0	25.6	74.4	17,639	4,884	12,755
Property crime[3]	716,254	116,753	599,501	100.0	16.3	83.7	78,824	16,710	62,114
Burglary	114,027	23,200	90,827	100.0	20.3	79.7	13,323	3,286	10,037
Larceny-theft	540,174	78,106	462,068	100.0	14.5	85.5	55,719	11,069	44,650
Motor vehicle theft	56,263	14,392	41,871	100.0	25.6	74.4	8,672	2,161	6,511
Arson	5,790	1,055	4,735	100.0	18.2	81.8	1,110	194	916
Other assaults	654,150	125,007	529,143	100.0	19.1	80.9	77,796	17,615	60,181
Forgery and counterfeiting	31,565	5,301	26,264	100.0	16.8	83.2	630	131	499
Fraud	74,521	9,636	64,885	100.0	12.9	87.1	3,047	433	2,614
Embezzlement	9,252	1,193	8,059	100.0	12.9	87.1	374	74	300
Stolen property; buying, receiving, possessing	57,379	11,278	46,101	100.0	19.7	80.3	5,709	1,222	4,487
Vandalism	112,716	21,479	91,237	100.0	19.1	80.9	19,361	3,953	15,408
Weapons; carrying, possessing, etc.	100,312	23,663	76,649	100.0	23.6	76.4	10,496	3,285	7,211
Prostitution and commercialized vice	21,484	4,379	17,105	100.0	20.4	79.6	177	35	142
Sex offenses (except forcible rape and prostitution)	28,928	7,398	21,530	100.0	25.6	74.4	4,538	1,065	3,473
Drug abuse violations	1,044,789	211,692	833,097	100.0	20.3	79.7	56,133	15,373	40,760
Gambling	1,390	341	1,049	100.0	24.5	75.5	77	10	67
Offenses against the family and children	51,589	5,999	45,590	100.0	11.6	88.4	1,892	301	1,591
Driving under the influence	604,136	147,221	456,915	100.0	24.4	75.6	3,222	882	2,340
Liquor laws	102,624	15,979	86,645	100.0	15.6	84.4	16,080	2,994	13,086
Drunkenness	233,325	52,491	180,834	100.0	22.5	77.5	2,321	862	1,459
Disorderly conduct	186,261	24,553	161,708	100.0	13.2	86.8	32,530	5,948	26,582
Vagrancy	16,649	2,557	14,092	100.0	15.4	84.6	394	86	308
All other offenses (except traffic)	1,947,281	317,928	1,629,353	100.0	16.3	83.7	82,061	17,815	64,246
Suspicion	390	15	375	100.0	3.8	96.2	25	2	23
Curfew and loitering law violations	14,661	3,030	11,631	100.0	20.7	79.3	14,661	3,030	11,631

Table 43A. Arrests, Distribution by Ethnicity, 2018—Continued

(Number, percent; 12,212 agencies; 2018 estimated population 247,752,415.)

Offense charged	Percent distribution[1]			Arrests 18 and over			Percent distribution[1]		
	Total[2]	Hispanic or Latino	Not Hispanic or Latino	Total[2]	Hispanic or Latino	Not Hispanic or Latino	Total[2]	Hispanic or Latino	Not Hispanic or Latino
Total	100.0	22.7	77.3	5,901,430	1,091,127	4,810,303	100.0	18.5	81.5
Violent crime[3]	100.0	26.3	73.7	302,122	75,060	227,062	100.0	24.8	75.2
Murder and nonnegligent manslaughter	100.0	27.9	72.1	6,515	1,323	5,192	100.0	20.3	79.7
Rape[4]	100.0	22.1	77.9	12,846	3,544	9,302	100.0	27.6	72.4
Robbery	100.0	24.9	75.1	45,786	10,021	35,765	100.0	21.9	78.1
Aggravated assault	100.0	27.7	72.3	236,975	60,172	176,803	100.0	25.4	74.6
Property crime[3]	100.0	21.2	78.8	637,430	100,043	537,387	100.0	15.7	84.3
Burglary	100.0	24.7	75.3	100,704	19,914	80,790	100.0	19.8	80.2
Larceny-theft	100.0	19.9	80.1	484,455	67,037	417,418	100.0	13.8	86.2
Motor vehicle theft	100.0	24.9	75.1	47,591	12,231	35,360	100.0	25.7	74.3
Arson	100.0	17.5	82.5	4,680	861	3,819	100.0	18.4	81.6
Other assaults	100.0	22.6	77.4	576,354	107,392	468,962	100.0	18.6	81.4
Forgery and counterfeiting	100.0	20.8	79.2	30,935	5,170	25,765	100.0	16.7	83.3
Fraud	100.0	14.2	85.8	71,474	9,203	62,271	100.0	12.9	87.1
Embezzlement	100.0	19.8	80.2	8,878	1,119	7,759	100.0	12.6	87.4
Stolen property; buying, receiving, possessing	100.0	21.4	78.6	51,670	10,056	41,614	100.0	19.5	80.5
Vandalism	100.0	20.4	79.6	93,355	17,526	75,829	100.0	18.8	81.2
Weapons; carrying, possessing, etc.	100.0	31.3	68.7	89,816	20,378	69,438	100.0	22.7	77.3
Prostitution and commercialized vice	100.0	19.8	80.2	21,307	4,344	16,963	100.0	20.4	79.6
Sex offenses (except forcible rape and prostitution)	100.0	23.5	76.5	24,390	6,333	18,057	100.0	26.0	74.0
Drug abuse violations	100.0	27.4	72.6	988,656	196,319	792,337	100.0	19.9	80.1
Gambling	100.0	13.0	87.0	1,313	331	982	100.0	25.2	74.8
Offenses against the family and children	100.0	15.9	84.1	49,697	5,698	43,999	100.0	11.5	88.5
Driving under the influence	100.0	27.4	72.6	600,914	146,339	454,575	100.0	24.4	75.6
Liquor laws	100.0	18.6	81.4	86,544	12,985	73,559	100.0	15.0	85.0
Drunkenness	100.0	37.1	62.9	231,004	51,629	179,375	100.0	22.3	77.7
Disorderly conduct	100.0	18.3	81.7	153,731	18,605	135,126	100.0	12.1	87.9
Vagrancy	100.0	21.8	78.2	16,255	2,471	13,784	100.0	15.2	84.8
All other offenses (except traffic)	100.0	21.7	78.3	1,865,220	300,113	1,565,107	100.0	16.1	83.9
Suspicion	100.0	8.0	92.0	365	13	352	100.0	3.6	96.4
Curfew and loitering law violations	100.0	20.7	79.3	NA	NA	NA	NA	NA	NA

NA = Not available.
1 Because of rounding, the percentages may not sum to 100.   2 The ethnicity totals are representative of those agencies that provided ethnicity breakdowns. Not all agencies provide ethnicity data; therefore, the race and ethnicity totals will not be equal.   3 Violent crimes are offenses of murder and nonnegligent manslaughter, rape, robbery, and aggravated assault. Property crimes are offenses of burglary, larceny-theft, motor vehicle theft, and arson.   4 The rape figures in this table are aggregate totals of the data submitted based on both the legacy and revised Uniform Crime Reporting definitions.

Table 44. Arrest Trends, Cities, 2017–2018

(Number, percent change; 8,353 agencies; 2018 estimated population 162,937,279; 2017 estimated population 161,952,747.)

Offense charged	Number of persons arrested								
	Total, all ages			Under 18 years of age			18 years of age and over		
	2017	2018	Percent change	2017	2018	Percent change	2017	2018	Percent change
Total[1]	5,432,009	5,266,216	-3.1	458,425	405,981	-11.4	4,973,584	4,860,235	-2.3
Violent crime[2]	287,227	288,923	+0.6	29,983	28,281	-5.7	257,244	260,642	+1.3
Murder and nonnegligent manslaughter	6,143	5,940	-3.3	469	475	+1.3	5,674	5,465	-3.7
Rape[3]	12,552	12,763	+1.7	2,188	2,061	-5.8	10,364	10,702	+3.3
Robbery	57,465	52,581	-8.5	11,779	10,301	-12.5	45,686	42,280	-7.5
Aggravated assault	211,067	217,639	+3.1	15,547	15,444	-0.7	195,520	202,195	+3.4
Property crime[2]	720,130	668,639	-7.2	97,526	76,229	-21.8	622,604	592,410	-4.8
Burglary	106,718	96,337	-9.7	16,987	12,431	-26.8	89,731	83,906	-6.5
Larceny-theft	562,312	521,359	-7.3	71,043	54,855	-22.8	491,269	466,504	-5.0
Motor vehicle theft	46,116	46,280	+0.4	8,172	7,973	-2.4	37,944	38,307	+1.0
Arson	4,984	4,663	-6.4	1,324	970	-26.7	3,660	3,693	+0.9
Other assaults	574,330	570,200	-0.7	66,838	65,755	-1.6	507,492	504,445	-0.6
Forgery and counterfeiting	29,452	26,510	-10.0	688	562	-18.3	28,764	25,948	-9.8
Fraud	62,837	61,470	-2.2	2,864	2,830	-1.2	59,973	58,640	-2.2
Embezzlement	9,270	8,626	-6.9	413	370	-10.4	8,857	8,256	-6.8
Stolen property; buying, receiving, possessing	52,375	50,516	-3.5	6,236	5,635	-9.6	46,139	44,881	-2.7
Vandalism	104,918	99,223	-5.4	20,627	16,972	-17.7	84,291	82,251	-2.4
Weapons; carrying, possessing, etc.	86,876	86,727	-0.2	10,261	9,449	-7.9	76,615	77,278	+0.9
Prostitution and commercialized vice	23,683	20,422	-13.8	201	149	-25.9	23,482	20,273	-13.7
Sex offenses (except forcible rape and prostitution)	24,692	23,958	-3.0	4,242	3,870	-8.8	20,450	20,088	-1.8
Drug abuse violations	827,924	829,358	+0.2	51,901	48,703	-6.2	776,023	780,655	+0.6
Gambling	1,234	1,057	-14.3	98	61	-37.8	1,136	996	-12.3
Offenses against the family and children	31,876	30,469	-4.4	2,012	1,671	-16.9	29,864	28,798	-3.6
Driving under the influence	414,105	406,674	-1.8	2,689	2,337	-13.1	411,416	404,337	-1.7
Liquor laws	115,550	95,175	-17.6	17,683	13,639	-22.9	97,867	81,536	-16.7
Drunkenness	226,713	206,506	-8.9	2,545	2,079	-18.3	224,168	204,427	-8.8
Disorderly conduct	207,049	192,786	-6.9	36,824	34,060	-7.5	170,225	158,726	-6.8
Vagrancy	15,325	15,889	+3.7	437	415	-5.0	14,888	15,474	+3.9
All other offenses (except traffic)	1,595,525	1,568,136	-1.7	83,439	77,962	-6.6	1,512,086	1,490,174	-1.4
Suspicion	276	153	-44.6	27	27	0.0	249	126	-49.4
Curfew and loitering law violations	20,918	14,952	-28.5	20,918	14,952	-28.5	NA	NA	NA

NA = Not available.

1 Does not include suspicion.   2 Violent crimes are offenses of murder and nonnegligent manslaughter, rape, robbery, and aggravated assault. Property crimes are offenses of burglary, larceny-theft, motor vehicle theft, and arson.   3 The rape figures in this table are aggregate totals of the data submitted based on both the legacy and revised Uniform Crime Reporting definitions.

Table 45. Arrest Trends, Cities, by Age and Sex, 2017–2018

(Number, percent change; 8,353 agencies; 2018 estimated population 162,937,279; 2017 estimated population 161,952,747.)

Offense charged	Male Total 2017	2018	Percent change	Male Under 18 2017	2018	Percent change	Female Total 2017	2018	Percent change	Female Under 18 2017	2018	Percent change
Total[1]	3,950,169	3,812,186	-3.5	323,926	283,885	-12.4	1,481,840	1,454,030	-1.9	134,499	122,096	-9.2
Violent crime[2]	227,016	226,883	-0.1	24,450	22,621	-7.5	60,211	62,040	+3.0	5,533	5,660	+2.3
Murder and nonnegligent manslaughter	5,405	5,226	-3.3	430	426	-0.9	738	714	-3.3	39	49	+25.6
Rape[3]	12,141	12,356	+1.8	2,091	1,964	-6.1	411	407	-1.0	97	97	0.0
Robbery	48,963	44,430	-9.3	10,496	9,089	-13.4	8,502	8,151	-4.1	1,283	1,212	-5.5
Aggravated assault	160,507	164,871	+2.7	11,433	11,142	-2.5	50,560	52,768	+4.4	4,114	4,302	+4.6
Property crime[2]	456,135	415,936	-8.8	66,940	51,108	-23.7	263,995	252,703	-4.3	30,586	25,121	-17.9
Burglary	86,164	76,824	-10.8	14,951	10,754	-28.1	20,554	19,513	-5.1	2,036	1,677	-17.6
Larceny-theft	330,296	299,763	-9.2	44,182	33,062	-25.2	232,016	221,596	-4.5	26,861	21,793	-18.9
Motor vehicle theft	35,712	35,755	+0.1	6,676	6,493	-2.7	10,404	10,525	+1.2	1,496	1,480	-1.1
Arson	3,963	3,594	-9.3	1,131	799	-29.4	1,021	1,069	+4.7	193	171	-11.4
Other assaults	407,269	403,669	-0.9	41,477	41,028	-1.1	167,061	166,531	-0.3	25,361	24,727	-2.5
Forgery and counterfeiting	19,492	17,644	-9.5	541	456	-15.7	9,960	8,866	-11.0	147	106	-27.9
Fraud	39,504	39,341	-0.4	1,917	1,949	+1.7	23,333	22,129	-5.2	947	881	-7.0
Embezzlement	4,741	4,270	-9.9	244	214	-12.3	4,529	4,356	-3.8	169	156	-7.7
Stolen property; buying, receiving, possessing	40,756	39,291	-3.6	5,271	4,729	-10.3	11,619	11,225	-3.4	965	906	-6.1
Vandalism	81,269	76,038	-6.4	16,950	13,691	-19.2	23,649	23,185	-2.0	3,677	3,281	-10.8
Weapons; carrying, possessing, etc.	79,046	78,604	-0.6	9,204	8,415	-8.6	7,830	8,123	+3.7	1,057	1,034	-2.2
Prostitution and commercialized vice	8,648	6,793	-21.5	59	50	-15.3	15,035	13,629	-9.4	142	99	-30.3
Sex offenses (except forcible rape and prostitution)	22,807	22,284	-2.3	3,715	3,454	-7.0	1,885	1,674	-11.2	527	416	-21.1
Drug abuse violations	631,504	627,864	-0.6	39,563	36,341	-8.1	196,420	201,494	+2.6	12,338	12,362	+0.2
Gambling	957	805	-15.9	85	56	-34.1	277	252	-9.0	13	5	-61.5
Offenses against the family and children	20,425	19,590	-4.1	1,258	986	-21.6	11,451	10,879	-5.0	754	685	-9.2
Driving under the influence	306,751	300,409	-2.1	2,013	1,732	-14.0	107,354	106,265	-1.0	676	605	-10.5
Liquor laws	80,524	66,192	-17.8	10,453	7,873	-24.7	35,026	28,983	-17.3	7,230	5,766	-20.2
Drunkenness	180,844	164,103	-9.3	1,798	1,450	-19.4	45,869	42,403	-7.6	747	629	-15.8
Disorderly conduct	145,432	135,001	-7.2	23,345	21,574	-7.6	61,617	57,785	-6.2	13,479	12,486	-7.4
Vagrancy	11,595	12,056	+4.0	343	324	-5.5	3,730	3,833	+2.8	94	91	-3.2
All other offenses (except traffic)	1,170,664	1,144,882	-2.2	59,510	55,303	-7.1	424,861	423,254	-0.4	23,929	22,659	-5.3
Suspicion	217	119	-45.2	20	17	-15.0	59	34	-42.4	7	10	+42.9
Curfew and loitering law violations	14,790	10,531	-28.8	14,790	10,531	-28.8	6,128	4,421	-27.9	6,128	4,421	-27.9

1 Does not include suspicion.   2 Violent crimes are offenses of murder and nonnegligent manslaughter, rape, robbery, and aggravated assault. Property crimes are offenses of burglary, larceny-theft, motor vehicle theft, and arson.   3 The rape figures in this table are aggregate totals of the data submitted based on both the legacy and revised Uniform Crime Reporting definitions.

Table 46. Arrests, Cities, Distribution by Age, 2018

(Number, percent; 8,967 agencies; 2018 estimated population 172,802,238.)

Offense charged	Total, all ages	Ages under 15	Ages under 18	Ages 18 and over	Under 10	10–12	13–14	15	16	17	18	19	20
Total	5,660,751	132,538	438,355	5,222,396	2,597	30,492	99,449	84,180	102,051	119,586	163,972	172,836	172,517
Total percent distribution[1]	100.0	2.3	7.7	92.3	*	0.5	1.8	1.5	1.8	2.1	2.9	3.1	3.0
Violent crime[2]	305,648	9,042	30,355	275,293	134	2,167	6,741	5,792	7,287	8,234	9,921	9,638	9,537
Violent crime percent distribution[1]	100.0	3.0	9.9	90.1	*	0.7	2.2	1.9	2.4	2.7	3.2	3.2	3.1
Murder and nonnegligent manslaughter	6,719	47	531	6,188	0	1	46	76	152	256	368	372	343
Rape[3]	13,740	929	2,194	11,546	16	291	622	378	439	448	531	476	467
Robbery	56,841	2,270	11,215	45,626	10	249	2,011	2,427	3,090	3,428	3,921	3,176	2,579
Aggravated assault	228,348	5,796	16,415	211,933	108	1,626	4,062	2,911	3,606	4,102	5,101	5,614	6,148
Property crime[2]	723,477	23,735	83,251	640,226	415	4,949	18,371	17,041	20,028	22,447	26,480	24,156	21,771
Property crime percent distribution[1]	100.0	3.3	11.5	88.5	0.1	0.7	2.5	2.4	2.8	3.1	3.7	3.3	3.0
Burglary	101,535	3,998	13,168	88,367	131	831	3,036	2,837	3,055	3,278	3,903	3,383	3,106
Larceny-theft	564,524	16,862	59,824	504,700	235	3,646	12,981	11,746	14,450	16,766	20,407	18,902	17,007
Motor vehicle theft	52,376	2,278	9,205	43,171	10	261	2,007	2,280	2,370	2,277	2,037	1,786	1,561
Arson	5,042	597	1,054	3,988	39	211	347	178	153	126	133	85	97
Other assaults	616,990	29,979	71,533	545,457	622	8,369	20,988	13,793	14,233	13,528	14,530	14,217	15,446
Forgery and counterfeiting	28,226	135	645	27,581	2	32	101	87	150	273	791	1,127	1,276
Fraud	66,364	713	2,995	63,369	7	126	580	571	714	997	1,510	1,754	2,076
Embezzlement	9,067	20	395	8,672	1	2	17	28	114	233	443	468	454
Stolen property; buying, receiving, possessing	53,149	1,288	5,943	47,206	10	151	1,127	1,278	1,618	1,759	2,112	2,068	1,919
Vandalism	107,028	7,157	18,346	88,682	294	2,088	4,775	3,566	3,889	3,734	3,841	3,498	3,234
Weapons; carrying, possessing, etc.	97,680	2,926	10,530	87,150	108	771	2,047	1,923	2,440	3,241	3,936	4,077	3,776
Prostitution and commercialized vice	20,966	25	155	20,811	0	3	22	22	38	70	669	706	811
Sex offenses (except forcible rape and prostitution)	25,439	1,937	4,076	21,363	51	508	1,378	758	686	695	688	650	549
Drug abuse violations	888,318	9,507	52,666	835,652	68	1,494	7,945	8,561	13,262	21,336	37,816	38,130	35,464
Gambling	1,909	22	116	1,793	1	3	18	15	27	52	66	63	56
Offenses against the family and children	33,590	690	1,878	31,712	26	170	494	401	409	378	550	590	630
Driving under the influence	429,437	58	2,523	426,914	3	7	48	126	590	1,749	5,310	7,097	8,812
Liquor laws	103,908	2,110	14,598	89,310	15	213	1,882	2,394	3,861	6,233	13,729	15,195	12,490
Drunkenness	217,976	334	2,153	215,823	7	30	297	329	514	976	2,887	3,677	3,961
Disorderly conduct	206,822	14,709	36,250	170,572	238	3,880	10,591	7,330	7,562	6,649	6,054	5,667	5,621
Vagrancy	16,254	113	420	15,834	2	15	96	95	111	101	268	221	236
All other offenses (except traffic)	1,692,876	23,229	84,035	1,608,841	501	4,527	18,201	16,621	20,436	23,749	32,367	39,836	44,392
Suspicion	165	13	30	135	0	3	10	3	5	9	4	1	6
Curfew and loitering law violations	15,462	4,796	15,462	NA	92	984	3,720	3,446	4,077	3,143	NA	NA	NA

Table 46. Arrests, Cities, Distribution by Age, 2018—Continued

(Number, percent; 8,967 agencies; 2018 estimated population 172,802,238.)

Offense charged	21	22	23	24	25–29	30–34	35–39	40–44	45–49	50–54	55–59	60–64	65 and over
Total	175,580	176,999	181,181	208,961	967,031	813,268	666,810	448,664	367,726	298,768	221,285	113,242	73,556
Total percent distribution[1]	3.1	3.1	3.2	3.7	17.1	14.4	11.8	7.9	6.5	5.3	3.9	2.0	1.3
Violent crime[2]	10,005	9,976	10,101	12,307	53,130	43,195	33,758	22,562	17,451	14,313	10,416	5,239	3,744
Violent crime percent distribution[1]	3.3	3.3	3.3	4.0	17.4	14.1	11.0	7.4	5.7	4.7	3.4	1.7	1.2
Murder and nonnegligent manslaughter	288	284	278	418	1,256	821	613	356	240	215	162	87	87
Rape[3]	460	390	363	429	1,770	1,668	1,482	1,068	787	618	502	267	268
Robbery	2,254	2,078	2,019	2,889	8,843	6,272	4,320	2,507	1,852	1,502	954	325	135
Aggravated assault	7,003	7,224	7,441	8,571	41,261	34,434	27,343	18,631	14,572	11,978	8,798	4,560	3,254
Property crime[2]	20,248	19,924	20,366	25,267	116,680	102,794	83,344	54,583	45,362	35,905	24,510	11,586	7,250
Property crime percent distribution[1]	2.8	2.8	2.8	3.5	16.1	14.2	11.5	7.5	6.3	5.0	3.4	1.6	1.0
Burglary	2,944	3,070	3,028	3,486	17,239	14,762	11,711	7,102	5,829	4,318	2,784	1,113	589
Larceny-theft	15,632	15,149	15,635	18,322	89,776	80,178	65,621	43,984	36,954	29,897	20,745	10,048	6,443
Motor vehicle theft	1,558	1,596	1,602	3,336	9,025	7,270	5,446	3,131	2,234	1,407	777	276	129
Arson	114	109	101	123	640	584	566	366	345	283	204	149	89
Other assaults	17,678	18,563	19,190	23,769	103,608	86,501	71,320	48,619	39,311	30,780	22,169	11,371	8,385
Forgery and counterfeiting	796	868	854	967	4,972	4,790	4,089	2,487	1,828	1,343	815	370	208
Fraud	1,864	2,001	2,128	2,212	11,974	11,059	8,954	5,939	4,482	3,385	2,182	1,099	750
Embezzlement	413	344	371	339	1,572	1,248	962	734	524	366	235	117	82
Stolen property; buying, receiving, possessing	1,666	1,642	1,731	1,902	9,709	8,150	6,467	3,771	2,689	1,780	1,021	413	166
Vandalism	3,797	3,599	3,597	4,375	18,146	13,836	10,515	6,494	4,990	3,801	2,760	1,304	895
Weapons; carrying, possessing, etc.	4,067	4,123	3,993	6,369	18,344	12,753	9,487	5,660	3,878	2,887	1,959	1,076	765
Prostitution and commercialized vice	922	944	939	912	4,160	2,983	2,324	1,657	1,385	1,049	645	366	339
Sex offenses (except forcible rape and prostitution)	603	564	575	584	2,966	2,752	2,599	1,969	1,844	1,612	1,425	915	1,068
Drug abuse violations	33,118	32,725	32,822	37,533	163,786	130,710	102,837	64,260	49,302	37,051	24,764	10,798	4,536
Gambling	70	74	76	321	296	196	158	120	90	75	55	39	38
Offenses against the family and children	738	822	906	1,123	6,297	6,077	5,195	3,177	2,198	1,627	939	527	316
Driving under the influence	14,474	15,772	16,447	16,956	79,252	63,020	51,012	38,302	33,721	28,241	23,456	13,987	11,055
Liquor laws	2,502	1,781	1,417	1,420	6,367	5,455	5,533	4,671	4,742	5,023	4,857	2,655	1,473
Drunkenness	6,655	6,351	6,430	6,554	33,085	29,757	26,834	20,987	20,120	19,033	16,429	8,480	4,583
Disorderly conduct	7,062	6,344	6,084	7,146	29,281	24,408	20,232	13,881	12,083	10,624	8,316	4,471	3,298
Vagrancy	244	246	326	335	1,990	1,989	2,103	1,595	1,775	1,723	1,466	851	466
All other offenses (except traffic)	48,652	50,331	52,824	58,566	301,396	261,568	219,075	147,188	119,941	98,136	72,858	37,574	24,137
Suspicion	6	5	4	4	20	27	12	8	10	14	8	4	2
Curfew and loitering law violations	NA	NA	NA	NA	NA	NA	NA	NA	NA	NA	NA	NA	NA

NA = Not available.
* = Less than one-tenth of one percent.
1 Because of rounding, the percentages may not sum to 100.   2 Violent crimes are offenses of murder and nonnegligent manslaughter, rape, robbery, and aggravated assault.   Property crimes are offenses of burglary, larceny-theft, motor vehicle theft, and arson.   3 The rape figures in this table are aggregate totals of the data submitted based on both the legacy and revised Uniform Crime Reporting definitions.

Table 47. Arrests, Cities, Persons Under 15, 18, 21, and 25 Years of Age, 2018

(Number; percent; 8,967 agencies; 2018 estimated population 172,802,238.)

Offense charged	Total, all ages	Number of persons arrested				Percent of total of all ages			
		Under 15	Under 18	Under 21	Under 25	Under 15	Under 18	Under 21	Under 25
Total	5,660,751	132,538	438,355	947,680	1,690,401	2.3	7.7	16.7	29.9
Violent crime[1]	305,648	9,042	30,355	59,451	101,840	3.0	9.9	19.5	33.3
Murder and nonnegligent manslaughter	6,719	47	531	1,614	2,882	0.7	7.9	24.0	42.9
Rape[2]	13,740	929	2,194	3,668	5,310	6.8	16.0	26.7	38.6
Robbery	56,841	2,270	11,215	20,891	30,131	4.0	19.7	36.8	53.0
Aggravated assault	228,348	5,796	16,415	33,278	63,517	2.5	7.2	14.6	27.8
Property crime[1]	723,477	23,735	83,251	155,658	241,463	3.3	11.5	21.5	33.4
Burglary	101,535	3,998	13,168	23,560	36,088	3.9	13.0	23.2	35.5
Larceny-theft	564,524	16,862	59,824	116,140	180,878	3.0	10.6	20.6	32.0
Motor vehicle theft	52,376	2,278	9,205	14,589	22,681	4.3	17.6	27.9	43.3
Arson	5,042	597	1,054	1,369	1,816	11.8	20.9	27.2	36.0
Other assaults	616,990	29,979	71,533	115,726	194,926	4.9	11.6	18.8	31.6
Forgery and counterfeiting	28,226	135	645	3,839	7,324	0.5	2.3	13.6	25.9
Fraud	66,364	713	2,995	8,335	16,540	1.1	4.5	12.6	24.9
Embezzlement	9,067	20	395	1,760	3,227	0.2	4.4	19.4	35.6
Stolen property; buying, receiving, possessing	53,149	1,288	5,943	12,042	18,983	2.4	11.2	22.7	35.7
Vandalism	107,028	7,157	18,346	28,919	44,287	6.7	17.1	27.0	41.4
Weapons; carrying, possessing, etc.	97,680	2,926	10,530	22,319	40,871	3.0	10.8	22.8	41.8
Prostitution and commercialized vice	20,966	25	155	2,341	6,058	0.1	0.7	11.2	28.9
Sex offenses (except forcible rape and prostitution)	25,439	1,937	4,076	5,963	8,289	7.6	16.0	23.4	32.6
Drug abuse violations	888,318	9,507	52,666	164,076	300,274	1.1	5.9	18.5	33.8
Gambling	1,909	22	116	301	842	1.2	6.1	15.8	44.1
Offenses against the family and children	33,590	690	1,878	3,648	7,237	2.1	5.6	10.9	21.5
Driving under the influence	429,437	58	2,523	23,742	87,391	*	0.6	5.5	20.4
Liquor laws	103,908	2,110	14,598	56,012	63,132	2.0	14.0	53.9	60.8
Drunkenness	217,976	334	2,153	12,678	38,668	0.2	1.0	5.8	17.7
Disorderly conduct	206,822	14,709	36,250	53,592	80,228	7.1	17.5	25.9	38.8
Vagrancy	16,254	113	420	1,145	2,296	0.7	2.6	7.0	14.1
All other offenses (except traffic)	1,692,876	23,229	84,035	200,630	411,003	1.4	5.0	11.9	24.3
Suspicion	165	13	30	41	60	7.9	18.2	24.8	36.4
Curfew and loitering law violations	15,462	4,796	15,462	15,462	15,462	31.0	100.0	100.0	100.0

* = Less than one-tenth of one percent.
1 Violent crimes are offenses of murder and nonnegligent manslaughter, rape, robbery, and aggravated assault. Property crimes are offenses of burglary, larceny-theft, motor vehicle theft, and arson.   2 The rape figures in this table are aggregate totals of the data submitted based on both the legacy and revised Uniform Crime Reporting definitions.

Table 48. Arrests, Cities, Distribution by Sex, 2018

(Number, percent; 8,967 agencies; 2018 estimated population 172,802,23.)

Offense charged	Number of persons arrested			Percent male	Percent female	Percent distribution[1]		
	Total	Male	Female			Total	Male	Female
Total	5,660,751	4,103,093	1,557,658	72.5	27.5	100.0	100.0	100.0
Violent crime[2]	305,648	240,665	64,983	78.7	21.3	5.4	5.9	4.2
Murder and nonnegligent manslaughter	6,719	5,912	807	88.0	12.0	0.1	0.1	0.1
Rape[3]	13,740	13,310	430	96.9	3.1	0.2	0.3	0.0
Robbery	56,841	48,236	8,605	84.9	15.1	1.0	1.2	0.6
Aggravated assault	228,348	173,207	55,141	75.9	24.1	4.0	4.2	3.5
Property crime[2]	723,477	451,024	272,453	62.3	37.7	12.8	11.0	17.5
Burglary	101,535	81,251	20,284	80.0	20.0	1.8	2.0	1.3
Larceny-theft	564,524	325,338	239,186	57.6	42.4	10.0	7.9	15.4
Motor vehicle theft	52,376	40,538	11,838	77.4	22.6	0.9	1.0	0.8
Arson	5,042	3,897	1,145	77.3	22.7	0.1	0.1	0.1
Other assaults	616,990	437,260	179,730	70.9	29.1	10.9	10.7	11.5
Forgery and counterfeiting	28,226	18,750	9,476	66.4	33.6	0.5	0.5	0.6
Fraud	66,364	42,581	23,783	64.2	35.8	1.2	1.0	1.5
Embezzlement	9,067	4,488	4,579	49.5	50.5	0.2	0.1	0.3
Stolen property; buying, receiving, possessing	53,149	41,352	11,797	77.8	22.2	0.9	1.0	0.8
Vandalism	107,028	81,939	25,089	76.6	23.4	1.9	2.0	1.6
Weapons; carrying, possessing, etc.	97,680	88,859	8,821	91.0	9.0	1.7	2.2	0.6
Prostitution and commercialized vice	20,966	7,012	13,954	33.4	66.6	0.4	0.2	0.9
Sex offenses (except forcible rape and prostitution)	25,439	23,636	1,803	92.9	7.1	0.4	0.6	0.1
Drug abuse violations	888,318	674,130	214,188	75.9	24.1	15.7	16.4	13.8
Gambling	1,909	1,623	286	85.0	15.0	*	*	*
Offenses against the family and children	33,590	21,405	12,185	63.7	36.3	0.6	0.5	0.8
Driving under the influence	429,437	317,280	112,157	73.9	26.1	7.6	7.7	7.2
Liquor laws	103,908	72,588	31,320	69.9	30.1	1.8	1.8	2.0
Drunkenness	217,976	173,210	44,766	79.5	20.5	3.9	4.2	2.9
Disorderly conduct	206,822	145,391	61,431	70.3	29.7	3.7	3.5	3.9
Vagrancy	16,254	12,337	3,917	75.9	24.1	0.3	0.3	0.3
All other offenses (except traffic)	1,692,876	1,236,563	456,313	73.0	27.0	29.9	30.1	29.3
Suspicion	165	129	36	78.2	21.8	*	*	*
Curfew and loitering law violations	15,462	10,871	4,591	70.3	29.7	0.3	0.3	0.3

* = Less than one-tenth of 1 percent.
1 Because of rounding, the percentages may not sum to 100.   2 Violent crimes are offenses of murder and nonnegligent manslaughter, rape, robbery, and aggravated assault.   Property crimes are offenses of burglary, larceny-theft, motor vehicle theft, and arson.   3 The rape figures in this table are aggregate totals of the data submitted based on both the legacy and revised Uniform Crime Reporting definitions.

Table 49. Arrests, Cities, Distribution by Race, 2018

(Number, percent; 8,967 agencies; 2018 estimated population 172,802,238.)

Offense charged	Total arrests — Total	White	Black	American Indian or Alaskan Native	Asian	Native Hawaiian or Other Pacific Islander	Percent distribution[1] — Total	White	Black	American Indian or Alaskan Native	Asian	Native Hawaiian or Other Pacific Islander	Arrests under 18 — Total	White	Black	American Indian or Alaskan Native	Asian	Native Hawaiian or Other Pacific Islander
Total	5,583,383	3,734,292	1,633,054	131,935	70,285	13,817	100.0	66.9	29.2	2.4	1.3	0.2	429,648	262,293	152,984	8,475	4,829	1,067
Violent crime[2]	302,505	168,500	121,232	6,184	5,185	1,404	100.0	55.7	40.1	2.0	1.7	0.5	29,930	14,306	14,773	375	356	120
Murder and nonnegligent manslaughter	6,634	2,590	3,859	81	80	24	100.0	39.0	58.2	1.2	1.2	0.4	528	194	323	5	3	3
Rape[3]	13,501	8,615	4,411	196	247	32	100.0	63.8	32.7	1.5	1.8	0.2	2,134	1,382	704	21	22	5
Robbery	56,271	24,076	30,825	564	572	234	100.0	42.8	54.8	1.0	1.0	0.4	11,086	3,777	7,084	60	108	57
Aggravated assault	226,099	133,219	82,137	5,343	4,286	1,114	100.0	58.9	36.3	2.4	1.9	0.5	16,182	8,953	6,662	289	223	55
Property crime[2]	710,768	469,017	219,015	13,162	8,002	1,572	100.0	66.0	30.8	1.9	1.1	0.2	81,456	44,465	34,237	1,442	1,071	241
Burglary	100,385	65,323	32,391	1,219	1,192	260	100.0	65.1	32.3	1.2	1.2	0.3	12,965	6,887	5,706	205	131	36
Larceny-theft	553,430	368,898	166,338	10,939	6,060	1,195	100.0	66.7	30.1	2.0	1.1	0.2	58,355	33,053	23,213	1,051	853	185
Motor vehicle theft	51,994	31,413	18,922	900	666	93	100.0	60.4	36.4	1.7	1.3	0.2	9,119	3,831	5,033	168	71	16
Arson	4,959	3,383	1,364	104	84	24	100.0	68.2	27.5	2.1	1.7	0.5	1,017	694	285	18	16	4
Other assaults	604,982	371,588	210,116	12,589	8,721	1,968	100.0	61.4	34.7	2.1	1.4	0.3	69,750	40,893	26,738	1,197	697	225
Forgery and counterfeiting	27,900	18,518	8,640	274	411	57	100.0	66.4	31.0	1.0	1.5	0.2	634	340	275	6	10	3
Fraud	65,376	41,534	21,728	1,156	833	125	100.0	63.5	33.2	1.8	1.3	0.2	2,945	1,110	1,740	56	35	4
Embezzlement	8,987	5,439	3,292	112	131	13	100.0	60.5	36.6	1.2	1.5	0.1	388	201	169	4	12	2
Stolen property; buying, receiving, possessing	52,172	31,664	18,815	701	679	313	100.0	60.7	36.1	1.3	1.3	0.6	5,789	2,106	3,494	63	84	42
Vandalism	105,051	68,936	32,184	2,458	1,281	192	100.0	65.6	30.6	2.3	1.2	0.2	17,850	11,986	5,269	409	165	21
Weapons; carrying, possessing, etc.	96,666	49,899	44,577	779	1,122	289	100.0	51.6	46.1	0.8	1.2	0.3	10,379	5,601	4,481	109	158	30
Prostitution and commercialized vice	20,789	11,421	8,168	81	1,064	55	100.0	54.9	39.3	0.4	5.1	0.3	155	88	64	1	1	1
Sex offenses (except forcible rape and prostitution)	25,136	17,460	6,507	475	624	70	100.0	69.5	25.9	1.9	2.5	0.3	3,970	2,861	985	33	75	16
Drug abuse violations	875,127	607,647	245,844	10,119	9,827	1,690	100.0	69.4	28.1	1.2	1.1	0.2	51,423	37,600	11,822	1,154	693	154
Gambling	1,902	677	1,076	8	131	10	100.0	35.6	56.6	0.4	6.9	0.5	116	28	87	1	0	0
Offenses against the family and children	33,207	21,800	9,347	1,638	387	35	100.0	65.6	28.1	4.9	1.2	0.1	1,854	1,220	459	160	14	1
Driving under the influence	423,592	342,123	62,752	8,826	7,929	1,962	100.0	80.8	14.8	2.1	1.9	0.5	2,487	2,149	181	103	45	9
Liquor laws	102,053	78,607	15,543	6,250	1,525	128	100.0	77.0	15.2	6.1	1.5	0.1	14,324	12,307	1,015	795	184	23
Drunkenness	216,892	163,662	33,622	16,787	2,436	385	100.0	75.5	15.5	7.7	1.1	0.2	2,123	1,683	275	133	28	4
Disorderly conduct	204,745	127,660	66,622	8,580	1,652	231	100.0	62.4	32.5	4.2	0.8	0.1	35,866	19,891	14,983	719	243	30
Vagrancy	16,187	11,476	3,982	457	249	23	100.0	70.9	24.6	2.8	1.5	0.1	418	206	199	8	3	2
All other offenses (except traffic)	1,673,879	1,118,228	493,420	40,997	17,947	3,287	100.0	66.8	29.5	2.4	1.1	0.2	82,464	54,862	25,199	1,466	806	131
Suspicion	172	64	43	65	0	0	100.0	37.2	25.0	37.8	0.0	0.0	32	18	10	4	0	0
Curfew and loitering law violations	15,295	8,372	6,529	237	149	8	100.0	54.7	42.7	1.5	1.0	0.1	15,295	8,372	6,529	237	149	8

Table 49. Arrests, Cities, Distribution by Race, 2018—Continued

(Number, percent; 8,967 agencies; 2018 estimated population 172,802,238.)

Offense charged	Percent distribution[1]						Arrests 18 and over						Percent distribution[1]					
	Total	White	Black	American Indian or Alaskan Native	Asian	Native Hawaiian or Other Pacific Islander	Total	White	Black	American Indian or Alaskan Native	Asian	Native Hawaiian or Other Pacific Islander	Total	White	Black	American Indian or Alaskan Native	Asian	Native Hawaiian or Other Pacific Islander
Total	100.0	61.0	35.6	2.0	1.1	0.2	5,153,735	3,471,999	1,480,070	123,460	65,456	12,750	100.0	67.4	28.7	2.4	1.3	0.2
Violent crime[2]	100.0	47.8	49.4	1.3	1.2	0.4	272,575	154,194	106,459	5,809	4,829	1,284	100.0	56.6	39.1	2.1	1.8	0.5
Murder and nonnegligent manslaughter	100.0	36.7	61.2	0.9	0.6	0.6	6,106	2,396	3,536	76	77	21	100.0	39.2	57.9	1.2	1.3	0.3
Rape[3]	100.0	64.8	33.0	1.0	1.0	0.2	11,367	7,233	3,707	175	225	27	100.0	63.6	32.6	1.5	2.0	0.2
Robbery	100.0	34.1	63.9	0.5	1.0	0.5	45,185	20,299	23,741	504	464	177	100.0	44.9	52.5	1.1	1.0	0.4
Aggravated assault	100.0	55.3	41.2	1.8	1.4	0.3	209,917	124,266	75,475	5,054	4,063	1,059	100.0	59.2	36.0	2.4	1.9	0.5
Property crime[2]	100.0	54.6	42.0	1.8	1.3	0.3	629,312	424,552	184,778	11,720	6,931	1,331	100.0	67.5	29.4	1.9	1.1	0.2
Burglary	100.0	53.1	44.0	1.6	1.0	0.3	87,420	58,436	26,685	1,014	1,061	224	100.0	66.8	30.5	1.2	1.2	0.3
Larceny-theft	100.0	56.6	39.8	1.8	1.5	0.3	495,075	335,845	143,125	9,888	5,207	1,010	100.0	67.8	28.9	2.0	1.1	0.2
Motor vehicle theft	100.0	42.0	55.2	1.8	0.8	0.2	42,875	27,582	13,889	732	595	77	100.0	64.3	32.4	1.7	1.4	0.2
Arson	100.0	68.2	28.0	1.8	1.6	0.4	3,942	2,689	1,079	86	68	20	100.0	68.2	27.4	2.2	1.7	0.5
Other assaults							535,232	330,695	183,378	11,392	8,024	1,743	100.0	61.8	34.3	2.1	1.5	0.3
Forgery and counterfeiting	100.0	58.6	38.3	1.7	1.0	0.3	27,266	18,178	8,365	268	401	54	100.0	66.7	30.7	1.0	1.5	0.2
Fraud	100.0	53.6	43.4	0.9	1.6	0.5	62,431	40,424	19,988	1,100	798	121	100.0	64.7	32.0	1.8	1.3	0.2
Embezzlement	100.0	37.7	59.1	1.9	1.2	0.1	8,599	5,238	3,123	108	119	11	100.0	60.9	36.3	1.3	1.4	0.1
Stolen property; buying, receiving, possessing	100.0	51.8	43.6	1.0	3.1	0.5	46,383	29,558	15,321	638	595	271	100.0	63.7	33.0	1.4	1.3	0.6
Vandalism	100.0	36.4	60.4	1.1	1.5	0.7	87,201	56,950	26,915	2,049	1,116	171	100.0	65.3	30.9	2.3	1.3	0.2
	100.0	67.1	29.5	2.3	0.9	0.1												
Weapons; carrying, possessing, etc.	100.0	54.0	43.2	1.1	1.5	0.3	86,287	44,298	40,096	670	964	259	100.0	51.3	46.5	0.8	1.1	0.3
Prostitution and commercialized vice	100.0	56.8	41.3	0.6	0.6	0.6	20,634	11,333	8,104	80	1,063	54	100.0	54.9	39.3	0.4	5.2	0.3
Sex offenses (except forcible rape and prostitution)	100.0	72.1	24.8	0.8	1.9	0.4	21,166	14,599	5,522	442	549	54	100.0	69.0	26.1	2.1	2.6	0.3
Drug abuse violations	100.0	73.1	23.0	2.2	1.3	0.3	823,704	570,047	234,022	8,965	9,134	1,536	100.0	69.2	28.4	1.1	1.1	0.2
Gambling	100.0	24.1	75.0	0.9	0.0	0.0	1,786	649	989	7	131	10	100.0	36.3	55.4	0.4	7.3	0.6
Offenses against the family and children	100.0	65.8	24.8	8.6	0.8	0.1	31,353	20,580	8,888	1,478	373	34	100.0	65.6	28.3	4.7	1.2	0.1
Driving under the influence	100.0	86.4	7.3	4.1	1.8	0.4	421,105	339,974	62,571	8,723	7,884	1,953	100.0	80.7	14.9	2.1	1.9	0.5
Liquor laws	100.0	85.9	7.1	5.6	1.3	0.2	87,729	66,300	14,528	5,455	1,341	105	100.0	75.6	16.6	6.2	1.5	0.1
Drunkenness	100.0	79.3	13.0	6.3	1.3	0.2	214,769	161,979	33,347	16,654	2,408	381	100.0	75.4	15.5	7.8	1.1	0.2
Disorderly conduct	100.0	55.5	41.8	2.0	0.7	0.1	168,879	107,769	51,639	7,861	1,409	201	100.0	63.8	30.6	4.7	0.8	0.1
Vagrancy	100.0	49.3	47.6	1.9	0.7	0.5	15,769	11,270	3,783	449	246	21	100.0	71.5	24.0	2.8	1.6	0.1
All other offenses (except traffic)	100.0	66.5	30.6	1.8	1.0	0.2	1,591,415	1,063,366	468,221	39,531	17,141	3,156	100.0	66.8	29.4	2.5	1.1	0.2
Suspicion	100.0	56.3	31.3	12.5	0.0	0.0	140	46	33	61	0	0	100.0	32.9	23.6	43.6	0.0	0.0
Curfew and loitering law violations	100.0	54.7	42.7	1.5	1.0	0.1	NA	NA	NA	NA	NA	NA	NA	NA	NA	NA	NA	NA

NA = Not available.
* = Less than one-tenth of one percent.
1 Because of rounding, the percentages may not sum to 100.   2 Violent crimes are offenses of murder and nonnegligent manslaughter, rape, robbery, and aggravated assault. Property crimes are offenses of burglary, larceny-theft, motor vehicle theft, and arson.   3 The rape figures in this table are aggregate totals of the data submitted based on both the legacy and revised Uniform Crime Reporting definitions.

Table 49A. Arrests, Cities, Distribution by Ethnicity, 2018

(Number, percent; 8,967 agencies; 2018 estimated population 172,802,238.)

Offense charged	Total arrests			Percent distribution[1]			Arrests under 18		
	Total[2]	Hispanic or Latino	Not Hispanic or Latino	Total[2]	Hispanic or Latino	Not Hispanic or Latino	Total[2]	Hispanic or Latino	Not Hispanic or Latino
Total	4,676,763	938,341	3,738,422	100.0	20.1	79.9	355,783	86,687	269,096
Violent crime[3]	262,335	69,591	192,744	100.0	26.5	73.5	25,867	7,272	18,595
Murder and nonnegligent manslaughter	5,261	1,135	4,126	100.0	21.6	78.4	433	119	314
Rape[4]	11,262	3,249	8,013	100.0	28.8	71.2	1,781	440	1,341
Robbery	48,355	11,293	37,062	100.0	23.4	76.6	9,549	2,466	7,083
Aggravated assault	197,457	53,914	143,543	100.0	27.3	72.7	14,104	4,247	9,857
Property crime[3]	584,289	101,509	482,780	100.0	17.4	82.6	65,773	14,753	51,020
Burglary	87,245	19,925	67,320	100.0	22.8	77.2	10,581	2,841	7,740
Larceny-theft	450,681	69,393	381,288	100.0	15.4	84.6	47,194	9,912	37,282
Motor vehicle theft	42,216	11,377	30,839	100.0	26.9	73.1	7,138	1,829	5,309
Arson	4,147	814	3,333	100.0	19.6	80.4	860	171	689
Other assaults	502,875	105,992	396,883	100.0	21.1	78.9	59,309	15,171	44,138
Forgery and counterfeiting	23,930	4,177	19,753	100.0	17.5	82.5	510	102	408
Fraud	55,586	7,704	47,882	100.0	13.9	86.1	2,616	376	2,240
Embezzlement	7,483	1,063	6,420	100.0	14.2	85.8	331	69	262
Stolen property; buying, receiving, possessing	43,794	9,074	34,720	100.0	20.7	79.3	4,847	1,060	3,787
Vandalism	88,167	18,331	69,836	100.0	20.8	79.2	15,262	3,461	11,801
Weapons; carrying, possessing, etc.	77,633	19,266	58,367	100.0	24.8	75.2	8,618	2,901	5,717
Prostitution and commercialized vice	19,343	4,010	15,333	100.0	20.7	79.3	148	31	117
Sex offenses (except forcible rape and prostitution)	21,372	5,879	15,493	100.0	27.5	72.5	3,388	895	2,493
Drug abuse violations	757,303	165,291	592,012	100.0	21.8	78.2	43,956	12,814	31,142
Gambling	1,016	234	782	100.0	23.0	77.0	60	9	51
Offenses against the family and children	26,894	3,915	22,979	100.0	14.6	85.4	1,486	241	1,245
Driving under the influence	359,971	91,364	268,607	100.0	25.4	74.6	2,082	637	1,445
Liquor laws	82,999	12,894	70,105	100.0	15.5	84.5	12,026	2,488	9,538
Drunkenness	201,622	45,479	156,143	100.0	22.6	77.4	2,009	782	1,227
Disorderly conduct	155,726	21,842	133,884	100.0	14.0	86.0	27,354	5,473	21,881
Vagrancy	15,093	2,268	12,825	100.0	15.0	85.0	360	73	287
All other offenses (except traffic)	1,375,605	245,572	1,130,033	100.0	17.9	82.1	66,183	15,197	50,986
Suspicion	149	6	143	100.0	4.0	96.0	20	2	18
Curfew and loitering law violations	13,578	2,880	10,698	100.0	21.2	78.8	13,578	2,880	10,698

Table 49A. Arrests, Cities, Distribution by Ethnicity, 2018—Continued

(Number, percent; 8,967 agencies; 2018 estimated population 172,802,238.)

Offense charged	Percent distribution[1]			Arrests 18 and over			Percent distribution[1]		
	Total[2]	Hispanic or Latino	Not Hispanic or Latino	Total[2]	Hispanic or Latino	Not Hispanic or Latino	Total[2]	Hispanic or Latino	Not Hispanic or Latino
Total	100.0	24.4	75.6	4,320,980	851,654	3,469,326	100.0	19.7	80.3
Violent crime[3]	100.0	28.1	71.9	236,468	62,319	174,149	100.0	26.4	73.6
Murder and nonnegligent manslaughter	100.0	27.5	72.5	4,828	1,016	3,812	100.0	21.0	79.0
Rape[4]	100.0	24.7	75.3	9,481	2,809	6,672	100.0	29.6	70.4
Robbery	100.0	25.8	74.2	38,806	8,827	29,979	100.0	22.7	77.3
Aggravated assault	100.0	30.1	69.9	183,353	49,667	133,686	100.0	27.1	72.9
Property crime[3]	100.0	22.4	77.6	518,516	86,756	431,760	100.0	16.7	83.3
Burglary	100.0	26.9	73.1	76,664	17,084	59,580	100.0	22.3	77.7
Larceny-theft	100.0	21.0	79.0	403,487	59,481	344,006	100.0	14.7	85.3
Motor vehicle theft	100.0	25.6	74.4	35,078	9,548	25,530	100.0	27.2	72.8
Arson	100.0	19.9	80.1	3,287	643	2,644	100.0	19.6	80.4
Other assaults				443,566	90,821	352,745	100.0	20.5	79.5
Forgery and counterfeiting	100.0	25.6	74.4	23,420	4,075	19,345	100.0	17.4	82.6
Fraud	100.0	20.0	80.0	52,970	7,328	45,642	100.0	13.8	86.2
Embezzlement	100.0	14.4	85.6	7,152	994	6,158	100.0	13.9	86.1
Stolen property; buying, receiving, possessing	100.0	20.8	79.2	38,947	8,014	30,933	100.0	20.6	79.4
Vandalism	100.0	21.9	78.1	72,905	14,870	58,035	100.0	20.4	79.6
	100.0	22.7	77.3						
Weapons; carrying, possessing, etc.	100.0	33.7	66.3	69,015	16,365	52,650	100.0	23.7	76.3
Prostitution and commercialized vice	100.0	20.9	79.1	19,195	3,979	15,216	100.0	20.7	79.3
Sex offenses (except forcible rape and prostitution)	100.0	26.4	73.6	17,984	4,984	13,000	100.0	27.7	72.3
Drug abuse violations	100.0	29.2	70.8	713,347	152,477	560,870	100.0	21.4	78.6
Gambling	100.0	15.0	85.0	956	225	731	100.0	23.5	76.5
Offenses against the family and children	100.0	16.2	83.8	25,408	3,674	21,734	100.0	14.5	85.5
Driving under the influence	100.0	30.6	69.4	357,889	90,727	267,162	100.0	25.4	74.6
Liquor laws	100.0	20.7	79.3	70,973	10,406	60,567	100.0	14.7	85.3
Drunkenness	100.0	38.9	61.1	199,613	44,697	154,916	100.0	22.4	77.6
Disorderly conduct	100.0	20.0	80.0	128,372	16,369	112,003	100.0	12.8	87.2
Vagrancy	100.0	20.3	79.7	14,733	2,195	12,538	100.0	14.9	85.1
All other offenses (except traffic)	100.0	23.0	77.0	1,309,422	230,375	1,079,047	100.0	17.6	82.4
Suspicion	100.0	10.0	90.0	129	4	125	100.0	3.1	96.9
Curfew and loitering law violations	100.0	21.2	78.8	NA	NA	NA	NA	NA	NA

NA = Not available.
1 Because of rounding, the percentages may not sum to 100. 2 The ethnicity totals are representative of those agencies that provided ethnicity breakdowns. Not all agencies provide ethnicity data; therefore, the race and ethnicity totals will not be equal. 3 Violent crimes are offenses of murder and nonnegligent manslaughter, rape, robbery, and aggravated assault. Property crimes are offenses of burglary, larceny-theft, motor vehicle theft, and arson. 4 The rape figures in this table are aggregate totals of the data submitted based on both the legacy and revised Uniform Crime Reporting definitions.

Table 50. Arrest Trends, Metropolitan Counties, 2017–2018

(Number, percent change; 1,296 agencies; 2018 estimated population 48,986,577; 2017 estimated population 48,991,999.)

Offense charged	Number of persons arrested								
	Total, all ages			Under 18 years of age			18 years of age and over		
	2017	2018	Percent change	2017	2018	Percent change	2017	2018	Percent change
Total[1]	1,412,921	1,395,666	-1.2	89,517	80,653	-9.9	1,323,404	1,315,013	-0.6
Violent crime[2]	63,898	63,652	-0.4	5,936	5,902	-0.6	57,962	57,750	-0.4
Murder and nonnegligent manslaughter	1,614	1,492	-7.6	84	103	+22.6	1,530	1,389	-9.2
Rape[3]	3,340	3,420	+2.4	595	628	+5.5	2,745	2,792	+1.7
Robbery	9,011	8,272	-8.2	1,791	1,680	-6.2	7,220	6,592	-8.7
Aggravated assault	49,933	50,468	+1.1	3,466	3,491	+0.7	46,467	46,977	+1.1
Property crime[2]	128,980	120,878	-6.3	16,547	13,013	-21.4	112,433	107,865	-4.1
Burglary	24,838	21,802	-12.2	3,420	2,495	-27.0	21,418	19,307	-9.9
Larceny-theft	90,480	85,738	-5.2	11,347	8,861	-21.9	79,133	76,877	-2.9
Motor vehicle theft	12,527	12,156	-3.0	1,537	1,420	-7.6	10,990	10,736	-2.3
Arson	1,135	1,182	+4.1	243	237	-2.5	892	945	+5.9
Other assaults	127,962	125,481	-1.9	17,003	16,970	-0.2	110,959	108,511	-2.2
Forgery and counterfeiting	7,528	6,750	-10.3	142	111	-21.8	7,386	6,639	-10.1
Fraud	16,962	15,917	-6.2	460	408	-11.3	16,502	15,509	-6.0
Embezzlement	1,912	1,605	-16.1	46	41	-10.9	1,866	1,564	-16.2
Stolen property; buying, receiving, possessing	12,950	12,456	-3.8	898	806	-10.2	12,052	11,650	-3.3
Vandalism	21,724	20,096	-7.5	4,484	3,399	-24.2	17,240	16,697	-3.1
Weapons; carrying, possessing, etc.	20,268	20,492	+1.1	2,044	1,851	-9.4	18,224	18,641	+2.3
Prostitution and commercialized vice	2,746	2,018	-26.5	28	33	+17.9	2,718	1,985	-27.0
Sex offenses (except forcible rape and prostitution)	6,924	6,634	-4.2	1,187	1,046	-11.9	5,737	5,588	-2.6
Drug abuse violations	237,224	240,586	+1.4	11,910	11,081	-7.0	225,314	229,505	+1.9
Gambling	477	414	-13.2	26	17	-34.6	451	397	-12.0
Offenses against the family and children	22,650	21,464	-5.2	549	452	-17.7	22,101	21,012	-4.9
Driving under the influence	186,883	190,174	+1.8	860	822	-4.4	186,023	189,352	+1.8
Liquor laws	19,223	15,562	-19.0	3,970	3,013	-24.1	15,253	12,549	-17.7
Drunkenness	23,240	22,893	-1.5	284	243	-14.4	22,956	22,650	-1.3
Disorderly conduct	27,365	26,200	-4.3	5,633	5,199	-7.7	21,732	21,001	-3.4
Vagrancy	1,604	1,492	-7.0	80	68	-15.0	1,524	1,424	-6.6
All other offenses (except traffic)	481,097	479,827	-0.3	16,126	15,103	-6.3	464,971	464,724	-0.1
Suspicion	80	238	+197.5	24	4	-83.3	56	234	+317.9
Curfew and loitering law violations	1,304	1,075	-17.6	1,304	1,075	-17.6	NA	NA	NA

NA = Not available.

1 Does not include suspicion.   2 Violent crimes in this table are offenses of murder and nonnegligent manslaughter, rape, robbery, and aggravated assault. Property crimes are offenses of burglary, larceny-theft, motor vehicle theft, and arson.   3 The rape figures in this table are aggregate totals of the data submitted based on both the legacy and revised Uniform Crime Reporting definitions.

Table 51. Arrest Trends, Metropolitan Counties, by Age and Sex, 2017–2018

(Number, percent change; 1,296 agencies; 2018 estimated population 48,986,577; 2017 estimated population 48,991,999.)

| | Male | | | | | | Female | | | | | |
| | Total | | | Under 18 | | | Total | | | Under 18 | | |
Offense charged	2017	2018	Percent change	2017	2018	Percent change	2017	2018	Percent change	2017	2018	Percent change
Total[1]	1,044,624	1,028,780	-1.5	64,382	57,321	-11.0	368,297	366,886	-0.4	25,135	23,332	-7.2
Violent crime[2]	51,398	50,970	-0.8	4,819	4,728	-1.9	12,500	12,682	+1.5	1,117	1,174	+5.1
Murder and nonnegligent manslaughter	1,398	1,309	-6.4	80	83	+3.8	216	183	-15.3	4	20	+400.0
Rape[3]	3,257	3,321	+2.0	581	609	+4.8	83	99	+19.3	14	19	+35.7
Robbery	7,729	7,036	-9.0	1,613	1,490	-7.6	1,282	1,236	-3.6	178	190	+6.7
Aggravated assault	39,014	39,304	+0.7	2,545	2,546	*	10,919	11,164	+2.2	921	945	+2.6
Property crime[2]	85,585	78,196	-8.6	11,900	8,999	-24.4	43,395	42,682	-1.6	4,647	4,014	-13.6
Burglary	20,332	17,712	-12.9	3,035	2,205	-27.3	4,506	4,090	-9.2	385	290	-24.7
Larceny-theft	54,532	50,207	-7.9	7,397	5,439	-26.5	35,948	35,531	-1.2	3,950	3,422	-13.4
Motor vehicle theft	9,790	9,348	-4.5	1,257	1,156	-8.0	2,737	2,808	+2.6	280	264	-5.7
Arson	931	929	-0.2	211	199	-5.7	204	253	+24.0	32	38	+18.8
Other assaults	92,026	89,831	-2.4	10,941	10,881	-0.5	35,936	35,650	-0.8	6,062	6,089	+0.4
Forgery and counterfeiting	4,998	4,453	-10.9	109	93	-14.7	2,530	2,297	-9.2	33	18	-45.5
Fraud	10,883	10,230	-6.0	308	266	-13.6	6,079	5,687	-6.4	152	142	-6.6
Embezzlement	987	864	-12.5	26	28	+7.7	925	741	-19.9	20	13	-35.0
Stolen property; buying, receiving, possessing	10,144	9,813	-3.3	742	666	-10.2	2,806	2,643	-5.8	156	140	-10.3
Vandalism	17,084	15,722	-8.0	3,676	2,789	-24.1	4,640	4,374	-5.7	808	610	-24.5
Weapons; carrying, possessing, etc.	18,213	18,395	+1.0	1,772	1,592	-10.2	2,055	2,097	+2.0	272	259	-4.8
Prostitution and commercialized vice	1,530	1,067	-30.3	14	21	+50.0	1,216	951	-21.8	14	12	-14.3
Sex offenses (except forcible rape and prostitution)	6,520	6,219	-4.6	1,080	950	-12.0	404	415	+2.7	107	96	-10.3
Drug abuse violations	178,584	180,039	+0.8	9,072	8,323	-8.3	58,640	60,547	+3.3	2,838	2,758	-2.8
Gambling	364	317	-12.9	20	15	-25.0	113	97	-14.2	6	2	-66.7
Offenses against the family and children	17,570	16,530	-5.9	348	305	-12.4	5,080	4,934	-2.9	201	147	-26.9
Driving under the influence	140,495	142,946	+1.7	666	634	-4.8	46,388	47,228	+1.8	194	188	-3.1
Liquor laws	13,100	10,726	-18.1	2,328	1,740	-25.3	6,123	4,836	-21.0	1,642	1,273	-22.5
Drunkenness	18,342	17,837	-2.8	189	153	-19.0	4,898	5,056	+3.2	95	90	-5.3
Disorderly conduct	19,269	18,691	-3.0	3,655	3,432	-6.1	8,096	7,509	-7.3	1,978	1,767	-10.7
Vagrancy	1,202	1,096	-8.8	63	45	-28.6	402	396	-1.5	17	23	+35.3
All other offenses (except traffic)	355,514	354,134	-0.4	11,838	10,957	-7.4	125,583	125,693	+0.1	4,288	4,146	-3.3
Suspicion	58	173	+198.3	17	3	-82.4	22	65	+195.5	7	1	-85.7
Curfew and loitering law violations	816	704	-13.7	816	704	-13.7	488	371	-24.0	488	371	-24.0

* = Less than one-tenth of one percent.
1 Does not include suspicion.   2 Violent crimes are offenses of murder and nonnegligent manslaughter, rape, robbery, and aggravated assault.   Property crimes are offenses of burglary, larceny-theft, motor vehicle theft, and arson.   3 The rape figures in this table are aggregate totals of the data submitted based on both the legacy and revised Uniform Crime Reporting definitions.

Table 52. Arrests, Metropolitan Counties, Distribution by Age, 2018

(Number, percent; 1,440 agencies; 2018 estimated population 55,828,114.)

Offense charged	Total, all ages	Ages under 15	Ages under 18	Ages 18 and over	Under 10	10–12	13–14	15	16	17	18	19	20
Total	1,536,169	26,080	91,083	1,445,086	645	6,148	19,287	16,058	21,523	27,422	37,207	41,955	43,907
Total percent distribution[1]	100.0	1.7	5.9	94.1	*	0.4	1.3	1.0	1.4	1.8	2.4	2.7	2.9
Violent crime[2]	71,516	2,000	6,806	64,710	37	489	1,474	1,225	1,691	1,890	2,129	2,025	2,141
Violent crime percent distribution[1]	100.0	2.8	9.5	90.5	0.1	0.7	2.1	1.7	2.4	2.6	3.0	2.8	3.0
Murder and nonnegligent manslaughter	1,755	15	126	1,629	0	2	13	15	38	58	85	92	85
Rape[3]	3,753	289	678	3,075	5	89	195	129	122	138	164	134	130
Robbery	9,434	340	1,947	7,487	1	33	306	345	602	660	659	544	482
Aggravated assault	56,574	1,356	4,055	52,519	31	365	960	736	929	1,034	1,221	1,255	1,444
Property crime[2]	136,876	4,165	14,699	122,177	64	883	3,218	2,680	3,530	4,324	5,017	4,698	4,237
Property crime percent distribution[1]	100.0	3.0	10.7	89.3	*	0.6	2.4	2.0	2.6	3.2	3.7	3.4	3.1
Burglary	24,780	887	2,879	21,901	19	198	670	522	662	808	933	834	803
Larceny-theft	97,589	2,749	9,999	87,590	32	589	2,128	1,788	2,398	3,064	3,641	3,394	2,987
Motor vehicle theft	13,191	358	1,551	11,640	2	44	312	337	440	416	407	432	409
Arson	1,316	171	270	1,046	11	52	108	33	30	36	36	38	38
Other assaults	141,785	7,670	19,215	122,570	197	2,187	5,286	3,629	4,030	3,886	2,959	2,917	3,084
Forgery and counterfeiting	7,550	20	122	7,428	3	1	16	7	26	69	168	300	357
Fraud	18,272	108	473	17,799	2	15	91	100	91	174	263	391	429
Embezzlement	1,766	0	41	1,725	0	0	0	2	12	27	77	79	79
Stolen property; buying, receiving, possessing	14,190	202	983	13,207	3	16	183	170	277	334	504	524	415
Vandalism	23,085	1,388	3,910	19,175	45	382	961	722	847	953	866	752	725
Weapons; carrying, possessing, etc.	23,014	715	2,163	20,851	33	229	453	383	470	595	752	798	764
Prostitution and commercialized vice	2,528	12	38	2,490	0	4	8	5	4	17	35	56	70
Sex offenses (except forcible rape and prostitution)	7,608	575	1,238	6,370	24	167	384	231	202	230	229	210	176
Drug abuse violations	265,238	1,811	12,769	252,469	14	241	1,556	1,793	3,204	5,961	10,505	11,574	11,440
Gambling	425	1	18	407	0	0	1	4	6	7	5	19	18
Offenses against the family and children	23,312	167	502	22,810	8	41	118	107	103	125	152	147	202
Driving under the influence	201,462	26	895	200,567	5	2	19	25	201	643	1,965	3,118	3,847
Liquor laws	17,026	420	3,295	13,731	1	44	375	491	914	1,470	2,292	2,302	2,002
Drunkenness	24,559	29	253	24,306	0	1	28	49	54	121	351	444	501
Disorderly conduct	30,511	2,251	5,851	24,660	77	583	1,591	1,127	1,325	1,148	773	663	645
Vagrancy	1,557	31	93	1,464	1	3	27	24	24	14	28	26	39
All other offenses (except traffic)	522,443	4,167	16,509	505,934	122	817	3,228	3,005	4,134	5,203	8,132	10,901	12,729
Suspicion	240	1	4	236	0	0	1	0	2	1	5	11	7
Curfew and loitering law violations	1,206	321	1,206	NA	9	43	269	279	376	230	NA	NA	NA

Table 52. Arrests, Metropolitan Counties, Distribution by Age, 2018—Continued

(Number, percent; 1,440 agencies; 2018 estimated population 55,828,114.)

Offense charged	21	22	23	24	25–29	30–34	35–39	40–44	45–49	50–54	55–59	60–64	65 and over
Total	46,356	48,706	50,162	52,735	274,298	233,431	195,334	130,595	104,758	80,872	56,799	28,494	19,477
Total percent distribution[1]	3.0	3.2	3.3	3.4	17.9	15.2	12.7	8.5	6.8	5.3	3.7	1.9	1.3
Violent crime[2]	2,224	2,271	2,243	2,301	11,914	10,132	8,343	5,626	4,467	3,760	2,675	1,383	1,076
Violent crime percent distribution[1]	3.1	3.2	3.1	3.2	16.7	14.2	11.7	7.9	6.2	5.3	3.7	1.9	1.5
Murder and nonnegligent manslaughter	86	71	70	67	302	238	179	107	83	54	54	22	34
Rape[3]	126	136	84	81	411	420	360	263	240	193	139	84	110
Robbery	376	375	356	332	1,574	1,028	642	419	287	223	133	42	15
Aggravated assault	1,636	1,689	1,733	1,821	9,627	8,446	7,162	4,837	3,857	3,290	2,349	1,235	917
Property crime[2]	3,937	4,019	3,923	4,221	22,836	19,941	16,375	10,501	8,374	6,526	4,251	2,049	1,272
Property crime percent distribution[1]	2.9	2.9	2.9	3.1	16.7	14.6	12.0	7.7	6.1	4.8	3.1	1.5	0.9
Burglary	717	758	741	785	4,373	3,883	3,086	1,804	1,361	963	507	230	123
Larceny-theft	2,804	2,799	2,737	2,960	15,748	13,792	11,476	7,661	6,233	5,089	3,489	1,681	1,099
Motor vehicle theft	396	434	418	459	2,532	2,105	1,672	954	688	392	211	102	29
Arson	20	28	27	17	183	161	141	82	92	82	44	36	21
Other assaults	3,487	3,815	3,786	4,062	21,511	19,382	17,052	11,878	10,001	7,874	5,467	2,921	2,374
Forgery and counterfeiting	220	237	254	243	1,351	1,205	1,023	707	520	388	261	135	59
Fraud	481	475	542	583	3,169	3,061	2,560	1,885	1,500	1,094	716	369	281
Embezzlement	60	71	66	59	330	226	190	168	136	86	47	27	24
Stolen property; buying, receiving, possessing	405	448	477	521	2,707	2,258	1,929	1,107	789	557	348	152	66
Vandalism	754	759	768	752	3,841	2,910	2,323	1,493	1,099	930	585	333	285
Weapons; carrying, possessing, etc.	882	914	904	893	4,288	3,265	2,515	1,599	1,187	895	632	326	237
Prostitution and commercialized vice	99	97	98	107	486	331	296	237	222	162	85	59	50
Sex offenses (except forcible rape and prostitution)	154	165	160	152	762	822	831	573	556	549	438	241	352
Drug abuse violations	10,969	10,679	10,593	10,704	50,919	39,011	30,387	19,093	14,539	10,502	7,189	3,052	1,313
Gambling	9	10	14	10	46	49	48	34	24	25	40	34	22
Offenses against the family and children	270	304	378	482	3,752	4,686	4,614	3,185	2,214	1,326	701	258	139
Driving under the influence	6,616	7,390	7,786	8,221	39,105	30,246	24,677	17,940	15,513	12,987	10,499	6,059	4,598
Liquor laws	359	274	258	263	1,156	974	854	689	661	649	556	290	152
Drunkenness	699	701	773	769	3,927	3,633	3,216	2,281	2,028	2,072	1,661	816	434
Disorderly conduct	696	750	756	842	4,161	3,545	3,205	2,312	2,030	1,688	1,299	701	594
Vagrancy	25	27	34	38	229	174	202	159	130	138	128	62	25
All other offenses (except traffic)	14,005	15,291	16,341	17,499	97,763	87,544	74,658	49,113	38,749	28,650	19,215	9,223	6,121
Suspicion	5	9	8	13	45	36	36	15	19	14	6	4	3
Curfew and loitering law violations	NA	NA	NA	NA	NA	NA	NA	NA	NA	NA	NA	NA	NA

NA = Not available.
* = Less than one-tenth of one percent.
1 Because of rounding, the percentages may not sum to 100.   2 Violent crimes are offenses of murder and nonnegligent manslaughter, rape, robbery, and aggravated assault. Property crimes are offenses of burglary, larceny-theft, motor vehicle theft, and arson.   3 The rape figures in this table are aggregate totals of the data submitted based on both the legacy and revised Uniform Crime Reporting definitions.

Table 53. Arrests, Metropolitan Counties, Persons Under 15, 18, 21, and 25 Years of Age, 2018

(Number, percent; 1,440 agencies; 2018 estimated population 55,828,114.)

Offense charged	Total, all ages	Number of persons arrested				Percent of total all ages			
		Under 15	Under 18	Under 21	Under 25	Under 15	Under 18	Under 21	Under 25
Total	1,536,169	26,080	91,083	214,152	412,111	1.7	5.9	13.9	26.8
Violent crime[1]	71,516	2,000	6,806	13,101	22,140	2.8	9.5	18.3	31.0
Murder and nonnegligent manslaughter	1,755	15	126	388	682	0.9	7.2	22.1	38.9
Rape[2]	3,753	289	678	1,106	1,533	7.7	18.1	29.5	40.8
Robbery	9,434	340	1,947	3,632	5,071	3.6	20.6	38.5	53.8
Aggravated assault	56,574	1,356	4,055	7,975	14,854	2.4	7.2	14.1	26.3
Property crime[1]	136,876	4,165	14,699	28,651	44,751	3.0	10.7	20.9	32.7
Burglary	24,780	887	2,879	5,449	8,450	3.6	11.6	22.0	34.1
Larceny-theft	97,589	2,749	9,999	20,021	31,321	2.8	10.2	20.5	32.1
Motor vehicle theft	13,191	358	1,551	2,799	4,506	2.7	11.8	21.2	34.2
Arson	1,316	171	270	382	474	13.0	20.5	29.0	36.0
Other assaults	141,785	7,670	19,215	28,175	43,325	5.4	13.6	19.9	30.6
Forgery and counterfeiting	7,550	20	122	947	1,901	0.3	1.6	12.5	25.2
Fraud	18,272	108	473	1,556	3,637	0.6	2.6	8.5	19.9
Embezzlement	1,766	0	41	276	532	0.0	2.3	15.6	30.1
Stolen property; buying, receiving, possessing	14,190	202	983	2,426	4,277	1.4	6.9	17.1	30.1
Vandalism	23,085	1,388	3,910	6,253	9,286	6.0	16.9	27.1	40.2
Weapons; carrying, possessing, etc.	23,014	715	2,163	4,477	8,070	3.1	9.4	19.5	35.1
Prostitution and commercialized vice	2,528	12	38	199	600	0.5	1.5	7.9	23.7
Sex offenses (except forcible rape and prostitution)	7,608	575	1,238	1,853	2,484	7.6	16.3	24.4	32.6
Drug abuse violations	265,238	1,811	12,769	46,288	89,233	0.7	4.8	17.5	33.6
Gambling	425	1	18	60	103	0.2	4.2	14.1	24.2
Offenses against the family and children	23,312	167	502	1,003	2,437	0.7	2.2	4.3	10.5
Driving under the influence	201,462	26	895	9,825	39,838	*	0.4	4.9	19.8
Liquor laws	17,026	420	3,295	9,891	11,045	2.5	19.4	58.1	64.9
Drunkenness	24,559	29	253	1,549	4,491	0.1	1.0	6.3	18.3
Disorderly conduct	30,511	2,251	5,851	7,932	10,976	7.4	19.2	26.0	36.0
Vagrancy	1,557	31	93	186	310	2.0	6.0	11.9	19.9
All other offenses (except traffic)	522,443	4,167	16,509	48,271	111,407	0.8	3.2	9.2	21.3
Suspicion	240	1	4	27	62	0.4	1.7	11.3	25.8
Curfew and loitering law violations	1,206	321	1,206	1,206	1,206	26.6	100.0	100.0	100.0

* = Less than one-tenth of one percent.
1 Violent crimes are offenses of murder and nonnegligent manslaughter, rape, robbery, and aggravated assault. Property crimes are offenses of burglary, larceny-theft, motor vehicle theft, and arson.   2 The rape figures in this table are aggregate totals of the data submitted based on both the legacy and revised Uniform Crime Reporting definitions.

Table 54. Arrests, Metropolitan Counties, Distribution by Sex, 2018

(Number, percent; 1,440 agencies; 2018 estimated population 55,828,114.)

Offense charged	Number of persons arrested			Percent male	Percent female	Percent distribution[1]		
	Total	Male	Female			Total	Male	Female
Total	1,536,169	1,132,058	404,111	73.7	26.3	100.0	100.0	100.0
Violent crime[2]	71,516	57,177	14,339	79.9	20.1	4.7	5.1	3.5
Murder and nonnegligent manslaughter	1,755	1,540	215	87.7	12.3	0.1	0.1	0.1
Rape[3]	3,753	3,646	107	97.1	2.9	0.2	0.3	0.0
Robbery	9,434	8,064	1,370	85.5	14.5	0.6	0.7	0.3
Aggravated assault	56,574	43,927	12,647	77.6	22.4	3.7	3.9	3.1
Property crime[2]	136,876	89,190	47,686	65.2	34.8	8.9	7.9	11.8
Burglary	24,780	20,227	4,553	81.6	18.4	1.6	1.8	1.1
Larceny-theft	97,589	57,761	39,828	59.2	40.8	6.4	5.1	9.9
Motor vehicle theft	13,191	10,169	3,022	77.1	22.9	0.9	0.9	0.7
Arson	1,316	1,033	283	78.5	21.5	0.1	0.1	0.1
Other assaults	141,785	101,228	40,557	71.4	28.6	9.2	8.9	10.0
Forgery and counterfeiting	7,550	5,004	2,546	66.3	33.7	0.5	0.4	0.6
Fraud	18,272	11,698	6,574	64.0	36.0	1.2	1.0	1.6
Embezzlement	1,766	950	816	53.8	46.2	0.1	0.1	0.2
Stolen property; buying, receiving, possessing	14,190	11,212	2,978	79.0	21.0	0.9	1.0	0.7
Vandalism	23,085	18,057	5,028	78.2	21.8	1.5	1.6	1.2
Weapons; carrying, possessing, etc.	23,014	20,630	2,384	89.6	10.4	1.5	1.8	0.6
Prostitution and commercialized vice	2,528	1,288	1,240	50.9	49.1	0.2	0.1	0.3
Sex offenses (except forcible rape and prostitution)	7,608	7,115	493	93.5	6.5	0.5	0.6	0.1
Drug abuse violations	265,238	198,488	66,750	74.8	25.2	17.3	17.5	16.5
Gambling	425	328	97	77.2	22.8	*	*	*
Offenses against the family and children	23,312	17,882	5,430	76.7	23.3	1.5	1.6	1.3
Driving under the influence	201,462	151,333	50,129	75.1	24.9	13.1	13.4	12.4
Liquor laws	17,026	11,726	5,300	68.9	31.1	1.1	1.0	1.3
Drunkenness	24,559	19,145	5,414	78.0	22.0	1.6	1.7	1.3
Disorderly conduct	30,511	21,717	8,794	71.2	28.8	2.0	1.9	2.2
Vagrancy	1,557	1,139	418	73.2	26.8	0.1	0.1	0.1
All other offenses (except traffic)	522,443	385,787	136,656	73.8	26.2	34.0	34.1	33.8
Suspicion	240	175	65	72.9	27.1	*	*	*
Curfew and loitering law violations	1,206	789	417	65.4	34.6	0.1	0.1	0.1

* = Less than one-tenth of one percent.
1 Because of rounding, the percentages may not sum to 100.   2 Violent crimes are offenses of murder and nonnegligent manslaughter, rape, robbery, and aggravated assault. Property crimes are offenses of burglary, larceny-theft, motor vehicle theft, and arson.   3 The rape figures in this table are aggregate totals of the data submitted based on both the legacy and revised Uniform Crime Reporting definitions.

Table 55. Arrests, Metropolitan Counties, Distribution by Race, 2018

(Number, percent; 1,440 agencies; 2018 estimated population 55,828,114.)

Offense charged	Total arrests						Percent distribution[1]						Arrests under 18					
	Total	White	Black	American Indian or Alaskan Native	Asian	Native Hawaiian or Other Pacific Islander	Total	White	Black	American Indian or Alaskan Native	Asian	Native Hawaiian or Other Pacific Islander	Total	White	Black	American Indian or Alaskan Native	Asian	Native Hawaiian or Other Pacific Islander
Total	1,524,774	1,086,539	400,923	14,369	18,412	4,531	100.0	71.3	26.3	0.9	1.2	0.3	90,135	54,948	33,047	859	935	346
Violent crime[2]	71,188	46,846	22,730	557	837	218	100.0	65.8	31.9	0.8	1.2	0.3	6,762	3,307	3,317	46	67	25
Murder and nonnegligent manslaughter	1,755	952	780	6	14	3	100.0	54.2	44.4	0.3	0.8	0.2	128	57	71	0	0	0
Rape[3]	3,710	2,835	805	17	36	17	100.0	76.4	21.7	0.5	1.0	0.5	669	494	166	1	7	1
Robbery	9,408	4,226	5,046	45	65	26	100.0	44.9	53.6	0.5	0.7	0.3	1,939	619	1,287	9	17	7
Aggravated assault	56,315	38,833	16,099	489	722	172	100.0	69.0	28.6	0.9	1.3	0.3	4,026	2,137	1,793	36	43	17
Property crime[2]	135,629	90,818	42,112	745	1,563	391	100.0	67.0	31.0	0.5	1.2	0.3	14,528	7,630	6,579	84	178	57
Burglary	24,650	18,040	6,217	114	209	70	100.0	73.2	25.2	0.5	0.8	0.3	2,857	1,615	1,183	22	22	15
Larceny-theft	96,539	62,075	32,541	527	1,202	194	100.0	64.3	33.7	0.5	1.2	0.2	9,864	5,044	4,615	40	143	22
Motor vehicle theft	13,134	9,735	3,039	97	141	122	100.0	74.1	23.1	0.7	1.1	0.9	1,542	799	689	22	12	20
Arson	1,306	968	315	7	11	5	100.0	74.1	24.1	0.5	0.8	0.4	265	172	92	0	1	0
Other assaults	140,377	98,833	38,525	1,189	1,479	351	100.0	70.4	27.4	0.8	1.1	0.3	19,018	10,540	8,118	200	122	38
Forgery and counterfeiting	7,514	4,730	2,620	27	131	6	100.0	62.9	34.9	0.4	1.7	0.1	120	82	37	0	1	0
Fraud	18,103	11,999	5,737	119	230	18	100.0	66.3	31.7	0.7	1.3	0.1	462	265	187	8	1	1
Embezzlement	1,750	1,089	627	7	25	2	100.0	62.2	35.8	0.4	1.4	0.1	40	21	19	0	0	0
Stolen property; buying, receiving, possessing	14,100	9,693	4,179	77	135	16	100.0	68.7	29.6	0.5	1.0	0.1	977	391	572	2	11	1
Vandalism	22,872	16,410	5,946	244	237	35	100.0	71.7	26.0	1.1	1.0	0.2	3,861	2,574	1,202	49	27	9
Weapons; carrying, possessing, etc.	22,877	13,778	8,648	140	230	81	100.0	60.2	37.8	0.6	1.0	0.4	2,145	1,151	943	18	25	8
Prostitution and commercialized vice	2,511	1,333	918	10	244	6	100.0	53.1	36.6	0.4	9.7	0.2	38	26	11	0	1	0
Sex offenses (except forcible rape and prostitution)	7,558	5,742	1,640	46	122	8	100.0	76.0	21.7	0.6	1.6	0.1	1,220	864	339	7	9	1
Drug abuse violations	263,201	186,174	71,975	1,618	2,917	517	100.0	70.7	27.3	0.6	1.1	0.2	12,616	9,143	3,123	94	194	62
Gambling	422	226	86	3	66	41	100.0	53.6	20.4	0.7	15.6	9.7	18	2	16	0	0	0
Offenses against the family and children	23,233	15,065	7,913	133	113	9	100.0	64.8	34.1	0.6	0.5	*	496	376	104	12	4	0
Driving under the influence	199,949	163,032	30,659	1,277	4,433	548	100.0	81.5	15.3	0.6	2.2	0.3	887	796	67	10	12	2
Liquor laws	16,793	13,584	2,620	281	272	36	100.0	80.9	15.6	1.7	1.6	0.2	3,253	2,941	193	51	49	19
Drunkenness	24,488	20,397	3,496	202	356	37	100.0	83.3	14.3	0.8	1.5	0.2	252	209	36	3	4	0
Disorderly conduct	30,345	20,069	9,670	331	216	59	100.0	66.1	31.9	1.1	0.7	0.2	5,826	2,799	2,926	59	38	4
Vagrancy	1,553	1,093	442	8	9	1	100.0	70.4	28.5	0.5	0.6	0.1	93	46	46	0	1	0
All other offenses (except traffic)	518,872	364,668	139,984	7,348	4,763	2,109	100.0	70.3	27.0	1.4	0.9	0.4	16,320	10,977	4,899	209	158	77
Suspicion	240	154	85	0	1	0	100.0	64.2	35.4	0.0	0.4	0.0	4	2	2	0	0	0
Curfew and loitering law violations	1,199	806	311	7	33	42	100.0	67.2	25.9	0.6	2.8	3.5	1,199	806	311	7	33	42

Table 55. Arrests, Metropolitan Counties, Distribution by Race, 2018—Continued

(Number, percent; 1,440 agencies; 2018 estimated population 55,828,114.)

Offense charged	Percent distribution[1]						Arrests 18 and over						Percent distribution[1]					
	Total	White	Black	American Indian or Alaskan Native	Asian	Native Hawaiian or Other Pacific Islander	Total	White	Black	American Indian or Alaskan Native	Asian	Native Hawaiian or Other Pacific Islander	Total	White	Black	American Indian or Alaskan Native	Asian	Native Hawaiian or Other Pacific Islander
Total	100.0	61.0	36.7	1.0	1.0	0.4	1,434,639	1,031,591	367,876	13,510	17,477	4,185	100.0	71.9	25.6	0.9	1.2	0.3
Violent crime[2]	100.0	48.9	49.1	0.7	1.0	0.4	64,426	43,539	19,413	511	770	193	100.0	67.6	30.1	0.8	1.2	0.3
Murder and nonnegligent manslaughter	100.0	44.5	55.5	0.0	0.0	0.0	1,627	895	709	6	14	3	100.0	55.0	43.6	0.4	0.9	0.2
Rape[3]	100.0	73.8	24.8	0.1	1.0	0.1	3,041	2,341	639	16	29	16	100.0	77.0	21.0	0.5	1.0	0.5
Robbery	100.0	31.9	66.4	0.5	0.9	0.4	7,469	3,607	3,759	36	48	19	100.0	48.3	50.3	0.5	0.6	0.3
Aggravated assault	100.0	53.1	44.5	0.9	1.1	0.4	52,289	36,696	14,306	453	679	155	100.0	70.2	27.4	0.9	1.3	0.3
Property crime[2]	100.0	52.5	45.3	0.6	1.2	0.4	121,101	83,188	35,533	661	1,385	334	100.0	68.7	29.3	0.5	1.1	0.3
Burglary	100.0	56.5	41.4	0.8	0.8	0.5	21,793	16,425	5,034	92	187	55	100.0	75.4	23.1	0.4	0.9	0.3
Larceny-theft	100.0	51.1	46.8	0.4	1.4	0.2	86,675	57,031	27,926	487	1,059	172	100.0	65.8	32.2	0.6	1.2	0.2
Motor vehicle theft	100.0	51.8	44.7	1.4	0.8	1.3	11,592	8,936	2,350	75	129	102	100.0	77.1	20.3	0.6	1.1	0.9
Arson	100.0	64.9	34.7	0.0	0.4	0.0	1,041	796	223	7	10	5	100.0	76.5	21.4	0.7	1.0	0.5
Other assaults	100.0	55.4	42.7	1.1	0.6	0.2	121,359	88,293	30,407	989	1,357	313	100.0	72.8	25.1	0.8	1.1	0.3
Forgery and counterfeiting	100.0	68.3	30.8	0.0	0.8	0.0	7,394	4,648	2,583	27	130	6	100.0	62.9	34.9	0.4	1.8	0.1
Fraud	100.0	57.4	40.5	1.7	0.2	0.2	17,641	11,734	5,550	111	229	17	100.0	66.5	31.5	0.6	1.3	0.1
Embezzlement	100.0	52.5	47.5	0.0	0.0	0.0	1,710	1,068	608	7	25	2	100.0	62.5	35.6	0.4	1.5	0.1
Stolen property; buying, receiving, possessing	100.0	40.0	58.5	0.2	1.1	0.1	13,123	9,302	3,607	75	124	15	100.0	70.9	27.5	0.6	0.9	0.1
Vandalism	100.0	66.7	31.1	1.3	0.7	0.2	19,011	13,836	4,744	195	210	26	100.0	72.8	25.0	1.0	1.1	0.1
Weapons; carrying, possession, etc.	100.0	53.7	44.0	0.8	1.2	0.4	20,732	12,627	7,705	122	205	73	100.0	60.9	37.2	0.6	1.0	0.4
Prostitution and commercialized vice	100.0	68.4	28.9	0.0	2.6	0.0	2,473	1,307	907	10	243	6	100.0	52.9	36.7	0.4	9.8	0.2
Sex offenses (except forcible rape and prostitution)	100.0	70.8	27.8	0.6	0.7	0.1	6,338	4,878	1,301	39	113	7	100.0	77.0	20.5	0.6	1.8	0.1
Drug abuse violations	100.0	72.5	24.8	0.7	1.5	0.5	250,585	177,031	68,852	1,524	2,723	455	100.0	70.6	27.5	0.6	1.1	0.2
Gambling	100.0	11.1	88.9	0.0	0.0	0.0	404	224	70	3	66	41	100.0	55.4	17.3	0.7	16.3	10.1
Offenses against the family and children	100.0	75.8	21.0	2.4	0.8	0.0	22,737	14,689	7,809	121	109	9	100.0	64.6	34.3	0.5	0.5	*
Driving under the influence	100.0	89.7	7.6	1.1	1.4	0.2	199,062	162,236	30,592	1,267	4,421	546	100.0	81.5	15.4	0.6	2.2	0.3
Liquor laws	100.0	90.4	5.9	1.6	1.5	0.6	13,540	10,643	2,427	230	223	17	100.0	78.6	17.9	1.7	1.6	0.1
Drunkenness	100.0	82.9	14.3	1.2	1.6	0.0	24,236	20,188	3,460	199	352	37	100.0	83.3	14.3	0.8	1.5	0.2
Disorderly conduct	100.0	48.0	50.2	1.0	0.7	0.1	24,519	17,270	6,744	272	178	55	100.0	70.4	27.5	1.1	0.7	0.2
Vagrancy	100.0	49.5	49.5	0.0	1.1	0.0	1,460	1,047	396	8	8	1	100.0	71.7	27.1	0.5	0.5	0.1
All other offenses (except traffic)	100.0	67.3	30.0	1.3	1.0	0.5	502,552	353,691	135,085	7,139	4,605	2,032	100.0	70.4	26.9	1.4	0.9	0.4
Suspicion	100.0	50.0	50.0	0.0	0.0	0.0	236	152	83	0	1	0	100.0	64.4	35.2	0.0	0.4	0.0
Curfew and loitering law violations	100.0	67.2	25.9	0.6	2.8	3.5	NA	NA	NA	NA	NA	NA	NA	NA	NA	NA	NA	NA

NA = Not available.

* = Less than one-tenth of one percent.

1 Because of rounding, the percentages may not sum to 100.   2 Violent crimes are offenses of murder and nonnegligent manslaughter, rape, robbery, and aggravated assault.   Property crimes are offenses of burglary, larceny-theft, motor vehicle theft, and arson.   3 The rape figures in this table are an aggregate total of the data submitted using both the revised and legacy Uniform Crime Reporting definitions.

Table 55A. Arrests, Metropolitan Counties, Distribution by Ethnicity, 2018

(Number, percent; 1,440 agencies; 2018 estimated population 55,828,114.)

Offense charged	Total arrests			Percent distribution[1]			Arrests under 18		
	Total[2]	Hispanic or Latino	Not Hispanic or Latino	Total[2]	Hispanic or Latino	Not Hispanic or Latino	Total[2]	Hispanic or Latino	Not Hispanic or Latino
Total	1,239,300	220,086	1,019,214	100.0	17.8	82.2	69,862	11,843	58,019
Violent crime[3]	58,468	12,680	45,788	100.0	21.7	78.3	5,338	1,032	4,306
Murder and nonnegligent manslaughter	1,356	301	1,055	100.0	22.2	77.8	75	24	51
Rape[4]	2,978	731	2,247	100.0	24.5	75.5	529	97	432
Robbery	7,898	1,464	6,434	100.0	18.5	81.5	1,664	327	1,337
Aggravated assault	46,236	10,184	36,052	100.0	22.0	78.0	3,070	584	2,486
Property crime[3]	107,033	13,730	93,303	100.0	12.8	87.2	11,212	1,799	9,413
Burglary	19,795	2,875	16,920	100.0	14.5	85.5	2,144	387	1,757
Larceny-theft	74,989	7,921	67,068	100.0	10.6	89.4	7,604	1,089	6,515
Motor vehicle theft	11,157	2,782	8,375	100.0	24.9	75.1	1,245	302	943
Arson	1,092	152	940	100.0	13.9	86.1	219	21	198
Other assaults	115,190	16,781	98,409	100.0	14.6	85.4	15,430	2,187	13,243
Forgery and counterfeiting	5,898	945	4,953	100.0	16.0	84.0	99	25	74
Fraud	14,663	1,669	12,994	100.0	11.4	88.6	369	52	317
Embezzlement	1,490	123	1,367	100.0	8.3	91.7	36	5	31
Stolen property; buying, receiving, possessing	11,021	2,069	8,952	100.0	18.8	81.2	734	148	586
Vandalism	19,373	2,879	16,494	100.0	14.9	85.1	3,296	435	2,861
Weapons; carrying, possessing, etc.	18,074	4,034	14,040	100.0	22.3	77.7	1,641	355	1,286
Prostitution and commercialized vice	2,054	363	1,691	100.0	17.7	82.3	28	4	24
Sex offenses (except forcible rape and prostitution)	5,882	1,395	4,487	100.0	23.7	76.3	903	157	746
Drug abuse violations	217,703	40,225	177,478	100.0	18.5	81.5	9,988	2,265	7,723
Gambling	289	90	199	100.0	31.1	68.9	17	1	16
Offenses against the family and children	18,863	1,683	17,180	100.0	8.9	91.1	334	45	289
Driving under the influence	175,064	49,871	125,193	100.0	28.5	71.5	726	189	537
Liquor laws	12,850	2,400	10,450	100.0	18.7	81.3	2,530	376	2,154
Drunkenness	22,953	6,074	16,879	100.0	26.5	73.5	228	67	161
Disorderly conduct	22,125	2,113	20,012	100.0	9.6	90.4	3,921	363	3,558
Vagrancy	1,391	257	1,134	100.0	18.5	81.5	31	13	18
All other offenses (except traffic)	407,795	60,558	347,237	100.0	14.9	85.1	12,106	2,186	9,920
Suspicion	229	8	221	100.0	3.5	96.5	3	0	3
Curfew and loitering law violations	892	139	753	100.0	15.6	84.4	892	139	753

Table 55A. Arrests, Metropolitan Counties, Distribution by Ethnicity, 2018—Continued

(Number, percent; 1,440 agencies; 2018 estimated population 55,828,114.)

Offense charged	Percent distribution[1]			Arrests 18 and over			Percent distribution[1]		
	Total[2]	Hispanic or Latino	Not Hispanic or Latino	Total[2]	Hispanic or Latino	Not Hispanic or Latino	Total[2]	Hispanic or Latino	Not Hispanic or Latino
Total	100.0	17.0	83.0	1,169,438	208,243	961,195	100.0	17.8	82.2
Violent crime[3]	100.0	19.3	80.7	53,130	11,648	41,482	100.0	21.9	78.1
Murder and nonnegligent manslaughter	100.0	32.0	68.0	1,281	277	1,004	100.0	21.6	78.4
Rape[4]	100.0	18.3	81.7	2,449	634	1,815	100.0	25.9	74.1
Robbery	100.0	19.7	80.3	6,234	1,137	5,097	100.0	18.2	81.8
Aggravated assault	100.0	19.0	81.0	43,166	9,600	33,566	100.0	22.2	77.8
Property crime[3]	100.0	16.0	84.0	95,821	11,931	83,890	100.0	12.5	87.5
Burglary	100.0	18.1	81.9	17,651	2,488	15,163	100.0	14.1	85.9
Larceny-theft	100.0	14.3	85.7	67,385	6,832	60,553	100.0	10.1	89.9
Motor vehicle theft	100.0	24.3	75.7	9,912	2,480	7,432	100.0	25.0	75.0
Arson	100.0	9.6	90.4	873	131	742	100.0	15.0	85.0
Other assaults	100.0	14.2	85.8	99,760	14,594	85,166	100.0	14.6	85.4
Forgery and counterfeiting	100.0	25.3	74.7	5,799	920	4,879	100.0	15.9	84.1
Fraud	100.0	14.1	85.9	14,294	1,617	12,677	100.0	11.3	88.7
Embezzlement	100.0	13.9	86.1	1,454	118	1,336	100.0	8.1	91.9
Stolen property; buying, receiving, possessing	100.0	20.2	79.8	10,287	1,921	8,366	100.0	18.7	81.3
Vandalism	100.0	13.2	86.8	16,077	2,444	13,633	100.0	15.2	84.8
Weapons; carrying, possessing, etc.	100.0	21.6	78.4	16,433	3,679	12,754	100.0	22.4	77.6
Prostitution and commercialized vice	100.0	14.3	85.7	2,026	359	1,667	100.0	17.7	82.3
Sex offenses (except forcible rape and prostitution)	100.0	17.4	82.6	4,979	1,238	3,741	100.0	24.9	75.1
Drug abuse violations	100.0	22.7	77.3	207,715	37,960	169,755	100.0	18.3	81.7
Gambling	100.0	5.9	94.1	272	89	183	100.0	32.7	67.3
Offenses against the family and children	100.0	13.5	86.5	18,529	1,638	16,891	100.0	8.8	91.2
Driving under the influence	100.0	26.0	74.0	174,338	49,682	124,656	100.0	28.5	71.5
Liquor laws	100.0	14.9	85.1	10,320	2,024	8,296	100.0	19.6	80.4
Drunkenness	100.0	29.4	70.6	22,725	6,007	16,718	100.0	26.4	73.6
Disorderly conduct	100.0	9.3	90.7	18,204	1,750	16,454	100.0	9.6	90.4
Vagrancy	100.0	41.9	58.1	1,360	244	1,116	100.0	17.9	82.1
All other offenses (except traffic)	100.0	18.1	81.9	395,689	58,372	337,317	100.0	14.8	85.2
Suspicion	100.0	0.0	100.0	226	8	218	100.0	3.5	96.5
Curfew and loitering law violations	100.0	15.6	84.4	NA	NA	NA	NA	NA	NA

NA = Not available.
1 Because of rounding, the percentages may not sum to 100.   2 The ethnicity totals are representative of those agencies that provided ethnicity breakdowns. Not all agencies provide ethnicity data; therefore, the race and ethnicity totals will not be equal.   3 Violent crimes are offenses of murder and nonnegligent manslaughter, rape, robbery, and aggravated assault. Property crimes are offenses of burglary, larceny-theft, motor vehicle theft, and arson.   4 The rape figures in this table are an aggregate total of the data submitted using both the revised and legacy Uniform Crime Reporting definitions.

Table 56. Arrest Trends, Nonmetropolitan Counties, 2017–2018

(Number, percent change; 1,617 agencies; 2018 estimated population 17,352,148; 2017 estimated population 17,344,934.)

| Offense charged | Number of persons arrested | | | | | | | | |
| | Total, all ages | | | Under 18 years of age | | | 18 years of age and over | | |
	2017	2018	Percent change	2017	2018	Percent change	2017	2018	Percent change
Total[1]	582,309	558,180	-4.1	24,032	22,229	-7.5	558,277	535,951	-4.0
Violent crime[2]	17,724	17,114	-3.4	1,157	1,009	-12.8	16,567	16,105	-2.8
Murder and nonnegligent manslaughter	486	506	+4.1	21	29	+38.1	465	477	+2.6
Rape[3]	1,612	1,502	-6.8	317	263	-17.0	1,295	1,239	-4.3
Robbery	932	954	+2.4	80	51	-36.3	852	903	+6.0
Aggravated assault	14,694	14,152	-3.7	739	666	-9.9	13,955	13,486	-3.4
Property crime[2]	34,217	31,421	-8.2	3,075	2,605	-15.3	31,142	28,816	-7.5
Burglary	9,684	8,599	-11.2	1,037	805	-22.4	8,647	7,794	-9.9
Larceny-theft	20,447	18,494	-9.6	1,498	1,311	-12.5	18,949	17,183	-9.3
Motor vehicle theft	3,660	3,671	+0.3	479	430	-10.2	3,181	3,241	+1.9
Arson	426	657	+54.2	61	59	-3.3	365	598	+63.8
Other assaults	48,002	46,086	-4.0	4,138	4,063	-1.8	43,864	42,023	-4.2
Forgery and counterfeiting	2,080	2,194	+5.5	26	24	-7.7	2,054	2,170	+5.6
Fraud	6,646	5,629	-15.3	110	90	-18.2	6,536	5,539	-15.3
Embezzlement	442	410	-7.2	7	7	0.0	435	403	-7.4
Stolen property; buying, receiving, possessing	3,553	3,196	-10.0	233	160	-31.3	3,320	3,036	-8.6
Vandalism	7,257	6,445	-11.2	1,250	1,024	-18.1	6,007	5,421	-9.8
Weapons; carrying, possessing, etc.	6,501	6,238	-4.0	313	272	-13.1	6,188	5,966	-3.6
Prostitution and commercialized vice	180	202	+12.2	2	6	+200.0	178	196	+10.1
Sex offenses (except forcible rape and prostitution)	2,283	2,300	+0.7	390	373	-4.4	1,893	1,927	+1.8
Drug abuse violations	89,975	88,262	-1.9	3,249	2,861	-11.9	86,726	85,401	-1.5
Gambling	114	97	-14.9	2	0	-100.0	112	97	-13.4
Offenses against the family and children	7,416	6,906	-6.9	77	81	+5.2	7,339	6,825	-7.0
Driving under the influence	105,293	103,148	-2.0	627	581	-7.3	104,666	102,567	-2.0
Liquor laws	11,145	9,363	-16.0	2,361	1,949	-17.5	8,784	7,414	-15.6
Drunkenness	10,484	9,766	-6.8	115	104	-9.6	10,369	9,662	-6.8
Disorderly conduct	13,649	12,661	-7.2	1,702	1,736	+2.0	11,947	10,925	-8.6
Vagrancy	76	253	+232.9	4	13	+225.0	72	240	+233.3
All other offenses (except traffic)	215,050	206,259	-4.1	4,972	5,041	+1.4	210,078	201,218	-4.2
Suspicion	24	22	-8.3	4	3	-25.0	20	19	-5.0
Curfew and loitering law violations	222	230	+3.6	222	230	+3.6	NA	NA	NA

NA = Not available.

1 Does not include suspicion.   2 Violent crimes are offenses of murder and nonnegligent manslaughter, rape, robbery, and aggravated assault. Property crimes are offenses of burglary, larceny-theft, motor vehicle theft, and arson.   3 The rape figures in this table are aggregate totals of the data submitted based on both the legacy and revised Uniform Crime Reporting definitions.

Table 57. Arrest Trends, Nonmetropolitan Counties, by Age and Sex, 2017–2018

(Number, percent; 1,617 agencies; 2018 estimated population 17,352,148; 2017 estimated population 17,344,934.)

Offense charged	Male						Female					
	Total			Under 18			Total			Under 18		
	2017	2018	Percent change	2017	2018	Percent change	2017	2018	Percent change	2017	2018	Percent change
Total[1]	427,036	408,305	-4.4	17,210	15,829	-8.0	155,273	149,875	-3.5	6,822	6,400	-6.2
Violent crime[2]	14,461	13,970	-3.4	962	829	-13.8	3,263	3,144	-3.6	195	180	-7.7
Murder and nonnegligent manslaughter	390	433	+11.0	19	29	+52.6	96	73	-24.0	2	0	-100.0
Rape[3]	1,561	1,437	-7.9	305	249	-18.4	51	65	+27.5	12	14	+16.7
Robbery	772	779	+0.9	74	47	-36.5	160	175	+9.4	6	4	-33.3
Aggravated assault	11,738	11,321	-3.6	564	504	-10.6	2,956	2,831	-4.2	175	162	-7.4
Property crime[2]	23,835	21,921	-8.0	2,413	2,018	-16.4	10,382	9,500	-8.5	662	587	-11.3
Burglary	7,794	6,968	-10.6	931	723	-22.3	1,890	1,631	-13.7	106	82	-22.6
Larceny-theft	12,871	11,679	-9.3	1,067	897	-15.9	7,576	6,815	-10.0	431	414	-3.9
Motor vehicle theft	2,828	2,768	-2.1	366	348	-4.9	832	903	+8.5	113	82	-27.4
Arson	342	506	+48.0	49	50	+2.0	84	151	+79.8	12	9	-25.0
Other assaults	35,192	33,880	-3.7	2,737	2,745	+0.3	12,810	12,206	-4.7	1,401	1,318	-5.9
Forgery and counterfeiting	1,254	1,392	+11.0	21	16	-23.8	826	802	-2.9	5	8	+60.0
Fraud	3,888	3,314	-14.8	78	66	-15.4	2,758	2,315	-16.1	32	24	-25.0
Embezzlement	210	219	+4.3	5	6	+20.0	232	191	-17.7	2	1	-50.0
Stolen property; buying, receiving, possessing	2,740	2,497	-8.9	181	127	-29.8	813	699	-14.0	52	33	-36.5
Vandalism	5,721	5,137	-10.2	1,044	853	-18.3	1,536	1,308	-14.8	206	171	-17.0
Weapons; carrying, possessing, etc.	5,862	5,592	-4.6	283	250	-11.7	639	646	+1.1	30	22	-26.7
Prostitution and commercialized vice	106	154	+45.3	2	3	+50.0	74	48	-35.1	0	3	
Sex offenses (except forcible rape and prostitution)	2,124	2,141	+0.8	340	341	+0.3	159	159	0.0	50	32	-36.0
Drug abuse violations	65,062	62,840	-3.4	2,344	2,007	-14.4	24,913	25,422	+2.0	905	854	-5.6
Gambling	74	64	-13.5	1	0	-100.0	40	33	-17.5	1	0	-100.0
Offenses against the family and children	5,504	5,142	-6.6	46	58	+26.1	1,912	1,764	-7.7	31	23	-25.8
Driving under the influence	79,873	78,192	-2.1	488	438	-10.2	25,420	24,956	-1.8	139	143	+2.9
Liquor laws	7,531	6,291	-16.5	1,354	1,140	-15.8	3,614	3,072	-15.0	1,007	809	-19.7
Drunkenness	7,663	7,082	-7.6	85	64	-24.7	2,821	2,684	-4.9	30	40	+33.3
Disorderly conduct	9,680	8,923	-7.8	1,188	1,196	+0.7	3,969	3,738	-5.8	514	540	+5.1
Vagrancy	56	187	+233.9	2	11	+450.0	20	66	+230.0	2	2	0.0
All other offenses (except traffic)	156,061	149,232	-4.4	3,497	3,526	+0.8	58,989	57,027	-3.3	1,475	1,515	+2.7
Suspicion	22	19	-13.6	4	3	-25.0	2	3	+50.0	0	0	
Curfew and loitering law violations	139	135	-2.9	139	135	-2.9	83	95	+14.5	83	95	+14.5

1 Does not include suspicion.   2 Violent crimes are offenses of murder and nonnegligent manslaughter, rape, robbery, and aggravated assault. Property crimes are offenses of burglary, larceny-theft, motor vehicle theft, and arson.   3 The rape figures in this table are aggregate totals of the data submitted based on both the legacy and revised Uniform Crime Reporting definitions.

Table 58. Arrests, Nonmetropolitan Counties, Distribution by Age, 2018

(Number, percent; 1,805 agencies; 2018 estimated population 19,122,063.)

Offense charged	Total, all ages	Ages under 15	Ages under 18	Ages 18 and over	Under 10	10–12	13–14	15	16	17	18	19	20
Total	614,165	6,724	24,182	589,983	259	1,664	4,801	3,910	5,504	8,044	13,953	16,298	17,452
Total percent distribution[1]	100.0	1.1	3.9	96.1	*	0.3	0.8	0.6	0.9	1.3	2.3	2.7	2.8
Violent crime[2]	19,101	379	1,122	17,979	7	99	273	197	245	301	482	466	499
Violent crime percent distribution[1]	100.0	2.0	5.9	94.1	*	0.5	1.4	1.0	1.3	1.6	2.5	2.4	2.6
Murder and nonnegligent manslaughter	575	5	37	538	0	1	4	9	7	16	21	15	21
Rape[3]	1,600	106	272	1,328	1	32	73	45	52	69	69	84	56
Robbery	1,122	5	58	1,064	0	1	4	9	12	32	61	44	52
Aggravated assault	15,804	263	755	15,049	6	65	192	134	174	184	331	323	370
Property crime[2]	34,634	863	2,793	31,841	41	205	617	468	630	832	1,147	1,063	981
Property crime percent distribution[1]	100.0	2.5	8.1	91.9	0.1	0.6	1.8	1.4	1.8	2.4	3.3	3.1	2.8
Burglary	9,603	251	886	8,717	10	67	174	139	224	272	395	364	328
Larceny-theft	20,404	447	1,399	19,005	22	103	322	233	286	433	594	587	529
Motor vehicle theft	3,935	130	446	3,489	3	17	110	87	112	117	138	102	98
Arson	692	35	62	630	6	18	11	9	8	10	20	10	26
Other assaults	50,275	1,685	4,368	45,907	81	476	1,128	828	914	941	1,028	1,092	1,078
Forgery and counterfeiting	2,352	2	25	2,327	0	0	2	2	10	11	32	44	61
Fraud	6,250	19	99	6,151	0	5	14	14	29	37	70	86	127
Embezzlement	445	0	7	438	0	0	0	2	1	4	4	14	12
Stolen property; buying, receiving, possessing	3,657	34	174	3,483	1	5	28	26	44	70	118	111	99
Vandalism	6,995	394	1,073	5,922	23	102	269	202	236	241	264	222	220
Weapons; carrying, possessing, etc.	6,894	103	318	6,576	14	30	59	60	63	92	139	184	185
Prostitution and commercialized vice	205	4	6	199	1	0	3	0	1	1	3	1	2
Sex offenses (except forcible rape and prostitution)	2,502	186	405	2,097	13	33	140	63	78	78	111	87	95
Drug abuse violations	98,296	440	3,177	95,119	2	83	355	400	735	1,602	3,519	4,106	4,071
Gambling	141	0	0	141	0	0	0	0	0	0	2	6	4
Offenses against the family and children	7,970	36	97	7,873	1	4	31	16	17	28	76	81	98
Driving under the influence	115,676	18	646	115,030	0	3	15	22	140	466	1,463	2,087	2,542
Liquor laws	9,987	237	2,029	7,958	2	23	212	301	566	925	1,483	1,641	1,443
Drunkenness	10,192	15	106	10,086	0	1	14	12	29	50	167	194	217
Disorderly conduct	13,849	824	1,973	11,876	25	229	570	346	399	404	359	306	288
Vagrancy	310	1	14	296	0	0	1	7	2	4	4	6	6
All other offenses (except traffic)	224,181	1,416	5,516	218,665	46	353	1,017	895	1,301	1,904	3,480	4,501	5,423
Suspicion	22	0	3	19	0	0	0	0	0	3	2	0	1
Curfew and loitering law violations	231	68	231	NA	2	13	53	49	64	50	NA	NA	NA

Table 58. Arrests, Nonmetropolitan Counties, Distribution by Age, 2018—Continued

(Number, percent; 1,805 agencies; 2018 estimated population 19,122,063.)

Offense charged	21	22	23	24	25–29	30–34	35–39	40–44	45–49	50–54	55–59	60–64	65 and over
Total	17,527	18,139	18,440	19,338	105,033	96,206	83,034	57,704	44,750	33,851	24,858	13,199	10,201
Total percent distribution[1]	2.9	3.0	3.0	3.1	17.1	15.7	13.5	9.4	7.3	5.5	4.0	2.1	1.7
Violent crime[2]	549	467	516	574	3,026	2,930	2,513	1,708	1,404	1,097	855	417	476
Violent crime percent distribution[1]	2.9	2.4	2.7	3.0	15.8	15.3	13.2	8.9	7.4	5.7	4.5	2.2	2.5
Murder and nonnegligent manslaughter	20	16	29	14	79	79	80	40	40	33	19	12	20
Rape[3]	62	30	34	41	176	194	155	112	89	77	66	34	49
Robbery	52	47	38	53	201	154	153	90	47	34	28	4	6
Aggravated assault	415	374	415	466	2,570	2,503	2,125	1,466	1,228	953	742	367	401
Property crime[2]	917	953	962	973	5,964	5,433	4,784	2,997	2,232	1,553	1,059	473	350
Property crime percent distribution[1]	2.6	2.8	2.8	2.8	17.2	15.7	13.8	8.7	6.4	4.5	3.1	1.4	1.0
Burglary	288	291	260	276	1,643	1,531	1,367	764	500	371	209	81	49
Larceny-theft	492	534	583	563	3,453	3,158	2,810	1,848	1,488	1,017	741	348	260
Motor vehicle theft	123	109	108	115	754	655	521	330	191	124	83	20	18
Arson	14	19	11	19	114	89	86	55	53	41	26	24	23
Other assaults	1,127	1,168	1,230	1,360	7,672	7,272	6,589	4,790	3,835	3,117	2,238	1,225	1,086
Forgery and counterfeiting	50	66	85	78	444	416	383	240	159	100	87	45	37
Fraud	117	148	153	159	946	1,026	1,032	707	571	426	263	175	145
Embezzlement	9	8	18	3	60	83	66	53	44	30	22	6	6
Stolen property; buying, receiving, possessing	106	130	110	120	654	648	535	339	217	147	89	35	25
Vandalism	247	191	210	194	1,105	957	742	482	398	291	187	107	105
Weapons; carrying, possessing, etc.	215	219	211	207	1,186	1,037	883	594	472	396	326	161	161
Prostitution and commercialized vice	5	5	6	5	32	31	27	18	17	10	15	16	6
Sex offenses (except forcible rape and prostitution)	57	59	50	48	234	251	254	195	176	146	140	72	122
Drug abuse violations	3,842	3,750	3,732	3,634	18,032	14,932	12,215	8,099	5,895	4,231	3,005	1,400	656
Gambling	1	5	5	6	24	11	16	17	8	7	17	6	6
Offenses against the family and children	130	147	153	217	1,332	1,549	1,572	1,067	657	407	213	96	78
Driving under the influence	3,617	3,936	3,897	4,059	20,077	16,382	13,611	10,465	9,606	8,366	7,082	4,342	3,498
Liquor laws	247	163	141	123	575	448	409	322	283	279	180	121	100
Drunkenness	239	243	232	264	1,561	1,567	1,442	1,089	938	856	598	317	162
Disorderly conduct	361	331	343	347	1,881	1,751	1,596	1,212	953	798	676	361	313
Vagrancy	7	5	4	8	60	43	52	20	22	29	19	9	2
All other offenses (except traffic)	5,683	6,145	6,381	6,959	40,164	39,433	34,313	23,288	16,862	11,565	7,786	3,815	2,867
Suspicion	1	0	1	0	4	6	0	2	1	0	1	0	0
Curfew and loitering law violations	NA	NA	NA	NA	NA	NA	NA	NA	NA	NA	NA	NA	NA

NA = Not available.

* = Less than one-tenth of one percent.

1 Because of rounding, the percentages may not sum to 100.   2 Violent crimes are offenses of murder and nonnegligent manslaughter, rape, robbery, and aggravated assault. Property crimes are offenses of burglary, larceny-theft, motor vehicle theft, and arson.   3 The rape figures in this table are aggregate totals of the data submitted based on both the legacy and revised Uniform Crime Reporting definitions.

Table 59. Arrests, Nonmetropolitan Counties, Persons Under 15, 18, 21, and 25 Years of Age, 2018

(Number, percent; 1,805 agencies; 2018 estimated population 19,122,063.)

Offense charged	Total, all ages	Number of persons arrested				Percent of total all ages			
		Under 15	Under 18	Under 21	Under 25	Under 15	Under 18	Under 21	Under 25
Total	614,165	6,724	24,182	71,885	145,329	1.1	3.9	11.7	23.7
Violent crime[1]	19,101	379	1,122	2,569	4,675	2.0	5.9	13.4	24.5
Murder and nonnegligent manslaughter	575	5	37	94	173	0.9	6.4	16.3	30.1
Rape[2]	1,600	106	272	481	648	6.6	17.0	30.1	40.5
Robbery	1,122	5	58	215	405	0.4	5.2	19.2	36.1
Aggravated assault	15,804	263	755	1,779	3,449	1.7	4.8	11.3	21.8
Property crime[1]	34,634	863	2,793	5,984	9,789	2.5	8.1	17.3	28.3
Burglary	9,603	251	886	1,973	3,088	2.6	9.2	20.5	32.2
Larceny-theft	20,404	447	1,399	3,109	5,281	2.2	6.9	15.2	25.9
Motor vehicle theft	3,935	130	446	784	1,239	3.3	11.3	19.9	31.5
Arson	692	35	62	118	181	5.1	9.0	17.1	26.2
Other assaults	50,275	1,685	4,368	7,566	12,451	3.4	8.7	15.0	24.8
Forgery and counterfeiting	2,352	2	25	162	441	0.1	1.1	6.9	18.8
Fraud	6,250	19	99	382	959	0.3	1.6	6.1	15.3
Embezzlement	445	0	7	37	75	0.0	1.6	8.3	16.9
Stolen property; buying, receiving, possessing	3,657	34	174	502	968	0.9	4.8	13.7	26.5
Vandalism	6,995	394	1,073	1,779	2,621	5.6	15.3	25.4	37.5
Weapons; carrying, possessing, etc.	6,894	103	318	826	1,678	1.5	4.6	12.0	24.3
Prostitution and commercialized vice	205	4	6	12	33	2.0	2.9	5.9	16.1
Sex offenses (except forcible rape and prostitution)	2,502	186	405	698	912	7.4	16.2	27.9	36.5
Drug abuse violations	98,296	440	3,177	14,873	29,831	0.4	3.2	15.1	30.3
Gambling	141	0	0	12	29	0.0	0.0	8.5	20.6
Offenses against the family and children	7,970	36	97	352	999	0.5	1.2	4.4	12.5
Driving under the influence	115,676	18	646	6,738	22,247	*	0.6	5.8	19.2
Liquor laws	9,987	237	2,029	6,596	7,270	2.4	20.3	66.0	72.8
Drunkenness	10,192	15	106	684	1,662	0.1	1.0	6.7	16.3
Disorderly conduct	13,849	824	1,973	2,926	4,308	5.9	14.2	21.1	31.1
Vagrancy	310	1	14	30	54	0.3	4.5	9.7	17.4
All other offenses (except traffic)	224,181	1,416	5,516	18,920	44,088	0.6	2.5	8.4	19.7
Suspicion	22	0	3	6	8	0.0	13.6	27.3	36.4
Curfew and loitering law violations	231	68	231	231	231	29.4	100.0	100.0	100.0

* = Less than one-tenth of one percent.
1 Violent crimes are offenses of murder and nonnegligent manslaughter, rape, robbery, and aggravated assault. Property crimes are offenses of burglary, larceny-theft, motor vehicle theft, and arson. 2 The rape figures in this table are aggregate totals of the data submitted based on both the legacy and revised Uniform Crime Reporting definitions.

Table 60. Arrests, Nonmetropolitan Counties, Distribution by Sex, 2018

(Number, percent; 1,805 agencies; 2018 estimated population 19,122,063.)

Offense charged	Number of persons arrested			Percent male	Percent female	Percent distribution[1]		
	Total	Male	Female			Total	Male	Female
Total	614,165	449,234	164,931	73.1	26.9	100.0	100.0	100.0
Violent crime[2]	19,101	15,569	3,532	81.5	18.5	3.1	3.5	2.1
Murder and nonnegligent manslaughter	575	492	83	85.6	14.4	0.1	0.1	0.1
Rape[3]	1,600	1,531	69	95.7	4.3	0.3	0.3	*
Robbery	1,122	912	210	81.3	18.7	0.2	0.2	0.1
Aggravated assault	15,804	12,634	3,170	79.9	20.1	2.6	2.8	1.9
Property crime[2]	34,634	24,220	10,414	69.9	30.1	5.6	5.4	6.3
Burglary	9,603	7,772	1,831	80.9	19.1	1.6	1.7	1.1
Larceny-theft	20,404	12,963	7,441	63.5	36.5	3.3	2.9	4.5
Motor vehicle theft	3,935	2,953	982	75.0	25.0	0.6	0.7	0.6
Arson	692	532	160	76.9	23.1	0.1	0.1	0.1
Other assaults	50,275	36,894	13,381	73.4	26.6	8.2	8.2	8.1
Forgery and counterfeiting	2,352	1,487	865	63.2	36.8	0.4	0.3	0.5
Fraud	6,250	3,692	2,558	59.1	40.9	1.0	0.8	1.6
Embezzlement	445	238	207	53.5	46.5	0.1	0.1	0.1
Stolen property; buying, receiving, possessing	3,657	2,847	810	77.9	22.1	0.6	0.6	0.5
Vandalism	6,995	5,561	1,434	79.5	20.5	1.1	1.2	0.9
Weapons; carrying, possessing, etc.	6,894	6,184	710	89.7	10.3	1.1	1.4	0.4
Prostitution and commercialized vice	205	156	49	76.1	23.9	*	*	*
Sex offenses (except forcible rape and prostitution)	2,502	2,331	171	93.2	6.8	0.4	0.5	0.1
Drug abuse violations	98,296	70,100	28,196	71.3	28.7	16.0	15.6	17.1
Gambling	141	99	42	70.2	29.8	*	*	*
Offenses against the family and children	7,970	5,916	2,054	74.2	25.8	1.3	1.3	1.2
Driving under the influence	115,676	87,618	28,058	75.7	24.3	18.8	19.5	17.0
Liquor laws	9,987	6,732	3,255	67.4	32.6	1.6	1.5	2.0
Drunkenness	10,192	7,400	2,792	72.6	27.4	1.7	1.6	1.7
Disorderly conduct	13,849	9,770	4,079	70.5	29.5	2.3	2.2	2.5
Vagrancy	310	238	72	76.8	23.2	0.1	*	*
All other offenses (except traffic)	224,181	162,027	62,154	72.3	27.7	36.5	36.1	37.7
Suspicion	22	19	3	86.4	13.6	*	*	*
Curfew and loitering law violations	231	136	95	58.9	41.1	*	*	0.1

* = Less than one-tenth of 1 percent.
1 Because of rounding, the percentages may not sum to 100.   2 Violent crimes are offenses of murder and nonnegligent manslaughter, rape, robbery, and aggravated assault. Property crimes are offenses of burglary, larceny-theft, motor vehicle theft, and arson.   3 The rape figures in this table are aggregate totals of the data submitted based on both the legacy and revised Uniform Crime Reporting definitions.

Table 61. Arrests, Nonmetropolitan Counties, Distribution by Race, 2018

(Number, percent; 1,805 agencies; 2018 estimated population 19,122,063.)

Offense charged	Total arrests						Percent distribution[1]						Arrests under 18					
	Total	White	Black	American Indian or Alaskan Native	Asian	Native Hawaiian or Other Pacific Islander	Total	White	Black	American Indian or Alaskan Native	Asian	Native Hawaiian or Other Pacific Islander	Total	White	Black	American Indian or Alaskan Native	Asian	Native Hawaiian or Other Pacific Islander
Total	602,743	498,823	81,404	18,126	4,040	350	100.0	82.8	13.5	3.0	0.7	0.1	23,459	18,786	3,565	1,012	76	20
Violent crime[2]	18,869	14,953	2,772	1,043	80	21	100.0	79.2	14.7	5.5	0.4	0.1	1,096	834	200	58	3	1
Murder and nonnegligent manslaughter	568	411	139	18	0	0	100.0	72.4	24.5	3.2	0.0	0.0	37	29	7	1	0	0
Rape[3]	1,565	1,344	160	54	6	1	100.0	85.9	10.2	3.5	0.4	0.1	267	241	14	11	1	0
Robbery	1,110	723	316	67	4	0	100.0	65.1	28.5	6.0	0.4	0.0	57	27	27	3	0	0
Aggravated assault	15,626	12,475	2,157	904	70	20	100.0	79.8	13.8	5.8	0.4	0.1	735	537	152	43	2	1
Property crime[2]	34,076	29,389	3,621	958	100	8	100.0	86.2	10.6	2.8	0.3	*	2,717	2,164	408	135	8	2
Burglary	9,507	8,218	1,009	257	21	2	100.0	86.4	10.6	2.7	0.2	*	877	681	140	53	2	1
Larceny-theft	20,014	17,220	2,207	521	62	4	100.0	86.0	11.0	2.6	0.3	*	1,356	1,096	203	52	5	0
Motor vehicle theft	3,874	3,364	344	154	11	1	100.0	86.8	8.9	4.0	0.3	*	428	346	58	22	1	1
Arson	681	587	61	26	6	1	100.0	86.2	9.0	3.8	0.9	0.1	56	41	7	8	0	0
Other assaults	49,428	41,604	5,719	1,933	148	24	100.0	84.2	11.6	3.9	0.3	*	4,237	3,253	818	149	13	4
Forgery and counterfeiting	2,310	1,892	377	34	6	1	100.0	81.9	16.3	1.5	0.3	*	25	23	2	0	0	0
Fraud	6,131	5,039	922	144	25	1	100.0	82.2	15.0	2.3	0.4	*	92	72	17	3	0	0
Embezzlement	437	395	36	3	3	0	100.0	90.4	8.2	0.7	0.7	*	7	7	0	0	0	0
Stolen property; buying, receiving, possessing	3,602	2,822	667	103	5	5	100.0	78.3	18.5	2.9	0.1	0.1	170	101	57	11	0	1
Vandalism	6,871	5,830	757	247	34	3	100.0	84.8	11.0	3.6	0.5	*	1,042	858	141	38	5	0
Weapons; carrying, possessing, etc.	6,789	5,079	1,490	175	38	7	100.0	74.8	21.9	2.6	0.6	0.1	316	231	77	7	1	0
Prostitution and commercialized vice	202	174	23	4	1	0	100.0	86.1	11.4	2.0	0.5	0.0	6	4	0	2	0	0
Sex offenses (except forcible rape and prostitution)	2,463	2,136	256	66	5	0	100.0	86.7	10.4	2.7	0.2	0.0	395	337	37	21	0	0
Drug abuse violations	95,850	77,474	15,294	2,411	601	70	100.0	80.8	16.0	2.5	0.6	0.1	3,057	2,568	359	109	15	6
Gambling	141	97	36	0	8	0	100.0	68.8	25.5	0.0	5.7	0.0	0	0	0	0	0	0
Offenses against the family and children	7,917	6,506	1,270	124	10	7	100.0	82.2	16.0	1.6	0.1	0.1	97	78	10	9	0	0
Driving under the influence	113,103	92,764	15,292	3,047	1,961	39	100.0	82.0	13.5	2.7	1.7	*	624	567	30	20	7	0
Liquor laws	9,607	8,496	580	442	79	10	100.0	88.4	6.0	4.6	0.8	0.1	1,953	1,773	52	113	11	4
Drunkenness	10,110	8,983	663	423	33	8	100.0	88.9	6.6	4.2	0.3	0.1	104	97	5	2	0	0
Disorderly conduct	13,626	10,804	1,900	859	58	5	100.0	79.3	13.9	6.3	0.4	*	1,929	1,327	508	89	5	0
Vagrancy	308	254	34	17	3	0	100.0	82.5	11.0	5.5	1.0	0.0	14	13	1	0	0	0
All other offenses (except traffic)	220,657	183,929	29,682	6,065	840	141	100.0	83.4	13.5	2.7	0.4	0.1	5,349	4,292	831	218	6	2
Suspicion	20	19	1	0	0	0	100.0	95.0	5.0	0.0	0.0	0.0	3	3	0	0	0	0
Curfew and loitering law violations	226	184	12	28	2	0	100.0	81.4	5.3	12.4	0.9	0.0	226	184	12	28	2	0

Table 61. Arrests, Nonmetropolitan Counties, Distribution by Race, 2018—Continued

(Number, percent; 1,805 agencies; 2018 estimated population 19,122,063.)

Offense charged	Percent distribution[1]						Arrests 18 and over						Percent distribution[1]					
	Total	White	Black	American Indian or Alaskan Native	Asian	Native Hawaiian or Other Pacific Islander	Total	White	Black	American Indian or Alaskan Native	Asian	Native Hawaiian or Other Pacific Islander	Total	White	Black	American Indian or Alaskan Native	Asian	Native Hawaiian or Other Pacific Islander
Total	100.0	80.1	15.2	4.3	0.3	0.1	579,284	480,037	77,839	17,114	3,964	330	100.0	82.9	13.4	3.0	0.7	0.1
Violent crime[2]	100.0	76.1	18.2	5.3	0.3	0.1	17,773	14,119	2,572	985	77	20	100.0	79.4	14.5	5.5	0.4	0.1
Murder and nonnegligent manslaughter	100.0	78.4	18.9	2.7	0.0	0.0	531	382	132	17	0	0	100.0	71.9	24.9	3.2	0.0	0.0
Rape[3]	100.0	90.3	5.2	4.1	0.4	0.0	1,298	1,103	146	43	5	1	100.0	85.0	11.2	3.3	0.4	0.1
Robbery	100.0	47.4	47.4	5.3	0.0	0.0	1,053	696	289	64	4	0	100.0	66.1	27.4	6.1	0.4	0.0
Aggravated assault	100.0	73.1	20.7	5.9	0.3	0.1	14,891	11,938	2,005	861	68	19	100.0	80.2	13.5	5.8	0.5	0.1
Property crime[2]	100.0	79.6	15.0	5.0	0.3	0.1	31,359	27,225	3,213	823	92	6	100.0	86.8	10.2	2.6	0.3	*
Burglary	100.0	77.7	16.0	6.0	0.2	0.1	8,630	7,537	869	204	19	1	100.0	87.3	10.1	2.4	0.2	*
Larceny-theft	100.0	80.8	15.0	3.8	0.4	0.0	18,658	16,124	2,004	469	57	4	100.0	86.4	10.7	2.5	0.3	*
Motor vehicle theft	100.0	80.8	13.6	5.1	0.2	0.2	3,446	3,018	286	132	10	0	100.0	87.6	8.3	3.8	0.3	0.0
Arson	100.0	73.2	12.5	14.3	0.0	0.0	625	546	54	18	6	1	100.0	87.4	8.6	2.9	1.0	0.2
Other assaults	100.0	76.8	19.3	3.5	0.3	0.1	45,191	38,351	4,901	1,784	135	20	100.0	84.9	10.8	3.9	0.3	*
Forgery and counterfeiting	100.0	92.0	8.0	0.0	0.0	0.0	2,285	1,869	375	34	6	1	100.0	81.8	16.4	1.5	0.3	*
Fraud	100.0	78.3	18.5	3.3	0.0	0.0	6,039	4,967	905	141	25	1	100.0	82.2	15.0	2.3	0.4	*
Embezzlement	100.0	100.0	0.0	0.0	0.0	0.0	430	388	36	3	3	0	100.0	90.2	8.4	0.7	0.7	0.0
Stolen property; buying, receiving, possessing	100.0	59.4	33.5	6.5	0.0	0.6	3,432	2,721	610	92	5	4	100.0	79.3	17.8	2.7	0.1	0.1
Vandalism	100.0	82.3	13.5	3.6	0.5	0.0	5,829	4,972	616	209	29	3	100.0	85.3	10.6	3.6	0.5	0.1
Weapons; carrying, possessing, etc.	100.0	73.1	24.4	2.2	0.3	0.0	6,473	4,848	1,413	168	37	7	100.0	74.9	21.8	2.6	0.6	0.1
Prostitution and commercialized vice	100.0	66.7	0.0	33.3	0.0	0.0	196	170	23	2	1	0	100.0	86.7	11.7	1.0	0.5	0.0
Sex offenses (except forcible rape and prostitution)	100.0	85.3	9.4	5.3	0.0	0.0	2,068	1,799	219	45	5	0	100.0	87.0	10.6	2.2	0.2	0.0
Drug abuse violations	100.0	84.0	11.7	3.6	0.5	0.2	92,793	74,906	14,935	2,302	586	64	100.0	80.7	16.1	2.5	0.6	0.1
Gambling	100.0						141	97	36	0	8	0	100.0	68.8	25.5	0.0	5.7	0.0
Offenses against the family and children	100.0	80.4	10.3	9.3	0.0	0.0	7,820	6,428	1,260	115	10	7	100.0	82.2	16.1	1.5	0.1	0.1
Driving under the influence	100.0	90.9	4.8	3.2	1.1	0.0	112,479	92,197	15,262	3,027	1,954	39	100.0	82.0	13.6	2.7	1.7	*
Liquor laws	100.0	90.8	2.7	5.8	0.6	0.2	7,654	6,723	528	329	68	6	100.0	87.8	6.9	4.3	0.9	0.1
Drunkenness	100.0	93.3	4.8	1.9	0.0	0.0	10,006	8,886	658	421	33	8	100.0	88.8	6.6	4.2	0.3	0.1
Disorderly conduct	100.0	68.8	26.3	4.6	0.3	0.0	11,697	9,477	1,392	770	53	5	100.0	81.0	11.9	6.6	0.5	*
Vagrancy	100.0	92.9	7.1	0.0	0.0	0.0	294	241	33	17	3	0	100.0	82.0	11.2	5.8	1.0	0.0
All other offenses (except traffic)	100.0	80.2	15.5	4.1	0.1	*	215,308	179,637	28,851	5,847	834	139	100.0	83.4	13.4	2.7	0.4	0.1
Suspicion	100.0	100.0	0.0	0.0	0.0	0.0	17	16	1	0	0	0	100.0	94.1	5.9	0.0	0.0	0.0
Curfew and loitering law violations	100.0	81.4	5.3	12.4	0.9	0.0	NA	NA	NA	NA	NA	NA	NA	NA	NA	NA	NA	NA

NA = Not available.
* = Less than one-tenth of one percent.
1 Because of rounding, the percentages may not sum to 100.   2 Violent crimes are offenses of murder and nonnegligent manslaughter, rape, robbery, and aggravated assault.   Property crimes are offenses of burglary, larceny-theft, motor vehicle theft, and arson.   3 The rape figures in this table are aggregate totals of the data submitted based on both the legacy and revised Uniform Crime Reporting definitions.

Table 61A. Arrests, Nonmetropolitan Counties, Distribution by Ethnicity, 2018

(Number, percent; 1,805 agencies; 2018 estimated population 19,122,063.)

Offense charged	Total arrests			Percent distribution[1]			Arrests under 18		
	Total[2]	Hispanic or Latino	Not Hispanic or Latino	Total[2]	Hispanic or Latino	Not Hispanic or Latino	Total[2]	Hispanic or Latino	Not Hispanic or Latino
Total	427,621	32,907	394,714	100.0	7.7	92.3	16,609	1,677	14,932
Violent crime[3]	13,225	1,170	12,055	100.0	8.8	91.2	701	77	624
Murder and nonnegligent manslaughter	433	36	397	100.0	8.3	91.7	27	6	21
Rape[4]	1,076	110	966	100.0	10.2	89.8	160	9	151
Robbery	795	66	729	100.0	8.3	91.7	49	9	40
Aggravated assault	10,921	958	9,963	100.0	8.8	91.2	465	53	412
Property crime[3]	24,932	1,514	23,418	100.0	6.1	93.9	1,839	158	1,681
Burglary	6,987	400	6,587	100.0	5.7	94.3	598	58	540
Larceny-theft	14,504	792	13,712	100.0	5.5	94.5	921	68	853
Motor vehicle theft	2,890	233	2,657	100.0	8.1	91.9	289	30	259
Arson	551	89	462	100.0	16.2	83.8	31	2	29
Other assaults	36,085	2,234	33,851	100.0	6.2	93.8	3,057	257	2,800
Forgery and counterfeiting	1,737	179	1,558	100.0	10.3	89.7	21	4	17
Fraud	4,272	263	4,009	100.0	6.2	93.8	62	5	57
Embezzlement	279	7	272	100.0	2.5	97.5	7	0	7
Stolen property; buying, receiving, possessing	2,564	135	2,429	100.0	5.3	94.7	128	14	114
Vandalism	5,176	269	4,907	100.0	5.2	94.8	803	57	746
Weapons; carrying, possessing, etc.	4,605	363	4,242	100.0	7.9	92.1	237	29	208
Prostitution and commercialized vice	87	6	81	100.0	6.9	93.1	1	0	1
Sex offenses (except forcible rape and prostitution)	1,674	124	1,550	100.0	7.4	92.6	247	13	234
Drug abuse violations	69,783	6,176	63,607	100.0	8.9	91.1	2,189	294	1,895
Gambling	85	17	68	100.0	20.0	80.0	0	0	0
Offenses against the family and children	5,832	401	5,431	100.0	6.9	93.1	72	15	57
Driving under the influence	69,101	5,986	63,115	100.0	8.7	91.3	414	56	358
Liquor laws	6,775	685	6,090	100.0	10.1	89.9	1,524	130	1,394
Drunkenness	8,750	938	7,812	100.0	10.7	89.3	84	13	71
Disorderly conduct	8,410	598	7,812	100.0	7.1	92.9	1,255	112	1,143
Vagrancy	165	32	133	100.0	19.4	80.6	3	0	3
All other offenses (except traffic)	163,881	11,798	152,083	100.0	7.2	92.8	3,772	432	3,340
Suspicion	12	1	11	100.0	8.3	91.7	2	0	2
Curfew and loitering law violations	191	11	180	100.0	5.8	94.2	191	11	180

Table 61A. Arrests, Nonmetropolitan Counties, Distribution by Ethnicity, 2018—Continued

(Number, percent; 1,805 agencies; 2018 estimated population 19,122,063.)

Offense charged	Percent distribution[1]				Arrests 18 and over			Percent distribution[1]	
	Total[2]	Hispanic or Latino	Not Hispanic or Latino	Total[2]	Hispanic or Latino	Not Hispanic or Latino	Total[2]	Hispanic or Latino	Not Hispanic or Latino
Total	100.0	10.1	89.9	411,012	31,230	379,782	100.0	7.6	92.4
Violent crime[3]	100.0	11.0	89.0	12,524	1,093	11,431	100.0	8.7	91.3
Murder and nonnegligent manslaughter	100.0	22.2	77.8	406	30	376	100.0	7.4	92.6
Rape[4]	100.0	5.6	94.4	916	101	815	100.0	11.0	89.0
Robbery	100.0	18.4	81.6	746	57	689	100.0	7.6	92.4
Aggravated assault	100.0	11.4	88.6	10,456	905	9,551	100.0	8.7	91.3
Property crime[3]	100.0	8.6	91.4	23,093	1,356	21,737	100.0	5.9	94.1
Burglary	100.0	9.7	90.3	6,389	342	6,047	100.0	5.4	94.6
Larceny-theft	100.0	7.4	92.6	13,583	724	12,859	100.0	5.3	94.7
Motor vehicle theft	100.0	10.4	89.6	2,601	203	2,398	100.0	7.8	92.2
Arson	100.0	6.5	93.5	520	87	433	100.0	16.7	83.3
Other assaults	100.0	8.4	91.6	33,028	1,977	31,051	100.0	6.0	94.0
Forgery and counterfeiting	100.0	19.0	81.0	1,716	175	1,541	100.0	10.2	89.8
Fraud	100.0	8.1	91.9	4,210	258	3,952	100.0	6.1	93.9
Embezzlement	100.0	0.0	100.0	272	7	265	100.0	2.6	97.4
Stolen property; buying, receiving, possessing	100.0	10.9	89.1	2,436	121	2,315	100.0	5.0	95.0
Vandalism	100.0	7.1	92.9	4,373	212	4,161	100.0	4.8	95.2
Weapons; carrying, possessing, etc.	100.0	12.2	87.8	4,368	334	4,034	100.0	7.6	92.4
Prostitution and commercialized vice	100.0	0.0	100.0	86	6	80	100.0	7.0	93.0
Sex offenses (except forcible rape and prostitution)	100.0	5.3	94.7	1,427	111	1,316	100.0	7.8	92.2
Drug abuse violations	100.0	13.4	86.6	67,594	5,882	61,712	100.0	8.7	91.3
Gambling	100.0			85	17	68	100.0	20.0	80.0
Offenses against the family and children	100.0	20.8	79.2	5,760	386	5,374	100.0	6.7	93.3
Driving under the influence	100.0	13.5	86.5	68,687	5,930	62,757	100.0	8.6	91.4
Liquor laws	100.0	8.5	91.5	5,251	555	4,696	100.0	10.6	89.4
Drunkenness	100.0	15.5	84.5	8,666	925	7,741	100.0	10.7	89.3
Disorderly conduct	100.0	8.9	91.1	7,155	486	6,669	100.0	6.8	93.2
Vagrancy	100.0	0.0	100.0	162	32	130	100.0	19.8	80.2
All other offenses (except traffic)	100.0	11.5	88.5	160,109	11,366	148,743	100.0	7.1	92.9
Suspicion	100.0	0.0	100.0	10	1	9	100.0	10.0	90.0
Curfew and loitering law violations	100.0	5.8	94.2	NA	NA	NA	NA	NA	NA

NA = Not available.
1 Because of rounding, the percentages may not sum to 100.   2 The ethnicity totals are representative of those agencies that provided ethnicity breakdowns. Not all agencies provide ethnicity data; therefore, the race and ethnicity totals will not be equal.   3 Violent crimes are offenses of murder and nonnegligent manslaughter, rape, robbery, and aggravated assault.   Property crimes are offenses of burglary, larceny-theft, motor vehicle theft, and arson.   4 The rape figures in this table are aggregate totals of the data submitted based on both the legacy and revised Uniform Crime Reporting definitions.

Table 62. Arrest Trends, Suburban Areas,[1] 2017–2018

(Number, percent change; 6,287 agencies; 2018 estimated population 97,716,355; 2017 estimated population 97,435,218.)

Offense charged	Number of persons arrested								
	Total, all ages			Under 18 years of age			18 years of age and over		
	2017	2018	Percent change	2017	2018	Percent change	2017	2018	Percent change
Total[2]	2,960,294	2,871,139	-3.0	231,733	207,158	-10.6	2,728,561	2,663,981	-2.4
Violent crime[3]	117,381	116,181	-1.0	12,322	12,250	-0.6	105,059	103,931	-1.1
Murder and nonnegligent manslaughter	2,388	2,296	-3.9	134	169	+26.1	2,254	2,127	-5.6
Rape[4]	6,172	6,352	+2.9	1,147	1,167	+1.7	5,025	5,185	+3.2
Robbery	18,618	16,489	-11.4	3,650	3,261	-10.7	14,968	13,228	-11.6
Aggravated assault	90,203	91,044	+0.9	7,391	7,653	+3.5	82,812	83,391	+0.7
Property crime[3]	339,162	313,822	-7.5	44,352	34,629	-21.9	294,810	279,193	-5.3
Burglary	50,751	44,123	-13.1	7,885	5,747	-27.1	42,866	38,376	-10.5
Larceny-theft	264,389	246,314	-6.8	32,599	25,390	-22.1	231,790	220,924	-4.7
Motor vehicle theft	21,631	21,085	-2.5	3,170	2,896	-8.6	18,461	18,189	-1.5
Arson	2,391	2,300	-3.8	698	596	-14.6	1,693	1,704	+0.6
Other assaults	267,234	262,547	-1.8	36,398	36,844	+1.2	230,836	225,703	-2.2
Forgery and counterfeiting	16,761	15,072	-10.1	420	301	-28.3	16,341	14,771	-9.6
Fraud	36,598	34,795	-4.9	1,215	1,003	-17.4	35,383	33,792	-4.5
Embezzlement	4,239	3,781	-10.8	137	137	0.0	4,102	3,644	-11.2
Stolen property; buying, receiving, possessing	26,883	25,270	-6.0	2,575	2,208	-14.3	24,308	23,062	-5.1
Vandalism	48,812	44,752	-8.3	11,074	8,752	-21.0	37,738	36,000	-4.6
Weapons; carrying, possessing, etc.	38,813	39,205	+1.0	4,597	4,255	-7.4	34,216	34,950	+2.1
Prostitution and commercialized vice	4,603	3,278	-28.8	64	47	-26.6	4,539	3,231	-28.8
Sex offenses (except forcible rape and prostitution)	13,143	13,079	-0.5	2,546	2,372	-6.8	10,597	10,707	+1.0
Drug abuse violations	488,831	489,260	+0.1	31,439	29,762	-5.3	457,392	459,498	+0.5
Gambling	598	553	-7.5	46	35	-23.9	552	518	-6.2
Offenses against the family and children	31,625	30,000	-5.1	1,001	851	-15.0	30,624	29,149	-4.8
Driving under the influence	330,171	331,305	+0.3	1,823	1,621	-11.1	328,348	329,684	+0.4
Liquor laws	62,867	49,180	-21.8	11,716	8,466	-27.7	51,151	40,714	-20.4
Drunkenness	80,985	76,042	-6.1	1,294	1,134	-12.4	79,691	74,908	-6.0
Disorderly conduct	98,973	92,504	-6.5	19,902	18,174	-8.7	79,071	74,330	-6.0
Vagrancy	3,787	3,462	-8.6	232	181	-22.0	3,555	3,281	-7.7
All other offenses (except traffic)	942,827	922,733	-2.1	42,579	39,818	-6.5	900,248	882,915	-1.9
Suspicion	159	285	+79.2	39	11	-71.8	120	274	+128.3
Curfew and loitering law violations	6,001	4,318	-28.0	6,001	4,318	-28.0	NA	NA	NA

NA = Not available.
1 Suburban areas include law enforcement agencies in cities with less than 50,000 inhabitants and county law enforcement agencies that are within a Metropolitan Statistical Area. Suburban areas exclude all metropolitan agencies associated with a principal city.   2 Does not include suspicion.   3 Violent crimes are offenses of murder and nonnegligent manslaughter, rape, robbery, and aggravated assault. Property crimes are offenses of burglary, larceny-theft, motor vehicle theft, and arson.   4 The rape figures in this table are aggregate totals of the data submitted based on both the legacy and revised Uniform Crime Reporting definitions.

Table 63. Arrest Trends, Suburban Areas¹, by Age and Sex, 2017–2018

(Number, percent change; 6,287 agencies; 2018 estimated population 97,716,355; 2017 estimated population 97,435,218.)

Offense charged	Male						Female					
	Total			Under 18			Total			Under 18		
	2017	2018	Percent change	2017	2018	Percent change	2017	2018	Percent change	2017	2018	Percent change
Total²	2,153,580	2,081,626	-3.3	165,099	145,708	-11.7	806,714	789,513	-2.1	66,634	61,450	-7.8
Violent crime³	93,636	92,437	-1.3	9,930	9,688	-2.4	23,745	23,744	*	2,392	2,562	+7.1
Murder and nonnegligent manslaughter	2,070	1,989	-3.9	128	141	+10.2	318	307	-3.5	6	28	+366.7
Rape⁴	5,999	6,169	+2.8	1,111	1,125	+1.3	173	183	+5.8	36	42	+16.7
Robbery	15,879	14,017	-11.7	3,281	2,894	-11.8	2,739	2,472	-9.7	369	367	-0.5
Aggravated assault	69,688	70,262	+0.8	5,410	5,528	+2.2	20,515	20,782	+1.3	1,981	2,125	+7.3
Property crime³	215,206	194,104	-9.8	31,127	23,431	-24.7	123,956	119,718	-3.4	13,225	11,198	-15.3
Burglary	41,495	35,729	-13.9	6,969	5,008	-28.1	9,256	8,394	-9.3	916	739	-19.3
Larceny-theft	154,986	140,305	-9.5	20,971	15,555	-25.8	109,403	106,009	-3.1	11,628	9,835	-15.4
Motor vehicle theft	16,770	16,278	-2.9	2,580	2,389	-7.4	4,861	4,807	-1.1	590	507	-14.1
Arson	1,955	1,792	-8.3	607	479	-21.1	436	508	+16.5	91	117	+28.6
Other assaults	190,571	186,730	-2.0	23,452	23,569	+0.5	76,663	75,817	-1.1	12,946	13,275	+2.5
Forgery and counterfeiting	11,169	10,048	-10.0	330	247	-25.2	5,592	5,024	-10.2	90	54	-40.0
Fraud	23,145	22,168	-4.2	788	670	-15.0	13,453	12,627	-6.1	427	333	-22.0
Embezzlement	2,148	1,919	-10.7	74	88	+18.9	2,091	1,862	-11.0	63	49	-22.2
Stolen property; buying, receiving, possessing	20,830	19,707	-5.4	2,150	1,845	-14.2	6,053	5,563	-8.1	425	363	-14.6
Vandalism	38,490	35,115	-8.8	9,193	7,260	-21.0	10,322	9,637	-6.6	1,881	1,492	-20.7
Weapons; carrying, possessing, etc.	34,768	35,147	+1.1	4,033	3,692	-8.5	4,045	4,058	+0.3	564	563	-0.2
Prostitution and commercialized vice	2,329	1,648	-29.2	36	30	-16.7	2,274	1,630	-28.3	28	17	-39.3
Sex offenses (except forcible rape and prostitution)	12,255	12,182	-0.6	2,250	2,110	-6.2	888	897	+1.0	296	262	-11.5
Drug abuse violations	366,593	364,164	-0.7	23,805	22,144	-7.0	122,238	125,096	+2.3	7,634	7,618	-0.2
Gambling	455	426	-6.4	32	31	-3.1	143	127	-11.2	14	4	-71.4
Offenses against the family and children	23,361	22,029	-5.7	643	556	-13.5	8,264	7,971	-3.5	358	295	-17.6
Driving under the influence	245,323	245,890	+0.2	1,367	1,228	-10.2	84,848	85,415	+0.7	456	393	-13.8
Liquor laws	42,687	33,497	-21.5	6,917	4,897	-29.2	20,180	15,683	-22.3	4,799	3,569	-25.6
Drunkenness	63,003	58,986	-6.4	884	750	-15.2	17,982	17,056	-5.1	410	384	-6.3
Disorderly conduct	69,534	65,182	-6.3	13,116	11,906	-9.2	29,439	27,322	-7.2	6,786	6,268	-7.6
Vagrancy	2,901	2,636	-9.1	183	133	-27.3	886	826	-6.8	49	48	-2.0
All other offenses (except traffic)	691,191	674,740	-2.4	30,804	28,562	-7.3	251,636	247,993	-1.4	11,775	11,256	-4.4
Suspicion	120	212	+76.7	29	7	-75.9	39	73	+87.2	10	4	-60.0
Curfew and loitering law violations	3,985	2,871	-28.0	3,985	2,871	-28.0	2,016	1,447	-28.2	2,016	1,447	-28.2

* = Less than one-tenth of one percent.
1 Suburban areas include law enforcement agencies in cities with less than 50,000 inhabitants and county law enforcement agencies that are within a Metropolitan Statistical Area. Suburban areas exclude all metropolitan agencies associated with a principal city.   2 Does not include suspicion.   3 Violent crimes are offenses of murder and nonnegligent manslaughter, rape, robbery, and aggravated assault. Property crimes are offenses of burglary, larceny-theft, motor vehicle theft, and arson.   4 The rape figures in this table are aggregate totals of the data submitted based on both the legacy and revised Uniform Crime Reporting definitions.

Table 64. Arrests, Suburban Areas,[1] Distribution by Age, 2018

(Number, percent; 6,757 agencies; 2018 estimated population 106,796,972.)

Offense charged	Total, all ages	Ages under 15	Ages under 18	Ages 18 and over	Under 10	10–12	13–14	15	16	17	18	19	20
Total	3,100,251	65,580	225,277	2,874,974	1,454	15,293	48,833	41,242	52,680	65,775	91,713	98,074	97,132
Total percent distribution[2]	100.0	2.1	7.3	92.7	*	0.5	1.6	1.3	1.7	2.1	3.0	3.2	3.1
Violent crime[3]	126,922	4,268	13,489	113,433	61	1,114	3,093	2,484	3,185	3,552	4,016	3,867	3,893
Violent crime percent distribution[2]	100.0	3.4	10.6	89.4	*	0.9	2.4	2.0	2.5	2.8	3.2	3.0	3.1
Murder and nonnegligent manslaughter	2,630	23	197	2,433	0	2	21	27	58	89	138	133	122
Rape[4]	6,816	513	1,239	5,577	7	157	349	242	227	257	324	268	259
Robbery	18,132	658	3,619	14,513	1	74	583	670	1,064	1,227	1,321	1,092	904
Aggravated assault	99,344	3,074	8,434	90,910	53	881	2,140	1,545	1,836	1,979	2,233	2,374	2,608
Property crime[3]	342,516	10,532	37,688	304,828	200	2,252	8,080	7,272	9,025	10,859	12,712	11,746	10,497
Property crime percent distribution[2]	100.0	3.1	11.0	89.0	0.1	0.7	2.4	2.1	2.6	3.2	3.7	3.4	3.1
Burglary	48,234	1,924	6,323	41,911	63	415	1,446	1,272	1,452	1,675	1,876	1,652	1,563
Larceny-theft	269,196	7,451	27,587	241,609	112	1,610	5,729	5,256	6,632	8,248	9,961	9,280	8,199
Motor vehicle theft	22,555	761	3,118	19,437	5	90	666	653	854	850	806	755	674
Arson	2,531	396	660	1,871	20	137	239	91	87	86	69	59	61
Other assaults	286,906	16,568	40,149	246,757	410	4,671	11,487	7,691	8,194	7,696	6,396	6,297	6,740
Forgery and counterfeiting	16,328	53	332	15,996	4	8	41	28	87	164	457	677	693
Fraud	38,972	252	1,118	37,854	3	45	204	192	247	427	739	965	1,105
Embezzlement	4,072	5	143	3,929	1	1	3	5	49	84	171	196	210
Stolen property; buying, receiving, possessing	27,778	534	2,444	25,334	6	71	457	444	675	791	1,041	1,064	834
Vandalism	49,295	3,626	9,623	39,672	137	1,023	2,466	1,819	2,074	2,104	2,039	1,772	1,583
Weapons; carrying, possessing, etc.	42,873	1,594	4,735	38,138	66	473	1,055	861	1,035	1,245	1,500	1,580	1,447
Prostitution and commercialized vice	3,850	13	53	3,797	0	5	8	8	8	24	56	76	97
Sex offenses (except forcible rape and prostitution)	14,380	1,229	2,621	11,759	50	341	838	477	448	467	458	432	346
Drug abuse violations	526,907	5,033	32,550	494,357	36	730	4,267	4,915	8,187	14,415	25,548	26,387	24,382
Gambling	674	2	38	636	0	0	2	8	11	17	19	26	33
Offenses against the family and children	32,385	302	923	31,462	13	78	211	179	213	229	291	307	382
Driving under the influence	349,935	35	1,738	348,197	7	2	26	56	383	1,264	3,514	5,381	6,787
Liquor laws	53,293	1,096	9,064	44,229	7	98	991	1,381	2,435	4,152	9,110	8,934	6,792
Drunkenness	80,130	199	1,161	78,969	1	20	178	189	273	500	1,406	1,683	1,705
Disorderly conduct	100,631	7,434	19,542	81,089	160	1,854	5,420	3,886	4,343	3,879	3,286	2,863	2,683
Vagrancy	3,619	62	209	3,410	2	11	49	45	61	41	89	58	80
All other offenses (except traffic)	993,863	11,454	43,015	950,848	274	2,338	8,842	8,204	10,452	12,905	18,857	23,751	26,834
Suspicion	292	5	12	280	0	0	5	1	3	3	8	12	9
Curfew and loitering law violations	4,630	1,284	4,630	NA	16	158	1,110	1,097	1,292	957	NA	NA	NA

Table 64. Arrests, Suburban Areas,[1] Distribution by Age, 2018—Continued

(Number, percent; 6,757 agencies; 2018 estimated population 106,796,972.)

Offense charged	21	22	23	24	25–29	30–34	35–39	40–44	45–49	50–54	55–59	60–64	65 and over
Total	97,372	98,472	100,162	104,230	532,850	450,235	373,839	250,148	204,141	160,701	115,779	58,890	41,236
Total percent distribution[2]	3.1	3.2	3.2	3.4	17.2	14.5	12.1	8.1	6.6	5.2	3.7	1.9	1.3
Violent crime[3]	4,002	3,951	3,964	4,100	20,921	17,561	14,355	9,816	7,812	6,499	4,522	2,316	1,838
Violent crime percent distribution[2]	3.2	3.1	3.1	3.2	16.5	13.8	11.3	7.7	6.2	5.1	3.6	1.8	1.4
Murder and nonnegligent manslaughter	117	97	106	106	473	336	268	165	114	85	74	42	57
Rape[4]	248	220	161	173	771	753	652	475	407	315	242	141	168
Robbery	727	717	667	602	2,925	1,974	1,287	828	593	475	280	85	36
Aggravated assault	2,910	2,917	3,030	3,219	16,752	14,498	12,148	8,348	6,698	5,624	3,926	2,048	1,577
Property crime[3]	9,684	9,630	9,483	10,208	55,737	49,220	40,562	26,266	21,513	17,046	11,406	5,433	3,685
Property crime percent distribution[2]	2.8	2.8	2.8	3.0	16.3	14.4	11.8	7.7	6.3	5.0	3.3	1.6	1.1
Burglary	1,427	1,412	1,391	1,504	8,256	7,214	5,759	3,431	2,648	1,905	1,132	459	282
Larceny-theft	7,497	7,437	7,383	7,928	43,032	38,248	31,835	21,082	17,568	14,320	9,798	4,751	3,290
Motor vehicle theft	711	724	665	733	4,156	3,483	2,720	1,598	1,132	672	373	165	70
Arson	49	57	44	43	293	275	248	155	165	149	103	58	43
Other assaults	7,417	7,867	7,882	8,352	43,496	38,759	33,509	23,433	19,769	15,557	10,945	5,734	4,604
Forgery and counterfeiting	475	517	539	577	2,900	2,638	2,232	1,480	1,082	824	528	246	131
Fraud	1,077	1,097	1,235	1,245	6,798	6,477	5,303	3,806	2,973	2,233	1,506	719	576
Embezzlement	157	159	154	140	704	529	431	367	290	185	109	70	57
Stolen property; buying, receiving, possessing	816	836	909	1,001	5,169	4,375	3,630	2,090	1,491	1,053	642	266	117
Vandalism	1,669	1,625	1,584	1,592	7,776	5,911	4,649	2,910	2,251	1,832	1,241	683	555
Weapons; carrying, possessing, etc.	1,653	1,691	1,645	1,617	7,801	5,849	4,512	2,808	2,114	1,649	1,133	645	494
Prostitution and commercialized vice	134	134	140	168	698	535	465	367	345	256	149	89	88
Sex offenses (except forcible rape and prostitution)	338	327	300	289	1,475	1,476	1,430	1,051	972	936	788	463	678
Drug abuse violations	22,293	21,357	20,837	20,799	97,763	74,740	57,683	35,391	26,819	19,352	13,115	5,490	2,401
Gambling	14	27	22	27	90	78	67	49	34	36	45	40	29
Offenses against the family and children	481	515	619	724	5,350	6,149	6,084	4,084	2,874	1,780	993	394	250
Driving under the influence	11,208	12,375	13,057	13,667	65,128	51,342	42,153	31,616	28,169	23,765	19,632	11,494	8,909
Liquor laws	1,159	821	729	690	2,994	2,479	2,201	1,783	1,751	1,825	1,644	836	481
Drunkenness	2,566	2,343	2,456	2,476	12,229	10,957	10,035	7,385	7,001	6,575	5,658	2,894	1,600
Disorderly conduct	3,193	2,898	2,790	2,822	13,438	11,185	9,584	6,787	6,082	5,277	4,106	2,248	1,847
Vagrancy	82	69	78	85	489	440	458	346	322	289	306	145	74
All other offenses (except traffic)	28,949	30,221	31,728	33,637	181,842	159,368	134,390	88,298	70,455	53,714	37,305	18,680	12,819
Suspicion	5	12	11	14	52	47	41	15	22	18	6	5	3
Curfew and loitering law violations	NA	NA	NA	NA	NA	NA	NA	NA	NA	NA	NA	NA	NA

NA = Not available.

* = Less than one-tenth of one percent.

1 Suburban areas include law enforcement agencies in cities with less than 50,000 inhabitants and county law enforcement agencies that are within a Metropolitan Statistical Area Suburban areas exclude all metropolitan agencies associated with a principal city.   2 Because of rounding, the percentages may not sum to 100.   3 Violent crimes are offenses of murder and nonnegligent manslaughter, rape, robbery, and aggravated assault. Property crimes are offenses of burglary, larceny-theft, motor vehicle theft, and arson.   4 The rape figures in this table are aggregate totals of the data submitted based on both the legacy and revised Uniform Crime Reporting definitions.

Table 65. Arrests, Suburban Areas,[1] Persons Under 15, 18, 21, and 25 Years of Age, 2018

(Number, percent; 6,757 agencies; 2018 estimated population 106,796,972.)

Offense charged	Total, all ages	Number of persons arrested				Percent of total all ages			
		Under 15	Under 18	Under 21	Under 25	Under 15	Under 18	Under 21	Under 25
Total	3,100,251	65,580	225,277	512,196	912,432	2.1	7.3	16.5	29.4
Violent crime[2]	126,922	4,268	13,489	25,265	41,282	3.4	10.6	19.9	32.5
Murder and nonnegligent manslaughter	2,630	23	197	590	1,016	0.9	7.5	22.4	38.6
Rape[3]	6,816	513	1,239	2,090	2,892	7.5	18.2	30.7	42.4
Robbery	18,132	658	3,619	6,936	9,649	3.6	20.0	38.3	53.2
Aggravated assault	99,344	3,074	8,434	15,649	27,725	3.1	8.5	15.8	27.9
Property crime[2]	342,516	10,532	37,688	72,643	111,648	3.1	11.0	21.2	32.6
Burglary	48,234	1,924	6,323	11,414	17,148	4.0	13.1	23.7	35.6
Larceny-theft	269,196	7,451	27,587	55,027	85,272	2.8	10.2	20.4	31.7
Motor vehicle theft	22,555	761	3,118	5,353	8,186	3.4	13.8	23.7	36.3
Arson	2,531	396	660	849	1,042	15.6	26.1	33.5	41.2
Other assaults	286,906	16,568	40,149	59,582	91,100	5.8	14.0	20.8	31.8
Forgery and counterfeiting	16,328	53	332	2,159	4,267	0.3	2.0	13.2	26.1
Fraud	38,972	252	1,118	3,927	8,581	0.6	2.9	10.1	22.0
Embezzlement	4,072	5	143	720	1,330	0.1	3.5	17.7	32.7
Stolen property; buying, receiving, possessing	27,778	534	2,444	5,383	8,945	1.9	8.8	19.4	32.2
Vandalism	49,295	3,626	9,623	15,017	21,487	7.4	19.5	30.5	43.6
Weapons; carrying, possessing, etc.	42,873	1,594	4,735	9,262	15,868	3.7	11.0	21.6	37.0
Prostitution and commercialized vice	3,850	13	53	282	858	0.3	1.4	7.3	22.3
Sex offenses (except forcible rape and prostitution)	14,380	1,229	2,621	3,857	5,111	8.5	18.2	26.8	35.5
Drug abuse violations	526,907	5,033	32,550	108,867	194,153	1.0	6.2	20.7	36.8
Gambling	674	2	38	116	206	0.3	5.6	17.2	30.6
Offenses against the family and children	32,385	302	923	1,903	4,242	0.9	2.9	5.9	13.1
Driving under the influence	349,935	35	1,738	17,420	67,727	*	0.5	5.0	19.4
Liquor laws	53,293	1,096	9,064	33,900	37,299	2.1	17.0	63.6	70.0
Drunkenness	80,130	199	1,161	5,955	15,796	0.2	1.4	7.4	19.7
Disorderly conduct	100,631	7,434	19,542	28,374	40,077	7.4	19.4	28.2	39.8
Vagrancy	3,619	62	209	436	750	1.7	5.8	12.0	20.7
All other offenses (except traffic)	993,863	11,454	43,015	112,457	236,992	1.2	4.3	11.3	23.8
Suspicion	292	5	12	41	83	1.7	4.1	14.0	28.4
Curfew and loitering law violations	4,630	1,284	4,630	4,630	4,630	27.7	100.0	100.0	100.0

* = Less than one-tenth of one percent.
1 Suburban areas include law enforcement agencies in cities with less than 50,000 inhabitants and county law enforcement agencies that are within a Metropolitan Statistical Area. Suburban areas exclude all metropolitan agencies associated with a principal city.   2 Violent crimes are offenses of murder and nonnegligent manslaughter, rape, robbery, and aggravated assault. Property crimes are offenses of burglary, larceny-theft, motor vehicle theft, and arson.   3 The rape figures in this table are aggregate totals of the data submitted based on both the legacy and revised Uniform Crime Reporting definitions.

Table 66. Arrests, Suburban Areas,[1] Distribution by Sex, 2018

(Number, percent; 6,757 agencies; 2018 estimated population 106,796,972.)

Offense charged	Number of persons arrested			Percent male	Percent female	Percent distribution[2]		
	Total	Male	Female			Total	Male	Female
Total	3,100,251	2,247,638	852,613	72.5	27.5	100.0	100.0	100.0
Violent crime[3]	126,922	100,938	25,984	79.5	20.5	4.1	4.5	3.0
Murder and nonnegligent manslaughter	2,630	2,281	349	86.7	13.3	0.1	0.1	*
Rape[4]	6,816	6,621	195	97.1	2.9	0.2	0.3	*
Robbery	18,132	15,456	2,676	85.2	14.8	0.6	0.7	0.3
Aggravated assault	99,344	76,580	22,764	77.1	22.9	3.2	3.4	2.7
Property crime[3]	342,516	212,502	130,014	62.0	38.0	11.0	9.5	15.2
Burglary	48,234	39,190	9,044	81.2	18.8	1.6	1.7	1.1
Larceny-theft	269,196	153,895	115,301	57.2	42.8	8.7	6.8	13.5
Motor vehicle theft	22,555	17,441	5,114	77.3	22.7	0.7	0.8	0.6
Arson	2,531	1,976	555	78.1	21.9	0.1	0.1	0.1
Other assaults	286,906	203,767	83,139	71.0	29.0	9.3	9.1	9.8
Forgery and counterfeiting	16,328	10,890	5,438	66.7	33.3	0.5	0.5	0.6
Fraud	38,972	24,952	14,020	64.0	36.0	1.3	1.1	1.6
Embezzlement	4,072	2,068	2,004	50.8	49.2	0.1	0.1	0.2
Stolen property; buying, receiving, possessing	27,778	21,708	6,070	78.1	21.9	0.9	1.0	0.7
Vandalism	49,295	38,654	10,641	78.4	21.6	1.6	1.7	1.2
Weapons; carrying, possessing, etc.	42,873	38,409	4,464	89.6	10.4	1.4	1.7	0.5
Prostitution and commercialized vice	3,850	1,896	1,954	49.2	50.8	0.1	0.1	0.2
Sex offenses (except forcible rape and prostitution)	14,380	13,376	1,004	93.0	7.0	0.5	0.6	0.1
Drug abuse violations	526,907	392,247	134,660	74.4	25.6	17.0	17.5	15.8
Gambling	674	527	147	78.2	21.8	*	*	*
Offenses against the family and children	32,385	23,745	8,640	73.3	26.7	1.0	1.1	1.0
Driving under the influence	349,935	259,679	90,256	74.2	25.8	11.3	11.6	10.6
Liquor laws	53,293	36,419	16,874	68.3	31.7	1.7	1.6	2.0
Drunkenness	80,130	62,178	17,952	77.6	22.4	2.6	2.8	2.1
Disorderly conduct	100,631	70,881	29,750	70.4	29.6	3.2	3.2	3.5
Vagrancy	3,619	2,754	865	76.1	23.9	0.1	0.1	0.1
All other offenses (except traffic)	993,863	726,750	267,113	73.1	26.9	32.1	32.3	31.3
Suspicion	292	219	73	75.0	25.0	*	*	*
Curfew and loitering law violations	4,630	3,079	1,551	66.5	33.5	0.1	0.1	0.2

* = Less than one-tenth of one percent.
1 Suburban areas include law enforcement agencies in cities with less than 50,000 inhabitants and county law enforcement agencies that are within a Metropolitan Statistical Area. Suburban areas exclude all metropolitan agencies associated with a principal city.   2 Because of rounding, the percentages may not sum to 100.   3 Violent crimes are offenses of murder and nonnegligent manslaughter, rape, robbery, and aggravated assault. Property crimes are offenses of burglary, larceny-theft, motor vehicle theft, and arson.   4 The rape figures in this table are aggregate totals of the data submitted based on both the legacy and revised Uniform Crime Reporting definitions.

Table 67. Arrests, Suburban Areas,[1] Distribution by Race, 2018

(Number, percent; 6,757 agencies; 2018 estimated population 106,796,972.)

Offense charged	Total arrests						Percent distribution[2]						Arrests under 18					
	Total	White	Black	American Indian or Alaskan Native	Asian	Native Hawaiian or Other Pacific Islander	Total	White	Black	American Indian or Alaskan Native	Asian	Native Hawaiian or Other Pacific Islander	Total	White	Black	American Indian or Alaskan Native	Asian	Native Hawaiian or Other Pacific Islander
Total	3,061,471	2,201,630	792,093	27,369	34,617	5,762	100.0	71.9	25.9	0.9	1.1	0.2	220,954	144,663	71,453	2,118	2,223	497
Violent crime[3]	125,749	82,627	40,273	968	1,575	306	100.0	65.7	32.0	0.8	1.3	0.2	13,312	6,965	6,082	95	129	41
Murder and nonnegligent manslaughter	2,609	1,354	1,210	14	26	5	100.0	51.9	46.4	0.5	1.0	0.2	198	83	113	1	0	1
Rape[4]	6,703	5,039	1,520	44	79	21	100.0	75.2	22.7	0.7	1.2	0.3	1,212	896	296	3	14	3
Robbery	17,987	8,354	9,365	86	138	44	100.0	46.4	52.1	0.5	0.8	0.2	3,586	1,230	2,301	17	25	13
Aggravated assault	98,450	67,880	28,178	824	1,332	236	100.0	68.9	28.6	0.8	1.4	0.2	8,316	4,756	3,372	74	90	24
Property crime[3]	335,593	228,229	100,952	2,462	3,434	516	100.0	68.0	30.1	0.7	1.0	0.2	36,750	20,411	15,560	277	423	79
Burglary	47,799	34,476	12,558	237	423	105	100.0	72.1	26.3	0.5	0.9	0.2	6,239	3,733	2,399	41	48	18
Larceny-theft	262,899	175,608	82,229	2,035	2,757	270	100.0	66.8	31.3	0.8	1.0	0.1	26,795	14,639	11,567	203	350	36
Motor vehicle theft	22,391	16,263	5,595	167	233	133	100.0	72.6	25.0	0.7	1.0	0.6	3,076	1,593	1,407	31	22	23
Arson	2,504	1,882	570	23	21	8	100.0	75.2	22.8	0.9	0.8	0.3	640	446	187	2	3	2
Other assaults	281,751	199,044	76,709	2,368	3,124	506	100.0	70.6	27.2	0.8	1.1	0.2	39,276	23,768	14,794	363	279	72
Forgery and counterfeiting	16,142	10,353	5,472	68	236	13	100.0	64.1	33.9	0.4	1.5	0.1	327	212	108	1	6	0
Fraud	38,431	25,379	12,257	295	458	42	100.0	66.0	31.9	0.8	1.2	0.1	1,084	600	455	9	17	3
Embezzlement	4,035	2,551	1,424	12	45	3	100.0	63.2	35.3	0.3	1.1	0.1	139	71	67	0	1	0
Stolen property; buying, receiving, possessing	27,365	18,247	8,677	159	254	28	100.0	66.7	31.7	0.6	0.9	0.1	2,392	965	1,393	8	24	2
Vandalism	48,398	35,168	12,137	549	483	61	100.0	72.7	25.1	1.1	1.0	0.1	9,376	6,624	2,523	151	64	14
Weapons; carrying, possessing, etc.	42,340	26,116	15,463	246	407	108	100.0	61.7	36.5	0.6	1.0	0.3	4,666	2,789	1,775	32	56	14
Prostitution and commercialized vice	3,794	2,165	1,221	16	383	9	100.0	57.1	32.2	0.4	10.1	0.2	53	33	19	0	1	0
Sex offenses (except forcible rape and prostitution)	14,199	10,670	3,150	97	265	17	100.0	75.1	22.2	0.7	1.9	0.1	2,551	1,870	631	13	32	5
Drug abuse violations	518,969	373,407	136,286	3,116	5,458	702	100.0	72.0	26.3	0.6	1.1	0.1	31,798	24,318	6,680	280	437	83
Gambling	670	352	198	4	74	42	100.0	52.5	29.6	0.6	11.0	6.3	38	14	23	1	0	0
Offenses against the family and children	32,153	21,849	9,747	341	201	15	100.0	68.0	30.3	1.1	0.6	*	912	677	190	36	9	0
Driving under the influence	346,858	286,138	50,964	2,299	6,753	704	100.0	82.5	14.7	0.7	1.9	0.2	1,720	1,539	134	20	22	5
Liquor laws	52,504	42,956	7,710	881	896	61	100.0	81.8	14.7	1.7	1.7	0.1	8,919	8,053	547	161	135	23
Drunkenness	79,693	66,844	10,985	845	930	89	100.0	83.9	13.8	1.1	1.2	0.1	1,151	920	204	12	15	0
Disorderly conduct	99,881	68,262	29,647	1,125	756	91	100.0	68.3	29.7	1.1	0.8	0.1	19,367	10,933	8,142	163	114	15
Vagrancy	3,607	2,412	1,126	22	42	5	100.0	66.9	31.2	0.6	1.2	0.1	209	117	90	1	1	0
All other offenses (except traffic)	984,462	695,385	266,421	11,469	8,785	2,402	100.0	70.6	27.1	1.2	0.9	0.2	42,321	30,485	10,867	469	401	99
Suspicion	298	186	110	1	1	0	100.0	62.4	36.9	0.3	0.3	0.0	14	9	5	0	0	0
Curfew and loitering law violations	4,579	3,290	1,164	26	57	42	100.0	71.8	25.4	0.6	1.2	0.9	4,579	3,290	1,164	26	57	42

Table 67. Arrests, Suburban Areas,[1] Distribution by Race, 2018—Continued

(Number, percent; 6,757 agencies; 2018 estimated population 106,796,972.)

Offense charged	Percent distribution[2]						Arrests 18 and over						Percent distribution[2]					
	Total	White	Black	American Indian or Alaskan Native	Asian	Native Hawaiian or Other Pacific Islander	Total	White	Black	American Indian or Alaskan Native	Asian	Native Hawaiian or Other Pacific Islander	Total	White	Black	American Indian or Alaskan Native	Asian	Native Hawaiian or Other Pacific Islander
Total	100.0	65.5	32.3	1.0	1.0	0.2	2,840,517	2,056,967	720,640	25,251	32,394	5,265	100.0	72.4	25.4	0.9	1.1	0.2
Violent crime[3]	100.0	52.3	45.7	0.7	1.0	0.3	112,437	75,662	34,191	873	1,446	265	100.0	67.3	30.4	0.8	1.3	0.2
Murder and nonnegligent manslaughter	100.0	41.9	57.1	0.5	0.0	0.5	2,411	1,271	1,097	13	26	4	100.0	52.7	45.5	0.5	1.1	0.2
Rape[4]	100.0	73.9	24.4	0.2	1.2	0.2	5,491	4,143	1,224	41	65	18	100.0	75.5	22.3	0.7	1.2	0.3
Robbery	100.0	34.3	64.2	0.5	0.7	0.4	14,401	7,124	7,064	69	113	31	100.0	49.5	49.1	0.5	0.8	0.2
Aggravated assault	100.0	57.2	40.5	0.9	1.1	0.3	90,134	63,124	24,806	750	1,242	212	100.0	70.0	27.5	0.8	1.4	0.2
Property crime[3]	100.0	55.5	42.3	0.8	1.2	0.2	298,843	207,818	85,392	2,185	3,011	437	100.0	69.5	28.6	0.7	1.0	0.1
Burglary	100.0	59.8	38.5	0.7	0.8	0.3	41,560	30,743	10,159	196	375	87	100.0	74.0	24.4	0.5	0.9	0.2
Larceny-theft	100.0	54.6	43.2	0.8	1.3	0.1	236,104	160,969	70,662	1,832	2,407	234	100.0	68.2	29.9	0.8	1.0	0.1
Motor vehicle theft	100.0	51.8	45.7	1.0	0.7	0.7	19,315	14,670	4,188	136	211	110	100.0	76.0	21.7	0.7	1.1	0.6
Arson	100.0	69.7	29.2	0.3	0.5	0.3	1,864	1,436	383	21	18	6	100.0	77.0	20.5	1.1	1.0	0.3
Other assaults	100.0	60.5	37.7	0.9	0.7	0.2	242,475	175,276	61,915	2,005	2,845	434	100.0	72.3	25.5	0.8	1.2	0.2
Forgery and counterfeiting	100.0	64.8	33.0	0.3	1.8	0.0	15,815	10,141	5,364	67	230	13	100.0	64.1	33.9	0.4	1.5	0.1
Fraud	100.0	55.4	42.0	0.8	1.6	0.3	37,347	24,779	11,802	286	441	39	100.0	66.3	31.6	0.8	1.2	0.1
Embezzlement	100.0	51.1	48.2	0.0	0.7	0.0	3,896	2,480	1,357	12	44	3	100.0	63.7	34.8	0.3	1.1	0.1
Stolen property; buying, receiving, possessing	100.0	40.3	58.2	0.3	1.0	0.1	24,973	17,282	7,284	151	230	26	100.0	69.2	29.2	0.6	0.9	0.1
Vandalism	100.0	70.6	26.9	1.6	0.7	0.1	39,022	28,544	9,614	398	419	47	100.0	73.1	24.6	1.0	1.1	0.1
Weapons; carrying, possessing, etc.	100.0	59.8	38.0	0.7	1.2	0.3	37,674	23,327	13,688	214	351	94	100.0	61.9	36.3	0.6	0.9	0.2
Prostitution and commercialized vice	100.0	62.3	35.8	0.0	1.9	0.0	3,741	2,132	1,202	16	382	9	100.0	57.0	32.1	0.4	10.2	0.2
Sex offenses (except forcible rape and prostitution)	100.0	73.3	24.7	0.5	1.3	0.2	11,648	8,800	2,519	84	233	12	100.0	75.5	21.6	0.7	2.0	0.1
Drug abuse violations	100.0	76.5	21.0	0.9	1.4	0.3	487,171	349,089	129,606	2,836	5,021	619	100.0	71.7	26.6	0.6	1.0	0.1
Gambling	100.0	36.8	60.5	2.6	0.0	0.0	632	338	175	3	74	42	100.0	53.5	27.7	0.5	11.7	6.6
Offenses against the family and children	100.0	74.2	20.8	3.9	1.0	0.0	31,241	21,172	9,557	305	192	15	100.0	67.8	30.6	1.0	0.6	*
Driving under the influence	100.0	89.5	7.8	1.2	1.3	0.3	345,138	284,599	50,830	2,279	6,731	699	100.0	82.5	14.7	0.7	2.0	0.2
Liquor laws	100.0	90.3	6.1	1.8	1.5	0.3	43,585	34,903	7,163	720	761	38	100.0	80.1	16.4	1.7	1.7	0.1
Drunkenness	100.0	79.9	17.7	1.0	1.3	0.0	78,542	65,924	10,781	833	915	89	100.0	83.9	13.7	1.1	1.2	0.1
Disorderly conduct	100.0	56.5	42.0	0.8	0.6	0.1	80,514	57,329	21,505	962	642	76	100.0	71.2	26.7	1.2	0.8	0.1
Vagrancy	100.0	56.0	43.1	0.5	0.5	0.0	3,398	2,295	1,036	21	41	5	100.0	67.5	30.5	0.6	1.2	0.1
All other offenses (except traffic)	100.0	72.0	25.7	1.1	0.9	0.2	942,141	664,900	255,554	11,000	8,384	2,303	100.0	70.6	27.1	1.2	0.9	0.2
Suspicion	100.0	64.3	35.7	0.0	0.0	0.0	284	177	105	1	1	0	100.0	62.3	37.0	0.4	0.4	*
Curfew and loitering law violations	100.0	71.8	25.4	0.6	1.2	0.9	NA	NA	NA	NA	NA	NA	NA	NA	NA	NA	NA	NA

NA = Not available.
* = Less than one-tenth of one percent.
1 Suburban areas include law enforcement agencies in cities with less than 50,000 inhabitants and county law enforcement agencies that are within a Metropolitan Statistical Area. Suburban areas exclude all metropolitan agencies associated with a principal city.   2 Because of rounding, the percentages may not sum to 100.   3 Violent crimes are offenses of murder and nonnegligent manslaughter, rape, robbery, and aggravated assault. Property crimes are offenses of burglary, larceny-theft, motor vehicle theft, and arson.   4 The rape figures in this table are aggregate totals of the data submitted based on both the legacy and revised Uniform Crime Reporting definitions.

Table 67A. Arrests, Suburban Areas,[1] Distribution by Ethnicity, 2018

(Number, percent; 6,757 agencies; 2018 estimated population 106,796,972.)

Offense charged	Total arrests			Percent distribution[2]			Arrests under 18		
	Total[3]	Hispanic or Latino	Not Hispanic or Latino	Total[3]	Hispanic or Latino	Not Hispanic or Latino	Total[3]	Hispanic or Latino	Not Hispanic or Latino
Total	2,529,971	429,677	2,100,294	100.0	17.0	83.0	179,985	35,435	144,550
Violent crime[4]	105,365	23,479	81,886	100.0	22.3	77.7	11,033	2,522	8,511
Murder and nonnegligent manslaughter	2,008	412	1,596	100.0	20.5	79.5	126	36	90
Rape[5]	5,491	1,358	4,133	100.0	24.7	75.3	984	200	784
Robbery	15,316	2,910	12,406	100.0	19.0	81.0	3,095	643	2,452
Aggravated assault	82,550	18,799	63,751	100.0	22.8	77.2	6,828	1,643	5,185
Property crime[4]	272,418	35,646	236,772	100.0	13.1	86.9	29,345	5,070	24,275
Burglary	39,881	6,777	33,104	100.0	17.0	83.0	4,933	1,088	3,845
Larceny-theft	211,229	23,951	187,278	100.0	11.3	88.7	21,364	3,307	18,057
Motor vehicle theft	19,156	4,596	14,560	100.0	24.0	76.0	2,501	605	1,896
Arson	2,152	322	1,830	100.0	15.0	85.0	547	70	477
Other assaults	235,359	37,321	198,038	100.0	15.9	84.1	33,274	6,507	26,767
Forgery and counterfeiting	13,280	2,055	11,225	100.0	15.5	84.5	279	59	220
Fraud	31,642	3,539	28,103	100.0	11.2	88.8	881	117	764
Embezzlement	3,320	280	3,040	100.0	8.4	91.6	124	16	108
Stolen property; buying, receiving, possessing	21,926	3,816	18,110	100.0	17.4	82.6	1,942	383	1,559
Vandalism	41,318	6,325	34,993	100.0	15.3	84.7	8,150	1,276	6,874
Weapons; carrying, possessing, etc.	34,577	7,548	27,029	100.0	21.8	78.2	3,886	1,050	2,836
Prostitution and commercialized vice	3,133	522	2,611	100.0	16.7	83.3	43	6	37
Sex offenses (except forcible rape and prostitution)	11,441	2,642	8,799	100.0	23.1	76.9	2,035	395	1,640
Drug abuse violations	440,291	79,752	360,539	100.0	18.1	81.9	26,749	6,680	20,069
Gambling	431	116	315	100.0	26.9	73.1	35	8	27
Offenses against the family and children	26,145	2,570	23,575	100.0	9.8	90.2	630	87	543
Driving under the influence	297,601	72,206	225,395	100.0	24.3	75.7	1,419	321	1,098
Liquor laws	41,473	5,964	35,509	100.0	14.4	85.6	7,373	1,063	6,310
Drunkenness	73,840	16,543	57,297	100.0	22.4	77.6	1,087	372	715
Disorderly conduct	78,284	8,588	69,696	100.0	11.0	89.0	14,896	2,108	12,788
Vagrancy	3,090	536	2,554	100.0	17.3	82.7	117	39	78
All other offenses (except traffic)	791,070	119,482	671,588	100.0	15.1	84.9	32,994	6,620	26,374
Suspicion	283	13	270	100.0	4.6	95.4	9	2	7
Curfew and loitering law violations	3,684	734	2,950	100.0	19.9	80.1	3,684	734	2,950

Table 67A. Arrests, Suburban Areas,[1] Distribution by Ethnicity, 2018—Continued

(Number, percent; 6,757 agencies; 2018 estimated population 106,796,972.)

Offense charged	Percent distribution[2]			Arrests 18 and over			Percent distribution[2]		
	Total[3]	Hispanic or Latino	Not Hispanic or Latino	Total[3]	Hispanic or Latino	Not Hispanic or Latino	Total[3]	Hispanic or Latino	Not Hispanic or Latino
Total	100.0	19.7	80.3	2,349,986	394,242	1,955,744	100.0	16.8	83.2
Violent crime[4]	100.0	22.9	77.1	94,332	20,957	73,375	100.0	22.2	77.8
Murder and nonnegligent manslaughter	100.0	28.6	71.4	1,882	376	1,506	100.0	20.0	80.0
Rape[5]	100.0	20.3	79.7	4,507	1,158	3,349	100.0	25.7	74.3
Robbery	100.0	20.8	79.2	12,221	2,267	9,954	100.0	18.6	81.4
Aggravated assault	100.0	24.1	75.9	75,722	17,156	58,566	100.0	22.7	77.3
Property crime[4]	100.0	17.3	82.7	243,073	30,576	212,497	100.0	12.6	87.4
Burglary	100.0	22.1	77.9	34,948	5,689	29,259	100.0	16.3	83.7
Larceny-theft	100.0	15.5	84.5	189,865	20,644	169,221	100.0	10.9	89.1
Motor vehicle theft	100.0	24.2	75.8	16,655	3,991	12,664	100.0	24.0	76.0
Arson	100.0	12.8	87.2	1,605	252	1,353	100.0	15.7	84.3
Other assaults	100.0	19.6	80.4	202,085	30,814	171,271	100.0	15.2	84.8
Forgery and counterfeiting	100.0	21.1	78.9	13,001	1,996	11,005	100.0	15.4	84.6
Fraud	100.0	13.3	86.7	30,761	3,422	27,339	100.0	11.1	88.9
Embezzlement	100.0	12.9	87.1	3,196	264	2,932	100.0	8.3	91.7
Stolen property; buying, receiving, possessing	100.0	19.7	80.3	19,984	3,433	16,551	100.0	17.2	82.8
Vandalism	100.0	15.7	84.3	33,168	5,049	28,119	100.0	15.2	84.8
Weapons; carrying, possessing, etc.	100.0	27.0	73.0	30,691	6,498	24,193	100.0	21.2	78.8
Prostitution and commercialized vice	100.0	14.0	86.0	3,090	516	2,574	100.0	16.7	83.3
Sex offenses (except forcible rape and prostitution)	100.0	19.4	80.6	9,406	2,247	7,159	100.0	23.9	76.1
Drug abuse violations	100.0	25.0	75.0	413,542	73,072	340,470	100.0	17.7	82.3
Gambling	100.0	22.9	77.1	396	108	288	100.0	27.3	72.7
Offenses against the family and children	100.0	13.8	86.2	25,515	2,483	23,032	100.0	9.7	90.3
Driving under the influence	100.0	22.6	77.4	296,182	71,885	224,297	100.0	24.3	75.7
Liquor laws	100.0	14.4	85.6	34,100	4,901	29,199	100.0	14.4	85.6
Drunkenness	100.0	34.2	65.8	72,753	16,171	56,582	100.0	22.2	77.8
Disorderly conduct	100.0	14.2	85.8	63,388	6,480	56,908	100.0	10.2	89.8
Vagrancy	100.0	33.3	66.7	2,973	497	2,476	100.0	16.7	83.3
All other offenses (except traffic)	100.0	20.1	79.9	758,076	112,862	645,214	100.0	14.9	85.1
Suspicion	100.0	22.2	77.8	274	11	263	100.0	4.0	96.0
Curfew and loitering law violations	100.0	19.9	80.1	NA	NA	NA	NA	NA	NA

NA = Not available.

1 Suburban areas include law enforcement agencies in cities with less than 50,000 inhabitants and county law enforcement agencies that are within a Metropolitan Statistical Area. Suburban areas exclude all metropolitan agencies associated with a principal city.   2 Because of rounding, the percentages may not sum to 100.   3 The ethnicity totals are representative of those agencies that provided ethnicity breakdowns. Not all agencies provide ethnicity data; therefore, the race and ethnicity totals will not be equal.   4 Violent crimes are offenses of murder and nonnegligent manslaughter, rape, robbery, and aggravated assault. Property crimes are offenses of burglary, larceny-theft, motor vehicle theft, and arson.   5 The rape figures in this table are aggregate totals of the data submitted based on both the legacy and revised Uniform Crime Reporting definitions.

Table 68. Police Disposition of Juvenile Offenders Taken into Custody, 2018

(Number, percent.)

Population group	Total[1]	Handled within department and released	Referred to juvenile court jurisdiction	Referred to welfare agency	Referred to other police agency	Referred to criminal or adult court	Referred to other authorities not specified	Number of agencies	Estimated population, 2018
Total Agencies									
Number	289,597	68,726	128,246	2,532	5,422	17,424	67,247	12,212	247,752,415
Percent[2]	100.0	23.7	44.3	0.9	1.9	6.0	23.2		
Total Cities									
Number	231,497	57,981	99,338	2,070	4,253	13,750	54,105	8,967	172,802,238
Percent[2]	100.0	25.0	42.9	0.9	1.8	5.9	23.4		
Group I (250,000 and over)									
Number	57,825	17,203	25,905	138	622	959	12,998	69	47,674,339
Percent[2]	100.0	29.8	44.8	0.2	1.1	1.7	22.5		
Group II (100,000 to 249,999)									
Number	33,400	6,454	13,595	70	125	360	12,796	184	27,136,228
Percent[2]	100.0	19.3	40.7	0.2	0.4	1.1	38.3		
Group III (50,000 to 99,999)									
Number	37,666	7,823	16,702	181	173	2,009	10,778	409	28,755,433
Percent[2]	100.0	20.8	44.3	0.5	0.5	5.3	28.6		
Group IV (25,000 to 49,999)									
Number	43,015	13,573	14,834	1,389	2,777	3,374	7,068	748	25,885,651
Percent[2]	100.0	31.6	34.5	3.2	6.5	7.8	16.4		
Group V (10,000 to 24,999)									
Number	31,349	6,780	14,337	90	176	3,246	6,720	1,525	24,273,410
Percent[2]	100.0	21.6	45.7	0.3	0.6	10.4	21.4		
Group VI (under 10,000)									
Number	28,242	6,148	13,965	202	380	3,802	3,745	6,032	19,077,177
Percent[2]	100.0	21.8	49.4	0.7	1.3	13.5	13.3		
Metropolitan Counties									
Number	48,878	8,630	25,041	374	1,026	2,713	11,094	1,440	55,828,114
Percent[2]	100.0	17.7	51.2	0.8	2.1	5.6	22.7		
Nonmetropolitan Counties									
Number	9,222	2,115	3,867	88	143	961	2,048	1,805	19,122,063
Percent[2]	100.0	22.9	41.9	1.0	1.6	10.4	22.2		
Suburban Areas[3]									
Number	121,446	27,900	54,763	1,992	4,177	10,930	21,684	6,757	106,796,972
Percent[2]	100.0	23.0	45.1	1.6	3.4	9.0	17.9		

1 Includes all offenses except traffic and neglect cases.　2 Because of rounding, the percentages may not sum to 100.　3 Suburban areas include law enforcement agencies in cities with less than 50,000 inhabitants and county law enforcement agencies that are within a Metropolitan Statistical Area. Suburban areas exclude all metropolitan agencies associated with a principal city. The agencies associated with suburban areas also appear in other groups within this table.

This page is intentionally left blank

Table 69. Arrests, by State, 2018

(Number)

State	Total, all classes[1]	Violent crime[2]	Property crime[2]	Murder and non-negligent man-slaughter	Rape[3]	Robbery	Aggra-vated assault	Burglary	Larceny-theft	Motor vehicle theft	Arson	Other assaults	Forgery and counter-feiting	Fraud	Embez-zlement	Stolen prop-erty; buying, receiving, possessing	Vandalism
Alabama																	
Under 18	3,578	296	959	13	22	111	150	212	627	112	8	608	2	19	0	92	82
Total, all ages	126,404	4,761	15,609	214	245	919	3,383	2,352	12,332	840	85	13,027	768	2,103	112	1,756	1,004
Alaska																	
Under 18	1,687	206	439	4	35	21	146	96	218	103	22	374	5	6	6	4	109
Total, all ages	30,620	2,686	3,763	38	149	367	2,132	602	2,392	726	43	4,943	154	201	54	120	(1,103
Arizona																	
Under 18	20,478	1,127	3,298	16	65	388	658	535	2,414	325	24	3,866	21	77	12	87	1,631
Total, all ages	256,785	11,628	32,622	281	328	1,940	9,079	3,883	26,621	1,711	407	25,198	1,121	2,055	854	1,087	10,177
Arkansas																	
Under 18	7,697	427	1,423	6	48	82	291	291	1,030	93	9	1,668	18	33	4	187	311
Total, all ages	120,240	4,650	12,516	141	238	474	3,797	1,748	10,118	594	56	11,688	820	852	49	1,736	1,544
California																	
Under 18	42,958	7,210	7,484	84	245	2,937	3,944	2,864	3,048	1,402	170	8,026	37	118	17	915	2,030
Total, all ages	1,093,080	110,236	97,247	1,409	2,539	16,670	89,618	35,230	42,468	18,020	1,529	81,812	4,118	6,105	921	16,227	16,652
Colorado																	
Under 18	17,906	758	3,161	18	90	211	439	338	2,455	314	54	1,895	4	78	13	22	700
Total, all ages	193,216	7,832	24,136	195	549	1,166	5,922	2,301	19,199	2,437	199	16,477	688	2,243	112	526	4,843
Connecticut																	
Under 18	7,106	325	1,359	6	27	153	139	206	862	273	18	1,763	10	41	1	135	284
Total, all ages	95,709	3,399	12,312	79	212	870	2,238	1,624	9,834	778	76	17,370	582	921	140	692	1,640
Delaware																	
Under 18	2,851	302	547	2	15	86	199	134	370	41	2	788	4	48	2	62	114
Total, all ages	28,742	1,965	5,337	33	77	391	1,464	688	4,511	116	22	6,121	210	1,348	163	324	755
District of Columbia[5]																	
Under 18	505	92	34	0	0	64	28	0	32	2	0	111	0	1	0	5	12
Total, all ages	13,682	185	86	0	2	113	70	0	76	9	1	411	3	3	0	14	35
Florida[6,7]																	
Under 18	48,213	3,218	12,686	46	253	1,090	1,829	3,040	7,380	2,209	57	8,152	48	401	32	119	890
Total, all ages	715,424	34,907	89,456	712	1,936	5,761	26,498	14,757	66,157	8,295	247	80,570	1,989	11,207	1,086	1,632	6,129
Georgia																	
Under 18	15,400	836	3,161	50	24	233	529	590	2,311	228	32	2,451	32	74	1	241	467
Total, all ages	200,643	7,920	22,314	307	168	990	6,455	2,689	18,597	913	115	16,260	1,573	2,298	127	2,147	2,919
Hawaii																	
Under 18	1,762	104	309	1	9	46	48	32	233	40	4	307	1	3	0	51	7
Total, all ages	24,487	828	2,413	40	75	204	509	290	1,844	252	27	2,968	51	109	0	449	92
Idaho																	
Under 18	5,993	192	978	2	57	19	114	136	766	48	28	759	5	30	7	14	257
Total, all ages	52,292	1,542	4,896	16	162	90	1,274	777	3,911	157	51	4,559	132	355	47	175	788
Illinois[6]																	
Under 18	7,366	786	1,876	18	29	564	175	143	897	826	10	1,297	2	14	0	45	264
Total, all ages	86,947	5,581	14,859	416	437	2,422	2,306	1,015	9,514	4,267	63	16,749	127	247	0	84	2,696
Indiana																	
Under 18	8,831	615	1,784	9	29	163	414	199	1,339	220	26	1,652	20	63	8	24	342
Total, all ages	125,536	7,236	14,135	184	212	1,118	5,722	1,617	11,037	1,408	73	10,492	968	1,434	210	289	1,054
Iowa[8]																	
Under 18																	
Total, all ages																	
Kansas																	
Under 18	1,639	43	105	0	12	4	27	17	77	10	1	165	0	2	7	8	42
Total, all ages	32,837	387	1,005	5	43	15	324	116	802	78	9	1,590	58	271	25	120	285
Kentucky																	
Under 18	2,985	161	691	9	24	59	69	125	428	107	31	767	6	12	16	86	77
Total, all ages	205,075	1,982	12,269	126	252	517	1,087	2,060	9,363	723	123	9,649	812	989	378	1,459	806
Louisiana																	
Under 18	16,533	1,175	3,683	31	97	202	845	1,099	2,223	328	33	3,231	52	33	0	408	390
Total, all ages	176,520	10,465	30,218	334	443	1,376	8,312	5,163	23,652	1,304	99	21,314	703	1,283	138	2,761	3,019
Maine																	
Under 18	2,845	51	673	3	9	16	23	96	532	39	6	531	6	16	3	11	205
Total, all ages	40,851	756	5,456	16	73	135	532	561	4,615	235	45	4,877	209	480	46	116	1,032
Maryland																	
Under 18	17,825	1,907	3,705	22	83	1,048	754	608	2,462	525	110	4,697	19	29	5	47	784
Total, all ages	181,434	10,327	21,592	266	477	3,283	6,301	3,851	15,404	2,030	307	21,826	440	866	103	337	2,527
Massachusetts																	
Under 18	4,508	464	615	0	17	88	359	132	428	39	16	1,343	6	25	1	67	299
Total, all ages	101,681	6,608	10,308	21	315	709	5,563	1,478	8,263	512	55	17,237	391	1,087	112	794	2,207
Michigan																	
Under 18	13,267	1,044	3,054	12	174	229	629	497	2,266	253	38	2,711	23	151	42	221	416
Total, all ages	235,757	12,793	23,212	299	970	1,190	10,334	3,034	18,770	1,201	207	29,164	702	3,767	1,149	2,019	2,873
Minnesota																	
Under 18	19,391	864	4,165	2	100	351	411	378	3,318	441	28	2,419	27	188	3	297	697
Total, all ages	147,370	5,482	23,768	101	588	1,005	3,788	2,014	20,063	1,595	96	14,842	1,075	3,428	15	1,964	2,662
Mississippi																	
Under 18	2,453	80	562	2	9	28	41	120	402	35	5	348	8	12	2	31	42
Total, all ages	60,902	1,201	7,352	58	67	322	754	1,003	5,998	314	37	4,884	303	704	275	642	571
Missouri																	
Under 18	15,560	893	2,886	32	102	265	494	408	2,156	280	42	2,821	19	50	14	367	697
Total, all ages	197,865	9,005	27,019	369	507	1,426	6,703	3,325	21,098	2,383	213	19,443	1,387	2,088	249	2,814	3,484

Table 69. Arrests, by State, 2018—Continued

(Number)

State	Weapons; carrying, possessing, etc.	Prostitution and commercialized vice	Sex offenses (except rape and prostitution)	Drug abuse violations	Gambling	Offenses against the family and children	Driving under the influence	Liquor laws	Drunkenness[4]	Disorderly conduct	Vagrancy	All other offenses (except traffic)	Suspicion	Curfew and loitering law violations	Number of agencies	Estimated population, 2018
Alabama																
Under 18	88	0	9	130	0	11	26	131	24	250	0	851	0	0	171	3,070,799
Total, all ages	1,585	0	446	8,217	0	420	6,391	1,434	5,300	1,815	34	61,622	0	0		
Alaska																
Under 18	18	0	34	183	0	3	35	65	1	10	0	184	0	5	32	733,747
Total, all ages	387	2	263	1,046	0	174	3,148	592	47	843	17	11,072	0	5		
Arizona																
Under 18	247	2	221	3,239	1	248	141	1,060	74	1,424	27	3,022	0	653	91	6,586,181
Total, all ages	3,093	349	1,386	32,272	2	2,448	19,200	7,082	11,514	14,723	567	78,700	54	653		
Arkansas																
Under 18	114	1	17	925	0	3	50	158	74	579	0	1,446	0	259	241	2,640,116
Total, all ages	1,112	136	83	17,954	6	434	5,761	1,265	5,035	2,301	303	51,736	0	259		
California																
Under 18	2,748	12	876	2,967	8	1	474	930	522	1,007	88	6,836	0	652	700	39,431,921
Total, all ages	28,290	6,418	8,901	219,251	403	268	127,250	5,948	58,286	3,451	7,290	293,353	1	652		
Colorado																
Under 18	279	2	145	2,257	0	37	217	1,056	0	1,762	0	4,747	0	773	180	4,952,541
Total, all ages	2,313	376	521	16,172	7	2,466	20,353	7,007	144	6,887	549	78,790	1	773		
Connecticut																
Under 18	153	0	64	489	1	34	18	18	0	1,460	0	950	0	1	104	3,457,743
Total, all ages	1,088	184	360	8,087	10	1,363	7,484	96	11	10,505	41	29,423	0	1		
Delaware																
Under 18	82	1	28	279	1	0	0	49	1	228	0	283	0	32	52	964,106
Total, all ages	322	121	107	3,707	9	185	427	669	323	1,164	164	5,289	0	32		
District of Columbia[5]																
Under 18	13	0	2	10	0	0	0	1	0	53	0	171	0	0	2	0
Total, all ages	42	0	20	290	0	2	9	817	49	300	13	11,403	0	0		
Florida[6,7]																
Under 18	799	0	290	5,399	4	0	69	405	0	0	0	15,701	0	0	596	21,278,278
Total, all ages	6,604	1,920	2,862	134,142	123	0	32,127	10,590	0	0	0	300,080	0	0		
Georgia																
Under 18	391	4	264	2,053	2	122	139	207	14	1,387	77	3,328	6	143	258	6,742,246
Total, all ages	2,619	322	1,629	37,291	152	2,607	23,449	1,467	1,273	9,230	366	64,518	19	143		
Hawaii																
Under 18	12	0	31	337	0	0	11	49	0	18	0	413	0	109	2	1,148,121
Total, all ages	185	104	125	1,873	149	17	4,288	319	0	463	0	9,945	0	109		
Idaho																
Under 18	94	1	71	928	0	7	78	196	25	188	0	2,046	3	114	74	1,554,954
Total, all ages	283	12	243	8,777	1	716	5,689	874	333	1,455	8	21,290	3	114		
Illinois[6]																
Under 18	620	0	17	834	47	6	1	27	0	564	0	916	0	50	2	2,865,349
Total, all ages	6,798	115	350	17,060	706	355	2,825	181	0	3,987	28	14,149	0	50		
Indiana																
Under 18	203	0	64	1,155	0	203	36	457	16	518	9	1,556	2	104	202	4,025,425
Total, all ages	2,024	204	540	25,058	7	912	11,890	2,824	3,261	3,177	39	39,648	30	104		
Iowa[8]																
Under 18																
Total, all ages																
Kansas																
Under 18	3	0	12	202	0	14	31	335	0	108	0	562	0	0	213	1,308,859
Total, all ages	83	1	44	2,242	0	152	4,554	1,971	119	946	0	18,984	0	0		
Kentucky																
Under 18	24	0	28	257	0	2	39	11	27	137	0	643	0	1	332	3,500,586
Total, all ages	508	95	237	19,355	1	4,729	14,812	168	14,231	3,664	23	118,907	0	1		
Louisiana																
Under 18	439	4	117	1,496	6	88	15	78	12	2,076	29	2,963	2	236	165	3,954,330
Total, all ages	3,648	405	1,102	30,437	33	1,727	5,650	1,287	2,880	7,178	250	51,773	13	236		
Maine																
Under 18	6	0	33	304	0	1	22	395	0	95	0	483	0	10	134	1,338,404
Total, all ages	144	54	167	3,692	2	137	5,811	2,049	15	1,360	1	14,432	5	10		
Maryland																
Under 18	615	5	153	2,046	19	13	41	311	1	967	16	2,369	8	68	153	5,879,299
Total, all ages	3,694	809	690	31,914	76	1,821	18,150	4,439	56	4,843	204	56,390	262	68		
Massachusetts																
Under 18	72	1	56	132	1	21	18	103	17	227	0	1,040	0	0	327	5,884,293
Total, all ages	913	360	304	7,125	9	1,185	8,280	1,280	5,168	3,554	3	34,756	0	0		
Michigan																
Under 18	284	5	110	1,668	0	4	166	282	0	498	0	2,338	0	250	611	9,857,904
Total, all ages	4,798	216	663	30,320	26	2,642	26,130	4,739	284	5,724	107	84,179	0	250		
Minnesota																
Under 18	316	0	105	1,698	2	15	154	1,609	0	2,110	108	4,154	0	460	378	5,570,925
Total, all ages	1,859	153	878	20,404	30	585	20,186	7,099	23	8,994	225	33,238	0	460		
Mississippi																
Under 18	69	0	8	190	0	197	41	27	15	301	4	432	0	84	53	1,161,807
Total, all ages	945	16	119	8,003	74	2,160	5,370	747	3,039	3,102	72	21,239	0	84		
Missouri																
Under 18	236	5	308	2,018	1	76	108	484	7	1,210	9	2,819	0	532	331	5,406,785
Total, all ages	3,565	269	1,089	32,982	38	2,128	11,874	2,985	197	6,333	773	69,611	0	532		

Table 69. Arrests, by State, 2018—Continued

(Number)

State	Total, all classes[1]	Violent crime[2]	Property crime[2]	Murder and non-negligent man-slaughter	Rape[3]	Robbery	Aggra-vated assault	Burglary	Larceny-theft	Motor vehicle theft	Arson	Other assaults	Forgery and counter-feiting	Fraud	Embez-zlement	Stolen prop-erty; buying, receiving, possessing	Vandalism
Montana																	
Under 18	3,722	81	666	1	11	10	59	58	546	57	5	501	1	10	2	0	189
Total, all ages	27,357	1,174	4,114	10	64	97	1,003	296	3,487	305	26	3,962	100	196	40	110	762
Nebraska																	
Under 18	6,985	207	1,426	6	46	90	65	65	1,222	121	18	1,255	5	61	4	105	394
Total, all ages	53,007	1,671	6,581	36	213	247	1,175	398	5,735	391	57	7,474	236	1,066	63	736	1,693
Nevada																	
Under 18	10,026	1,340	1,262	24	70	304	942	266	855	121	20	1,944	5	45	12	169	261
Total, all ages	140,967	8,012	10,245	191	408	1,411	6,002	3,103	6,314	749	79	17,883	428	1,813	282	1,850	1,635
New Hampshire																	
Under 18	3,283	59	349	0	8	16	35	39	278	23	9	600	2	12	6	37	205
Total, all ages	46,413	872	3,681	10	76	144	642	309	3,186	165	21	5,668	237	758	91	553	1,254
New Jersey																	
Under 18	11,513	870	1,819	11	44	369	446	305	1,382	97	35	1,003	24	65	12	325	398
Total, all ages	226,427	7,146	20,307	115	274	1,699	5,058	2,982	16,659	540	126	16,839	852	3,558	214	1,826	2,474
New Mexico																	
Under 18	3,203	231	478	7	10	22	192	69	360	40	9	664	1	7	4	45	86
Total, all ages	74,786	4,232	7,309	67	103	425	3,637	916	5,993	359	41	8,588	171	324	123	1,015	1,015
New York[6]																	
Under 18	14,434	1,207	3,468	22	166	466	553	499	2,536	370	63	2,249	56	96	1	328	1,449
Total, all ages	244,041	11,433	40,466	244	933	2,630	7,626	4,291	34,122	1,786	267	26,623	2,019	3,749	27	2,752	12,509
North Carolina																	
Under 18	11,088	757	2,673	30	13	412	302	708	1,655	290	20	2,013	20	118	22	351	478
Total, all ages	200,411	9,180	26,731	351	165	2,177	6,487	5,451	20,037	1,115	128	22,676	863	4,412	799	2,682	3,006
North Dakota																	
Under 18	4,009	91	435	0	19	9	63	44	338	51	2	498	4	20	2	21	122
Total, all ages	33,210	724	3,100	10	47	63	604	254	2,622	215	9	2,846	140	369	34	278	438
Ohio																	
Under 18	20,003	873	2,995	17	79	275	502	396	2,351	199	49	4,360	14	119	0	337	760
Total, all ages	218,433	8,085	29,413	237	470	1,548	5,830	3,354	25,004	777	278	30,939	770	2,089	14	2,701	3,142
Oklahoma																	
Under 18	7,701	392	1,641	11	20	93	268	306	1,218	81	36	824	8	32	18	307	194
Total, all ages	101,053	4,859	14,717	138	216	642	3,863	2,388	11,304	856	169	7,785	539	1,332	362	2,932	1,224
Oregon																	
Under 18	8,618	351	1,720	4	32	110	205	196	1,310	157	57	1,117	9	55	3	32	553
Total, all ages	125,230	4,232	18,015	55	217	824	3,136	1,725	14,123	1,911	256	10,735	616	1,871	54	611	3,677
Pennsylvania																	
Under 18	36,034	2,558	4,540	19	225	772	1,542	617	3,338	520	65	4,986	50	948	34	302	1,353
Total, all ages	345,822	19,536	44,478	444	1,132	3,915	14,045	5,185	36,453	2,508	332	40,984	2,222	8,126	446	2,119	6,267
Rhode Island																	
Under 18	2,373	121	406	0	13	44	64	70	302	30	4	441	1	16	3	33	138
Total, all ages	25,996	954	2,660	4	77	194	679	498	1,992	158	12	4,169	125	551	75	352	915
South Carolina																	
Under 18	10,803	616	2,328	28	106	179	303	455	1,692	148	33	1,969	8	50	21	151	299
Total, all ages	152,664	6,970	22,900	287	532	1,209	4,942	3,116	18,578	1,070	136	15,413	1,115	3,333	348	2,366	2,473
South Dakota																	
Under 18	4,886	92	657	1	8	17	66	89	506	55	7	689	2	63	4	26	196
Total, all ages	44,268	1,046	2,866	11	43	72	920	294	2,348	201	23	4,451	124	816	31	152	536
Tennessee																	
Under 18	19,692	1,421	3,843	46	103	410	862	506	2,690	624	23	3,922	59	111	26	147	777
Total, all ages	330,989	14,353	38,557	380	435	1,797	11,741	4,458	30,141	3,822	136	30,862	1,690	5,043	716	1,611	4,177
Texas																	
Under 18	55,458	3,946	10,127	67	363	1,242	2,274	1,560	7,577	926	64	11,680	121	320	36	157	1,525
Total, all ages	729,902	34,166	74,627	747	2,068	5,708	25,643	9,009	60,263	4,952	403	92,541	4,332	6,320	447	862	7,246
Utah																	
Under 18	12,307	374	2,523	6	76	93	199	148	2,187	163	25	1,238	11	43	4	113	732
Total, all ages	104,886	2,327	14,038	36	306	398	1,587	890	12,545	541	62	7,972	704	1,007	35	940	2,868
Vermont																	
Under 18	702	40	100	0	16	4	20	13	74	9	4	163	0	8	2	3	75
Total, all ages	14,334	684	1,637	11	86	38	549	220	1,343	54	20	1,519	52	306	56	98	321
Virginia																	
Under 18	15,864	719	2,994	18	90	330	281	314	2,420	217	43	2,694	19	126	25	176	515
Total, all ages	268,094	7,090	26,694	356	558	1,431	4,745	2,309	23,014	1,180	191	30,541	1,572	4,868	1,272	1,085	3,490
Washington																	
Under 18	10,996	866	2,274	19	81	323	443	411	1,617	216	30	2,764	8	17	1	165	798
Total, all ages	171,466	8,384	25,722	150	536	1,767	5,931	4,292	19,762	1,504	164	24,701	677	1,130	55	3,245	4,798
West Virginia																	
Under 18	496	38	55	1	2	3	32	9	44	2	0	121	0	1	1	2	22
Total, all ages	29,202	1,173	3,757	28	55	56	1,034	440	3,112	181	24	2,825	214	265	41	263	468
Wisconsin																	
Under 18	35,109	1,023	4,622	14	220	258	531	472	3,531	578	41	2,419	37	96	36	335	1,443
Total, all ages	245,015	7,907	25,731	171	925	1,172	5,639	2,080	22,087	1,431	133	16,251	899	2,220	368	1,125	5,531
Wyoming																	
Under 18	3,191	52	391	0	1	1	50	62	299	23	7	404	0	5	0	6	108
Total, all ages	28,437	600	2,197	12	26	21	541	239	1,811	128	19	1,902	36	127	6	80	421

Table 69. Arrests, by State, 2018—Continued

(Number)

State	Weapons; carrying, possessing, etc.	Prostitution and commercialized vice	Sex offenses (except rape and prostitution)	Drug abuse violations	Gambling	Offenses against the family and children	Driving under the influence	Liquor laws	Drunkenness[4]	Disorderly conduct	Vagrancy	All other offenses (except traffic)	Suspicion	Curfew and loitering law violations	Number of agencies	Estimated population, 2018
Montana																
Under 18	15	0	15	358	0	35	38	499	0	254	0	760	0	298	97	995,183
Total, all ages	75	12	81	2,732	0	321	3,794	1,406	0	2,003	10	6,167	0	298		
Nebraska																
Under 18	78	0	66	1,006	0	199	63	504	1	341	0	1,142	0	128	118	1,516,162
Total, all ages	775	92	314	8,993	0	945	4,630	2,355	1	1,851	13	13,390	0	128		
Nevada																
Under 18	231	55	74	1,244	2	23	70	430	125	615	2	1,757	0	360	47	3,013,371
Total, all ages	2,240	2,859	903	11,238	23	961	10,984	3,720	362	2,213	3,182	59,772	2	360		
New Hampshire																
Under 18	4	0	31	344	0	5	29	267	209	68	0	1,026	0	30	184	1,317,257
Total, all ages	146	24	130	6,522	5	187	5,053	1,989	3,844	884	99	14,386	0	30		
New Jersey																
Under 18	470	4	94	2,769	0	13	42	395	0	992	23	1,892	0	303	478	7,844,556
Total, all ages	2,766	522	895	48,008	41	7,297	17,230	1,356	24	9,922	197	84,648	2	303		
New Mexico																
Under 18	66	1	10	472	0	18	53	132	7	161	0	765	1	1	59	1,406,211
Total, all ages	535	87	70	5,375	3	1,388	6,464	1,333	568	1,497	30	34,655	3	1		
New York[6]																
Under 18	288	3	279	2,643	1	9	59	126	0	393	9	1,770	0	0	505	9,571,301
Total, all ages	3,156	561	1,705	69,571	45	470	25,094	943	0	4,273	580	38,065	0	0		
North Carolina																
Under 18	386	0	72	1,414	0	18	141	173	0	686	2	1,759	0	5	204	5,380,474
Total, all ages	4,052	148	608	26,936	39	3,181	27,915	1,490	0	4,183	15	61,490	0	5		
North Dakota																
Under 18	23	0	30	429	0	243	41	385	1	644	0	914	0	106	103	757,131
Total, all ages	340	11	81	5,448	1	356	5,136	2,623	263	1,583	4	9,329	0	106		
Ohio																
Under 18	327	5	92	1,675	5	138	61	409	41	1,722	1	5,685	2	382	417	9,011,984
Total, all ages	3,948	792	451	39,708	23	1,275	13,723	4,793	5,855	9,835	20	60,471	4	382		
Oklahoma																
Under 18	147	0	35	1,146	11	7	70	83	217	567	0	1,350	0	652	400	3,847,775
Total, all ages	2,418	7	376	17,766	28	630	8,660	1,198	10,698	2,195	13	22,658	4	652		
Oregon																
Under 18	97	0	49	1,653	0	2	104	632	0	546	0	1,388	0	307	194	3,710,013
Total, all ages	2,113	281	348	13,605	1	342	13,707	2,891	29	6,210	3	45,582	0	307		
Pennsylvania																
Under 18	710	5	477	3,231	0	26	280	1,696	128	6,882	34	2,980	0	4,814	1,375	12,629,530
Total, all ages	4,921	1,182	2,286	61,934	34	1,806	43,798	6,716	19,808	31,264	234	42,847	0	4,814		
Rhode Island																
Under 18	85	0	11	104	0	25	2	21	0	552	0	396	0	18	48	1,057,315
Total, all ages	347	63	82	2,049	4	74	2,423	337	11	2,269	0	8,518	0	18		
South Carolina																
Under 18	415	1	48	1,957	0	11	69	283	64	1,103	0	1,377	0	33	373	4,408,967
Total, all ages	2,594	285	284	34,105	70	1,167	15,188	4,092	5,722	8,101	588	25,517	0	33		
South Dakota																
Under 18	95	0	10	819	0	242	51	447	0	408	0	1,010	0	75	114	816,012
Total, all ages	250	15	51	8,108	1	490	5,891	2,164	99	2,409	616	14,077	0	75		
Tennessee																
Under 18	423	0	105	2,380	9	30	104	394	165	1,422	0	3,517	0	837	437	6,363,426
Total, all ages	2,869	527	545	47,876	71	4,361	19,108	3,245	13,627	5,968	10	134,936	0	837		
Texas																
Under 18	895	34	380	9,893	15	153	349	1,072	567	1,144	21	11,378	0	1,645	876	26,829,159
Total, all ages	12,968	3,987	2,442	139,188	304	3,931	69,643	8,237	54,286	7,549	497	204,684	0	1,645		
Utah																
Under 18	140	14	262	2,258	1	24	92	670	57	354	0	3,075	1	321	109	2,670,944
Total, all ages	839	374	686	19,562	1	1,428	7,119	3,826	2,677	2,280	63	35,815	4	321		
Vermont																
Under 18	12	0	9	38	0	5	15	45	0	79	0	108	0	0	72	615,720
Total, all ages	36	1	38	902	0	201	2,576	82	0	853	0	4,972	0	0		
Virginia																
Under 18	294	4	109	2,132	0	36	49	503	68	588	0	4,293	0	520	389	8,240,312
Total, all ages	4,062	373	597	45,409	12	1,536	20,885	4,131	19,398	2,844	46	91,669	0	520		
Washington																
Under 18	215	4	140	1,053	0	4	152	554	10	263	0	1,699	0	9	198	6,423,244
Total, all ages	1,824	211	550	11,283	7	257	27,632	1,721	78	2,460	120	56,599	3	9		
West Virginia																
Under 18	9	0	6	67	0	0	6	13	7	15	0	124	0	9	131	1,052,107
Total, all ages	281	60	63	6,044	2	86	3,141	555	727	689	8	8,531	0	9		
Wisconsin																
Under 18	444	5	521	3,150	1	96	213	1,786	0	6,994	27	10,437	0	1,424	422	5,730,204
Total, all ages	3,683	451	1,587	31,066	19	2,116	24,368	10,654	0	31,008	530	78,077	0	1,424		
Wyoming																
Under 18	16	21	21	580	0	9	50	364	15	104	41	906	12	86	54	507,616
Total, all ages	52	53	109	4,895	0	433	3,432	1,725	3,062	840	166	8,198	17	86		

NOTE: Because the number of agencies submitting arrest data varies from year to year, users are cautioned about making direct comparisons between 2018 arrest totals and those published in previous years' editions of Crime in the United States. Further, arrest figures may vary widely from state to state because some Part II crimes are not considered crimes in some states.
1 Does not include traffic arrests.   2 Violent crimes are offenses of murder and nonnegligent manslaughter, rape, robbery, and aggravated assault. Property crimes are offenses of burglary, larceny-theft, motor vehicle theft, and arson.   3 The rape figures in this table are aggregate totals of the data submitted based on both the legacy and revised Uniform Crime Reporting definitions.   4 Drunkenness is not considered a crime in some states; therefore, the figures vary widely from state to state.   5 Includes arrests reported by the District of Columbia Fire and Emergency Medical Services: Arson Investigation Unit and the Metro Transit Police. These agencies have no population associated with them.   6 See 2018 arrest data for details.   7 The Florida arrest counts for offenses against the family and children, drunkenness, disorderly conduct, vagrancy, suspicion, and curfew and loitering law violations are included under the category All other offenses (except for the data submitted by two Bureau of Indian Affairs agencies that provided data using those specific breakdowns).   8 Limited data for 2018 were available for Iowa.

SECTION V

LAW ENFORCEMENT PERSONNEL

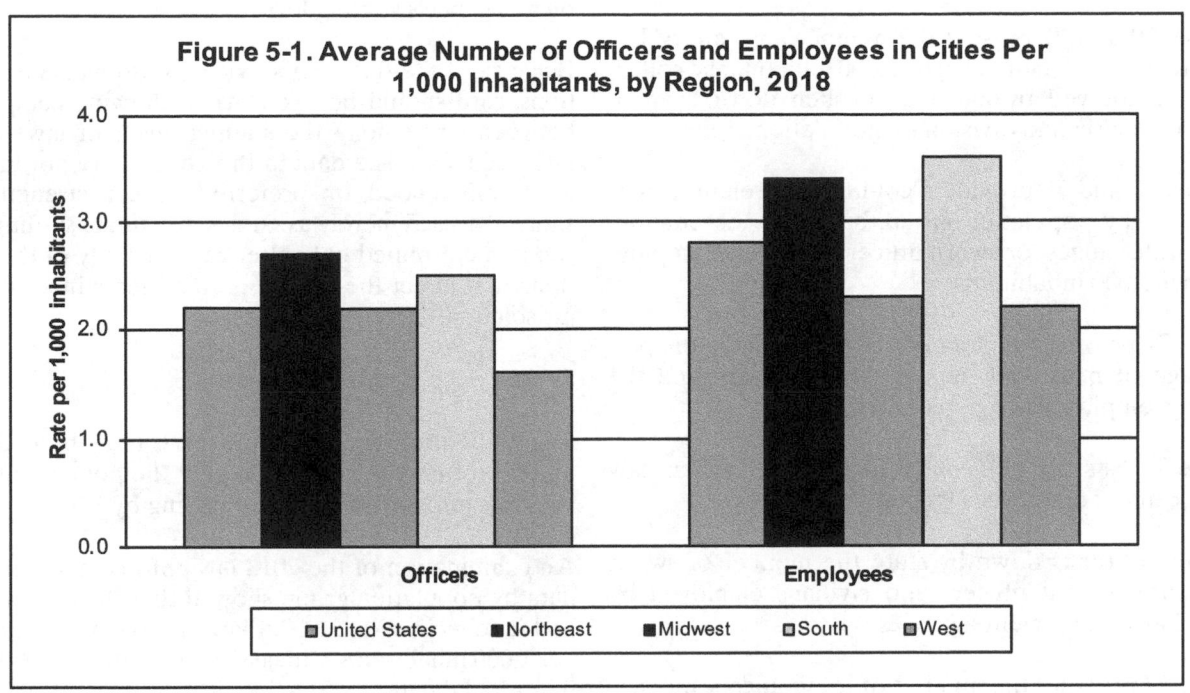

Figure 5-1. Average Number of Officers and Employees in Cities Per 1,000 Inhabitants, by Region, 2018

The Uniform Crime Reporting (UCR) program defines law enforcement officers as individuals who ordinarily carry a firearm and a badge, have full arrest powers, and are paid from government funds set aside specifically for sworn law enforcement representatives. Because of law enforcement's varied service requirements and functions, as well as the distinct demographic traits and characteristics of jurisdictions, readers should use caution when comparing staffing levels between agencies based on police employment data from the UCR program. In addition, the data presented here reflect existing staff levels and should not be interpreted as preferred officer strengths recommended by the Federal Bureau of Investigation (FBI). Also, readers should note that the totals given for sworn officers for any particular agency reflect both patrol officers on the street and officers assigned to various other duties, such as administrative and investigative positions and assignments to special teams.

Each year, law enforcement agencies across the United States report the total number of sworn law enforcement officers and civilians in their agencies as of October 31 to the UCR program. Civilian employees include personnel such as clerks, radio dispatchers, meter attendants,

stenographers, jailers, correctional officers, and mechanics, (provided that they are full-time employees of the agency).

This section of *Crime in the United States* presents those data as the number and rate of law enforcement officers and civilian employees throughout the United States. In 2018, 686,665 sworn officers and 288,640 civilians provided law enforcement services to more than 287 million people nationwide. These law enforcement personnel were employed by 13,497 state, city, university/college, metropolitan/nonmetropolitan county, and other designated law enforcement agencies. Of the slightly less than 1 million law enforcement employees, 73.3 percent were male. (Table 74)

The data in this section are broken down by geographic region and division, population group, state, city, university/college, metropolitan/nonmetropolitan county, and other law enforcement agency groups. (Information about geographic regions and divisions and population groups can be found in Appendix III.) UCR program staff compute the rate of sworn officers and law enforcement employees by taking the number of employees (sworn officers only or in combination with civilians), dividing by the population for which the agency provides law enforcement service, and multiplying by 1,000.

- Tables 70 and 71 present the number and rate of law enforcement personnel per 1,000 inhabitants collectively employed by agencies, broken down by geographic region and division by population group

- Tables 72 and 73 provide a count of law enforcement agencies by population group, based on the employment rate ranges for sworn officer and civilian employees per 1,000 inhabitants

- Table 74 provides the number of total officers, the percentage of male and female sworn officers, and the civilian employees by population group

- Table 75 lists the percentage of full-time civilian law enforcement employees by population group

- Table 76 breaks down by state the number of sworn law enforcement officers and civilians employed by state law enforcement agencies

- Table 77 provides the number of total officers, the percentage of male and female sworn officers, and the civilian employees by state

- Tables 78 to 80 list the number of law enforcement employees for cities, universities and colleges, and metropolitan and nonmetropolitan counties

- Table 81 supplies employee data for those law enforcement agencies that serve selected transit systems, parks and forests, schools and school districts, hospitals, etc., in the nation

The demographic traits and characteristics of a jurisdiction affect its requirements for law enforcement service. For instance, a village between two large cities may require more law enforcement than a community of the same size with no urban center nearby. A town with legal gambling may have different law enforcement needs than a town near a military base. A city largely made up of college students may have different law enforcement needs than a city whose residents are mainly retirees.

Similarly, the functions of law enforcement agencies are diverse. Employees of these agencies patrol local streets and major highways, protect citizens in the nation's smallest towns and largest cities, and conduct investigations on offenses at the local and state levels. State police in one area may enforce traffic laws on state highways and interstates; in another area, they may be responsible for investigating violent crimes. Sheriff's departments may collect tax monies, serve as the enforcement authority for local and state courts, administer jail facilities, or carry out some combination of these duties. This has an impact on an agency's staffing levels.

Because of the differing service requirements and functions, care should be taken when drawing comparisons between and among the staffing levels of law enforcement agencies. The data in this section are not intended as recommended or preferred officer strength; they should be used merely as guides. Adequate staffing levels can be determined only after careful study of the conditions that affect the service requirements in a particular jurisdiction.

RATE

The UCR program computes these rates by taking the number of employees, dividing by the population of the agency's jurisdiction, and multiplying by 1,000.

An examination of the 2018 law enforcement employee data by population group showed that the nation's cities had a collective rate of 2.8 law enforcement employees per 1,000 inhabitants. Cities with fewer than 10,000 inhabitants had the highest rate of law enforcement employees, with a rate of 4.9 per 1,000 inhabitants. Cities with 25,000 to 49,999 inhabitants and 50,000 to 99,999 inhabitants had the lowest rate of law enforcement employees (2.1 per 1,000 in population for each). The nation's largest cities, those with 250,000 or more inhabitants, averaged 3.3 law enforcement employees for every 1,000 inhabitants. (Table 70)

Sworn Personnel

An analysis of the 2018 data showed that law enforcement agencies in the cities in the Northeast had the highest rate of sworn officers—2.7 per 1,000 inhabitants, followed by the South (2.5), the Midwest (2.2), and the West (1.6). (Table 71)

By population group in 2018, there were 2.2 sworn officers for each 1,000 resident population. This rate remained static from 2016 to 2018. Cities with fewer than 10,000 inhabitants had the highest rate at 3.8 sworn officers per 1,000 inhabitants, unchanged from 2017. The nation's largest cities, those with 250,000 or more inhabitants, averaged 2.6 officers per 1,000 inhabitants, the same as in 2017. The lowest rates were in cities with 50,000 to 99,999 inhabitants (1.6 per 1,000 resident population). (Table 71)

Males accounted for 87.4 percent of all full-time sworn law enforcement officers in 2018. Cities with populations of 1 million and over employed the highest percentage (18.2 percent) of full-time female officers. Of the city population groups and subsets, cities with populations of 10,000 to 24,999 inhabitants employed the highest percentage (91.0 percent) of male officers. In metropolitan counties, 85.9 percent of officers were male; in nonmetropolitan counties, 91.9 percent of officers were male; and in suburban areas, 87.6 percent of officers were male. (Table 74)

Civilian Employees

Civilian employees provide a myriad of services to the nation's law enforcement and criminal justice agencies. Among other duties, they dispatch officers, provide administrative and record keeping support, and query local, state, and national databases.

In 2018, 29.6 percent of all law enforcement employees in the nation were civilians. Male employees accounted for 39.7 percent of all full-time civilian law enforcement employees in 2018. In cities, civilians made up 21.9 percent of law enforcement agency employees. Civilians made up 40.0 percent of law enforcement employees in metropolitan and nonmetropolitan counties and 33.3 percent of law enforcement employees in suburban areas. (Table 74)

Table 70. Full-Time Law Enforcement Employees,[1] by Region and Geographic Division and Population Group, 2018

(Number, rate per 1,000 inhabitants.)

Region/geographic division	Total (10,420 cities; population 197,821,036)	Group I (84 cities, 250,000 and over; population 62,552,350)	Group II (202 cities, 100,000 to 249,999; population 30,038,031)	Group III (442 cities, 50,000 to 99,999; population 30,878,709)	Group IV (787 cities, 25,000 to 49,999; population 27,144,313)	Group V (1,634 cities, 10,000 to 24,999; population 25,900,835)	Group VI (7,271 cities, under 10,000; population 21,306,798)	Total city agencies	2018 estimated city population	County[2] (3,077 agencies; population 89,881,260)	Total city and county agencies	2018 estimated total agency population	Suburban areas[3] (7,234 agencies; population 121,529,639)
Total													
Number of employees	558,583	208,397	64,905	63,808	57,819	60,082	103,572	10,420	197,821,036	416,722	13,497	287,702,296	453,018
Average number of employees per 1,000 inhabitants	2.8	3.3	2.2	2.1	2.1	2.3	4.9			4.6			3.7
Northeast													
Number of employees	152,527	66,776	8,440	16,041	18,642	18,864	23,764	2,641	45,277,838				
Average number of employees per 1,000 inhabitants	3.4	5.6	2.9	2.4	2.2	2.1	3.7						
New England													
Number of employees	34,420	2,715	4,416	6,435	7,369	7,046	6,439	794	13,036,890				
Average number of employees per 1,000 inhabitants	2.6	3.9	2.9	2.3	2.2	2.3	3.8						
Middle Atlantic													
Number of employees	118,107	64,061	4,024	9,606	11,273	11,818	17,325	1,847	32,240,948				
Average number of employees per 1,000 inhabitants	3.7	5.7	2.9	2.5	2.1	2.0	3.7						
Midwest													
Number of employees	102,771	37,023	6,894	13,010	12,947	13,739	19,158	2,656	39,761,438				
Average number of employees per 1,000 inhabitants	2.6	3.7	2.0	1.8	1.9	2.1	3.3						
East North Central													
Number of employees	69,456	29,472	4,016	8,502	9,649	8,139	9,678	1,439	25,931,951				
Average number of employees per 1,000 inhabitants	2.7	4.1	2.0	1.9	1.9	2.0	3.0						
West North Central													
Number of employees	33,315	7,551	2,878	4,508	3,298	5,600	9,480	1,217	13,829,487				
Average number of employees per 1,000 inhabitants	2.4	2.8	1.9	1.7	1.9	2.1	3.7						
South													
Number of employees	187,857	54,512	29,281	19,406	17,453	20,766	46,439	3,723	59,379,495				
Average number of employees per 1,000 inhabitants	3.2	2.8	2.5	2.5	2.6	2.9	6.8						
South Atlantic													
Number of employees	91,937	22,718	15,012	11,053	9,233	9,961	23,960	1,708	26,360,842				
Average number of employees per 1,000 inhabitants	3.5	3.5	2.6	2.6	2.7	3.0	8.0						
East South Central													
Number of employees	32,470	6,601	4,977	2,486	4,046	4,317	10,043	892	9,498,849				
Average number of employees per 1,000 inhabitants	3.4	2.8	3.1	2.6	2.8	3.1	5.9						
West South Central													
Number of employees	63,450	25,193	9,292	5,867	4,174	6,488	12,436	1,123	23,519,804				
Average number of employees per 1,000 inhabitants	2.7	2.4	2.3	2.3	2.3	2.7	5.9						
West													
Number of employees	115,428	50,086	20,290	15,351	8,777	6,713	14,211	1,400	53,402,265				
Average number of employees per 1,000 inhabitants	2.2	2.4	1.7	1.7	1.7	2.0	6.1						
Mountain													
Number of employees	41,073	16,482	6,693	4,681	3,504	2,457	7,256	630	17,094,219				
Average number of employees per 1,000 inhabitants	2.4	2.4	1.9	2.0	1.8	2.3	6.0						
Pacific													
Number of employees	74,355	33,604	13,597	10,670	5,273	4,256	6,955	770	36,308,046				
Average number of employees per 1,000 inhabitants	2.0	2.4	1.6	1.6	1.6	1.9	6.2						

1 Full-time law enforcement employees include civilians.   2 The designation county is a combination of both metropolitan and nonmetropolitan counties.   3 Suburban areas include law enforcement agencies in cities with less than 50,000 inhabitants and county law enforcement agencies that are within a Metropolitan Statistical Area. Suburban areas exclude all metropolitan agencies associated with a principal city. The agencies associated with suburban areas also appear in other groups within this table.

Table 71. Full-Time Law Enforcement Officers, by Region, Geographic Division, and Population Group, 2018

(Number, rate per 1,000 inhabitants.)

Region/geographic division	Total (10,420 cities; population 197,821,036)	Group I (84 cities, 250,000 and over; population 62,552,350)	Group II (202 cities, 100,000 to 249,999; population 30,038,031)	Group III (442 cities, 50,000 to 99,999; population 30,878,709)	Group IV (787 cities, 25,000 to 49,999; population 27,144,313)	Group V (1,634 cities, 10,000 to 24,999; population 25,900,835)	Group VI (7,271 cities, under 10,000; population 21,306,798)	Total city agencies	2018 estimated city population	County[1] (3,077 agencies; population 89,881,260)	Total city and county agencies	2018 estimated total agency population	Suburban areas[2] (7,234 agencies; population 121,529,639)
Total													
Number of officers	436,603	160,641	49,636	49,670	46,443	49,118	81,095	10,420	197,821,036	250,062	13,497	287,702,296	302,056
Average number of officers per 1,000 inhabitants	2.2	2.6	1.7	1.6	1.7	1.9	3.8			2.8			2.5
Northeast													
Number of officers	120,668	48,608	7,176	13,389	15,758	16,073	19,664	2,641	45,277,838				
Average number of officers per 1,000 inhabitants	2.7	4.1	2.5	2.0	1.8	1.8	3.1						
New England													
Number of officers	28,252	2,122	3,827	5,447	6,121	5,699	5,036	794	13,036,890				
Average number of officers per 1,000 inhabitants	2.2	3.1	2.5	2.0	1.9	1.9	2.9						
Middle Atlantic													
Number of officers	92,416	46,486	3,349	7,942	9,637	10,374	14,628	1,847	32,240,948				
Average number of officers per 1,000 inhabitants	2.9	4.1	2.4	2.1	1.8	1.8	3.1						
Midwest													
Number of officers	86,036	31,748	5,769	10,649	10,459	11,449	15,962	2,656	39,761,438				
Average number of officers per 1,000 inhabitants	2.2	3.2	1.6	1.5	1.5	1.7	2.8						
East North Central													
Number of officers	59,261	25,909	3,441	7,055	7,828	6,854	8,174	1,439	25,931,951				
Average number of officers per 1,000 inhabitants	2.3	3.6	1.7	1.6	1.6	1.7	2.6						
West North Central													
Number of officers	26,775	5,839	2,328	3,594	2,631	4,595	7,788	1,217	13,829,487				
Average number of officers per 1,000 inhabitants	1.9	2.2	1.5	1.4	1.5	1.7	3.0						
South													
Number of officers	146,409	43,205	22,255	14,924	13,816	16,543	35,666	3,723	59,379,495				
Average number of officers per 1,000 inhabitants	2.5	2.2	1.9	1.9	2.1	2.3	5.2						
South Atlantic													
Number of officers	71,972	17,608	11,716	8,576	7,405	8,042	18,625	1,708	26,360,842				
Average number of officers per 1,000 inhabitants	2.7	2.7	2.0	2.0	2.2	2.5	6.2						
East South Central													
Number of officers	25,553	5,287	3,835	1,988	3,198	3,485	7,760	892	9,498,849				
Average number of officers per 1,000 inhabitants	2.7	2.3	2.4	2.1	2.2	2.5	4.5						
West South Central													
Number of officers	48,884	20,310	6,704	4,360	3,213	5,016	9,281	1,123	23,519,804				
Average number of officers per 1,000 inhabitants	2.1	1.9	1.6	1.7	1.8	2.1	4.4						
West													
Number of officers	83,490	37,080	14,436	10,708	6,410	5,053	9,803	1,400	53,402,265				
Average number of officers per 1,000 inhabitants	1.6	1.7	1.2	1.2	1.2	1.5	4.2						
Mountain													
Number of officers	29,644	11,822	4,931	3,289	2,644	1,897	5,061	630	17,094,219				
Average number of officers per 1,000 inhabitants	1.7	1.7	1.4	1.4	1.4	1.8	4.2						
Pacific													
Number of officers	53,846	25,258	9,505	7,419	3,766	3,156	4,742	770	36,308,046				
Average number of officers per 1,000 inhabitants	1.5	1.8	1.1	1.1	1.2	1.4	4.2						

1 The designation county is a combination of both metropolitan and nonmetropolitan counties.   2 Suburban areas include law enforcement agencies in cities with less than 50,000 inhabitants and county law enforcement agencies that are within a Metropolitan Statistical Area. Suburban areas exclude all metropolitan agencies associated with a principal city. The agencies associated with suburban areas also appear in other groups within this table.

Table 72. Full-Time Law Enforcement Employees,[1] Range in Rate, by Population Group, 2018

(Number, rate per 1,000 inhabitants.)

Rate range	Total cities[2] (9,148 cities; population 197,821,036)	Group I (84 cities, 250,000 and over; population 62,552,350)	Group II (202 cities, 100,000 to 249,999; population 30,038,031)	Group III (442 cities, 50,000 to 99,999; population 30,878,709)	Group IV (787 cities, 25,000 to 49,999; population 27,144,313)	Group V (1,634 cities, 10,000 to 24,999; population 25,900,835)	Group VI (5,999 cities, under 10,000; population 21,306,798)
Total Cities							
Number	9,148	84	202	442	787	1,634	5,999
Percent[3]	100.0	100.0	100.0	100.0	100.0	100.0	100.0
0.1–0.5							
Number	85	0	0	0	1	4	80
Percent	0.9	0.0	0.0	0.0	0.1	0.2	1.3
0.6–1.0							
Number	463	0	1	10	27	54	371
Percent	5.1	0.0	0.5	2.3	3.4	3.3	6.2
1.1–1.5							
Number	1,215	5	47	102	148	220	693
Percent	13.3	6.0	23.3	23.1	18.8	13.5	11.6
1.6–2.0							
Number	1,829	17	57	129	227	384	1,015
Percent	20.0	20.2	28.2	29.2	28.8	23.5	16.9
2.1–2.5							
Number	1,688	29	43	106	180	419	911
Percent	18.5	34.5	21.3	24.0	22.9	25.6	15.2
2.6–3.0							
Number	1,217	7	29	60	115	291	715
Percent	13.3	8.3	14.4	13.6	14.6	17.8	11.9
3.1–3.5							
Number	784	7	17	18	57	122	563
Percent	8.6	8.3	8.4	4.1	7.2	7.5	9.4
3.6–4.0							
Number	545	10	6	7	22	69	431
Percent	6.0	11.9	3.0	1.6	2.8	4.2	7.2
4.1–4.5							
Number	340	2	1	6	2	30	299
Percent	3.7	2.4	0.5	1.4	0.3	1.8	5.0
4.6–5.0							
Number	230	2	1	2	4	18	203
Percent	2.5	2.4	0.5	0.5	0.5	1.1	3.4
5.1 and over							
Number	752	5	0	2	4	23	718
Percent	8.2	6.0	0.0	0.5	0.5	1.4	12.0

1 Full-time law enforcement employees include civilians.   2 The number of agencies used to compile these figures differs from other tables that include data about law enforcement employees because agencies with no resident population are excluded from this table. Agencies not included in this table are associated with universities and colleges (see Table 79) and other agencies (see Table 81), as well as some state agencies that have concurrent jurisdiction with other local law enforcement.   3 Because of rounding, the percentages may not sum to 100.

Table 73. Full-Time Law Enforcement Officers, Range in Rate, by Population Group, 2018

(Number, rate per 1,000 inhabitants.)

Rate range	Total cities[1] (9,148 cities; population 197,821,036)	Group I (84 cities, 250,000 and over; population 62,552,350)	Group II (202 cities, 100,000 to 249,999; population 30,038,031)	Group III (442 cities, 50,000 to 99,999; population 30,878,709)	Group IV (787 cities, 25,000 to 49,999; population 27,144,313)	Group V (1,634 cities, 10,000 to 24,999; population 25,900,835)	Group VI (5,999 cities, under 10,000; population 21,306,798)
Total Cities							
Number	9,148	84	202	442	787	1,634	5,999
Percent[2]	100.0	100.0	100.0	100.0	100.0	100.0	100.0
0.1–0.5							
Number	102	0	0	1	3	7	91
Percent	1.1	0.0	0.0	0.2	0.4	0.4	1.5
0.6–1.0							
Number	702	4	34	84	74	92	414
Percent	7.7	4.8	16.8	19.0	9.4	5.6	6.9
1.1–1.5							
Number	1,798	21	75	134	255	402	911
Percent	19.7	25.0	37.1	30.3	32.4	24.6	15.2
1.6–2.0							
Number	2,236	26	47	141	257	546	1,219
Percent	24.4	31.0	23.3	31.9	32.7	33.4	20.3
2.1–2.5							
Number	1,554	11	23	56	126	349	989
Percent	17.0	13.1	11.4	12.7	16.0	21.4	16.5
2.6–3.0							
Number	945	5	17	15	54	141	713
Percent	10.3	6.0	8.4	3.4	6.9	8.6	11.9
3.1–3.5							
Number	615	8	4	8	12	56	527
Percent	6.7	9.5	2.0	1.8	1.5	3.4	8.8
3.6–4.0							
Number	338	3	2	0	3	26	304
Percent	3.7	3.6	1.0	0.0	0.4	1.6	5.1
4.1–4.5							
Number	239	4	0	2	1	5	227
Percent	2.6	4.8	0.0	0.5	0.1	0.3	3.8
4.6–5.0							
Number	136	1	0	0	1	4	130
Percent	1.5	1.2	0.0	0.0	0.1	0.2	2.2
5.1 and over							
Number	483	1	0	1	1	6	474
Percent	5.3	1.2	0.0	0.2	0.1	0.4	7.9

1 The number of agencies used to compile these figures differs from other tables that include data about law enforcement officers because agencies with no resident population are excluded from this table. Agencies not included in this table are associated with universities and colleges (see Table 79) and other agencies (see Table 81), as well as some state agencies that have concurrent jurisdiction with other local law enforcement.   2 Because of rounding, the percentages may not sum to 100.

Table 74. Full-Time Law Enforcement Employees, by Population Group, Percent Male and Female, 2018

(Number, percent.)

Population group	Total law enforcement employees (number)	Law enforcement employees (percent)		Total officers (number)	Officers (percent)		Civilians (number) Total civilians	Civilians (percent)		Agencies (number)	Population, 2018, estimated
		Male	Female		Male	Female		Male	Female		
Total Agencies	975,305	73.3	26.7	686,665	87.4	12.6	288,640	39.7	60.3	13,497	287,702,296
Total Cities	558,583	75.3	24.7	436,603	87.2	12.8	121,980	32.7	67.3	10,420	197,821,036
Group I (250,000 and over)	208,397	72.0	28.0	160,641	83.0	17.0	47,756	35.1	64.9	84	62,552,350
1,000,000 and over (Group I subset)	111,889	70.6	29.4	85,136	81.8	18.2	26,753	34.7	65.3	11	27,887,008
500,000 to 999,999 (Group I subset)	53,983	74.7	25.3	42,308	84.2	15.8	11,675	40.2	59.8	25	18,176,452
250,000 to 499,999 (Group I subset)	42,525	72.5	27.5	33,197	84.5	15.5	9,328	29.8	70.2	48	16,488,890
Group II (100,000 to 249,999)	64,905	73.3	26.7	49,636	87.7	12.3	15,269	26.5	73.5	202	30,038,031
Group III (50,000 to 99,999)	63,808	75.8	24.2	49,670	89.2	10.8	14,138	29.0	71.0	442	30,878,709
Group IV (25,000 to 49,999)	57,819	78.2	21.8	46,443	90.5	9.5	11,376	28.1	71.9	787	27,144,313
Group V (10,000 to 24,999)	60,082	79.3	20.7	49,118	91.0	9.0	10,964	27.0	73.0	1,634	25,900,835
Group VI (under 10,000)	103,572	78.9	21.1	81,095	89.9	10.1	22,477	39.2	60.8	7,271	21,306,798
Metropolitan Counties	297,199	69.8	30.2	178,402	85.9	14.1	118,797	45.7	54.3	1,277	67,869,144
Nonmetropolitan Counties	119,523	72.2	27.8	71,660	91.9	8.1	47,863	42.8	57.2	1,800	22,012,116
Suburban Areas[1]	453,018	72.9	27.1	302,056	87.6	12.4	150,962	43.5	56.5	7,234	121,529,639

1 Suburban areas include law enforcement agencies in cities with less than 50,000 inhabitants and county law enforcement agencies that are within a Metropolitan Statistical Area. Suburban areas exclude all metropolitan agencies associated with a principal city. The agencies associated with suburban areas also appear in other groups within this table.

Table 75. Full-Time Civilian Law Enforcement Employees, by Population Group, 2018

(Number, percent.)

Population group	Civilian employees (percent)	Agencies (number)	Population, 2018, estimated
Total Agencies	29.6	13,497	287,702,296
Total Cities	21.8	10,420	197,821,036
Group I (250,000 and over)	22.9	84	62,552,350
1,000,000 and over (Group I subset)	23.9	11	27,887,008
500,000 to 999,999 (Group I subset)	21.6	25	18,176,452
250,000 to 499,999 (Group I subset)	21.9	48	16,488,890
Group II (100,000 to 249,999)	23.5	202	30,038,031
Group III (50,000 to 99,999)	22.2	442	30,878,709
Group IV (25,000 to 49,999)	19.7	787	27,144,313
Group V (10,000 to 24,999)	18.2	1,634	25,900,835
Group VI (under 10,000)	21.7	7,271	21,306,798
Metropolitan Counties	40.0	1,277	67,869,144
Nonmetropolitan Counties	40.0	1,800	22,012,116
Suburban Areas[1]	33.3	7,234	121,529,639

[1]Suburban areas include law enforcement agencies in cities with less than 50,000 inhabitants and county law enforcement agencies that are within a Metropolitan Statistical Area. Suburban areas exclude all metropolitan agencies associated with a principal city. The agencies associated with suburban areas also appear in other groups within this table.

Table 76. Full-Time State Law Enforcement Employees, by Selected State, 2018

(Number.)

State/agency	Law enforcement employees	Officers		Civilians	
		Male	Female	Male	Female
Alabama					
Other state agencies	39	32	0	0	7
Alaska					
State Troopers	597	334	24	107	132
Arizona					
Department of Public Safety	1,944	1,115	46	312	471
Arkansas					
State Patrol	942	497	21	130	294
Other state agencies	33	29	2	0	2
California					
Highway Patrol	10,529	6,832	454	1,392	1,851
Other state agencies	1,430	1,107	210	39	74
Colorado					
State Police	1,016	743	55	67	151
Other state agencies	371	54	9	107	201
Connecticut					
State Police	1,137	836	81	83	137
Other state agencies	106	79	6	13	8
Delaware					
State Police	964	635	97	87	145
Other state agencies	728	240	26	146	316
Florida					
Highway Patrol	2,311	1,657	181	143	330
Other state agencies	2,305	1,300	212	264	529
Georgia					
Department of Public Safety	1,628	1,152	31	150	295
Other state agencies	1,224	381	98	222	523
Idaho					
State Police	531	278	16	67	170
Illinois					
State Police	2,785	1,525	171	483	606
Other state agencies	220	112	7	67	34
Indiana					
State Police	1,653	1,160	55	152	286
Other state agencies	10	9	0	0	1
Iowa					
Department of Public Safety	831	497	34	151	149
Kansas					
Highway Patrol	788	491	21	102	174
Other state agencies	260	219	11	8	22
Kentucky					
State Police	1,796	1,005	22	358	411
Other state agencies	207	188	7	2	10
Louisiana[1]					
Other state agencies	3	2	0	0	1
Maine					
State Police	441	291	24	54	72
Other state agencies	61	28	1	17	15
Maryland					
State Police	2,196	1,392	100	338	366
Other state agencies	1,478	911	139	190	238
Massachusetts					
State Police	2,601	1,995	121	158	327
Other state agencies	261	223	29	4	5
Michigan					
State Police	3,085	1,840	195	432	618
Minnesota					
State Patrol	674	487	54	57	76
Other state agencies	404	242	36	68	58
Mississippi[1]					
Other state agencies	120	93	6	3	18

Table 76. Full-Time State Law Enforcement Employees, by Selected State, 2018—Continued

(Number.)

State/agency	Law enforcement employees	Officers		Civilians	
		Male	Female	Male	Female
Missouri					
State Highway Patrol	2,309	1,160	61	519	569
Other state agencies	115	104	9	0	2
Montana					
Highway Patrol	286	217	15	12	42
Other state agencies	43	16	2	10	15
Nebraska					
State Patrol	678	410	27	82	159
Nevada					
Highway Patrol	604	432	83	36	53
Other state agencies	116	77	10	7	22
New Hampshire					
State Police	526	337	32	48	109
Other state agencies	29	14	4	4	7
New Jersey					
State Police	4,032	2,660	136	585	651
Other state agencies	571	453	46	36	36
Port Authority of New York and New Jersey[2]	1,914	1,530	209	88	87
New Mexico					
State Police	1,051	620	48	157	226
New York					
State Police	5,769	4,379	515	314	561
Other state agencies	332	259	38	14	21
North Carolina					
Highway Patrol	2,109	1,563	45	291	210
Other state agencies	1,160	702	131	137	190
North Dakota					
Highway Patrol	189	145	6	12	26
Ohio					
State Highway Patrol	2,596	1,482	153	473	488
Oklahoma					
Highway Patrol	1,404	785	17	262	340
Other state agencies	121	67	4	41	9
Oregon					
State Police	1,217	615	56	187	359
Other state agencies	77	51	19	1	6
Pennsylvania					
State Police	4,314	3,341	225	332	416
Other state agencies	453	331	28	60	34
Rhode Island					
State Police	286	208	21	28	29
Other state agencies	77	55	5	11	6
South Carolina					
Highway Patrol	1,283	929	54	109	191
Other state agencies	568	471	46	21	30
South Dakota					
Highway Patrol	254	170	11	46	27
Other state agencies	175	46	3	50	76
Tennessee					
Department of Safety	1,716	821	48	262	585
Other state agencies	1,200	688	187	121	204
Texas					
Department of Public Safety	9,474	3,858	306	1,856	3,454
Other state agencies	108	71	20	7	10
Utah					
Highway Patrol	634	491	25	21	97
Other state agencies	127	118	6	1	2
Vermont					
State Police	664	435	60	49	120
Other state agencies	118	88	9	10	11
Virginia					
State Police	2,669	1,805	123	248	493
Other state agencies	856	534	58	109	155

Table 76. Full-Time State Law Enforcement Employees, by Selected State, 2018—Continued

(Number.)

State/agency	Law enforcement employees	Officers		Civilians	
		Male	Female	Male	Female
Washington					
State Patrol	2,262	941	91	617	613
Other state agencies	113	49	16	12	36
West Virginia					
State Patrol	1,002	614	21	128	239
Other state agencies	219	177	1	19	22
Wisconsin					
State Patrol	627	438	40	75	74
Other state agencies	317	256	23	19	19
Wyoming					
Highway Patrol	334	185	7	52	90

Note: Caution should be used when comparing data from one state to that of another. The responsibilities of the various state police, highway patrol, and department of public safety agencies range from full law enforcement duties to only traffic patrol, which can impact both the level of employment for agencies as well as the ratio of sworn officers to civilians employed. Any valid comparison must take these factors and the other identified variables affecting crime into consideration.
1 Police employee data were not received from the State Police/Highway Patrol/Department of Public Safety for the state.   2 Data reported are the number of law enforcement employees for the state of New Jersey.

Table 77. Full-Time Law Enforcement Employees, by State, 2018

(Number.)

State	Total law enforcement employees	Total officers		Total civilians		Total agencies	Population, 2018, estimated
		Male	Female	Male	Female		
Alabama	15,855	9,763	898	2,000	3,194	376	4,764,354
Alaska	1,985	1,162	124	263	436	38	737,438
Arizona	22,428	11,357	1,399	4,417	5,255	114	7,170,315
Arkansas	10,628	6,123	620	1,533	2,352	303	3,009,746
California	120,041	68,663	10,478	15,339	25,561	465	33,867,039
Colorado	18,510	10,791	1,721	2,181	3,817	239	5,690,128
Connecticut	9,283	6,970	822	596	895	106	3,572,665
Delaware	3,305	2,043	272	377	613	55	964,931
District of Columbia	5,145	3,417	976	320	432	3	702,455
Florida	68,605	36,327	6,553	9,951	15,774	333	19,436,120
Georgia	36,833	22,481	4,769	3,048	6,535	527	10,012,759
Hawaii	3,624	2,544	300	243	537	4	1,420,491
Idaho	5,567	2,689	205	1,134	1,539	108	1,751,570
Illinois	36,749	22,164	4,580	5,343	4,662	371	8,323,221
Indiana	12,513	8,208	1,141	1,322	1,842	121	4,230,746
Iowa	7,530	4,350	366	1,213	1,601	219	2,710,078
Kansas	8,992	5,887	688	819	1,598	305	2,578,157
Kentucky	9,588	6,897	489	869	1,333	273	3,691,938
Louisiana	18,554	10,990	2,970	1,592	3,002	185	4,200,142
Maine	2,932	2,162	187	214	369	133	1,331,125
Maryland	19,916	13,353	2,057	1,620	2,886	149	6,041,598
Massachusetts	20,340	15,220	1,497	1,505	2,118	306	6,428,834
Michigan	23,991	15,076	2,153	3,559	3,203	609	9,334,869
Minnesota	15,264	8,755	1,172	2,429	2,908	396	5,605,723
Mississippi	4,240	2,413	287	595	945	62	1,048,379
Missouri	20,226	12,943	1,485	2,301	3,497	503	5,980,758
Montana	2,902	1,706	133	472	591	100	1,017,708
Nebraska	5,398	3,370	427	559	1,042	162	1,912,427
Nevada	9,110	5,588	685	847	1,990	50	3,034,392
New Hampshire	3,689	2,572	266	254	597	174	1,279,586
New Jersey	40,847	28,659	3,158	3,521	5,509	531	8,638,529
New Mexico	3,877	2,433	277	433	734	100	994,639
New York	84,204	53,072	9,255	7,860	14,017	412	18,697,787
North Carolina	34,100	21,179	2,825	4,565	5,531	520	10,377,256
North Dakota	2,477	1,562	214	251	450	106	759,138
Ohio	19,868	13,323	1,653	1,847	3,045	287	6,795,599
Oklahoma	13,016	8,107	786	1,616	2,507	414	3,938,268
Oregon	10,664	5,856	697	1,757	2,354	206	4,111,065
Pennsylvania	29,181	22,863	2,642	1,282	2,394	1,074	9,791,899
Rhode Island	3,113	2,296	198	245	374	49	1,057,315
South Carolina	15,215	9,999	1,554	1,292	2,370	335	4,651,913
South Dakota	3,008	1,615	156	585	652	129	862,436
Tennessee	27,737	15,610	1,753	4,876	5,498	454	6,766,324
Texas	70,186	38,960	5,897	10,239	15,090	570	20,609,733
Utah	7,235	4,728	378	893	1,236	134	3,146,133
Vermont	1,815	1,242	150	139	284	86	606,587
Virginia	24,272	16,719	2,539	1,344	3,670	284	8,516,800
Washington	15,873	9,754	1,066	2,071	2,982	257	7,507,712
West Virginia	4,538	3,463	129	359	587	291	1,795,624
Wisconsin	18,013	11,028	1,676	2,260	3,049	413	5,708,284
Wyoming	2,323	1,358	132	292	541	56	519,563

Table 78. Full-Time Law Enforcement Employees, by Selected State and City, 2018

(Number.)

State/city	Population	Total law enforcement employees	Total officers	Total civilians
ALABAMA				
Abbeville	2,551	8	7	1
Adamsville	4,323	29	17	12
Addison	725	5	4	1
Alabaster	33,501	84	67	17
Alexander City	14,548	66	50	16
Aliceville	2,315	7	6	1
Altoona	914	2	2	0
Andalusia	8,753	38	29	9
Anderson	275	1	1	0
Anniston	21,592	90	85	5
Arab	8,311	34	27	7
Ardmore	1,428	10	7	3
Argo	4,296	9	9	0
Arley	344	2	2	0
Ashford	2,145	6	5	1
Ashland	1,918	14	9	5
Ashville	2,302	5	5	0
Athens	26,177	59	48	11
Atmore	9,847	36	27	9
Attalla	5,797	29	23	6
Auburn	65,585	143	134	9
Autaugaville	852	1	1	0
Baker Hill	252	3	3	0
Bay Minette	9,304	30	22	8
Bayou La Batre	2,500	20	15	5
Bear Creek	1,038	2	2	0
Berry	1,092	5	3	2
Bessemer	26,240	159	114	45
Birmingham	210,564	977	762	215
Blountsville	1,668	7	6	1
Boaz	9,678	30	21	9
Brantley	785	4	4	0
Brent	4,853	7	7	0
Brewton	5,212	29	21	8
Bridgeport	2,298	17	8	9
Brighton	2,782	5	5	0
Brilliant	867	2	2	0
Brookwood	1,861	6	6	0
Brundidge	1,935	18	13	5
Butler	1,718	8	8	0
Calera	14,334	38	30	8
Camden	1,824	8	7	1
Camp Hill	958	6	6	0
Carbon Hill	1,915	4	4	0
Carrollton	961	2	2	0
Cedar Bluff	1,794	5	5	0
Centre	3,500	13	12	1
Centreville	2,667	7	7	0
Chatom	1,200	5	5	0
Cherokee	999	4	4	0
Chickasaw	5,754	35	30	5
Childersburg	4,870	19	17	2
Clanton	8,773	29	29	0
Clayton	2,854	4	4	0
Cleveland	1,309	3	3	0
Clio	1,491	4	4	0
Coaling	1,661	4	4	0
Collinsville	1,967	9	4	5
Columbia	728	2	2	0
Columbiana	4,720	13	9	4
Coosada	1,291	4	4	0
Cordova	1,938	11	5	6
Cottonwood	1,251	2	2	0
Courtland	586	1	1	0
Creola	2,006	13	9	4
Crossville	1,845	4	4	0
Cuba	298	2	2	0
Cullman	15,470	73	52	21
Dadeville	3,091	13	12	1
Daleville	5,096	23	16	7
Daphne	26,618	95	54	41
Dauphin Island	1,274	18	10	8
Decatur	54,207	148	134	14
Demopolis	6,770	26	21	5
Dora	1,897	9	5	4
Dothan	68,530	233	165	68
Double Springs	1,030	7	7	0
Douglas	771	4	4	0
East Brewton	2,373	15	5	10
Eclectic	1,022	9	8	1
Elba	3,864	18	10	8
Elberta	1,742	9	8	1
Enterprise	28,464	68	56	12
Eufaula	11,905	56	35	21

Table 78. Full-Time Law Enforcement Employees, by Selected State and City, 2018—Continued

(Number.)

State/city	Population	Total law enforcement employees	Total officers	Total civilians
Eutaw	2,656	9	8	1
Evergreen	3,639	25	19	6
Excel	647	2	2	0
Fairfield	10,625	67	38	29
Fairhope	21,688	62	38	24
Falkville	1,243	6	6	0
Fayette	4,313	11	11	0
Flomaton	1,382	12	7	5
Florala	1,903	5	5	0
Florence	39,925	134	106	28
Foley	18,740	92	64	28
Fort Payne	14,066	37	32	5
Franklin	126	1	1	0
Frisco City	1,175	2	2	0
Fultondale	9,312	32	25	7
Fyffe	1,018	4	4	0
Gadsden	35,204	135	100	35
Gardendale	13,907	39	30	9
Geneva	4,353	13	12	1
Georgiana	1,618	11	6	5
Geraldine	900	3	3	0
Glencoe	5,151	8	8	0
Goodwater	1,310	12	4	8
Gordo	1,629	4	4	0
Gordon	325	2	2	0
Grant	910	2	2	0
Greensboro	2,290	9	9	0
Greenville	7,564	33	28	5
Grove Hill	1,441	6	5	1
Guin	2,260	9	7	2
Gulf Shores	12,014	64	47	17
Guntersville	8,462	46	35	11
Hackleburg	1,460	4	4	0
Haleyville	3,957	15	10	5
Hamilton	6,611	13	11	2
Hanceville	3,423	18	12	6
Harpersville	1,721	7	7	0
Hartford	2,587	16	11	5
Hartselle	14,385	6	6	0
Hayneville	806	2	2	0
Headland	4,706	17	9	8
Heflin	3,415	13	12	1
Helena	19,387	28	23	5
Henagar	2,354	10	6	4
Hillsboro	514	1	1	0
Hokes Bluff	4,267	7	7	0
Hollywood	965	3	2	1
Homewood	25,523	121	82	39
Hoover	85,521	230	168	62
Hueytown	15,367	45	36	9
Huntsville	196,620	633	434	199
Ider	716	13	5	8
Irondale	12,486	39	31	8
Jackson	4,733	21	20	1
Jacksons Gap	813	3	3	0
Jacksonville	12,534	38	30	8
Jasper	13,512	69	50	19
Jemison	2,628	13	13	0
Killen	969	4	4	0
Kimberly	3,246	7	7	0
Kinsey	2,181	2	2	0
Kinston	545	1	1	0
LaFayette	2,937	12	11	1
Lake View	2,349	5	3	2
Lanett	6,245	31	29	2
Leeds	12,065	28	25	3
Leesburg	1,021	3	3	0
Leighton	705	3	3	0
Level Plains	2,023	5	5	0
Lexington	714	1	1	0
Lincoln	6,725	21	19	2
Linden	1,912	6	6	0
Lineville	2,246	13	9	4
Lipscomb	2,145	12	6	6
Littleville	985	4	4	0
Livingston	3,317	5	5	0
Louisville	462	3	3	0
Loxley	2,462	21	16	5
Luverne	2,767	13	12	1
Madison	49,709	112	84	28
Maplesville	702	6	6	0
Margaret	4,870	2	2	0
Marion	3,265	10	9	1
McIntosh	221	8	8	0
McKenzie	497	3	3	0

Table 78. Full-Time Law Enforcement Employees, by Selected State and City, 2018—Continued

(Number.)

State/city	Population	Total law enforcement employees	Total officers	Total civilians
Mentone	369	1	1	0
Midfield	5,056	21	16	5
Midland City	2,387	8	5	3
Millbrook	15,410	45	33	12
Millport	982	5	5	0
Millry	505	2	2	0
Mobile	245,475	715	494	221
Monroeville	5,852	28	23	5
Montevallo	6,683	18	14	4
Montgomery	198,662	566	474	92
Moody	13,134	20	20	0
Morris	1,987	6	6	0
Moulton	3,229	12	12	0
Moundville	2,449	10	9	1
Mountain Brook	20,373	71	57	14
Mount Vernon	1,491	14	6	8
Munford	1,261	1	1	0
Muscle Shoals	14,143	43	35	8
Napier Field	340	6	1	5
New Hope	2,846	6	6	0
New Site	755	2	2	0
Newton	1,457	4	4	0
Newville	510	1	1	0
Northport	25,353	79	53	26
Notasulga	827	5	1	4
Oakman	727	1	1	0
Odenville	3,781	9	9	0
Ohatchee	1,157	8	8	0
Oneonta	6,646	24	23	1
Opelika	30,822	100	81	19
Opp	6,441	27	19	8
Orange Beach	6,116	78	52	26
Owens Crossroads	2,002	5	5	0
Oxford	21,149	74	63	11
Ozark	14,358	40	34	6
Parrish	938	3	3	0
Pelham	23,785	85	70	15
Pell City	13,817	47	38	9
Phenix City	36,668	94	73	21
Phil Campbell	1,269	1	1	0
Pickensville	577	3	2	1
Piedmont	4,583	17	12	5
Pine Hill	870	5	4	1
Pleasant Grove	10,105	20	15	5
Powell	966	1	1	0
Prattville	35,697	87	79	8
Priceville	3,592	5	5	0
Prichard	21,615	47	34	13
Ragland	1,692	5	5	0
Rainbow City	9,546	33	24	9
Rainsville	5,050	12	12	0
Ranburne	404	2	2	0
Red Bay	3,075	13	9	4
Reform	1,577	5	5	0
Repton	265	2	2	0
Riverside	2,306	3	3	0
Roanoke	5,914	29	23	6
Robertsdale	6,220	29	17	12
Rogersville	1,226	5	5	0
Russellville	9,676	27	23	4
Samson	1,880	7	7	0
Saraland	14,704	57	46	11
Sardis City	1,809	4	4	0
Satsuma	6,153	16	12	4
Scottsboro	14,443	71	44	27
Selma	18,049	43	43	0
Shorter	409	9	5	4
Silverhill	917	4	4	0
Sipsey	412	2	2	0
Skyline	823	1	1	0
Slocomb	1,916	6	6	0
Snead	841	14	13	1
Somerville	723	5	3	2
Southside	8,774	18	13	5
Spanish Fort	8,923	26	23	3
Springville	4,257	11	11	0
Steele	1,074	8	8	0
Stevenson	1,950	6	4	2
St. Florian	653	3	3	0
Sulligent	1,835	5	5	0
Sumiton	2,348	16	7	9
Summerdale	1,467	7	6	1
Sylacauga	12,186	72	37	35
Sylvania	1,884	3	3	0
Talladega	15,341	40	36	4

Table 78. Full-Time Law Enforcement Employees, by Selected State and City, 2018—Continued

(Number.)

State/city	Population	Total law enforcement employees	Total officers	Total civilians
Tallassee	4,650	26	20	6
Tarrant	6,175	24	19	5
Taylor	2,399	4	4	0
Thomaston	382	1	1	0
Thomasville	3,909	25	20	5
Thorsby	2,061	6	6	0
Town Creek	1,044	3	3	0
Trafford	628	5	5	0
Triana	544	1	1	0
Trinity	2,165	8	8	0
Troy	19,159	77	76	1
Tuscaloosa	101,764	349	274	75
Tuscumbia	8,370	28	21	7
Tuskegee	8,373	27	14	13
Union Springs	3,510	19	11	8
Uniontown	2,271	7	4	3
Valley	9,230	32	30	2
Valley Head	549	2	2	0
Vance	1,626	5	5	0
Vernon	1,861	8	8	0
Vestavia Hills	34,368	95	92	3
Wadley	710	1	1	0
Warrior	3,213	19	12	7
Weaver	3,067	11	8	3
Wedowee	796	9	8	1
West Blocton	1,251	2	2	0
Wetumpka	8,377	32	30	2
White Hall	767	3	1	2
Winfield	4,441	12	11	1
Woodstock	1,621	4	4	0
York	2,245	4	4	0
ALASKA				
Anchorage	291,992	574	427	147
Bethel	6,509	22	12	10
Bristol Bay Borough	843	8	3	5
Cordova	2,179	11	5	6
Craig	1,285	10	5	5
Dillingham	2,365	19	8	11
Fairbanks	31,635	43	39	4
Haines	2,508	10	5	5
Homer	5,797	21	11	10
Hoonah	778	8	4	4
Juneau	31,922	76	47	29
Kenai	7,888	24	16	8
Ketchikan	8,300	35	23	12
Klawock	831	3	3	0
Kodiak	5,995	41	17	24
Kotzebue	3,273	15	7	8
Nome	3,874	13	8	5
North Pole	2,096	14	12	2
North Slope Borough	9,743	70	42	28
Palmer	7,403	25	15	10
Petersburg	3,262	12	7	5
Sand Point	1,089	6	5	1
Seldovia	279	1	1	0
Seward	2,850	21	9	12
Sitka	8,588	25	13	12
Skagway	1,177	11	4	7
Soldotna	4,731	16	14	2
St. Paul	508	9	3	6
Unalaska	4,546	22	10	12
Valdez	3,845	12	12	0
Wasilla	10,522	58	24	34
Whittier	206	8	8	0
Wrangell	2,521	12	6	6
ARIZONA				
Apache Junction	41,245	88	58	30
Avondale	85,204	185	122	63
Benson	4,804	22	15	7
Bisbee	5,135	19	15	4
Buckeye	71,318	125	91	34
Bullhead City	40,354	110	68	42
Camp Verde	11,249	32	19	13
Casa Grande	56,479	102	80	22
Chandler	255,986	494	332	162
Chino Valley	11,840	30	24	6
Clarkdale	4,367	10	9	1
Clifton	3,743	12	7	5
Colorado City	4,839	12	5	7
Coolidge	12,815	39	26	13
Cottonwood	12,146	55	33	22
Douglas	15,970	44	32	12
Eagar	4,876	8	6	2

Table 78. Full-Time Law Enforcement Employees, by Selected State and City, 2018—Continued
(Number.)

State/city	Population	Total law enforcement employees	Total officers	Total civilians
El Mirage	35,733	64	46	18
Eloy	19,549	41	30	11
Flagstaff	72,852	158	111	47
Florence	25,987	40	30	10
Fredonia	1,300	3	3	0
Gilbert	247,463	386	232	154
Glendale	249,799	561	426	135
Globe	7,330	16	13	3
Goodyear	82,159	148	110	38
Hayden	970	8	8	0
Holbrook	5,048	14	11	3
Huachuca City	1,711	9	5	4
Kearny	2,116	10	5	5
Kingman	29,669	70	51	19
Lake Havasu City	54,678	110	69	41
Mammoth	1,626	4	3	1
Marana	46,447	120	91	29
Maricopa	48,660	88	68	20
Mesa	504,873	1,202	779	423
Miami	1,764	10	5	5
Nogales	19,973	65	48	17
Oro Valley	44,844	127	98	29
Page	7,576	33	20	13
Paradise Valley	14,519	42	31	11
Parker	3,060	14	11	3
Payson	15,549	43	26	17
Peoria	170,177	278	196	82
Phoenix	1,653,080	3,902	2,919	983
Pima	2,533	6	6	0
Pinetop-Lakeside	4,371	17	14	3
Prescott	43,172	81	69	12
Prescott Valley	45,337	96	75	21
Quartzsite	3,695	12	10	2
Safford	9,657	24	21	3
Sahuarita	29,896	50	40	10
San Luis	33,074	54	34	20
Scottsdale	254,961	608	381	227
Sedona	10,379	35	25	10
Show Low	11,156	39	29	10
Sierra Vista	42,574	86	60	26
Snowflake-Taylor	9,971	21	13	8
Somerton	16,380	27	16	11
South Tucson	5,643	20	19	1
Springerville	1,955	7	5	2
St. Johns	3,510	9	6	3
Superior	3,095	9	8	1
Surprise	136,611	193	139	54
Tempe	188,543	488	346	142
Thatcher	5,048	12	11	1
Tolleson	7,305	49	32	17
Tombstone	1,283	9	7	2
Tucson	537,392	1,015	807	208
Wellton	3,003	7	6	1
Wickenburg	7,042	28	20	8
Willcox	3,465	17	9	8
Williams	3,176	23	12	11
Winslow	9,361	33	23	10
Yuma	96,121	269	173	96
ARKANSAS				
Alexander	3,078	8	8	0
Alma	5,772	24	16	8
Amity	678	1	1	0
Arkadelphia	10,647	29	23	6
Arkansas City	320	1	1	0
Ashdown	4,389	12	11	1
Ash Flat	1,090	4	4	0
Atkins	3,041	9	8	1
Augusta	1,958	6	6	0
Austin	3,508	3	3	0
Bald Knob	2,879	13	9	4
Barling	4,972	11	11	0
Batesville	10,782	28	27	1
Bay	1,806	4	4	0
Bearden	865	1	1	0
Beebe	8,268	21	15	6
Bella Vista	28,798	49	34	15
Benton	36,556	93	67	26
Bentonville	51,607	104	75	29
Berryville	5,470	15	13	2
Bethel Heights	2,825	7	6	1
Black Rock	613	1	1	0
Blytheville	13,843	49	34	15
Bono	2,405	4	4	0
Booneville	3,837	12	8	4

Table 78. Full-Time Law Enforcement Employees, by Selected State and City, 2018—Continued

(Number.)

State/city	Population	Total law enforcement employees	Total officers	Total civilians
Bradford	742	3	3	0
Brinkley	2,658	15	10	5
Brookland	3,582	6	6	0
Bryant	20,738	57	44	13
Bull Shoals	1,943	4	4	0
Cabot	26,459	55	44	11
Caddo Valley	591	6	4	2
Camden	10,880	36	19	17
Cammack Village	732	4	3	1
Caraway	1,253	3	3	0
Carlisle	2,177	10	6	4
Cave City	1,911	5	5	0
Cave Springs	4,981	7	7	0
Cedarville	1,401	2	2	0
Centerton	14,791	24	22	2
Charleston	2,458	5	5	0
Cherokee Village	4,637	8	7	1
Cherry Valley	593	1	1	0
Clarendon	1,415	4	4	0
Clarksville	9,679	23	18	5
Clinton	2,471	8	7	1
Concord	235	1	1	0
Conway	66,720	173	127	46
Corning	3,102	12	8	4
Cotter	935	3	2	1
Crossett	4,920	27	17	10
Damascus	372	1	1	0
Danville	2,422	8	7	1
Dardanelle	4,535	15	9	6
Decatur	1,814	6	6	0
Dell	193	1	1	0
De Queen	6,588	17	14	3
Dermott	2,566	13	7	6
Des Arc	1,618	6	6	0
DeWitt	3,058	12	8	4
Diamond City	794	1	1	0
Diaz	1,215	2	2	0
Dierks	1,098	3	3	0
Dover	1,411	5	5	0
Dumas	4,179	22	11	11
Dyer	900	1	1	0
Earle	2,221	2	2	0
El Dorado	17,916	68	51	17
Elkins	3,111	7	7	0
England	2,732	12	7	5
Etowah	317	1	1	0
Eudora	1,970	6	4	2
Eureka Springs	2,073	17	13	4
Fairfield Bay	2,189	17	7	10
Farmington	7,032	14	13	1
Fayetteville	87,008	178	128	50
Flippin	1,324	7	7	0
Fordyce	3,852	12	8	4
Forrest City	14,144	44	33	11
Fort Smith	88,290	181	143	38
Gassville	2,145	4	4	0
Gentry	3,842	10	8	2
Glenwood	2,107	2	2	0
Gosnell	3,225	7	7	0
Gravette	3,328	11	10	1
Greenbrier	5,592	15	9	6
Green Forest	2,682	13	11	2
Greenland	1,422	4	4	0
Greenwood	9,454	23	21	2
Greers Ferry	854	4	3	1
Gurdon	2,080	5	4	1
Guy	786	2	2	0
Hamburg	2,672	7	6	1
Hampton	1,274	3	3	0
Hardy	759	2	2	0
Harrisburg	2,353	5	5	0
Harrison	13,100	46	34	12
Haskell	4,649	8	8	0
Hazen	1,372	7	6	1
Heber Springs	6,929	27	16	11
Helena-West Helena	10,477	33	17	16
Higginson	670	1	1	0
Highfill	663	3	3	0
Highland	1,104	3	3	0
Hope	9,744	36	24	12
Hot Springs	37,006	129	101	28
Hoxie	2,611	4	4	0
Hughes	1,254	3	3	0
Huntington	623	1	1	0
Jacksonville	28,530	62	50	12

Table 78. Full-Time Law Enforcement Employees, by Selected State and City, 2018—Continued

(Number.)

State/city	Population	Total law enforcement employees	Total officers	Total civilians
Jasper	437	2	2	0
Johnson	3,716	11	11	0
Jonesboro	77,134	173	160	13
Judsonia	1,988	4	3	1
Kensett	1,629	3	3	0
Lake City	2,507	4	4	0
Lakeview	713	2	2	0
Lake Village	2,293	16	10	6
Lamar	1,729	3	3	0
Lavaca	2,464	3	3	0
Leachville	1,766	5	4	1
Lepanto	1,825	7	3	4
Lincoln	2,489	6	5	1
Little Flock	2,787	6	6	0
Little Rock	199,288	701	575	126
Lonoke	4,247	16	11	5
Lowell	9,522	26	20	6
Luxora	1,044	1	1	0
Madison	680	3	3	0
Magnolia	11,425	23	21	2
Malvern	10,881	23	21	2
Mammoth Spring	931	2	2	0
Mansfield	1,094	4	4	0
Marianna	3,492	23	12	11
Marion	12,426	31	29	2
Marked Tree	2,493	9	5	4
Marmaduke	1,260	4	4	0
Marvell	960	7	4	3
Maumelle	18,356	48	38	10
Mayflower	2,511	9	9	0
McCrory	1,532	6	5	1
McGehee	3,775	25	9	16
McRae	665	3	2	1
Mena	5,546	15	14	1
Mineral Springs	1,160	3	2	1
Monette	1,601	4	4	0
Monticello	9,630	28	21	7
Morrilton	6,633	27	24	3
Mountainburg	614	2	2	0
Mountain Home	12,315	35	27	8
Mountain View	2,867	14	13	1
Mulberry	1,640	4	4	0
Murfreesboro	1,542	3	3	0
Nashville	4,454	17	16	1
Newport	7,654	24	17	7
North Little Rock	66,424	219	185	34
Ola	1,219	4	3	1
Osceola	6,819	37	25	12
Ozark	3,598	13	11	2
Pangburn	584	2	2	0
Paragould	28,827	58	53	5
Paris	3,379	14	9	5
Parkin	1,005	1	1	0
Pea Ridge	5,873	15	14	1
Perryville	1,432	6	6	0
Piggott	3,575	8	8	0
Pine Bluff	42,195	150	129	21
Plainview	584	1	1	0
Plumerville	775	2	2	0
Pocahontas	6,478	17	16	1
Pottsville	3,246	8	6	2
Prairie Grove	5,921	13	13	0
Prescott	2,993	11	10	1
Quitman	719	4	4	0
Ravenden	447	1	1	0
Redfield	1,578	7	6	1
Rison	1,244	2	2	0
Rogers	68,026	150	109	41
Rose Bud	486	4	3	1
Russellville	29,455	59	53	6
Salem	1,605	4	3	1
Searcy	24,058	69	51	18
Shannon Hills	3,912	6	6	0
Sheridan	4,922	27	14	13
Sherwood	31,284	99	74	25
Siloam Springs	17,102	52	37	15
Springdale	80,895	201	141	60
Stamps	1,482	3	3	0
Star City	2,099	7	6	1
St. Charles	211	1	1	0
Stuttgart	8,696	32	23	9
Sulphur Springs	543	3	3	0
Swifton	738	2	2	0
Texarkana	30,300	93	84	9
Trumann	7,071	27	19	8

Table 78. Full-Time Law Enforcement Employees, by Selected State and City, 2018—Continued

(Number.)

State/city	Population	Total law enforcement employees	Total officers	Total civilians
Tuckerman	1,708	3	3	0
Tyronza	746	2	2	0
Van Buren	23,608	61	49	12
Vilonia	4,648	9	9	0
Waldron	3,375	10	9	1
Walnut Ridge	5,013	8	8	0
Ward	5,278	11	9	2
Warren	5,608	20	13	7
Weiner	687	1	1	0
West Fork	2,623	7	6	1
West Memphis	24,668	108	87	21
White Hall	4,987	19	17	2
Wilson	845	1	1	0
Wynne	7,907	22	20	2
CALIFORNIA				
Alameda	79,951	113	80	33
Albany	20,379	30	22	8
Alhambra	85,718	122	77	45
Alturas	2,501	9	8	1
Anaheim	354,743	597	419	178
Anderson	10,433	29	21	8
Angels Camp	3,808	5	4	1
Antioch	112,956	133	97	36
Arcadia	59,151	94	68	26
Arcata	18,073	37	25	12
Arroyo Grande	18,244	25	21	4
Arvin	21,560	22	15	7
Atascadero	30,716	36	24	12
Atherton	7,285	27	19	8
Atwater	29,565	33	23	10
Auburn	14,094	25	18	7
Avenal	12,084	19	17	2
Azusa	50,393	88	60	28
Bakersfield	385,609	537	398	139
Baldwin Park	76,541	101	68	33
Banning	31,451	37	24	13
Barstow	24,095	51	35	16
Bear Valley	5,500	5	4	1
Beaumont	48,559	60	43	17
Bell	35,857	36	27	9
Bell Gardens	42,845	68	48	20
Belmont	27,325	42	29	13
Belvedere	2,134	8	7	1
Benicia	28,536	49	31	18
Berkeley	123,735	247	153	94
Beverly Hills	34,557	215	133	82
Bishop	3,744	20	12	8
Blythe	19,517	30	21	9
Brawley	26,590	48	34	14
Brea	43,279	90	61	29
Brentwood	64,118	91	63	28
Brisbane	4,786	19	15	4
Broadmoor	4,440	10	9	1
Buena Park	83,336	125	86	39
Burbank	105,041	231	148	83
Burlingame	30,959	54	35	19
Calexico	40,596	34	21	13
California City	14,051	20	12	8
Calipatria	7,549	5	5	0
Calistoga	5,289	12	8	4
Campbell	41,853	68	41	27
Capitola	10,218	26	19	7
Carlsbad	116,739	162	117	45
Carmel	3,921	23	15	8
Cathedral City	55,056	72	48	24
Central Marin	35,033	46	42	4
Ceres	49,101	62	47	15
Chico	94,273	141	91	50
Chino	91,535	153	102	51
Chowchilla	18,551	27	19	8
Chula Vista	274,370	305	221	84
Citrus Heights	88,603	133	86	47
Claremont	36,178	62	39	23
Clayton	12,330	13	11	2
Clearlake	15,037	31	19	12
Cloverdale	8,826	22	14	8
Clovis	111,759	166	101	65
Coalinga	16,593	23	15	8
Colma	1,524	25	19	6
Colton	55,203	77	51	26
Colusa	5,961	9	8	1
Concord	130,855	197	145	52
Corcoran	21,487	26	15	11
Corning	7,580	21	12	9

Table 78. Full-Time Law Enforcement Employees, by Selected State and City, 2018—Continued

(Number.)

State/city	Population	Total law enforcement employees	Total officers	Total civilians
Corona	170,041	209	148	61
Coronado	24,491	62	42	20
Costa Mesa	114,358	188	128	60
Cotati	7,509	15	10	5
Covina	48,557	83	57	26
Crescent City	6,245	12	11	1
Culver City	39,335	138	103	35
Cypress	49,223	68	54	14
Daly City	107,928	124	98	26
Davis	69,486	91	57	34
Delano	53,141	67	49	18
Del Rey Oaks	1,696	10	10	0
Desert Hot Springs	28,991	33	25	8
Dinuba	24,411	42	32	10
Dixon	20,472	29	24	5
Dos Palos	5,518	13	8	5
Downey	113,277	165	116	49
East Palo Alto	29,991	43	35	8
El Cajon	104,497	182	119	63
El Centro	44,609	67	43	24
El Cerrito	25,793	47	40	7
Elk Grove	174,651	226	139	87
El Monte	116,464	162	119	43
El Segundo	16,881	79	51	28
Emeryville	12,016	52	38	14
Escalon	7,653	11	10	1
Escondido	153,073	209	155	54
Etna	718	3	3	0
Eureka	27,174	68	46	22
Exeter	10,583	19	17	2
Fairfax	7,620	16	11	5
Fairfield	117,883	177	119	58
Farmersville	10,806	14	13	1
Ferndale	1,373	5	5	0
Firebaugh	8,438	16	11	5
Folsom	78,916	101	70	31
Fontana	213,964	290	183	107
Fort Bragg	7,317	18	12	6
Fortuna	12,228	25	19	6
Foster City	34,993	53	39	14
Fountain Valley	56,433	75	57	18
Fowler	6,627	12	11	1
Fremont	238,024	278	181	97
Fresno	531,818	1,063	811	252
Fullerton	141,132	189	124	65
Galt	26,548	47	31	16
Gardena	60,423	121	94	27
Garden Grove	174,661	213	155	58
Gilroy	59,033	98	61	37
Glendale	204,724	323	223	100
Glendora	52,727	79	48	31
Gonzales	8,521	15	12	3
Grass Valley	13,004	29	26	3
Greenfield	17,680	26	22	4
Gridley	6,612	18	13	5
Grover Beach	13,694	24	15	9
Guadalupe	7,411	15	13	2
Gustine	5,890	7	6	1
Hanford	56,805	82	57	25
Hawthorne	88,372	134	86	48
Hayward	162,881	292	177	115
Healdsburg	11,917	25	17	8
Hemet	86,047	104	71	33
Hercules	25,750	26	23	3
Hermosa Beach	19,737	62	35	27
Hillsborough	11,580	36	28	8
Hollister	38,930	40	32	8
Huntington Beach	203,428	349	215	134
Huntington Park	58,922	90	60	30
Huron	7,396	20	12	8
Imperial	17,976	20	16	4
Indio	91,346	103	64	39
Inglewood	110,726	235	185	50
Ione	7,848	7	7	0
Irvine	288,052	310	216	94
Irwindale	1,467	33	26	7
Jackson	4,752	9	8	1
Kensington	5,400	6	6	0
Kerman	15,128	23	20	3
King City	14,228	17	15	2
Kingsburg	12,089	20	17	3
Laguna Beach	23,202	94	55	39
La Habra	62,769	97	63	34
Lakeport	4,763	12	11	1
Lake Shastina	2,563	5	5	0

Table 78. Full-Time Law Enforcement Employees, by Selected State and City, 2018—Continued

(Number.)

State/city	Population	Total law enforcement employees	Total officers	Total civilians
La Mesa	60,442	96	68	28
La Palma	15,747	28	21	7
La Verne	32,656	57	40	17
Lemoore	26,626	41	33	8
Lincoln	48,364	29	21	8
Lindsay	13,542	18	15	3
Livermore	91,612	141	92	49
Livingston	14,301	29	19	10
Lodi	66,416	98	66	32
Lompoc	43,719	59	43	16
Long Beach	470,445	1,164	824	340
Los Alamitos	11,629	20	17	3
Los Altos	30,989	44	31	13
Los Angeles	4,029,741	13,010	9,974	3,036
Los Banos	39,651	66	40	26
Los Gatos	30,899	57	38	19
Madera	66,098	94	63	31
Mammoth Lakes	8,118	16	13	3
Manhattan Beach	36,038	97	59	38
Manteca	81,080	99	68	31
Marina	22,511	29	22	7
Martinez	38,699	42	31	11
Marysville	12,459	25	18	7
McFarland	15,475	16	11	5
Mendota	11,476	14	12	2
Menlo Park	34,694	66	45	21
Merced	83,659	129	92	37
Mill Valley	14,418	25	19	6
Milpitas	79,895	108	85	23
Modesto	215,822	301	217	84
Monrovia	37,128	79	48	31
Montclair	39,648	60	44	16
Montebello	63,291	85	61	24
Monterey	28,744	64	48	16
Monterey Park	61,160	106	70	36
Moraga	17,866	12	11	1
Morgan Hill	46,142	59	38	21
Morro Bay	10,692	18	16	2
Mountain View	82,518	131	85	46
Mount Shasta	3,289	10	7	3
Murrieta	114,706	129	88	41
Napa	80,145	119	71	48
National City	61,763	122	83	39
Nevada City	3,146	12	11	1
Newark	48,276	75	54	21
Newman	11,525	14	11	3
Newport Beach	86,276	213	137	76
Novato	56,577	84	59	25
Oakdale	23,504	29	18	11
Oakland	430,230	1,010	731	279
Oceanside	177,464	293	207	86
Ontario	177,542	381	280	101
Orange	141,108	218	152	66
Orange Cove	9,682	12	11	1
Orland	7,697	12	10	2
Oroville	19,186	35	19	16
Oxnard	211,737	357	239	118
Pacifica	39,339	34	31	3
Pacific Grove	15,788	33	22	11
Palm Springs	48,644	145	95	50
Palo Alto	67,560	137	77	60
Palos Verdes Estates	13,559	31	21	10
Paradise	26,755	34	20	14
Parlier	15,356	23	18	5
Pasadena	143,448	333	222	111
Paso Robles	32,228	47	32	15
Petaluma	61,289	85	60	25
Piedmont	11,478	27	17	10
Pinole	19,509	42	26	16
Pismo Beach	8,323	35	23	12
Pittsburg	73,462	100	78	22
Placentia	52,324	62	41	21
Placerville	11,018	25	19	6
Pleasant Hill	35,252	56	41	15
Pleasanton	84,992	110	76	34
Pomona	153,496	269	146	123
Porterville	59,394	89	58	31
Port Hueneme	22,417	29	20	9
Red Bluff	14,315	40	26	14
Redding	92,068	135	104	31
Redlands	71,954	123	82	41
Redondo Beach	68,048	149	96	53
Redwood City	88,161	118	82	36
Reedley	25,809	46	30	16
Rialto	104,173	125	96	29

Table 78. Full-Time Law Enforcement Employees, by Selected State and City, 2018—Continued

(Number.)

State/city	Population	Total law enforcement employees	Total officers	Total civilians
Richmond	110,982	253	181	72
Ridgecrest	29,055	50	32	18
Rio Dell	3,413	3	3	0
Rio Vista	9,268	15	13	2
Ripon	15,878	30	23	7
Riverside	331,022	522	370	152
Rocklin	65,969	82	57	25
Rohnert Park	43,129	85	61	24
Roseville	137,706	185	122	63
Ross	2,487	8	8	0
Sacramento	507,037	948	651	297
Salinas	158,590	204	151	53
San Bernardino	217,986	394	238	156
San Bruno	43,621	62	46	16
Sand City	395	11	10	1
San Diego	1,436,495	2,332	1,731	601
San Fernando	24,869	40	26	14
San Francisco	889,282	2,913	2,306	607
San Gabriel	40,637	63	48	15
Sanger	25,287	41	37	4
San Jose	1,047,305	1,550	1,113	437
San Leandro	91,359	127	87	40
San Luis Obispo	47,885	80	57	23
San Marino	13,358	31	24	7
San Mateo	105,839	148	107	41
San Pablo	31,403	72	49	23
San Rafael	59,254	87	63	24
San Ramon	76,569	82	65	17
Santa Ana	335,403	533	313	220
Santa Barbara	92,630	199	134	65
Santa Clara	128,682	222	150	72
Santa Cruz	65,680	123	93	30
Santa Maria	108,100	170	121	49
Santa Monica	92,674	397	218	179
Santa Paula	30,456	41	29	12
Santa Rosa	176,325	246	170	76
Sausalito	7,167	25	19	6
Scotts Valley	11,998	28	20	8
Seal Beach	24,356	49	34	15
Seaside	34,303	43	33	10
Sebastopol	7,705	21	14	7
Selma	24,979	45	34	11
Shafter	19,986	34	25	9
Sierra Madre	11,055	19	16	3
Signal Hill	11,711	46	31	15
Simi Valley	127,222	162	109	53
Soledad	26,313	21	17	4
Sonora	4,851	17	10	7
South Gate	95,570	124	78	46
South Lake Tahoe	22,060	56	32	24
South Pasadena	25,924	46	31	15
South San Francisco	67,973	112	75	37
Stallion Springs	2,645	4	4	0
St. Helena	6,251	17	12	5
Stockton	313,158	671	469	202
Suisun City	29,859	33	22	11
Sunnyvale	155,637	282	217	65
Susanville	15,017	15	13	2
Sutter Creek	2,584	5	5	0
Taft	9,449	25	15	10
Tehachapi	12,402	26	19	7
Tiburon	9,195	17	13	4
Torrance	146,968	316	212	104
Tracy	91,988	136	89	47
Truckee	16,609	36	23	13
Tulare	64,509	108	66	42
Tulelake	991	2	2	0
Turlock	74,267	114	72	42
Tustin	81,243	139	92	47
Ukiah	16,037	46	27	19
Union City	76,198	92	74	18
Upland	77,453	99	65	34
Vacaville	101,146	157	103	54
Vallejo	122,974	150	107	43
Ventura	111,272	176	136	40
Vernon	113	49	38	11
Visalia	134,224	212	146	66
Walnut Creek	70,587	118	82	36
Watsonville	54,513	93	69	24
Weed	2,682	14	10	4
West Covina	107,806	153	95	58
Westminster	91,821	118	79	39
Westmorland	2,291	5	5	0
West Sacramento	54,215	94	72	22
Wheatland	3,892	9	8	1

Table 78. Full-Time Law Enforcement Employees, by Selected State and City, 2018—Continued

(Number.)

State/city	Population	Total law enforcement employees	Total officers	Total civilians
Whittier	87,055	164	117	47
Williams	5,380	13	11	2
Willits	4,875	15	10	5
Winters	7,371	13	11	2
Woodlake	7,700	12	11	1
Woodland	60,679	78	64	14
Yreka	7,573	21	14	7
Yuba City	67,035	88	58	30
COLORADO				
Alamosa	9,955	27	23	4
Arvada	120,631	220	174	46
Aspen	7,465	36	27	9
Ault	1,792	8	7	1
Aurora	372,824	857	723	134
Avon	6,565	21	18	3
Basalt	4,219	12	11	1
Bayfield	2,738	8	7	1
Black Hawk	128	35	25	10
Blue River	927	2	2	0
Boulder	108,380	262	173	89
Breckenridge	4,981	27	23	4
Brighton	41,613	91	65	26
Broomfield	70,307	207	107	100
Brush	5,347	13	10	3
Buena Vista	2,842	11	9	2
Burlington	3,057	8	6	2
Calhan	835	4	4	0
Canon City	16,557	41	33	8
Carbondale	6,882	15	12	3
Castle Rock	64,526	102	75	27
Cedaredge	2,226	9	6	3
Centennial	111,646	163	122	41
Center	2,282	17	11	6
Cherry Hills Village	6,740	27	23	4
Collbran	702	1	1	0
Colorado Springs	471,124	995	702	293
Columbine Valley	1,469	8	8	0
Commerce City	57,474	132	96	36
Cortez	8,738	47	29	18
Craig	8,848	25	20	5
Crested Butte	1,668	8	7	1
Cripple Creek	1,206	22	14	8
Dacono	5,774	16	13	3
De Beque	500	4	4	0
Del Norte	1,563	3	2	1
Delta	8,819	20	17	3
Denver	720,745	1,824	1,517	307
Dillon	971	10	9	1
Durango	18,717	62	53	9
Eagle	6,921	12	11	1
Eaton	5,355	11	10	1
Edgewater	5,328	17	17	0
Elizabeth	1,416	8	7	1
Empire	304	1	1	0
Englewood	35,029	108	76	32
Erie	25,233	37	31	6
Estes Park	6,399	32	20	12
Evans	20,744	37	35	2
Fairplay	742	2	2	0
Federal Heights	12,929	38	26	12
Firestone	14,419	32	27	5
Florence	3,919	14	13	1
Fort Collins	168,163	302	207	95
Fort Lupton	8,273	20	17	3
Fort Morgan	11,267	33	27	6
Fountain	30,367	57	50	7
Fowler	1,138	2	2	0
Fraser/Winter Park	2,320	10	9	1
Frederick	13,390	22	19	3
Frisco	3,196	11	8	3
Fruita	13,390	20	17	3
Garden City	267	4	4	0
Georgetown	1,077	3	3	0
Glendale	5,293	39	28	11
Glenwood Springs	10,022	34	27	7
Golden	20,768	63	49	14
Granby	2,110	9	7	2
Grand Junction	62,974	182	104	78
Greeley	107,325	208	156	52
Green Mountain Falls	699	1	1	0
Greenwood Village	15,989	82	60	22
Gunnison	6,627	30	14	16
Gypsum	7,210	4	4	0
Haxtun	909	3	3	0

Table 78. Full-Time Law Enforcement Employees, by Selected State and City, 2018—Continued

(Number.)

State/city	Population	Total law enforcement employees	Total officers	Total civilians
Hayden	1,952	6	4	2
Holyoke	2,199	4	4	0
Hotchkiss	922	4	4	0
Hudson	1,578	6	5	1
Hugo	746	3	3	0
Idaho Springs	1,792	11	8	3
Ignacio	733	8	8	0
Johnstown	16,490	19	17	2
Keenesburg	1,224	9	9	0
Kersey	1,633	4	4	0
Kiowa	757	2	2	0
Kremmling	1,491	4	4	0
Lafayette	28,914	48	41	7
La Junta	6,867	21	15	6
Lakeside	8	5	4	1
Lakewood	156,779	409	285	124
Lamar	7,552	29	15	14
La Salle	2,385	8	8	0
La Veta	777	1	1	0
Leadville	2,785	8	7	1
Limon	1,937	6	5	1
Littleton	48,632	98	77	21
Lochbuie	6,613	12	10	2
Log Lane Village	867	2	2	0
Lone Tree	13,933	60	49	11
Longmont	95,534	245	169	76
Louisville	21,545	42	35	7
Loveland	78,192	159	107	52
Mancos	1,426	4	3	1
Manitou Springs	5,365	13	12	1
Manzanola	421	3	2	1
Mead	4,761	6	6	0
Meeker	2,274	6	6	0
Milliken	7,238	13	9	4
Monte Vista	4,136	17	13	4
Montrose	19,335	57	41	16
Monument	7,594	19	16	3
Morrison	435	10	9	1
Mountain View	541	8	7	1
Mountain Village	1,405	8	5	3
Mount Crested Butte	849	9	8	1
Nederland	1,554	4	3	1
New Castle	4,863	9	8	1
Northglenn	39,383	74	57	17
Oak Creek	933	3	3	0
Olathe	1,809	6	6	0
Ouray	1,015	5	5	0
Pagosa Springs	1,974	7	6	1
Palisade	2,693	11	10	1
Palmer Lake	2,774	2	2	0
Paonia	1,416	5	5	0
Parachute	1,120	6	5	1
Parker	55,573	106	66	40
Platteville	3,887	10	9	1
Pueblo	111,756	279	219	60
Rangely	2,323	6	3	3
Ridgway	986	3	3	0
Rifle	9,711	24	19	5
Rocky Ford	3,808	11	11	0
Salida	5,951	20	18	2
Sanford	875	1	1	0
Sheridan	6,159	32	31	1
Silt	3,160	6	6	0
Silverthorne	4,775	15	11	4
Simla	641	2	2	0
Snowmass Village	2,762	13	10	3
South Fork	353	2	2	0
Springfield	1,358	3	3	0
Steamboat Springs	13,100	37	24	13
Sterling	13,928	28	22	6
Stratton	651	1	1	0
Telluride	2,456	16	11	5
Thornton	139,697	313	233	80
Timnath	4,174	8	7	1
Trinidad	7,947	30	20	10
Vail	5,511	51	25	26
Walsh	509	1	1	0
Westminster	113,751	247	174	73
Wheat Ridge	31,452	96	78	18
Wiggins	886	3	3	0
Windsor	26,441	39	33	6
Woodland Park	7,709	32	22	10
Wray	2,368	5	4	1
Yuma	3,509	8	7	1

Table 78. Full-Time Law Enforcement Employees, by Selected State and City, 2018—Continued

(Number.)

State/city	Population	Total law enforcement employees	Total officers	Total civilians
CONNECTICUT				
Ansonia	18,751	55	46	9
Avon	18,379	41	33	8
Berlin	20,593	54	41	13
Bethel	19,974	46	37	9
Bloomfield	21,541	61	48	13
Branford	28,121	66	51	15
Bridgeport	146,819	445	392	53
Bristol	60,184	144	119	25
Brookfield	17,230	44	34	10
Canton	10,298	20	15	5
Cheshire	29,337	58	48	10
Clinton	12,917	36	27	9
Coventry	12,438	21	16	5
Cromwell	13,950	35	26	9
Danbury	85,818	150	145	5
Darien	22,050	61	51	10
Derby	12,535	36	34	2
East Hampton	12,893	18	16	2
East Hartford	50,184	150	120	30
East Haven	28,805	57	53	4
East Lyme	18,744	28	22	6
Easton	7,590	17	15	2
East Windsor	11,425	37	28	9
Enfield	44,574	106	87	19
Fairfield	62,452	111	105	6
Farmington	25,602	62	48	14
Glastonbury	34,593	76	57	19
Granby	11,367	21	16	5
Greenwich	63,075	178	152	26
Groton	9,051	33	26	7
Groton Long Point	510	5	5	0
Groton Town	29,372	79	62	17
Guilford	22,268	46	38	8
Hamden	61,234	133	104	29
Hartford	123,117	425	394	31
Ledyard	14,808	30	21	9
Madison	18,184	38	28	10
Manchester	57,884	151	110	41
Meriden	59,792	131	118	13
Middlebury	7,746	14	12	2
Middletown	46,314	127	112	15
Milford	54,754	126	109	17
Monroe	19,653	55	43	12
Naugatuck	31,400	68	57	11
New Britain	72,630	169	161	8
New Canaan	20,461	50	45	5
New Haven	131,181	460	406	54
Newington	30,382	66	52	14
New London	26,995	85	69	16
New Milford	26,956	57	45	12
Newtown	28,015	48	45	3
North Branford	14,179	29	23	6
North Haven	23,703	60	51	9
Norwalk	89,442	213	177	36
Norwich	39,318	96	83	13
Old Saybrook	10,117	29	22	7
Orange	14,002	55	43	12
Plainfield	15,049	21	18	3
Plainville	17,701	47	38	9
Plymouth	11,646	31	23	8
Portland	9,340	13	12	1
Putnam	9,325	17	14	3
Redding	9,242	22	16	6
Ridgefield	25,260	46	41	5
Rocky Hill	20,163	50	36	14
Seymour	16,589	39	37	2
Shelton	41,657	60	50	10
Simsbury	25,164	45	36	9
Southington	43,960	87	66	21
South Windsor	25,968	54	40	14
Stamford	132,007	304	282	22
Stonington	18,602	50	39	11
Stratford	52,472	114	105	9
Suffield	15,688	24	20	4
Thomaston	7,563	29	16	13
Torrington	34,286	87	77	10
Trumbull	36,167	85	74	11
Vernon	29,304	61	48	13
Wallingford	44,680	93	71	22
Waterbury	108,378	315	264	51
Waterford	18,937	50	45	5
Watertown	21,631	46	37	9
West Hartford	63,085	142	123	19
West Haven	54,738	117	109	8

Table 78. Full-Time Law Enforcement Employees, by Selected State and City, 2018—Continued

(Number.)

State/city	Population	Total law enforcement employees	Total officers	Total civilians
Weston	10,351	17	16	1
Westport	28,278	76	64	12
Wethersfield	26,127	63	48	15
Willimantic	17,691	47	42	5
Wilton	18,654	46	43	3
Winchester	10,669	28	23	5
Windsor	28,867	65	52	13
Windsor Locks	12,560	35	28	7
Wolcott	16,666	34	24	10
Woodbridge	8,832	32	24	8
DELAWARE				
Bethany Beach	1,224	11	10	1
Blades	1,444	3	3	0
Bridgeville	2,368	7	7	0
Camden	3,497	8	7	1
Cheswold	1,596	5	5	0
Clayton	3,297	9	8	1
Dagsboro	902	4	4	0
Delaware City	1,835	4	3	1
Delmar	1,810	14	13	1
Dewey Beach	388	10	8	2
Dover	37,778	133	101	32
Ellendale	439	1	1	0
Elsmere	6,033	12	11	1
Felton	1,414	4	4	0
Fenwick Island	437	8	7	1
Georgetown	7,419	23	19	4
Greenwood	1,116	4	3	1
Harrington	3,659	14	13	1
Laurel	4,394	17	16	1
Lewes	3,134	14	13	1
Middletown	22,350	39	33	6
Milford	11,301	41	30	11
Millsboro	4,439	17	16	1
Milton	2,966	9	8	1
Newark	34,207	88	70	18
New Castle	5,351	18	17	1
Newport	1,038	6	6	0
Ocean View	2,146	12	11	1
Rehoboth Beach	1,522	29	17	12
Seaford	7,876	38	27	11
Selbyville	2,494	9	8	1
Smyrna	11,791	30	23	7
South Bethany	519	4	4	0
Wilmington	71,157	338	292	46
Wyoming	1,531	4	4	0
DISTRICT OF COLUMBIA				
Washington	702,455	4,520	3,841	679
FLORIDA				
Altamonte Springs	44,664	115	97	18
Apalachicola	2,306	8	7	1
Apopka	53,106	139	102	37
Arcadia	8,082	22	18	4
Atlantic Beach	13,750	39	27	12
Atlantis	2,151	20	15	5
Auburndale	16,358	44	36	8
Aventura	38,544	122	85	37
Bal Harbour Village	3,116	35	23	12
Bartow	19,954	56	37	19
Bay Harbor Islands	6,074	26	22	4
Belleair	4,121	15	13	2
Belle Isle	7,151	16	15	1
Belleview	5,026	16	14	2
Biscayne Park	3,199	10	10	0
Boca Raton	100,162	302	200	102
Bonifay	2,712	7	6	1
Bowling Green	2,918	7	7	0
Boynton Beach	79,142	196	144	52
Bradenton	57,647	146	119	27
Bradenton Beach	1,284	10	10	0
Bunnell	2,939	11	9	2
Cape Coral	187,869	311	228	83
Casselberry	28,744	60	52	8
Cedar Key	688	3	3	0
Center Hill	1,435	2	2	0
Chiefland	2,172	14	12	2
Clearwater	116,504	321	233	88
Clermont	36,233	82	75	7
Clewiston	7,807	17	12	5
Cocoa	18,739	93	62	31
Coconut Creek	62,237	129	95	34
Cooper City	36,896	77	59	18

Table 78. Full-Time Law Enforcement Employees, by Selected State and City, 2018—Continued

(Number.)

State/city	Population	Total law enforcement employees	Total officers	Total civilians
Coral Gables	51,716	255	182	73
Coral Springs	134,640	307	210	97
Crescent City	1,540	4	3	1
Crestview	24,293	55	43	12
Dade City	7,238	30	23	7
Dania Beach	32,376	84	76	8
Davenport	4,849	11	10	1
Davie	107,120	258	187	71
Daytona Beach	69,030	292	245	47
Daytona Beach Shores	4,549	39	31	8
Deerfield Beach	81,371	137	128	9
DeFuniak Springs	6,646	27	20	7
DeLand	33,384	81	61	20
Delray Beach	69,970	229	164	65
Doral	63,680	172	127	45
Eatonville	2,289	14	12	2
Edgewater	22,643	32	27	5
Edgewood	2,996	15	12	3
El Portal	2,503	14	7	7
Eustis	21,182	48	36	12
Fellsmere	5,803	8	7	1
Fernandina Beach	12,411	42	37	5
Flagler Beach	5,152	17	14	3
Fort Lauderdale	182,150	679	525	154
Fort Myers	82,805	285	209	76
Fort Pierce	46,109	137	111	26
Fort Walton Beach	22,263	56	43	13
Fruitland Park	9,093	18	17	1
Gainesville	133,400	330	262	68
Golden Beach	972	24	18	6
Graceville	2,188	7	6	1
Groveland	14,342	46	31	15
Gulfport	12,424	36	32	4
Gulf Stream	888	12	12	0
Haines City	24,887	62	49	13
Hialeah	241,778	335	269	66
Hialeah Gardens	24,510	61	41	20
Highland Beach	3,838	16	15	1
High Springs	6,147	15	13	2
Hillsboro Beach	2,038	19	15	4
Holly Hill	12,302	28	24	4
Hollywood	155,503	394	300	94
Holmes Beach	4,325	26	17	9
Homestead	71,314	150	112	38
Howey-in-the-Hills	1,176	7	7	0
Indialantic	2,920	15	10	5
Indian Creek Village	93	15	10	5
Indian Harbour Beach	8,617	25	18	7
Indian Shores	3,809	24	21	3
Interlachen	1,384	4	4	0
Jacksonville	903,213	3,032	1,724	1,308
Jacksonville Beach	23,842	84	63	21
Jasper	3,894	8	7	1
Jennings	872	2	2	0
Juno Beach	3,682	17	15	2
Jupiter	66,457	145	118	27
Jupiter Inlet Colony	459	5	5	0
Jupiter Island	922	23	18	5
Key Biscayne	13,299	47	36	11
Key Colony Beach	837	5	5	0
Key West	25,286	122	94	28
Kissimmee	72,894	209	133	76
Lady Lake	15,517	29	23	6
Lake Alfred	6,084	16	12	4
Lake City	12,182	53	35	18
Lake Clarke Shores	3,632	12	11	1
Lake Hamilton	1,418	8	7	1
Lakeland	109,616	351	241	110
Lake Mary	16,896	50	41	9
Lake Placid	2,282	10	8	2
Lake Wales	16,349	48	43	5
Lantana	12,006	37	29	8
Largo	85,568	186	145	41
Lauderdale-by-the-Sea	6,615	23	21	2
Lauderdale Lakes	36,575	46	44	2
Lauderhill	72,694	137	112	25
Lawtey	722	2	2	0
Leesburg	23,029	88	65	23
Lighthouse Point	11,372	39	30	9
Live Oak	6,902	22	19	3
Longboat Key	7,351	22	19	3
Longwood	15,273	46	41	5
Lynn Haven	21,285	43	33	10
Maitland	17,846	60	52	8
Marco Island	18,122	38	35	3

Table 78. Full-Time Law Enforcement Employees, by Selected State and City, 2018—Continued

(Number.)

State/city	Population	Total law enforcement employees	Total officers	Total civilians
Margate	59,186	146	111	35
Marianna	7,251	21	16	5
Mascotte	5,693	11	10	1
Melbourne	82,844	208	151	57
Melbourne Beach	3,304	11	9	2
Mexico Beach	1,217	8	8	0
Miami	473,047	1,741	1,309	432
Miami Beach	92,928	508	393	115
Miami Gardens	114,670	264	214	50
Miami Shores	10,673	46	37	9
Miami Springs	14,508	54	43	11
Milton	10,158	23	16	7
Miramar	143,103	290	215	75
Mount Dora	14,179	60	44	16
Naples	22,308	93	66	27
Neptune Beach	7,317	28	20	8
New Port Richey	16,459	61	44	17
New Smyrna Beach	26,937	57	40	17
Niceville	15,621	35	25	10
North Bay Village	8,499	37	29	8
North Lauderdale	44,650	59	52	7
North Miami Beach	44,485	140	104	36
North Palm Beach	13,214	38	33	5
North Port	67,682	140	108	32
Oakland	3,066	14	13	1
Oakland Park	45,564	95	84	11
Ocala	59,505	253	172	81
Ocean Ridge	1,966	21	15	6
Ocoee	48,128	90	77	13
Orange City	11,805	30	26	4
Orange Park	8,750	34	26	8
Orlando	286,679	944	729	215
Ormond Beach	43,315	85	64	21
Oviedo	41,937	75	68	7
Palatka	10,365	39	32	7
Palm Bay	112,902	209	152	57
Palm Beach	8,837	93	62	31
Palm Beach Gardens	55,999	170	116	54
Palm Beach Shores	1,260	15	10	5
Palmetto	13,807	48	35	13
Palm Springs	25,146	60	42	18
Panama City	37,318	142	102	40
Panama City Beach	12,935	82	64	18
Parkland	33,760	44	40	4
Pembroke Pines	173,053	361	267	94
Pensacola	52,672	197	150	47
Perry	6,926	23	21	2
Pinellas Park	53,383	123	106	17
Plantation	95,204	277	183	94
Plant City	39,305	86	68	18
Pompano Beach	112,045	258	231	27
Ponce Inlet	3,272	14	12	2
Port Orange	64,208	109	88	21
Port Richey	2,855	22	17	5
Port St. Lucie	193,137	299	232	67
Punta Gorda	20,170	53	36	17
Riviera Beach	34,991	157	119	38
Rockledge	27,852	67	47	20
Sanford	60,154	149	130	19
Sanibel	7,498	40	26	14
Satellite Beach	11,197	32	23	9
Sea Ranch Lakes	749	11	7	4
Sebastian	25,672	59	39	20
Sebring	10,741	39	33	6
Sewall's Point	2,221	10	9	1
Shalimar	821	5	4	1
South Daytona	13,038	35	29	6
South Miami	12,365	58	50	8
South Palm Beach	1,453	8	8	0
Starke	5,361	18	17	1
St. Augustine Beach	7,120	22	19	3
St. Cloud	53,560	123	84	39
St. Petersburg	265,942	781	549	232
Stuart	16,689	60	42	18
Sunny Isles Beach	22,563	62	50	12
Sunrise	95,812	230	145	85
Surfside	5,878	37	31	6
Tallahassee	192,443	447	377	70
Tamarac	66,454	100	80	20
Tampa	392,945	1,206	946	260
Tavares	17,318	31	28	3
Temple Terrace	26,777	60	43	17
Tequesta	6,161	24	19	5
Titusville	46,650	127	81	46
Treasure Island	6,972	22	18	4

Table 78. Full-Time Law Enforcement Employees, by Selected State and City, 2018—Continued

(Number.)

State/city	Population	Total law enforcement employees	Total officers	Total civilians
Trenton	2,106	3	2	1
Umatilla	3,786	10	9	1
Valparaiso	4,936	16	11	5
Vero Beach	17,172	75	53	22
Village of Pinecrest	19,854	66	45	21
Virginia Gardens	2,486	7	6	1
Wauchula	4,927	18	14	4
Welaka	701	1	1	0
West Melbourne	22,665	53	45	8
West Miami	8,486	23	19	4
Weston	71,744	108	89	19
West Palm Beach	111,659	377	287	90
West Park	15,297	43	39	4
White Springs	768	4	4	0
Wildwood	7,120	46	37	9
Williston	2,702	18	12	6
Wilton Manors	12,941	46	32	14
Windermere	3,478	15	14	1
Winter Garden	44,921	95	67	28
Winter Haven	42,268	113	85	28
Winter Park	31,323	107	82	25
Winter Springs	37,137	59	45	14
Zephyrhills	15,504	45	30	15
GEORGIA				
Abbeville	2,772	5	5	0
Acworth	23,028	63	45	18
Adairsville	4,879	16	15	1
Adel	5,316	21	18	3
Adrian	642	2	2	0
Alamo	3,408	3	3	0
Alapaha	667	2	1	1
Albany	72,594	183	148	35
Alma	3,486	10	8	2
Alpharetta	67,051	139	105	34
Alto	1,178	6	2	4
Americus	15,184	45	39	6
Aragon	1,249	9	3	6
Arcade	1,905	4	4	0
Arlington	1,375	4	4	0
Ashburn	3,623	17	15	2
Athens-Clarke County	127,014	278	218	60
Atlanta	496,106	1,987	1,535	452
Auburn	7,706	21	16	5
Austell	7,301	29	20	9
Avondale Estates	3,205	12	12	0
Bainbridge	12,033	46	38	8
Baldwin	3,329	14	9	5
Ball Ground	2,147	4	4	0
Barnesville	6,487	21	20	1
Baxley	4,718	16	12	4
Berlin	561	2	2	0
Blackshear	3,526	17	14	3
Blairsville	610	8	7	1
Blakely	4,603	33	16	17
Bloomingdale	2,767	16	13	3
Blue Ridge	1,418	9	8	1
Blythe	704	3	3	0
Bowdon	2,107	10	8	2
Braselton	11,537	20	19	1
Braswell	384	3	2	1
Bremen	6,456	23	21	2
Brookhaven	54,138	77	66	11
Brooklet	1,647	3	2	1
Broxton	1,197	5	4	1
Brunswick	16,431	62	59	3
Buchanan	1,166	7	6	1
Buena Vista	2,081	4	4	0
Butler	1,798	8	7	1
Byron	5,258	23	19	4
Cairo	9,407	25	22	3
Calhoun	16,513	54	46	8
Camilla	5,016	19	16	3
Canon	831	1	1	0
Canton	28,685	53	48	5
Carrollton	27,189	81	67	14
Cartersville	21,156	66	57	9
Cave Spring	1,131	2	2	0
Cecil	279	4	2	2
Cedartown	9,959	36	32	4
Centerville	7,795	22	19	3
Chamblee	29,818	85	63	22
Chatsworth	4,301	20	18	2
Chattahoochee Hills	2,982	10	9	1
Chickamauga	3,149	6	6	0

Table 78. Full-Time Law Enforcement Employees, by Selected State and City, 2018—Continued

(Number.)

State/city	Population	Total law enforcement employees	Total officers	Total civilians
Clarkesville	1,843	7	6	1
Clarkston	12,957	21	17	4
Claxton	2,240	14	11	3
Clayton	2,264	12	12	0
Cleveland	3,956	16	15	1
Cochran	4,882	13	12	1
College Park	15,034	116	89	27
Colquitt	1,863	9	8	1
Columbus	194,135	503	403	100
Commerce	6,927	24	19	5
Conyers	16,128	87	64	23
Coolidge	524	2	1	1
Cordele	10,669	31	26	5
Cornelia	4,278	19	16	3
Covington	14,178	66	56	10
Cumming	6,414	23	14	9
Cuthbert	3,585	8	4	4
Dallas	13,496	34	24	10
Dalton	33,831	97	85	12
Danielsville	587	3	3	0
Darien	1,836	12	12	0
Davisboro	1,704	1	1	0
Dawson	4,103	17	12	5
Decatur	24,491	58	46	12
Demorest	1,951	8	7	1
Dillard	369	4	3	1
Doerun	753	5	4	1
Donalsonville	2,524	13	11	2
Doraville	10,625	59	42	17
Douglasville	34,076	111	91	20
Dublin	15,756	70	58	12
Duluth	29,882	76	60	16
Dunwoody	50,095	73	60	13
East Ellijay	573	9	8	1
Eastman	5,038	14	12	2
East Point	35,486	114	80	34
Eatonton	6,614	28	19	9
Edison	1,459	5	4	1
Elberton	4,300	24	22	2
Ellaville	1,874	5	5	0
Ellijay	1,733	12	11	1
Emerson	1,610	7	7	0
Eton	923	3	3	0
Euharlee	4,321	11	10	1
Fairburn	15,904	42	37	5
Fairmount	741	4	4	0
Fayetteville	18,042	55	47	8
Fitzgerald	8,673	30	25	5
Flowery Branch	7,760	18	16	2
Folkston	4,664	6	6	0
Forest Park	20,024	82	60	22
Forsyth	4,082	14	13	1
Fort Oglethorpe	9,912	28	26	2
Fort Valley	8,675	28	23	5
Franklin	953	8	8	0
Franklin Springs	1,161	3	3	0
Gainesville	41,368	109	96	13
Garden City	9,008	42	33	9
Glennville	5,083	13	11	2
Gordon	1,869	11	6	5
Graham	295	1	1	0
Grantville	3,250	14	13	1
Gray	3,188	13	12	1
Greensboro	3,354	19	16	3
Greenville	838	6	5	1
Griffin	22,707	80	70	10
Grovetown	14,543	27	20	7
Guyton	1,996	5	4	1
Hahira	2,988	10	8	2
Hampton	7,841	19	17	2
Hapeville	6,607	35	24	11
Harlem	3,214	7	6	1
Hartwell	4,468	26	21	5
Hazlehurst	4,143	14	12	2
Helen	547	9	8	1
Hephzibah	3,944	4	4	0
Hiawassee	916	5	5	0
Hinesville	33,163	91	76	15
Hiram	4,046	23	18	5
Hoboken	529	3	1	2
Hogansville	3,116	25	13	12
Holly Springs	12,369	33	32	1
Homeland	909	7	7	0
Homerville	2,394	9	8	1
Ivey	912	2	2	0

Table 78. Full-Time Law Enforcement Employees, by Selected State and City, 2018—Continued

(Number.)

State/city	Population	Total law enforcement employees	Total officers	Total civilians
Jackson	5,101	11	10	1
Jefferson	11,394	26	24	2
Jesup	9,698	32	30	2
Johns Creek	85,446	84	75	9
Jonesboro	4,760	30	25	5
Kennesaw	34,907	73	65	8
Kingsland	17,251	36	34	2
Kingston	655	1	1	0
LaFayette	7,210	24	22	2
LaGrange	30,611	106	88	18
Lake City	2,838	18	17	1
Lake Park	909	4	4	0
Lavonia	2,163	15	14	1
Lawrenceville	30,247	95	69	26
Leary	577	1	1	0
Leslie	369	4	3	1
Lilburn	12,847	37	32	5
Locust Grove	6,852	24	21	3
Loganville	12,308	25	23	2
Lookout Mountain	1,565	7	7	0
Louisville	2,209	6	6	0
Ludowici	2,289	11	5	6
Lumber City	1,247	1	1	0
Lumpkin	1,162	7	6	1
Lyons	4,284	20	18	2
Madison	4,098	15	13	2
Manchester	3,966	17	12	5
Marietta	61,675	180	135	45
Marshallville	1,258	4	3	1
Maysville	1,956	3	3	0
McDonough	25,151	53	44	9
McIntyre	602	5	5	0
Metter	3,981	13	12	1
Midville	258	1	1	0
Midway	2,026	8	6	2
Milledgeville	18,620	62	38	24
Millen	2,769	11	11	0
Milton	39,848	43	38	5
Molena	372	1	1	0
Monroe	13,573	50	46	4
Montezuma	3,030	14	11	3
Morrow	7,632	25	24	1
Moultrie	14,136	32	29	3
Mountain City	1,076	3	3	0
Mount Zion	1,811	3	3	0
Nahunta	1,065	2	1	1
Nashville	4,839	17	14	3
Newnan	39,830	96	81	15
Newton	593	1	1	0
Norcross	17,089	57	42	15
Norman Park	976	3	2	1
Oakwood	4,179	15	14	1
Ocilla	3,653	14	13	1
Oglethorpe	1,160	5	4	1
Omega	1,221	4	4	0
Oxford	2,250	1	1	0
Palmetto	4,752	16	13	3
Peachtree City	35,374	63	58	5
Pelham	3,511	12	11	1
Pembroke	2,581	10	8	2
Pine Lake	770	4	3	1
Pine Mountain	1,383	9	7	2
Plains	720	1	1	0
Pooler	24,656	59	52	7
Porterdale	1,489	6	6	0
Port Wentworth	9,105	33	28	5
Poulan	787	6	5	1
Powder Springs	15,214	32	30	2
Quitman	3,692	14	12	2
Ray City	1,065	5	3	2
Remerton	1,097	9	8	1
Reynolds	991	7	6	1
Richland	1,488	5	5	0
Richmond Hill	13,157	40	34	6
Rincon	10,039	21	19	2
Ringgold	3,600	12	11	1
Riverdale	16,618	44	38	6
Roberta	970	6	6	0
Rochelle	1,104	7	5	2
Rockmart	4,281	21	19	2
Rossville	3,967	12	11	1
Roswell	95,677	175	134	41
Royston	2,577	12	9	3
Sandersville	5,527	20	18	2
Sandy Springs	108,654	157	139	18

Table 78. Full-Time Law Enforcement Employees, by Selected State and City, 2018—Continued

(Number.)

State/city	Population	Total law enforcement employees	Total officers	Total civilians
Sardis	967	7	6	1
Savannah-Chatham Metropolitan	242,265	687	519	168
Screven	765	4	3	1
Senoia	4,352	17	15	2
Shiloh	476	3	1	2
Sky Valley	267	3	3	0
Smyrna	57,498	136	91	45
Snellville	19,947	56	44	12
Social Circle	4,517	16	15	1
Soperton	3,015	8	7	1
Sparks	2,012	3	3	0
Sparta	1,232	13	7	6
Springfield	4,192	8	7	1
Statesboro	31,819	84	67	17
Statham	2,722	5	4	1
St. Marys	18,130	16	13	3
Stone Mountain	6,447	17	16	1
Summerville	4,275	18	16	2
Suwanee	20,227	47	37	10
Swainsboro	7,501	24	21	3
Sylvania	2,433	13	10	3
Sylvester	5,835	26	20	6
Talbotton	843	15	5	10
Tallapoosa	3,159	11	10	1
Tallulah Falls	168	2	1	1
Temple	4,462	17	14	3
Tennille	1,977	4	4	0
Thomaston	8,703	33	30	3
Thomasville	18,507	64	57	7
Thunderbolt	2,697	10	8	2
Tifton	16,779	49	41	8
Toccoa	8,310	32	31	1
Toomsboro	426	2	1	1
Trenton	2,224	8	8	0
Trion	1,744	11	10	1
Tunnel Hill	873	5	3	2
Twin City	1,692	5	4	1
Tybee Island	3,148	36	25	11
Tyrone	7,390	17	17	0
Union City	21,647	64	59	5
Valdosta	56,250	164	138	26
Vidalia	10,488	35	27	8
Vienna	3,663	7	6	1
Villa Rica	15,536	49	41	8
Wadley	1,896	7	6	1
Warner Robins	75,668	148	106	42
Warrenton	1,714	6	6	0
Warwick	393	4	2	2
Waverly Hall	756	4	3	1
Waycross	13,771	59	48	11
Waynesboro	5,462	23	16	7
West Point	3,766	25	17	8
Whigham	469	4	3	1
Willacoochee	1,373	6	5	1
Winder	16,514	44	37	7
Winterville	1,239	2	2	0
Woodbury	887	10	10	0
Woodstock	32,850	62	54	8
Wrens	1,974	10	9	1
Wrightsville	3,643	6	5	1
Zebulon	1,174	6	6	0
HAWAII				
Honolulu	982,019	2,434	1,942	492
IDAHO				
Aberdeen	1,943	5	5	0
American Falls	4,253	9	7	2
Bellevue	2,368	3	3	0
Blackfoot	11,910	30	27	3
Boise	229,265	376	292	84
Bonners Ferry	2,618	7	7	0
Buhl	4,399	10	9	1
Caldwell	55,936	80	68	12
Chubbuck	14,998	36	22	14
Coeur d'Alene	51,650	109	87	22
Cottonwood	926	1	1	0
Emmett	6,871	15	13	2
Filer	2,813	5	5	0
Fruitland	5,308	16	12	4
Garden City	12,025	34	26	8
Gooding	3,433	9	7	2
Grangeville	3,168	6	6	0
Hagerman	869	1	1	0
Hailey	8,334	14	13	1

Table 78. Full-Time Law Enforcement Employees, by Selected State and City, 2018—Continued

(Number.)

State/city	Population	Total law enforcement employees	Total officers	Total civilians
Heyburn	3,364	8	7	1
Homedale	2,645	6	5	1
Idaho City	452	1	1	0
Idaho Falls	61,643	131	89	42
Jerome	11,738	20	16	4
Kamiah	1,290	3	3	0
Kellogg	2,074	7	7	0
Ketchum	2,771	13	11	2
Kimberly	3,943	9	8	1
Lewiston	32,949	68	45	23
McCall	3,413	14	12	2
Meridian	103,774	135	105	30
Middleton	7,762	10	9	1
Montpelier	2,517	7	5	2
Moscow	25,339	40	34	6
Mountain Home	14,220	36	27	9
Nampa	95,386	178	123	55
Orofino	3,020	7	6	1
Osburn	1,515	2	2	0
Parma	2,123	6	6	0
Payette	7,430	16	14	2
Pocatello	55,317	131	89	42
Ponderay	1,116	7	6	1
Post Falls	34,144	75	45	30
Preston	5,411	8	7	1
Priest River	1,822	7	5	2
Rathdrum	8,508	17	14	3
Rexburg	28,765	39	31	8
Rigby	4,076	7	6	1
Rupert	5,845	12	11	1
Salmon	3,103	8	8	0
Sandpoint	8,533	24	19	5
Shelley	4,412	8	8	0
Shoshone	1,505	5	5	0
Soda Springs	3,036	5	5	0
Spirit Lake	2,378	8	7	1
St. Anthony	3,546	6	6	0
Sun Valley	1,443	13	12	1
Twin Falls	49,908	95	75	20
Weiser	5,349	14	11	3
Wendell	2,692	4	4	0
Wilder	1,748	5	5	0
ILLINOIS				
Addison	36,791	130	68	62
Alsip	19,050	44	41	3
Altamont	2,274	5	5	0
Alton	26,563	78	61	17
Arlington Heights	75,688	130	106	24
Arthur	2,248	6	6	0
Ashland	1,203	1	1	0
Assumption	1,083	2	2	0
Auburn	4,695	6	6	0
Aviston	2,117	1	1	0
Barrington Hills	4,219	21	17	4
Batavia	26,614	47	39	8
Beardstown	5,507	10	9	1
Beecher	4,486	9	8	1
Bensenville	18,324	41	35	6
Bethalto	9,300	17	12	5
Bethany	1,265	1	1	0
Bloomingdale	22,008	55	44	11
Bloomington	78,097	163	126	37
Bolingbrook	75,451	129	112	17
Bourbonnais	18,388	26	25	1
Braidwood	6,217	23	18	5
Brighton	2,136	4	4	0
Brooklyn	706	9	9	0
Burbank	28,771	57	49	8
Burr Ridge	10,852	30	27	3
Byron	3,588	7	6	1
Cahokia	14,004	34	28	6
Cambridge	2,090	1	1	0
Campton Hills	11,305	5	5	0
Carbondale	25,816	76	61	15
Carlinville	5,499	17	12	5
Carol Stream	40,019	87	69	18
Carpentersville	38,220	60	56	4
Carrollton	2,434	6	6	0
Carthage	2,466	4	4	0
Casey	2,649	8	8	0
Caseyville	4,038	13	12	1
Catlin	1,958	1	1	0
Centralia	12,372	30	21	9
Centreville	4,969	8	7	1

Table 78. Full-Time Law Enforcement Employees, by Selected State and City, 2018—Continued

(Number.)

State/city	Population	Total law enforcement employees	Total officers	Total civilians
Champaign	88,326	149	125	24
Channahon	12,837	25	23	2
Chatham	12,770	20	14	6
Chenoa	3,142	3	3	0
Cherry Valley	3,067	15	14	1
Chester	8,505	12	9	3
Chicago	2,719,151	14,086	13,138	948
Chicago Ridge	14,167	35	31	4
Christopher	2,717	6	6	0
Cicero	82,310	179	157	22
Coal City	5,338	11	10	1
Cobden	1,094	3	3	0
Columbia	10,356	23	16	7
Cortland	4,342	6	6	0
Countryside	5,969	27	24	3
Crest Hill	21,221	32	30	2
Crete	8,147	21	19	2
Crystal Lake	40,345	73	64	9
Dallas City	880	2	2	0
Dana	153	1	1	0
Danville	31,203	73	60	13
Decatur	71,625	154	147	7
Deer Creek	668	1	1	0
Deerfield	19,049	53	40	13
DeKalb	43,064	78	64	14
Delavan	1,612	4	4	0
De Soto	1,534	3	2	1
Des Plaines	58,155	116	97	19
Downers Grove	49,626	78	65	13
Du Quoin	5,770	15	10	5
East Alton	6,073	12	9	3
East Dubuque	1,592	4	4	0
East Peoria	22,640	51	48	3
Effingham	12,624	39	25	14
Elgin	113,060	233	181	52
Elizabeth	729	1	1	0
Elk Grove Village	32,723	103	89	14
Elmhurst	47,025	106	85	21
Elmwood	2,054	2	2	0
Elwood	2,262	10	10	0
Erie	1,519	2	2	0
Essex	767	1	1	0
Eureka	5,335	6	6	0
Evanston	74,780	215	160	55
Fairfield	5,013	14	10	4
Fairmount	612	1	1	0
Farmington	2,257	5	5	0
Fisher	1,973	2	2	0
Flora	4,856	18	12	6
Flossmoor	9,315	25	20	5
Fox Lake	10,535	32	25	7
Fox River Grove	4,639	9	9	0
Freeburg	4,246	10	9	1
Freeport	23,887	65	48	17
Galena	3,198	11	10	1
Galesburg	30,573	72	48	24
Georgetown	3,265	4	4	0
Germantown	1,278	1	1	0
Gibson City	3,292	8	7	1
Gilman	1,687	2	2	0
Glendale Heights	34,030	71	56	15
Glenwood	8,864	25	22	3
Golf	499	1	1	0
Goodfield	999	1	1	0
Grafton	636	2	2	0
Granite City	28,593	68	55	13
Grayville	1,586	4	3	1
Greenfield	995	2	2	0
Greenup	1,487	5	5	0
Gurnee	30,698	96	62	34
Hamel	814	2	2	0
Hampshire	6,466	12	12	0
Hampton	1,807	3	3	0
Hanover Park	37,971	81	58	23
Hartford	1,359	5	4	1
Harvard	9,144	19	17	2
Harwood Heights	8,490	29	27	2
Hawthorn Woods	8,504	13	12	1
Herrin	12,930	25	18	7
Highland	9,812	27	20	7
Highland Park	29,764	69	57	12
Highwood	5,307	12	11	1
Hillsdale	510	1	1	0
Hinckley	2,045	3	3	0
Hinsdale	17,831	24	21	3

Table 78. Full-Time Law Enforcement Employees, by Selected State and City, 2018—Continued

(Number.)

State/city	Population	Total law enforcement employees	Total officers	Total civilians
Hodgkins	1,897	23	21	2
Homer	1,168	1	1	0
Homewood	19,056	46	41	5
Hoopeston	5,078	16	10	6
Inverness	7,523	14	12	2
Itasca	9,531	25	22	3
Jacksonville	18,320	43	39	4
Joliet	148,553	340	269	71
Kankakee	26,032	69	65	4
Kansas	720	1	1	0
Kenilworth	2,521	9	8	1
Kildeer	4,060	10	8	2
Kincaid	1,397	2	2	0
La Grange	15,583	31	27	4
Lake Bluff	5,654	17	15	2
Lake Villa	8,726	17	16	1
Lakewood	3,945	9	8	1
Lake Zurich	19,930	48	31	17
Leland	921	1	1	0
Libertyville	20,499	47	40	7
Lincolnshire	7,343	24	21	3
Lindenhurst	14,450	15	13	2
Lockport	25,510	44	38	6
Lombard	43,794	77	64	13
Lovington	1,061	2	2	0
Lyons	10,563	10	8	2
Machesney Park	22,627	26	25	1
Macomb	18,124	28	25	3
Maple Park	1,327	1	1	0
Marengo	7,470	15	13	2
Marissa	1,820	3	3	0
Marquette Heights	2,669	4	4	0
Marseilles	4,869	11	10	1
Mascoutah	8,078	15	14	1
Mattoon	17,794	42	38	4
McHenry	26,893	76	48	28
Melrose Park	25,164	85	72	13
Mendota	7,062	17	15	2
Metropolis	6,076	16	14	2
Midlothian	14,607	28	26	2
Milan	5,046	20	15	5
Millstadt	3,856	8	8	0
Minier	1,196	2	2	0
Minonk	1,996	5	5	0
Mokena	20,507	33	30	3
Moline	42,051	100	81	19
Momence	3,127	7	7	0
Morris	14,798	29	25	4
Morrison	4,054	6	6	0
Morton	16,302	23	21	2
Morton Grove	23,123	58	46	12
Mount Carmel	6,931	15	10	5
Mount Carroll	1,588	3	3	0
Mount Morris	2,803	5	4	1
Mount Olive	1,956	6	4	2
Mount Prospect	53,888	102	83	19
Mount Pulaski	1,484	2	2	0
Mount Zion	5,816	12	10	2
Moweaqua	1,712	2	2	0
Murphysboro	7,511	23	16	7
New Athens	1,903	4	4	0
New Baden	3,268	6	6	0
Niles	29,433	69	55	14
Nokomis	2,124	5	4	1
Normal	54,525	91	81	10
Northbrook	33,424	91	65	26
Northfield	5,472	22	19	3
North Pekin	1,543	7	7	0
Oak Brook	8,103	43	40	3
Oak Forest	27,644	53	42	11
Oak Park	52,313	131	107	24
Oakwood	1,523	2	2	0
Oblong	1,381	1	1	0
O'Fallon	29,354	69	50	19
Okawville	1,368	4	4	0
Olney	8,919	12	11	1
Orion	1,810	2	2	0
Orland Park	59,064	124	97	27
Ottawa	18,096	49	34	15
Palatine	68,648	128	106	22
Palestine	1,285	1	1	0
Palos Hills	17,338	34	31	3
Paris	8,253	24	16	8
Pawnee	2,667	7	7	0
Pekin	32,541	59	52	7

Table 78. Full-Time Law Enforcement Employees, by Selected State and City, 2018—Continued

(Number.)

State/city	Population	Total law enforcement employees	Total officers	Total civilians
Peoria	112,595	226	207	19
Peotone	4,152	11	10	1
Plainfield	44,525	71	55	16
Plano	11,692	24	22	2
Pontiac	11,795	18	17	1
Posen	5,903	17	15	2
Princeton	7,538	18	17	1
Quincy	40,249	88	75	13
Rantoul	12,741	38	31	7
Richmond	1,926	7	7	0
Ridge Farm	828	1	1	0
River Forest	11,125	29	27	2
Riverton	3,427	9	9	0
Rochester	3,733	7	7	0
Rockdale	1,939	5	5	0
Rockford	146,198	339	299	40
Rock Island	37,985	108	81	27
Rockton	7,443	17	15	2
Rolling Meadows	23,970	57	50	7
Roscoe	10,466	15	13	2
Round Lake	18,454	30	26	4
Round Lake Beach	27,534	42	39	3
Round Lake Heights	2,689	5	5	0
Roxana	1,455	7	6	1
Royalton	1,122	3	3	0
Rushville	2,936	4	4	0
Salem	7,131	23	15	8
Sandwich	7,382	24	17	7
San Jose	607	2	2	0
Sauget	148	9	9	0
Savanna	2,818	7	7	0
Schiller Park	11,617	35	32	3
Seneca	2,255	8	7	1
Shorewood	17,482	33	29	4
Silvis	7,578	22	16	6
Sleepy Hollow	3,314	8	7	1
Smithton	3,822	6	6	0
Somonauk	1,878	9	9	0
South Beloit	7,642	14	13	1
South Elgin	22,627	35	31	4
Southern View	1,590	3	3	0
South Roxana	1,968	5	5	0
Springfield	114,623	268	239	29
Spring Valley	5,196	11	10	1
St. Anne	1,183	3	3	0
St. Charles	32,764	62	53	9
St. Elmo	1,378	3	3	0
Stockton	1,730	6	5	1
Streator	13,038	25	23	2
Sullivan	4,459	11	9	2
Summit	11,310	33	31	2
Swansea	13,506	23	21	2
Thayer	664	1	1	0
Thornton	2,457	11	10	1
Tilton	2,565	4	4	0
Tinley Park	56,638	89	76	13
Tolono	3,447	2	2	0
Trenton	2,605	5	5	0
Vernon Hills	26,429	67	43	24
Vienna	1,729	3	3	0
Villa Park	21,806	49	39	10
Virden	3,344	10	7	3
Walnut	1,324	2	2	0
Warren	1,319	4	3	1
Warrenville	13,280	39	31	8
Waterloo	10,408	18	17	1
Waukegan	87,530	190	147	43
West Chicago	27,174	50	44	6
West City	648	12	7	5
West Dundee	7,354	22	20	2
Western Springs	13,554	24	21	3
West Frankfort	7,921	20	15	5
Westville	3,017	3	3	0
Wheaton	53,418	79	65	14
Wheeling	38,687	88	56	32
White Hall	2,352	7	5	2
Willow Springs	5,639	10	8	2
Wilmette	27,467	58	44	14
Winnebago	2,973	6	6	0
Winnetka	12,518	31	26	5
Winthrop Harbor	6,727	15	10	5
Wood Dale	13,800	43	35	8
Woodstock	25,353	41	37	4
Zion	23,885	50	46	4

Table 78. Full-Time Law Enforcement Employees, by Selected State and City, 2018—Continued
(Number.)

State/city	Population	Total law enforcement employees	Total officers	Total civilians
INDIANA				
Albion	2,324	6	6	0
Anderson	54,925	124	102	22
Auburn	13,220	25	24	1
Bargersville	7,695	13	12	1
Batesville	6,616	17	12	5
Bedford	13,282	39	30	9
Berne	4,155	8	7	1
Bloomington	85,730	157	97	60
Bluffton	10,046	32	19	13
Bremen	4,507	17	12	5
Brownsburg	26,525	49	43	6
Cannelton	1,496	3	3	0
Carmel	94,128	140	115	25
Cedar Lake	12,602	25	20	5
Chesterton	13,561	26	22	4
Clinton	4,707	10	8	2
Columbia City	9,082	20	19	1
Columbus	47,595	94	84	10
Crawfordsville	16,207	41	36	5
Crown Point	29,884	51	45	6
Cumberland	5,739	15	13	2
Dyer	15,880	35	31	4
East Chicago	28,010	76	69	7
Edinburgh	4,607	13	12	1
Elkhart	52,659	161	137	24
Ellettsville	6,740	12	11	1
Elwood	8,405	16	15	1
Fairmount	2,771	7	6	1
Fishers	94,035	125	114	11
Fort Wayne	267,634	531	470	61
Frankfort	15,744	35	32	3
Franklin	25,288	57	51	6
Gary	75,426	192	171	21
Goshen	33,386	71	64	7
Greenfield	22,292	45	42	3
Greenwood	58,312	69	61	8
Griffith	16,050	39	33	6
Hagerstown	1,678	5	5	0
Hammond	76,050	240	210	30
Hartford City	5,736	14	12	2
Highland	22,428	47	40	7
Hobart	28,101	77	67	10
Huntingburg	6,135	15	14	1
Indianapolis	877,584	3,153	2,616	537
Jasper	15,583	26	23	3
Jeffersonville	47,709	90	85	5
Kendallville	9,850	27	18	9
Knox	3,528	7	7	0
Kokomo	57,804	97	81	16
Lafayette	72,904	188	142	46
Lake Station	11,880	23	23	0
Lawrence	49,093	82	63	19
Lawrenceburg	5,033	25	21	4
Ligonier	4,369	11	10	1
Logansport	17,681	42	41	1
Lowell	9,711	17	16	1
Marion	28,116	78	63	15
Merrillville	34,858	64	57	7
Mooresville	9,681	27	21	6
Muncie	68,406	114	100	14
Munster	22,596	47	42	5
New Haven	15,669	29	21	8
New Whiteland	6,182	9	8	1
Noblesville	63,315	92	82	10
North Vernon	6,694	20	18	2
Peru	10,973	32	30	2
Plainfield	33,668	58	53	5
Plymouth	9,948	22	20	2
Portage	36,646	74	67	7
Rensselaer	5,864	17	11	6
Roseland	632	5	4	1
Rushville	6,009	17	12	5
Sellersburg	8,935	18	16	2
Seymour	19,681	60	41	19
Shelbyville	19,075	61	45	16
South Bend	102,397	283	237	46
Speedway	12,187	50	35	15
St. John	17,615	23	20	3
Terre Haute	60,773	136	129	7
Valparaiso	33,610	63	57	6
Walkerton	2,285	8	6	2
Westfield	41,037	56	52	4
West Lafayette	46,906	70	50	20
Westville	5,664	8	8	0

Table 78. Full-Time Law Enforcement Employees, by Selected State and City, 2018—Continued

(Number.)

State/city	Population	Total law enforcement employees	Total officers	Total civilians
Whitestown	9,388	26	25	1
Whiting	4,802	20	18	2
Zionsville	27,185	38	36	2
IOWA				
Adel	4,490	10	9	1
Albia	3,760	7	6	1
Algona	5,456	14	10	4
Altoona	19,361	34	31	3
Ames	67,636	77	54	23
Anamosa	5,369	9	8	1
Ankeny	65,235	65	58	7
Atlantic	6,632	13	12	1
Audubon	1,907	4	4	0
Belle Plaine	2,429	4	4	0
Bettendorf	36,190	51	45	6
Bloomfield	2,680	7	6	1
Boone	12,492	19	18	1
Burlington	24,946	48	43	5
Camanche	4,285	6	6	0
Carlisle	4,290	9	8	1
Cedar Falls	41,901	55	54	1
Cedar Rapids	133,039	279	212	67
Centerville	5,420	18	11	7
Charles City	7,334	19	12	7
Cherokee	4,854	9	8	1
Clarinda	5,301	11	10	1
Clarion	2,759	8	7	1
Clear Lake	7,533	22	16	6
Clinton	25,289	50	43	7
Colfax	2,060	4	4	0
Coralville	21,178	38	34	4
Council Bluffs	62,309	133	113	20
Creston	7,842	16	11	5
Davenport	102,706	193	170	23
Decorah	7,641	20	13	7
Denison	8,367	20	14	6
DeWitt	5,204	11	10	1
Dubuque	58,362	111	105	6
Eagle Grove	3,408	5	5	0
Eldora	2,642	5	5	0
Eldridge	6,679	10	9	1
Emmetsburg	3,754	7	6	1
Estherville	5,719	13	13	0
Fairfield	10,565	19	13	6
Forest City	4,085	8	8	0
Fort Dodge	24,191	43	40	3
Fort Madison	10,448	19	17	2
Glenwood	5,317	12	10	2
Grinnell	9,000	16	14	2
Grundy Center	2,686	4	4	0
Hampton	4,205	8	7	1
Harlan	4,850	9	8	1
Hiawatha	7,401	14	14	0
Humboldt	4,585	6	6	0
Independence	6,062	13	12	1
Indianola	16,163	23	20	3
Iowa City	76,984	105	84	21
Iowa Falls	5,021	14	10	4
Jefferson	4,122	8	8	0
Johnston	22,242	31	28	3
Keokuk	10,284	27	24	3
Knoxville	7,166	12	11	1
Lansing	932	3	3	0
Le Claire	4,003	8	7	1
Le Mars	9,989	16	14	2
Lisbon	2,253	3	3	0
Manchester	4,993	16	10	6
Maquoketa	5,891	17	11	6
Marengo	2,441	4	4	0
Marion	40,034	60	47	13
Marshalltown	27,238	47	42	5
Mason City	27,308	53	49	4
Mechanicsville	1,119	1	1	0
Mount Pleasant	8,476	16	14	2
Mount Vernon	4,426	6	6	0
Muscatine	23,785	43	40	3
Nevada	6,773	12	10	2
New Hampton	3,393	6	6	0
Newton	15,091	26	21	5
North Liberty	19,698	23	21	2
Norwalk	11,192	19	18	1
Oelwein	5,899	15	10	5
Ogden	2,019	2	2	0
Onawa	2,783	5	5	0

Table 78. Full-Time Law Enforcement Employees, by Selected State and City, 2018—Continued

(Number.)

State/city	Population	Total law enforcement employees	Total officers	Total civilians
Orange City	6,152	7	7	0
Osage	3,567	7	6	1
Osceola	5,094	12	11	1
Oskaloosa	11,550	17	15	2
Ottumwa	24,371	49	38	11
Pella	10,208	23	17	6
Perry	7,487	19	12	7
Pleasant Hill	10,030	20	18	2
Polk City	4,848	6	6	0
Postville	2,077	4	4	0
Prairie City	1,734	3	3	0
Princeton	952	1	1	0
Red Oak	5,374	12	10	2
Rock Valley	3,798	6	6	0
Sac City	2,081	4	4	0
Sergeant Bluff	4,765	9	8	1
Sheldon	5,049	7	7	0
Shenandoah	4,877	12	10	2
Sigourney	1,994	4	3	1
Sioux Center	7,656	7	7	0
Sioux City	82,470	150	125	25
Spencer	11,020	28	19	9
Spirit Lake	5,131	10	9	1
State Center	1,457	2	2	0
Storm Lake	10,602	23	19	4
Story City	3,390	6	6	0
Tama	2,762	6	6	0
Tipton	3,218	7	6	1
Toledo	2,141	5	5	0
University Heights	1,073	5	5	0
Urbandale	44,212	60	51	9
Van Meter	1,147	2	2	0
Vinton	5,095	10	9	1
Walcott	1,643	3	3	0
Washington	7,414	12	11	1
Waukee	21,845	25	23	2
Waukon	3,666	8	8	0
Webster City	7,751	17	12	5
West Branch	2,403	4	4	0
West Burlington	2,916	10	10	0
West Des Moines	66,966	89	76	13
West Union	2,327	5	5	0
Williamsburg	3,149	7	7	0
Windsor Heights	4,963	14	13	1
Winterset	5,287	8	8	0
KANSAS				
Abilene	6,315	17	14	3
Altamont	1,018	3	3	0
Andover	13,307	34	26	8
Argonia	479	1	1	0
Arkansas City	11,791	29	25	4
Arma	1,432	5	5	0
Atchison	10,589	24	24	0
Attica	563	1	1	0
Atwood	1,196	2	2	0
Augusta	9,387	29	20	9
Baldwin City	4,661	12	10	2
Basehor	6,239	15	14	1
Baxter Springs	3,919	14	10	4
Bel Aire	8,092	13	12	1
Belle Plaine	1,568	5	5	0
Belleville	1,885	5	5	0
Beloit	3,695	7	5	2
Benton	872	3	3	0
Blue Rapids	959	2	2	0
Bonner Springs	7,826	28	25	3
Buhler	1,283	3	3	0
Burlington	2,537	9	7	2
Burrton	870	2	2	0
Caldwell	1,001	3	3	0
Caney	2,000	10	6	4
Canton	703	1	1	0
Carbondale	1,357	3	3	0
Cedar Vale	519	1	1	0
Chanute	9,046	17	15	2
Chapman	1,363	3	3	0
Cheney	2,180	5	5	0
Cherokee	706	1	1	0
Cherryvale	2,154	7	6	1
Claflin	614	1	1	0
Clay Center	3,930	7	6	1
Clearwater	2,529	6	5	1
Coffeyville	9,375	29	21	8
Colby	5,355	18	12	6

Table 78. Full-Time Law Enforcement Employees, by Selected State and City, 2018—Continued

(Number.)

State/city	Population	Total law enforcement employees	Total officers	Total civilians
Columbus	3,066	8	7	1
Colwich	1,417	4	4	0
Concordia	5,059	16	9	7
Council Grove	2,030	7	6	1
Derby	23,842	55	45	10
Dodge City	27,756	58	44	14
Eastborough	751	6	6	0
Edwardsville	4,505	19	18	1
El Dorado	12,960	25	24	1
Elkhart	1,825	3	3	0
Ellinwood	1,992	5	5	0
Ellis	1,978	4	4	0
Ellsworth	3,044	7	6	1
Elwood	1,199	3	3	0
Emporia	24,698	50	42	8
Erie	1,078	4	3	1
Eudora	6,354	12	12	0
Fredonia	2,243	7	6	1
Frontenac	3,409	9	7	2
Galena	2,871	12	11	1
Galva	864	1	1	0
Garden City	26,902	76	52	24
Garden Plain	905	3	3	0
Gardner	21,945	39	34	5
Garnett	3,231	6	6	0
Girard	2,696	8	6	2
Goddard	4,795	14	13	1
Goodland	4,400	10	9	1
Grandview Plaza	1,627	8	7	1
Great Bend	15,251	37	33	4
Greensburg	775	1	1	0
Halstead	2,050	6	5	1
Harper	1,340	3	3	0
Hays	20,892	42	37	5
Haysville	11,343	28	21	7
Hesston	3,791	8	7	1
Hiawatha	3,132	10	9	1
Highland	1,003	2	2	0
Hill City	1,409	3	3	0
Hillsboro	2,829	5	5	0
Hoisington	2,539	7	6	1
Holton	3,258	6	6	0
Holyrood	431	1	1	0
Horton	1,687	10	6	4
Howard	590	1	1	0
Hoxie	1,194	2	2	0
Hugoton	3,816	8	6	2
Humboldt	1,783	4	3	1
Hutchinson	40,573	97	63	34
Independence	8,629	26	19	7
Inman	1,328	2	2	0
Iola	5,306	17	16	1
Junction City	22,875	62	45	17
Kechi	2,020	4	3	1
Kingman	2,895	7	7	0
Kiowa	955	2	2	0
La Cygne	1,122	2	2	0
Lansing	12,043	18	17	1
Larned	3,828	7	7	0
Lawrence	98,219	180	153	27
Leavenworth	36,331	76	54	22
Leawood	35,070	81	58	23
Lenexa	54,349	130	87	43
Liberal	19,725	49	36	13
Lindsborg	3,247	7	6	1
Little River	524	1	1	0
Louisburg	4,512	11	10	1
Lyndon	998	2	2	0
Lyons	3,540	13	6	7
Macksville	531	1	1	0
Maize	4,735	12	11	1
Marion	1,784	3	3	0
Marquette	605	1	1	0
Marysville	3,268	9	8	1
McLouth	843	1	1	0
McPherson	13,211	37	29	8
Meade	1,610	4	3	1
Medicine Lodge	1,886	4	4	0
Merriam	11,238	36	31	5
Minneapolis	1,949	5	5	0
Mission	9,421	33	28	5
Mission Hills	3,587	3	3	0
Moran	511	1	1	0
Mound City	680	1	1	0
Moundridge	1,875	5	5	0

Table 78. Full-Time Law Enforcement Employees, by Selected State and City, 2018—Continued
(Number.)

State/city	Population	Total law enforcement employees	Total officers	Total civilians
Mulberry	519	1	1	0
Mulvane	6,391	21	15	6
Neodesha	2,292	9	7	2
Newton	18,830	42	38	4
North Newton	1,774	4	4	0
Norton	2,760	7	6	1
Oakley	2,102	10	5	5
Oberlin	1,730	4	4	0
Olathe	139,154	211	182	29
Osage City	2,777	7	7	0
Osawatomie	4,278	18	13	5
Osborne	1,326	3	3	0
Oswego	1,703	4	4	0
Ottawa	12,300	32	28	4
Overbrook	1,008	2	2	0
Overland Park	193,877	295	237	58
Oxford	1,007	3	3	0
Paola	5,574	22	16	6
Park City	7,785	17	15	2
Parsons	9,664	33	25	8
Peabody	1,111	3	2	1
Pittsburg	20,210	65	48	17
Plainville	1,832	5	5	0
Pleasanton	1,182	3	3	0
Pratt	6,737	20	14	6
Roeland Park	6,777	17	15	2
Rose Hill	3,986	8	7	1
Rossville	1,135	2	2	0
Russell	4,454	9	8	1
Sabetha	2,569	10	6	4
Salina	46,862	102	73	29
Scott City	3,854	13	8	5
Sedan	1,023	1	1	0
Sedgwick	1,661	3	3	0
Seneca	2,044	6	6	0
Shawnee	65,983	114	93	21
South Hutchinson	2,515	4	4	0
Spearville	811	1	1	0
Spring Hill	6,806	10	9	1
Stafford	958	3	3	0
Sterling	2,214	5	5	0
St. Francis	1,301	3	2	1
St. George	1,028	1	1	0
St. John	1,187	3	3	0
St. Marys	2,646	5	5	0
Stockton	1,285	5	5	0
Tonganoxie	5,508	11	10	1
Topeka	126,399	324	267	57
Troy	976	1	1	0
Udall	713	2	2	0
Ulysses	5,878	11	10	1
Valley Center	7,370	19	17	2
Valley Falls	1,131	2	2	0
Victoria	1,191	2	2	0
Wamego	4,748	13	8	5
Wellington	7,775	19	16	3
Wellsville	1,803	4	4	0
Westwood	2,276	9	8	1
Wichita	391,726	824	648	176
Wilson	750	1	1	0
Winfield	12,072	29	24	5
Yates Center	1,323	3	3	0
KENTUCKY				
Adairville	878	1	1	0
Albany	2,019	16	16	0
Alexandria	9,583	19	15	4
Ashland	20,525	46	42	4
Auburn	1,377	2	2	0
Audubon Park	1,506	3	3	0
Bancroft	517	1	1	0
Bardstown	13,244	30	28	2
Beaver Dam	3,587	6	6	0
Bellefonte	836	4	4	0
Bellevue	5,746	12	11	1
Benham	434	1	1	0
Benton	4,495	7	7	0
Booneville	125	1	1	0
Bowling Green	68,268	147	113	34
Brandenburg	2,852	5	5	0
Burgin	968	1	1	0
Burkesville	1,473	6	6	0
Burnside	905	6	5	1
Cadiz	2,637	9	8	1
Calvert City	2,513	8	7	1

Table 78. Full-Time Law Enforcement Employees, by Selected State and City, 2018—Continued

(Number.)

State/city	Population	Total law enforcement employees	Total officers	Total civilians
Carlisle	1,957	9	4	5
Carrollton	3,820	19	12	7
Catlettsburg	1,766	8	8	0
Cave City	2,425	9	9	0
Central City	5,746	12	12	0
Clinton	1,277	2	2	0
Cloverport	1,145	1	1	0
Cold Spring	6,430	11	11	0
Covington	40,448	122	111	11
Cumberland	1,967	7	7	0
Cynthiana	6,362	28	18	10
Danville	16,801	44	31	13
Dayton	5,464	14	13	1
Eddyville	2,569	5	5	0
Edgewood	8,736	16	16	0
Edmonton	1,583	7	7	0
Elizabethtown	30,180	72	52	20
Elkhorn City	893	2	2	0
Elkton	2,106	7	7	0
Elsmere	8,680	15	15	0
Eminence	2,581	6	6	0
Erlanger	22,993	45	41	4
Evarts	816	3	3	0
Falmouth	2,100	8	6	2
Flatwoods	7,136	12	12	0
Fleming-Neon	689	2	2	0
Flemingsburg	2,822	8	8	0
Florence	32,701	68	64	4
Fort Mitchell	8,260	15	15	0
Fort Wright	5,737	13	13	0
Frankfort	27,664	72	57	15
Franklin	8,829	21	20	1
Fulton	2,175	11	10	1
Georgetown	34,351	60	56	4
Glasgow	14,411	39	31	8
Grayson	3,983	12	11	1
Greenville	4,239	11	11	0
Guthrie	1,388	4	4	0
Hardinsburg	2,320	5	5	0
Harlan	1,526	11	10	1
Harrodsburg	8,399	22	19	3
Hawesville	1,001	1	1	0
Hazard	5,035	22	18	4
Highland Heights	7,112	12	11	1
Hillview	9,163	17	16	1
Hodgenville	3,223	6	6	0
Hopkinsville	30,606	111	76	35
Hyden	341	1	1	0
Independence	28,052	38	36	2
Indian Hills	3,002	7	7	0
Irvine	2,330	5	5	0
Irvington	1,173	4	4	0
Jackson	2,029	10	9	1
Jamestown	1,790	5	5	0
Jeffersontown	27,443	58	48	10
Jenkins	1,981	4	4	0
Junction City	2,300	3	3	0
La Grange	8,995	16	15	1
Lakeside Park-Crestview Hills	6,107	13	12	1
Lancaster	3,866	12	12	0
Lawrenceburg	11,378	20	13	7
Lebanon	5,668	28	18	10
Leitchfield	6,914	20	19	1
Lewisburg	804	1	1	0
Lexington	325,579	701	611	90
Livingston	217	1	1	0
London	8,008	35	32	3
Louisa	2,405	6	6	0
Louisville Metro	682,005	1,538	1,246	292
Loyall	613	2	2	0
Ludlow	4,502	12	11	1
Madisonville	18,959	58	46	12
Marion	2,916	7	7	0
Mayfield	9,819	28	26	2
Maysville	8,770	35	25	10
Middletown	7,962	4	3	1
Monticello	6,101	11	10	1
Morehead	7,869	28	21	7
Morganfield	3,454	7	7	0
Mount Sterling	7,253	23	21	2
Mount Vernon	2,437	8	8	0
Mount Washington	14,704	20	19	1
Muldraugh	984	3	3	0
Murray	19,402	48	40	8
Newport	14,972	42	39	3

Table 78. Full-Time Law Enforcement Employees, by Selected State and City, 2018—Continued

(Number.)

State/city	Population	Total law enforcement employees	Total officers	Total civilians
Nicholasville	30,922	65	57	8
Oak Grove	7,232	19	13	6
Olive Hill	1,569	7	7	0
Owensboro	59,686	131	94	37
Owingsville	1,575	5	5	0
Paducah	24,933	82	74	8
Paintsville	4,061	9	9	0
Park Hills	2,982	7	7	0
Pembroke	872	1	1	0
Pikeville	6,641	33	22	11
Pioneer Village	2,914	5	5	0
Pippa Passes	677	7	1	6
Powderly	736	2	2	0
Prestonsburg	3,404	19	13	6
Princeton	6,075	16	15	1
Prospect	4,956	7	6	1
Providence	2,994	3	3	0
Ravenna	571	1	1	0
Russell	3,203	13	13	0
Russell Springs	2,588	11	10	1
Russellville	7,088	23	22	1
Science Hill	696	3	3	0
Scottsville	4,478	16	15	1
Sebree	1,535	1	1	0
Shively	15,876	34	28	6
Simpsonville	2,871	8	8	0
Smiths Grove	789	1	1	0
Somerset	11,453	45	37	8
Southgate	3,908	8	8	0
Springfield	3,157	16	10	6
Stamping Ground	782	1	1	0
St. Matthews	18,228	44	38	6
Taylor Mill	6,781	10	9	1
Vanceburg	1,403	7	7	0
Versailles	26,552	37	36	1
Villa Hills	7,455	14	14	0
Vine Grove	6,237	6	5	1
Warsaw	1,693	2	2	0
West Buechel	1,287	9	9	0
West Point	858	4	4	0
Whitesburg	1,885	8	7	1
Wilder	3,068	9	9	0
Williamsburg	5,299	17	17	0
Williamstown	3,932	8	7	1
Wilmore	6,406	9	8	1
Winchester	18,505	35	32	3
Worthington	1,519	4	4	0
LOUISIANA				
Abbeville	12,279	33	29	4
Addis	5,505	12	11	1
Alexandria	47,238	180	147	33
Baker	13,487	31	21	10
Ball	4,018	10	8	2
Basile	1,810	9	7	2
Bastrop	10,270	32	32	0
Baton Rouge	224,790	795	631	164
Bernice	1,630	4	4	0
Berwick	4,537	12	12	0
Blanchard	3,168	6	5	1
Bogalusa	11,730	53	35	18
Bossier City	69,551	192	156	36
Breaux Bridge	8,349	26	25	1
Broussard	12,672	34	30	4
Brusly	2,773	9	9	0
Carencro	9,174	27	25	2
Church Point	4,440	13	13	0
Clinton	1,516	6	6	0
Cottonport	1,927	4	3	1
Coushatta	1,787	5	5	0
Covington	10,658	40	33	7
Crowley	12,779	44	36	8
Denham Springs	9,761	37	29	8
De Ridder	10,820	30	25	5
Epps	820	2	1	1
Erath	2,083	11	7	4
Eunice	10,073	42	30	12
Farmerville	3,805	12	12	0
Ferriday	3,256	17	13	4
Florien	607	3	3	0
Folsom	860	5	4	1
Franklin	6,874	22	22	0
Franklinton	3,771	26	20	6
Georgetown	324	4	3	1
Golden Meadow	1,985	7	5	2

Table 78. Full-Time Law Enforcement Employees, by Selected State and City, 2018—Continued

(Number.)

State/city	Population	Total law enforcement employees	Total officers	Total civilians
Gonzales	10,916	49	44	5
Gramercy	3,382	8	8	0
Greensburg	659	5	5	0
Greenwood	3,183	11	10	1
Gretna	17,965	129	96	33
Hammond	20,550	102	77	25
Harahan	9,424	23	18	5
Haughton	3,425	13	12	1
Hodge	437	5	5	0
Houma	33,226	92	75	17
Ida	208	1	1	0
Independence	1,911	9	9	0
Iowa	3,322	14	10	4
Jennings	9,949	31	26	5
Kenner	67,556	229	162	67
Kentwood	2,434	11	10	1
Killian	1,302	5	5	0
Krotz Springs	1,221	7	7	0
Lafayette	127,592	332	283	49
Lake Arthur	2,757	11	11	0
Lake Providence	3,551	11	6	5
Leesville	5,999	31	30	1
Lutcher	3,266	4	4	0
Mamou	3,170	13	12	1
Mandeville	12,371	48	37	11
Mansfield	4,741	17	12	5
Many	2,714	12	12	0
Marion	750	1	1	0
Marksville	5,450	27	20	7
Minden	12,215	33	32	1
Monroe	48,291	175	132	43
Montgomery	721	2	2	0
Moreauville	889	2	2	0
Morgan City	11,066	50	40	10
Natchitoches	17,981	70	57	13
New Orleans	396,374	1,457	1,209	248
Oak Grove	1,581	7	7	0
Oil City	995	4	4	0
Olla	1,362	2	2	0
Opelousas	16,262	57	40	17
Patterson	5,964	25	25	0
Pearl River	2,641	15	11	4
Pineville	14,415	72	64	8
Plaquemine	6,660	28	25	3
Ponchatoula	7,369	28	22	6
Port Allen	5,011	18	17	1
Port Vincent	751	3	3	0
Rayne	8,184	21	20	1
Rayville	3,557	7	7	0
Ringgold	1,396	10	5	5
Ruston	22,274	49	36	13
Scott	8,810	28	26	2
Shreveport	190,808	721	524	197
Sibley	1,161	3	3	0
Slidell	27,973	73	60	13
Springhill	4,891	18	18	0
Sterlington	2,731	8	8	0
St. Gabriel	7,399	13	13	0
Sulphur	20,250	70	46	24
Tallulah	6,777	16	12	4
Thibodaux	14,745	60	48	12
Tickfaw	783	5	5	0
Vidalia	3,948	36	29	7
Ville Platte	7,130	26	25	1
Walker	6,286	21	17	4
Washington	940	6	6	0
Welsh	3,230	15	15	0
Westlake	4,627	18	18	0
West Monroe	12,594	73	72	1
Westwego	8,551	39	36	3
Winnfield	4,376	16	10	6
Youngsville	14,370	29	25	4
Zachary	17,884	42	41	1
Zwolle	1,922	6	6	0
MAINE				
Ashland	1,214	3	3	0
Auburn	23,031	56	50	6
Augusta	18,523	59	45	14
Baileyville	1,446	5	5	0
Bangor	31,746	91	73	18
Bar Harbor	5,464	27	18	9
Bath	8,293	23	18	5
Berwick	7,738	13	12	1
Biddeford	21,519	77	54	23

Table 78. Full-Time Law Enforcement Employees, by Selected State and City, 2018—Continued

(Number.)

State/city	Population	Total law enforcement employees	Total officers	Total civilians
Boothbay Harbor	2,193	7	6	1
Brewer	8,984	20	19	1
Bridgton	5,391	10	9	1
Brunswick	20,672	46	33	13
Bucksport	4,914	12	8	4
Buxton	8,285	15	8	7
Calais	2,970	9	9	0
Camden	4,856	13	11	2
Cape Elizabeth	9,358	15	14	1
Caribou	7,617	16	15	1
Carrabassett Valley	777	1	1	0
Clinton	3,342	4	4	0
Cumberland	8,274	12	11	1
Damariscotta	2,134	5	4	1
Dexter	3,707	6	6	0
Dixfield	2,465	4	4	0
Dover-Foxcroft	4,023	5	5	0
East Millinocket	2,929	3	3	0
Eastport	1,258	4	4	0
Eliot	6,651	8	7	1
Ellsworth	8,008	20	17	3
Fairfield	6,539	11	10	1
Falmouth	12,307	28	19	9
Farmington	7,617	13	12	1
Fort Fairfield	3,279	4	4	0
Fort Kent	3,895	9	5	4
Freeport	8,542	16	14	2
Fryeburg	3,437	5	5	0
Gardiner	5,673	13	12	1
Gorham	17,609	26	24	2
Gouldsboro	1,745	2	2	0
Greenville	1,588	2	2	0
Hallowell	2,363	5	5	0
Hampden	7,336	12	11	1
Holden	3,061	4	4	0
Houlton	5,770	18	12	6
Islesboro	568	1	1	0
Jay	4,606	7	6	1
Kennebunk	11,463	25	22	3
Kennebunkport	3,632	19	14	5
Kittery	9,755	25	18	7
Lewiston	36,170	94	81	13
Limestone	2,174	3	3	0
Lincoln	4,891	8	7	1
Lisbon	8,869	19	14	5
Livermore Falls	3,120	6	6	0
Machias	2,086	3	3	0
Madawaska	3,750	8	7	1
Mechanic Falls	2,973	5	5	0
Mexico	2,600	5	5	0
Milbridge	1,286	2	2	0
Millinocket	4,264	6	6	0
Milo	2,262	2	2	0
Monmouth	4,103	3	3	0
Newport	3,273	6	6	0
North Berwick	4,707	9	8	1
Norway	4,948	10	9	1
Oakland	6,253	11	10	1
Ogunquit	925	12	11	1
Old Orchard Beach	8,890	23	20	3
Old Town	7,450	17	16	1
Orono	11,451	15	14	1
Oxford	4,049	9	8	1
Paris	5,145	8	7	1
Phippsburg	2,246	1	1	0
Pittsfield	3,999	6	6	0
Portland	66,997	214	154	60
Presque Isle	8,997	22	16	6
Rangeley	1,150	3	3	0
Richmond	3,423	4	4	0
Rockland	7,171	18	16	2
Rockport	3,384	7	6	1
Rumford	5,712	13	13	0
Sabattus	5,057	9	8	1
Saco	19,628	45	32	13
Sanford	21,062	42	38	4
Scarborough	20,072	59	40	19
Searsport	2,668	4	4	0
Skowhegan	8,223	16	15	1
South Berwick	7,500	10	9	1
South Portland	25,557	57	51	6
Southwest Harbor	1,779	9	5	4
Thomaston	2,772	4	4	0
Topsham	8,780	17	16	1
Van Buren	2,002	3	3	0

Table 78. Full-Time Law Enforcement Employees, by Selected State and City, 2018—Continued

(Number.)

State/city	Population	Total law enforcement employees	Total officers	Total civilians
Veazie	1,819	5	5	0
Waldoboro	5,015	6	5	1
Washburn	1,550	1	1	0
Waterville	16,729	41	31	10
Wells	10,412	30	22	8
Westbrook	18,915	44	39	5
Wilton	3,939	6	6	0
Windham	18,230	30	27	3
Winslow	7,589	12	11	1
Winthrop	6,007	10	9	1
Wiscasset	3,678	5	4	1
Yarmouth	8,510	14	13	1
York	13,170	38	27	11
MARYLAND				
Aberdeen	16,210	50	37	13
Annapolis	39,461	150	119	31
Baltimore	605,436	2,935	2,488	447
Baltimore City Sheriff	0	195	151	44
Bel Air	10,027	39	30	9
Berlin	4,660	19	14	5
Berwyn Heights	3,300	9	8	1
Bladensburg	9,518	29	19	10
Boonsboro	3,569	3	2	1
Bowie	59,356	79	60	19
Brentwood	3,513	3	2	1
Brunswick	6,322	16	16	0
Cambridge	12,364	48	44	4
Capitol Heights	4,587	12	10	2
Centreville	4,844	13	13	0
Chestertown	5,035	13	12	1
Cheverly	6,519	15	11	4
Chevy Chase Village	2,094	17	11	6
Colmar Manor	1,476	5	3	2
Cottage City	1,375	5	5	0
Crisfield	2,587	14	11	3
Cumberland	19,555	51	46	5
Delmar	3,227	14	13	1
Denton	4,485	14	13	1
District Heights	6,062	12	11	1
Easton	16,550	53	45	8
Edmonston	1,508	5	4	1
Elkton	15,681	47	41	6
Fairmount Heights	1,545	1	1	0
Federalsburg	2,656	7	6	1
Forest Heights	2,588	9	7	2
Frederick	72,299	184	139	45
Frostburg	8,591	16	12	4
Fruitland	5,349	21	19	2
Glenarden	6,258	16	14	2
Greenbelt	23,661	59	46	13
Greensboro	1,882	3	3	0
Hagerstown	40,384	109	90	19
Hampstead	6,364	8	7	1
Hancock	1,546	4	3	1
Havre de Grace	13,655	42	34	8
Hurlock	2,023	10	9	1
Hyattsville	18,448	51	38	13
Landover Hills	1,679	4	3	1
La Plata	9,449	21	20	1
Laurel	26,038	83	64	19
Luke	60	1	1	0
Manchester	4,837	6	6	0
Morningside	1,594	9	7	2
Mount Airy	9,434	12	9	3
Mount Rainier	8,198	14	13	1
New Carrollton	13,115	26	19	7
North East	3,642	11	10	1
Oakland	1,829	2	2	0
Ocean City	6,950	128	98	30
Ocean Pines	12,244	19	15	4
Oxford	601	3	3	0
Perryville	4,424	13	12	1
Pocomoke City	4,044	19	12	7
Princess Anne	3,600	13	12	1
Ridgely	1,638	5	5	0
Rising Sun	2,800	5	5	0
Riverdale Park	7,330	26	18	8
Rock Hall	1,263	3	3	0
Salisbury	33,183	112	88	24
Seat Pleasant	4,857	18	17	1
Smithsburg	2,977	5	4	1
Snow Hill	2,044	5	5	0
St. Michaels	1,028	8	7	1
Sykesville	3,941	8	7	1

Table 78. Full-Time Law Enforcement Employees, by Selected State and City, 2018—Continued

(Number.)

State/city	Population	Total law enforcement employees	Total officers	Total civilians
Takoma Park	18,049	57	38	19
Taneytown	6,795	15	13	2
Thurmont	6,712	13	10	3
University Park	2,670	9	8	1
Upper Marlboro	676	4	3	1
Westminster	18,603	56	43	13
MASSACHUSETTS				
Abington	16,443	27	25	2
Acton	24,038	54	43	11
Acushnet	10,576	22	19	3
Agawam	28,955	61	46	15
Amesbury	17,623	40	33	7
Amherst	40,242	64	47	17
Andover	36,324	73	54	19
Aquinnah	329	4	4	0
Arlington	45,876	81	65	16
Ashburnham	6,335	17	12	5
Ashby	3,243	10	5	5
Ashland	17,860	33	27	6
Attleboro	44,719	95	81	14
Auburn	16,771	49	37	12
Avon	4,514	17	13	4
Ayer	8,246	32	20	12
Barnstable	44,015	139	113	26
Barre	5,592	10	9	1
Becket	1,716	4	4	0
Bedford	14,319	37	29	8
Belchertown	15,165	25	19	6
Bellingham	17,184	40	32	8
Belmont	26,700	59	46	13
Berkley	6,748	10	10	0
Berlin	3,222	11	10	1
Bernardston	2,108	3	3	0
Beverly	42,114	73	69	4
Billerica	44,482	77	63	14
Blackstone	9,345	22	18	4
Bolton	5,335	13	12	1
Boston	694,673	2,715	2,122	593
Bourne	19,894	51	43	8
Boxborough	6,634	19	13	6
Boxford	8,355	13	13	0
Boylston	4,674	13	10	3
Braintree	37,345	101	85	16
Brewster	9,831	30	23	7
Brockton	95,922	207	183	24
Brookfield	3,444	5	5	0
Brookline	59,199	170	132	38
Buckland	1,871	2	2	0
Burlington	27,562	72	66	6
Cambridge	114,881	320	277	43
Canton	23,709	43	43	0
Carlisle	5,289	15	10	5
Carver	11,743	19	15	4
Chatham	6,174	28	22	6
Chelmsford	35,264	68	52	16
Chelsea	40,974	117	110	7
Cheshire	3,129	1	1	0
Chester	1,388	1	1	0
Chicopee	55,639	133	130	3
Clinton	14,009	38	28	10
Cohasset	8,665	18	17	1
Concord	19,459	42	32	10
Cummington	882	1	1	0
Dalton	6,556	12	10	2
Danvers	27,703	53	41	12
Dartmouth	34,322	87	71	16
Dedham	25,437	60	57	3
Deerfield	5,012	10	9	1
Dennis	13,872	53	44	9
Dighton	7,807	21	14	7
Douglas	8,925	19	15	4
Dover	6,104	17	16	1
Dracut	31,917	45	41	4
Dudley	11,807	15	14	1
Dunstable	3,407	8	7	1
East Bridgewater	14,558	27	23	4
Eastham	4,871	21	16	5
Easthampton	16,050	33	28	5
East Longmeadow	16,398	26	24	2
Easton	25,225	48	36	12
Egremont	1,202	3	3	0
Erving	1,762	5	5	0
Essex	3,782	13	12	1
Everett	47,005	136	117	19

Table 78. Full-Time Law Enforcement Employees, by Selected State and City, 2018—Continued

(Number.)

State/city	Population	Total law enforcement employees	Total officers	Total civilians
Fairhaven	16,076	39	34	5
Fall River	89,475	289	229	60
Falmouth	31,033	62	59	3
Fitchburg	40,836	96	78	18
Foxborough	17,667	47	36	11
Framingham	72,510	151	131	20
Franklin	33,156	54	47	7
Freetown	9,404	19	19	0
Gardner	20,704	51	33	18
Georgetown	8,757	18	13	5
Gill	1,498	2	2	0
Gloucester	30,356	66	60	6
Goshen	1,067	2	2	0
Grafton	18,900	24	20	4
Granby	6,347	14	10	4
Great Barrington	6,821	17	16	1
Greenfield	17,443	45	34	11
Groton	11,462	26	19	7
Groveland	6,833	12	10	2
Hadley	5,347	20	15	5
Halifax	7,901	12	11	1
Hamilton	8,088	18	13	5
Hampden	5,213	15	11	4
Hanson	10,858	25	20	5
Hardwick	3,029	5	5	0
Harwich	12,130	40	32	8
Haverhill	64,012	113	99	14
Hingham	23,588	53	51	2
Holbrook	11,052	24	23	1
Holland	2,502	3	3	0
Holliston	14,924	29	23	6
Holyoke	40,470	126	110	16
Hopedale	5,984	16	12	4
Hopkinton	18,516	37	27	10
Hudson	20,060	42	32	10
Ipswich	14,107	30	25	5
Kingston	13,700	32	24	8
Lakeville	11,525	23	18	5
Lancaster	8,074	12	11	1
Lanesboro	2,948	6	6	0
Lawrence	80,669	164	142	22
Leicester	11,435	21	20	1
Lenox	4,941	10	10	0
Leominster	41,727	95	77	18
Lexington	34,050	63	47	16
Lincoln	6,839	19	13	6
Littleton	10,292	27	19	8
Longmeadow	15,898	30	24	6
Lowell	111,989	316	241	75
Ludlow	21,590	49	38	11
Lunenburg	11,498	16	15	1
Lynn	94,558	179	161	18
Lynnfield	13,141	27	22	5
Malden	61,469	112	102	10
Mansfield	24,050	51	37	14
Marblehead	20,652	43	33	10
Marion	5,134	16	16	0
Marlborough	40,052	80	68	12
Marshfield	25,922	43	40	3
Mashpee	14,215	43	34	9
Mattapoisett	6,369	20	20	0
Maynard	10,744	27	21	6
Medford	57,997	111	107	4
Medway	13,406	24	23	1
Melrose	28,552	48	47	1
Mendon	6,130	19	14	5
Methuen	50,676	114	95	19
Middleboro	25,125	46	40	6
Middleton	9,991	18	16	2
Milford	29,056	59	49	10
Millbury	13,802	25	20	5
Millville	3,260	6	5	1
Montague	8,235	20	16	4
Nahant	3,513	13	12	1
Natick	36,717	73	57	16
Needham	31,264	54	45	9
New Bedford	95,106	299	254	45
Newton	89,505	188	145	43
Norfolk	11,872	26	20	6
North Adams	12,858	33	24	9
Northampton	28,587	70	65	5
North Andover	31,394	51	39	12
North Attleboro	29,208	58	43	15
Northborough	15,124	27	22	5
Northbridge	16,759	27	20	7

Table 78. Full-Time Law Enforcement Employees, by Selected State and City, 2018—Continued

(Number.)

State/city	Population	Total law enforcement employees	Total officers	Total civilians
North Reading	15,849	33	31	2
Norton	19,983	35	34	1
Norwell	11,144	26	23	3
Norwood	29,267	70	61	9
Orange	7,625	14	13	1
Orleans	5,809	27	21	6
Oxford	14,015	29	23	6
Palmer	12,320	27	20	7
Paxton	4,888	20	15	5
Peabody	53,209	110	95	15
Pelham	1,326	1	1	0
Pembroke	18,446	33	31	2
Pepperell	12,234	17	16	1
Petersham	1,252	2	2	0
Phillipston	1,752	2	2	0
Pittsfield	42,298	109	88	21
Plymouth	60,349	144	128	16
Plympton	2,988	9	9	0
Princeton	3,458	7	6	1
Provincetown	2,960	24	17	7
Quincy	94,388	244	212	32
Randolph	34,535	64	58	6
Raynham	14,320	34	27	7
Reading	26,293	59	46	13
Rehoboth	12,268	34	28	6
Revere	54,296	110	103	7
Rochester	5,623	13	12	1
Rowley	6,392	17	12	5
Salem	43,634	107	97	10
Sandwich	20,248	36	35	1
Saugus	28,471	76	64	12
Scituate	18,761	37	35	2
Seekonk	15,820	39	36	3
Sharon	18,373	33	30	3
Sherborn	4,351	13	12	1
Shrewsbury	37,631	61	47	14
Somerset	18,166	37	32	5
Somerville	82,161	158	124	34
Southborough	10,187	23	18	5
Southbridge	16,933	44	36	8
South Hadley	17,799	33	27	6
Southwick	9,810	22	17	5
Spencer	11,989	21	17	4
Springfield	155,179	552	489	63
Stockbridge	1,900	9	8	1
Stoneham	22,135	50	39	11
Stoughton	28,729	77	66	11
Stow	7,171	11	11	0
Sturbridge	9,626	25	19	6
Sudbury	19,037	40	29	11
Sunderland	3,638	6	5	1
Sutton	9,527	20	16	4
Swampscott	15,380	32	31	1
Swansea	16,619	37	31	6
Taunton	57,304	121	115	6
Templeton	8,156	14	9	5
Tewksbury	31,561	75	62	13
Topsfield	6,628	12	11	1
Townsend	9,600	13	12	1
Truro	2,004	17	12	5
Wakefield	27,447	44	43	1
Walpole	25,204	55	44	11
Waltham	62,655	171	138	33
Wareham	22,747	55	45	10
Watertown	36,320	80	67	13
Wayland	14,088	31	22	9
Webster	17,051	34	32	2
Wellesley	29,681	55	38	17
Wellfleet	2,733	18	13	5
Wenham	5,299	9	8	1
Westborough	19,226	31	29	2
West Brookfield	3,789	6	6	0
Westfield	41,854	88	82	6
Westford	24,649	50	46	4
Westminster	7,835	14	12	2
West Newbury	4,694	15	10	5
Weston	12,264	34	24	10
Westport	15,959	34	29	5
West Springfield	28,802	96	89	7
West Tisbury	2,920	10	9	1
Westwood	16,267	39	33	6
Weymouth	57,069	112	93	19
Whitman	15,093	27	26	1
Wilbraham	14,760	28	27	1
Williamsburg	2,493	1	1	0

Table 78. Full-Time Law Enforcement Employees, by Selected State and City, 2018—Continued

(Number.)

State/city	Population	Total law enforcement employees	Total officers	Total civilians
Williamstown	7,845	12	11	1
Wilmington	24,005	51	48	3
Winchendon	10,933	19	14	5
Winchester	23,036	47	38	9
Winthrop	18,783	35	34	1
Woburn	39,895	81	76	5
Worcester	186,188	495	445	50
Wrentham	11,952	20	19	1
Yarmouth	23,269	76	61	15
MICHIGAN				
Adrian	20,624	32	30	2
Adrian Township	6,264	1	1	0
Akron	374	1	1	0
Albion	8,241	17	16	1
Allegan	5,051	10	9	1
Allen Park	27,020	44	40	4
Alma	8,944	15	13	2
Almont	2,820	7	7	0
Alpena	9,934	19	17	2
Ann Arbor	122,571	145	119	26
Argentine Township	6,526	6	5	1
Armada	1,734	2	2	0
Auburn Hills	23,579	54	49	5
Au Gres	835	1	1	0
Augusta	905	2	1	1
Bad Axe	2,933	8	7	1
Bancroft	497	1	1	0
Bangor	1,831	6	6	0
Baraga	1,970	2	2	0
Baroda-Lake Township	3,826	7	5	2
Barryton	353	1	1	0
Barry Township	3,476	3	3	0
Bath Township	12,984	13	12	1
Battle Creek	60,615	139	108	31
Bay City	32,953	57	52	5
Beaverton	1,047	3	3	0
Belding	5,737	8	8	0
Bellaire	1,065	2	2	0
Belleville	3,855	23	23	0
Bellevue	1,285	2	2	0
Benton Harbor	9,836	26	22	4
Benton Township	14,382	28	23	5
Berkley	15,382	34	28	6
Berrien Springs-Oronoko Township	8,961	9	8	1
Beverly Hills	10,450	26	24	2
Big Rapids	10,369	21	19	2
Birch Run	1,465	6	5	1
Birmingham	21,295	42	31	11
Blackman Township	36,884	35	34	1
Bloomfield Hills	4,009	27	24	3
Bloomfield Township	42,199	89	69	20
Boyne City	3,741	7	6	1
Breckenridge	1,273	1	1	0
Bridgeport Township	9,853	9	8	1
Bridgman	2,231	5	5	0
Brighton	7,635	20	18	2
Bronson	2,297	4	4	0
Brown City	1,238	2	2	0
Brownstown Township	31,912	39	31	8
Buchanan	4,293	10	9	1
Buena Vista Township	8,146	10	9	1
Burton	28,464	33	31	2
Byron	554	1	1	0
Cadillac	10,455	17	15	2
Calumet	694	1	1	0
Cambridge Township	5,656	4	4	0
Canton Township	92,055	119	82	37
Capac	1,831	1	1	0
Carleton	2,364	3	2	1
Caro	3,993	7	7	0
Carrollton Township	5,675	6	6	0
Carson City	1,112	1	1	0
Caseville	729	2	2	0
Caspian-Gaastra	1,166	1	1	0
Cass City	2,281	4	4	0
Cassopolis	1,694	5	5	0
Center Line	8,275	25	20	5
Central Lake	934	1	1	0
Charlevoix	2,491	8	7	1
Charlotte	9,053	17	16	1
Cheboygan	4,690	8	8	0
Chelsea	5,248	14	10	4
Chesaning	2,251	2	1	1
Chesterfield Township	45,686	58	44	14

Table 78. Full-Time Law Enforcement Employees, by Selected State and City, 2018—Continued

(Number.)

State/city	Population	Total law enforcement employees	Total officers	Total civilians
Chocolay Township	5,936	5	4	1
Clare	3,055	8	8	0
Clawson	11,962	18	17	1
Clayton Township	7,121	6	5	1
Clay Township	8,849	20	16	4
Clinton	2,281	4	4	0
Clinton Township	101,279	101	93	8
Clio	2,491	4	4	0
Coldwater	10,736	21	18	3
Coleman	1,193	2	2	0
Coloma Township	6,369	10	8	2
Colon	1,157	2	2	0
Columbia Township	7,356	6	6	0
Constantine	2,103	5	5	0
Corunna	3,359	3	3	0
Covert Township	2,849	9	9	0
Croswell	2,267	6	6	0
Crystal Falls	1,365	2	2	0
Davison	4,893	7	6	1
Davison Township	19,177	21	19	2
Dearborn	94,022	224	191	33
Dearborn Heights	55,495	95	83	12
Decatur	1,737	5	5	0
Denton Township	5,384	4	4	0
Detroit	671,275	3,019	2,398	621
DeWitt	4,742	7	6	1
DeWitt Township	15,194	17	16	1
Dowagiac	5,738	15	14	1
Dryden Township	4,744	4	4	0
Dundee	4,432	3	3	0
Durand	3,296	5	5	0
East Grand Rapids	11,886	30	28	2
East Jordan	2,343	4	4	0
Eastpointe	32,526	41	37	4
Eaton Rapids	5,194	10	9	1
Eau Claire	603	1	1	0
Ecorse	9,184	18	16	2
Elk Rapids	1,614	5	5	0
Elkton	751	1	1	0
Elsie	977	1	1	0
Emmett Township	11,619	15	13	2
Erie Township	4,338	4	3	1
Escanaba	12,169	41	31	10
Essexville	3,306	8	8	0
Evart	1,860	2	2	0
Fair Haven Township	1,038	1	1	0
Farmington	10,605	23	22	1
Farmington Hills	81,239	140	104	36
Fennville	1,419	1	1	0
Fenton	11,225	17	14	3
Ferndale	20,095	51	40	11
Flat Rock	9,967	18	18	0
Flint	95,677	119	106	13
Flint Township	30,378	50	43	7
Flushing	7,890	9	9	0
Flushing Township	10,179	9	8	1
Forsyth Township	6,199	9	8	1
Fowlerville	2,953	7	6	1
Frankenmuth	5,290	7	7	0
Frankfort	1,279	3	3	0
Franklin	3,266	10	10	0
Fraser	14,626	28	27	1
Freeport	493	1	1	0
Fremont	4,008	8	7	1
Fruitport Township	14,168	10	10	0
Gagetown	362	1	1	0
Gaines Township	6,100	1	1	0
Galien	535	2	1	1
Garden City	26,520	33	31	2
Garfield Township	829	1	1	0
Gaylord	3,693	11	10	1
Gerrish Township	2,919	7	7	0
Gibraltar	4,474	10	9	1
Gladwin	2,874	5	5	0
Grand Blanc	7,841	18	16	2
Grand Blanc Township	36,489	47	40	7
Grand Haven	10,984	36	31	5
Grand Ledge	7,804	14	14	0
Grand Rapids	200,428	335	276	59
Grandville	16,057	25	23	2
Grant	882	1	1	0
Grayling	1,837	7	6	1
Green Oak Township	18,874	19	16	3
Greenville	8,437	19	17	2
Grosse Ile Township	10,128	24	17	7

Table 78. Full-Time Law Enforcement Employees, by Selected State and City, 2018—Continued

(Number.)

State/city	Population	Total law enforcement employees	Total officers	Total civilians
Grosse Pointe	5,157	22	22	0
Grosse Pointe Farms	9,116	37	32	5
Grosse Pointe Park	11,069	38	33	5
Grosse Pointe Shores	2,907	18	18	0
Grosse Pointe Woods	15,497	36	30	6
Hamburg Township	22,024	18	17	1
Hampton Township	9,458	9	9	0
Hamtramck	21,668	34	29	5
Hancock	4,545	8	8	0
Harbor Beach	1,591	4	4	0
Harbor Springs	1,205	8	7	1
Harper Woods	13,674	33	30	3
Hart	2,101	5	5	0
Hartford	2,595	6	6	0
Hastings	7,310	14	12	2
Hazel Park	16,501	37	32	5
Hesperia	934	2	2	0
Highland Park	10,794	10	9	1
Hillsdale	8,120	14	13	1
Holly	6,170	8	8	0
Home Township	1,367	1	1	0
Hopkins	612	1	1	0
Houghton	7,914	10	9	1
Howell	9,532	18	16	2
Hudson	2,221	2	2	0
Huntington Woods	6,328	18	17	1
Huron Township	15,930	26	20	6
Imlay City	3,579	11	8	3
Inkster	24,334	36	26	10
Ionia	11,170	17	15	2
Iron Mountain	7,327	12	12	0
Iron River	2,818	4	4	0
Ironwood	4,915	8	8	0
Ishpeming	6,441	12	11	1
Ishpeming Township	3,528	1	1	0
Jackson	32,602	59	45	14
Jonesville	2,206	3	3	0
Kalamazoo	76,020	251	231	20
Kalamazoo Township	24,623	33	30	3
Kalkaska	2,068	2	2	0
Keego Harbor	3,465	5	5	0
Kentwood	52,192	79	69	10
Kinde	418	1	1	0
Kingsford	4,960	17	17	0
Kinross Township	7,432	2	2	0
Laingsburg	1,277	1	1	0
Lake Angelus	309	1	1	0
Lake Linden	969	1	1	0
Lake Odessa	2,031	3	3	0
Lake Orion	3,118	5	4	1
Lakeview	1,005	2	2	0
L'Anse	1,884	4	4	0
Lansing	117,380	213	188	25
Lansing Township	8,213	16	15	1
Lapeer	8,697	22	20	2
Lapeer Township	5,036	4	2	2
Lathrup Village	4,130	10	9	1
Laurium	1,924	4	4	0
Lawton	1,847	5	5	0
Leslie	1,889	3	3	0
Lexington	1,107	3	3	0
Lincoln Park	36,466	56	47	9
Lincoln Township	14,585	13	12	1
Linden	3,884	5	5	0
Litchfield	1,336	2	2	0
Livonia	93,740	167	133	34
Lowell	4,138	6	5	1
Ludington	8,058	14	13	1
Luna Pier	1,408	2	2	0
Mackinac Island	467	8	8	0
Mackinaw City	794	6	6	0
Madison Heights	30,100	62	50	12
Madison Township	8,341	4	4	0
Mancelona	1,361	1	1	0
Manistee	6,091	13	13	0
Manistique	2,907	8	8	0
Manton	1,489	1	1	0
Marenisco Township	1,626	1	1	0
Marine City	4,083	4	4	0
Marlette	1,757	4	4	0
Marquette	20,529	38	33	5
Marysville	9,674	16	14	2
Mason	8,431	12	11	1
Mattawan	1,971	6	6	0
Mayville	888	1	1	0

Table 78. Full-Time Law Enforcement Employees, by Selected State and City, 2018—Continued

(Number.)

State/city	Population	Total law enforcement employees	Total officers	Total civilians
Melvindale	10,291	24	24	0
Memphis	1,190	1	1	0
Mendon	854	2	2	0
Menominee	8,089	17	16	1
Meridian Township	43,072	41	37	4
Metamora Township	4,279	4	4	0
Metro Police Authority of Genesee County	19,887	25	22	3
Michiana	181	3	3	0
Midland	41,961	50	48	2
Milan	6,079	16	12	4
Milford	16,808	20	18	2
Millington	1,000	2	2	0
Monroe	19,754	45	40	5
Montague	2,350	5	5	0
Montrose Township	7,459	9	8	1
Morenci	2,159	2	2	0
Morrice	894	2	2	0
Mount Morris	2,860	4	4	0
Mount Morris Township	20,295	31	28	3
Mount Pleasant	25,828	34	28	6
Munising	2,186	4	4	0
Muskegon	38,125	83	76	7
Muskegon Heights	10,720	25	22	3
Muskegon Township	17,879	15	14	1
Napoleon Township	6,751	3	3	0
Nashville	1,660	4	4	0
Negaunee	4,554	9	9	0
Newaygo	2,043	7	7	0
New Baltimore	12,423	18	17	1
New Buffalo	1,875	6	5	1
New Era	442	1	1	0
New Lothrop	557	1	1	0
Niles	11,154	27	17	10
Northfield Township	8,741	13	11	2
North Muskegon	3,794	8	8	0
Northville	5,992	12	12	0
Northville Township	28,939	42	29	13
Norton Shores	24,578	32	30	2
Norway	2,746	6	6	0
Novi	60,378	94	71	23
Oak Park	29,688	60	48	12
Olivet	1,695	2	2	0
Ontwa Township-Edwardsburg	6,493	7	7	0
Orchard Lake	2,465	9	8	1
Oscoda Township	6,771	11	10	1
Otisville	822	1	1	0
Otsego	4,000	7	6	1
Ovid	1,618	2	2	0
Owendale	225	1	1	0
Owosso	14,455	17	17	0
Oxford	3,561	4	4	0
Paw Paw	3,404	9	8	1
Pentwater	849	3	3	0
Perry	2,085	4	4	0
Petoskey	5,733	19	18	1
Pigeon	1,126	1	1	0
Pinckney	2,479	4	4	0
Pinconning	1,241	1	1	0
Pittsfield Township	39,314	42	41	1
Plainwell	3,810	9	8	1
Plymouth	9,142	17	16	1
Plymouth Township	27,032	42	29	13
Portage	49,175	66	53	13
Port Austin	622	1	1	0
Port Huron	28,907	56	49	7
Portland	3,927	7	7	0
Port Sanilac	579	1	1	0
Potterville	2,678	2	2	0
Prairieville Township	3,509	2	2	0
Quincy	1,610	3	3	0
Raisin Township	7,716	5	5	0
Reading	1,045	1	1	0
Redford Township	46,899	68	60	8
Reed City	2,380	3	3	0
Reese	1,372	2	2	0
Richfield Township, Roscommon County	3,633	6	5	1
Richland	807	3	3	0
Richland Township, Saginaw County	3,934	3	3	0
Richmond	5,918	17	12	5
River Rouge	7,426	20	18	2
Riverview	12,058	22	21	1
Rochester	13,075	30	22	8
Rockford	6,345	11	10	1
Rockwood	3,169	14	7	7

Table 78. Full-Time Law Enforcement Employees, by Selected State and City, 2018—Continued

(Number.)

State/city	Population	Total law enforcement employees	Total officers	Total civilians
Rogers City	2,676	6	6	0
Romeo	3,623	11	8	3
Romulus	23,389	57	41	16
Roosevelt Park	3,793	5	5	0
Roseville	47,524	72	69	3
Rothbury	445	1	1	0
Royal Oak	59,383	93	76	17
Saginaw	48,302	61	51	10
Saginaw Township	39,198	48	43	5
Saline	9,358	17	13	4
Sand Lake	532	2	1	1
Sandusky	2,515	6	5	1
Sault Ste. Marie	13,557	24	22	2
Schoolcraft	1,566	3	3	0
Scottville	1,218	2	2	0
Sebewaing	1,638	3	3	0
Shelby	2,019	3	3	0
Shelby Township	79,878	86	68	18
Shepherd	1,503	2	2	0
Somerset Township	4,553	3	3	0
Southfield	73,418	133	114	19
Southgate	28,959	44	40	4
South Haven	4,340	24	20	4
South Lyon	11,803	17	16	1
South Rockwood	1,657	2	2	0
Sparta	4,380	5	5	0
Spring Arbor Township	8,044	2	2	0
Springport Township	2,144	2	2	0
Stanton	1,430	1	1	0
St. Charles	1,910	3	3	0
St. Clair	5,316	7	7	0
St. Clair Shores	59,618	88	83	5
Sterling Heights	133,055	168	146	22
St. Ignace	2,311	5	5	0
St. Johns	7,890	11	10	1
St. Joseph	8,364	22	21	1
St. Joseph Township	9,773	12	11	1
St. Louis	7,274	8	7	1
Stockbridge	1,237	2	2	0
Sturgis	10,796	25	20	5
Sumpter Township	9,362	17	15	2
Sylvan Lake	1,860	4	4	0
Tawas	4,487	5	4	1
Taylor	61,037	91	75	16
Tecumseh	8,363	14	13	1
Thetford Township	6,699	1	1	0
Thomas Township	11,488	8	8	0
Three Rivers	7,673	17	16	1
Tittabawassee Township	9,819	6	5	1
Traverse City	15,630	31	29	2
Trenton	18,176	35	34	1
Troy	84,221	152	105	47
Tuscarora Township	2,928	9	8	1
Ubly	800	1	1	0
Unadilla Township	3,465	3	3	0
Union City	1,564	5	5	0
Utica	4,949	18	14	4
Van Buren Township	28,210	52	41	11
Vassar	2,543	5	5	0
Vernon	776	1	1	0
Vicksburg	3,443	5	5	0
Walker	25,010	40	36	4
Walled Lake	7,170	6	6	0
Warren	135,160	246	207	39
Waterford Township	73,066	70	54	16
Watervliet	1,658	3	3	0
Wayland	4,260	8	6	2
Wayne	16,862	19	19	0
West Bloomfield Township	65,928	103	75	28
West Branch	2,051	6	5	1
Westland	81,438	102	79	23
White Cloud	1,377	2	2	0
White Lake Township	31,236	38	28	10
White Pigeon	1,521	4	4	0
Williamston	3,924	8	7	1
Wixom	13,876	22	19	3
Wolverine Lake	4,686	7	7	0
Woodhaven	12,435	31	29	2
Woodland Township	2,097	2	1	1
Wyandotte	24,862	45	35	10
Wyoming	76,498	101	86	15
Yale	1,883	3	3	0
Ypsilanti	21,298	30	25	5
Zeeland	5,567	11	10	1
Zilwaukee	1,538	2	2	0

Table 78. Full-Time Law Enforcement Employees, by Selected State and City, 2018—Continued

(Number.)

State/city	Population	Total law enforcement employees	Total officers	Total civilians
MINNESOTA				
Adrian	1,223	2	2	0
Aitkin	1,998	7	6	1
Akeley	438	1	1	0
Albany	2,711	5	4	1
Albert Lea	17,655	30	27	3
Alexandria	13,759	27	24	3
Annandale	3,389	6	5	1
Anoka	17,574	41	31	10
Appleton	1,333	3	3	0
Apple Valley	52,922	61	53	8
Arlington	2,141	3	3	0
Atwater	1,115	1	1	0
Audubon	532	1	1	0
Austin	24,935	36	32	4
Avon	1,573	4	3	1
Babbitt	1,510	5	5	0
Bagley	1,419	3	3	0
Barnesville	2,586	5	5	0
Battle Lake	925	2	2	0
Baxter	8,372	16	15	1
Bayport	3,774	6	6	0
Becker	4,880	8	7	1
Belgrade/Brooten	1,523	3	3	0
Belle Plaine	7,189	12	10	2
Bemidji	15,528	35	32	3
Benson	3,072	8	7	1
Big Lake	11,036	15	13	2
Blackduck	768	2	2	0
Blaine	65,649	81	60	21
Blooming Prairie	1,980	3	3	0
Bloomington	86,279	152	118	34
Blue Earth	3,112	5	5	0
Bovey	789	2	2	0
Braham	1,788	4	4	0
Brainerd	13,404	30	24	6
Breckenridge	3,200	7	7	0
Breezy Point	2,390	7	6	1
Breitung Township	608	2	2	0
Brooklyn Center	31,128	60	48	12
Brooklyn Park	81,263	140	106	34
Brownton	727	1	1	0
Buffalo	16,304	21	17	4
Buffalo Lake	680	2	2	0
Burnsville	61,592	86	75	11
Caledonia	2,736	7	6	1
Callaway	232	1	1	0
Cambridge	8,905	16	15	1
Canby	1,688	3	3	0
Cannon Falls	4,060	10	8	2
Centennial Lakes	11,062	17	15	2
Champlin	25,304	31	26	5
Chaska	26,962	32	26	6
Chisholm	4,908	13	12	1
Clara City	1,287	2	2	0
Clearbrook	530	1	1	0
Cloquet	11,911	26	24	2
Cold Spring/Richmond	5,572	10	9	1
Coleraine	1,970	2	2	0
Columbia Heights	21,119	31	25	6
Coon Rapids	62,818	74	64	10
Corcoran	5,988	9	8	1
Cottage Grove	37,102	49	42	7
Crookston	7,779	18	16	2
Crosby	2,338	8	8	0
Crosslake	2,266	5	5	0
Crystal	23,310	38	33	5
Danube	457	1	1	0
Dawson/Boyd	1,549	3	3	0
Dayton	5,970	8	7	1
Deephaven	3,951	8	7	1
Deer River	933	4	4	0
Detroit Lakes	9,289	19	17	2
Dilworth	4,474	7	6	1
Duluth	86,048	172	147	25
Dundas	1,544	2	2	0
Eagan	66,981	86	73	13
Eagle Lake	3,129	3	3	0
East Grand Forks	8,632	25	23	2
East Range	3,614	8	8	0
Eden Prairie	64,917	86	66	20
Eden Valley	1,033	1	1	0
Edina	52,544	75	52	23
Elko New Market	4,809	4	4	0
Elk River	24,724	43	34	9

Table 78. Full-Time Law Enforcement Employees, by Selected State and City, 2018—Continued
(Number.)

State/city	Population	Total law enforcement employees	Total officers	Total civilians
Elmore	619	1	1	0
Ely	3,377	8	7	1
Eveleth	3,609	11	10	1
Fairfax	1,130	2	2	0
Fairmont	10,053	20	18	2
Faribault	23,806	43	35	8
Farmington	23,355	26	23	3
Fergus Falls	13,839	29	24	5
Floodwood	520	4	3	1
Foley	2,635	3	3	0
Forest Lake	20,097	26	24	2
Frazee	1,397	3	3	0
Fridley	27,943	47	42	5
Fulda	1,222	2	2	0
Gaylord	2,211	4	4	0
Gilbert	1,796	7	7	0
Glencoe	5,480	9	8	1
Glenwood	2,523	6	5	1
Golden Valley	21,688	38	30	8
Goodhue	1,176	2	2	0
Goodview	4,125	5	4	1
Grand Rapids	11,297	23	20	3
Granite Falls	2,712	7	6	1
Hallock	898	1	1	0
Hastings	22,799	32	28	4
Hawley	2,209	4	4	0
Hector	1,047	2	2	0
Henning	811	2	2	0
Hermantown	9,525	18	15	3
Hibbing	15,998	27	24	3
Hill City	586	1	1	0
Hokah	549	1	1	0
Hopkins	18,838	37	29	8
Houston	958	2	2	0
Howard Lake	2,066	3	3	0
Hutchinson	13,862	35	23	12
International Falls	5,933	12	11	1
Inver Grove Heights	35,592	45	40	5
Isanti	5,787	9	8	1
Isle	801	4	4	0
Janesville	2,259	4	4	0
Jordan	6,375	13	11	2
Kasson	6,444	9	8	1
Keewatin	1,021	3	3	0
Kenyon	1,805	3	3	0
Kimball	795	3	3	0
La Crescent	5,012	9	8	1
Lake Benton	634	1	1	0
Lake City	5,116	11	10	1
Lake Crystal	2,487	3	3	0
Lakefield	1,615	3	3	0
Lake Park	804	2	2	0
Lakes Area	9,679	15	13	2
Lake Shore	1,052	2	2	0
Lakeville	64,914	66	57	9
Lamberton	768	1	1	0
Le Center	2,469	3	3	0
Lester Prairie	1,710	3	3	0
Le Sueur	4,004	8	7	1
Lewiston	1,557	2	2	0
Lino Lakes	21,577	29	26	3
Litchfield	6,615	11	10	1
Little Falls	8,683	16	14	2
Long Prairie	3,305	6	6	0
Lonsdale	4,038	8	7	1
Madelia	2,228	4	4	0
Madison Lake	1,183	3	3	0
Mankato	42,606	65	57	8
Maple Grove	72,502	81	67	14
Mapleton	1,696	3	3	0
Maplewood	41,339	55	50	5
Marshall	13,713	24	21	3
Medina	6,721	11	10	1
Melrose	3,622	6	5	1
Menahga	1,315	3	3	0
Mendota Heights	11,381	20	19	1
Milaca	2,880	7	6	1
Minneapolis	428,261	1,037	849	188
Minneota	1,368	1	1	0
Minnesota Lake	641	1	1	0
Minnetonka	53,573	63	55	8
Minnetrista	10,357	16	13	3
Montevideo	5,101	9	8	1
Montgomery	2,950	8	7	1
Moorhead	43,657	70	54	16

Table 78. Full-Time Law Enforcement Employees, by Selected State and City, 2018—Continued

(Number.)

State/city	Population	Total law enforcement employees	Total officers	Total civilians
Moose Lake	2,795	6	5	1
Morris	5,300	9	7	2
Motley	651	1	1	0
Mounds View	13,235	22	20	2
Mountain Lake	2,054	4	4	0
Nashwauk	945	3	3	0
New Brighton	22,978	34	29	5
New Hope	21,168	43	34	9
New Prague	7,884	11	9	2
New Richland	1,184	2	2	0
New Ulm	13,202	24	22	2
New York Mills	1,228	3	3	0
Nisswa	2,045	6	6	0
North Branch	10,511	13	11	2
Northfield	20,535	27	22	5
North Mankato	13,794	16	15	1
North St. Paul	12,588	16	14	2
Oakdale	28,178	39	31	8
Oak Park Heights	4,991	11	10	1
Olivia	2,328	5	5	0
Onamia	858	3	3	0
Orono	20,225	31	27	4
Ortonville	1,788	4	4	0
Osakis	1,700	3	3	0
Osseo	2,820	6	5	1
Owatonna	25,829	38	34	4
Parkers Prairie	998	2	2	0
Park Rapids	4,046	11	10	1
Paynesville	2,503	5	5	0
Pelican Rapids	2,467	5	5	0
Pequot Lakes	2,321	7	6	1
Perham	3,484	7	6	1
Pike Bay	1,673	1	1	0
Pine River	925	2	2	0
Plainview	3,284	8	7	1
Plymouth	79,559	93	77	16
Preston	1,295	3	3	0
Princeton	4,666	14	12	2
Prior Lake	26,925	30	26	4
Proctor	3,058	9	7	2
Ramsey	27,023	28	25	3
Red Wing	16,405	35	30	5
Redwood Falls	4,952	13	11	2
Renville	1,178	3	3	0
Rice	1,354	3	3	0
Richfield	36,300	52	43	9
Robbinsdale	14,629	29	24	5
Rochester	117,037	198	137	61
Rogers	13,257	22	19	3
Roseau	2,704	6	5	1
Rosemount	24,707	30	25	5
Roseville	36,701	60	47	13
Rushford	1,713	3	3	0
Sartell	18,014	24	21	3
Sauk Centre	4,389	8	7	1
Sauk Rapids	13,853	18	17	1
Savage	32,029	41	32	9
Sebeka	670	6	6	0
Shakopee	41,424	56	46	10
Sherburn	1,089	4	4	0
Silver Bay	1,753	5	5	0
Silver Lake	820	2	2	0
Slayton	2,004	5	4	1
Sleepy Eye	3,378	7	7	0
South Lake Minnetonka	12,731	18	15	3
South St. Paul	20,260	34	30	4
Springfield	2,006	4	4	0
Spring Grove	1,276	2	2	0
Spring Lake Park	6,515	14	11	3
St. Anthony	9,205	23	20	3
Staples	2,947	7	6	1
Starbuck	1,246	4	4	0
St. Charles	3,759	6	6	0
St. Cloud	68,282	134	107	27
St. Francis	7,728	14	11	3
Stillwater	19,467	27	22	5
St. James	4,375	8	7	1
St. Joseph	7,212	10	9	1
St. Louis Park	49,595	69	54	15
St. Paul	309,756	768	631	137
St. Paul Park	5,409	9	9	0
St. Peter	12,012	18	13	5
Thief River Falls	8,865	19	17	2
Tracy	2,049	3	3	0
Tri-City	1,397	3	3	0

Table 78. Full-Time Law Enforcement Employees, by Selected State and City, 2018—Continued

(Number.)

State/city	Population	Total law enforcement employees	Total officers	Total civilians
Trimont	702	1	1	0
Truman	1,046	2	2	0
Twin Valley	778	2	2	0
Two Harbors	3,486	9	8	1
Tyler	1,074	2	2	0
Verndale	568	1	1	0
Virginia	8,458	23	23	0
Wabasha	2,475	8	7	1
Wadena	4,076	10	9	1
Waite Park	7,512	21	18	3
Walker	930	3	3	0
Warroad	1,758	6	5	1
Waseca	8,918	19	17	2
Waterville	1,866	4	4	0
Wayzata	6,582	15	13	2
Wells	2,176	5	5	0
West Concord	774	1	1	0
West Hennepin	5,663	11	9	2
West St. Paul	19,798	35	31	4
Wheaton	1,303	3	3	0
White Bear Lake	26,187	34	30	4
Willmar	19,635	38	34	4
Windom	4,401	10	9	1
Winnebago	1,339	3	3	0
Winona	26,840	42	38	4
Winsted	2,280	4	4	0
Woodbury	70,900	84	72	12
Worthington	13,309	31	21	10
Wyoming	7,900	11	10	1
Zumbrota	3,428	6	6	0
MISSISSIPPI				
Ackerman	1,444	6	6	0
Amory	6,911	32	25	7
Batesville	7,212	55	42	13
Biloxi	46,148	183	130	53
Booneville	8,688	25	18	7
Brandon	24,283	48	35	13
Brookhaven	12,125	44	36	8
Byram	11,692	39	27	12
Clinton	25,137	74	54	20
D'Iberville	11,928	39	36	3
Edwards	1,006	1	1	0
Florence	4,468	24	19	5
Flowood	9,243	66	51	15
Gautier	18,501	47	37	10
Grenada	12,436	45	39	6
Gulfport	72,402	214	162	52
Hattiesburg	46,461	177	104	73
Heidelberg	672	5	4	1
Holly Springs	7,614	21	17	4
Laurel	18,486	73	52	21
Leakesville	896	2	2	0
Madison	25,832	79	58	21
Magee	4,252	21	15	6
Meridian	37,500	107	85	22
Natchez	14,765	50	40	10
New Albany	8,867	28	26	2
Ocean Springs	17,726	52	39	13
Oxford	24,369	91	77	14
Pascagoula	21,654	79	56	23
Pass Christian	6,082	23	19	4
Philadelphia	7,243	30	23	7
Starkville	25,559	70	59	11
Summit	1,593	8	7	1
Vicksburg	22,298	85	62	23
Waveland	6,343	20	20	0
West Point	10,593	33	29	4
Wiggins	4,561	19	14	5
Yazoo City	10,931	24	18	6
MISSOURI				
Adrian	1,599	3	3	0
Advance	1,348	3	3	0
Anderson	1,975	6	6	0
Annapolis	341	2	2	0
Appleton City	1,064	2	2	0
Archie	1,209	4	4	0
Arnold	21,151	59	52	7
Ash Grove	1,448	5	5	0
Ashland	3,956	9	8	1
Aurora	7,478	23	16	7
Ava	2,883	11	6	5
Ballwin	30,151	60	48	12
Bates City	216	1	1	0

Table 78. Full-Time Law Enforcement Employees, by Selected State and City, 2018—Continued

(Number.)

State/city	Population	Total law enforcement employees	Total officers	Total civilians
Battlefield	6,218	9	9	0
Bella Villa	736	5	5	0
Belle	1,490	5	5	0
Bellefontaine Neighbors	10,597	32	30	2
Bel-Nor	1,453	6	6	0
Bel-Ridge	2,661	18	16	2
Belton	23,526	57	37	20
Berkeley	8,892	29	23	6
Bertrand	756	1	1	0
Bethany	3,107	6	6	0
Billings	1,100	2	2	0
Blue Springs	55,277	141	94	47
Bolivar	10,966	27	21	6
Bonne Terre	7,305	11	11	0
Boonville	8,434	28	21	7
Bourbon	1,598	6	6	0
Bowling Green	5,577	12	9	3
Branson	11,589	65	46	19
Branson West	450	6	6	0
Braymer	849	2	2	0
Breckenridge Hills	4,612	18	17	1
Brentwood	7,991	28	27	1
Bridgeton	11,663	63	52	11
Brookfield	4,291	18	11	7
Buckner	3,053	9	8	1
Buffalo	3,057	7	6	1
Bunker	388	1	1	0
Butler	4,025	13	9	4
Butterfield Village	472	1	1	0
Byrnes Mill	3,016	4	4	0
Cabool	2,119	11	7	4
California	4,425	8	7	1
Calverton Park	1,276	8	8	0
Camdenton	4,106	20	17	3
Cameron	9,736	23	15	8
Campbell	1,858	4	4	0
Canton	2,335	5	4	1
Cape Girardeau	39,303	114	79	35
Cardwell	658	1	1	0
Carl Junction	7,921	15	11	4
Carrollton	3,508	7	7	0
Carterville	1,919	5	5	0
Carthage	14,342	37	28	9
Caruthersville	5,640	17	16	1
Cassville	3,311	12	12	0
Center	506	1	1	0
Centralia	4,255	13	8	5
Charleston	5,599	19	13	6
Chesterfield	47,602	108	98	10
Chillicothe	9,699	27	18	9
Clarkton	1,189	3	3	0
Claycomo	1,496	12	12	0
Clayton	16,935	56	48	8
Cleveland	660	1	1	0
Clever	2,743	6	5	1
Clinton	8,897	23	22	1
Cole Camp	1,106	3	3	0
Columbia	123,586	195	158	37
Concordia	2,362	6	6	0
Conway	773	1	1	0
Cottleville	5,670	12	12	0
Country Club Hills	1,258	7	7	0
Country Club Village	2,474	2	2	0
Crestwood	11,864	33	26	7
Creve Coeur	18,831	50	47	3
Crocker	1,022	4	4	0
Crystal City	4,726	22	16	6
Cuba	3,302	15	14	1
Delta	439	1	1	0
Desloge	4,861	12	11	1
Des Peres	8,601	48	41	7
Dexter	7,839	23	19	4
Diamond	928	3	2	1
Dixon	1,429	9	5	4
Doolittle	602	1	1	0
Drexel	950	2	2	0
Duenweg	1,348	4	4	0
Duquesne	1,736	10	9	1
Edina	1,122	1	1	0
Edmundson	831	12	11	1
Eldon	4,632	13	12	1
El Dorado Springs	3,568	12	8	4
Ellisville	9,842	25	24	1
Elsberry	2,022	4	4	0
Eminence	582	1	1	0

Table 78. Full-Time Law Enforcement Employees, by Selected State and City, 2018—Continued

(Number.)

State/city	Population	Total law enforcement employees	Total officers	Total civilians
Eureka	10,626	28	24	4
Everton	304	1	1	0
Excelsior Springs	11,626	33	23	10
Exeter	771	2	2	0
Fair Grove	1,473	6	6	0
Fair Play	476	1	1	0
Farmington	18,740	36	27	9
Fayette	2,713	6	6	0
Ferguson	20,663	48	40	8
Festus	12,092	36	27	9
Flordell Hills	801	9	9	0
Florissant	51,326	112	89	23
Foristell	578	6	6	0
Forsyth	2,437	7	6	1
Fredericktown	4,014	13	12	1
Frontenac	3,875	22	21	1
Fulton	12,856	34	28	6
Gallatin	1,759	2	2	0
Garden City	1,626	3	3	0
Gerald	1,311	3	3	0
Gideon	985	2	2	0
Gladstone	27,382	61	45	16
Glendale	5,881	14	11	3
Goodman	1,244	2	2	0
Gower	1,476	3	3	0
Grain Valley	14,165	28	23	5
Granby	2,100	5	5	0
Grandview	25,256	67	55	12
Greenfield	1,309	2	2	0
Hallsville	1,562	6	3	3
Hamilton	1,694	5	5	0
Hannibal	17,545	50	39	11
Hardin	534	1	1	0
Harrisonville	10,113	31	23	8
Hartville	606	2	2	0
Hayti	2,644	8	7	1
Hazelwood	25,234	77	66	11
Henrietta	355	1	1	0
Herculaneum	4,067	8	7	1
Hermann	2,327	12	7	5
Higginsville	4,606	24	11	13
Highlandville	1,021	1	1	0
Hillsdale	1,567	11	10	1
Holcomb	592	2	2	0
Holden	2,232	6	6	0
Hollister	4,561	19	13	6
Holts Summit	4,599	13	11	2
Houston	2,091	8	8	0
Howardville	346	2	1	1
Humansville	1,048	1	1	0
Huntsville	1,512	1	1	0
Iberia	745	1	1	0
Independence	117,368	285	200	85
Indian Point	519	4	4	0
Ironton	1,389	3	3	0
Jackson	15,101	33	26	7
Jasper	942	2	2	0
Jefferson City	42,856	126	88	38
Joplin	52,492	134	100	34
Kahoka	1,987	2	2	0
Kansas City	493,115	1,819	1,299	520
Kearney	10,300	17	16	1
Kennett	10,326	29	22	7
Kimberling City	2,306	6	6	0
Kirksville	17,539	29	26	3
Kirkwood	27,670	79	60	19
Knob Noster	2,763	11	7	4
Laddonia	500	1	1	0
Ladue	8,625	32	26	6
La Grange	915	5	5	0
Lake Lotawana	2,119	4	4	0
Lake Ozark	1,822	18	12	6
Lakeshire	1,397	4	4	0
Lake St. Louis	16,134	40	31	9
Lake Tapawingo	725	4	3	1
Lake Winnebago	1,175	4	4	0
Lamar	4,303	16	14	2
Lanagan	416	5	5	0
Lathrop	2,028	5	5	0
Laurie	935	5	5	0
Lawson	2,382	7	6	1
Leadington	606	4	4	0
Leadwood	1,165	11	8	3
Lebanon	14,622	40	29	11
Lee's Summit	98,144	201	145	56

Table 78. Full-Time Law Enforcement Employees, by Selected State and City, 2018—Continued

(Number.)

State/city	Population	Total law enforcement employees	Total officers	Total civilians
Leeton	552	1	1	0
Lexington	4,531	8	7	1
Liberal	717	2	2	0
Liberty	31,842	56	42	14
Licking	3,094	5	5	0
Lilbourn	1,082	1	1	0
Lincoln	1,179	3	3	0
Linn	1,517	4	4	0
Linn Creek	252	2	2	0
Lone Jack	1,266	8	7	1
Louisiana	3,282	10	5	5
Macon	5,368	12	10	2
Malden	3,943	16	14	2
Manchester	18,114	37	34	3
Mansfield	1,249	5	5	0
Maplewood	8,130	33	31	2
Marceline	2,122	9	9	0
Marionville	2,186	4	4	0
Marshall	12,655	27	22	5
Marshfield	7,442	12	11	1
Marston	456	1	1	0
Maryland Heights	26,930	96	78	18
Maryville	11,716	24	18	6
Matthews	606	3	3	0
Memphis	1,864	3	3	0
Mexico	11,507	28	27	1
Milan	1,799	5	5	0
Miller	685	1	1	0
Miner	947	12	8	4
Moberly	13,750	36	25	11
Moline Acres	2,382	10	9	1
Monett	8,984	23	21	2
Monroe City	2,424	9	8	1
Montgomery City	2,630	6	6	0
Morehouse	880	2	2	0
Moscow Mills	3,004	6	6	0
Mound City	1,026	2	2	0
Mountain Grove	4,659	16	12	4
Mountain View	2,645	9	8	1
Mount Vernon	4,525	11	11	0
Neosho	12,057	29	27	2
Nevada	8,116	29	23	6
Newburg	435	1	1	0
New Franklin	1,074	4	3	1
New Haven	2,076	5	5	0
New London	973	2	2	0
New Madrid	2,870	16	8	8
Nixa	21,653	38	32	6
Noel	1,815	2	2	0
Normandy	7,488	26	25	1
North Kansas City	4,552	50	39	11
Northwoods	4,404	16	15	1
Oak Grove	8,151	16	15	1
Oakland	1,368	79	60	19
Odessa	5,184	11	10	1
O'Fallon	88,763	154	117	37
Old Monroe	282	1	1	0
Olivette	7,843	24	23	1
Oran	1,240	1	1	0
Oregon	754	1	1	0
Oronogo	2,578	5	5	0
Orrick	802	1	1	0
Osage Beach	4,582	33	20	13
Osceola	895	2	2	0
Overland	15,660	52	39	13
Owensville	2,576	8	8	0
Ozark	20,203	34	30	4
Pacific	7,241	25	17	8
Pagedale	3,292	17	17	0
Palmyra	3,598	9	8	1
Park Hills	8,528	16	15	1
Parkville	6,963	17	16	1
Peculiar	5,192	10	9	1
Perry	694	1	1	0
Perryville	8,495	30	24	6
Pevely	5,883	21	15	6
Piedmont	1,947	6	6	0
Pierce City	1,302	3	3	0
Pilot Grove	760	1	1	0
Pilot Knob	718	3	3	0
Pineville	790	5	5	0
Platte City	4,979	14	14	0
Platte Woods	407	2	2	0
Plattsburg	2,262	5	5	0
Pleasant Hill	8,606	19	14	5

Table 78. Full-Time Law Enforcement Employees, by Selected State and City, 2018—Continued

(Number.)

State/city	Population	Total law enforcement employees	Total officers	Total civilians
Pleasant Hope	615	2	2	0
Pleasant Valley	3,059	12	8	4
Polo	536	1	1	0
Poplar Bluff	17,074	60	45	15
Portageville	3,019	15	11	4
Potosi	2,623	13	12	1
Purdy	1,096	2	2	0
Queen City	607	1	1	0
Qulin	453	1	1	0
Raymore	21,452	39	26	13
Raytown	29,173	46	34	12
Reeds Spring	880	3	2	1
Republic	16,495	25	20	5
Rich Hill	1,323	1	1	0
Richland	1,759	6	6	0
Richmond	5,636	14	12	2
Richmond Heights	8,342	42	41	1
Risco	315	2	1	1
Riverside	3,417	34	25	9
Riverview	2,772	12	12	0
Rockaway Beach	866	2	2	0
Rock Hill	4,599	11	10	1
Rock Port	1,212	3	3	0
Rogersville	3,739	9	8	1
Rolla	20,385	56	33	23
Salem	4,910	18	13	5
Salisbury	1,524	4	3	1
Sarcoxie	1,296	2	2	0
Savannah	5,202	8	7	1
Scott City	4,486	18	13	5
Sedalia	21,590	57	40	17
Seligman	844	1	1	0
Senath	1,652	4	4	0
Seneca	2,389	5	5	0
Seymour	2,003	6	6	0
Shelbina	1,602	6	5	1
Shrewsbury	6,108	24	22	2
Sikeston	16,129	80	61	19
Silex	301	2	2	0
Smithville	10,012	19	19	0
Southwest City	951	3	3	0
Sparta	1,907	2	2	0
Springfield	168,537	409	335	74
St. Ann	12,698	73	45	28
St. Charles	70,925	149	109	40
St. Clair	4,702	16	14	2
Steele	1,991	5	5	0
Steelville	1,677	6	6	0
Ste. Genevieve	4,443	11	11	0
St. James	4,059	12	11	1
St. John	6,344	22	21	1
St. Joseph	76,409	173	130	43
St. Louis	306,875	1,608	1,189	419
St. Marys	346	1	1	0
Stover	1,063	2	2	0
St. Peters	57,838	121	93	28
Strafford	2,408	4	4	0
St. Robert	6,006	24	17	7
Sugar Creek	3,303	22	17	5
Sullivan	7,156	26	19	7
Summersville	491	2	2	0
Sunrise Beach	493	2	2	0
Sunset Hills	8,492	33	26	7
Tarkio	1,453	3	3	0
Tipton	3,387	4	4	0
Town and Country	11,154	30	29	1
Trenton	5,800	17	10	7
Troy	12,226	24	22	2
Truesdale	813	1	1	0
Union	11,710	27	25	2
University City	34,438	88	67	21
Urbana	414	1	1	0
Vandalia	4,215	7	6	1
Velda City	1,378	9	9	0
Verona	608	1	1	0
Versailles	2,426	11	10	1
Viburnum	665	3	3	0
Vienna	588	2	2	0
Vinita Park	11,003	64	62	2
Walnut Grove	807	1	1	0
Warrensburg	20,355	41	36	5
Warrenton	8,283	25	22	3
Warsaw	2,184	7	7	0
Warson Woods	1,915	8	8	0
Washington	13,964	32	29	3

Table 78. Full-Time Law Enforcement Employees, by Selected State and City, 2018—Continued

(Number.)

State/city	Population	Total law enforcement employees	Total officers	Total civilians
Waverly	835	2	1	1
Weatherby Lake	2,034	5	5	0
Webb City	11,379	27	23	4
Webster Groves	22,873	49	47	2
Wellsville	1,132	3	3	0
Wentzville	41,057	87	67	20
Weston	1,804	5	5	0
West Plains	12,277	31	25	6
Wheaton	690	1	1	0
Willard	5,447	11	10	1
Willow Springs	2,110	8	7	1
Winona	1,299	1	1	0
Woodson Terrace	4,032	19	17	2
Wright City	3,777	13	12	1
MONTANA				
Baker	1,960	5	5	0
Belgrade	8,724	22	18	4
Billings	110,397	185	148	37
Bozeman	48,101	68	58	10
Bridger	760	3	3	0
Chinook	1,256	2	2	0
Colstrip	2,324	12	7	5
Columbia Falls	5,456	10	9	1
Columbus	2,046	9	7	2
Cut Bank	3,013	9	8	1
Deer Lodge	2,902	6	6	0
Dillon	4,281	11	10	1
East Helena	2,075	5	5	0
Ennis	936	1	1	0
Fairview	899	4	4	0
Fort Benton	1,450	4	4	0
Glasgow	3,325	11	7	4
Glendive	5,132	14	9	5
Great Falls	58,828	128	88	40
Hamilton	4,794	15	14	1
Havre	9,821	24	18	6
Helena	31,898	77	52	25
Hot Springs	565	2	2	0
Kalispell	23,700	51	41	10
Laurel	6,800	17	13	4
Lewistown	5,899	24	13	11
Libby	2,698	6	6	0
Livingston	7,608	14	14	0
Manhattan	1,787	4	4	0
Miles City	8,496	15	14	1
Missoula	74,300	128	104	24
Plains	1,101	3	3	0
Polson	4,928	16	15	1
Red Lodge	2,310	5	5	0
Ronan City	2,110	6	6	0
Sidney	6,490	12	11	1
Stevensville	2,011	3	2	1
St. Ignatius	838	2	2	0
Thompson Falls	1,386	5	5	0
Troy	907	3	3	0
West Yellowstone	1,379	11	6	5
Whitefish	7,801	20	17	3
Wolf Point	2,782	9	7	2
NEBRASKA				
Albion	1,606	3	3	0
Alliance	8,122	25	18	7
Ashland	2,586	5	4	1
Aurora	4,488	10	9	1
Bayard	1,130	4	4	0
Beatrice	12,244	36	22	14
Bellevue	53,683	108	94	14
Bennington	1,532	1	1	0
Blair	8,103	18	16	2
Boys Town	631	13	13	0
Broken Bow	3,546	7	6	1
Burwell	1,190	2	2	0
Central City	2,918	6	5	1
Chadron	5,621	19	13	6
Columbus	23,257	50	35	15
Cozad	3,791	8	8	0
Crete	7,185	15	14	1
Emerson	798	1	1	0
Fairbury	3,677	4	3	1
Falls City	4,167	12	8	4
Fremont	26,465	41	36	5
Gering	8,291	20	18	2
Gordon	1,537	7	6	1
Gothenburg	3,458	7	6	1

Table 78. Full-Time Law Enforcement Employees, by Selected State and City, 2018—Continued

(Number.)

State/city	Population	Total law enforcement employees	Total officers	Total civilians
Grand Island	51,768	102	83	19
Harvard	959	1	1	0
Hastings	24,963	51	38	13
Holdrege	5,432	17	10	7
Imperial	2,061	4	4	0
Kearney	34,261	68	54	14
Kimball	2,342	5	4	1
Laurel	922	1	1	0
La Vista	17,177	43	38	5
Lexington	9,996	22	20	2
Lincoln	288,589	479	344	135
Madison	2,352	3	3	0
McCook	7,518	21	16	5
Milford	2,078	4	4	0
Minden	2,981	5	5	0
Mitchell	1,654	4	4	0
Nebraska City	7,316	13	12	1
Neligh	1,501	2	2	0
Norfolk	24,458	52	36	16
North Platte	23,774	65	42	23
Ogallala	4,512	10	9	1
Omaha	469,351	1,016	879	137
O'Neill	3,625	9	8	1
Ord	2,097	4	4	0
Papillion	19,588	46	42	4
Pierce	1,724	3	3	0
Plattsmouth	6,444	17	14	3
Ralston	7,535	15	13	2
Schuyler	6,210	11	9	2
Scottsbluff	16,029	36	30	6
Scribner	816	2	2	0
Seward	7,209	14	12	2
Sidney	6,602	15	13	2
South Sioux City	12,845	28	27	1
St. Paul	2,347	4	4	0
Superior	1,848	4	4	0
Sutton	1,419	2	2	0
Tekamah	1,709	4	4	0
Tilden	929	1	1	0
Valentine	2,791	7	6	1
Valley	2,334	5	5	0
Wahoo	4,464	6	6	0
Waterloo	926	4	4	0
Wayne	5,468	12	7	5
West Point	3,335	6	6	0
York	7,875	18	15	3
NEVADA				
Boulder City	16,112	48	32	16
Carlin	2,319	7	5	2
Elko	20,764	46	39	7
Fallon	8,383	34	21	13
Henderson	309,586	664	380	284
Las Vegas Metropolitan Police Department	1,644,390	4,535	2,962	1,573
Lovelock	1,775	7	5	2
Mesquite	19,055	46	38	8
North Las Vegas	246,951	420	296	124
Reno	252,341	386	320	66
Sparks	102,354	162	112	50
West Wendover	4,290	19	11	8
Winnemucca	7,832	26	23	3
Yerington	3,134	6	5	1
NEW HAMPSHIRE				
Alexandria	1,611	2	2	0
Allenstown	4,365	12	10	2
Alstead	1,902	2	2	0
Alton	5,353	14	12	2
Amherst	11,232	19	18	1
Antrim	2,673	6	5	1
Ashland	2,056	5	5	0
Atkinson	6,970	7	6	1
Auburn	5,564	12	10	2
Barnstead	4,674	5	5	0
Barrington	9,122	11	10	1
Bartlett	2,784	4	4	0
Bedford	22,640	49	36	13
Belmont	7,329	18	14	4
Bennington	1,483	2	2	0
Berlin	10,263	31	23	8
Bethlehem	2,550	6	6	0
Boscawen	4,022	8	7	1
Bow	7,860	13	11	2
Bradford	1,690	3	3	0

Table 78. Full-Time Law Enforcement Employees, by Selected State and City, 2018—Continued

(Number.)

State/city	Population	Total law enforcement employees	Total officers	Total civilians
Brentwood	4,740	5	5	0
Bristol	3,047	9	9	0
Brookline	5,351	9	8	1
Campton	3,281	7	6	1
Canaan	3,875	6	6	0
Candia	3,959	7	6	1
Canterbury	2,434	3	3	0
Carroll	730	3	3	0
Center Harbor	1,109	3	3	0
Charlestown	4,988	10	6	4
Chester	5,201	8	7	1
Chesterfield	3,561	6	5	1
Chichester	2,661	4	4	0
Claremont	12,930	28	22	6
Colebrook	2,117	5	5	0
Concord	43,071	94	82	12
Conway	10,153	32	23	9
Danville	4,595	5	5	0
Deerfield	4,536	9	8	1
Deering	1,938	2	2	0
Derry	33,724	67	54	13
Dover	31,600	72	48	24
Dublin	1,531	4	3	1
Dunbarton	2,829	5	5	0
Durham	16,813	23	20	3
East Kingston	2,437	4	4	0
Effingham	1,458	2	2	0
Enfield	4,536	8	7	1
Epping	7,114	16	15	1
Epsom	4,707	6	5	1
Exeter	15,305	35	25	10
Farmington	6,902	15	14	1
Fitzwilliam	2,343	3	3	0
Franconia	1,101	3	3	0
Franklin	8,621	23	18	5
Freedom	1,532	2	2	0
Fremont	4,821	4	3	1
Gilford	7,216	23	18	5
Gilmanton	3,757	4	3	1
Goffstown	17,978	45	30	15
Gorham	2,578	10	6	4
Grantham	2,954	5	4	1
Greenland	4,139	9	8	1
Hampstead	8,696	9	9	0
Hampton	15,679	45	35	10
Hampton Falls	2,380	4	4	0
Hancock	1,639	3	3	0
Hanover	11,519	31	20	11
Haverhill	4,557	10	8	2
Henniker	4,948	10	9	1
Hillsborough	5,936	22	14	8
Hinsdale	3,855	10	9	1
Holderness	2,091	6	6	0
Hollis	7,851	16	14	2
Hooksett	14,283	39	28	11
Hopkinton	5,680	8	7	1
Hudson	25,232	65	48	17
Jackson	824	3	3	0
Jaffrey	5,232	12	11	1
Keene	22,870	53	38	15
Kensington	2,135	6	5	1
Kingston	6,308	9	8	1
Laconia	16,658	49	39	10
Lancaster	3,226	6	5	1
Lebanon	13,578	46	33	13
Lee	4,435	9	8	1
Lincoln	1,772	15	10	5
Lisbon	1,574	3	3	0
Litchfield	8,535	14	12	2
Littleton	5,872	15	13	2
Londonderry	26,627	76	63	13
Loudon	5,523	8	7	1
Lyndeborough	1,720	1	1	0
Madison	2,561	4	4	0
Manchester	111,422	279	227	52
Marlborough	2,054	3	3	0
Meredith	6,446	18	14	4
Merrimack	25,683	52	40	12
Middleton	1,820	4	4	0
Milford	15,497	31	26	5
Milton	4,636	7	6	1
Mont Vernon	2,555	3	3	0
Moultonborough	4,098	8	7	1
Nashua	88,596	234	170	64
New Boston	5,706	10	9	1

Table 78. Full-Time Law Enforcement Employees, by Selected State and City, 2018—Continued

(Number.)

State/city	Population	Total law enforcement employees	Total officers	Total civilians
Newbury	2,211	5	5	0
New Castle	988	4	4	0
New Durham	2,680	4	4	0
Newfields	1,736	3	3	0
New Hampton	2,215	6	6	0
Newington	800	12	11	1
New Ipswich	5,302	6	5	1
New London	4,405	14	9	5
Newmarket	9,160	20	13	7
Newport	6,347	17	12	5
Newton	4,995	8	7	1
Northfield	4,864	10	9	1
North Hampton	4,510	13	12	1
Northumberland	2,112	1	1	0
Northwood	4,326	7	6	1
Nottingham	5,130	8	7	1
Ossipee	4,335	9	8	1
Pelham	13,795	30	23	7
Pembroke	7,157	13	11	2
Peterborough	6,536	14	12	2
Pittsburg	806	1	1	0
Pittsfield	4,101	4	4	0
Plainfield	2,355	3	3	0
Plaistow	7,773	26	18	8
Plymouth	6,722	19	12	7
Portsmouth	22,038	90	69	21
Raymond	10,485	24	16	8
Rindge	6,235	9	8	1
Rochester	30,947	63	52	11
Rollinsford	2,567	5	5	0
Rye	5,501	9	8	1
Salem	29,297	80	64	16
Sanbornton	2,992	6	5	1
Sandown	6,501	8	8	0
Sandwich	1,332	2	2	0
Seabrook	8,941	30	23	7
Somersworth	11,920	32	25	7
South Hampton	827	2	2	0
Springfield	1,329	2	2	0
Strafford	4,132	5	5	0
Stratham	7,484	11	10	1
Sugar Hill	572	2	2	0
Sunapee	3,462	5	5	0
Tamworth	3,009	3	3	0
Thornton	2,492	6	5	1
Tilton	3,581	21	17	4
Troy	2,072	2	2	0
Tuftonboro	2,372	3	3	0
Wakefield	5,708	11	10	1
Warner	2,924	4	3	1
Washington	1,103	1	1	0
Waterville Valley	242	7	6	1
Weare	8,990	12	11	1
Webster	1,923	2	2	0
Whitefield	2,201	6	6	0
Wilton	3,704	7	6	1
Winchester	4,160	9	8	1
Windham	14,811	27	20	7
Wolfeboro	6,286	19	13	6
Woodstock	1,362	6	6	0
NEW JERSEY				
Aberdeen Township	18,378	45	38	7
Absecon	8,252	30	25	5
Allendale	6,865	20	15	5
Allenhurst	488	13	9	4
Allentown	1,809	6	5	1
Alpine	1,873	12	12	0
Andover Township	5,936	17	12	5
Asbury Park	15,717	95	91	4
Atlantic City	38,271	224	190	34
Atlantic Highlands	4,302	18	13	5
Audubon	8,599	19	18	1
Avalon	1,258	29	21	8
Avon-by-the-Sea	1,780	11	11	0
Barnegat Township	22,777	51	49	2
Barrington	6,661	15	15	0
Bay Head	971	9	8	1
Bayonne	66,824	248	189	59
Beach Haven	1,169	14	13	1
Beachwood	11,146	22	20	2
Bedminster Township	8,126	18	16	2
Belleville	36,075	123	115	8
Bellmawr	11,312	24	23	1
Belmar	5,666	31	25	6

Table 78. Full-Time Law Enforcement Employees, by Selected State and City, 2018—Continued

(Number.)

State/city	Population	Total law enforcement employees	Total officers	Total civilians
Belvidere	2,592	6	6	0
Bergenfield	27,684	53	46	7
Berkeley Heights Township	13,646	33	27	6
Berkeley Township	41,331	97	76	21
Berlin	7,495	18	17	1
Berlin Township	5,532	18	17	1
Bernards Township	26,813	42	38	4
Bernardsville	7,742	26	20	6
Beverly	2,497	8	8	0
Blairstown Township	5,787	9	8	1
Bloomfield	50,777	150	125	25
Bloomingdale	8,211	18	17	1
Bogota	8,499	18	13	5
Boonton	8,236	28	23	5
Boonton Township	4,299	13	13	0
Bordentown City	3,823	14	14	0
Bordentown Township	12,323	24	23	1
Bound Brook	10,360	29	24	5
Bradley Beach	4,214	21	18	3
Branchburg Township	14,577	28	26	2
Brick Township	74,712	208	142	66
Bridgeton	24,386	80	66	14
Bridgewater Township	45,050	81	74	7
Brielle	4,719	16	15	1
Brigantine	8,896	44	34	10
Brooklawn	1,904	7	7	0
Burlington City	9,817	35	33	2
Burlington Township	22,857	56	44	12
Butler	7,679	17	16	1
Byram Township	7,925	14	14	0
Caldwell	7,999	22	22	0
Camden County Police Department	73,140	413	370	43
Cape May	3,463	27	22	5
Carlstadt	6,252	34	28	6
Carney's Point Township	7,655	19	18	1
Carteret	23,921	72	63	9
Cedar Grove Township	12,566	32	31	1
Chatham	8,793	23	19	4
Chatham Township	10,288	22	20	2
Cherry Hill Township	70,578	162	135	27
Chesilhurst	1,617	10	9	1
Chesterfield Township	7,567	11	10	1
Chester Township	7,809	23	22	1
Cinnaminson Township	16,630	28	28	0
Clark Township	16,079	49	38	11
Clayton	8,624	17	16	1
Clementon	4,887	13	12	1
Cliffside Park	25,001	51	44	7
Clifton	85,732	188	148	40
Clinton	2,699	10	10	0
Clinton Township	12,824	23	22	1
Closter	8,691	22	21	1
Collingswood	13,843	30	26	4
Colts Neck Township	9,944	22	21	1
Cranbury Township	3,900	20	19	1
Cranford Township	24,353	67	51	16
Cresskill	8,862	27	22	5
Deal	730	22	18	4
Delanco Township	4,509	13	12	1
Delaware Township	4,461	8	7	1
Delran Township	16,579	34	30	4
Demarest	4,977	13	13	0
Denville Township	16,737	42	33	9
Deptford Township	30,137	74	68	6
Dover	17,982	40	35	5
Dumont	17,825	40	32	8
Dunellen	7,328	16	16	0
Eastampton Township	5,940	18	17	1
East Brunswick Township	48,342	109	84	25
East Greenwich Township	10,504	19	17	2
East Hanover Township	11,084	33	33	0
East Newark	2,740	7	7	0
East Orange	64,625	261	202	59
East Rutherford	9,941	39	34	5
East Windsor Township	27,401	50	44	6
Eatontown	12,364	44	37	7
Edgewater	12,318	36	31	5
Edgewater Park Township	8,713	16	15	1
Edison Township	101,309	219	170	49
Egg Harbor City	4,162	18	17	1
Egg Harbor Township	43,276	113	85	28
Elizabeth	129,080	411	313	98
Elk Township	4,116	12	11	1
Elmer	1,301	2	2	0
Elmwood Park	20,277	46	42	4

Table 78. Full-Time Law Enforcement Employees, by Selected State and City, 2018—Continued

(Number.)

State/city	Population	Total law enforcement employees	Total officers	Total civilians
Emerson	7,679	24	21	3
Englewood	28,988	101	77	24
Englewood Cliffs	5,395	26	25	1
Englishtown	1,959	7	7	0
Essex Fells	2,109	13	13	0
Evesham Township	45,354	99	89	10
Ewing Township	36,142	102	82	20
Fairfield Township, Essex County	7,528	40	36	4
Fair Haven	5,927	13	13	0
Fair Lawn	33,413	68	59	9
Fairview	14,428	36	32	4
Fanwood	7,768	18	17	1
Far Hills	918	6	6	0
Flemington	4,627	15	15	0
Florence Township	12,748	30	28	2
Florham Park	11,602	38	32	6
Fort Lee	37,729	116	98	18
Franklin	4,735	17	16	1
Franklin Lakes	11,191	28	23	5
Franklin Township, Gloucester County	16,225	41	37	4
Franklin Township, Hunterdon County	3,238	6	6	0
Franklin Township, Somerset County	66,624	119	101	18
Freehold Borough	11,873	30	27	3
Freehold Township	34,896	71	67	4
Frenchtown	1,363	3	3	0
Galloway Township	36,467	79	61	18
Garfield	32,203	69	59	10
Garwood	4,370	20	16	4
Gibbsboro	2,211	8	8	0
Glassboro	19,938	51	45	6
Glen Ridge	7,622	29	23	6
Glen Rock	11,937	26	23	3
Gloucester City	11,167	34	32	2
Gloucester Township	63,198	152	131	21
Green Brook Township	7,138	24	23	1
Greenwich Township, Gloucester County	4,769	18	17	1
Greenwich Township, Warren County	5,510	12	12	0
Guttenberg	11,602	28	25	3
Hackensack	44,926	115	100	15
Hackettstown	9,530	18	17	1
Haddonfield	11,253	23	21	2
Haddon Heights	7,497	15	14	1
Haddon Township	14,500	27	26	1
Haledon	8,363	18	18	0
Hamburg	3,109	9	8	1
Hamilton Township, Atlantic County	26,380	80	56	24
Hamilton Township, Mercer County	87,889	206	171	35
Hammonton	14,311	35	28	7
Hanover Township	14,583	38	31	7
Harding Township	3,824	12	11	1
Hardyston Township	7,823	24	18	6
Harrington Park	4,802	11	11	0
Harrison	18,058	50	38	12
Harrison Township	12,915	24	23	1
Harvey Cedars	338	8	8	0
Hasbrouck Heights	12,163	31	29	2
Haworth	3,463	13	12	1
Hawthorne	18,874	38	32	6
Hazlet Township	19,970	47	39	8
High Bridge	3,528	7	7	0
Highland Park	13,989	32	26	6
Highlands	4,794	17	14	3
Hightstown	5,289	13	12	1
Hillsborough Township	39,796	62	53	9
Hillsdale	10,484	23	19	4
Hillside Township	22,078	79	67	12
Hi-Nella	855	13	13	0
Hoboken	55,096	152	134	18
Ho-Ho-Kus	4,139	19	16	3
Holland Township	5,128	7	6	1
Holmdel Township	16,621	50	43	7
Hopatcong	14,183	31	24	7
Hopewell Township	18,000	39	30	9
Howell Township	52,672	104	88	16
Independence Township	5,495	10	9	1
Irvington	54,220	223	168	55
Island Heights	1,652	6	6	0
Jackson Township	56,706	113	90	23
Jamesburg	6,006	20	16	4
Jefferson Township	21,071	43	35	8
Jersey City	270,175	955	886	69
Keansburg	9,766	38	32	6
Kearny	42,339	153	109	44
Kenilworth	8,249	31	26	5
Keyport	7,065	24	20	4

Table 78. Full-Time Law Enforcement Employees, by Selected State and City, 2018—Continued

(Number.)

State/city	Population	Total law enforcement employees	Total officers	Total civilians
Kinnelon	10,080	17	16	1
Lacey Township	28,654	57	43	14
Lakehurst	2,672	16	14	2
Lakewood Township	102,915	171	137	34
Lambertville	3,811	12	9	3
Laurel Springs	1,856	7	7	0
Lavallette	1,824	14	12	2
Lawnside	2,875	9	9	0
Lawrence Township, Mercer County	32,644	62	58	4
Lebanon Township	6,070	11	10	1
Leonia	9,175	22	19	3
Lincoln Park	10,308	29	23	6
Linden	42,806	165	136	29
Lindenwold	17,204	44	41	3
Linwood	6,822	19	18	1
Little Egg Harbor Township	21,087	56	43	13
Little Falls Township	14,306	34	28	6
Little Ferry	10,895	33	28	5
Little Silver	5,898	23	18	5
Livingston Township	29,820	85	70	15
Lodi	24,720	48	46	2
Logan Township	5,844	22	21	1
Long Beach Township	3,029	48	36	12
Long Branch	30,750	117	94	23
Long Hill Township	8,587	25	23	2
Longport	873	13	13	0
Lopatcong Township	8,384	17	16	1
Lower Alloways Creek Township	1,676	13	13	0
Lower Township	21,617	53	47	6
Lumberton Township	12,253	22	20	2
Lyndhurst Township	22,384	49	46	3
Madison	15,832	38	30	8
Magnolia	4,237	12	12	0
Mahwah Township	26,501	62	53	9
Manalapan Township	40,150	59	56	3
Manasquan	5,903	21	16	5
Manchester Township	42,939	89	70	19
Mansfield Township, Burlington County	8,577	15	14	1
Mansfield Township, Warren County	7,431	16	15	1
Mantoloking	249	10	9	1
Mantua Township	14,772	33	30	3
Manville	10,308	27	24	3
Maple Shade Township	18,772	39	35	4
Maplewood Township	24,635	76	64	12
Margate City	6,045	36	28	8
Marlboro Township	40,338	110	80	30
Matawan	8,864	23	22	1
Maywood	9,763	26	22	4
Medford Lakes	3,995	10	9	1
Medford Township	23,558	41	37	4
Mendham	4,905	13	12	1
Mendham Township	5,757	16	15	1
Merchantville	3,712	15	14	1
Metuchen	14,262	34	28	6
Middlesex Borough	13,704	34	31	3
Middle Township	18,358	70	56	14
Middletown Township	65,469	124	112	12
Midland Park	7,313	17	16	1
Millburn Township	20,250	60	54	6
Milltown	7,099	18	16	2
Millville	27,837	91	81	10
Monmouth Beach	3,231	10	9	1
Monroe Township, Gloucester County	36,498	74	66	8
Monroe Township, Middlesex County	45,597	79	60	19
Montclair	38,893	130	110	20
Montgomery Township	23,515	40	34	6
Montvale	8,729	25	23	2
Montville Township	21,396	46	40	6
Moonachie	2,774	24	21	3
Moorestown Township	20,510	38	33	5
Morris Plains	5,509	20	18	2
Morristown	18,860	62	58	4
Morris Township	22,183	39	33	6
Mountain Lakes	4,308	14	13	1
Mountainside	6,925	22	17	5
Mount Arlington	5,914	15	14	1
Mount Ephraim	4,565	14	13	1
Mount Holly Township	9,658	30	26	4
Mount Laurel Township	41,629	77	69	8
Mount Olive Township	28,994	59	50	9
Mullica Township	6,005	13	12	1
Neptune City	4,694	19	17	2
Neptune Township	27,825	92	78	14
Netcong	3,182	10	10	0
Newark	282,258	1,490	1,155	335

Table 78. Full-Time Law Enforcement Employees, by Selected State and City, 2018—Continued

(Number.)

State/city	Population	Total law enforcement employees	Total officers	Total civilians
New Brunswick	56,577	170	147	23
New Hanover Township	7,504	3	3	0
New Milford	16,701	42	36	6
New Providence	13,283	35	33	2
Newton	7,824	25	24	1
North Arlington	15,868	36	29	7
North Bergen Township	63,166	128	113	15
North Brunswick Township	42,205	102	84	18
North Caldwell	6,716	18	14	4
Northfield	8,324	22	21	1
North Haledon	8,469	24	19	5
North Hanover Township	7,518	11	10	1
North Plainfield	21,834	55	47	8
Northvale	4,965	14	14	0
North Wildwood	3,816	33	26	7
Norwood	5,836	17	16	1
Nutley Township	28,596	81	70	11
Oakland	13,102	32	27	5
Oaklyn	3,934	16	15	1
Ocean City	11,138	72	59	13
Ocean Gate	2,001	10	9	1
Oceanport	5,742	15	14	1
Ocean Township, Monmouth County	26,947	79	63	16
Ocean Township, Ocean County	9,045	30	21	9
Ogdensburg	2,262	6	6	0
Old Bridge Township	66,321	117	95	22
Old Tappan	5,998	15	14	1
Oradell	8,243	24	23	1
Orange City	30,449	140	114	26
Palisades Park	20,888	45	34	11
Palmyra	7,198	19	18	1
Paramus	26,744	110	91	19
Park Ridge	8,858	21	20	1
Parsippany-Troy Hills Township	52,447	116	104	12
Passaic	70,435	189	165	24
Paterson	146,893	526	419	107
Paulsboro	5,812	20	18	2
Peapack-Gladstone	2,588	9	8	1
Pemberton Borough	1,331	7	6	1
Pemberton Township	27,212	47	42	5
Pennington	2,554	6	5	1
Pennsauken Township	35,420	81	73	8
Penns Grove	4,790	16	15	1
Pennsville Township	12,378	24	22	2
Pequannock Township	15,177	39	34	5
Perth Amboy	52,347	163	132	31
Phillipsburg	14,395	37	36	1
Pine Beach	2,148	7	6	1
Pine Hill	10,431	23	21	2
Pine Valley	11	6	6	0
Piscataway Township	57,342	101	82	19
Pitman	8,696	19	18	1
Plainfield	50,820	153	125	28
Plainsboro Township	23,243	47	36	11
Pleasantville	20,799	65	53	12
Plumsted Township	8,460	16	15	1
Pohatcong Township	3,217	12	12	0
Point Pleasant	18,474	43	33	10
Point Pleasant Beach	4,472	29	23	6
Pompton Lakes	11,062	27	23	4
Princeton	31,856	60	52	8
Prospect Park	5,893	18	17	1
Rahway	30,113	93	76	17
Ramsey	15,126	39	33	6
Randolph Township	25,552	39	34	5
Raritan	8,098	21	20	1
Raritan Township	22,092	36	33	3
Readington Township	15,941	26	23	3
Red Bank	12,128	45	39	6
Ridgefield	11,329	32	30	2
Ridgefield Park	13,028	39	31	8
Ridgewood	25,429	52	47	5
Ringwood	12,303	26	21	5
Riverdale	4,293	21	17	4
River Edge	11,611	28	25	3
Riverside Township	7,875	15	15	0
Riverton	2,698	6	6	0
River Vale Township	10,157	21	20	1
Robbinsville Township	14,710	38	29	9
Rochelle Park Township	5,648	24	20	4
Rockaway	6,388	16	15	1
Rockaway Township	25,328	59	48	11
Roseland	5,867	25	25	0
Roselle	21,787	70	57	13
Roselle Park	13,698	41	34	7

Table 78. Full-Time Law Enforcement Employees, by Selected State and City, 2018—Continued

(Number.)

State/city	Population	Total law enforcement employees	Total officers	Total civilians
Roxbury Township	23,010	45	42	3
Rumson	6,835	20	16	4
Runnemede	8,261	17	16	1
Rutherford	18,617	42	40	2
Saddle Brook Township	14,037	39	34	5
Saddle River	3,230	23	18	5
Salem	4,726	21	19	2
Sayreville	45,062	107	92	15
Scotch Plains Township	24,423	52	49	3
Sea Bright	1,379	20	11	9
Sea Girt	1,766	12	11	1
Sea Isle City	2,061	30	23	7
Seaside Heights	2,872	28	21	7
Seaside Park	1,526	12	11	1
Secaucus	20,482	88	73	15
Ship Bottom	1,129	12	11	1
Shrewsbury	4,170	22	17	5
Somerdale	5,484	18	17	1
Somers Point	10,436	31	24	7
Somerville	12,326	33	31	2
South Amboy	8,764	34	28	6
South Bound Brook	4,621	13	12	1
South Brunswick Township	46,340	109	82	27
South Hackensack Township	2,473	24	21	3
South Harrison Township	3,118	5	5	0
South Orange Village	16,880	52	45	7
South Plainfield	24,238	67	54	13
South River	16,159	42	32	10
South Toms River	3,740	13	12	1
Sparta Township	18,694	44	31	13
Spotswood	8,364	30	26	4
Springfield Township, Burlington County	3,280	11	10	1
Springfield Township, Union County	17,762	48	44	4
Spring Lake	2,958	13	13	0
Spring Lake Heights	4,607	15	15	0
Stafford Township	27,141	70	54	16
Stanhope	3,306	10	9	1
Stone Harbor	816	19	17	2
Stratford	6,913	15	15	0
Summit	22,125	52	47	5
Surf City	1,174	10	10	0
Teaneck Township	40,939	109	92	17
Tenafly	14,742	39	33	6
Teterboro	68	24	21	3
Tewksbury Township	5,825	11	10	1
Tinton Falls	17,754	43	41	2
Toms River Township	92,191	181	160	21
Totowa	10,666	32	28	4
Trenton	83,753	359	287	72
Tuckerton	3,336	13	12	1
Union Beach	5,469	17	17	0
Union City	69,950	215	167	48
Union Township	58,861	183	132	51
Upper Saddle River	8,330	21	17	4
Ventnor City	10,182	51	38	13
Vernon Township	22,057	41	32	9
Verona	13,437	35	30	5
Vineland	60,330	172	145	27
Voorhees Township	29,071	63	56	7
Waldwick	10,019	25	20	5
Wallington	11,676	24	23	1
Wall Township	25,955	84	68	16
Wanaque	11,960	29	24	5
Warren Township	15,951	37	30	7
Washington Township, Bergen County	9,299	19	19	0
Washington Township, Gloucester County	47,024	87	79	8
Washington Township, Morris County	18,484	30	29	1
Washington Township, Warren County	6,434	28	27	1
Watchung	5,939	38	31	7
Waterford Township	10,641	29	28	1
Wayne Township	54,340	147	120	27
Weehawken Township	15,567	74	52	22
Westampton Township	8,752	26	23	3
West Amwell Township	2,757	6	6	0
West Caldwell Township	10,912	30	25	5
West Deptford Township	20,889	46	43	3
Westfield	30,011	70	57	13
West Long Branch	7,957	22	21	1
West Milford Township	26,560	50	43	7
West New York	54,095	125	114	11
West Orange	48,071	109	96	13
Westville	4,121	12	11	1
West Wildwood	561	5	5	0
West Windsor Township	28,277	60	48	12

Table 78. Full-Time Law Enforcement Employees, by Selected State and City, 2018—Continued

(Number.)

State/city	Population	Total law enforcement employees	Total officers	Total civilians
Westwood	11,219	33	27	6
Wharton	6,482	22	21	1
Wildwood	5,035	54	44	10
Wildwood Crest	3,116	27	21	6
Willingboro Township	32,124	76	66	10
Winfield Township	1,514	10	10	0
Winslow Township	38,382	81	74	7
Woodbridge Township	100,884	264	196	68
Woodbury	9,746	32	29	3
Woodbury Heights	2,944	8	7	1
Woodcliff Lake	5,844	19	18	1
Woodland Park	12,799	30	26	4
Woodlynne	2,902	8	6	2
Wood-Ridge	9,105	24	20	4
Woodstown	3,447	10	9	1
Woolwich Township	12,636	25	24	1
Wyckoff Township	17,161	26	26	0
NEW MEXICO				
Alamogordo	31,332	84	57	27
Anthony	9,313	11	10	1
Artesia	12,007	47	30	17
Aztec	6,538	17	14	3
Bayard	2,166	7	6	1
Belen	7,061	26	23	3
Bernalillo	9,841	24	21	3
Bloomfield	7,922	14	12	2
Bosque Farms	3,789	14	13	1
Capitan	1,402	3	2	1
Carlsbad	29,158	92	63	29
Carrizozo	928	4	3	1
Clayton	2,735	13	7	6
Cloudcroft	689	3	3	0
Clovis	39,063	77	54	23
Corrales	8,577	18	15	3
Cuba	750	5	4	1
Deming	14,094	40	36	4
Dexter	1,242	6	5	1
Edgewood	3,911	13	12	1
Estancia	1,581	3	2	1
Eunice	2,961	11	6	5
Gallup	21,980	79	63	16
Grants	8,982	24	18	6
Hatch	1,607	9	8	1
Hobbs	38,320	103	73	30
Hope	105	1	1	0
Hurley	1,199	5	3	2
Jal	2,072	14	7	7
Logan	962	4	4	0
Lordsburg	2,421	13	10	3
Los Alamos	18,883	71	34	37
Los Lunas	15,568	43	39	4
Lovington	11,175	33	23	10
Magdalena	874	2	2	0
Milan	3,644	11	9	2
Moriarty	1,777	11	9	2
Peralta	3,572	14	13	1
Questa	1,749	4	3	1
Raton	5,960	22	13	9
Red River	466	11	4	7
Rio Rancho	97,394	214	125	89
Ruidoso	7,718	36	24	12
Ruidoso Downs	2,557	10	5	5
Santa Clara	1,786	5	4	1
Santa Fe	84,176	196	150	46
Santa Rosa	2,691	15	9	6
San Ysidro	197	3	2	1
Socorro	8,363	16	14	2
Springer	903	2	2	0
Taos	5,662	27	21	6
Taos Ski Valley	67	3	3	0
Tatum	813	8	3	5
Texico	1,113	4	3	1
Truth or Consequences	5,875	16	13	3
Tularosa	2,939	12	6	6
NEW YORK				
Addison Town and Village	2,490	3	3	0
Akron Village	2,872	1	1	0
Albany	98,322	404	316	88
Albion Village	5,878	13	12	1
Alfred Village	4,022	5	5	0
Allegany Village	1,702	2	2	0
Altamont Village	1,707	1	1	0
Amherst Town	121,343	181	151	30

Table 78. Full-Time Law Enforcement Employees, by Selected State and City, 2018—Continued

(Number.)

State/city	Population	Total law enforcement employees	Total officers	Total civilians
Amityville Village	9,526	24	23	1
Amsterdam	17,737	42	40	2
Arcade Village	1,951	6	6	0
Ardsley Village	4,614	19	19	0
Asharoken Village	650	2	2	0
Attica Village	2,426	2	2	0
Auburn	26,570	70	64	6
Avon Village	3,235	4	4	0
Baldwinsville Village	7,976	11	10	1
Ballston Spa Village	5,329	3	3	0
Batavia	14,565	34	31	3
Bath Village	5,498	11	10	1
Beacon	14,241	36	34	2
Bedford Town	18,034	43	38	5
Belmont Village	913	1	1	0
Bethlehem Town	35,704	53	38	15
Binghamton	44,876	146	133	13
Blooming Grove Town	11,888	13	11	2
Bolivar Village	989	1	1	0
Boonville Village	2,022	2	2	0
Briarcliff Manor Village	8,044	21	21	0
Brighton Town	36,470	45	39	6
Brockport Village	8,290	16	15	1
Bronxville Village	6,584	23	21	2
Buffalo	258,219	973	784	189
Cairo Town	6,404	1	1	0
Caledonia Village	2,140	3	3	0
Cambridge Village	1,809	3	3	0
Camden Village	2,184	3	3	0
Camillus Town and Village	24,462	27	24	3
Canajoharie Village	2,129	4	4	0
Canandaigua	10,252	26	24	2
Canastota Village	4,536	5	4	1
Canisteo Village	2,156	2	2	0
Canton Village	6,510	11	10	1
Carmel Town	34,382	41	34	7
Carthage Village	3,392	4	4	0
Catskill Village	3,803	16	15	1
Cayuga Heights Village	3,753	7	6	1
Cazenovia Village	2,842	5	4	1
Central Square Village	1,768	3	3	0
Centre Island Village	414	7	7	0
Cheektowaga Town	77,648	158	123	35
Chester Town	8,053	12	12	0
Chester Village	4,157	12	11	1
Chittenango Village	4,861	3	2	1
Clarkstown Town	81,994	176	152	24
Clayton Village	1,860	8	7	1
Cobleskill Village	4,534	13	13	0
Coeymans Town	7,416	4	3	1
Cohoes	16,979	39	35	4
Colchester Town	1,978	2	2	0
Colonie Town	79,842	153	114	39
Cooperstown Village	1,757	5	4	1
Corning	10,643	23	19	4
Cornwall-on-Hudson Village	2,935	3	3	0
Cornwall Town	9,558	12	9	3
Cortland	18,631	46	43	3
Crawford Town	9,217	12	11	1
Croton-on-Hudson Village	8,284	21	19	2
Cuba Town	3,110	4	4	0
Deerpark Town	7,759	3	3	0
Delhi Village	3,116	4	4	0
Depew Village	15,159	36	30	6
DeWitt Town	25,268	44	42	2
Dobbs Ferry Village	11,182	27	27	0
Dolgeville Village	2,084	3	3	0
Dryden Village	2,201	4	4	0
Dunkirk	11,755	37	36	1
East Aurora-Aurora Town	13,900	20	15	5
Eastchester Town	20,452	50	48	2
East Fishkill Town	29,623	34	27	7
East Greenbush Town	16,331	33	24	9
East Hampton Town	19,992	92	67	25
East Hampton Village	1,130	26	23	3
East Rochester Village	6,580	9	8	1
Eden Town	7,667	5	4	1
Ellenville Village	4,023	11	10	1
Ellicott Town	5,060	12	12	0
Ellicottville	1,583	3	3	0
Elmira Heights Village	3,865	9	9	0
Elmira Town	5,665	4	4	0
Elmsford Village	5,379	25	21	4
Endicott Village	12,754	30	29	1
Evans Town	16,220	29	22	7

Table 78. Full-Time Law Enforcement Employees, by Selected State and City, 2018—Continued

(Number.)

State/city	Population	Total law enforcement employees	Total officers	Total civilians
Fairport Village	5,388	11	10	1
Fallsburg Town	12,207	21	21	0
Floral Park Village	16,131	46	35	11
Florida Village	2,872	1	1	0
Fort Edward Village	3,277	5	5	0
Fort Plain Village	2,218	3	3	0
Freeport Village	43,597	114	99	15
Garden City Village	22,749	62	50	12
Gates Town	28,717	35	32	3
Geddes Town	10,177	16	14	2
Geneseo Village	8,184	8	8	0
Geneva	12,841	36	34	2
Glens Falls	14,403	32	30	2
Glenville Town	21,670	25	23	2
Gloversville	14,860	37	34	3
Goshen Town	8,703	8	8	0
Goshen Village	5,373	20	17	3
Gouverneur Village	3,702	8	5	3
Granville Village	2,446	15	15	0
Great Neck Estates Village	2,898	16	13	3
Greece Town	96,650	106	99	7
Greenburgh Town	45,723	137	105	32
Greene Village	1,432	2	2	0
Greenwich Village	1,721	1	1	0
Greenwood Lake Village	3,099	6	5	1
Guilderland Town	34,260	50	36	14
Hamburg Town	46,490	67	64	3
Hamburg Village	9,735	15	14	1
Hamilton Village	4,091	5	5	0
Harriman Village	2,461	7	7	0
Harrison Town	28,741	76	65	11
Hastings-on-Hudson Village	8,030	21	21	0
Haverstraw Town	37,750	67	62	5
Hempstead Village	56,059	148	123	25
Highland Falls Village	3,838	9	6	3
Holley Village	1,691	1	1	0
Homer Village	3,104	6	5	1
Hoosick Falls Village	3,386	1	1	0
Hornell	8,161	22	21	1
Horseheads Village	6,464	9	8	1
Hudson	6,173	30	25	5
Hudson Falls Village	7,071	10	10	0
Huntington Bay Village	1,436	4	4	0
Hyde Park Town	21,046	17	14	3
Ilion Village	7,736	20	18	2
Inlet Town	307	1	1	0
Irondequoit Town	50,212	60	50	10
Irvington Village	6,631	22	22	0
Ithaca	31,145	73	68	5
Jamestown	29,384	72	62	10
Johnson City Village	14,418	42	37	5
Johnstown	8,265	27	25	2
Kenmore Village	15,178	25	25	0
Kensington Village	1,192	6	6	0
Kent Town	13,326	24	19	5
Kingston	23,077	73	68	5
Kirkland Town	8,355	5	5	0
Lackawanna	17,904	47	47	0
Lake Placid Village	2,398	14	11	3
Lake Success Village	3,170	28	24	4
Lakewood-Busti	7,260	11	10	1
Lancaster Town	37,776	67	51	16
Larchmont Village	6,200	25	22	3
Lewisboro Town	12,823	3	3	0
Lewiston Town and Village	15,922	12	11	1
Liberty Village	4,092	18	16	2
Little Falls	4,684	12	11	1
Liverpool Village	2,238	4	4	0
Lloyd Harbor Village	3,697	14	12	2
Lloyd Town	10,510	14	11	3
Lockport	20,486	50	48	2
Long Beach	33,801	83	67	16
Lowville Village	3,347	5	5	0
Lynbrook Village	19,745	58	50	8
Macedon Town and Village	8,960	7	6	1
Malone Village	5,641	12	12	0
Malverne Village	8,626	22	22	0
Mamaroneck Town	12,336	34	34	0
Mamaroneck Village	19,496	57	50	7
Manchester Village	1,630	1	1	0
Manlius Town	24,417	44	38	6
Marlborough Town	8,663	10	8	2
Massena Village	10,291	25	20	5
Maybrook Village	3,667	4	4	0
Medina Village	5,687	13	12	1

Table 78. Full-Time Law Enforcement Employees, by Selected State and City, 2018—Continued

(Number.)

State/city	Population	Total law enforcement employees	Total officers	Total civilians
Menands Village	3,940	14	11	3
Middleport Village	1,756	4	4	0
Middletown	27,885	82	69	13
Mohawk Village	2,554	4	4	0
Monroe Village	8,665	20	16	4
Montgomery Town	9,122	15	13	2
Montgomery Village	4,682	4	4	0
Monticello Village	6,414	23	22	1
Moriah Town	3,532	2	2	0
Mount Hope Town	6,978	3	3	0
Mount Pleasant Town	26,506	50	42	8
Mount Vernon	68,889	269	207	62
Newark Village	8,864	15	14	1
New Berlin Town	1,512	1	1	0
Newburgh	28,282	94	82	12
Newburgh Town	31,200	57	46	11
New Castle Town	18,197	39	37	2
New Hartford Town and Village	20,232	24	20	4
New Paltz Town and Village	14,075	24	21	3
New Rochelle	80,340	218	160	58
New Windsor Town	28,137	55	44	11
New York	8,523,171	52,278	36,134	16,144
New York Mills Village	3,265	4	4	0
Niagara Falls	48,225	164	146	18
Niagara Town	8,014	9	8	1
Niskayuna Town	22,486	30	28	2
Nissequogue Village	1,751	1	1	0
North Greenbush Town	12,216	18	16	2
Northport Village	7,362	21	17	4
North Syracuse Village	6,730	11	10	1
North Tonawanda	30,325	52	48	4
Norwich	6,656	19	19	0
Ocean Beach Village	83	4	4	0
Ogdensburg	10,629	31	27	4
Ogden Town	20,288	14	11	3
Old Brookville Village	2,220	34	26	8
Old Westbury Village	4,763	30	25	5
Olean	13,615	40	34	6
Oneida	10,940	27	23	4
Oneonta City	14,073	28	23	5
Orangetown Town	37,973	89	82	7
Orchard Park Town	29,760	42	32	10
Ossining Village	25,452	65	57	8
Oswego City	17,370	52	46	6
Owego Village	3,898	3	2	1
Oyster Bay Cove Village	4,342	14	14	0
Palmyra Village	3,345	6	5	1
Peekskill	24,365	60	51	9
Pelham Manor Village	5,660	24	23	1
Pelham Village	7,036	28	25	3
Penn Yan Village	4,946	14	13	1
Perry Village	3,474	4	4	0
Piermont Village	2,585	8	8	0
Plattsburgh City	19,651	51	45	6
Pleasantville Village	7,352	22	20	2
Port Chester Village	29,814	64	62	2
Port Dickinson Village	1,553	5	4	1
Port Jervis	8,599	32	31	1
Port Washington	19,555	70	62	8
Potsdam Village	9,723	18	14	4
Poughkeepsie	30,580	114	84	30
Pound Ridge Town	5,257	2	1	1
Quogue Village	1,019	14	13	1
Rensselaer City	9,249	33	27	6
Riverhead Town	33,812	101	85	16
Rochester	207,701	863	747	116
Rockville Centre Village	24,960	64	55	9
Rome	32,298	75	73	2
Rosendale Town	5,889	1	1	0
Rotterdam Town	29,882	44	41	3
Rye	16,050	37	33	4
Rye Brook Village	9,622	27	26	1
Sag Harbor Village	2,310	13	12	1
Salamanca	5,495	15	15	0
Sands Point Village	2,926	21	21	0
Saranac Lake Village	5,265	11	11	0
Saratoga Springs	28,237	83	71	12
Saugerties Town	19,136	27	23	4
Scarsdale Village	18,214	48	44	4
Schenectady	65,550	182	154	28
Schodack Town	11,747	11	11	0
Scotia Village	7,700	14	13	1
Seneca Falls Town	8,670	18	16	2
Shelter Island Town	2,425	9	8	1
Sherrill	3,031	3	3	0

Table 78. Full-Time Law Enforcement Employees, by Selected State and City, 2018—Continued

(Number.)

State/city	Population	Total law enforcement employees	Total officers	Total civilians
Shortsville Village	1,422	1	1	0
Sidney Village	3,621	8	8	0
Skaneateles Village	2,486	1	1	0
Solvay Village	6,307	15	14	1
Southampton Town	51,231	131	98	33
Southampton Village	3,335	48	33	15
South Glens Falls Village	3,628	6	6	0
South Nyack Village	3,556	5	5	0
Southold Town	20,092	68	48	20
Spring Valley Village	32,909	59	52	7
Stony Point Town	15,667	26	25	1
Suffern Village	11,032	26	22	4
Syracuse	143,129	488	418	70
Tarrytown Village	11,617	36	33	3
Ticonderoga Town	4,853	6	6	0
Tonawanda	14,868	35	29	6
Tonawanda Town	57,256	151	105	46
Troy	49,491	134	124	10
Trumansburg Village	1,818	1	1	0
Tuckahoe Village	6,677	26	23	3
Tupper Lake Village	3,503	9	9	0
Tuxedo Park Village	603	3	3	0
Tuxedo Town	2,924	7	7	0
Ulster Town	12,600	28	24	4
Utica	60,413	174	159	15
Vestal Town	28,223	38	35	3
Walden Village	6,727	15	12	3
Wallkill Town	29,123	45	44	1
Walton Village	2,820	5	5	0
Warsaw Village	3,317	5	5	0
Warwick Town	18,450	38	33	5
Washingtonville Village	5,755	17	17	0
Waterloo Village	4,906	9	8	1
Watertown	25,525	71	68	3
Watervliet	10,115	23	22	1
Watkins Glen Village	1,929	3	3	0
Waverly Village	4,123	11	10	1
Wayland Village	1,769	1	1	0
Webb Town	1,795	6	6	0
Webster Town and Village	45,023	34	31	3
Wellsville Village	4,420	12	11	1
Westfield Village	3,012	6	6	0
Westhampton Beach Village	1,819	15	13	2
West Seneca Town	45,721	77	64	13
White Plains	59,350	198	190	8
Whitesboro Village	3,655	6	6	0
Whitestown Town	9,175	6	6	0
Windham Town	1,671	1	1	0
Woodbury Town	11,114	26	22	4
Woodstock Town	5,819	10	10	0
Yonkers	202,827	669	587	82
Yorktown Town	37,101	65	56	9
Yorkville Village	2,600	4	4	0
NORTH CAROLINA				
Aberdeen	7,821	30	28	2
Ahoskie	4,850	18	16	2
Albemarle	15,991	52	41	11
Andrews	1,824	5	5	0
Angier	5,203	14	14	0
Apex	52,577	96	78	18
Archdale	11,529	32	26	6
Asheboro	25,922	80	73	7
Asheville	93,186	283	222	61
Atlantic Beach	1,493	17	16	1
Aurora	511	1	1	0
Ayden	5,162	22	18	4
Badin	1,958	4	4	0
Bakersville	443	1	1	0
Bald Head Island	179	27	22	5
Banner Elk	1,146	9	8	1
Beaufort	4,178	17	16	1
Beech Mountain	323	14	10	4
Belhaven	1,565	7	6	1
Belmont	12,331	42	35	7
Benson	3,795	11	10	1
Bessemer City	5,493	15	14	1
Bethel	1,616	4	4	0
Beulaville	1,317	4	4	0
Biltmore Forest	1,432	14	13	1
Biscoe	1,675	9	8	1
Black Creek	773	3	3	0
Black Mountain	8,195	23	19	4
Bladenboro	1,644	4	4	0
Blowing Rock	1,267	11	10	1

Table 78. Full-Time Law Enforcement Employees, by Selected State and City, 2018—Continued

(Number.)

State/city	Population	Total law enforcement employees	Total officers	Total civilians
Boiling Spring Lakes	6,126	10	9	1
Boiling Springs	4,696	9	9	0
Boone	19,524	48	36	12
Boonville	1,164	4	4	0
Brevard	7,921	31	24	7
Bridgeton	438	1	1	0
Broadway	1,270	4	4	0
Bryson City	1,459	9	8	1
Bunn	369	2	2	0
Burgaw	4,147	13	12	1
Burlington	53,385	168	134	34
Burnsville	1,630	8	8	0
Butner	7,803	42	35	7
Candor	826	4	4	0
Canton	4,283	21	16	5
Cape Carteret	2,071	7	7	0
Carolina Beach	6,352	33	31	2
Carrboro	21,841	38	35	3
Carthage	2,488	12	11	1
Cary	170,518	231	190	41
Caswell Beach	425	4	4	0
Chadbourn	1,730	7	6	1
Chapel Hill	60,225	105	93	12
Charlotte-Mecklenburg[1]	931,235	2,342	1,817	525
Cherryville	6,012	19	14	5
China Grove	4,209	13	13	0
Chocowinity	792	3	3	0
Claremont	1,404	10	9	1
Clayton	22,258	47	44	3
Cleveland	876	4	4	0
Clinton	8,522	31	27	4
Clyde	1,290	5	5	0
Coats	2,484	6	6	0
Columbus	991	9	8	1
Concord	94,022	189	170	19
Conover	8,391	29	26	3
Conway	738	2	2	0
Cooleemee	965	1	1	0
Cornelius	29,850	73	59	14
Cramerton	4,405	14	13	1
Creedmoor	4,576	19	15	4
Dallas	4,732	17	12	5
Davidson	12,954	22	20	2
Dobson	1,552	7	7	0
Drexel	1,858	5	5	0
Duck	387	13	12	1
Dunn	9,793	43	38	5
Durham	273,759	641	530	111
East Bend	576	3	2	1
East Spencer	1,550	7	7	0
Eden	14,952	50	46	4
Edenton	4,671	18	16	2
Elizabeth City	17,629	63	53	10
Elizabethtown	3,452	18	17	1
Elkin	3,973	21	17	4
Elon	10,354	21	18	3
Emerald Isle	3,685	19	18	1
Enfield	2,322	10	9	1
Erwin	4,991	10	9	1
Fair Bluff	889	3	3	0
Fairmont	2,604	9	8	1
Farmville	4,712	23	16	7
Fayetteville	210,117	582	428	154
Fletcher	8,392	18	17	1
Forest City	7,175	33	31	2
Four Oaks	2,106	6	6	0
Foxfire Village	1,019	3	3	0
Franklin	4,025	18	17	1
Franklinton	2,148	9	9	0
Fremont	1,266	4	4	0
Fuquay-Varina	29,665	51	44	7
Garner	29,309	73	65	8
Garysburg	929	2	2	0
Gaston	1,034	2	2	0
Gastonia	77,316	193	169	24
Gibsonville	7,193	19	18	1
Glen Alpine	1,476	5	4	1
Goldsboro	35,159	108	96	12
Graham	14,886	39	36	3
Granite Falls	4,653	16	12	4
Granite Quarry	2,987	8	8	0
Greensboro	293,298	781	630	151
Greenville	93,235	232	187	45
Grifton	2,669	7	7	0
Hamlet	6,278	23	19	4

Table 78. Full-Time Law Enforcement Employees, by Selected State and City, 2018—Continued

(Number.)

State/city	Population	Total law enforcement employees	Total officers	Total civilians
Havelock	19,870	34	24	10
Haw River	2,497	8	8	0
Henderson	14,780	44	39	5
Hendersonville	14,081	57	42	15
Hertford	2,121	4	3	1
Hickory	40,701	138	106	32
Highlands	942	13	12	1
High Point	112,526	289	237	52
Hillsborough	7,323	29	27	2
Holden Beach	647	8	8	0
Holly Ridge	2,584	11	10	1
Holly Springs	37,008	67	52	15
Hope Mills	16,219	44	39	5
Hot Springs	576	1	1	0
Hudson	3,690	15	14	1
Huntersville	57,677	100	92	8
Indian Beach	117	5	5	0
Jackson	460	1	1	0
Jacksonville	71,715	154	121	33
Jefferson	1,519	6	6	0
Jonesville	2,226	8	7	1
Kannapolis	49,750	103	76	27
Kenansville	837	3	3	0
Kenly	1,544	8	8	0
Kernersville	24,571	83	66	17
Kill Devil Hills	7,179	34	28	6
King	6,911	24	21	3
Kings Mountain	10,808	39	32	7
Kinston	20,341	73	58	15
Kitty Hawk	3,529	18	16	2
Knightdale	16,588	34	32	2
Kure Beach	2,118	13	12	1
Lake Lure	1,148	10	9	1
Lake Royale	2,730	3	3	0
Lake Waccamaw	1,400	4	4	0
Landis	3,119	10	10	0
Laurel Park	2,338	7	7	0
Laurinburg	15,052	43	41	2
Leland	21,008	34	32	2
Lenoir	17,904	66	48	18
Lewiston Woodville	491	1	1	0
Lexington	18,754	65	55	10
Liberty	2,659	10	9	1
Lilesville	481	1	1	0
Lillington	3,639	14	13	1
Lincolnton	10,839	36	32	4
Littleton	603	3	3	0
Locust	3,214	13	13	0
Long View	4,889	15	15	0
Louisburg	3,549	16	15	1
Lowell	3,672	6	6	0
Lumberton	20,966	97	88	9
Madison	2,119	18	17	1
Maggie Valley	1,208	10	9	1
Magnolia	950	2	2	0
Maiden	3,431	16	15	1
Manteo	1,451	10	9	1
Marion	7,582	27	25	2
Marshall	907	4	4	0
Mars Hill	2,157	5	5	0
Marshville	2,728	11	11	0
Matthews	32,873	79	59	20
Maxton	2,375	10	6	4
Mayodan	2,399	15	15	0
Maysville	950	3	3	0
Mebane	15,566	39	35	4
Micro	515	1	1	0
Middlesex	824	4	4	0
Mint Hill	27,375	32	29	3
Misenheimer	669	5	5	0
Mocksville	5,303	23	22	1
Monroe	35,393	103	88	15
Montreat	766	4	4	0
Mooresville	38,340	108	84	24
Morehead City	9,393	43	38	5
Morganton	16,478	88	54	34
Morrisville	27,799	36	34	2
Mount Airy	10,208	51	40	11
Mount Gilead	1,159	7	7	0
Mount Holly	15,940	37	31	6
Mount Olive	4,656	18	17	1
Murfreesboro	2,984	9	8	1
Murphy	1,640	9	8	1
Nags Head	2,925	20	18	2
Nashville	5,485	16	15	1

Table 78. Full-Time Law Enforcement Employees, by Selected State and City, 2018—Continued

(Number.)

State/city	Population	Total law enforcement employees	Total officers	Total civilians
Navassa	1,963	3	3	0
New Bern	29,600	107	83	24
Newland	683	5	5	0
Newport	4,691	8	8	0
Newton	13,121	44	35	9
Newton Grove	562	3	3	0
Norlina	1,055	5	5	0
North Topsail Beach	723	14	13	1
Northwest	785	2	2	0
North Wilkesboro	4,277	26	25	1
Norwood	2,413	8	8	0
Oakboro	1,878	8	8	0
Oak Island	7,939	24	22	2
Ocean Isle Beach	624	14	13	1
Old Fort	916	4	4	0
Oriental	856	2	2	0
Oxford	8,793	29	27	2
Parkton	420	2	2	0
Pembroke	3,011	18	14	4
Pikeville	677	3	3	0
Pilot Mountain	1,427	9	8	1
Pinebluff	1,515	3	3	0
Pinehurst	16,213	30	25	5
Pine Knoll Shores	1,330	7	7	0
Pine Level	1,962	5	5	0
Pinetops	1,259	6	6	0
Pineville	8,939	50	39	11
Pink Hill	514	2	2	0
Pittsboro	4,289	12	12	0
Plymouth	3,448	13	12	1
Polkton	3,099	2	2	0
Princeton	1,355	4	4	0
Raeford	4,976	19	17	2
Raleigh	473,765	855	732	123
Ramseur	1,690	6	6	0
Randleman	4,133	16	16	0
Ranlo	3,623	9	8	1
Red Springs	3,397	16	14	2
Reidsville	13,774	49	43	6
Richlands	1,719	8	8	0
Rich Square	842	1	1	0
River Bend	3,057	6	6	0
Roanoke Rapids	14,664	43	36	7
Robbins	1,212	4	4	0
Robersonville	1,359	7	7	0
Rockingham	8,754	39	34	5
Rockwell	2,146	7	7	0
Rocky Mount	54,085	188	152	36
Rolesville	8,481	20	19	1
Rose Hill	1,636	6	6	0
Rowland	1,010	7	6	1
Roxboro	8,284	37	29	8
Rutherfordton	4,014	15	14	1
Salisbury	33,901	93	86	7
Saluda	695	4	4	0
Sanford	29,483	102	80	22
Scotland Neck	1,880	7	6	1
Seagrove	227	1	1	0
Selma	6,776	25	23	2
Seven Devils	206	6	6	0
Shallotte	4,183	15	14	1
Sharpsburg	2,016	4	4	0
Shelby	19,978	88	75	13
Siler City	8,225	17	13	4
Smithfield	12,507	41	37	4
Snow Hill	1,516	6	6	0
Southern Pines	14,271	49	41	8
Southern Shores	2,907	12	11	1
Southport	3,856	7	7	0
Sparta	1,741	6	6	0
Spencer	3,254	13	13	0
Spindale	4,203	11	11	0
Spring Hope	1,305	7	7	0
Spring Lake	12,744	30	27	3
Spruce Pine	2,130	10	10	0
Stallings	15,927	26	23	3
Stanfield	1,521	5	5	0
Stanley	3,727	13	12	1
Stantonsburg	780	4	4	0
Star	855	4	4	0
Statesville	26,975	96	74	22
Stoneville	1,243	4	4	0
St. Pauls	2,344	14	10	4
Sugar Mountain	197	5	5	0
Sunset Beach	3,943	13	13	0

Table 78. Full-Time Law Enforcement Employees, by Selected State and City, 2018—Continued

(Number.)

State/city	Population	Total law enforcement employees	Total officers	Total civilians
Surf City	2,412	21	20	1
Swansboro	3,292	10	9	1
Sylva	2,691	14	14	0
Tabor City	3,909	11	10	1
Tarboro	10,780	35	29	6
Taylorsville	2,192	13	13	0
Taylortown	838	2	2	0
Thomasville	26,591	74	68	6
Topsail Beach	428	10	9	1
Trent Woods	4,064	6	6	0
Troutman	2,714	13	13	0
Troy	3,275	13	12	1
Tryon	1,612	10	8	2
Valdese	4,427	12	11	1
Vanceboro	977	3	3	0
Vass	783	4	4	0
Wadesboro	5,207	25	21	4
Wagram	780	1	1	0
Wake Forest	44,318	91	71	20
Wallace	3,923	18	14	4
Walnut Creek	867	4	3	1
Warrenton	838	5	4	1
Warsaw	3,106	15	13	2
Washington	9,532	40	31	9
Waxhaw	16,112	24	22	2
Waynesville	9,991	44	34	10
Weaverville	3,946	15	14	1
Weldon	1,510	9	9	0
Wendell	7,485	16	15	1
West Jefferson	1,287	7	7	0
Whispering Pines	3,348	9	8	1
Whitakers	708	3	3	0
White Lake	762	6	6	0
Whiteville	5,401	26	25	1
Wilkesboro	3,482	25	23	2
Williamston	5,243	20	19	1
Wilmington	120,920	333	268	65
Wilson	49,367	127	111	16
Wilson's Mills	2,678	5	5	0
Windsor	3,259	9	9	0
Wingate	4,034	7	7	0
Winston-Salem	246,759	686	502	184
Winterville	9,712	21	20	1
Woodfin	6,541	15	15	0
Woodland	709	2	1	1
Wrightsville Beach	2,558	22	20	2
Yadkinville	2,879	14	13	1
Youngsville	1,331	12	11	1
Zebulon	5,396	22	21	1
NORTH DAKOTA				
Arnegard	158	2	2	0
Belfield	1,006	4	3	1
Berthold	503	1	1	0
Beulah	3,288	6	5	1
Bismarck	74,644	157	127	30
Bowman	1,661	5	4	1
Burlington	1,227	2	2	0
Carrington	2,007	5	5	0
Cavalier	1,264	3	3	0
Devils Lake	7,314	21	19	2
Dickinson	22,878	61	41	20
Ellendale	1,158	2	2	0
Emerado	453	1	1	0
Fargo	124,906	196	174	22
Fessenden	449	1	1	0
Grafton	4,216	10	9	1
Grand Forks	57,662	103	88	15
Harvey	1,715	3	3	0
Hazen	2,366	4	4	0
Jamestown	15,378	35	31	4
Kenmare	1,027	2	2	0
Killdeer	1,219	5	5	0
Lincoln	3,956	4	4	0
Lisbon	2,063	3	3	0
Mandan	22,743	41	35	6
Medora	135	2	2	0
Minot	48,829	106	83	23
Napoleon	773	1	1	0
New Town	2,626	8	7	1
Northwood	897	2	2	0
Oakes	1,703	3	3	0
Powers Lake	284	1	1	0
Ray	813	1	1	0
Rolla	1,314	3	3	0

Table 78. Full-Time Law Enforcement Employees, by Selected State and City, 2018—Continued

(Number.)

State/city	Population	Total law enforcement employees	Total officers	Total civilians
Rugby	2,679	5	5	0
Stanley	2,883	5	5	0
Steele	716	1	1	0
Surrey	1,453	3	3	0
Thompson	1,014	1	1	0
Tioga	1,542	5	3	2
Valley City	6,423	15	14	1
Wahpeton	7,836	17	15	2
Watford City	7,931	30	26	4
West Fargo	37,385	74	61	13
Williston	27,390	82	60	22
Wishek	927	2	2	0
OHIO				
Ada	5,556	9	8	1
Addyston	944	1	1	0
Akron	197,690	475	442	33
American Township	12,094	1	1	0
Amherst	12,100	26	19	7
Archbold	4,302	10	10	0
Ashland	20,446	37	30	7
Aurora	16,047	36	28	8
Austintown	35,029	56	40	16
Bainbridge Township	11,477	28	23	5
Barberton	26,060	44	42	2
Bath Township, Summit County	9,689	27	20	7
Bay Village	15,328	26	22	4
Beavercreek	47,203	67	50	17
Beaver Township	6,437	14	10	4
Bellefontaine	13,137	38	31	7
Belpre	6,402	16	11	5
Berea	18,838	32	30	2
Bethel	2,796	6	5	1
Bexley	13,893	36	31	5
Blanchester	4,246	7	7	0
Blue Ash	12,227	40	34	6
Bluffton	4,117	9	9	0
Boston Heights	1,297	9	9	0
Bowling Green	32,017	55	40	15
Brecksville	13,652	37	30	7
Brimfield Township	10,330	18	16	2
Brooklyn	10,759	35	31	4
Brunswick	34,954	52	40	12
Burton	1,454	3	3	0
Butler Township	7,802	18	17	1
Cambridge	10,369	32	26	6
Canal Fulton	5,450	12	11	1
Canfield	7,220	24	17	7
Canton	70,605	188	156	32
Carey	3,564	16	13	3
Carlisle	5,393	8	7	1
Catawba Island Township	3,540	5	5	0
Celina	10,273	21	16	5
Chagrin Falls	3,973	14	13	1
Chester Township	10,310	14	13	1
Cincinnati	301,952	1,167	1,032	135
Circleville	13,993	31	23	8
Clearcreek Township	15,765	20	14	6
Cleveland	384,666	1,675	1,462	213
Cleveland Heights	44,413	111	101	10
Clyde	6,182	20	16	4
Colerain Township	59,312	55	51	4
Columbiana	6,218	18	14	4
Columbus	892,576	2,255	1,870	385
Columbus Grove	2,068	3	3	0
Conneaut	12,616	25	18	7
Copley Township	17,307	23	22	1
Cortland	6,759	10	10	0
Covington	2,666	7	6	1
Cridersville	1,808	4	4	0
Dayton	140,094	424	358	66
Deer Park	5,671	14	10	4
Defiance	16,620	33	29	4
Delaware	39,944	58	51	7
Delhi Township	29,700	34	32	2
Dublin	48,570	107	71	36
East Cleveland	17,127	44	41	3
Eastlake	18,111	32	20	12
East Palestine	4,455	8	6	2
Elida	1,810	4	2	2
Elyria	53,796	94	80	14
Englewood	13,474	26	20	6
Evendale	2,863	22	20	2
Fairborn	33,604	72	48	24
Fairfield	42,568	78	59	19

Table 78. Full-Time Law Enforcement Employees, by Selected State and City, 2018—Continued

(Number.)

State/city	Population	Total law enforcement employees	Total officers	Total civilians
Fairfield Township	22,789	23	21	2
Fairview Park	16,248	29	27	2
Fayette	1,246	4	4	0
Findlay	41,351	82	65	17
Forest Park	18,686	43	36	7
Fort Loramie	1,522	2	2	0
Fostoria	13,232	25	21	4
Fremont	16,125	33	27	6
Gahanna	35,596	71	57	14
Garrettsville	2,315	5	5	0
Germantown	5,499	12	11	1
German Township, Montgomery County	2,886	6	6	0
Glenwillow	948	4	4	0
Grandview Heights	7,977	24	19	5
Greenhills	3,595	11	10	1
Green Springs	1,310	2	2	0
Greenville	12,707	32	24	8
Harrison	11,513	25	22	3
Heath	10,774	27	20	7
Hicksville	3,431	8	7	1
Highland Heights	8,438	29	22	7
Hilliard	37,184	76	63	13
Hiram	1,122	3	3	0
Holland	1,645	9	9	0
Huber Heights	37,969	68	52	16
Hunting Valley	725	11	11	0
Independence	7,135	45	32	13
Indian Hill	5,883	25	20	5
Kent	30,065	56	42	14
Kenton	8,114	16	16	0
Kirtland	6,819	14	9	5
Kirtland Hills	641	8	7	1
Lake Township	8,281	16	15	1
Lakewood	50,078	113	94	19
Lancaster	40,498	79	64	15
Lexington	4,666	14	10	4
Lordstown	3,252	13	9	4
Loudonville	2,621	8	7	1
Louisville	9,347	14	13	1
Lyndhurst	13,519	37	29	8
Macedonia	12,056	31	22	9
Mansfield	45,941	118	82	36
Mariemont	3,438	11	10	1
Mason	33,583	52	47	5
Mentor-on-the-Lake	7,399	13	8	5
Miamisburg	19,954	42	40	2
Middletown	48,837	104	68	36
Mifflin Township	2,620	5	5	0
Milan	1,331	3	3	0
Milford	6,914	20	18	2
Milton Township	2,446	4	4	0
Minerva Park	1,328	10	9	1
Mingo Junction	3,236	4	4	0
Mogadore	3,821	7	7	0
Monroe	16,310	41	32	9
Montgomery	10,807	24	21	3
Montpelier	3,934	10	9	1
Mount Healthy	6,058	14	11	3
Mount Vernon	16,607	34	31	3
Napoleon	8,236	20	16	4
Navarre	1,893	6	6	0
Newark	49,687	78	66	12
New Boston	2,103	14	10	4
New Bremen	2,972	7	7	0
Newcomerstown	3,756	8	5	3
New London	2,369	4	4	0
Newton Falls	4,516	5	5	0
Newtown	2,664	9	8	1
Niles	18,370	40	35	5
North Baltimore	3,545	5	5	0
North Olmsted	31,653	62	48	14
North Ridgeville	34,025	47	40	7
Northwood	5,421	23	18	5
Norton	12,003	17	16	1
Norwalk	16,800	30	24	6
Oak Harbor	2,716	9	6	3
Oak Hill	1,512	3	3	0
Oberlin	8,262	25	17	8
Olmsted Falls	8,912	10	10	0
Olmsted Township	13,425	16	16	0
Orrville	8,472	16	15	1
Ottawa	4,346	8	8	0
Owensville	821	3	3	0
Pandora	1,128	2	2	0
Peninsula	562	3	3	0

Table 78. Full-Time Law Enforcement Employees, by Selected State and City, 2018—Continued

(Number.)

State/city	Population	Total law enforcement employees	Total officers	Total civilians
Perkins Township	11,701	23	22	1
Perrysburg Township	12,935	31	24	7
Perry Township, Franklin County	3,773	12	11	1
Pierce Township	11,669	17	16	1
Plain City	4,401	10	9	1
Poland Township	11,888	12	12	0
Port Clinton	5,899	21	16	5
Powell	13,455	22	20	2
Reading	10,991	24	20	4
Reynoldsburg	38,126	75	57	18
Rittman	6,574	12	10	2
Roaming Shores Village	1,451	4	4	0
Rockford	1,107	2	2	0
Rossford	6,551	16	15	1
Ross Township	8,879	1	1	0
Russell Township	5,216	11	10	1
Sebring	4,217	11	7	4
Seven Hills	11,662	16	15	1
Shaker Heights	27,343	84	68	16
Sharonville	13,835	45	36	9
Shawnee Hills	804	5	5	0
Shawnee Township	12,061	18	12	6
Sidney	20,537	45	36	9
Silver Lake	2,496	9	8	1
Smithville	1,265	6	6	0
Solon	22,948	64	46	18
South Charleston	1,614	2	2	0
South Russell	3,781	9	9	0
South Zanesville	1,994	2	2	0
Springboro	18,789	29	25	4
Springfield	59,016	135	125	10
Springfield Township, Mahoning County	6,448	11	11	0
St. Clairsville	5,030	10	9	1
Steubenville	17,913	44	39	5
St. Henry	2,543	3	3	0
Streetsboro	16,411	37	29	8
Strongsville	44,819	91	74	17
Struthers	10,193	22	17	5
Sugarcreek	2,211	7	7	0
Sylvania	18,945	40	33	7
Tallmadge	17,550	28	25	3
Thornville	1,000	1	1	0
Tiffin	17,492	39	30	9
Toledo	275,023	686	590	96
Trotwood	24,380	31	29	2
Troy	25,960	46	43	3
Uhrichsville	5,343	9	9	0
Union Township, Clermont County	48,187	62	47	15
Urbana	11,337	19	17	2
Valley View, Cuyahoga County	2,005	21	19	2
Van Wert	10,631	28	21	7
Wadsworth	23,744	38	29	9
Walton Hills	2,298	15	11	4
Wapakoneta	9,771	19	14	5
Warren	39,280	75	70	5
Washington Court House	14,210	27	22	5
Waterville	5,490	12	11	1
Wauseon	7,345	18	15	3
West Carrollton	12,893	24	22	2
West Chester Township	62,063	109	84	25
Westlake	32,292	72	54	18
West Liberty	1,783	4	4	0
West Salem	1,477	2	2	0
West Union	3,141	5	4	1
Whitehall	19,024	70	50	20
Whitehouse	4,823	12	12	0
Wickliffe	12,734	39	29	10
Wilmington	12,386	31	22	9
Wooster	26,688	44	39	5
Worthington	14,805	42	33	9
Xenia	26,691	72	45	27
Yellow Springs	3,768	11	8	3
Zanesville	25,371	95	57	38
OKLAHOMA				
Achille	531	3	2	1
Ada	17,339	36	32	4
Allen	929	3	2	1
Altus	18,712	51	39	12
Alva	5,112	10	10	0
Amber	456	3	2	1
Anadarko	6,598	23	18	5
Antlers	2,300	10	5	5
Apache	1,411	2	2	0
Ardmore	24,817	56	51	5

Table 78. Full-Time Law Enforcement Employees, by Selected State and City, 2018—Continued

(Number.)

State/city	Population	Total law enforcement employees	Total officers	Total civilians
Arkoma	1,894	4	2	2
Atoka	3,086	15	15	0
Avant	302	1	1	0
Barnsdall	1,160	2	2	0
Bartlesville	36,473	79	57	22
Beaver	1,391	2	2	0
Beggs	1,245	6	4	2
Bennington	361	1	1	0
Bernice	577	2	2	0
Bethany	19,448	39	29	10
Big Cabin	252	3	2	1
Binger	642	2	1	1
Bixby	27,654	42	33	9
Blackwell	6,684	19	13	6
Blanchard	8,886	16	12	4
Boise City	1,071	2	2	0
Bokchito	678	6	5	1
Bokoshe	492	2	2	0
Boley	1,176	3	3	0
Boswell	687	1	1	0
Bristow	4,214	15	11	4
Broken Arrow	109,663	198	146	52
Broken Bow	4,069	18	12	6
Burns Flat	1,924	4	4	0
Cache	2,864	5	4	1
Caddo	1,076	3	3	0
Calera	2,338	13	10	3
Caney	198	4	3	1
Canton	594	3	3	0
Carnegie	1,664	6	3	3
Carney	662	1	1	0
Cashion	864	3	3	0
Catoosa	7,006	15	14	1
Cement	484	2	2	0
Chandler	3,127	13	9	4
Chattanooga	448	3	1	2
Checotah	3,138	14	10	4
Chelsea	1,913	4	4	0
Cherokee	1,568	3	3	0
Chickasha	16,314	31	24	7
Choctaw	12,724	18	17	1
Chouteau	2,076	9	8	1
Claremore	18,748	45	38	7
Clayton	793	6	2	4
Cleveland	3,164	8	8	0
Clinton	9,163	23	16	7
Coalgate	1,827	6	6	0
Colbert	1,231	3	2	1
Colcord	836	5	4	1
Collinsville	7,098	17	10	7
Comanche	1,554	5	5	0
Commerce	2,408	5	5	0
Cordell	2,757	5	4	1
Coweta	9,706	26	19	7
Crescent	1,539	6	4	2
Cushing	7,687	24	16	8
Cyril	1,032	1	1	0
Davenport	823	1	1	0
Davis	2,861	10	8	2
Del City	21,859	48	36	12
Depew	483	1	1	0
Dewar	862	2	2	0
Dewey	3,477	10	9	1
Dibble	862	3	3	0
Dickson	1,252	9	8	1
Drumright	2,832	5	5	0
Duncan	22,351	61	43	18
Durant	18,043	43	38	5
Earlsboro	647	3	3	0
Edmond	93,557	166	127	39
Elgin	3,279	5	5	0
Elk City	11,544	39	28	11
Elmore City	711	5	4	1
El Reno	19,272	59	38	21
Enid	50,214	119	93	26
Erick	993	2	2	0
Eufaula	2,898	12	8	4
Fairfax	1,287	3	1	2
Fairland	1,036	3	3	0
Fairview	2,623	9	5	4
Fletcher	1,139	1	1	0
Forest Park	1,080	4	2	2
Fort Cobb	618	1	1	0
Fort Gibson	4,021	12	11	1
Fort Towson	492	1	1	0

Table 78. Full-Time Law Enforcement Employees, by Selected State and City, 2018—Continued

(Number.)

State/city	Population	Total law enforcement employees	Total officers	Total civilians
Frederick	3,603	10	7	3
Gans	300	1	1	0
Geary	1,271	9	4	5
Glenpool	14,273	29	21	8
Goodwell	1,307	4	4	0
Gore	945	4	3	1
Grandfield	949	1	1	0
Granite	1,972	3	3	0
Grove	7,122	30	21	9
Guthrie	11,519	31	23	8
Guymon	11,546	22	14	8
Haileyville	760	2	2	0
Harrah	6,504	11	10	1
Hartshorne	1,952	4	4	0
Haskell	1,940	6	6	0
Healdton	2,708	4	4	0
Heavener	3,272	9	8	1
Hennessey	2,223	8	4	4
Henryetta	5,628	19	13	6
Hinton	3,247	6	6	0
Hobart	3,476	12	6	6
Holdenville	5,514	14	9	5
Hollis	1,872	10	6	4
Hominy	3,412	11	6	5
Hooker	1,923	3	3	0
Howe	788	2	1	1
Hugo	5,166	24	17	7
Hulbert	593	4	3	1
Hydro	943	3	3	0
Idabel	6,860	27	21	6
Jay	2,532	14	9	5
Jenks	23,473	28	21	7
Jennings	359	1	1	0
Jones	3,159	8	7	1
Kellyville	1,159	3	3	0
Kiefer	2,010	4	4	0
Kingfisher	4,912	15	12	3
Kingston	1,644	4	4	0
Kiowa	674	7	5	2
Konawa	1,232	3	3	0
Krebs	1,931	8	6	2
Lahoma	629	1	1	0
Lamont	400	2	2	0
Langley	819	3	3	0
Langston	1,845	3	2	1
Lawton	93,140	278	189	89
Lexington	2,150	9	4	5
Lindsay	2,818	14	8	6
Locust Grove	1,392	9	5	4
Lone Grove	5,090	9	7	2
Luther	1,772	5	5	0
Madill	3,957	12	11	1
Mangum	2,746	10	5	5
Mannford	3,195	11	8	3
Marietta	2,751	8	7	1
Marlow	4,410	10	10	0
Maud	1,064	2	2	0
Maysville	1,225	6	4	2
McAlester	17,999	46	43	3
McCurtain	508	5	3	2
McLoud	4,708	11	10	1
Medicine Park	454	2	2	0
Meeker	1,163	5	5	0
Miami	13,162	32	30	2
Midwest City	57,710	125	96	29
Minco	1,635	5	5	0
Moore	62,453	91	86	5
Mooreland	1,204	3	2	1
Morris	1,445	3	3	0
Mounds	1,253	2	2	0
Mountain View	740	2	2	0
Muldrow	3,203	12	7	5
Muskogee	37,659	93	86	7
Mustang	21,809	37	25	12
Nash	198	1	1	0
Newcastle	10,266	23	16	7
Newkirk	2,207	3	3	0
Nichols Hills	3,912	22	16	6
Nicoma Park	2,492	6	6	0
Ninnekah	1,037	3	3	0
Noble	6,772	17	12	5
Norman	124,577	239	176	63
North Enid	928	4	4	0
Nowata	3,635	8	5	3
Oilton	1,015	3	3	0

Table 78. Full-Time Law Enforcement Employees, by Selected State and City, 2018—Continued

(Number.)

State/city	Population	Total law enforcement employees	Total officers	Total civilians
Okarche	1,338	5	5	0
Okemah	3,190	14	9	5
Oklahoma City	652,936	1,382	1,102	280
Okmulgee	11,919	27	24	3
Olustee	567	1	1	0
Oologah	1,172	5	5	0
Owasso	37,220	76	56	20
Paoli	617	2	2	0
Pauls Valley	6,180	20	15	5
Pawhuska	3,349	13	9	4
Pawnee	2,128	5	5	0
Perkins	2,842	8	8	0
Perry	4,908	19	12	7
Piedmont	8,080	12	10	2
Pocola	4,072	11	7	4
Ponca City	24,066	66	44	22
Pond Creek	834	2	2	0
Porum	707	3	3	0
Poteau	8,913	33	26	7
Prague	2,415	13	8	5
Pryor Creek	9,369	33	25	8
Purcell	6,470	23	18	5
Quinton	985	3	3	0
Ramona	550	3	2	1
Ringling	977	2	2	0
Roland	3,794	12	9	3
Rush Springs	1,254	4	4	0
Salina	1,385	6	6	0
Sallisaw	8,427	31	23	8
Sand Springs	20,056	42	32	10
Sapulpa	20,948	55	43	12
Savanna	653	6	5	1
Sawyer	315	3	2	1
Sayre	4,508	11	6	5
Seminole	7,237	15	12	3
Shady Point	993	1	1	0
Shattuck	1,284	1	1	0
Shawnee	31,422	87	67	20
Skiatook	8,020	24	19	5
Snyder	1,295	6	3	3
South Coffeyville	748	5	5	0
Spencer	4,009	4	3	1
Sperry	1,315	3	3	0
Spiro	2,164	4	4	0
Sportsmen Acres	309	1	1	0
Stigler	2,742	11	9	2
Stillwater	50,445	116	78	38
Stilwell	4,007	23	14	9
Stonewall	476	4	2	2
Stratford	1,541	4	4	0
Stringtown	402	3	3	0
Stroud	2,747	14	9	5
Sulphur	5,005	11	9	2
Tahlequah	16,877	49	40	9
Talala	275	2	2	0
Talihina	1,076	10	5	5
Tecumseh	6,628	12	11	1
Texhoma	939	2	2	0
Thackerville	483	2	2	0
The Village	9,475	27	22	5
Thomas	1,200	2	2	0
Tipton	772	2	2	0
Tishomingo	3,077	8	7	1
Tonkawa	3,040	11	8	3
Tryon	501	1	1	0
Tulsa	403,147	987	807	180
Tupelo	311	2	2	0
Tushka	304	3	3	0
Tuttle	7,318	17	12	5
Tyrone	778	1	1	0
Union City	2,125	9	9	0
Valley Brook	774	10	9	1
Valliant	734	4	4	0
Velma	596	2	2	0
Verden	525	2	2	0
Verdigris	4,580	7	6	1
Vian	1,363	5	5	0
Vici	708	2	2	0
Vinita	5,348	23	16	7
Wagoner	8,986	21	16	5
Wakita	332	1	1	0
Walters	2,399	4	4	0
Warner	1,605	4	4	0
Warr Acres	10,372	31	25	6
Washington	662	3	2	1

Table 78. Full-Time Law Enforcement Employees, by Selected State and City, 2018—Continued

(Number.)

State/city	Population	Total law enforcement employees	Total officers	Total civilians
Watonga	2,848	9	7	2
Watts	308	2	1	1
Waukomis	1,314	4	4	0
Waurika	1,937	2	2	0
Waynoka	931	3	3	0
Weatherford	11,981	38	23	15
Webbers Falls	601	5	4	1
Weleetka	969	8	6	2
West Siloam Springs	867	12	11	1
Westville	1,534	9	5	4
Wetumka	1,192	6	2	4
Wewoka	3,300	7	6	1
Wilburton	2,615	7	6	1
Wilson	1,707	4	4	0
Wister	1,056	2	2	0
Woodward	12,323	23	21	2
Wright City	736	2	2	0
Wyandotte	329	5	4	1
Wynnewood	2,218	5	4	1
Yale	1,200	7	4	3
Yukon	27,452	64	46	18
OREGON				
Albany	53,973	96	64	32
Amity	1,699	9	2	7
Ashland	21,269	35	28	7
Astoria	9,918	26	16	10
Aumsville	4,186	7	6	1
Baker City	9,779	14	12	2
Bandon	3,119	7	7	0
Beaverton	98,616	183	142	41
Bend	97,403	133	101	32
Black Butte		7	6	1
Boardman	3,343	11	10	1
Brookings	6,453	21	14	7
Burns	2,768	4	4	0
Canby	17,914	29	25	4
Cannon Beach	1,733	10	8	2
Carlton	2,168	4	3	1
Central Point	18,402	33	26	7
Coburg	1,117	4	3	1
Columbia City	2,043	8	5	3
Coos Bay	16,343	34	22	12
Coquille	3,909	8	7	1
Corvallis	58,491	93	58	35
Cottage Grove	10,241	30	17	13
Dallas	16,561	26	20	6
Eagle Point	9,236	12	11	1
Enterprise	1,952	4	4	0
Eugene	170,771	306	181	125
Florence	9,016	20	13	7
Forest Grove	24,560	35	29	6
Gearhart	1,613	3	3	0
Gervais	2,742	6	5	1
Gladstone	12,310	19	17	2
Gold Beach	2,286	9	6	3
Grants Pass	37,814	91	62	29
Gresham	111,797	163	132	31
Hermiston	17,517	33	27	6
Hillsboro	109,121	182	135	47
Hood River	7,767	16	14	2
Hubbard	3,549	4	3	1
Independence	10,280	19	14	5
Jacksonville	2,910	6	5	1
John Day	1,657	10	10	0
Junction City	6,214	9	7	2
Keizer	39,727	47	39	8
King City	4,014	8	7	1
Klamath Falls	22,242	40	36	4
La Grande	13,186	29	18	11
Lake Oswego	39,557	65	42	23
Lakeview	2,299	2	1	1
Lebanon	17,080	39	27	12
Lincoln City	8,998	35	25	10
Madras	6,919	11	10	1
Malin	808	7	7	0
Manzanita	659	4	4	0
McMinnville	34,669	48	42	6
Medford	82,800	150	104	46
Milton-Freewater	7,021	17	11	6
Milwaukie	20,873	42	37	5
Molalla	9,322	17	15	2
Monmouth	10,457	14	13	1
Mount Angel	3,559	7	5	2
Myrtle Creek	3,483	9	7	2

Table 78. Full-Time Law Enforcement Employees, by Selected State and City, 2018—Continued

(Number.)

State/city	Population	Total law enforcement employees	Total officers	Total civilians
Myrtle Point	2,533	6	5	1
Newberg-Dundee	27,122	45	32	13
Newport	10,684	29	22	7
North Bend	9,705	31	24	7
North Plains	2,190	3	3	0
Nyssa	3,166	8	7	1
Oakridge	3,308	7	5	2
Ontario	10,958	25	21	4
Oregon City	36,918	54	46	8
Pendleton	16,681	29	24	5
Philomath	4,787	9	8	1
Phoenix	4,597	11	9	2
Pilot Rock	1,504	3	3	0
Portland	657,260	1,177	922	255
Port Orford	1,143	5	5	0
Prineville	10,184	32	19	13
Rainier	1,992	6	5	1
Redmond	30,597	48	39	9
Reedsport	4,117	18	11	7
Rockaway Beach	1,414	3	3	0
Rogue River	2,318	8	5	3
Roseburg	22,366	36	32	4
Salem	172,022	318	190	128
Sandy	11,382	18	15	3
Scappoose	7,345	11	10	1
Seaside	6,745	25	19	6
Sherwood	19,647	25	22	3
Silverton	10,477	19	17	2
Stanfield	2,085	3	3	0
Stayton	8,195	13	11	2
St. Helens	13,800	19	17	2
Sunriver		12	11	1
Sutherlin	8,052	18	14	4
Sweet Home	9,712	22	15	7
Talent	6,556	10	8	2
The Dalles	15,740	27	23	4
Tigard	53,880	89	72	17
Tillamook	5,295	9	8	1
Toledo	3,625	11	6	5
Tualatin	27,671	46	38	8
Turner	2,131	2	2	0
Umatilla	7,162	11	9	2
Vernonia	2,251	4	3	1
Warrenton	5,688	13	12	1
West Linn	26,934	31	28	3
Winston	5,463	10	8	2
Woodburn	26,031	40	32	8
Yamhill	1,175	9	3	6
PENNSYLVANIA				
Abington Township, Montgomery County	55,631	109	89	20
Adams Township, Butler County	14,105	14	14	0
Adams Township, Cambria County	5,581	5	5	0
Akron	4,015	5	5	0
Albion	1,466	1	1	0
Alburtis	2,663	4	4	0
Aldan	4,157	5	5	0
Aleppo Township	1,876	17	14	3
Aliquippa	8,946	17	16	1
Allegheny Township, Blair County	6,573	8	7	1
Allegheny Township, Westmoreland County	8,093	10	9	1
Allentown	121,743	232	211	21
Altoona	43,840	66	58	8
Ambler	6,532	13	12	1
Ambridge	6,679	11	11	0
Amity Township	13,076	14	13	1
Annville Township	4,968	10	8	2
Archbald	6,947	18	18	0
Arnold	4,868	8	8	0
Ashland	2,680	2	2	0
Ashley	2,709	4	4	0
Aspinwall	2,722	5	5	0
Aston Township	16,708	18	16	2
Athens	3,192	5	4	1
Athens Township	5,079	11	10	1
Avalon	4,569	6	5	1
Avis	1,500	2	2	0
Avoca	2,625	2	2	0
Baden	3,928	3	3	0
Baldwin Borough	19,586	25	24	1
Baldwin Township	1,932	5	5	0
Bally	1,275	2	2	0
Bangor	5,222	11	10	1
Beaver	4,320	10	9	1

Table 78. Full-Time Law Enforcement Employees, by Selected State and City, 2018—Continued

(Number.)

State/city	Population	Total law enforcement employees	Total officers	Total civilians
Beaver Falls	9,588	19	18	1
Beaver Meadows	832	1	1	0
Bedford	2,709	4	4	0
Bedminster Township	7,241	7	6	1
Bell Acres	1,387	3	3	0
Bellefonte	6,325	13	10	3
Bellevue	8,130	16	13	3
Bellwood	1,735	3	3	0
Ben Avon	1,750	17	14	3
Ben Avon Heights	364	17	14	3
Bensalem Township	60,588	127	100	27
Bentleyville	2,492	1	1	0
Berlin	1,973	2	2	0
Bern Township	7,025	12	12	0
Bernville	956	1	1	0
Berwick	10,030	18	16	2
Bethel Park	32,417	44	38	6
Bethel Township, Berks County	4,154	3	3	0
Bethlehem	75,809	165	145	20
Bethlehem Township	23,983	35	34	1
Biglerville	1,213	2	2	0
Birdsboro	5,167	8	7	1
Birmingham Township	4,201	3	3	0
Blairsville	3,248	5	5	0
Blair Township	4,503	5	5	0
Blakely	6,201	6	6	0
Blawnox	1,391	3	3	0
Bloomsburg Town	14,145	23	18	5
Blossburg	1,478	2	2	0
Bonneauville	1,824	1	1	0
Boyertown	4,058	8	7	1
Brackenridge	3,168	2	2	0
Braddock Hills	1,824	2	2	0
Bradford	8,244	18	18	0
Bradford Township	4,724	5	5	0
Branch Township	1,747	2	2	0
Brecknock Township, Berks County	4,640	14	14	0
Brentwood	9,364	15	13	2
Briar Creek Township	2,974	4	4	0
Bridgeport	4,596	8	7	1
Bridgeville	5,005	9	8	1
Bridgewater	772	2	2	0
Brighton Township	8,297	11	11	0
Bristol	9,618	16	14	2
Bristol Township	53,684	71	62	9
Brockway	2,004	3	2	1
Brookhaven	8,042	8	7	1
Brookville	3,807	8	7	1
Brownsville	2,238	2	2	0
Bryn Athyn	1,409	4	4	0
Buckingham Township	20,311	24	22	2
Buffalo Township	7,294	5	5	0
Buffalo Valley Regional	12,660	15	14	1
Bushkill Township	8,528	16	15	1
Butler	13,017	24	23	1
Butler Township, Butler County	16,542	23	21	2
Butler Township, Luzerne County	9,788	12	11	1
Butler Township, Schuylkill County	5,625	13	4	9
Caernarvon Township, Berks County	4,129	8	7	1
California	6,738	7	6	1
Caln Township	14,316	24	22	2
Cambria Township	5,768	4	4	0
Cambridge Springs	2,648	3	3	0
Camp Hill	7,946	12	11	1
Canonsburg	8,815	18	16	2
Canton	1,881	1	1	0
Carbondale	8,386	10	10	0
Carlisle	19,335	34	31	3
Carnegie	7,888	14	13	1
Carrolltown	796	6	6	0
Carroll Township, Washington County	5,481	3	3	0
Carroll Township, York County	6,440	12	12	0
Carroll Valley	3,928	5	4	1
Castle Shannon	8,153	15	14	1
Catasauqua	6,619	8	7	1
Catawissa	1,484	3	3	0
Cecil Township	12,633	21	20	1
Center Township	11,439	20	19	1
Centerville	3,159	2	2	0
Central Berks Regional	13,309	21	20	1
Central Bucks Regional	15,584	30	27	3
Chambersburg	20,962	37	34	3
Charleroi Regional	6,519	9	8	1
Chartiers Township	7,937	12	12	0
Cheltenham Township	37,501	79	71	8

Table 78. Full-Time Law Enforcement Employees, by Selected State and City, 2018—Continued

(Number.)

State/city	Population	Total law enforcement employees	Total officers	Total civilians
Chester	34,087	96	87	9
Chester Township	4,102	13	12	1
Cheswick	1,697	1	1	0
Chippewa Township	7,995	9	8	1
Churchill	2,928	9	9	0
Clairton	6,587	8	8	0
Clarion	5,316	9	8	1
Clarks Summit	6,210	5	5	0
Clearfield	5,874	11	7	4
Cleona	2,197	4	4	0
Clifton Heights	6,709	11	10	1
Clymer	1,272	1	1	0
Coaldale	2,150	3	3	0
Coal Township	10,329	12	11	1
Cochranton	1,090	2	2	0
Colebrookdale District	6,014	11	9	2
Collegeville	5,134	8	8	0
Collier Township	8,324	17	16	1
Collingdale	8,793	9	8	1
Colonial Regional	17,966	27	25	2
Columbia	10,436	22	19	3
Conemaugh Township, Cambria County	1,854	1	1	0
Conemaugh Township, Somerset County	6,865	6	6	0
Conewago Township, Adams County	7,184	10	9	1
Conewango Township	3,362	4	4	0
Conneaut Lake Regional	3,482	4	3	1
Connellsville	7,331	16	15	1
Conoy Township	3,484	19	17	2
Conshohocken	8,081	19	19	0
Conway	2,090	4	4	0
Conyngham	1,860	3	3	0
Coopersburg	2,509	7	7	0
Coplay	3,274	6	5	1
Coraopolis	5,510	13	9	4
Cornwall	4,326	6	5	1
Corry	6,311	11	10	1
Coudersport	2,430	4	4	0
Covington Township	2,243	2	2	0
Crafton	6,223	10	9	1
Cranberry Township	31,154	34	31	3
Crescent Township	2,569	3	3	0
Cresson	1,576	10	10	0
Cresson Township	2,536	5	4	1
Croyle Township	2,232	1	1	0
Cumberland Township, Adams County	6,236	6	6	0
Cumberland Township, Greene County	6,221	5	5	0
Cumru Township	15,387	25	24	1
Curwensville	2,397	4	3	1
Dallas	2,753	4	4	0
Dallas Township	9,259	11	10	1
Dalton	1,190	2	2	0
Danville	4,621	9	7	2
Darby	10,702	18	17	1
Darby Township	9,282	15	14	1
Decatur Township	4,660	1	1	0
Delmont	2,570	4	4	0
Derry	2,540	2	2	0
Derry Township, Dauphin County	25,131	59	40	19
Dickson City	5,761	8	7	1
Donegal Township	3,252	2	2	0
Donora	4,584	6	6	0
Dormont	8,347	14	13	1
Douglass Township, Berks County	3,597	6	6	0
Douglass Township, Montgomery County	10,644	13	12	1
Downingtown	7,933	19	16	3
Doylestown Township	17,430	22	20	2
Dublin Borough	2,149	3	2	1
DuBois	7,409	14	13	1
Duboistown	1,180	1	1	0
Duncansville	1,174	1	1	0
Dunmore	12,933	20	20	0
Dunnstable Township	1,011	2	2	0
Dupont	2,670	2	2	0
Duquesne	5,544	13	13	0
Duryea	4,857	3	3	0
East Bangor	1,705	1	1	0
East Berlin	1,539	3	1	2
East Brandywine Township	8,765	14	13	1
East Coventry Township	6,778	8	7	1
East Deer Township	1,450	1	1	0
East Earl Township	6,903	8	8	0
Eastern Adams Regional	7,379	6	6	0
Eastern Pike Regional	4,604	11	10	1
East Fallowfield Township	7,584	7	7	0
East Franklin Township	3,854	1	1	0

Table 78. Full-Time Law Enforcement Employees, by Selected State and City, 2018—Continued

(Number.)

State/city	Population	Total law enforcement employees	Total officers	Total civilians
East Hempfield Township	24,694	37	33	4
East Lampeter Township	17,133	39	36	3
East Lansdowne	2,670	5	3	2
East Marlborough Township	7,416	1	1	0
East McKeesport	2,636	3	3	0
East Norriton Township	14,085	29	27	2
Easton	27,158	66	61	5
East Pennsboro Township	21,750	22	21	1
East Pikeland Township	7,345	9	9	0
East Pittsburgh	1,768	1	1	0
Easttown Township	10,668	14	13	1
East Union Township	1,586	2	2	0
East Vincent Township	7,232	7	7	0
East Whiteland Township	12,085	19	17	2
Ebensburg	3,093	5	5	0
Economy	9,205	13	12	1
Eddystone	2,412	10	9	1
Edgewood	3,022	9	9	0
Edgeworth	1,653	13	4	9
Edinboro	5,902	8	8	0
Edwardsville	4,687	5	5	0
Elizabeth	1,980	2	2	0
Elizabethtown	11,591	19	17	2
Elizabeth Township	13,087	12	12	0
Elkland	1,736	2	2	0
Ellwood City	7,445	12	10	2
Emmaus	11,490	22	20	2
Emporium	1,851	2	2	0
Emsworth	2,379	17	14	3
Ephrata	13,956	38	34	4
Erie	96,758	198	174	24
Etna	3,348	7	6	1
Evans City-Seven Fields Regional	4,488	3	3	0
Everett	1,737	3	3	0
Everson	760	2	2	0
Exeter Township, Berks County	25,956	33	31	2
Exeter Township, Luzerne County	2,358	1	1	0
Fairview Township, Luzerne County	4,485	7	7	0
Fairview Township, York County	17,555	18	15	3
Falls Township, Bucks County	33,854	61	53	8
Farrell	4,651	14	13	1
Fawn Township	2,326	2	1	1
Ferguson Township	19,551	24	22	2
Ferndale	1,503	2	2	0
Findlay Township	5,867	24	17	7
Fleetwood	4,087	6	6	0
Folcroft	6,615	12	11	1
Ford City	2,788	1	1	0
Forest City	1,770	2	2	0
Forest Hills	6,331	9	9	0
Forks Township	15,545	22	21	1
Forty Fort	4,092	5	5	0
Forward Township	3,295	1	1	0
Foster Township, McKean County	4,080	5	5	0
Fountain Hill	4,721	11	10	1
Fox Chapel	5,297	11	11	0
Frackville	3,624	5	5	0
Franconia Township	13,343	12	11	1
Franklin	6,081	23	17	6
Franklin Park	14,706	13	12	1
Franklin Township, Beaver County	3,893	4	4	0
Franklin Township, Carbon County	4,132	4	4	0
Franklin Township, Columbia County	585	5	5	0
Frazer Township	1,130	2	2	0
Freedom Township	3,352	3	3	0
Freeland	3,441	4	4	0
Freemansburg	2,620	3	3	0
Galeton	1,095	1	1	0
Gallitzin	1,779	6	6	0
Geistown	2,281	3	3	0
Gettysburg	7,637	12	11	1
Girard	2,959	4	4	0
Glassport	4,351	7	7	0
Glenolden	7,163	11	10	1
Granville Township	5,000	10	8	2
Greencastle	4,030	5	4	1
Greene County Regional Police Department	4,492	1	1	0
Greenfield Township	2,004	1	1	0
Greenfield Township, Blair County	3,981	2	2	0
Greensburg	14,217	38	28	10
Green Tree	4,966	11	10	1
Greenville	5,472	8	7	1
Grove City	7,969	12	11	1
Hamburg	4,427	7	6	1

Table 78. Full-Time Law Enforcement Employees, by Selected State and City, 2018—Continued

(Number.)

State/city	Population	Total law enforcement employees	Total officers	Total civilians
Hampden Township	30,399	26	25	1
Hampton Township	18,318	19	18	1
Hanover	15,653	28	25	3
Hanover Township, Luzerne County	10,843	17	16	1
Harmar Township	3,046	9	8	1
Harmony Township	3,033	5	5	0
Harrisburg	49,147	168	139	29
Harrison Township	10,353	21	18	3
Harveys Lake	2,782	2	2	0
Hastings	2,154	1	1	0
Hatboro	7,446	18	14	4
Hatfield Township	21,048	29	27	2
Haverford Township	49,422	82	70	12
Hazleton	24,637	44	40	4
Hegins Township	3,391	2	2	0
Heidelberg	1,219	3	3	0
Heidelberg Township, Berks County	1,742	1	1	0
Hellam Township	8,645	12	12	0
Hellertown	5,840	11	10	1
Hemlock Township	2,242	9	9	0
Hempfield Township, Mercer County	3,614	7	6	1
Hermitage	15,531	33	30	3
Highspire	2,369	15	15	0
Hilltown Township	15,467	20	17	3
Hollidaysburg	5,763	10	8	2
Homer City	1,597	2	2	0
Homestead	3,162	14	13	1
Honesdale	4,208	5	5	0
Honey Brook	1,752	1	1	0
Hooversville	601	1	1	0
Hopewell Township	12,711	16	15	1
Horsham Township	26,615	48	40	8
Houston	1,239	2	2	0
Hughestown	1,373	1	1	0
Hughesville	2,050	3	3	0
Hummelstown	4,648	7	6	1
Huntingdon	6,946	12	12	0
Independence Township, Beaver County	2,409	2	2	0
Indiana	13,039	22	20	2
Indiana Township	7,195	10	10	0
Indian Lake	380	1	1	0
Ingram	3,236	4	4	0
Irwin	3,758	4	4	0
Jackson Township, Butler County	3,953	10	8	2
Jackson Township, Cambria County	4,083	2	2	0
Jackson Township, Luzerne County	4,631	2	2	0
Jeannette	9,127	17	14	3
Jefferson Hills Borough	11,309	16	15	1
Jefferson Township, Mercer County	1,829	2	2	0
Jenkins Township	4,475	4	4	0
Jenkintown	4,442	17	17	0
Jermyn	2,053	2	2	0
Jim Thorpe	4,613	8	7	1
Johnsonburg	2,291	3	3	0
Johnstown	20,877	43	38	5
Kane	3,489	3	3	0
Kenhorst	2,874	182	160	22
Kennedy Township	8,183	10	8	2
Kennett Square	6,192	16	13	3
Kennett Township	8,317	9	8	1
Kidder Township	1,919	5	5	0
Kilbuck Township	721	17	14	3
Kingston	12,836	21	19	2
Kingston Township	6,898	11	11	0
Kiskiminetas Township	4,496	9	9	0
Kittanning	3,764	9	8	1
Kline Township	1,366	2	1	1
Knox	1,074	2	2	0
Koppel	723	2	2	0
Kulpmont	2,787	1	1	0
Kutztown	5,066	14	12	2
Lake City	2,906	2	2	0
Lancaster	59,761	163	139	24
Lancaster Township, Butler County	2,577	3	3	0
Langhorne Borough	1,592	1	1	0
Lansdale	16,633	32	23	9
Lansdowne	10,650	18	15	3
Lansford	3,778	6	6	0
Larksville	4,390	7	7	0
Latimore Township	2,613	1	1	0
Latrobe	7,896	14	13	1
Laureldale	3,899	5	5	0
Lawrence Park Township	3,794	9	8	1
Lawrence Township, Clearfield County	7,581	9	8	1
Lebanon	25,816	44	41	3

Table 78. Full-Time Law Enforcement Employees, by Selected State and City, 2018—Continued

(Number.)

State/city	Population	Total law enforcement employees	Total officers	Total civilians
Leechburg	2,002	3	3	0
Leetsdale	1,183	5	5	0
Leet Township	1,585	5	5	0
Lehighton	5,277	12	11	1
Lehigh Township, Northampton County	10,479	13	12	1
Lehman Township	3,470	4	4	0
Lewistown	8,188	12	11	1
Liberty	2,477	1	1	0
Liberty Township, Adams County	1,252	1	1	0
Ligonier	1,525	2	2	0
Ligonier Township	6,400	6	6	0
Limerick Township	19,144	32	30	2
Lincoln	1,038	2	2	0
Linesville	992	7	7	0
Lititz	9,448	17	15	2
Littlestown	4,489	9	8	1
Lock Haven	9,218	12	10	2
Locust Township	1,399	5	5	0
Logan Township	12,364	18	16	2
Loretto	1,289	5	5	0
Lower Allen Township	19,539	25	22	3
Lower Burrell	11,155	18	17	1
Lower Chichester Township	3,471	5	5	0
Lower Frederick Township	4,884	4	4	0
Lower Gwynedd Township	11,543	19	18	1
Lower Heidelberg Township	6,071	11	10	1
Lower Makefield Township	32,768	42	38	4
Lower Merion Township	59,262	149	133	16
Lower Moreland Township	13,204	12	9	3
Lower Paxton Township	49,296	65	58	7
Lower Pottsgrove Township	12,128	19	17	2
Lower Providence Township	27,051	33	31	2
Lower Salford Township	15,440	21	19	2
Lower Saucon Township	10,824	17	15	2
Lower Southampton Township	19,230	33	30	3
Lower Swatara Township	8,904	14	13	1
Lower Windsor Township	7,574	10	9	1
Lykens	1,770	1	1	0
Macungie	3,179	4	4	0
Mahanoy City	3,958	4	4	0
Mahanoy Township	3,186	1	1	0
Mahoning Township, Carbon County	4,209	6	6	0
Mahoning Township, Lawrence County	2,911	1	1	0
Mahoning Township, Montour County	4,163	7	6	1
Malvern	3,510	8	7	1
Manheim	4,890	18	17	1
Manheim Township	40,395	76	64	12
Manor	3,369	3	3	0
Manor Township, Armstrong County	4,074	1	1	0
Manor Township, Lancaster County	21,090	21	19	2
Mansfield	3,034	5	5	0
Marcus Hook	2,402	5	4	1
Marietta	2,627	19	17	2
Marion Township, Beaver County	878	2	2	0
Marlborough Township	3,366	3	3	0
Marple Township	23,872	32	29	3
Mars	1,628	1	1	0
Martinsburg	1,873	2	2	0
Marysville	2,553	2	2	0
Masontown	3,305	5	5	0
Mayfield	1,697	2	2	0
McAdoo	2,166	4	4	0
McCandless	28,475	30	28	2
McDonald Borough	2,066	5	4	1
McKeesport	20,915	55	52	3
McKees Rocks	5,929	9	8	1
McSherrystown	3,076	4	4	0
Meadville	12,917	28	22	6
Mechanicsburg	9,021	16	15	1
Media	5,367	22	14	8
Mercer	1,876	5	5	0
Mercersburg	1,552	2	2	0
Meshoppen	1,442	2	2	0
Middleburg	1,308	3	2	1
Middlesex Township, Butler County	5,636	4	4	0
Middlesex Township, Cumberland County	7,499	10	9	1
Middletown	9,319	13	12	1
Middletown Township	45,185	63	57	6
Midland	2,495	3	3	0
Mifflinburg	3,512	10	9	1
Mifflin County Regional	16,941	13	13	0
Milford	973	2	2	0
Millbourne	1,159	1	1	0
Millcreek Township, Erie County	53,422	81	63	18

Table 78. Full-Time Law Enforcement Employees, by Selected State and City, 2018—Continued

(Number.)

State/city	Population	Total law enforcement employees	Total officers	Total civilians
Millcreek Township, Lebanon County	5,714	2	2	0
Millersburg	2,541	3	2	1
Millersville	8,380	15	13	2
Millvale	3,635	6	6	0
Milton	6,819	9	8	1
Minersville	4,160	6	6	0
Mohnton	3,064	4	4	0
Monaca	5,492	8	8	0
Monessen	7,287	12	11	1
Monongahela	4,125	8	7	1
Monroeville	27,628	56	45	11
Montgomery	1,518	1	1	0
Montgomery Township	26,299	45	36	9
Montoursville	4,420	7	6	1
Montour Township	1,299	3	3	0
Montrose	1,484	4	4	0
Moon Township	25,758	34	29	5
Moore Township	9,343	11	10	1
Morris-Cooper Regional		1	1	0
Morrisville	8,557	13	11	2
Morton	2,686	5	4	1
Moscow	1,927	3	3	0
Mount Carmel	5,618	8	8	0
Mount Carmel Township	3,007	6	6	0
Mount Gretna Borough	206	6	5	1
Mount Holly Springs	2,049	3	3	0
Mount Joy	8,332	13	12	1
Mount Lebanon	32,239	54	45	9
Mount Oliver	3,303	10	10	0
Mount Pleasant	4,273	3	3	0
Mount Pleasant Township	3,503	5	5	0
Mount Union	2,367	5	5	0
Muhlenberg Township	20,303	31	29	2
Muncy	2,419	3	3	0
Muncy Township	1,063	2	2	0
Munhall	11,123	25	23	2
Murrysville	19,759	23	21	2
Nanticoke	10,253	15	14	1
Nanty Glo	2,512	1	1	0
Narberth	4,363	7	6	1
Nazareth	5,706	7	6	1
Neshannock Township	9,223	7	7	0
Nesquehoning	3,231	4	4	0
Nether Providence Township	13,770	16	15	1
Neville Township	1,057	17	14	3
Newberry Township	15,749	18	16	2
New Bethlehem	2,716	3	3	0
New Brighton	8,807	9	7	2
New Britain Township	11,252	15	14	1
New Cumberland	7,323	10	9	1
New Florence	653	1	1	0
New Hanover Township	13,201	10	9	1
New Holland	5,507	14	13	1
New Hope	2,515	11	9	2
New Kensington	12,377	22	22	0
Newport Township	5,386	2	2	0
New Sewickley Township	7,249	11	10	1
Newtown	2,251	5	5	0
Newtown Township, Bucks County	22,880	32	28	4
Newtown Township, Delaware County	13,571	20	18	2
Newville	1,345	2	2	0
New Wilmington	2,188	5	5	0
Norristown	34,531	81	69	12
Northampton	9,884	14	12	2
Northampton Township	39,289	49	43	6
North Belle Vernon	1,861	2	2	0
North Braddock	4,713	3	3	0
North Catasauqua	2,837	5	5	0
North Cornwall Township	7,868	9	9	0
North Coventry Township	8,012	12	11	1
North East, Erie County	4,105	7	7	0
Northeastern Regional	11,878	13	12	1
Northern Berks Regional	13,366	16	15	1
Northern Cambria Borough	3,546	2	2	0
Northern Lancaster County Regional	36,089	26	24	2
Northern Regional	35,447	31	29	2
Northern York County Regional	69,814	55	51	4
North Fayette Township	14,935	26	21	5
North Franklin Township	4,542	10	10	0
North Hopewell Township	2,804	1	1	0
North Huntingdon Township	30,414	31	25	6
North Lebanon Township	12,042	14	12	2
North Londonderry Township	8,523	10	9	1
North Middleton Township	11,682	11	10	1
North Sewickley Township	5,406	1	1	0

Table 78. Full-Time Law Enforcement Employees, by Selected State and City, 2018—Continued

(Number.)

State/city	Population	Total law enforcement employees	Total officers	Total civilians
North Strabane Township	14,703	20	19	1
Northumberland	3,655	5	5	0
North Versailles Township	12,127	24	19	5
North Wales	3,271	4	4	0
Northwest Lancaster County Regional	20,029	21	19	2
Norwood	5,896	7	6	1
Oakland	566	2	2	0
Oakmont	6,466	7	7	0
O'Hara Township	8,724	17	16	1
Ohio Township	6,874	17	14	3
Ohioville	3,382	2	2	0
Oil City	9,769	22	16	6
Old Forge	7,885	5	5	0
Old Lycoming Township	4,927	9	8	1
Olyphant	5,026	8	4	4
Orangeville Area	1,731	1	1	0
Orwigsburg	2,956	5	5	0
Overfield Township	2,751	1	1	0
Oxford	5,648	11	10	1
Palmerton	5,289	10	9	1
Palmer Township	21,512	36	34	2
Palmyra	7,556	9	8	1
Palo Alto	982	1	1	0
Parkesburg	3,876	9	8	1
Parkside	2,331	3	3	0
Parks Township	2,571	2	2	0
Patterson Township	4,218	4	4	0
Patton	1,627	2	2	0
Patton Township	16,142	21	19	2
Penbrook	2,985	6	6	0
Penndel	2,185	1	1	0
Penn Hills	41,143	53	50	3
Pennridge Regional	11,013	15	13	2
Penn Township, Butler County	4,916	4	3	1
Penn Township, Westmoreland County	19,297	23	21	2
Penn Township, York County	16,511	25	23	2
Pequea Township	5,022	5	5	0
Perkasie	8,561	20	18	2
Perryopolis	1,690	2	2	0
Peters Township	22,136	23	21	2
Philadelphia	1,586,916	7,366	6,577	789
Phoenixville	17,012	31	30	1
Pine Creek Township	3,271	2	2	0
Pine Grove	2,079	2	2	0
Pitcairn	3,197	3	3	0
Pittsburgh	302,544	999	950	49
Pittston	7,689	9	9	0
Pittston Township	3,389	3	2	1
Plains Township	9,725	19	18	1
Pleasant Hills	8,113	20	18	2
Plum	27,274	30	24	6
Plumstead Township	14,244	18	16	2
Plymouth	5,789	4	4	0
Plymouth Township, Montgomery County	17,756	53	46	7
Pocono Mountain Regional	42,712	41	36	5
Pocono Township	10,855	19	18	1
Point Township	3,633	6	6	0
Polk	778	2	2	0
Portage	2,419	2	2	0
Port Allegany	2,021	3	3	0
Port Carbon	1,786	2	2	0
Portland	516	2	2	0
Port Vue	3,686	2	2	0
Pottstown	22,792	56	44	12
Pottsville	13,529	24	24	0
Pringle	957	21	19	2
Prospect Park	6,496	9	9	0
Pulaski Township, Lawrence County	3,290	2	2	0
Punxsutawney	5,764	10	8	2
Pymatuning Township	3,090	7	6	1
Quakertown	8,824	20	18	2
Quarryville	2,787	4	4	0
Raccoon Township	2,925	4	4	0
Radnor Township	31,935	46	42	4
Ralpho Township	4,242	6	6	0
Rankin	2,059	1	1	0
Reading	88,466	182	160	22
Reading Township	5,837	2	2	0
Redstone Township	4,225	3	3	0
Reilly Township	688	2	2	0
Renovo	1,219	1	1	0
Reserve Township	3,238	4	4	0
Reynoldsville	2,660	1	1	0
Rice Township	3,559	6	6	0

Table 78. Full-Time Law Enforcement Employees, by Selected State and City, 2018—Continued

(Number.)

State/city	Population	Total law enforcement employees	Total officers	Total civilians
Richland Township, Bucks County	13,388	16	14	2
Richland Township, Cambria County	11,940	23	22	1
Ridgway	3,764	7	6	1
Ridley Park	7,045	13	10	3
Ridley Township	31,190	37	32	5
Riverside	1,873	3	3	0
Roaring Brook Township	1,941	1	1	0
Roaring Creek Township	534	5	5	0
Roaring Spring	2,467	3	3	0
Robeson Township	7,432	7	6	1
Robinson Township, Allegheny County	13,673	31	29	2
Rochester	3,477	8	7	1
Rochester Township	2,667	4	4	0
Rockledge	2,542	4	4	0
Ross Township	30,541	45	43	2
Rostraver Township	11,023	17	16	1
Royalton	1,041	5	5	0
Rural Valley	820	1	1	0
Rush Township	3,260	1	1	0
Sadsbury Township, Chester County	4,017	3	3	0
Salem Township, Luzerne County	4,192	5	5	0
Salisbury Township	13,977	22	20	2
Sandy Lake	635	1	1	0
Sandy Township	10,475	11	10	1
Saxonburg	1,456	1	1	0
Saxton	698	3	3	0
Sayre	6,410	13	10	3
Schuylkill Haven	5,116	8	8	0
Schuylkill Township, Chester County	8,658	13	11	2
Scottdale	4,151	6	6	0
Scott Township, Allegheny County	16,567	23	22	1
Scott Township, Columbia County	5,016	6	6	0
Scott Township, Lackawanna County	4,753	4	4	0
Scranton	77,827	170	150	20
Selinsgrove	5,962	7	6	1
Seward	469	1	1	0
Sewickley	4,381	11	11	0
Sewickley Heights	810	3	3	0
Shaler Township	28,039	28	26	2
Shamokin	7,020	11	10	1
Shamokin Dam	1,751	3	3	0
Sharon	13,154	29	28	1
Sharon Hill	5,705	10	9	1
Sharpsburg	3,344	6	6	0
Shenandoah	4,779	5	5	0
Shenango Township, Lawrence County	7,253	7	7	0
Shenango Township, Mercer County	3,720	10	10	0
Shillington	5,289	9	8	1
Shinglehouse	1,068	1	1	0
Shippensburg	5,584	10	9	1
Shippingport	199	1	1	0
Shiremanstown	1,576	2	2	0
Shohola Township	2,399	1	1	0
Silver Lake Township	1,600	1	1	0
Silver Spring Township	18,078	25	24	1
Sinking Spring	4,128	6	5	1
Slate Belt Regional	12,451	23	23	0
Slatington	4,322	6	6	0
Slippery Rock	3,537	4	4	0
Smethport	1,541	2	2	0
Smith Township	4,367	3	3	0
Solebury Township	8,585	16	14	2
Somerset	5,899	8	7	1
Souderton	7,063	6	5	1
South Abington Township	8,904	12	11	1
South Annville Township	2,992	2	2	0
South Beaver Township	2,613	4	4	0
South Buffalo Township	2,533	2	2	0
South Centre Township	4,191	4	4	0
South Coatesville	1,467	2	2	0
Southern Chester County Regional	14,974	18	16	2
Southern Regional York County	11,515	16	14	2
South Fayette Township	15,788	18	17	1
South Fork	851	1	1	0
South Greensburg	2,003	2	2	0
South Heidelberg Township	7,378	8	8	0
South Lebanon Township	9,935	8	7	1
South Londonderry Township	8,427	8	8	0
South Park Township	13,332	17	16	1
South Pymatuning Township	2,553	3	3	0
South Strabane Township	9,467	20	19	1
Southwestern Regional	17,789	15	14	1
Southwest Greensburg	2,033	2	2	0
Southwest Regional, Fayette County	2,677	3	2	1
Southwest Regional, Washington County	132	2	2	0

Table 78. Full-Time Law Enforcement Employees, by Selected State and City, 2018—Continued

(Number.)

State/city	Population	Total law enforcement employees	Total officers	Total civilians
South Whitehall Township	19,918	41	39	2
South Williamsport	6,109	9	7	2
Spring City	3,329	3	3	0
Springdale	3,318	4	4	0
Springdale Township	1,590	3	3	0
Springettsbury Township	26,833	33	30	3
Springfield Township, Bucks County	5,045	4	4	0
Springfield Township, Delaware County	24,259	37	32	5
Springfield Township, Montgomery County	19,751	30	29	1
Spring Garden Township	13,120	22	19	3
Spring Township, Berks County	27,528	30	29	1
Spring Township, Centre County	7,905	8	7	1
State College	58,781	71	61	10
St. Clair Boro	2,835	5	5	0
Steelton	5,944	14	12	2
St. Marys City	12,279	16	15	1
Stoneboro	990	1	1	0
Stonycreek Township	2,613	4	4	0
Stowe Township	6,179	9	8	1
Strasburg	2,988	5	5	0
Stroud Area Regional	34,887	59	52	7
Sugarcreek	4,969	6	2	4
Sugarloaf Township, Luzerne County	3,982	5	5	0
Sugar Notch	960	2	2	0
Summerhill Township	2,281	2	2	0
Summit Hill	2,934	6	4	2
Sunbury	9,469	19	15	4
Susquehanna Regional	8,455	19	17	2
Susquehanna Township, Dauphin County	25,197	45	42	3
Swarthmore	6,266	9	9	0
Swatara Township	26,532	52	49	3
Sweden Township	828	1	1	0
Swissvale	8,713	27	25	2
Swoyersville	4,949	5	5	0
Sykesville	1,116	1	1	0
Tamaqua	6,698	9	8	1
Tarentum	4,401	8	7	1
Tatamy	1,135	1	1	0
Taylor	5,889	7	7	0
Telford	4,849	6	5	1
Throop	3,892	8	8	0
Tiadaghton Valley Regional	7,586	11	10	1
Tilden Township	3,607	4	4	0
Tinicum Township, Bucks County	3,970	5	5	0
Tinicum Township, Delaware County	4,108	18	16	2
Titusville	5,286	10	10	0
Towamencin Township	18,443	24	21	3
Towanda	2,828	7	7	0
Trafford	3,065	4	4	0
Trainer	1,847	4	4	0
Tredyffrin Township	29,575	48	42	6
Tremont	1,675	1	1	0
Troy	1,246	2	2	0
Tullytown	1,839	7	6	1
Tulpehocken Township	3,368	3	3	0
Tunkhannock	1,730	3	3	0
Tunkhannock Township, Wyoming County	6,147	6	6	0
Turtle Creek	5,192	5	5	0
Tyrone	5,210	14	11	3
Union City	3,162	4	3	1
Uniontown	9,751	21	20	1
Union Township, Lawrence County	4,921	7	7	0
Upland	3,250	6	5	1
Upper Allen Township	20,123	24	23	1
Upper Burrell Township	2,231	2	2	0
Upper Chichester Township	17,002	22	21	1
Upper Darby Township	82,931	145	126	19
Upper Dublin Township	26,432	46	40	6
Upper Gwynedd Township	15,958	24	21	3
Upper Macungie Township	24,995	32	30	2
Upper Makefield Township	8,479	16	15	1
Upper Merion Township	30,673	85	68	17
Upper Moreland Township	24,182	43	37	6
Upper Nazareth Township	6,947	9	8	1
Upper Perkiomen	3,877	5	5	0
Upper Pottsgrove Township	5,617	10	9	1
Upper Providence Township, Delaware County	10,478	15	15	0
Upper Providence Township, Montgomery County	24,445	32	29	3
Upper Saucon Township	17,121	21	20	1
Upper Southampton Township	15,038	25	22	3
Upper St. Clair Township	19,758	34	27	7

Table 78. Full-Time Law Enforcement Employees, by Selected State and City, 2018—Continued

(Number.)

State/city	Population	Total law enforcement employees	Total officers	Total civilians
Upper Uwchlan Township	11,506	11	11	0
Upper Yoder Township	5,093	13	13	0
Uwchlan Township	19,044	22	21	1
Valley Township	7,869	5	5	0
Vandergrift	4,917	9	8	1
Vernon Township	5,432	5	5	0
Verona	2,402	4	3	1
Versailles	1,471	2	2	0
Walnutport	2,088	4	4	0
Warminster Township	32,395	49	44	5
Warren	9,088	20	16	4
Warrington Township	24,582	35	32	3
Warwick Township, Bucks County	14,618	19	18	1
Washington Township, Fayette County	3,662	4	4	0
Washington Township, Franklin County	14,671	9	7	2
Washington Township, Northampton County	5,228	6	5	1
Washington Township, Westmoreland County	7,103	7	7	0
Washington, Washington County	13,505	33	31	2
Watsontown	2,275	5	5	0
Waverly Township	1,674	4	4	0
Waynesboro	10,920	22	20	2
Waynesburg	3,960	8	8	0
Weatherly	2,443	4	4	0
Wellsboro	3,228	7	7	0
Wesleyville	3,157	8	7	1
West Brandywine Township	7,495	9	8	1
West Brownsville	965	3	2	1
West Caln Township	9,087	3	3	0
West Carroll Township	1,212	2	2	0
West Chester	20,299	64	47	17
West Conshohocken	1,415	13	12	1
West Cornwall Township	2,038	6	5	1
West Deer Township	11,973	12	11	1
West Earl Township	8,503	6	6	0
Western Berks Regional	4,833	6	5	1
West Fallowfield Township	2,597	2	2	0
Westfield	1,030	2	2	0
West Goshen Township	23,160	36	31	5
West Hazleton	4,466	4	3	1
West Hempfield Township	16,598	24	21	3
West Hills Regional	10,032	12	11	1
West Homestead	1,891	7	6	1
West Lampeter Township	16,092	16	15	1
West Mahanoy Township	2,723	3	3	0
West Manchester Township	18,833	30	27	3
West Manheim Township	8,497	8	8	0
West Mead Township	5,082	2	2	0
West Mifflin	19,773	38	31	7
West Newton	2,484	2	2	0
West Norriton Township	15,708	28	25	3
West Penn Township	4,259	2	2	0
West Pikeland Township	4,085	4	4	0
West Pike Run	1,546	1	1	0
West Pittston	4,741	2	2	0
West Pottsgrove Township	3,885	8	8	0
West Reading	4,209	16	14	2
West Sadsbury Township	2,479	4	4	0
West Salem Township	3,404	8	7	1
West Shore Regional	7,745	11	10	1
Westtown-East Goshen Regional	32,253	32	29	3
West View	6,578	13	11	2
West Vincent Township	5,572	7	6	1
West Whiteland Township	18,393	27	25	2
West York	4,578	8	8	0
Whitehall	13,703	25	20	5
Whitehall Township	27,679	51	46	5
White Haven Borough	1,096	3	3	0
Whitemarsh Township	17,966	41	36	5
White Oak	7,646	14	13	1
Whitpain Township	19,326	38	32	6
Wiconisco Township	1,199	1	1	0
Wilkes-Barre	40,710	81	77	4
Wilkes-Barre Township	2,889	15	14	1
Wilkinsburg	15,502	25	23	2
Wilkins Township	6,184	12	12	0
Williamsburg	1,193	2	2	0
Williamsport	28,331	54	50	4
Willistown Township	10,983	20	18	2
Wilson	7,808	13	12	1
Windber	3,867	3	2	1
Womelsdorf	2,878	1	1	0
Woodward Township	2,378	2	2	0
Wrightsville	2,293	3	3	0

Table 78. Full-Time Law Enforcement Employees, by Selected State and City, 2018—Continued

(Number.)

State/city	Population	Total law enforcement employees	Total officers	Total civilians
Wright Township	5,611	7	6	1
Wyoming	3,008	4	4	0
Wyomissing	10,454	24	23	1
Yardley	2,489	4	4	0
Yeadon	11,512	14	13	1
York	44,170	120	105	15
York Area Regional	55,386	50	45	5
Youngsville	1,617	2	2	0
Zelienople	3,639	10	9	1
Zerbe Township	1,795	1	1	0
RHODE ISLAND				
Barrington	16,112	31	24	7
Bristol	22,131	47	38	9
Burrillville	16,781	31	24	7
Central Falls	19,293	44	36	8
Charlestown	7,810	25	20	5
Coventry	34,814	72	57	15
Cranston	81,059	180	149	31
Cumberland	35,018	54	43	11
East Greenwich	13,051	40	33	7
East Providence	47,526	111	92	19
Foster	4,735	13	9	4
Glocester	10,158	20	15	5
Hopkinton	8,109	19	14	5
Jamestown	5,537	19	14	5
Johnston	29,317	77	66	11
Lincoln	21,900	43	36	7
Little Compton	3,511	14	10	4
Middletown	16,030	42	39	3
Narragansett	15,448	52	39	13
Newport	24,863	98	80	18
New Shoreham	1,034	8	4	4
North Kingstown	26,101	60	48	12
North Providence	32,475	83	65	18
North Smithfield	12,469	27	26	1
Pawtucket	71,892	171	137	34
Portsmouth	17,474	38	36	2
Providence	180,169	505	410	95
Richmond	7,627	19	14	5
Scituate	10,617	28	17	11
Smithfield	21,746	54	41	13
South Kingstown	30,816	70	53	17
Tiverton	15,835	41	29	12
Warren	10,393	29	24	5
Warwick	80,380	207	162	45
Westerly	22,537	59	49	10
West Greenwich	6,227	19	13	6
West Warwick	28,464	60	48	12
Woonsocket	41,707	113	100	13
SOUTH CAROLINA				
Aiken	30,881	118	90	28
Allendale	2,970	6	6	0
Anderson	27,415	129	93	36
Andrews	2,878	10	9	1
Aynor	904	4	4	0
Bamberg	3,239	11	8	3
Barnwell	4,385	17	15	2
Batesburg-Leesville	5,380	27	24	3
Beaufort	13,920	57	52	5
Belton	4,402	15	13	2
Bennettsville	7,898	34	32	2
Bishopville	3,089	13	11	2
Blacksburg	1,899	13	12	1
Blackville	2,217	7	6	1
Bluffton	22,578	52	48	4
Bonneau	490	2	2	0
Bowman	907	3	3	0
Branchville	956	3	2	1
Briarcliffe Acres	576	1	1	0
Burnettown	2,824	2	2	0
Calhoun Falls	1,925	4	4	0
Camden	7,215	36	34	2
Cameron	403	1	1	0
Campobello	575	14	12	2
Cayce	14,238	82	68	14
Central	5,180	7	6	1
Chapin	1,629	8	7	1
Charleston	137,092	514	410	104
Cheraw	5,611	28	22	6
Chester	5,394	29	27	2
Clemson	17,080	44	33	11
Clinton	8,498	30	29	1
Clio	670	4	4	0

Table 78. Full-Time Law Enforcement Employees, by Selected State and City, 2018—Continued

(Number.)

State/city	Population	Total law enforcement employees	Total officers	Total civilians
Clover	6,234	24	19	5
Columbia	133,540	454	363	91
Conway	24,784	59	55	4
Cottageville	738	6	6	0
Coward	767	1	1	0
Cowpens	2,348	10	8	2
Darlington	5,960	30	30	0
Dillon	6,392	28	25	3
Due West	1,289	5	5	0
Duncan	3,480	19	18	1
Easley	21,203	57	46	11
Edgefield	4,756	10	10	0
Edisto Beach	405	7	7	0
Ehrhardt	491	3	2	1
Elgin	1,587	7	6	1
Elloree	652	6	3	3
Estill	1,807	15	13	2
Eutawville	294	1	1	0
Fairfax	1,706	6	5	1
Florence	37,819	101	85	16
Folly Beach	2,746	30	18	12
Forest Acres	10,375	31	25	6
Fort Lawn	878	2	2	0
Fort Mill	18,618	56	49	7
Fountain Inn	8,846	33	25	8
Gaffney	12,816	45	41	4
Gaston	1,690	4	4	0
Georgetown	8,819	34	30	4
Gifford	264	3	2	1
Goose Creek	43,545	93	67	26
Greenville	69,608	244	200	44
Greenwood	23,265	57	51	6
Greer	31,722	79	55	24
Hampton	2,527	14	13	1
Hanahan	26,060	42	32	10
Hardeeville	6,561	25	23	2
Harleyville	691	3	3	0
Hartsville	7,608	40	37	3
Holly Hill	1,190	6	6	0
Honea Path	3,782	12	11	1
Inman	2,341	14	12	2
Irmo	12,413	27	22	5
Isle of Palms	4,396	27	20	7
Iva	1,302	10	10	0
Jackson	1,781	3	3	0
Johnsonville	1,493	6	5	1
Johnston	2,327	8	8	0
Jonesville	841	5	3	2
Kingstree	3,065	17	14	3
Lake City	6,668	25	24	1
Lancaster	9,040	44	33	11
Landrum	2,586	11	11	0
Lane	456	4	1	3
Latta	1,296	9	9	0
Laurens	8,868	34	29	5
Lexington	21,680	60	57	3
Liberty	3,161	15	11	4
Loris	2,722	14	12	2
Manning	3,958	17	16	1
Marion	6,416	21	18	3
Mauldin	25,418	63	52	11
McCormick	2,446	7	7	0
Moncks Corner	11,484	33	30	3
Mount Pleasant	89,733	183	158	25
Mullins	4,350	17	17	0
Myrtle Beach	33,687	326	247	79
Newberry	10,293	28	25	3
New Ellenton	2,164	4	4	0
Ninety Six	2,037	7	7	0
North	719	5	5	0
North Augusta	23,161	89	65	24
North Charleston	112,840	389	323	66
North Myrtle Beach	16,688	150	81	69
Norway	313	1	1	0
Olar	229	1	1	0
Orangeburg	12,820	91	61	30
Pacolet	2,440	7	7	0
Pageland	2,680	14	10	4
Pamplico	1,232	4	4	0
Pawleys Island	106	7	5	2
Pickens	3,170	15	15	0
Port Royal	13,227	24	23	1
Prosperity	1,222	4	4	0
Quinby	931	1	1	0
Ridgeland	4,072	14	13	1

Table 78. Full-Time Law Enforcement Employees, by Selected State and City, 2018—Continued

(Number.)

State/city	Population	Total law enforcement employees	Total officers	Total civilians
Ridge Spring	755	1	1	0
Ridgeville	1,727	2	2	0
Rock Hill	74,049	192	145	47
Salem	154	1	1	0
Salley	420	2	1	1
Santee	908	5	5	0
Scranton	823	2	1	1
Sellers	204	1	1	0
Seneca	8,371	44	32	12
Simpsonville	22,641	52	42	10
South Congaree	2,466	6	6	0
Spartanburg	37,601	143	123	20
Springdale	2,760	7	7	0
Springfield	488	4	4	0
St. Stephen	1,828	7	5	2
Sullivans Island	1,942	12	11	1
Summerton	954	5	4	1
Summerville	51,565	133	109	24
Sumter	39,898	149	104	45
Swansea	941	4	3	1
Tega Cay	10,763	28	25	3
Travelers Rest	5,183	18	12	6
Trenton	193	1	1	0
Union	7,748	27	24	3
Varnville	1,990	6	6	0
Wagener	837	2	2	0
Walhalla	4,327	13	12	1
Walterboro	5,083	31	28	3
Wellford	2,629	10	9	1
West Columbia	17,368	60	49	11
Westminster	2,536	5	5	0
West Pelzer	939	3	3	0
West Union	319	2	2	0
Whitmire	1,473	4	4	0
Williamston	4,216	20	19	1
Williston	2,941	10	9	1
Winnsboro	3,197	20	19	1
Woodruff	4,253	8	7	1
Yemassee	958	12	9	3
York	8,203	39	33	6
SOUTH DAKOTA				
Aberdeen	28,713	53	44	9
Alcester	727	2	2	0
Avon	597	1	1	0
Belle Fourche	5,544	11	10	1
Beresford	1,944	1	1	0
Box Elder	9,761	19	17	2
Brandon	10,107	14	13	1
Brookings	24,206	43	34	9
Canton	3,481	6	6	0
Chamberlain	2,388	6	6	0
Clark	1,035	2	2	0
Deadwood	1,305	16	13	3
Eagle Butte	1,349	2	2	0
Elk Point	1,809	4	4	0
Faith	417	2	2	0
Flandreau	2,332	8	7	1
Freeman	1,286	2	2	0
Gregory	1,250	3	3	0
Groton	1,514	4	4	0
Hot Springs	3,426	8	6	2
Huron	13,193	27	26	1
Jefferson	495	2	2	0
Kadoka	711	1	1	0
Kimball	677	1	1	0
Lead	2,957	6	5	1
Lennox	2,424	4	4	0
Madison	7,441	14	13	1
Martin	1,066	3	3	0
Menno	618	1	1	0
Milbank	3,103	7	7	0
Miller	1,361	4	4	0
Mitchell	15,653	28	28	0
Mobridge	3,528	13	7	6
Murdo	447	1	1	0
North Sioux City	2,821	8	7	1
Parkston	1,495	2	2	0
Philip	785	2	2	0
Pierre	14,050	40	26	14
Platte	1,278	1	1	0
Rapid City	75,290	165	128	37
Scotland	814	1	1	0
Sioux Falls	180,335	293	256	37
Sisseton	2,395	7	7	0

Table 78. Full-Time Law Enforcement Employees, by Selected State and City, 2018—Continued

(Number.)

State/city	Population	Total law enforcement employees	Total officers	Total civilians
Spearfish	11,763	32	22	10
Sturgis	6,949	17	14	3
Summerset	2,690	3	3	0
Tea	5,725	7	7	0
Tripp	630	1	1	0
Tyndall	1,041	2	2	0
Vermillion	10,804	20	19	1
Wagner	1,589	6	6	0
Watertown	22,323	62	42	20
Webster	1,757	5	5	0
Whitewood	949	4	4	0
Winner	2,832	10	10	0
Yankton	14,523	30	28	2
TENNESSEE				
Adamsville	2,199	6	5	1
Alamo	2,324	4	4	0
Alcoa	10,506	51	43	8
Alexandria	1,000	3	3	0
Algood	4,517	13	13	0
Ardmore	1,236	12	7	5
Ashland City	4,641	18	16	2
Athens	13,627	32	30	2
Atoka	9,305	20	19	1
Baileyton	441	3	3	0
Bartlett	59,407	163	123	40
Baxter	1,453	5	5	0
Bean Station	3,094	6	6	0
Belle Meade	2,917	22	15	7
Bells	2,477	5	5	0
Benton	1,277	7	6	1
Berry Hill	524	16	12	4
Big Sandy	517	1	1	0
Blaine	1,880	4	4	0
Bluff City	1,660	8	8	0
Bolivar	4,954	22	19	3
Bradford	974	4	4	0
Brentwood	43,507	79	63	16
Brighton	2,910	4	4	0
Bristol	26,863	86	66	20
Brownsville	9,490	38	34	4
Bruceton	1,403	4	4	0
Burns	1,509	1	1	0
Calhoun	492	3	3	0
Camden	3,500	18	13	5
Carthage	2,258	12	8	4
Caryville	2,146	6	6	0
Celina	1,458	8	6	2
Centerville	3,557	17	15	2
Chapel Hill	1,511	6	6	0
Charleston	686	3	3	0
Chattanooga	180,397	601	490	111
Church Hill	6,664	11	9	2
Clarksville	156,264	342	278	64
Cleveland	44,954	108	96	12
Clifton	2,676	6	6	0
Clinton	10,137	41	34	7
Collegedale	12,189	22	22	0
Collierville	50,985	136	99	37
Collinwood	944	4	4	0
Columbia	38,802	94	84	10
Cookeville	33,785	94	72	22
Coopertown	4,552	4	3	1
Cornersville	1,243	2	2	0
Covington	8,794	31	30	1
Cowan	1,650	2	2	0
Crossville	11,535	45	42	3
Crump	1,463	1	1	0
Cumberland City	303	2	2	0
Dandridge	2,981	12	11	1
Dayton	7,365	18	18	0
Decatur	1,629	6	6	0
Decaturville	865	1	1	0
Decherd	2,388	13	12	1
Dickson	15,637	61	53	8
Dover	1,461	5	5	0
Dresden	2,902	9	8	1
Dunlap	5,111	14	12	2
Dyer	2,193	8	7	1
Dyersburg	16,382	65	57	8
Eagleville	687	3	3	0
East Ridge	21,135	50	45	5
Elizabethton	13,657	45	41	4
Elkton	541	2	2	0
Englewood	1,518	4	3	1

Table 78. Full-Time Law Enforcement Employees, by Selected State and City, 2018—Continued

(Number.)

State/city	Population	Total law enforcement employees	Total officers	Total civilians
Erin	1,274	7	5	2
Erwin	5,840	14	14	0
Estill Springs	2,012	7	7	0
Ethridge	482	1	1	0
Etowah	3,461	9	8	1
Fairview	8,898	21	21	0
Fayetteville	7,024	30	24	6
Franklin	80,825	143	130	13
Friendship	679	1	1	0
Gadsden	467	1	1	0
Gainesboro	940	4	4	0
Gallatin	38,450	93	80	13
Gallaway	652	6	6	0
Gatlinburg	4,192	53	43	10
Germantown	39,179	127	102	25
Gibson	385	4	4	0
Gleason	1,365	3	3	0
Goodlettsville	17,000	57	43	14
Gordonsville	1,210	6	6	0
Grand Junction	269	3	3	0
Graysville	1,553	5	5	0
Greenbrier	6,899	15	14	1
Greeneville	14,867	53	51	2
Greenfield	2,067	4	3	1
Halls	2,118	4	4	0
Harriman	6,132	21	20	1
Henderson	6,234	15	15	0
Hendersonville	58,437	136	121	15
Henry	474	2	2	0
Hohenwald	3,671	14	14	0
Hollow Rock	674	1	1	0
Hornbeak	385	1	1	0
Humboldt	8,110	30	24	6
Huntingdon	3,807	14	10	4
Huntland	843	2	2	0
Jacksboro	1,918	6	6	0
Jackson	66,848	248	218	30
Jamestown	1,956	9	9	0
Jasper	3,317	8	8	0
Jefferson City	8,361	28	26	2
Jellico	2,198	8	7	1
Johnson City	66,795	172	144	28
Jonesborough	5,446	22	17	5
Kenton	1,201	3	3	0
Kimball	1,398	9	9	0
Kingsport	53,465	140	102	38
Kingston	5,794	13	12	1
Kingston Springs	2,776	6	5	1
Knoxville	188,653	502	387	115
Lafayette	5,318	24	17	7
La Follette	6,722	31	23	8
La Vergne	36,167	75	60	15
Lawrenceburg	10,807	37	32	5
Lebanon	33,181	110	84	26
Lenoir City	9,284	27	25	2
Lewisburg	11,967	36	35	1
Lexington	7,673	34	29	5
Livingston	4,016	25	20	5
Lookout Mountain	1,873	21	16	5
Loretto	1,769	5	5	0
Loudon	5,815	15	14	1
Madisonville	4,754	20	17	3
Manchester	10,719	38	34	4
Martin	10,418	38	30	8
Maryville	28,961	64	58	6
Mason	1,571	7	7	0
Maury City	669	1	1	0
Maynardville	2,351	4	4	0
McEwen	1,723	5	5	0
McKenzie	5,392	20	15	5
McMinnville	13,668	41	37	4
Medina	4,313	8	8	0
Memphis	652,226	2,605	1,995	610
Metropolitan Nashville Police Department	686,492	1,757	1,435	322
Middleton	636	4	4	0
Milan	7,640	31	25	6
Millersville	6,914	18	16	2
Millington	11,016	40	29	11
Minor Hill	520	2	2	0
Monteagle	1,173	8	7	1
Monterey	2,875	9	9	0
Morristown	29,884	92	86	6
Moscow	522	4	4	0
Mountain City	2,395	8	8	0
Mount Carmel	5,345	5	5	0

Table 78. Full-Time Law Enforcement Employees, by Selected State and City, 2018—Continued

(Number.)

State/city	Population	Total law enforcement employees	Total officers	Total civilians
Mount Juliet	36,397	74	61	13
Mount Pleasant	4,924	20	14	6
Munford	6,090	16	14	2
Murfreesboro	140,702	292	242	50
Newbern	3,334	13	13	0
New Johnsonville	1,905	5	5	0
New Market	1,353	4	4	0
Newport	6,770	32	28	4
New Tazewell	2,709	10	10	0
Niota	723	4	3	1
Nolensville	8,545	11	10	1
Norris	1,640	6	6	0
Oakland	8,107	20	18	2
Oak Ridge	29,067	79	62	17
Obion	1,049	3	3	0
Oliver Springs	3,256	13	9	4
Oneida	3,673	17	12	5
Paris	10,088	36	25	11
Parsons	2,316	8	8	0
Petersburg	552	1	1	0
Pigeon Forge	6,291	74	59	15
Pikeville	1,626	3	3	0
Piperton	1,757	7	7	0
Pittman Center	583	4	4	0
Plainview	2,091	2	2	0
Pleasant View	4,449	6	6	0
Portland	12,887	34	31	3
Pulaski	7,650	28	25	3
Puryear	667	1	1	0
Red Bank	11,768	22	20	2
Red Boiling Springs	1,148	6	5	1
Ridgely	1,662	4	4	0
Ridgetop	2,071	6	6	0
Ripley	7,977	25	18	7
Rockwood	5,417	15	14	1
Rocky Top	1,774	10	7	3
Rogersville	4,264	17	13	4
Rossville	890	6	6	0
Rutherford	1,077	5	4	1
Rutledge	1,358	2	2	0
Savannah	6,968	21	19	2
Scotts Hill	974	3	3	0
Selmer	4,445	19	17	2
Sevierville	16,999	71	55	16
Sharon	914	2	2	0
Shelbyville	21,708	51	41	10
Signal Mountain	8,602	17	15	2
Smithville	4,783	15	14	1
Smyrna	51,489	102	81	21
Soddy-Daisy	13,804	37	30	7
Somerville	3,213	11	11	0
South Carthage	1,356	4	4	0
South Fulton	2,200	8	8	0
South Pittsburg	3,031	8	8	0
Sparta	4,951	14	13	1
Spencer	1,641	2	2	0
Spring City	1,856	8	8	0
Springfield	16,896	38	34	4
Spring Hill	41,354	56	52	4
St. Joseph	811	1	1	0
Surgoinsville	1,770	1	1	0
Sweetwater	5,873	20	19	1
Tazewell	2,278	6	6	0
Tellico Plains	945	8	4	4
Tiptonville	4,304	7	7	0
Townsend	446	4	4	0
Tracy City	1,394	5	5	0
Trenton	4,043	23	17	6
Trezevant	839	2	2	0
Trimble	615	1	1	0
Troy	1,269	5	5	0
Tullahoma	19,321	42	34	8
Tusculum	2,695	2	2	0
Union City	10,358	40	31	9
Vonore	1,517	9	9	0
Wartburg	898	5	5	0
Wartrace	679	2	1	1
Watertown	1,537	4	4	0
Waverly	4,093	14	13	1
Waynesboro	2,322	6	6	0
Westmoreland	2,325	10	9	1
White Bluff	3,535	5	5	0
White House	11,818	24	21	3
White Pine	2,288	11	10	1
Whiteville	4,500	5	5	0

Table 78. Full-Time Law Enforcement Employees, by Selected State and City, 2018—Continued

(Number.)

State/city	Population	Total law enforcement employees	Total officers	Total civilians
Whitwell	1,706	5	4	1
Winchester	8,504	26	24	2
Woodbury	2,815	10	9	1
TEXAS				
Abernathy	2,743	5	5	0
Abilene	122,480	268	202	66
Addison	15,839	73	62	11
Alamo Heights	8,629	34	21	13
Alice	18,925	43	33	10
Allen	103,168	190	134	56
Alvarado	4,179	21	19	2
Angleton	19,650	53	39	14
Aransas Pass	8,280	39	26	13
Archer City	1,742	2	2	0
Arlington	400,920	871	673	198
Arp	1,009	4	4	0
Athens	12,704	32	25	7
Austin	973,344	2,422	1,851	571
Azle	12,741	35	26	9
Balcones Heights	3,361	24	19	5
Bastrop	9,050	26	22	4
Bedford	49,841	129	79	50
Beeville	12,951	24	17	7
Bellaire	19,076	60	44	16
Bellville	4,257	12	11	1
Belton	22,248	47	36	11
Benbrook	23,924	47	37	10
Bertram	1,454	4	4	0
Blanco	2,062	10	9	1
Boerne	17,008	61	41	20
Borger	12,675	33	31	2
Breckenridge	5,396	17	12	5
Bridge City	8,208	22	16	6
Bridgeport	6,691	21	14	7
Brookshire	5,346	25	18	7
Brownsboro	1,259	4	4	0
Brownsville	184,461	299	197	102
Brownwood	18,772	60	38	22
Bryan	85,152	180	147	33
Buda	18,028	21	19	2
Bulverde	5,257	17	16	1
Burkburnett	11,221	28	19	9
Burleson	47,612	82	62	20
Cactus	3,268	10	8	2
Caldwell	4,361	9	8	1
Calvert	1,149	4	4	0
Carrollton	138,216	218	165	53
Castle Hills	4,508	28	22	6
Castroville	3,064	11	10	1
Cedar Hill	49,253	91	66	25
Cedar Park	79,087	126	91	35
Celina	10,559	24	23	1
Chandler	3,055	8	8	0
Cibolo	30,768	43	38	5
Cisco	3,789	13	11	2
Cleburne	30,317	68	49	19
Clifton	3,390	8	7	1
Clute	11,695	38	25	13
College Station	116,565	214	143	71
Colleyville	27,262	40	36	4
Collinsville	1,816	3	3	0
Colorado City	3,915	14	8	6
Comanche	4,188	13	10	3
Commerce	9,307	20	16	4
Conroe	87,544	166	123	43
Converse	24,185	58	47	11
Coppell	42,415	71	63	8
Copperas Cove	32,754	65	48	17
Corinth	21,352	39	34	5
Corpus Christi	328,614	652	443	209
Corrigan	1,581	18	13	5
Crandall	3,721	18	18	0
Crane	3,692	15	9	6
Crockett	6,470	18	14	4
Crowell	854	1	1	0
Crowley	15,777	38	27	11
Cuero	8,300	16	15	1
Cuney	140	3	2	1
Daingerfield	2,394	6	5	1
Dallas	1,362,465	3,581	3,007	574
Dalworthington Gardens	2,405	15	10	5
Dayton	8,070	31	22	9
Deer Park	34,155	88	59	29
De Leon	2,169	3	3	0

Table 78. Full-Time Law Enforcement Employees, by Selected State and City, 2018—Continued

(Number.)

State/city	Population	Total law enforcement employees	Total officers	Total civilians
Denton	139,262	227	174	53
DeSoto	54,201	107	65	42
Diboll	5,289	20	15	5
Dickinson	20,600	44	29	15
Donna	16,761	48	34	14
Double Oak	3,108	8	8	0
Driscoll	747	5	4	1
Dublin	3,604	12	9	3
Dumas	14,790	23	20	3
Eastland	3,929	12	10	2
Edna	5,811	11	9	2
El Campo	11,764	42	27	15
Electra	2,699	12	7	5
Elgin	9,918	29	20	9
El Paso	688,442	1,341	1,103	238
Everman	6,382	18	14	4
Fairfield	2,913	10	6	4
Fair Oaks Ranch	9,516	24	22	2
Farmersville	3,489	11	9	2
Fate	13,003	17	16	1
Ferris	2,651	17	12	5
Flatonia	1,449	8	8	0
Florence	1,280	2	2	0
Flower Mound	78,542	132	94	38
Floydada	2,717	6	6	0
Forney	21,464	43	29	14
Fort Stockton	8,365	35	23	12
Fort Worth	893,756	2,132	1,694	438
Frankston	1,183	7	6	1
Fredericksburg	11,490	35	30	5
Freeport	12,185	46	31	15
Friendswood	40,419	74	56	18
Frisco	187,889	285	186	99
Fulshear	13,790	19	17	2
Fulton	1,642	1	1	0
Gainesville	16,478	54	40	14
Galena Park	11,000	23	18	5
Galveston	50,896	200	142	58
Garden Ridge	4,055	14	13	1
Garland	239,577	471	344	127
Gatesville	12,377	26	16	10
Georgetown	74,709	129	84	45
George West	2,601	8	7	1
Giddings	5,141	19	14	5
Gilmer	5,226	18	13	5
Gladewater	6,402	20	15	5
Gonzales	7,687	24	16	8
Gorman	1,038	4	2	2
Graham	8,656	24	22	2
Grand Prairie	196,535	506	260	246
Grand Saline	3,120	9	8	1
Granite Shoals	5,144	9	8	1
Grapevine	55,130	143	96	47
Greenville	27,713	67	49	18
Groesbeck	4,316	9	9	0
Haltom City	44,708	74	69	5
Hamilton	2,994	9	8	1
Harker Heights	31,710	55	45	10
Harlingen	65,525	178	134	44
Haskell	3,204	6	5	1
Helotes	9,456	23	21	2
Hemphill	1,203	4	4	0
Hereford	14,812	33	27	6
Hewitt	14,556	35	26	9
Highland Park	9,302	74	61	13
Highland Village	16,805	40	30	10
Hill Country Village	1,098	11	11	0
Hillsboro	8,422	41	27	14
Hitchcock	8,038	16	15	1
Hollywood Park	3,400	16	15	1
Horseshoe Bay	3,936	21	18	3
Houston	2,344,966	6,258	5,229	1,029
Hughes Springs	1,734	4	4	0
Hurst	39,292	121	75	46
Hutchins	5,671	27	20	7
Hutto	26,924	48	45	3
Ingleside	10,453	28	20	8
Ingram	1,863	7	6	1
Irving	243,940	530	354	176
Itasca	1,692	6	6	0
Jacinto City	10,675	26	21	5
Jacksonville	14,960	37	28	9
Jarrell	1,643	3	3	0
Jasper	7,602	29	23	6
Jersey Village	7,974	28	26	2

Table 78. Full-Time Law Enforcement Employees, by Selected State and City, 2018—Continued

(Number.)

State/city	Population	Total law enforcement employees	Total officers	Total civilians
Jonestown	2,109	9	8	1
Josephine	1,701	2	2	0
Jourdanton	4,403	10	9	1
Katy	18,965	74	58	16
Keller	48,439	78	48	30
Kermit	6,131	22	13	9
Kerrville	23,532	65	49	16
Kilgore	14,978	44	34	10
Killeen	148,007	322	251	71
Kirby	8,807	22	15	7
Knox City	1,137	2	2	0
Kyle	46,155	66	45	21
Lacy-Lakeview	6,630	28	19	9
La Feria	7,384	14	13	1
Lago Vista	6,923	24	18	6
La Grange	4,686	10	10	0
Laguna Vista	3,206	8	8	0
Lake Dallas	8,084	18	15	3
Lakeside	1,404	5	5	0
Lakeview, Harrison County	6,388	13	12	1
Lakeway	15,722	47	32	15
Lake Worth	5,002	34	26	8
La Marque	17,107	37	33	4
Lampasas	7,992	32	21	11
Lancaster	39,772	66	60	6
La Porte	35,591	103	75	28
Lavon	3,299	10	9	1
Leander	53,637	79	60	19
Leon Valley	11,598	42	40	2
Levelland	13,646	35	23	12
Lewisville	107,560	217	144	73
Liberty Hill	2,119	11	10	1
Lindale	6,268	24	17	7
Littlefield	5,934	20	13	7
Live Oak	16,230	48	33	15
Llano	3,533	9	8	1
Lockhart	13,944	38	26	12
Longview	81,660	214	168	46
Lorena	1,771	8	7	1
Lubbock	257,372	534	432	102
Lufkin	35,937	97	75	22
Lyford	2,546	5	5	0
Manor	10,102	31	25	6
Mansfield	70,851	200	99	101
Manvel	11,097	23	18	5
Marble Falls	6,579	36	24	12
Marshall	23,146	66	48	18
McAllen	144,363	427	285	142
McGregor	5,134	19	11	8
McKinney	189,555	273	212	61
Meadows Place	4,621	16	15	1
Melissa	10,107	13	13	0
Mesquite	144,558	311	228	83
Midlothian	26,346	77	53	24
Miles	856	1	1	0
Milford	750	3	3	0
Missouri City	75,628	132	94	38
Montgomery	1,034	8	8	0
Morgans Point Resort	4,499	9	9	0
Mount Pleasant	16,291	42	29	13
Murphy	21,084	31	21	10
Nacogdoches	33,703	90	65	25
Naples	1,319	5	4	1
Nash	3,483	8	8	0
Nassau Bay	4,058	13	12	1
Navasota	7,677	25	18	7
New Boston	4,642	19	14	5
Nixon	2,506	6	6	0
Nolanville	5,380	9	9	0
Northeast	3,106	12	11	1
North Richland Hills	71,498	189	112	77
Odessa	119,545	212	160	52
Olmos Park	2,434	13	12	1
Olney	3,078	5	4	1
Onalaska	2,771	7	7	0
Orange	19,137	56	42	14
Oyster Creek	1,163	13	9	4
Paducah	1,076	1	1	0
Palestine	18,238	47	33	14
Panhandle	2,337	4	4	0
Parker	4,746	11	10	1
Pearland	124,179	223	163	60
Pearsall	10,525	17	15	2
Penitas	4,961	15	13	2
Perryton	8,675	21	13	8

Table 78. Full-Time Law Enforcement Employees, by Selected State and City, 2018—Continued

(Number.)

State/city	Population	Total law enforcement employees	Total officers	Total civilians
Pharr	80,814	161	125	36
Pinehurst	2,070	8	6	2
Pittsburg	4,668	14	11	3
Plano	289,897	585	408	177
Pleasanton	10,627	29	22	7
Ponder	2,049	6	5	1
Port Aransas	4,245	30	20	10
Port Arthur	55,643	152	121	31
Port Lavaca	12,214	25	19	6
Port Neches	12,881	23	20	3
Poteet	3,436	11	10	1
Pottsboro	2,381	10	8	2
Princeton	10,749	19	18	1
Prosper	22,570	35	26	9
Queen City	1,449	5	5	0
Ralls	1,852	2	2	0
Rancho Viejo	2,483	8	8	0
Red Oak	13,095	29	27	2
Refugio	2,826	9	8	1
Reno, Lamar County	3,318	6	5	1
Richardson	119,480	253	159	94
Richmond	12,130	44	33	11
Riesel	1,026	3	3	0
Rio Grande City	14,617	35	26	9
River Oaks	7,743	30	18	12
Roanoke	8,489	40	29	11
Robinson	11,774	31	22	9
Robstown	11,373	34	26	8
Rockdale	5,663	14	9	5
Rockport	10,734	29	26	3
Roma	11,506	42	31	11
Rosenberg	38,541	111	87	24
Round Rock	127,354	241	169	72
Rowlett	63,863	108	81	27
Royse City	13,104	24	21	3
Sabinal	1,696	5	4	1
Sachse	26,839	47	32	15
Saginaw	23,495	47	37	10
Salado	2,308	5	5	0
San Antonio	1,539,328	2,991	2,352	639
San Augustine	1,856	8	7	1
San Diego	4,261	7	6	1
San Marcos	66,157	146	102	44
Schertz	41,383	83	56	27
Schulenburg	2,915	8	7	1
Seabrook	13,958	34	26	8
Seagraves	2,875	6	5	1
Sealy	6,544	23	20	3
Seguin	29,487	82	54	28
Selma	11,742	34	29	5
Seymour	2,606	7	4	3
Shallowater	2,545	5	5	0
Shavano Park	3,913	20	19	1
Sherman	42,448	89	66	23
Sinton	5,424	12	11	1
Somerset	1,893	4	4	0
Somerville	1,445	5	5	0
Sour Lake	1,860	7	6	1
South Houston	17,619	42	29	13
Spearman	3,267	4	4	0
Splendora	2,109	11	10	1
Spring Valley	4,363	29	23	6
Stafford	18,393	76	58	18
Stamford	2,933	7	6	1
Stephenville	21,400	54	37	17
Sugar Land	89,919	188	165	23
Sullivan City	4,172	16	10	6
Sulphur Springs	16,111	39	28	11
Sunset Valley	693	14	13	1
Sweeny	3,753	8	8	0
Sweetwater	10,530	30	24	6
Taft	2,924	5	5	0
Tahoka	2,617	4	4	0
Tatum	1,386	6	6	0
Taylor	17,225	40	29	11
Teague	3,498	7	6	1
Temple	75,706	174	140	34
Terrell	18,104	61	42	19
Texarkana	37,460	98	87	11
Texas City	49,044	110	84	26
Thorndale	1,302	3	3	0
Thrall	951	1	1	0
Three Rivers	1,957	12	11	1
Tioga	1,009	4	4	0
Trophy Club	13,090	20	16	4

Table 78. Full-Time Law Enforcement Employees, by Selected State and City, 2018—Continued

(Number.)

State/city	Population	Total law enforcement employees	Total officers	Total civilians
Tulia	4,690	17	9	8
Universal City	20,825	43	32	11
University Park	25,516	53	39	14
Van	2,742	9	9	0
Van Alstyne	4,115	13	8	5
Venus	3,683	12	12	0
Vidor	10,875	32	31	1
Waco	138,091	347	249	98
Waelder	1,129	5	5	0
Wake Village	5,416	9	8	1
Waller	3,546	12	12	0
Watauga	24,757	43	33	10
Webster	11,194	64	46	18
Weimar	2,189	8	7	1
West	2,990	8	8	0
West Columbia	3,899	17	11	6
West Lake Hills	3,444	13	12	1
Westover Hills	701	16	12	4
Westworth	2,763	17	12	5
Wichita Falls	104,738	272	190	82
Willis	6,515	19	17	2
Wills Point	3,639	11	10	1
Windcrest	5,936	37	25	12
Wolfforth	5,131	12	11	1
Woodway	8,878	47	36	11
Wylie	51,051	68	62	6
Yoakum	5,983	17	12	5
UTAH				
Alta	385	8	4	4
American Fork/Cedar Hills	40,366	46	39	7
Big Water	500	1	1	0
Blanding	3,737	5	5	0
Bluffdale	14,648	12	12	0
Bountiful	44,317	57	38	19
Brian Head	91	5	5	0
Brigham City	19,362	28	24	4
Cedar City	32,242	45	39	6
Centerville	18,013	19	16	3
Clearfield	31,558	40	28	12
Clinton	22,179	19	18	1
Cottonwood Heights	34,054	49	40	9
Draper	48,518	56	44	12
East Carbon	1,558	4	4	0
Enoch	6,892	7	5	2
Ephraim	7,302	7	6	1
Fairview	1,314	1	1	0
Farmington	25,006	24	21	3
Fountain Green	1,134	1	1	0
Garland	2,541	3	3	0
Grantsville	11,326	15	13	2
Gunnison	3,539	6	4	2
Harrisville	6,678	11	10	1
Heber	16,527	27	22	5
Helper	2,075	6	5	1
Hildale	2,949	12	7	5
Hurricane	17,676	28	25	3
Kamas	2,226	2	2	0
Kanab	4,729	8	7	1
Kaysville	32,404	29	26	3
La Verkin	4,387	5	4	1
Layton	78,052	110	80	30
Lehi	65,125	59	53	6
Lindon	11,099	17	15	2
Logan	51,508	83	53	30
Lone Peak	29,969	27	22	5
Mapleton	10,041	10	9	1
Moab	5,274	21	16	5
Monticello	1,995	3	3	0
Mount Pleasant	3,440	4	4	0
Murray	49,675	87	74	13
Naples	2,098	8	7	1
Nephi	6,037	13	10	3
North Ogden	19,771	20	17	3
North Park	15,713	10	8	2
North Salt Lake	21,190	28	24	4
Ogden	87,616	174	139	35
Orem	99,221	119	86	33
Park City	8,491	36	32	4
Parowan	3,073	6	5	1
Payson	20,079	23	20	3
Perry	5,043	8	7	1
Pleasant Grove	39,641	37	28	9
Pleasant View	10,663	9	9	0
Price	8,201	20	18	2

Table 78. Full-Time Law Enforcement Employees, by Selected State and City, 2018—Continued

(Number.)

State/city	Population	Total law enforcement employees	Total officers	Total civilians
Provo	117,986	127	101	26
Richfield	7,777	16	15	1
Riverdale	8,795	22	19	3
Roosevelt	6,962	12	11	1
Roy	38,834	44	38	6
Salem	8,496	11	10	1
Salina	2,560	4	4	0
Salt Lake City	202,633	583	474	109
Sandy	97,057	126	100	26
Santa Clara/Ivins	16,671	15	14	1
Santaquin/Genola	13,584	14	13	1
Saratoga Springs	31,786	28	25	3
Smithfield	11,637	10	9	1
South Jordan	74,321	65	58	7
South Ogden	17,174	25	22	3
South Salt Lake	25,160	68	57	11
Spanish Fork	40,095	40	36	4
Spring City	1,053	1	1	0
Springdale	601	9	8	1
Springville	33,824	35	25	10
St. George	86,202	158	109	49
Stockton	680	1	1	0
Sunset	5,304	9	8	1
Syracuse	30,301	26	24	2
Tooele	35,065	41	35	6
Tremonton	8,764	12	10	2
Vernal	10,484	23	20	3
Washington	27,705	33	24	9
West Bountiful	5,705	11	10	1
West Jordan	115,392	146	114	32
West Valley	137,132	250	207	43
Willard	1,872	8	7	1
Woods Cross	11,600	19	17	2
VERMONT				
Barre	8,605	21	20	1
Barre Town	7,693	8	7	1
Bellows Falls	2,993	11	10	1
Bennington	14,900	32	24	8
Berlin	2,796	9	8	1
Bradford	2,697	2	2	0
Brandon	3,766	7	6	1
Brattleboro	11,410	37	24	13
Brighton	1,182	1	1	0
Bristol	3,891	3	3	0
Burlington	42,212	135	98	37
Canaan	927	1	1	0
Castleton	4,595	5	5	0
Chester	3,006	6	5	1
Colchester	17,313	35	27	8
Dover	1,057	7	6	1
Essex	21,803	33	27	6
Fair Haven	2,574	4	4	0
Hardwick	2,849	8	7	1
Hartford	9,567	29	20	9
Hinesburg	4,577	4	4	0
Killington	765	2	2	0
Ludlow	1,870	10	6	4
Lyndonville	1,157	3	3	0
Manchester	4,230	12	9	3
Middlebury	8,613	17	15	2
Milton	11,024	18	17	1
Montpelier	7,434	24	15	9
Morristown	5,450	10	10	0
Newport	4,248	17	14	3
Northfield	6,006	8	7	1
Norwich	3,304	5	4	1
Pittsford	2,806	1	1	0
Richmond	4,148	4	4	0
Royalton	2,835	1	1	0
Rutland	15,300	51	39	12
Rutland Town	4,078	3	3	0
Shelburne	7,817	19	11	8
South Burlington	19,318	47	39	8
Springfield	8,864	21	15	6
St. Albans	6,777	30	22	8
St. Johnsbury	7,158	15	9	6
Stowe	4,495	12	12	0
Swanton	6,560	7	6	1
Thetford	2,557	3	3	0
Vergennes	2,547	7	7	0
Weathersfield	2,745	2	2	0
Williston	9,778	18	15	3
Wilmington	1,796	6	4	2
Windsor	3,377	10	10	0

Table 78. Full-Time Law Enforcement Employees, by Selected State and City, 2018—Continued

(Number.)

State/city	Population	Total law enforcement employees	Total officers	Total civilians
Winhall	730	9	8	1
Winooski	7,233	20	16	4
Woodstock	2,917	7	6	1
VIRGINIA				
Abingdon	7,949	27	24	3
Alexandria	162,588	408	320	88
Altavista	3,417	12	11	1
Amherst	2,194	6	6	0
Appalachia	1,568	3	3	0
Ashland	7,876	27	24	3
Bedford	6,532	28	25	3
Berryville	4,361	10	9	1
Big Stone Gap	5,215	13	12	1
Blacksburg	44,853	76	64	12
Blackstone	3,367	13	11	2
Bluefield	4,624	20	15	5
Bowling Green	1,175	1	1	0
Bridgewater	6,125	9	9	0
Bristol	16,613	72	52	20
Broadway	3,908	5	5	0
Brookneal	1,102	1	1	0
Buena Vista	6,272	17	16	1
Burkeville	402	1	1	0
Cape Charles	1,009	6	6	0
Cedar Bluff	1,011	2	2	0
Charlottesville	48,585	140	114	26
Chase City	2,219	10	9	1
Chatham	1,434	3	3	0
Chesapeake	242,310	519	373	146
Chilhowie	1,718	6	6	0
Chincoteague	2,881	14	10	4
Christiansburg	22,444	66	61	5
Clarksville	1,175	8	7	1
Clifton Forge	3,524	12	10	2
Clintwood	1,311	4	4	0
Coeburn	1,881	7	6	1
Colonial Beach	3,584	12	10	2
Colonial Heights	17,857	56	52	4
Covington	5,462	27	18	9
Crewe	2,151	7	6	1
Culpeper	18,671	54	45	9
Damascus	788	4	4	0
Danville	40,781	134	122	12
Dayton	1,615	3	3	0
Dublin	2,667	8	7	1
Dumfries	5,265	14	14	0
Elkton	2,860	5	4	1
Emporia	5,184	36	26	10
Exmore	1,386	6	6	0
Fairfax City	24,259	81	62	19
Falls Church	14,884	40	32	8
Farmville	7,778	29	27	2
Franklin	8,100	37	27	10
Fredericksburg	28,919	94	69	25
Front Royal	15,356	51	38	13
Galax	6,559	39	23	16
Gate City	1,888	4	4	0
Glade Spring	1,424	1	1	0
Glasgow	1,106	1	1	0
Glen Lyn	100	1	1	0
Gordonsville	1,606	7	7	0
Gretna	1,205	3	3	0
Grottoes	2,813	5	5	0
Grundy	917	6	6	0
Halifax	1,219	5	5	0
Hampton	133,965	371	270	101
Harrisonburg	54,869	121	101	20
Haymarket	1,744	6	6	0
Haysi	480	3	2	1
Herndon	24,697	67	53	14
Hillsville	2,644	11	10	1
Honaker	1,343	4	3	1
Hopewell	22,562	79	59	20
Hurt	1,235	3	3	0
Independence	895	2	2	0
Jonesville	938	3	3	0
Kenbridge	1,198	5	5	0
Kilmarnock	1,407	5	5	0
La Crosse	574	1	1	0
Lawrenceville	1,004	6	6	0
Lebanon	3,184	14	13	1
Leesburg	56,030	95	79	16
Lexington	7,098	21	18	3
Louisa	1,678	6	6	0

Table 78. Full-Time Law Enforcement Employees, by Selected State and City, 2018—Continued

(Number.)

State/city	Population	Total law enforcement employees	Total officers	Total civilians
Luray	4,806	13	12	1
Lynchburg	81,603	188	166	22
Manassas	41,888	118	90	28
Manassas Park	16,882	38	30	8
Marion	5,615	22	21	1
Martinsville	13,025	50	45	5
Middleburg	879	7	6	1
Middletown	1,365	4	3	1
Mount Jackson	2,100	6	6	0
Narrows	1,950	5	5	0
New Market	2,245	5	5	0
Newport News	178,734	567	421	146
Norfolk	244,347	801	702	99
Norton	3,914	24	17	7
Occoquan	1,097	1	1	0
Onancock	1,218	5	5	0
Onley	502	5	5	0
Orange	5,016	17	15	2
Parksley	817	3	3	0
Pearisburg	2,643	7	7	0
Pembroke	1,084	3	3	0
Pennington Gap	1,732	6	6	0
Petersburg	31,568	111	87	24
Poquoson	12,011	24	23	1
Portsmouth	94,218	350	232	118
Pound	939	3	3	0
Pulaski	8,720	32	28	4
Purcellville	10,090	17	14	3
Quantico	529	1	1	0
Radford	17,797	47	35	12
Remington	645	1	1	0
Rich Creek	744	1	1	0
Richlands	5,256	22	17	5
Richmond	229,927	841	737	104
Roanoke	100,042	309	263	46
Rocky Mount	4,762	25	23	2
Rural Retreat	1,459	1	1	0
Salem	25,942	84	59	25
Saltville	1,927	7	7	0
Shenandoah	2,316	6	5	1
Smithfield	8,392	23	19	4
South Boston	7,721	31	28	3
South Hill	4,345	23	21	2
Stanley	1,651	5	5	0
Staunton	24,584	63	50	13
Stephens City	2,024	4	4	0
St. Paul	877	6	6	0
Strasburg	6,643	19	18	1
Suffolk	90,817	231	178	53
Tangier	708	1	1	0
Tappahannock	2,417	10	9	1
Tazewell	4,185	15	13	2
Timberville	2,662	6	6	0
Victoria	1,631	4	4	0
Vienna	16,660	51	41	10
Vinton	8,077	26	24	2
Virginia Beach	451,001	953	778	175
Warrenton	9,912	22	20	2
Warsaw	1,484	5	5	0
Waverly	1,976	13	7	6
Waynesboro	22,470	58	47	11
Weber City	1,224	4	4	0
West Point	3,311	11	10	1
White Stone	332	2	2	0
Williamsburg	15,191	41	38	3
Winchester	28,128	85	76	9
Windsor	2,731	6	6	0
Wise	2,965	13	12	1
Woodstock	5,232	20	18	2
Wytheville	7,969	28	25	3
WASHINGTON				
Aberdeen	16,404	53	39	14
Airway Heights	9,085	21	20	1
Algona	3,207	10	8	2
Anacortes	17,130	33	25	8
Arlington	19,394	32	27	5
Asotin	1,301	2	2	0
Auburn	82,381	133	113	20
Bainbridge Island	24,739	26	22	4
Battle Ground	21,002	28	24	4
Bellevue	146,913	210	172	38
Bellingham	90,208	174	115	59
Black Diamond	4,476	10	9	1
Blaine	5,402	14	12	2

Table 78. Full-Time Law Enforcement Employees, by Selected State and City, 2018—Continued

(Number.)

State/city	Population	Total law enforcement employees	Total officers	Total civilians
Bonney Lake	21,192	34	27	7
Bothell	46,387	89	61	28
Bremerton	41,527	64	52	12
Brewster	2,339	6	5	1
Brier	6,975	8	7	1
Buckley	5,402	11	9	2
Burien	52,189	76	53	23
Burlington	8,839	25	20	5
Camas	23,865	30	26	4
Carnation	2,224	3	2	1
Castle Rock	2,251	5	4	1
Centralia	17,299	36	27	9
Chehalis	7,573	22	17	5
Cheney	12,715	23	17	6
Chewelah	2,643	6	5	1
Clarkston	7,417	16	14	2
Cle Elum	2,966	9	8	1
Clyde Hill	3,367	10	9	1
Colfax	2,917	5	5	0
College Place	9,325	16	13	3
Colville	4,777	12	10	2
Connell	5,765	7	6	1
Cosmopolis	1,620	6	5	1
Coulee Dam	1,076	2	2	0
Coupeville	1,942	2	2	0
Covington	21,436	24	18	6
Des Moines	31,460	46	35	11
Dupont	9,678	10	8	2
Duvall	7,980	14	13	1
East Wenatchee	14,097	24	21	3
Eatonville	3,027	6	5	1
Edgewood	11,510	10	10	0
Edmonds	42,565	63	51	12
Ellensburg	20,616	35	29	6
Elma	3,089	7	6	1
Enumclaw	11,882	30	17	13
Ephrata	8,062	18	15	3
Everett	111,091	230	194	36
Everson	4,325	7	6	1
Federal Way	97,762	155	126	29
Ferndale	14,439	23	20	3
Fife	10,300	39	30	9
Fircrest	6,839	9	9	0
Forks	3,874	11	5	6
Gig Harbor	9,909	20	18	2
Goldendale	3,496	11	9	2
Grand Coulee	2,047	8	8	0
Grandview	11,163	23	19	4
Granger	3,850	6	6	0
Hoquiam	8,469	24	23	1
Issaquah	38,606	72	41	31
Kalama	2,737	7	6	1
Kelso	12,164	30	26	4
Kenmore	23,219	20	16	4
Kennewick	82,687	116	101	15
Kent	129,870	197	143	54
Kettle Falls	1,616	4	3	1
Kirkland	89,805	134	98	36
Kittitas	1,510	1	1	0
La Center	3,258	10	8	2
Lacey	50,844	62	50	12
Lake Forest Park	13,504	20	17	3
Lake Stevens	33,491	40	32	8
Lakewood	60,694	118	101	17
Langley	1,140	4	4	0
Liberty Lake	10,272	12	11	1
Long Beach	1,416	8	7	1
Longview	37,720	72	60	12
Lynden	14,612	18	14	4
Lynnwood	38,620	105	70	35
Mabton	2,283	1	1	0
Maple Valley	26,212	24	19	5
Marysville	70,204	95	69	26
Mattawa	4,586	6	5	1
McCleary	1,697	3	3	0
Medina	3,311	10	8	2
Mercer Island	25,641	34	30	4
Mill Creek	21,234	28	24	4
Milton	8,366	14	14	0
Monroe	19,003	41	32	9
Montesano	3,959	9	8	1
Morton	1,164	3	3	0
Moses Lake	23,763	44	36	8
Mountlake Terrace	21,549	35	27	8
Mount Vernon	35,550	57	43	14

Table 78. Full-Time Law Enforcement Employees, by Selected State and City, 2018—Continued

(Number.)

State/city	Population	Total law enforcement employees	Total officers	Total civilians
Moxee	4,114	7	6	1
Mukilteo	21,638	36	29	7
Napavine	1,908	3	2	1
Newcastle	11,878	12	10	2
Normandy Park	6,693	11	10	1
Oak Harbor	23,330	37	24	13
Ocean Shores	5,977	11	10	1
Odessa	871	2	2	0
Olympia	52,312	107	74	33
Omak	4,784	12	11	1
Oroville	1,669	6	5	1
Orting	8,179	11	10	1
Othello	8,247	23	16	7
Pacific	7,269	12	11	1
Palouse	1,064	3	3	0
Pasco	74,582	87	78	9
Pe Ell	656	1	1	0
Port Angeles	19,992	57	32	25
Port Orchard	14,269	24	22	2
Port Townsend	9,615	18	14	4
Poulsbo	10,886	23	20	3
Prosser	6,342	15	14	1
Pullman	33,896	42	28	14
Puyallup	41,572	80	59	21
Quincy	7,598	26	21	5
Raymond	2,928	7	6	1
Reardan	584	1	1	0
Redmond	65,827	117	82	35
Renton	102,749	154	124	30
Republic	1,062	2	2	0
Richland	57,450	79	65	14
Ridgefield	8,552	12	11	1
Ritzville	1,631	4	4	0
Roy	826	2	2	0
Royal City	2,212	3	3	0
Ruston	840	5	5	0
Sammamish	65,604	39	31	8
SeaTac	29,463	60	42	18
Seattle	742,759	1,954	1,420	534
Sedro Woolley	11,953	20	17	3
Selah	7,932	18	15	3
Sequim	7,183	23	19	4
Shelton	10,188	21	18	3
Shoreline	56,637	69	50	19
Snohomish	10,227	20	18	2
Snoqualmie	13,947	26	22	4
Soap Lake	1,583	5	4	1
South Bend	1,654	5	4	1
Spokane	218,222	410	326	84
Spokane Valley	99,020	133	103	30
Springdale	294	1	1	0
Stanwood	7,225	13	11	2
Steilacoom	6,389	11	10	1
Sumas	1,488	7	6	1
Sumner	10,191	23	19	4
Sunnyside	16,468	48	29	19
Tacoma	215,687	386	346	40
Tenino	1,851	5	4	1
Tieton	1,310	2	2	0
Toledo	755	3	2	1
Tonasket	1,123	4	3	1
Toppenish	8,898	16	11	5
Tukwila	20,288	85	67	18
Tumwater	23,405	36	29	7
Twisp	961	3	3	0
Union Gap	6,163	21	17	4
University Place	33,743	17	16	1
Vancouver	177,580	258	205	53
Walla Walla	32,906	77	47	30
Wapato	5,045	8	7	1
Warden	2,733	4	3	1
Washougal	15,949	26	21	5
Wenatchee	34,169	50	40	10
Westport	2,047	8	7	1
West Richland	15,012	23	19	4
White Salmon	2,583	6	5	1
Winlock	1,357	2	2	0
Winthrop	444	3	2	1
Woodinville	12,153	19	15	4
Woodland	6,228	11	9	2
Yakima	93,959	173	129	44
Yelm	9,498	17	15	2
Zillah	3,139	9	8	1

Table 78. Full-Time Law Enforcement Employees, by Selected State and City, 2018—Continued

(Number.)

State/city	Population	Total law enforcement employees	Total officers	Total civilians
WEST VIRGINIA				
Alderson	1,151	4	4	0
Anmoore	745	2	2	0
Ansted	1,345	3	2	1
Athens	905	1	1	0
Barboursville	4,256	24	22	2
Barrackville	1,298	3	2	1
Beckley	16,234	69	50	19
Belington	1,856	3	3	0
Belle	1,149	4	4	0
Benwood	1,292	11	6	5
Berkeley Springs	599	2	2	0
Bethlehem	2,339	5	5	0
Bluefield	9,789	33	27	6
Bradshaw	279	1	1	0
Bramwell	343	2	2	0
Bridgeport	8,708	35	31	4
Buckhannon	5,516	12	11	1
Burnsville	487	1	1	0
Cameron	861	2	2	0
Cedar Grove	932	1	1	0
Ceredo	1,339	8	4	4
Chapmanville	1,124	6	6	0
Charleston	47,470	187	163	24
Charles Town	6,060	18	16	2
Chesapeake	1,443	2	2	0
Chester	2,429	6	5	1
Clarksburg	15,489	42	39	3
Clendenin	1,131	4	4	0
Danville	621	2	2	0
Davy	347	1	1	0
Delbarton	506	2	2	0
Dunbar	7,262	12	11	1
Eleanor	1,609	2	2	0
Elkins	7,029	14	12	2
Fairmont	18,430	43	37	6
Fairview	408	1	1	0
Farmington	368	1	1	0
Fayetteville	2,750	11	10	1
Follansbee	2,736	7	7	0
Fort Gay	668	3	3	0
Gary	809	1	1	0
Gassaway	868	1	1	0
Gauley Bridge	564	1	1	0
Gilbert	397	2	2	0
Glasgow	854	3	3	0
Glen Dale	1,398	11	6	5
Glenville	1,462	3	3	0
Grafton	5,065	8	7	1
Grantsville	527	1	1	0
Grant Town	599	1	1	0
Granville	3,138	16	16	0
Hamlin	1,063	3	2	1
Harpers Ferry/Bolivar	1,310	3	2	1
Harrisville	1,722	1	1	0
Hartford City	593	1	1	0
Hinton	2,417	8	6	2
Hundred	269	1	1	0
Huntington	46,787	100	97	3
Hurricane	6,579	22	20	2
Iaeger	249	1	1	0
Kenova	2,979	14	10	4
Kermit	359	1	1	0
Keyser	5,029	15	10	5
Kimball	158	1	1	0
Kingwood	2,927	3	3	0
Lewisburg	3,917	14	12	2
Logan	1,508	11	8	3
Lumberport	844	1	1	0
Mabscott	1,284	1	1	0
Madison	2,764	8	7	1
Man	652	3	3	0
Mannington	2,040	4	4	0
Marmet	1,397	5	5	0
Martinsburg	17,428	60	47	13
Mason	941	5	4	1
Matewan	434	1	1	0
McMechen	1,755	4	4	0
Milton	2,641	10	9	1
Monongah	1,135	1	1	0
Montgomery	1,537	8	7	1
Moorefield	2,417	11	9	2
Morgantown	30,855	83	71	12
Moundsville	8,417	21	17	4
Mount Hope	1,297	4	3	1
Mullens	1,343	2	2	0

Table 78. Full-Time Law Enforcement Employees, by Selected State and City, 2018—Continued

(Number.)

State/city	Population	Total law enforcement employees	Total officers	Total civilians
New Cumberland	1,043	1	1	0
New Haven	1,492	1	1	0
New Martinsville	5,107	14	10	4
Nitro	6,509	19	17	2
Nutter Fort	1,532	5	5	0
Oak Hill	8,264	21	17	4
Oceana	1,226	4	4	0
Paden City	2,396	5	4	1
Parkersburg	29,933	86	73	13
Parsons	1,407	1	1	0
Paw Paw	489	2	1	1
Pennsboro	1,032	1	1	0
Petersburg	2,621	2	2	0
Philippi	3,446	6	6	0
Piedmont	805	1	1	0
Pineville	590	3	3	0
Point Pleasant	4,126	10	5	5
Pratt	571	3	3	0
Princeton	5,780	22	20	2
Rainelle	1,481	5	4	1
Ranson	5,292	16	15	1
Ravenswood	3,720	11	10	1
Reedsville	600	1	1	0
Rhodell	160	2	1	1
Richwood	1,887	3	3	0
Ridgeley	624	3	2	1
Ripley	3,229	11	10	1
Rivesville	914	1	1	0
Romney	1,723	5	4	1
Ronceverte	1,710	6	6	0
Rupert	915	1	1	0
Salem	1,479	5	4	1
Shepherdstown	1,757	6	5	1
Shinnston	2,118	7	7	0
Sistersville	1,282	4	4	0
Smithers	746	4	3	1
Sophia	1,264	2	2	0
South Charleston	12,357	47	44	3
Spencer	2,086	6	6	0
St. Albans	10,161	29	26	3
Star City	1,986	7	7	0
St. Marys	1,778	4	4	0
Stonewood	1,727	2	2	0
Summersville	3,332	15	14	1
Sutton	987	1	1	0
Sylvester	140	1	1	0
Terra Alta	1,503	3	3	0
Triadelphia	753	1	1	0
Vienna	10,306	24	20	4
War	697	2	2	0
Wayne	1,397	1	1	0
Webster Springs	677	5	4	1
Weirton	18,542	37	34	3
Welch	1,663	7	6	1
Wellsburg	2,560	7	6	1
West Liberty	1,427	1	1	0
West Logan	365	1	1	0
West Milford	606	2	2	0
Weston	3,953	7	5	2
Westover	4,208	13	12	1
Wheeling	26,855	81	69	12
White Hall	661	5	5	0
White Sulphur Springs	2,419	7	6	1
Whitesville	443	2	2	0
Williamson	2,745	6	5	1
Williamstown	2,906	8	7	1
Winfield	2,367	6	6	0
WISCONSIN				
Adams	1,852	3	3	0
Albany	999	3	3	0
Algoma	3,071	5	5	0
Altoona	7,827	15	14	1
Amery	2,809	6	6	0
Antigo	7,720	18	15	3
Appleton	74,931	135	109	26
Arcadia	3,065	4	4	0
Ashland	7,770	21	19	2
Ashwaubenon	17,316	58	51	7
Athens	1,086	1	1	0
Balsam Lake	977	2	2	0
Bangor	1,472	3	3	0
Baraboo	12,178	33	27	6
Barneveld	1,240	1	1	0
Barron	3,300	6	6	0

Table 78. Full-Time Law Enforcement Employees, by Selected State and City, 2018—Continued

(Number.)

State/city	Population	Total law enforcement employees	Total officers	Total civilians
Bayfield	471	3	3	0
Bayside	4,375	14	13	1
Beaver Dam	16,394	37	33	4
Belleville	2,432	6	5	1
Beloit	36,746	79	68	11
Beloit Town	7,688	14	12	2
Berlin	5,365	13	12	1
Big Bend	1,395	6	3	3
Birchwood	428	1	1	0
Black River Falls	3,488	7	6	1
Blair	1,365	3	3	0
Bloomer	3,491	7	6	1
Bloomfield	6,323	8	8	0
Blue Mounds	988	2	2	0
Boscobel	3,104	6	6	0
Boyceville	1,098	2	2	0
Brillion	3,116	8	8	0
Brodhead	3,247	12	8	4
Brookfield	38,065	82	66	16
Brookfield Township	6,295	17	16	1
Brown Deer	11,963	33	30	3
Brownsville	573	1	1	0
Burlington	11,039	21	20	1
Butler	1,812	9	8	1
Caledonia	25,047	35	33	2
Campbellsport	1,963	2	2	0
Campbell Township	4,366	5	5	0
Cashton	1,103	2	2	0
Cedarburg	11,469	26	19	7
Chenequa	597	9	8	1
Chetek	2,141	5	4	1
Chilton	3,798	7	7	0
Chippewa Falls	14,084	26	23	3
Cleveland	1,457	3	2	1
Clinton	2,124	5	5	0
Clintonville	4,332	15	11	4
Colfax	1,142	2	2	0
Columbus	5,037	12	10	2
Cornell	1,412	2	2	0
Cottage Grove	7,024	15	13	2
Crandon	1,833	4	3	1
Cross Plains	4,331	7	6	1
Cuba City	2,037	4	4	0
Cudahy	18,290	39	30	9
Cumberland	2,112	6	6	0
Darlington	2,351	5	5	0
Deforest	10,557	19	17	2
Delafield	7,588	18	16	2
Delavan	9,938	28	22	6
Delavan Town	5,322	12	11	1
De Pere	25,199	40	36	4
Dodgeville	4,734	10	10	0
Durand	1,805	4	4	0
Eagle River	1,514	7	6	1
Eagle Village	2,086	4	2	2
East Troy	4,333	7	7	0
Eau Claire	68,923	130	94	36
Edgar	1,452	1	1	0
Edgerton	5,602	9	8	1
Eleva	664	1	1	0
Elkhart Lake	1,022	3	3	0
Elkhorn	9,934	17	15	2
Elk Mound	875	1	1	0
Ellsworth	3,287	5	5	0
Elm Grove	6,205	25	17	8
Elroy	1,355	3	3	0
Evansville	5,379	10	9	1
Everest Metropolitan	17,392	31	27	4
Fall Creek	1,309	1	1	0
Fall River	1,703	2	2	0
Fennimore	2,478	5	5	0
Fitchburg	30,151	59	46	13
Fond du Lac	42,777	81	73	8
Fontana	1,719	8	7	1
Fort Atkinson	12,495	26	20	6
Fox Crossing	19,323	32	27	5
Fox Lake	1,452	2	2	0
Fox Point	6,671	18	17	1
Fox Valley Metro	22,006	28	26	2
Franklin	36,251	73	60	13
Frederic	1,098	2	1	1
Freedom	6,231	2	2	0
Galesville	1,585	4	4	0
Geneva Town	5,032	7	6	1
Genoa City	3,005	7	6	1

Table 78. Full-Time Law Enforcement Employees, by Selected State and City, 2018—Continued

(Number.)

State/city	Population	Total law enforcement employees	Total officers	Total civilians
Germantown	20,014	43	32	11
Gillett	1,313	4	4	0
Gilman	392	2	1	1
Glendale	12,710	47	42	5
Grafton	11,662	28	22	6
Grand Chute	22,865	39	35	4
Grand Rapids	7,385	8	6	2
Grantsburg	1,287	6	3	3
Green Bay	105,281	220	180	40
Greendale	14,181	40	30	10
Greenfield	36,850	76	57	19
Green Lake	925	3	3	0
Hales Corners	7,640	17	16	1
Hammond	1,887	4	3	1
Hartford	15,183	31	27	4
Hartland	9,302	19	17	2
Hayward	2,296	6	5	1
Hazel Green	1,230	2	2	0
Highland	834	1	1	0
Hillsboro	1,401	2	2	0
Hobart-Lawrence	14,667	11	10	1
Holmen	9,993	13	12	1
Horicon	3,605	8	7	1
Hortonville	2,776	7	6	1
Hudson	13,848	28	25	3
Hurley	1,426	7	6	1
Independence	1,305	3	3	0
Iron Ridge	895	1	1	0
Iron River	1,133	3	3	0
Jackson	7,156	12	11	1
Janesville	64,471	114	103	11
Jefferson	8,021	17	14	3
Juneau	2,662	5	4	1
Kaukauna	16,172	27	26	1
Kenosha	99,948	207	196	11
Kewaskum	4,139	8	8	0
Kewaunee	2,856	6	6	0
Kiel	3,780	8	7	1
Kohler	2,077	8	7	1
Kronenwetter	7,813	9	8	1
La Crosse	51,901	116	95	21
Ladysmith	3,120	7	6	1
La Farge	766	1	1	0
Lake Delton	3,005	24	21	3
Lake Geneva	7,907	33	24	9
Lake Hallie	6,742	10	9	1
Lake Mills	5,925	11	9	2
Lancaster	3,717	7	6	1
Lena	539	1	1	0
Linn Township	2,403	12	6	6
Lodi	3,058	13	6	7
Lomira	2,366	4	3	1
Luxemburg	2,562	1	1	0
Lyndon Station	479	1	1	0
Madison	258,455	595	482	113
Manawa	1,284	1	1	0
Manitowoc	32,557	74	64	10
Maple Bluff	1,333	5	5	0
Marathon City	1,506	3	3	0
Marinette	10,561	28	24	4
Marion	1,191	8	4	4
Markesan	1,399	4	4	0
Marshall Village	3,988	8	7	1
Marshfield	18,309	48	40	8
Mauston	4,390	10	9	1
Mayville	4,862	8	7	1
McFarland	8,544	19	17	2
Medford	4,294	10	9	1
Menasha	17,788	38	31	7
Menomonee Falls	37,712	67	54	13
Menomonie	16,450	33	27	6
Mequon	24,311	49	37	12
Merrill	9,091	25	22	3
Middleton	19,970	48	39	9
Milton	5,585	13	11	2
Milwaukee	595,619	2,305	1,851	454
Mineral Point	2,478	6	6	0
Minocqua	4,380	18	11	7
Mishicot	1,381	3	3	0
Mondovi	2,613	4	4	0
Monona	8,183	25	20	5
Monroe	10,575	33	25	8
Monticello	1,204	2	2	0
Mosinee	4,003	8	7	1
Mount Horeb	7,462	12	12	0

Table 78. Full-Time Law Enforcement Employees, by Selected State and City, 2018—Continued

(Number.)

State/city	Population	Total law enforcement employees	Total officers	Total civilians
Mount Pleasant	26,571	56	51	5
Mukwonago	8,034	19	12	7
Mukwonago Town	8,146	7	6	1
Muscoda	1,253	3	3	0
Muskego	25,118	47	39	8
Neenah	26,016	50	40	10
Neillsville	2,410	6	5	1
Nekoosa	2,408	7	7	0
New Berlin	39,763	81	69	12
New Glarus	2,148	2	2	0
New Holstein	3,098	7	6	1
New Lisbon	2,500	4	4	0
New London	7,083	19	17	2
New Richmond	9,052	19	18	1
Niagara	1,543	4	4	0
North Fond du Lac	5,079	10	8	2
North Hudson	3,801	5	4	1
Oak Creek	36,643	82	58	24
Oconomowoc	16,850	30	23	7
Oconomowoc Lake	600	6	6	0
Oconomowoc Town	8,692	12	11	1
Oconto	4,421	9	9	0
Oconto Falls	2,810	6	6	0
Omro	3,590	7	6	1
Onalaska	18,841	31	28	3
Oregon	10,549	21	19	2
Osceola	2,500	5	4	1
Oshkosh	66,736	118	104	14
Osseo	1,671	4	4	0
Palmyra	1,766	6	6	0
Park Falls	2,227	7	7	0
Pepin	775	1	1	0
Peshtigo	3,355	6	6	0
Pewaukee Village	8,172	21	19	2
Phillips	1,345	5	5	0
Pittsville	833	1	1	0
Plainfield	834	1	1	0
Platteville	12,642	25	19	6
Pleasant Prairie	20,911	37	34	3
Plover	12,853	23	20	3
Plymouth	8,554	16	16	0
Portage	10,496	26	22	4
Port Edwards	1,772	4	3	1
Port Washington	11,831	25	20	5
Poynette	2,489	5	4	1
Prairie du Chien	5,618	13	12	1
Prescott	4,273	9	8	1
Princeton	1,165	3	3	0
Pulaski	3,581	8	7	1
Racine	77,373	229	195	34
Reedsburg	9,518	29	22	7
Rhinelander	7,535	20	17	3
Rib Lake	875	1	1	0
Rice Lake	8,332	18	18	0
Richland Center	4,968	13	11	2
Rio	1,040	2	2	0
Ripon	7,823	19	14	5
Ripon Town	1,381	1	1	0
River Falls	15,578	27	24	3
River Hills	1,590	11	11	0
Rome Town	2,670	6	6	0
Rosendale	1,032	1	1	0
Rothschild	5,334	13	11	2
Sauk Prairie	4,611	16	13	3
Saukville	4,415	12	10	2
Seymour	3,460	12	6	6
Sharon	1,572	6	5	1
Shawano	8,936	22	20	2
Sheboygan	48,195	102	82	20
Sheboygan Falls	7,945	16	14	2
Shiocton	920	2	1	1
Shorewood	13,368	29	25	4
Shorewood Hills	2,101	9	7	2
Shullsburg	1,203	1	1	0
Siren	773	4	3	1
Slinger	5,476	11	10	1
South Milwaukee	20,972	41	35	6
Sparta	9,681	22	20	2
Spencer	1,908	4	4	0
Spooner	2,583	8	7	1
Spring Green	1,641	4	3	1
Spring Valley	1,374	1	1	0
Stanley	3,671	5	5	0
St. Croix Falls	2,036	6	5	1
Stevens Point	26,233	48	44	4

Table 78. Full-Time Law Enforcement Employees, by Selected State and City, 2018—Continued

(Number.)

State/city	Population	Total law enforcement employees	Total officers	Total civilians
St. Francis	9,459	22	21	1
Stoughton	13,149	29	23	6
Strum	1,094	2	2	0
Sturgeon Bay	8,889	22	20	2
Sturtevant	6,966	12	11	1
Summit	4,947	10	10	0
Sun Prairie	33,390	72	52	20
Superior	26,054	66	61	5
Theresa	1,206	1	1	0
Thiensville	3,137	8	7	1
Thorp	1,623	3	3	0
Three Lakes	2,088	5	5	0
Tomah	9,394	22	20	2
Tomahawk	3,147	9	8	1
Town of East Troy	4,058	7	6	1
Town of Madison	6,942	13	12	1
Trempealeau	1,645	3	3	0
Twin Lakes	6,077	18	13	5
Two Rivers	11,077	29	26	3
Verona	13,490	25	23	2
Viroqua	4,461	11	9	2
Walworth	2,849	8	7	1
Washburn	2,039	5	5	0
Waterloo	3,337	8	7	1
Watertown	23,628	54	40	14
Waukesha	72,672	152	117	35
Waunakee	14,000	21	19	2
Waupaca	5,859	16	15	1
Waupun	11,260	17	16	1
Wausau	38,682	85	74	11
Wautoma	2,130	9	9	0
Wauwatosa	48,562	120	94	26
Webster	619	2	2	0
West Allis	59,887	157	126	31
West Bend	31,651	71	54	17
Westby	2,255	3	3	0
Westfield	1,244	1	1	0
West Milwaukee	4,152	24	19	5
West Salem	5,055	8	7	1
Whitefish Bay	13,933	25	24	1
Whitehall	1,582	4	4	0
Whitewater	14,561	32	23	9
Wild Rose	700	2	2	0
Williams Bay	2,600	9	8	1
Wilton	498	1	1	0
Winneconne	2,429	6	5	1
Wisconsin Dells	3,018	20	15	5
Wisconsin Rapids	17,725	41	37	4
Woodruff	1,952	6	5	1
WYOMING				
Afton	2,018	4	4	0
Buffalo	4,583	21	12	9
Casper	58,200	136	101	35
Cheyenne	64,178	126	107	19
Cody	9,935	24	21	3
Diamondville	761	2	2	0
Douglas	6,386	19	17	2
Evanston	11,797	30	25	5
Evansville	3,001	12	10	2
Gillette	30,659	80	53	27
Glenrock	2,584	11	6	5
Green River	12,025	33	25	8
Greybull	1,864	6	5	1
Hanna	787	2	2	0
Jackson	10,671	40	33	7
Kemmerer	2,761	6	6	0
Lander	7,542	20	19	1
Laramie	32,509	72	45	27
Lusk	1,539	6	6	0
Mills	3,966	21	15	6
Moorcroft	1,060	4	3	1
Newcastle	3,370	16	8	8
Pine Bluffs	1,143	2	2	0
Powell	6,458	24	17	7
Rawlins	8,806	27	17	10
Riverton	11,076	24	24	0
Rock Springs	23,405	56	42	14
Saratoga	1,651	8	3	5
Sheridan	17,919	44	28	16
Sundance	1,276	3	3	0
Thermopolis	2,919	13	7	6
Torrington	6,699	24	17	7
Wheatland	3,557	10	9	1
Worland	5,148	13	12	1

1 The employee data presented in this table for Charlotte-Mecklenburg represent only Charlotte-Mecklenburg Police Department and exclude Mecklenburg County Sheriff's Office.

Table 79. Full-Time Law Enforcement Employees, by Selected State and University or College, 2018

(Number.)

State and university/college	Student enrollment[1]	Law enforcement employees	Officers	Civilians
ALABAMA				
Alabama A&M University	6,392	41	16	25
Alabama State University	5,916	30	24	6
Auburn University, Montgomery	5,775	22	14	8
Bevill State Community College	5,505	4	2	2
Bishop State Community College	4,763	7	7	0
Calhoun Community College	15,185	12	11	1
Coastal Alabama Community College	7,048	6	6	0
Jacksonville State University	10,166	35	30	5
Jefferson State Community College	13,564	12	10	2
Lawson State Community College	4,588	8	8	0
Samford University	5,956	17	14	3
Southern Union State Community College	7,071	4	4	0
Troy University	22,125	16	12	4
Tuskegee University	3,219	26	11	15
University of Alabama				
Huntsville	9,897	27	17	10
Tuscaloosa	41,834	162	85	77
University of Montevallo	3,063	20	10	10
University of North Alabama	8,315	17	15	2
University of South Alabama	18,481	32	25	7
University of West Alabama	6,029	15	9	6
Wallace Community College				
Dothan	6,098	8	8	0
Selma	2,765	8	8	0
Wallace State Community College	7,270	8	7	1
ALASKA				
University of Alaska				
Anchorage	25,009	19	12	7
Fairbanks	13,263	11	8	3
ARIZONA				
Arizona State University, Main Campus	118,390	148	84	64
Arizona Western College	11,653	13	8	5
Central Arizona College	9,741	11	10	1
Northern Arizona University	34,554	37	22	15
Pima Community College	34,308	48	28	20
University of Arizona	47,648	114	59	55
Yavapai College	10,000	9	7	2
ARKANSAS				
Arkansas State University				
Beebe	5,491	6	5	1
Jonesboro	19,148	25	20	5
Newport	4,943	3	3	0
Arkansas Tech University	13,677	24	21	3
Henderson State University	4,043	9	8	1
Northwest Arkansas Community College	11,225	18	13	5
Southern Arkansas University	5,683	9	8	1
Southern Arkansas University Tech	2,056	3	3	0
University of Arkansas				
Fayetteville	29,958	54	34	20
Little Rock	14,292	35	24	11
Medical Sciences	3,147	62	36	26
Monticello	4,702	10	9	1
Pine Bluff	3,106	16	12	4
University of Arkansas Community College at				
Morrilton	2,684	3	3	0
University of Central Arkansas	13,347	37	26	11
CALIFORNIA				
Allan Hancock College	17,716	7	3	4
California State Polytechnic University				
Pomona	26,669	50	19	31
San Luis Obispo	22,168	42	20	22
California State University				
Bakersfield	11,152	21	13	8
Channel Islands	7,161	29	14	15
Chico	19,004	25	15	10
Dominguez Hills	15,580	30	22	8
East Bay	17,600	26	14	12
Fresno	26,380	38	25	13
Fullerton	44,790	39	29	10
Long Beach	40,641	38	22	16
Los Angeles	29,181	36	20	16
Monterey Bay	7,801	25	15	10
Northridge	41,909	35	19	16
Sacramento	33,379	42	23	19
San Bernardino	21,914	32	17	15
San Jose	34,035	74	28	46
San Marcos	13,615	26	19	7
Stanislaus	10,627	19	11	8
Chaffey College	28,430	13	13	0
College of the Sequoias	15,236	7	6	1

Table 79. Full-Time Law Enforcement Employees, by Selected State and University or College, 2018—Continued

(Number.)

State and university/college	Student enrollment[1]	Law enforcement employees	Officers	Civilians
Contra Costa Community College	52,597	32	21	11
Cuesta College	14,878	10	6	4
El Camino College	33,150	22	14	8
Foothill-De Anza College	63,210	16	12	4
Humboldt State University	9,171	20	12	8
Irvine Valley College	21,294	14	8	6
Marin Community College	7,905	8	6	2
Pasadena Community College	38,096	15	10	5
Riverside Community College	58,507	27	22	5
San Bernardino Community College	26,697	17	7	10
San Diego State University	36,908	50	27	23
San Francisco State University	33,036	48	22	26
San Jose/Evergreen Community College	26,585	18	7	11
Sonoma County Junior College	30,921	24	12	12
Sonoma State University	10,041	13	11	2
State Center Community College District	60,065	20	15	5
University of California				
Berkeley	42,684	110	50	60
Davis	38,778	65	43	22
Irvine	34,754	58	39	19
Los Angeles	46,298	96	61	35
Merced	7,703	26	15	11
Riverside	24,371	41	32	9
San Diego	36,785	74	38	36
San Francisco	3,176	151	50	101
Santa Barbara	25,833	66	44	22
Santa Cruz	19,912	36	19	17
Ventura County Community College District	49,927	15	14	1
West Valley-Mission College	25,905	13	8	5
COLORADO				
Adams State University	4,343	5	4	1
Arapahoe Community College	14,866	11	8	3
Auraria Higher Education Center[2]		45	28	17
Colorado School of Mines	6,910	11	10	1
Colorado State University, Fort Collins	36,966	45	32	13
Fort Lewis College	3,936	10	8	2
Pikes Peak Community College	18,666	20	18	2
Red Rocks Community College	13,644	10	7	3
University of Colorado				
Boulder	37,921	72	34	38
Colorado Springs	16,743	30	18	12
Denver	31,281	59	26	33
University of Northern Colorado	15,365	21	13	8
CONNECTICUT				
Central Connecticut State University	13,930	25	19	6
Eastern Connecticut State University	6,068	20	11	9
Southern Connecticut State University	11,978	30	25	5
University of Connecticut, Storrs, Avery Point, and Hartford[2]		130	96	34
Western Connecticut State University	6,853	19	13	6
Yale University	13,613	109	91	18
DELAWARE				
Delaware State University	5,162	37	14	23
University of Delaware	24,855	74	46	28
FLORIDA				
Florida A&M University	10,797	46	29	17
Florida Atlantic University	37,793	63	33	30
Florida Gulf Coast University	16,732	26	19	7
Florida International University	68,005	98	61	37
Florida Polytechnic University	1,370	13	10	3
Florida SouthWestern State College	21,624	28	14	14
New College of Florida	899	20	16	4
Northwest Florida State College	8,079	4	4	0
Pensacola State College	13,602	24	9	15
Santa Fe College	20,335	22	16	6
Tallahassee Community College	16,979	24	12	12
University of Central Florida	75,824	129	75	54
University of Florida	58,993	136	82	54
University of North Florida	19,013	41	30	11
University of South Florida				
St. Petersburg	5,731	22	15	7
Tampa	50,961	81	55	26
University of West Florida	16,517	27	20	7
GEORGIA				
Abraham Baldwin Agricultural College	4,012	14	13	1
Agnes Scott College	981	14	7	7
Albany State University	9,171	33	29	4
Albany Technical College	4,798	3	3	0
Andrew College	320	2	2	0
Athens Technical College	5,859	2	2	0

Table 79. Full-Time Law Enforcement Employees, by Selected State and University or College, 2018—Continued

(Number.)

State and university/college	Student enrollment[1]	Law enforcement employees	Officers	Civilians
Atlanta Metropolitan State College	4,068	12	6	6
Augusta Technical College	6,284	7	7	0
Augusta University	8,998	53	37	16
Bainbridge State College	3,193	7	5	2
Berry College	2,339	17	12	5
Chattahoochee Technical College	14,643	13	10	3
Clark Atlanta University	4,263	44	19	25
Clayton State University	8,590	25	13	12
College of Coastal Georgia	4,372	12	12	0
Columbus State University	10,295	37	26	11
Dalton State College	6,043	16	13	3
East Georgia State College	3,777	8	8	0
Emory University	15,653	71	52	19
Fort Valley State University	3,044	34	13	21
Georgia College and State University	7,989	24	16	8
Georgia Gwinnett College	14,770	27	22	5
Georgia Institute of Technology	31,513	108	79	29
Georgia Military College	14,343	5	3	2
Georgia Southern University	23,596	70	49	21
Georgia Southwestern State University	3,646	12	12	0
Georgia State University	38,370	268	124	144
Gordon State College	4,523	14	14	0
Gwinnett Technical College	11,152	3	3	0
Kennesaw State University	40,676	96	57	39
Middle Georgia State University	9,429	34	31	3
Morehouse College	2,219	21	6	15
Piedmont College	3,088	6	4	2
Savannah State University	5,488	44	27	17
Savannah Technical College	6,050	12	11	1
Southern Crescent Technical College	6,558	5	5	0
Spelman College	2,166	32	22	10
University of Georgia	40,462	105	85	20
University of North Georgia	21,419	45	35	10
University of West Georgia	15,672	42	32	10
Valdosta State University	13,710	31	24	7
Wesleyan College	848	6	6	0
West Georgia Technical College	9,696	7	7	0
Young Harris College	1,336	4	4	0
ILLINOIS				
Eastern Illinois University	8,590	14	12	2
Elgin Community College	15,211	17	15	2
John Wood Community College	2,925	5	4	1
Joliet Junior College	22,351	25	15	10
Lewis University	8,101	19	9	10
Lincoln Land Community College	11,353	13	11	2
Millikin University	2,258	15	5	10
Parkland College	12,686	18	14	4
Rend Lake College	5,773	5	5	0
Southern Illinois University				
Carbondale	17,873	51	35	16
School of Medicine[2]		6	6	0
University of Illinois				
Springfield	5,428	22	15	7
Urbana	46,951	96	60	36
Springfield	6,590	24	17	7
Urbana	50,885	94	60	34
Waubonsee Community College	18,016	8	8	0
INDIANA				
Ball State University	26,419	37	31	6
Indiana University				
Indianapolis	34,984	64	48	16
Southeast	7,159	13	12	1
Purdue University	44,190	53	39	14
IOWA				
Iowa State University	39,729	52	37	15
University of Iowa	35,671	55	37	18
KANSAS				
Butler Community College	12,885	10	9	1
Emporia State University	7,160	10	9	1
Fort Hays State University	17,429	10	9	1
Garden City Community College	3,262	2	1	1
Kansas City Kansas Community College	8,340	17	16	1
Kansas State University	25,775	38	22	16
University of Kansas				
Main Campus	31,201	67	28	39
Medical Center[2]		142	47	95
Washburn University	7,702	22	17	5
Wichita State University	15,758	42	29	13
KENTUCKY				
Eastern Kentucky University	19,517	27	22	5

Table 79. Full-Time Law Enforcement Employees, by Selected State and University or College, 2018—Continued

(Number.)

State and university/college	Student enrollment[1]	Law enforcement employees	Officers	Civilians
Morehead State University	12,390	21	14	7
Murray State University	11,950	26	16	10
Northern Kentucky University	16,475	21	15	6
Transylvania University	983	12	9	3
University of Kentucky	31,564	166	52	114
University of Louisville	25,091	78	43	35
Western Kentucky University	25,038	38	25	13
LOUISIANA				
Delgado Community College	21,530	36	23	13
Grambling State University	6,941	25	15	10
Louisiana State University				
Baton Rouge	33,801	68	50	18
Health Sciences Center, New Orleans	3,116	30	30	0
Health Sciences Center, Shreveport	1,011	54	39	15
Shreveport	6,375	10	9	1
McNeese State University	8,689	14	8	6
Nicholls State University	7,333	15	12	3
Northwestern State University	12,260	29	23	6
Southeastern Louisiana University	17,788	24	24	0
Southern University and A&M College				
New Orleans	3,113	20	17	3
Shreveport	4,654	9	7	2
Tulane University	14,066	79	65	14
University of Louisiana				
Lafayette	19,297	35	33	2
Monroe	10,087	25	24	1
University of New Orleans	10,011	23	18	5
MAINE				
University of Maine				
Farmington	2,351	5	4	1
Orono	12,693	25	16	9
University of Southern Maine	10,156	17	11	6
MARYLAND				
Bowie State University	6,570	28	14	14
Coppin State University	3,442	31	19	12
Frostburg State University	6,455	22	18	4
Hagerstown Community College	5,827	3	3	0
Morgan State University	8,522	55	36	19
Prince George's County Community College	17,365	19	14	5
Salisbury University	9,800	36	18	18
St. Mary's College	1,779	13	10	3
Towson University	25,467	46	35	11
University of Baltimore	7,008	37	17	20
University of Maryland				
Baltimore City	7,158	144	53	91
Baltimore County	15,700	34	25	9
College Park	43,691	125	79	46
Eastern Shore	4,258	17	14	3
MASSACHUSETTS				
Amherst College	1,945	19	14	5
Assumption College	2,913	21	15	6
Babson College	3,726	28	18	10
Becker College	2,675	18	12	6
Bentley University	5,771	35	24	11
Boston College	15,649	74	51	23
Boston University	40,807	66	51	15
Brandeis University	6,325	23	21	2
Bridgewater State University	13,289	20	19	1
Bunker Hill Community College	18,428	17	16	1
Clark University	3,524	16	12	4
College of the Holy Cross	2,806	28	21	7
Dean College	1,568	16	1	15
Emerson College	4,774	25	22	3
Fitchburg State University	11,434	23	19	4
Framingham State University	9,304	21	15	6
Gordon College	2,465	10	10	0
Harvard University	38,934	106	80	26
Holyoke Community College	7,650	13	13	0
Massachusetts Bay Community College	7,695	6	6	0
Massachusetts College of Art	2,383	28	9	19
Massachusetts College of Liberal Arts	2,249	15	10	5
Massachusetts Institute of Technology	12,144	78	64	14
Massasoit Community College	10,613	17	16	1
Merrimack College	4,683	19	14	5
Mount Holyoke College	2,599	43	30	13
Mount Wachusett Community College	5,315	11	10	1
Northeastern University	27,486	98	63	35
North Shore Community College	8,852	19	15	4
Quinsigamond Community College	10,602	13	11	2
Salem State University	11,057	25	22	3

Table 79. Full-Time Law Enforcement Employees, by Selected State and University or College, 2018—Continued

(Number.)

State and university/college	Student enrollment[1]	Law enforcement employees	Officers	Civilians
Springfield College	3,290	46	18	28
Springfield Technical Community College	7,713	17	14	3
Stonehill College	2,536	20	16	4
Tufts University, Medford	12,802	80	50	30
University of Massachusetts				
Amherst	34,778	78	62	16
Dartmouth	9,997	30	19	11
Medical Center, Worcester	1,171	32	25	7
Wellesley College	2,688	20	15	5
Wentworth Institute of Technology	4,778	24	17	7
Western New England University	4,201	27	18	9
Westfield State University	8,017	23	17	6
Wheaton College	1,695	17	14	3
Worcester Polytechnic Institute	7,288	24	16	8
Worcester State University	10,679	22	17	5
MICHIGAN				
Central Michigan University	28,486	31	23	8
Delta College	12,428	8	5	3
Eastern Michigan University	24,545	49	38	11
Ferris State University	16,828	19	15	4
Grand Rapids Community College	20,473	17	13	4
Grand Valley State University	28,875	38	21	17
Kalamazoo Valley Community College	12,245	8	6	2
Kellogg Community College	5,672	3	3	0
Kirtland Community College	2,014	1	1	0
Lansing Community College	19,206	15	10	5
Macomb Community College	30,719	30	25	5
Michigan State University	55,545	118	87	31
Michigan Technological University	7,784	18	12	6
Mott Community College	10,769	30	20	10
Northern Michigan University	9,235	24	21	3
Oakland Community College	29,644	23	22	1
Oakland University	23,532	32	23	9
Saginaw Valley State University	10,320	9	8	1
Schoolcraft College	17,861	15	11	4
University of Michigan				
Ann Arbor	46,316	76	60	16
Dearborn	10,714	26	13	13
Flint	9,455	31	19	12
Western Michigan University	26,096	39	32	7
MINNESOTA				
University of Minnesota				
Duluth	11,613	13	11	2
Morris	1,912	5	3	2
Twin Cities	64,860	67	51	16
MISSISSIPPI				
Coahoma Community College	2,940	10	9	1
Jackson State University	11,185	68	38	30
Mississippi State University	23,820	48	33	15
Northeast Mississippi Community College	4,403	8	8	0
University of Mississippi, Oxford	25,877	48	29	19
MISSOURI				
Jefferson College	6,046	8	8	0
Lincoln University	3,289	16	12	4
Metropolitan Community College	22,584	36	28	8
Mineral Area College	4,858	11	2	9
Missouri Southern State University	7,031	8	7	1
Missouri University of Science and Technology	9,547	22	12	10
Missouri Western State University	6,145	11	8	3
Northwest Missouri State University	7,556	13	9	4
Southeast Missouri State University	13,984	14	13	1
St. Charles Community College	9,689	14	12	2
St. Louis Community College, Meramec	29,716	34	28	6
Truman State University	6,918	12	10	2
University of Central Missouri	18,509	25	14	11
University of Missouri				
Columbia	36,780	70	47	23
Kansas City	19,796	39	29	10
St. Louis	20,987	26	20	6
Washington University	16,703	56	37	19
MONTANA				
Montana State University	18,420	30	19	11
University of Montana	14,683	25	16	9
NEBRASKA				
Metropolitan Community College, Douglas County	25,030	25	20	5
University of Nebraska				
Kearney	8,264	12	9	3
Lincoln	28,550	76	36	40

Table 79. Full-Time Law Enforcement Employees, by Selected State and University or College, 2018—Continued

(Number.)

State and university/college	Student enrollment[1]	Law enforcement employees	Officers	Civilians
NEVADA				
College of Southern Nevada	47,602	18	17	1
University of Nevada				
Las Vegas	34,647	53	36	17
Reno	24,118	35	27	8
NEW HAMPSHIRE				
University of New Hampshire	16,599	31	18	13
NEW JERSEY				
Brookdale Community College	18,974	13	12	1
Essex County College	12,638	55	12	43
Kean University	16,633	42	21	21
Middlesex County College	17,304	19	12	7
Monmouth University	7,049	52	19	33
Montclair State University	23,989	49	37	12
New Jersey Institute of Technology	13,130	74	37	37
Princeton University	8,483	92	26	66
Rowan University	19,833	87	31	56
Rutgers University				
Camden	7,675	79	21	58
New Brunswick	56,027	135	64	71
Newark	15,098	186	68	118
Stevens Institute of Technology	7,723	21	19	2
Stockton University	10,221	42	27	15
The College of New Jersey	8,792	30	19	11
William Paterson University	12,687	43	29	14
NEW MEXICO				
Eastern New Mexico University	7,440	10	9	1
New Mexico Military Institute	457	5	5	0
New Mexico State University	16,895	32	17	15
University of New Mexico	31,224	58	39	19
Western New Mexico University	4,454	7	6	1
NEW YORK				
Cornell University	22,820	68	45	23
Ithaca College	7,184	41	23	18
State University of New York Police				
Albany	19,834	59	40	19
Alfred	4,198	16	11	5
Binghamton	18,758	57	42	15
Brockport	9,340	22	16	6
Buffalo	33,647	76	64	12
Buffalo State College	10,918	36	31	5
Canton	5,183	10	9	1
Cortland	7,827	26	19	7
Delhi	4,093	15	12	3
Downstate Medical	2,071	103	20	83
Environmental Science	2,295	13	9	4
Farmingdale	12,307	31	21	10
Fredonia	4,935	15	14	1
Geneseo	5,941	24	17	7
Maritime	2,007	14	9	5
Morrisville	3,713	14	10	4
New Paltz	8,940	26	22	4
Old Westbury	5,636	25	20	5
Oneonta	6,593	25	16	9
Optometry	402	17	7	10
Oswego	9,566	26	21	5
Plattsburgh	6,271	20	15	5
Polytechnic Institute	3,060	16	11	5
Potsdam	4,119	15	12	3
Purchase	4,815	31	23	8
Stony Brook	29,798	150	63	87
Upstate Medical	1,581	111	20	91
NORTH CAROLINA				
Appalachian State University	19,974	43	26	17
Beaufort County Community College	1,995	4	4	0
Belmont Abbey College	1,633	5	5	0
Davidson College	1,959	10	9	1
Duke University	16,599	167	65	102
East Carolina University	32,388	70	54	16
Elizabeth City State University	1,495	22	12	10
Elon University	7,084	42	20	22
Fayetteville State University	7,618	39	19	20
Meredith College	2,143	14	3	11
Methodist University	2,761	24	10	14
North Carolina Agricultural and Technical State University	12,566	49	21	28
North Carolina Central University	9,263	48	21	27
North Carolina School of the Arts	1,070	21	15	6
North Carolina State University, Raleigh	38,431	67	51	16
Queens University	2,869	12	7	5

Table 79. Full-Time Law Enforcement Employees, by Selected State and University or College, 2018—Continued

(Number.)

State and university/college	Student enrollment[1]	Law enforcement employees	Officers	Civilians
Saint Augustine's University	1,032	18	3	15
University of North Carolina				
Asheville	4,461	20	12	8
Chapel Hill	31,720	104	50	54
Charlotte	33,351	53	45	8
Greensboro	22,138	55	34	21
Pembroke	7,389	25	19	6
Wilmington	18,287	50	33	17
Wake Forest University	8,478	51	24	27
Western Carolina University	12,280	24	24	0
Winston-Salem State University	5,884	40	17	23
NORTH DAKOTA				
Bismarck State College	5,067	3	2	1
North Dakota State College of Science	3,683	4	3	1
North Dakota State University	15,816	23	15	8
University of North Dakota	18,104	19	18	1
OHIO				
Capital University	3,367	16	10	6
Columbus State Community College	46,559	41	22	19
Kent State University	35,611	41	31	10
Lakeland Community College	10,630	14	10	4
Miami University	21,717	38	28	10
Notre Dame College	2,296	8	8	0
Sinclair Community College	30,680	18	17	1
University of Cincinnati	42,252	137	62	75
University of Toledo	23,248	40	32	8
OKLAHOMA				
Bacone College	1,094	4	4	0
Cameron University	5,918	13	13	0
East Central University	4,962	6	5	1
Eastern Oklahoma State College	2,104	4	4	0
Langston University	2,879	17	12	5
Mid-America Christian University	2,936	3	3	0
Northeastern Oklahoma A&M College	2,649	6	6	0
Northeastern State University, Tahlequah	9,556	19	14	5
Northwestern Oklahoma State University	2,623	4	4	0
Oklahoma City Community College	18,552	30	22	8
Oklahoma City University	3,420	10	6	4
Oklahoma State University				
Main Campus	28,608	44	32	12
Okmulgee	3,268	7	6	1
Tulsa	1,037	10	8	2
Rogers State University	4,795	9	9	0
Seminole State College	2,275	3	3	0
Southeastern Oklahoma State University	4,631	7	6	1
Southwestern Oklahoma State University	6,247	7	6	1
Tulsa Community College	24,245	30	24	6
University of Central Oklahoma	19,428	24	16	8
University of Oklahoma				
Health Sciences Center	3,872	66	40	26
Norman	32,274	69	38	31
OREGON				
Portland State University	36,762	27	12	15
University of Oregon	26,968	33	23	10
PENNSYLVANIA				
Bloomsburg University	10,656	21	13	8
California University	9,869	21	18	3
Cheyney University	846	11	8	3
Clarion University	6,240	16	11	5
Dickinson College	2,422	20	15	5
East Stroudsburg University	7,899	16	11	5
Edinboro University	7,245	15	14	1
Indiana University	14,728	27	22	5
Kutztown University	9,467	20	17	3
Lehigh University	7,586	35	25	10
Lock Haven University	4,701	12	9	3
Mansfield University	2,403	12	9	3
Millersville University	9,502	16	14	2
Moravian College	2,781	16	13	3
Pennsylvania State University				
Abington	4,599	7	4	3
Altoona	3,607	10	9	1
Beaver	800	5	5	0
Behrend	4,832	11	7	4
Berks	3,163	8	7	1
Brandywine	1,533	5	5	0
Dubois	727	1	1	0
Fayette	693	1	1	0
Great Valley	562	2	2	0
Greater Allegheny	612	5	5	0

Table 79. Full-Time Law Enforcement Employees, by Selected State and University or College, 2018—Continued

(Number.)

State and university/college	Student enrollment[1]	Law enforcement employees	Officers	Civilians
Harrisburg	5,645	9	8	1
Hazleton	959	5	5	0
Lehigh Valley	1,075	2	1	1
Mont Alto	999	6	6	0
New Kensington	833	2	2	0
Schuylkill	884	4	4	0
University Park	50,920	89	52	37
Wilkes-Barre	576	1	1	0
Worthington Scranton	1,123	3	3	0
York	1,231	4	3	1
Shippensburg University	7,812	17	14	3
Slippery Rock University	10,516	13	12	1
University of Pittsburgh				
Bradford	1,575	8	6	2
Greensburg	1,589	10	9	1
Johnstown	2,883	13	12	1
Pittsburgh	31,947	144	81	63
Titusville	358	6	5	1
West Chester University	19,348	47	26	21
RHODE ISLAND				
Brown University	10,335	87	55	32
University of Rhode Island	19,699	36	32	4
SOUTH CAROLINA				
Benedict College	2,552	16	13	3
Bob Jones University	3,375	3	3	0
Clemson University	24,758	40	28	12
Coastal Carolina University	11,988	87	36	51
College of Charleston	13,539	39	26	13
Columbia College	2,101	8	6	2
Denmark Technical College	996	3	3	0
Erskine College	911	3	2	1
Francis Marion University	4,476	15	9	6
Greenville Technical College	15,978	13	8	5
Lander University	3,017	16	10	6
Medical University of South Carolina	3,454	75	55	20
Midlands Technical College	14,388	10	9	1
Orangeburg-Calhoun Technical College	3,533	9	8	1
Presbyterian College	1,434	8	7	1
South Carolina State University	3,208	27	11	16
Spartanburg Methodist College	778	4	4	0
The Citadel	4,212	19	19	0
Tri-County Technical College	7,906	12	9	3
Trident Technical College	18,925	26	22	4
University of South Carolina				
Aiken	4,081	7	6	1
Beaufort	2,270	17	15	2
Columbia	36,813	110	82	28
Upstate	7,040	17	13	4
Winthrop University	7,223	20	14	6
SOUTH DAKOTA				
South Dakota State University	15,209	17	14	3
TENNESSEE				
Austin Peay State University	12,144	24	15	9
Chattanooga State Community College	11,237	12	5	7
Christian Brothers University	2,597	17	8	9
Cleveland State Community College	4,270	4	3	1
Columbia State Community College	7,392	5	1	4
East Tennessee State University	16,026	28	20	8
Jackson State Community College	6,331	3	2	1
Lincoln Memorial University	4,847	29	8	21
Middle Tennessee State University	26,214	45	35	10
Motlow State Community College	7,198	4	4	0
Northeast State Community College	7,608	7	7	0
Pellissippi State Community College	14,241	13	11	2
Roane State Community College	7,227	8	7	1
Southwest Tennessee Community College	12,453	24	20	4
Tennessee State University	9,820	76	32	44
Tennessee Technological University	11,507	20	13	7
University of Memphis	24,809	67	38	29
University of Tennessee				
Chattanooga	12,844	28	16	12
Health Science Center	3,250	69	28	41
Knoxville	30,680	93	55	38
Martin	7,789	16	12	4
University of the South	2,035	15	11	4
Vanderbilt University	13,397	244	83	161
Volunteer State Community College	11,544	12	9	3
Walters State Community College	7,285	9	8	1
TEXAS				
Alamo Colleges District	107,934	102	82	20
Alvin Community College	8,818	10	9	1

Table 79. Full-Time Law Enforcement Employees, by Selected State and University or College, 2018—Continued

(Number.)

State and university/college	Student enrollment[1]	Law enforcement employees	Officers	Civilians
Amarillo College	13,023	14	11	3
Austin College	1,304	8	7	1
Baylor University, Waco	18,094	63	38	25
Central Texas College	32,309	7	6	1
Cisco College	4,503	1	1	0
College of the Mainland	5,575	14	14	0
Hardin-Simmons University	2,441	5	5	0
Lubbock Christian University	2,239	6	2	4
Midwestern State University	7,024	14	9	5
Paris Junior College	6,895	5	5	0
Prairie View A&M University	9,861	33	26	7
Rice University	7,251	45	27	18
Southern Methodist University	13,012	38	29	9
Southwestern University	1,536	9	6	3
Tarleton State University	14,978	19	15	4
Texas A&M International University	8,459	27	20	7
Texas A&M University	7,390	29	20	9
College Station	70,245	146	72	74
Commerce	16,132	27	20	7
Texas State Technical College				
Harlingen[2]		12	9	3
Waco[2]		11	9	2
West Texas[2]		6	6	0
Texas State University, San Marcos	43,018	57	34	23
Texas Tech University, Lubbock	40,105	142	64	78
Texas Woman's University	18,819	41	19	22
University of Houston				
Central Campus	50,293	176	61	115
Downtown Campus	17,513	48	25	23
University of North Texas, Denton	43,725	65	44	21
University of Texas				
Austin	55,008	111	92	19
Dallas	29,645	76	28	48
Health Science Center, Tyler	42	24	7	17
Rio Grande Valley	32,508	80	44	36
Southwestern Medical School	2,456	137	43	94
Tyler	12,052	27	12	15
West Texas A&M University	11,757	23	16	7
UTAH				
Brigham Young University	39,582	42	28	14
Dixie State University	11,441	9	7	2
Southern Utah University	15,098	6	5	1
University of Utah	37,585	45	33	12
Utah State University				
Eastern[2]		2	2	0
Logan	34,904	21	14	7
Utah Valley University	45,411	15	11	4
Weber State University	33,339	15	13	2
VERMONT				
University of Vermont	15,069	29	17	12
VIRGINIA				
Bridgewater College	1,959	8	7	1
Christopher Newport University	5,215	31	21	10
College of William and Mary	9,767	28	20	8
Eastern Virginia Medical School	1,334	49	21	28
Emory and Henry College	1,257	3	3	0
Ferrum College	1,338	9	9	0
George Mason University	46,266	61	45	16
Germanna Community College	9,135	9	3	6
Hampton University	4,874	47	27	20
James Madison University	23,354	44	34	10
J. Sargeant Reynolds Community College	15,028	19	13	6
Longwood University	5,721	25	18	7
Lord Fairfax Community College	9,129	4	4	0
Norfolk State University	6,168	31	18	13
Northern Virginia Community College	74,283	54	42	12
Old Dominion University	28,758	56	42	14
Radford University	10,254	31	23	8
Richard Bland College	2,808	5	4	1
Thomas Nelson Community College	13,121	12	9	3
University of Mary Washington	5,276	24	18	6
University of Richmond	4,811	34	22	12
University of Virginia	27,960	118	52	66
University of Virginia's College at Wise	3,474	10	9	1
Virginia Commonwealth University	34,271	119	91	28
Virginia Military Institute	1,766	12	11	1
Virginia Polytechnic Institute and State University	34,947	65	46	19
Virginia State University	5,137	37	21	16
Virginia Western Community College	10,802	8	8	0
WASHINGTON				
Central Washington University	17,163	16	14	2
Eastern Washington University	15,602	16	14	2

Table 79. Full-Time Law Enforcement Employees, by Selected State and University or College, 2018—Continued

(Number.)

State and university/college	Student enrollment[1]	Law enforcement employees	Officers	Civilians
Evergreen State College	4,996	12	6	6
University of Washington	55,073	78	43	35
Washington State University				
Pullman	33,974	26	21	5
Vancouver[2]		6	3	3
Western Washington University	17,475	23	15	8
WEST VIRGINIA				
Bluefield State College	1,558	3	3	0
Concord University	2,803	7	4	3
Fairmont State University	4,558	11	9	2
Glenville State College	2,123	6	3	3
Marshall University	17,198	21	20	1
Potomac State College	1,658	7	6	1
Shepherd University	4,641	12	10	2
West Liberty University	2,541	7	7	0
West Virginia State University	4,175	7	5	2
West Virginia University	31,900	69	49	20
WISCONSIN				
University of Wisconsin				
Eau Claire	11,836	11	11	0
Green Bay	8,412	12	11	1
La Crosse	11,943	20	13	7
Madison	46,350	126	65	61
Milwaukee	30,031	45	33	12
Oshkosh	16,213	17	14	3
Parkside	5,217	11	8	3
Platteville	9,916	10	8	2
River Falls	6,633	7	5	2
Stevens Point	9,703	12	8	4
Stout	11,232	11	9	2
Superior	3,040	7	2	5
Whitewater	14,456	19	15	4
WYOMING				
University of Wyoming	13,975	22	13	9

1 The student enrollment figures provided by the United States Department of Education are for the 2017 school year, the most recent available. The enrollment figures include full-time and part-time students.   2 Student enrollment figures were not available.

Table 80. Full-Time Law Enforcement Employees, by Selected State Metropolitan and Nonmetropolitan Counties, 2018

(Number.)

State/county	Law enforcement employees	Officers	Civilians
ALABAMA			
Metropolitan Counties			
Autauga	45	35	10
Baldwin	307	125	182
Bibb	12	11	1
Blount	49	45	4
Calhoun	89	49	40
Chilton	73	29	44
Colbert	38	33	5
Elmore	119	58	61
Etowah	164	68	96
Geneva	28	14	14
Greene	30	7	23
Hale	14	12	2
Henry	22	18	4
Houston	162	67	95
Jefferson	703	539	164
Lauderdale	45	39	6
Lawrence	39	18	21
Lee	165	78	87
Limestone	126	56	70
Lowndes	32	14	18
Madison	189	131	58
Mobile	521	175	346
Montgomery	330	118	212
Morgan	169	44	125
Russell	118	39	79
Shelby	211	86	125
St. Clair	117	66	51
Tuscaloosa	209	101	108
Washington	22	10	12
Nonmetropolitan Counties			
Barbour	9	7	2
Bullock	6	5	1
Butler	14	12	2
Chambers	59	25	34
Cherokee	29	29	0
Choctaw	15	7	8
Clarke	41	12	29
Clay	25	11	14
Cleburne	28	11	17
Conecuh	33	11	22
Coosa	23	10	13
Covington	28	25	3
Crenshaw	24	11	13
Cullman	146	80	66
Dale	52	26	26
Dallas	48	22	26
DeKalb	81	30	51
Escambia	58	25	33
Fayette	21	12	9
Franklin	53	21	32
Jackson	81	32	49
Lamar	20	9	11
Macon	44	25	19
Marengo	26	12	14
Marion	30	15	15
Marshall	47	30	17
Monroe	52	15	37
Perry	18	7	11
Randolph	39	20	19
Sumter	13	7	6
Talladega	85	37	48
Tallapoosa	53	22	31
ARIZONA			
Metropolitan Counties			
Cochise	200	88	112
Coconino	243	61	182
Maricopa	3,252	680	2,572
Mohave	250	80	170
Pima	1,395	504	891
Pinal	470	198	272
Yavapai	173	119	54
Yuma	332	85	247
Nonmetropolitan Counties			
Apache	56	26	30
Gila	128	50	78
Graham	80	23	57
Greenlee	48	17	31
La Paz	59	34	25

Table 80. Full-Time Law Enforcement Employees, by Selected State Metropolitan and Nonmetropolitan Counties, 2018—Continued

(Number.)

State/county	Law enforcement employees	Officers	Civilians
Navajo	133	47	86
Santa Cruz	84	34	50
ARKANSAS			
Metropolitan Counties			
Benton	248	115	133
Cleveland	14	8	6
Craighead	118	40	78
Crawford	69	35	34
Crittenden	139	32	107
Faulkner	157	50	107
Franklin	27	11	16
Garland	179	73	106
Grant	21	18	3
Jefferson	122	36	86
Lincoln	27	12	15
Little River	31	14	17
Lonoke	70	35	35
Madison	21	9	12
Miller	37	26	11
Perry	14	12	2
Poinsett	41	14	27
Pulaski	427	126	301
Saline	103	53	50
Sebastian	147	45	102
Washington	305	154	151
Nonmetropolitan Counties			
Arkansas	11	11	0
Ashley	43	21	22
Baxter	54	33	21
Boone	56	26	30
Bradley	9	5	4
Calhoun	12	6	6
Carroll	62	20	42
Chicot	8	7	1
Clark	31	15	16
Clay	27	13	14
Cleburne	45	26	19
Columbia	38	20	18
Conway	43	21	22
Cross	42	17	25
Dallas	18	6	12
Desha	7	6	1
Drew	14	13	1
Fulton	17	7	10
Greene	30	22	8
Hempstead	49	21	28
Hot Spring	30	16	14
Howard	23	10	13
Independence	38	34	4
Izard	31	20	11
Jackson	35	12	23
Johnson	42	16	26
Lafayette	14	9	5
Lawrence	38	15	23
Lee	11	6	5
Logan	18	14	4
Marion	21	19	2
Mississippi	92	39	53
Monroe	16	9	7
Montgomery	20	11	9
Nevada	14	7	7
Newton	19	10	9
Ouachita	49	20	29
Phillips	21	14	7
Pike	23	10	13
Polk	27	15	12
Pope	87	34	53
Prairie	24	7	17
Randolph	13	10	3
Scott	28	9	19
Searcy	16	7	9
Sevier	36	16	20
Sharp	26	14	12
St. Francis	37	18	19
Stone	22	11	11
Union	64	33	31
Van Buren	37	23	14
White	103	53	50
Woodruff	19	6	13
Yell	29	16	13

Table 80. Full-Time Law Enforcement Employees, by Selected State Metropolitan and Nonmetropolitan Counties, 2018—Continued

(Number.)

State/county	Law enforcement employees	Officers	Civilians
CALIFORNIA			
Metropolitan Counties			
Alameda	1,537	939	598
Butte	263	98	165
Contra Costa	961	647	314
El Dorado	341	150	191
Fresno	1,152	430	722
Imperial	275	187	88
Kern	1,163	806	357
Kings	286	83	203
Los Angeles	15,754	9,426	6,328
Madera	116	85	31
Marin	291	196	95
Merced	249	117	132
Monterey	426	304	122
Napa	135	99	36
Orange	3,735	1,880	1,855
Placer	543	260	283
Riverside	3,530	1,795	1,735
Sacramento	1,898	1,302	596
San Benito	54	24	30
San Bernardino	3,407	2,018	1,389
San Diego	4,283	2,572	1,711
San Francisco	1,045	860	185
San Joaquin	740	302	438
San Luis Obispo	409	305	104
San Mateo	734	348	386
Santa Barbara	624	454	170
Santa Clara	1,694	1,279	415
Santa Cruz	328	140	188
Shasta	198	138	60
Solano	507	123	384
Sonoma	608	232	376
Stanislaus	681	508	173
Sutter	132	107	25
Tulare	761	536	225
Ventura	1,232	760	472
Yolo	259	84	175
Yuba	155	118	37
Nonmetropolitan Counties			
Alpine	15	12	3
Amador	90	46	44
Calaveras	99	48	51
Colusa	58	40	18
Del Norte	53	23	30
Glenn	68	33	35
Humboldt	240	186	54
Inyo	77	36	41
Lake	68	49	19
Lassen	84	57	27
Mariposa	74	60	14
Mendocino	197	135	62
Modoc	28	19	9
Mono	41	21	20
Nevada	151	62	89
Plumas	62	33	29
Sierra	13	9	4
Siskiyou	99	44	55
Tehama	114	79	35
Trinity	42	30	12
Tuolumne	131	62	69
COLORADO			
Metropolitan Counties			
Adams	566	369	197
Arapahoe	547	378	169
Boulder	385	104	281
Clear Creek	64	29	35
Douglas	498	328	170
Elbert	45	36	9
El Paso	792	515	277
Gilpin	57	39	18
Jefferson	793	483	310
Larimer	312	196	116
Mesa	227	128	99
Park	32	18	14
Pueblo	356	172	184
Teller	80	48	32
Weld	388	133	255
Nonmetropolitan Counties			
Alamosa	51	28	23

Table 80. Full-Time Law Enforcement Employees, by Selected State Metropolitan and Nonmetropolitan Counties, 2018—Continued

(Number.)

State/county	Law enforcement employees	Officers	Civilians
Archuleta	43	13	30
Baca	13	4	9
Bent	20	8	12
Chaffee	54	21	33
Cheyenne	9	5	4
Conejos	27	9	18
Costilla	7	7	0
Crowley	15	7	8
Custer	23	11	12
Delta	65	31	34
Dolores	8	5	3
Eagle	80	45	35
Fremont	84	36	48
Garfield	132	101	31
Grand	52	23	29
Gunnison	28	12	16
Hinsdale	5	4	1
Huerfano	44	20	24
Jackson	7	3	4
Kiowa	8	5	3
Kit Carson	27	5	22
Lake	20	9	11
La Plata	121	91	30
Las Animas	32	12	20
Lincoln	24	10	14
Logan	49	22	27
Mineral	7	4	3
Moffat	37	34	3
Montezuma	66	28	38
Montrose	90	45	45
Morgan	46	37	9
Otero	22	20	2
Ouray	8	8	0
Phillips	3	3	0
Pitkin	57	23	34
Prowers	30	10	20
Rio Blanco	27	13	14
Rio Grande	33	28	5
Routt	51	23	28
Saguache	19	7	12
San Juan	4	4	0
San Miguel	35	15	20
Sedgwick	4	3	1
Summit	70	52	18
Washington	38	9	29
Yuma	20	17	3
DELAWARE			
Metropolitan Counties			
New Castle County Police Department	417	377	40
FLORIDA			
Metropolitan Counties			
Baker	65	45	20
Bay	275	213	62
Brevard	1,321	526	795
Charlotte	396	264	132
Citrus	325	203	122
Clay	589	292	297
Collier	891	564	327
Escambia	662	409	253
Flagler	282	212	70
Gadsden	72	47	25
Gilchrist	61	37	24
Hernando	538	244	294
Highlands	345	152	193
Hillsborough	3,325	1,210	2,115
Indian River	480	189	291
Jefferson	41	25	16
Lake	674	278	396
Lee	1,504	670	834
Levy	147	70	77
Manatee	1,148	757	391
Marion	450	340	110
Martin	375	251	124
Miami-Dade	3,933	2,878	1,055
Nassau	243	133	110
Okaloosa	436	306	130
Orange	2,201	1,537	664
Osceola	641	405	236
Palm Beach	3,538	1,596	1,942
Pinellas	2,347	796	1,551
Polk	1,160	661	499

Table 80. Full-Time Law Enforcement Employees, by Selected State Metropolitan and Nonmetropolitan Counties, 2018—Continued

(Number.)

State/county	Law enforcement employees	Officers	Civilians
Santa Rosa	415	207	208
Sarasota	965	415	550
Seminole	1,226	434	792
St. Johns	668	318	350
St. Lucie	801	293	508
Volusia	719	414	305
Wakulla	136	97	39
Nonmetropolitan Counties			
Bradford	91	44	47
Calhoun	33	26	7
Columbia	187	103	84
DeSoto	131	64	67
Dixie	72	28	44
Glades	143	33	110
Gulf	43	29	14
Hamilton	58	19	39
Hardee	102	74	28
Holmes	60	33	27
Jackson	79	57	22
Lafayette	32	12	20
Liberty	27	20	7
Madison	82	63	19
Monroe	497	194	303
Okeechobee	135	94	41
Putnam	201	108	93
Suwannee	116	57	59
Taylor	77	55	22
GEORGIA			
Metropolitan Counties			
Barrow	191	123	68
Bartow	223	181	42
Bibb	516	430	86
Brantley	48	20	28
Brooks	49	25	24
Bryan	60	40	20
Burke	108	70	38
Butts	100	55	45
Carroll	179	102	77
Catoosa	114	68	46
Chatham	573	396	177
Chatham County Police Department	133	119	14
Chattahoochee	13	8	5
Cherokee	394	332	62
Clarke	160	130	30
Clayton	423	285	138
Clayton County Police Department	434	321	113
Cobb	675	437	238
Cobb County Police Department	720	647	73
Columbia	381	300	81
Coweta	255	172	83
Crawford	31	15	16
Dade	47	44	3
Dawson	97	58	39
DeKalb	711	508	203
DeKalb County Police Department	958	729	229
Dougherty	210	195	15
Douglas	341	302	39
Echols	9	8	1
Effingham	124	84	40
Fayette	216	140	76
Floyd	141	76	65
Floyd County Police Department	81	76	5
Forsyth	429	351	78
Fulton	972	746	226
Fulton County Police Department	71	38	33
Glynn	43	34	9
Glynn County Police Department	128	120	8
Gwinnett County Police Department	975	726	249
Hall	433	271	162
Haralson	78	73	5
Harris	70	68	2
Heard	36	19	17
Henry	276	254	22
Henry County Police Department	253	214	39
Houston	331	125	206
Jasper	43	29	14
Jones	78	43	35
Lamar	58	34	24
Lanier	17	15	2
Lee	77	52	25
Liberty	134	125	9

Table 80. Full-Time Law Enforcement Employees, by Selected State Metropolitan and Nonmetropolitan Counties, 2018—Continued

(Number.)

State/county	Law enforcement employees	Officers	Civilians
Lincoln	24	11	13
Long	34	30	4
Lowndes	242	211	31
Madison	81	71	10
Marion	15	7	8
McDuffie	55	28	27
McIntosh	60	38	22
Meriwether	50	25	25
Monroe	95	54	41
Murray	77	45	32
Muscogee	312	289	23
Newton	248	139	109
Oconee	96	63	33
Oglethorpe	48	21	27
Paulding	264	227	37
Peach	63	33	30
Pickens	86	81	5
Pike	37	26	11
Spalding	184	103	81
Stewart	7	6	1
Talbot	12	7	5
Terrell	33	31	2
Twiggs	43	31	12
Walker	107	66	41
Walton	206	187	19
Whitfield	207	176	31
Worth	42	28	14
Nonmetropolitan Counties			
Appling	61	23	38
Atkinson	21	9	12
Bacon	12	10	2
Baker	6	5	1
Baldwin	124	60	64
Banks	64	58	6
Ben Hill	48	27	21
Berrien	43	38	5
Bleckley	41	16	25
Bulloch	130	119	11
Calhoun	15	7	8
Camden	118	65	53
Candler	29	16	13
Charlton	31	19	12
Chattooga	48	30	18
Clay	5	4	1
Clinch	13	10	3
Coffee	124	53	71
Colquitt	99	96	3
Cook	47	28	19
Crisp	98	60	38
Decatur	60	48	12
Dodge	55	20	35
Dooly	80	37	43
Early	36	18	18
Elbert	66	35	31
Evans	17	13	4
Fannin	52	38	14
Franklin	73	40	33
Gilmer	104	79	25
Glascock	6	5	1
Gordon	117	79	38
Grady	23	20	3
Greene	37	32	5
Habersham	56	52	4
Hancock	40	23	17
Hart	33	28	5
Irwin	23	15	8
Jackson	106	91	15
Jeff Davis	28	16	12
Jefferson	42	39	3
Laurens	106	63	43
Lumpkin	82	72	10
Miller	21	11	10
Mitchell	46	21	25
Pierce	50	22	28
Polk	76	37	39
Polk County Police Department	45	41	4
Pulaski	29	16	13
Quitman	6	4	2
Rabun	55	53	2
Schley	8	4	4
Screven	15	9	6
Seminole	24	15	9

Table 80. Full-Time Law Enforcement Employees, by Selected State Metropolitan and Nonmetropolitan Counties, 2018—Continued

(Number.)

State/county	Law enforcement employees	Officers	Civilians
Stephens	71	38	33
Sumter	95	42	53
Tattnall	47	21	26
Taylor	21	11	10
Thomas	88	84	4
Tift	99	82	17
Toombs	73	26	47
Towns	40	19	21
Treutlen	23	12	11
Troup	84	75	9
Turner	38	21	17
Union	46	41	5
Upson	62	36	26
Ware	128	49	79
Warren	8	8	0
Washington	49	23	26
Webster	5	5	0
Wheeler	13	13	0
White	75	46	29
Wilcox	15	11	4
Wilkes	26	25	1
Wilkinson	31	18	13
HAWAII			
Metropolitan Counties			
Maui Police Department	446	343	103
Nonmetropolitan Counties			
Hawaii Police Department	554	422	132
Kauai Police Department	190	137	53
IDAHO			
Metropolitan Counties			
Ada	690	160	530
Bannock	125	42	83
Boise	23	15	8
Bonneville	185	72	113
Butte	14	4	10
Canyon	260	68	192
Franklin	17	11	6
Gem	34	13	21
Jefferson	60	22	38
Jerome	44	19	25
Kootenai	288	90	198
Nez Perce	77	23	54
Owyhee	28	13	15
Power	26	9	17
Twin Falls	120	42	78
Nonmetropolitan Counties			
Adams	22	7	15
Bear Lake	14	7	7
Benewah	27	12	15
Bingham	81	35	46
Blaine	51	18	33
Bonner	96	38	58
Boundary	27	8	19
Camas	6	4	2
Caribou	23	7	16
Cassia	77	33	44
Clark	7	3	4
Clearwater	29	15	14
Custer	17	9	8
Elmore	75	30	45
Fremont	37	21	16
Gooding	34	16	18
Idaho	38	18	20
Latah	51	27	24
Lemhi	23	8	15
Lewis	11	5	6
Lincoln	13	10	3
Madison	62	23	39
Minidoka	30	20	10
Oneida	12	8	4
Payette	46	16	30
Shoshone	37	15	22
Teton	16	9	7
Valley	46	18	28
Washington	31	12	19
ILLINOIS			
Metropolitan Counties			
Champaign	142	54	88

Table 80. Full-Time Law Enforcement Employees, by Selected State Metropolitan and Nonmetropolitan Counties, 2018—Continued

(Number.)

State/county	Law enforcement employees	Officers	Civilians
Cook	5,504	1,649	3,855
DuPage	485	183	302
Fulton	44	20	24
Grundy	46	31	15
Henry	63	22	41
Jackson	89	31	58
Kendall	57	50	7
Madison	164	85	79
Marshall	17	8	9
McHenry	371	102	269
McLean	138	50	88
Rock Island	151	63	88
Sangamon	193	66	127
Stark	11	4	7
Vermilion	88	41	47
Will	594	229	365
Winnebago	289	96	193
Nonmetropolitan Counties			
Adams	30	28	2
Cass	7	6	1
Clay	17	10	7
Crawford	22	15	7
Cumberland	15	6	9
Effingham	47	20	27
Ford	27	22	5
Franklin	16	16	0
Gallatin	3	3	0
Hardin	11	4	7
Jefferson	60	21	39
Jo Daviess	37	17	20
Knox	67	23	44
Livingston	68	27	41
Logan	17	15	2
Mason	22	9	13
McDonough	21	11	10
Montgomery	35	11	24
Morgan	33	14	19
Perry	31	12	19
Schuyler	6	5	1
Scott	6	2	4
Shelby	25	15	10
Stephenson	33	26	7
Wabash	9	4	5
Whiteside	64	21	43
INDIANA			
Metropolitan Counties			
Bartholomew	102	42	60
Brown	42	15	27
Delaware	124	44	80
Floyd	125	43	82
Franklin	15	13	2
Hancock	77	40	37
Lake	519	154	365
La Porte	158	65	93
Monroe	55	45	10
Porter	75	66	9
Shelby	98	33	65
St. Joseph	278	112	166
Vigo	88	39	49
Warrick	82	42	40
Nonmetropolitan Counties			
Clinton	46	21	25
Daviess	78	21	57
Gibson	44	15	29
Greene	53	19	34
Huntington	16	16	0
Jackson	67	17	50
Jay	47	13	34
Jefferson	19	18	1
Jennings	20	17	3
Miami	42	17	25
Starke	33	13	20
Wabash	38	34	4
Wayne	120	80	40
Wells	15	15	0
IOWA			
Metropolitan Counties			
Black Hawk	132	78	54
Boone	31	12	19

Table 80. Full-Time Law Enforcement Employees, by Selected State Metropolitan and Nonmetropolitan Counties, 2018—Continued

(Number.)

State/county	Law enforcement employees	Officers	Civilians
Bremer	35	13	22
Dallas	66	28	38
Dubuque	92	78	14
Grundy	16	12	4
Guthrie	14	9	5
Harrison	11	10	1
Jasper	47	17	30
Johnson	93	70	23
Jones	26	11	15
Linn	193	127	66
Mills	26	12	14
Polk	507	157	350
Pottawattamie	195	51	144
Scott	151	40	111
Story	84	30	54
Warren	36	20	16
Washington	48	17	31
Woodbury	116	40	76
Nonmetropolitan Counties			
Adair	15	6	9
Allamakee	18	8	10
Appanoose	16	8	8
Audubon	9	5	4
Buchanan	30	13	17
Buena Vista	27	14	13
Butler	19	12	7
Calhoun	12	7	5
Carroll	16	9	7
Cass	12	9	3
Cedar	39	13	26
Cerro Gordo	79	20	59
Cherokee	19	7	12
Chickasaw	16	9	7
Clarke	23	7	16
Clay	24	11	13
Clayton	27	13	14
Clinton	46	25	21
Crawford	15	10	5
Davis	17	6	11
Decatur	21	6	15
Delaware	21	14	7
Des Moines	25	21	4
Dickinson	21	10	11
Emmet	17	9	8
Fayette	35	12	23
Franklin	8	5	3
Fremont	28	10	18
Greene	25	16	9
Hamilton	28	9	19
Hancock	9	8	1
Hardin	31	10	21
Henry	31	11	20
Howard	15	8	7
Humboldt	23	16	7
Ida	17	9	8
Iowa	29	14	15
Jackson	17	10	7
Jefferson	30	11	19
Kossuth	24	9	15
Lee	35	17	18
Lucas	12	5	7
Lyon	21	12	9
Mahaska	23	10	13
Marion	38	16	22
Marshall	55	19	36
Mitchell	17	7	10
Monona	18	8	10
Monroe	17	5	12
Muscatine	81	23	58
O'Brien	27	9	18
Osceola	13	8	5
Page	16	8	8
Palo Alto	17	8	9
Plymouth	33	11	22
Pocahontas	16	7	9
Poweshiek	25	12	13
Ringgold	11	5	6
Sac	22	9	13
Shelby	10	9	1
Sioux	39	14	25
Tama	22	13	9
Taylor	13	9	4

Table 80. Full-Time Law Enforcement Employees, by Selected State Metropolitan and Nonmetropolitan Counties, 2018—Continued

(Number.)

State/county	Law enforcement employees	Officers	Civilians
Union	11	5	6
Van Buren	12	6	6
Wapello	42	12	30
Webster	36	15	21
Winnebago	13	7	6
Winneshiek	26	11	15
Worth	25	13	12
Wright	22	10	12
KANSAS			
Metropolitan Counties			
Butler	97	59	38
Doniphan	16	6	10
Douglas	154	84	70
Harvey	23	21	2
Jefferson	39	24	15
Johnson	638	482	156
Leavenworth	97	74	23
Linn	32	19	13
Miami	67	35	32
Pottawatomie	39	28	11
Riley County Police Department	204	109	95
Shawnee	174	108	66
Sumner	33	28	5
Wabaunsee	23	9	14
Wyandotte	95	66	29
Nonmetropolitan Counties			
Allen	30	13	17
Anderson	9	9	0
Atchison	17	16	1
Barton	19	18	1
Bourbon	15	12	3
Brown	24	9	15
Chase	9	3	6
Chautauqua	15	6	9
Cherokee	36	25	11
Clark	10	5	5
Cloud	10	9	1
Coffey	18	13	5
Cowley	46	22	24
Crawford	40	35	5
Decatur	4	4	0
Dickinson	23	20	3
Edwards	10	6	4
Elk	9	4	5
Ellis	37	19	18
Ellsworth	19	7	12
Ford	36	26	10
Franklin	38	28	10
Gove	6	4	2
Graham	8	3	5
Grant	14	5	9
Gray	16	10	6
Greeley	8	4	4
Greenwood	16	11	5
Haskell	16	11	5
Hodgeman	10	5	5
Jewell	9	5	4
Kearny	16	9	7
Kingman	16	7	9
Kiowa	18	7	11
Labette	20	18	2
Lane	10	5	5
Lincoln	11	8	3
Logan	5	5	0
Lyon	31	25	6
Marion	10	9	1
Marshall	24	10	14
McPherson	22	19	3
Meade	18	8	10
Mitchell	10	9	1
Morris	12	7	5
Morton	11	5	6
Nemaha	27	10	17
Neosho	30	17	13
Ness	10	4	6
Norton	10	5	5
Osborne	9	7	2
Ottawa	19	5	14
Pawnee	10	9	1
Phillips	14	9	5
Pratt	18	12	6

Table 80. Full-Time Law Enforcement Employees, by Selected State Metropolitan and Nonmetropolitan Counties, 2018—Continued

(Number.)

State/county	Law enforcement employees	Officers	Civilians
Rawlins	8	3	5
Reno	69	58	11
Republic	10	9	1
Rice	7	5	2
Rooks	15	6	9
Rush	12	7	5
Russell	17	11	6
Saline	50	38	12
Scott	9	4	5
Smith	5	5	0
Stafford	10	5	5
Stanton	10	6	4
Stevens	18	7	11
Thomas	22	8	14
Trego	6	4	2
Wallace	7	3	4
Washington	16	9	7
Wichita	8	4	4
Woodson	11	6	5
KENTUCKY			
Metropolitan Counties			
Allen	25	14	11
Boone	158	153	5
Bracken	6	5	1
Bullitt	68	49	19
Butler	10	8	2
Carter	9	6	3
Christian	39	29	10
Clark	17	13	4
Daviess	42	36	6
Edmonson	8	6	2
Grant	17	15	2
Greenup	17	17	0
Hardin	46	39	7
Henderson	26	20	6
Jefferson	272	224	48
Jefferson County Police Department	30	29	1
Kenton	43	35	8
Kenton County Police Department	38	36	2
Larue	8	6	2
Oldham	16	13	3
Oldham County Police Department	40	37	3
Pendleton	16	7	9
Scott	44	40	4
Shelby	25	22	3
Trigg	11	8	3
Woodford	17	9	8
Nonmetropolitan Counties			
Adair	8	6	2
Anderson	16	14	2
Ballard	10	9	1
Barren	22	17	5
Bath	8	7	1
Bell	18	9	9
Boyle	17	16	1
Breckinridge	19	13	6
Caldwell	10	8	2
Calloway	34	16	18
Carlisle	3	2	1
Carroll	12	5	7
Casey	8	6	2
Clay	14	11	3
Clinton	6	4	2
Crittenden	4	3	1
Elliott	3	2	1
Estill	6	4	2
Fleming	7	6	1
Fulton	5	4	1
Garrard County Police Department	10	10	0
Graves	17	14	3
Grayson	19	10	9
Green	4	4	0
Harrison	11	10	1
Hart	11	9	2
Hickman	3	2	1
Hopkins	34	29	5
Jackson	9	8	1
Knott	6	6	0
Knox	16	12	4
Laurel	46	33	13
Lee	4	2	2

Table 80. Full-Time Law Enforcement Employees, by Selected State Metropolitan and Nonmetropolitan Counties, 2018—Continued

(Number.)

State/county	Law enforcement employees	Officers	Civilians
Leslie	5	3	2
Letcher	9	5	4
Lewis	7	5	2
Lincoln	8	7	1
Logan	29	22	7
Lyon	7	6	1
Madison	34	31	3
Marion	8	5	3
Martin	9	6	3
Mason	16	12	4
McCracken	47	42	5
McCreary	5	4	1
Menifee	5	4	1
Metcalfe	7	6	1
Monroe	6	5	1
Muhlenberg	14	12	2
Nelson	28	23	5
Nicholas	2	1	1
Ohio	21	18	3
Owen	5	4	1
Pike	26	11	15
Powell	5	3	2
Pulaski	68	46	22
Rockcastle	6	5	1
Rowan	28	12	16
Russell	8	7	1
Simpson	15	14	1
Trimble	2	2	0
Union	10	8	2
Washington	10	6	4
Wayne	13	12	1
Webster	9	7	2
Whitley	18	14	4
LOUISIANA			
Metropolitan Counties			
Acadia	101	58	43
Ascension	337	276	61
Assumption	83	60	23
Bossier	384	303	81
Calcasieu	870	595	275
Cameron	79	66	13
East Baton Rouge	826	706	120
East Feliciana	55	55	0
Grant	78	78	0
Iberia	175	116	59
Iberville	143	80	63
Jefferson	1,447	1,016	431
Livingston	293	293	0
Morehouse	161	161	0
Ouachita	387	387	0
Plaquemines	275	275	0
Pointe Coupee	102	54	48
Rapides	505	410	95
St. Bernard	258	232	26
St. Charles	398	220	178
St. Helena	46	27	19
St. John the Baptist	237	236	1
St. Martin	176	102	74
St. Tammany	671	444	227
Tangipahoa	255	134	121
Terrebonne	215	162	53
Union	42	26	16
Vermilion	124	100	24
West Baton Rouge	198	63	135
West Feliciana	69	32	37
Nonmetropolitan Counties			
Avoyelles	89	65	24
Beauregard	91	72	19
Bienville	69	41	28
Caldwell	27	27	0
Catahoula	89	22	67
Claiborne	84	42	42
Concordia	221	27	194
East Carroll	48	14	34
Evangeline	44	16	28
Franklin	98	98	0
Jackson	180	44	136
Jefferson Davis	78	78	0
La Salle	78	28	50
Lincoln	83	60	23
Natchitoches	163	96	67

Table 80. Full-Time Law Enforcement Employees, by Selected State Metropolitan and Nonmetropolitan Counties, 2018—Continued

(Number.)

State/county	Law enforcement employees	Officers	Civilians
Red River	66	40	26
Richland	139	113	26
Sabine	82	65	17
St. Landry	205	80	125
St. Mary	138	138	0
Tensas	36	19	17
Vernon	126	68	58
Washington	104	92	12
Webster	124	107	17
West Carroll	18	10	8
Winn	32	14	18
MAINE			
Metropolitan Counties			
Androscoggin	22	20	2
Cumberland	74	62	12
Penobscot	37	32	5
Sagadahoc	21	19	2
York	35	32	3
Nonmetropolitan Counties			
Aroostook	28	21	7
Franklin	20	19	1
Hancock	21	19	2
Kennebec	26	23	3
Knox	20	19	1
Lincoln	25	23	2
Oxford	27	24	3
Piscataquis	9	8	1
Somerset	28	24	4
Waldo	25	23	2
Washington	15	13	2
MARYLAND			
Metropolitan Counties			
Allegany	34	32	2
Anne Arundel	103	79	24
Anne Arundel County Police Department	950	710	240
Baltimore County	75	65	10
Baltimore County Police Department	2,081	1,865	216
Calvert	133	106	27
Carroll	157	125	32
Cecil	108	90	18
Charles	420	286	134
Frederick	246	179	67
Harford	390	292	98
Howard	72	53	19
Howard County Police Department	671	469	202
Montgomery	188	156	32
Montgomery County Police Department	1,812	1,292	520
Prince George's County Police Department	1,866	1,632	234
Queen Anne's	67	55	12
Somerset	30	24	6
St. Mary's	208	138	70
Washington	259	106	153
Wicomico	110	89	21
Worcester	64	52	12
Nonmetropolitan Counties			
Caroline	38	34	4
Dorchester	44	40	4
Garrett	52	35	17
Kent	26	22	4
Talbot	38	35	3
MICHIGAN			
Metropolitan Counties			
Bay	87	40	47
Berrien	156	75	81
Calhoun	186	81	105
Cass	69	32	37
Clinton	61	26	35
Genesee	268	116	152
Ingham	157	79	78
Ionia	59	29	30
Jackson	136	53	83
Kalamazoo	232	160	72
Kent	548	207	341
Lapeer	80	47	33
Livingston	168	52	116
Macomb	528	257	271
Monroe	154	74	80
Montcalm	45	20	25

Table 80. Full-Time Law Enforcement Employees, by Selected State Metropolitan and Nonmetropolitan Counties, 2018—Continued

(Number.)

State/county	Law enforcement employees	Officers	Civilians
Muskegon	107	44	63
Oakland	1,073	891	182
Ottawa	239	141	98
Saginaw	105	57	48
Shiawassee	51	21	30
St. Clair	208	83	125
Washtenaw	303	128	175
Wayne	920	629	291
Nonmetropolitan Counties			
Alcona	24	11	13
Alger	13	8	5
Allegan	105	57	48
Alpena	27	13	14
Antrim	50	20	30
Arenac	20	11	9
Baraga	8	6	2
Barry	52	30	22
Benzie	34	16	18
Branch	33	12	21
Charlevoix	38	21	17
Cheboygan	37	20	17
Chippewa	38	13	25
Crawford	28	15	13
Delta	10	10	0
Emmet	49	26	23
Gladwin	39	15	24
Gogebic	25	17	8
Grand Traverse	123	66	57
Gratiot	40	38	2
Hillsdale	38	24	14
Houghton	28	19	9
Huron	36	20	16
Iosco	24	5	19
Iron	19	10	9
Isabella	49	21	28
Kalkaska	34	15	19
Keweenaw	6	6	0
Lake	72	16	56
Leelanau	37	20	17
Lenawee	110	38	72
Luce	6	5	1
Mackinac	26	14	12
Manistee	36	16	20
Marquette	64	24	40
Mason	40	20	20
Mecosta	49	21	28
Menominee	15	15	0
Missaukee	26	13	13
Montmorency	13	13	0
Newaygo	63	27	36
Oceana	35	21	14
Ogemaw	37	15	22
Ontonagon	10	6	4
Osceola	21	18	3
Oscoda	16	12	4
Otsego	27	11	16
Presque Isle	14	14	0
Roscommon	39	25	14
Sanilac	57	27	30
Schoolcraft	11	4	7
St. Joseph	58	27	31
Tuscola	47	22	25
Van Buren	111	66	45
Wexford	48	23	25
MINNESOTA			
Metropolitan Counties			
Anoka	254	128	126
Benton	70	24	46
Blue Earth	75	38	37
Carlton	55	25	30
Carver	144	73	71
Chisago	98	43	55
Clay	84	33	51
Dakota	198	80	118
Dodge	38	24	14
Fillmore	31	20	11
Hennepin	819	318	501
Houston	34	13	21
Isanti	61	22	39
Lake	29	16	13
Le Sueur	38	20	18

Table 80. Full-Time Law Enforcement Employees, by Selected State Metropolitan and Nonmetropolitan Counties, 2018—Continued

(Number.)

State/county	Law enforcement employees	Officers	Civilians
Mille Lacs	82	37	45
Nicollet	42	16	26
Olmsted	174	71	103
Polk	53	33	20
Ramsey	468	224	244
Scott	131	44	87
Sherburne	294	81	213
Stearns	200	66	134
St. Louis	258	104	154
Wabasha	50	18	32
Washington	247	108	139
Wright	250	145	105
Nonmetropolitan Counties			
Aitkin	47	17	30
Becker	60	21	39
Beltrami	78	30	48
Big Stone	7	5	2
Brown	34	14	20
Cass	72	43	29
Chippewa	19	8	11
Clearwater	23	10	13
Cook	22	14	8
Cottonwood	22	10	12
Crow Wing	126	40	86
Douglas	79	35	44
Faribault	28	12	16
Freeborn	80	25	55
Goodhue	105	40	65
Grant	17	11	6
Hubbard	49	18	31
Itasca	76	33	43
Jackson	28	15	13
Kanabec	54	21	33
Kandiyohi	104	34	70
Kittson	11	5	6
Koochiching	20	10	10
Lac qui Parle	12	6	6
Lake of the Woods	14	7	7
Lincoln	13	7	6
Lyon	50	17	33
Mahnomen	19	12	7
Marshall	21	12	9
Martin	34	13	21
McLeod	56	24	32
Meeker	47	21	26
Morrison	56	21	35
Mower	70	24	46
Murray	19	12	7
Nobles	33	13	20
Norman	12	7	5
Otter Tail	84	37	47
Pennington	33	10	23
Pine	80	33	47
Pipestone	24	14	10
Pope	15	8	7
Red Lake	11	9	2
Redwood	28	13	15
Renville	36	15	21
Rice	58	30	28
Rock	17	12	5
Roseau	19	9	10
Sibley	26	12	14
Steele	28	22	6
Stevens	17	7	10
Swift	17	9	8
Todd	34	16	18
Traverse	14	6	8
Wadena	20	11	9
Waseca	29	13	16
Watonwan	22	8	14
Wilkin	18	7	11
Winona	65	17	48
Yellow Medicine	21	10	11
MISSISSIPPI			
Metropolitan Counties			
DeSoto	290	156	134
Hancock	139	70	69
Harrison	318	129	189
Hinds	395	98	297
Lamar	53	46	7
Madison	77	73	4
Tunica	104	49	55

Table 80. Full-Time Law Enforcement Employees, by Selected State Metropolitan and Nonmetropolitan Counties, 2018—Continued

(Number.)

State/county	Law enforcement employees	Officers	Civilians
Nonmetropolitan Counties			
Chickasaw	15	14	1
Claiborne	29	10	19
Greene	18	6	12
Kemper	14	12	2
Lauderdale	123	48	75
Lee	128	115	13
Lincoln	51	25	26
Marion	21	15	6
Panola	77	40	37
Washington	47	34	13
MISSOURI			
Metropolitan Counties			
Andrew	35	16	19
Bates	41	16	25
Bollinger	17	12	5
Boone	82	63	19
Buchanan	106	69	37
Caldwell	49	10	39
Callaway	31	28	3
Cape Girardeau	78	42	36
Cass	112	85	27
Christian	136	98	38
Clay	205	140	65
Clinton	19	15	4
Cole	83	49	34
Cooper	11	9	2
Dallas	25	17	8
DeKalb	12	6	6
Franklin	129	118	11
Greene	347	138	209
Howard	13	9	4
Jackson	135	96	39
Jasper	133	83	50
Jefferson	218	146	72
Lafayette	45	29	16
Lincoln	107	55	52
Moniteau	12	11	1
Newton	70	59	11
Osage	14	7	7
Platte	136	88	48
Polk	37	23	14
Ray	28	15	13
St. Charles	44	31	13
St. Charles County Police Department	156	123	33
St. Louis County Police Department	1,236	931	305
Warren	51	31	20
Webster	34	19	15
Nonmetropolitan Counties			
Adair	23	12	11
Atchison	11	6	5
Audrain	40	29	11
Barry	25	22	3
Benton	28	18	10
Butler	43	30	13
Camden	113	71	42
Carroll	9	8	1
Carter	14	6	8
Cedar	38	13	25
Clark	11	6	5
Crawford	32	17	15
Dade	12	8	4
Dent	21	16	5
Douglas	12	7	5
Dunklin	23	14	9
Gasconade	12	11	1
Gentry	5	5	0
Grundy	14	4	10
Harrison	12	5	7
Hickory	14	9	5
Holt	12	6	6
Howell	41	27	14
Iron	12	8	4
Johnson	61	34	27
Knox	3	2	1
Laclede	34	23	11
Lawrence	35	26	9
Lewis	13	7	6
Linn	10	9	1
Livingston	11	10	1
Macon	22	12	10

Table 80. Full-Time Law Enforcement Employees, by Selected State Metropolitan and Nonmetropolitan Counties, 2018—Continued

(Number.)

State/county	Law enforcement employees	Officers	Civilians
Madison	11	9	2
Maries	10	7	3
Marion	39	17	22
McDonald	28	19	9
Mercer	10	4	6
Miller	33	19	14
Mississippi	19	9	10
Monroe	9	8	1
Montgomery	20	18	2
Morgan	54	26	28
Nodaway	14	11	3
Oregon	10	6	4
Ozark	16	9	7
Pemiscot	54	18	36
Perry	34	23	11
Pettis	60	37	23
Phelps	72	34	38
Pulaski	39	21	18
Putnam	4	4	0
Ralls	14	12	2
Randolph	42	26	16
Reynolds	10	9	1
Ripley	13	11	2
Saline	34	21	13
Schuyler	9	5	4
Scotland	5	2	3
Shannon	9	4	5
Shelby	7	5	2
St. Clair	66	19	47
Ste. Genevieve	70	45	25
St. Francois	74	61	13
Stoddard	30	15	15
Stone	59	48	11
Sullivan	4	4	0
Taney	60	43	17
Texas	13	13	0
Vernon	43	17	26
Washington	38	22	16
Wayne	17	7	10
Worth	4	3	1
Wright	14	7	7
MONTANA			
Metropolitan Counties			
Carbon	21	11	10
Cascade	147	36	111
Missoula	74	54	20
Stillwater	16	10	6
Yellowstone	161	54	107
Nonmetropolitan Counties			
Beaverhead	16	5	11
Big Horn	31	16	15
Blaine	11	6	5
Broadwater	24	10	14
Carter	3	3	0
Chouteau	24	9	15
Custer	18	7	11
Dawson	8	7	1
Deer Lodge	22	22	0
Fallon	9	4	5
Fergus	22	10	12
Flathead	108	56	52
Gallatin	122	58	64
Garfield	4	3	1
Glacier	26	13	13
Golden Valley	2	2	0
Granite	10	6	4
Hill	29	11	18
Jefferson	27	13	14
Judith Basin	6	5	1
Lake	42	21	21
Lincoln	38	18	20
Madison	12	11	1
McCone	4	4	0
Meagher	8	3	5
Mineral	6	6	0
Musselshell	8	8	0
Park	24	15	9
Phillips	13	7	6
Pondera	7	6	1
Powder River	5	4	1
Powell	11	7	4

Table 80. Full-Time Law Enforcement Employees, by Selected State Metropolitan and Nonmetropolitan Counties, 2018—Continued

(Number.)

State/county	Law enforcement employees	Officers	Civilians
Prairie	4	3	1
Ravalli	75	35	40
Richland	12	10	2
Roosevelt	44	15	29
Rosebud	25	13	12
Sanders	12	12	0
Sheridan	8	6	2
Silver Bow	95	51	44
Sweet Grass	13	7	6
Teton	13	10	3
Toole	22	13	9
Valley	18	8	10
Wheatland	12	6	6
NEBRASKA			
Metropolitan Counties			
Cass	74	41	33
Dakota	20	18	2
Dixon	13	8	5
Douglas	212	131	81
Hall	42	32	10
Howard	11	4	7
Lancaster	104	85	19
Merrick	17	9	8
Sarpy	211	120	91
Saunders	19	13	6
Seward	26	14	12
Washington	53	29	24
Nonmetropolitan Counties			
Adams	32	16	16
Antelope	18	4	14
Arthur	1	1	0
Boone	12	5	7
Box Butte	20	5	15
Boyd	3	3	0
Buffalo	46	29	17
Burt	10	5	5
Butler	11	10	1
Cedar	7	7	0
Chase	8	4	4
Cherry	6	5	1
Cheyenne	21	10	11
Clay	14	8	6
Colfax	17	9	8
Cuming	6	5	1
Custer	8	7	1
Dawes	15	7	8
Dawson	67	28	39
Deuel	6	5	1
Dodge	24	21	3
Dundy	8	5	3
Fillmore	12	6	6
Franklin	8	4	4
Frontier	8	4	4
Furnas	14	8	6
Gage	18	15	3
Garden	11	4	7
Garfield	2	2	0
Gosper	6	5	1
Grant	2	2	0
Hamilton	22	9	13
Harlan	8	4	4
Hayes	1	1	0
Hitchcock	8	5	3
Holt	7	6	1
Hooker	2	2	0
Jefferson	27	17	10
Johnson	13	7	6
Kearney	10	5	5
Keith	16	8	8
Keya Paha	1	1	0
Kimball	9	4	5
Knox	14	4	10
Lincoln	61	24	37
Logan	2	2	0
Madison	63	34	29
McPherson	1	1	0
Morrill	14	9	5
Nance	9	6	3
Nemaha	10	10	0
Nuckolls	10	5	5
Otoe	29	14	15

Table 80. Full-Time Law Enforcement Employees, by Selected State Metropolitan and Nonmetropolitan Counties, 2018—Continued

(Number.)

State/county	Law enforcement employees	Officers	Civilians
Pawnee	5	4	1
Perkins	7	6	1
Phelps	25	6	19
Pierce	6	3	3
Platte	64	19	45
Polk	11	7	4
Red Willow	21	6	15
Richardson	27	10	17
Rock	8	3	5
Saline	25	19	6
Scotts Bluff	24	17	7
Sheridan	15	5	10
Sherman	5	4	1
Stanton	9	8	1
Thayer	11	6	5
Thurston	13	9	4
Valley	10	5	5
Wayne	7	6	1
Webster	10	5	5
Wheeler	2	2	0
York	26	10	16
NEVADA			
Metropolitan Counties			
Carson City	137	95	42
Storey	29	27	2
Washoe	682	416	266
Nonmetropolitan Counties			
Churchill	46	38	8
Douglas	121	107	14
Elko	79	64	15
Esmeralda	16	11	5
Eureka	15	9	6
Humboldt	55	34	21
Lander	32	20	12
Lincoln	30	25	5
Lyon	106	77	29
Mineral	19	13	6
Nye	134	106	28
Pershing	20	13	7
White Pine	33	27	6
NEW HAMPSHIRE			
Metropolitan Counties			
Rockingham	48	26	22
Strafford	40	26	14
Nonmetropolitan Counties			
Carroll	24	12	12
Cheshire	21	9	12
Grafton	25	10	15
Merrimack	29	16	13
NEW JERSEY			
Metropolitan Counties			
Atlantic	133	109	24
Bergen	585	481	104
Burlington	88	70	18
Camden	201	171	30
Cape May	162	138	24
Cumberland	63	63	0
Essex	466	394	72
Gloucester	108	94	14
Hudson	406	277	129
Hunterdon	33	28	5
Mercer	184	143	41
Middlesex	230	187	43
Monmouth	625	427	198
Morris	122	90	32
Ocean	259	147	112
Passaic	706	554	152
Salem	243	210	33
Somerset	218	181	37
Sussex	141	119	22
Union	256	205	51
Warren	24	20	4
NEW MEXICO			
Metropolitan Counties			
Sandoval	61	54	7
San Juan	122	95	27
Santa Fe	125	95	30
Torrance	19	15	4

Table 80. Full-Time Law Enforcement Employees, by Selected State Metropolitan and Nonmetropolitan Counties, 2018—Continued

(Number.)

State/county	Law enforcement employees	Officers	Civilians
Nonmetropolitan Counties			
Catron	11	7	4
Chaves	43	35	8
Cibola	20	16	4
Colfax	12	11	1
Curry	27	15	12
De Baca	2	2	0
Eddy	71	52	19
Grant	41	36	5
Hidalgo	11	9	2
Lincoln	31	21	10
Luna	33	26	7
McKinley	42	29	13
Mora	8	4	4
Otero	57	40	17
Quay	8	7	1
Rio Arriba	28	26	2
San Miguel	11	9	2
Sierra	16	14	2
Socorro	16	14	2
Taos	31	26	5
Union	7	5	2
NEW YORK			
Metropolitan Counties			
Albany	193	131	62
Broome	65	56	9
Chemung	48	43	5
Dutchess	146	109	37
Erie	192	148	44
Herkimer	15	5	10
Jefferson	58	43	15
Livingston	73	48	25
Madison	49	38	11
Monroe	333	273	60
Nassau	3,337	2,424	913
Niagara	157	106	51
Onondaga	235	205	30
Ontario	122	75	47
Orleans	26	26	0
Oswego	86	68	18
Putnam	94	77	17
Rensselaer	42	34	8
Rockland	154	77	77
Saratoga	187	166	21
Schoharie	31	17	14
Suffolk	390	270	120
Suffolk County Police Department	3,027	2,519	508
Tompkins	44	40	4
Ulster	59	56	3
Warren	105	68	37
Washington	45	39	6
Wayne	80	69	11
Westchester Public Safety	370	296	74
Yates	26	23	3
Nonmetropolitan Counties			
Allegany	34	11	23
Cattaraugus	76	50	26
Cayuga	35	31	4
Clinton	39	26	13
Columbia	71	57	14
Cortland	42	39	3
Delaware	23	17	6
Essex	20	17	3
Franklin	7	5	2
Fulton	46	27	19
Greene	30	28	2
Hamilton	7	6	1
Lewis	30	20	10
Montgomery	35	22	13
Otsego	21	19	2
Schuyler	22	19	3
Steuben	50	34	16
St. Lawrence	31	31	0
Sullivan	50	50	0
Wyoming	43	32	11
NORTH CAROLINA			
Metropolitan Counties			
Alamance	279	138	141
Alexander	71	37	34
Anson	58	32	26

Table 80. Full-Time Law Enforcement Employees, by Selected State Metropolitan and Nonmetropolitan Counties, 2018—Continued

(Number.)

State/county	Law enforcement employees	Officers	Civilians
Brunswick	296	183	113
Buncombe	375	225	150
Burke	109	86	23
Cabarrus	320	181	139
Caldwell	122	81	41
Camden	20	17	3
Catawba	192	142	50
Chatham	140	99	41
Craven	132	74	58
Cumberland	560	301	259
Currituck	98	63	35
Davidson	172	122	50
Davie	91	54	37
Durham	442	180	262
Edgecombe	127	56	71
Forsyth	510	208	302
Franklin	125	85	40
Gaston	214	111	103
Gaston County Police Department	222	131	91
Gates	13	12	1
Granville	62	56	6
Guilford	614	257	357
Harnett	259	160	99
Haywood	140	66	74
Henderson	211	142	69
Hoke	104	57	47
Iredell	210	145	65
Johnston	184	117	67
Jones	29	18	11
Lincoln	169	115	54
Madison	41	24	17
Mecklenburg[1]	1,093	279	814
Nash	137	89	48
New Hanover	511	360	151
Onslow	259	129	130
Orange	133	88	45
Pamlico	49	22	27
Pender	115	70	45
Person	86	49	37
Pitt	321	136	185
Randolph	242	182	60
Rockingham	141	93	48
Rowan	192	126	66
Stokes	73	52	21
Union	299	207	92
Wake	992	375	617
Wayne	131	124	7
Yadkin	76	40	36
Nonmetropolitan Counties			
Alleghany	35	20	15
Ashe	63	29	34
Avery	52	31	21
Beaufort	90	52	38
Bertie	44	23	21
Bladen	100	54	46
Carteret	99	60	39
Caswell	56	37	19
Cherokee	71	31	40
Chowan	38	19	19
Clay	35	19	16
Cleveland	183	109	74
Columbus	119	76	43
Dare	143	67	76
Duplin	94	65	29
Graham	28	15	13
Greene	45	22	23
Halifax	92	62	30
Hertford	53	24	29
Hyde	15	13	2
Jackson	83	58	25
Lee	100	69	31
Lenoir	70	62	8
Macon	73	53	20
Martin	43	40	3
McDowell	65	42	23
Mitchell	19	18	1
Montgomery	57	30	27
Moore	151	80	71
Northampton	59	35	24
Pasquotank	51	46	5
Perquimans	19	17	2
Polk	35	35	0

Table 80. Full-Time Law Enforcement Employees, by Selected State Metropolitan and Nonmetropolitan Counties, 2018—Continued

(Number.)

State/county	Law enforcement employees	Officers	Civilians
Richmond	91	58	33
Robeson	207	121	86
Rutherford	132	77	55
Sampson	132	90	42
Scotland	63	36	27
Stanly	89	48	41
Surry	120	74	46
Swain	48	28	20
Transylvania	84	61	23
Tyrrell	14	12	2
Vance	102	47	55
Warren	64	34	30
Washington	46	24	22
Watauga	73	43	30
Wilkes	130	72	58
Wilson	153	92	61
Yancey	38	19	19
NORTH DAKOTA			
Metropolitan Counties			
Burleigh	146	54	92
Cass	171	111	60
Grand Forks	39	33	6
Morton	45	36	9
Oliver	5	4	1
Nonmetropolitan Counties			
Adams	6	6	0
Barnes	10	9	1
Benson	4	4	0
Billings	6	6	0
Bottineau	21	11	10
Bowman	4	3	1
Burke	4	3	1
Cavalier	12	6	6
Dickey	4	3	1
Divide	6	6	0
Dunn	18	16	2
Eddy	6	5	1
Emmons	6	5	1
Foster	4	3	1
Golden Valley	5	4	1
Grant	5	5	0
Griggs	3	3	0
Hettinger	5	4	1
Kidder	4	3	1
Lamoure	6	5	1
Logan	3	3	0
McHenry	8	8	0
McIntosh	3	3	0
McKenzie	50	33	17
McLean	41	25	16
Mercer	34	20	14
Mountrail	24	12	12
Nelson	6	5	1
Pembina	16	9	7
Pierce	38	4	34
Ramsey	8	7	1
Ransom	5	4	1
Renville	6	6	0
Richland	37	18	19
Rolette	22	6	16
Sargent	6	5	1
Sheridan	3	3	0
Sioux	1	1	0
Slope	1	1	0
Stark	28	23	5
Steele	3	3	0
Stutsman	14	12	2
Towner	6	6	0
Traill	15	10	5
Walsh	19	12	7
Ward	93	37	56
Wells	4	3	1
Williams	84	41	43
OHIO			
Metropolitan Counties			
Allen	148	65	83
Brown	45	29	16
Carroll	36	20	16
Delaware	207	97	110
Fulton	23	21	2

Table 80. Full-Time Law Enforcement Employees, by Selected State Metropolitan and Nonmetropolitan Counties, 2018—Continued

(Number.)

State/county	Law enforcement employees	Officers	Civilians
Geauga	117	50	67
Greene	151	67	84
Hocking	39	33	6
Jefferson	40	33	7
Madison	41	29	12
Medina	144	56	88
Miami	106	50	56
Morrow	58	29	29
Ottawa	64	25	39
Perry	21	15	6
Pickaway	81	37	44
Portage	140	75	65
Richland	129	51	78
Stark	259	130	129
Summit	402	331	71
Union	63	46	17
Warren	194	101	93
Wood	122	56	66
Nonmetropolitan Counties			
Ashland	84	44	40
Ashtabula	86	34	52
Athens	33	28	5
Champaign	25	22	3
Clinton	74	36	38
Darke	66	34	32
Fayette	40	24	16
Hancock	99	40	59
Highland	47	28	19
Knox	75	49	26
Marion	57	32	25
Meigs	24	18	6
Mercer	68	33	35
Noble	28	13	15
Scioto	74	38	36
Washington	95	52	43
Wayne	75	49	26
Wyandot	28	15	13
OKLAHOMA			
Metropolitan Counties			
Canadian	101	61	40
Cleveland	163	61	102
Comanche	41	30	11
Cotton	7	3	4
Creek	86	36	50
Garfield	29	21	8
Grady	24	22	2
Lincoln	32	18	14
Logan	72	38	34
McClain	35	21	14
Oklahoma	603	417	186
Okmulgee	17	15	2
Osage	76	38	38
Pawnee	23	9	14
Rogers	80	56	24
Sequoyah	25	21	4
Tulsa	585	218	367
Wagoner	74	38	36
Nonmetropolitan Counties			
Adair	10	10	0
Alfalfa	11	7	4
Atoka	23	9	14
Beaver	13	7	6
Beckham	42	14	28
Blaine	18	9	9
Bryan	18	15	3
Caddo	34	16	18
Carter	59	21	38
Cherokee	32	22	10
Choctaw	13	6	7
Cimarron	7	3	4
Coal	14	9	5
Craig	29	12	17
Custer	37	12	25
Delaware	45	17	28
Dewey	12	7	5
Ellis	18	8	10
Garvin	29	14	15
Grant	11	6	5
Greer	6	2	4
Harmon	4	3	1

Table 80. Full-Time Law Enforcement Employees, by Selected State Metropolitan and Nonmetropolitan Counties, 2018—Continued

(Number.)

State/county	Law enforcement employees	Officers	Civilians
Harper	7	4	3
Haskell	18	9	9
Hughes	23	11	12
Jackson	39	14	25
Jefferson	13	3	10
Johnston	23	7	16
Kay	25	18	7
Kingfisher	21	11	10
Kiowa	13	5	8
Latimer	13	7	6
Le Flore	20	16	4
Love	27	10	17
Major	18	7	11
Marshall	27	6	21
Mayes	55	27	28
McCurtain	26	22	4
McIntosh	17	11	6
Murray	12	6	6
Muskogee	83	28	55
Noble	19	9	10
Nowata	16	6	10
Okfuskee	22	7	15
Ottawa	36	15	21
Payne	89	35	54
Pittsburg	35	23	12
Pontotoc	41	18	23
Pottawatomie	32	28	4
Pushmataha	22	15	7
Roger Mills	13	8	5
Seminole	19	17	2
Stephens	26	23	3
Texas	35	13	22
Tillman	10	5	5
Washington	60	27	33
Washita	29	7	22
Woods	8	7	1
Woodward	17	13	4
OREGON			
Metropolitan Counties			
Benton	81	67	14
Clackamas	441	197	244
Columbia	57	44	13
Deschutes	219	167	52
Jackson	148	113	35
Josephine	109	60	49
Lane	290	67	223
Linn	170	71	99
Marion	318	94	224
Multnomah	775	131	644
Polk	36	27	9
Washington	562	400	162
Yamhill	79	67	12
Nonmetropolitan Counties			
Baker	41	39	2
Clatsop	75	26	49
Coos	89	60	29
Crook	32	13	19
Curry	38	16	22
Douglas	142	64	78
Gilliam	7	6	1
Grant	18	18	0
Harney	19	13	6
Hood River	53	27	26
Jefferson	43	17	26
Klamath	92	28	64
Lake	21	20	1
Lincoln	87	31	56
Malheur	63	40	23
Morrow	38	25	13
Sherman	7	6	1
Tillamook	52	41	11
Umatilla	109	54	55
Union	32	15	17
Wallowa	13	5	8
Wasco	28	15	13
Wheeler	5	4	1
PENNSYLVANIA			
Metropolitan Counties			
Adams	17	14	3
Allegheny	195	163	32
Allegheny County Police Department	276	219	57

Table 80. Full-Time Law Enforcement Employees, by Selected State Metropolitan and Nonmetropolitan Counties, 2018—Continued

(Number.)

State/county	Law enforcement employees	Officers	Civilians
Beaver	24	20	4
Berks	109	97	12
Blair	27	24	3
Bucks	80	65	15
Butler	30	27	3
Centre	27	23	4
Chester	90	72	18
Cumberland	37	30	7
Erie	45	38	7
Franklin	26	22	4
Lancaster	65	56	9
Lycoming	21	15	6
Mercer	18	14	4
Monroe	49	24	25
Montgomery	125	100	25
Northampton	69	64	5
Pike	25	21	4
Washington	32	29	3
Westmoreland	61	53	8
Wyoming	6	4	2
York	108	98	10
Nonmetropolitan Counties			
Bedford	12	9	3
Bradford	13	11	2
Clarion	10	7	3
Elk	6	5	1
Greene	8	6	2
Indiana	21	18	3
Jefferson	9	8	1
Lawrence	23	18	5
Northumberland	12	9	3
Schuylkill	17	14	3
Snyder	7	7	0
Tioga	10	8	2
Union	9	8	1
Warren	12	10	2
Wayne	16	13	3
SOUTH CAROLINA			
Metropolitan Counties			
Aiken	244	135	109
Anderson	365	267	98
Beaufort	300	219	81
Berkeley	188	161	27
Charleston	720	276	444
Clarendon	66	64	2
Darlington	73	68	5
Fairfield	48	44	4
Florence	229	190	39
Greenville	548	445	103
Horry County Police Department	269	242	27
Jasper	43	38	5
Kershaw	71	67	4
Lancaster	172	125	47
Laurens	119	111	8
Lexington	440	284	156
Pickens	147	113	34
Richland	615	582	33
Saluda	65	25	40
Spartanburg	342	315	27
Sumter	196	100	96
Nonmetropolitan Counties			
Bamberg	13	13	0
Barnwell	91	32	59
Cherokee	111	57	54
Colleton	120	57	63
Dillon	83	36	47
Georgetown	158	93	65
Greenwood	155	79	76
Hampton	42	41	1
Marion	66	30	36
McCormick	40	19	21
Newberry	107	51	56
Oconee	177	105	72
Orangeburg	118	90	28
Union	31	28	3
Williamsburg	39	35	4
SOUTH DAKOTA			
Metropolitan Counties			
Lincoln	21	19	2
McCook	9	8	1

Table 80. Full-Time Law Enforcement Employees, by Selected State Metropolitan and Nonmetropolitan Counties, 2018—Continued

(Number.)

State/county	Law enforcement employees	Officers	Civilians
Meade	50	18	32
Minnehaha	213	96	117
Pennington	406	98	308
Turner	10	8	2
Union	28	8	20
Nonmetropolitan Counties			
Aurora	4	3	1
Beadle	23	5	18
Bennett	4	3	1
Bon Homme	8	3	5
Brookings	24	15	9
Brown	60	19	41
Brule	11	4	7
Buffalo	1	1	0
Butte	7	5	2
Campbell	3	3	0
Charles Mix	20	6	14
Clark	3	3	0
Clay	13	8	5
Codington	28	9	19
Corson	5	4	1
Custer	12	11	1
Davison	10	7	3
Day	5	3	2
Deuel	6	5	1
Dewey	3	3	0
Douglas	4	4	0
Edmunds	9	4	5
Fall River	17	6	11
Faulk	15	4	11
Grant	11	4	7
Gregory	5	4	1
Haakon	2	2	0
Hamlin	4	4	0
Hand	4	2	2
Hanson	3	3	0
Harding	3	2	1
Hughes	48	6	42
Hutchinson	3	3	0
Hyde	2	2	0
Jackson	3	2	1
Jerauld	4	4	0
Jones	1	1	0
Kingsbury	6	5	1
Lake	18	8	10
Lawrence	38	15	23
Lyman	5	4	1
Marshall	12	6	6
McPherson	4	4	0
Miner	4	3	1
Moody	10	5	5
Oglala Lakota	1	1	0
Perkins	8	7	1
Potter	3	2	1
Roberts	29	5	24
Sanborn	3	2	1
Spink	12	7	5
Stanley	6	5	1
Sully	3	3	0
Tripp	6	3	3
Walworth	16	3	13
Yankton	35	12	23
Ziebach	3	3	0
TENNESSEE			
Metropolitan Counties			
Anderson	174	67	107
Blount	303	173	130
Bradley	219	112	107
Campbell	83	43	40
Cannon	37	16	21
Carter	134	72	62
Cheatham	91	49	42
Chester	50	16	34
Crockett	34	16	18
Dickson	133	59	74
Fayette	91	42	49
Gibson	80	33	47
Grainger	50	27	23
Hamblen	96	44	52
Hamilton	412	172	240
Hartsville/Trousdale	49	22	27
Hawkins	106	61	45
Jefferson	105	50	55

Table 80. Full-Time Law Enforcement Employees, by Selected State Metropolitan and Nonmetropolitan Counties, 2018—Continued

(Number.)

State/county	Law enforcement employees	Officers	Civilians
Knox	1,027	404	623
Loudon	85	51	34
Macon	63	28	35
Madison	281	120	161
Marion	62	33	29
Maury	155	86	69
Montgomery	355	112	243
Morgan	47	20	27
Polk	66	27	39
Roane	75	41	34
Robertson	164	61	103
Rutherford	462	233	229
Sequatchie	45	19	26
Shelby	1,835	616	1,219
Smith	64	27	37
Stewart	53	20	33
Sullivan	302	142	160
Sumner	301	107	194
Tipton	105	61	44
Unicoi	42	25	17
Union	60	35	25
Washington	216	97	119
Williamson	278	189	89
Wilson	256	135	121
Nonmetropolitan Counties			
Bedford	101	54	47
Benton	60	21	39
Bledsoe	42	16	26
Carroll	65	27	38
Claiborne	95	42	53
Clay	21	13	8
Cocke	76	46	30
Coffee	115	45	70
Cumberland	113	55	58
Decatur	29	13	16
DeKalb	48	25	23
Dyer	98	36	62
Fentress	49	20	29
Franklin	80	44	36
Giles	58	29	29
Greene	157	62	95
Grundy	39	17	22
Hancock	37	15	22
Hardeman	78	30	48
Hardin	51	23	28
Haywood	45	21	24
Henderson	73	35	38
Henry	65	31	34
Hickman	45	25	20
Houston	24	11	13
Humphreys	41	27	14
Jackson	36	15	21
Johnson	44	16	28
Lake	9	7	2
Lauderdale	62	24	38
Lawrence	97	57	40
Lewis	33	16	17
Lincoln	86	39	47
Marshall	56	31	25
McMinn	87	38	49
McNairy	37	18	19
Meigs	36	16	20
Monroe	58	50	8
Moore	34	14	20
Obion	63	26	37
Overton	56	26	30
Perry	27	15	12
Pickett	23	14	9
Putnam	158	69	89
Rhea	56	55	1
Scott	67	29	38
Sevier	205	106	99
Van Buren	24	8	16
Warren	99	51	48
Wayne	44	11	33
Weakley	45	23	22
White	76	41	35
TEXAS			
Metropolitan Counties			
Bandera	69	33	36
Bastrop	201	76	125
Bowie	44	37	7

Table 80. Full-Time Law Enforcement Employees, by Selected State Metropolitan and Nonmetropolitan Counties, 2018—Continued

(Number.)

State/county	Law enforcement employees	Officers	Civilians
Brazos	239	102	137
Burleson	39	20	19
Caldwell	93	34	59
Callahan	15	6	9
Cameron	505	120	385
Carson	20	7	13
Clay	23	14	9
Collin	502	399	103
Comal	273	136	137
Coryell	82	38	44
Crosby	17	6	11
Dallas	1,940	422	1,518
Denton	569	407	162
Ellis	219	80	139
Grayson	177	67	110
Gregg	241	104	137
Guadalupe	224	97	127
Hardin	72	34	38
Harrison	111	56	55
Hays	346	166	180
Hidalgo	792	279	513
Hunt	61	45	16
Johnson	128	94	34
Kaufman	252	93	159
Kendall	94	49	45
Lampasas	37	17	20
McLennan	120	100	20
Medina	76	40	36
Montgomery	909	499	410
Oldham	12	7	5
Parker	132	94	38
Potter	203	98	105
Randall	210	96	114
Robertson	32	14	18
Rusk	78	43	35
Smith	355	165	190
Sterling	5	5	0
Tarrant	1,452	1,245	207
Taylor	233	82	151
Tom Green	165	78	87
Travis	1,704	348	1,356
Victoria	188	107	81
Wichita	219	60	159
Williamson	529	223	306
Wilson	81	38	43
Wise	130	60	70
Nonmetropolitan Counties			
Andrews	39	13	26
Aransas	71	23	48
Bailey	23	6	17
Bee	52	19	33
Blanco	31	14	17
Borden	3	2	1
Bosque	40	19	21
Briscoe	3	3	0
Brooks	37	33	4
Brown	68	30	38
Burnet	151	49	102
Camp	18	7	11
Cass	50	21	29
Castro	19	6	13
Cherokee	69	30	39
Collingsworth	11	5	6
Comanche	32	10	22
Cooke	87	84	3
Crane	11	6	5
Dawson	21	9	12
Deaf Smith	38	13	25
DeWitt	53	20	33
Dickens	6	3	3
Dimmit	66	32	34
Donley	10	6	4
Eastland	28	11	17
Erath	57	24	33
Fannin	31	21	10
Fayette	49	27	22
Franklin	26	11	15
Freestone	38	28	10
Gaines	37	16	21
Gillespie	54	30	24
Gonzales	52	20	32
Grimes	59	57	2

Table 80. Full-Time Law Enforcement Employees, by Selected State Metropolitan and Nonmetropolitan Counties, 2018—Continued

(Number.)

State/county	Law enforcement employees	Officers	Civilians
Hale	60	60	0
Hartley	7	6	1
Henderson	153	68	85
Hockley	29	12	17
Hopkins	64	24	40
Houston	48	20	28
Jack	29	12	17
Jackson	34	12	22
Jeff Davis	5	4	1
Karnes	61	29	32
Kenedy	18	11	7
Kent	6	3	3
Kerr	107	51	56
King	1	1	0
Kinney	13	5	8
Kleberg	69	24	45
Knox	9	3	6
Lamb	27	10	17
Lee	42	14	28
Limestone	84	22	62
Lipscomb	11	6	5
Llano	50	25	25
Madison	31	13	18
Matagorda	73	38	35
McMullen	12	10	2
Montague	28	8	20
Nacogdoches	88	40	48
Nolan	36	13	23
Palo Pinto	57	24	33
Rains	31	12	19
Real	11	5	6
Red River	31	12	19
Refugio	42	16	26
Runnels	29	6	23
Sabine	19	9	10
Scurry	39	7	32
Shackelford	16	7	9
Shelby	30	15	15
Somervell	45	24	21
Starr	106	51	55
Stephens	20	5	15
Terry	33	10	23
Titus	60	26	34
Trinity	17	11	6
Uvalde	80	27	53
Val Verde	67	47	20
Van Zandt	71	37	34
Walker	77	38	39
Wharton	73	41	32
Wilbarger	18	7	11
Willacy	42	13	29
Yoakum	21	9	12
Young	33	26	7
UTAH			
Metropolitan Counties			
Box Elder	79	26	53
Cache	131	43	88
Davis	303	196	107
Juab	27	16	11
Morgan	13	11	2
Salt Lake County Unified Police Department	560	406	154
Tooele	93	26	67
Utah	389	152	237
Washington	156	44	112
Weber	63	62	1
Nonmetropolitan Counties			
Beaver	72	21	51
Carbon	52	28	24
Daggett	4	3	1
Duchesne	63	28	35
Garfield	30	17	13
Grand	31	17	14
Iron	82	35	47
Kane	47	22	25
Millard	54	31	23
Piute	5	4	1
Rich	10	4	6
San Juan	29	13	16
Sanpete	58	25	33
Sevier	62	26	36
Summit	97	56	41

Table 80. Full-Time Law Enforcement Employees, by Selected State Metropolitan and Nonmetropolitan Counties, 2018—Continued

(Number.)

State/county	Law enforcement employees	Officers	Civilians
Uintah	73	24	49
Wasatch	59	29	30
Wayne	6	5	1
VERMONT			
Metropolitan Counties			
Chittenden	16	13	3
Franklin	11	11	0
Grand Isle	1	1	0
Nonmetropolitan Counties			
Addison	6	6	0
Bennington	15	12	3
Caledonia	11	10	1
Essex	4	4	0
Lamoille	24	8	16
Orange	16	10	6
Orleans	9	7	2
Rutland	20	15	5
Washington	11	9	2
Windham	17	11	6
Windsor	15	14	1
VIRGINIA			
Metropolitan Counties			
Albemarle County Police Department	170	138	32
Amelia	29	17	12
Amherst	49	44	5
Appomattox	24	22	2
Arlington County Police Department	452	347	105
Augusta	83	72	11
Bedford	97	88	9
Botetourt	116	94	22
Campbell	74	65	9
Charles City	20	13	7
Chesterfield County Police Department	603	496	107
Clarke	28	16	12
Craig	14	9	5
Culpeper	100	87	13
Dinwiddie	41	39	2
Fairfax County Police Department	1,727	1,417	310
Fauquier	176	133	43
Fluvanna	49	34	15
Franklin	101	80	21
Frederick	137	127	10
Giles	37	24	13
Gloucester	98	82	16
Goochland	53	37	16
Greene	42	25	17
Hanover	260	241	19
Henrico County Police Department	817	654	163
Isle of Wight	54	50	4
James City County Police Department	107	101	6
King and Queen	21	13	8
King William	35	22	13
Loudoun	639	527	112
Madison	26	20	6
Mathews	18	11	7
Montgomery	116	107	9
Nelson	23	17	6
New Kent	47	34	13
Powhatan	47	42	5
Prince George County Police Department	72	53	19
Prince William County Police Department	783	654	129
Pulaski	50	48	2
Rappahannock	21	17	4
Roanoke County Police Department	154	140	14
Rockingham	81	64	17
Scott	37	30	7
Southampton	87	69	18
Spotsylvania	251	200	51
Stafford	244	179	65
Sussex	47	43	4
Warren	79	61	18
Washington	88	70	18
York	99	91	8
Nonmetropolitan Counties			
Accomack	68	58	10
Alleghany	69	49	20
Bath	21	14	7
Bland	21	12	9
Brunswick	46	34	12

Table 80. Full-Time Law Enforcement Employees, by Selected State Metropolitan and Nonmetropolitan Counties, 2018—Continued

(Number.)

State/county	Law enforcement employees	Officers	Civilians
Buchanan	48	35	13
Buckingham	26	19	7
Caroline	76	54	22
Carroll	41	36	5
Charlotte	40	37	3
Cumberland	22	17	5
Dickenson	35	20	15
Essex	21	13	8
Floyd	33	24	9
Grayson	33	27	6
Greensville	37	23	14
Halifax	38	31	7
Henry	134	122	12
Highland	13	8	5
King George	58	41	17
Lancaster	39	30	9
Lee	34	34	0
Louisa	65	48	17
Lunenburg	19	13	6
Mecklenburg	52	50	2
Middlesex	40	29	11
Northampton	81	67	14
Northumberland	33	22	11
Nottoway	23	14	9
Orange	43	40	3
Page	73	55	18
Patrick	71	55	16
Pittsylvania	122	105	17
Prince Edward	32	32	0
Richmond	21	13	8
Rockbridge	41	38	3
Russell	49	34	15
Shenandoah	66	60	6
Smyth	47	40	7
Surry	14	13	1
Tazewell	73	51	22
Westmoreland	41	27	14
Wise	71	53	18
Wythe	44	35	9
WASHINGTON			
Metropolitan Counties			
Asotin	30	13	17
Benton	193	63	130
Chelan	80	60	20
Clark	234	141	93
Cowlitz	51	41	10
Douglas	34	28	6
Franklin	81	27	54
King	295	226	69
Kitsap	232	116	116
Pierce	337	278	59
Skagit	131	52	79
Skamania	34	17	17
Snohomish	360	290	70
Spokane	152	122	30
Stevens	58	27	31
Thurston	228	92	136
Walla Walla	35	28	7
Whatcom	189	84	105
Yakima	85	59	26
Nonmetropolitan Counties			
Adams	34	15	19
Clallam	44	36	8
Columbia	10	10	0
Ferry	26	8	18
Garfield	13	7	6
Grant	121	52	69
Grays Harbor	78	61	17
Island	66	35	31
Jefferson	42	22	20
Kittitas	77	35	42
Klickitat	39	20	19
Lewis	107	38	69
Lincoln	29	16	13
Mason	90	45	45
Okanogan	33	28	5
Pacific	46	15	31
Pend Oreille	32	12	20
San Juan	29	16	13
Wahkiakum	16	6	10
Whitman	35	18	17

Table 80. Full-Time Law Enforcement Employees, by Selected State Metropolitan and Nonmetropolitan Counties, 2018—Continued

(Number.)

State/county	Law enforcement employees	Officers	Civilians
WEST VIRGINIA			
Metropolitan Counties			
Berkeley	68	60	8
Boone	28	22	6
Brooke	31	17	14
Cabell	47	41	6
Clay	5	5	0
Fayette	41	35	6
Hampshire	21	18	3
Hancock	33	29	4
Jackson	16	15	1
Jefferson	39	32	7
Kanawha	132	104	28
Lincoln	7	6	1
Marshall	37	32	5
Mineral	21	14	7
Monongalia	42	39	3
Morgan	11	10	1
Ohio	37	35	2
Preston	22	19	3
Putnam	63	42	21
Raleigh	72	54	18
Wayne	23	20	3
Wirt	3	3	0
Wood	51	35	16
Nonmetropolitan Counties			
Barbour	10	7	3
Braxton	10	9	1
Calhoun	3	2	1
Doddridge	10	8	2
Gilmer	4	4	0
Grant	14	10	4
Greenbrier	38	27	11
Hardy	12	11	1
Harrison	57	53	4
Lewis	19	14	5
Logan	22	20	2
Marion	46	31	15
Mason	27	18	9
McDowell	14	12	2
Mercer	41	29	12
Mingo	19	17	2
Monroe	7	7	0
Nicholas	23	20	3
Pendleton	3	3	0
Pleasants	7	6	1
Pocahontas	11	6	5
Randolph	15	14	1
Ritchie	13	9	4
Roane	10	7	3
Summers	7	6	1
Taylor	12	6	6
Tucker	6	4	2
Tyler	12	10	2
Upshur	14	12	2
Webster	6	4	2
Wetzel	15	13	2
Wyoming	20	19	1
WISCONSIN			
Metropolitan Counties			
Brown	330	159	171
Calumet	54	26	28
Chippewa	75	26	49
Columbia	100	42	58
Dane	573	465	108
Douglas	78	29	49
Eau Claire	110	42	68
Fond du Lac	126	59	67
Green	56	31	25
Iowa	22	20	2
Kenosha	342	121	221
Kewaunee	34	32	2
La Crosse	112	42	70
Lincoln	67	30	37
Marathon	177	69	108
Milwaukee	613	292	321
Oconto	63	29	34
Outagamie	176	70	106
Ozaukee	106	78	28
Pierce	53	39	14
Racine	246	148	98

Table 80. Full-Time Law Enforcement Employees, by Selected State Metropolitan and Nonmetropolitan Counties, 2018—Continued

(Number.)

State/county	Law enforcement employees	Officers	Civilians
Rock	129	100	29
Sheboygan	168	70	98
St. Croix	92	84	8
Washington	168	72	96
Waukesha	337	164	173
Winnebago	193	136	57
Nonmetropolitan Counties			
Adams	59	28	31
Ashland	46	24	22
Barron	72	29	43
Bayfield	43	20	23
Buffalo	26	11	15
Burnett	18	17	1
Clark	51	24	27
Crawford	30	24	6
Dodge	159	64	95
Door	54	50	4
Dunn	61	27	34
Florence	21	21	0
Forest	37	19	18
Grant	54	30	24
Green Lake	43	18	25
Iron	22	11	11
Jackson	45	23	22
Juneau	55	42	13
Lafayette	22	21	1
Langlade	41	18	23
Manitowoc	104	64	40
Marinette	77	32	45
Marquette	45	23	22
Menominee	14	6	8
Monroe	78	25	53
Oneida	87	37	50
Pepin	18	7	11
Portage	104	48	56
Price	28	20	8
Richland	32	32	0
Rusk	31	17	14
Sauk	144	48	96
Sawyer	45	37	8
Shawano	110	39	71
Taylor	41	19	22
Trempealeau	56	26	30
Vernon	47	23	24
Vilas	63	38	25
Walworth	202	82	120
Washburn	31	15	16
Waupaca	107	44	63
Waushara	54	27	27
Wood	68	41	27
WYOMING			
Metropolitan Counties			
Natrona	148	109	39
Nonmetropolitan Counties			
Albany	48	45	3
Big Horn	37	13	24
Campbell	155	60	95
Carbon	54	18	36
Crook	21	14	7
Fremont	40	35	5
Goshen	29	19	10
Hot Springs	13	5	8
Johnson	32	29	3
Lincoln	46	20	26
Niobrara	16	4	12
Park	60	20	40
Platte	38	24	14
Sheridan	59	20	39
Sublette	70	54	16
Sweetwater	101	42	59
Uinta	47	34	13
Washakie	8	8	0
Weston	6	6	0

1 The employee data presented in this table for Mecklenburg represent only Mecklenburg County Sheriff's Office employees and exclude Charlotte-Mecklenburg Police Department employees.

Table 81. Full-Time Law Enforcement Employees, by Selected State and Agency, 2018

(Number.)

State/agency	Law enforcement employees	Officers	Civilians
ALABAMA			
State Agencies			
State Fire Marshal	37	31	6
Taylor Hardin Secure Medical Facility	2	1	1
Tribal Agencies			
Poarch Creek Tribal	53	46	7
Other Agencies			
Huntsville International Airport	20	19	1
Mobile Regional Airport	18	15	3
ALASKA			
Other Agencies			
Fairbanks International Airport	31	24	7
Ted Stevens Anchorage International Airport	72	59	13
ARIZONA			
Tribal Agencies			
Ak-Chin Tribal	80	21	59
Cocopah Tribal	24	17	7
Colorado River Agency	2	2	0
Colorado River Tribal	54	20	34
Fort Apache Agency	4	4	0
Hopi Tribal	43	15	28
Kaibab Paiute Tribal	1	1	0
Navajo Nation	328	219	109
Pascua Yaqui Tribal	83	28	55
Quechan Tribal	7	7	0
Salt River Tribal	150	117	33
Truxton Canon Agency	9	5	4
White Mountain Apache Tribal	44	24	20
Yavapai-Apache Nation	20	16	4
Yavapai-Prescott Tribal	15	12	3
Other Agencies			
Tucson Airport Authority	40	20	20
ARKANSAS			
State Agencies			
Camp Robinson	11	11	0
State Capitol Police	22	20	2
Other Agencies			
Northwest Arkansas Regional Airport	14	11	3
CALIFORNIA			
State Agencies			
Atascadero State Hospital	187	173	14
California State Fair	5	4	1
Coalinga State Hospital	261	244	17
Department of Parks and Recreation, Capital	514	493	21
Fairview Developmental Center	10	8	2
Metropolitan State Hospital	126	111	15
Napa State Hospital	129	118	11
Patton State Hospital	123	106	17
Porterville Developmental Center	61	55	6
Sonoma Developmental Center	14	5	9
Tribal Agencies			
Blue Lake Tribal	3	3	0
Hoopa Valley Tribal	16	9	7
La Jolla Tribal	3	3	0
Los Coyotes Tribal	3	3	0
Table Mountain Rancheria	24	17	7
Yurok Tribal	5	4	1
Other Agencies			
East Bay Regional Park District	89	62	27
Fontana Unified School District	76	16	60
Kern High School District	31	28	3
Port of San Diego Harbor	170	125	45
San Bernardino Unified School District	98	29	69
San Francisco Bay Area Rapid Transit, Contra Costa County	337	229	108
Shasta County Marshal	25	19	6
Stockton Unified School District	43	34	9
Twin Rivers Unified School District	25	18	7
COLORADO			
State Agencies			
Colorado Bureau of Investigation	265	41	224
Colorado Mental Health Institute	106	22	84

Table 81. Full-Time Law Enforcement Employees, by Selected State and Agency, 2018—Continued

(Number.)

State/agency	Law enforcement employees	Officers	Civilians
Tribal Agencies			
Southern Ute Tribal	37	20	17
Ute Mountain Tribal	13	8	5
Other Agencies			
All Crimes Enforcement Team	3	3	0
CONNECTICUT			
State Agencies			
Department of Motor Vehicles	63	53	10
State Capitol Police	43	32	11
Tribal Agencies			
Mashantucket Pequot Tribal	38	28	10
Mohegan Tribal	28	27	1
Other Agencies			
Metropolitan Transportation Authority	37	36	1
DELAWARE			
State Agencies			
Alcohol and Tobacco Enforcement	16	14	2
Animal Welfare, New Castle County	16	16	0
Attorney General			
Kent County	76	9	67
New Castle County	293	28	265
Sussex County	54	2	52
Environmental Control	11	9	2
Fish and Wildlife	35	26	9
Park Rangers	21	21	0
River and Bay Authority	65	55	10
State Capitol Police	89	66	23
State Fire Marshal	52	20	32
Other Agencies			
Amtrak Police	59	28	31
Wilmington Fire Department	15	9	6
DISTRICT OF COLUMBIA			
Other Agencies			
District of Columbia Fire and Emergency Medical			
Services, Arson Investigation Unit	16	16	0
Metro Transit Police	609	536	73
FLORIDA			
State Agencies			
Capitol Police	78	59	19
Department of Corrections, Office of the Inspector			
General, Leon County	141	116	25
Department of Law Enforcement			
Duval County, Jacksonville	131	43	88
Escambia County, Pensacola	94	31	63
Hillsborough County, Tampa	176	59	117
Lee County, Fort Myers	91	40	51
Miami-Dade County, Miami	101	73	28
Orange County, Orlando	176	58	118
Division of Alcoholic Beverages and Tobacco, Leon			
County	169	99	70
Department of Investigative and Forensic Services	307	236	71
Broward County	12	9	3
Duval County	13	12	1
Escambia County	7	5	2
Hillsborough County	18	15	3
Lee County	6	5	1
Miami-Dade County	27	24	3
Orange County	21	18	3
Palm Beach County	20	17	3
Pinellas County	8	6	2
Fish and Wildlife Conservation Commission, Leon			
County	1,016	823	193
Tribal Agencies			
Miccosukee Tribal	61	41	20
Seminole Tribal	206	129	77
Other Agencies			
Florida School for the Deaf and Blind	18	9	9
Fort Lauderdale Airport	113	92	21
Jacksonville Aviation Authority	51	37	14
Lee County Port Authority	57	37	20
Melbourne International Airport	14	12	2
Miami-Dade County Public Schools	219	179	40
Northwest Florida Beaches International Airport	21	15	6
Palm Beach County School District	203	181	22
Port Everglades	80	57	23
Sarasota-Manatee Airport Authority	11	10	1

Table 81. Full-Time Law Enforcement Employees, by Selected State and Agency, 2018—Continued

(Number.)

State/agency	Law enforcement employees	Officers	Civilians
Tampa International Airport	171	72	99
Volusia County Beach Safety	54	50	4
GEORGIA			
State Agencies			
Department of Transportation, Office of Investigations	3	3	0
Georgia Bureau of Investigation, Headquarters	820	282	538
Georgia Forestry Commission	6	5	1
Georgia Public Safety Training Center	186	67	119
Georgia World Congress	72	24	48
Ports Authority, Savannah	126	93	33
State Board of Workers Compensation Fraud Investigation Division	11	5	6
Other Agencies			
Appling County Board of Education	2	2	0
Atlanta Public Schools	75	72	3
Augusta Board of Education	33	29	4
Bibb County Board of Education	28	22	6
Chatham County Board of Education	90	48	42
Cherokee County Board of Education	23	19	4
Cherokee County Marshal	19	13	6
Cobb County Board of Education	66	64	2
Decatur County Schools	5	5	0
DeKalb County School System	192	75	117
Dougherty County Board of Education	22	19	3
Fayette County Marshal	4	4	0
Forsyth County Fire Investigation Unit	3	3	0
Fulton County Marshal	68	54	14
Fulton County School System	66	64	2
Glynn County School System	24	24	0
Gwinnett County Public Schools	100	89	11
Hall County Marshal	14	13	1
Hartsfield-Jackson Atlanta International Airport	171	162	9
Lanier County Board of Education	2	2	0
Metropolitan Atlanta Rapid Transit Authority	378	318	60
Muscogee City Marshal	24	20	4
Richmond County Marshal	62	48	14
Stone Mountain Park	24	21	3
Troup County Marshal	7	6	1
Turner County Schools	2	2	0
Twiggs County Board of Education	1	1	0
Washington County Board of Education	6	6	0
IDAHO			
Tribal Agencies			
Kootenai Tribal	2	2	0
Nez Perce Tribal	23	18	5
ILLINOIS			
State Agencies			
Secretary of State Police	220	119	101
Other Agencies			
Alton & Southern Railway	7	7	0
Capitol Airport Authority	5	5	0
Crystal Lake Park District	1	1	0
Decatur Park District	4	4	0
Fon du Lac Park District	2	2	0
Indiana Harbor Belt Railroad	12	12	0
Kane County Forest Preserve	6	6	0
Lake County Forest Preserve	20	18	2
McHenry County Conservation District	12	11	1
Norfolk Southern Railway			
Cook County	40	40	0
Macon County	2	2	0
Madison County	5	5	0
Pekin Park District	1	1	0
Rockford Park District	14	13	1
Springfield Park District	4	4	0
Terminal Railroad Association	6	6	0
INDIANA			
State Agencies			
Northern Indiana Commuter Transportation District	10	9	1
KANSAS			
State Agencies			
Kansas Department of Wildlife and Parks	160	158	2
Kansas Lottery Security Division	8	4	4
Kansas Racing Commission, Security Division	74	52	22
Securities Office, Investigation Section	5	4	1
State Fire Marshal	13	12	1

Table 81. Full-Time Law Enforcement Employees, by Selected State and Agency, 2018—Continued

(Number.)

State/agency	Law enforcement employees	Officers	Civilians
Tribal Agencies			
Iowa Tribal	6	6	0
Kickapoo Tribal	4	4	0
Potawatomi Tribal	21	11	10
Sac and Fox Tribal	5	4	1
Other Agencies			
Blue Valley School District	9	8	1
El Dorado School District	2	2	0
Johnson County Park	23	22	1
Metropolitan Topeka Airport Authority	22	17	5
Shawnee Mission Public Schools	9	8	1
Topeka Fire Department Arson Investigation	4	4	0
Unified School District			
Auburn-Washburn	4	2	2
Goddard	5	5	0
Kansas City	38	35	3
Seaman	4	4	0
Shawnee Heights	1	1	0
KENTUCKY			
State Agencies			
Alcohol Beverage Control, Investigative Division	13	7	6
Department of Agriculture Animal Health			
Enforcement Division	4	4	0
Department of Insurance Fraud Unit	16	12	4
Fish and Wildlife Enforcement	117	115	2
Kentucky Horse Park	8	8	0
Park Security	46	46	0
Unlawful Narcotics Investigation Treatment and			
Education	3	3	0
Other Agencies			
Barren County Drug Task Force	2	1	1
Cincinnati-Northern Kentucky International Airport	69	50	19
Clark County School System	6	6	0
FIVCO Area Drug Task Force	4	4	0
Greater Hardin County Narcotics Task Force	14	12	2
Jefferson County School District	27	20	7
Louisville Fire Department Arson Division	11	10	1
Louisville Regional Airport Authority	41	36	5
McCracken County Public Schools	8	8	0
Norfolk Southern Railway	3	3	0
Northern Kentucky Drug Strike Force	3	2	1
South Central Kentucky Drug Task Force	8	7	1
LOUISIANA			
State Agencies			
Tensas Basin Levee District	3	2	1
Tribal Agencies			
Chitimacha Tribal	15	15	0
Tunica-Biloxi Tribal	15	13	2
Other Agencies			
Tensas Basin Levee District	3	2	1
MAINE			
State Agencies			
Bureau of Capitol Police	21	13	8
Drug Enforcement Agency	3	1	2
State Fire Marshal	37	15	22
Tribal Agencies			
Passamaquoddy Indian Township	10	5	5
Passamaquoddy Pleasant Point Tribal	7	7	0
Penobscot Nation	10	6	4
MARYLAND			
State Agencies			
Comptroller of the Treasury, Field Enforcement			
Division	58	24	34
Department of Public Safety and Correctional			
Services, Internal Investigations Unit	75	38	37
General Services			
Internal Investigation Division	75	38	37
Annapolis, Anne Arundel County	58	28	30
Baltimore City	88	66	22
Natural Resources Police	307	255	52
Springfield Hospital	44	6	38
State Fire Marshal	61	37	24
Transit Administration	227	167	60
Transportation Authority	560	429	131

Table 81. Full-Time Law Enforcement Employees, by Selected State and Agency, 2018—Continued

(Number.)

State/agency	Law enforcement employees	Officers	Civilians
Other Agencies			
Maryland-National Capital Park Police			
Montgomery County	104	84	20
Prince George's County	148	121	27
MASSACHUSETTS			
State Agencies			
Massachusetts Bay Transportation Authority,			
Suffolk County	261	252	9
Tribal Agencies			
Wampanoag Tribe of Gay Head	2	2	0
Other Agencies			
Beth Israel Deaconess Medical Center	57	14	43
Massachusetts General Hospital	139	65	74
MICHIGAN			
Tribal Agencies			
Gun Lake Tribal	17	12	5
Nottawaseppi Huron Band of Potawatomi	18	17	1
Other Agencies			
Bishop International Airport	8	7	1
Capitol Region Airport Authority	17	9	8
Genessee County Parks and Recreation	9	9	0
Gerald R. Ford International Airport	18	17	1
Huron-Clinton Metropolitan Authority			
Hudson Mills Metropark	3	3	0
Kensington Metropark	8	8	0
Lower Huron Metropark	9	9	0
Stony Creek Metropark	11	11	0
Wayne County Airport	104	100	4
MINNESOTA			
State Agencies			
Bureau of Criminal Apprehension	105	73	32
Capitol Security, St. Paul	82	21	61
Department of Natural Resources Enforcement			
Division	217	184	33
Tribal Agencies			
Fond du Lac Tribal	21	19	2
Mille Lacs Tribal	28	22	6
Upper Sioux Community	8	8	0
White Earth Tribal	34	28	6
Other Agencies			
Metropolitan Transit Commission	164	128	36
Minneapolis-St. Paul International Airport	160	87	73
Three Rivers Park District	12	11	1
MISSISSIPPI			
State Agencies			
Department of Marine Resources	36	30	6
State Capitol Police	84	69	15
MISSOURI			
State Agencies			
Gaming Commission, Enforcement Division	115	113	2
Other Agencies			
Clay County Park Authority	8	7	1
Jackson County Park Rangers	17	15	2
Kansas City International Airport	95	50	45
Lambert-St. Louis International Airport	71	61	10
Logan-Rogersville School District	1	1	0
Springfield-Branson Airport	14	11	3
Springfield-Greene County Park Rangers	7	7	0
St. Charles County Park Rangers	10	10	0
Terminal Railroad	6	6	0
MONTANA			
State Agencies			
Gambling Investigations Bureau	43	18	25
Tribal Agencies			
Blackfeet Agency	30	24	6
Fort Belknap Tribal	14	10	4
Rocky Boy's Tribal	21	14	7
NEBRASKA			
Tribal Agencies			
Santee Tribal	5	5	0
Winnebago Tribal	8	4	4

Table 81. Full-Time Law Enforcement Employees, by Selected State and Agency, 2018—Continued

(Number.)

State/agency	Law enforcement employees	Officers	Civilians
NEVADA			
State Agencies			
Capitol Police	17	17	0
Department of Public Safety, Investigative Division	46	28	18
Department of Wildlife, Law Enforcement Division	44	33	11
Secretary of State Securities Division Enforcement			
Section	3	3	0
State Fire Marshal	6	6	0
Tribal Agencies			
Eastern Nevada Agency	18	4	14
Reno-Sparks Indian Colony	15	14	1
Walker River Tribal	6	6	0
Western Nevada Agency	8	5	3
Western Shoshone Tribal	1	1	0
Other Agencies			
Clark County School District	193	158	35
Las Vegas Fire and Rescue, Arson Bomb Unit	1	1	0
North Las Vegas Fire Department Arson			
Investigations	1	1	0
Reno Municipal Court Marshal	14	11	3
Reno Tahoe Airport Authority	23	22	1
Washoe County School District	44	37	7
NEW HAMPSHIRE			
State Agencies			
Liquor Commission	44	37	7
NEW JERSEY			
State Agencies			
Department of Human Services	77	76	1
Division of Fish and Wildlife	50	47	3
New Jersey Transit Police	322	260	62
Palisades Interstate Parkway	30	26	4
Port Authority of New York and New Jersey	1,914	1,739	175
State Park Police	92	90	2
Other Agencies			
Park Police			
Morris County	28	27	1
Union County	118	72	46
Prosecutor			
Atlantic County	170	73	97
Bergen County	256	102	154
Burlington County	126	43	83
Camden County	264	182	82
Cape May County	91	43	48
Cumberland County	116	41	75
Essex County	371	249	122
Gloucester County	102	36	66
Hudson County	265	99	166
Hunterdon County	54	27	27
Mercer County	181	61	120
Middlesex County	205	69	136
Monmouth County	281	78	203
Morris County	155	66	89
Ocean County	174	71	103
Passaic County	185	73	112
Salem County	57	21	36
Somerset County	123	55	68
Sussex County	56	36	20
Union County	184	77	107
Warren County	63	22	41
NEW MEXICO			
Tribal Agencies			
Acoma Tribal	27	13	14
Isleta Tribal	43	28	15
Jicarilla Apache Tribal	29	18	11
Laguna Tribal	49	36	13
Mescalero Tribal	19	10	9
Northern Pueblos Agency	9	8	1
Pojoaque Tribal	16	9	7
Ramah Navajo Tribal	16	8	8
Santa Ana Tribal	21	20	1
Santa Clara Pueblo	15	8	7
Southern Pueblos Agency	22	14	8
Taos Pueblo	12	8	4
Tesuque Pueblo	10	5	5
NEW YORK			
State Agencies			
State Park			
Allegany Region	12	9	3

Table 81. Full-Time Law Enforcement Employees, by Selected State and Agency, 2018—Continued

(Number.)

State/agency	Law enforcement employees	Officers	Civilians
Central Region	20	15	5
Finger Lakes Region	14	11	3
Genesee Region	15	13	2
Long Island Region	62	58	4
New York City Region	22	18	4
Niagara Region	32	32	0
Palisades Region	39	35	4
Saratoga/Capital Region	87	79	8
Taconic Region	13	12	1
Thousand Island Region	16	15	1
Tribal Agencies			
Oneida Indian Nation	42	36	6
St. Regis Tribal	33	27	6
Other Agencies			
New York City Department of Environmental Protection Police, Ashokan Precinct	252	221	31
New York City Metropolitan Transportation Authority	816	743	73
Onondaga County Parks	1	1	0
NORTH CAROLINA			
State Agencies			
Cherry Hospital	15	9	6
Department of Health and Human Resources	6	6	0
Department of Wildlife	215	203	12
Division of Alcohol Law Enforcement	105	96	9
Division of Marine Fisheries	61	54	7
North Carolina Arboretum	4	4	0
North Carolina State Bureau of Investigation	412	228	184
State Capitol Police	83	53	30
State Fairgrounds	8	2	6
State Park Rangers			
Carolina Beach	6	4	2
Carvers Creek	2	2	0
Chimney Rock	8	5	3
Cliffs of the Neuse	3	3	0
Crowders Mountain	12	7	5
Dismal Swamp	4	3	1
Elk Knob	3	3	0
Eno River	5	5	0
Falls Lake Recreation Area	14	12	2
Fort Fisher	3	3	0
Fort Macon	5	4	1
Goose Creek	3	2	1
Gorges	7	2	5
Grandfather Mountain	6	4	2
Hammocks Beach	10	5	5
Hanging Rock	6	6	0
Haw River	3	3	0
Jockey's Ridge	6	5	1
Jones Lake	5	4	1
Jordan Lake State Recreation Area	15	13	2
Kerr Lake	12	10	2
Lake James	4	4	0
Lake Norman	6	4	2
Lake Waccamaw	9	4	5
Lumber River	5	2	3
Mayo River	4	2	2
Medoc Mountain	3	3	0
Merchants Millpond	3	2	1
Morrow Mountain	7	4	3
Mount Mitchell	8	4	4
New River-Mount Jefferson	8	8	0
Pettigrew	3	2	1
Pilot Mountain	5	5	0
Raven Rock	5	3	2
Singletary Lake	5	2	3
South Mountains	9	8	1
Stone Mountain	11	6	5
Weymouth Woods/Sandhills Nature Preserve	5	3	2
William B. Umstead	13	7	6
Tribal Agencies			
Cherokee Tribal	88	63	25
Other Agencies			
Asheville Regional Airport	14	12	2
Beaufort County Alcoholic Beverage Control Enforcement	1	1	0
Durham County Alcoholic Beverage Control Law Enforcement Office	3	3	0
Nash County Alcoholic Beverage Control Enforcement	1	1	0
Piedmont Triad International Airport	37	25	12

Table 81. Full-Time Law Enforcement Employees, by Selected State and Agency, 2018—Continued

(Number.)

State/agency	Law enforcement employees	Officers	Civilians
Raleigh-Durham International Airport	43	41	2
Triad Municipal Alcoholic Beverage Control Law Enforcement	5	4	1
University of North Carolina Hospitals	95	34	61
WakeMed Campus Police	86	48	38
Wilmington International Airport	14	10	4
NORTH DAKOTA			
Tribal Agencies			
Fort Totten Agency	18	8	10
Three Affiliated Tribes	54	38	16
OHIO			
Other Agencies			
Cleveland Metropolitan Park District	90	76	14
Hamilton County Park District	32	29	3
Holden Arboretum	2	2	0
Johnny Appleseed Metropolitan Park District	2	2	0
Muskingum Watershed Conservancy District	25	25	0
Preservation Parks of Delaware County	6	6	0
Sandusky County Park District	5	5	0
Wood County Park District	6	6	0
OKLAHOMA			
State Agencies			
Capitol Park Police	68	18	50
State Park Rangers	53	53	0
Tribal Agencies			
Absentee Shawnee Tribal	12	11	1
Anadarko Agency	15	9	6
Cherokee Nation	40	32	8
Chickasaw Nation	62	52	10
Choctaw Nation	44	42	2
Citizen Potawatomi Nation	42	26	16
Comanche Nation	37	26	11
Concho Agency	8	8	0
Eastern Shawnee Tribal	17	16	1
Iowa Tribal	16	10	6
Kaw Tribal	8	8	0
Kickapoo Tribal	14	13	1
Miami Agency	5	5	0
Miami Tribal	9	9	0
Muscogee Nation Tribal	58	47	11
Otoe-Missouria Tribal	14	7	7
Pawnee Tribal	6	5	1
Ponca Tribal	4	4	0
Sac and Fox Tribal	11	11	0
Seminole Nation Lighthorse	8	7	1
Tonkawa Tribal	8	6	2
Wyandotte Nation	5	4	1
Other Agencies			
Jenks Public Schools	9	8	1
Lawton Public Schools	14	14	0
Muskogee City Schools	8	6	2
Putnam City Campus	16	12	4
OREGON			
State Agencies			
Liquor Commission			
Benton County	1	1	0
Clackamas County	7	7	0
Columbia County	1	1	0
Coos County	1	1	0
Crook County	1	1	0
Deschutes County	5	4	1
Douglas County	1	1	0
Grant County	1	1	0
Jackson County	8	7	1
Josephine County	4	4	0
Klamath County	1	1	0
Lane County	13	12	1
Lincoln County	1	1	0
Marion County	6	5	1
Multnomah County	17	14	3
Polk County	1	1	0
Umatilla County	2	2	0
Washington County	4	4	0
Wheeler County	1	1	0
Yamhill County	1	1	0
Tribal Agencies			
Burns Paiute Tribal	4	3	1
Columbia River Inter-Tribal Fisheries Enforcement	22	14	8
Coos, Lower Umpqua, and Siuslaw Tribal	5	4	1

Table 81. Full-Time Law Enforcement Employees, by Selected State and Agency, 2018—Continued

(Number.)

State/agency	Law enforcement employees	Officers	Civilians
Coquille Tribal	4	4	0
Grand Ronde Tribal	10	8	2
Umatilla Tribal	27	21	6
Other Agencies			
Hillsboro School District	1	1	0
Port of Portland	70	54	16
PENNSYLVANIA			
State Agencies			
Pennsylvania Fish and Boat Commission	85	76	9
State Capitol Police	109	106	3
State Park Rangers			
Bald Eagle	3	3	0
Beltzville	2	2	0
Ben Rush	5	2	3
Bendigo	1	1	0
Black Moshannon	2	2	0
Caledonia	1	1	0
Canoe Creek	1	1	0
Chapman	2	2	0
Codorus	12	2	10
Colonel Denning	6	1	5
Cook Forest	5	5	0
Cowans Gap	2	2	0
Delaware Canal	5	5	0
Evansburg	3	2	1
Fort Washington	2	2	0
Frances Slocum	1	1	0
French Creek	10	10	0
Gifford Pinchot	3	1	2
Greenwood Furnace	3	3	0
Hickory Run	9	9	0
Hills Creek	2	2	0
Jacobsburg Environmental Education Center	1	1	0
Jennings Environmental Education Center	6	6	0
Kettle Creek	1	1	0
Keystone	3	3	0
Kings Gap Environmental Education Center	1	1	0
Lackawanna	4	4	0
Laurel Hill	5	5	0
Linn Run	1	1	0
Little Buffalo	4	4	0
Little Pine	1	1	0
Lyman Run	1	1	0
Marsh Creek	10	10	0
Maurice K. Goddard	2	1	1
Memorial Lake	3	1	2
Moraine	6	6	0
Mount Pisgah	1	1	0
Neshaminy	5	2	3
Nockamixon	3	3	0
Ohiopyle	14	5	9
Oil Creek	2	1	1
Ole Bull	1	1	0
Parker Dam	8	2	6
Pine Grove Furnace	1	1	0
Point	2	2	0
Presque Isle	9	9	0
Prince Gallitzin	20	8	12
Promised Land	1	1	0
Pymatuning	8	6	2
Raccoon Creek	14	4	10
Raymond B. Winter	1	1	0
Reeds Gap	1	1	0
Ricketts Glen	4	4	0
Ridley Creek	2	2	0
Ryerson Station	4	1	3
Samuel S. Lewis	1	1	0
Shawnee	2	2	0
Shikellamy	1	1	0
Sinnemahoning	5	1	4
Sizerville	1	1	0
Susquehannock	1	1	0
Tobyhanna	1	1	0
Trough Creek	1	1	0
Tuscarora	1	1	0
Tyler	5	2	3
White Clay	2	2	0
Worlds End	7	2	5
Yellow Creek	1	1	0
Other Agencies			
Allegheny County District Attorney, Criminal Investigation Division	39	29	10
Allegheny County Housing Authority	7	6	1

Table 81. Full-Time Law Enforcement Employees, by Selected State and Agency, 2018—Continued

(Number.)

State/agency	Law enforcement employees	Officers	Civilians
Allegheny County Port Authority	51	40	11
County Detective			
Adams County	2	2	0
Beaver County	9	8	1
Berks County	38	32	6
Bucks County	23	22	1
Butler County	4	4	0
Chester County	26	21	5
Cumberland County	10	6	4
Dauphin County	11	9	2
Erie County	11	9	2
Lackawanna County	13	13	0
Lancaster County	32	30	2
Lawrence County	7	6	1
Lebanon County	7	5	2
Lehigh County	29	26	3
Luzerne County	10	10	0
McKean County	2	2	0
Monroe County	8	6	2
Montgomery County	53	38	15
Montour County	1	1	0
Pike County	3	3	0
Schuylkill County	21	5	16
Wayne County	3	3	0
Westmoreland County	56	15	41
Wyoming County	4	4	0
York County	11	10	1
Delaware County District Attorney, Criminal Investigation Division	46	36	10
Delaware County Park	56	55	1
Erie Municipal Airport Authority	8	8	0
Fort Indiantown Gap	25	18	7
Franklin County Drug Task Force	5	3	2
Harrisburg International Airport	18	13	5
Lehigh Valley International Airport	11	11	0
Westmoreland County Park	33	32	1
Wyoming Area School District	1	1	0
RHODE ISLAND			
State Agencies			
Department of Environmental Management	42	32	10
Rhode Island State Airport	35	28	7
Tribal Agencies			
Narragansett Tribal	4	4	0
SOUTH CAROLINA			
State Agencies			
Bureau of Protective Services	58	58	0
Department of Natural Resources			
Abbeville County	3	3	0
Aiken County	2	2	0
Allendale County	2	2	0
Anderson County	6	6	0
Bamberg County	3	3	0
Barnwell County	2	2	0
Beaufort County	7	7	0
Berkeley County	5	5	0
Calhoun County	4	4	0
Charleston County	25	25	0
Cherokee County	4	4	0
Chester County	3	3	0
Chesterfield County	4	4	0
Clarendon County	3	3	0
Colleton County	4	4	0
Darlington County	4	4	0
Dillon County	3	3	0
Dorchester County	3	3	0
Edgefield County	4	4	0
Fairfield County	4	4	0
Florence County	7	7	0
Georgetown County	7	7	0
Greenville County	5	5	0
Greenwood County	2	2	0
Hampton County	4	4	0
Horry County	6	6	0
Jasper County	4	4	0
Kershaw County	3	3	0
Lancaster County	2	2	0
Laurens County	4	4	0
Lee County	3	3	0
Lexington County	5	5	0
Marion County	3	3	0
Marlboro County	3	3	0
McCormick County	3	3	0

Table 81. Full-Time Law Enforcement Employees, by Selected State and Agency, 2018—Continued

(Number.)

State/agency	Law enforcement employees	Officers	Civilians
Newberry County	3	3	0
Oconee County	4	4	0
Orangeburg County	3	3	0
Pickens County	8	8	0
Richland County	49	49	0
Saluda County	4	4	0
Spartanburg County	4	4	0
Sumter County	3	3	0
Union County	3	3	0
Williamsburg County	6	6	0
York County	2	2	0
Department of Public Safety, Illegal Immigration Enforcement Unit	8	7	1
Forestry Commission			
Aiken County	1	1	0
Anderson County	2	1	1
Bamberg County	1	1	0
Berkeley County	1	1	0
Cherokee County	1	1	0
Chesterfield County	3	3	0
Colleton County	1	1	0
Darlington County	2	2	0
Fairfield County	1	1	0
Florence County	1	1	0
Horry County	1	1	0
Kershaw County	2	2	0
Laurens County	1	1	0
Lexington County	3	3	0
Marlboro County	1	1	0
Newberry County	1	1	0
Oconee County	1	1	0
Orangeburg County	2	2	0
Pickens County	1	1	0
Richland County	3	3	0
Spartanburg County	1	1	0
Sumter County	2	2	0
Williamsburg County	2	2	0
Santee Cooper	10	10	0
State Museum	4	1	3
State Ports Authority	48	36	12
State Transport Police	5	5	0
Abbeville County	2	2	0
Allendale County	1	1	0
Anderson County	3	3	0
Barnwell County	1	1	0
Beaufort County	3	3	0
Berkeley County	1	1	0
Charleston County	1	1	0
Chesterfield County	2	2	0
Colleton County	2	2	0
Darlington County	1	1	0
Dillon County	1	1	0
Dorchester County	6	5	1
Edgefield County	1	1	0
Fairfield County	1	1	0
Florence County	5	4	1
Greenville County	3	3	0
Greenwood County	7	7	0
Hampton County	2	2	0
Kershaw County	2	2	0
Lancaster County	2	2	0
Laurens County	1	1	0
Lexington County	11	9	2
Marion County	3	3	0
Newberry County	2	2	0
Oconee County	3	3	0
Orangeburg County	1	1	0
Richland County	24	7	17
Saluda County	3	3	0
Spartanburg County	8	7	1
Sumter County	2	2	0
Williamsburg County	1	1	0
York County	5	5	0
United States Department of Energy Savannah River Plant	49	37	12
Other Agencies			
15th Circuit Drug Enforcement Unit	4	3	1
Charleston County Aviation Authority	51	35	16
Columbia Metropolitan Airport	17	17	0
Greenville Hospital			
Greenville	31	31	0
Laurens	4	4	0
Oconee	4	4	0
Greenville-Spartanburg International Airport	20	19	1
Lexington County Medical Center	45	24	21

Table 81. Full-Time Law Enforcement Employees, by Selected State and Agency, 2018—Continued

(Number.)

State/agency	Law enforcement employees	Officers	Civilians
SOUTH DAKOTA			
State Agencies			
Division of Criminal Investigation	175	49	126
Tribal Agencies			
Crow Creek Tribal	12	8	4
Flandreau Santee Sioux Tribal	4	4	0
Lower Brule Tribal	23	7	16
Pine Ridge Sioux Tribal	81	60	21
Rosebud Tribal	44	28	16
Yankton Tribal	14	10	4
TENNESSEE			
State Agencies			
Alcoholic Beverage Commission	40	39	1
Department of Agriculture, Agricultural Crime Unit	7	7	0
Department of Correction, Internal Affairs	96	25	71
State Fire Marshal	26	22	4
State Park Rangers			
Bicentennial Capitol Mall	6	6	0
Big Hill Pond	2	2	0
Big Ridge	4	4	0
Bledsoe Creek	2	2	0
Booker T. Washington	4	4	0
Burgess Falls Natural Area	4	4	0
Cedars of Lebanon	5	5	0
Chickasaw	4	4	0
Cordell Hull Birthplace	2	2	0
Cove Lake	4	4	0
Cumberland Mountain	4	4	0
Cumberland Trail	8	8	0
Cummins Falls	3	3	0
David Crockett	4	4	0
Davy Crockett Birthplace	3	3	0
Dunbar Cave Natural Area	3	3	0
Edgar Evins	3	3	0
Fall Creek Falls	10	10	0
Fort Loudon State Historic Park	4	4	0
Fort Pillow State Historic Park	2	2	0
Frozen Head Natural Area	5	5	0
Harpeth Scenic Rivers	4	4	0
Harrison Bay	4	4	0
Henry Horton	8	6	2
Hiwassee/Ocoee State Scenic Rivers	6	6	0
Indian Mountain	2	2	0
Johnsonville State Historic Park	3	3	0
Long Hunter	5	5	0
Meeman-Shelby Forest	5	5	0
Montgomery Bell	6	6	0
Mousetail Landing	3	3	0
Natchez Trace	5	5	0
Nathan Bedford Forrest	3	3	0
Norris Dam	4	4	0
Old Stone Fort State Archaeological Park	3	3	0
Panther Creek	3	3	0
Paris Landing	5	5	0
Pickett	5	5	0
Pickwick Landing	5	5	0
Pinson Mounds State Archaeological Park	2	2	0
Radnor Lake Natural Area	5	5	0
Red Clay State Historic Park	2	2	0
Reelfoot Lake	4	4	0
Roan Mountain	4	4	0
Rock Island	4	4	0
Rocky Fork	2	2	0
Seven Islands Birding Park	2	2	0
Sgt. Alvin C. York	2	2	0
South Cumberland Recreation Area	9	9	0
Standing Stone	3	3	0
Sycamore Shoals State Historic Park	3	3	0
Tim's Ford	3	3	0
T.O. Fuller	3	3	0
Warrior's Path	5	5	0
TennCare Office of Inspector General	41	16	25
Tennessee Bureau of Investigation	514	322	192
Tennessee Department of Revenue, Special Investigations Unit	46	33	13
Wildlife Resources Agency			
Region 1	45	42	3
Region 2	67	59	8
Region 3	49	46	3
Region 4	51	48	3
Other Agencies			
Chattanooga Housing Authority	6	5	1
Chattanooga Metropolitan Airport	11	10	1

Table 81. Full-Time Law Enforcement Employees, by Selected State and Agency, 2018—Continued

(Number.)

State/agency	Law enforcement employees	Officers	Civilians
Dickson Parks and Recreation	1	1	0
Drug Task Force			
1st Judicial District	4	1	3
3rd Judicial District	4	4	0
4th Judicial District	2	1	1
8th Judicial District	2	1	1
9th Judicial District	4	4	0
10th Judicial District	6	5	1
12th Judicial District	3	3	0
14th Judicial District	1	1	0
15th Judicial District	3	2	1
17th Judicial District	6	6	0
18th Judicial District	4	3	1
21st Judicial District	8	7	1
22nd Judicial District	1	1	0
23rd Judicial District	9	9	0
24th Judicial District	9	8	1
25th Judicial District	1	1	0
31st Judicial District	1	1	0
Knoxville Metropolitan Airport	45	27	18
Memphis-Shelby County Airport Authority	58	46	12
Metropolitan Nashville Park Police	20	20	0
Nashville International Airport	96	64	32
Tri-Cities Regional Airport	15	14	1
West Tennessee Violent Crime Task Force	7	6	1
TEXAS			
State Agencies			
Texas Comptroller of Public Accounts Criminal Investigation Division	108	91	17
Tribal Agencies			
Ysleta del Sur Pueblo Tribal	13	11	2
Other Agencies			
Amarillo International Airport	13	13	0
Dallas-Fort Worth International Airport	196	183	13
Hospital District			
Dallas County	157	91	66
Tarrant County	75	49	26
Independent School District			
Austin	107	75	32
Bastrop	14	6	8
Brazosport	22	21	1
Brownsville	160	52	108
Calhoun County	2	2	0
Columbia-Brazoria	5	5	0
Conroe	82	61	21
Corpus Christi	66	42	24
Corsicana	14	11	3
East Central	13	11	2
Edinburg	116	82	34
El Paso	56	44	12
Galveston	16	10	6
Hallsville	5	5	0
Houston	242	192	50
Idalou	1	1	0
Judson	30	29	1
Killeen	21	21	0
Pasadena	42	34	8
Raymondville	7	6	1
Rio Grande City	78	18	60
Santa Fe	26	14	12
Santa Rosa	5	3	2
Socorro	49	43	6
Taft	3	3	0
United	218	84	134
Port of Brownsville	20	12	8
Port of Houston Authority	52	39	13
UTAH			
State Agencies			
Parks and Recreation	57	56	1
Wildlife Resources	70	68	2
Tribal Agencies			
Uintah and Ouray Tribal	17	15	2
Other Agencies			
Cache-Rich Drug Task Force	7	6	1
Granite School District	33	26	7
Unified Fire Authority Investigations Bureau	7	6	1
Utah County Attorney, Investigations Division	7	5	2
Utah Transit Authority	90	81	9

Table 81. Full-Time Law Enforcement Employees, by Selected State and Agency, 2018—Continued

(Number.)

State/agency	Law enforcement employees	Officers	Civilians
VERMONT			
State Agencies			
Attorney General	4	4	0
Capitol Police	4	4	0
Department of Liquor Control, Division of			
Enforcement and Licensing	17	14	3
Department of Motor Vehicles	43	29	14
Fish and Wildlife Department, Law Enforcement			
Division	43	41	2
Secretary of State, Investigations Unit	7	5	2
VIRGINIA			
State Agencies			
Alcoholic Beverage Control Commission	146	96	50
Department of Conservation and Recreation	263	104	159
Department of Game and Inland Fisheries,			
Enforcement Division	195	176	19
Department of Motor Vehicles	90	74	16
Virginia Marine Resources Commission Law			
Enforcement Division	73	65	8
Virginia State Capitol	89	77	12
Other Agencies			
Norfolk Airport Authority	45	37	8
Port Authority, Norfolk	49	36	13
Reagan National Airport	265	217	48
Richmond International Airport	43	32	11
WASHINGTON			
State Agencies			
State Gambling Commission, Enforcement Unit	103	59	44
State Insurance Commissioner, Special			
Investigations Unit	10	6	4
Tribal Agencies			
Chehalis Tribal	37	18	19
Colville Tribal	38	27	11
Jamestown S'Klallam Tribal	42	37	5
Kalispel Tribal	19	17	2
La Push Tribal	3	3	0
Lower Elwha Klallam Tribal	13	11	2
Lummi Tribal	27	24	3
Makah Tribal	15	10	5
Muckleshoot Tribal	14	12	2
Nisqually Tribal	16	12	4
Nooksack Tribal	8	8	0
Port Gamble S'Klallam Tribal	12	12	0
Puyallup Tribal	48	28	20
Quinault Indian Nation	15	8	7
Sauk-Suiattle Tribal	8	7	1
Shoalwater Bay Tribal	5	5	0
Skokomish Tribal	8	7	1
Snoqualmie Tribal	4	4	0
Spokane Agency	19	11	8
Squaxin Island Tribal	14	11	3
Stillaguamish Tribal	8	8	0
Suquamish Tribal	16	14	2
Swinomish Tribal	19	15	4
Tulalip Tribal	57	42	15
Upper Skagit Tribal	7	7	0
Yakama Nation	85	38	47
Other Agencies			
Port of Seattle	152	110	42
WEST VIRGINIA			
State Agencies			
Capitol Protective Services	47	30	17
Department of Natural Resources			
Barbour County	1	1	0
Berkeley County	2	2	0
Boone County	1	1	0
Braxton County	2	2	0
Brooke County	2	2	0
Cabell County	2	2	0
Calhoun County	1	1	0
Clay County	1	1	0
Doddridge County	1	1	0
Fayette County	2	2	0
Gilmer County	1	1	0
Grant County	2	2	0
Greenbrier County	2	2	0
Hampshire County	7	6	1
Hancock County	1	1	0
Hardy County	2	2	0

Table 81. Full-Time Law Enforcement Employees, by Selected State and Agency, 2018—Continued

(Number.)

State/agency	Law enforcement employees	Officers	Civilians
Harrison County	2	2	0
Jackson County	3	3	0
Jefferson County	1	1	0
Kanawha County	14	9	5
Lewis County	2	2	0
Lincoln County	1	1	0
Logan County	2	2	0
Marion County	5	4	1
Marshall County	1	1	0
Mason County	2	2	0
McDowell County	1	1	0
Mercer County	3	3	0
Mineral County	1	1	0
Mingo County	3	3	0
Monongalia County	2	2	0
Monroe County	1	1	0
Morgan County	1	1	0
Nicholas County	3	3	0
Ohio County	1	1	0
Pendleton County	1	1	0
Pleasants County	1	1	0
Pocahontas County	1	1	0
Preston County	3	3	0
Putnam County	2	2	0
Raleigh County	8	7	1
Randolph County	2	2	0
Ritchie County	1	1	0
Roane County	1	1	0
Summers County	2	2	0
Taylor County	1	1	0
Tucker County	1	1	0
Tyler County	1	1	0
Upshur County	5	4	1
Wayne County	2	2	0
Webster County	1	1	0
Wetzel County	1	1	0
Wirt County	1	1	0
Wood County	6	5	1
Wyoming County	2	2	0
State Fire Marshall, Kanawha County	50	36	14
Other Agencies			
Central West Virginia Drug Task Force	2	1	1
Eastern Panhandle Drug and Violent Crime Task Force	12	11	1
Greenbrier County Drug and Violent Crime Task Force	4	3	1
Hancock/Brooke/Weirton Drug Task Force	7	7	0
Harrison County Drug and Violent Crime Task Force	7	7	0
Huntington Drug and Violent Crime Task Force	4	3	1
Kanawha County Parks and Recreation	3	3	0
Logan County Drug and Violent Crime Task Force	10	9	1
Metropolitan Drug Enforcement Network Team	3	3	0
Mon Valley Drug Task Force	9	8	1
Ohio Valley Drug and Violent Crime Task Force	4	4	0
Parkersburg Narcotics and Violent Crime Task Force	9	8	1
Potomac Highlands Drug and Violent Crime Task Force	2	2	0
Southern Regional Drug and Violent Crime Task Force	5	5	0
Three Rivers Drug and Violent Crime Task Force	2	2	0
WISCONSIN			
State Agencies			
Capitol Police	50	39	11
Department of Natural Resources	260	234	26
State Fair Park Police	7	6	1
Tribal Agencies			
Bad River Tribal	5	4	1
Lac Courte Oreilles Tribal	12	10	2
Lac du Flambeau Tribal	15	13	2
Menominee Tribal	26	19	7
Oneida Tribal	26	19	7
St. Croix Tribal	12	8	4
PUERTO RICO AND OTHER OUTLYING AREAS			
Puerto Rico	13,292	12,568	724

SECTION VI

HATE CRIMES

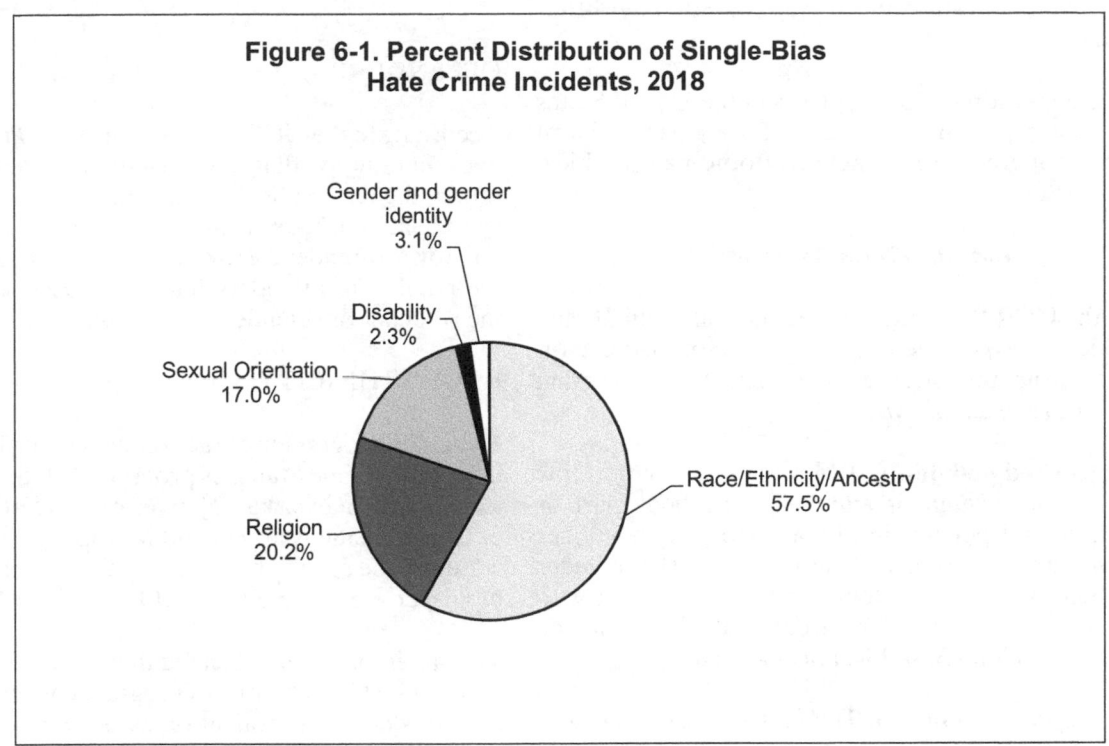

Figure 6-1. Percent Distribution of Single-Bias Hate Crime Incidents, 2018

Gender and gender identity
3.1%

Disability
2.3%

Sexual Orientation
17.0%

Religion
20.2%

Race/Ethnicity/Ancestry
57.5%

The Federal Bureau of Investigation (FBI) began the procedures for implementing, collecting, and managing hate crime data after Congress passed the Hate Crime Statistics Act in 1990. This act required the collection of data "about crimes that manifest evidence of prejudice based on race, religion, sexual orientation, or ethnicity." Beginning in 2013, law enforcement agencies could submit hate crime data in accordance with a number of program modifications. In 1994, the Hate Crime Statistics Act was amended to include bias against persons with disabilities. The Church Arson Prevention Act, which was signed into law in July 1996, removed the sunset clause from the original statute and mandated that the collection of hate crime data become a permanent part of the UCR program. In 2009, Congress further amended the Hate Crime Statistics Act by passing the Matthew Shepard and James Byrd, Jr., Hate Crime Prevention Act. The amendment includes the collection of data for crimes motivated by bias against a particular gender and gender identity, as well as for crimes committed by, and crimes directed against, juveniles. In response to the Shepard/Byrd Act, the FBI modified its data collection so that reporting

agencies could indicate whether hate crimes were committed by, or directed against, juveniles.

Definitions

Hate crimes include any crime motivated by bias against race, religion, sexual orientation, ethnicity/national origin, and/or disability. Because motivation is subjective, it is sometimes difficult to know with certainty whether a crime resulted from the offender's bias. Moreover, the presence of bias alone does not necessarily mean that a crime can be considered a hate crime. Only when law enforcement investigation reveals sufficient evidence to lead a reasonable and prudent person to conclude that the offender's actions were motivated, in whole or in part, by his or her bias should an incident be reported as a hate crime.

Data Collection

The UCR (Uniform Crime Reporting) program collects data about both single-bias and multiple-bias hate crimes. A single-bias incident is defined as an incident in which one or more offense types are motivated by the same bias. A multiple-bias incident is defined as an incident in which more than one offense type occurs and at least two offense types are motivated by different biases.

A table enumerating selected places in the United States that did not report hate crimes in 2018 is available at https://ucr.fbi.gov/hate-crime/2018/topic-pages/tables/table-14.xls/view.

Important Note: Rape Data

In 2014, the UCR Program initiated the collection of rape data under a revised definition and removed the term "forcible" from the offense name. The UCR Program now defines rape as follows:

- **Rape (revised definition):** Penetration, no matter how slight, of the vagina or anus with any body part or object, or oral penetration by a sex organ of another person, without the consent of the victim. (This includes the offenses of rape, sodomy, and sexual assault with an object as converted from data submitted via the National Incident-Based Reporting System.)

- **Rape (legacy definition):** The carnal knowledge of a female forcibly and against her will. For tables within this publication that present data for 2018 only or provide a 2-year trend, the rape figures are an aggregate total of the data submitted based on both the legacy and revised UCR definitions. For 5- and 10-year trend tables, the rape figures for the previous year (2014 or 2009) are based on the legacy definition and the 2018 rape figures are an aggregate total based on both the legacy and revised definitions. For this reason, a percent change is not provided.

CRIMES AGAINST PERSONS, PROPERTY, OR SOCIETY

The UCR program's data collection guidelines stipulate that a hate crime may involve multiple offenses, victims, and offenders within one incident; therefore, the Hate Crime Statistics program is incident-based. According to UCR counting guidelines:

- One offense is counted for each victim in *crimes against persons*

- One offense is counted for each offense type in *crimes against property*

- One offense is counted for each offense type in *crimes against society*

VICTIMS

In the UCR program, the victim of a hate crime may be an individual, a business, an institution, or society as a whole.

OFFENDERS

According to the UCR program, the term *known offender* does not imply that the suspect's identity is known; rather, the term indicates that some aspect of the suspect was identified, thus distinguishing the suspect from an unknown offender. Law enforcement agencies specify the number of offenders, and when possible, the race of the offender or offenders as a group.

RACE/ETHNICITY

The UCR program uses the following racial designations in its Hate Crime Statistics program: White; Black; American Indian or Alaskan Native; Asian; Native Hawaiian or Other Pacific Islander; and Multiple Races, Group. In addition, the UCR program uses the ethnic designations of Hispanic or Latino and Not Hispanic or Latino.

The law enforcement agencies that voluntarily participate in the Hate Crime Statistics program collect details about an offender's bias motivation associated with 11 offense types already being reported to the UCR program: murder and nonnegligent manslaughter, rape, aggravated assault, simple assault, and intimidation (crimes against persons); and robbery, burglary, larceny-theft, motor vehicle theft, arson, and destruction/damage/vandalism (crimes against property). The law enforcement agencies that participate in the UCR program via the National Incident-Based Reporting System (NIBRS) collect data about additional offenses for *crimes against persons* and *crimes against property*. These data appear in the category of other. These agencies also collect hate crime data for the category called *crimes against society*, which includes drug or narcotic offenses, gambling offenses, prostitution offenses, and weapon law violations.

NATIONAL VOLUME AND PERCENT DISTRIBUTION

In 2018, 2,026 law enforcement agencies (out of 16,039 participating agencies) reported 7,120 hate crime incidents involving 8,496 offenses. Of these, 7,036 were single-bias offenses. An analysis of the single-bias incidents revealed that 57.5 percent were racially/ethnically/ancestrally motivated, 20.2 percent were motivated by religious bias, 17.0 percent resulted from sexual orientation bias, 3.1 percent were motivated by gender and gender-identity bias, and 2.3 percent were prompted by a disability bias. (Table 82)

The majority of the 4,954 hate crime offenses that were racially motivated resulted from an anti-Black or African American bias (46.9 percent) followed by an anti-White basis (20.2 percent). Bias against people of more than one race accounted for 3.4 percent of offenses, while anti-Asian bias accounted for 3.5 percent of racially motivated offenses, anti-Arab bias accounted for 2.0 percent of these offenses, anti–Native Hawaiian and Other Pacific Islander accounted for 0.5 percent of these offenses, and anti–American Indian or Alaska Native bias accounted for 4.1 percent of these offenses. Approximately 13.0 percent of crimes were classified as an anti-Hispanic or Latino bias. (Table 82)

Hate crimes motivated by religious bias accounted for 1,550 offenses reported by law enforcement. A breakdown of these offenses revealed 57.4 percent were motivated by anti-Jewish bias, 14.5 percent by anti-Islamic (Muslim) bias, 3.2 percent were anti–multiple religions or groups, 3.8 percent had an anti-Catholic bias, 2.5 percent were anti-Protestant, 2.1 percent were anti–Eastern Orthodox (Russian, Greek, or other), 2.78 percent were anti–other Christian, 0.4 percent were anti-atheism/agnosticism/etc., 0.6 percent were anti-Mormon, 0.9 percent were anti-Hindu, 0.6 percent were anti–Jehovah's Witness, 0.6 percent were anti-Buddhist, 4.1 percent were anti-Sikh, and the remainder, 6.2 percent, of offenses were based on a bias against other religions—those not specified. (Table 82)

In 2018, 1,404 offenses were committed on the basis of sexual orientation bias. Of the offenses based on sexual orientation, 25.1 percent were classified as having an anti–lesbian, gay, bisexual, or transgender (mixed group) bias; 59.8 percent were classified as having an anti-gay bias; 12.2 percent had an anti-lesbian bias; 1.5 percent had an anti-bisexual bias; and 1.4 percent had an anti-heterosexual bias. (Table 82)

Hate crime offenses committed based on disability totaled 177 offenses. The majority (62.1 percent) were classified as anti-mental disability, with the rest (37.9 percent) classified as anti–physical disability. (Table 82)

Of the 184 gender identity bias offenses reported, 157 were anti-transgender and 27 were anti–gender nonconforming. Of the 58 gender bias offenses reported, 32 were anti-female and 26 were anti-male. (Table 82)

CRIMES AGAINST PERSONS

Law enforcement agencies reported 5,566 hate crime offenses against persons in 2018. Approximately 46.0 percent involved intimidation, 34.0 percent involved simple assault, and 18.4 percent involved aggravated assault. There were 24 murders and 22 rapes. (Table 83)

CRIMES AGAINST PROPERTY

In 2018, hate crime offences against property totaled 2,641. Approximately 71.0 percent of offenses involved destruction/damage or vandalism. The remaining 29.0 percent of crimes against property consisted of robbery, burglary, larceny-theft, motor vehicle theft, arson, and other crimes. (Table 83)

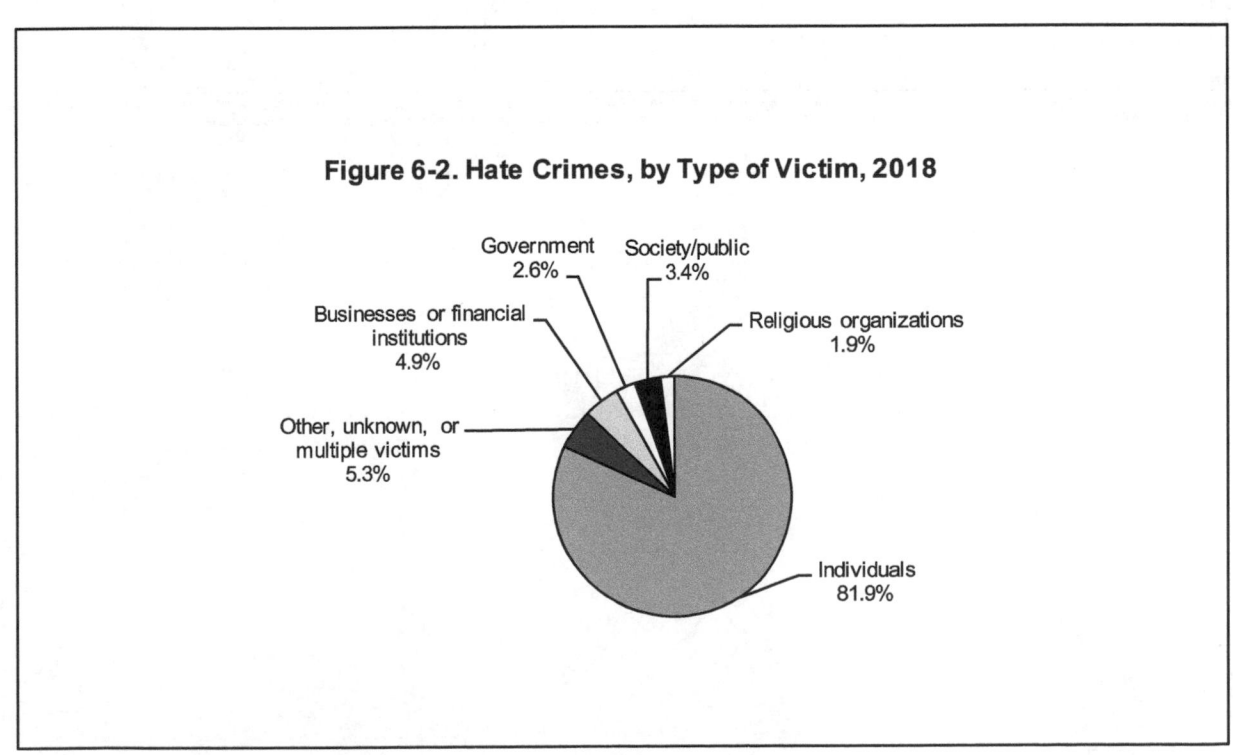

Figure 6-2. Hate Crimes, by Type of Victim, 2018

Government 2.6%
Society/public 3.4%
Businesses or financial institutions 4.9%
Religious organizations 1.9%
Other, unknown, or multiple victims 5.3%
Individuals 81.9%

Table 82. Incidents, Offenses, Victims, and Known Offenders, by Bias Motivation, 2018

(Number.)

Bias motivation	Incidents	Offenses	Victims[1]	Known offenders[2]
Total	7,120	8,496	8,819	6,266
Single-Bias Incidents	7,036	8,327	8,646	6,188
Race/Ethnicity/Ancestry	4,047	4,954	5,155	3,634
Anti-White	762	1,001	1,038	754
Anti-Black or African American	1,943	2,325	2,426	1,707
Anti-American Indian or Alaska Native	194	204	209	163
Anti-Asian	148	171	177	125
Anti-Native Hawaiian or Other Pacific Islander	20	26	26	15
Anti-Multiple Races, Group	137	166	174	91
Anti-Arab	82	100	100	80
Anti-Hispanic or Latino	485	644	671	495
Anti-Other Race/Ethnicity/Ancestry	276	317	334	204
Religion	1,419	1,550	1,617	917
Anti-Jewish	835	896	920	484
Anti-Catholic	53	59	63	36
Anti-Protestant	34	38	39	22
Anti-Islamic (Muslim)	188	225	236	153
Anti-Other Religion	91	96	109	60
Anti-Multiple Religions, Group	46	50	52	18
Anti-Mormon	9	9	11	8
Anti-Jehovah's Witness	9	9	9	4
Anti-Eastern Orthodox (Russian, Greek, Other)	31	32	33	26
Anti-Other Christian	35	42	43	25
Anti-Buddhist	10	10	11	9
Anti-Hindu	12	14	14	10
Anti-Sikh	60	64	69	49
Anti-Atheism/Agnosticism/etc.	6	6	8	13
Sexual Orientation	1,196	1,404	1,445	1,268
Anti-Gay (Male)	726	839	863	841
Anti-Lesbian	129	171	177	105
Anti-Lesbian, Gay, Bisexual, or Transgender (Mixed Group)	303	353	360	294
Anti-Heterosexual	17	20	24	13
Anti-Bisexual	21	21	21	15
Disability	159	177	179	151
Anti-Physical	60	67	68	52
Anti-Mental	99	110	111	99
Gender	47	58	61	38
Anti-Male	22	26	28	21
Anti-Female	25	32	33	17
Gender Identity	168	184	189	180
Anti-Transgender	142	157	160	156
Anti-Gender Non-Conforming	26	27	29	24
Multiple-Bias Incidents[3]	84	169	173	78

1 The term victim may refer to an individual, business/financial institution, government entity, religious organization, or society/public as a whole.   2 The term known offender does not imply the suspect's identity is known; rather, the term indicates some aspect of the suspect was identified, thus distinguishing the suspect from an unknown offender.   3 A multiple-bias incident is an incident in which one or more offense types are motivated by two or more biases.

Table 83. Incidents, Offenses, Victims, and Known Offenders, by Offense Type, 2018

(Number.)

Offense type	Incidents[1]	Offenses	Victims[2]	Known offenders[3]
Total	7,120	8,496	8,819	6,266
Crimes Against Persons	4,571	5,566	5,566	4,738
Murder and nonnegligent manslaughter	13	24	24	12
Rape [4]	22	22	22	21
Aggravated assault	818	1,026	1,026	997
Simple assault	1,653	1,895	1,895	1,991
Intimidation	2,039	2,560	2,560	1,688
Other[5]	26	39	39	29
Crimes Against Property	2,641	2,641	2,964	1,627
Robbery	132	132	169	203
Burglary	131	131	166	76
Larceny-theft	330	330	357	198
Motor vehicle theft	42	42	43	18
Arson	43	43	53	22
Destruction/damage/vandalism	1,876	1,876	2,080	1,052
Other[5]	87	87	96	58
Crimes Against Society[5]	289	289	289	323

1 The actual number of incidents is 7,120. However, the column figures will not add to the total because incidents may include more than one offense type, and these are counted in each appropriate offense type category.   2 The term victim may refer to an individual, business/financial institution, government entity, religious organization, or society/public as a whole.   3 The term known offender does not imply the suspect's identity is known; rather, the term indicates some aspect of the suspect was identified, thus distinguishing the suspect from an unknown offender. The actual number of known offenders is 6,266. However, the column figures will not add to the total because some offenders are responsible for more than one offense type, and are, therefore, counted more than once in this table.   4 Only the revised Uniform Crime Reporting definition of rape was used for the figures reported in this row.   5 The figures shown include additional offenses collected in the National Incident-Based Reporting System.

Table 84. Offenses, Known Offender's Race and Ethnicity, by Offense Type, 2018

(Number.)

Bias motivation	Total offenses	Known offender's race							Known offender's ethnicity[1]				Unknown offender
		White	Black or African American	American Indian or Alaska Native	Asian	Native Hawaiian or Other Pacific Islander	Group of multiple races	Unknown race	Hispanic or Latino	Not Hispanic or Latino	Group of multiple ethnicities	Unknown ethnicity	
Total	8,496	3,511	1,605	64	95	19	285	718	412	1,847	51	3,065	2,199
Crimes Against Persons	5,566	2,772	1,311	49	78	13	231	285	331	1,485	41	2,351	827
Murder and nonnegligent manslaughter	24	18	4	0	0	0	1	0	1	19	0	3	1
Rape [2]	22	11	8	1	0	0	0	0	2	6	0	12	2
Aggravated assault	1,026	532	289	9	15	4	51	60	107	326	10	396	66
Simple assault	1,895	966	534	19	32	7	95	115	133	488	13	858	127
Intimidation	2,560	1,216	468	20	31	2	83	110	87	624	18	1,067	630
Other[3]	39	29	8	0	0	0	1	0	1	22	0	15	1
Crimes Against Property	2,641	554	223	13	12	6	47	431	70	243	10	572	1,355
Robbery	132	35	54	2	1	0	15	13	11	22	1	56	12
Burglary	131	37	17	0	0	0	1	4	4	23	1	29	72
Larceny-theft	330	99	41	3	2	0	5	11	9	45	1	91	169
Motor vehicle theft	42	6	5	0	0	0	0	3	0	4	0	10	28
Arson	43	8	7	0	0	0	0	4	2	2	0	8	24
Destruction/damage/ vandalism	1,876	325	94	8	9	6	24	396	42	137	7	339	1,014
Other[3]	87	44	5	0	0	0	2	0	2	10	0	39	36
Crimes Against Society[3]	289	185	71	2	5	0	7	2	11	119	0	142	17

1 The sum of offenses by the known offender's ethnicity does not equal the sum of offenses by the known offender's race because not all law enforcement agencies that report offender race data also report offender ethnicity data.   2 Only the revised Uniform Crime Reporting definition of rape was used for the figures reported in this row.   3 Includes additional offenses collected in the National Incident-Based Reporting System.

Table 85. Offenses, Offense Type, by Bias Motivation, 2018

(Number.)

Bias motivation	Total offenses	Crimes against persons					
		Murder and nonnegligent manslaughter	Rape[1]	Aggravated assault	Simple assault	Intimidation	Other[2]
Total	8,496	24	22	1,026	1,895	2,560	39
Single-Bias Incidents	8,327	24	22	1,017	1,882	2,468	39
Race/Ethnicity/Ancestry	4,954	8	9	659	1,121	1,627	21
Anti-White	1,001	3	6	114	250	289	9
Anti-Black or African American	2,325	4	2	323	486	908	2
Anti-American Indian or Alaska Native	204	0	0	6	30	11	5
Anti-Asian	171	0	0	18	46	60	0
Anti-Native Hawaiian or Other Pacific Islander	26	0	0	5	6	7	0
Anti-Multiple Races, Group	166	0	0	7	16	60	0
Anti-Arab	100	0	0	18	17	37	0
Anti-Hispanic or Latino	644	1	0	129	197	190	4
Anti-Other Race/Ethnicity/Ancestry	317	0	1	39	73	65	1
Religion	1,550	12	0	63	161	406	11
Anti-Jewish	896	11	0	24	65	243	8
Anti-Catholic	59	0	0	3	3	11	0
Anti-Protestant	38	0	0	4	4	3	0
Anti-Islamic (Muslim)	225	0	0	14	53	102	0
Anti-Other Religion	96	1	0	3	9	21	1
Anti-Multiple Religions, Group	50	0	0	1	3	11	0
Anti-Mormon	9	0	0	0	1	0	0
Anti-Jehovah's Witness	9	0	0	1		2	0
Anti-Eastern Orthodox (Russian, Greek, Other)	32	0	0	4	1	0	2
Anti-Other Christian	42	0	0	3	4	6	0
Anti-Buddhist	10	0	0	1	2	1	0
Anti-Hindu	14	0	0	0	5	2	0
Anti-Sikh	64	0	0	5	10	4	0
Anti-Atheism/Agnosticism/etc.	6	0	0	0	1	0	0
Sexual Orientation	1,404	3	5	245	468	356	3
Anti-Gay (Male)	839	2	2	160	297	198	2
Anti-Lesbian	171	1	1	28	44	63	0
Anti-Lesbian, Gay, Bisexual, or Transgender (Mixed Group)	353	0	0	53	119	84	1
Anti-Heterosexual	20	0	1	2	5	5	0
Anti-Bisexual	21	0	1	2	3	6	0
Disability	177	0	4	16	55	19	2
Anti-Physical	67	0	1	4	22	7	1
Anti-Mental	110	0	3	12	33	12	1
Gender	58	1	2	5	13	20	2
Anti-Male	26	0	2	5	5	6	1
Anti-Female	32	1	0	0	8	14	1
Gender Identity	184	0	2	29	64	40	0
Anti-Transgender	157	0	1	26	56	37	0
Anti-Gender Non-Conforming	27	0	1	3	8	3	0
Multiple-Bias Incidents[3]	169	0	0	9	13	92	0

Table 85. Offenses, Offense Type, by Bias Motivation, 2018—Continued

(Number.)

Bias motivation	Crimes against property							Crimes against society[2]
	Robbery	Burglary	Larceny-theft	Motor vehicle theft	Arson	Destruction/ damage/ vandalism	Other[2]	
Total	132	131	330	42	43	1,876	87	289
Single-Bias Incidents	131	129	325	42	43	1,830	86	289
Race/Ethnicity/Ancestry	68	76	195	26	16	854	50	224
Anti-White	15	24	79	8	1	91	20	92
Anti-Black or African American	14	24	22	3	10	474	3	50
Anti-American Indian or Alaska Native	2	8	49	9	1	14	12	57
Anti-Asian	4	2	5	0	0	30	2	4
Anti-Native Hawaiian or Other Pacific Islander	0	0	3	0	0	3	1	1
Anti-Multiple Races, Group	1	3	5	1	1	68	0	4
Anti-Arab	2	2	4	0	1	8	2	9
Anti-Hispanic or Latino	23	8	8	4	1	73	3	3
Anti-Other Race/Ethnicity/Ancestry	7	5	20	1	1	93	7	4
Religion	12	25	50	8	24	723	16	39
Anti-Jewish	5	2	3	1	10	522	0	2
Anti-Catholic	0	2	3	1	5	24	3	4
Anti-Protestant	0	0	7	1	2	15	0	2
Anti-Islamic (Muslim)	4	2	3	0	2	44	0	1
Anti-Other Religion	1	3	7	1	2	43	1	3
Anti-Multiple Religions, Group	0	2	2	0	2	24	0	5
Anti-Mormon	0	0	1	1	0	5	0	1
Anti-Jehovah's Witness	0	0	1	0	1	4	0	0
Anti-Eastern Orthodox (Russian, Greek, Other)	0	1	5	1	0	5	4	9
Anti-Other Christian	1	4	1	0	0	21	0	2
Anti-Buddhist	1	2	1	0	0	1	0	1
Anti-Hindu	0	0	1	0	0	5	1	0
Anti-Sikh	0	7	14	2	0	7	6	9
Anti-Atheism/Agnosticism/etc.	0	0	1	0	0	3	1	0
Sexual Orientation	32	18	44	5	3	214	3	5
Anti-Gay (Male)	23	10	15	3	1	125	0	1
Anti-Lesbian	2	3	2	0	1	23	1	2
Anti-Lesbian, Gay, Bisexual, or Transgender (Mixed Group)	7	4	21	1	1	60	1	1
Anti-Heterosexual	0	0	3	1	0	2	1	0
Anti-Bisexual	0	1	3	0	0	4	0	1
Disability	3	7	29	2	0	12	13	15
Anti-Physical	2	1	13	0	0	6	4	6
Anti-Mental	1	6	16	2	0	6	9	9
Gender	2	0	3	0	0	5	3	2
Anti-Male	2	0	1	0	0	1	2	1
Anti-Female	0	0	2	0	0	4	1	1
Gender Identity	14	3	4	1	0	22	1	4
Anti-Transgender	14	2	2	1	0	15	1	2
Anti-Gender Non-Conforming	0	1	2	0	0	7	0	2
Multiple-Bias Incidents[3]	1	2	5	0	0	46	1	0

1 Only the revised Uniform Crime Reporting definition of rape was used for the figures reported in this column.   2 Includes additional offenses collected in the National Incident-Based Reporting System.   3 A multiple-bias incident is an incident in which one or more offense types are motivated by two or more biases.

Table 86. Offenses, Known Offender's Race, by Bias Motivation, 2018

(Number.)

Bias motivation	Total offenses	Known offender's race							Known offender's ethnicity[1]				Unknown offender
		White	Black or African American	American Indian or Alaska Native	Asian	Native Hawaiian or Other Pacific Islander	Group of multiple races	Unknown race	Hispanic or Latino	Not Hispanic or Latino	Group of multiple ethnicities	Unknown ethnicity	
Total	8,496	3,511	1,605	64	95	19	285	718	412	1,847	51	3,065	2,199
Single-Bias Incidents	8,327	3,462	1,536	64	93	19	282	714	402	1,765	49	3,032	2,157
Race/Ethnicity/Ancestry	4,954	2,309	907	46	62	9	185	276	218	1,180	27	1,939	1,160
Anti-White	1,001	252	492	20	6	1	23	36	40	287	12	431	171
Anti-Black or African American	2,325	1,330	115	16	34	3	100	149	106	491	7	918	578
Anti-American Indian or Alaska Native	204	106	27	1	2	0	7	2	8	39	0	97	59
Anti-Asian	171	70	33	0	14	2	4	6	8	42	0	59	42
Anti-Native Hawaiian or Other Pacific Islander	26	8	11	0	0	2	0	0	0	13	0	7	5
Anti-Multiple Races, Group	166	45	8	0	2	0	15	11	2	22	3	42	85
Anti-Arab	100	62	17	0	1	0	1	4	3	29	0	40	15
Anti-Hispanic or Latino	644	322	152	8	2	1	24	47	41	212	1	240	88
Anti-Other Race/Ethnicity/Ancestry	317	114	52	1	1	0	11	21	10	45	4	105	117
Religion	1,550	439	122	6	16	6	30	306	28	193	10	360	625
Anti-Jewish	896	179	41	1	7	0	14	258	7	82	3	143	396
Anti-Catholic	59	26	3	1	1	0	0	5	3	10	0	16	23
Anti-Protestant	38	13	3	0	0	0	2	1	2	3	0	14	19
Anti-Islamic (Muslim)	225	98	32	0	5	0	6	22	7	31	4	88	62
Anti-Other Religion	96	31	12	0	1	5	2	8	2	11	0	33	37
Anti-Multiple Religions, Group	50	12	6	0	0	0	0	3	0	2	0	15	29
Anti-Mormon	9	4	0	0	0	1	0	0	0	1	0	2	4
Anti-Jehovah's Witness	9	3	0	1	0	0	0	0	1	2	0	1	5
Anti-Eastern Orthodox (Russian, Greek, Other)	32	19	4	1	0	0	0	1	1	12	0	12	7
Anti-Other Christian	42	11	5	0	1	0	5	5	2	8	0	8	15
Anti-Buddhist	10	4	3	0	1	0	0	0	0	7	0	1	2
Anti-Hindu	14	8	1	0	0	0	0	3	1	2	0	8	2
Anti-Sikh	64	30	10	2	0	0	1	0	2	21	3	17	21
Anti-Atheism/Agnosticism/etc.	6	1	2	0	0	0	0	0	0	1	0	2	3
Sexual Orientation	1,404	535	380	11	12	4	56	110	130	299	11	531	296
Anti-Gay (Male)	839	307	245	6	6	3	39	83	94	205	9	284	150
Anti-Lesbian	171	80	36	0	2	0	5	7	18	35	1	60	41
Anti-Lesbian, Gay, Bisexual, or Transgender (Mixed Group)	353	128	92	5	4	1	12	19	18	53	1	167	92
Anti-Heterosexual	20	14	1	0	0	0	0	0	0	2	0	12	5
Anti-Bisexual	21	6	6	0	0	0	0	1	0	4	0	8	8
Disability	177	92	37	1	3	0	3	4	8	37	1	92	37
Anti-Physical	67	30	15	0	2	0	1	1	4	9	1	33	18
Anti-Mental	110	62	22	1	1	0	2	3	4	28	0	59	19
Gender	58	30	14	0	0	0	1	0	1	9	0	32	13
Anti-Male	26	13	8	0	0	0	1	0	1	8	0	13	4
Anti-Female	32	17	6	0	0	0	0	0	0	1	0	19	9
Gender Identity	184	57	76	0	0	0	7	18	17	47	0	78	26
Anti-Transgender	157	50	65	0	0	0	7	16	17	36	0	72	19
Anti-Gender Non-Conforming	27	7	11	0	0	0	0	2	0	11	0	6	7
Multiple-Bias Incidents[2]	169	49	69	0	2	0	3	4	10	82	2	33	42

1 The aggregate of offenses by the known offender's ethnicity does not equal the aggregate of offenses by the known offender's race because not all law enforcement agencies that report offender race data also report offender ethnicity data. 2 A multiple-bias incident is an incident in which one or more offense types are motivated by two or more biases.

Table 87. Offenses, Victim Type, by Offense Type, 2018

(Number.)

Offense type	Total offenses	Victim type					
		Individual	Business/ financial institution	Government	Religious organization	Society/ public[1]	Other/ unknown/ multiple
Total	8,496	6,961	414	221	161	289	450
Crimes against persons[2]	5,566	5,566	NA	NA	NA	NA	NA
Crimes against property	2,641	1,395	414	221	161	0	450
Robbery	132	105	2	0	0	0	25
Burglary	131	101	10	4	12	0	4
Larceny-theft	330	227	79	1	9	0	14
Motor vehicle theft	42	38	3	0	0	0	1
Arson	43	19	3	0	12	0	9
Destruction/damage/vandalism	1,876	835	305	212	128	0	396
Other[2]	87	70	12	4	0	0	1
Crimes against society[2]	289	NA	NA	NA	NA	289	NA

NA = Not available.
1 The victim type society/public is collected only in the National Incident-Based Reporting System (NIBRS).   2 Includes additional offenses collected in the NIBRS.

Table 88. Victims, Offense Type, by Bias Motivation, 2018

(Number.)

Bias motivation	Total victims[1]	Total number of adult victims[2]	Total number of juvenile victims[2]	Crimes against persons					
				Murder and nonnegligent manslaughter	Rape[3]	Aggravated assault	Simple assault	Intimidation	Other[4]
Total	8,819	5,986	712	24	22	1,026	1,895	2,560	39
Single-Bias Incidents	8,646	5,864	704	24	22	1,017	1,882	2,468	39
Race/Ethnicity/Ancestry	5,155	3,656	457	8	9	659	1,121	1,627	21
Anti-White	1,038	759	75	3	6	114	250	289	9
Anti-Black or African American	2,426	1,707	258	4	2	323	486	908	2
Anti-American Indian or Alaska Native	209	115	15	0	0	6	30	11	5
Anti-Asian	177	136	8	0	0	18	46	60	0
Anti-Native Hawaiian or Other Pacific Islander	26	19	6	0	0	5	6	7	0
Anti-Multiple Races, Group	174	94	7	0	0	7	16	60	0
Anti-Arab	100	69	10	0	0	18	17	37	0
Anti-Hispanic or Latino	671	536	60	1	0	129	197	190	4
Anti-Other Race/Ethnicity/Ancestry	334	221	18	0	1	39	73	65	1
Religion	1,617	779	86	12	0	63	161	406	11
Anti-Jewish	920	398	38	11	0	24	65	243	8
Anti-Catholic	63	29	1	0	0	3	3	11	0
Anti-Protestant	39	20	1	0	0	4	4	3	0
Anti-Islamic (Muslim)	236	145	33	0	0	14	53	102	0
Anti-Other Religion	109	55	2	1	0	3	9	21	1
Anti-Multiple Religions, Group	52	16	2	0	0	1	3	11	0
Anti-Mormon	11	6	0	0	0	0	1	0	0
Anti-Jehovah's Witness	9	3	0	0	0	1	0	2	0
Anti-Eastern Orthodox (Russian, Greek, Other)	33	23	2	0	0	4	1	0	2
Anti-Other Christian	43	11	2	0	0	3	4	6	0
Anti-Buddhist	11	8	0	0	0	1	2	1	0
Anti-Hindu	14	10	0	0	0	0	5	2	0
Anti-Sikh	69	48	4	0	0	5	10	4	0
Anti-Atheism/Agnosticism/etc.	8	7	1	0	0	0	1	0	0
Sexual Orientation	1,445	1,116	113	3	5	245	468	356	3
Anti-Gay (Male)	863	677	67	2	2	160	297	198	2
Anti-Lesbian	177	126	20	1	1	28	44	63	0
Anti-Lesbian, Gay, Bisexual, or Transgender (Mixed Group)	360	281	23	0	0	53	119	84	1
Anti-Heterosexual	24	16	3	0	1	2	5	5	0
Anti-Bisexual	21	16	0	0	1	2	3	6	0
Disability	179	119	26	0	4	16	55	19	2
Anti-Physical	68	51	5	0	1	4	22	7	1
Anti-Mental	111	68	21	0	3	12	33	12	1
Gender	61	51	6	1	2	5	13	20	2
Anti-Male	28	24	2	0	2	5	5	6	1
Anti-Female	33	27	4	1	0	0	8	14	1
Gender Identity	189	143	16	0	2	29	64	40	0
Anti-Transgender	160	127	13	0	1	26	56	37	0
Anti-Gender Non-Conforming	29	16	3	0	1	3	8	3	0
Multiple-Bias Incidents[5]	173	122	8	0	0	9	13	92	0

Table 88. Victims, Offense Type, by Bias Motivation, 2018—Continued
(Number.)

Bias motivation	Crimes against property							Crimes against society[4]
	Robbery	Burglary	Larceny-theft	Motor vehicle theft	Arson	Destruction/ damage/ vandalism	Other[4]	
Total	169	166	357	43	53	2,080	96	289
Single-Bias Incidents	165	164	352	43	53	2,033	95	289
Race/Ethnicity/Ancestry	95	97	213	27	24	976	54	224
Anti-White	23	31	86	8	1	104	22	92
Anti-Black or African American	18	32	26	3	16	553	3	50
Anti-American Indian or Alaska Native	3	8	52	9	1	15	12	57
Anti-Asian	7	4	5	0	0	31	2	4
Anti-Native Hawaiian or Other Pacific Islander	0	0	3	0	0	3	1	1
Anti-Multiple Races, Group	1	4	5	1	2	74	0	4
Anti-Arab	2	2	4	0	1	8	2	9
Anti-Hispanic or Latino	32	10	11	5	1	83	5	3
Anti-Other Race/Ethnicity/Ancestry	9	6	21	1	2	105	7	4
Religion	15	33	54	8	26	771	18	39
Anti-Jewish	5	3	3	1	11	544		2
Anti-Catholic	0	2	4	1	6	25	4	4
Anti-Protestant	0	0	8	1	2	15	0	2
Anti-Islamic (Muslim)	6	6	3	0	2	49	0	1
Anti-Other Religion	1	3	7	1	2	56	1	3
Anti-Multiple Religions, Group	0	2	2	0	2	26	0	5
Anti-Mormon	0	0	2	1	0	6	0	1
Anti-Jehovah's Witness	0	0	1	0	1	4	0	0
Anti-Eastern Orthodox (Russian, Greek, Other)	0	1	5	1	0	6	4	9
Anti-Other Christian	1	4	1	0	0	22	0	2
Anti-Buddhist	2	2	1	0	0	1	0	1
Anti-Hindu	0	0	1	0	0	5	1	0
Anti-Sikh	0	10	15	2	0	7	7	9
Anti-Atheism/Agnosticism/etc.	0	0	1	0	0	5	1	0
Sexual Orientation	33	23	49	5	3	244	3	5
Anti-Gay (Male)	24	12	19	3	1	142	0	1
Anti-Lesbian	2	5	2	0	1	27	1	2
Anti-Lesbian, Gay, Bisexual, or Transgender (Mixed Group)	7	5	22	1	1	65	1	1
Anti-Heterosexual	0	0	3	1	0	6	1	0
Anti-Bisexual	0	1	3	0	0	4	0	1
Disability	3	8	29	2	0	13	13	15
Anti-Physical	2	1	13	0	0	7	4	6
Anti-Mental	1	7	16	2	0	6	9	9
Gender	2	0	3	0	0	5	6	2
Anti-Male	2	0	1	0	0	1	4	1
Anti-Female	0	0	2	0	0	4	2	1
Gender Identity	17	3	4	1	0	24	1	4
Anti-Transgender	17	2	2	1	0	15	1	2
Anti-Gender Non-Conforming	0	1	2	0	0	9	0	2
Multiple-Bias Incidents[5]	4	2	5	0	0	47	1	0

NOTE: The aggregate of adult and juvenile individual victims does not equal the total number of victims because total victims include individuals, businesses/financial institutions, government entities, religious organizations, and society/public as a whole. In addition, the aggregate of adult and juvenile individual victims does not equal the aggregate of victims of crimes against persons because not all law enforcement agencies report the ages of individual victims.
1 A victim can be an individual, a business, an institution, or society as a whole.   2 The figures shown in this column are individual victims only.   3 Only the revised Uniform Crime Reporting definition of rape is used for the figures reported in this column.   4 Includes additional offenses collected in the National Incident-Based Reporting System.   5 A multiple-bias incident is an incident in which one or more offense types are motivated by two or more biases.

Table 89. Incidents, Victim Type, by Bias Motivation, 2018

(Number.)

Bias motivation	Total incidents	Victim type					
		Individual	Business/ financial institution	Government	Religious organization	Society/ public[1]	Other/ unknown/ multiple
Total	7,120	5,581	381	214	153	257	534
Single-Bias Incidents	7,036	5,532	371	204	151	257	521
Race/Ethnicity/Ancestry	4,047	3,334	189	97	14	195	218
Religion	1,419	784	128	91	127	37	252
Sexual Orientation	1,196	1,091	36	14	10	5	40
Disability	159	131	11	1	0	15	1
Gender	47	43	0	1	0	1	2
Gender Identity	168	149	7	0	0	4	8
Multiple-Bias Incidents[2]	84	49	10	10	2	0	13

1 The victim type society/public is collected only in the National Incident-Based Reporting System.   2 A multiple-bias incident is an incident in which one or more offense types are motivated by two or more biases.

Table 90. Known Offenders,[1] by Known Offender's Race, Ethnicity, and Age, 2018

(Number.)

Race/ethnicity/age	Total
Race	6,266
White	3,359
Black or African American	1,506
American Indian or Alaska Native	60
Asian	80
Native Hawaiian or Other Pacific Islander	19
Group of multiple races[2]	432
Unknown race	810
Ethnicity[3]	5,349
Hispanic or Latino	477
Not Hispanic or Latino	1,601
Group of multiple ethnicities[4]	88
Unknown ethnicity	3,183
Age[3]	5,589
Total known offenders 18 and over	4,734
Total known offenders under 18	855

1 The term known offender does not imply the suspect's identity is known; rather, the term indicates some aspect of the suspect was identified, thus distinguishing the suspect from an unknown offender.   2 The term group of multiple races is used to describe a group of offenders of varying races.   3 The total number of known offenders by age and the total number of known offenders by ethnicity do not equal the total number of known offenders by race because not all law enforcement agencies report the age and/or ethnicity of the known offenders.   4 The term group of multiple ethnicities is used to describe a group of offenders of varying ethnicities.

Table 91. Incidents, Bias Motivation, by Location, 2018

(Number.)

Location	Total incidents	Bias motivation						Multiple-bias incidents[1]
		Race/ethnicity/ ancestry	Religion	Sexual orientation	Disability	Gender	Gender identity	
Total	7,120	4,047	1,419	1,196	159	47	168	84
Abandoned/condemned structure	4	3	1	0	0	0	0	0
Air/bus/train terminal	113	67	2	34	1	1	6	2
Amusement park	3	2	0	0	0	0	1	0
Arena/stadium/fairgrounds/coliseum	7	2	1	3	0	0	1	0
ATM separate from bank	2	1	0	0	0	0	1	0
Auto dealership new/used	8	5	1	2	0	0	0	0
Bank/savings and loan	28	14	8	2	3	0	1	0
Bar/nightclub	119	53	3	59	1	0	2	1
Camp/campground	4	4	0	0	0	0	0	0
Church/synagogue/temple/mosque	263	29	219	12	0	0	0	3
Commercial office building	145	97	22	16	1	3	4	2
Community center	20	8	5	4	1	0	1	1
Construction site	20	13	4	2	0	0	0	1
Convenience store	141	100	13	19	4	0	5	0
Cyberspace	23	15	4	2	1	0	0	1
Daycare facility	2	2	0	0	0	0	0	0
Department/discount store	111	63	20	11	4	2	6	5
Dock/wharf/freight/modal terminal	1	1	0	0	0	0	0	0
Drug store/doctor's office/hospital	93	63	12	7	7	0	2	2
Farm facility	5	3	1	1	0	0	0	0
Field/woods	47	31	5	7	2	0	1	1
Gambling facility/casino/race track	3	3	0	0	0	0	0	0
Government/public building	163	116	22	12	4	2	2	5
Grocery/supermarket	98	75	5	10	3	0	5	0
Highway/road/alley/street/sidewalk	1,328	846	143	259	23	4	42	11
Hotel/motel/etc.	67	41	6	17	2	0	1	0
Industrial site	7	5	0	0	1	1	0	0
Jail/prison/penitentiary/corrections facility	69	45	3	19	1	0	1	0
Lake/waterway/beach	8	4	1	2	0	0	0	1
Liquor store	13	6	0	4	0	1	2	0
Military installation	0	0	0	0	0	0	0	0
Park/playground	106	68	15	20	0	0	3	0
Parking/drop lot/garage	380	245	57	59	8	3	7	1
Rental storage facility	12	8	3	0	1	0	0	0
Residence/home	1,832	1,044	303	352	66	18	33	16
Rest area	8	2	6	0	0	0	0	0
Restaurant	189	136	15	30	0	1	6	1
School/college[2]	69	35	17	11	1	0	4	1
School—college/university	314	155	88	53	5	5	3	5
School—elementary/secondary	273	153	59	33	6	0	5	17
Service/gas station	91	63	12	10	2	0	4	0
Shelter—mission/homeless	18	9	4	2	0	0	3	0
Shopping mall	21	14	1	5	0	0	0	1
Specialty store (TV, fur, etc.)	79	56	10	7	1	1	2	2
Tribal lands	1	1	0	0	0	0	0	0
Other/unknown	800	334	327	108	9	5	13	4
Multiple locations	12	7	1	2	1	0	1	0

1 A multiple-bias incident is an incident in which one or more offense types are motivated by two or more biases. 2 The location designation school/college has been retained for agencies that have not updated their records management systems to include the new location designations of School—college/university and school—elementary/secondary, which allow for more specificity in reporting.

Table 92. Offenses, Offense Type, by Participating State/Federal,[1] 2018

(Number.)

State	Total offenses	Crimes against persons						Crimes against property							Crimes against society[3]
		Murder and nonnegligent manslaughter	Rape[2]	Aggravated assault	Simple assault	Intimidation	Other[3]	Robbery	Burglary	Larceny-theft	Motor vehicle theft	Arson	Destruction/damage/vandalism	Other[3]	
Total	8,496	24	22	1,026	1,895	2,560	39	132	131	330	42	43	1,876	87	289
Alabama	0	0	0	0	0	0	0	0	0	0	0	0	0	0	0
Alaska	8	0	0	2	1	2	0	1	0	0	0	0	2	0	0
Arizona	211	0	1	29	59	62	0	0	2	4	1	0	50	1	2
Arkansas	14	0	0	1	2	2	0	0	2	1	0	0	5	0	1
California	1,222	0	1	237	286	273	0	35	9	11	4	10	356	0	0
Colorado	176	0	0	32	37	69	8	0	4	2	0	0	23	0	1
Connecticut	92	0	0	3	15	35	0	0	2	5	1	0	28	1	2
Delaware	18	0	0	0	2	3	0	1	1	0	0	0	11	0	0
District of Columbia	236	0	0	27	122	34	0	11	0	4	0	0	38	0	0
Florida	166	0	0	47	45	30	0	4	5	1	0	1	33	0	0
Georgia	41	0	0	5	17	14	0	0	0	1	0	0	4	0	0
Hawaii	48	0	0	5	18	22	0	0	0	1	1	0	0	0	1
Idaho	26	0	0	4	6	10	0	0	0	0	0	0	6	0	0
Illinois	139	0	0	29	29	52	0	3	0	1	0	1	24	0	0
Indiana	226	0	0	16	16	150	1	4	5	5	1	1	21	1	5
Iowa	16	0	0	2	1	8	0	0	1	0	0	0	4	0	0
Kansas	87	1	0	17	17	11	2	2	4	9	0	0	14	3	7
Kentucky	288	1	0	14	35	89	2	3	11	27	4	3	45	11	43
Louisiana	59	0	0	14	11	2	1	0	2	6	2	1	6	3	11
Maine	22	0	0	6	8	6	0	0	0	0	0	0	2	0	0
Maryland	52	0	0	6	17	6	0	1	0	1	0	0	19	1	1
Massachusetts	474	1	0	66	76	207	1	4	2	3	0	0	112	2	0
Michigan	495	0	7	62	124	155	4	3	6	16	0	2	77	14	25
Minnesota	159	0	0	11	37	66	1	2	2	2	0	1	36	1	0
Mississippi	5	0	0	0	3	0	0	0	0	0	0	1	0	1	0
Missouri	80	0	0	11	24	25	0	1	2	1	0	2	9	2	3
Montana	7	0	0	0	2	0	0	0	0	1	0	0	4	0	0
Nebraska	35	0	0	4	6	5	0	0	3	2	1	0	13	1	0
Nevada	37	0	0	11	9	5	0	0	0	0	0	0	12	0	0
New Hampshire	19	0	0	0	3	8	1	0	1	1	0	0	5	0	0
New Jersey	577	1	1	6	31	458	0	1	0	1	0	0	78	0	0
New Mexico	34	0	0	10	13	3	0	0	1	0	0	0	6	1	0
New York	525	0	0	41	160	2	0	16	1	13	0	4	288	0	0
North Carolina	202	0	3	24	41	75	0	0	5	5	2	0	47	0	0
North Dakota	10	0	0	1	1	3	0	0	0	0	0	1	4	0	0
Ohio	390	0	2	19	50	135	2	8	11	52	9	1	67	10	24
Oklahoma	25	2	0	3	5	12	0	0	0	0	0	0	3	0	0
Oregon	139	0	0	11	40	37	0	4	1	2	0	0	41	0	3
Pennsylvania	75	0	0	5	13	23	0	1	1	0	0	7	24	0	1
Rhode Island	15	0	0	2	4	3	0	1	1	0	0	0	4	0	0
South Carolina	123	0	0	6	29	20	2	2	5	17	0	1	23	2	16
South Dakota	26	0	0	0	9	1	0	1	1	3	1	0	7	1	2
Tennessee	207	0	2	38	47	56	3	0	1	10	0	0	29	4	17
Texas	500	0	1	31	127	60	4	5	23	59	5	0	87	10	88
Utah	36	0	0	5	11	7	0	0	0	3	0	0	7	3	0
Vermont	48	0	1	3	12	1	0	0	2	10	0	0	12	3	4
Virginia	159	0	0	7	50	28	0	0	2	5	0	1	54	0	12
Washington	666	0	3	99	178	183	6	18	5	27	9	1	121	6	10
West Virginia	51	0	0	6	14	2	1	0	5	7	1	0	3	4	8
Wisconsin	59	0	0	10	17	7	0	0	1	11	0	0	10	1	2
Wyoming	0	0	0	0	0	0	0	0	0	0	0	0	0	0	0
Federal															
Federal Bureau of Investigation, Field Offices	171	18	0	38	15	93	0	0	1	0	0	4	2	0	0

1 Federal includes only the Federal Bureau of Investigation field offices.   2 Only the revised Uniform Crime Reporting definition of rape was used for the figures shown in this column.   3 Includes additional offenses collected in the National Incident-Based Reporting System.

Table 93. Agency Hate Crime Reporting, by Participating State/Territory and Federal,[1] 2018

(Number.)

State	Number of participating agencies	Population covered	Agencies submitting incident reports	Total number of incidents reported
Total	16,039	306,874,326	2,026	7,120
Alabama	98	1,865,517	0	0
Alaska	32	733,747	4	7
Arizona	102	7,135,285	19	166
Arkansas	286	2,874,960	9	13
California	736	39,520,441	220	1,063
Colorado	217	5,512,017	37	121
Connecticut	97	3,150,064	34	81
Delaware	63	962,453	10	16
District of Columbia	2	702,455	2	213
Florida	651	20,922,562	54	141
Georgia	487	8,497,512	9	35
Hawaii	1	982,019	1	44
Idaho	106	1,738,946	13	23
Illinois	738	11,942,645	31	107
Indiana	161	3,004,204	24	107
Iowa	228	3,042,074	9	10
Kansas	367	2,561,072	38	69
Kentucky	414	4,448,098	97	235
Louisiana	147	3,528,527	18	45
Maine	133	1,338,404	7	20
Maryland	155	6,039,822	20	49
Massachusetts	359	6,730,168	79	352
Michigan	633	9,948,030	190	431
Minnesota	385	5,484,503	38	126
Mississippi	35	720,646	4	5
Missouri	604	5,919,676	22	64
Montana	108	1,062,359	5	7
Nebraska	116	1,781,091	14	34
Nevada	56	3,034,392	7	33
New Hampshire	184	1,317,257	11	13
New Jersey	577	8,908,520	180	561
New Mexico	110	1,915,743	3	28
New York	572	19,348,748	59	523
North Carolina	531	10,330,057	42	140
North Dakota	109	760,650	8	10
Ohio	547	9,774,082	116	350
Oklahoma	417	3,621,189	17	20
Oregon	222	4,012,987	33	118
Pennsylvania	1,480	12,712,213	15	67
Rhode Island	48	1,056,281	9	13
South Carolina	439	4,960,159	52	111
South Dakota	130	806,540	13	20
Tennessee	466	6,737,273	67	170
Texas	1,028	27,845,758	127	455
Utah	126	3,068,388	18	33
Vermont	89	630,980	27	45
Virginia	415	8,510,090	53	143
Washington	248	7,479,358	73	506
West Virginia	251	1,573,786	21	43
Wisconsin	436	5,767,760	27	52
Wyoming	57	552,818	0	0
Federal				
Federal Bureau of Investigation, Field Offices[2]	40	0	40	82

1 Federal includes only the Federal Bureau of Investigation field offices.   2 Population estimates are not attributed to the Federal Bureau of Investigation field offices.

Table 94. Hate Crime Incidents Per Bias Motivation and Quarter, by Selected State and Agency and Federal,[1] 2018

(Number.)

State/agency	Number of incidents per bias motivation						Number of incidents per quarter				Population[2]
	Race/ Ethnicity/ Ancestry	Religion	Sexual orientation	Disability	Gender	Gender Identity	1st quarter	2nd quarter	3rd quarter	4th quarter	
ALASKA **Total**	4	2	0	1	0	0					
Cities	4	2	0	1	0	0					
Anchorage	1	0	0	0	0	0	0	0	1	0	291,992
Fairbanks	2	0	0	1	0	0	1	1	1	0	31,635
Juneau	0	2	0	0	0	0	0	0	2	0	31,922
Kotzebue	1	0	0	0	0	0	0	1	0	0	3,273
ARIZONA **Total**	95	34	37	2	2	3					
Cities	93	33	37	2	2	3					
Avondale	1	0	0	0	0	0		1	0	0	85,204
Coolidge	2	0	0	0	0	0	0	0	0	2	12,815
Flagstaff	1	0	1	0	0	0	0	2	0	0	72,852
Gilbert	1	0	0	0	0	0	0	0	1	0	247,463
Glendale	7	0	1	0	0	0	3	1	1	3	249,799
Maricopa	1	0	0	0	0	0	0	1	0	0	48,660
Mesa	2	0	1	0	0	0	2	1	0	0	504,873
Page	2	0	1	0	0	0	1	1	1	0	7,576
Peoria	1	0	0	0	0	0	0	1	0	0	170,177
Phoenix[3]	59	24	25	1	1	2	35	26	18	27	1,653,080
Prescott	1	0	0	0	0	0	1	0	0	0	43,172
Scottsdale	2	2	1	0	0	0	1	1	1	2	254,961
St. Johns	0	1	0	0	0	0	0	0	1	0	3,510
Surprise	1	2	0	0	0	0	0	1	2	0	136,611
Tempe[3]	0	1	0	0	0	0	1	0	0	0	188,543
Tucson[3]	7	2	6	1	1	1	5	4	8	0	537,392
Yuma	5	1	1	0	0	0	1	2	2	2	96,121
Universities and Colleges	1	1	0	0	0	0					
University of Arizona	1	1	0	0	0	0	1	1	0	0	47,648
Nonmetropolitan Counties	1	0	0	0	0	0					
La Paz	1	0	0	0	0	0	0	0	0	1	
ARKANSAS **Total**	10	1	1	1	0	0					
Cities	8	1	1	1	0	0					
Benton	1	0	0	0	0	0	0	1	0	0	36,556
Fort Smith	2	0	1	0	0	0	2	1	0	0	88,290
Hot Springs	1	0	0	0	0	0	1	0	0	0	37,006
Newport	1	0	0	0	0	0	0	0	0	1	7,654
Rogers	2	0	0	0	0	0	0	1	1	0	68,026
Sherwood	1	1	0	0	0	0	0	1	0	1	31,284
Springdale	0	0	0	1	0	0	1	0	0	0	73,496
Metropolitan Counties	1	0	0	0	0	0					
Pulaski	1	0	0	0	0	0	0	0	1	0	
Nonmetropolitan Counties	1	0	0	0	0	0					
Sevier	1	0	0	0	0	0	0	1	0	0	
CALIFORNIA **Total**	5	0	1	1	0	0					
Cities	5	0	1	0	0	0					
Benton	1	0	0	0	0	0	0	0	1	0	36,702
Fayetteville	0	0	1	0	0	0	0	0	0	1	85,592
Fort Smith	4	0	0	0	0	0	0	1	1	2	88,437
Nonmetropolitan Counties	0	0	0	1	0	0					
Boone	0	0	0	1	0	0	0	1	0	0	
CALIFORNIA **Total**	596	199	239	7	4	20					
Cities	538	183	209	5	3	16					
Alameda	3	3	1	0	0	0	3	2	2	0	79,951
Albany	2	1	1	0	0	0	2	0	0	2	20,379
American Canyon	0	1	0	0	0	0	0	1	0	0	20,339
Anaheim	0	0	2	0	0	0	1	0	1	0	354,743
Antioch	1	1	0	0	0	0	0	1	0	1	112,956
Apple Valley	1	0	0	0	0	0	1	0	0	0	73,631
Arvin	1	0	0	0	0	0	0	0	1	0	21,560
Azusa	3	0	0	0	0	0	0	1	1	1	50,393
Bakersfield	3	6	1	0	0	0	6	2	2	0	385,609

Table 94. Hate Crime Incidents Per Bias Motivation and Quarter, by Selected State and Agency and Federal,[1] 2018—Continued

(Number.)

State/agency	Number of incidents per bias motivation						Number of incidents per quarter				Population[2]
	Race/ Ethnicity/ Ancestry	Religion	Sexual orientation	Disability	Gender	Gender Identity	1st quarter	2nd quarter	3rd quarter	4th quarter	
Baldwin Park	1	0	0	0	0	0	1	0	0	0	76,541
Beaumont	1	0	0	0	0	0	0	1	0	0	48,559
Bell	1	0	1	0	0	0	1	0	0	1	35,857
Bellflower	1	0	0	0	0	0	0	1	0	0	77,937
Bell Gardens	1	0	0	0	0	0	1	0	0	0	42,845
Berkeley	8	5	4	0	0	0	5	3	5	4	123,735
Beverly Hills	2	3	0	0	0	0	0	1	2	2	34,557
Brea	0	1	0	0	0	0	0	0	1	0	43,279
Brentwood	3	0	0	0	0	0	0	3	0	0	64,118
Buena Park	1	0	1	0	0	0	0	0	0	2	83,336
Burbank	4	4	2	0	0	0	5	0	1	4	105,041
Calabasas	0	2	0	0	0	0	0	1	1	0	24,309
Calimesa	1	0	0	0	0	0	0	0	1	0	8,953
Camarillo	2	0	0	0	0	0	1	1	0	0	68,218
Capitola	0	0	1	0	0	0	1	0	0	0	10,218
Carlsbad	4	2	0	0	0	0	3	1	2	0	116,739
Carson	1	0	0	0	0	0	1	0	0	0	92,895
Central Marin	1	0	0	0	0	0	1	0	0	0	35,033
Chino Hills	1	0	0	0	0	0	1	0	0	0	81,177
Chula Vista	1	1	0	0	0	0	0	0	1	1	274,370
Citrus Heights	3	0	0	0	0	0	1	0	2	0	88,603
Claremont	1	0	0	0	0	0	0	0	0	1	36,178
Clayton	1	0	0	0	0	0	0	0	1	0	12,330
Clearlake	2	0	0	0	0	0	1	0	1	0	15,037
Clovis	0	0	0	0	0	1	1	0	0	0	111,759
Commerce	0	0	1	0	0	0	0	1	0	0	12,961
Compton	3	0	0	0	0	0	0	1	2	0	97,775
Corning	0	0	1	0	0	0	1	0	0	0	7,580
Corona	1	1	0	0	0	0	1	0	1	0	170,041
Cupertino	0	1	1	0	0	0	1	0	0	1	61,078
Cypress	2	0	0	0	0	0	0	2	0	0	49,223
Daly City	1	0	0	0	0	0	0	0	1	0	107,928
Davis	8	4	1	1	0	0	1	7	4	2	69,486
Downey	0	0	1	0	0	0	0	1	0	0	113,277
Eastvale	0	1	0	0	0	0	1	0	0	0	64,642
El Cajon	3	0	1	0	0	0	1	0	2	1	104,497
El Cerrito	1	1	0	0	0	0	0	2	0	0	25,793
Elk Grove	2	0	2	0	0	0	0	1	3	0	174,651
El Monte	5	0	0	0	0	0	2	2	1	0	116,464
El Segundo	1	0	0	0	0	0	0	0	1	0	16,881
Encinitas	0	3	0	0	0	0	2	0	0	1	63,700
Escalon	1	0	0	0	0	0	0	0	0	1	7,653
Escondido	2	0	0	0	0	0	1	1	0	0	153,073
Eureka	0	0	1	0	0	0	0	1	0	0	27,174
Fairfield	1	0	1	0	0	0	0	1	0	1	117,883
Fillmore	0	0	1	0	0	0	0	0	1	0	15,928
Folsom	1	0	0	0	0	0	1	0	0	0	78,916
Fontana	1	0	0	0	0	0	0	0	1	0	213,964
Fort Bragg	0	1	0	0	0	0	1	0	0	0	7,317
Foster City	0	2	0	0	0	0	0	0	0	2	34,993
Fountain Valley	0	0	1	0	0	0	1	0	0	0	56,433
Fremont	6	0	0	0	0	0	4	1	1	0	238,024
Fresno	19	3	5	0	0	0	5	0	8	14	531,818
Galt	1	0	0	0	0	0	0	1	0	0	26,548
Gardena	0	1	1	0	0	0	2	0	0	0	60,423
Garden Grove	1	0	0	0	0	0	0	0	1	0	174,661
Glendale	4	0	0	0	0	0	3	0	0	1	204,724
Glendora	1	0	0	0	0	0	1	0	0	0	52,727
Gridley	1	0	0	0	0	0	1	0	0	0	6,612
Hawaiian Gardens	2	0	0	0	0	0	0	0	1	1	14,474
Hawthorne	3	2	1	0	0	0	0	0	2	4	88,372
Hayward	3	1	0	0	0	0	1	1	1	1	162,881
Hemet	1	0	0	0	0	0	1	0	0	0	86,047
Hesperia	1	0	0	0	0	0	0	1	0	0	95,519
Huntington Beach	2	2	0	0	0	0	0	1	2	1	203,428
Huntington Park	3	0	1	0	0	0	1	0	2	1	58,922
Imperial Beach	1	0	0	0	0	0	0	0	0	1	27,569
Inglewood	1	0	0	0	0	0	0	1	0	0	110,726
Irvine	1	1	0	0	0	0	0	0	1	1	288,052
Jurupa Valley	1	0	0	0	0	0	0	0	1	0	107,605
Laguna Woods	0	0	1	0	0	0	0	0	1	0	16,219
Lakeport	0	0	1	0	0	0	0	1	0	0	4,763
La Mesa	1	0	0	0	0	0	1	0	0	0	60,442
Lancaster	9	0	2	0	0	0	1	3	4	3	160,818
Lawndale	1	0	0	0	0	0	0	0	0	1	33,121
Livermore	3	2	1	0	0	0	1	3	1	1	91,612
Lodi	1	1	0	0	0	0	0	0	1	1	66,416
Long Beach	6	0	3	0	0	0	2	2	3	2	470,445
Los Angeles[3]	136	63	74	0	0	10	45	78	89	70	4,029,741

Table 94. Hate Crime Incidents Per Bias Motivation and Quarter, by Selected State and Agency and Federal,[1] 2018—Continued

(Number.)

State/agency	Number of incidents per bias motivation						Number of incidents per quarter				Population[2]
	Race/ Ethnicity/ Ancestry	Religion	Sexual orientation	Disability	Gender	Gender Identity	1st quarter	2nd quarter	3rd quarter	4th quarter	
Los Banos	0	0	1	0	0	0	1	0	0	0	39,651
Lynwood	1	0	0	0	0	0	1	0	0	0	71,315
Malibu	1	0	0	0	0	0	0	0	0	1	12,911
Marysville	1	0	0	0	0	0	0	1	0	0	12,459
Menifee	2	0	0	0	0	0	2	0	0	0	92,540
Modesto	2	1	2	0	2	0	1	1	4	1	215,822
Monterey	2	0	0	0	0	0	0	1	1	0	28,744
Moreno Valley	1	0	0	0	0	0	1	0	0	0	209,145
Morro Bay	0	0	1	0	0	0	0	1	0	0	10,692
Mountain View	1	0	0	0	0	0	0	0	1	0	82,518
Newark	1	0	0	0	0	0	0	0	1	0	48,276
Newport Beach	1	0	2	0	0	1	3	1	0	0	86,276
Norwalk	3	0	0	0	0	0	0	0	2	1	106,158
Oakland	3	5	5	1	0	1	3	3	5	4	430,230
Oceanside	2	0	0	0	0	0	1	0	0	1	177,464
Orange	2	0	0	0	0	0	1	1	0	0	141,108
Oroville	1	0	0	0	0	0	0	0	1	0	19,186
Oxnard	0	1	1	0	0	0	0	1	1	0	211,737
Pacifica	0	1	2	0	0	0	0	0	2	1	39,339
Palmdale	1	0	0	0	0	0	0	1	0	0	158,177
Palm Springs	1	0	3	0	0	0	0	1	1	2	48,644
Palo Alto	2	2	1	0	0	0	2	3	0	0	67,560
Paramount	1	0	1	0	0	0	0	1	1	0	55,023
Parlier	1	0	0	0	0	0	0	1	0	0	15,356
Pasadena	1	2	0	0	0	0	1	0	1	1	143,448
Perris	1	0	0	0	0	0	1	0	0	0	79,238
Petaluma	1	0	0	0	0	0	0	0	1	0	61,289
Pinole	1	0	0	0	0	0	0	1	0	0	19,509
Pittsburg	1	0	0	0	0	0	0	0	1	0	73,462
Placentia	3	1	1	0	0	0	0	2	1	2	52,324
Pleasanton	1	0	0	0	0	0	0	1	0	0	84,992
Poway	0	1	0	0	0	0	0	0	0	1	50,346
Rancho Cucamonga	2	0	0	0	0	0	0	0	0	2	179,114
Rancho Santa Margarita	1	0	0	0	0	0	0	1	0	0	48,918
Red Bluff	2	0	0	0	0	0	0	1	0	1	14,315
Redding	9	0	0	0	0	0	1	3	3	2	92,068
Redlands	1	0	0	0	0	0	0	0	1	0	71,954
Redwood City	1	1	0	0	0	0	2	0	0	0	88,161
Rialto	1	0	0	0	0	0	0	1	0	0	104,173
Richmond	11	1	0	0	0	0	3	3	6	0	110,982
Rio Vista	0	1	0	0	0	0	0	1	0	0	9,268
Ripon	1	0	0	0	0	0	0	0	1	0	15,878
Riverside	9	1	0	0	0	0	0	2	5	3	331,022
Roseville	5	0	0	0	0	0	2	1	2	0	137,706
Sacramento	4	1	6	0	0	0	1	5	1	4	507,037
Salinas	0	0	1	0	0	0	0	0	0	1	158,590
San Bernardino	4	0	0	0	0	0	1	3	0	0	217,986
San Bruno	0	0	1	0	0	0	1	0	0	0	43,621
San Clemente	1	0	1	0	0	0	0	0	2	0	65,509
San Diego	20	8	12	0	0	0	10	11	8	11	1,436,495
San Dimas	0	1	0	0	0	0	1	0	0	0	34,463
San Francisco	41	8	17	0	0	2	20	22	11	15	889,282
San Gabriel	2	0	0	0	0	0	1	1	0	0	40,637
San Jacinto	2	0	0	0	0	0	0	1	0	1	48,830
San Jose	22	6	9	0	0	0	7	10	10	10	1,047,305
San Leandro	1	1	0	0	0	0	1	1	0	0	91,359
San Luis Obispo	4	0	0	1	1	0	1	1	1	3	47,885
San Marcos	1	0	0	0	0	0	0	1	0	0	98,088
San Mateo	0	0	1	0	0	0	0	1	0	0	105,839
San Pablo	0	1	0	0	0	0	0	1	0	0	31,403
San Rafael	3	1	0	0	0	0	2	1	1	0	59,254
San Ramon	0	1	0	0	0	0	1	0	0	0	76,569
Santa Ana	6	6	1	0	0	0	1	2	8	2	335,403
Santa Barbara	2	0	0	0	0	0	2	0	0	0	92,630
Santa Clarita	0	0	1	0	0	0	0	0	0	1	216,589
Santa Cruz[3]	5	2	3	0	0	0	2	4	1	2	65,680
Santa Maria	1	0	0	0	0	0	0	1	0	0	108,100
Santa Monica	1	0	0	0	0	0	0	0	1	0	92,674
Santa Rosa	2	1	3	0	0	0	0	1	3	2	176,325
Santee	1	0	0	0	0	0	0	0	0	1	58,781
Scotts Valley	0	0	1	0	0	0	0	1	0	0	11,998
Seaside	1	0	0	0	0	0	0	0	0	1	34,303
Simi Valley	4	2	1	0	0	0	1	2	2	2	127,222
South Gate	1	0	0	0	0	0	0	1	0	0	95,570
South Lake Tahoe	0	2	3	0	0	0	0	3	2	0	22,060
South Pasadena	1	0	0	0	0	0	1	0	0	0	25,924
Stockton	2	1	1	0	0	0	0	2	1	1	313,158
Sunnyvale	2	2	0	0	0	0	0	1	0	3	155,637
Thousand Oaks	1	0	0	0	0	0	1	0	0	0	129,319

Table 94. Hate Crime Incidents Per Bias Motivation and Quarter, by Selected State and Agency and Federal,[1] 2018—Continued

(Number.)

State/agency	Number of incidents per bias motivation						Number of incidents per quarter				Population[2]
	Race/ Ethnicity/ Ancestry	Religion	Sexual orientation	Disability	Gender	Gender Identity	1st quarter	2nd quarter	3rd quarter	4th quarter	
Torrance	0	0	2	0	0	0	1	1	0	0	146,968
Tracy	0	0	2	0	0	0	1	0	0	1	91,988
Turlock	1	0	1	0	0	0	0	1	1	0	74,267
Union City	1	0	0	0	0	0	0	0	0	1	76,198
Upland	2	0	0	0	0	0	0	1	1	0	77,453
Vallejo	1	0	0	0	0	0	0	1	0	0	122,974
Ventura	4	0	0	0	0	0	2	0	0	2	111,272
Victorville	3	0	0	2	0	0	0	2	1	2	123,343
Vista	0	0	1	0	0	0	0	0	1	0	102,742
Walnut Creek	1	0	0	0	0	0	0	1	0	0	70,587
West Covina	3	0	0	0	0	0	1	1	0	1	107,806
West Hollywood	6	1	4	0	0	1	3	5	4	0	37,478
Williams	0	0	1	0	0	0	1	0	0	0	5,380
Yucaipa	1	0	0	0	0	0	0	1	0	0	54,001
Yucca Valley	1	0	0	0	0	0	0	1	0	0	21,895
Universities and Colleges	7	5	6	0	1	1					
California State University											
Fresno	1	0	0	0	0	0	1	0	0	0	26,380
Northridge	1	2	1	0	0	0	0	1	1	2	41,909
Foothill-De Anza College	0	0	0	0	0	1	1	0	0	0	63,210
Humboldt State University	1	1	0	0	1	0	0	0	0	3	9,171
San Francisco State University	0	1	1	0	0	0	0	0	1	1	33,036
State Center Community College District	0	0	1	0	0	0	0	1			60,065
University of California											
Davis	0	0	1	0	0	0	0	1	0	0	38,778
Los Angeles	1	1	1	0	0	0	1	1	0	1	46,298
San Diego	3	0	0	0	0	0	0	0	2	1	36,785
Santa Barbara	0	0	1	0	0	0	0	0	0	1	25,833
Metropolitan Counties	40	11	21	2	0	2					
El Dorado	1	0	0	0	0	0	0	0	1	0	
Fresno	1	0	0	0	0	0	0	0	1	0	
Imperial	1	0	0	0	0	0	0	1	0	0	
Kern	3	1	0	0	0	0	1	2	1	0	
Los Angeles	9	1	7	0	0	2	5	7	5	2	
Monterey	0	0	1	0	0	0	1	0	0	0	
Napa	1	0	0	0	0	0	0	1	0	0	
Orange	1	0	0	0	0	0	1	0	0	0	
Riverside	2	0	1	0	0	0	0	1	2	0	
Sacramento	3	1	0	0	0	0	2	2	0	0	
San Bernardino	1	0	0	0	0	0	0	1	0	0	
San Diego	2	1	3	0	0	0	0	4	0	2	
San Mateo	1	0	1	1	0	0	2	0	1	0	
Santa Clara	2	2	2	1	0	0	2	0	4	1	
Santa Cruz	6	5	2	0	0	0	3	3	4	3	
Solano	3	0	2	0	0	0	2	2		1	
Ventura	0	0	1	0	0	0	1	0	0	0	
Yuba	3	0	1	0	0	0	2	1	1	0	
Nonmetropolitan Counties	4	0	0	0	0	0					
Calaveras	1	0	0	0	0	0	0	1	0	0	
Lassen	1	0	0	0	0	0	0	0	1	0	
Mendocino	2	0	0	0	0	0	2	0	0	0	
Other Agencies	7	0	3	0	0	1					
California State Fair	0	0	0	0	0	1	0	0	1	0	
Los Angeles Transportation Services Bureau	2	0	1	0	0	0	0	1	1	1	
Port of San Diego Harbor	2	0	1	0	0	0	0	2	1		
San Francisco Bay Area Rapid Transit											
Alameda County	1	0	0	0	0	0	0	1	0	0	
Contra Costa County	0	0	1	0	0	0	0	0	1	0	
Santa Clara Transit District	1	0	0	0	0	0	1	0	0	0	
Twin Rivers Unified School District	1	0	0	0	0	0	0	1	0	0	
COLORADO											
Total	78	16	24	2	0	3					
Cities	55	10	15	1	0	3					
Aurora	8	2	0	0	0	0	2	4	2	2	324,276
Boulder	2	0	0	0	0	0	1	0	0	1	108,380
Brighton[3]	2	0	2	0	0	0	0	0	1	2	40,696
Canon City	2	0	0	0	0	0	0	2	0	0	16,557
Centennial	2	1	2	0	0	0	2	1	1	1	111,646
Colorado Springs	7	3	0	0	0	0	1	4	2	3	471,124
Commerce City	1	0	0	0	0	0	0	1	0	0	57,474
Denver[3]	15	3	8	1	0	3	4	12	8	5	720,745
Fort Collins	4	0	1	0	0	0	2	2	0	1	168,163
Golden	0	0	1	0	0	0	0	0	0	1	20,768

Table 94. Hate Crime Incidents Per Bias Motivation and Quarter, by Selected State and Agency and Federal,[1] 2018—Continued

(Number.)

State/agency	Number of incidents per bias motivation						Number of incidents per quarter				Population[2]
	Race/ Ethnicity/ Ancestry	Religion	Sexual orientation	Disability	Gender	Gender Identity	1st quarter	2nd quarter	3rd quarter	4th quarter	
Grand Junction	2	0	0	0	0	0	1	1	0	0	62,974
Lafayette	1	0	1	0	0	0	1	1	0	0	28,914
Lone Tree	1	0	0	0	0	0	0	0	1	0	13,933
Longmont	2	0	0	0	0	0	0	1	0	1	95,217
Louisville	1	0	0	0	0	0	0	0	0	1	21,545
Rifle	2	0	0	0	0	0	0	1	1	0	9,711
Silverthorne	0	1	0	0	0	0	0	0	1	0	4,775
Sterling	1	0	0	0	0	0	0	0	0	1	13,928
Trinidad	1	0	0	0	0	0	1	0	0	0	7,947
Woodland Park	1	0	0	0	0	0	0	1	0	0	7,709
Universities and Colleges	2	2	4	0	0	0					
Auraria Higher Education Center[4]	1	0	0	0	0	0	0	0	1	0	
Colorado State University, Fort Collins	1	2	0	0	0	0	0	3	0	0	36,966
University of Colorado:											
Boulder	0	0	2	0	0	0	0	0	2	0	37,921
Colorado Springs	0	0	2	0	0	0	0	0	2	0	16,743
Metropolitan Counties	16	2	3	1	0	0					
Adams	1	0	0	0	0	0	1	0	0	0	
Arapahoe	5	1	1	0	0	0	1	1	0	5	
Boulder	1	0	0	0	0	0	0	0	1	0	
El Paso	2	1	0	0	0	0	1	2	0	0	
Jefferson	3	0	0	1	0	0	1	2	1	0	
Larimer	4	0	1	0	0	0	2	1	1	1	
Mesa	0	0	1	0	0	0	0	0	1	0	
Nonmetropolitan Counties	5	2	2	0	0	0					
Archuleta	0	0	1	0	0	0	0	0	0	1	
Custer	0	0	1	0	0	0	0	1	0	0	
Logan	0	1	0	0	0	0	0	0	1	0	
Montezuma	1	0	0	0	0	0	0	0	1	0	
Summit	3	1	0	0	0	0	2	1	0	1	
Washington	1	0	0	0	0	0	0	0	1	0	
CONNECTICUT											
Total	54	13	12	1	1	0					
Cities	51	10	9	1	1	0					
Berlin	1	0	0	0	0	0	0	1	0	0	20,593
Bethel	0	0	0	1	0	0	0	0	0	1	19,974
Bridgeport	4	0	0	0	0	0		1	1	2	146,819
Bristol	1	0	0	0	0	0	0	0	0	1	60,184
Danbury	2	0	1	0	0	0	2	0	1	0	85,818
East Hartford	1	0	0	0	0	0	0	1	0	0	50,184
Fairfield	1	1	0	0	0	0	0	0	1	1	62,452
Glastonbury	2	1	1	0	0	0	0	2	1	1	34,593
Groton	0	1	0	0	0	0	0	0	1	0	9,051
Guilford	1	0	0	0	0	0	0	0	0	1	22,268
Middletown	4	0	0	0	0	0	0	1	1	2	46,314
New Haven	5	2	0	0	0	0	1	2	3	1	131,181
New Milford	1	0	0	0	0	0	0	0	1	0	26,956
Norwalk	1	1	0	0	0	0	0	0	0	2	89,442
Norwich	6	0	0	0	1	0	2	0	4	1	39,318
Old Saybrook	5	0	0	0	0	0	2	2	0	1	10,117
Orange	1	0	0	0	0	0	0	0	0	1	14,002
Putnam	1	0	0	0	0	0	0	1	0	0	9,325
Ridgefield	1	0	0	0	0	0	0	1	0	0	25,260
Rocky Hill	1	1	0	0	0	0	0	1	0	1	20,163
Southington	1	0	1	0	0	0	0	0	2	0	43,960
South Windsor	0	0	1	0	0	0	0	1	0	0	25,968
Stamford	4	2	2	0	0	0	1	1	2	4	132,007
Stratford	1	0	0	0	0	0	0	1	0	0	52,472
Torrington	2	0	1	0	0	0	1	0	0	2	34,286
Trumbull	0	1	0	0	0	0	0	0	0	1	36,167
Vernon	0	0	1	0	0	0	0	0	0	1	29,304
Waterbury	2	0	0	0	0	0	0	2	0	0	108,378
Willimantic	0	0	1	0	0	0	0	1	0	0	17,691
Windsor	1	0	0	0	0	0	0	1	0	0	28,867
Woodbridge	1	0	0	0	0	0	0	1	0	0	8,832
Universities and Colleges	1	0	0	0	0	0					
Southern Connecticut State University	1	0	0	0	0	0	0	0	1	0	11,978
State Police Agencies	1	3	3	0	0	0					
Connecticut State Police	1	3	3	0	0	0	4	0	2	1	
Tribal Agencies	1	0	0	0	0	0					
Mashantucket Pequot Tribal	1	0	0	0	0	0	0	0	1	0	

Table 94. Hate Crime Incidents Per Bias Motivation and Quarter, by Selected State and Agency and Federal,[1] 2018—Continued

(Number.)

State/agency	Number of incidents per bias motivation						Number of incidents per quarter				Population[2]
	Race/Ethnicity/Ancestry	Religion	Sexual orientation	Disability	Gender	Gender Identity	1st quarter	2nd quarter	3rd quarter	4th quarter	
DELAWARE											
Total	13	1	2	0	0	0					
Cities	5	0	0	0	0	0					
Dover	1	0	0	0	0	0	0	1	0	0	37,778
Felton	1	0	0	0	0	0	0	0	1	0	1,414
Newark	1	0	0	0	0	0	0	1	0	0	34,207
Seaford	1	0	0	0	0	0	1	0	0	0	7,876
Wilmington	1	0	0	0	0	0	0	1	0	0	71,157
Universities and Colleges	4	0	0	0	0	0					
Delaware State University	1	0	0	0	0	0	1	0	0	0	5,162
University of Delaware	3	0	0	0	0	0	1	0	1	1	24,855
Metropolitan Counties	3	0	2	0	0	0					
New Castle County Police Department	3	0	2	0	0	0	1	2	0	2	
State Police Agencies	1	1	0	0	0	0					
State Police											
Kent County	1	0	0	0	0	0	0	0	0	1	
New Castle County	0	1	0	0	0	0	1	0	0	0	
DISTRICT OF COLUMBIA											
Total	99	12	68	0	1	33					
Cities											
Washington	88	12	60	0	1	33	32	49	58	55	702,455
Other Agencies	11	0	8	0	0	0					
Metro Transit Police	11	0	8	0	0	0	2	5	6	6	
FLORIDA											
Total	71	29	35	1	0	5					
Cities	39	22	26	0	0	4					
Boca Raton	1	1	0	0	0	0	2	0	0	0	100,162
Cape Coral	1	0	0	0	0	0	0	0	0	1	187,869
Coral Gables	0	1	0	0	0	0	0	1	0	0	51,716
Davie	2	1	0	0	0	0	0	2	1		107,120
Deerfield Beach	0	1	1	0	0	0		1	0	1	81,371
Fort Lauderdale	3	0	2	0	0	0	0	5	0	0	182,150
Fort Myers	0	0	1	0	0	0	0	1	0	0	82,805
Gainesville	1	2	0	0	0	0	1	0	1	1	133,400
Groveland	1	0	0	0	0	0	0	0	0	1	14,342
Jacksonville	4	0	0	0	0	0	1	1	2	0	903,213
Key West	0	0	1	0	0	0	0	0	1	0	25,286
Largo	1	0	0	0	0	0	0	0	0	1	85,568
Lauderdale Lakes	3	0	0	0	0	0	1	0	1	1	36,575
Miami	3	1	4	0	0	2	3	1	3	3	473,047
Miami Beach	1	11	7	0	0	1	5	4	7	4	92,928
Minneola	1	0	0	0	0	0	1	0	0	0	11,859
North Miami	0	0	1	0	0	0	1	0	0	0	62,585
Ocala	1	0	0	0	0	0	0	1	0	0	59,505
Orlando	2	0	2	0	0	0	1	0	2	1	286,679
Palm Bay	6	0	0	0	0	0	1	0	3	2	112,902
Parkland	0	1	0	0	0	0	0	0	1	0	33,760
Pembroke Pines	0	1	0	0	0	0	0	1	0	0	173,053
Pompano Beach	0	0	2	0	0	1	0	0	3	0	112,045
Port St. Lucie	1	0	2	0	0	0	0	0	0	3	193,137
Sebastian	0	0	1	0	0	0	0	0	0	1	25,672
Sunrise	2	0	0	0	0	0	0	1	1	0	95,812
Tallahassee	1	0	0	0	0	0	0	1	0	0	192,443
Tampa	1	1	0	0	0	0	0	0	0	2	392,945
Temple Terrace	2	0	0	0	0	0	1	0	1	0	26,777
Weston	0	1	0	0	0	0	0	0	1	0	71,744
West Palm Beach	1	0	1	0	0	0	0	0	2	0	111,659
Wilton Manors	0	0	1	0	0	0	0	0	1	0	12,941
Universities and Colleges	3	0	0	0	0	0					
Pensacola State College	3	0	0	0	0	0	2	0	1	0	13,602
Metropolitan Counties	29	7	9	1	0	1					
Alachua	0	0	0	0	0	1	0	0	1	0	
Bay	0	0	1	0	0	0	0	1	0	0	
Brevard	1	0	0	0	0	0	0	1	0	0	
Broward	3	0	0	0	0	0	0	0	2	1	
Clay	1	0	1	0	0	0	0	0	0	2	
Collier	0	1	0	0	0	0	0	0	0	1	
Flagler	1	0	0	0	0	0	0	0	0	1	

Table 94. Hate Crime Incidents Per Bias Motivation and Quarter, by Selected State and Agency and Federal,[1] 2018—Continued

(Number.)

State/agency	Number of incidents per bias motivation						Number of incidents per quarter				Population[2]
	Race/ Ethnicity/ Ancestry	Religion	Sexual orientation	Disability	Gender	Gender Identity	1st quarter	2nd quarter	3rd quarter	4th quarter	
Lake	2	0	0	0	0	0	0	0	1	1	
Lee	5	0	1	0	0	0	1	2	1	2	
Leon	0	1	0	0	0	0	1	0	0	0	
Manatee	1	0	0	0	0	0	0	0	1	0	
Martin	1	1	0	0	0	0	1	1	0	0	
Miami-Dade	2	2	1	1	0	0	2	3	0	1	
Orange	4	1	2	0	0	0	1	2	4	0	
Palm Beach	0	1	0	0	0	0	0	1	0	0	
Pinellas	1	0	0	0	0	0	0	0	0	1	
Polk	1	0	1	0	0	0	0	1	0	1	
Seminole	2	0	0	0	0	0	0	0	2	0	
St. Johns	1	0	1	0	0	0	0	1	1	0	
Sumter	1	0	1	0	0	0	1	0	1	0	
Volusia	2	0	0	0	0	0	1	0	0	1	
GEORGIA											
Total	28	4	3	0	0	0					
Cities	8	2	1	0	0	0					
Atlanta	1	1	0	0	0	0	0	2	0	0	461,405
Columbus	4	1	1	0	0	0	4	1	0	1	194,135
Conyers	1	0	0	0	0	0	0	0	1	0	16,128
Woodstock	2	0	0	0	0	0	1	1	0	0	32,850
Universities and Colleges	1	0	0	0	0	0					
University of Georgia	1	0	0	0	0	0	0	0	1	0	40,462
Metropolitan Counties	19	2	2	0	0	0					
Chatham County Police Department	1	0	0	0	0	0	0	0	1	0	
Cobb County Police Department	14	2	1	0	0	0	4	7	2	4	
Gwinnett County Police Department	3	0	1	0	0	0	0	2	2	0	
Henry County Police Department	1	0	0	0	0	0	0	0	0	1	
HAWAII											
Total	33	1	10	0	0	0					
Cities	33	1	10	0	0	0					
Honolulu	33	1	10	0	0	0	4	10	12	18	982,019
IDAHO											
Total	15	6	2	0	0	0					
Cities	14	6	2	0	0	0					
Boise	3	1	0	0	0	0	0	1	1	2	229,265
Chubbuck	1	0	0	0	0	0	1	0	0	0	14,998
Coeur d'Alene	2	0	1	0	0	0	0	1	1	1	51,650
Filer	1	0	0	0	0	0	1	0	0	0	2,813
Idaho Falls	1	1	0	0	0	0	1	0	1	0	61,643
Jerome	1	0	0	0	0	0	0	0	0	1	11,738
Ketchum	1	0	0	0	0	0	0	0	0	1	2,771
Lewiston	2	0	0	0	0	0	0	0	1	1	32,949
Meridian	0	0	1	0	0	0	0	0	0	1	103,774
Nampa	2	0	0	0	0	0	1	0	1	0	95,386
Pocatello	0	1	0	0	0	0	0	0	0	1	55,304
Twin Falls	0	3	0	0	0	0	0	0	1	2	49,908
Nonmetropolitan Counties	1	0	0	0	0	0					
Cassia	1	0	0	0	0	0	0	1	0		
ILLINOIS	14	6	2	0	0	0					
Total	62	20	20	0	0	6					
Cities	59	20	19	0	0	6					
Addison	1	0	0	0	0	0	0	1	0	0	36,791
Aurora	1	0	0	0	0	0	0	0	0	1	133,546
Bartlett	1	0	0	0	0	0	0	0	0	1	24,369
Calumet City	1	0	0	0	0	0	1	0	0	0	36,560
Champaign	0	0	1	0	0	0	0	0	1	0	88,326
Chicago	36	10	13	0	0	3	11	21	20	10	2,719,151
Crete	1	0	0	0	0	0	0	1	0	0	8,147
DeKalb	3	0	0	0	0	0	1	1	1	0	43,064
East Peoria	1	0	0	0	0	0	0	0	1	0	22,640
Elgin	0	1	1	0	0	0	0	0	1	1	87,989
Evanston	0	0	1	0	0	0	0	0	1	0	74,780
Galesburg	2	0	0	0	0	0	0	1	0	1	30,573
Harwood Heights	1	0	0	0	0	0	0	1	0	0	8,490
Herscher	1	0	0	0	0	0	0	0	1	0	1,515
Joliet	0	3	1	0	0	0	0	0	0	3	137,970
Marengo	0	0	1	0	0	0	0	0	1	0	7,470
Normal	2	0	0	0	0	0	0	0	1	1	54,525

Table 94. Hate Crime Incidents Per Bias Motivation and Quarter, by Selected State and Agency and Federal,[1] 2018—Continued

(Number.)

State/agency	Number of incidents per bias motivation						Number of incidents per quarter				Population[2]
	Race/ Ethnicity/ Ancestry	Religion	Sexual orientation	Disability	Gender	Gender Identity	1st quarter	2nd quarter	3rd quarter	4th quarter	
Orland Park	0	4	0	0	0	0	0	1	1	2	58,873
Peoria	1	0	0	0	0	1	1	1	0	0	112,595
Plainfield	1	0	0	0	0	1	2	0	0	0	42,281
Quincy	1	0	0	0	0	0	0	1	0	0	40,249
Rockford[3]	3	0	2	0	0	0	0	2	1	1	146,196
Rolling Meadows	0	1	0	0	0	0	0	1	0	0	23,970
Romeoville	1	0	0	0	0	0	0	0	1		39,625
Skokie	0	1	0	0	0	0	0	1	0	0	63,849
Watseka	0	0	0	0	0	1	0	0	1		4,868
Willow Springs	1	0	0	0	0	0	0	1	0	0	5,639
Universities and Colleges	0	0	1	0	0	0					
Western Illinois University	0	0	1	0	0	0	1	0	0		11,951
Metropolitan Counties	2	0	0	0	0	0					
Kankakee	1	0	0	0	0	0	0	0	1	0	
Will	1	0	0	0	0	0	1	0	0	0	
Nonmetropolitan Counties	1	0	0	0	0	0					
Perry	1	0	0	0	0	0	1	0	0	0	
INDIANA	0	1	0	0	0	0					
Total	75	20	11	1	2	2	0				
Cities	69	13	10	1	2	1					
Bloomington	6	1	0	0	0	0	1	3	1	2	85,730
Columbus	2	0	0	0	0	0		2			47,595
Fort Wayne	0	1	0	0	0	0	0	0	1	0	267,634
Greenfield	1	0	0	0	0	0	0	1	0	0	22,292
Hammond	4	0	0	0	0	0		1	2	1	76,050
Indianapolis[3]	22	5	5	0	2	0	3	13	10	5	877,584
Jasper	0	1	0	0	0	0		0	0	1	15,583
Lafayette	5	0	0	0	0	0	1		3	1	72,904
Lawrence	3	0	1	0	0	1	0	2	1	2	49,093
Plainfield	2	0	0	0	0	0	1			1	33,668
South Bend[3]	18	2	3	1	0	0	4	6	7	6	102,397
Terre Haute	6	3	1	0	0	0	3	3	2	2	60,773
Universities and Colleges	2	1	1	0	0	1					
Indiana University, Bloomington	1	1	0	0	0	1	1		2		53,254
Purdue University	1	0	1	0	0	0	2				44,190
Metropolitan Counties	1	0	0	0	0	0					
Madison	1	0	0	0	0	0	0	0	0	1	
State Police Agencies	3	6	0	0	0	0					
Clark County	0	1	0	0	0	0	0	1	0	0	
Floyd County	0	1	0	0	0	0	0	0	0	1	
Lake County	0	1	0	0	0	0	0	0	1	0	
Marion County	1	0	0	0	0	0	0	0	1	0	
Miami County	1	0	0	0	0	0	0	1	0	0	
Monroe County	0	1	0	0	0	0	0	0	1	0	
Orange County	0	1	0	0	0	0	0	0	0	1	
Spencer County	1	0	0	0	0	0	0	1	0	0	
St. Joseph County	0	1	0	0	0	0	0	1	0	0	
IOWA	0	1	0	0	0	0					
Total	4	2	2	2	0	0					
Cities	2	1	2	2	0	0					
Des Moines	0	1	0	0	0	0	0	1	0	0	219,159
Dubuque	1	0	0	0	0	0	0	0	1	0	58,362
Grinnell	1	0	0	0	0	0	0	0	1	0	9,000
Le Mars	0	0	0	1	0	0	0	1	0		9,989
Mount Vernon	0	0	1	0	0	0	0	1			4,426
Pella	0	0	1	0	0	0	0	0	1	0	10,208
Pleasant Hill	0	0	0	1	0	0	1	0	0	0	10,030
Universities and Colleges	1	0	0	0	0	0					
University of Iowa	1	0	0	0	0	0	1	0	0		35,671
Metropolitan Counties	1	1	0	0	0	0					
Dubuque	1	1	0	0	0	0	1	0	1	0	
KANSAS	1	0	0	0	0	0					
Total	35	18	9	7	0	0					
Cities	19	16	6	6	0	0					
Bel Aire	0	1	0	0	0	0	0	0	0	1	8,092
Burlington	0	0	1	0	0	0	1	0	0	0	2,537

Table 94. Hate Crime Incidents Per Bias Motivation and Quarter, by Selected State and Agency and Federal,[1] 2018—Continued

(Number.)

State/agency	Number of incidents per bias motivation						Number of incidents per quarter				Population[2]
	Race/Ethnicity/Ancestry	Religion	Sexual orientation	Disability	Gender	Gender Identity	1st quarter	2nd quarter	3rd quarter	4th quarter	
Chanute	1	0	0	0	0	0	1	0			9,046
Dodge City	1	1	0	0	0	0	0	0	1	1	27,756
Garden City	0	0	0	1	0	0	0	0	1	0	26,902
Goodland	0	1	0	0	0	0	1	0	0	0	4,400
Great Bend	1	0	1	0	0	0	0	0	1	1	15,251
Hutchinson	4	0	0	1	0	0	1	2	1	1	40,573
Iola	1	0	0	0	0	0	0	1	0	0	5,306
Liberal	2	1	2	1	0	0	1	3	1	1	19,725
Olathe	1	0	0	0	0	0	0	0	1	0	139,154
Ottawa	1	0	1	0	0	0	1	1	0	0	12,300
Overland Park	1	1	0	0	0	0	1	0	1	0	193,877
Pittsburg	0	1	0	0	0	0	0	0	1	0	20,210
Salina	2	0	1	1	0	0	1	0	2	1	46,862
Shawnee	1	0	0	0	0	0	0	0	0	1	65,983
St. Marys	0	1	0	0	0	0	0	0	0	1	2,646
Topeka	2	1	0	0	0	0	0	0	3	0	126,399
Valley Center	0	0	0	2	0	0	2	0	0	0	7,370
Wellington	0	3	0	0	0	0	0	0	0	3	7,775
Wichita	1	2	0	0	0	0	1	0	1	1	391,726
Winfield	0	3	0	0	0	0	0	0	0	3	12,072
Universities and Colleges	2	0	2	0	0	0					
Kansas State University	1	0	0	0	0	0	0	0	1	0	25,775
University of Kansas:											
Main Campus	0	0	1	0	0	0	0	0	0	1	31,201
Medical Center[4]	1	0	1	0	0	0	1	0	1	0	
Metropolitan Counties	7	2	0	0	0	0					
Jefferson	2	1	0	0	0	0	2	0	0	1	
Johnson	1	0	0	0	0	0	0	0	1	0	
Riley County Police Department	2	0	0	0	0	0	0	0	1	1	
Sedgwick	1	1	0	0	0	0	1	1	0	0	
Wyandotte	1	0	0	0	0	0	1	0	0	0	
Nonmetropolitan Counties	6	0	1	0	0	0					
Crawford	2	0	0	0	0	0	0	1	1	0	
Dickinson	1	0	0	0	0	0	0	1	0	0	
Franklin	1	0	0	0	0	0	1	0	0	0	
Montgomery	1	0	0	0	0	0	1	0	0	0	
Pratt	1	0	0	0	0	0	0	0	1	0	
Saline	0	0	1	0	0	0	1	0	0	0	
State Police Agencies	1	0	0	0	0	0					
Highway Patrol, Troop E	1	0	0	0	0	0	0	1	0	0	
	0	0	0	1	0	0					
Tribal Agencies											
Potawatomi Tribal	0	0	0	1	0	0	0	1	0	0	
KENTUCKY											
Total	189	16	22	3	8	2					
Cities	132	9	21	3	5	2					
Ashland	2	0	1	0	0	0	0	1	1	1	20,525
Berea	1	0	0	0	0	0	1	0	0	0	15,893
Bowling Green	8	2	0	0	2	0	6	3	1	2	68,268
Cadiz	0	0	0	0	1	0	0	0	0	1	2,637
Calvert City	1	0	0	0	0	0	0	0	0	1	2,513
Campbellsville	2	0	0	0	0	0	1	0	1	0	11,503
Columbia	1	0	0	0	0	0	0	1	0	0	4,927
Corbin	1	0	0	0	0	0	1	0	0	0	5,517
Covington	4	1	1	0	0	1	1	1	3	2	40,448
Cynthiana	1	0	0	1	0	0	1	0	0	1	6,362
Danville	2	0	0	0	0	0	0	1	1	0	16,801
Dawson Springs	2	0	0	0	0	0	0	0	2	0	2,665
Elizabethtown	1	0	0	0	0	0	0	1	0	0	30,180
Erlanger	1	0	0	0	0	0	1	0	0	0	22,993
Falmouth	0	0	1	0	0	0	0	0	0	1	2,100
Florence	4	0	0	0	0	0	2	1	0	1	32,701
Fort Mitchell	1	0	0	0	0	0	0	1	0	0	8,260
Fort Thomas	1	0	0	0	0	0	0	0	1	0	16,274
Frankfort	6	0	0	0	0	0	0	0	4	2	27,664
Fulton	1	0	0	0	0	0	0	0	1	0	2,175
Georgetown	7	0	0	0	0	0	2	2	3	0	34,351
Glasgow	2	0	0	0	0	0	0	2	0	0	14,411
Henderson	2	0	0	0	0	0	0	0	1	1	28,618
Highland Heights	1	0	0	0	0	0	1	0	0	0	7,112
Hopkinsville	2	0	1	0	0	0	0	0	2	1	30,606
Independence	1	0	0	0	0	0	0	0	0	0	28,052
Jeffersontown	3	0	0	0	0	0	0	1	1	1	27,443

Table 94. Hate Crime Incidents Per Bias Motivation and Quarter, by Selected State and Agency and Federal,[1] 2018—Continued

(Number.)

State/agency	Number of incidents per bias motivation						Number of incidents per quarter				Population[2]
	Race/ Ethnicity/ Ancestry	Religion	Sexual orientation	Disability	Gender	Gender Identity	1st quarter	2nd quarter	3rd quarter	4th quarter	
La Grange[3]	1	0	0	0	1	0	0	0	1	0	8,995
Lancaster	1	0	0	0	0	0	0	0	1	0	3,866
Lawrenceburg	1	0	0	0	0	0	1	0	0	0	11,378
Lebanon	1	0	0	0	0	0	0	0	1	0	5,668
Lexington[3]	23	3	7	1	1	0	5	7	6	15	325,579
London	1	0	1	0	0	0	1	1	0	0	8,008
Louisville Metro	9	0	2	1	0	1	5	1	1	6	682,005
Mount Washington	1	0	0	0	0	0	0	0	1	0	14,704
Murray	0	1	0	0	0	0	0	0	0	1	19,402
Newport	1	0	0	0	0	0	0	1	0	0	14,972
Nicholasville[3]	4	0	1	0	0	0	0	2	1	1	30,922
Oak Grove	1	0	2	0	0	0	1	0	0	2	7,232
Owensboro	4	0	0	0	0	0	0	2	1	1	59,686
Owingsville	1	0	0	0	0	0	0	0	1	0	1,575
Paducah	4	1	1	0	0	0	3	1	2	0	24,933
Paris[3]	3	0	1	0	0	0	2	1	0	0	9,809
Radcliff	3	0	0	0	0	0	0	1	2	0	22,576
Richmond	3	0	0	0	0	0	0	3	0	0	35,952
Russell Springs	1	0	0	0	0	0	0	0	1	0	2,588
Russellville	1	0	0	0	0	0	0	0	1	0	7,088
Shelbyville	1	0	0	0	0	0	0	0	0	1	16,138
St. Matthews	1	0	0	0	0	0	0	1	0	0	18,228
Taylorsville	1	0	0	0	0	0	0	1	0	0	1,262
Tompkinsville	1	0	0	0	0	0	0	0	0	1	2,267
Uniontown	1	0	0	0	0	0	1	0	0	0	943
Versailles	2	1	0	0	0	0	0	0	1	2	26,552
Vine Grove	1	0	0	0	0	0	0	1	0	0	6,237
Williamsburg	1	0	0	0	0	0	0	0	1	0	5,299
Wilmore	1	0	1	0	0	0	1	0	1	0	6,406
Winchester	0	0	1	0	0	0	0	1	0	0	18,505
Universities and Colleges	3	0	0	0	1	0					
Morehead State University	1	0	0	0	0	0	1	0	0	0	12,390
University of Kentucky	0	0	0	0	1	0	0	0	0	1	31,564
University of Louisville	2	0	0	0	0	0	0	1	1	0	25,091
Metropolitan Counties	18	4	0	0	0	0					
Boone	6	1	0	0	0	0	1	2	0	4	
Bourbon	0	1	0	0	0	0	0	0	1	0	
Boyd	3	1	0	0	0	0	0	2	1	1	
Campbell County Police Department	2	0	0	0	0	0	0	0	1	1	
Gallatin	1	0	0	0	0	0	0	0	1	0	
Jessamine	1	0	0	0	0	0	0	0	1	0	
Oldham County Police Department	1	1	0	0	0	0	1	0	0	1	
Scott	1	0	0	0	0	0	0	0	0	1	
Shelby	1	0	0	0	0	0	0	0	0	1	
Warren	2	0	0	0	0	0	2	0	0	0	
Nonmetropolitan Counties	10	2	1	0	2	0					
Boyle	2	0	0	0	0	0	0	0	2	0	
Clay	0	1	0	0	0	0	0	0	0	1	
Franklin	1	0	0	0	0	0	0	1	0	0	
Garrard County Police Department	0	0	1	0	0	0	0	1	0	0	
Hart	1	0	0	0	0	0	0	1	0	0	
Laurel	0	1	0	0	0	0	1	0	0	0	
Lee	1	0	0	0	0	0	0	0	1	0	
McCracken	1	0	0	0	2	0	1	0	2	0	
Montgomery	1	0	0	0	0	0	1	0	0	0	
Pulaski	2	0	0	0	0	0	1	0	0	1	
Whitley	1	0	0	0	0	0	0	0	1	0	
State Police Agencies	19	1	0	0	0	0					
Ashland	0	1	0	0	0	0	1	0	0	0	
Bowling Green	1	0	0	0	0	0	0	0	0	1	
Campbellsburg	3	0	0	0	0	0	1	0	2	0	
Cannabis Suppression Section	1	0	0	0	0	0	0	0	1	0	
Dry Ridge	1	0	0	0	0	0	0	0	1	0	
Elizabethtown	3	0	0	0	0	0	1	1	0	1	
Frankfort	2	0	0	0	0	0	0	1	1	0	
Hazard	3	0	0	0	0	0	0	0	2	1	
Madisonville	1	0	0	0	0	0	0	1	0	0	
Morehead	2	0	0	0	0	0	0	1	1	0	
West Drug Enforcement Branch	2	0	0	0	0	0	0	0	1	1	
Other Agencies	7	0	0	0	0	0					
Cincinnati-Northern Kentucky International Airport	1	0	0	0	0	0	1	0	0	0	
Fayette County Schools	1	0	0	0	0	0	0	0	0	1	
Greater Hardin County Narcotics Task Force	1	0	0	0	0	0	1	0	0	0	
Jefferson County School District	1	0	0	0	0	0	1	0	0	0	
South Central Kentucky Drug Task Force	3	0	0	0	0	0	0	0	3	0	

Table 94. Hate Crime Incidents Per Bias Motivation and Quarter, by Selected State and Agency and Federal,[1] 2018—Continued

(Number.)

State/agency	Number of incidents per bias motivation						Number of incidents per quarter				Population[2]
	Race/Ethnicity/Ancestry	Religion	Sexual orientation	Disability	Gender	Gender Identity	1st quarter	2nd quarter	3rd quarter	4th quarter	
LOUISIANA											
Total	25	13	6	0	1	0					
Cities	4	0	0	0	0	0					
Franklinton	1	0	0	0	0	0	0		1	0	3,771
Gonzales	1	0	0	0	0	0	0	0	1	0	10,916
Monroe	1	3	0	0	0	0	1	1	1	1	48,291
New Orleans	2	0	0	0	0	0	1	1	0	0	396,374
Tallulah	1	0	0	0	0	0	0	1	0	0	6,777
Westlake	1	0	0	0	0	0	1	0	0		4,627
Universities and Colleges											
Southern University and A&M College, New Orleans	0	0	1	0	0	0	0	0	0	1	3,113
Metropolitan Counties	6	11	1	0	0	0					
Bossier	2	2	0	0	0	0	0	2	2	0	
Calcasieu	2	5	2	0	0	0	4	2	3	0	
Lafourche	1	0	3	0	0	0	4	0	0	0	
Morehouse	0	0	0	0	1	0	0	1	0	0	
Ouachita	0	2	0	0	0	0	0	0	1	1	
Rapides	2	0	0	0	0	0	1	1	0	0	
St. John the Baptist	1	0	0	0	0	0	0	0	1	0	
Nonmetropolitan Counties	3	0	0	0	0	0					
Concordia	1	1	0	0	0	0	1	0	0	1	
Evangeline	6	0	0	0	0	0	0	0	6	0	
Madison	2	0	0	0	0	0	0	1	0	1	
Washington	1	0	0	0	0	0	1	0	0	0	
MAINE											
Total	11	1	6	1	0	1					
Cities	16	5	2	0	0	1					
Cities	11	1	5	1	0	0					
Biddeford	1	0	0	0	0	0	0	1	0	0	21,519
Eastport	1	0	0	0	0	0	0	0	1	0	1,258
Lewiston	0	0	1	0	0	0	0	0	1	0	36,170
Portland	7	1	3	1	0	0	3	5	2	2	66,997
Saco	1	0	1	0	0	0	0	1	0	1	19,628
South Portland	1	0	0	0	0	0	1	0	0	0	25,557
State Police Agencies	0	0	1	0	0	1					
Maine State Police	0	0	1	0	0	1	2	0	0	0	
MARYLAND											
Total	27	7	9	2	0	5					
Cities	3	2	2	0	0	0					
Baltimore	0	0	1	0	0	0	0	0	1	0	605,436
Denton	1	0	0	0	0	0	0	1	0	0	4,485
Laurel	0	1	0	0	0	0	0	1	0	0	26,038
Riverdale Park[3]	1	1	0	0	0	0	0	0	0	1	7,330
Takoma Park	0	0	1	0	0	0	0	1	0	0	18,049
Taneytown	1	0	0	0	0	0	0	0	0	1	6,795
Universities and Colleges	3	0	1	0	0	0					
Towson University	1	0	0	0	0	0	0	0	0	1	25,467
University of Maryland											
Baltimore County	2	0	0	0	0	0	0	0	2	0	15,700
College Park	0	0	1	0	0	0	0	0	0	1	43,691
Metropolitan Counties	16	5	6	2	0	5					
Anne Arundel County Police Department	3	0	1	0	0	2	2	1	3	0	
Baltimore County Police Department	1	0	2	0	0	0		0	3	0	
Calvert	1	0	0	0	0	0	0	0	1	0	
Charles	1	0	0	0	0	0	0	1	0		
Howard County Police Department	0	0	1	0	0	0	0	0	1	0	
Montgomery County Police Department	8	3	0	2	0	3	11	2	2	1	
Prince George's County Police Department	2	2	2	0	0	0	1	1	3	1	
Nonmetropolitan Counties	2	0	0	0	0	0					
Kent	2	0	0	0	0	0	0	1	0	1	
State Police Agencies	1	0	0	0	0	0					
State Police, Wicomico County	1	0	0	0	0	0	0	1	0	0	
Other Agencies	2	0	0	0	0	0					
Natural Resources Police	1	0	0	0	0	0	0	0	0	1	
Transit Administration	1	0	0	0	0	0	0	0	1	0	

Table 94. Hate Crime Incidents Per Bias Motivation and Quarter, by Selected State and Agency and Federal,[1] 2018—Continued

(Number.)

State/agency	Number of incidents per bias motivation						Number of incidents per quarter				Population[2]
	Race/ Ethnicity/ Ancestry	Religion	Sexual orientation	Disability	Gender	Gender Identity	1st quarter	2nd quarter	3rd quarter	4th quarter	
MASSACHUSETTS **Total**	200	86	69	6	5	7					
Cities	179	79	63	5	5	5					
Acton	0	1	0	0	0	0	0	1	0	0	24,038
Amherst	2	1	0	0	0	0	0	2	1	0	40,242
Andover	0	3	0	0	0	0	1	1	0	1	36,324
Arlington	4	4	1	0	0	0	4	2	3	0	45,876
Ashburnham	0	1	0	0	0	0	0	1	0	0	6,335
Ashland	0	0	0	1	0	0	1	0	0	0	17,860
Ayer	1	1	0	0	0	0	1	1	0	0	8,246
Barnstable	1	2	0	0	0	0	0	0	1	2	44,015
Belmont[3]	2	0	1	0	0	0	0	0	1	1	26,700
Boston[3]	89	18	39	0	0	2	25	37	43	39	694,673
Boxford	0	1	0	0	0	0	0	0	0	1	8,355
Braintree	1	2	0	0	0	0	0	0	2	1	37,345
Brockton	1	1	0	0	0	0	1	1	0	0	95,922
Brookline	2	0	0	0	0	0	1	1	0	0	59,199
Cambridge[3]	6	8	0	1	1	1	6	3	3	4	114,881
Chelmsford	2	1	0	0	0	0	1	1	0	1	35,264
Chicopee	1	0	0	0	0	0	0	0	1	0	55,639
Chilmark	0	0	0	0	1	0	1	0	0	0	923
Cohasset	1	0	0	0	0	0	0	1	0	0	8,665
Concord[3]	1	1	0	0	0	0	0	0	0	4	19,459
Danvers	1	1	0	0	1	0	0	0	2	1	27,703
Dracut	1	0	0	0	0	0	0	1	0	0	31,917
Easthampton[3]	1	1	1	0	0	0	0	0	1	1	16,050
Easton	1	0	0	0	0	0	0	0	0	1	25,225
Edgartown	1	0	0	1	0	0	0	0	1	1	4,357
Everett	0	1	0	0	0	0	0	1	0	0	47,005
Falmouth[3]	1	1	0	0	0	0	1	0	0	0	31,033
Framingham	3	3	0	0	0	0	1	3	2	0	72,510
Great Barrington	0	1	0	0	0	0	1	0	0	0	6,821
Groton	0	1	0	0	0	0	0	0	1	0	11,462
Haverhill[3]	6	2	1	1	0	1	3	2	2	3	64,012
Holbrook	1	1	0	0	0	0	0	0	0	2	11,052
Lawrence	0	0	1	0	0	0	1	0	0	0	80,669
Lynn	0	1	0	0	0	1	0	0	2	0	94,558
Malden	1	0	0	0	0	0	0	0	1	0	61,469
Medford	0	0	0	1	0	0	0	1	0	0	57,997
Melrose[3]	1	1	1	0	0	0	0	1	0	0	28,552
Milford	1	0	0	0	0	0	0	0	0	1	29,056
Millbury	0	1	0	0	0	0	0	1	0	0	13,802
Monson	0	1	0	0	0	0	0	1	0	0	8,890
Nantucket	1	0	0	0	0	0	1	0	0	0	11,388
Natick	1	0	0	0	0	0	0	1	0	0	36,717
Newton	2	3	2	0	0	0	0	3	1	3	89,505
Northampton	1	0	0	0	0	0	1	0	0	0	28,587
North Andover	1	0	0	0	0	0	0	0	0	1	31,394
Oak Bluffs	0	1	0	0	0	0	0	1	0	0	4,699
Palmer	1	0	0	0	0	0	0	1	0	0	12,320
Pittsfield[3]	2	1	0	0	0	0	0	1	0	1	42,298
Provincetown	0	0	2	0	0	0	0	1	1	0	2,960
Quincy	7	2	0	0	0	0	2	1	2	4	94,388
Revere	2	0	2	0	0	0	0	0	3	1	54,296
Salem	2	1	2	0	0	0	0	1	1	3	43,634
Somerville[3]	5	1	3	0	1	0	1	5	2	1	82,161
South Hadley	2	0	0	0	0	0	0	1	1	0	17,799
Spencer	0	0	1	0	0	0	0	0	1	0	11,989
Springfield	6	1	3	0	0	0	3	1	3	3	155,179
Sturbridge[3]	2	1	0	0	0	0	1	0	0	1	9,626
Swampscott[3]	2	3	0	0	0	0	0	3	0	0	15,380
Tisbury	1	0	1	0	0	0	1	0	1	0	4,131
Wales	0	0	0	0	1	0	0	1	0	0	1,902
Waltham	4	2	1	0	0	0	3	1	1	2	62,655
Watertown	0	1	0	0	0	0	0	1	0	0	36,320
Westfield	1	0	0	0	0	0	1	0	0	0	41,854
West Tisbury	1	0	0	0	0	0	0	0	0	1	2,920
Winchester	1	0	0	0	0	0	0	1	0	0	23,036
Winthrop	0	1	0	0	0	0	1	0	0	0	18,783
Worcester	1	0	1	0	0	0	0	1	1	0	186,188
Universities and Colleges	13	5	2	1	0	2					
Assumption College	1	0	0	0	0	0	0	1	0	0	2,913
Boston University	2	0	0	0	0	0	0	0	2	0	40,807
College of the Holy Cross	1	1	1	0	0	0	1	1	0	1	2,806
Dean College	1	0	0	0	0	0	0	0	1	0	1,568
Massasoit Community College[3]	1	1	0	0	0	0	0	0	0	1	10,613

Table 94. Hate Crime Incidents Per Bias Motivation and Quarter, by Selected State and Agency and Federal,[1] 2018—Continued

(Number.)

State/agency	Race/ Ethnicity/ Ancestry	Religion	Sexual orientation	Disability	Gender	Gender Identity	1st quarter	2nd quarter	3rd quarter	4th quarter	Population[2]
Northeastern University[3]	2	1	1	1	0	1	1	0	1	2	27,486
Springfield Technical Community College	0	1	0	0	0	0	0	0	1	0	7,713
University of Massachusetts, Amherst	2	1	0	0	0	1	1	0	2	1	34,778
Westfield State University	3	0	0	0	0	0	0	2	0	1	8,017
Other Agencies	8	2	4	0	0	0					
Massachusetts Bay Transportation Authority:											
Essex County	0	0	1	0	0	0	0	0	0	1	
Norfolk County[3]	2	1	1	0	0	0	1		2		
Suffolk County[3]	6	1	2	0	0	0	2	1	1	4	
Worcester[2]	5	1	0	0	0	0	2	2	0	1	185,107
Wrentham	0	1	0	0	0	0	0	0	0	1	11,838
MICHIGAN											
Total	282	48	70	19	12	0					
Cities	182	31	55	14	8	0					
Allen Park	1	0	0	0	0	0	0	0	1	0	27,020
Ann Arbor	3	5	1	0	0	0	3	5	1	0	122,571
Auburn Hills	1	0	0	0	0	0	0	0	0	1	23,579
Bad Axe	1	0	0	0	0	0	0	0	1	0	2,933
Battle Creek	0	0	2	0	0	0	0	2	0	0	60,615
Bay City	0	0	2	0	0	0	0	0	2	0	32,953
Belding	0	0	1	0	0	0	1	0	0	0	5,737
Benton Township	1	0	1	0	0	0	0	1	0	1	14,382
Bloomfield Township	1	0	0	0	0	0	0	0	1	0	42,199
Bridgeport Township	1	0	0	0	0	0	0	1	0	0	9,853
Brighton	0	0	1	0	0	0	0	1	0	0	7,635
Bronson	0	1	0	0	0	0	0	1	0	0	2,297
Burton	4	0	1	0	0	0	0	2	0	3	28,464
Cadillac	0	2	1	0	0	0	0	1	2	0	10,455
Canton Township	2	0	0	0	0	0	1	0	1	0	92,055
Chelsea	1	0	0	0	0	0	0	0	1	0	5,248
Chocolay Township	0	0	1	0	0	0	0	0	0	1	5,936
Clare	1	0	0	0	0	0	0	1	0	0	2,990
Clinton Township	2	0	0	0	0	0	1	0	0	1	101,279
Coloma Township	0	0	0	1	0	0	0	0	0	1	6,369
Dearborn	1	1	0	0	0	0	0	0	1	1	94,022
Dearborn Heights	1	1	0	1	0	0	0	1	1	1	55,495
Detroit	28	1	18	5	2	0	12	16	14	12	671,275
DeWitt Township	0	0	0	1	0	0	0	1	0	0	15,194
Dowagiac	1	0	0	0	0	0	0	0	0	1	5,738
East Lansing	0	1	1	0	0	0	0	0	1	1	46,913
Elkton	0	1	0	0	0	0	0	1	0	0	751
Escanaba	4	0	1	0	0	0	1	1	2	1	12,169
Farmington Hills	0	1	0	0	0	0	0	0	1	0	81,239
Ferndale	0	0	1	0	0	0	0	1	0	0	20,095
Flat Rock	0	1	0	0	0	0	1	0	0	0	9,967
Flint	9	0	0	0	1	0	3	0	0	7	95,677
Flint Township	1	0	0	0	0	0	0	0	0	1	30,378
Fowlerville	0	0	0	0	2	0	0	0	0	2	2,953
Frankenmuth	1	0	0	0	0	0	0	0	1	0	5,290
Fruitport Township	2	0	0	0	0	0	0	1	0	1	14,168
Garden City	2	0	0	0	0	0	1	0	0	1	26,520
Gladstone	1	0	0	0	0	0	0	0	1	0	4,721
Gladwin	1	0	0	0	0	0	0	0	1	0	2,874
Grand Blanc Township	1	0	0	0	0	0	0	1	0	0	36,489
Grand Rapids	5	0	1	0	0	0	1	1	0	4	200,428
Grandville	1	0	0	0	0	0	0	0	0	1	16,057
Grant	1	0	0	0	0	0	0	0	1	0	882
Grosse Ile Township	0	0	1	0	0	0	0	0	1	0	10,128
Hamburg Township	1	0	0	0	0	0	0	1	0	0	22,024
Hampton Township	1	0	0	0	0	0	0	1	0	0	9,458
Hamtramck	0	1	0	0	0	0	0	0	0	1	21,668
Harbor Beach	0	0	1	0	0	0	0	0	1	0	1,591
Harper Woods	1	0	0	0	0	0	0	0	0	1	13,674
Highland Park	5	1	1	0	3	0	1	4	0	5	10,794
Holland	1	2	0	0	0	0	1	1	1	0	26,322
Huntington Woods	2	0	0	0	0	0	0	0	1	1	6,328
Inkster	1	0	1	0	0	0	0	1	0	1	24,334
Kalamazoo	1	0	1	0	0	0	1	0	0	1	76,020
Kentwood	1	0	0	0	0	0	0	0	0	1	52,192
Kingsford	0	0	0	1	0	0	1	0	0	0	4,960
Lansing	2	0	0	0	0	0	1	0	0	1	112,534
Lansing Township	1	0	0	0	0	0	0	0	0	1	8,213
Litchfield	1	0	0	0	0	0	0	0	1	0	1,336
Livonia	0	0	1	0	0	0	0	1	0	0	93,740
Lowell	1	0	0	0	0	0	0	1	0	0	4,138
Ludington	1	0	0	0	0	0	0	1	0	0	8,058

Table 94. Hate Crime Incidents Per Bias Motivation and Quarter, by Selected State and Agency and Federal,[1] 2018—Continued

(Number.)

State/agency	Number of incidents per bias motivation						Number of incidents per quarter				Population[2]
	Race/ Ethnicity/ Ancestry	Religion	Sexual orientation	Disability	Gender	Gender Identity	1st quarter	2nd quarter	3rd quarter	4th quarter	
Mackinac Island	1	0	0	0	0	0	0	1	0	0	467
Madison Heights	1	0	0	0	0	0	0	0	1	0	30,100
Marquette	1	0	0	0	0	0	0	0	1	0	20,529
Marshall	0	0	1	0	0	0	0	0	0	1	6,986
Melvindale	1	0	0	0	0	0	0	1	0	0	10,291
Menominee	0	0	0	1	0	0	0	0	0	1	8,089
Meridian Township	2	0	1	0	0	0	0	1	1	1	43,072
Metro Police Authority of Genesee County	1	0	0	0	0	0	1	0	0	0	19,887
Midland	2	2	0	0	0	0	2	0	1	1	41,798
Milan	0	1	0	0	0	0	0	0	0	1	4,018
Monroe	1	0	0	0	0	0	0	1	0	0	19,754
Muskegon Township	1	0	0	0	0	0	0	0	0	1	17,879
Northfield Township	1	0	0	0	0	0	0	1	0	0	8,741
Northville Township	0	1	0	0	0	0	1	0	0	0	28,939
Norton Shores	1	0	0	0	0	0	0	0	0	1	24,578
Oak Park	0	0	1	0	0	0	1	0	0	0	29,688
Ontwa Township-Edwardsburg	1	0	0	0	0	0	0	1	0	0	6,493
Orchard Lake	1	0	0	0	0	0	0	0	0	1	2,465
Orion Township	1	0	0	0	0	0	0	0	0	1	36,193
Owosso	0	0	1	0	0	0	0	0	0	1	14,455
Pinckney	0	0	0	1	0	0	0	0	1	0	2,479
Pontiac	1	0	0	0	0	0	0	0	0	1	59,817
Port Huron	1	0	0	0	0	0	0	0	1	0	28,907
Redford Township	2	0	1	0	0	0	0	0	2	1	46,899
Richmond	0	0	0	1	0	0	0	0	1	0	5,916
Romulus	5	0	0	0	0	0	0	1	3	1	23,389
Roseville	4	1	1	0	0	0	0	2	2	2	47,524
Royal Oak	1	1	0	0	0	0	1	0	1	0	59,383
Saginaw	1	0	1	0	0	0	0	2	0	0	48,302
Saginaw Township	1	0	0	0	0	0	0	1	0	0	39,198
Sault Ste. Marie	1	0	0	0	0	0	0	1	0	0	13,557
Shelby	0	0	0	1	0	0	0	0	0	1	2,019
Shelby Township	2	0	0	0	0	0	2	0	0	0	79,878
Southfield	2	0	1	0	0	0	0	0	2	1	73,418
Southgate	2	0	1	0	0	0	3	0	0	0	28,959
South Haven	2	0	0	0	0	0	1	0	0	1	4,337
St. Clair Shores	5	0	0	0	0	0	2	0	2	1	59,618
St. Joseph	1	0	0	0	0	0	0	1	0	0	8,364
Sturgis	1	0	0	0	0	0	0	1	0	0	10,796
Tawas	1	0	1	0	0	0	2	0	0	0	4,487
Tecumseh	1	0	0	0	0	0	0	0	0	1	8,363
Thomas Township	1	0	0	0	0	0	0	1	0	0	11,488
Traverse City	2	0	1	0	0	0	0	2	1	0	15,441
Trenton	1	0	0	0	0	0	1	0	0	0	18,176
Troy	5	0	0	0	0	0	3	1	0	1	84,221
Unadilla Township	0	0	1	0	0	0	0	1	0	0	3,465
Walker	1	0	1	0	0	0	0	0	0	2	25,010
Warren	9	2	0	0	0	0	1	2	7	1	135,160
Waterford Township	2	0	2	0	0	0	0	1	0	3	73,066
Wayland	0	0	1	0	0	0	0	0	1	0	4,260
Wayne	1	0	0	0	0	0	1	0	0	0	16,862
West Bloomfield Township	2	1	0	0	0	0	0	1	1	1	65,928
Williamston	1	0	0	0	0	0	0	0	0	1	3,924
Wyandotte	0	1	0	0	0	0	0	0	1	0	24,862
Wyoming	5	2	0	1	0	0	1	2	2	3	76,498
Ypsilanti	3	0	0	0	0	0	1	0	2	0	21,298
Universities and Colleges	9	3	4	0	1	0					
Eastern Michigan University	1	1	0	0	0	0	0	0	1	1	24,545
Ferris State University	0	0	1	0	0	0	0	1	0	0	16,828
Michigan State University	1	0	1	0	1	0	1	0	1	1	55,545
Mott Community College	0	0	1	0	0	0	0	1	0	0	10,769
Oakland Community College	1	0	0	0	0	0	0	1	0	0	29,644
Saginaw Valley State University	1	0	0	0	0	0	1	0	0	0	10,320
University of Michigan:											
Ann Arbor	4	1	0	0	0	0	0	1	2	2	46,316
Dearborn	0	1	0	0	0	0	0	1	0	0	10,714
Flint	1	0	1	0	0	0	2	0	0	0	9,455
Metropolitan Counties	28	5	4	3	1	0					
Bay	1	0	0	0	0	0	0	1	0	0	
Calhoun	1	0	0	2	0	0	2	1	0	0	
Eaton	1	0	0	1	0	0	0	0	2	0	
Genesee	4	1	0	0	1	0	0	5	0	1	
Ingham	1	0	0	0	0	0	0	0	0	1	
Ionia	6	0	0	0	0	0	0	1	3	2	
Kent	3	0	3	0	0	0	0	1	4	1	
Lapeer	0	1	0	0	0	0	0	1	0	0	
Livingston	1	0	0	0	0	0	0	1	0	0	

Table 94. Hate Crime Incidents Per Bias Motivation and Quarter, by Selected State and Agency and Federal,[1] 2018—Continued

(Number.)

State/agency	Number of incidents per bias motivation						Number of incidents per quarter				Population[2]
	Race/Ethnicity/Ancestry	Religion	Sexual orientation	Disability	Gender	Gender Identity	1st quarter	2nd quarter	3rd quarter	4th quarter	
Monroe	3	0	0	0	0	0	2	0	1	0	
Muskegon	1	0	0	0	0	0	1	0	0	0	
Ottawa	5	2	0	0	0	0	6	0	1	0	
Saginaw	0	0	1	0	0	0	0	1	0	0	
Washtenaw	1	1	0	0	0	0	1	1	0	0	
Nonmetropolitan Counties	11	4	4	1	2	0					
Allegan	0	0	1	0	0	0	0	1	0	0	
Alpena	0	0	0	0	1	0	0	0	0	1	
Barry	3	0	0	0	0	0	1	0	2	0	
Charlevoix	0	0	1	0	0	0	0	1	0	0	
Chippewa	1	0	0	1	0	0	1	1	0	0	
Delta	0	0	0	0	1	0	1	0	0	0	
Gladwin	0	0	1	0	0	0	0	0	1	0	
Isabella	2	0	0	0	0	0	0	1	0	1	
Luce	1	0	0	0	0	0	0	1	0	0	
Newaygo	0	1	0	0	0	0	0	0	1	0	
Oceana	1	0	0	0	0	0	1	0	0	0	
Osceola	0	0	1	0	0	0	1	0	0	0	
St. Joseph	1	0	0	0	0	0	0	1	0	0	
Tuscola	1	0	0	0	0	0	0	0	0	1	
Van Buren	1	3	0	0	0	0	2	0	1	1	
State Police Agencies	50	5	3	1	0	0					
Alger County	0	1	0	0	0	0	1	0	0	0	
Allegan County	1	0	0	0	0	0	0	1	0	0	
Alpena County	1	1	0	0	0	0	0	1	0	1	
Arenac County	1	0	0	0	0	0	0	0	1	0	
Barry County	1	0	0	0	0	0	0	1	0	0	
Berrien County	3	0	0	0	0	0	0	0	3	0	
Calhoun County	4	0	0	0	0	0	1	1	1	1	
Chippewa County	3	0	1	0	0	0	2	0	1	1	
Delta County	1	0	0	0	0	0	0	0	0	1	
Eaton County	1	0	0	0	0	0	0	0	1	0	
Genesee County	1	0	0	0	0	0	1	0	0	0	
Hillsdale County	1	0	0	0	0	0	1	0	0	0	
Ionia County	1	0	0	0	0	0	1	0	0	0	
Iosco County	1	0	0	0	0	0	0	1	0	0	
Isabella County	1	0	0	0	0	0	0	1	0	0	
Jackson County	2	1	1	0	0	0	1	1	1	1	
Kalamazoo County	2	0	0	0	0	0	0	2	0	0	
Livingston County	2	0	0	0	0	0	2	0	0	0	
Macomb County	1	0	0	0	0	0	0	0	1	0	
Mecosta County	1	0	0	0	0	0	0	0	1	0	
Montcalm County	4	2	0	0	0	0	2	1	1	2	
Muskegon County	1	0	0	1	0	0	1	1	0	0	
Oakland County	0	0	1	0	0	0	0	0	1	0	
Saginaw County	2	0	0	0	0	0	0	0	1	1	
Schoolcraft County	2	0	0	0	0	0	0	2	0	0	
Shiawassee County	3	0	0	0	0	0	0	2	1	0	
St. Clair County	1	0	0	0	0	0	0	0	0	1	
St. Joseph County	1	0	0	0	0	0	0	0	1	0	
Van Buren County	1	0	0	0	0	0	1	0	0	0	
Washtenaw County	2	0	0	0	0	0	1	1	0	0	
Wayne County	3	0	0	0	0	0	2	0	0	1	
Wexford County	1	0	0	0	0	0	0	1	0	0	
Tribal Agencies	1	0	0	0	0	0					
Little River Band of Ottawa Indians	1	0	0	0	0	0	0	0	0	1	
Other Agencies	1	0	0	0	0	0					
Gerald R. Ford International Airport	1	0	0	0	0	0	0	0	1	0	
MINNESOTA											
Total	72	26	25	3	0	0					
Cities	62	24	23	2	0	0					
Blaine	1	0	0	0	0	0	0	0	1	0	65,649
Brooklyn Park	2	1	1	0	0	0	1	2	1	0	81,263
Columbia Heights	1	0	0	0	0	0	0	0	1	0	21,119
Coon Rapids	2	0	1	0	0	0	1	1	0	1	62,818
Detroit Lakes	0	1	0	1	0	0	0	1	1	0	9,289
Eden Prairie	0	1	0	0	0	0	0	0	0	1	64,917
Fairmont	1	0	0	0	0	0	0	0	1	0	10,053
Fergus Falls	1	0	0	0	0	0	1	0	0	0	13,839
Inver Grove Heights	1	0	0	0	0	0	0	0	0	1	35,592
Janesville	1	0	0	0	0	0	0	0	0	1	2,259
Lakeville	4	1	1	0	0	0	1	0	3	2	64,914
Mankato	7	1	0	0	0	0	1	0	4	3	42,606

Table 94. Hate Crime Incidents Per Bias Motivation and Quarter, by Selected State and Agency and Federal,[1] 2018—Continued

(Number.)

State/agency	Number of incidents per bias motivation						Number of incidents per quarter				Population[2]
	Race/ Ethnicity/ Ancestry	Religion	Sexual orientation	Disability	Gender	Gender Identity	1st quarter	2nd quarter	3rd quarter	4th quarter	
Maple Grove	1	0	0	0	0	0	1	0	0	0	72,502
Maplewood	2	2	1	0	0	0	0	1	4	0	41,339
Mendota Heights	0	1	0	0	0	0	0	0	0	1	11,381
Minneapolis	8	1	14	0	0	0	4	7	7	5	428,261
Minnetonka	0	1	0	0	0	0	0	1	0	0	53,573
Moorhead	2	0	1	0	0	0	2	0	0	1	43,657
Mounds View	1	0	0	0	0	0	0	0	1	0	13,235
New Brighton	2	0	0	0	0	0	0	0	2	0	22,978
North Branch	1	0	0	0	0	0	0	0	1	0	10,511
Northfield	1	0	0	0	0	0	0	0	1	0	19,327
Prior Lake	2	0	0	0	0	0	0	0	0	2	26,925
Red Wing	2	0	0	0	0	0	1	0	0	1	16,405
Rochester	2	3	0	0	0	0	3	2	0	0	117,037
St. Cloud	5	3	1	0	0	0	1	2	3	3	54,591
St. Louis Park	4	1	0	0	0	0	2	1	0	1	49,595
St. Paul	6	7	2	0	0	0	5	1	0	9	309,756
St. Peter	0	0	1	0	0	0	0	1	0	0	12,012
West St. Paul	1	0	0	0	0	0	1	0	0	0	19,798
Winnebago	0	0	0	1	0	0	0	0	1	0	1,339
Woodbury	1	0	0	0	0	0	1	0	0	0	70,900
Universities and Colleges	3	0	0	0	0	0					
University of Minnesota, Twin Cities	3	0	0	0	0	0	0	0	3	0	64,860
Metropolitan Counties	5	1	2	1	0	0					
Carver	1	0	1	0	0	0	1	1	0	0	
Ramsey	4	1	0	1	0	0	0	0	5	1	
Sherburne	0	0	1	0	0	0	0	0	0	1	
Nonmetropolitan Counties	0	1	0	0	0	0					
Waseca	0	1	0	0	0	0	0	1	0	0	
Tribal Agencies	2	0	0	0	0	0					
White Earth Tribal	2	0	0	0	0	0	0	0	2	0	
MISSISSIPPI											
Total	2	1	2	0	0	0					
Cities	2	1	1	0	0	0					
Brandon	2	0	0	0	0	0	0	1	0	1	24,283
Clinton	0	0	1	0	0	0	0	0	0	1	25,137
Holly Springs	0	1	0	0	0	0			1		7,614
Metropolitan Counties	0	0	1	0	0	0					
DeSoto	0	0	1	0	0	0	1	0	0	0	
MISSOURI											
Total	50	3	8	2	0	1					
Cities	44	2	6	2	0	1					
Belton	2	0	0	0	0	0	0	0	1	1	23,526
Blue Springs	4	0	0	0	0	0	1	1	1	1	55,277
Duquesne	0	0	0	1	0	0	0	0	1	0	1,736
Fulton	1	0	0	0	0	0	0	1	0	0	12,856
Gladstone	0	1	0	0	0	0	0	0	0	1	27,382
Grain Valley	1	0	0	0	0	0	0	0	1	0	14,165
Independence	1	0	2	0	0	0	0	3	0	0	117,368
Jefferson City	1	0	0	0	0	0	0	0	1	0	42,834
Kansas City	29	0	3	0	0	1	9	10	7	7	317,135
Lexington	1	0	0	0	0	0	0	0	0	1	4,531
Lilbourn	0	0	0	1	0	0	0	0	1	0	1,082
Macon	1	0	0	0	0	0	1	0	0	0	5,368
Smithville	1	0	0	0	0	0	1	0	0	0	10,012
St. Louis	1	0	1	0	0	0	0	0	1	1	306,875
Wentzville	0	1	0	0	0	0	0	1	0	0	41,057
West Plains	1	0	0	0	0	0	0	1	0	0	12,277
Metropolitan Counties	3	0	0	0	0	0					
St. Louis County Police Department	3	0	0	0	0	0		0	1	2	
Nonmetropolitan Counties	3	1	2	0	0	0					
Dade	2	0	0	0	0	0	0	1	1	0	
Henry	1	0	0	0	0	0	0	0	0	4	
Laclede	0	0	1	0	0	0	0	0	0	1	
Ste. Genevieve	0	1	0	0	0	0	0	1	0	0	
Wayne	0	0	1	0	0	0	0	0	1	0	
MONTANA											
Total	1	0	6	0	0	0					

Table 94. Hate Crime Incidents Per Bias Motivation and Quarter, by Selected State and Agency and Federal,[1] 2018—Continued

(Number.)

State/agency	Number of incidents per bias motivation						Number of incidents per quarter				Population[2]
	Race/ Ethnicity/ Ancestry	Religion	Sexual orientation	Disability	Gender	Gender Identity	1st quarter	2nd quarter	3rd quarter	4th quarter	
Cities	0	0	5	0	0	0					
Billings	0	0	1	0	0	0	1	0	0	0	110,397
Bozeman	0	0	1	0	0	0	0	0	0	1	48,101
Missoula	0	0	3	0	0	0	0	0	3	0	74,300
Universities and Colleges	1	0	0	0	0	0					
University of Montana	1	0	0	0	0	0	0	1	0	0	14,683
Metropolitan Counties	0	0	1	0	0	0					
Yellowstone	0	0	1	0	0	0	0	0	0	1	
NEBRASKA											
Total	22	2	5	4	0	1					
Cities	15	2	4	3	0	1					
Bellevue	0	0	0	1	0	0	0	0	1	0	53,683
Grand Island	0	0	2	0	0	0	0	2	0	0	51,768
La Vista	0	0	0	2	0	0	2	0	0	0	17,177
Lincoln	10	0	1	0	0	1	4	6	1	1	288,589
North Platte	0	0	1	0	0	0	0	0	1	0	23,774
Ogallala	1	0	0	0	0	0	1	0	0	0	4,512
Omaha	3	2	0	0	0	0	1	1	3	0	469,351
Valley	1	0	0	0	0	0		0	0	1	2,334
Metropolitan Counties	5	0	1	1	0	0					
Cass	0	0	1	0	0	0	0	0	1	0	
Douglas	1	0	0	1	0	0	0	2	0	0	
Howard	2	0	0	0	0	0	0	0	1	1	
Merrick	2	0	0	0	0	0	2	0	0	0	
Nonmetropolitan Counties	2	0	0	0	0	0					
Perkins	1	0	0	0	0	0	0	0	0	1	
Thurston	1	0	0	0	0	0	0	1	0	0	
NEVADA											
Total	15	11	8	0	0	0					
Cities	13	7	7	0	0	0					
Boulder City	0	0	1	0	0	0	1	0	0	0	16,112
Henderson	3	2	0	0	0	0	1	1	3	0	309,586
Las Vegas Metropolitan Police Department	7	4	5	0	0	0	5	2	5	4	1,644,390
North Las Vegas	3	0	0	0	0	0	0	1	2	0	246,951
Reno	0	1	1	0	0	0	0	0	1	1	252,341
Universities and Colleges	1	4	1	0	0	0					
University of Nevada, Las Vegas[3]	1	4	1	0	0	0	1	0	1	3	34,647
Nonmetropolitan Counties	1	0	0	0	0	0					
Clark County School District	1	0	0	0	0	0	1	0			
NEW HAMPSHIRE											
Total	7	2	3	1	0	0					
Cities	6	1	2	1	0	0					
Bedford	0	1	0	0	0	0	0	1	0	0	22,640
Carroll	0	0	1	0	0	0	0	0	0	1	730
Goffstown	1	0	0	0	0	0	0	0	0	1	17,978
Hinsdale	1	0	0	0	0	0	0	0	1	0	3,855
Lincoln	0	0	1	0	0	0	0	1	0	0	1,772
Manchester	2	0	0	0	0	0	1	0	1	0	111,422
Northumberland	1	0	0	0	0	0	0	0	0	1	2,112
Pelham	1	0	0	0	0	0	0	0	1	0	13,795
Seabrook	0	0	0	1	0	0	0	0	0	1	8,941
Universities and Colleges	0	1	1	0	0	0					
University of New Hampshire	0	1	1	0	0	0	0	1	1	0	16,599
Nonmetropolitan Counties	1	0	0	0	0	0					
Grafton	1	0	0	0	0	0	0	0	0	1	
NEW JERSEY											
Total	308	198	53	4	1	7					
Cities	277	183	46	4	1	7					
Aberdeen Township	2	0	1	0	0	2	1	2	0	2	18,378
Barnegat Township	0	0	0	1	0	0	0	0	1	0	22,777
Berkeley Heights Township	1	0	0	0	0	0	0	0	0	1	13,646
Berlin	1	0	0	0	0	0	0	0	0	1	7,495
Beverly	1	0	0	0	0	0	0	0	0	1	2,497

Table 94. Hate Crime Incidents Per Bias Motivation and Quarter, by Selected State and Agency and Federal,[1] 2018—Continued

(Number.)

State/agency	Number of incidents per bias motivation						Number of incidents per quarter				Population[2]
	Race/ Ethnicity/ Ancestry	Religion	Sexual orientation	Disability	Gender	Gender Identity	1st quarter	2nd quarter	3rd quarter	4th quarter	
Bloomingdale	1	0	0	0	0	0	0	1	0	0	8,211
Boonton	3	2	0	0	0	0	0	2	2	1	8,236
Bordentown Township	1	0	0	0	0	0	0	1	0	0	12,323
Brick Township	0	1	0	0	0	0	0	0	1	0	74,712
Bridgeton	4	1	4	0	0	0	5	0	1	3	24,386
Bridgewater Township	1	0	1	0	0	0	2	0	0	0	45,050
Brooklawn	1	0	0	0	0	0	0	0	0	1	1,904
Burlington City	1	0	0	0	0	0	1	0	0	0	9,817
Camden County Police Department	0	1	0	0	0	0	1	0	0	0	73,140
Carteret	0	1	0	0	0	0	0	1	0	0	23,921
Cedar Grove Township	0	1	0	0	0	0	0	1	0	0	12,566
Chatham	1	0	0	0	0	0	1	0	0	0	8,793
Cherry Hill Township	2	2	2	0	0	0	4	0	2	0	70,578
Cinnaminson Township	1	0	0	0	0	0	0	1	0	0	16,630
Clifton	2	2	0	0	0	0	2	1	1	0	85,732
Closter	1	1	0	1	0	0	0	0	1	2	8,691
Colts Neck Township	0	1	0	0	0	0	0	0	0	1	9,944
Cranbury Township	1	0	0	0	0	0	0	0	1	0	3,900
Deal	1	0	0	0	0	0	1	0	0	0	730
Delanco Township	2	0	0	0	0	0	2	0	0	0	4,509
Denville Township	1	0	0	0	0	0	0	1	0	0	16,737
Dover	2	0	0	0	0	0	0	0	1	1	17,982
Dumont	1	1	0	0	0	0	0	0	0	2	17,825
East Brunswick Township[3]	7	5	3	0	0	0	3	4	3	4	48,342
East Hanover Township	1	0	0	0	0	0	0	0	1	0	11,084
East Orange	0	1	0	0	0	0	0	0	0	1	64,625
East Rutherford	0	1	0	0	0	0	0	0	1	0	9,941
Edison Township	0	4	0	0	0	0	2	0	0	2	101,309
Egg Harbor Township	2	0	0	0	0	0	1	1	0	0	43,276
Elizabeth	1	0	0	0	0	0	0	0	1	0	129,080
Emerson	1	0	0	0	0	0	0	1	0	0	7,679
Englewood	6	1	0	0	0	0	1	3	1	2	28,988
Evesham Township[3]	12	10	1	0	0	0	7	8	5	2	45,354
Fair Lawn	0	2	0	0	0	0	1	0	1	0	33,413
Fort Lee	3	2	0	0	0	0	1	2	1	1	37,729
Franklin Lakes	0	5	0	0	0	0	2	1	1	1	11,191
Franklin Township, Somerset County	1	0	0	0	0	0	0	0	1	0	66,624
Freehold Borough	0	1	0	0	0	0	0	0	0	1	11,873
Freehold Township	1	2	1	0	0	0	0	2	2	0	34,896
Galloway Township	2	0	0	0	0	0	0	0	1	1	36,467
Glen Ridge	1	0	0	0	0	0	0	0	1	0	7,622
Gloucester City	1	0	0	0	0	0	0	0	0	1	11,167
Hackensack	3	1	0	0	0	0	1	2	0	1	44,926
Haddonfield	1	1	0	0	0	0	1	1	0	0	11,253
Hamilton Township, Atlantic County	1	0	0	0	0	0	0	0	0	1	87,889
Hamilton Township, Mercer County[3]	2	1	0	0	0	0	0	1	0	1	26,380
Hanover Township	1	2	0	0	0	0	1	2	0	0	14,583
Hardyston Township	1	0	0	0	0	0	0	1	0	0	7,823
Harrison Township	1	0	0	0	0	0	1	0	0	0	12,915
Haworth	0	2	0	0	0	0	0	0	0	2	3,463
Highland Park	0	1	0	0	0	0	1	0	0	0	13,989
Highlands	1	0	0	0	0	0	1	0	0	0	4,794
Hightstown	2	0	0	0	0	0	0	0	1	1	5,289
Hillsborough Township	0	0	1	0	0	0	1	0	0	0	39,796
Hillsdale	2	7	0	0	0	0	1	0	1	7	10,484
Hoboken	3	1	3	0	0	0	2	4	1	0	55,096
Holmdel Township	1	1	0	0	0	0	0	0	0	2	16,621
Hopewell Township	4	0	0	0	0	0	0	0	0	4	18,000
Howell Township	11	2	1	0	0	0	2	8	1	3	52,672
Jackson Township	0	1	0	0	0	0	1	0	0	0	56,706
Jefferson Township	0	0	1	0	0	0	1	0	0	0	21,071
Jersey City	3	1	0	0	0	0	0	1	3	0	270,175
Keansburg	7	1	3	0	0	0	3	2	3	3	9,766
Lakewood Township	2	16	0	0	0	0	3	3	11	1	102,915
Lambertville	0	0	1	0	0	0	0	1	0	0	3,811
Leonia	0	1	0	0	0	0	0	0	0	1	9,175
Lincoln Park	1	0	0	0	0	0	0	0	1	0	10,308
Linden	2	0	0	0	0	0	0	0	0	2	42,806
Little Egg Harbor Township	1	0	0	0	0	0	0	0	0	1	21,087
Little Falls Township	2	0	0	0	0	0	1	1	0	0	14,306
Livingston Township	1	1	0	0	0	0	1	1	0	0	29,820
Lodi	0	0	2	0	0	0	0	1	1	0	24,720
Long Branch	1	0	0	0	0	0	0	1	0	0	30,750
Lower Township	1	0	0	0	0	0	0	0	1	0	21,617
Madison	12	1	0	0	0	0	1	0	1	11	15,832
Mahwah Township	1	0	0	0	0	0	0	0	0	1	26,501
Manalapan Township	4	5	1	0	0	0	3	3	2	2	40,150
Mansfield Township, Burlington County	3	0	0	0	0	0	0	1	0	2	8,577
Maple Shade Township	3	0	0	0	0	0	3	0	0	0	18,772

Table 94. Hate Crime Incidents Per Bias Motivation and Quarter, by Selected State and Agency and Federal,[1] 2018—Continued

(Number.)

State/agency	Race/ Ethnicity/ Ancestry	Religion	Sexual orientation	Disability	Gender	Gender Identity	1st quarter	2nd quarter	3rd quarter	4th quarter	Population[2]
Maplewood Township	1	0	0	0	0	0	0	1	0	0	24,635
Marlboro Township	3	3	0	0	0	0	0	0	4	2	40,338
Medford Township	4	3	0	0	0	0	2	1	1	3	23,558
Mendham	0	1	0	0	0	0	1	0	0	0	4,905
Merchantville	1	0	0	0	0	0	1	0	0	0	3,712
Metuchen	0	1	0	0	0	0	0	1	0	0	14,262
Middle Township	0	0	1	0	0	0	1	0	0	0	18,358
Middletown Township	1	2	1	0	0	0	0	3	0	1	65,469
Millburn Township	0	2	0	0	0	0	0	0	0	2	20,250
Millville	1	0	1	0	0	0	0	1	1	0	27,837
Monmouth Beach	0	1	0	0	0	0	0	1	0	0	3,231
Monroe Township, Gloucester County	1	1	0	0	0	2	2	1	0	1	36,498
Monroe Township, Middlesex County	1	3	0	0	0	0	0	1	2	1	45,597
Montclair	2	1	0	0	0	0	1	0	1	1	38,893
Montgomery Township	2	0	0	0	0	0	0	0	1	1	23,515
Montville Township	0	1	0	0	0	0	1	0	0	0	21,396
Moorestown Township	6	1	0	0	0	0	2	1	3	1	20,510
Morris Township	0	1	0	0	0	0	1	0	0	0	22,183
Mountainside	0	1	0	0	0	0	0	1	0	0	6,925
Mount Holly Township	1	0	0	0	0	0	0	1	0	0	9,658
Mount Laurel Township	1	1	0	0	0	0	0	0	1	1	41,629
Neptune Township	8	8	2	0	0	1	0	0	2	17	27,825
New Brunswick	0	0	1	0	0	0	0	0	0	1	56,577
New Milford	1	1	0	0	0	0	0	0	0	2	16,701
New Providence	2	1	0	1	0	0	1	1	0	2	13,283
Newton	1	0	1	0	0	0	1	1	0	0	7,824
North Arlington	0	1	0	0	0	0	0	0	0	1	15,868
North Bergen Township[3]	1	3	0	0	0	0	0	0	1	2	63,166
Northfield	1	0	0	0	0	0	1	0	0	0	8,324
North Haledon	1	0	1	0	0	0	1	1	0	0	8,469
Ocean Township, Monmouth County	2	2	1	0	0	0	1	2	0	2	26,947
Old Bridge Township	3	1	0	0	0	0	2	1	0	1	66,321
Oradell	0	1	0	0	0	0	0	1	0	0	8,243
Paramus	1	1	0	0	0	0	0	0	0	2	26,744
Parsippany-Troy Hills Township	1	0	0	0	0	0	1	0	0	0	52,447
Paulsboro	1	0	0	0	0	0	0	0	0	1	5,812
Pemberton Township	1	0	0	0	0	0	1	0	0	0	27,212
Pennsauken Township	1	0	0	0	0	0	1	0	0	0	35,420
Piscataway Township	0	3	0	0	0	0	2	1	0	0	57,342
Pitman	3	0	0	0	0	0	0	0	0	3	8,696
Pleasantville	0	1	0	0	0	0	0	0	0	1	20,799
Point Pleasant Beach	1	0	0	0	0	0	0	0	1	0	4,472
Pompton Lakes	1	3	1	0	0	0	1	1	2	1	11,062
Princeton	0	0	1	0	0	0	1	0	0	0	31,856
Rahway	2	0	0	0	0	0	0	0	0	2	30,113
Randolph Township	2	2	0	0	0	0	1	3	0	0	25,552
Raritan Township	1	0	0	0	0	0	0	1	0	0	22,092
Ridgefield Park	1	0	0	0	0	0	0	0	0	1	13,028
Ridgewood	1	4	0	0	0	0	1	1	0	3	25,429
Riverside Township	1	0	0	0	0	0	0	0	0	1	7,875
River Vale Township	0	1	0	0	0	0	0	0	0	1	10,157
Rockaway Township	9	3	2	0	0	0	9	2	1	2	25,328
Roselle	2	0	0	0	0	0	0	1	1	0	21,787
Scotch Plains Township	0	1	0	0	0	0	0	0	0	1	24,423
Sea Girt	1	0	0	0	0	0	0	1	0	0	1,766
Secaucus	1	0	0	0	0	0	0	0	0	1	20,482
Shrewsbury	1	0	0	0	0	0	0	0	0	1	4,170
South Brunswick Township[3]	4	4	0	0	0	0	2	3	1	1	46,340
South Orange Village	2	1	0	0	0	0	0	1	2	0	16,880
South Plainfield	1	0	0	0	0	0	1	0	0	0	24,238
Sparta Township	2	0	0	0	0	0	1	0	0	1	18,694
Spotswood	1	0	1	0	0	0	1	1	0	0	8,364
Stanhope	0	1	0	0	0	0	0	0	0	1	3,306
Summit	1	4	0	0	0	0	1	0	0	4	22,125
Teaneck Township	0	1	0	0	0	2	0	1	1	1	40,939
Tenafly	0	1	0	0	0	0	0	1	0	0	14,742
Tinton Falls	2	0	0	0	1	0	1	0	2	0	17,754
Toms River Township	1	5	0	0	0	0	0	3	1	2	92,191
Totowa	1	0	0	0	0	0	1	0	0	0	10,666
Tuckerton	1	0	0	0	0	0	0	1	0	0	3,336
Union City	1	1	0	0	0	0	0	1	1	0	69,950
Verona	0	1	0	0	0	0	1	0	0	0	13,437
Vineland	2	0	0	0	0	0	0	0	2	0	60,330
Voorhees Township[3]	2	1	0	0	0	0	1	0	0	1	29,071
Washington Township, Gloucester County	0	1	0	0	0	0	0	0	1	0	47,024
Washington Township, Morris County	0	1	0	0	0	0	0	0	0	1	18,484
Washington Township, Warren County	1	0	0	0	0	0	0	0	1	0	6,434
Wayne Township	2	2	0	0	0	0	0	0	1	3	54,340

Table 94. Hate Crime Incidents Per Bias Motivation and Quarter, by Selected State and Agency and Federal,[1] 2018—Continued

(Number.)

State/agency	Number of incidents per bias motivation						Number of incidents per quarter				Population[2]
	Race/ Ethnicity/ Ancestry	Religion	Sexual orientation	Disability	Gender	Gender Identity	1st quarter	2nd quarter	3rd quarter	4th quarter	
Weehawken Township	1	0	0	0	0	0	1	0	0	0	15,567
Westampton Township	1	0	0	0	0	0	0	0	1	0	8,752
Westfield[3]	4	4	0	0	0	0	0	0	0	5	30,011
West New York	1	0	1	0	0	0	1	1	0	0	54,095
West Orange	3	1	0	0	0	0	1	2	0	1	48,071
West Windsor Township	3	0	0	0	0	0	0	2	1	0	28,277
Willingboro Township	0	0	1	0	0	0	0	1	0	0	32,124
Winslow Township	1	0	0	0	0	0	1	0	0	0	38,382
Woodbridge Township	1	0	1	0	0	0	0	1	0	1	100,884
Woodbury	12	0	3	1	0	0	3	4	4	5	9,746
Universities and Colleges	29	15	7	0	0	0					
Monmouth University	1	0	1	0	0	0	0	0	0	2	7,049
Montclair State University	6	3	0	0	0	0	3	1	0	5	23,989
Princeton University	4	0	0	0	0	0	0	1	1	2	8,483
Rutgers University											
Newark	1	0	0	0	0	0	0	0	1	0	15,098
New Brunswick[3]	12	12	6	0	0	0	7	7	9	6	56,027
The College of New Jersey	5	0	0	0	0	0	1	0	0	4	8,792
State Police Agencies	1	0	0	0	0	0					
State Police, Atlantic County	1	0	0	0	0	0	0	1	0	0	
Other Agencies	1	0	0	0	0	0					
New Jersey Transit Police	1	0	0	0	0	0	1	0	0	0	
NEW MEXICO											
Total	21	3	3	0	0	1					
Cities	20	3	3	0	0	1					
Albuquerque	19	3	3	0	0	1	8	8	9	1	560,235
Belen	1	0	0	0	0	0	1	0	0	0	7,061
Metropolitan Counties	1	0	0	0	0	0					
Bernalillo	1	0	0	0	0	0		1			
NEW YORK											
Total	153	286	69	1	1	13					
Cities	117	235	51	0	0	12					
Albany	5	4	3	0	0	0	2	3	6	1	98,322
Amherst Town	5	0	0	0	0	0	1	1	3	0	121,343
Binghamton	1	1	0	0	0	0	1	0	0	1	44,876
Buffalo	5	0	0	0	0	1	0	1	3	2	258,219
Colonie Town	1	0	1	0	0	0	1	0	1	0	79,842
DeWitt Town	0	0	1	0	0	0	0	1	0	0	25,268
Endicott Village	1	0	1	0	0	0	0	0	1	1	12,754
Hamburg Town	1	0	0	0	0	0	0	0	0	1	46,490
Hastings-on-Hudson Village	0	6	0	0	0	0	2	0	0	4	8,030
Hempstead Village	1	0	0	0	0	0	0	0	0	1	56,059
Hoosick Falls Village	0	1	0	0	0	0	0	0	1	0	3,386
Kingston	0	1	0	0	0	0	1	0	0	0	23,077
Larchmont Village	0	1	0	0	0	0	1	0	0	0	6,200
Monroe Village	1	0	0	0	0	0	1	0	0	0	8,665
Mount Vernon	3	1	0	0	0	0	2	1	1	0	68,889
Newburgh	0	0	1	0	0	0	0	1	0	0	28,282
New York	84	216	41	0	0	10	62	80	89	120	8,523,171
Niagara Falls	1	0	0	0	0	0	1	0	0	0	48,225
Pelham Village	0	1	0	0	0	0	0	0	0	1	7,036
Ramapo Town	0	1	0	0	0	0	0	1	0	0	95,068
Rochester	4	0	1	0	0	0	1	3	1	0	207,701
Rosendale Town	0	0	0	0	0	1	1	0	0	0	5,889
Saugerties Town	1	0	0	0	0	0	0	0	1	0	19,136
Southampton Town	0	1	0	0	0	0	0	0	0	1	51,231
Spring Valley Village	1	0	0	0	0	0	0	1	0	0	32,909
Tarrytown Village	0	0	1	0	0	0	0	1	0	0	11,617
Watervliet	0	0	1	0	0	0	0	0	1	0	10,115
Westhampton Beach Village	0	1	0	0	0	0	0	1	0	0	1,819
Yonkers	2	0	0	0	0	0	1	0	1	0	202,827
Universities and Colleges	6	4	0	0	0	0					
State University of New York Police:											
Alfred	1	0	0	0	0	0	1	0	0	0	4,198
Canton	1	0	0	0	0	0	0	0	0	1	5,183
Geneseo	1	0	0	0	0	0	1	0	0	0	5,941
Maritime	0	1	0	0	0	0	0	0	0	1	2,007
Purchase	0	1	0	0	0	0	0	0	0	1	4,815
Stony Brook	3	2	0	0	0	0	0	2	2	1	29,798

Table 94. Hate Crime Incidents Per Bias Motivation and Quarter, by Selected State and Agency and Federal,[1] 2018—Continued

(Number.)

State/agency	Number of incidents per bias motivation						Number of incidents per quarter				Population[2]
	Race/ Ethnicity/ Ancestry	Religion	Sexual orientation	Disability	Gender	Gender Identity	1st quarter	2nd quarter	3rd quarter	4th quarter	
Metropolitan Counties	10	21	13	1	1	0					
Dutchess	0	1	2	0	0	0	1	0	2	0	
Nassau	5	14	0	0	0	0	3	5	3	8	
Ontario	0	0	0	0	1	0	0	0	1	0	
Oswego	0	0	1	0	0	0	1	0	0	0	
Suffolk County Police Department	5	6	9	1	0	0	7	3	5	6	
Westchester Public Safety	0	0	1	0	0	0	0	0	1	0	
	10	9	3	0	0	1					
State Police Agencies											
Cayuga County	1	0	0	0	0	0	0	0	0	1	
Clinton County	1	0	1	0	0	0	0	2	0	0	
Dutchess County	0	0	1	0	0	0	0	0	1	0	
Herkimer County	0	2	0	0	0	0	1	1	0	0	
Onondaga County	1	1	0	0	0	0	0	0	0	2	
Oswego County	0	0	1	0	0	0	0	1	0	0	
Putnam County	1	0	0	0	0	0	0	0	1	0	
Rockland County	0	1	0	0	0	0	0	0	0	1	
Saratoga County	0	1	0	0	0	0	1	0	0	0	
Schoharie County	2	0	0	0	0	0	0	1	1	0	
Seneca County	1	0	0	0	0	0	0	1	0	0	
Tompkins County	0	2	0	0	0	0	2	0	0	0	
Ulster County	0	0	0	0	0	1	1	0	0	0	
Wayne County	3	0	0	0	0	0	0	0	3	0	
Westchester County	0	2	0	0	0	0	2	0	0	0	
Other Agencies	10	17	2	0	0	0					
New York City Department of Environmental Protection Police, Eastview Precinct	0	1	1	0	0	0	0	0	0	2	
New York City Metropolitan Transportation Authority	9	16	1	0	0	0	6	9	7	4	
State Park, Central Region	1	0	0	0	0	0	0	1	0	0	
NORTH CAROLINA											
Total	83	27	29	3	0	0					
Cities	70	24	22	2	0	0					
Apex	1	0	0	0	0	0	0	0	0	1	52,577
Asheville	2	1	0	0	0	0	1	1	1	0	93,186
Boone	1	0	2	0	0	0	0	0	1	2	19,524
Carolina Beach	3	0	0	0	0	0	0	1	0	2	6,352
Cary	0	5	0	0	0	0	0	0	0	5	168,700
Charlotte-Mecklenburg	13	6	4	1	0	0	6	6	5	6	931,235
Dunn	0	0	0	1	0	0	0	0	1	0	9,793
Durham	8	3	1	0	0	0	1	9	0	2	273,726
Fayetteville	3	0	0	0	0	0	1	1	1	0	210,117
Greensboro	8	0	3	0	0	0	2	1	4	4	293,298
Hendersonville	1	0	0	0	0	0	1	0	0	0	14,081
Hickory	0	1	0	0	0	0	0	0	0	1	40,617
Hope Mills	1	0	0	0	0	0	0	0	1	0	16,219
Huntersville	1	1	1	0	0	0	1	0	0	1	57,677
Jacksonville	1	0	1	0	0	0	1	0	1	0	71,715
Lexington	1	0	0	0	0	0	0	0	0	1	18,754
Mocksville	2	0	0	0	0	0	0	0	1	1	5,303
Mooresville	2	0	1	0	0	0	1	1	1	0	38,340
Morganton	1	0	1	0	0	0	0	1	1	0	16,478
New Bern	2	0	0	0	0	0	0	2	0	0	29,600
Newton	2	0	0	0	0	0	0	0	2	0	13,121
Pittsboro	3	0	0	0	0	0	1	1	1	0	4,289
Raleigh	3	4	3	0	0	0	2	1	3	4	472,472
Roanoke Rapids	4	0	1	0	0	0	1	3	1	0	14,664
Salisbury	2	0	1	0	0	0	1	0	1	1	33,901
Southern Shores	0	0	1	0	0	0	0	1	0	0	2,907
Statesville	0	0	1	0	0	0	0	0	1	0	26,975
Wilmington	5	3	1	0	0	0	1	4	0	4	120,920
Universities and Colleges	1	2	1	0	0	0					
Duke University	1	1	0	0	0	0	0	0	1	1	16,599
East Carolina University	0	1	0	0	0	0	1	0	0	0	32,388
University of North Carolina, Wilmington	0	0	1	0	0	0	0	1	0	0	18,287
Metropolitan Counties	11	1	5	1	0	0					
Buncombe	1	0	0	0	0	0	0	1	0	0	
Currituck	0	0	0	1	0	0	0	0	1	0	
Forsyth	1	0	1	0	0	0	0	1	0	1	
Franklin	2	0	0	0	0	0	0	1	1	0	
Lincoln	2	0	0	0	0	0	0	1	1	0	
New Hanover	2	0	0	0	0	0	1	1	0	0	
Pitt	1	0	3	0	0	0	0	0	1	3	
Wake	1	1	1	0	0	0	1	1	1	0	
Wayne	1	0	0	0	0	0	0	0	0	1	

Table 94. Hate Crime Incidents Per Bias Motivation and Quarter, by Selected State and Agency and Federal,[1] 2018—Continued

(Number.)

State/agency	Number of incidents per bias motivation						Number of incidents per quarter				Population[2]
	Race/ Ethnicity/ Ancestry	Religion	Sexual orientation	Disability	Gender	Gender Identity	1st quarter	2nd quarter	3rd quarter	4th quarter	
Nonmetropolitan Counties	1	0	1	0	0	0					
Greene	1	0	0	0	0	0	1	0	0	0	
Martin	0	0	1	0	0	0	0	0	1	0	
NORTH DAKOTA											
Total	4	3	3	0	0	0					
Cities	3	2	3	0	0	0					
Bismarck	1	0	1	0	0	0	0	0	1	1	74,644
Devils Lake	0	0	1	0	0	0	0	0	1	0	7,314
Dickinson	1	0	0	0	0	0	0	0	1	0	22,878
Fargo	0	1	1	0	0	0	0	0	2	0	124,906
Grand Forks	0	1	0	0	0	0	0	0	0	1	57,662
Williston	1	0	0	0	0	0	0	1	0	0	27,390
Universities and Colleges	1	0	0	0	0	0					
University of North Dakota	1	0	0	0	0	0	1	0	0	0	18,104
Metropolitan Counties	0	1	0	0	0	0					
Morton	0	1	0	0	0	0	0	1	0	0	
OHIO											
Total	218	40	54	32	2	4					
Cities	187	29	48	31	1	4					
Akron	5	0	2	1	0	0	0	2	5	1	197,690
Ashland	0	0	1	1	0	0	0	0	2	0	20,446
Austintown	0	0	1	0	0	0	0	0	1	0	35,029
Barberton	1	0	0	2	0	0	1	1	1	0	26,060
Bellefontaine	0	0	0	0	0	1	0	0	1	0	13,137
Boardman	1	0	0	0	0	0	1	0	0	0	39,121
Brunswick	1	0	0	0	0	0	0	1	0	0	34,954
Canton	2	0	0	0	0	0	0	0	2	0	70,605
Cincinnati	24	4	2	0	0	0	10	6	7	7	301,952
Circleville	0	1	0	0	0	0	0	0	1	0	13,993
Cleveland	25	4	3	4	1	1	7	5	11	15	384,666
Colerain Township	1	0	0	0	0	0	0	1	0	0	59,312
Columbus	42	6	19	4	0	0	11	23	22	15	873,582
Copley Township	1	0	0	1	0	0	1	0	1		17,307
Dayton	2	1	0	0	0	0	0	1	2	0	140,094
Defiance	0	0	0	0	0	1	0	1	0	0	16,620
Delaware	0	1	0	0	0	0	1	0	0	0	39,944
Delhi Township	0	0	1	0	0	0	0	1	0	0	29,700
Elyria	0	0	1	0	0	0	1	0			53,796
Englewood	0	1	0	1	0	0	1	0	1	0	13,474
Fairborn	1	0	0	0	0	0	1	0	0	0	33,604
Findlay	1	0	0	0	0	0	0	0	1	0	41,351
Girard	2	0	0	0	0	0	0	2	0	0	9,304
Green Township	2	0	0	0	0	0	0	0	0	2	59,132
Grove City	1	0	0	0	0	0	0	0	0	1	41,833
Hamilton	4	0	0	1	0	0	1	3	1	0	62,059
Huber Heights	2	1	2	0	0	0	0	3	1	1	36,964
Jackson Township, Stark County	1	1	0	0	0	0	0	1	0	1	40,416
Johnstown	1	0	0	0	0	0	0	0	1	0	5,054
Lancaster	1	0	1	0	0	0	0	1	1	0	40,498
Lebanon	0	0	0	1	0	0	0	0	0	1	20,696
Liberty Township	1	0	0	0	0	0	0	0	0	1	11,456
Lockland	1	0	0	0	0	0	0	0	0	1	3,462
Madison Township, Franklin County	0	0	0	3	0	0	0	0	2	1	19,241
Madison Township, Lake County	0	0	0	0	0	1	1	0	0	0	15,626
Mansfield	3	0	1	0	0	0	1	0	1	2	45,941
Marietta	1	0	0	0	0	0	0	0	1	0	13,618
Massillon	1	1	0	1	0	0	0	1	2	0	32,361
Maumee	0	0	1	0	0	0	0	0	1	0	13,720
Mayfield Heights	0	0	0	1	0	0	0	0	1	0	18,648
Medina	1	1	0	0	0	0	0	1	1	0	26,128
Mentor-on-the-Lake	2	0	0	0	0	0	0	1	0	1	7,399
Miami Township, Clermont County	2	0	0	0	0	0	1	0	1	0	42,493
Miami Township, Montgomery County	2	0	0	0	0	0	0	1	0	1	29,065
Middletown	4	0	0	1	0	0		2	2	1	46,084
Monroe	0	0	0	2	0	0	2	0	0	0	16,168
Montgomery	1	0	0	0	0	0	0	0	0	1	10,807
Montville Township	1	0	0	0	0	0	0	1	0	0	11,831
Mount Healthy	0	0	1	0	0	0	1	0	0	0	6,058
Mount Orab	0	0	1	0	0	0	0	0	1	0	3,485
Napoleon	0	0	1	0	0	0	0	0	0	1	8,236
New Albany	1	0	0	0	0	0	0	0	0	1	10,997
Newton Falls	3	1	0	0	0	0	0	1	2	1	4,516
North Canton	1	0	1	0	0	0	0	0	2	0	17,265

Table 94. Hate Crime Incidents Per Bias Motivation and Quarter, by Selected State and Agency and Federal,[1] 2018—Continued

(Number.)

State/agency	Race/ Ethnicity/ Ancestry	Religion	Sexual orientation	Disability	Gender	Gender Identity	1st quarter	2nd quarter	3rd quarter	4th quarter	Population[2]
North College Hill	1	0	0	0	0	0	0	0	1	0	9,299
Norton	1	0	0	0	0	0	0	1	0	0	11,999
Norwood	1	0	0	0	0	0	0	1	0	0	19,976
Oak Harbor	2	0	0	0	0	0	0	0	2	0	2,716
Ontario	0	0	0	1	0	0	0	0	0	1	6,056
Pickerington	1	0	0	0	0	0	0	1	0	0	20,631
Poland Township	1	0	0	0	0	0	0	0	1	0	11,888
Portsmouth	0	1	2	0	0	0	0	2	1	0	20,473
Reading	1	0	0	0	0	0	0	0	1	0	10,991
Reynoldsburg	1	0	0	0	0	0	0	0	1	0	28,025
Riverside	1	0	0	0	0	0	0	0	0	1	25,083
Ross Township	1	0	0	0	0	0	0	0	0	1	8,879
Shelby	1	0	0	0	0	0	0	1	0	0	8,984
Sidney	0	1	0	0	0	0	0	1	0	0	20,537
Solon	1	0	0	0	0	0	0	1	0	0	22,948
Springfield Township, Summit County	1	0	0	0	0	0	0	0	0	1	14,572
Sylvania Township	1	0	0	0	0	0	0	0	1	0	29,574
Tipp City	0	1	0	0	0	0	0	1	0	0	9,995
Toledo	5	0	2	0	0	0	1	1	3	2	275,023
Trotwood	3	0	0	0	0	0	0	2	1	0	24,380
Upper Arlington	2	0	0	0	0	0	1	0	1	0	35,572
Urbana	2	1	0	1	0	0	1	3	0	0	11,337
Van Wert	2	1	0	0	0	0	0	1	2	0	10,631
Village of Leesburg	1	0	0	0	0	0	0	1	0	0	1,301
Wapakoneta	0	0	0	1	0	0	1	0	0	0	9,771
Washington Court House	1	0	0	0	0	0	0	0	0	1	14,210
Wauseon	0	1	0	0	0	0	0	0	1	0	7,345
Weathersfield	4	0	0	0	0	0				4	7,988
Wilmington	3	0	0	0	0	0	0	1	1	1	12,386
Wooster	0	0	1	2	0	0	0	1	1	1	26,688
Youngstown	1	0	1	0	0	0	0	0	1	1	64,271
Zanesville	2	0	3	2	0	0	1	3	2	1	25,371
Universities and Colleges	5	4	1	0	1	0					
Bowling Green State University	2	1	1	0	0	0	2	0	2	0	20,395
Notre Dame College	1	0	0	0	0	0	1	0	0	0	2,296
Ohio State University, Columbus	2	3	0	0	1	0	0	1	1	4	64,723
Metropolitan Counties	12	3	3	1	0	0					
Clark	1	0	0	0	0	0	0	1	0	0	
Clermont	1	0	0	0	0	0	0	0	1	0	
Cuyahoga	1	0	0	0	0	0	0	0	1	0	
Fairfield	0	0	0	1	0	0	0	1	0	0	
Greene	1	0	0	0	0	0	1	0	0	0	
Hocking	0	0	1	0	0	0	1	0	0	0	
Licking	0	1	0	0	0	0	1				
Lorain	1	0	0	0	0	0	0	1	0	0	
Montgomery	1	0	2	0	0	0	1	2	0	0	
Stark	3	0	0	0	0	0	1	0	0	2	
Summit	2	0	0	0	0	0	0	0	1	1	
Trumbull	1	0	0	0	0	0	0	1	0	0	
Warren	0	2	0	0	0	0	1	0	1	0	
Nonmetropolitan Counties	10	4	2	0	0	0					
Hardin	0	1	0	0	0	0	1	0	0	0	
Logan	1	0	0	0	0	0	0	0	0	1	
Morgan	1	0	0	0	0	0	0	0	1	0	
Pike	1	0	0	0	0	0	0	1	0	0	
Preble	0	0	1	0	0	0	0	0	1	0	
Ross	4	2	0	0	0	0	2	0	2	2	
Van Wert	1	0	0	0	0	0	0	1	0	0	
Vinton	2	0	0	0	0	0	0	1	0	1	
Washington	0	0	1	0	0	0	0	0	0	1	
Wayne	0	1	0	0	0	0	0	0	0	1	
State Police Agencies	1	0	0	0	0	0					
Ohio State Highway Patrol	1	0	0	0	0	0	0	0	0	1	
Other Agencies	3	0	0	0	0	0					
Cleveland Metropolitan Park District	1	0	0	0	0	0	0	0	0	1	
Greater Cleveland Regional Transit Authority	1	0	0	0	0	0	0	0	1	0	
Ohio Department of Natural Resources	1	0	0	0	0	0	0	0	1	0	
OKLAHOMA											
Total	16	1	3	0	0	0					
Cities	9	1	3	0	0	0					
Cushing	0	1	0	0	0	0	0	0	0	1	7,687
Enid	2	0	0	0	0	0	0	0	2	0	50,214

Table 94. Hate Crime Incidents Per Bias Motivation and Quarter, by Selected State and Agency and Federal,[1] 2018—Continued

(Number.)

State/agency	Number of incidents per bias motivation						Number of incidents per quarter				Population[2]
	Race/ Ethnicity/ Ancestry	Religion	Sexual orientation	Disability	Gender	Gender Identity	1st quarter	2nd quarter	3rd quarter	4th quarter	
Jay	1	0	0	0	0	0	0	1	0	0	2,532
Maud	0	0	1	0	0	0	1	0	0	0	706
Muskogee	1	0	1	0	0	0	1	0	1	0	37,659
Norman	1	0	0	0	0	0	0	0	0	1	124,577
North Enid	0	0	1	0	0	0	0	0	1	0	928
Oklahoma City	1	0	0	0	0	0	0	0	1	0	526,630
Owasso	1	0	0	0	0	0	0	0	0	1	34,036
Tulsa	1	0	0	0	0	0	0	0	1	0	397,021
Woodward	1	0	0	0	0	0	0	0	1	0	12,323
Metropolitan Counties	4	0	0	0	0	0					
Logan	1	0	0	0	0	0	0	0	1	0	
Okmulgee	1	0	0	0	0	0	1	0	0	0	
Rogers	2	0	0	0	0	0	0	0	1	1	
Nonmetropolitan Counties	3	0	0	0	0	0					
Cherokee	1	0	0	0	0	0	0	0	0	1	
Kingfisher	1	0	0	0	0	0	0	0	0	1	
Okfuskee	1	0	0	0	0	0	0	1	0	0	
OREGON											
Total	71	16	23	2	0	8					
Cities	56	14	18	2	0	8					
Albany	1	0	0	0	0	0	0	1	0	0	46,472
Ashland	0	0	1	0	0	0	0	0	0	1	21,269
Astoria	2	0	0	0	0	0	0	2	0	0	9,918
Baker City	2	0	0	0	0	0	1	0	1	0	9,779
Bend	1	0	0	0	0	0	0	1	0	0	97,403
Corvallis	1	0	0	0	0	0	1	0	0	0	58,491
Eugene	18	7	9	1	0	4	11	15	6	7	170,771
Grants Pass	1	0	0	0	0	0	0	0	0	1	37,814
Hermiston	1	0	0	0	0	0	1	0	0	0	17,517
Hillsboro	3	1	1	0	0	0	2	1	0	2	109,121
Klamath Falls	2	0	0	1	0	0	1	1	0	1	22,242
McMinnville	1	0	0	0	0	0	0	0	0	1	34,669
Medford	0	1	0	0	0	0	0	1	0	0	82,800
Milwaukie	2	0	0	0	0	1	0	0	3	0	20,873
Newberg-Dundee	1	0	0	0	0	0	1	0	0	0	27,122
North Bend	1	0	0	0	0	0	0	1	0	0	9,705
Oregon City[3]	3	1	0	0	0	0	0	0	3	0	36,918
Portland	8	0	4	0	0	3	2	3	8	2	654,636
Reedsport	1	0	0	0	0	0	0	0	0	1	4,117
Salem	3	0	2	0	0	0	2	2	1	0	144,501
Springfield	2	0	0	0	0	0	0	1	1	0	62,786
Tigard	1	1	1	0	0	0	1	0	1	1	53,880
West Linn	1	2	0	0	0	0	0	1	1	1	26,934
Woodburn	0	1	0	0	0	0	1	0	0	0	26,031
Universities and Colleges	1	1	0	0	0	0					
Portland State University	1	1	0	0	0	0	0	0	1	1	36,762
Metropolitan Counties											
Universities and Colleges	13	1	4	0	0	0					
Clackamas[3]	5	0	1	0	0	0	2	1	1	1	
Jackson	1	0	0	0	0	0	0	0	0	1	
Lane	0	0	1	0	0	0	0	0	0	1	
Linn	2	0	0	0	0	0	0	1	1	0	
Washington	5	0	2	0	0	0	0	3	2	2	
Yamhill	0	1	0	0	0	0	1	0	0	0	
Nonmetropolitan Counties	1	0	1	0	0	0					
Morrow	1	0	0	0	0	0	0	1	0	0	
Wasco	0	0	1	0	0	0	1	0	0	0	
PENNSYLVANIA											
Total	43	19	5	0	0	0					
Cities	37	18	4	0	0	0					
Bethlehem	1	0	0	0	0	0	1	0	0	0	55,878
Horsham Township	0	1	0	0	0	0	0	0	0	1	26,615
Northern York County Regional	1	0	0	0	0	0	0	1	0	0	69,814
Old Lycoming Township	0	0	1	0	0	0	0	0	1	0	4,927
Philadelphia	24	14	3	0	0	0	8	6	5	22	1,586,916
Pittsburgh	7	2	0	0	0	0	0	2	3	4	302,544
State College	1	0	0	0	0	0	1	0	0	0	58,781
Washington Township, Franklin County	2	1	0	0	0	0	0	2	0	1	14,671
Watsontown	1	0	0	0	0	0	1	0	0	0	2,275

Table 94. Hate Crime Incidents Per Bias Motivation and Quarter, by Selected State and Agency and Federal,[1] 2018—Continued

(Number.)

State/agency	Number of incidents per bias motivation						Number of incidents per quarter				Population[2]
	Race/ Ethnicity/ Ancestry	Religion	Sexual orientation	Disability	Gender	Gender Identity	1st quarter	2nd quarter	3rd quarter	4th quarter	
Universities and Colleges	4	1	1	0	0	0					
California University	0	0	1	0	0	0	0	0	1	0	9,869
Lehigh University	1	0	0	0	0	0	0	1	0	0	7,586
Pennsylvania State University, University Park	2	1	0	0	0	0	0	1	1	0	50,920
University of Pittsburgh, Pittsburgh	1	0	0	0	0	0	0	1	0	0	31,947
State Police Agencies	2	0	0	0	0	0					
Snyder County	1	0	0	0	0	0	0	0	1	0	
York County	1	0	0	0	0	0	1	0	0	0	
RHODE ISLAND											
Total	6	3	4	0	0	0					
Cities	5	3	4	0	0	0					
Coventry	1	0	0	0	0	0	1	0	0	0	34,814
Cumberland	1	0	0	0	0	0	0	1	0	0	35,018
Johnston	0	0	1	0	0	0	1	0	0	0	29,317
Newport	0	0	1	0	0	0	0	1	0	0	24,863
North Kingstown	0	1	0	0	0	0	0	0	0	1	26,101
Pawtucket	1	0	0	0	0	0	0	1	0	0	71,892
Providence	2	2	1	0	0	0	0	1	2	2	180,169
South Kingstown	0	0	1	0	0	0	0	1	0	0	30,816
State Police Agencies	1	0	0	0	0	0					
State Police, Hope Valley	1	0	0	0	0	0	0	1	0	0	
SOUTH CAROLINA											
Total	67	28	8	2	0	6					
Cities	40	7	6	2	0	0					
Beaufort	1	0	0	0	0	0	0	1	0	0	13,920
Blacksburg	0	0	1	0	0	0	0	0	0	1	1,899
Bluffton	0	1	0	0	0	0	0	0	0	1	22,578
Calhoun Falls	5	0	0	1	0	0	0	1	2	3	1,925
Cayce	1	0	0	0	0	0	0	1	0	0	13,481
Chapin	1	0	0	0	0	0	0	0	1	0	1,629
Conway	0	1	1	0	0	0	0	1	1	0	24,784
Duncan	0	0	1	0	0	0	0	0	1	0	3,480
Easley	1	0	0	0	0	0	0	0	1	0	21,144
Elloree	4	0	0	0	0	0	0	1	0	3	652
Estill	0	0	1	0	0	0	0	0	1	0	1,807
Forest Acres	1	0	0	0	0	0	0	1	0	0	10,375
Georgetown	1	1	0	0	0	0	0	0	1	1	8,819
Greenville	1	0	0	0	0	0	1	0	0	0	69,608
Greer	2	0	0	0	0	0	1	0	1	0	23,691
Hartsville	1	1	0	0	0	0	2	0	0	0	7,608
Holly Hill	1	0	0	0	0	0	0	1	0	0	1,190
Inman	1	0	0	0	0	0	0	0	0	1	2,341
Lane	0	0	0	1	0	0	1	0	0	0	456
Manning	1	0	0	0	0	0	0	0	1	0	3,958
Myrtle Beach	1	0	0	0	0	0	0	0	0	1	33,687
North Charleston	2	0	0	0	0	0	0	1	0	1	90,159
Pickens	1	0	0	0	0	0	0	0	0	1	3,170
Rock Hill	3	1	0	0	0	0	1	1	1	1	74,049
South Congaree	1	0	1	0	0	0	0	2	0	0	2,466
Springfield	2	0	0	0	0	0	0	0	0	2	488
Summerville	1	2	0	0	0	0	0	0	1	2	45,656
Winnsboro	5	0	0	0	0	0	1	0	2	2	3,197
Yemassee	0	0	1	0	0	0	0	0	0	1	825
York	2	0	0	0	0	0	0	1	1	0	8,203
Universities and Colleges	4	0	0	0	0	0					
Benedict College	3	0	0	0	0	0	1	1	1	0	2,552
Medical University of South Carolina	1	0	0	0	0	0	0	0	0	1	3,454
Metropolitan Counties	16	6	1	0	0	1					
Anderson	0	1	0	0	0	0	0	0	1	0	
Beaufort	1	1	1	0	0	0	1	0	1	1	
Calhoun	1	0	0	0	0	0	0	0	1	0	
Charleston	4	0	0	0	0	0	1	0	1	2	
Fairfield	0	0	0	0	0	1	0	0	0	1	
Florence	3	0	0	0	0	0	2	0	0	1	
Horry County Police Department	1	0	0	0	0	0	0	0	0	1	
Kershaw	1	1	0	0	0	0	1	0	0	1	
Laurens	2	0	0	0	0	0	0	1	1	0	
Pickens	3	3	0	0	0	0	0	0	2	4	
Nonmetropolitan Counties	6	15	1	0	0	5					
Bamberg	0	7	0	0	0	0	1	3	3	0	
Cherokee	0	1	0	0	0	0	1	0	0	0	

Table 94. Hate Crime Incidents Per Bias Motivation and Quarter, by Selected State and Agency and Federal,[1] 2018—Continued

(Number.)

State/agency	Number of incidents per bias motivation						Number of incidents per quarter				Population[2]
	Race/ Ethnicity/ Ancestry	Religion	Sexual orientation	Disability	Gender	Gender Identity	1st quarter	2nd quarter	3rd quarter	4th quarter	
Colleton	2	1	0	0	0	0	0	3	0	0	
Dillon	1	0	0	0	0	0	0	0	1	0	
Georgetown	0	0	1	0	0	1	0	1	0	1	
Greenwood	1	2	0	0	0	4	2	2	1	2	
Hampton	1	0	0	0	0	0	0	0	1	0	
Marlboro	1	0	0	0	0	0	0	1	0	0	
Oconee	0	4	0	0	0	0	0	2	0	2	
Other Agencies	1	0	0	0	0	0					
Lexington County Medical Center	1	0	0	0	0	0	0	0	0	1	
SOUTH DAKOTA											
Total	17	0	3	0	0	0					
Cities	13	0	2	0	0	0					
Box Elder	1	0	0	0	0	0	1	0	0	0	6,508
Brookings	1	0	1	0	0	0	0	0	0	2	24,206
Flandreau	2	0	0	0	0	0	0	1	0	1	2,332
Huron	1	0	0	0	0	0	0	1	0	0	13,193
Rapid City	1	0	0	0	0	0	1	0	0	0	75,290
Sioux Falls	5	0	1	0	0	0	1	1	2	2	152,374
Vermillion	1	0	0	0	0	0	0	0	1	0	10,804
Watertown	1	0	0	0	0	0	0	0	0	1	22,323
Metropolitan Counties	2	0	0	0	0	0					
Meade	1	0	0	0	0	0	0	0	1	0	
Turner	1	0	0	0	0	0	0	0	1	0	
Nonmetropolitan Counties	2	0	1	0	0	0					
Brookings	1	0	0	0	0	0	0	1	0	0	
Custer	0	0	1	0	0	0	0	1	0	0	
Jones	1	0	0	0	0	0	0	0	0	1	
TENNESSEE											
Total	100	26	29	13	2	4	0				
Cities	60	15	21	8	0	4					
Alcoa	1	2	0	0	0	0	0	0	1	2	10,506
Algood	0	0	0	1	0	0	0	1	0	0	4,517
Bartlett[3]	3	1	0	0	0	0	1	0	2	0	59,407
Brighton	1	0	0	0	0	0	0	1	0	0	2,910
Chattanooga	4	3	1	1	0	1	0	1	5	4	180,397
Clarksville	4	0	0	0	0	0	0	3	0	1	156,264
Cleveland	3	0	1	0	0	0	1	1	0	2	44,954
Clifton	0	1	0	0	0	0	1	0	0	0	2,676
Clinton	1	0	0	0	0	0	0	0	1	0	10,137
Covington	0	0	0	1	0	0	0	0	1	0	8,794
Crossville	1	0	0	0	0	0	0	0	1	0	11,535
Dandridge	0	0	1	0	0	0	0	0	1	0	2,981
Dover	0	1	0	0	0	0	1	0	0	0	1,461
Dyersburg	0	0	2	0	0	0	0	0	0	2	16,382
Elizabethton	2	0	1	0	0	0	1	0	0	2	13,657
Franklin	0	2	2	0	0	0	1	2	0	1	80,825
Germantown	1	0	0	0	0	0	0	0	1	0	39,179
Greenbrier	0	0	0	0	0	1	0	1	0	0	6,899
Greeneville	2	0	0	1	0	0	0	0	3	0	14,867
Hendersonville	1	0	0	0	0	0	0	0	1	0	58,437
Jackson	1	0	0	0	0	0	1	0	0	0	66,848
Kingsport	2	0	0	0	0	0	0	0	0	2	50,565
Knoxville	4	2	3	1	0	0	5	3	1	1	188,653
Lebanon	5	0	0	0	0	0	1	1	3	0	33,181
Maryville	2	0	0	0	0	0	0	2	0	0	28,961
McMinnville	1	0	0	0	0	0	1	0	0	0	13,668
Memphis	3	0	3	0	0	0	0	2	2	2	652,226
Metropolitan Nashville Police Department	3	0	0	0	0	2	3	0	1	1	686,492
Millington	3	0	0	2	0	0	2	0	2	1	11,016
Morristown	1	0	1	0	0	0	0	1	1	0	29,859
Mount Juliet	1	1	0	0	0	0	0	0	1	1	36,397
Munford	1	0	0	0	0	0	0	1	0	0	6,090
Murfreesboro	2	0	3	0	0	0	0	1	1	3	140,702
Oak Ridge	2	0	1	0	0	0	0	1	0	2	26,053
Pigeon Forge	1	0	0	0	0	0	0	0	0	1	6,291
Ripley	0	1	0	0	0	0	0	1	0	0	7,977
Sevierville	0	0	1	0	0	0	0	1	0	0	16,999
Shelbyville	0	0	1	0	0	0	1	0	0	0	21,708
Springfield	0	1	0	0	0	0	0	1	0	0	16,896
Spring Hill	3	0	0	0	0	0	0	2	1	0	31,100
Trenton	1	0	0	0	0	0	1	0	0	0	4,043
Whitwell	0	0	0	1	0	0	1	0	0	0	1,706

Table 94. Hate Crime Incidents Per Bias Motivation and Quarter, by Selected State and Agency and Federal,[1] 2018—Continued

(Number.)

State/agency	Number of incidents per bias motivation						Number of incidents per quarter				Population[2]
	Race/ Ethnicity/ Ancestry	Religion	Sexual orientation	Disability	Gender	Gender Identity	1st quarter	2nd quarter	3rd quarter	4th quarter	
Universities and Colleges	2	0	1	0	0	0					
Tennessee State University	0	0	1	0	0	0	0	0	0	1	9,820
Vanderbilt University	2	0	0	0	0	0	1	0	1	0	13,397
Metropolitan Counties	23	7	4	4	1	0					
Blount	1	0	2	0	0	0	0	0	3	0	
Bradley	3	1	0	0	0	0	1	1	2	0	
Carter	0	0	1	0	0	0	0	0	1	0	
Gibson	6	1	0	0	0	0	2	1	2	2	
Hamilton	0	2	0	0	0	0	1	1	0	0	
Jefferson	0	1	0	0	0	0	0	0	0	1	
Maury	1	0	0	0	0	0	0	1	0	0	
Montgomery[3]	1	0	1	0	1	0	0	1	1	0	
Robertson	0	1	0	0	0	0	0	0	1	0	
Rutherford	1	0	0	0	0	0	0	1	0	0	
Shelby	5	0	0	1	0	0	1	2	0	3	
Sullivan	1	1	0	3	0	0	0	0	3	2	
Washington	3	0	0	0	0	0	0	1	1	1	
Williamson	1	0	0	0	0	0	0	1	0	0	
Nonmetropolitan Counties	4	2	2	1	0	0					
Benton	0	1	0	0	0	0	1	0	0	0	
Hardeman	0	1	0	0	0	0	0	0	0	1	
Hickman	0	0	0	1	0	0	0	0	0	1	
McMinn	1	0	0	0	0	0	0	1	0	0	
Meigs	1	0	1	0	0	0	2	0	0	0	
Monroe	1	0	1	0	0	0	0	0	2	0	
Sevier	1	0	0	0	0	0	1	0	0	0	
State Police Agencies	10	2	1	0	1	0					
Department of Safety[3]	10	2	1	0	1	0	6	4	1	1	
Other Agencies	1	0	0	0	0	0					
Tennessee Bureau of Investigation	1	0	0	0	0	0	0	1	0	0	
TEXAS **Total**	314	59	50	16	3	15					
Cities	241	50	42	14	3	14					
Abilene	3	2	0	0	0	0	0	1	1	3	116,805
Addison	0	0	0	0	0	1	0	0	0	1	15,839
Arlington	8	2	1	0	0	0	0	2	2	7	400,920
Austin	13	0	4	1	0	1	7	5	4	3	919,709
Balch Springs	1	0	0	0	0	0	0	1	0	0	25,565
Bellmead	1	0	0	0	0	0	0	0	1	0	10,587
Blanco	1	0	0	0	0	0	0	0	1	0	2,062
Borger	1	0	0	0	0	0	1	0	0	0	12,675
Breckenridge	1	0	0	0	0	0	0	1	0	0	5,396
Brenham	3	1	1	0	0	0	0	2	1	2	17,116
Bridgeport	0	0	1	0	0	0	1	0	0	0	6,691
Brownsville	1	0	0	0	0	0	0	0	1	0	184,461
Brownwood	1	0	0	0	0	0	0	0	1	0	18,772
Burleson	1	0	0	0	0	0	1	0	0	0	37,451
Canyon	1	1	0	0	0	0	0	0	1	1	15,608
Carrollton	1	0	0	0	0	0	0	0	0	1	81,238
Carthage	1	0	0	0	0	0	0	0	0	1	6,555
Cedar Park	2	0	0	3	0	0	0	0	0	5	70,496
Cisco	0	0	0	0	1	0	0	0	1	0	3,789
Conroe	0	1	0	0	0	0	0	0	0	1	87,544
Corpus Christi	1	0	0	0	0	0	0	1	0	0	328,614
Dallas	15	4	7	2	0	3	1	3	14	13	1,278,345
Dayton	0	1	0	0	0	0	0	1	0	0	8,070
Decatur	9	0	0	0	0	0	4	2	2	1	6,826
Del Rio	0	0	1	0	0	0	0	1	0	0	36,007
Denton	3	0	1	0	0	0	2	1	1	0	139,262
DeSoto	0	0	1	0	0	0	0	1	0	0	54,201
Dumas	8	1	0	0	0	0	4	3	1	1	14,790
El Campo	2	0	0	0	0	0	0	0	0	2	11,764
Elgin	1	0	0	0	0	0	0	1	0	0	8,874
El Paso	0	1	1	0	0	0	1	1	0	0	688,442
Ennis	6	1	0	0	0	1	2	0	3	3	19,367
Ferris	1	0	0	0	0	0	0	1	0	0	2,649
Fort Worth[3]	18	2	5	1	0	0	5	13	6	0	884,233
Freeport	13	0	0	1	0	0	5	2	7	0	12,185
Frisco	0	0	1	0	0	0	0	0	0	1	115,650
Garland	1	0	0	0	0	0	0	0	0	1	239,220
Georgetown	1	0	0	0	0	0	0	1	0	0	74,709
Gladewater	1	0	0	0	0	0	0	0	0	1	3,847

Table 94. Hate Crime Incidents Per Bias Motivation and Quarter, by Selected State and Agency and Federal,[1] 2018—Continued

(Number.)

State/agency	Number of incidents per bias motivation						Number of incidents per quarter				Population[2]
	Race/ Ethnicity/ Ancestry	Religion	Sexual orientation	Disability	Gender	Gender Identity	1st quarter	2nd quarter	3rd quarter	4th quarter	
Graham	2	0	0	0	0	0	1	0	1	0	8,656
Grand Prairie	3	0	0	1	0	0	1	2	0	1	135,214
Hamilton	1	0	0	0	0	0	1	0	0	0	2,994
Harlingen	2	1	0	0	0	0	0	0	1	2	65,525
Hedwig Village	1	0	0	0	0	0	0	0	1	0	2,685
Henderson	3	1	0	0	0	0	0	2	0	2	13,241
Highland Village	0	0	1	0	0	0	0	0	0	1	16,805
Hillsboro	3	0	0	0	0	0	0	0	3	0	8,422
Horseshoe Bay	0	1	0	0	0	0	1	0	0	0	3,097
Houston	13	4	6	0	0	2	10	3	9	3	2,296,862
Iowa Park	1	0	0	0	0	0	0	0	1	0	6,352
Jacksonville	2	0	0	0	0	0	1	0	1	0	14,960
Katy	2	0	0	0	0	0	0	1	0	1	14,964
Keller	0	0	1	0	0	0	0	1	0	0	48,439
Kyle	1	0	1	0	0	0	0	1	1	0	46,155
Lampasas	1	0	0	0	0	0	1	0	0	0	7,992
League City	2	0	0	0	0	0	0	0	2	0	106,264
Leander	0	0	0	1	0	0	0	0	0	1	51,602
Levelland	1	0	0	0	0	0	0	0	1	0	13,646
Livingston	0	1	0	0	0	0	0	1	0	0	5,128
Longview	2	0	0	0	0	1	1	1	1	0	79,705
Lubbock	4	1	2	0	0	0	0	0	5	2	257,372
Lyford	1	0	0	0	0	0	1	0	0	0	2,546
Manor	1	0	0	0	0	0	1	0	0	0	10,102
Mesquite	1	0	0	0	0	0	0	0	0	1	144,425
Mineral Wells	0	2	0	0	0	0	1	0	0	1	14,572
Mont Belvieu	4	0	0	0	0	0	3	0	0	1	6,301
Nacogdoches	2	0	0	0	0	0	0	0	2	0	33,703
New Braunfels	2	1	0	1	0	0	1	1	2	0	68,300
North Richland Hills	2	0	0	0	0	1	1	0	0	2	71,498
Oak Ridge North	4	0	0	0	0	0	1	1	2	0	3,143
Odessa	6	2	1	0	0	0	0	3	5	1	117,453
Orange	7	1	0	0	0	0	1	3	3	1	19,137
Palestine	2	0	0	0	0	0	0	0	2	0	18,238
Pampa	0	0	1	0	0	1	1	1	0	0	17,412
Pearland	1	0	1	0	0	0	0	1	1	0	117,846
Pflugerville	6	0	1	0	1	1	2	4	2	1	65,556
Plainview	12	9	0	2	0	2	6	6	6	7	20,569
Port Isabel	2	0	0	0	0	0	2	0	0	0	5,064
Rockwall	0	1	0	0	0	0	0	1	0	0	45,183
Rosenberg	2	0	1	0	0	0	0	2	0	1	38,541
Rusk	2	0	0	0	0	0	0	0	1	1	5,539
San Antonio	3	2	1	0	0	0	1	2	1	2	1,539,300
Sanger	1	0	0	0	0	0	0	1	0	0	8,457
San Juan	1	0	0	0	0	0	0	0	1	0	37,398
San Saba	0	1	0	0	0	0	1	0	0	0	3,059
Seven Points	1	0	0	0	0	0	1	0	0	0	1,424
Silsbee	2	1	0	0	0	0	0	1	2	0	6,734
Stafford	0	1	0	0	1	0	1	1	0	0	18,079
Sweetwater	1	0	0	0	0	0	1	0	0	0	10,530
Teague	1	0	0	0	0	0	0	0	0	1	3,498
Temple	3	0	0	0	0	0	0	0	2	1	75,706
Tyler	1	0	0	0	0	0	0	1	0	0	106,159
Victoria	1	0	0	1	0	0	1	0	0	1	67,766
Vidor	1	1	0	0	0	0	0	1	0	1	10,875
Waco[3]	1	2	1	0	0	0	0	1	2	0	138,091
Watauga	1	0	0	0	0	0	0	0	1	1	24,757
Wichita Falls	2	0	0	0	0	0	0	0	2	0	104,738
Universities and Colleges	5	0	2	1	0	0					
Angelo State University	1	0	1	0	0	0	1	0	1	0	11,025
Stephen F. Austin State University	1	0	0	0	0	0	0	0	0	1	14,493
University of Houston, Central Campus	2	0	0	0	0	0	1	1	0	0	50,293
University of Texas:											
Arlington	0	0	1	0	0	0	0	0	0	1	59,019
Houston	1	0	0	1	0	0	1	0	0	1	6,634
Metropolitan Counties	55	4	5	1	0	0					
Brazoria	0	0	1	0	0	0	0	0	0	1	
Chambers	0	0	1	0	0	0	0	1	0	0	
Fort Bend	2	0	0	0	0	0	0	2	0	0	
Hudspeth	48	0	0	0	0	0	0	14	14	20	
Liberty	2	0	0	0	0	0	0	1	0	1	
Lubbock	1	0	0	0	0	0	1	0	0	0	
Parker	0	1	1	0	0	0	1	0	0	1	
Potter	1	1	1	0	0	0	0	1	0	2	
Smith	1	0	0	0	0	0	0	0	1	0	
Travis	0	1	1	0	0	0	0	2	0	0	
Williamson	0	0	0	1	0	0	0	0	0	1	
Wise	0	1	0	0	0	0	0	0	1	0	

Table 94. Hate Crime Incidents Per Bias Motivation and Quarter, by Selected State and Agency and Federal,[1] 2018—Continued

(Number.)

State/agency	Number of incidents per bias motivation						Number of incidents per quarter				Population[2]
	Race/ Ethnicity/ Ancestry	Religion	Sexual orientation	Disability	Gender	Gender Identity	1st quarter	2nd quarter	3rd quarter	4th quarter	
Nonmetropolitan Counties	12	4	1	0	0	0					
Bee	2	0	0	0	0	0	0	1	1	0	
Cherokee	3	1	0	0	0	0	2	0	1	1	
Deaf Smith	1	0	0	0	0	0		0	0	1	
Delta	1	0	0	0	0	0	0	0	1	0	
Erath	0	0	1	0	0	0	0	0	1	0	
Floyd	2	0	0	0	0	0	1	1	0	0	
Houston	2	1	0	0	0	0	1	0	1	1	
Navarro	0	1	0	0	0	0	1	0	0	0	
Ward	1	0	0	0	0	0	0	0	0	1	
Washington	0	1	0	0	0	0	0	1	0	0	
Other Agencies	1	1	0	0	0	1					
Independent School District											
Calhoun County	0	1	0	0	0	0	1	0	0	0	
Pflugerville	0	0	0	0	0	1	0	0	0	1	
Spring Branch	1	0	0	0	0	0	0	1	0	0	
UTAH											
Total	20	7	4	1	0	1					
Cities	18	4	4	1	0	0					
Bountiful	0	0	1	0	0	0	1	0	0	0	44,317
Clearfield	1	0	0	0	0	0	0	0	1	0	31,558
Draper	1	0	0	0	0	0	0	0	0	1	46,257
Farmington	0	1	0	0	0	0	0	0	0	1	25,006
Hurricane	0	1	0	0	0	0	1	0	0	0	17,676
Layton	3	0	0	1	0	0	2	0	1	1	78,052
Price	4	1	0	0	0	0	2	0	3	0	8,201
Salt Lake City	2	0	2	0	0	0	0	1	2	1	202,633
Saratoga Springs	1	0	0	0	0	0	0	0	1	0	31,786
South Salt Lake	1	0	0	0	0	0	0	1	0	0	25,160
St. George	1	0	0	0	0	0	0	1	0	0	86,202
Vernal	1	1	0	0	0	0	0	0	0	2	10,484
Washington	1	0	0	0	0	0	0	0	1	0	27,705
West Bountiful	1	0	1	0	0	0	0	0	0	2	5,705
Woods Cross	1	0	0	0	0	0	0	0	0	1	11,600
Nonmetropolitan Counties	0	1	0	0	0	0					
Wayne	0	1	0	0	0	0	0	1	0	0	
State Police Agencies	1	0	0	0	0	0					
Utah Highway Patrol	1	0	0	0	0	0	0	0	1	0	
Other Agencies	1	2	0	0	0	1					
Utah Transit Authority	1	2	0	0	0	1	3	0	0	1	
VERMONT											
Total	30	11	3	1	0	0					
Cities	25	8	1	1	0	0					
Barre	1	0	0	0	0	0	0	0	0	1	8,605
Barre Town	1	0	0	0	0	0	0	1	0	0	7,693
Bellows Falls	0	0	1	0	0	0	0	1	0	0	2,993
Brandon	1	0	0	0	0	0	0	1	0	0	3,766
Brattleboro	1	2	0	0	0	0	0	0	2	1	11,410
Burlington	7	1	0	0	0	0	5	1	1	1	42,212
Essex	1	0	0	0	0	0	0	0	1	0	21,803
Hartford	1	0	0	0	0	0	0	1	0	0	9,567
Lyndonville	1	0	0	0	0	0	1	0	0	0	1,157
Milton	0	0	0	1	0	0	0	0	1	0	11,024
Montpelier	1	0	0	0	0	0	0	0	0	1	7,434
Morristown	1	1	0	0	0	0	0	1	1	0	5,450
South Burlington	1	2	0	0	0	0	2	0	1	0	19,318
Springfield	1	0	0	0	0	0	1	0	0	0	8,864
St. Albans	1	0	0	0	0	0	0	0	0	1	6,777
St. Johnsbury	1	0	0	0	0	0	0	1	0	0	7,158
Stowe	1	0	0	0	0	0	0	1	0	0	4,495
Swanton	0	1	0	0	0	0	0	1	0	0	6,560
Williston	1	1	0	0	0	0	1	0	1	0	9,778
Winhall	3	0	0	0	0	0	0	0	3	0	730
Universities and Colleges	1	2	1	0	0	0					
University of Vermont	1	2	1	0	0	0	4	0	0	0	15,069
Metropolitan Counties	1	0	0	0	0	0					
Chittenden	1	0	0	0	0	0	0	1	0	0	
Nonmetropolitan Counties	1	0	0	0	0	0					
Windham	1	0	0	0	0	0	0	0	1	0	

Table 94. Hate Crime Incidents Per Bias Motivation and Quarter, by Selected State and Agency and Federal,[1] 2018—Continued

(Number.)

State/agency	Number of incidents per bias motivation						Number of incidents per quarter				Population[2]
	Race/ Ethnicity/ Ancestry	Religion	Sexual orientation	Disability	Gender	Gender Identity	1st quarter	2nd quarter	3rd quarter	4th quarter	
State Police Agencies	2	1	1	0	0	0					
State Police											
Middlesex	0	0	1	0	0	0	0	0	1	0	
Rutland	1	0	0	0	0	0	0	0	1	0	
Shaftsbury	0	1	0	0	0	0	0	0	1	0	
Vermont State Police Headquarters Bureau of Criminal Investigations	1	0	0	0	0	0	0	1	0	0	
VIRGINA											
Total	85	25	23	9	1	0					
Cities	20	4	3	2	0	0					
Alexandria	2	0	0	0	0	0	0	1	0	1	162,588
Bristol	0	1	0	0	0	0	0	0	0	1	16,613
Charlottesville	4	1	0	0	0	0	1	0	3	1	48,585
Chesapeake	2	0	0	0	0	0	0	0	0	2	242,310
Fairfax City	1	0	0	0	0	0	1	0	0	0	24,259
Falls Church	1	0	0	0	0	0	0	0	0	1	14,884
Front Royal	0	0	1	0	0	0	0	1	0	0	15,356
Hampton	1	0	1	1	0	0	0	1	1	1	133,965
Middleburg	1	0	0	0	0	0	0	0	0	1	879
Newport News	4	0	1	0	0	0	2	0	1	2	178,734
Orange	1	0	0	0	0	0	1	0	0	0	5,016
Petersburg	0	0	0	1	0	0	0	0	0	1	31,568
Suffolk	1	0	0	0	0	0	0	0	1	0	90,817
Vienna	1	0	0	0	0	0	1	0	0	0	16,660
Virginia Beach	1	1	0	0	0	0	0	0	1	1	451,001
Williamsburg	0	1	0	0	0	0	0	0	0	1	15,191
Universities and Colleges	6	2	2	2	0	0					
George Mason University	2	0	0	0	0	0	1	0	0	1	46,266
Northern Virginia Community College	2	1	0	0	0	0	0	0	2	1	74,283
Old Dominion University	0	0	2	0	0	0	0	1	1	0	28,758
University of Mary Washington	0	0	0	1	0	0	0	0	0	1	5,276
University of Virginia	1	1	0	1	0	0	0	2	1	0	27,960
Virginia Commonwealth University	1	0	0	0	0	0	0	0	0	1	34,271
Metropolitan Counties	58	18	15	3	1	0					
Albemarle County Police Department	1	0	0	1	0	0	0	0	0	2	
Arlington County Police Department	4	0	1	0	0	0	2	0	1	2	
Bedford	1	0	0	2	0	0	0	0	0	3	
Campbell	1	0	0	0	0	0	0	0	1	0	
Chesterfield County Police Department	4	3	0	0	0	0	3	2	1	1	
Dinwiddie	2	1	0	0	0	0	2	0	0	1	
Fairfax County Police Department	16	5	5	0	0	0	3	4	11	8	
Fluvanna	1	0	0	0	0	0	1	0	0	0	
Franklin	1	0	0	0	0	0	0	0	1	0	
Frederick	0	0	1	0	0	0	0	1	0	0	
Giles	1	0	0	0	0	0	0	0	1	0	
Gloucester	1	0	1	0	0	0	1	0	0	1	
Henrico County Police Department	2	0	0	0	0	0	0	1	1	0	
King William	0	0	0	0	1	0	1	0	0	0	
Loudoun	13	6	1	0	0	0	8	3	1	8	
Nelson	1	0	0	0	0	0	0	1	0	0	
Prince William County Police Department	5	2	0	0	0	0	3	2	0	2	
Pulaski	0	0	1	0	0	0	0	0	1	0	
Roanoke County Police Department	1	0	0	0	0	0	0	1	0	0	
Rockingham	0	0	2	0	0	0	0	1	1	0	
Southampton	0	0	1	0	0	0	0	0	1	0	
Spotsylvania	2	1	0	0	0	0	0	0	1	2	
Stafford	1	0	1	0	0	0	0	1	1	0	
York	0	0	1	0	0	0	0	0	1	0	
Nonmetropolitan Counties	1	1	1	0	0	0					
Accomack	1	0	0	0	0	0	1	0	0	0	
Page	0	1	0	0	0	0	1	0	0	0	
Surry	0	0	1	0	0	0	0	0	1	0	
State Police Agencies	0	0	2	2	0	0					
State Police											
Amherst County	0	0	0	1	0	0	0	1	0	0	
Fairfax County	0	0	0	1	0	0	0	0	0	1	
Virginia Beach	0	0	1	0	0	0	0	0	0	1	
Winchester	0	0	1	0	0	0	0	0	0	1	
WASHINGTON											
Total	299	72	106	6	5	19					

Table 94. Hate Crime Incidents Per Bias Motivation and Quarter, by Selected State and Agency and Federal,[1] 2018—Continued

(Number.)

State/agency	Number of incidents per bias motivation						Number of incidents per quarter				Population[2]
	Race/ Ethnicity/ Ancestry	Religion	Sexual orientation	Disability	Gender	Gender Identity	1st quarter	2nd quarter	3rd quarter	4th quarter	
Cities	270	55	102	6	4	18					
Airway Heights	1	0	0	0	0	0	1	0	0	0	9,085
Auburn	4	0	0	0	0	0	3	0	0	1	72,392
Bellevue	3	2	3	0	0	0	2	3	2	1	146,913
Bellingham	1	4	0	1	0	0	2	2	1	1	90,208
Bothell	0	0	0	0	0	1	0	1	0	0	28,325
Castle Rock	0	0	1	0	0	0	0	0	0	1	2,251
Centralia	2	0	1	0	0	0	0	2	1	0	17,299
Cheney	1	0	0	0	0	0	0	0	1	0	12,715
Clarkston	1	0	0	0	0	0	1	0	0	0	7,417
Dupont	1	0	0	0	0	0	0	0	1	0	9,678
Edgewood	1	0	0	0	0	0	0	1	0	0	11,510
Edmonds	2	1	0	0	0	0	2	1	0	0	42,565
Everett	7	0	0	0	0	0	2	2	1	2	111,091
Fircrest	1	0	0	0	0	0	0	0	1	0	6,839
Issaquah	1	0	2	0	0	0	0	3	0	0	38,606
Kennewick	1	0	0	0	0	0	0	0	0	1	82,687
Kent	11	3	3	0	0	1	4	5	4	5	129,870
Kirkland	0	0	0	0	0	1	0	1	0	0	89,805
Lacey	1	0	0	0	0	0	1	0	0	0	50,844
Lake Forest Park	1	0	0	0	0	0	1	0	0	0	13,504
Lake Stevens	1	0	0	0	0	0	0	0	0	1	33,491
Lakewood	6	0	0	0	0	0	1	2	2	1	60,694
Longview	3	0	0	0	0	0	1	1	0	1	37,720
Lynden	1	0	0	0	0	0	0	0	1	0	14,612
Lynnwood	2	0	0	0	0	0	1	0	0	1	38,620
Marysville	4	1	0	0	0	0	2	2	0	1	70,204
Mill Creek	1	0	0	0	0	0	1	0	0	0	21,234
Monroe	3	0	0	0	0	0	2	0	1	0	19,003
Morton	0	0	2	0	0	0	1	1	0	0	1,164
Mountlake Terrace	1	0	0	0	0	0	0	0	1	0	21,549
Mount Vernon	1	0	0	0	0	0	0	1	0	0	35,550
Newcastle	1	0	0	0	0	0	0	0	1	0	11,878
Oak Harbor	2	0	0	0	0	0	0	1	0	1	23,330
Ocean Shores	0	0	1	0	0	0	0	0	1	0	5,977
Olympia	1	1	0	0	0	0	0	0	1	1	52,312
Port Angeles	1	0	0	0	0	0	0	0	1	0	19,992
Port Townsend	1	0	0	1	0	0	1	0	1	0	9,615
Pullman	0	0	0	0	1	0	0	1	0	0	33,896
Puyallup	1	0	0	0	0	0	0	0	1	0	41,572
Redmond	0	1	0	0	0	0	0	1	0	0	65,827
Renton	3	0	0	0	0	0	0	2	0	1	102,749
Sammamish	1	0	0	0	0	0	0	0	0	1	65,604
SeaTac	0	1	0	0	0	0	0	1	0	0	29,463
Seattle	159	33	81	4	3	11	57	79	90	64	742,759
Sedro Woolley	1	0	0	0	0	0	0	0	1	0	11,953
Spokane	22	3	3	0	0	3	2	10	13	6	218,222
Spokane Valley	2	0	1	0	0	0	1	0	2	0	99,020
Tacoma	4	0	1	0	0	0	0	3	1	1	215,687
Tukwila[3]	3	3	1	0	0	0	1	1	3	1	20,288
Tumwater	0	0	0	0	0	1	0	1	0	0	23,405
Vancouver	1	1	0	0	0	0	0	2	0	0	177,580
Walla Walla	1	1	0	0	0	0	0	1	0	1	32,906
Woodland	1	0	0	0	0	0	0	0	1	0	6,137
Yakima	2	0	2	0	0	0	0	0	1	3	93,959
Universities and Colleges	1	3	0	0	0	0					
University of Washington	1	0	0	0	0	0	0	0	1	0	55,073
Western Washington University	0	3	0	0	0	0	3	0	0	0	17,475
Metropolitan Counties	25	14	3	0	1	0					
Chelan	2	0	0	0	0	0	1	0	0	1	
Clark	1	1	0	0	0	0	1	1	0	0	
Cowlitz	0	1	0	0	0	0	1	0	0	0	
King	6	1	0	0	0	0	1	1	0	5	
Pierce	5	3	0	0	0	0	1	4	3	0	
Skagit	0	0	1	0	0	0	0	0	0	1	
Snohomish	2	5	0	0	0	0	3	1	1	2	
Spokane	2	1	2	0	0	0	2	2	0	1	
Thurston	1	2	0	0	0	0	0	1	2	0	
Walla Walla	0	0	0	0	1	0	0	0	0	1	
Whatcom	4	0	0	0	0	0	1	0	0	3	
Yakima	2	0	0	0	0	0	1	1	0	0	
Nonmetropolitan Counties	3	0	0	0	0	1					
Island	1	0	0	0	0	0	1	0	0	0	
Mason	1	0	0	0	0	0	0	0	0	1	
Okanogan	1	0	0	0	0	0	0	0	0	1	
San Juan	0	0	0	0	0	1	1	0			

Table 94. Hate Crime Incidents Per Bias Motivation and Quarter, by Selected State and Agency and Federal,[1] 2018—Continued

(Number.)

State/agency	Number of incidents per bias motivation						Number of incidents per quarter				Population[2]
	Race/ Ethnicity/ Ancestry	Religion	Sexual orientation	Disability	Gender	Gender Identity	1st quarter	2nd quarter	3rd quarter	4th quarter	
Other Agencies	0	0	1	0	0	0					
Port of Seattle	0	0	1	0	0	0	0	0	0	1	
WEST VIRGINIA											
Total	28	10	3	1	1	0					
	16	4	2	0	0	0					
Buckhannon	4	0	0	0	0	0	0	0	3	1	5,516
Charleston	2	4	1	0	0	0	3	1	1	2	47,470
Fairmont	3	0	0	0	0	0	1	1	1	0	18,430
Huntington	1	0	0	0	0	0	0	0	0	1	43,203
Kenova	0	0	1	0	0	0	0	0	0	1	2,979
Moundsville	1	0	0	0	0	0	1	0	0	0	8,417
Parkersburg	1	0	0	0	0	0	0	0	0	1	29,933
Ranson	2	0	0	0	0	0	0	1	0	1	5,292
Ravenswood	1	0	0	0	0	0	0	1	0	0	3,720
Vienna	1	0	0	0	0	0	0	0	0	1	10,306
Metropolitan Counties	3	3	0	1	0	0					
Berkeley	1	3	0	0	0	0	2	0	0	2	
Brooke	1	0	0	0	0	0	1	0	0	0	
Hancock	0	0	0	1	0	0	1	0	0	0	
Marshall	1	0	0	0	0	0	0	1	0	0	
Nonmetropolitan Counties	8	2	1	0	1	0					
Lewis	1	1	0	0	1	0	0	0	1	2	
Mason	5	0	0	0	0	0	0	2	2	1	
McDowell	2	0	0	0	0	0	0	1	0	1	
Mercer	0	1	0	0	0	0	0	1	0	0	
Pocahontas	0	0	1	0	0	0	0	0	1	0	
State Police Agencies	1	1	0	0	0	0					
State Police											
Madison	1	0	0	0	0	0	1	0	0	0	
Parkersburg	0	1	0	0	0	0	1	0	0	0	
WISCONSIN											
Total	26	8	14	3	0	2					
Cities	12	6	11	2	0	1					
Appleton	0	1	0	0	0	0	1	0	0	0	62,164
Ashwaubenon	1	0	0	0	0	0	1	0	0	0	17,316
Beaver Dam	1	0	0	0	0	0	0	0	0	1	16,394
Fox Valley Metro	0	1	0	0	0	0	0	1	0	0	22,006
Hudson	0	1	9	0	0	0	10	0	0	0	13,848
Janesville	2	1	0	0	0	0	2	0	1	0	64,471
Lake Delton	0	0	1	0	0	0	0	0	0	1	3,005
Marshall Village	1	0	0	0	0	0	1	0	0	0	3,988
Mayville	1	0	0	0	0	0	0	1	0	0	4,862
McFarland	0	0	0	0	0	1	0	1	0	0	8,544
Merrill	1	0	0	0	0	0	0	0	1	0	9,091
Milwaukee	2	0	1	0	0	0	0	2	0	1	595,619
New London	0	1	0	0	0	0	1	0	0	0	5,465
Phillips	0	0	0	1	0	0	0	1	0	0	1,345
Seymour	1	0	0	0	0	0	0	0	0	1	3,460
Sheboygan	0	0	0	1	0	0	0	0	0	1	48,195
Stevens Point	2	0	0	0	0	0	0	0	0	2	26,233
Waterloo	0	1	0	0	0	0	1	0	0	0	3,337
Universities and Colleges	1	0	0	0	0	0					
University of Wisconsin, Platteville	1	0	0	0	0	0	1	0	0	0	9,916
Metropolitan Counties	5	1	1	0	0	1					
Eau Claire	1	0	0	0	0	0	1	0	0	0	
Rock[3]	4	1	1	0	0	1	1	3	2	0	
Nonmetropolitan Counties	8	0	2	1	0	0					
Burnett	1	0	0	1	0	0	0	1	1	0	
Clark	1	0	0	0	0	0	0	0	1	0	
Dodge	2	0	1	0	0	0	2	1	0	0	
Oneida	4	0	0	0	0	0	2	0	1	1	
Wood	0	0	1	0	0	0	0	1	0	0	
Tribal Agencies	0	1	0	0	0	0					
Oneida Tribal	0	1	0	0	0	0	0	1	0	0	
FEDERAL											
Federal Agencies	40	28	15	1	0	0					
Federal Bureau of Investigation Field Offices											

Table 94. Hate Crime Incidents Per Bias Motivation and Quarter, by Selected State and Agency and Federal,[1] 2018—Continued

(Number.)

State/agency	Number of incidents per bias motivation						Number of incidents per quarter				Population[2]
	Race/ Ethnicity/ Ancestry	Religion	Sexual orientation	Disability	Gender	Gender Identity	1st quarter	2nd quarter	3rd quarter	4th quarter	
Albany, NY	0	0	1	0	0	0	1				
Albuquerque, NM	1	0	0	0	0	0				1	
Atlanta, GA	1	1	0	0	0	0	1	1			
Baltimore, MD	2	1	0	0	0	0			1	2	
Birmingham, AL	1	0	0	0	0	0	1		.		
Boston, MA	1	0	0	0	0	0		1			
Buffalo, NY	0	0	1	0	0	0				1	
Charlotte, NC	0	1	0	0	0	0				1	
Chicago, IL	0	1	0	0	0	0				1	
Cincinnati, OH	1	0	0	0	0	0	1				
Cleveland, OH	0	1	0	0	0	0	1				
Columbia, SC	2	0	1	0	0	0	1	1	1		
Dallas, TX	1	0	0	0	0	0			1		
Detroit, MI	1	0	0	0	0	0				1	
El Paso, TX[3]	2	2	0	0	0	0	2			1	
Indianapolis, IN	0	1	0	0	0	0			1		
Kansas City, MO	5	2	0	0	0	0	2	1	3	1	
Knoxville, TN	0	1	0	0	0	0	1				
Los Angeles, CA	1	1	1	0	0	0	2		1		
Louisville, KY	2	0	0	0	0	0	1			1	
Memphis, TN	0	0	1	0	0	0			1		
Miami, FL	0	2	2	0	0	0		2	2		
Milwaukee, WI	0	1	0	0	0	0		1			
Mobile, AL	1	0	0	0	0	0		1			
Newark, NJ	0	1	0	0	0	0			1		
New Orleans, LA	2	0	0	0	0	0	1		1		
Oklahoma City, OK	0	1	0	0	0	0	1				
Omaha, NB	0	1	0	0	0	0			1		
Philadelphia, PA	0	0	0	1	0	0		1			
Phoenix, AZ	0	0	1	0	0	0		1			
Pittsburgh, PA	2	1	0	0	0	0			2	1	
Portland, OR	3	1	0	0	0	0			2	2	
Sacramento, CA[3]	2	2	2	0	0	0	2	1	1	1	
Salt Lake City, UT	2	1	1	0	0	0	2	1		1	
San Francisco, CA	0	1	1	0	0	0	2				
Seattle, WA	2	3	1	0	0	0	2		1	3	
Springfield, IL	1	0	0	0	0	0	1				
St. Louis, MO	1	0	1	0	0	0		1		1	
Tampa, FL	1	1	0	0	0	0	1	1			
Washington, D.C.	2	0	1	0	0	0	1	2			

1 Federal includes only the Federal Bureau of Investigation field offices.   2 Population figures are published only for the cities. The figures listed for the universities and colleges are student enrollment and were provided by the United States Department of Education for the 2017 school year, the most recent available. The enrollment figures include full-time and part-time students.   3 The figures shown include one incident reported with more than one bias motivation.   4 Student enrollment figures were not available.

Table 95. Participation Table, Number of Participating Agencies and Population Covered, by Population Group and Federal, 2018

(Number.)

Population group	Number of participating agencies	Population covered
Total	16,039	306,874,326
Group I (cities 250,000 and over)	86	62,760,666
Group II (cities 100,000-249,999)	219	31,826,315
Group III (cities 50,000-99,999)	491	34,086,636
Group IV (cities 25,000-49,999)	872	29,934,423
Group V (cities 10,000-24,999)	1,771	28,121,786
Group VI1 (cities under 10,000)	8,187	23,169,515
Metropolitan counties[1]	2,002	73,662,889
Nonmetropolitan counties[1]	2,371	23,312,096
Federal		
Federal Bureau of Investigations, Field Offices[2]	40	

1 Includes universities and colleges, state police agencies, and/or other agencies to which no population is attributed.   2 Population estimates are not attributed to the Federal Bureau of Investigation field offices.

APPENDIXES

APPENDIX I. METHODOLOGY

Submitting UCR data to the FBI is a collective effort on the part of city, university/college, county, state, tribal, and federal law enforcement agencies to present a nationwide view of crime. Participating agencies throughout the country voluntarily provide reports on crimes known to the police and on persons arrested. For the most part, agencies submit monthly crime reports, using uniform offense definitions, to a centralized repository within their state. The state UCR Program then forwards the data to the FBI's UCR Program. Agencies in states that do not have a state UCR Program submit their data directly to the FBI. Staff members review the information for accuracy and reasonableness. [The FBI distributes the data presentations, special studies, and other publications compiled from the data to all who are interested in knowing about crime in the nation.] The national UCR Program is housed in the Operational Programs (OP) Branch of the FBI's Criminal Justice Information Services (CJIS) Division. Within the OP Branch, four units (the Crime Statistics Management Unit [CSMU], the CJIS Audit Unit, the Multimedia Productions Group [MPG]), and the CJIS Training and Advisory Process [CTAP] Unit), are involved in the day-to-day administration of the program.

Criteria for State UCR programs

The criteria established for state programs ensure consistency and comparability in the data submitted to the national program, as well as regular and timely reporting. These criteria are:

1. A UCR Program must conform to the FBI UCR Program's submission standards, definitions, specifications, and required deadlines.

2. A UCR Program must establish data integrity procedures and have personnel assigned to assist contributing agencies in quality assurance practices and crime reporting procedures. Data integrity procedures should include crime trend assessments, offense classification verification, and technical specification validation.

3. A UCR Program's submissions must cover more than 50 percent of the law enforcement agencies within its established reporting domain and be willing to cover any and all UCR-contributing agencies that wish to use the UCR Program from within its domain. (An agency wishing to become a UCR Program must be willing to report for all of the agencies within the state.)

4. A UCR Program must furnish the FBI UCR Program with all of the UCR data collected by the law enforcement agencies within its domain.

These requirements do not prohibit the state from gathering other statistical data beyond the national collection.

Data Completeness and Quality

National program staff members contact the state UCR program in connection with crime-reporting matters and, when necessary and approved by the state, they contact individual contributors within the state. To fulfill its responsibilities in connection with the UCR program, the FBI reviews and edits individual agency reports for completeness and quality. Upon request, they conduct training programs within the state on law enforcement record-keeping and crime-reporting procedures. The FBI conducts an audit of each state's UCR data collection procedures once every three years, in accordance with audit standards established by the federal government. Should circumstances develop in which the state program does not comply with the aforementioned requirements, the national program may institute a direct collection of data from law enforcement agencies within the state.

During a review of publication processes, the UCR Program staff analyzed Web statistics from previous editions of *Crime in the United States* (*CIUS*) to determine the tables that users access the most. Based on these criteria, the UCR Program streamlined the 2016 edition by reducing the number of tables from 81 to 29. The publication, however, still presents the major topics (offenses known, clearances, and persons arrested) that readers have come to expect. On June 30, 2017, the UCR Program launched the Crime Data Explorer (CDE), which provides law enforcement and the general public with crime data at the agency, state, and national levels. Offering multiple pathways to reported crime data, the CDE provides data visualizations of high-level trends and incident data with more detailed perspectives through downloads and a system enabling developers to create software applications. Planned enhancements to the CDE include additional tools to create dynamic data presentations, progressing beyond the static data tables of *CIUS* and the National Incident-Based Reporting System (NIBRS).

Beginning January 1, 2017, the UCR Program discontinued collecting rape data via the SRS according to the legacy definition. Therefore, the 2016 editions of *CIUS* and *Hate Crime Statistics* are the final publications which include the legacy definition of rape. Only rape data submitted under the revised definition will be published for 2017 and subsequent years. This change did not affect agencies that submit rape data via NIBRS.

Reporting Procedures

Offenses known and value of property–Law enforcement agencies tabulate the number of Part I offenses reported based on records of all reports of crime received from victims, officers who discover infractions, or other sources, and submit these reports each month to the FBI directly or through their state UCR programs. Part I offenses include murder and nonnegligent manslaughter, forcible rape, robbery, aggravated assault, burglary, larceny-theft, motor vehicle theft, and arson. Each month, law enforcement agencies also submit to the FBI the value of property stolen and recovered in connection with the offenses and detailed information pertaining to criminal homicide.

Unfounded offenses and clearances—When, through investigation, an agency determines that complaints of crimes are unfounded or false, the agency eliminates that offense from its crime tally through an entry on the monthly report. The report also provides the total number of actual Part I offenses, the number of offenses cleared, and the number of clearances that involve only offenders under the age of 18. (Law enforcement can clear crimes in one of two ways: by the arrest of at least one person who is charged and turned over to the court for prosecution or by exceptional means—when some element beyond law enforcement's control precludes the arrest of a known offender.)

Persons arrested—In addition to reporting Part I offenses each month, law enforcement agencies also provide data on the age, sex, and race of persons arrested for Part I and Part II offenses. Part II offenses encompass all crimes, except traffic violations, that are not classified as Part I offenses.

Officers killed or assaulted—Each month, law enforcement agencies also report information to the UCR program regarding law enforcement officers killed or assaulted, and each year they report the number of full-time sworn and civilian law enforcement personnel employed as of October 31.

Hate crimes—At the end of each quarter, law enforcement agencies report summarized data on hate crimes; that is specific offenses that were motivated by an offender's bias against the perceived race, religion, ethnic or national origin, sexual orientation, or physical or mental disability of the victim. Those agencies participating in the UCR program's National Incident-Based Reporting System (NIBRS) submit hate crime data monthly.

Editing Procedures

The UCR program thoroughly examines each report it receives for arithmetical accuracy and for deviations in crime data from month to month and from present to past years that may indicate errors. UCR staff members compare an agency's monthly reports with its previous submissions and with reports from similar agencies to identify any unusual fluctuations in the agency's crime count. Considerable variations in crime levels may indicate modified records procedures, incomplete reporting, or changes in the jurisdiction's geopolitical structure.

Evaluation of trends—Data reliability is a high priority of the FBI, which brings any deviations or arithmetical adjustments to the attention of state UCR programs or the submitting agencies. Typically, FBI staff members study the monthly reports to evaluate periodic trends prepared for individual reporting units. Any significant increase or decrease becomes the subject of a special inquiry. Changes in crime reporting procedures or annexations that affect an agency's jurisdiction can influence the level of reported crime. When this occurs, the FBI excludes the figures for specific crime categories or totals, if necessary, from the trend tabulations.

Training for contributors—In addition to the evaluation of trends, the FBI provides training seminars and instructional materials on crime reporting procedures to assist contributors in complying with UCR standards. Throughout the country, representatives from the national program coordinate with representatives of state programs and law enforcement personnel and hold training sessions to explain the purpose of the program, the rules of uniform classification and scoring, and the methods of assembling the information for reporting. When an individual agency has specific problems with compiling its crime statistics and its remedial efforts are unsuccessful, personnel from the FBI's Criminal Justice Information Services Division may visit the contributor to aid in resolving the problems.

UCR Handbook—The national UCR program publishes the *Uniform Crime Reporting (UCR) Handbook*, which details procedures for classifying and scoring offenses and serves as the contributing agencies' basic resource for preparing reports. The national staff also produces letters to UCR contributors, state program bulletins, and UCR newsletters as needed. These publications provide policy updates and new information, as well as clarification of reporting issues.

The final responsibility for data submissions rests with the individual contributing law enforcement agency. Although the FBI makes every effort through its editing procedures, training practices, and correspondence to ensure the validity of the data it receives, the accuracy of the statistics depends primarily on the adherence of each contributor to the established standards of reporting. Deviations from these established standards that cannot be resolved by the national UCR program may be brought to the attention of the Criminal Justice Information Systems Committees of the International Association of Chiefs of Police and the National Sheriffs' Association.

NIBRS Conversion

Thirty-three state programs are certified to provide their UCR data in the expanded National Incident-Based Reporting System (NIBRS) format. For presentation in this book, the NIBRS data were converted to the historical Summary Reporting System data. The UCR program staff constructed the NIBRS database to allow for such conversion so that UCR's long-running time series could continue.

Crime Trends

By showing fluctuations from year to year, trend statistics offer the data user an added perspective from which to study crime. Percent change tabulations in this publication are computed only for reporting agencies that provided comparable data for the periods under consideration. The FBI excludes from the trend calculations all figures except those received for common months from common agencies. Also excluded are unusual fluctuations of data that the FBI determines are the result of such variables as improved records procedures, annexations, and so on.

Caution to Users

Data users should exercise care in making any direct comparison between data in this publication and those in prior issues of *Crime in the United States*. Because of differing levels of participation from year to year and reporting problems that require the FBI to estimate crime counts for certain contributors, some data may not be comparable. In addition, this publication may contain updates to data provided in prior years' publications.

Offense Estimation

Some tables in this publication contain statistics for the entire United States. Because not all law enforcement agencies provide data for complete reporting periods, the FBI includes estimated crime numbers in these presentations. The FBI estimates data for three areas: Metropolitan Statistical Areas (MSAs), cities outside MSAs, and nonmetropolitan counties; and computes estimates for participating agencies that do not provide 12 months of complete data. For agencies supplying 3 to 11 months of data, the national UCR program estimates for the missing data by following a standard estimation procedure using the data provided by the agency. If an agency has supplied less than 3 months of data, the FBI computes estimates by using the known crime figures of similar areas within a state and assigning the same proportion of crime volumes to nonreporting agencies. The estimation process considers the following: population size covered by the agency; type of jurisdiction; for example, police department versus sheriff's office; and geographic location.

Estimation of State-Level Data

In response to various circumstances, the FBI calculates estimated offense totals for certain states. For example, some states do not provide forcible rape figures in accordance with UCR guidelines. In addition, problems at the state level have, at times, resulted in no useable data. Also, the conversion of the National Incident-Based Reporting System (NIBRS) data to Summary data has contributed to the need for unique estimation procedures.

APPENDIX II. OFFENSE DEFINITIONS

The Uniform Crime Reporting (UCR) program divides offenses into two groups. Contributing agencies submit information on the number of Part I offenses known to law enforcement; those offenses cleared by arrest or exceptional means; and the age, sex, and race of persons arrested for each of these offenses. Contributors provide only arrest data for Part II offenses. These are definitions of offenses set forth by the UCR.

The UCR program collects data on Part I offenses to measure the level and scope of crime occurring throughout the nation. The program's founders chose these offenses because (1) they are serious crimes, (2) they occur with regularity in all areas of the country, and (3) they are likely to be reported to police.

Part I offenses include criminal homicide, forcible rape, robbery, aggravated assault, burglary, larceny-theft, motor vehicle theft, and arson.

Criminal homicide—a.) Murder and nonnegligent manslaughter: the willful (nonnegligent) killing of one human being by another. Deaths caused by negligence, attempts to kill, assaults to kill, suicides, and accidental deaths are excluded. The program classifies justifiable homicides separately and limits the definition to (1) the killing of a felon by a law enforcement officer in the line of duty; or (2) the killing of a felon, during the commission of a felony, by a private citizen. b.) Manslaughter by negligence: the killing of another person through gross negligence. Deaths of persons due to their own negligence, accidental deaths not resulting from gross negligence, and traffic fatalities are excluded.

Rape—In 2013, the FBI UCR Program began collecting rape data under a revised definition within the Summary Reporting System. Previously, offense data for forcible rape were collected under the legacy UCR definition: the carnal knowledge of a female forcibly and against her will. Beginning with the 2013 data year, the term "forcible" was removed from the offense title, and the definition was changed. The revised UCR definition of rape is: penetration, no matter how slight, of the vagina or anus with any body part or object, or oral penetration by a sex organ of another person, without the consent of the victim. Attempts or assaults to commit rape are also included in the statistics presented here; however, statutory rape and incest are excluded. In 2016, the FBI director approved the recommendation to discontinue the reporting of rape data using the UCR legacy definition beginning in 2017. However, to maintain the 20-year trend in Table 1, national estimates for rape under the legacy definition are provided along with estimates under the revised definition for 2017. The UCR Program counts one offense for each victim of a rape, attempted rape, or assault with intent to rape, regardless of the victim's age. Non-consensual sexual relations involving a familial member is considered rape, not incest. All other crimes of a sexual nature are considered to be Part II offenses; as such, the UCR Program collects only arrest data for those crimes. The offense of statutory rape, in which no force is used but the female victim is under the age of consent, is included in the arrest total for the sex offenses category.

Robbery—The taking or attempted taking of anything of value from the care, custody, or control of a person or persons by force or threat of force or violence and/or by putting the victim in fear.

Aggravated assault—An unlawful attack by one person upon another for the purpose of inflicting severe or aggravated bodily injury. This type of assault usually is accompanied by the use of a weapon or by means likely to produce death or great bodily harm. Simple assaults are excluded.

Burglary (breaking or entering)—The unlawful entry of a structure to commit a felony or a theft. Attempted forcible entry is included.

Larceny-theft (except motor vehicle theft)—The unlawful taking, carrying, leading, or riding away of property from the possession or constructive possession of another. Examples are thefts of bicycles or automobile parts and accessories, shoplifting, pocket-picking, or the stealing of any property or article that is not taken by force and violence or by fraud. Attempted larcenies are included. Embezzlement, confidence games, forgery, worthless checks, and the like, are excluded.

Motor vehicle theft—The theft or attempted theft of a motor vehicle. A motor vehicle is self-propelled and runs on land surface and not on rails. Motorboats, construction equipment, airplanes, and farming equipment are specifically excluded from this category.

Arson—Any willful or malicious burning or attempt to burn, with or without intent to defraud, a dwelling house, public building, motor vehicle, aircraft, personal property of another, and the like.

The **Part II** offenses for which only arrest data are collected, are:

Other assaults, also known as other assaults (simple)—Assaults and attempted assaults that are not of an aggravated nature and do not result in serious injury to the victim. Included in this category are stalking, intimidation, coercion, and hazing.

Forgery and counterfeiting—The altering, copying, or imitating of something, without authority or right, with the intent to deceive or defraud by passing the copy or thing altered or imitated as that which is original or genuine; or the selling, buying, or possession of an altered, copied, or imitated thing with the intent to deceive or defraud. Attempts are included.

Fraud—The intentional perversion of the truth for the purpose of inducing another person or other entity in reliance upon it to part with something of value or to surrender a legal right. Fraudulent conversion and obtaining of money or property by false pretenses. Confidence games and bad checks, except forgeries and counterfeiting, are included.

Embezzlement—The unlawful misappropriation or misapplication by an offender of money, property, or some other thing of value entrusted to that offender's care, custody, or control.

Stolen property; buying, receiving, possessing—Buying, receiving, possessing, selling, concealing, or transporting any property with the knowledge that it has been unlawfully taken, as by burglary, embezzlement, fraud, larceny, robbery, and the like. Attempts are included.

Vandalism—To willfully or maliciously destroy, injure, disfigure, or deface any public or private property, real or personal, without the consent of the owner or person having custody or control by cutting, tearing, breaking, marking, painting, drawing, covering with filth, or any other such means as may be specified by local law. Attempts are included.

Weapons; carrying, possessing, and the like—The violation of laws or ordinances prohibiting the manufacture, sale, purchase, transportation, possession, concealment, or use of firearms, cutting instruments, explosives, incendiary devices, or other deadly weapons. Attempts are included.

Prostitution and commercialized vice—The unlawful promotion of or participation in sexual activities for profit, including attempts. To solicit customers or transport persons for prostitution purposes; to own, manage, or operate a dwelling or other establishment for the purposes of providing a place where prostitution is performed; or to otherwise assist or promote prostitution.

Sex offenses (except forcible rape, prostitution, and commercialized vice)—Offenses against chastity, common decency, morals, and the like. Incest, indecent exposure, and statutory rape, as well as attempts are included.

Drug abuse violations—The violation of laws prohibiting the production, distribution, and/or use of certain controlled substances. The unlawful cultivation, manufacture, distribution, sale, purchase, use, possession, transportation, or importation of any controlled drug or narcotic substance. Arrests for violations of state and local laws, specifically those relating to the unlawful possession, sale, use, growing, manufacturing, and making of narcotic drugs. The following drug categories are specified: opium or cocaine and their derivatives (morphine, heroin, codeine); marijuana; synthetic narcotics—manufactured narcotics that can cause true addiction (demerol, methadone); and dangerous nonnarcotic drugs (barbiturates, benzedrine).

Gambling—To unlawfully bet or wager money or something else of value; assist, promote, or operate a game of chance for money or some other stake; possess or transmit wagering information; manufacture, sell, purchase, possess, or transport gambling equipment, devices, or goods; or tamper with the outcome of a sporting event or contest to gain a gambling advantage.

Offenses against the family and children—Unlawful nonviolent acts by a family member (or legal guardian) that threaten the physical, mental, or economic well-being or morals of another family member and that are not classifiable as other offenses, such as assault or sex offenses. Attempts are included.

Driving under the influence—Driving or operating a motor vehicle or common carrier while mentally or physically impaired as the result of consuming an alcoholic beverage or using a drug or narcotic.

Liquor laws—The violation of state or local laws or ordinances prohibiting the manufacture, sale, purchase, transportation, possession, or use of alcoholic beverages, not including driving under the influence and drunkenness. Federal violations are excluded.

Drunkenness—To drink alcoholic beverages to the extent that one's mental faculties and physical coordination are substantially impaired. Excludes driving under the influence.

Disorderly conduct—Any behavior that tends to disturb the public peace or decorum, scandalize the community, or shock the public sense of morality.

Vagrancy—The violation of a court order, regulation, ordinance, or law requiring the withdrawal of persons from the streets or other specified areas; prohibiting persons from remaining in an area or place in an idle or aimless manner; or prohibiting persons from going from place to place without visible means of support.

All other offenses—All violations of state or local laws not specifically identified as Part I or Part II offenses, except traffic violations.

Suspicion—Arrested for no specific offense and released without formal charges being placed.

Curfew and loitering laws (persons under 18 years of age)—Violations by juveniles of local curfew or loitering ordinances.

APPENDIX III. GEOGRAPHIC AREA DEFINITIONS

The program collects crime data and supplemental information that make it possible to generate a variety of statistical compilations, including data presented by reporting areas. These statistics enable data users to analyze local crime data in conjunction with those for areas of similar geographic location or population size. The reporting areas that the program uses in its data breakdowns include community types, population groups, and regions and divisions. For community types, the program considers proximity to metropolitan areas using the designations established by the U.S. Office of Management and Budget (OMB). (Generally, sheriffs, county police, and state police report crimes within counties but outside of cities; local police report crimes within city limits.) The number of inhabitants living in a locale (based on the U.S. Census Bureau's figures) determines the population group into which the program places it. For its geographic breakdowns, the program divides the United States into regions and divisions.

Regions and Divisions

The map below illustrates the nine divisions that make up the four regions of the United States. The program uses this widely recognized geographic organization when compiling the nation's crime data. The regions and divisions are as follows:

NORTHEAST

New England—Connecticut, Maine, Massachusetts, New Hampshire, Rhode Island, and Vermont

Middle Atlantic—New York, New Jersey, and Pennsylvania

MIDWEST

East North Central—Illinois, Indiana, Michigan, Ohio, and Wisconsin

West North Central—Iowa, Kansas, Minnesota, Missouri, Nebraska, North Dakota, and South Dakota

SOUTH

South Atlantic—Delaware, District of Columbia, Florida, Georgia, Maryland, North Carolina, South Carolina, Virginia, and West Virginia

East South Central—Alabama, Kentucky, Mississippi, and Tennessee

West South Central—Arkansas, Louisiana, Oklahoma, and Texas

WEST

Mountain—Arizona, Colorado, Idaho, Montana, Nevada, New Mexico, Utah, and Wyoming

Pacific—Alaska, California, Hawaii, Oregon, and Washington

Community Types

To assist data users who wish to analyze and present uniform statistical data about metropolitan areas, the program uses reporting units that represent major population centers. The program compiles data for the following three types of communities:

Metropolitan Statistical Areas (MSAs)—Each MSA contains a principal city or urbanized area with a population of at least 50,000 inhabitants. MSAs include the principal city, the county in which the city is located, and other adjacent counties that have a high degree of economic and social integration with the principal city and county (as defined by the OMB), which is measured through commuting. In the program, counties within an MSA are considered metropolitan counties. In addition, MSAs may cross state boundaries.

Some presentations in this publication refer to Metropolitan Divisions, which are subdivisions of an MSA that consists of a core with "a population of at least 2.5 million persons. A Metropolitan Division consists of one or more main/secondary counties that represent an employment center or centers, plus adjacent counties associated with the main county or counties through commuting ties," (*Federal Register* 65 [249]). Also, some tables reference suburban areas, which are subdivisions of MSAs that exclude the principal cities but include all the remaining cities (those having fewer than 50,000 inhabitants) and the unincorporated areas of the MSAs.

Because the elements that comprise MSAs, particularly the geographic compositions, are subject to change, the program discourages data users from making year-to-year comparisons of MSA data.

Cities Outside MSAs—Ordinarily, cities outside MSAs are incorporated areas. In 2013, cities outside MSAs made up 6.0 percent of the nation's population.

Nonmetropolitan Counties Outside MSAs—Most nonmetropolitan counties are composed of unincorporated areas.

Metropolitan and nonmetropolitan community types are further illustrated in the following table:

Metropolitan	Nonmetropolitan
Principal cities (50,000+ inhabitants)	Cities outside metropolitan areas
Suburban cities	
Metropolitan counties	Nonmetropolitan counties

The Department of Justice administers two statistical programs to measure the magnitude, nature, and impact of crime in the nation: the Uniform Crime Reporting (UCR) program and the National Crime Victimization Survey (NCVS). Each of these programs produces valuable information about aspects of the nation's crime problem. Because the UCR and NCVS programs are conducted for different purposes, use different methods, and focus on somewhat different aspects of crime, the information they produce together provides a more comprehensive panorama of the nation's crime problem than either could produce alone.

Uniform Crime Reporting (UCR) program

The UCR program, administered by the Federal Bureau of Investigation (FBI), was created in 1929 and collects information on the following crimes reported to law enforcement authorities: murder and nonnegligent manslaughter, forcible rape, robbery, aggravated assault, burglary, larceny-theft, motor vehicle theft, and arson. Law enforcement agencies also report arrest data for 20 additional crime categories.

The UCR program compiles data from monthly law enforcement reports and from individual crime incident records transmitted directly to the FBI or to centralized state agencies that report to the FBI. The program thoroughly examines each report it receives for reasonableness, accuracy, and deviations that may indicate errors. Large variations in crime levels may indicate modified records procedures, incomplete reporting, or changes in a jurisdiction's boundaries. To identify any unusual fluctuations in an agency's crime counts, the program compares monthly reports to previous submissions of the agency and to those for similar agencies.

The FBI annually publishes its findings in a preliminary release in the spring of the following calendar year, followed by a detailed annual report, *Crime in the United States*, issued in the fall. (The printed copy of *Crime in the United States* is now published by Bernan.) In addition to crime counts and trends, this report includes data on crimes cleared, persons arrested (age, sex, and race), law enforcement personnel (including the number of sworn officers killed or assaulted), and the characteristics of homicides (including age, sex, and race of victims and offenders; victim-offender relationships; weapons used; and circumstances surrounding the homicides). Other periodic reports are also available from the UCR program.

The state and local law enforcement agencies participating in the UCR program are continually converting to the more comprehensive and detailed National Incident-Based Reporting System (NIBRS).

The UCR program presents crime counts for the nation as a whole, as well as for regions, states, counties, cities, towns, tribal law enforcement areas, and colleges and universities. This allows for studies among neighboring jurisdictions and among those with similar populations and other common characteristics.

National Crime Victimization Survey

The NCVS, conducted by the Bureau of Justice Statistics (BJS), began in 1973. It provides a detailed picture of crime incidents, victims, and trends. After a substantial period of research, the BJS completed an intensive methodological redesign of the survey in 1993. It conducted this redesign to improve the questions used to uncover crime, update the survey methods, and broaden the scope of crimes measured. The redesigned survey collects detailed information on the frequency and nature of the crimes of rape, sexual assault, personal robbery, aggravated and simple assault, household burglary, theft, and motor vehicle theft. It does not measure homicide or commercial crimes (such as burglaries of stores).

Twice a year, Census Bureau personnel interview household members in a nationally representative sample of approximately 90,000 households (about 160,000 people). Households stay in the sample for 3 years, and new households rotate into the sample on an ongoing basis.

The NCVS collects information on crimes suffered by individuals and households, whether or not those crimes were reported to law enforcement. It estimates the proportion of each crime type reported to law enforcement, and it summarizes the reasons that victims give for reporting or not reporting.

The survey provides information about victims (age, sex, race, ethnicity, marital status, income, and educational level); offenders (sex, race, approximate age, and victim-offender relationship); and crimes (time and place of occurrence, use of weapons, nature of injury, and economic consequences). Questions also cover victims' experiences with the criminal justice system, self-protective measures used by victims, and possible substance abuse by offenders. Supplements are added to the survey periodically to obtain detailed information on specific topics, such as school crime.

The BJS published the first data from the redesigned NCVS in a June 1995 bulletin. The publication of NCVS data includes *Criminal Victimization in the United States*, an annual report that covers the broad range of detailed information collected by the NCVS. The bureau also publishes detailed reports on topics such as crime against women, urban crime, and gun use in crime. The National Archive of Criminal Justice Data at the University of Michigan archives the NCVS data files to help researchers perform independent analyses.

Comparing the UCR program and the NCVS

Because the BJS designed the NCVS to complement the UCR program, the two programs share many similarities. As much as their different collection methods permit, the two measure the same subset of serious crimes with the same definitions. Both programs cover rape, robbery, aggravated assault, burglary, theft, and motor vehicle theft; both define rape, robbery, theft, and motor vehicle theft virtually identically. (Although rape is defined analogously, the UCR program measures the crime against women only, and the NCVS measures it against both sexes.)

There are also significant differences between the two programs. First, the two programs were created to serve different purposes. The UCR program's primary objective is to provide a reliable set of criminal justice statistics for law enforcement administration, operation, and management. The BJS established the NCVS to provide previously unavailable information about crime (including crime not reported to police), victims, and offenders.

Second, the two programs measure an overlapping but nonidentical set of crimes. The NCVS includes crimes both reported and not reported to law enforcement. The NCVS excludes—but the UCR program includes—homicide, arson, commercial crimes, and crimes committed against children under 12 years of age. The UCR program captures crimes reported to law enforcement but collects only arrest data for simple assaults and sexual assaults other than forcible rape.

Third, because of methodology, the NCVS and UCR have different definitions of some crimes. For example, the UCR defines burglary as the unlawful entry or attempted entry of a structure to commit a felony or theft. The NCVS, not wanting to ask victims to ascertain offender motives, defines burglary as the entry or attempted entry of a residence by a person who had no right to be there.

Fourth, for property crimes (burglary, theft, and motor vehicle theft), the two programs calculate crime rates using different bases. The UCR program rates for these crimes are per capita (number of crimes per 100,000 persons), whereas the NCVS rates for these crimes are per household (number of crimes per 1,000 households).

Because the number of households may not grow at the same annual rate as the total population, trend data for rates of property crimes measured by the two programs may not be comparable. In addition, some differences in the data from the two programs may result from sampling variation in the NCVS and from estimating for nonresponsiveness in the UCR program.

The BJS derives the NCVS estimates from interviewing a sample and are, therefore, subject to a margin of error. The bureau uses rigorous statistical methods to calculate confidence intervals around all survey estimates, and describes trend data in the NCVS reports as genuine only if there is at least a 90-percent certainty that the measured changes are not the result of sampling variation. The UCR program bases its data on the actual counts of offenses reported by law enforcement agencies. In some circumstances, the UCR program estimates its data for nonparticipating agencies or those reporting partial data. Apparent discrepancies between statistics from the two programs can usually be accounted for by their definitional and procedural differences, or resolved by comparing NCVS sampling variations (confidence intervals) of crimes said to have been reported to police with UCR program statistics.

For most types of crimes measured by both the UCR program and the NCVS, analysts familiar with the programs can exclude those aspects of crime not common to both from analysis. Resulting long-term trend lines can be brought into close concordance. The impact of such adjustments is most striking for robbery, burglary, and motor vehicle theft, whose definitions most closely coincide.

With robbery, the BJS bases the NCVS victimization rates on only those robberies reported to the police. It is also possible to remove UCR program robberies of commercial establishments, such as gas stations, convenience stores, and banks, from analysis. When users compare the resulting NCVS police-reported robbery rates and the UCR program noncommercial robbery rates, the results reveal closely corresponding long-term trends.

Conclusion

Each program has unique strengths. The UCR program provides a measure of the number of crimes reported to law enforcement agencies throughout the country. The program's Supplementary Homicide Reports provide the most reliable, timely data on the extent and nature of homicides in the nation. The NCVS is the primary source of information on the characteristics of criminal victimization and on the number and types of crimes not reported to law enforcement authorities.

By understanding the strengths and limitations of each program, it is possible to use the UCR program and NCVS to achieve a greater understanding of crime trends and the nature of crime in the United States. For example, changes in police procedures, shifting attitudes towards crime and police, and other societal changes can affect the extent to which people report and law enforcement agencies record crime. NCVS and UCR program data can be used in concert to explore why trends in reported and police-recorded crime may differ.